2-10-06

2-10-06

Financial Aid
for Hispanic Americans
2003-2005

RSP FINANCIAL AID DIRECTORIES
OF INTEREST TO MINORITIES

College Student's Guide to Merit and Other No-Need Funding, 2002-2004
Selected as one of the "Outstanding Titles of the Year" by *Choice,* this directory describes 1,300 no-need funding opportunities for college students. 488 pages. ISBN 1-58841-041-2. $32, plus $5 shipping.

Directory of Financial Aids for Women, 2003-2005
Nearly 1,600 funding programs set aside for women are described in this biennial directory, which *School Library Journal* calls "the cream of the crop." 582 pages. ISBN 1-58841-067-6. $45, plus $5 shipping.

Financial Aid for African Americans, 2003-2005
More than 1,400 scholarships, fellowships, loans, grants, and internships open to African Americans are described in this award-winning directory. 522 pages. ISBN 1-58841-068-5. $40, plus $5 shipping.

Financial Aid for Asian Americans, 2003-2005
This is the source to use if you are looking for financial aid for Asian Americans; nearly 1,000 funding opportunities are described. 346 pages. ISBN 1-58841-069-2. $37.50, plus $5 shipping.

Financial Aid for Hispanic Americans, 2003-2005
Nearly 1,300 funding programs open to Americans of Mexican, Puerto Rican, Central American, or other Latin American heritage are described here. 492 pages. ISBN 1-58841-070-6. $40, plus $5 shipping.

Financial Aid for Native Americans, 2003-2005
Detailed information is provided on 1,500 funding opportunities open to American Indians, Native Alaskans, and Native Pacific Islanders. 546 pages. ISBN 1-58841-071-4. $40, plus $5 shipping.

Financial Aid for Research and Creative Activities Abroad, 2002-2004
Described here are 1,300 scholarships, fellowships, grants, etc. available to support research, professional, or creative activities abroad. 378 pages. ISBN 1-58841-062-5. $45, plus $5 shipping.

Financial Aid for Study and Training Abroad, 2001-2003
This directory, which *Children's Bookwatch* calls "invaluable," describes more than 1,100 financial aid opportunities available to support study abroad. 398 pages. ISBN 1-58841-031-5. $39.50, plus $5 shipping.

Financial Aid for the Disabled and Their Families, 2002-2004
Named one of the "Best Reference Books of the Year" by *Library Journal,* this directory describes in detail more than 1,100 funding opportunities. 484 pages. ISBN 1-58841-042-0. $40, plus $5 shipping.

Financial Aid for Veterans, Military Personnel, and Their Dependents, 2002-2004
According to *Reference Book Review,* this directory (with its 1,100 entries) is "the most comprehensive guide available on the subject." 392 pages. ISBN 1-58841-043-9. $40, plus $5 shipping.

High School Senior's Guide to Merit and Other No-Need Funding, 2002-2004
Here's your guide to 1,100 funding programs that *never* look at income level when making awards to college-bound high school seniors. 400 pages. ISBN 1-58841-044-7. $29.95, plus $5 shipping.

How to Pay for Your Degree in Education & Related Fields, 2002-2004
Here's hundreds of funding opportunities to support undergraduate and graduate students preparing for a career in teaching, guidance, etc. 250 pages. ISBN 1-58841-063-3. $30, plus $5 shipping.

How to Pay for Your Degree in Journalism & Related Fields, 2002-2004
If you need funding for an undergraduate or graduate degree in journalism, or a related field, this is the directory to use (500+ funding programs described). 250 pages. ISBN 1-58841-064-1. $30, plus $5 shipping.

Money for Graduate Students in the Social & Behavioral Sciences, 2003-2005
Described here are the 1,100 biggest and best funding opportunities available to students working on a graduate degree in the social or behavioral sciences. 332 pages. ISBN 1-58841-078-1. $42.50, plus $5 shipping.

RSP Funding for Engineering Students, 2002-2004
Covered here are the 700 biggest and best scholarships, fellowships, awards, and grants for undergraduate or graduate students in engineering. 230 pages. ISBN 1-58841-045-5. $30, plus $5 shipping.

RSP Funding for Nursing Students, 2002-2004
You'll find 500+ scholarships, fellowships, loans, grants, and awards here that can be used for study, research, professional, or other nursing activities. 189 pages. ISBN 1-58841-045-5. $30, plus $5 shipping.

Financial Aid for Hispanic Americans 2003-2005

Gail Ann Schlachter
R. David Weber

A List of: Scholarships, Fellowships, Loans, Grants, Awards, and Internships Open Primarily or Exclusively to Hispanic Americans

Reference Service Press
El Dorado Hills, California

ISBN: 1-58841-070-6

10 9 8 7 6 5 4 3 2 1

Reference Service Press (RSP) began in 1977 with a single financial aid publication *(The Directory of Financial Aids for Women)* and now specializes in the development of financial aid resources in multiple formats, including books, large print books, disks, CD-ROMs, print-on-demand reports, eBooks, and online sources. Long recognized as a leader in the field, RSP has been called, by the *Simba Report on Directory Publishing* "a true success in the world of independent directory publishers." Kaplan Educational Centers hailed RSP as "the leading authority on scholarships.

Reference Service Press
El Dorado Hills Business Park
5000 Windplay Drive, Suite 4
El Dorado Hills, CA 95762
>   **(916) 939-9620**
>   **Fax: (916) 939-9626**
>   **E-mail: findaid@aol.com**
Visit our web site:
>   **http://www.rspfunding.com**

Manufactured in the United States of America
Price: $40.00, plus $5 shipping.

Contents

Introduction

PURPOSE OF THE DIRECTORY

Despite the recent steps taken to curtail affirmative action and equal opportunity programs, the financial aid picture for minorities has never looked brighter. Currently, billions of dollars are available for Hispanic Americans and other minorities. This funding is open to applicants at any level (high school through postdoctoral and professional) for study, research, travel, training, career development, or innovative effort.

While numerous directories have been prepared to identify and describe general financial aid programs (those open to all segments of society), they have never covered more than a small portion of the programs designed primarily or exclusively for minorities. Before *Financial Aid for Hispanic Americans* and its predecessor, the *Directory of Financial Aids for Minorities,* was published, many advisors, librarians, scholars, researchers, and students were unaware of the extensive funding opportunities available to Hispanic Americans and other minorities. Now, with the ongoing publication of *Financial Aid for Hispanic Americans,* up-to-date and comprehensive information is available in a single volume about the special resources set aside for members of this group.

Financial Aid for Hispanic Americans is prepared biennially as part of Reference Service Press' four-volume *Minority Funding Set* (the other volumes cover funding for African Americans, Asian Americans, and Native Americans). Each of the volumes in this set is sold separately, or the complete set can be purchased at a discounted price (for more information contact Reference Service Press's marketing department). No other source offers the coverage provided by these titles. That's why the Grantsmanship Center called the set "a must for every organization serving minorities" and *Reference Books Bulletin* selected each of the volumes in the *Minority Funding Set* as the "Editor's Choice." Perhaps *College Spotlight* sums up the critical reaction best: "the top of all books of this sort."

EXTENT OF UPDATING IN THE 2003-2005 EDITION

The 2003-2005 edition of *Financial Aid for Hispanic Americans* completely revises and updates the previous edition. Programs that have ceased operations have been dropped from the listing. Profiles of continuing programs have been rewritten to reflect operations in 2003-2005; nearly 80 percent of the continuing programs reported substantive changes in their locations, requirements (particularly application deadline), or benefits since 2001. In addition, more than 375 new entries have been added to the program section of the directory. The resulting listing describes more than 1,350 scholarships, fellowships, loans, grants, awards, internships, and general financial aid directories.

SCOPE OF THE DIRECTORY

This 2003-2005 edition of *Financial Aid for Hispanic Americans* will help Hispanic Americans (persons whose origins are from Mexico, Central America, Puerto Rico, Cuba, or other Latin American countries) tap into the billions of dollars available to them, as minorities, to support study, research, creative activities, past accomplishments, future projects, professional development, and work experience. The listings cover every major subject area, are sponsored by nearly 900 different private and public agencies and organizations, and are open to Hispanic Americans at any level—from high school through postdoctorate and professional. This approach is unique. No other single source provides this type of comprehensive and current coverage of funding opportunities available exclusively to Hispanic Americans or to minority pools that specifically include Hispanic Americans.

In addition to its comprehensive coverage, *Financial Aid for Hispanic Americans* offers several other unique features. Covered here are hundreds of funding opportunities not listed in any other source. Unlike other funding directories, which generally follow a straight alphabetical arrangement, this one groups entries by type, thus facilitating your search for appropriate programs. The same convenience is offered in the indexes, where title, organization, geographic, subject, and deadline date entries are each subdivided by type of program. Finally, we have tried to anticipate all the ways you might wish to search for funding. The volume is organized so you can identify programs not only by type, but by specific subject, sponsoring organization, program title, residency requirements, where the money can be spent, and even deadline date. Plus, we've included all the information you'll need to decide if a program is right for you: purpose, eligibility requirements, financial data, duration, special features, limitations, number awarded, and application date. You even get fax numbers, toll-free numbers, e-mail addresses, and web sites (when available), along with complete contact information.

COMPILATION OF THE DIRECTORY

To compile the 2003-2005 edition of *Financial Aid for Hispanic Americans,* we first reviewed and updated all relevant programs included in the previous edition of the directory. Next, we collected information on all programs open to Hispanic Americans that were added to Reference Service Press' funding database since the last edition of the directory. Then, we searched extensively for new program leads in a variety of sources, including printed directories, news reports, journals, newsletters, house organs, annual reports, and sites on the Internet.

Finally, we contacted the sponsoring organizations identified in this process (up to four times in writing and, if necessary, up to 3 times by telephone) and requested descriptions of their funding programs so we could prepare the entries for this book (no information is ever taken from secondary sources). Unfortunately, despite our best efforts, some sponsoring organizations failed to respond to our data requests; consequently, their programs are not included in this edition of the directory.

ARRANGEMENT OF THE DIRECTORY

Financial Aid for Hispanic Americans is divided into three separate sections: descriptions of more than 1,300 funding opportunities open to Hispanic Americans, an annotated bibliography of directories listing general financial aid programs, and a set of six indexes.

Financial Aid Programs Open to Hispanic Americans.   The first section of the directory describes 1,313 funding opportunities open to Hispanic Americans. The programs described here are sponsored by nearly 900 government agencies, professional organizations, corporations, sororities and fraternities, foundations, religious groups, educational associations, and military/veterans organizations. They are open to Hispanic Americans at any level (high school through postdoctoral) for education, research, travel, training, career development, or innovative effort. All areas of the sciences, social sciences, and humanities are covered. The focus is on programs open to American citizens or permanent residents and tenable in the United States.

Entries in this section are grouped in the following six categories to facilitate your search for a specific kind of financial assistance (e.g., a scholarship for undergraduate study, a grant for independent research, an award for outstanding literary achievement):

> ***Scholarships:***   Programs that support studies at the undergraduate level in the United States. Usually no return of service or repayment is required. For information on funding for research on the undergraduate level, see the Grants category below.

> ***Fellowships:***   Programs that support studies at the graduate level in the United States, including work on a master's degree, doctorate, professional degree (e.g., law, medicine), or a specialist's certificate. Usually no return of service or repayment is required. For information on funding for research on the graduate level, see the Grants category below.

Loans: Programs that provide money that eventually must be repaid—in cash or in service and with or without interest. Forgivable loans (along with scholarship/loans and loans-for-service) are also described in this part of the directory.

Grants: Programs that provide funds to support Hispanic Americans' innovative efforts, travel, projects, creative activities, or research on any level (from undergraduate to postdoctorate, professional, or other). In a number of cases, proposals must be submitted by institutions or organizations only; in others, individual minority group members may submit proposals directly.

Awards: Competitions, prizes, and honoraria granted in recognition of Hispanic Americans' personal accomplishments, professional contributions, or public service. Prizes received solely as the result of entering contests are excluded.

Internships: Work experience programs for Hispanic American undergraduates, graduate students, and recent graduates. Only salaried positions are described.

Programs that supply more than one type of assistance are listed in all relevant subsections. For example, both undergraduate and graduate students may apply for the ABC Hispanic Scholarship Fund, so the program is described in the scholarship and in the fellowship subsections.

Each program entry has been designed to provide a concise profile that includes information (when available) on program title, organization address and telephone numbers (including toll-free and fax numbers), e-mail and web site addresses, purpose, eligibility, remuneration, duration, special features, limitations, number of awards, and application deadline. (Refer to the sample on page xiii). The information reported for each of the programs in this section was supplied in response to research inquiries distributed through the middle of 2003. While this listing is intended to be as comprehensive as possible, some sponsoring organizations did not respond to our research requests and, consequently, are not included in this edition of the directory.

The focus of the directory is on noninstitution-specific programs open exclusively to Hispanic Americans or to minority pools that specifically include Hispanic Americans. Excluded from this listing are:

Awards for which American citizens would be ineligible: Programs open only to nationals from other countries (e.g., Hispanic nations) are not covered.

Awards tenable only outside the United States: Since there are comprehensive and up-to-date directories that describe all available funding for study and research abroad (see the Annotated Bibliography section), only programs that fund activities in the United States are covered here.

Minority programs that specifically exclude Hispanic Americans: Programs that are open to specific minority groups, but not to Hispanic Americans (e.g., programs only for Asian Americans), are excluded.

Programs that are open equally to all segments of the population: See the Annotated Bibliography section for the names of publications that list and describe these unrestricted programs.

Programs that offer small monetary awards: The emphasis here is on programs that offer significant compensation. If the maximum a program offers is less than $500, it is not included in this listing.

Programs open to residents in a very restricted geographic location: In general, programs are excluded if they are open only to the residents of midsize or smaller counties or cities. a

Programs administered by individual academic institutions solely for their own students: The directory identifies "portable" programs—ones that can be used at any number of schools. Financial aid administered by individual schools specifically for their currently-enrolled students is not covered. Write directly to the schools you are considering to get information on their offerings.

Annotated Bibliography of General Financial Aid Directories. While this directory is the only comprehensive and current listing of financial aid programs available to Hispanic Americans, there are numerous other publications that describe the thousands of resources open equally to all segments of American society. The second section of the directory provides an annotated list of nearly 50 key directories published in the past five years or so that any individual (Hispanic American or not) can use to locate additional sources of financial assistance. The directories are listed by type (general directories; subject or activity directories; directories for special groups; directories listing contests and awards; directories listing internships; nothing over $4.95; and cyberspace sites). Each entry contains basic bibliographic information and an annotation specifying scope, arrangement, publication history, and special features of the source. If a more comprehensive listing of available directories is required, the reader is directed to the evaluative guide published by Reference Service Press: *How to Find Out About Financial Aid and Funding: A Guide to Print, Electronic, and Internet Resources Listing Scholarships, Fellowships, Loans, Grants, Awards, and Internships.*

Indexes.   The six indexes included in *Financial Aid for Hispanic Americans* will facilitate your search for appropriate financial aid opportunities. Program Title, Sponsoring Organization, Residency, Tenability, Subject, and Calendar Indexes follow a word-by-word alphabetical arrangement and pinpoint the entry numbers (not page numbers) that you should check.

> *Program Title Index.*   If you know the name of a particular funding program and want to find out where it is covered in the directory, use the Program Title Index. Here, program names are arranged alphabetically, word by word. To assist you in your search, every program is listed by all its known names, former names, and abbreviations. Since one program can be listed in several subsections (e.g., a program providing assistance to both undergraduate and graduate students is described in both the scholarships and the fellowships subsections), each entry number in the index has been coded to indicate program type (e.g., "F" = Fellowships; "A" = Awards). By using this coding system, you can avoid duplicate entries and turn directly to the programs that match your financial interests.

> *Sponsoring Organization Index.*   This index makes it easy to identify agencies that offer funding primarily or exclusively to Hispanic Americans. Nearly 900 organizations are listed alphabetically, word by word. As in the Program Title Index, we've used a code to help you determine which organizations offer scholarships, fellowships, loans, grants, awards, and/or internships.

> *Residency Index.*   Some programs listed in this book are restricted to Hispanic Americans in a particular city, county, state, or region. Others are open to Hispanic Americans wherever they live. This index helps you identify programs available only to residents in your area as well as programs that have no residency requirements. Further, to assist you in your search, we've also indicated the type of funding offered to residents in each of the areas listed in the index.

> *Tenability Index.*   This index identifies the geographic locations where the funding described in *Financial Aid for Hispanic Americans* may be used. Index entries (city, county, state, province, region, country, continent) are arranged alphabetically (word by word) and subdivided by program type. Use this index when you are looking for money to support your activities in a particular geographic area.

> *Subject Index.*   This index allows you to identify the subject focus of each of the financial aid opportunities described in *Financial Aid for Hispanic Americans* Nearly 300 different subject terms are listed. Extensive "see" and "see also" references, as well as type-of-program subdivisions, will help you in your search for appropriate funding opportunities.

> *Calendar Index.*   Since most financial aid programs have specific deadline dates, some may have closed by the time you begin to look for funding. You can use the Calendar Index to determine which programs are still open. This index is arranged by program type (e.g., scholarship, loan, internship) and subdivided by month during which the deadline falls. Filing dates can and quite often do vary from year to year; consequently, this index should be used only as a guide for deadlines beyond 2005.

HOW TO USE THE DIRECTORY

To Locate Programs Offering a Particular Type of Assistance.   If you are looking for programs offering a particular type of financial aid (e.g., a scholarship for undergraduate courses, a grant for independent research, an award for outstanding literary achievement), first read the definitions of the various

SAMPLE ENTRY

(1) **[61]**

(2) **COLLEGE SCHOLARSHIP PROGRAM OF THE HISPANIC SCHOLARSHIP FUND**

(3) Hispanic Scholarship Fund
Attn: Selection Committee
55 Second Street, Suite 1500
San Francisco, CA 94105
(877) HSF-INFO   Fax: (415) 808-2302
E-mail: info@hsf.net
Web: www.hsf.net

(4) **Purpose** To provide financial assistance for college or graduate school to Hispanic American students.

(5) **Eligibility** This program is open to U.S. citizens, permanent residents, and visitors with a passport stamped I-551. Applicants must be of Hispanic heritage (each parent half Hispanic or 1 parent fully Hispanic) and enrolled full time in a degree-seeking program at an accredited college or university in the United States or Puerto Rico. They may be undergraduate or graduate students, but they must have completed at least 12 undergraduate units with a GPA of 2.7 or higher. Along with their application, they must submit a 2-page essay that addresses the following topics: their Hispanic heritage and family background, personal and academic achievements, academic plans and career goals, efforts toward making a difference in the community, and financial need.

(6) **Financial data** Stipends normally range from $1,000 to $3,000 per year.

(7) **Duration** 1 year; recipients may reapply.

(8) **Additional information** Since this program began in 1975, more than $47 million has been awarded to more than 40,000 Hispanic students. Requests for applications must be accompanied by a self-addressed stamped envelope.

(9) **Number awarded** More than 4,000 each year.

(10) **Deadline** October of each year.

DEFINITION

(1) **Entry number:** Consecutive number assigned to the references and used to index the entry.

(2) **Program title:** Title of scholarship, fellowship, loan, grant, award, or internship.

(3) **Sponsoring organization:** Name, address, and telephone number, toll-free number, fax number, e-mail address, and/or web site (when information was available) for organization sponsoring the program.

(4) **Purpose:** Identifies the major program requirements; read the rest of the entry for additional detail.

(5) **Eligibility:** Qualifications required of applicants.

(6) **Financial data:** Financial details of the program, including fixed sum, average amount, or range of funds offered, expenses for which funds may and may not be applied, and cash-related benefits supplied (e.g., room and board).

(7) **Duration:** Period for which support is provided; renewal prospects.

(8) **Additional information:** Any unusual (generally nonmonetary) benefits, features, restrictions, or limitations associated with the program.

(9) **Number awarded:** Total number of recipients each year or other specified period.

(10) **Deadline:** The month by which applications must be submitted.

program types described on page x in the Introduction and then turn to the appropriate category in the first section of the directory (scholarships, fellowships, loans, grants, awards, or internships). Since programs with multiple purposes are listed in every appropriate location, each of these subsections functions as a self-contained entity. In fact, you can browse through any of the sections or subsections in the directory without first consulting an index.

To Locate a Particular Financial Aid Program. If you know the name of a particular financial aid program, and the type of assistance offered by the program (scholarship, fellowship, grant, etc.), then go directly to the appropriate category in the first section of the directory, where you will find the program profiles arranged alphabetically by title. But be careful: program titles can be misleading. For example, the Cesar Chavez Memorial Leadership Award is actually a scholarship, not an award, while the CLA Scholarship for Minority Students in Memory of Edna Yelland is a fellowship rather than a scholarship. So, if you are looking for a specific program and do not find it in the subsection you have checked, be sure to refer to the Program Title Index to see if it is covered elsewhere in the directory. To save time, always check the Program Title Index first if you know the name of a specific award but are not sure under which subsection it has been listed. Since we index each program by all its known names and abbreviations, you'll also be able to track down a program there when you only know the popular rather than official name.

To Locate Programs Sponsored by a Particular Organization. The Sponsoring Organization Index makes it easy to identify agencies that provide financial assistance to Hispanic Americans or to identify specific financial aid programs offered by a particular organization. Each entry number in the index is coded to identify program type, so that you can easily target appropriate entries.

To Browse Quickly Through the Listings. Turn to the type of funding that interests you (scholarships, fellowships, awards, etc.) and read the "Purpose" paragraph in each entry. In seconds, you'll know if this is an opportunity that you might want to pursue. If it is, be sure to read the rest of the information in the entry, to make sure you meet all of the program requirements before writing or going on the Internet for an application form.

To Locate Funding Available to Hispanic Americans from or Tenable in a Particular City, County, or State. The Residency Index identifies financial aid programs open to Hispanic Americans in a particular city, county, state, region, or country. The Tenability Index shows where the money can be spent. In both indexes, "see" and "see also" references are used liberally, and index entries for a particular geographic area are subdivided by type of program (scholarships, fellowships, loans, grants, awards, internships) to help you identify the funding that's right for you. When using these indexes, always check the listings under the term "United States," since the programs indexed there have no geographic restrictions and can be used in any area.

To Locate Financial Aid Programs Open to Hispanic Americans in a Particular Subject Area. Turn to the Subject Index first if you are interested in identifying financial aid programs for Hispanic Americans in a particular subject area (nearly 300 different subject fields are listed there). To facilitate your search, the type of funding available (scholarships, fellowships, loans, grants, awards, internships) is clearly identified. Extensive cross-references are provided. As part of your search, be sure to check the listings in the index under the heading "General Programs;" those programs provide funding in any subject area (although they may be restricted in other ways).

To Locate Financial Aid Programs for Hispanic Americans by Deadline Date. If you are working with specific time constraints and want to weed out the financial aid programs whose filing dates you won't be able to meet, turn first to the Calendar Index and check the program references listed under the appropriate program type and month. Remember, not all sponsoring organizations supplied deadline information, so not all programs are indexed in this section. To identify every relevant financial aid program, regardless of filing date, read through all the entries in each of the program categories (Scholarships, Fellowships, etc.) that apply.

To Locate Financial Aid Programs Open to All Segments of the Population. Only programs available to Hispanic Americans are listed in this publication. However, there are thousands of other programs that are open equally to all segments of the population. To identify these programs, use the resources described in the second section of the directory, talk to your local librarian, check with your financial aid office on campus, or use a computerized scholarship or grant search service.

PLANS TO UPDATE THE DIRECTORY

This volume, covering 2003-2005, is the fourth edition of *Financial Aid for Hispanic Americans.* The next biennial edition will cover the years 2005-2007 and will be issued in mid-2005.

OTHER RELATED PUBLICATIONS

In addition to *Financial Aid for Hispanic Americans,* Reference Service Press publishes several other titles dealing with fundseeking, including the award-winning *Directory of Financial Aids for Women; Financial Aid for the Disabled and Their Families;* and *Financial Aid for Veterans, Military Personnel, and Their Dependents.* Since each of these titles focuses on a separate population group, there is very little duplication in the listings. For more information on Reference Service Press' publications, write to the company at 5000 Windplay Drive, Suite 4, El Dorado Hills, CA 95762, call us at (916) 939-9620, fax us at (916) 939-9626, send us an e-mail at findaid@aol.com, or visit us on the web: www.rspfunding.com.

ACKNOWLEDGEMENTS

A debt of gratitude is owed all the organizations that contributed information to the 2003-2005 edition of *Financial Aid for Hispanic Americans.* Their generous cooperation has helped to make this publication a current and comprehensive survey of awards.

ABOUT THE AUTHORS

Dr. Gail Ann Schlachter has worked for nearly three decades as a library administrator, a library educator, and an administrator of library-related publishing companies. Among the reference books to her credit are the biennially-issued *Directory of Financial Aids for Women* and two award-winning bibliographic guides: *Minorities and Women: A Guide to Reference Literature in the Social Sciences* (which was chosen as an "outstanding reference book of the year" by *Choice)* and *Reference Sources in Library and Information Services* (which won the first Knowledge Industry Publications "Award for Library Literature"). She was the reference book review editor for *RQ* (now *Reference and User Services Quarterly)* for 10 years, is a past president of the American Library Association's Reference and User Services Association, and is the former editor-in-chief of the *Reference and User Services Association Quarterly.* In recognition of her outstanding contributions to reference service, Dr. Schlachter has been awarded both the Isadore Gilbert Mudge Citation and the Louis Shores/Oryx Press Award.

Dr. R. David Weber teaches economics and history at East Los Angeles College (Wilmington, California), where he directed the Honors Program for many years. He has written a number of critically-acclaimed reference works, including *Dissertations in Urban History* and the three-volume *Energy Information Guide.* With Gail Schlachter, he is the author of Reference Service Press' *Financial Aid for the Disabled and Their Families,* which was selected by *Library Journal* as one of the "best reference books of the year," and a number of other financial aid titles, including the *College Student's Guide to Merit and Other No-Need Funding,* which was selected as one of the "outstanding reference books of the year" by *Choice.*

Financial Aid Programs
Open to Hispanic Americans

- Scholarships
- Fellowships
- Loans
- Grants
- Awards
- Internships

Scholarships

Described here are 384 funding programs open to Hispanic Americans that are available to fund studies on the undergraduate level in the United States. Usually no return of service or repayment is required. Note: other funding opportunities for Hispanic American undergraduates are also described in the Loans, Grants, Awards, and Internships sections. So, if you are looking for a particular program and don't find it in this section, be sure to check the Program Title Index to see if it is covered elsewhere in the directory.

[1]
AAHCPA LOS ANGELES CHAPTER SCHOLARSHIPS

American Association of Hispanic Certified Public
  Accountants–Los Angeles Chapter
P.O. Box 71235
Los Angeles, CA 90071-0235
(213) 688-5160   E-mail: info@aahcpa-la.org
Web: www.aahcpa-la.org

Purpose To provide financial assistance to Hispanic undergraduate accounting students in southern California.

Eligibility This program is open to undergraduate students at colleges and universities in southern California who have demonstrated an interest in accounting. Applicants must be of Hispanic descent and have completed or be enrolled in an intermediate accounting course. Selection is based on academic achievement, financial need, and community involvement.

Financial data The stipends depend on the availability of funds and the need of the recipient.

Duration 1 year.

Additional information Information is also available from Erika Rodriguez, Director of Scholarships, (213) 356-6159.

Number awarded 1 or more each year.

[2]
AAHCPA NORTHERN CALIFORNIA CHAPTER SCHOLARSHIP

American Association of Hispanic Certified Public
  Accountants–Northern California Chapter
c/o Reynaldo E. Arellano, CPA
BoostWorks, Inc.
221 Main Street, Suite 770
San Francisco, CA 94126-6109
(415) 546-9100, ext. 104   Fax: (415) 354-3324
E-mail: rarellano@boostworks.com
Web: www.Hispanic-cpa.org

Purpose To provide financial assistance to Hispanic American college students in the San Francisco Bay area who are interested in majoring in accounting.

Eligibility Hispanic American students at accredited San Francisco Bay area 4-year colleges and universities are eligible to apply if they are majoring or minoring in accounting. Applicants must be juniors or seniors in college and be enrolled in or have completed intermediate accounting. They must have at least a 3.0 GPA and be taking at least 3 courses each semester. Selection is based on academic record, financial need, extracurricular activities, and an essay on 1) the most significant challenges they had to overcome; 2) their 3 most important academic and/or professional goals; or 3) the 2 most influential individuals in their lives.

Financial data The stipend is $1,000.

Duration 1 year. Recipients must either be members of the American Association of Hispanic CPA's Northern California Chapter or join the chapter before receiving scholarship funds.

Number awarded 1 or more each year.

Deadline October of each year.

[3]
ABC HISPANIC SCHOLARSHIP FUNDS

American Baptist Churches USA
Attn: Educational Ministries
P.O. Box 851
Valley Forge, PA 19482-0851
(610) 768-2067   (800) ABC-3USA, ext. 2067
Fax: (610) 768-2056   E-mail: paula.weiss@abc-usa.org
Web: www.abc-em.org

Purpose To provide financial assistance to Hispanic Americans who are interested in preparing for or furthering a church career in the American Baptist Church (ABC).

Eligibility This program is open to Hispanic American members of the church or its recognized institutions who demonstrate financial need. They must be enrolled on at least a two-thirds basis in an accredited institution, working on an undergraduate degree or first professional degree in a seminary. Applicants must be currently serving or planning to serve in a vocation with the church or with its recognized institutions. They must be U.S. citizens who have been a member of an American Baptist Church for at least 1 year.

Financial data The stipend is $500 per year.

Duration 1 year; may be renewed.

Deadline May of each year.

[4]
ACCOUNTANCY BOARD OF OHIO EDUCATIONAL ASSISTANCE PROGRAM

Accountancy Board of Ohio
77 South High Street, 18th Floor
Columbus, OH 43266-0301
(614) 466-4135   Fax: (614) 466-2628
Web: www.state.oh.us./acc/educasst.html

Purpose To provide financial assistance to minority and financially disadvantaged students enrolled in an accounting education program at Ohio academic institutions approved by the Accountancy Board of Ohio.

Eligibility Minority and financially disadvantaged students in Ohio may apply if they are beginning their sophomore year. Minority is defined as people with significant ancestry from Africa (excluding the Middle East), Asia (excluding the Middle East), Central America and the Caribbean islands, South America, and the islands of the Pacific Ocean. Students who remain in good standing at their institutions and who enter a qualified fifth year program may receive a scholarship award. The criteria that must be met for a student to qualify for the scholarship are: enrolled full time in an accredited Ohio college or university, submit the initial application when a sophomore or junior, be majoring in accounting or a comparable program leading to a CPA certificate, and be in good standing academically.

Financial data The amount of the stipend is determined annually but is intended to provide substantive relief from the cost of study.

Duration 1 year.

Number awarded Several each year.

Deadline May or November of each year.

[5]
¡ADELANTE! FUND SCHOLARSHIP PROGRAM

¡Adelante! U.S. Education Leadership Fund
8415 Datapoint Drive, Suite 400
San Antonio, TX 78229
(210) 692-1971   Fax: (210) 692-1951
E-mail: rubeng@dcci.com

Purpose To provide financial aid, internships, and leadership training to upper-division Hispanic students enrolled in Hispanic Serving Institutions (HSIs).

Eligibility This program is open to Hispanic students currently enrolled in HSIs. Applicants must have a GPA of 3.0 or higher, be eligible to receive financial aid, be juniors or seniors in college, agree to attend the Adelante Leadership Institute, be eligible to participate in a summer internship, exhibit leadership, and provide 2 letters of recommendation. Most recipients are the first in their families to complete a college education.

Financial data The maximum stipend is $3,000 per year.

Duration 1 year.

Additional information This fund was established by the Hispanic Association of Colleges and Universities in 1997 and became a separate organization in 1999. Recipients must participate in a summer internship and the Adelante Leadership Institute.

Number awarded Varies each year; recently, 22 students received scholarships.

[6]
AIA/AAF MINORITY/DISADVANTAGED SCHOLARSHIP PROGRAM

American Institute of Architects
Attn: American Architectural Foundation
1735 New York Avenue, N.W.
Washington, DC 20006-5292
(202) 626-7318   Fax: (202) 626-7420
E-mail: info@archfoundation.org
Web: www.archfoundation.org/scholarships/index.htm

Purpose To provide financial assistance to high school and college students from minority and/or disadvantaged backgrounds who are interested in studying architecture in college.

Eligibility This program is open to students from minority and/or disadvantaged backgrounds who are high school seniors, students in a community college or technical school transferring to an accredited architectural program, or college freshmen entering a professional degree program at an accredited program of architecture. Students who have completed 1 or more years of a 4-year college curriculum are not eligible. Initially, candidates must be nominated by 1 of the following organizations or persons: an individual architect or firm, a component of the American Institute of Architects (AIA), a community design center, a guidance counselor or teacher, the dean or professor at an accredited school of architecture, or the director of a community or civic organization. Nominees are reviewed and eligible candidates are invited to complete an application form in which they write an essay describing the reasons they are interested in becoming an architect and provide documentation of academic excellence and financial need. Selection is based primarily on financial need.

Financial data Awards range from $500 to $2,500 per year, depending upon individual need. Students must apply for supplementary funds from other sources.

Duration 9 months; may be renewed for up to 2 additional years.

Additional information This program is offered jointly by the American Architectural Foundation (AAF) and the AIA.

Number awarded 20 each year.

Deadline Nominations are due by December of each year; final applications must be submitted in January.

[7]
AIR FORCE ROTC HOST MINORITY SCHOLARSHIP PROGRAM

U.S. Air Force
Attn: Headquarters AFROTC/RRUC
551 East Maxwell Boulevard
Maxwell AFB, AL 36112-6106
(334) 953-2091   (800) 522-0033, ext. 2091
Fax: (334) 953-5271
Web: www.afrotc.com

Purpose To provide financial assistance to students at designated predominantly Hispanic universities who are willing to serve as Air Force officers following completion of their bachelor's degree.

Eligibility Applicants must be U.S. citizens at least 17 years of age who are currently enrolled or have been accepted as sophomores or juniors at a designated predominantly Hispanic university that has an Air Force ROTC unit on campus. They must have completed 1 or 2 years of study at the university and have a cumulative GPA of 2.5 or higher. At the time of graduation with a bachelor's degree, applicants may be no more than 27 years of age. They must agree to serve for at least 4 years as active-duty Air Force officers following graduation from college.

Financial data Currently, awards are type 2 AFROTC scholarships that provide for payment of tuition and fees, to a maximum of $15,000 per year, plus an annual book allowance of $510. All recipients are also awarded a tax-free subsistence allowance for 10 months of each year that is $250 per month during the sophomore year, $300 during the junior year, and $350 during the senior year.

Duration 2 to 3 years, until completion of a bachelor's degree.

Additional information Currently, the designated universities are New Mexico State University, the University of New Mexico, the University of Puerto Rico at Rio Piedras, the University of Puerto Rico at Mayaguez, and the University of Texas at San Antonio. While scholarship recipients can major in any subject, they must complete 4 years of aerospace studies courses. They must also attend a 4-week summer training camp at an Air Force base, usually between their sophomore and junior years; 2-year scholarship awardees attend in the summer after their junior year. Current military personnel are eligible for early release from active duty in order to enter the Air Force ROTC program. Following completion of their bachelor's degree, scholarship recipients earn a commission as a second lieutenant in the Air Force and serve at least 4 years.

[8]
ALICE NEWELL JOSLYN MEDICAL FUND

Beca Foundation
Attn: Ana Garcia, Operations Manager
830 East Grand Avenue, Suite B
Escondido, CA 92025
(760) 741-8246   Fax: (760) 741-8716

Purpose To provide financial assistance to Latino students in

San Diego County, California who are interested in preparing for a career in the health field.

Eligibility This program is open to Latino students living or attending college in San Diego County. They may be high school seniors planning to enter the medical/health care profession (i.e., nursing, dental/medical assistance, physical therapy) or students already in college and majoring in the health field. Selection is based on financial need, scholastic abilities, and contributions, both now and in the future, to the Latino community.

Financial data Stipends range from $1,000 to $2,000 per year.

Duration 1 year; may be renewed up to 3 additional years depending on scholastic progress.

Number awarded 1 or more each year.

Deadline February of each year.

[9]
ALLFIRST/HCF SCHOLARSHIP PROGRAM

Hispanic College Fund
Attn: National Director
1717 Pennsylvania Avenue, N.W., Suite 460
Washington, D.C. 20006
(800) 644-4223   Fax: (202) 296-3774
E-mail: hispaniccollegefund@earthlink.net
Web: www.hispanicfund.org

Purpose To provide financial assistance to Hispanic American undergraduate students from designated areas of Maryland, Virginia, and Pennsylvania who are interested in preparing for a career in business, computer science, or engineering.

Eligibility This program is open to U.S. citizens of Hispanic background who are entering their freshman, sophomore, junior, or senior year of college. Residency in the following areas is required: Maryland, northern Virginia (Loudoun or Fairfax counties), or south central Pennsylvania (Adams, Berks, Chester, Cumberland, Dauphin, Franklin, Lancaster, Lebanon, Lehigh, Montgomery, Northampton, or York counties). Applicants must be working on a bachelor's degree in business, computer science, engineering, or a business-related major and have a cumulative GPA of 3.0 or higher. They must be applying to or enrolled in a college or university in the 50 states or Puerto Rico as a full-time student. Financial need is considered in the selection process.

Financial data Stipends range from $500 to $5,000, depending on the need of the recipient. The sponsor's goal is to have the average award be $3,000. Funds are paid directly to the recipient's college or university to help cover tuition and fees.

Duration 1 year; recipients may reapply.

Additional information This program is sponsored by Allfirst Financial Inc. and administered by the Hispanic College Fund (HCF).

Number awarded Varies each year; recently, 6 of these scholarships were awarded.

Deadline April of each year.

[10]
AMELIA KEMP MEMORIAL SCHOLARSHIP

Women of the Evangelical Lutheran Church in America
Attn: Scholarships
8765 West Higgins Road
Chicago, IL 60631-4189
(773) 380-2730   (800) 638-3522, ext. 2730
Fax: (773) 380-2419   E-mail: womenelca@elca.org
Web: www.elca.org/wo/index.html

Purpose To provide financial assistance to lay women of color who are members of Evangelical Lutheran Church of America (ELCA) congregations and who wish to study on the undergraduate, graduate, professional, or vocational school level.

Eligibility These scholarships are available to ELCA lay women of color who are at least 21 years of age and have experienced an interruption of at least 2 years in their education since high school. Applicants must have been admitted to an educational institution to prepare for a career in other than a church-certified profession. U.S. citizenship is required.

Financial data The amount of the award varies, depending on the availability of funds.

Duration Up to 2 years.

Number awarded Varies each year, depending upon the funds available.

Deadline February of each year.

[11]
AMERICAN ASSOCIATION OF BLACKS IN ENERGY SCHOLARSHIP

American Association of Blacks in Energy
Attn: Scholarship Committee
927 15th Street, N.W., Suite 200
Washington, DC 20005
(202) 371-9530   Fax: (202) 371-9218
E-mail: aabe@aabe.org
Web: www.aabe.org/mission/scholarships.html

Purpose To provide financial assistance to underrepresented minority high school seniors who are interested in majoring in engineering, mathematics, or physical science in college.

Eligibility This program is open to members of minority groups underrepresented in the energy industry (African Americans, Hispanics, and Native Americans) who are graduating high school seniors. Applicants must have a "B" academic average overall and a "B" average in mathematics and science courses. They must be planning to attend an accredited college or university to major in engineering, mathematics, or the physical sciences. Along with their application, they must submit a 350-word essay covering why they should receive this scholarship, their professional career objectives, and any other pertinent information. Financial need is also considered in the selection process. The applicant who demonstrates the most outstanding achievement and promise is presented with the Premier Award. All applications must be submitted to the local office of the sponsoring organization in the student's state. For a list of local offices, contact the scholarship committee at the national office.

Financial data The stipends are $1,500. The Premier Award is an additional $3,000. All funds are paid directly to the students upon proof of enrollment at an accredited college or university.

Duration 1 year; nonrenewable.

Number awarded 6 each year (1 in each of the organization's regions); of those 6 winners, 1 is chosen to receive the Premier Award.

Deadline   February of each year.

[12]
AMERICAN CHEMICAL SOCIETY SCHOLARS PROGRAM

American Chemical Society
Attn: Department of Diversity Programs
1155 16th Street, N.W.
Washington, DC 20036
(202) 872-6250   (800) 227-5558, ext. 6250
Fax: (202) 776-8003   E-mail: scholars@acs.org
Web: www.acs.org/scholars

Purpose   To provide financial assistance to underrepresented minority students with a strong interest in chemistry and a desire to pursue a career in a chemically-related science.

Eligibility   This program is open to high school seniors and college freshmen, sophomores, and juniors intending to enroll or already enrolled full time at an accredited college, university, or community college. Applicants must be African American, Hispanic/Latino, or American Indian. They must be majoring or planning to major in chemistry, biochemistry, chemical engineering, or other chemically-related fields such as environmental science, materials science, or toxicology, and planning to pursue a career in 1 of those fields. Students interested in 2-year chemical technology programs and careers in that field are also eligible. Students planning careers in medicine or pharmacy are not eligible. U.S. citizenship or permanent resident status is required. Selection is based on academic merit (GPA of 3.0 or higher) and financial need.

Financial data   The maximum stipend is $2,500 for the freshman year in college or $3,000 per year for sophomores, juniors, and seniors.

Duration   1 year; nonrenewable.

Number awarded   More than 200 each year.

Deadline   February of each year.

[13]
AMERICAN DENTAL HYGIENISTS' ASSOCIATION INSTITUTE MINORITY SCHOLARSHIP

American Dental Hygienists' Association
Attn: Institute for Oral Health
444 North Michigan Avenue, Suite 3400
Chicago, IL 60611
(312) 440-8944   (800) 735-4916
Fax: (312) 440-8929   E-mail: institute@adha.net
Web: www.adha.org

Purpose   To provide financial assistance to minority students and males of any race enrolled in certificate/associate programs in dental hygiene.

Eligibility   This program is open to members of groups currently underrepresented in the dental hygiene profession: Native Americans, African Americans, Hispanics, Asians, and males. Applicants must have completed 1 year in a dental hygiene curriculum at the certificate/associate level with at least a 3.0 GPA. They must intend to be full-time students and be able to demonstrate financial need.

Financial data   The amount of the award depends on the need of the recipient, to a maximum of $1,500.

Duration   1 year; nonrenewable.

Number awarded   2 each year.

Deadline   May of each year.

[14]
AMERICAN DIETETIC ASSOCIATION BACCALAUREATE OR COORDINATED PROGRAM

American Dietetic Association
Attn: Accreditation, Education Programs, and Student Operations
216 West Jackson Boulevard, Suite 800
Chicago, IL 60606-6995
(312) 899-0040   (800) 877-1600, ext. 5400
Fax: (312) 899-4817   E-mail: education@eatright.org
Web: www.eatright.org

Purpose   To provide financial assistance to students who will be at least juniors in a CADE-approved college or university program in dietetics.

Eligibility   Applicants must have completed the academic requirements in a CADE-accredited/approved college or university program for at least junior status in the dietetics program. All applicants must be U.S. citizens or permanent residents and show promise of being a valuable, contributing member of the profession. Some scholarships require membership in the association, specific dietetic practice group membership, residency in a specific state, or underrepresented minority group status. The same application form can be used for all categories.

Financial data   Awards range from $500 to $5,000.

Duration   1 year.

Number awarded   Varies each year, depending upon the funds available. Recently, the sponsoring organization awarded 209 scholarships for all its programs.

Deadline   February of each year.

[15]
AMERICAN GI FORUM OF THE UNITED STATES SCHOLARSHIPS

American GI Forum of the United States
Attn: Hispanic Education Foundation
P.O. Box 952
Ulysses, KS 67880
(620) 356-4070   Fax: (620) 424-2745

Purpose   To provide financial assistance for postsecondary education to needy and qualified students of Hispanic descent.

Eligibility   High school seniors, high school graduates, and college students are eligible to apply if they need money to attend college. Selection is based on academic achievement, financial need, general leadership qualities, and career aspirations. Each local chapter administers its own program; for the chapter chair in your area, contact the national office.

Financial data   The amount awarded varies, depending upon the availability of funds and the recipient's financial need.

Duration   1 year; recipients may reapply.

Additional information   Chapters are located in Arizona, California, Colorado, Idaho, Illinois, Kansas, Michigan, Nebraska, New Mexico, Oklahoma, Nevada, Texas, Utah, Washington, and Washington, D.C.

Number awarded   Varies each year.

Deadline   Each chapter sets its own application deadline.

[16]
AMERICAN METEOROLOGICAL SOCIETY UNDERGRADUATE SCHOLARSHIPS

American Meteorological Society
Attn: Fellowship/Scholarship Coordinator
45 Beacon Street
Boston, MA 02108-3693
(617) 227-2426, ext. 246   Fax: (617) 742-8718
E-mail: amsinfo@ametsoc.org
Web: www.ametsoc.org

Purpose To provide financial assistance to undergraduates majoring in meteorology or some aspect of atmospheric sciences.

Eligibility This program is open to undergraduate students entering their final year of study and majoring in meteorology or some aspect of the atmospheric or related oceanic and hydrologic sciences. Applicants must intend to make atmospheric or related sciences their career. They must be U.S. citizens or permanent residents, be enrolled full time in an accredited U.S. institution, and have a cumulative GPA of 3.0 or higher. Along with their application, they must submit a 100-word essay on their most important achievements that qualify them for this scholarship and a 500-word essay on their career goals in the atmospheric or related oceanic or hydrologic fields. Selection is based on academic excellence and achievement; financial need is not considered. The sponsor specifically encourages applications from women, minorities, and students with disabilities who are traditionally underrepresented in the atmospheric and related oceanic sciences.

Financial data Stipends range from $700 to $5,000 per year.

Duration 1 year.

Additional information This program includes the following named scholarships: the Howard H. Hanks, Jr. Scholarship in Meteorology ($700), the AMS 75th Anniversary Scholarship ($2,000), the Ethan and Allan Murphy Memorial Scholarship ($2,000), the Howard T. Orville Scholarship in Meteorology ($2,000), the Dr. Pedro Grau Undergraduate Scholarship ($2,500, 2 awarded), the Guillermo Salazar Rodriguez Scholarship ($2,500, 2 awarded), the John R. Hope Scholarship ($2,500), the Richard and Helen Hagemeyer Scholarship ($3,000), and the Werner A. Baum Undergraduate Scholarship ($5,000). Requests for an application must be accompanied by a self-addressed stamped envelope.

Number awarded 11 each year.

Deadline February of each year.

[17]
AMERICAN PHILOLOGICAL ASSOCIATION MINORITY SCHOLARSHIP

American Philological Association
Attn: Executive Director
University of Pennsylvania
291 Logan Hall
249 South 36th Street
Philadelphia, PA 19104-6304
(215) 898-4975   Fax: (215) 573-7874
E-mail: apaclassics@sas.upenn.edu
Web: www.apaclassics.org

Purpose To prepare minority undergraduates during the summer for advanced work in the classics.

Eligibility Eligible to apply are minority (African American, Hispanic American, Asian American, and Native American) under-graduate students who wish to engage in summer study as preparation for graduate work in the classics. Applicants may propose participation in summer programs in Italy, Greece, Egypt, or other classical centers; language training at institutions in the United States or Canada; or other relevant courses of study. Selection is based on academic qualifications, especially in classics; demonstrated ability in at least 1 classical language; quality of the proposal for study with respect to preparation for a career in classics; and financial need. Applications must be endorsed by a member of the American Philological Association (APA).

Financial data The maximum award is $3,000.

Duration 1 summer.

Additional information Information is also available from Professor T. Davina McClain, Loyola University, Department of Classical Studies, 6363 St. Charles Avenue, Box 113, New Orleans, LA 70118, (504) 865-3683, Fax: (504) 865-2257, E-mail: mcclain@loyno.edu.

Number awarded 1 each year.

Deadline February of each year.

[18]
ANHEUSER-BUSCH FOUNDATION SCHOLARSHIPS

Chicago Urban League
Attn: Scholarship Coordinator
4510 South Michigan Avenue
Chicago, IL 60653-3898
(773) 451-3567   Fax: (773) 285-7772
E-mail: info@cul-chicago.org
Web: www.cul-chicago.org

Purpose To provide financial assistance to Illinois residents of color interested in full-time study at a 4-year college or university.

Eligibility This program is open to minority residents of Illinois who will be full-time freshmen at a 4-year college or university. Applicants must have a GPA of 2.5 or higher and be able to demonstrate financial need. An interview is required.

Financial data The stipend is $2,500 per year.

Duration 4 years.

Additional information This program is supported by the Anheuser-Busch Foundation, which makes the final decision on selection of recipients.

Number awarded Varies each year.

Deadline May of each year.

[19]
ANNA GRACE SAWYER MINORITY SCHOLARSHIP

Presbytery of Chicago
Attn: Scholarship Coordinator
100 South Morgan Street
Chicago, IL 60607-2619
(312) 243-8300   Fax: (312) 243-8409
E-mail: roseblaney@chicagopresbytery.org
Web: www.chicagopresbytery.org

Purpose To provide financial assistance for college to minority students from the Chicago area who are affiliated with the Presbyterian Church (USA).

Eligibility This program is open to confirmed members of a Presbyterian Church in the Chicago Presbytery and, for nonmembers, participants in the youth program of those churches. Applicants must be African Americans, Hispanic Americans, Asian Americans, or Native Americans who have been accepted or are currently enrolled as a full-time undergraduate at an accredited college, university, or vocational school. They must demonstrate a volunteer spirit through service to others. Selection is based on the applicant's personal and financial situation and current and potential service to others.

Financial data   Stipends range from $100 to $1,000. The exact amount awarded depends on the availability of funds.

Duration   1 year; recipients may reapply.

Additional information   The Presbytery of Chicago covers Cook, DuPage, and Lake counties.

Number awarded   1 or more each year.

Deadline   April of each year.

[20]
APPRAISAL INSTITUTE MINORITIES AND WOMEN EDUCATIONAL SCHOLARSHIP PROGRAM

Appraisal Institute
Attn: Minorities and Women Scholarship Fund
875 North Michigan Avenue, Suite 2400
Chicago, IL 60611-1980
(312) 335-4121   Fax: (312) 335-4200
E-mail: sbarnes@appraisalinstitute.org
Web: www.appraisalinstitute.org

Purpose   To provide financial assistance to women and minority undergraduate students majoring in real estate or allied fields.

Eligibility   This program is open to members of ethnic, racial, and gender minority groups underrepresented in the real estate appraisal profession. Those groups include women, American Indians, Alaska Natives, Asians, Black or African Americans, Hispanics or Latinos, and Native Hawaiians or other Pacific Islanders. Applicants must be full- or part-time students enrolled in real estate courses within a degree-granting college, university, or junior college. They must submit evidence of demonstrated financial need and a GPA of 2.5 or higher.

Financial data   The stipend is $1,000 per year. Funds are paid directly to the recipient's institution to be used for tuition and fees.

Duration   1 year.

Number awarded   At least 1 each year.

Deadline   April of each year.

[21]
ARKANSAS FRESHMAN/SOPHOMORE MINORITY GRANT PROGRAM

Arkansas Department of Higher Education
Attn: Financial Aid Division
114 East Capitol Avenue
Little Rock, AR 72201-3818
(501) 371-2050   (800) 54-STUDY
Fax: (501) 371-2001   E-mail: finaid@adhe.arknet.edu
Web: www.arscholarships.com/minoritygrant.html

Purpose   To provide financial assistance to minority college students in Arkansas who want to become teachers.

Eligibility   This program is open to minority (African American, Hispanic, or Asian American) residents of Arkansas who are full-time freshmen and sophomores in college and interested in teacher education programs. Applicants must be attending an approved Arkansas public or private college or university. They must sign a statement of interest in teaching and participate in pre-service internships in public school settings.

Financial data   The stipend is $1,000 per year.

Duration   1 year; may be renewed for 1 additional year.

Additional information   Information is available from the teacher certifying official at 4-year institutions or the vice president for academic affairs, academic dean, or dean of instruction at 2-year institutions.

Number awarded   Varies each year; recently, 250 of these scholarships were awarded.

[22]
ARTHUR GOODMAN MEMORIAL SCHOLARSHIPS

San Diego Foundation
Attn: Scholarship Committee
1420 Kettner Boulevard, Suite 500
P.O. Box 81107
San Diego, CA 92138-1107
(619) 235-2300, ext. 133   Fax: (619) 239-1710
E-mail: sdf@sdfoundation.org
Web: www.sdfoundation.org

Purpose   To provide financial assistance to women and minority college students from southern California who are interested in preparing for a career related to economic and community development.

Eligibility   This program is open to women and minority residents of Imperial, Orange, Riverside, and San Diego counties who have completed 2 years of community college study and are ready to transfer to a 4-year college or university. Applicants must be interested in studying fields related to economic and community development, including public finance, social services, housing, and small business lending. They must have a GPA of 3.0 or higher and be able to submit a letter of recommendation from a supervisor or mentor of a community service or economic development project with which they have worked.

Financial data   The stipend averages $1,000.

Duration   1 year.

Number awarded   4 each year.

Deadline   March of each year.

[23]
ASCE MAINE SECTION SCHOLARSHIP

American Society of Civil Engineers-Maine Section
c/o Holly Anderson, P.E.
Maine Department of Transportation
Highway Design Division
16 State House Section
Augusta, ME 04333-0016
(207) 287-2126   E-mail: holly.anderson@state.me.us

Purpose   To provide financial assistance to high school seniors in Maine who are interested in studying civil engineering in college.

Eligibility   This program is open to graduating high school seniors who are Maine residents and who intend to study civil engineering in college. Women and minorities are especially encouraged to apply. Selection is based on academic performance, extracurricular activities, letters of recommendation, and statement of interest in civil engineering as a career.

Financial data   The stipend is $1,000.

Duration   1 year; nonrenewable.

Number awarded   1 each year.

Deadline   January of each year.

[24]
ASOCIACION SALVADORENA AMERICANA DE VIRGINIA SCHOLARSHIP

Asociación Salvadoreña Americana de Virginia
Attn: Scholarship Committee
859 North Larrimore Street
Arlington, VA 22205
(703) 538-5909

Purpose To provide financial assistance for college to residents of Salvadoran descent in the Washington, D.C. metropolitan area.

Eligibility Applicants must be of Salvadoran descent and residents of the metropolitan Washington, D.C. area. They must have a basic knowledge of Spanish and have limited financial resources (copies of their previous year's tax return must be provided). There are no age restrictions; graduating high school seniors, high school graduates, and currently-enrolled or returning college students (including adults) may apply. As part of the application process, students must submit a completed application form and a 500-word essay (preferably in Spanish) that answers the following: "As someone of Salvadoran descent, keeping in mind the crisis that El Salvador is going through, how have you helped or are going to help in the process of reconstruction of the country?"

Financial data A stipend is awarded (amount not specified).

Duration 1 year.

Number awarded 1 or more each year.

Deadline August of each year.

[25]
ASSOCIATED COLLEGES OF ILLINOIS SCHOLARSHIP PROGRAM

Associated Colleges of Illinois
Attn: Executive Director
20 North Wacker Drive, Suite 4114
Chicago, IL 60606
(312) 263-2391, ext. 23   Fax: (312) 263-3424
E-mail: aci@acifund.org
Web: www.acifund.org/pages/programs/scholarships.htm

Purpose To provide financial assistance to students attending or planning to attend an academic institution affiliated with the Associated Colleges of Illinois (ACI).

Eligibility Eligible to apply are students entering or currently enrolled at the 24 private colleges and universities that are members of ACI. The program includes 5 categories of awards: 1) first-generation and minority scholarships, to support students who are the first in their family to attend college and encourage minority achievement and graduation; 2) college-to-work scholarships, to attract more students to specific fields of study and career paths; 3) basic needs scholarships, to address students' unmet financial needs; 4) emergency assistance scholarships, to direct critical financial support to students experiencing personal or family emergencies; and 5) academic merit scholarships, to reward the best and the brightest students.

Financial data Awards depend on the availability of funds and the need of the recipient.

Duration 1 year; may be renewed.

Additional information Members of ACI are Augustana College, Aurora University, Barat College, Concordia University, Dominican University, Elmhurst College, Eureka College, Greenville College, Illinois College, Illinois Wesleyan University, Knox College, Lake Forest College, Lewis University, McKendree College, Millikin University, Monmouth College, North Central College, North Park University, Olivet Nazarene University, Principia College, Quincy University, Saint Xavier University, Trinity Christian College, and University of St. Francis. This program includes the following named scholarships: the A. Montgomery Ward Scholarship, the Aileen S. Andrew Foundation, the Betty A. DeVries Memorial Fund, the Carole B. Whitcomb Endowed Scholarship, the Catherine McGuire Memorial Fund, the CBS Scholarship Program of the Westinghouse Foundation, the Frank J. Lewis Scholarship, the James R. Donnelley Scholarship, the Jay Frey Scholarship, the Grover Hermann Foundation Scholarship, the McGraw Foundation Emergency Award, the Michele and Peter Willmott Fund for Minority Leadership, the Motorola Scholarship, the Motorola Minority Scholarship, the Pepper Family Foundation Scholarship, the Polk Brothers Minority Scholarship, the Sean M. Staudt Memorial Scholarship, the Sterling/Rock Falls Scholarship, the Toni S. Smith Scholarship, and the UPS Scholarship.

Number awarded Varies each year; recently, 139 scholarships worth nearly $250,000 were awarded.

[26]
ASSOCIATION OF CUBAN ENGINEERS SCHOLARSHIPS

Association of Cuban Engineers
Attn: President
P.O. Box 557575
Miami, FL 33255-7575
(305) 649-7429

Purpose To provide financial assistance to undergraduate and graduate students of Cuban American heritage and others who are interested in preparing for a career in engineering.

Eligibility This program is open to U.S. citizens and legal residents who have completed at least 50 units of college work in the United States and are majoring or planning to major in some aspect of engineering. Applicants must be attending an ABET-accredited college or university within the United States or Puerto Rico as a full-time student. They must be of Cuban American heritage. If an insufficient number of qualified Cuban American students apply, scholarships may be made available to other Hispanic, African American, and women applicants. Selection is based on GPA (up to 35 points, 3.0 or higher), financial need (up to 25 points for an applicant needing $5,470), participation in extracurricular activities (up to 25 points), and student class standing (3.75 points for sophomores, 7.5 points for juniors, 11.25 points for seniors, and 15 points for graduate students).

Financial data Stipends range from $500 to $1,000 per year.

Duration 1 year.

Additional information This program includes the Luciano Goicochea Award (for the top-rated Cuban American student at Florida International University) and the Noel Betancourt Award (for the top-rated Cuban American student at the University of Miami).

Number awarded Up to 20 each year.

Deadline October of each year.

[27]
ASSOCIATION OF LATINO PROFESSIONALS IN FINANCE AND ACCOUNTING SCHOLARSHIPS

Association of Latino Professionals in Finance and
    Accounting
Attn: National Executive Director
510 West Sixth Street, Suite 400
Los Angeles, CA 90017
(213) 243-0004   Fax: (213) 243-0006
E-mail: scholarships.national@alpfa.org
Web: www.alpfa.org

Purpose　To provide financial assistance to undergraduate and graduate students of Hispanic descent who are preparing for a career in a field related to finance or accounting.

Eligibility　This program is open to full-time undergraduate and graduate students who have completed at least 15 undergraduate units at a college or university in the United States or Puerto Rico with a GPA of 3.0 or higher. Applicants must be of Hispanic heritage, defined as having 1 parent fully Hispanic or both parents half Hispanic. They must be pursuing a degree in accounting, finance, or a related field. Along with their application, they must submit a 2-page personal statement that addresses their Hispanic heritage and family background, personal and academic achievements, academic plans and career goals, efforts and plans for making a difference in their community, and financial need. U.S. citizenship or permanent resident status is required.

Financial data　The stipend is at least $1,250 per year.

Duration　1 year.

Additional information　The sponsoring organization was formerly named the American Association of Hispanic Certified Public Accountants. This program is administered by the Hispanic Scholarship Fund, 55 Second Street, Suite 1500, San Francisco, CA 94105, (877) HSF-INFO, E-mail: specialprograms@hsf.net.

Number awarded　Varies each year; recently, 78 of these scholarships, worth $195,000, were awarded.

Deadline　May of each year.

[28]
ASTRAZENECA PHARMACEUTICALS SCHOLARS PROGRAM

American Chemical Society
Attn: Department of Diversity Programs
1155 16th Street, N.W.
Washington, DC 20036
(202) 872-6250   (800) 227-5558, ext. 6250
Fax: (202) 776-8003   E-mail: scholars@acs.org
Web: www.acs.org/scholars

Purpose　To provide financial assistance to underrepresented minority undergraduates from designated states with a strong interest in organic chemistry and a desire to prepare for a career in a chemically-related science.

Eligibility　This program is open to college sophomores with an interest in synthetic organic chemistry who are enrolled in a 4-year undergraduate program. Applicants must be African American, Hispanic/Latino, or American Indian. They must be attending a college or university in or near any of the following locations: Wilmington, Delaware; New Jersey; northeastern Maryland; eastern Pennsylvania; southeastern New York; or Washington, D.C. Students planning careers in medicine or pharmacy are not eligible. U.S. citizenship or permanent resident status is required. Selection is based on academic merit (GPA of 3.0 or higher) and financial need.

Financial data　The maximum stipend is $3,000 per year.

Duration　1 year.

Additional information　This program is offered by the American Chemical Society in cooperation with AstraZeneca Pharmaceuticals, L.P.

Number awarded　Varies each year.

Deadline　February of each year.

[29]
AVON GRANT SCHOLARSHIPS

Chicago Urban League
Attn: Scholarship Coordinator
4510 South Michigan Avenue
Chicago, IL 60653-3898
(773) 451-3567   Fax: (773) 285-7772
E-mail: info@cul-chicago.org
Web: www.cul-chicago.org

Purpose　To provide financial assistance to Illinois residents who are women of color interested in full-time study at a 4-year college or university.

Eligibility　This program is open to minority women residents of Illinois who will be full-time freshmen at a 4-year college or university. Applicants must have a GPA of 2.5 or higher, be a head of household, and be able to demonstrate financial need. An interview is required.

Financial data　The stipend is $1,000 per year.

Duration　1 year.

Number awarded　2 each year.

Deadline　May of each year.

[30]
AZTEC SCHOLARSHIP PROGRAM

Spanish Speaking Citizens' Foundation
Attn: Education Coordinator
1470 Fruitvale Avenue
Oakland, CA 94601
(510) 261-7839   Fax: (510) 261-2968
E-mail: salomon@sscf.org
Web: www.sscf.org/afterschool/mainframe.php3

Purpose　To provide financial assistance to Hispanic seniors in northern California who are interested in going to college.

Eligibility　Awards are limited to residents of Oakland, California, of Hispanic descent, who are high school seniors and planning to attend an accredited public or private university, community college, or vocational school. Applicants must complete an essay in which they describe their family and cultural background, involvement in school and community activities, and plans to become involved in the future development of the Raza/Latino community. Selection is based on scholastic achievement and financial need.

Financial data　The stipend is $750 per year.

Duration　1 year.

Number awarded　10 each year.

Deadline　June of each year.

[31]
BANK OF AMERICA MINORITY STUDENT SCHOLARSHIP

Community Foundation for Palm Beach and Martin Counties
700 South Dixie Highway, Suite 200
West Palm Beach, FL 33401
(561) 659-6800   (888) 853-GIFT (within FL)
Fax: (561) 832-6542   E-mail: info@cfpbmc.org
Web: www.cfpbmc.org

Purpose To provide financial assistance to minority high school seniors in selected areas of Florida who are interested in preparing for a career in business.

Eligibility Applicants must be minority residents of Palm Beach, Martin, or Hendry counties in Florida. Priority is given to economically disadvantaged students in good academic standing who intend to major in business.

Financial data Varies; recently, the stipend was $4,500.

Duration 4 years.

Additional information The funds for this program, established in 1986, are provided by Bank of America, formerly NationsBank and prior to that the Barnett Bank of Palm Beach County.

Number awarded 1 each year.

Deadline February of each year.

[32]
BANK ONE/UNCF CORPORATE SCHOLARS PROGRAM

United Negro College Fund
Attn: Program Services Department
8260 Willow Oaks Corporate Drive
P.O. Box 10444
Fairfax, VA 22031-8044
(703) 205-3490   (866) 671-7237
Fax: (703) 205-3550   E-mail: internship@uncf.org
Web: www.uncf.org/Scholarship/CorporateScholars.asp

Purpose To provide financial assistance and work experience to minority undergraduates who are interested in preparing for a career in banking.

Eligibility This program is open to African American, Asian/Pacific Islander, Hispanic, and Native American/Alaskan Native students at targeted colleges and universities and those that are members of the United Negro College Fund (UNCF). Applicants must be sophomores or juniors with a GPA of 3.0 or higher. All majors are welcome; degrees in accounting, business administration, finance, and retail management are preferred. Along with their application, students must submit an official school transcript, a letter of recommendation from a faculty member, a resume, a personal statement of career interest, and a financial need statement. Finalists are interviewed by representatives of Bank One, the program's sponsor.

Financial data Recipients are assigned paid internships at a Bank One location in the areas of accounting, business administration, and finance. Following successful completion of the internship, they receive a scholarship up to $10,000 to cover school expenses.

Duration 8 weeks for the internship; 1 academic year for the scholarship.

Number awarded 12 each year.

Deadline January of each year.

[33]
BARBARA JORDAN MEMORIAL SCHOLARSHIP

Association of Texas Professional Educators
Attn: Scholarships
305 East Huntland Drive, Suite 300
Austin, TX 78752-3792
(512) 467-0071   (800) 777-ATPE
Fax: (512) 467-2203
Web: www.atpe.org/AboutATPE/bjordaninfo.htm

Purpose To provide financial assistance to undergraduate and graduate students enrolled in educator preparation programs at predominantly ethnic minority institutions in Texas.

Eligibility This program is open to juniors, seniors, and graduate students enrolled in educator preparation programs at predominantly ethnic minority institutions in Texas. Applicants must submit a 2-page essay on their personal philosophy toward education, why they want to become an educator, who influenced them the most in making their career decision, and why they are applying for the scholarship. Financial need is not considered in the selection process.

Financial data The stipend is $1,500 per year.

Duration 1 year.

Additional information The qualifying institutions are Huston-Tillotson College, Jarvis Christian College, Our Lady of the Lake University, Paul Quinn College, Prairie View A&M University, St. Mary's University of San Antonio, Sul Ross State University, Sul Ross State University Rio Grande College, Texas A&M International University, Texas A&M-Kingsville, Texas Southern University, University of Houston, University of Houston-Downtown, University of St. Thomas, University of Texas at Brownsville and Texas Southmost College, University of Texas at El Paso, University of Texas at San Antonio, University of Texas-Pan American, University of the Incarnate Word, and Wiley College.

Number awarded Up to 4 each year.

Deadline November of each year.

[34]
BOOKER T. WASHINGTON SCHOLARSHIPS

National FFA Organization
Attn: Scholarship Office
6060 FFA Drive
P.O. Box 68960
Indianapolis, IN 46268-0960
(317) 802-4321   Fax: (317) 802-5321
E-mail: scholarships@ffa.org
Web: www.ffa.org

Purpose To provide financial assistance to minority FFA members who are interested in studying agriculture in college.

Eligibility This program is open to members who are graduating high school seniors planning to enroll full time in college. Applicants must be members of a minority ethnic group (African American, Asian American, Pacific Islander, Hispanic, Alaska Native, or American Indian) planning to pursue a 4-year college degree in agriculture. Selection is based on academic achievement (10 points for GPA, 10 points for SAT or ACT score, 10 points for class rank), leadership in FFA activities (30 points), leadership in community activities (10 points), and participation in the Supervised Agricultural Experience (SAE) program (30 points). U.S. citizenship is required.

Financial data Scholarships are either $10,000 or $5,000. Funds are paid directly to the recipient.

Duration 1 year; may be renewed for up to 3 additional years, if the recipients attend college full time and maintain at least a 2.0 GPA.

Number awarded 4 each year: 1 at $10,000 and 3 at $5,000.

Deadline February of each year.

[35]
BREAKTHROUGH TO NURSING SCHOLARSHIPS FOR ETHNIC PEOPLE OF COLOR

National Student Nurses' Association
Attn: NSNA Foundation
555 West 57th Street, Suite 1327
New York, NY 10019
(212) 581-2215   Fax: (212) 581-2368
E-mail: nsna@nsna.org
Web: www.nsna.org

Purpose To provide financial assistance to minority undergraduate and graduate students who wish to prepare for careers in nursing.

Eligibility Minority undergraduate students (Black, Native American, Spanish surname, Asian, or Polynesian) currently enrolled in state-approved schools of nursing or pre-nursing associate degree, baccalaureate, diploma, generic doctorate, and generic master's programs are eligible to apply. Although graduate students in other disciplines are also eligible if they wish to study nursing or pre-nursing, no funds can be used for graduate education in nursing. Graduating high school seniors are not eligible. Selection is based on academic achievement, financial need, and involvement in student nursing organizations and community health activities.

Financial data The stipend awarded ranges from $1,000 to $2,000. A total of $50,000 is awarded each year by the foundation for all its scholarship programs.

Duration 1 year.

Additional information Applications must be accompanied by a $10 processing fee.

Number awarded 13 to 15 each year.

Deadline January of each year.

[36]
BROWN FOUNDATION COLLEGE SCHOLARSHIPS

Brown Foundation for Educational Equity, Excellence and
    Research
P.O. Box 4862
Topeka, KS 66604
(785) 235-3939   Fax: (785) 235-1001
E-mail: brownfound@juno.com
Web: brownvboard.org

Purpose To provide financial assistance to currently-enrolled college juniors of color who are interested in preparing for a teaching career.

Eligibility To be eligible for this scholarship, applicants must meet the following requirements: be a minority; be a college junior; be admitted to a teacher education program; be enrolled in an institution of higher education with an accredited program in education; have at least a 3.0 GPA; be enrolled at least half time; and submit 2 recommendations (from a teacher, counselor, or other school official and from a person familiar with the applicant). Selection is based on GPA, extracurricular activities, career plans, essays, and recommendations.

Financial data The stipend is $1,000 per year.

Duration 2 years (junior and senior years).

Additional information The first Brown Foundation Scholarships were awarded in 1989.

Number awarded 2 each year.

Deadline April of each year.

[37]
BUFFETT FOUNDATION SCHOLARSHIP PROGRAM

Buffett Foundation
Attn: Scholarship Office
P.O. Box 4508
Decatur, IL 62525
(402) 451-6011   E-mail: buffettfound@aol.com
Web: www.BuffettScholarships.org

Purpose To provide financial assistance to entering or currently-enrolled college students in Nebraska.

Eligibility This program is open to U.S. citizens who are Nebraska residents. Applicants must be entering or currently enrolled in a Nebraska state school or a 2-year college or trade school in Nebraska. They must be in financial need, be the only family member presently receiving a grant from the foundation, have at least a 2.5 GPA, and have applied for federal financial aid. Selection is based on academic performance and financial need. Preference is given to minority students, students with disabilities, and married or unmarried students with dependents.

Financial data Up to $2,300 per semester. Funds are sent directly to the recipient's school and must be used to pay tuition and fees; funds may not be used to pay for books or other expenses.

Duration Up to 5 years for a 4-year college, or up to 3 years for a 2-year school. Students on scholarship may not drop out for a period of time and be reinstated as a scholarship recipient; they must reapply along with first-time students. Students on a 12-month program or the quarter system may use the scholarship for summer tuition; students on the semester system may not use funds for summer school. Students who are not working must enroll in at least 12 credit hours; students who are working must enroll in at least 9 credit hours.

Deadline Generally, April of each year.

[38]
BUREAU OF LAND MANAGEMENT AWARD

Hispanic Association of Colleges and Universities
Attn: Scholarship Programs
8415 Datapoint Drive, Suite 400
San Antonio, TX 78229
(210) 692-3805   Fax: (210) 692-0823
E-mail: hacu@hacu.net
Web: www.hacu.net/student_resources/index.shtml

Purpose To provide financial assistance to undergraduate students at institutions that are members of the Hispanic Association of Colleges and Universities (HACU).

Eligibility This program is open to full-time undergraduate students at HACU member and partner colleges and universities who are majoring in natural resources, sciences, or forestry. Applicants must submit an essay of 200 to 250 words that describes their academic and/or career goals, where they expect to be and what they expect to be doing 10 years from now, and what skills they can bring to an employer. They must be able to demonstrate financial need and a GPA of 3.2 or higher.

Financial data The stipend is $3,000 per year.

Duration 1 year; nonrenewable.

Additional information This program is sponsored by the U.S. Bureau of Land Management and administered by HACU.

Number awarded 1 or more each year.

Deadline June of each year.

[39]
CALIFORNIA REAL ESTATE ENDOWMENT FUND SCHOLARSHIP PROGRAM

California Community Colleges
Attn: Student Financial Assistance Programs
1102 Q Street
Sacramento, CA 95814-6511
(916) 445-8752
Web: www.cccco.edu

Purpose To provide financial assistance to disadvantaged California community college students who are studying real estate.

Eligibility This program is open to students at community colleges in California who are majoring in real estate or (if their college does not offer a real estate major) business administration with a concentration in real estate. Applicants must have completed at least a 3-unit college course in real estate with a grade of "C" or better and must be enrolled in at least 6 semester units of real estate for the semester of the scholarship. Students must meet 1 of the following financial need criteria: 1) have completed the Free Application for Federal Student Aid (FAFSA) and been determined by their college to have financial need; 2) come from a family with an income less than $10,625 for 1 person, $21,250 for 2 persons, $23,250 for 3 persons, or an additional $2,000 for each additional family member; or 3) come from a family with an income less than $50,000 and be from a disadvantaged group (have low economic status and/or have been denied opportunities in society for reasons of gender, race, ethnicity, economics, language, education, physical disabilities, or other mitigating factors). Scholarships are awarded on a first-come, first-served basis.

Financial data Awards up to $500 per semester are available.

Duration 1 semester; may be renewed if the student remains enrolled in at least 6 units of real estate with a GPA of at least 2.0. Students apply to their community college, not to the sponsoring organization.

Number awarded From 90 to 120 each year; approximately $90,000 per year is available for this program.

Deadline April of each year.

[40]
CALIFORNIA TABLE GRAPE WORKERS' SCHOLARSHIP PROGRAM

California Table Grape Commission
Attn: Scholarship Committee
392 West Fallbrook, Suite 101
Fresno, CA 93711-6150
(559) 447-8350   (800) 813-8478
Fax: (559) 447-9184   E-mail: adrienne@tablegrape.com
Web: www.tablegrape.com

Purpose To provide financial assistance to the children of California table grape field workers who are interested in attending a branch of the California State University system.

Eligibility To be eligible, applicants must be high school graduates or seniors graduating in June. They, or their parents, must have worked in the last table grape harvest or verify employment for the upcoming season. Farmers and their families, raisin and wine grape workers, students currently enrolled in college, permanent staff and members of the California Table Grade Commission and their families, and commission suppliers are not eligible. All applicants must intend to attend a branch of the California State University system. Selection is based on academic performance, financial need, obstacles overcome, leadership ability and/or community service, and ability to succeed.

Additional information The stipend is $3,000 per year.

Duration 4 years, provided the recipient maintains a GPA of 2.0 or higher. Recipients must attend a branch of the California State University on a full-time basis.

Number awarded Varies; generally, 3 each year.

Deadline March of each year.

[41]
CALIFORNIA WINE GRAPE GROWERS FOUNDATION SCHOLARSHIPS

California Association of Winegrape Growers
Attn: California Wine Grape Growers Foundation
601 University Avenue, Suite 135
Sacramento, CA 95825
(916) 924-5370   (800) 241-1800
E-mail: info@cawg.org
Web: www.cawg.org/services/scholarship.htm

Purpose To provide financial assistance for college to high school seniors in California whose parent(s) work in the grape wine vineyards.

Eligibility This program is open to high school seniors in California who plan to attend a branch of the University of California, a branch of the California State University system, or a community college in the state. Applicants must have a parent or legal guardian who was employed as a vineyard worker by a winegrape grower during either or both of the 2 preceding seasons. Applications are available in either English or Spanish. Along with their application, they must submit a high school transcript, a copy of their SAT or ACT scores (if they are planning to attend a 4-year university), a letter of recommendation from a school official, an endorsement from a member of the California Association of Winegrape Growers (CAWG), and a 2-page essay on themselves and their career goals. Selection is based on financial need, demonstrated academic ability, community involvement and leadership and/or work history, and determination to succeed.

Financial data The stipend is $1,000 per year at a 4-year university or $500 per year at a community college.

Duration 4 years at branches of the University of California or California State University system; 2 years at community colleges.

Number awarded 6 each year: 2 at 4-year universities and 4 at community colleges.

Deadline April of each year.

[42]
CAMP SCHOLARSHIPS

College Assistance Migrant Program
Attn: LCSC-CAMP Office
500 Eighth Avenue, RCH 212
Lewiston, ID 83501
(208) 792-2101   Fax: (208) 792-2550
E-mail: ggalindo@campaa.org
Web: campaa.org/Scholarships.html

Purpose To provide financial assistance for college to high school students from migrant or seasonal farmworker families.

Eligibility This program is open to migrant and seasonal farmworkers and their families working in agricultural activities directly related to the production of crops, dairy products, poultry, or livestock; the cultivation or harvesting of trees; or fish farms. Applicants may verify eligibility in 1 of 3 ways: 1) participation during high school or eligibility to participate in a Title 1 Migrant Education Program; 2) participation or eligibility to participate in the Workforce Investment Act (WIA); or 3) verification that they or their parents have spent at least 75 days during the past 24 months as a migrant and/or seasonal (not year-round) farmworker as their primary employment. They must also plan to enroll in a college or university that participates in the College Assistance Migrant Program (CAMP) of the U.S. Department of Education to complete a bachelor's degree, be a U.S. citizen or permanent resident, and be able to document financial need.

Financial data The maximum stipend is $5,000 per year.

Duration 1 year.

Additional information Currently, 43 colleges and universities participate in the CAMP program, including schools in California, Colorado, Florida, Georgia, Idaho, Kansas, Michigan, Mississippi, Missouri, New Mexico, New York, Ohio, Oregon, Pennsylvania, Puerto Rico, Texas, Washington, and Wisconsin.

Number awarded Approximately 2,000 each year.

Deadline February of each year.

[43]
CANFIT PROGRAM SCHOLARSHIPS

California Adolescent Nutrition and Fitness Program
2140 Shattuck Avenue, Suite 610
Berkeley, CA 94704
(510) 644-1533   (800) 200-3131
Fax: (510) 644-1535   E-mail: info@canfit.org
Web: www.canfit.org

Purpose To provide financial assistance to minority undergraduate and graduate students who are studying nutrition or physical education in California.

Eligibility Eligible to apply are American Indians/Alaska Natives, African Americans, Asians/Pacific Islanders, and Latinos/Hispanics who are enrolled in either: 1) an approved master's or doctoral graduate program in nutrition, public health nutrition, or physical education or in a preprofessional practice program approved by the American Dietetic Association at an accredited university in California; or, 2) an approved bachelor's or professional certificate program in culinary arts, nutrition, or physical education at an accredited university or college in California. Graduate student applicants must have completed at least 12 units of graduate course work and have a cumulative GPA of 3.0 or higher; undergraduate applicants must have completed 50 semester units or the equivalent of college credits and have a cumulative GPA of 2.5 or higher. Selection is based on financial need, academic goals, and community nutrition or physical education activities.

Financial data Graduate stipends are $1,000 each and undergraduate stipends are $500 per year.

Additional information A goal of the California Adolescent Nutrition and Fitness (CANFit) program is to improve the nutritional status and physical fitness of California's low-income multiethnic youth aged 10 to 14. By offering these scholarships, the program hopes to encourage more students to consider careers in adolescent nutrition and fitness.

Number awarded 5 graduate scholarships and 10 undergraduate scholarships are available each year.

Deadline March of each year.

[44]
CARBONE PUBLIC SERVICE SCHOLARSHIP

Vermont Student Assistance Corporation
Champlain Mill
1 Main Street, Fourth Floor
P.O. Box 2000
Winooski, VT 05404-2601
(802) 655-9602   (800) 642-3177
Fax: (802) 654-3765   TDD: (802) 654-3766
TDD: (800) 281-3341 (within VT)   E-mail: info@vsac.org
Web: www.vsac.org

Purpose To provide financial assistance to residents of Vermont from diverse backgrounds who are interested in preparing for a career in public service.

Eligibility This program is open to residents of Vermont who are graduating high school seniors, high school graduates, or GED recipients. Applicants must be interested in attending an accredited postsecondary institution to pursue a degree in public administration or services, including but not limited to human services, public administration, public policy analysis, social work, or community organization services. Selection is based on a letter of recommendation, required essays, and financial need. Preference is given to women and minority applicants.

Financial data The stipend is $500 per year.

Duration 1 year.

Additional information This program was established in 2002.

Number awarded 1 each year.

Deadline June of each year.

[45]
CARL A. SCOTT BOOK FELLOWSHIPS

Council on Social Work Education
Attn: Chair, Carl A. Scott Memorial Fund
1725 Duke Street, Suite 500
Alexandria, VA 22314-3457
(703) 683-8080   Fax: (703) 683-8099
E-mail: eafrancis@cswe.org
Web: www.cswe.org

Purpose To provide financial assistance to ethnic minority social work students in their last year of study for a baccalaureate or master's degree.

Eligibility This program is open to students from ethnic groups of color (African American, Asian American, Mexican American, Puerto Rican, and American Indian) who are in the last year of study for a social work degree in an accredited baccalaureate or master's degree program. Applicants must have a cumulative GPA of 3.0 or higher and be enrolled full time. They must demonstrate a commitment to work for equity and social justice in social work.

Financial data The award is $500.

Duration This is a 1-time award.

Number awarded 2 each year.

Deadline May of each year.

[46]
CAROLE SIMPSON SCHOLARSHIPS

Radio and Television News Directors Foundation
1000 Connecticut Avenue, N.W., Suite 615
Washington, DC 20036-5302
(202) 467-5218   Fax: (202) 223-4007
E-mail: karenb@rtndf.org
Web: www.rtndf.org/asfi/scholarships/undergrad.shtml

Purpose To provide financial assistance to outstanding undergraduate students, especially minorities, who are interested in preparing for a career in electronic journalism.

Eligibility Eligible are sophomore or more advanced undergraduate students enrolled in an electronic journalism sequence at an accredited or nationally-recognized college or university. Applicants must submit 1 to 3 examples of reporting or producing skills on audio or video cassette tapes (no more than 15 minutes total), a description of their role on each story and a list of who worked on each story and what they did, a statement explaining why they are seeking a career in broadcast or cable journalism, and a letter of endorsement from a faculty sponsor that verifies the applicant has at least 1 year of school remaining. Preference is given to undergraduate students of color.

Financial data The stipend is $2,000, paid in semiannual installments of $1,000 each.

Duration 1 year.

Additional information The Radio and Television News Directors Foundation (RTNDF) also provides an expense-paid trip to the Radio-Television News Directors Association (RTNDA) annual international conference. It defines electronic journalism to include radio, television, cable, and online news. Previous winners of any RTNDF scholarship or internship are not eligible.

Number awarded 1 each year.

Deadline April of each year.

[47]
CARSON PURIEFOY MEMORIAL FUND

Philadelphia Foundation
1234 Market Street, Suite 1800
Philadelphia, PA 19107-3794
(215) 563-6417   Fax: (215) 563-6882
Web: www.philafound.org

Purpose To provide financial assistance for college to high school seniors from the Philadelphia area who are minority group members involved in golf.

Eligibility This program is open to minority seniors graduating from high schools in the Philadelphia area. Applicants must be involved in golf.

Financial data A stipend is awarded (amount not specified).

Duration 1 year.

Additional information This fund was established in 1998.

Number awarded 1 or more each year.

[48]
CATHY L. BROCK MEMORIAL SCHOLARSHIP

Institute for Diversity in Health Management
Attn: Education Program Coordinator
One North Franklin Street, 30th Floor
Chicago, IL 60606
(800) 233-0996   Fax: (312) 422-4566
E-mail: clopez@aha.org
Web: www.diversityconnection.com

Purpose To provide financial assistance to minority upper-division and graduate students in health care management or business management.

Eligibility This program is open to members of ethnic minority groups who are college juniors, seniors, or graduate students. Applicants must be accepted or enrolled in an accredited program in health care management or business management and have a GPA of 3.0 or higher. They must demonstrate commitment to a career in health services administration, financial need, solid extracurricular and community service activities, and a strong interest and experience in finance. U.S. citizenship or permanent resident status is required.

Financial data The stipend is $1,000.

Duration 1 year.

Number awarded 1 or more each year, depending on the availability of funds.

Deadline June of each year.

[49]
CEDAR VALLEY CHAPTER #132 SCHOLARSHIP

Association for Facilities Engineering
Cedar Valley Chapter #132
c/o Joe Zachar, Special Events Chair
1203 Forest Glen Court, S.E.
Cedar Rapids, IA 52403
E-mail: Jzachar@acmeelectric.com

Purpose To provide financial assistance to currently-enrolled engineering majors in Iowa who are preparing for a career in facilities management or facilities maintenance.

Eligibility Applicants must be enrolled (full or part time) in an engineering program at an accredited college or university in Iowa, working on an associate or bachelor's degree. They must be employed in the facilities management or facilities maintenance field, have a GPA of 2.5 or higher, be a U.S. citizen, and be an Iowa resident. Special consideration is given to applicants who are minorities, can demonstrate financial need, have a committed interest in the facilities management or facilities maintenance field, are members of the Association for Facilities Engineering (AFE), are relatives of an AFE member, or are residents of a county where any member of the chapter is a resident.

Financial data The stipend is $250 per semester ($500 per year). Funds are paid directly to the recipient's school.

Duration 2 semesters (1 year).

Number awarded 2 each year.

Deadline April of each year.

[50]
CESAR CHAVEZ MEMORIAL LEADERSHIP AWARD

TELACU Education Foundation
5400 East Olympic Boulevard, Suite 300
Los Angeles, CA 90022
(323) 721-1655   Fax: (323) 724-3372
E-mail: info@telacu.com
Web: www.telacu.com

Purpose To provide financial assistance for college to outstanding Latino students in the Los Angeles area.

Eligibility This program is open to Latino undergraduate college or university students residing in unincorporated areas of east Los Angeles, as well as the cities of Bell Gardens, Commerce, Huntington Park, Los Angeles, Montebello, Monterey Park, Pico Rivera, Santa Ana, and South Gate. Applicants must 1) be a first-generation college student; 2) be from a low-income family; 3) have a GPA of 2.5 or higher; and 4) be a U.S. citizen or permanent resident. They must be attending or planning to transfer to 1 of 23 participating institutions in southern California. Full-time enrollment is required. The scholarship is awarded to a student who exhibits outstanding leadership abilities as evidenced by both academic accomplishments and community activities. Selection is based on an interview and 2 essays: 1 that addresses their goals and ambitions, reasons for pursuing a degree in the field they have chosen, commitment to their community, and how they plan to help their community after graduation, and 1 that describes why they should be considered for this special award.

Financial data The stipend is $2,500.

Duration 1 year.

Number awarded 1 each year.

Deadline April of each year.

[51]
CHARLESTON GAZETTE MINORITY SCHOLARSHIPS

Charleston Gazette
Attn: Managing Editor
1001 Virginia Street, East
Charleston, WV 25301
(304) 348-1723   (800) 982-6397
Fax: (304) 348-1233   E-mail: earle@wvgazette.com
Web: www.wvgazette.com

Purpose To provide financial assistance for college to minority high school seniors from southern and central West Virginia.

Eligibility This program is open to minority students who are graduating seniors at high schools in southern and central West Virginia. Applicants must submit a photograph; a letter of recommendation from a faculty member; an acceptance letter from an accredited college, university, or community college; copies of their ACT or SAT scores; and their most recent grade transcripts (at least a 2.0 GPA).

Financial data The stipend is $1,000 per year.

Duration 1 year; may be renewed up to 3 additional years if the recipient maintains a GPA of 2.0 or higher.

Number awarded 1 or more each year.

[52]
CHARLOTTE OBSERVER MINORITY SCHOLARSHIPS

Charlotte Observer
Attn: Zaira Goodman
600 South Tryon Street
P.O. Box 30308
Charlotte, NC 28230-3038
(704) 358-5715 E-mail: zgoodman@charlotteobserver.com
Web: www.charlotteobserver.com

Purpose To provide financial assistance to minority high school seniors in North and South Carolina who are interested in pursuing a career in the newspaper field.

Eligibility This program is open to minority seniors at high schools in the service area of the *Charlotte Observer* (North and South Carolina). Applicants must submit an original essay explaining why they want to pursue a career in newspapering, what they know about Knight Ridder and how they see themselves contributing to the company in the future, 2 letters of recommendation, a transcript, SAT/ACT scores, and up to 3 samples of work with bylines.

Financial data The stipend is $500 per year.

Duration 1 year.

Additional information The recipients of these scholarships are automatically entered into competition for the Knight Ridder Minority Scholarship Program of $10,000 per year for 4 years.

Number awarded 1 or more each year.

Deadline November of each year.

[53]
CHEERIOS BRAND HEALTH INITIATIVE SCHOLARSHIP

Congressional Black Caucus Foundation, Inc.
Attn: Director, Educational Programs
1004 Pennsylvania Avenue, S.E.
Washington, DC 20003
(202) 675-6739   (800) 784-2577
Fax: (202) 547-3806   E-mail: spouses@cbcfonline.org
Web: www.cbcfonline.org/cbcspouses/scholarship.html

Purpose To provide financial assistance to minority and other undergraduate and graduate students who reside in a congressional district represented by an African American and are interested in preparing for a health-related career.

Eligibility This program is open to 1) minority and other graduating high school seniors planning to attend an accredited institution of higher education and 2) currently-enrolled full-time undergraduate, graduate, and doctoral students in good academic standing with a GPA of 2.5 or higher. Applicants must reside, attend school, or have attended high school in a congressional district represented by an African American member of Congress. They must be interested in pursuing a career in a health-related field, including pre-medicine, nursing, chemistry, biology, physical education, and engineering. As part of the application process, they must include a 250-word personal statement describing how this scholarship will assist them in their educational career.

Financial data The program provides tuition assistance.

Duration 1 year.

Additional information The program was established in 1998 with support from General Mills, Inc.

Number awarded Varies each year.

Deadline May or September of each year.

[54]
CHEN SCHOLARSHIP

Coors Hispanic Employee Network
P.O. Box 1454
Golden, CO 80401
E-mail: paulandchris@prodigy.net

Purpose To provide financial assistance for college to high school seniors in Colorado who are of Hispanic descent.

Eligibility Applicants must be U.S. citizens, be Colorado residents, be of Hispanic heritage, be high school seniors, have a GPA of 2.5 or higher, and be planning to attend college after graduation. Selection is based on academic record, financial need, and educational plans. To apply, students must submit a signed application, a personal statement, a transcript, and 2 letters of recommendation.

Financial data The stipend is $1,000 per year.

Duration 1 year.

Additional information This program was established in 1991. Additional information is available from Grace Valdez at (303) 277-5258 or Ron Martinez at (303) 277-5037.

Number awarded Several each year.

Deadline February of each year.

[55]
CHICAGO SUN-TIMES MINORITY SCHOLARSHIP AND INTERNSHIP PROGRAM

Chicago Sun-Times
Attn: Director of Editorial Administration
401 North Wabash Avenue
Chicago, IL 60611
(312) 321-3000

Purpose To provide financial assistance and work experience to minority college students in the Chicago area who are interested in preparing for a career in print journalism.

Eligibility This program is open to minority college students and recent graduates who graduated from a Chicago-area high school or have lived in the Chicago metropolitan area for the past 5 years. Applicants must have demonstrated an interest in print journalism, including reporting, editing, graphics, or photography. They must submit a 500-word essay about themselves, explaining why they want to become a newspaper reporter, editor, or photographer.

Financial data Students selected for this program receive a $1,500 scholarship plus a paid internship at the *Chicago Sun-Times.*

Duration 1 year for the scholarship; 12 weeks during the summer for the internship.

Additional information The Chicago metropolitan area includes Cook, DuPage, Kane, Lake, McHenry, and Will counties in Illinois and Lake and Porter counties in Indiana. Recipients may use the scholarship at any school of their choosing. For the summer internships, assignments are available in reporting, editing, graphics, or photography.

Number awarded 1 or more each year.

Deadline December of each year.

[56]
CHICANA/LATINA FOUNDATION SCHOLARSHIP COMPETITION

Chicana/Latina Foundation
Attn: Scholarship Program
P.O. Box 1941
El Cerrito, CA 94530-4941
(510) 526-5861   E-mail: info@chicanalatina.org
Web: www.chicanalatina.org/scholarship.html

Purpose To provide financial assistance for college or graduate school to Latina women in the San Francisco Bay area.

Eligibility This program is open to Latina women who either have resided for at least 2 years in or are currently enrolled in accredited colleges, universities, or community colleges in the following California counties: Alameda, Contra Costa, Marin, Monterey, Napa, San Francisco, San Mateo, Santa Clara, Santa Cruz, Solano, or Sonoma. Undergraduate students must have completed at least 15 college units, must be enrolled as full-time students, must have a GPA of 2.5 or higher, and must complete 3 essays (on their family background, their community activities, and their career goals). Graduate students must verify acceptance to a graduate school and complete a supplementary application that requires 3 essays: on an issue affecting the Latina community in the Bay area, on their personal background, and on their leadership of their younger Chicana/Latina sisters so they stay in school and graduate. Selection is based on commitment to Latina women's progress and development, demonstrated leadership qualities, involvement within the Latino community, clarity of direction and goals, academic achievement, and letters of recommendation. Students who received a scholarship from the foundation within the past 4 years are not eligible.

Financial data The stipend is $1,000 per year.

Duration 1 year.

Additional information The foundation was formerly known as the Chicana Foundation of Northern California. Requests for applications must be accompanied by a self-addressed stamped envelope.

Number awarded Varies each year; recently, 18 of these scholarships were awarded.

Deadline March of each year.

[57]
CHIPS QUINN SCHOLARS PROGRAM

Freedom Forum
Attn: Chips Quinn Scholars Program
1101 Wilson Boulevard
Arlington, VA 22209
(703) 284-2863   Fax: (703) 284-3543
E-mail: chipsquinnscholars@freedomforum.org
Web: www.chipsquinn.org

Purpose To provide work experience, career mentoring, and scholarship support to minority college students and recent graduates who are majoring in journalism.

Eligibility This program is open to students enrolled at an historically Black college or university or a college or university that has significant numbers of students who are members of ethnic or racial minority groups. Deans of the journalism schools at those colleges and universities are invited to nominate up to 4 juniors, seniors, or recent graduates who are majoring or minoring in journalism or have clearly demonstrated an interest in journalism as a career. Nominees must also apply for an internship. Scholars who subsequently work for at least 3 years in newspaper newsrooms are eligible to apply for additional funding to participate in journalism seminars, such as those at the American Press Institute, Poynter Institute, Northwestern University Media Management Center, or Maynard Institute for Journalism Education.

Financial data Students chosen for this program receive a travel stipend to attend a workshop at the Freedom Forum in Arlington, Virginia and, upon completion of the internship, a $1,000 scholarship. Scholars selected to participate in a journalism seminar receive an additional $2,500 in funding.

Duration 1 year, including the internship.

Additional information Students are invited to the workshop at the Freedom Forum and then work as an intern during the summer at a newspaper where they are linked with a mentor editor. This program was established in 1991 in memory of the late John D. Quinn Jr., managing editor of the *Poughkeepsie Journal.* Funding is provided by the Freedom Forum, formerly the Gannett Foundation.

Number awarded Approximately 150 each year. From all participants in the program, 12 are selected each year to attend a journalism seminar.

Deadline March of each year for programs to begin in fall or spring; October of each year for programs to begin in summer.

[58]
COLEMAN A. YOUNG SCHOLARS PROGRAM

Coleman A. Young Foundation
Attn: Scholarship Program Manager
2921 East Jefferson Avenue, Suite 200
Detroit, MI 48207-4267
(313) 963-3030   E-mail: thelmabush@cayf.org
Web: www.cayf.org

Purpose To provide financial assistance for college to minority and other disadvantaged high school seniors in Detroit.

Eligibility This program is open to minority and other disadvantaged high school seniors in Detroit who can and will 1) excel academically, 2) set up career goals that meet the needs of the Detroit community, 3) develop strong leadership skills, and 4) become Detroit's future leading citizens.

Financial data The stipend is $5,000 per year.

Duration 1 year; renewable for up to 3 additional years.

Additional information This program was established in 1986. The foundation has awarded more than $2 million in scholarships since then. The relationship between the recipients and the Young Foundation is intended to be ongoing. During their entire undergraduate career, scholars receive support and guidance. During the summer, they participate in bi-weekly seminars, to enrich and strengthen their academic, administrative, and technological skills, and are offered employment assistance.

Number awarded Varies; generally, 10 or more each year.

Deadline April of each year.

[59]
COLGATE "BRIGHT SMILES, BRIGHT FUTURES" MINORITY SCHOLARSHIPS

American Dental Hygienists' Association
Attn: Institute for Oral Health
444 North Michigan Avenue, Suite 3400
Chicago, IL 60611
(312) 440-8944   (800) 735-4916
Fax: (312) 440-8929   E-mail: institute@adha.net
Web: www.adha.org

Purpose To provide financial assistance to minority group students enrolled in certificate/associate programs in dental hygiene.

Eligibility This program is open to members of groups currently underrepresented in the dental hygiene profession: Native Americans, African Americans, Hispanics, Asians, and males. Applicants must have completed at least 1 year in a dental hygiene curriculum at the certificate/associate level, have earned at least a 3.0 GPA, and be able to demonstrate financial need. They must intend to be full-time students in the academic year for which they are applying.

Financial data The amount of the award depends on the need of the recipient, to a maximum of $1,250.

Duration 1 year.

Additional information These scholarships are sponsored by the Colgate-Palmolive Company.

Number awarded 2 each year.

Deadline May of each year.

[60]
COLLEGE FUND/COCA-COLA CORPORATE INTERN PROGRAM

United Negro College Fund
Attn: Corporate Scholars Program
P.O. Box 1435
Alexandria, VA 22313-9998
(866) 671-7237   E-mail: internship@uncf.org
Web: www.uncf.org/Scholarship/CorporateScholars.asp

Purpose To provide financial assistance and work experience to students of color majoring in designated fields and interested in an internship at Coca-Cola Company's corporate headquarters in Atlanta, Georgia.

Eligibility This program is open to students of color, including African Americans, Hispanic Americans, Asian/Pacific Islander Americans, and American Indians/Alaskan Natives, who attend member institutions of the United Negro College Fund (UNCF), the Hispanic Association of Colleges and Universities (HACU), other targeted Historically Black Colleges and Universities (HBCUs), and designated majority institutions. Applicants must be sophomores majoring in business (sales interest), chemistry, communications, engineering, finance, human resources, information technology, or marketing with a GPA of 3.0 or higher. They must be a U.S. citizen, permanent resident, asylee, refugee, or lawful temporary resident under amnesty programs. Along with their application, they must submit a 1-page essay about themselves and their career goals, including information about their personal background and any particular challenges they have faced. Interviews are required.

Financial data The program provides a stipend of $2,500 per month during the internship, housing accommodations in Atlanta, round-trip transportation to and from Atlanta, local transportation to and from the internship site, and (based on successful internship performance) a $10,000 scholarship.

Duration 8 to 10 weeks for the internship; 1 year for the scholarship.

Number awarded Approximately 50 each year.

Deadline December of each year.

[61]
COLLEGE SCHOLARSHIP PROGRAM OF THE HISPANIC SCHOLARSHIP FUND

Hispanic Scholarship Fund
Attn: Selection Committee
55 Second Street, Suite 1500
San Francisco, CA 94105
(877) HSF-INFO   Fax: (415) 808-2302
E-mail: info@hsf.net
Web: www.hsf.net

Purpose To provide financial assistance for college or graduate school to Hispanic American students.

Eligibility This program is open to U.S. citizens, permanent residents, and visitors with a passport stamped I-551. Applicants must be of Hispanic heritage (each parent half Hispanic or 1 parent fully Hispanic) and enrolled full time in a degree-seeking program at an accredited college or university in the United States or Puerto Rico. They may be undergraduate or graduate students, but they must have completed at least 12 undergraduate units with a GPA of 2.7 or higher. Along with their application, they must submit a 2-page essay that addresses the following topics: their Hispanic heritage and family background, personal and academic achievements, academic plans and career goals, efforts toward making a difference in the community, and financial need.

Financial data Stipends normally range from $1,000 to $3,000 per year.

Duration 1 year; recipients may reapply.

Additional information Since this program began in 1975, more than $47 million has been awarded to more than 40,000 Hispanic students. Requests for applications must be accompanied by a self-addressed stamped envelope.

Number awarded More than 4,000 each year.

Deadline October of each year.

[62]
COLORADO SOCIETY OF CPAS ETHNIC DIVERSITY SCHOLARSHIPS FOR COLLEGE STUDENTS

Colorado Society of Certified Public Accountants
Attn: Educational Foundation
7979 East Tufts Avenue, Suite 500
Denver, CO 80237-2843
(303) 741-8613   (800) 523-9082 (within CO)
Fax: (303) 773-6344
E-mail: cpa-staff@cscpa.denver.co.us
Web: www.cocpa.org

Purpose To provide financial assistance to minority undergraduate or graduate students in Colorado who are studying accounting.

Eligibility This program is open to African American, Hispanic, Asian American, American Indian, and Pacific Islander students studying at a college or university in Colorado at the associate, baccalaureate, or graduate level. Applicants must have completed at least 1 intermediate accounting class, be declared accounting majors, have completed at least 8 semester hours of accounting classes, and have a GPA of at least 3.0. Selection is

based first on scholastic achievement and second on financial need.

Financial data The stipend is $1,000.

Duration 1 year; recipients may reapply.

Number awarded 2 each year.

Deadline November of each year.

[63]
COLORADO SOCIETY OF CPAS ETHNIC DIVERSITY SCHOLARSHIPS FOR HIGH SCHOOL STUDENTS

Colorado Society of Certified Public Accountants
Attn: Educational Foundation
7979 East Tufts Avenue, Suite 500
Denver, CO 80237-2843
(303) 741-8613   (800) 523-9082 (within CO)
Fax: (303) 773-6344
E-mail: cpa-staff@cscpa.denver.co.us
Web: www.cocpa.org

Purpose To provide financial assistance to minority high school seniors in Colorado who plan to study accounting in college.

Eligibility This program is open to African American, Hispanic, Asian American, American Indian, and Pacific Islander high school seniors planning to major in accounting at a college or university in Colorado. Applicants must have a GPA of at least 3.0. Selection is based primarily on scholastic achievement.

Financial data The stipend is $1,000.

Duration 1 year; nonrenewable.

Number awarded 3 each year.

Deadline February of each year.

[64]
COMISION FEMENIL DE LOS ANGELES SCHOLARSHIP

Comisión Femenil de Los Angeles
Attn: Scholarship Committee
P.O. Box 86013
Los Angeles, CA 90086
(818) 549-9530

Purpose To provide financial assistance to Latinas in southern California interested in working on an undergraduate or graduate degree.

Eligibility This program is open to Latinas who reside in the Los Angeles County area. Applicants must be interested in attending a 2-year or 4-year college, university, trade school, or professional school (e.g., law school, medical school) in southern California. They must submit a 1-page biographical essay and a 1-page essay on topics relating to their goals and aspirations. Finalists are interviewed. Selection is based on academic achievement (at least a 3.0 GPA), evidence of character and promise, demonstration of leadership, the essays, letters of recommendation, the interview, and financial need.

Financial data The amount awarded depends upon the needs of the recipient. Funds are paid in 2 installments: the first half is issued when verification of enrollment is received; the second is issued upon satisfactory completion of the first term.

Duration 1 year.

Number awarded Varies each year.

Deadline July of each year.

[65]
COMMUNITY COLLEGE ORANGE COUNTY HISPANIC EDUCATION ENDOWMENT FUND AWARDS

Orange County Community Foundation
Attn: Scholarship Coordinator
2081 Business Center Drive, Suite 100
Irvine, CA 92612-1115
(949) 553-4202, ext. 22　　　　　　Fax: (949) 553-4211
E-mail: occf@oc-communityfoundation.org
Web: www.oc-communityfoundation.org/grantsscholar

Purpose　To provide financial assistance to Hispanic community college students from Orange County, California who plan to transfer to a 4-year university.

Eligibility　This program is open to Hispanic students in Orange County, California who are currently enrolled in a community college and planning to transfer to a 4-year college or university. Selection is based on financial need, extracurricular activities, academic ability, and community service.

Financial data　The stipend is $1,000 per year.

Duration　1 year.

Number awarded　20 each year.

Deadline　February of each year.

[66]
COMMUNITY COLLEGE TRANSFER PROGRAM OF THE HISPANIC SCHOLARSHIP FUND

Hispanic Scholarship Fund
Attn: Selection Committee
55 Second Street, Suite 1500
San Francisco, CA 94105
(877) HSF-INFO　　　　　　　　Fax: (415) 808-2302
E-mail: info@hsf.net
Web: www.hsf.net

Purpose　To provide financial assistance to Hispanic American students who are attending a community college and interested in transferring to a 4-year institution.

Eligibility　This program is open to U.S. citizens, permanent residents, and visitors with a passport stamped I-551. Applicants must be of Hispanic heritage (each parent half Hispanic or 1 parent fully Hispanic) and part-time or full-time community college students with a GPA of 3.0 or higher. They must be planning to transfer and enroll full time at an accredited 4-year college or university in the United States. Along with their application, they must submit a 2-page essay that addresses the following topics: their Hispanic heritage and family background, personal and academic achievements, academic plans and career goals, efforts toward making a difference in the community, and financial need.

Financial data　Stipends range from $1,000 to $2,500 per year.

Duration　1 year; may reapply. Requests for applications must be accompanied by a self-addressed stamped envelope.

Number awarded　At least 600 each year.

Deadline　February of each year.

[67]
CONGRESSIONAL BLACK CAUCUS SPOUSES SCHOLARSHIP FUND PROGRAM

Congressional Black Caucus Foundation, Inc.
Attn: Director, Educational Programs
1004 Pennsylvania Avenue, S.E.
Washington, DC 20003
(202) 675-6739　　　　　　　　　(800) 784-2577
Fax: (202) 547-3806　　　E-mail: spouses@cbcfonline.org
Web: www.cbcfonline.org/cbcspouses/scholarship.html

Purpose　To provide financial assistance to minority and other undergraduate and graduate students who reside in a congressional district represented by an African American.

Eligibility　This program is open to 1) minority and other graduating high school seniors planning to attend an accredited institution of higher education and 2) currently-enrolled full-time undergraduate, graduate, and doctoral students in good academic standing with a GPA of 2.5 or higher. Applicants must reside, attend school, or have attended high school in a congressional district represented by an African American member of Congress. Relatives of caucus members, spouses, and staff are not eligible.

Financial data　The program provides tuition assistance.

Duration　1 year.

Additional information　The program was established in 1988.

Number awarded　Varies each year.

Deadline　May or September of each year.

[68]
CONGRESSIONAL HISPANIC CAUCUS INSTITUTE SCHOLARSHIP AWARDS

Congressional Hispanic Caucus Institute, Inc.
504 C Street, N.E.
Washington, DC 20002
(202) 543-1771　　　　　　　　　(800) EXCEL-DC
Fax: (202) 546-2143　　　　　E-mail: chci@chci.org
Web: www.chci.org

Purpose　To provide financial assistance for college or graduate school to students of Hispanic descent.

Eligibility　This program is open to U.S. citizens and permanent residents who are Hispanic as defined by the U.S. Census Bureau (individuals of Mexican, Puerto Rican, Cuban, Central and South American, and other Spanish and Latin American descent). Applicants must be attending or planning to attend an accredited community college, 4-year university, or professional or graduate program. They must submit evidence of financial need, consistent and active participation in public service activities, and 3 1-page essays on 1) how effective the public education system has been in addressing the needs of the Latino community and what policy recommendations they suggest to improve the system; 2) the field of study they plan to pursue and how the Latino community will benefit; and 3) their definition of leadership and which Latino leader best exemplifies their definition of leadership.

Financial data　The stipend is $5,000 at 4-year and graduate institutions or $1,500 at 2-year community colleges.

Duration　1 year.

Number awarded　Varies each year; recently, 40 undergraduates and 15 graduate students received these scholarships.

Deadline　April of each year.

[69]
CONNECTICUT ASSOCIATION OF LATIN AMERICANS IN HIGHER EDUCATION SCHOLARSHIPS

Hartford Foundation for Public Giving
85 Gillett Street
Hartford, CT 06105
(860) 548-1888   Fax: (860) 524-8346
E-mail: hfpg2@hfpg.org
Web: www.hfpg.org

Purpose To provide financial assistance for college to Latino residents of Connecticut.

Eligibility This program is open to Connecticut residents who are graduating high school seniors or currently enrolled in college. Applicants must come from a Latino background and have a GPA of 3.0 or higher. Selection is based on academic achievement, financial need, community service, and an essay on "How do you feel education is going to impact your ability to continue assisting others to pursue an education?"

Financial data The stipend is $500 per year.

Duration 1 year.

Additional information Funding for this program is provided by the Connecticut Association of Latin Americans in Higher Education, c/o Dr. Wilson Luna, P.O. Box 382, Milford, CT 06460-0382, (203) 789-7011, Fax: (203) 285-2142, E-mail: wilsonluna@aol.com.

Number awarded 5 each year.

Deadline April of each year.

[70]
CONNECTICUT EDUCATION FOUNDATION SCHOLARSHIPS FOR MINORITY COLLEGE STUDENTS

Connecticut Education Foundation, Inc.
c/o Connecticut Education Association
21 Oak Street, Suite 500
Hartford, CT 06106-8001
(860) 525-5641   (800) 842-4316
Fax: (860) 725-6388   E-mail: phila@cea.org
Web: www.cea.org

Purpose To provide financial assistance to minority college students in Connecticut who are interested in preparing for a teaching career.

Eligibility This program is open to minority students (Blacks, Native Americans or Alaskan Natives, Asian or Pacific Islanders, and Hispanics or Latinos) who have been accepted into a teacher preparation program at an accredited college or university in Connecticut. Applicants must have earned a GPA of 2.75 or higher. Finalists may be interviewed. Financial need is considered in the selection process.

Financial data The stipend is $750.

Duration 1 year; may be renewed.

Number awarded At least 1 each year.

Deadline April of each year.

[71]
CONNECTICUT EDUCATION FOUNDATION SCHOLARSHIPS FOR MINORITY HIGH SCHOOL STUDENTS

Connecticut Education Foundation, Inc.
c/o Connecticut Education Association
21 Oak Street, Suite 500
Hartford, CT 06106-8001
(860) 525-5641   (800) 842-4316
Fax: (860) 725-6388   E-mail: phila@cea.org
Web: www.cea.org

Purpose To provide financial assistance to minority high school students in Connecticut who are interested in preparing for a teaching career.

Eligibility This program is open to minority students (Blacks, Native Americans or Alaskan Natives, Asian or Pacific Islanders, and Hispanics or Latinos) who have been accepted at an accredited 2- or 4-year college or university in Connecticut. Applicants must intend to enter the teaching profession. They must have earned a GPA of 2.75 or higher. Finalists may be interviewed. Financial need is considered in the selection process.

Financial data The stipend is $500.

Duration 1 year; may be renewed.

Number awarded At least 1 each year.

Deadline April of each year.

[72]
CONNECTICUT MINORITY TEACHER INCENTIVE PROGRAM

Connecticut Department of Higher Education
Attn: Office of Student Financial Aid
61 Woodland Street
Hartford, CT 06105-2326
(860) 947-1855   Fax: (860) 947-1838
E-mail: mtip@ctdhe.org
Web: www.ctdhe.org

Purpose To provide financial assistance and loan repayment to minority upper-division college students in Connecticut who are interested in teaching at public schools in the state.

Eligibility This program is open to minority juniors and seniors enrolled full time in Connecticut college and university teacher preparation programs. Applicants must be nominated by the education dean at their institution.

Financial data The maximum stipend is $5,000 per year. If recipients complete a credential and teach at a public school in Connecticut, they may receive up to $2,500 per year, for up to 4 years, to help pay off college loans.

Duration Up to 2 years.

Number awarded Varies each year.

Deadline October of each year.

[73]
CONNTESOL SCHOLARSHIPS

Connecticut Teachers of English to Speakers of Other
　Languages
c/o Sue Goldstein
42 Crosswinds Drive
Noank, CT 06340
E-mail: goldstei@galaxyinternet.net

Purpose To provide financial assistance for college to Connecticut high school seniors whose native language is not English.

Eligibility This program is open to seniors graduating from high schools in Connecticut whose first language is not English. Selection is based on academic achievement, community service, an essay, and financial need.

Financial data The stipend is at least $250 for students at 2-year colleges or $500 for students at 4-year colleges and universities.

Duration 1 year.

Number awarded 2 each year.

[74]
COORS LIGHT ACADEMIC SUCCESS IN EDUCATION (CLASE) SCHOLARSHIP AWARD

Hispanic Association of Colleges and Universities
Attn: Scholarship Programs
8415 Datapoint Drive, Suite 400
San Antonio, TX 78229
(210) 692-3805　　　　　Fax: (210) 692-0823
E-mail: hacu@hacu.net
Web: www.hacu.net/student_resources/index.shtml

Purpose To provide financial assistance to undergraduate and graduate students at institutions in the United States, Puerto Rico, and Mexico that are members of the Hispanic Association of Colleges and Universities (HACU).

Eligibility This program is open to full-time undergraduate and graduate students at HACU member and partner colleges. Students in the United States and Puerto Rico may study at their home institution or at an HACU-member institution in Mexico. Students in Mexico may study at a U.S. HACU-member institution. All academic majors are eligible. Applicants must submit an essay of 200 to 250 words that describes their academic and/or career goals, where they expect to be and what they expect to be doing 10 years from now, and what skills they can bring to an employer. They must be able to demonstrate financial need and a GPA of 3.2 or higher.

Financial data The stipend is $1,000 per year.

Duration 1 year; nonrenewable.

Additional information This program is sponsored by the Coors Brewing Company and administered by HACU. Recently, the sponsor provided additional funding in conjunction with the concert tour of the musical group *Maná Revolución de Amor*. For every concert ticket sold, the group donated $0.50 and Coors matched with an additional $0.50, to a combined maximum contribution of $200,000.

Number awarded Up to 200 each year.

Deadline June of each year.

[75]
CORPORATE-SPONSORED SCHOLARSHIPS FOR MINORITY UNDERGRADUATE STUDENTS WHO MAJOR IN PHYSICS

American Physical Society
Attn: Committee on Minorities
One Physics Ellipse
College Park, MD 20740-3844
(301) 209-3200　　　　　Fax: (301) 209-0865
Web: www.aps.org/educ/com/scholars/index.html

Purpose To provide financial assistance to underrepresented minority students interested in studying physics on the undergraduate level.

Eligibility Any African American, Hispanic American, or Native American who plans to major in physics and who is a high school senior or college freshman or sophomore may apply. U.S. citizenship or permanent resident status is required. The selection committee especially encourages applications from students who are attending or planning to attend institutions with historically or predominantly Black, Hispanic, or Native American enrollment. Selection is based on commitment to the study of physics and plans to pursue a physics baccalaureate degree.

Financial data Stipends are $2,000 per year in the first year or $3,000 in the second year; funds must be used for tuition, room, and board. In addition, $500 is awarded to the host department.

Duration 1 year; renewable for 1 additional year with the approval of the APS selection committee.

Additional information APS conducts the scholarship program in conjunction with the Corporate Associates of the American Institute of Physics. Each scholarship is sponsored by a corporation, which is normally designated as the sponsor. A corporation generally sponsors from 1 to 10 scholarships, depending upon its size and utilization of physics in the business.

Number awarded Varies each year; recently, 26 of these scholarships were awarded.

Deadline January of each year.

[76]
CRISTINA SARALEGUI SCHOLARSHIP PROGRAM

National Association of Hispanic Journalists
Attn: Scholarship Committee
1000 National Press Building
529 14th Street, N.W.
Washington, DC 20045-2001
(202) 662-7145　　　　　(888) 346-NAHJ
Fax: (202) 662-7144　　　　E-mail: nahj@nahj.org
Web: www.nahj.org/scholarship.html

Purpose To provide financial assistance and work experience to Hispanic American undergraduate students interested in preparing for careers in the media.

Eligibility College sophomores are eligible to apply if they are of Hispanic descent, fluent in Spanish, and planning to pursue a career in broadcast journalism. Applicants must submit an official transcript of grades; a 1-page resume with their educational background, work history, awards, internships, other scholarships, language proficiency, and any work done for their school newspaper, radio, and/or television station; samples of their work; 2 reference letters; a 500-word autobiography in third person in the form of a news story; and documentation of financial need.

Financial data The stipend is $5,000 per year; the program also provides funding to attend the association's convention and an internship during the summer following the junior year.

Duration 2 years.

Additional information This program, which began in 2000, is sponsored by the Spanish language talk show host Cristina Saralegüi and administered by the National Association of Hispanic Journalists (NAHJ) as part of its Rubén Salazar Scholarship Fund. The recipient participates in a summer internship on the Cristina Saralegüi show.

Number awarded 1 each year.

Deadline January of each year.

[77]
C.T. LANG JOURNALISM MINORITY SCHOLARSHIP AND INTERNSHIP

Albuquerque Journal
Attn: Scholarship Committee
7777 Jefferson Street, N.E.
P.O. Drawer J
Albuquerque, NM 87103
(505) 823-7777

Purpose To provide financial assistance and work experience to minority undergraduates in journalism programs at universities in New Mexico.

Eligibility This program is open to minority students majoring or minoring in journalism at a New Mexico university in their junior year with a GPA of 2.5 or higher. Applicants must be enrolled full time. They must be planning a career in newswriting, photography, design, copy editing, or online. Selection is based on clips of published stories, a short autobiography that explains the applicant's interest in the field, a grade transcript, and a letter of recommendation.

Financial data The scholarship is $1,000 per semester; the recipient also receives a paid internship and moving expenses.

Duration The scholarship is for 2 semesters (fall and spring). The internship is for 1 semester.

Additional information This program is funded by the *Albuquerque Journal,* where the internship takes place.

Number awarded 1 each year.

Deadline February of each year.

[78]
CUBAN AMERICAN SCHOLARSHIP PROGRAM

Cuban American Scholarship Fund
Attn: Victor Cueto
P.O. Box 6422
Santa Ana, CA 92706
(714) 835-7676

Purpose To provide financial assistance for postsecondary education to Cuban American students in California.

Eligibility This program is open to students who are California residents, U.S. citizens or permanent residents, of Cuban descent, and enrolled or planning to enroll as a full-time student in an accredited college or university. A GPA of 3.0 or higher is required. Selection is based on a statement describing Cuban and family background, personal and academic achievements, current educational status, career goals, community involvement, and financial need.

Financial data The stipend depends on the need of the recipient and the availability of funds.

Duration 1 year.

Number awarded 1 or more each year.

Deadline April of each year.

[79]
CUBAN-AMERICAN TEACHERS ASSOCIATION SCHOLARSHIPS

Cuban-American Teachers Association
c/o Alberto C. del Calvo
9727 Garnish Drive
Downey, CA 90240-3002
(562) 923-0204   E-mail: cubacata@aol.com

Purpose To provide financial assistance to high school seniors of Cuban heritage in southern California who are interested in attending college.

Eligibility High school seniors who reside in Los Angeles County are eligible to apply if they are of Cuban descent, have earned a GPA of 3.0 or higher, can demonstrate an interest in Cuban heritage and the Cuban American community, and speak Spanish fluently (as determined by interviews). Financial need is not considered.

Financial data Stipends are either $300 or $500 per year.

Duration 1 year.

Number awarded Varies; 1 at $500 and others at $300, depending on the availability of funds.

Deadline March of each year.

[80]
DAISY AND L.C. BATES MINORITY SCHOLARSHIP PROGRAM

Southwestern Bell Foundation
P.O. Box 165316
Little Rock, AR 72216

Purpose To provide financial assistance for college to minority high school seniors in Arkansas.

Eligibility This program is open to minority high school seniors in Arkansas who are planning to attend a 4-year academic institution in the state. As part of the application process, they must submit a short essay on "the importance of a college education." Selection is based on academic achievement, community service, school activities, leadership qualities, financial need, and written communication skills.

Financial data The stipend is $2,500 per year.

Duration 1 year; nonrenewable.

Additional information Recipients must attend a 4-year academic institution in Arkansas.

Number awarded 10 each year.

Deadline March of each year.

[81]
DAMON P. MOORE SCHOLARSHIP

Indiana State Teachers Association
Attn: Scholarships
150 West Market Street, Suite 900
Indianapolis, IN 46204
(317) 263-3400   (800) 382-4037
E-mail: kmcallen@ista-in.org
Web: www.ista-in.org

Purpose   To provide financial assistance to ethnic minority high school seniors in Indiana who are interested in studying education in college.

Eligibility   This program is open to ethnic minority public high school seniors in Indiana who are interested in studying education in college. Selection is based on academic achievement, leadership ability as expressed through co-curricular activities and community involvement, recommendations, and an essay.

Financial data   The stipend is $1,000.

Duration   1 year; may be renewed for 2 additional years.

Number awarded   1 each year.

Deadline   February of each year.

[82]
DANIEL GUTIERREZ MEMORIAL GENERAL SCHOLARSHIP

Beca Foundation
Attn: Ana Garcia, Operations Manager
830 East Grand Avenue, Suite B
Escondido, CA 92025
(760) 741-8246   Fax: (760) 741-8716

Purpose   To provide financial assistance to Latino high school students from the San Diego area who plan to attend college.

Eligibility   Eligible are graduating seniors from high schools in San Diego County who plan to attend college in the following fall. Applicants may pursue their education anywhere in the United States and major in any subject. Selection is based on financial need, scholastic abilities, and contribution, both now and in the future, to the Latino community.

Financial data   Awards range from $500 to $1,000 per year.

Duration   1 year; nonrenewable.

Number awarded   1 or more each year.

Deadline   February of each year.

[83]
DELL/UNCF CORPORATE SCHOLARS PROGRAM

United Negro College Fund
Attn: Corporate Scholars Program
P.O. Box 1435
Alexandria, VA 22313-9998
(866) 671-7237   E-mail: internship@uncf.org
Web: www.uncf.org/Scholarship/CorporateScholars.asp

Purpose   To provide financial assistance and work experience to undergraduate and graduate students, especially minorities, majoring in designated fields and interested in an internship at Dell Computer Corporation's corporate headquarters near Austin, Texas.

Eligibility   This program is open to rising juniors and graduate students who are African Americans, Hispanics, Asian/Pacific Islanders, Caucasians, and Native Americans. Applicants must be enrolled full time at institutions that are members of the United Negro College Fund (UNCF) or at other targeted colleges and universities. They must be majoring in business administration, computer science, engineering (computer, electrical, or mechanical), finance, human resources, management information systems, marketing, or supply chain management with a GPA of 3.0 or higher. Along with their application, they must submit a 1-page essay about themselves and their career goals, including information about their personal background and any particular challenges they have faced. Finalists are interviewed by a team of representatives from Dell, the program's sponsor.

Financial data   The program provides a paid summer internship, housing accommodations in Austin, round-trip transportation to and from Austin, and (based on financial need and successful internship performance) a $10,000 scholarship.

Duration   8 to 10 weeks for the internship; 1 year for the scholarship.

Number awarded   Varies each year.

Deadline   February of each year.

[84]
DENNY'S GRAND SLAM SCHOLARS

Hispanic College Fund
Attn: National Director
1717 Pennsylvania Avenue, N.W., Suite 460
Washington, D.C. 20006
(800) 644-4223   Fax: (202) 296-3774
E-mail: hispaniccollegefund@earthlink.net
Web: www.hispanicfund.org

Purpose   To provide financial assistance to Hispanic American undergraduate students who are interested in preparing for a career in business, computer science, or engineering.

Eligibility   This program is open to U.S. citizens of Hispanic background who are entering their freshman, sophomore, junior, or senior year of college. Applicants must be working on a bachelor's degree in business, computer science, engineering, or a business-related major and have a cumulative GPA of 3.0 or higher. They must be applying to or enrolled in a college or university in the 50 states or Puerto Rico as a full-time student. Financial need is considered in the selection process.

Financial data   Stipends range from $500 to $5,000, depending on the need of the recipient. The sponsor's goal is to have the average award be $3,000. Funds are paid directly to the recipient's college or university to help cover tuition and fees.

Duration   1 year; recipients may reapply.

Additional information   This program, which began in 1996, is sponsored by Denny's.

Number awarded   Varies each year; recently, 44 of these scholarships were awarded.

Deadline   April of each year.

[85]
DIETETIC TECHNICIAN PROGRAM SCHOLARSHIPS

American Dietetic Association
Attn: Accreditation, Education Programs, and Student
  Operations
216 West Jackson Boulevard, Suite 800
Chicago, IL 60606-6995
(312) 899-0040   (800) 877-1600, ext. 5400
Fax: (312) 899-4817   E-mail: education@eatright.org
Web: www.eatright.org

Purpose To provide financial assistance to students who are in the first year of a dietetic technician program.
Eligibility Applicants must be in the first year of study in a CADE-approved or accredited dietetic technician program. All applicants must be U.S. citizens or permanent residents and show promise of being a valuable, contributing member of the profession. Some scholarships require membership in the association, specific dietetic practice group membership, residency in a specific state, or underrepresented minority group status. The same application form can be used for all categories.
Financial data Awards range from $500 to $5,000.
Duration 1 year.
Additional information Funds must be used for the second year of study.
Number awarded Varies each year, depending upon the funds available. Recently, the sponsoring organization awarded 209 scholarships for all its programs.
Deadline February of each year.

[86]
DISTRICT OF COLUMBIA SPACE GRANT CONSORTIUM AWARDS

District of Columbia Space Grant Consortium
c/o American University
Department of Physics
McKinley Building, Suite 106
4400 Massachusetts Avenue, N.W.
Washington, DC 20016-8058
(202) 885-2780   Fax: (202) 885-2723
E-mail: SpaceGrant@aol.com
Web: www.DCSpaceGrant.org

Purpose To provide financial assistance to undergraduate and graduate students studying space-related fields at member institutions of the District of Columbia Space Grant Consortium.
Eligibility This program is open to students at member institutions of the consortium. Each participating university conducts its own program. The consortium is a component of the Space Grant program of the U.S. National Aeronautics and Space Administration (NASA), which encourages participation by women, underrepresented minorities, and persons with disabilities.
Financial data Each university determines the amount of the awards.
Additional information Institutions participating in the consortium include American University, Gallaudet University, George Washington University, Howard University, and the University of the District of Columbia. Funding for this program is provided by NASA.
Number awarded Varies each year.

[87]
DON SAHLI–KATHY WOODALL MINORITY STUDENT SCHOLARSHIPS

Tennessee Education Association
801 Second Avenue North
Nashville, TN 37201-1099
(615) 242-8392   (800) 342-8262
Fax: (615) 259-4581
Web: www.teateachers.org

Purpose To provide financial assistance to minority high school seniors in Tennessee who are interested in majoring in education.
Eligibility This program is open to minority high school seniors in Tennessee who are planning to major in education. Application must be made by either a Future Teachers of America chapter affiliated with the Tennessee Education Association (TEA) or by the student with the recommendation of an active TEA member. Selection is based on academic record, leadership ability, economic need, and demonstrated interest in becoming a teacher.
Financial data The stipend is $1,000.
Duration 1 year.
Number awarded 1 each year.

[88]
DOUVAS MEMORIAL SCHOLARSHIP

Wyoming Department of Education
Attn: Director, Programs Unit
2300 Capitol Avenue
Cheyenne, WY 82002-0050
(307) 777-7168   Fax: (307) 777-6234
E-mail: psoumo@educ.state.wy.us
Web: www.k12.wy.us/ADMIN/awards/douvasmemorial.htm

Purpose To provide financial assistance to high school seniors or students in Wyoming who are first-generation Americans.
Eligibility This program is open to first-generation youth in Wyoming who demonstrate need and are motivated to attend college. First-generation Americans are those born in the United States but whose parents were not born here. Applicants must be high school seniors or between the ages of 18 and 22. They must be Wyoming residents and be willing to use the scholarship at Wyoming's community colleges or the University of Wyoming.
Financial data The stipend is $500, payable in 2 equal installments. Funds are paid directly to the recipient's school.
Duration 1 year.
Additional information This scholarship was first awarded in 1995.
Number awarded 1 each year.
Deadline April of each year.

[89]
DR. JUAN ANDRADE, JR. SCHOLARSHIP FOR YOUNG HISPANIC LEADERS

United States Hispanic Leadership Institute
431 South Dearborn Street, Suite 1203
Chicago, IL 60605
(312) 427-8683   Fax: (312) 427-5183
E-mail: ushli@aol.com
Web: www.ushli.com/aScholarship.htm

Purpose To provide financial assistance for college to Hispanic students in the United States.

Eligibility This program is open to U.S. citizens and permanent residents who are enrolled or accepted for enrollment as full-time students at a 4-year college or university in the United States. Applicants must have at least 1 parent of Hispanic ancestry. They must be able to demonstrate financial need. Along with their application, they must submit 1) a 250- to 500-word essay on their family history, life and/or work experiences that have influenced them, pertinent extracurricular and community involvement activities, and a self-description; 2) a 500- to 750-word essay on the future of Hispanics in America, the kind of leadership needed, and any role they hope to play in providing such leadership; 3) a transcript; and 4) 3 letters of reference.

Financial data The stipend is at least $1,000.

Duration 1 year.

Additional information This program began in 1994. Recipients are expected to pay for their own travel expenses to Chicago to attend a luncheon of the sponsor where they are introduced. Expenses for lodging and meals are covered by the sponsor.

Number awarded 1 or more each year.

Deadline July of each year.

[90]
DR. JUAN D. VILLARREAL–HDA FOUNDATION SCHOLARSHIPS

Hispanic Dental Association
Attn: HDA Foundation
188 West Randolph Street, Suite 415
Chicago, IL 60601
(312) 577-4013   (800) 852-7921
Fax: (312) 577-0052   E-mail: hdassoc1@qwest.net
Web: www.hdassoc.org

Purpose To provide financial assistance to Hispanic dental hygiene and dental students at institutions in Texas.

Eligibility This program is open to Hispanic dental hygiene and dental students. Applicants must have been accepted or be currently enrolled at an accredited dental school in Texas.

Financial data Stipends are $1,000 or $500.

Duration 1 year.

Number awarded 1 or more each year.

Deadline June of each year.

[91]
DR. SCHOLL FOUNDATION SCHOLARSHIPS

Chicago Urban League
Attn: Scholarship Coordinator
4510 South Michigan Avenue
Chicago, IL 60653-3898
(773) 451-3567   Fax: (773) 285-7772
E-mail: info@cul-chicago.org
Web: www.cul-chicago.org

Purpose To provide financial assistance to Illinois residents of color enrolled at a 4-year college or university.

Eligibility This program is open to Illinois residents of color who are full-time undergraduate students at a 4-year college or university with at least a 2.5 GPA. Applicants may be majoring in any field. Financial need must be demonstrated.

Financial data The stipend is $2,000 per year.

Duration 1 year.

Additional information This program is offered as part of the Chicago Urban League's Whitney M. Young, Jr. Memorial Schol-

arship Fund, established in 1970. It is sponsored by the Dr. Scholl Foundation.

Number awarded Varies each year.

Deadline May of each year.

[92]
DVSGC UNDERGRADUATE TUITION SCHOLARSHIPS

Delaware Valley Space Grant College Consortium
c/o University of Delaware
Bartol Research Institute
104 Center Mall, #217
Newark, DE 19716-4793
(302) 831-1094   Fax: (302) 831-1843
E-mail: nfness@bartol.udel.edu
Web: www.delspace.org

Purpose To provide financial support to undergraduate students in Delaware and Pennsylvania involved in space-related studies.

Eligibility This program is open to undergraduate students in aerospace engineering and space science-related fields studying at institutions belonging to the Delaware Valley Space Grant College (DVSGC) Consortium. U.S. citizenship is required. As a component of the U.S. National Aeronautics and Space Administration (NASA) Space Grant program, this program encourages applications from women, minorities, and persons with disabilities.

Financial data This program provides tuition assistance up to $4,000 per year.

Duration 1 year; may be renewed.

Additional information This program is funded by NASA. Members of the consortium include Delaware State University (Dover, Delaware), Delaware Technical and Community College (Dover, Delaware), Franklin and Marshall College (Lancaster, Pennsylvania), Gettysburg College (Gettysburg, Pennsylvania), Lehigh University (Bethlehem, Pennsylvania), Lincoln University (Lincoln University, Pennsylvania), Swarthmore College (Swarthmore, Pennsylvania), University of Delaware–Bartol Research Institute (Newark, Delaware), University of Pennsylvania (Philadelphia, Pennsylvania), Villanova University (Villanova, Pennsylvania), and Wilmington College (New Castle, Delaware).

Number awarded Varies each year; recently, 11 students received these scholarships.

Deadline February of each year.

[93]
EARL P. ANDREWS, JR. MEMORIAL SCHOLARSHIP

Central Alabama Community Foundation
412 North Hull Street
P.O. Box 11587
Montgomery, AL 36111
(334) 264-6223   Fax: (334) 263-6225

Purpose To provide financial assistance for college to minority high school seniors in central Alabama.

Eligibility This program is open to minority high school seniors in central Alabama who have at least a 3.5 GPA and a minimum ACT score of 23 or the SAT equivalent. To apply, students must submit a completed application form, a high school transcript, and an essay outlining career goals. Finalists are interviewed. Selection is based on academic achievement and financial need.

Financial data The stipend ranges from $500 to $1,000 per year.

Duration 1 year.

Additional information This program was funded in 1989.

Number awarded 1 each year.

Deadline March of each year.

[94]
EARL PHILLIPS SCHOLARSHIP

YMCA of Greater Seattle
Human Resources Department
Attn: Scholarship Committee
909 Fourth Avenue
Seattle, WA 98104
(206) 382-5003

Purpose To provide financial assistance for college to Christian minority students in Washington state who are preparing for a career with the YMCA.

Eligibility This program is open to minority students in Washington state who are Christians and preparing for employment with the YMCA or a related organization. Appropriate courses of study in college include: human services, child development, physical education, health/fitness, psychology, education, recreation, sociology, business administration, and related fields. Applicants must be able to demonstrate leadership in the YMCA, school, or other organizations. They may be high school seniors, high school/GED program graduates, or currently-enrolled college undergraduates. Selection is based on leadership and participation in school, YMCA, and community activities; academic achievement and honors; financial need; work experience; statement of career and educational goals; and recommendations. Finalists may be interviewed.

Financial data Up to $1,000 per year.

Duration Up to a maximum of 4 years.

Number awarded The number of scholarships awarded varies each year; not all applicants receive awards.

Deadline Students must request application materials in January or February. The completed application must be returned by the end of March.

[95]
EAST OHIO CONFERENCE BOARD OF ORDAINED MINISTRY ETHNIC MINORITY GRANTS

East Ohio Conference Board of Ordained Ministry
c/o Preston Forbes, Grant/Scholarship Secretary
9071 Inverrary Drive
Warren, OH 44484
(330) 856-2631   E-mail: forbes@onecom.com

Purpose To provide financial assistance to ethnic minority undergraduate and graduate students who are preparing for ordained ministry in the East Ohio Conference.

Eligibility This program is open to ethnic minority college and graduate students who are preparing for ordained ministry in the East Ohio Conference. Students must be recommended to receive this aid either by their District Superintendent or by the District Committee on Ordained Ministry where they hold their relationship. Applicants must attend a college or seminary that is fully accredited by the University Senate. They do not need to be certified candidates. Ethnic minority undergraduate pre-theological students are also eligible.

Financial data The stipend is $500 per year.

Duration 1 year.

Number awarded 1 or more each year.

Deadline September of each year.

[96]
EATON MULTICULTURAL ENGINEERING SCHOLARS PROGRAM

Eaton Corporation
c/o INROADS
The Lorenzo Carter Building
1360 West Ninth Street, Suite 260
Cleveland, OH 44113
(216) 623-1010
Web: www.eaton.com

Purpose To provide financial assistance and work experience to minority college students interested in a career as an engineer.

Eligibility This program is open to full-time minority engineering students who are U.S. citizens or permanent residents. Applicants must have completed 1 year in an accredited engineering program and have 3 remaining years of course work before completing a bachelor's degree. They must have a GPA of 2.8 or higher and an expressed interest in at least 1 of the following areas of engineering as a major: computer, electrical, electronic, industrial, manufacturing, materials, mechanical, or software. Selection is based on academic performance, the student's school recommendation, and an expressed interest in pursuing challenging and rewarding internship assignments.

Financial data Stipends up to $2,500 per year are provided. Funds are paid directly to the recipient's university to cover the cost of tuition, books, supplies, equipment, and fees.

Duration 3 years.

Additional information In addition to the scholarships, recipients are offered paid summer internships at company headquarters in Cleveland. The target schools participating in this program are Cornell, Detroit-Mercy, Florida A&M, Georgia Tech, Illinois at Chicago, Illinois at Urbana-Champaign, Lawrence Technological, Marquette, Massachusetts Institute of Technology, Michigan at Ann Arbor, Michigan at Dearborn, Michigan State, Milwaukee School of Engineering, Minnesota, Morehouse College, North Carolina A&T State, North Carolina State, Northwestern, Notre Dame, Ohio State, Purdue, Southern, Tennessee, Western Michigan, and Wisconsin at Madison. This program was established in 1994. Until 2002, it was known as the Eaton Minority Engineering Scholars Program.

Number awarded Varies each year.

Deadline January of each year.

[97]
ED BRADLEY SCHOLARSHIP

Radio and Television News Directors Foundation
1000 Connecticut Avenue, N.W., Suite 615
Washington, DC 20036-5302
(202) 467-5218   Fax: (202) 223-4007
E-mail: karenb@rtndf.org
Web: www.rtndf.org/asfi/scholarships/undergrad.shtml

Purpose To provide financial assistance to outstanding undergraduate students, especially minorities, who are preparing for a career in electronic journalism.

Eligibility Eligible are sophomore or more advanced undergraduate students enrolled in an electronic journalism sequence at an accredited or nationally-recognized college or university.

Applicants must submit 1 to 3 examples of reporting or producing skills on audio or video cassette tapes (no more than 15 minutes total), a statement explaining why they are interested in a career in broadcast or cable journalism, and a letter of endorsement from a faculty sponsor that verifies the applicant has at least 1 year of school remaining. Preference is given to undergraduate students of color.

Financial data The stipend is $10,000, paid in semiannual installments of $5,000 each.

Duration 1 year.

Additional information The Radio and Television News Directors Foundation (RTNDF) also provides an expense-paid trip to the Radio-Television News Directors Association (RTNDA) annual international conference. It defines electronic journalism to include radio, television, cable, and online news. Previous winners of any RTNDF scholarship or internship are not eligible.

Number awarded 1 each year.

Deadline April of each year.

[98]
EDISON INTERNATIONAL SCHOLARSHIPS

TELACU Education Foundation
5400 East Olympic Boulevard, Suite 300
Los Angeles, CA 90022
(323) 721-1655   Fax: (323) 724-3372
E-mail: info@telacu.com
Web: www.telacu.com

Purpose To provide financial assistance to Latinos in southern California who wish to pursue careers in teaching.

Eligibility Applicants must be high school seniors who are citizens or permanent residents of the United States, attending school or living in an area served by Edison International, and planning a career in teaching. Selection is based on an interview and 2 essays: 1 that addresses their goals and ambitions, reasons for pursuing a degree in the field they have chosen, commitment to their community, and how they plan to help their community after graduation, and 1 that describes why they should be considered for this special award.

Financial data The award is $1,000 per year.

Duration 4 years.

Number awarded 2 each year.

Deadline April of each year.

[99]
EDUCATIONAL ADVANCEMENT BSN COMPLETION SCHOLARSHIPS

American Association of Critical-Care Nurses
Attn: Educational Advancement Scholarships
101 Columbia
Aliso Viejo, CA 92656-4109
(949) 362-2000, ext. 338   (800) 899-AACN, ext. 338
Fax: (949) 362-2020   E-mail: info@aacn.org
Web: www.aacn.org

Purpose To provide financial assistance to members of the American Association of Critical-Care Nurses (AACN) who are working on a B.S.N. degree in nursing.

Eligibility Registered nurses who are current members of the association and enrolled in an accredited program in nursing leading to a B.S.N. degree are eligible to apply. This program is open to nurses who hold an active R.N. license and are currently working in critical care or have 1 year's experience in the last 3

years. They must have a cumulative GPA of 3.0 or higher and plan to hold junior or upper-division status in the fall semester. As part of the application process, they must describe their contributions to critical care nursing, including work, community, and profession-related activities. Financial need is not considered in the selection process. Qualified ethnic minority candidates receive at least 20% of these awards.

Financial data The stipend is $1,500 per year. The funds are sent directly to the recipient's college or university and may be used only for tuition, fees, books, and supplies.

Duration 1 year; recipients may reapply.

Number awarded Varies each year; recently, 25 of these scholarships were awarded.

Deadline March of each year.

[100]
EDWARD D. STONE, JR. AND ASSOCIATES MINORITY SCHOLARSHIP

Landscape Architecture Foundation
Attn: Scholarship Program
636 Eye Street, N.W.
Washington, DC 20001-3736
(202) 216-2356   Fax: (202) 898-1185
E-mail: msippel@asla.org
Web: www.laprofession.org

Purpose To provide financial assistance to minority college students who wish to study landscape architecture.

Eligibility This program is open to African American, Hispanic, Native American, and minority college students of other cultural and ethnic backgrounds, if they are entering their final 2 years of undergraduate study in landscape architecture. Applicants must submit a 500-word essay on a design or research effort they wish to pursue (explaining how it will contribute to the advancement of the profession and to their ethnic heritage), 4 to 8 35mm color slides or black-and-white photographs of their best work, and 2 letters of recommendation. Selection is based on professional experience, community involvement, extracurricular activities, and financial need.

Financial data The stipend is $1,000.

Duration 1 year.

Number awarded 2 each year.

Deadline March of each year.

[101]
EDWARD DAVIS SCHOLARSHIP FUND

Auto Industry Diversity Efforts
65 Cadillac Square, Suite 2815
Detroit, MI 48226
(313) 963-2209   (877) 847-9060
Web: www.automag.com

Purpose To provide financial assistance to minority students interested in preparing for a career in an automotive-related profession.

Eligibility Applicants must be minority high school seniors or currently-enrolled college students who are interested in preparing for a career in the automotive industry. High school students must have a GPA of 3.0 or higher; college students must have at least a 2.5. To apply, students must complete an application; provide proof of acceptance or enrollment in an accredited college, university, vocational institute, or technical school; and submit an essay (up to 200 words) on "The Importance of Diversity in the Automobile Industry."

Financial data A stipend is awarded (amount not specified).

Duration 1 year.

Additional information This scholarship, established in 1999, honors the first African American to own a new car dealership.

[102]
EDWARD S. ROTH MANUFACTURING ENGINEERING SCHOLARSHIP

Society of Manufacturing Engineers
Attn: SME Education Foundation
One SME Drive
P.O. Box 930
Dearborn, MI 48121-0930
(313) 271-1500, ext. 1707   (800) 733-4763
Fax: (313) 271-2861   E-mail: monzcyn@sme.org
Web: www.sme.org

Purpose To provide financial assistance to students enrolled or planning to enroll in a degree program in manufacturing engineering at selected universities.

Eligibility This program is open to U.S. citizens who are graduating high school seniors or currently-enrolled undergraduate or graduate students. Applicants must be enrolled or planning to enroll as a full-time student at 1 of 13 selected 4-year universities to pursue a bachelor's or master's degree in manufacturing engineering. They must have a GPA of 3.0 or higher. Preference is given to 1) students demonstrating financial need, 2) minority students, and 3) students participating in a co-op program.

Financial data The stipend is $2,500.

Duration 1 year; may be renewed.

Additional information The eligible institutions are California Polytechnic State University at San Luis Obispo, California State Polytechnic State University at Pomona, University of Miami (Florida), Bradley University, Central State University (Ohio), Miami University (Ohio), Boston University, Worcester Polytechnic Institute, University of Massachusetts, St. Cloud State University, University of Texas-Pan American, Brigham Young University, and Utah State University.

Number awarded 1 each year.

Deadline January of each year.

[103]
EISENHOWER HISPANIC-SERVING INSTITUTIONS FELLOWSHIPS

Department of Transportation
Federal Highway Administration
Attn: National Highway Institute
4600 North Fairfax Drive, Suite 800
Arlington, VA 22203-1553
(703) 235-0538   Fax: (703) 235-0593
E-mail: ilene.payne@fhwa.dov.gov
Web: www.nhi.fhwa.dot.gov/fellowships.html

Purpose To provide financial assistance for undergraduate study in transportation-related fields to students at Hispanic Serving Institutions.

Eligibility These fellowships are intended for students who are enrolled at federally-designated 4-year Hispanic-Serving Institutions (HSIs) and who are working on a degree in a transportation-related field (i.e., engineering, accounting, business, architecture,

environmental sciences, etc.). Applicants must have entered their junior year, have at least a 3.0 GPA, and have a faculty sponsor.

Financial data The stipend covers the fellow's full cost of education, including tuition and fees.

Duration 1 year.

Number awarded Varies each year; recently, 18 students received support from this program.

Deadline February of each year.

[104]
ELLEN MASIN PERSINA SCHOLARSHIP

National Press Club
Attn: General Manager's Office
529 14th Street, N.W.
Washington, DC 20045
(202) 662-7532   E-mail: jbooze@press.org
Web: www.press.org/programs/aboutscholarship.shtml

Purpose To provide funding to minority high school seniors interested in preparing for a journalism career in college.

Eligibility This program is open to minority high school seniors who have been accepted to college and plan to pursue a career in journalism. Applicants must 1) demonstrate an ongoing interest in journalism through work in high school and/or other media; 2) submit a 1-page essay on why they want to pursue a career in journalism; and 3) have a GPA of 2.75 or higher in high school. Financial need is considered in the selection process.

Financial data The stipend is $5,000 per year.

Duration 4 years.

Additional information The program began in 1991. In the past, the Press Club has drawn on the Washington Association of Black Journalists and Youth Connections (a nationwide organization that produces free papers written by high school students).

Number awarded 1 or more each year.

Deadline February of each year.

[105]
ENGINEERING VANGUARD PROGRAM SCHOLARSHIPS

National Action Council for Minorities in Engineering
350 Fifth Avenue, Suite 2212
New York, NY 10118-2299
(212) 279-2626   Fax: (212) 629-5178
E-mail: awalter@nacme.org
Web: www.nacme.org/prec/scol/vanguard.html

Purpose To provide financial assistance to underrepresented minority high school seniors who are interested in studying engineering or a related field at designated universities.

Eligibility This program is open to African American, Latino, and American Indian high school seniors who are U.S. citizens or permanent residents. Applicants must be interested in majoring at a participating partner university in 1 of the following fields: architectural engineering, aerospace engineering, agricultural engineering, biomedical engineering, chemical engineering, civil engineering, computer engineering, computer science, electrical engineering, engineering science, engineering technology, environmental engineering, environmental science, industrial engineering, information systems and technology, manufacturing engineering, materials science, mathematics, mechanical engineering, metallurgical engineering, nuclear engineering, operations research, petroleum engineering, physics, or systems engineering. Students with substantial financial need are given priority.

Financial data This program provides full payment of tuition and room costs at participating universities.

Duration 1 year; may be renewed until completion of a bachelor's degree as long as the recipient maintains full-time enrollment and a GPA of 2.5 or higher.

Additional information The current partner institutions include Clarkson University (for New York residents only), Drexel University, Howard University, New Jersey Institute of Technology, Polytech University, Renselaer Polytechnic University, Rochester Institute of Technology, and the University of Colorado at Boulder (for Colorado residents only).

Number awarded Varies each year.

Deadline October of each year.

[106]
ENVIRONMENTAL EDUCATIONAL SCHOLARSHIP PROGRAM

Missouri Department of Natural Resources
P.O. Box 176
Jefferson City, MO 65102
(573) 751-2518   (800) 334-6946
TDD: (800) 379-2419
Web: dnr.state.mo.us/eesp

Purpose To provide financial assistance to underrepresented and minority students from Missouri who are studying an environmental field in college or graduate school.

Eligibility This program is open to minority and underrepresented residents of Missouri who have graduated from an accredited high school with a GPA of 3.0 or higher. Students who are already enrolled in college must have a GPA of 2.5 or higher and must be full-time students. Applicants may be 1) engineering students pursuing undergraduate and graduate degrees in civil, chemical, mechanical, or agricultural engineering; 2) environmental students pursuing undergraduate or graduate degrees in geology, biology, wildlife management, planning, natural resources, or a closely-related course of study; 3) chemistry students pursuing undergraduate or graduate degrees in the field of environmental chemistry; or 4) law enforcement students pursuing undergraduate or graduate degrees in environmental law enforcement. Selection is based on GPA and test scores, school and community activities, leadership and character, and a 1-page essay.

Financial data A stipend is awarded (amount not specified).

Duration 1 year; may be renewed if the recipient maintains a GPA of 2.5 or higher and full-time enrollment.

Number awarded Varies each year.

Deadline November of each year.

[107]
ENVIRONMENTAL MANAGEMENT SCHOLARSHIP

Hispanic Scholarship Fund Institute
1001 Connecticut Avenue, N.W., Suite 632
Washington, DC 20036
(202) 296-0009   Fax: (202) 296-3633
E-mail: info@hsfi.org
Web: www.hsfi.org/sch_energy.html

Purpose To provide financial assistance to Hispanic undergraduate students majoring in designated business, engineering, and science fields related to the U.S. Department of Energy (DOE) goal of environmental restoration and waste management.

Eligibility This program is open to U.S. citizens and permanent residents of Hispanic background who have completed at least 12 undergraduate college credits with a GPA of 2.8 or higher. Applicants must be interested in pursuing a career supportive of the DOE goal of environmental restoration and waste management. Eligible academic majors are in the fields of business (management and system analysis), engineering (agricultural, chemical, civil, electrical, environmental, industrial, mechanical, metallurgical, nuclear, and petroleum), and science (applied math/physics, chemistry, computer science, ecology, environmental, epidemiology, geology, health physics, hydrology, radiochemistry, radio-ecology, and toxicology). Along with their application, they must submit a 2-page essay on why a career in public service interests them, how their academic major connects with their stated DOE career goal, why the DOE should invest in them through this program, and how they believe the DOE will benefit from this investment. Selection is based on academic achievement, financial need, and demonstrated commitment to a career in public service.

Financial data The stipend is $3,000 per year for 4-year university students or $2,000 per year for community college students.

Duration 1 year.

Additional information This program, which began in 1990, is sponsored by DOE's Office of Environmental Management. Recipients must enroll full time at a college or university in the United States.

Number awarded Varies each year.

Deadline February of each year.

[108]
ESPERANZA SCHOLARSHIP FUND

Esperanza, Inc.
Attn: Executive Director
4115 Bridge Avenue
Cleveland, OH 44113
(216) 651-7178   Fax: (216) 651-7183
E-mail: hope4edu@aol.com
Web: www.esperanza.org

Purpose To provide financial assistance for postsecondary education to students of Hispanic descent in the Cleveland area.

Eligibility This program is open to Hispanic students in Ashtabula, Cuyahoga, Geauga, Lake, Lorain, Medina, Portage, Stark, and Summit counties (Ohio) who wish to enroll as full-time students in a college, university, trade apprenticeship program, or accredited technical institute. They must be graduating high school seniors, high school graduates, GED recipients, or current college or university students. Financial need must be demonstrated.

Financial data Stipends range from $500 to $2,500. Funds must be used for tuition, room and board, educational expenses, or books at an accredited college or university.

Duration 1 year; may be renewed for up to 3 additional years if the recipient maintains at least a 2.0 GPA in college.

Additional information This organization was formerly known as the Cleveland Hispanic Scholarship Fund. The program defines Hispanic students as those who have at least 1 parent who is of Puerto Rican, Mexican, Dominican, Cuban, Central American, South American, or Spanish origin.

Number awarded Approximately 35 each year.

Deadline February of each year.

[109]
ETHNIC MINORITY BACHELOR'S SCHOLARSHIPS IN ONCOLOGY NURSING

Oncology Nursing Society
Attn: ONS Foundation
501 Holiday Drive
Pittsburgh, PA 15220-2749
(412) 921-7373, ext. 231   Fax: (412) 921-6565
E-mail: foundation@ons.org
Web: www.ons.org

Purpose To provide financial assistance to ethnic minorities interested in pursuing undergraduate studies in oncology nursing.
Eligibility The candidate must 1) demonstrate an interest in and commitment to cancer nursing; 2) be enrolled in an undergraduate nursing degree program at an NLN- or CCNE-accredited school of nursing (the program must have application to oncology nursing); 3) have a current license to practice as a registered nurse or a practical (vocational) nurse; 4) not have previously received a bachelor's scholarship from this sponsor; and 5) be a member of an ethnic minority group (Native American, African American, Asian American, Pacific Islander, Hispanic/Latino, or other ethnic minority background). Applicants must submit an essay of 250 words or less on their role in caring for persons with cancer and a statement of their professional goals and their relationship to the advancement of oncology nursing. Financial need is not considered in the selection process.
Financial data The stipend is $2,000.
Duration 1 year.
Additional information This program includes a mentoring component with an individual in the applicant's area of clinical interest. When appropriate, efforts are made to match the applicant and mentor by ethnicity. At the end of each year of scholarship participation, recipients must submit a summary describing their educational activities. Applications must be accompanied by a $5 fee.
Number awarded 3 each year.
Deadline January of each year.

[110]
ETHNIC MISSIONS SCHOLARSHIP PROGRAM

Baptist General Convention of Texas
State Missions Commission
Attn: Ethnic Missions
333 North Washington
Dallas, TX 75246-1798
(214) 828-5342   (800) 352-5342
Fax: (214) 828-5284   E-mail: deleon@bgct.org
Web: www.bgct.org/ethnic_missions

Purpose To provide financial assistance for college or seminary education to ethnic and deaf students in Texas who are members of Texas Baptist ethnic congregations.
Eligibility This program is open to members of Texas Baptist congregations who are Asian, Hispanic, or deaf and have a "sense of call" as a lay person or minister. Applicants must be U.S. citizens or permanent residents, have resided in Texas for at least 1 year, demonstrate financial need, and plan to attend or be attending a Texas Baptist university or the Southwestern Baptist Theological Seminary. Students still in high school must have a GPA of at least 3.0; students previously enrolled in a college or seminary must have at least a 2.0 GPA. Applicants must submit brief essays on what they, as a Baptist, believe about God, Jesus, sin, salvation, church membership, and baptism.

They must also explain how they became a Christian, why they are seeking a Christian university education, and what they plan to do following graduation.
Financial data The grant for full-time students is $800 per year or $400 per semester. Part-time students receive $27 per credit hour.
Duration 1 year; may be renewed.
Additional information The scholarships are funded through the Week of Prayer and the Mary Hill Davis Offering for state missions sponsored annually by Women's Missionary Union of Texas.

[111]
FALU FOUNDATION SCHOLARSHIP

Falú Foundation
c/o Universal Business and Media School
220 East 106th Street
New York, NY 10029
(212) 360-1210   Fax: (212) 360-1231
E-mail: falu@ubms.edu
Web: www.ubms.edu/FaluFoundation.html

Purpose To provide funding to Hispanic students interested in preparing for a career in technology.
Eligibility This program is open to Hispanic students who are interested in preparing for a career in computer technology or information technology. Applicants must be enrolled in or admitted to an accredited business school, college, or university.
Financial data The stipend is $1,000.
Number awarded 1 or more each year.

[112]
FIRST IN MY FAMILY SCHOLARSHIP PROGRAM

Hispanic College Fund
Attn: National Director
1717 Pennsylvania Avenue, N.W., Suite 460
Washington, D.C. 20006
(800) 644-4223   Fax: (202) 296-3774
E-mail: hispaniccollegefund@earthlink.net
Web: www.hispanicfund.org

Purpose To provide financial assistance to Hispanic American undergraduate students who are the first in their family to attend college and are majoring in business, computer science, or engineering.
Eligibility This program is open to U.S. citizens of Hispanic background who are entering their freshman, sophomore, junior, or senior year of college and are the first member of their family to attend college. Applicants must be working on a bachelor's degree in business, computer science, engineering, or a business-related major and have a cumulative GPA of 3.0 or higher. They must be applying to or enrolled in a college or university in the 50 states or Puerto Rico as a full-time student. Financial need is considered in the selection process.
Financial data Stipends range from $1,000 to $5,000, depending on the need of the recipient. Funds are paid directly to the recipient's college or university to help cover tuition and fees.
Duration 1 year; recipients may reapply.
Additional information This program is sponsored by the Sallie Mae Community Foundation for the National Capital Region and Sallie Mae.
Number awarded Varies each year.
Deadline April of each year.

[113]
FISHER BROADCASTING SCHOLARSHIPS FOR MINORITIES

Fisher Broadcasting Company
600 University Street, Suite 1525
Seattle, WA 98101
(206) 404-6048
Web: www.fsci.com/broadcasting/scholarship.htm

Purpose To provide financial assistance to minority college students in selected states who are interested in preparing for a career in broadcasting, marketing, or journalism.

Eligibility This program is open to minority students (Blacks, Hispanics, Native Americans, or Asian/Pacific Islanders) who are U.S. citizens, have a GPA of 2.5 or higher, and are sophomores enrolled in 1) a broadcasting, marketing, or journalism curriculum leading to a bachelor's degree at an accredited 4-year college or university; 2) a broadcast curriculum at an accredited community college, transferable to a 4-year baccalaureate degree program; or 3) a broadcast curriculum at an accredited vocational/technical school. Applicants must be 1) residents of Washington, Oregon, Idaho, Montana, or Georgia, or 2) attending a school in those states. They must submit an essay that explains their financial need, education and career goals, and school activities; a copy of their college transcript; and 2 letters of recommendation.

Financial data Awards provide assistance in payment of tuition.

Duration 1 year; recipients may reapply.

Additional information This program began in 1987.

Number awarded Several each year.

Deadline April of each year.

[114]
FLEMING/BLASZCAK SCHOLARSHIP

Society of Plastics Engineers
Attn: SPE Foundation
14 Fairfield Drive
Brookfield, CT 06804
(203) 740-5434   Fax: (203) 775-8490
E-mail: foundation@4spe.org
Web: www.4spe.org

Purpose To provide college scholarships to Mexican American undergraduate and graduate students who have a career interest in the plastics industry.

Eligibility This program is open to full-time undergraduate and graduate students of Mexican descent who are enrolled in a 4-year college or university. Applicants must be U.S. citizens or legal residents. They must have a demonstrated or expressed interest in the plastics industry and should be taking classes that would be beneficial to a career in the plastics industry (e.g., plastics engineering, polymer sciences, chemistry, physics, chemical engineering, mechanical engineering, industrial engineering, and business administration). Financial need must be documented. Along with their application, students must submit 3 letters of recommendation; a high school and/or college transcript; a 1- to 2-page statement telling why they are interested in the scholarship, their qualifications, and their career goals in the plastics industry; and documentation of their Mexican heritage.

Financial data The stipend is $2,000 per year.

Duration 1 year.

Additional information This program is sponsored by Cal Mold Inc. and Formula Plastics.

Number awarded 1 each year.

Deadline December of each year.

[115]
FLORIDA NICARAGUAN AND HAITIAN SCHOLARSHIPS

Florida Department of Education
Attn: Office of Student Financial Assistance
1940 North Monroe Street, Suite 70
Tallahassee, FL 32303-4759
(850) 410-5185   (888) 827-2004
Fax: (850) 488-3612   E-mail: osfa@mail.doe.state.fl.us
Web: www.firn.edu/doe/osfa

Purpose To provide financial assistance for undergraduate and graduate studies to residents of Florida who were born in Nicaragua or Haiti.

Eligibility This program is open to residents of Florida who are citizens of, or were born in, Nicaragua or Haiti. Applicants must be enrolled or planning to enroll in an undergraduate or graduate level program of study at a state university in Florida. They must have at least a 3.0 cumulative GPA either in high school (if a graduating senior) or in college (if currently enrolled). Selection is based on academic achievement and community service.

Financial data The stipend ranges from $4,000 to $5,000 per year.

Duration 1 year; nonrenewable, although recipients may reapply in subsequent years.

Number awarded 2 each year: 1 to a Nicaraguan and 1 to a Haitian.

Deadline June of each year.

[116]
FLORIDA SOCIETY OF NEWSPAPER EDITORS MINORITY SCHOLARSHIP PROGRAM

Florida Society of Newspaper Editors
c/o Kevin Walsh, Scholarship Committee
Florida Press Association
122 South Calhoun Street
Tallahassee, FL 32301-1554
(850) 222-5790   Fax: (850) 224-6012
E-mail: info@fsne.org
Web: www.fsne.org/minorityscholar.html

Purpose To provide financial assistance and summer work experience to minority upper-division students majoring in journalism at a college or university in Florida.

Eligibility This program is open to minority students in accredited journalism or mass communication programs at Florida 4-year colleges and universities. Applicants must be full-time students in their junior year, have at least a 3.0 GPA, and be willing to participate in a paid summer internship at a Florida newspaper. As part of the application process, they must write a 300-word autobiographical essay explaining why they want to pursue a career in print journalism and provide a standard resume, references, and clips or examples of relevant classroom work.

Financial data Winners are given a paid summer internship at a participating newspaper between their junior and senior year. Upon successfully completing the internship, the students are awarded a $3,600 scholarship (paid in 2 equal installments) to be used during their senior year.

Duration 1 summer for the internship; 1 academic year for the scholarship.

Deadline December of each year.

[117]
FOOD MARKETING INSTITUTE SCHOLARSHIPS

DECA
1908 Association Drive
Reston, VA 20191-1594
(703) 860-5000 Fax: (703) 860-4013
E-mail: decainc@aol.com
Web: www.deca.org/scholarships/index.html

Purpose To provide financial assistance to DECA members who are women or minorities and interested in attending college to prepare for a marketing career.

Eligibility This program is open to DECA members who are minorities and/or women intending to pursue a career in marketing, business, or marketing education. Applicants must be able to demonstrate supermarket industry experience, DECA activities, grades, and leadership ability. Awards are made on the basis of merit, not financial need.

Financial data The stipend is $1,000.

Duration 1 year.

Additional information This program is sponsored by the Food Marketing Institute.

Number awarded 5 each year.

Deadline February of each year.

[118]
FORD/HENAAC SCHOLARS PROGRAM

Hispanic Engineer National Achievement Awards Conference
3900 Whiteside Street
Los Angeles, CA 90063
(323) 262-0997 Fax: (323) 262-0946
E-mail: info@henaac.org
Web: www.henaac.org/scholarships.htm

Purpose To provide financial assistance to Hispanic undergraduate students majoring in engineering and related fields.

Eligibility This program is open to Hispanic undergraduate students who are majoring in computer science or the following engineering fields: aeronautical, electrical, industrial, and, mechanical. Applicants must have a GPA of 3.0 or higher. Academic achievement and campus community activities are considered in the selection process.

Financial data The stipend is $5,000.

Duration 1 year.

Additional information This program is sponsored by Ford Motor Company as part of its effort to support the mission of the Hispanic Engineer National Achievement Awards Conference (HENAAC) to promote technical excellence and leadership in the Hispanic community.

Number awarded 5 each year.

Deadline April of each year.

[119]
FORE DIVERSITY SCHOLARSHIPS

American Health Information Management Association
Attn: Foundation of Research and Education
233 North Michigan Avenue, Suite 2150
Chicago, IL 60601-5519
(312) 233-1168 Fax: (312) 233-1090
E-mail: fore@ahima.org
Web: www.ahima.org/fore/programs.html

Purpose To provide financial assistance to minority members of the American Health Information Management Association (AHIMA) who are interested in working on an undergraduate degree in health information administration or technology.

Eligibility This program is open to AHIMA members who are enrolled in a health information administration or health information technology program accredited by the Commission on Accreditation of Allied Health Education Programs. Applicants must be minorities, be pursuing a degree on at least a half-time basis, and have a GPA of 3.0 or higher. U.S. citizenship is required. Selection is based on GPA and academic achievement, volunteer and work experience, commitment to the health information management profession, suitability to the health information management profession, quality and suitability of references provided, and clarity of application.

Financial data Stipends range from $1,000 to $5,000.

Duration 1 year; nonrenewable.

Number awarded Varies each year; recently, 2 of these scholarships were awarded.

Deadline May of each year.

[120]
FORUM FOR CONCERNS OF MINORITIES SCHOLARSHIPS

American Society for Clinical Laboratory Science
Attn: Forum for Concerns of Minorities
6701 Democracy Boulevard, Suite 300
Bethesda, MD 20817
(301) 657-2768 Fax: (301) 657-2909
E-mail: ascls@ascls.org
Web: www.ascls.org/leadership/awards/fcm.htm

Purpose To provide financial assistance to minority students in clinical laboratory scientist and clinical laboratory technician programs.

Eligibility This program is open to minority students who are enrolled in a program in clinical laboratory science, including clinical laboratory science/medical technology (CLS/MT) and clinical laboratory technician/medical laboratory technician (CLT/MLT). Applicants must be able to demonstrate financial need. Membership in the American Society for Clinical Laboratory Science is encouraged but not required.

Financial data Stipends depend on the need of the recipients and the availability of funds.

Duration 1 year.

Additional information Information is also available from the Scholarship Chair, Ms. A. Casey Ceasor, P.O. Box 9006, Ocala, FL 34479, E-mail: acasey@dellnet.com

Number awarded 2 each year: 1 to a CLS/MT student and 1 to a CLT/MLT student.

Deadline March of each year.

[121]
FOUNDERS SCHOLARSHIP

Society of Mexican American Engineers and Scientists
Attn: National Office Director
13337 South Street, Suite 349
Cerritos, CA 90703
E-mail: maes@tamu.edu
Web: www.maes-natl.org

Purpose To provide financial assistance to undergraduate and graduate student members of the Society of Mexican American Engineers and Scientists (MAES).

Eligibility This program is open to MAES student members who are full-time undergraduate or graduate students at a college or university in the United States. Community college students must be enrolled in majors that can transfer to a 4-year institution offering a baccalaureate degree. All applicants must be majoring in a field of science or engineering. U.S. citizenship or permanent resident status is required. Selection is based on financial need; academic achievement; personal qualities, strengths, and leadership abilities; and timeliness and completeness of the application.

Financial data The stipend is $2,000.

Duration 1 year.

Additional information Information is also available from José M. Hernández, Chair, MAES Scholarship Committee, 4015 North Water Iris Cort, Houston, TX 77059. Recipients must attend the MAES International Symposium's Medalla de Oro Banquet in October.

Number awarded 1 each year.

Deadline October of each year.

[122]
FRANK KAZMIERCZAK MEMORIAL MIGRANT SCHOLARSHIP

BOCES Geneseo Migrant Center
27 Lackawanna Avenue
Mount Morris, NY 14510-1096
(585) 658-7960   (800) 245-5681
Fax: (585) 658-7969   E-mail: info@migrant.net
Web: www.migrant.net/sch_kazmierczak.htm

Purpose To provide financial assistance for college to migrant farmworker youth interested in preparing for a career in teaching.

Eligibility This program is open to migrant farmworkers and their children who are interested in preparing for a career as a teacher. Priority is given to applicants who have experienced mobility within the past 3 years. They must submit a personal essay of 300 to 500 words on their reasons for wanting to become a teacher, 2 letters of recommendation, and an official school transcript. Selection is based on financial need, academic achievement, and history of migration for agricultural employment.

Financial data The stipend is $1,000.

Duration 1 year.

Number awarded 1 each year.

Deadline January of each year.

[123]
FULFILLING OUR DREAMS SCHOLARSHIP PROGRAM

Salvadoran American Leadership and Educational Fund
Attn: Education and Youth Programs Manager
1625 West Olympic Boulevard, Suite 718
Los Angeles, CA 90015
(213) 480-1052   Fax: (213) 487-2530
E-mail: info@salef.org
Web: www.salef.org

Purpose To provide financial assistance for college and graduate school to Salvadoran Americans and other Americans of Hispanic descent.

Eligibility This program is open to high school seniors and graduates who have been accepted at a 4-year university, undergraduates in 2- and 4-year colleges and universities, and graduate students. Applicants do not need to provide proof of documented immigrant status, but they must be of Salvadoran, Central American, or other Latino background. Along with their application, they must submit a 750-word statement on their goals, aspirations, and ambitions; ways to give back to the community; leadership involvement; why they chose their field of study; and short- and long-term goals and how they plan to contribute to the community after graduation. They must be able to demonstrate financial need, have a GPA of at least 2.5, and have a history of community service and involvement. An interview may be required.

Financial data Stipends range from $500 to $2,500.

Duration 1 year.

Additional information This program began in 1998. Recipients are paired with a professional in their field of study who serves as a mentor, providing moral support and direction. Funding for this program comes from the Bank of America Foundation and the Los Angeles Department of Water and Power.

Number awarded 50 each year.

Deadline June of each year.

[124]
FUTURE LEADERS OF AMERICA SCHOLARSHIP

Orange County Community Foundation
Attn: Scholarship Coordinator
2081 Business Center Drive, Suite 100
Irvine, CA 92612-1115
(949) 553-4202, ext. 22   Fax: (949) 553-4211
E-mail: occf@oc-communityfoundation.org
Web: www.oc-communityfoundation.org/grantsscholar

Purpose To provide financial assistance for college to Hispanic students from Orange County, California who have demonstrated outstanding community service.

Eligibility This program is open to Hispanics who are seniors graduating from high schools in Orange County, California. Applicants must have demonstrated community leadership by volunteering at least 30 hours at a community-based nonprofit organization. Other selection criteria include academic ability and financial need.

Financial data The stipend is $500 per year.

Duration 1 year.

Number awarded 1 each year.

Deadline February of each year.

[125]
GARTH REEVES JR. MEMORIAL SCHOLARSHIP

Society of Professional Journalists-South Florida Chapter
c/o Oline Cogdill
The Sun-Sentinel
200 East Las Olas Boulevard
Fort Lauderdale, FL 33301
(954) 356-4513   E-mail: ocogdill@sun-sentinel.com
Web: www.netrox.net/~dali/spj/contest.htm

Purpose To provide financial assistance to south Florida minority undergraduates interested in journalism as a career.

Eligibility Minority students committed to careers in print or broadcast journalism are eligible for these scholarships if they reside in south Florida and can demonstrate financial need. Selection is based on academic performance, quality of work for student or professional news media, and teachers' recommendations.

Financial data The stipend ranges from $500 to $1,000 per year, depending upon the recipient's educational requirements and financial need.

Duration 1 year; recipients may reapply.

Number awarded 1 or more each year.

Deadline February of each year.

[126]
GATES MILLENNIUM UNDERGRADUATE SCHOLARS PROGRAM

Bill and Melinda Gates Foundation
P.O. Box 10500
Fairfax, VA 22031-8044
(877) 690-GMSP
Web: www.gmsp.org

Purpose To provide financial assistance for college to outstanding low-income minority students.

Eligibility This program is open to African Americans, Alaska Natives, American Indians, Hispanic Americans, and Asian Pacific Islander Americans who are graduating high school seniors with a GPA of 3.3 or higher. Principals, teachers, guidance counselors, tribal higher education representatives, and other professional educators are invited to nominate students with outstanding academic qualifications, especially those likely to succeed in the fields of mathematics, science, engineering, education, or library science. Nominees should have significant financial need and demonstrated leadership abilities through participation in community service, extracurricular, or other activities. U.S. citizenship or permanent resident status is required. Nominees must be planning to enter an accredited college or university as a full-time, degree-seeking freshman in the following fall.

Financial data The program covers the cost of tuition, fees, books, and living expenses not paid for by grants and scholarships already committed as part of the recipient's financial aid package.

Duration 4 years or the completion of the undergraduate degree, if the recipient maintains at least a 3.0 GPA.

Additional information This program, established in 1999, is funded by the Bill and Melinda Gates Foundation and administered by the United Negro College Fund with support from the American Indian Graduate Center, the Hispanic Scholarship Fund, and the Organization of Chinese Americans.

Number awarded Under the Gates Millennium Scholars Program, a total of 4,000 students receive support each year.

Deadline January of each year.

[127]
GENERAL ELECTRIC FUND/LEAGUE OF UNITED LATIN AMERICAN CITIZENS SCHOLARSHIPS

League of United Latin American Citizens
Attn: LULAC National Education Service Centers
2000 L Street, N.W., Suite 610
Washington, DC 20036
(202) 833-6130   Fax: (202) 833-6135
E-mail: LNESCAward@aol.com
Web: www.lulac.org/Programs/Scholar.html

Purpose To provide financial assistance to minority students who are studying engineering or business in college.

Eligibility Eligible to apply are minority students who will be enrolled as college sophomores pursuing full-time studies in a program leading to a baccalaureate degree in engineering or business at colleges or universities in the United States approved by the League of United Latin American Citizens (LULAC) and General Electric. They must have a GPA of 3.25 or higher and be U.S. citizens or legal residents. Selection is based on academic performance, likelihood of pursuing a career in business or engineering, performance in business or engineering subjects, writing ability, extracurricular activities, and community involvement.

Financial data The stipends are $5,000 per year. The funds are to be used to pay for tuition, required fees, room and board, and required educational materials and books. The funds are sent directly to the college or university and deposited in the scholarship recipient's name.

Duration 1 year; may be renewed if the recipient maintains a GPA of 3.0 or higher.

Additional information Funding for this program is provided by the General Electric Fund. All requests for applications or information must include a self-addressed stamped envelope.

Number awarded 2 each year.

Deadline July of each year.

[128]
GENERAL MOTORS ENGINEERING EXCELLENCE AWARD

Hispanic Association of Colleges and Universities
Attn: Scholarship Programs
8415 Datapoint Drive, Suite 400
San Antonio, TX 78229
(210) 692-3805   Fax: (210) 692-0823
E-mail: hacu@hacu.net
Web: www.hacu.net/student_resources/index.shtml

Purpose To provide financial assistance to undergraduate and graduate engineering students at institutions that are members of the Hispanic Association of Colleges and Universities (HACU).

Eligibility This program is open to full-time undergraduate and graduate students at 4-year HACU member and partner colleges and universities who are working on an engineering degree. Applicants must submit an essay of 200 to 250 words that describes their academic and/or career goals, where they expect to be and what they expect to be doing 10 years from now, and what skills they can bring to an employer. They must be able to demonstrate financial need and a GPA of 3.2 or higher.

Financial data The stipend is $2,000 per year.

Duration 1 year; may be renewed.

Additional information   This program is sponsored by General Motors and administered by HACU.

Number awarded   1 or more each year.

Deadline   June of each year.

[129]
GENERAL MOTORS/LEAGUE OF UNITED LATIN AMERICAN CITIZENS SCHOLARSHIPS

League of United Latin American Citizens
Attn: LULAC National Education Service Centers
2000 L Street, N.W., Suite 610
Washington, DC 20036
(202) 833-6130   Fax: (202) 833-6135
E-mail: LNESCAward@aol.com
Web: www.lulac.org/Programs/Scholar.html

Purpose   To encourage outstanding Latino students to complete their college education in engineering.

Eligibility   Eligible to apply are Latino students who are enrolled or planning to enroll as full-time students in a program leading to a baccalaureate degree in engineering at colleges or universities in the United States approved by the League of United Latin American Citizens (LULAC) and General Motors. Continuing college students must have a GPA of 3.2 or better; entering college freshmen must have a high school GPA of 3.5 or higher and either an ACT composite score of at least 23 or an SAT combined score of at least 970. Selection is based on academic performance; likelihood of pursuing a career in engineering; performance in science, mathematics, and engineering skills; writing ability; extracurricular activities; and community involvement.

Financial data   The stipends are $2,000 per year. The funds are to be used to pay for tuition, required fees, room and board, and required educational materials and books. The funds are sent directly to the college or university and deposited in the scholarship recipient's name.

Duration   1 year.

Additional information   All requests for applications or information must include a self-addressed stamped envelope.

Number awarded   20 each year.

Deadline   July of each year.

[130]
GEORGE M. BROOKER COLLEGIATE SCHOLARSHIP FOR MINORITIES

Institute of Real Estate Management Foundation
Attn: Foundation Coordinator
430 North Michigan Avenue
Chicago, IL 60611-4090
(312) 329-6008   Fax: (312) 410-7908
E-mail: kholmes@irem.org
Web: www.irem.org

Purpose   To provide financial assistance to minorities interested in preparing (on the undergraduate or graduate level) for a career in the real estate management industry.

Eligibility   This program is open to junior, senior, and graduate minority (non-Caucasian) students majoring in real estate, preferably with an emphasis on management, asset management, or related fields. Applicants must be interested in entering a career in real estate management upon graduation. They must have earned a GPA of 3.0 or higher in their major, have completed at least 2 college courses in real estate, and write an essay (up to 500 words) on why they want to follow a career in real estate

management. U.S. citizenship is required. Selection is based on academic success and a demonstrated commitment to a career in real estate management.

Financial data   The stipend for undergraduates is $1,000; the stipend for graduate students is $2,500. Funds are disbursed to the institution the student attends to be used only for tuition expenses.

Duration   1 year; nonrenewable.

Number awarded   3 each year: 2 undergraduate awards and 1 graduate award.

Deadline   February of each year.

[131]
GILLETTE/NATIONAL URBAN LEAGUE SCHOLARSHIP FOR MINORITY STUDENTS

National Urban League
Attn: Scholarship Coordinator
120 Wall Street
New York, NY 10005
(212) 558-5300   (888) 839-0467
Fax: (212) 344-5332   E-mail: info@nul.org
Web: www.nul.org/caaa/scholarship/gillette_schol.html

Purpose   To provide financial assistance to minority students who are interested in completing their college education in designated areas of business and engineering.

Eligibility   Eligible to apply are minority students who are pursuing full-time studies leading to a bachelor's degree at an accredited institution of higher learning. They must be juniors or third-year students at the time the scholarship award begins, have a GPA of 3.0 or higher, be U.S. citizens or permanent residents or have a student visa, be able to demonstrate financial need, and be majoring in business-related fields (e.g., accounting, business administration, economics, engineering, finance, human resource management, ITS, manufacturing operations, marketing, MIS, public relations). Applications must be endorsed by an Urban League affiliate.

Financial data   The stipend is $2,500 per year. Funds must be used for tuition, room, board, and the purchase of required educational materials and books.

Duration   2 years.

Number awarded   Approximately 5 each year.

Deadline   January of each year.

[132]
GLAXOSMITHKLINE ACS SCHOLARS PROGRAM

American Chemical Society
Attn: Department of Diversity Programs
1155 16th Street, N.W.
Washington, DC 20036
(202) 872-6250   (800) 227-5558, ext. 6250
Fax: (202) 776-8003   E-mail: scholars@acs.org
Web: www.acs.org/scholars

Purpose   To provide financial assistance to underrepresented minority students enrolled in an undergraduate program in chemistry and interested in a possible summer internship.

Eligibility   This program is open to college freshmen, sophomores, and juniors enrolled in a 4-year program in chemistry and interested in a possible summer internship at GlaxoSmithKline in Research Triangle Park, North Carolina. Applicants must be African American, Hispanic/Latino, or American Indian. Students planning careers in medicine or pharmacy are not eligible. U.S.

citizenship or permanent resident status is required. Selection is based on academic merit (GPA of 3.0 or higher) and financial need.

Financial data The maximum stipend is $3,000 per year.

Duration 1 year; nonrenewable.

Number awarded 1 or more each year.

Deadline February of each year.

[133]
GLORIA AND JOSEPH MATTERA NATIONAL SCHOLARSHIP FUND FOR MIGRANT CHILDREN

BOCES Geneseo Migrant Center
27 Lackawanna Avenue
Mount Morris, NY 14510-1096
(585) 658-7960 (800) 245-5681
Fax: (585) 658-7969 E-mail: info@migrant.net
Web: www.migrant.net/sch_mattera.htm

Purpose To provide financial assistance for college to migrant farmworker youth.

Eligibility This program is open to migrant farmworker youth. Priority is given to current interstate migrant youth. Applicants must be 1) enrolled in or accepted at an accredited public or private college, technical school, or vocational school, or 2) a dropout or a potential dropout from high school who shows promise of ability to continue schooling. They must submit a personal essay telling about their background, career and personal goals, and why they should receive this assistance. Selection is based on the essay, background in migrant farmwork, potential, and financial need.

Financial data The amount varies, depending upon the financial need and potential of the recipient. Generally, awards range from $150 to $500 per year.

Duration 1 year; may be renewed.

Number awarded Approximately 100 each year.

Deadline Applications may be submitted at any time.

[134]
HACE NATIONAL SCHOLARSHIP PROGRAM

Hispanic Alliance for Career Enhancement
Attn: Student Development Program
14 East Jackson Avenue, Suite 1310
Chicago, IL 60604
(312) 435-0498, ext. 21 Fax: (312) 435-1494
E-mail: haceorg@enteract.com
Web: www.hace-usa.org/programs/scholar.htm

Purpose To provide financial assistance to Hispanic students working on an undergraduate or graduate degree.

Eligibility Applicants may be undergraduate or graduate students who are enrolled full time in an institution of higher education in the United States. They must be working on a bachelor's degree or higher. Undergraduates must have completed at least 12 credit hours of college course work before applying. All applicants must have a GPA of 2.5 or higher. Selection is based on academic achievement, letters of recommendation, community involvement, leadership skills, and financial need.

Financial data A stipend is awarded (amount not specified).

Duration 1 year; nonrenewable.

Number awarded Several each year.

Deadline August of each year.

[135]
HENAAC STUDENT LEADERSHIP AWARDS

Hispanic Engineer National Achievement Awards Conference
3900 Whiteside Street
Los Angeles, CA 90063
(323) 262-0997 Fax: (323) 262-0946
E-mail: info@henaac.org
Web: www.henaac.org/scholarships.htm

Purpose To provide financial assistance to Hispanic undergraduate and graduate students majoring in engineering and related fields.

Eligibility This program is open to Hispanic undergraduate and graduate students who are majoring in computer science, engineering, material science, or mathematics. Applicants must have a GPA of 3.0 or higher. Academic achievement and campus community activities are considered in the selection process.

Financial data The stipend is $5,000.

Duration 1 year.

Additional information This program is sponsored by the Hispanic Engineer National Achievement Awards Conference (HENAAC) to promote technical excellence and leadership in the Hispanic community.

Number awarded 2 each year: 1 undergraduate and 1 graduate student.

Deadline April of each year.

[136]
HERCULES MINORITY ENGINEERS DEVELOPMENT PROGRAM

Hercules Incorporated
Attn: Human Resources Department
Hercules Plaza
1313 North Market Street
Wilmington, DE 19894-0001
(302) 594-6030 Fax: (302) 594-6483
Web: www.herc.com

Purpose To provide financial assistance and summer work experience to minority undergraduates interested in preparing for a career in engineering.

Eligibility Eligible are minority group members who have completed at least 1 semester of university study before applying, are interested in careers in engineering, have earned at least a 3.0 GPA, and attend 1 of the 5 schools participating in the program (Georgia Institute of Technology, University of Delaware, North Carolina State University, Virginia Polytechnic Institute and State University, and Pennsylvania State University).

Financial data The scholarship stipend is $4,000 per year.

Duration 1 year; renewable for up to 3 additional years.

Additional information Recipients are eligible to work as interns during the summer months throughout their undergraduate years. Information about the scholarship/internship program can be obtained by writing to Hercules Incorporated or contacting the participating university. Candidates must be nominated by their Dean of Engineering.

Deadline Varies from school to school.

[137]
HIGH SCHOOL JUNIOR ORANGE COUNTY HISPANIC EDUCATION ENDOWMENT FUND AWARDS

Orange County Community Foundation
Attn: Scholarship Coordinator
2081 Business Center Drive, Suite 100
Irvine, CA 92612-1115
(949) 553-4202, ext. 22   Fax: (949) 553-4211
E-mail: occf@oc-communityfoundation.org
Web: www.oc-communityfoundation.org/grantsscholar

Purpose   To provide financial assistance for college to Hispanic high school juniors from Orange County, California.

Eligibility   This program is open to Hispanic students in Orange County, California who are high school juniors planning to attend a trade school, college, or university after graduating. Selection is based on financial need, extracurricular activities, academic ability, and community service.

Financial data   The stipend is $500 per year. Funds are paid when the student enters a postsecondary institution.

Duration   1 year.

Number awarded   20 each year.

Deadline   February of each year.

[138]
HIGH SCHOOL SCHOLARSHIP PROGRAMS OF THE HISPANIC SCHOLARSHIP FUND

Hispanic Scholarship Fund
Attn: Selection Committee
55 Second Street, Suite 1500
San Francisco, CA 94105
(877) HSF-INFO   Fax: (415) 808-2302
E-mail: info@hsf.net
Web: www.hsf.net

Purpose   To provide financial assistance to Hispanic American high school seniors who are interested in attending college.

Eligibility   This program is open to U.S. citizens, permanent residents, and visitors with a passport stamped I-551. Applicants must be of Hispanic heritage (each parent half Hispanic or 1 parent fully Hispanic) and seniors in high schools in the United States. They must have a high school GPA of 3.0 or higher and plan to enroll full time at an accredited college or university for the following fall. As part of the application process, they must submit a 2-page essay that addresses the following topics: their Hispanic heritage and family background, personal and academic achievements, academic plans and career goals, efforts toward making a difference in the community, and financial need.

Financial data   The stipends range from $1,000 to $2,500 per year.

Duration   1 year.

Additional information   This program includes a number of named HSF Scholarships: Stockton Unified School (Stockton, California), Bassett Unified (Bassett Senior High School in La Puente, California), East Side Union High School District (San Jose, California), Jeff Garcia (public and private schools in south San Francisco Bay area of Santa Clara, Santa Cruz, and San Mateo counties), Albino R. Pineda (Santa Paula High School in Santa Paula, California), Los Angeles Unified School District (Los Angeles, California), Noche de Becas Coalition (Stanislaus County, California), California State University at Sacramento College Assistance Migrant Program (high school students who have been admitted to the College Assistance Migrant Program at CSU

Sacramento), Hispanic Chamber of Commerce (Sonoma County, California), Summer Search Foundation (participants in the Summer Search Program), Hispanic Alliance for Culture, Education and Recognition (Tulare, California), Kern County Hispanic Chamber of Commerce Foundation (Kern County, California), Sacramento Hispanic Chamber of Commerce Mayor Joe Serna, Jr. (Sacramento, Yuba, Yolo, Sutter, Placer, and El Dorado counties, California), Oakland Raiders Offensive Lineman & Wells Fargo (Contra Costa and Alameda counties, California), Wells Fargo (Alameda, Contra Costa, Los Angeles, Marin, Napa, San Francisco, San Mateo, Santa Clara, Solano, and Sonoma counties, California), Telemundo Channel 52 (Los Angeles County, California), Telemundo Channel 48 (Alameda, Contra Costa, Marin, Napa, San Francisco, San Mateo, Santa Clara, Solano, and Sonoma county, California), Georgia (high school seniors in Georgia who plan to enroll in an accredited 4-year university and participate in a Summer Bridge Program and an annual Leadership Development/Academic Skills Workshop), Coca-Cola Scholarship Classic (private and public schools in Georgia), Chicago Public Schools (Chicago, Illinois), New Mexico Alliance for Hispanic Education (Taos County, New Mexico), Dallas Independent School District (Dallas, Texas), Greater Dallas Hispanic Chamber of Commerce Foundation (Dallas County, Texas), Northside Independent School District (San Antonio, Texas), Rio Grande City Consolidated Independent School District (Rio Grande City, Texas), Laredo Independent School District (Laredo, Texas), Laredo Hispanic Chamber of Commerce (Laredo, Texas), LULAC Council #2 Reina Feria de las Flores (San Antonio, Texas), YES College Preparatory School (Houston, Texas), YES Academy (Dallas, Texas), Fort Worth Hispanic Chamber of Commerce (Tarrant County, Texas), Yakima Hispanic Academic Achievers Program (Yakima, Washington), Hispanic Business/Professional Association (Spokane County, Washington), Women of Spanish Origin (Broward County, Florida). Requests for applications must be accompanied by a self-addressed stamped envelope.

Number awarded   Varies each year.

Deadline   February of each year.

[139]
HIGH SCHOOL SENIOR ORANGE COUNTY HISPANIC EDUCATION ENDOWMENT FUND AWARDS

Orange County Community Foundation
Attn: Scholarship Coordinator
2081 Business Center Drive, Suite 100
Irvine, CA 92612-1115
(949) 553-4202, ext. 22   Fax: (949) 553-4211
E-mail: occf@oc-communityfoundation.org
Web: www.oc-communityfoundation.org/grantsscholar

Purpose   To provide financial assistance for college to Hispanic high school seniors from Orange County, California.

Eligibility   This program is open to Hispanic students in Orange County, California who are high school seniors planning to enter a trade school, college, or university in the following fall. Selection is based on financial need, extracurricular activities, academic ability, and community service.

Financial data   Stipends range from $1,000 to $2,500 per year.

Duration   1 year.

Additional information   This program includes scholarships sponsored by the Hispanic Chamber of Commerce, Hispanic Realtors, and the Association of Hispanic Professionals for Education.

Number awarded 54 each year.
Deadline February of each year.

[140]
H.I.S. SCHOLARS PROGRAM

Hispanic College Fund
Attn: National Director
1717 Pennsylvania Avenue, N.W., Suite 460
Washington, D.C. 20006
(800) 644-4223   Fax: (202) 296-3774
E-mail: hispaniccollegefund@earthlink.net
Web: www.hispanicfund.org

Purpose To provide financial assistance and summer work experience to Hispanic American undergraduate students who are interested in preparing for a career in telecommunications.
Eligibility This program is open to U.S. citizens of Hispanic background who are entering their freshman, sophomore, junior, or senior year of college. Applicants must be working on a bachelor's degree in accounting, business administration, computer science, economics, engineering specialties, finance, information systems, management, or other relevant technology or business fields. They must have an interest in telecommunications, have a cumulative GPA of 3.0 or higher, and be available to complete at least 2 consecutive summer internships before graduating from college. Financial need is considered in the selection process.
Financial data Stipends range from $500 to $5,000, depending on need and academic achievement. Funds are paid directly to the recipient's college or university to help cover tuition and fees.
Duration 1 year; recipients may reapply.
Additional information This program is a joint venture of the Hispanic College Fund (which provides scholarships), INROADS (which provides monthly coaching, leadership development, community service, and mentorship), and Sprint (which provides 10- to 12-week paid summer internships).
Number awarded Varies each year.
Deadline April of each year.

[141]
HISPANIC CHURCH MULTIPLICATION TEAM SCHOLARSHIPS

Southern Baptist Convention
Attn: North American Mission Board
4200 North Point Parkway
Alpharetta, GA 30022-4176
(770) 410-6227   Fax: (770) 410-6012
E-mail: mrodriguez@namb.net
Web: www.namb.net

Purpose To provide financial assistance to Hispanic American Baptists interested in religious vocations.
Eligibility This program is open to Hispanic Americans who are U.S. citizens involved in some type of approved Baptist ministry. Applicants must be able to demonstrate financial need. Only students in accredited institutions working toward a basic college (bachelor's) or seminary (M.Div.) degree are eligible. As part of the selection process, applicants must submit an essay describing their interest in and commitment to a Christian vocation.
Financial data The maximum grants are $500 per year for students attending accredited colleges, $600 per year for students in non-Southern Baptist Convention seminaries, and $850 per

year for students at 1 of the 6 Southern Baptist Convention seminaries.
Duration 1 year; renewable.
Additional information The 6 Southern Baptist seminaries are Golden Gate Baptist Theological Seminary (Mill Valley, California), Midwestern Baptist Theological Seminary (Kansas City, Missouri), New Orleans Baptist Theological Seminary (New Orleans, Louisiana), Southeastern Baptist Theological Seminary (Wake Forest, North Carolina), Southern Baptist Theological Seminary (Louisville, Kentucky), and Southwestern Baptist Theological Seminary (Fort Worth, Texas).
Number awarded Varies each year.
Deadline Applications may be submitted at any time, but they must be received at least 1 month (preferably sooner) before the student enrolls in a school.

[142]
HISPANIC COLLEGE FUND SCHOLARSHIPS

Hispanic College Fund
Attn: National Director
1717 Pennsylvania Avenue, N.W., Suite 460
Washington, D.C. 20006
(800) 644-4223   Fax: (202) 296-3774
E-mail: hispaniccollegefund@earthlink.net
Web: www.hispanicfund.org

Purpose To provide financial assistance to Hispanic American undergraduate students who are interested in preparing for a career in business, computer science, or engineering.
Eligibility This program is open to U.S. citizens of Hispanic background who are entering their freshman, sophomore, junior, or senior year of college. Applicants must be working on a bachelor's degree in business, computer science, engineering, or a business-related major, and have a cumulative GPA of 3.0 or higher. They must be applying to or enrolled in a college or university in the 50 states or Puerto Rico as a full-time student. Financial need is considered in the selection process.
Financial data Stipends range from $500 to $5,000, depending on the need of the recipient. The sponsor's goal is to have the average award be $3,000. Funds are paid directly to the recipient's college or university to help cover tuition and fees.
Duration 1 year; recipients may reapply.
Number awarded Varies each year; recently, 208 students were supported by this program, including 70 freshmen, 57 sophomores, 47 juniors, and 34 seniors.
Deadline April of each year.

[143]
HISPANIC DESIGNERS FOUNDERS SCHOLARSHIPS

Hispanic Designers, Inc.
Attn: National Hispanic Education and Communications
    Projects
1101 30th Street, N.W., Suite 500
Washington, DC 20007
(202) 337-9636   Fax: (202) 337-9635
E-mail: HispDesign@aol.com
Web: www.hispanicdesigners.org

Purpose To provide financial assistance to Hispanic students enrolled in fashion design schools.
Eligibility Applicants must be Hispanic or of Hispanic descent, be able to demonstrate financial need, be U.S. citizens or residents, have participated in an internship or work training program

in the field of fashion, and have a GPA of 3.0 or higher. They must be enrolled in an accredited postsecondary institution studying for a degree or in a certified program in fashion design or a related field. As part of the selection process, they must submit samples of design work which are judged on the basis of creativity and originality.

Financial data The stipend is $5,000.

Duration 1 year.

Additional information This program was established in 1999 with a grant from Absolut Vodka. The program includes the following named scholarships: the Adolfo Founders Scholarship (for the best knitwear collection design), the Paloma Picasso Founders Scholarship (for the best accessory or jewelry collection design), the Fernando Sanchez Founders Scholarship (for the best at-home and leisure collection design), the Oscar de La Renta Founders Scholarship (for the best design of an evening wear collection following the "Oscar" style), and the Carolina Herrera Founders Scholarship (for the best design of an evening wear collection with the "CH" look). No telephone inquiries are accepted.

Number awarded 5 each year.

Deadline August of each year.

[144]
HISPANIC DESIGNERS GENERAL SCHOLARSHIPS

Hispanic Designers, Inc.
Attn: National Hispanic Education and Communications
    Projects
1101 30th Street, N.W., Suite 500
Washington, DC 20007
(202) 337-9636   Fax: (202) 337-9635
E-mail: HispDesign@aol.com
Web: www.hispanicdesigners.org

Purpose To provide financial assistance to Hispanic students enrolled in fashion design schools.

Eligibility This program is open to students who are Hispanic or of Hispanic descent enrolled in accredited fashion design schools or other accredited institutions for a degree or certified program in fashion design, fashion merchandising, illustration, jewelry design, interior design, apparel manufacturing or management, marketing management, merchandising communications, theater costume design, or special event/fashion show production. Applicants must have documented evidence of extracurricular activities in the field of fashion through an internship or work training program, a GPA of 3.0 or higher, and financial need. U.S. citizenship or permanent resident status is required.

Financial data Stipends range from $500 to $2,500 per year; awards are paid directly to the recipient's school.

Duration 1 year. No telephone inquiries are accepted.

Number awarded Varies each year; recently, 34 scholarships were awarded.

Deadline August of each year.

[145]
HISPANIC OUTLOOK SCHOLARSHIP FUND

Hispanic Outlook in Higher Education
210 Route 4 East, Suite 310
P.O. Box 68
Paramus, NJ 07652-0068
(201) 587-8800   Fax: (201) 587-9105
Web: www.hispanicoutlook.com/scholar.html

Purpose To provide financial assistance for college to high school seniors of Hispanic descent.

Eligibility Applicants must be high school seniors of Hispanic descent, with at least 1 parent from a Spanish-speaking Latin American country or Spain. They must be legal residents or citizens of the United States, have earned at least a 3.5 GPA, and be entering as a full-time student at a 2-year or 4-year accredited college recommended in the *Hispanic Outlook in Higher Education Magazine's* "Publisher's Picks List." To apply, students must submit a completed application form, a letter of acceptance from the college they will be attending, a copy of their high school transcripts, and a letter of recommendation from their high school counselor. Scholarships are awarded on the basis of merit.

Financial data The stipend is $1,000.

Duration 1 year; renewable if the recipient maintains a GPA of 3.5 or higher. This scholarship is not transferable; students who change schools lose the scholarship.

Deadline April of each year.

[146]
HISPANIC SCHOLARSHIP FUND/FORD MOTOR COMPANY CORPORATE SCHOLARSHIP PROGRAM

Hispanic Scholarship Fund
Attn: Selection Committee
55 Second Street, Suite 1500
San Francisco, CA 94105
(877) HSF-INFO   Fax: (415) 808-2302
E-mail: specialprograms@hsf.net
Web: www.hsf.net/scholarship/Special.htm

Purpose To provide financial assistance to Hispanic college juniors who are majoring in business, computer science, or engineering.

Eligibility This program is open to U.S. citizens and permanent residents who are of Hispanic heritage (each parent half Hispanic or 1 parent fully Hispanic). Applicants must be juniors attending a U.S. accredited college or university on a full-time basis and majoring in business, computer science, or engineering with a GPA of 3.0 or higher. As part of the application process, they must submit a 2-page essay that addresses the following topics: their Hispanic heritage and family background, personal and academic achievements, academic plans and career goals, efforts toward making a difference in their community, and financial need.

Financial data Stipends range up to $15,000 per year, depending on the unmet financial need of the recipient.

Duration 1 year; may be renewed up to 2 additional years if the recipient continues to meet eligibility requirements.

Additional information This program is sponsored by Ford Motor Company, which may also offer a summer internship to recipients.

Number awarded Varies each year.

Deadline March of each year.

[147]
HISPANIC SCHOLARSHIP FUND/SOUTH TEXAS SCHOLARSHIP PROGRAM

L&F Distributors
3900 North McColl Road
McAllen, TX 78501
(956) 687-7751   E-mail: specialprograms@hsf.net
Web: www.hsf.net/scholarship/Special.htm

Purpose To provide financial assistance to Hispanic undergraduate and graduate students from designated counties in south Texas.

Eligibility This program is open to community college, undergraduate, and graduate students who are residents of south Texas. Applicants must be U.S. citizens or permanent residents of Hispanic heritage (each parent half Hispanic or 1 parent fully Hispanic). They must have earned at least 12 undergraduate units, have a GPA of 2.7 or higher, and be enrolled full time in a degree program at an accredited U.S. college or university. As part of the application process, they must submit a 2-page essay that addresses the following topics: their Hispanic heritage and family background, personal and academic achievements, academic plans and career goals, efforts toward making a difference in their community, and financial need.

Financial data Stipends range from $1,000 to $2,500.

Duration 1 year.

Additional information South Texas is defined to include the following counties: Aransas, Bee, Brooks, Cameron, Duval, Goliad, Hidalgo, Jim Hogg, Jim Wells, Karnes, Kenedy, Kleberg, La Salle, Live Oak, McMullen, Nueces, Refugio, San Patricio, Starr, Webb, Willacy, and Zapata. This program is administered by the Hispanic Scholarship Fund (HSF), 55 Second Street, Suite 1500, San Francisco, CA 94105, (877) HSF-INFO, Fax: (415) 808-2302.

Number awarded Varies each year.

Deadline September of each year

[148]
H.O.R.I.S.O.N.S. SCHOLARSHIPS

Pueblo Hispanic Education Foundation
Administration Building, Room 325
2200 Bonforte Boulevard
Pueblo, CO 81001
(719) 546-2563   Fax: (719) 546-0504
E-mail: pphef@aol.com
Web: www.phef.net

Purpose To provide financial assistance to Hispanic undergraduate students from Colorado.

Eligibility This program is open to full-time undergraduate students of Hispanic descent who are residents of Colorado. Applicants must submit an essay on their career and educational goals, school activities and awards, interests, community service and volunteer work, and work experience. Selection is based on financial need, proven ability, GPA, community and volunteer service, and educational desire. Preference is given to students of low to moderate income, continuing students, and single parents.

Financial data Stipends are generally $1,000 per year.

Duration 1 year. Recipients may reapply if they maintain a cumulative GPA of 2.0 or higher as first-time freshmen and 2.5 or higher as continuing students.

Additional information The title of this program stands for "Hispanic Outreach In Search of New Scholars."

Number awarded Varies each year; recently, 63 of these scholarships were awarded.

Deadline February of each year.

[149]
HP SCHOLAR PROGRAM

Hewlett-Packard Company
Attn: Scholar Program Manager
8000 Foothills Boulevard
MS 5214
Roseville, CA 95747
(916) 785-3809   E-mail: sandy.brooks2@hp.com
Web: www.hp.com/go/hpscholars

Purpose To provide financial assistance and summer work experience to underrepresented minority high school seniors and community college transfer students who are interested in studying computer engineering, electrical engineering, or computer science at designated universities.

Eligibility This program is open to graduating high school seniors and community college students who are members of an underrepresented minority group (African American, Latino, or American Indian). Applicants must be planning to major in electrical engineering, computer engineering, or computer science at the University of California at Los Angeles, San Jose State University, North Carolina A&T University, or Morgan State University. They must be interested in working during the summer at a major Hewlett-Packard (HP) location in California, Colorado, Idaho, Massachusetts, Oregon, or Washington. Selection is based on academic achievement, financial need, family's educational history (priority is given to first-generation students), letters of recommendation, a personal statement (communication skills, personal and professional qualities, community involvement), connections to HP Philanthropy and Education Partnerships, and demonstrated interest in math, science, and engineering.

Financial data The stipend is $3,000 per year. In addition, students receive a salary when they work at HP facilities during the summer. The total value of the award exceeds $40,000 per student.

Duration 4 years of university study plus 3 summers of internships.

Additional information Applications must be submitted to the school the student wishes to attend.

Number awarded Varies each year.

Deadline March of each year.

[150]
HYATT HOTEL FUND FOR MINORITY LODGING MANAGEMENT STUDENTS

American Hotel & Lodging Educational Foundation
Attn: Manager of Foundation Programs
1201 New York Avenue, N.W., Suite 600
Washington, DC 20005-3931
(202) 289-3181   Fax: (202) 289-3199
E-mail: ahlef@ahlef.org
Web: www.ahlf.org/scholarships

Purpose To provide financial assistance to minority college students working on a degree in hotel management.

Eligibility Applicants must be attending a 4-year college or university that is a member of the Council on Hotel, Restaurant and Institutional Education. They must be minorities and majoring in

hotel management. Each member university may nominate 1 student. The most outstanding students receive this scholarship.
Financial data The stipend is $2,000.
Duration 1 year.
Additional information Funding for this program is provided by Hyatt Hotels & Resorts.
Number awarded Varies each year; recently, 18 of these scholarships were awarded.
Deadline March of each year.

[151]
IAN M. ROLLAND SCHOLARSHIP

Lincoln Financial Group
Attn: Director of Actuarial Development
1300 South Clinton Street, 1H25
Fort Wayne, IN 46801
(219) 455-2390   (800) 2-LINCOLN, ext. 2390
Fax: (219) 455-9974   E-mail: ljjackson@lnc.com
Web: www.lfg.com

Purpose To provide financial assistance to minority high school seniors who are interested in preparing for a career as an actuary.
Eligibility This program is open to high school seniors who are members of minority groups underrepresented in the actuarial field. Applicants must rank in the top 10% of their class, have a combined verbal and math SAT score of at least 1200, and have a math SAT score of at least 650. Preference is given to applicants who choose a university with an actuarial program and major in actuarial science.
Financial data The stipend is $5,000 per year, paid to the university that the student attends.
Duration 1 year; may be renewed if the recipient maintains a cumulative GPA of 3.5 or higher while in college, passes course 1 of the actuarial exams by the beginning of the junior year, and passes course 2 of the actuarial exams by January of the senior year.
Additional information This program was established in 1999. Recipients who attend a university with an actuarial science program are expected to major in that field. Recipients who attend a university that does not have an actuarial science program are expected to major in a field consistent with a career in actuarial science; generally, that means a mathematics major with supporting course work in business, computer science, and economics.
Number awarded 1 each year.
Deadline January of each year.

[152]
IBERO AMERICAN ACTION LEAGUE HISPANIC SCHOLARSHIP ENDOWMENT

Rochester Area Community Foundation
Attn: Scholarship Manager
500 East Avenue
Rochester, NY 14607-1912
(585) 271-4100, ext. 4306   Fax: (585) 271-4292
E-mail: brainey@racf.org
Web: www.racf.org/scholarships

Purpose To provide financial assistance to Hispanic students in upstate New York who are interested in pursuing postsecondary education.
Eligibility Hispanic high school students in New York are eligible for consideration if they are interested in going to college and

are residents of Genesee, Livingston, Monroe, Ontario, Orleans, or Wayne counties.
Financial data The amount awarded varies, depending upon the needs of the recipient.
Duration 1 year; renewable.
Additional information Information is also available from Ibero American Action League, Inc., 817 East Main Street, Rochester, NY 14605. This program was established in 1990.
Number awarded Varies each year.

[153]
IDAHO MIGRANT COUNCIL HISPANIC SCHOLARSHIP FUND

Idaho Migrant Council, Inc.
Attn: Employment and Training Grants Specialist
317 Happy Day Boulevard, Suite 250
Caldwell, ID 83607
(208) 454-1652   Fax: (208) 459-0448

Purpose To provide financial assistance for college to Hispanic high school seniors in Idaho.
Eligibility This program is open to residents of Idaho who are of Hispanic origin. Applicants must be planning to enter college in Idaho as freshmen in the following fall. They must have a GPA of 2.5 or higher. Selection is based on a 1-page statement on educational goals, high school transcripts, 3 letters of recommendation, and financial need.
Financial data The stipend is $1,000.
Duration 1 year; nonrenewable.
Additional information Recipients are expected to attend the sponsor's annual meeting in September to accept their award.
Number awarded 5 or 6 each year.
Deadline April of each year.

[154]
IDAHO MINORITY AND "AT RISK" STUDENT SCHOLARSHIP

Idaho State Board of Education
Len B. Jordan Office Building
650 West State Street, Room 307
P.O. Box 83720
Boise, ID 83720-0037
(208) 334-2270   Fax: (208) 334-2632
E-mail: board@osbe.state.id.us
Web: www.sde.state.id.us/osbe/Scholarships/minority.htm

Purpose To help talented disabled and other "at risk" high school seniors in Idaho pursue a college education.
Eligibility This program focuses on talented students who may be at risk of failing to meet their ambitions because of physical, economic, or cultural limitations. Applicants must be high school graduates, be Idaho residents, and meet at least 3 of the following 5 requirements: 1) have a disability; 2) be a member of an ethnic minority group historically underrepresented in higher education; 3) have substantial financial need; 4) be a first-generation college student; 5) be a migrant farm worker or a dependent of a farm worker.
Financial data The stipend is up to $3,000 per year.
Duration 1 year; may be renewed for up to 3 additional years.
Additional information This program was established in 1991 by the Idaho state legislature. Information is also available from high school counselors and financial aid offices of colleges and

universities in Idaho. Recipients must plan to attend or be attending 1 of 8 participating postsecondary institutions in the state on a full-time basis. For a list of those schools, write to the State of Idaho Board of Education.

Number awarded Varies each year.

[155]
IDAHO SPACE GRANT CONSORTIUM SCHOLARSHIP PROGRAM

Idaho Space Grant Consortium
c/o University of Idaho
College of Engineering
P.O. Box 441011
Moscow, ID 83844-1011
(208) 885-6438   Fax: (208) 885-6645
E-mail: isgc@uidaho.edu
Web: ivc.uidaho.edu/isgc/fellow.html

Purpose To provide financial assistance for study in space-related fields to undergraduate students at institutions belonging to the Idaho Space Grant Consortium (ISGC).

Eligibility This program is open to undergraduate students at ISGC member institutions. Applicants must be majoring in engineering, mathematics, science, or science/math education and have a cumulative GPA of 3.0 or higher. They should be planning to pursue a 4-year degree in a space-related field. Along with their application, they must submit a 500-word essay on their future career and educational goals and why they believe the U.S. National Aeronautics and Space Administration (NASA) should support their education. U.S. citizenship is required. As a component of the NASA Space Grant program, the ISGC encourages participation by women, underrepresented minorities, and persons with disabilities.

Financial data The stipend is $1,000 per year.

Duration 1 year; may be renewed.

Additional information Members of the consortium include Albertson College of Idaho, Boise State University, College of Southern Idaho, Idaho State University, Lewis Clark State College, North Idaho College, Northwest Nazarene College, Brigham Young University of Idaho, and the University of Idaho. This program is funded by NASA.

Number awarded Varies each year.

Deadline February of each year.

[156]
ILLINOIS MINORITY REAL ESTATE SCHOLARSHIP

Illinois Association of Realtors
Attn: Illinois Real Estate Educational Foundation
3180 Adloff Lane, Suite 400
P.O. Box 19451
Springfield, IL 62794-9451
(217) 529-2600   E-mail: IARaccess@iar.org
Web: www.illinoisrelator.org/iar/about/scholarships.htm

Purpose To provide financial assistance to Illinois residents who are members of minority groups and preparing for a career in real estate.

Eligibility This program is open to residents of Illinois who are African American, Hispanic or Latino, Native American, or Asian. Applicants must be interested in preparing for a career in real estate by pursuing: 1) courses to meet Illinois salesperson license requirement; 2) course work to meet Illinois broker license requirement; 3) course work required for Illinois appraisal licens-

ing/certification; 4) professional development unrelated to obtaining license/certification; or 5) undergraduate or graduate studies. Along with their application, they must submit information on their employment history, transcripts, evidence of financial need, and an essay that describes their career goals and explains why they believe they should receive scholarship assistance through this program.

Financial data A stipend is awarded (amount not specified); checks are made payable to the school, not to the recipient.

Duration Funds must be used within 24 months of the award date.

Deadline Applications may be submitted at any time, but they must be received at least 12 weeks prior to the beginning of the school term for which financial assistance is requested.

[157]
IMA DIVERSITY SCHOLARSHIP PROGRAM

Institute of Management Accountants
Attn: Committee on Students
10 Paragon Drive
Montvale, NJ 07645-1760
(201) 573-9000   (800) 638-4427, ext. 1543
Fax: (201) 573-8438   E-mail: students@imanet.org
Web: www.imanet.org

Purpose To provide financial assistance to minority and disabled student members of the Institute of Management Accountants (IMA) who are interested in working on an undergraduate or graduate degree in management accounting or financial management.

Eligibility This program is open to undergraduate and graduate students of American Indian/Alaska Native, Asian/Pacific Islander, Black, or Hispanic heritage and students with physical disabilities (defined as hearing impairment, vision impairment, missing extremities, partial paralysis, complete paralysis, or severe distortion of limbs and/or spine). Applicants must be in their sophomore, junior, or senior year or in a graduate program with a major in management accounting, financial management, or information technology. Selection is based on 1) academic merit; 2) quality of their application presentation; 3) demonstrated community leadership; 4) potential for success in expressed career goals in a financial management position; 5) a written statement from applicants expressing their short-term and long-term career goals and objectives, including their participation in the IMA; and 6) letters of recommendation.

Financial data Stipends are $3,000 per year.

Duration 1 year.

Additional information Up to 15 finalists in each category (including the scholarship winners) receive a scholarship to take 5 parts of the CMA and/or CFM examination within a year of graduation.

Number awarded At least 13 each year.

Deadline February of each year.

[158]
INDIANA PROFESSIONAL CHAPTER OF SPJ DIVERSITY IN JOURNALISM SCHOLARSHIP

Society of Professional Journalists-Indiana Chapter
c/o Deborah K. Perkins
Assistant to the Dean and Academic Advisor
Indiana University School of Journalism
902 West New York Street, ES4104
Indianapolis, IN 46202-5154
(317) 274-2776   Fax: (317) 274-2786
E-mail: dperkins@iupui.edu

Purpose To provide financial assistance to minority college students in Indiana who are preparing for a career in journalism.

Eligibility This program is open to minority students majoring in journalism and entering their sophomore, junior, or senior year at a college or university in Indiana. Minorities are defined as U.S. citizens who are African American, Hispanic, Asian American, Native American, or Pacific Islander. Applicants must submit an essay of 200 to 500 words on their personal background and journalistic views, an official college transcript, 3 examples of their journalistic work, a letter of recommendation from a college instructor, and (if they have had a professional internship) a letter of recommendation from their employer.

Financial data The stipend is $1,000.

Duration 1 year; recipients may reapply.

Number awarded At least 2 each year.

Deadline April of each year.

[159]
INDUSTRY MINORITY SCHOLARSHIPS

American Meteorological Society
Attn: Fellowship/Scholarship Coordinator
45 Beacon Street
Boston, MA 02108-3693
(617) 227-2426, ext. 246   Fax: (617) 742-8718
E-mail: amsinfo@ametsoc.org
Web: www.ametsoc.org

Purpose To provide financial assistance to underrepresented minority students entering college and planning to major in meteorology or some aspect of atmospheric sciences.

Eligibility Candidates must be entering their freshman year at a 4-year college or university and planning to pursue careers in the atmospheric or related oceanic and hydrologic sciences. They must be minority students traditionally underrepresented in the sciences (Hispanic, Native American, and Black/African American students). Applicants must submit an official high school transcript showing grades from the past 3 years, a letter of recommendation from a high school teacher or guidance counselor, a copy of scores from an SAT or similar national entrance exam, and a 500-word essay on how they would use their college education in atmospheric sciences (or a closely-related field) to make their community a better place in which to live. Half of the application evaluation is based on the essay.

Financial data The stipend is $3,000 per year.

Duration 1 year; may be renewed for the second year of college study.

Additional information This program is funded by grants from industry and by donations from members of the Programs in Support of Science and Education of the American Meteorological Society (AMS). Requests for an application must be accompanied by a self-addressed stamped envelope.

Number awarded Varies each year; recently, 12 of these scholarships were awarded.

Deadline February of each year.

[160]
INDUSTRY UNDERGRADUATE SCHOLARSHIPS

American Meteorological Society
Attn: Fellowship/Scholarship Coordinator
45 Beacon Street
Boston, MA 02108-3693
(617) 227-2426, ext. 246   Fax: (617) 742-8718
E-mail: amsinfo@ametsoc.org
Web: www.ametsoc.org

Purpose To encourage outstanding undergraduate students to pursue careers in the atmospheric and related oceanic and hydrologic sciences.

Eligibility This program is open to full-time students entering their junior year who are either 1) enrolled or planning to enroll in a course of study leading to a bachelor's degree in the atmospheric or related oceanic or hydrologic sciences, or 2) enrolled in a program leading to a bachelor's degree in science or engineering who have demonstrated a clear intent to pursue a career in the atmospheric or related oceanic or hydrologic sciences following completion of appropriate specialized education at the graduate level. Applicants must have a GPA of 3.0 or higher and be U.S. citizens or permanent residents. Along with their application, they must submit 2 essays of 100 words or less: 1 on their career goals in the atmospheric or related oceanographic or hydrologic fields and 1 on their most important achievements that qualify them for this scholarship. The sponsor specifically encourages applications from women, minorities, and students with disabilities who are traditionally underrepresented in the atmospheric and related oceanic sciences. Selection is based on merit and potential for accomplishment in the field.

Financial data The stipend is $2,000 per academic year.

Duration 1 year; may be renewed for the final year of college study. Requests for an application must be accompanied by a self-addressed stamped envelope.

Number awarded Varies each year; recently, 9 of these scholarships were awarded.

Deadline February of each year.

[161]
INSTITUTE FOR INTERNATIONAL PUBLIC POLICY FELLOWSHIPS

United Negro College Fund Special Programs Corporation
2750 Prosperity Avenue, Suite 600
Fairfax, VA 22031
(703) 205-7624   (800) 530-6232
Fax: (703) 205-7645   E-mail: iipp@uncfsp.org
Web: www.uncfsp.org/iipp

Purpose To provide financial assistance and work experience to minority students who are interested in preparing for a career in international affairs.

Eligibility This program is open to full-time sophomores at 4-year institutions who have a GPA of 3.2 or higher and are nominated by the president of their institution. Applicants must be African American, Hispanic/Latino American, Asian American, American Indian, Alaskan Native, Native Hawaiian, or Pacific Islander. They must be interested in participating in policy institutes, study abroad, language training, internships, and graduate education that will prepare them for a career in international service. U.S. citizenship or permanent resident status is required. Preference is given to students interested in pursuing advanced language and area studies in targeted world areas who are supported by Title VI fellowships. Targeted languages include Arabic, Azeri, Armenian, Dari, Hindi, Kazakh, Kyrgyz, Persian, Pashto, Tajik, Turkish, Turkmen, Uzbek, Urdu, and other languages spoken in central and south Asia, the Middle East, and Russia/eastern Europe.

Financial data For the sophomore summer policy institute, fellows receive student housing and meals in a university facility, books and materials, all field trips and excursions, and a $1,050 stipend. For the junior year study abroad component, half the expenses for 1 semester are provided. For the junior summer policy institute, fellows receive student housing and meals in a university facility, books and materials, travel to and from the institute, and a $1,000 stipend. For the summer language institute, fellows receive tuition and fees, books and materials, room and board, travel to and from the institute, and a $1,000 stipend. During the internship, a stipend of up to $3,500 is paid. During the graduate school period, fellowships are funded jointly by this program and the participating graduate school. The program provides $15,000 toward a master's degree in international affairs with the expectation that the graduate school will provide $15,000 in matching funds.

Duration 2 years of undergraduate work and 2 years of graduate work, as well as the intervening summers.

Additional information This program consists of 6 components: 1) a sophomore year summer policy institute based at Clark Atlanta University's Department of International Affairs and Development, comprised of lectures, discussions, and group assignments, complemented by guest speakers and local site visits to international agencies and organizations in Washington, D.C. and New York; the program of study includes international politics, research methods, U.S. foreign policy, international business, economics, and selected area studies; 2) a junior year study abroad program at an accredited overseas institution; 3) a junior year summer institute of intensive academic preparation for graduate school, with course work in economics, mathematics, communication skills, and policy analysis; 4) for students without established foreign language competency, a summer language institute following the senior year; 5) fellows with previously established foreign language competence participate in a post-baccalaureate internship to provide the practical experience needed for successful graduate studies in international affairs; and 6) a master's degree in international affairs (for students who are admitted to such a program). This program is administered by the United Negro College Fund Special Programs Corporation in partnership with the Hispanic Scholarship Fund Institute and the Association of Professional Schools of International Affairs; funding is provided by a grant from the U.S. Department of Education.

Number awarded 20 each year.

Deadline February of each year.

[162]
JACKIE ROBINSON SCHOLARSHIP

Jackie Robinson Foundation
Attn: Scholarship Program
3 West 35th Street, 11th Floor
New York, NY 10001-2204
(212) 290-8600   Fax: (212) 290-8081
Web: www.jackierobinson.org

Purpose To provide financial assistance for college to minority high school seniors.

Eligibility To apply for the scholarship, students must be members of an ethnic minority group, U.S. citizens, high school seniors, and accepted at a 4-year college or university. They must be able to demonstrate high academic achievement (SAT score of 900 or higher or ACT score of 23 or higher), financial need, and leadership potential.

Financial data Up to $6,000 per year.

Duration 4 years.

Additional information The program also offers personal and career counseling on a year-round basis, a week of interaction with other scholarship students from around the country, and assistance in obtaining summer jobs and permanent employment after graduation. It was established in 1973 by a grant from Chesebrough-Pond.

Number awarded 100 or more each year.

Deadline March of each year.

[163]
JAMES CARLSON MEMORIAL SCHOLARSHIP

Oregon Student Assistance Commission
Attn: Private Awards Grant Department
1500 Valley River Drive, Suite 100
Eugene, OR 97401-2146
(541) 687-7395   (800) 452-8807, ext. 7395
Fax: (541) 687-7419
E-mail: awardinfo@mercury.osac.state.or.us
Web: www.osac.state.or.us

Purpose To provide financial assistance to Oregon residents majoring in education on the undergraduate or graduate school level.

Eligibility This program is open to residents of Oregon who are U.S. citizens or permanent residents. Applicants must be college seniors or fifth-year students majoring in elementary or secondary education, or graduate students pursuing an elementary or secondary certificate. Full-time enrollment and financial need are required. Priority is given to 1) members of African American, Asian American, Hispanic, or Native American ethnic groups; 2) dependents of members of the Oregon Education Association; and 3) applicants committed to teaching autistic children.

Financial data Scholarship amounts vary, depending upon the needs of the recipient.

Duration 1 year.

Number awarded Varies each year.

Deadline February of each year.

[164]
JAMES ECHOLS SCHOLARSHIP

California Association for Health, Physical Education,
  Recreation and Dance
Attn: Chair, Scholarship Committee
1501 El Camino Avenue, Suite 3
Sacramento, CA 95815-2748
(916) 922-3596   (800) 499-3596 (within CA)
Fax: (916) 922-0133   E-mail: cahperd@aol.com
Web: www.cahperd.org

Purpose To provide financial assistance to minority student members of the California Association for Health, Physical Education, Recreation and Dance.

Eligibility This program is open to California residents who have been members of the association for at least 60 days and are attending a 2-year or 4-year college or university in California. Applicants must be undergraduate or graduate students majoring in health, physical education, recreation, or dance and have completed at least 60 semester hours of college work. Selection is based on scholastic proficiency (a GPA of 3.0 or higher); leadership ability in school, community, and professional activities; and personal qualities of enthusiasm, cooperativeness, responsibility, initiative, and ability to work with others. This scholarship is awarded to the highest-ranked minority (Asian, African American, Latino, or Native American) applicant.

Financial data The stipend is $750.

Duration 1 year.

Number awarded 1 each year.

Deadline January of each year.

[165]
JAMES J. WYCHOR SCHOLARSHIPS

Minnesota Broadcasters Association
Attn: Scholarship Program
3033 Excelsior Boulevard, Suite 301
Minneapolis, MN 55416
(612) 926-8123   (800) 245-5838
Fax: (612) 926-9761
E-mail: jdubois@minnesotabroadcasters.com
Web: www.minnesotabroadcasters.com

Purpose To provide financial assistance to Minnesota residents interested in studying broadcasting in college.

Eligibility This program is open to residents of Minnesota who are accepted or enrolled at an accredited postsecondary institution offering a broadcast-related curriculum. Applicants must have a high school or college GPA of 2.5 or higher and must submit a 200-word essay on why they wish to pursue a career in broadcasting or electronic media. Employment in the broadcasting industry is not required, but students who are employed must include a letter from their general manager describing the duties they have performed as a radio or television station employee and evaluating their potential for success in the industry. Financial need is not considered in the selection process. Some of the scholarships are awarded only to minority and women candidates.

Financial data The stipend is $1,500.

Duration 1 year; recipients who are college seniors may reapply for an additional 1-year renewal.

Number awarded 10 each year, distributed as follows: 3 within the 7-county metro area, 5 allocated geographically throughout the state (northeast, northwest, central, southeast, southwest), and 2 reserved specifically for women and minority applicants.

Deadline May of each year.

[166]
JEAN MARSHALL MINORITY SCHOLARSHIPS

New Jersey State Nurses Association
Attn: Institute for Nursing
1479 Pennington Road
Trenton, NJ 08618-2661
(609) 883-5335, ext. 21   (888) UR-NJSNA, ext. 21
Fax: (609) 883-5343   E-mail: ita@njsna.org
Web: www.njsna.org/institute/institute.htm

Purpose To provide financial assistance to minority undergraduates in New Jersey who are preparing for a career as a nurse.

Eligibility All applicants must be New Jersey residents currently enrolled in an associate degree, baccalaureate, or diploma nursing program located in New Jersey. They must be members of 1 of the following groups: African American, Hispanic, American Indian or Alaskan Native, Asian, or Pacific Islander. Applicants who are R.N.s must be members of the New Jersey State Nurses Association (a copy of their membership card must be submitted with their application). Selection is based on financial need, GPA, and leadership potential.

Financial data A stipend is awarded (amount not specified).

Duration 1 year.

Additional information Applications must be typed or reproduced by computer; handwritten applications are not accepted.

Number awarded Varies each year; recently, 1 of these scholarships was awarded.

Deadline December of each year.

[167]
JERRY JUNKINS MINORITY SCHOLARSHIP

Communities Foundation of Texas
4605 Live Oak Street
Dallas, TX 75204-7099
(214) 826-5231   Fax: (214) 823-7737
E-mail: grants@cftexas.org
Web: www.cftexas.org

Purpose To provide financial assistance to undergraduates (particularly minorities and women) in the Dallas, Texas area who are interested in preparing for a management career in construction.

Eligibility High school and currently-enrolled college students, particularly minorities and women, are eligible to apply if they reside in the Dallas, Texas area and are interested in preparing for a management career in construction.

Financial data The stipend is $1,500 per year. Funds are to be used for tuition, fees, and books.

Duration 1 year.

Additional information Recipients must attend a community college or college or university in Texas.

Number awarded Up to 10 each year.

Deadline March of each year.

[168]
JEWEL OSCO SCHOLARSHIPS

Chicago Urban League
Attn: Scholarship Coordinator
4510 South Michigan Avenue
Chicago, IL 60653-3898
(773) 451-3567 Fax: (773) 285-7772
E-mail: info@cul-chicago.org
Web: www.cul-chicago.org

Purpose To provide financial assistance for college to Illinois residents of color who are also interested in interning at Jewel Osco.

Eligibility This program is open to Illinois residents of color who are graduating high school seniors with a GPA of 2.5 or higher and planning to enroll as full-time undergraduate students at a 4-year college or university. Applicants must agree to complete a summer internship with Jewel Osco. The selection process includes an interview with a representative of Jewel Osco. Financial need must be demonstrated.

Financial data The stipend is $2,000 per year.

Duration 1 year; nonrenewable.

Additional information This program is offered as part of the Chicago Urban League's Whitney M. Young, Jr. Memorial Scholarship Fund, established in 1970.

Number awarded 2 each year.

Deadline May of each year.

[169]
JIMMY A. YOUNG MEMORIAL EDUCATION RECOGNITION AWARD

American Respiratory Care Foundation
Attn: Administrative Coordinator
11030 Ables Lane
Dallas, TX 75229-4593
(972) 243-2272 Fax: (972) 484-2720
E-mail: info@aarc.org
Web: www.aarc.org/awards

Purpose To provide financial assistance to college students, especially minorities, interested in becoming respiratory therapists.

Eligibility Candidates must be enrolled in an accredited respiratory therapy program, have completed at least 1 semester/quarter of the program, and have earned a GPA of 3.0 or higher. Preference is given to nominees of minority origin. Applications must include 6 copies of an original referenced paper on some aspect of respiratory care and letters of recommendation. The foundation prefers that the candidates be nominated by a school or program, but any student may initiate a request for sponsorship by a school (in order that a deserving candidate is not denied the opportunity to compete simply because the school does not initiate the application).

Financial data The stipend is $1,000. The award also provides airfare, 1 night's lodging, and registration for the association's international congress.

Duration 1 year.

Number awarded 1 each year.

Deadline May of each year.

[170]
JOEL ATLAS SKIRBLE FOUNDATION SCHOLARSHIPS

Joel Atlas Skirble Foundation, Inc.
6316 Castle Place, Suite 300
Falls Church, VA 22044
(703) 237-8486 Fax: (703) 237-8540

Purpose To provide financial assistance for college to Hispanic immigrants in the Baltimore and Washington, D.C. area.

Eligibility This program is open to graduating seniors or recent graduates from Baltimore and Washington, D.C. metropolitan area high schools. Applicants must have been born or be descendants of persons born in Spanish-speaking countries. They must be planning to begin or continue college or university education. As part of the application process, students must submit an essay of between 1,500 and 2,500 words, in both English and Spanish, on "How immigrating to the U.S. has changed my life and that of my family." Selection is based on the presentation, grammar, and content of the essay; financial need; and an interview.

Financial data The amounts of the awards depend on the number of persons selected to receive assistance and their financial need. Funds are paid directly to the recipient's college or university, to be used for tuition or other educationally-related expenses.

Duration 1 year.

Additional information This program is cosponsored by the Joel Atlas Skirble Foundation and Univision Washington D.C.

Number awarded Varies; a total of $50,000 is available for these scholarships each year.

Deadline May of each year.

[171]
JOEL GARCIA MEMORIAL SCHOLARSHIPS

California Chicano News Media Association
c/o University of Southern California
Annenberg School for Communication
3800 South Figueroa Street
Los Angeles, CA 90037-1206
(213) 743-4960 Fax: (213) 743-4989
E-mail: info@ccnma.org
Web: www.ccnma.org

Purpose To provide financial assistance to deserving young Latino Americans in California interested in preparing for a career in journalism.

Eligibility The competition is open to all high school seniors and college students of Latino descent in California who are interested in pursuing journalism or communications careers (although they may major in any area). Applicants must submit 1) an essay of 300 to 500 words explaining their family background, including any hardships they have experienced, and what they believe is the role of Latino journalists in the news media; and 2) samples of their journalism-related work (e.g., news articles, news scripts, photographs, or audio and videotapes). Finalists are interviewed. Selection is based on academic achievement, commitment to the journalism field, awareness of the community in which they live, and financial need.

Financial data Scholarships range from $500 to $2,000.

Duration 1 year. Recipients must attend college on a full-time basis.

Number awarded 20 to 30 each year.

Deadline April of each year.

[172]
JOHN AND MURIEL LANDIS SCHOLARSHIPS

American Nuclear Society
Attn: Scholarship Program
555 North Kensington Avenue
La Grange Park, IL 60526-5592
(708) 352-6611   Fax: (708) 352-0499
E-mail: outreach@ans.org
Web: www.ans.org/honors/scholarships

Purpose To provide financial assistance to undergraduate or graduate students (particularly minorities) who are interested in pursuing a career in nuclear-related fields.

Eligibility This program is open to undergraduate and graduate students at colleges or universities located in the United States who are pursuing, or planning to pursue, a career in nuclear science, nuclear engineering, or a nuclear-related field. Qualified high school seniors are also eligible. Applicants must have greater than average financial need and "have experienced circumstances that render them disadvantaged." U.S. citizenship is not required. Selection is primarily based on financial need and potential for academic and professional success. Applicants must be sponsored by an organization within the American Nuclear Society (ANS). If the student does not know of a sponsoring organization, the society will help to establish contact. Augmentation of this scholarship program with matching or supplemental funds by the sponsoring organization is encouraged (though not required).

Financial data The stipend is $3,000, to be used to cover tuition, books, fees, room, and board.

Duration 1 year. Requests for an application must be accompanied by a self-addressed stamped envelope.

Number awarded Up to 8 each year.

Deadline January of each year.

[173]
JOSE MARTI SCHOLARSHIP CHALLENGE GRANT FUND

Florida Department of Education
Attn: Office of Student Financial Assistance
1940 North Monroe Street, Suite 70
Tallahassee, FL 32303-4759
(850) 410-5185   (888) 827-2004
Fax: (850) 488-3612   E-mail: osfa@mail.doe.state.fl.us
Web: www.firn.edu/doe/osfa

Purpose To provide financial assistance to Hispanic American high school seniors and graduate students in Florida.

Eligibility This program is open to Florida residents of Spanish culture who were born in, or whose natural parent was born in, Mexico, Spain, or a Hispanic country of the Caribbean, Central America, or South America. Applicants must be citizens or eligible noncitizens of the United States, be enrolled or planning to enroll as full-time undergraduate or graduate students at an eligible postsecondary school in Florida, be able to demonstrate financial need as determined by a nationally-recognized needs analysis service, and have earned a cumulative GPA of 3.0 or higher in high school or, if a graduate school applicant, in undergraduate course work.

Financial data The grant is $2,000 per academic year. Available funds are contingent upon matching contributions from private sources.

Duration 1 year; may be renewed if the student maintains full-time enrollment and a GPA of 3.0 or higher and continues to demonstrate financial need.

Number awarded Varies each year; recently, this program presented 98 awards.

Deadline March of each year.

[174]
JUAN EUGENE RAMOS SCHOLARSHIP

Hispanic Designers, Inc.
Attn: National Hispanic Education and Communications Projects
1101 30th Street, N.W., Suite 500
Washington, DC 20007
(202) 337-9636   Fax: (202) 337-9635
E-mail: HispDesign@aol.com
Web: www.hispanicdesigners.org

Purpose To provide financial assistance to Hispanic students enrolled in a fashion design school.

Eligibility Applicants must be Hispanic or of Hispanic descent, be able to demonstrate financial need, be U.S. citizens or residents, have participated in an internship or work training program in the field of fashion, and have a GPA of 3.0 or higher. They must be enrolled in an accredited postsecondary institution and studying for a degree or certified program that incorporates the importance of marketing and merchandising in fashion design.

Financial data The stipend is $5,000 per year; awards are paid directly to the institution.

Duration 1 year.

Additional information This program was established in 1995. No telephone inquiries are accepted.

Number awarded 1 each year.

Deadline August of each year.

[175]
JUDGE SIDNEY M. ARONOVITZ SCHOLARSHIP

Dade Community Foundation
Attn: Director of Development
200 South Biscayne Boulevard, Suite 2780
Miami, FL 33131-2343
(305) 371-2711   Fax: (305) 371-5342
E-mail: Dadecomfnd@aol.com

Purpose To provide financial assistance for college to minority students graduating from high school in Dade County, Florida.

Eligibility Eligible to apply for this support are minority students who are high school seniors or GED recipients in a Miami-Dade County (Florida) public school. Applicants must be planning to continue their education on the university level and pursue a career in south Florida. They must have at least a 3.0 GPA.

Financial data The stipend is $1,000.

Duration 1 year.

Number awarded 1 each year.

Deadline March of each year.

[176]
JUSTICIA EN DIVERSIDAD SCHOLARSHIP

Justicia en Diversidad Foundation, Inc.
Attn: Scholarship & Mentorship Program
c/o La Alianza
23 Everett Street
Cambridge, MA 02138
E-mail: scholarship@jdfoundation.org
Web: www.jdfoundation.org/scholarship

Purpose To provide financial assistance to Latino high school seniors who are planning to attend college to prepare for a career in a field related to law.

Eligibility This program is open to students of Latino heritage at high schools in the United States. Applicants must have a GPA of 2.5 or higher and be planning to attend an accredited 2-year or 4-year college or university on a full-time basis. They must show a strong interest in pursuing a career in law. Along with their application, they must submit a 2-page personal statement on the following topic: "What are your goals and aspirations, and how will a legal education help you achieve them?" Financial need is also considered in the selection process.

Financial data The stipend is $1,000.

Duration 1 year.

Additional information This program began in 2002. In addition to receiving financial support, the recipient is paired with a Harvard Law School student or Harvard Law School graduate mentor of Latino heritage who can address questions and concerns that may arise.

Number awarded 1 each year.

Deadline March of each year.

[177]
KANSAS CITY HISPANIC SCHOLARSHIP FUND

Greater Kansas City Community Foundation
Attn: Scholarship Coordinator
1055 Broadway, Suite 130
Kansas City, MO 64105-1595
(816) 842-0944   Fax: (816) 842-8079
E-mail: scholars@gkccf.org
Web: www.gkccf.org

Purpose To provide financial assistance for college or graduate school to Hispanic students from the greater Kansas City area.

Eligibility This program is open to Hispanic students who are permanent residents of the greater Kansas City area (including Cass, Clay, Jackson, and Platte counties in Missouri and Johnson and Wyandotte counties in Kansas). Applicants must be or plan to be full-time undergraduate or graduate students.

Financial data The stipends range from $250 to $1,200 per year.

Duration 1 year.

Additional information Further information is available from the LULAC Educational Center, 301 East Armour Boulevard, Suite 460, Kansas City, MO 64111, (816) 561-0227, Fax: (816) 561-8319, E-mail: lnesc@latino-net.org.

Number awarded 1 or more each year, depending on the availability of funds.

Deadline February of each year.

[178]
KANSAS ETHNIC MINORITY SCHOLARSHIP PROGRAM

Kansas Board of Regents
Attn: Student Financial Aid
1000 S.W. Jackson Street, Suite 520
Topeka, KS 66612-1368
(785) 296-3518   Fax: (785) 296-0983
E-mail: dlindeman@ksbor.org
Web: www.kansasregents.com

Purpose To provide financial assistance to minority students who are interested in attending college in Kansas.

Eligibility Eligible to apply are Kansas residents who fall into 1 of these minority groups: American Indian, Alaskan Native, African American, Asian, Pacific Islander, or Hispanic. Applicants may be current college students (enrolled in community colleges, colleges, or universities in Kansas), but high school seniors graduating in the current year receive priority consideration. Minimum academic requirements include 1 of the following: 1) ACT score of 21 or higher or SAT score of 816 or higher; 2) cumulative GPA of 3.0 or higher; 3) high school rank in upper one third; 4) completion of the Regents Scholars Curriculum (4 years of English, 3 years of mathematics, 3 years of science, 3 years of social studies, and 2 years of foreign language); 5) selection by the National Merit Corporation in any category; or 6) selection by the College Board as a Hispanic Scholar.

Financial data A stipend of up to $1,850 is provided, depending on financial need and availability of state funds.

Duration 1 year; may be renewed for up to 3 additional years (4 additional years for designated 5-year programs) if the recipient maintains a 2.0 cumulative GPA and has financial need. There is a $10 application fee.

Number awarded Approximately 200 each year.

Deadline March of each year.

[179]
KANSAS SPACE GRANT CONSORTIUM PROGRAM

Kansas Space Grant Consortium
c/o University of Kansas
135 Nichols Hall
2335 Irving Hill Road
Lawrence, KS 66045-7612
(785) 864-7401   Fax: (785) 864-3361
E-mail: ksgc@ukans.edu
Web: www.ksgc.org

Purpose To provide funding for space-related activities to students and faculty at member institutions of the Kansas Space Grant Consortium.

Eligibility This program is open to faculty and students at member institutions. Support is provided for undergraduate research scholarships, graduate research assistantships, undergraduate and graduate student participation in activities sponsored by the U.S. National Aeronautics and Space Administration (NASA), faculty participation in NASA research projects, and other activities in fields of interest to NASA. The consortium is a component of NASA's Space Grant program, which encourages participation by women, underrepresented minorities, and persons with disabilities.

Financial data Each participating institution determines the amounts of its awards.

Additional information The member institutions of the consortium are Emporia State University, Fort Hayes State University,

Haskell Indian Nations University, Kansas State University, Pittsburgh State University, University of Kansas, and Wichita State University. Funding for this program is provided by NASA.

Number awarded Varies each year.

Deadline Each participating institution establishes its own deadlines.

[180]
KATU THOMAS R. DARGAN MINORITY SCHOLARSHIP

KATU Channel 2 Portland
Attn: Human Resources
P.O. Box 2
Portland, OR 97207-0002
(503) 231-4222
Web: www.katu.com

Purpose To provide financial assistance and work experience to minority students from Oregon and Washington who are studying broadcasting or communications in college.

Eligibility This program is open to Native Americans, African Americans, Hispanic Americans, or Asian Americans who are U.S. citizens, currently enrolled in the first, second, or third year at a 4-year college or university or an accredited community college in Oregon or Washington, or, if a resident of Oregon or Washington, at a school in any state. Applicants must be majoring in broadcasting or communications and have a GPA of 3.0 or higher. Community college students must be enrolled in a broadcast curriculum that is transferable to a 4-year accredited university. Finalists will be interviewed. Selection is based on financial need, academic achievement, and an essay on personal and professional goals.

Financial data The stipend is $4,000. Funds are sent directly to the recipient's school.

Duration 1 year; recipients may reapply if they have maintained a GPA of 3.0 or higher.

Additional information Winners are also eligible for a paid internship in selected departments at Fisher Broadcasting/KATU in Portland, Oregon.

Number awarded 1 or more each year.

Deadline April of each year.

[181]
KEN INOUYE SCHOLARSHIP

Society of Professional Journalists-Greater Los Angeles
    Professional Chapter
c/o Christopher Burnett, Scholarship Chair
California State University at Long Beach
Department of Journalism
1250 Bellflower Boulevard
Long Beach, CA 90840-4601
(562) 985-5779   E-mail: cburnett@csulb.edu
Web: www.spj.org/losangeles

Purpose To provide financial assistance to minority undergraduate and graduate students in southern California who are interested in pursuing careers in journalism.

Eligibility Minority college juniors, seniors, or graduate students who are interested in careers in journalism (but not public relations, advertising, publicity, law, or a related field) are eligible to apply if they are residents of or attending school in Los Angeles, Ventura, or Orange counties, California. Applicants should be enrolled as journalism majors, but if their university does not offer

such a major they may present other evidence of intent to pursue a career in the field. Selection is based on evidence of unusual accomplishment and potential to advance in a news career; financial need is considered only if 2 applicants are equally qualified.

Financial data The stipend is $1,000 per year.

Duration 1 year; may be renewed. The sponsor reserves the right to split the scholarship equally if 2 or more applicants appear equally qualified or to make no award if there are no promising applicants.

Number awarded 1 each year.

Deadline March of each year.

[182]
KEN KASHIWAHARA SCHOLARSHIP

Radio and Television News Directors Foundation
1000 Connecticut Avenue, N.W., Suite 615
Washington, DC 20036-5302
(202) 467-5218   Fax: (202) 223-4007
E-mail: karenb@rtndf.org
Web: www.rtndf.org/asfi/scholarships/undergrad.shtml

Purpose To provide financial assistance to outstanding undergraduate students, especially minorities, who are interested in preparing for a career in electronic journalism.

Eligibility Eligible are sophomore or more advanced undergraduate students enrolled in an electronic journalism sequence at an accredited or nationally-recognized college or university. Applicants must submit 1 to 3 examples of reporting or producing skills on audio or video cassette tapes (no more than 15 minutes total), a description of their role on each story and a list of who worked on each story and what they did, a statement explaining why they are seeking a career in broadcast or cable journalism, and a letter of endorsement from a faculty sponsor that verifies the applicant has at least 1 year of school remaining. Preference is given to undergraduate students of color.

Financial data The stipend is $2,500, paid in semiannual installments of $1,250 each.

Duration 1 year.

Additional information The Radio and Television News Directors Foundation (RTNDF) also provides an expense-paid trip to the Radio-Television News Directors Association (RTNDA) annual international conference. It defines electronic journalism to include radio, television, cable, and online news. Previous winners of any RTNDF scholarship or internship are not eligible.

Number awarded 1 each year.

Deadline April of each year.

[183]
KENTUCKY SPACE GRANT CONSORTIUM UNDERGRADUATE SCHOLARSHIPS

Kentucky Space Grant Consortium
c/o Western Kentucky University
Department of Physics and Astronomy, TCCW 246
Hardin Planetarium and Astrophysical Observatory
One Big Red Way
Bowling Green, KY 42101-3576
(270) 745-4156   Fax: (270) 745-4255
E-mail: Richard.Hackney@wku.edu
Web: www.wku.edu/KSGC

Purpose To provide financial assistance to undergraduate students at member institutions of the Kentucky Space Grant Consortium (KSGC) interested in pursuing education and research in space-related fields.

Eligibility This program is open to undergraduate students at member institutions of the KSGC. Applicants must be enrolled in a baccalaureate degree program in a space-related field or teaching specialization. As part of the program, a faculty member must agree to serve as a mentor on a research project. U.S. citizenship is required. Selection is based on academic qualifications of the applicant, quality of the proposed research program and its relevance to space-related science and technology, and applicant's motivation for a space-related career as expressed in an essay on interests and goals. Applications are encouraged from women, underrepresented minorities, and students involved in projects of the U.S. National Aeronautics and Space Administration (NASA) such as NASA EPSCoR and SHARP.

Financial data The stipend is $3,000 per year, with an additional $500 to support the student's mentored research project. Matching grants of at least $3,000 are required. Preference is given to applicants from schools that agree to waive tuition for the scholar as part of the program.

Duration 1 year; may be renewed depending on the quality of the student's research and satisfactory performance in the program of study as evidenced by grades, presentation of research results, and evaluation of progress by the mentor.

Additional information This program is funded by NASA. The KSGC member institutions are Centre College, Eastern Kentucky University, Kentucky State University, Morehead State University, Murray State University, Northern Kentucky University, Transylvania University, University of Kentucky, University of Louisville, and Western Kentucky University.

Number awarded Varies each year.

Deadline April of each year.

[184]
KNIGHT RIDDER MINORITY SCHOLARS PROGRAM

Knight Ridder, Inc.
Attn: Office of Diversity
50 West San Fernando Street, Suite 1200
San Jose, CA 95113
(408) 938-7734   Fax: (408) 938-7755
Web: www.kri.com/working/interns.html

Purpose To provide financial assistance and work experience to minority high school seniors who are interested in going to college to prepare for a career in journalism.

Eligibility Graduating minority high school seniors are eligible to apply if they are attending a school in an area served by Knight Ridder and are interested in majoring in journalism in college. Candidates first apply to their local Knight Ridder newspaper and compete for local scholarships; selected winners are then nominated for this award.

Financial data The stipend is up to $10,000 per year.

Duration 1 year; may be renewed for up to 3 additional years, if the recipient maintains a GPA of 3.0 or higher.

Additional information Scholarship recipients are offered an internship opportunity at a Knight Ridder newspaper during the summer. At the end of the program, recipients must work at a Knight Ridder newspaper for 1 year.

Number awarded 4 each year.

[185]
LAGRANT FOUNDATION SCHOLARSHIPS

LAGRANT FOUNDATION
555 South Flower Street, Suite 700
Los Angeles, CA 90071-2423
(323) 469-8680   Fax: (323) 469-8683
Web: www.lagrantfoundation.org

Purpose To provide financial assistance to minority high school seniors or college students who are interested in majoring in advertising, public relations, or marketing.

Eligibility This program is open to African Americans, Asian Pacific Americans, Hispanics, or Native Americans who are full-time students at a 4-year accredited institution or high school seniors planning to attend a 4-year accredited institution on a full-time basis. Applicants must have a GPA of 2.5 or higher and be majoring or planning to major in advertising, marketing, or public relations. They must submit 1) a 1- to 2-page essay outlining their career goals, their accomplishments, why they should be selected as a scholarship recipient, and, as a person of color, describing they steps they will take to increase ethnic representation in the fields of advertising, marketing, and public relations; 2) a paragraph explaining how they are financing or planning to finance their education and why they need financial assistance; 3) a paragraph explaining the high school, college, and/or community activities in which they are involved; 4) a brief paragraph describing any honors and awards they have received; 5) if they are currently employed, a paragraph indicating the hours worked each week, responsibilities, and if the job will be kept while attending school; 6) a resume; and 7) an official transcript.

Financial data The stipend is $5,000 per year.

Duration 1 year.

Number awarded 10 each year.

Deadline March of each year.

[186]
LANDMARK SCHOLARS PROGRAM

Landmark Publishing Group
Attn: Director of Recruiting
150 West Brambleton Avenue
Norfolk, VA 23510
(757) 446-2456   (800) 446-2004, ext. 2456
Fax: (757) 446-2414   E-mail: csage@lcimedia.com
Web: www.landmarkcom.com

Purpose To provide work experience and financial aid to minority undergraduates who are interested in preparing for a career in journalism.

Eligibility This program is open to minority college sophomores, preferably those with ties to the mid-Atlantic/southern region. Applicants must be interested in pursuing a career in journalism. They must also be interested in internships as reporters, photographers, graphic artists, sports writers, copy editors, or page designers.

Financial data The stipend is $5,000 per year. During the summers between the sophomore and junior years and between the junior and seniors years, recipients are provided with paid internships. Following graduation, they are offered a 1-year internship with full benefits and the possibility of continued employment.

Duration 2 years (the junior and senior years of college).

Additional information The internships are offered at the *News & Record* in Greensboro, North Carolina, the *Virginian-Pilot* in Norfolk, Virginia, or the *Roanoke Times* in Roanoke, Virginia.

Number awarded 1 or more each year.

Deadline November of each year.

[187]
L.A.S.O. SCHOLARSHIP

Latin American Support Organization
c/o Denver Water
1600 West 12th Avenue
Denver, CO 80204
(303) 628-6810   E-mail: bar.maccoy@denverwater.org

Purpose To provide financial assistance for college to Colorado residents who are Hispanic Americans and relatives of members of the Latin American Support Organization (L.A.S.O.).

Eligibility To be eligible for this scholarship, students must be relatives of members of L.A.S.O., be Colorado residents, have at least 50% Hispanic heritage, be accepted at an accredited postsecondary institution, exhibit "unmet" financial need, and have a GPA of 2.5 or higher. To apply, students must submit a complete application form, a statement on personal background and activities (including activities that have benefited the Hispanic community), a current picture, 3 letters of reference, an official grade transcript, and the family's federal income tax returns for the past 2 years.

Financial data Stipends range from $250 to $1,500.

Duration 1 year.

Additional information Recipients must agree to volunteer a minimum of 8 hours at an L.A.S.O. fundraiser.

Number awarded Several each year.

Deadline April of each year.

[188]
LATIN AMERICAN EDUCATIONAL FOUNDATION SCHOLARSHIPS

Latin American Educational Foundation
Attn: Scholarship Selection Committee
924 West Colfax Avenue, Suite 103
Denver, CO 80204
(303) 446-0541   Fax: (303) 446-0526
E-mail: laefaa@uswest.net
Web: www.laef.org

Purpose To provide financial aid to Hispanic American undergraduate students in Colorado.

Eligibility This program is open to Colorado residents who are of Hispanic heritage and/or actively involved in the Hispanic community. Applicants must have been accepted at an accredited college, university, or vocational school and must have a cumulative GPA of 3.0 or higher. Selection is based on community involvement, academic achievement, letters of recommendation, a personal essay, an interview, and financial need.

Financial data The amount of the award depends on the need of the recipient, ranging from $500 to $3,000. Scholarships may be used at Colorado colleges and universities or at out-of-state institutions. Most colleges and universities within Colorado participate in the Colorado Higher Education Partnership; member institutions provide additional funds to match the award granted by this foundation.

Duration 1 year; recipients may reapply. Recipients are required to perform 10 hours of community service during the academic year.

Number awarded Varies each year; recently, 227 of these scholarships were awarded.

Deadline February of each year.

[189]
LATINGIRL SCHOLARSHIP

Latingirl: The Hispanic Teen Magazine
Attn: Latingirl Scholarship
P.O. Box 625
Hoboken, NJ 07030-0625
Fax: (201) 876-9640   E-mail: editor@latingirlmag.com
Web: www.latingirlmag.com

Purpose To provide financial assistance for college to Hispanic women graduating from high school.

Eligibility This program is open to women of Hispanic descent who are graduating high school seniors. Applicants must submit a 300-word essay on their background and their potential contribution to the Hispanic community. Selection is based on the essay, academic achievement, and financial need.

Financial data The stipend is $1,000.

Duration 1 year.

Additional information These scholarships were first offered in 1999.

Number awarded 10 each year.

Deadline April of each year.

[190]
LATINO COLLEGE EXPO SCHOLARSHIP AWARDS

Latino College Expo, Inc.
Attn: Scholarship Committee
511 Avenue of the Americas
PMB 192
New York, NY 10011
(212) 677-1108, ext. 156   E-mail: LatinoExpo@aol.com
Web: www.latinocollegeexpo.org

Purpose To provide financial assistance for college to Latino high school seniors in the New York tri-state area.

Eligibility This program is open to Latino seniors at high schools in the New York tri-state area. Applicants must be U.S. citizens or permanent residents planning to attend a college or university as a full-time student in the following fall. They must submit high school transcripts (with a 4-year high school average of 85% or higher), SAT score (1000 or higher), a list of academic accomplishments and honors (including any advanced placement courses completed with grades), 2 teacher recommendations, and a 250-word essay.

Financial data The stipend is $500.

Duration 1 year.

Number awarded 4 each year.

Deadline March of each year.

[191]
LAWRENCE WADE JOURNALISM FELLOWSHIP

Heritage Foundation
Attn: Selection Committee
214 Massachusetts Avenue, N.E.
Washington, DC 20002-4999
(202) 546-4400   Fax: (202) 546-8328
E-mail: info@heritage.org
Web: www.heritage.org

Purpose To provide financial assistance and work experience to undergraduate or graduate students who are interested in a career in journalism.

Eligibility This program is open to undergraduate or graduate students who are currently enrolled full time and are interested in a career as a journalist upon graduation. Applicants need not be majoring in journalism, but they must submit writing samples of published news stories, editorial commentaries, or broadcast scripts. Preference is given to candidates who are Asian Americans, African Americans, Hispanic Americans, or Native Americans.

Financial data The winner receives a $1,000 scholarship and participates in a 10-week salaried internship at the Heritage Foundation.

Duration 1 year.

Additional information This program was established in 1991.

Number awarded 1 each year.

Deadline February of each year.

[192]
LEADERSHIP FOR DIVERSITY SCHOLARSHIP

California School Library Association
717 K Street, Suite 515
Sacramento, CA 95814
(916) 447-2684   Fax: (916) 447-2695
E-mail: csla@pacbell.net
Web: www.schoollibrary.org

Purpose To encourage underrepresented minority students to get a credential as a library media teacher in California.

Eligibility This program is open to students who are members of a traditionally underrepresented group enrolled in a college or university library media teacher credential program in California. Applicants must intend to work as a library media teacher in a California school library media center for a minimum of 3 years. Financial need is considered in awarding the scholarship.

Financial data The stipend is $1,000.

Duration 1 year.

Number awarded 1 each year.

Deadline May of each year.

[193]
LEE ENTERPRISES COLLEGE-TO-WORK SCHOLARSHIP

Wisconsin Foundation for Independent Colleges, Inc.
735 North Water Street, Suite 800
Milwaukee, WI 53202-4100
(414) 273-5980   Fax: (414) 273-5995
E-mail: info@wficweb.org
Web: www.wficweb.org/documents/coll_work.htm

Purpose To provide financial assistance and work experience to minority students majoring in fields related to business or news at private colleges in Wisconsin.

Eligibility This program is open to full-time minority sophomores, juniors, and seniors at the 20 independent colleges and universities in Wisconsin. Applicants may be majoring in any liberal arts field, but they must be preparing for a career in accounting, information technology, computers, graphic design, sales, marketing, news reporting, or communications. They must have a GPA of 3.0 or higher and be interested in an internship at 1 of the 3 Lee newspapers in the state: the *Wisconsin State Journal,* the *La Crosse Tribune,* or the *Racine Journal Times.* Along with their application, they must submit a 1-page autobiography, transcripts, a list of campus involvement and academic honors, a resume including 3 references, and 2 letters of recommendation.

Financial data The stipends are $3,500 for the scholarship and $1,500 for the internship.

Duration 1 year for the scholarship; 10 weeks for the internship.

Additional information The participating schools are Alverno College, Beloit College, Cardinal Stritch University, Carroll College, Carthage College, Concordia University of Wisconsin, Edgewood College, Lakeland College, Lawrence University, Marian College, Marquette University, Milwaukee Institute of Art & Design, Milwaukee School of Engineering, Mount Mary College, Northland College, Ripon College, St. Norbert College, Silver Lake College, Viterbo University, and Wisconsin Lutheran College. This program is sponsored by Lee Enterprises/Madison Newspapers, Inc. (www.lee.net).

Number awarded 3 each year.

Deadline January of each year.

[194]
LEON WILLIAMS SCHOLARSHIP

San Diego Foundation
Attn: Scholarship Committee
1420 Kettner Boulevard, Suite 500
P.O. Box 81107
San Diego, CA 92138-1107
(619) 235-2300, ext. 133   Fax: (619) 239-1710
E-mail: sdf@sdfoundation.org
Web: www.sdfoundation.org

Purpose To provide financial assistance to minority high school seniors in San Diego County, California who are interested in preparing for a career in health care.

Eligibility This program is open to minority students from high schools in San Diego County who are planning to work on a college degree in health care at a 4-year university. Applicants must have a GPA of 3.0 or higher and be able to demonstrate financial need. Along with other application material, they must submit an essay on improving the health of our underserved community.

Financial data The stipend averages $1,000.

Duration 1 year.

Number awarded 2 each year.

Deadline March of each year.

[195]
LEONARD M. PERRYMAN COMMUNICATIONS SCHOLARSHIP FOR ETHNIC MINORITY STUDENTS

United Methodist Communications
Attn: Communications Resourcing Team
810 12th Avenue South
P.O. Box 320
Nashville, TN 37202-0320
(615) 742-5481   (888) CRT-4UMC
Fax: (615) 742-5485   E-mail: scholarships@umcom.org
Web: www.umcom.org

Purpose To provide financial assistance to minority college students who are interested in careers in religious communications.

Eligibility Applicants must be minorities who are enrolled in accredited institutions of higher education as juniors or seniors and are interested in pursuing careers in religious communications. For the purposes of this program, "communications" is meant to cover audiovisual, electronic, and print journalism. Selection is based on Christian commitment and involvement in

the life of the church, academic achievement, journalistic experience, clarity of purpose, and professional potential as a religious journalist.
Financial data The stipend is $2,500 per year.
Duration 1 year.
Additional information The scholarship may be used at any accredited institution of higher education.
Number awarded 2 each year: 1 to the best overall candidate of any Christian denomination and 1 to the best United Methodist candidate.
Deadline March of each year.

[196]
LEXINGTON HERALD-LEADER MINORITY SCHOLARSHIP

Lexington Herald-Leader
Attn: Educational Outreach Manager
100 Midland Avenue
Lexington, KY 40508
(859) 231-3104   E-mail: kaldridge@herald-leader.com
Web: www.kentucky.com/mld/heraldleader

Purpose To provide financial assistance for college to minority high school seniors in eastern and central Kentucky, especially those interested in studying journalism.
Eligibility This program is open to minority high school seniors from eastern and central Kentucky who are planning to attend college. Applicants must submit 2 letters of recommendation, transcripts, SAT/ACT scores, and an essay explaining why they want to go to college and the kind of career they hope to pursue upon graduation. Students who intend to pursue a career in journalism are considered for additional scholarships; they should also submit 5 samples of their writing. Financial need is not considered in the selection process.
Financial data The stipend is $1,000 per year.
Duration 1 year; nonrenewable.
Additional information If the recipients of these scholarships indicate an interest in a journalism career, they are automatically entered into competition for the 4-year $10,000 Knight Ridder Minority Scholarship Program.
Number awarded 2 each year.
Deadline January of each year.

[197]
LINC SCHOLARSHIPS

Latino Initiatives for the Next Century
Attn: Scholarship Program
2500 South St. Louis Avenue, Second Floor
Chicago, IL 60623
(773) 762-8970   (800) 510-LINC
Fax: (773) 762-8971   E-mail: admin@linc-usa.org
Web: linc-usa.org/ed/overv.html

Purpose To provide financial assistance for college to Latino undergraduate students from designated states.
Eligibility This program is open to Latinos who are first-generation college students from California, Illinois, New York, or Texas. Applicants must be enrolled or planning to enroll full time at an approved college or technical school. Most, but not all, of the approved institutions are in their home state; contact the sponsor for a list of colleges and universities for each state. Applicants must be a high school graduate or GED recipient, have a GPA of 2.5 or higher, be a U.S. citizen or permanent resident, and

be able to demonstrate an unmet financial need. Selection is based on academic achievement, financial need, community service, letters of recommendation, and the applicant's understanding of the issues confronting the Latino community.
Financial data The stipend depends on the unmet financial need of the recipient.
Duration 1 year; may be renewed as long as recipients maintain a GPA of 2.5 or higher, provide the sponsor with official transcripts and a personal report on their academic progress, participate in the sponsor's academic support programs, and provide 10 hours of community service per academic year.
Additional information Applicants from Illinois and New York should contact the Chicago office. For applicants in California and Texas, information is available from LINC-TELACU, Attn: Scholarship Program, 5400 East Olympic Boulevard, Suite 300, Los Angeles, CA 90022 (323) 721-1655, Fax: (323) 724-3372. This program was established in 2002 by the TELACU Education Foundation.
Number awarded More than 500 each year.
Deadline July of each year.

[198]
LOUIS B. RUSSELL, JR. MEMORIAL SCHOLARSHIP

Indiana State Teachers Association
Attn: Scholarships
150 West Market Street, Suite 900
Indianapolis, IN 46204
(317) 263-3400   (800) 382-4037
E-mail: kmcallen@ista-in.org
Web: www.ista-in.org

Purpose To provide financial assistance to ethnic minority high school seniors in Indiana who are interested in pursuing vocational education.
Eligibility This program is open to ethnic minority high school seniors in Indiana who are interested in continuing their education in the area of industrial arts, vocational education, or technical preparation at an accredited postsecondary institution. Selection is based on academic achievement, leadership ability as expressed through co-curricular activities and community involvement, recommendations, and an essay.
Financial data The stipend is $1,000.
Duration 1 year; may be renewed for 1 additional year.
Number awarded 1 each year.
Deadline February of each year.

[199]
LOWRIDER MAGAZINE SCHOLARSHIP FUND

Lowrider Magazine
P.O. Box 6930
Fullerton, CA 92834-6930
(714) 213-1000

Purpose To assist Chicano/Latino students who are interested in finishing their college education.
Eligibility Applicants must be of Latino descent, have a GPA of 3.0 or higher, and be currently enrolled as college sophomores, juniors, or seniors. They must submit an official transcript, 2 letters of recommendation, a 1-page essay outlining their financial situation, and a 2-page essay on 1 of 3 topics that change annually.
Financial data Stipends are available for tuition and books only.

Duration 1 year.

Additional information This program started in 1990. No phone calls are accepted. Requests for applications must be accompanied by a self-addressed stamped envelope.

Number awarded Varies each year.

Deadline May of each year.

[200]
LULAC GENERAL AWARDS

League of United Latin American Citizens
Attn: LULAC National Education Service Centers
2000 L Street, N.W., Suite 610
Washington, DC 20036
(202) 833-6130   Fax: (202) 833-6135
E-mail: LNESCAward@aol.com
Web: www.lulac.org/Programs/Scholar.html

Purpose To provide financial assistance to Hispanic American undergraduate and graduate students.

Eligibility This program is open to Hispanic Americans who are U.S. citizens or permanent residents currently enrolled or planning to enroll at an accredited college or university as a graduate or undergraduate student. Although grades are considered in the selection process, emphasis is placed on the applicant's motivation, sincerity, and integrity, as revealed through a personal interview and in an essay. Need, community involvement, and leadership activities are also considered. Candidates must live near a participating local council of the League of United Latin American Citizens (LULAC) and must apply directly to that council.

Financial data The stipend ranges from $250 to $1,000 per year, depending on the need of the recipient.

Duration 1 year.

Additional information This program represents an attempt to forge a partnership between the corporate world and the community. Under its fundsharing concept, LULAC's National Education Service Center gathers contributions nationally from corporations, while LULAC councils raise money locally. The total corporate donations are then apportioned back to the councils according to effort. Applications must be obtained directly from participating LULAC councils; for a list, send a self-addressed stamped envelope to the sponsor.

Number awarded Varies; approximately 500 each year.

Deadline March of each year.

[201]
LULAC HONORS AWARDS

League of United Latin American Citizens
Attn: LULAC National Education Service Centers
2000 L Street, N.W., Suite 610
Washington, DC 20036
(202) 833-6130   Fax: (202) 833-6135
E-mail: LNESCAward@aol.com
Web: www.lulac.org/Programs/Scholar.html

Purpose To provide financial assistance to Hispanic American undergraduate and graduate students.

Eligibility This program is open to Hispanic Americans who are U.S. citizens or permanent residents currently enrolled or planning to enroll at an accredited college or university as a graduate or undergraduate student. Applicants who are already in college must have a GPA of 3.25 or higher. Entering freshmen must have ACT scores of 20 or higher or SAT scores of 840 or higher. In addition, applicants must demonstrate motivation, sincerity, and

integrity through a personal interview and in an essay. Need, community involvement, and leadership activities are also considered. Candidates must live near a participating local council of the League of United Latin American Citizens (LULAC) and must apply directly to that council.

Financial data The stipend ranges from $250 to $1,000 per year, depending on the need of the recipient.

Duration 1 year.

Additional information This program represents an attempt to forge a partnership between the corporate world and the community. Under its fundsharing concept, LULAC's National Education Service Center gathers contributions nationally from corporations, while LULAC councils raise money locally. The total corporate donations are then apportioned back to the councils according to effort. Applications must be obtained directly from participating LULAC councils; for a list, send a self-addressed stamped envelope to the sponsor.

Number awarded Varies each year.

Deadline March of each year.

[202]
LULAC NATIONAL SCHOLASTIC ACHIEVEMENT AWARDS

League of United Latin American Citizens
Attn: LULAC National Education Service Centers
2000 L Street, N.W., Suite 610
Washington, DC 20036
(202) 833-6130   Fax: (202) 833-6135
E-mail: LNESCAward@aol.com
Web: www.lulac.org/Programs/Scholar.html

Purpose To provide financial assistance to Hispanic American undergraduate and graduate students.

Eligibility This program is open to Hispanic Americans who are U.S. citizens or permanent residents currently enrolled or planning to enroll at an accredited college or university as a graduate or undergraduate student. Applicants who are already in college must have a GPA of 3.5 or higher. Entering freshmen must have ACT scores of 23 or higher or SAT scores of 970 or higher. In addition, applicants must demonstrate motivation, sincerity, and integrity through a personal interview and in an essay. Need, community involvement, and leadership activities are also considered. Candidates must live near a participating local council of the League of United Latin American Citizens (LULAC) and must apply directly to that council.

Financial data Stipends are at least $1,000 per year.

Duration 1 year.

Additional information This program represents an attempt to forge a partnership between the corporate world and the community. Under its fundsharing concept, LULAC's National Education Service Center gathers contributions nationally from corporations, while LULAC councils raise money locally. The total corporate donations are then apportioned back to the councils according to effort. Applications must be obtained directly from participating LULAC councils; for a list, send a self-addressed stamped envelope to the sponsor.

Number awarded Varies each year.

Deadline March of each year.

[203]
MAES GENERAL SCHOLARSHIPS

Society of Mexican American Engineers and Scientists
Attn: National Office Director
13337 South Street, Suite 349
Cerritos, CA 90703
E-mail: maes@tamu.edu
Web: www.maes-natl.org

Purpose To provide financial assistance to undergraduate and graduate student members of the Society of Mexican American Engineers and Scientists (MAES).

Eligibility This program is open to MAES student members who are full-time undergraduate or graduate students at a college or university in the United States. Community college students must be enrolled in majors that can transfer to a 4-year institution offering a baccalaureate degree. All applicants must be majoring in a field of science or engineering. U.S. citizenship or permanent resident status is required. Selection is based on financial need; academic achievement; personal qualities, strengths, and leadership abilities; and timeliness and completeness of the application.

Financial data The stipend is $1,000.

Duration 1 year.

Additional information Information is also available from José M. Hernández, Chair, MAES Scholarship Committee, 4015 North Water Iris Cort, Houston, TX 77059.

Number awarded 1 or more each year.

Deadline October of each year.

[204]
MARGARET GONZALES SCHOLARSHIP

Las Mujeres de LULAC
Attn: Scholarship Committee
P.O. Box 2203
Albuquerque, NM 87103

Purpose To provide financial assistance to nontraditional Hispanic women to continue their college education in New Mexico.

Eligibility This program is open to Hispanic women who are residents of New Mexico; are enrolled in an accredited college, university, community college, vocational school, or certified career enhancement program in the state; and are nontraditional students who are returning to school to complete a degree, for career development, or for employment training. A personal interview may be required. Financial need is considered in the selection process.

Financial data A stipend is awarded (amount not specified).

Duration 1 year.

Number awarded 1 or more each year.

Deadline May of each year.

[205]
MARTIN LUTHER KING, JR. MEMORIAL SCHOLARSHIP FUND

California Teachers Association
Attn: Human Rights Department
P.O. Box 921
Burlingame, CA 94011-0921
(650) 697-1400   E-mail: scholarships@cta.org
Web: www.cta.org

Purpose To provide financial assistance to racial and ethnic minority group members in California needing a year to prepare for leadership roles in education.

Eligibility Applicants must be members of a racial or ethnic minority group; U.S. citizens and California residents; graduating high seniors, current college undergraduate students, or current graduate students; pursuing a degree or credential for a teaching-related career in public education at an accredited institution of higher education; and active members of the California Teachers Association (CTA), members of the Student CTA, or dependents of active, retired, or deceased CTA members.

Financial data Stipends vary each year, depending upon the amount of contributions received and the financial need of individual recipients.

Duration The fellowship is awarded annually.

Number awarded Varies; up to 7 each year.

Deadline March of each year.

[206]
MARTIN LUTHER KING, JR. SCHOLARSHIP

North Carolina Association of Educators.
Attn: Minority Affairs Commission
700 South Salisbury Street
P.O. Box 27347
Raleigh, NC 27611-7347
(919) 832-3000, ext. 211   (800) 662-7924, ext. 211
Fax: (919) 839-8229
Web: www.ncae.org

Purpose To provide financial assistance for college to minority and other high school seniors in North Carolina.

Eligibility Applicants must be North Carolina residents enrolled as seniors in high school. They must be planning to continue their education upon graduation. Applications are considered and judged by members of the association's Minority Affairs Commission. Selection is based on character, personality, and scholastic achievement.

Financial data The amount of the stipend depends on the availability of funding.

Duration 1 year.

Number awarded 1 each year.

Deadline January of each year.

[207]
MARYLAND SPACE SCHOLARS PROGRAM

Maryland Space Grant Consortium
c/o Johns Hopkins University
Bloomberg Center for Physics and Astronomy
3400 North Charles Street, Room 207
Baltimore, MD 21218-2686
(410) 516-7350   Fax: (410) 516-4109
E-mail: henry@pha.jhu.edu
Web: henry.pha.jhu.edu/msgc/scholarships.html

Purpose To provide financial assistance to undergraduates who are interested in studying space-related fields at selected universities in Maryland that are members of the Maryland Space Grant Consortium.

Eligibility This program is open to undergraduate students who are enrolled or accepted at member institutions. Applicants must be interested in majoring in a field related to space (previous majors have included aerospace engineering, chemistry, civil engineering, computer engineering, computer science, electrical engineering, electronic engineering, industrial engineering, and information systems). This program is a component of the U.S. National Aeronautics and Space Administration (NASA) Space Grant program, which encourages participation by women, underrepresented minorities, and persons with disabilities.

Financial data Scholars receive full payment of tuition at the participating university they attend.

Duration 4 years.

Additional information The participating universities are Hagerstown Community College, Johns Hopkins University, Morgan State University, Towson University, the United States Naval Academy, the University of Maryland at College Park, and Washington College. Funding for this program is provided by NASA.

Number awarded Varies each year; recently 21 of these scholarships were awarded (3 at Johns Hopkins University, 5 at Morgan State University, 3 at Hagerstown Community College, 2 at Towson University, and 8 at the University of Maryland at College Park).

[208]
MAS FAMILY SCHOLARSHIP PROGRAM

Jorge Mas Canosa Freedom Foundation
P.O. Box 440069
Miami, FL 33144-9926
(305) 592-7768

Purpose To provide financial assistance to students of Cuban descent who are working on an undergraduate or graduate degree in selected subject areas.

Eligibility This program is open to students who are direct descendants of those who left Cuba or were born in Cuba themselves. Applicants must be or have been in the top 10% of their high school graduating class and have a college GPA of 3.5 or higher. They must be able to meet federal standards of financial need. At least 1 parent or 2 grandparents must have been born in Cuba. Both undergraduate and graduate students may apply, provided they are majoring in 1 of the following subjects: engineering, business, international relations, economics, communications, or journalism. Selection is based on academic performance, leadership qualities, financial need, potential to contribute to the advancement of a free society, and the likelihood of succeeding in their chosen field. Finalists may be interviewed.

Financial data The amount of the award depends on the cost of tuition at the recipient's selected institution, on the family's situation, and on the amount of funds received from other sources. The amount of the yearly award cannot exceed $10,000. Full scholarships are not awarded to students who will be receiving full tuition scholarships and/or stipendiary support from other sources.

Duration 1 year; recipients may reapply and are given preference over other candidates.

Additional information This program was previously offered by the Cuban American National Foundation.

Deadline March of each year.

[209]
MAYOR JOE SERNA, JR. SCHOLARSHIP PROGRAM

Sacramento Hispanic Chamber of Commerce
Attn: Education Committee
2848 Arden Way, Suite 230
Sacramento, CA 95825
(916) 488-7700   Fax: (916) 488-7728
E-mail: valentin@sachcc.org
Web: www.sachcc.org/htmls/events/scholarship/index.htm

Purpose To provide financial assistance for college to Hispanic high school seniors in selected northern California counties.

Eligibility This program is open to high school seniors of Hispanic background in El Dorado, Placer, Sacramento, Sutter, Yolo, or Yuba counties of California accepted for enrollment in an accredited 2-year or 4-year college anywhere in the United States. Applicants must plan full-time study in business, computer science, engineering, health services, or programs leading to a professional career. Along with their application, they must submit a 2-page statement on their cultural background, achievements, financial need, current education status, career goals, school involvement, significant hobbies or interests, and community involvement.

Financial data The stipends are $500.

Duration 1 year; may be renewed.

Additional information Recipients are required to complete 30 hours of community service during the year they receive the scholarship.

Number awarded 30 each year.

Deadline April of each year.

[210]
MEFUSA SCHOLARSHIPS FOR LATINO/AS

Minority Educational Foundation of the United States of America
Attn: Scholarship Program
3160 Wedgewood Court
Reno, NV 89509-7103

Purpose To provide financial assistance to Latino/a high school seniors who are interested in attending a community college.

Eligibility This program is open to Latino/as graduating from high schools anywhere in the United States. Applicants must be planning to attend a community college on a full-time basis. As part of the selection process, they must submit a 1,000-word essay on their educational and career goals, how a community college education will help them to achieve those goals, and how they plan to serve the Latino community after completing their education. Selection is based on the essay, high school GPA (2.5 or higher), SAT or ACT scores, involvement in the Latino community, and financial need.

Financial data The stipend is $5,000 per year.

Duration 1 year; may be renewed 1 additional year if the recipient maintains full-time enrollment and a GPA of 2.5 or higher.

Additional information The Minority Educational Foundation of the United States of America (MEFUSA) was established in 2001 to meet the needs of minority students who "show a determination to get a college degree," but who, for financial or other personal reasons, are not able to attend a 4-year college or university. Requests for applications should be accompanied by a self-addressed stamped envelope, the student's e-mail address, and the source where they found the scholarship information.

Number awarded Up to 100 each year.

Deadline April of each year.

[211]
MENTOR GRAPHICS SCHOLARSHIPS

Oregon Student Assistance Commission
Attn: Private Awards Grant Department
1500 Valley River Drive, Suite 100
Eugene, OR 97401-2146
(541) 687-7395   (800) 452-8807, ext. 7395
Fax: (541) 687-7419
E-mail: awardinfo@mercury.osac.state.or.us
Web: www.osac.state.or.us

Purpose To provide financial assistance to Oregon residents who are seeking a college degree in computer science or engineering.

Eligibility This program is open to residents of Oregon who are U.S. citizens or permanent residents. Applicants must be full-time students in their junior or senior year of college and majoring in electrical engineering or computer science/engineering. Preference is given to female, African American, Native American, or Hispanic applicants. Financial need must be demonstrated.

Financial data Scholarship amounts vary, depending upon the needs of the recipient.

Duration 1 year.

Number awarded Varies each year.

Deadline February of each year.

[212]
MERCEDES BENZ SCHOLARSHIPS

Chicago Urban League
Attn: Scholarship Coordinator
4510 South Michigan Avenue
Chicago, IL 60653-3898
(773) 451-3567   Fax: (773) 285-7772
E-mail: info@cul-chicago.org
Web: www.cul-chicago.org

Purpose To provide financial assistance to Illinois residents of color interested in studying a field related to automotive technology in college.

Eligibility This program is open to Illinois residents of color who are graduating high school seniors with a GPA of 2.5 or higher and planning to enroll as full-time undergraduate students at a 4-year college or university, Triton College, or 1 of the City Colleges of Chicago. Applicants must be planning to major in automotive technology or a field related to the automotive industry (e.g., engineering, computer science, business, or accounting). Financial need must be demonstrated.

Financial data The stipend is $1,000 per year.

Duration 4 years.

Additional information This program is offered as part of the Chicago Urban League's Whitney M. Young, Jr. Memorial Scholarship Fund, established in 1970.

Number awarded 4 each year.

Deadline May of each year.

[213]
MERCURY NEWS MINORITY BUSINESS/FINANCE SCHOLARSHIP

Mercury News
Attn: Employee Relations and Services
750 Ridder Park Drive
San Jose, CA 95190
(408) 920-5821   Fax: (408) 271-3689
E-mail: jshaffran@sjmercury.com
Web: www.sjmercury.com

Purpose To provide financial assistance to minority students in northern California who are interested in preparing for newspaper careers in business or finance.

Eligibility Minority high school seniors in the San Francisco/San Jose area are eligible to apply if they are interested in majoring in business or finance in college and pursuing a career in newspaper production, finance, circulation management, human resources, marketing, electronic media, or advertising. They must submit a 500-word essay on why they want to pursue a career in newspaper business or finance. Financial need is not considered in the selection process.

Financial data The stipend is $1,000.

Duration 1 year.

Additional information The *Mercury News* selects its winners by February of each year and submits their applications to the Knight Ridder Minority Scholarship Program. These winners are given the chance to compete for a 4-year Knight Ridder scholarship/internship of up to $10,000 per year and the promise of a job in journalism upon graduation. The internship takes place at a Knight Ridder paper in the recipient's community; interns work each year, during the summer.

Number awarded 1 each year.

Deadline January of each year.

[214]
MERCURY NEWS MINORITY JOURNALISM SCHOLARSHIP

Mercury News
Attn: Employee Relations and Services
750 Ridder Park Drive
San Jose, CA 95190
(408) 920-5821   Fax: (408) 271-3689
E-mail: jshaffran@sjmercury.com
Web: www.sjmercury.com

Purpose To provide financial assistance to minority students in northern California who are interested in preparing for careers in journalism.

Eligibility Minority high school seniors in the San Francisco/San Jose area are eligible to apply if they are interested in majoring in journalism in college and pursuing a career as a reporter, editor, copy editor, photographer, or graphic artist. They must have professional experience or high school newspaper/yearbook experience, be nominated by their journalism advisor or teacher, send up to 5 samples of their work, and submit a 500-word essay on why they want to pursue a career in journalism. Financial need is not considered in the selection process.

Financial data The stipend is $1,000.

Duration 1 year.

Additional information The *Mercury News* selects its winners by February of each year and submits their applications to the Knight Ridder Minority Scholarship Program. These winners are given the chance to compete for a 4-year Knight Ridder scholarship/internship of up to $10,000 per year and the promise of a job in journalism upon graduation. The internship takes place at a Knight Ridder paper in the recipient's community; interns work each year, during the summer.

Number awarded 1 each year.

Deadline January of each year.

[215]
MEXICAN AMERICAN ENGINEERS AND SCIENTISTS PRESIDENTIAL SCHOLARSHIP

Society of Mexican American Engineers and Scientists
Attn: National Office Director
13337 South Street, Suite 349
Cerritos, CA 90703
E-mail: maes@tamu.edu
Web: www.maes-natl.org

Purpose To provide financial assistance to undergraduate and graduate student members of the Society of Mexican American Engineers and Scientists (MAES).

Eligibility This program is open to MAES student members who are full-time undergraduate or graduate students at a college or university in the United States. Community college students must be enrolled in majors that can transfer to a 4-year institution offering a baccalaureate degree. All applicants must be majoring in a field of science or engineering. U.S. citizenship or permanent resident status is required. Selection is based on financial need; academic achievement; personal qualities, strengths, and leadership abilities; and timeliness and completeness of the application.

Financial data The stipend is $2,000.

Duration 1 year.

Additional information Information is also available from José M. Hernández, Chair, MAES Scholarship Committee, 4015 North Water Iris Cort, Houston, TX 77059. Recipients must attend the MAES International Symposium's Medalla de Oro Banquet in October.

Number awarded 1 each year.

Deadline October of each year.

[216]
MEXICAN AMERICAN GROCERS ASSOCIATION SCHOLARSHIP PROGRAM

Mexican American Grocers Association
405 North San Fernando Road
Los Angeles, CA 90031-1798
(323) 227-1565   Fax: (323) 227-6935
Web: www.maga.org

Purpose To provide financial assistance to Latino/Hispanic students interested in preparing for a business career.

Eligibility This program is open to Latino/Hispanic full-time undergraduate students who are at least sophomores attending a community college or a 4-year accredited college or university. Applicants must have a GPA of 2.5 or higher and a major in business administration or a business-related field (e.g., finance, economics, international business). They must demonstrate genuine financial need.

Financial data Stipends range from $500 to $1,500.

Duration 1 year; may be renewed for up to 2 additional years.

Additional information To date, more than $500,000 has been distributed through this program. Requests for applications must be accompanied by a self-addressed stamped envelope.

Recipients from southern California must attend the scholarship awards banquet in September.

Number awarded Varies; generally more than 50 each year.

Deadline July of each year.

[217]
MEXICAN FIESTA SCHOLARSHIPS

Wisconsin Hispanic Scholarship Foundation, Inc.
1220 West Windlake Avenue
Milwaukee, WI 53215
(414) 383-7066   Fax: (414) 383-6677
E-mail: mexicanf@aol.com
Web: www.mexicanfiesta.org

Purpose To provide financial assistance to Hispanic American students in Wisconsin who are interested in attending college or graduate school.

Eligibility Applicants must be at least 50% Hispanic, be high school seniors or full-time undergraduate or graduate students, have earned a GPA of 2.75 or higher, be Wisconsin residents, and be bilingual in Spanish and English.

Financial data The amount of the stipend depends on the number of students selected.

Duration 1 year; recipients may reapply.

Additional information Recipients can attend college in any state. Funds for this program are raised each year at the Mexican Fiesta, held in Milwaukee for 3 days each August. Recipients must perform 20 hours of volunteer work in the Hispanic community.

Number awarded Varies; a total of $20,000 is awarded in scholarships each year.

Deadline May of each year.

[218]
MICHAEL BAKER CORPORATION SCHOLARSHIP PROGRAM FOR DIVERSITY IN ENGINEERING

Association of Independent Colleges and Universities of Pennsylvania
101 North Front Street
Harrisburg, PA 17101-1405
(717) 232-8649   Fax: (717) 233-8574
E-mail: info@aicup.org
Web: www.aicup.org

Purpose To provide financial assistance to women and minority students at member institutions of the Association of Independent Colleges and Universities of Pennsylvania (AICUP) who are majoring in engineering.

Eligibility This program is open to full-time undergraduate students at designated AICUP colleges and universities who are women and/or members of the following minority groups: American Indians, Alaska Natives, Asians, Blacks/African Americans, Hispanics/Latinos, Native Hawaiians, or Pacific Islanders. Applicants must be juniors or seniors majoring in engineering with a GPA of 3.0 or higher. Along with their application, they must submit an essay on what they believe will be the greatest challenge facing the engineering profession over the next decade, and why.

Financial data The stipend is $1,000.

Duration 1 year; may be renewed 1 additional year if the recipient maintains appropriate academic standards.

Additional information This program, sponsored by the Michael Baker Corporation, is available at the following AICUP colleges and universities: Bucknell University, Carnegie Mellon

University, Drexel University, Duquesne University, Gannon University, Geneva College, Grove City College, Lafayette College, Lehigh University, Messiah College, Philadelphia University, Robert Morris University, Saint Vincent College, Swarthmore College, University of Scranton, Villanova University, Widener University, Wilkes University, and York College.

Number awarded Varies each year; recently, 2 of these scholarships were awarded.

Deadline October of each year.

[219]
MICROSOFT NATIONAL SCHOLARSHIPS

Microsoft Corporation
Attn: National Minority Technical Scholarship
One Microsoft Way
Redmond, WA 98052-8303
(425) 882-8080   TTY: (800) 892-9811
E-mail: scholars@microsoft.com
Web: www.microsoft.com/college/scholarships/general.asp

Purpose To provide financial assistance and summer work experience to undergraduate students, especially underrepresented minorities and women, interested in preparing for a career in computer science or other related technical fields.

Eligibility This program is open to students who are enrolled full time and making satisfactory progress toward an undergraduate degree in computer science, computer engineering, or a related technical discipline (such as math or physics) with a demonstrated interest in computer science. Applicants must be enrolled in their sophomore or junior year and have earned a GPA of 3.0 or higher. Although all students who meet the eligibility criteria may apply, a large majority of scholarships are awarded to female and underrepresented minority (African American, Hispanic, and Native American) students. Along with their application, students must submit an essay that describes the following 4 items: 1) how they demonstrate their passion for technology outside the classroom; 2) the toughest technical problem they have worked on, how they addressed the problem, their role in reaching the outcome if it was team-based, and the final outcome; 3) a situation that demonstrates initiative and their willingness to go above and beyond; and 4) how they are currently funding their college education.

Financial data Scholarships cover 100% of the tuition as posted by the financial aid office of the university or college the recipient designates. Scholarships are made through that school and are not transferable to other academic institutions. Funds may be used for tuition only and may not be used for other costs on the recipient's bursar bill.

Duration 1 year.

Additional information Selected recipients are offered a paid summer internship where they will have a chance to develop Microsoft products.

Number awarded Varies. A total of $540,000 is available for this program each year.

Deadline January of each year.

[220]
MICROSOFT SCHOLARSHIP PROGRAM OF THE HISPANIC SCHOLARSHIP FUND

Hispanic Scholarship Fund
Attn: Selection Committee
55 Second Street, Suite 1500
San Francisco, CA 94105
(877) HSF-INFO   Fax: (415) 808-2302
E-mail: info@hsf.net
Web: www.hsf.net

Purpose To provide financial assistance to Hispanic American high school seniors who are interested in majoring in computer science, computer engineering, or mathematics in college.

Eligibility This program is open to U.S. citizens, permanent residents, and visitors with a passport stamped I-551. Applicants must be of Hispanic heritage (each parent half Hispanic or 1 parent fully Hispanic) and seniors in high schools in the United States. They must have a high school GPA of 3.0 or higher and plan to enroll full time at an accredited college or university to major in a computer-related science, computer engineering, or mathematics. As part of the application process, they must submit a 2-page essay that addresses the following topics: their Hispanic heritage and family background, personal and academic achievements, academic plans and career goals, efforts toward making a difference in the community, and financial need.

Eligibility This program is open to U.S. citizens or permanent residents of at least half Hispanic background who are high school seniors. Applicants must be planning to major in computer science, engineering, or mathematics as a full-time 4-year college student. They must have a GPA of 3.0 or higher in high school and be accepted at an accredited 4-year institution for the following fall. As part of the application process, they must submit a 2-page essay on their Hispanic background and potential contribution to the Hispanic community; their current high school status, activities, and achievements; and career goals. In addition to that essay, selection is based on academic achievement, a letter of recommendation, and financial need.

Financial data The stipend is $2,500.

Duration 1 year.

Additional information Funding for this program is provided by Microsoft Corporation. Requests for applications must be accompanied by a self-addressed stamped envelope.

Number awarded Varies each year.

Deadline February of each year.

[221]
MIGRANT FARMWORKER BACCALAUREATE SCHOLARSHIP

BOCES Geneseo Migrant Center
27 Lackawanna Avenue
Mount Morris, NY 14510-1096
(585) 658-7960   (800) 245-5681
Fax: (585) 658-7969   E-mail: info@migrant.net
Web: www.migrant.net/sch_mfb.htm

Purpose To provide financial assistance to migrant farmworkers who are currently enrolled in college.

Eligibility This program is open to migrant farmworker students with a history of migrating for employment in agriculture. Applicants must have completed at least 1 year of college. Along with their application, they must submit a statement of at least 500 words on their background, career and personal goals, and why they should receive this assistance; 3 letters of recommendation; a college transcript; and documentation of financial need.

Financial data The stipend is $2,000 per year. These funds are intended to be in addition to any that the student receives through federal, state, or other scholarship assistance as an undergraduate. The same annual amount is available for graduate study or loan repayment.

Duration 1 year; may be renewed for an additional 2 years of undergraduate study. Recipients also have the option of an additional 2 years of graduate support or 3 years of loan repayment.

Additional information Following completion of their baccalaureate degree, recipients may apply for additional support as a graduate student or for assistance in repayment of educational loans.

Number awarded 1 each year.

Deadline June of each year.

[222]
MIKE CARONA FOUNDATION LAW ENFORCEMENT SCHOLARSHIPS

Orange County Community Foundation
Attn: Scholarship Coordinator
2081 Business Center Drive, Suite 100
Irvine, CA 92612-1115
(949) 553-4202, ext. 22   Fax: (949) 553-4211
E-mail: occf@oc-communityfoundation.org
Web: www.oc-communityfoundation.org/grantsscholar

Purpose To provide financial assistance for college to Hispanic high school seniors from Orange County, California who are interested in preparing for a career in law enforcement.

Eligibility This program is open to Hispanic graduating seniors from high schools in Orange County, California. Applicants must be interested in preparing for a career in a facet of law enforcement. Selection is based on financial need, extracurricular activities, academic ability, and community service.

Financial data The stipend is $1,000 per year.

Duration 1 year; may be renewed upon reapplication.

Number awarded 1 or 2 each year.

Deadline February of each year.

[223]
MINNESOTA SPACE GRANT CONSORTIUM SCHOLARSHIPS AND FELLOWSHIPS

Minnesota Space Grant Consortium
c/o University of Minnesota
Department of Aerospace Engineering and Mechanics
107 Akerman Hall
110 Union Street S.E.
Minneapolis, MN 55455
(612) 625-8000   Fax: (612) 626-1558
E-mail: mnsgc@aem.umn.edu
Web: www.aem.umn.edu/msgc/awards

Purpose To provide financial assistance for space-related science and engineering studies to undergraduate and graduate students in Minnesota.

Eligibility This program is open to graduate and undergraduate students at institutions that are affiliates of the Minnesota Space Grant Consortium. U.S. citizenship and a GPA of 3.2 or higher are required. The Minnesota Space Grant Consortium is a component of the U.S. National Aeronautics and Space Administration (NASA) Space Grant program, which encourages participa-

tion by women, underrepresented minorities, and persons with disabilities.

Financial data More than $50,000 is available from this program each year for scholarships and fellowships. The amounts of the awards are set by each of the participating institutions, which augment funding from this program with institutional resources.

Duration 1 year; renewable.

Additional information This program is funded by NASA. The member institutions are: Augsburg College, Bethel College, Bemidji State University, College of St. Catherine, Carleton College, Fond du Lac Tribal and Community College, Leech Lake Tribal College, Macalester College, Normandale Community College, Southwest State University, University of Minnesota at Duluth, University of Minnesota at Twin Cities, and University of St. Thomas.

Number awarded 8 to 12 undergraduate scholarships and 2 to 3 graduate fellowships are awarded each year.

Deadline February of each year.

[224]
MINORITIES IN GOVERNMENT FINANCE SCHOLARSHIP

Government Finance Officers Association
Attn: Scholarship Committee
180 North Michigan Avenue, Suite 800
Chicago, IL 60601-7476
(312) 977-9700   Fax: (312) 977-4806
Web: www.gfoa.org

Purpose To provide financial assistance to minority undergraduate and graduate students who are preparing for a career in state and local government finance.

Eligibility This program is open to upper-division undergraduate and graduate students who are enrolled in a full-time program and preparing for a career in public finance. Applicants must be members of a minority group, citizens or permanent residents of the United States or Canada, and able to provide a letter of recommendation from the dean of their school. Selection is based on career plans, academic record, plan of study, letters of recommendation, and GPA. Financial need is not considered.

Financial data The stipend is $5,000.

Duration 1 year.

Additional information Funding for this program is provided by Fidelity Investments Tax-Exempt Services Company.

Number awarded 1 or more each year.

Deadline February of each year.

[225]
MINORITY ACADEMIC INSTITUTIONS UNDERGRADUATE STUDENT FELLOWSHIPS

Environmental Protection Agency
Attn: National Center for Environmental Research
Ariel Rios Building - 8723R
1200 Pennsylvania Avenue, N.W.
Washington, DC 20460
(202) 564-6926   E-mail: boddie.georgette@epa.gov
Web: es.epa.gov/ncer/rfa

Purpose To provide financial assistance and summer internships to undergraduates at minority academic institutions (MAIs) who are interested in majoring in fields related to the environment.

Eligibility Applicants for this program must be U.S. citizens or permanent residents who are enrolled full time with a minimum GPA of 3.0 in an accredited 4-year institution that meets the definition of the Environmental Protection Agency (EPA) as an MAI: Historically Black Colleges and Universities (HBCUs), Hispanic Serving Institutions (HSIs), Tribal Colleges (TCs), Native Hawaiian Serving Institutions (NHSIs), and Alaska Native Serving Institutions (ANSIs). Students must have at least 2 years remaining for completion of a bachelor's degree and must be majoring in environmental science, physical sciences, natural and life sciences, mathematics and computer science, social sciences, economics, or engineering. They must be available to work as interns at an EPA facility during the summer between their junior and senior years.

Financial data The fellowship provides up to $17,000 per year, including up to $10,000 for tuition and academic fees, a stipend of $4,500 ($500 per month for 9 months), and an expense allowance of up to $2,500 for items and activities for the direct benefit of the student's education, such as books, supplies, and travel to professional conferences and workshops. The summer internship grant is $7,500, including a stipend of $6,000, an allowance of $1,000 for travel to and from the site, and an allowance of $500 for travel while at the site.

Duration The final 2 years of baccalaureate study, including 12 weeks during the summer between those years.

Additional information This program began in 1982. It was formerly known as Culturally Diverse Academic Institutions Undergraduate Student Fellowships program.

Number awarded Approximately 25 each year.

Deadline November of each year.

[226]
MINORITY COMMUNITY COLLEGE TRANSFER SCHOLARSHIPS

State University System of Florida
Attn: Office of Academic and Student Services
325 West Gaines Street, Suite 1501
Tallahassee, FL 32399-1950
(850) 201-7216   Fax: (850) 201-7185
E-mail: lpage@borfl.org
Web: www.borfl.org

Purpose To provide financial assistance to minority community college students in Florida who are interested in transferring to a school within the State University System of Florida (SUS).

Eligibility This program is open to minority community college students who complete A.A. or A.S. degrees from an accredited Florida community college between December and August of the current year. Applicants must have been admitted as degree-seeking junior-level students at an SUS institution. All recipients must have participated in, received a waiver for, or passed the College-Level Academic Skills Test program. In addition, male applicants must have complied with the Selective Service System registration requirements. Students may apply for need awards, merit/need awards, or merit awards. The minimum cumulative GPA on postsecondary credits is 2.0 for need-based applicants or 3.0 for merit/need and merit applicants.

Financial data A stipend is awarded (amount not specified); funds are paid in 2 equal installments.

Duration Up to 6 semesters, provided the need recipient maintains at least a 2.0 GPA and the need/merit or merit recipient maintains at least a 3.0 average.

Additional information This program is administered by the equal opportunity program at each of the 10 public 4-year institutions in Florida. Contact that office for further information.

Number awarded Several each year.

Deadline May of each year.

[227]
MINORITY GEOSCIENCE UNDERGRADUATE SCHOLARSHIPS

American Geological Institute
Attn: Minority Participation Program
4220 King Street
Alexandria, VA 22302-1502
(703) 379-2480   Fax: (703) 379-7563
Web: www.agiweb.org/education/mpp/ugradmpp.html

Purpose To provide financial assistance to underrepresented minority undergraduate students interested in working on a degree in the geosciences.

Eligibility This program is open to members of ethnic minority groups underrepresented in the geosciences (Blacks, Hispanics, American Indians, Eskimos, Hawaiians, and Samoans). U.S. citizenship is required. Applicants must be full-time undergraduate students enrolled in an accredited institution with a major in the geosciences, including geology, geophysics, hydrology, meteorology, physical oceanography, planetary geology, and earth science education; students in other natural sciences, mathematics, or engineering are not eligible. Selection is based on a 250-word essay on career goals and why the applicant has chosen a geoscience as a major, work experience, recommendations, honors and awards, extracurricular activities, and financial need.

Financial data Up to $10,000 per year.

Duration 1 academic year; renewable if the recipient maintains satisfactory performance.

Additional information Funding for this program is provided by a grant from the National Science Foundation.

Number awarded Varies each year; recently, 11 of these scholarships were awarded.

Deadline February of each year.

[228]
MINORITY NURSE MAGAZINE SCHOLARSHIP PROGRAM

Minority Nurse
Attn: CASS Recruitment Media
1800 Sherman Avenue, Suite 404
Evanston, IL 60201
(847) 448-1011   E-mail: pam.chwedyk@careermedia.com
Web: www.minoritynurse.com

Purpose To provide financial assistance to members of minority groups who are working on a bachelor's degree in nursing.

Eligibility This program is open to third- and fourth-year minority nursing students currently enrolled in an accredited B.S.N. program. Selection is based on academic excellence (GPA of 3.0 or higher), demonstrated commitment of service to the student's minority community, and financial need.

Financial data The stipends are $1,000 or $500.

Duration 1 year.

Additional information These scholarships were first offered in 2000. Winners are announced in the fall issue of *Minority Nurse*.

Number awarded 4 each year: 2 at $1,000 and 2 at $500.

Deadline June of each year.

[229]
MINORITY SCHOLARSHIP AWARD IN PHYSICAL THERAPY

American Physical Therapy Association
Attn: Department of Minority/International Affairs
1111 North Fairfax Street
Alexandria, VA 22314-1488
(703) 706-3144   Fax: (703) 838-8910
E-mail: min-intl@apta.org
Web: www.apta.org/min-intl

Purpose To provide financial assistance to minority students who are interested in becoming a physical therapist or physical therapy assistant.

Eligibility This program is open to minority students who will graduate from professional physical therapy education or physical therapy assistant education programs at any time during the year following the submission of an application. Selection is based on academic excellence, professional and leadership potential, and commitment to minority issues.

Financial data The minimum award is $1,500 for physical therapy students or $750 for physical therapy assistant students. Applications are distributed to all physical therapy programs; they are not accepted directly from students.

Number awarded 10 each year: 6 for physical therapy students and 4 for physical therapy assistant students.

Deadline Nominations must be submitted by the end of November of each year.

[230]
MINORITY SCHOLARSHIP AWARDS FOR COLLEGE STUDENTS IN CHEMICAL ENGINEERING

American Institute of Chemical Engineers
Attn: Awards Administrator
Three Park Avenue
New York, NY 10016-5991
(212) 591-7478   Fax: (212) 591-8882
E-mail: awards@aiche.org
Web: www.aiche.org/awards

Purpose To provide financial assistance for study in chemical engineering to underrepresented minority college student members of the American Institute of Chemical Engineers (AIChE).

Eligibility This program is open to undergraduate student AIChE members who are also members of a disadvantaged minority group that is underrepresented in chemical engineering (African Americans, Hispanics, Native Americans, and Alaskan Natives). Each AIChE chapter may nominate 1 member. Selection is based on academic record (including a GPA of 3.0 or higher), participation in AIChE student and professional activities, a 300-word letter on career objectives and plans, and financial need.

Financial data Each scholarship is $1,000.

Duration 1 year; nonrenewable.

Number awarded Varies each year; recently, 16 of these scholarships were awarded.

Deadline Nominations must be submitted by April of each year.

[231]
MINORITY SCHOLARSHIP AWARDS FOR INCOMING COLLEGE FRESHMEN IN CHEMICAL ENGINEERING

American Institute of Chemical Engineers
Attn: Awards Administrator
Three Park Avenue
New York, NY 10016-5991
(212) 591-7478   Fax: (212) 591-8882
E-mail: awards@aiche.org
Web: www.aiche.org/awards

Purpose To provide financial assistance for study in chemical engineering to incoming minority freshmen.

Eligibility Eligible are members of a disadvantaged minority group that is underrepresented in chemical engineering (African Americans, Hispanics, Native Americans, and Alaskan Natives). Applicants must be graduating high school seniors planning to enroll in a 4-year university with a major in chemical engineering. They must be nominated by an American Institute of Chemical Engineers (AIChE) local section. Selection is based on academic record (including a GPA of 3.0 or higher), participation in school and/or necessary work activities, a 300-word letter outlining the reasons for choosing chemical engineering, and financial need.

Financial data Each scholarship is $1,000.

Duration 1 year; nonrenewable.

Number awarded Varies each year; recently, 14 of these scholarships were awarded.

Deadline Nominations must be submitted by April of each year.

[232]
MISSISSIPPI SPACE GRANT CONSORTIUM CAMPUS ACTIVITIES

Mississippi Space Grant Consortium
c/o University of Mississippi
217 Vardaman Hall
P.O. Box 1848
University, MS 38677-1848
(662) 915-1187   Fax: (662) 915-3927
E-mail: arandle@olemiss.edu
Web: www.olemiss.edu/programs/nasa/spacegrant.html

Purpose To provide funding to undergraduate and graduate students for space-related activities at colleges and universities that are members of the Mississippi Space Grant Consortium.

Eligibility This program is open to undergraduate and graduate students at member institutions of the Mississippi consortium. Each participating college or university establishes its own program and criteria for admission, but all activities are in engineering, mathematics, and science fields of interest to the U.S. National Aeronautics and Space Administration (NASA). U.S. citizenship is required. The consortium is a component of NASA's Space Grant program, which encourages participation by women, underrepresented minorities, and persons with disabilities.

Financial data Each participating institution establishes the amounts of the awards. Recently, the average undergraduate award was $1,308 and the average graduate award was $2,975. A total of $96,350 was awarded.

Additional information Consortium members include Alcorn State University, Coahoma Community College, Delta State University, Hinds Community College (Utica Campus), Itawamba Community College, Jackson State University, Meridian Community College, Mississippi Delta Community College, Mississippi Gulf Coast Community College (Jackson County Campus), Mississippi State University, Mississippi University for Women, Mississippi Valley State University, Northeast Mississippi Community College, Pearl River Community College, the University of Mississippi, and the University of Southern Mississippi. This program is funded by NASA.

Number awarded Varies each year; recently, a total of 66 students received support through this program.

[233]
MONSIGNOR PHILIP KENNEY SCHOLARSHIP FUND

New Hampshire Charitable Foundation
37 Pleasant Street
Concord, NH 03301-4005
(603) 225-6641　　　　　　　　　　(800) 464-6641
Fax: (603) 225-1700　　　　　　　E-mail: info@nhcf.org
Web: www.nhcf.org

Purpose To provide financial assistance for college to minority and other students from New Hampshire.

Eligibility This program is open to New Hampshire students who are economically disadvantaged, with a preference for Hispanics and other minorities who are enrolled in undergraduate study. Nontraditional students, both full and part time, are encouraged to apply. At least 1 scholarship is designated for a minority student from Merrimack County.

Financial data The scholarship designated for a minority student from Merrimack has a stipend of $1,000. Other stipends vary.

Duration 1 year; recipients may reapply.

Number awarded Varies; in addition to the 1 scholarship for a minority student from Merrimack County, a total of $8,500 is available each year.

Deadline April of each year.

[234]
MONTANA SPACE GRANT CONSORTIUM UNDERGRADUATE SCHOLARSHIPS

Montana Space Grant Consortium
c/o Montana State University
261 EPS Building
P.O. Box 173835
Bozeman, MT 59717-3835
(406) 994-4223　　　　　　　　　Fax: (406) 994-4452
E-mail: msgc@montana.edu
Web: www.montana.edu

Purpose To provide financial assistance to students in Montana who are interested in working on an undergraduate degree in the space sciences and/or engineering.

Eligibility This program is open to full-time undergraduate students at member institutions of the Montana Space Grant Consortium (MSGC) majoring in fields related to space sciences and engineering. Those fields include, but are not limited to, astronomy, biological and life sciences, chemical engineering, chemistry, civil engineering, computer sciences, electrical engineering, geological sciences, mechanical engineering, and physics. Priority is given to students who have been involved in aerospace-related research. U.S. citizenship is required. The MSGC is a component of the U.S. National Aeronautics and Space Administration (NASA) Space Grant program, which encourages participation by women, underrepresented minorities, and persons with disabilities. Financial need is not considered in the selection process.

Financial data The stipend is $1,000 per year.

Duration 1 year; may be renewed.

Additional information The MSGC member institutions are Blackfeet Community College, Carroll College, Chief Dull Knife College, Fort Belknap College, Fort Peck Community College, Little Big Horn College, Montana State University at Billings, Montana State University at Bozeman, Montana State University-Northern, Montana Tech, Rocky Mountain College, Salish Kootenai College, Stone Child College, the University of Montana, and the University of Montana-Western.

Additional information Funding for this program is provided by NASA.

Number awarded Varies each year; recently, 26 of these scholarships were awarded.

Deadline March of each year.

[235]
MORRIS SCHOLARSHIP

Morris Scholarship Fund
Attn: Scholarship Selection Committee
525 S.W. Fifth Street, Suite A
Des Moines, IA 50309-4501
(515) 282-8192　　　　　　　　　Fax: (515) 282-9117
E-mail: morris@assoc-mgmt.com
Web: www.morrisscholarship.org

Purpose To provide financial assistance to minority undergraduate and graduate students in Iowa.

Eligibility This program is open to minority students (African Americans, Asian/Pacific Islanders, Hispanics, or Native Americans) who are interested in studying at a college, graduate school, or law school. Applicants must be either Iowa residents and high school graduates who are attending a college or university anywhere in the United States or non-Iowa residents who are attending a college or university in Iowa; preference is given to native Iowans who are attending an Iowa college or university. Selection is based on academic achievement (GPA of 2.5 or higher), a statement of educational and career goals, community service, and financial need.

Financial data The stipend is $1,500 per year.

Duration 1 year; may be renewed.

Additional information This fund was established in 1977 in honor of the J.B. Morris family, who founded the Iowa branches of the National Association for the Advancement of Colored People and published the *Iowa Bystander* newspaper.

Number awarded 30 each year.

Deadline February of each year.

[236]
MSCPA MINORITY HIGH SCHOOL SCHOLARSHIPS

Missouri Society of Certified Public Accountants
Attn: Educational Foundation
275 North Lindbergh Boulevard, Suite 10
St. Louis, MO 63141-7809
(314) 997-7966　　　　　　　　　(800) 264-7966 (within MO)
Fax: (314) 997-2592　　　　　　　E-mail: member@mocpa.org
Web: www.mocpa.org/scholarships.html

Purpose To provide financial assistance to minority high school seniors in Missouri who are interested in studying accounting in college.

Eligibility This program is open to seniors at high schools in Missouri and Metro Kansas City who are minorities, plan to enroll in a 2-year or 4-year Missouri college or university, and plan to major in accounting. Selection is based on leadership and financial need.

Financial data The stipend is $500 the first year, $300 the second year, and $200 the third year.

Duration 3 years.

Number awarded 3 each year.

Deadline February of each year.

[237]
MVSNA STUDENT SCHOLARSHIP

Missouri Vocational Special Need Association
c/o Cindy Grizzell, Awards Chair
Waynesville Technical Academy
810 Roosevelt
Waynesville, MO 65583
(573) 774-6101   E-mail: cgrizzell@waynesville.k12.mo.us

Purpose To provide financial assistance to vocational/technical students in Missouri who are members of designated special populations.

Eligibility This program is open to Missouri vocational/technical students who are members of special populations, defined as individuals who are academically or economically disadvantaged, have limited English proficiency, or are nontraditional, disabled, pregnant teenagers, single/teen parents, or foster children. Applicants must submit brief essays on their professional or career goals; the challenges they have had to overcome to reach their educational goals; how they have received help from their school, teachers, or community; and how the award will help them in pursuing continued education. Selection is based on realism of career goal, financial need, unusual circumstances, and personal references.

Financial data A stipend is awarded (amount not specified).

Duration 1 year.

Number awarded 1 each year.

Deadline April of each year.

[238]
NACME SCHOLARS PROGRAM

National Action Council for Minorities in Engineering
350 Fifth Avenue, Suite 2212
New York, NY 10118-2299
(212) 279-2626   Fax: (212) 629-5178
E-mail: awalter@nacme.org
Web: www.nacme.org/univ/scol/nacmescholars.html

Purpose To provide financial assistance to underrepresented minority undergraduates majoring in engineering.

Eligibility This program is open to African Americans, Latinos, and American Indians who are currently enrolled full time in an undergraduate engineering program. Applicants must have completed at least 1 semester of study and have completed calculus, chemistry, or physics with a GPA of 2.7 or higher. They must be able to demonstrate financial need and provide recommendations from an engineering dean, program director, and/or mathematics, science, or engineering faculty member. U.S. citizenship or permanent resident status is required.

Financial data Stipends range up to $5,000 per year and average $3,000.

Duration 1 year; may be renewed if the recipient maintains a GPA of 2.7 or higher.

Additional information The National Action Council for Minorities in Engineering (NACME) works with its corporate sponsors and with government agencies to help scholars gain work experience through summer internships.

Number awarded Varies each year; recently, more than 700 new and continuing students were being supported at approximately 75 institutions.

Deadline February of each year.

[239]
NACME/NASA UNDERGRADUATE STUDENT AWARDS FOR RESEARCH

National Action Council for Minorities in Engineering
350 Fifth Avenue, Suite 2212
New York, NY 10118-2299
(212) 279-2626   Fax: (212) 629-5178
E-mail: awalter@nacme.org
Web: www.nacme.org/univ/scol/nasa.html

Purpose To provide financial assistance and research internships to undergraduates majoring in science and engineering fields at designated minority institutions.

Eligibility This program is open to students majoring in mathematics, computer science, engineering (aeronautical, astronautical, chemical, civil, electrical, materials, mechanical, metallurgical), environmental sciences (atmospheric sciences, geological sciences), life sciences (agricultural sciences, biological sciences, environmental biology, medical sciences), and physical sciences (astronomy, chemistry, physics) at 21 designated minority institutions. Applicants must have a GPA of 3.0 or higher, be enrolled full time, have earned no more than 39 credit hours, be able to demonstrate financial need, and be U.S. citizens. They must be nominated by the National Aeronautics and Space Administration (NASA) liaison at their university.

Financial data Awards provide support for tuition during the academic year and for a research internship during the summer.

Duration 1 year; may be renewed up to 3 additional years if the recipient maintains a GPA of 3.0 or higher and satisfactory progress toward a degree in an engineering, mathematics, or science field relevant to the mission of NASA.

Additional information Students submit applications through participating universities; currently, those are California State University at Los Angeles, City College of New York, D-Q University (Davis, California), Gallaudet University (Washington, D.C.), Florida A&M University/Florida State University (Tallahassee, Florida), Fayetteville State University (Fayetteville, North Carolina), LaGuardia Community College (Long Island City, New York), Morgan State University (Baltimore, Maryland), Morehouse College (Atlanta, Georgia), University of New Mexico (Albuquerque, New Mexico), New Mexico Highlands University (Las Vegas, New Mexico), New Mexico State University (Las Cruces, New Mexico), North Carolina A&T University (Greensboro, North Carolina), University of North Carolina at Pembroke, Shaw University (Raleigh, North Carolina), Southern University and A&M College (Baton Rouge, Louisiana), Spelman College (Atlanta, Georgia), Tennessee State University (Nashville, Tennessee), University of Texas–Pan American (Edinburg, Texas), University of Texas at San Antonio, and Winston-Salem State University (Winston-Salem, North Carolina). The National Action Council for Minorities in Engineering (NACME), in consultation with NASA, selects the recipients. NACME has administered this program since 1998, Students are required to participate in a research project at a

NASA facility during each summer they receive support from this program.

Number awarded Varies each year.

Deadline Nominations are usually made between the months of March and May.

[240]
NAHJ SCHOLARSHIPS

National Association of Hispanic Journalists
Attn: Scholarship Committee
1000 National Press Building
529 14th Street, N.W.
Washington, DC 20045-2001
(202) 662-7145   (888) 346-NAHJ
Fax: (202) 662-7144   E-mail: nahj@nahj.org
Web: www.nahj.org/scholarship.html

Purpose To provide financial assistance to Hispanic American undergraduate and graduate students interested in preparing for careers in the media.

Eligibility Hispanic American high school seniors, undergraduates, and graduate students are eligible to apply for this support. They must be interested in majoring in print, broadcast (radio or television), or photojournalism (broadcast or print); students majoring in other fields must be able to demonstrate a strong interest in preparing for a career in journalism. Applicants must submit an official transcript; a 1-page resume with their educational background, work history, awards, internships, other scholarships, language proficiency, and any work done for their school newspaper, radio, and/or television station; samples of their work; 2 reference letters; a 500-word autobiography in third person in the form of a news story; and documentation of financial need.

Financial data Stipends range from $1,000 to $2,000.

Duration 1 year.

Additional information This program is administered by the National Association of Hispanic Journalists (NAHJ) as a component of its Rubén Salazar Scholarship Fund.

Number awarded Varies each year; recently 35 scholarships were awarded through this program, including 4 for radio broadcasting, 10 for television broadcasting, 33 for print journalism, and 2 for photography.

Deadline January of each year.

[241]
NAMEPA BEGINNING FRESHMEN AWARD

National Association of Minority Engineering Program
   Administrators, Inc.
1133 West Morse Boulevard, Suite 201
Winter Park, FL 32789
(407) 647-8839   Fax: (407) 629-2502
E-mail: namepa@namepa.org
Web: www.namepa.org/pages/awards.htm

Purpose To provide financial assistance to underrepresented minority high school seniors who are planning to major in engineering.

Eligibility This program is open to African American, Hispanic, and American Indian high school seniors who have been approved for admission to an engineering program at an institution affiliated with the National Association of Minority Engineering Program Administrators (NAMEPA). For a list of affiliated schools, write to the sponsor. Applicants must have a GPA of 3.0 or higher and minimum cumulative scores of 25 on the ACT or

1000 on the SAT. They must submit a copy of their high school transcript; test scores; a letter of recommendation; and a 1-page essay on why they have chosen engineering as a profession, why they think they should be selected, and an overview of their future aspirations as an engineer. Financial need is not considered in the selection process.

Financial data The stipend is $1,000, paid in 2 equal installments.

Duration 1 year; nonrenewable.

Deadline March of each year.

[242]
NATA UNDERGRADUATE SCHOLARSHIPS

National Athletic Trainers' Association
Attn: Research and Education Foundation
2952 Stemmons Freeway, Suite 200
Dallas, TX 75247-6103
(214) 637-6282   (800) TRY-NATA, ext. 121
Fax: (214) 637-2206   E-mail: briana@nata.org
Web: www.nata.org

Purpose To provide financial aid to undergraduate student members of the National Athletic Trainers' Association (NATA).

Eligibility Applicants must be members of the association who are recommended by an NATA certified athletic trainer, have a GPA of 3.2 or higher, and intend to pursue athletic training as a profession. Students enrolled in baccalaureate programs requiring 4 years may apply after their sophomore year; students enrolled in baccalaureate programs requiring more than 4 years may apply after the third year. Several designated scholarships are set aside specifically for ethnic minority students (African Americans, Asians, Hispanics, and Native Americans). The main criteria in selection are service in the applicant's student athletic trainer program and (considered equally) academic achievement; a secondary consideration is participation in campus activities other than academic and athletic training. Financial need is not considered.

Financial data The stipend is $2,000 per year.

Number awarded At least 50 each year.

Deadline January of each year.

[243]
NATIONAL ASSOCIATION OF HISPANIC FEDERAL EXECUTIVES SCHOLARSHIP

National Association of Hispanic Federal Executives
Attn: NAHFE Scholarship Foundation Inc.
P.O. Box 469
Herndon, VA 20172-0469
(703) 787-0291   Fax: (703) 787-4675
E-mail: NAHFE@cs.com
Web: www.nahfe.org/scholars.htm

Purpose To provide financial assistance for college to Hispanic American high school seniors.

Eligibility Eligible to apply are graduating high school seniors of Hispanic American descent. Scholarships are awarded in 3 categories: 1) deserving Hispanic high school seniors on the basis of outstanding academic achievement (GPA of 3.5 or higher), community service, and financial need; 2) deserving Hispanic high school seniors on the basis of satisfactory academic achievement (GPA from 2.8 to 3.5), community involvement, and financial need; and 3) deserving Hispanic high school seniors on the basis of academic merit only (GPA of 3.5 or higher). As part of the application process, students must submit a completed application form, a copy of their high school transcript, 2 letters of recommendation, and a 300-word essay describing their professional or career goals. For scholarships in the first 2 categories listed above, students must also provide proof of financial need (e.g., a copy of the most recent income tax return).

Financial data A stipend is awarded (amount not specified).

Duration Up to 4 years.

Additional information This program was established in 1999. Information is also available from Bill Rodriguez, 5717 Marble Arch Way, Alexandria, VA 22315, (703) 971-3204, E-mail: BillRodriguez@compuserve.com.

Deadline May of each year.

[244]
NATIONAL ASSOCIATION OF HISPANIC NURSES SCHOLARSHIPS

National Association of Hispanic Nurses
Attn: National Awards and Scholarship Committee Chair
1501 16th Street, N.W.
Washington, DC 20036
(202) 387-2477   Fax: (202) 483-7183
E-mail: thehispanicnurses@earthlink.net
Web: www.thehispanicnurses.org

Purpose To provide financial assistance for nursing education to members of the National Association of Hispanic Nurses (NAHN).

Eligibility Eligible are members of the association enrolled in associate, diploma, baccalaureate, graduate, or practical/vocational nursing programs at NLN-accredited schools of nursing. Applicants must submit a 1-page essay that reflects their qualifications and potential for leadership in nursing for the Hispanic community. Selection is based on academic excellence (preferably a GPA of 3.0 or higher), potential for leadership in nursing, and financial need.

Financial data The stipend is $1,000.

Duration 1 year.

Number awarded Varies each year, depending on the availability of funds.

Deadline April of each year.

[245]
NATIONAL HISPANIC EXPLORERS SCHOLARSHIP PROGRAM

Hispanic College Fund
Attn: National Director
1717 Pennsylvania Avenue, N.W., Suite 460
Washington, D.C. 20006
(800) 644-4223   Fax: (202) 296-3774
E-mail: hispaniccollegefund@earthlink.net
Web: www.hispanicfund.org

Purpose To provide financial assistance to Hispanic American undergraduate students who are interested in preparing for a career in a field of interest to the U.S. National Aeronautics and Space Administration (NASA).

Eligibility This program is open to U.S. citizens of Hispanic background who are entering their freshman, sophomore, junior, or senior year of college. Applicants must be working on a bachelor's degree in science, computer science, engineering, or a NASA-related major and have a cumulative GPA of 3.0 or higher. They must be applying to or enrolled in a college or university in

the 50 states or Puerto Rico as a full-time student. Financial need is considered in the selection process.

Financial data Stipends range from $1,000 to $5,000, depending on the need of the recipient. Funds are paid directly to the recipient's college or university to help cover tuition and fees.

Duration 1 year; recipients may reapply.

Additional information This program is sponsored by NASA.

Number awarded Varies each year.

Deadline April of each year.

[246]
NATIONAL OCEANIC AND ATMOSPHERIC ADMINISTRATION EDUCATIONAL PARTNERSHIP PROGRAM WITH MINORITY SERVING INSTITUTIONS UNDERGRADUATE SCHOLARSHIPS

Oak Ridge Institute for Science and Education
Attn: Education and Training Division
P.O. Box 117
Oak Ridge, TN 37831-0117
(865) 576-9272   Fax: (865) 241-5220
E-mail: babcockc@orau.gov
Web: www.orau.gov/orise.htm

Purpose To provide financial assistance and research experience to undergraduate students at minority serving institutions who are majoring in scientific fields of interest to the National Oceanic and Atmospheric Administration (NOAA).

Eligibility This program is open to juniors and seniors at minority serving institutions, including Hispanic Serving Institutions (HSIs), Historically Black Colleges and Universities (HBCUs), and Tribal Colleges and Universities (TCUs). Applicants must be majoring in atmospheric science, biology, cartography, chemistry, computer science, engineering, environmental science, geodesy, geography, marine science, mathematics, meteorology, photogrammetry, physical science, physics, or remote sensing. They must also be interested in pursuing a research internship during the summer at a NOAA site.

Financial data This program provides payment of tuition and fees (to a maximum of $4,000 per year) and a stipend during the internship of $650 per week.

Duration 2 years.

Additional information This program is funded by NOAA through an interagency agreement with the U.S. Department of Energy and administered by the Education and Training Division (ETD) of Oak Ridge Institute for Science and Education (ORISE).

Number awarded 10 each year.

Deadline January of each year.

[247]
NAVESNP/PINEY MOUNTAIN PRESS STUDENT AWARD

National Association of Vocational Education Special Needs Personnel
c/o Zipura Matias, Awards Chair
Swann Special Care Center
109 Kenwood Road
Champaign, IL 61821-2905
(217) 356-5164   E-mail: zipuram@yahoo.com
Web: www.navesnp.org/awards.htm

Purpose To provide financial assistance to vocational/technical students who are members of a special population.

Eligibility This program is open to vocational/technical students who are members of a special population, defined to include those who are academically or economically disadvantaged, limited English proficient, nontraditional, disabled, pregnant teenagers, single/teen parents, or foster children. Applicants must demonstrate how they have overcome barriers to achieve their highest potential for success. Selection is based on their choice of a realistic career goal, financial need, unusual circumstances, and letters of reference.

Financial data The stipend is $1,000.

Duration 1 year.

Additional information Piney Mountain Press supports half the stipend.

Number awarded 1 each year.

Deadline October of each year.

[248]
NEBRASKA SPACE GRANT STATEWIDE SCHOLARSHIP COMPETITION

Nebraska Space Grant Consortium
c/o University of Nebraska at Omaha
Allwine Hall 422
6001 Dodge Street
Omaha, NE 68182-0406
(402) 554-3772   (800) 858-8648, ext. 4-3772 (within NE)
Fax: (402) 554-3781   E-mail: nasa@unomaha.edu
Web: www.unomaha.edu/~nasa/funding/ssc.html

Purpose To provide financial assistance to undergraduate and graduate students in Nebraska interested in aerospace-related study or research.

Eligibility This program is open to undergraduate and graduate students at schools that are members of the Nebraska Space Grant Consortium. Applicants must be U.S. citizens participating in approved aviation or aerospace-related research or course work. Selection is based primarily on past academic performance in the classroom. Special attention is given to applications submitted by women, underrepresented minorities, and persons with disabilities.

Financial data Maximum awards are $500 per semester for undergraduate or graduate course work, $750 per semester for undergraduate research, or $2,500 per semester for graduate research.

Duration 1 semester; may be renewed if the recipient maintains a GPA of 3.0 or higher.

Additional information The following schools are members of the Nebraska Space Grant Consortium: University of Nebraska at Omaha, University of Nebraska at Lincoln, University of Nebraska at Kearney, University of Nebraska Medical Center, Creighton University, Western Nebraska Community College, Chadron State College, College of St. Mary, Metropolitan Community College, Grace University, Hastings College, Little Priest Tribal College, and Nebraska Indian Community College. Funding for this program is provided by the National Aeronautics and Space Administration.

Deadline April of each year.

[249]
NEVADA SPACE GRANT CONSORTIUM UNDERGRADUATE SCHOLARSHIP PROGRAM

Nevada Space Grant Consortium
c/o University of Nevada at Reno
1664 North Virginia Street
MS/172
Reno, NV 89557-0138
(775) 784-6261   Fax: (775) 327-2235
E-mail: nvsg@mines.unr.edu
Web: www.unr.edu/spacegrant

Purpose To provide financial assistance for space-related study to undergraduate students at institutions that are members of the Nevada Space Grant Consortium (NSGC).

Eligibility This program is open to undergraduate students at NSGC member institutions. Applicants must be pursuing a degree in an aerospace-related field (including the behavioral sciences, biological sciences, business, communications, computer science, economics, education, engineering, international affairs, law, natural sciences, physical sciences, publication administration, and sociology) that is concerned with or likely to improve the understanding, assessment, development, and utilization of space. They must be U.S. citizens and enrolled full time. This program is part of the Space Grant program of the U.S. National Aeronautics and Space Administration (NASA), which encourages participation by members of underrepresented groups (African Americans, Hispanics, American Indians, Pacific Islanders, physically disabled people, and women of all races).

Financial data The stipend is $2,500 per year. Funds may be used for tuition or registration fees. Funds may not be regarded as payment for research work or any other work.

Duration 1 year; may be renewed.

Additional information Members of the NSGC include all state institutes of higher learned in Nevada: 2 Ph.D.-granting universities (the University of Nevada at Las Vegas and the University of Nevada at Reno), 4 community colleges (Southern Nevada, Great Basin, Truckee Meadows, and Western Nevada), and the system's research organization, the Desert Research Institute. Funding for this program is provided by NASA.

Number awarded Varies each year.

Deadline March of each year.

[250]
NEW HORIZONS SCHOLARSHIPS

New Horizons Scholars Program
55 Second Street, 15th Floor
San Francisco, CA 94105-3491
(866) 3-HORIZON
Web: www.hsf.net/DOC-PDF/NewHorizons.pdf

Purpose To provide financial assistance for college to Hispanic and African American high school seniors who are infected with Hepatitis C or who are dependents of someone with Hepatitis C.

Eligibility This program is open to high school seniors planning to enroll full time at a 4-year college or university in the following fall. Applicants must be of African American heritage or of Hispanic heritage (each parent half Hispanic or 1 parent fully Hispanic) and have a high school GPA of 3.0 or higher. Along with their application, they must submit 1) verification by a physician that they have Hepatitis C or are the dependent of a person with Hepatitis C; 2) transcripts; 3) a letter of recommendation; 4) documentation of financial need; and 5) a personal statement that addresses the following topics: heritage and family background, personal and academic achievements, academic plans and career goals, efforts toward making a difference in the community, and financial need.

Financial data A stipend is awarded (amount not specified).

Duration 1 year.

Additional information This program began in 2003 as the result of a partnership of the Thurgood Marshall Scholarship Fund and the Hispanic Scholarship Fund, with support from the Roche Foundation.

Number awarded 1 or more each year.

Deadline February of each year.

[251]
NEW JERSEY UTILITIES ASSOCIATION SCHOLARSHIPS

New Jersey Utilities Association
50 West State Street, Suite 1006
Trenton, NJ 08608
(609) 392-1000   Fax: (609) 396-4231
Web: www.njua.org

Purpose To provide financial assistance to minority, female, and disabled high school seniors in New Jersey interested in majoring in selected subjects in college.

Eligibility Eligible to apply for this scholarship are women, minorities (Black, Hispanic, American Indian/Alaska Native, or Asian American/Pacific Islander), and persons with disabilities who are high school seniors in New Jersey. They must be able to demonstrate financial need, be planning to enroll on a full-time basis at an institute of higher education, and be planning to work on a bachelor's degree in engineering, environmental science, chemistry, biology, business administration, or accounting. Children of employees of any New Jersey Utilities Association-member company are ineligible. Selection is based on overall academic excellence and demonstrated financial need.

Financial data The stipend is $1,500 per year.

Duration 4 years.

Number awarded 2 each year.

[252]
NEW YORK STATE MIGRANT STUDENT SCHOLARSHIP

BOCES Geneseo Migrant Center
27 Lackawanna Avenue
Mount Morris, NY 14510-1096
(585) 658-7960   (800) 245-5681
Fax: (585) 658-7969   E-mail: info@migrant.net
Web: www.migrant.net/sch_nys.htm

Purpose To provide financial assistance for college to migrant farmworker high school seniors from New York.

Eligibility This program is open to migrant farmworker students with a history of migration to and/or within New York state. Applicants must have senior status in high school and plans to attend a postsecondary institution or other advanced training. Along with their application, they must submit a statement of at least 250 words on their background and interest in higher education, at least 1 letter of recommendation, and a copy of their current Migrant Certificate of Eligibility (COE). Selection is based on demonstrated commitment to educational goals, participation in school and Migrant Education Outreach Program (MEOP) activities, participation in community and/or non-school activities, citi-

zenship, evidence of high mobility (interstate or intrastate), record of overcoming unusual obstacles, and financial need.

Financial data The stipend is $500 or $250.

Duration 1 year.

Number awarded 1 at $500 or 2 at $250 each year.

Deadline April of each year.

[253]
NEWHOUSE SCHOLARSHIP PROGRAM

National Association of Hispanic Journalists
Attn: Scholarship Committee
1000 National Press Building
529 14th Street, N.W.
Washington, DC 20045-2001
(202) 662-7145   (888) 346-NAHJ
Fax: (202) 662-7144   E-mail: nahj@nahj.org
Web: www.nahj.org/scholarship.html

Purpose To provide financial assistance and summer work experience to Hispanic American undergraduate students interested in preparing for careers in the media.

Eligibility College juniors and seniors are eligible to apply if they are of Hispanic descent and are interested in majoring in print journalism. Applicants must submit an official transcript; a 1-page resume with their educational background, work history, awards, internships, other scholarships, language proficiency, and any work done for their school newspaper, radio, and/or television station; samples of their work; 2 reference letters; a 500-word autobiography in third person written as a news story; and documentation of financial need.

Financial data The stipend is $5,000 per year; the program also provides funding to attend the association's convention and an internship during the summer between the junior and senior year.

Duration 2 years.

Additional information This program, which began in 1994, is sponsored by the Newhouse Foundation and administered by the National Association of Hispanic Journalists (NAHJ) as part of its Rubén Salazar Scholarship Fund. The recipient participates in a summer internship at a Newhouse Newspaper.

Number awarded 1 each year.

Deadline January of each year.

[254]
NEWSROOM DIVERSITY SCHOLARSHIP

Society of Professional Journalists-Kansas Professional
     Chapter
c/o Lillian Martell
The Wichita Eagle
P.O. Box 820
Wichita, KS 67201-0820
Fax: (316) 268-6627
Web: www.spj.org/kansas/scholarship.htm

Purpose To provide financial assistance to minority students at colleges and universities in Kansas who are interested in a career in journalism.

Eligibility This program is open to members of racial minority groups who are juniors and seniors at colleges and universities in Kansas. Sophomores may apply, designating the award for their junior year. Applicants do not have to be journalism or communication majors, but they must demonstrate a strong and sincere interest in print journalism, broadcast journalism, or photojournalism. They must have a GPA of 2.5 or higher and participate in outside journalism-related activities demonstrated by involvement in student or trade organizations and/or student or other news organizations or publications. Along with their application, they must submit 4 to 6 examples of their best work (clips or stories, copies of photographs, tapes or transcripts of broadcasts). Selection is based on the quality of work submitted, academic standing, references, and financial need.

Financial data The stipend is $1,000.

Duration 1 year.

Number awarded 1 each year.

Deadline February of each year.

[255]
NEXT GENERATION OF PUBLIC SERVANTS SCHOLARSHIP

Hispanic Scholarship Fund Institute
1001 Connecticut Avenue, N.W., Suite 632
Washington, DC 20036
(202) 296-0009   Fax: (202) 296-3633
E-mail: info@hsfi.org
Web: www.hsfi.org/sch_nextgen.html

Purpose To provide financial assistance to Hispanic and other students majoring in designated business, engineering, social science, and science fields and interested in employment with the U.S. Department of Energy (DOE).

Eligibility This program is open to U.S. citizens enrolled full time as sophomores with a GPA of 2.8 or higher. Applicants must be interested in pursuing a career with the DOE in an energy-related field. Eligible academic majors are in the fields of business (accounting, business administration, finance, and management), engineering (biomedical, chemical, civil, computer, electrical, environmental, industrial, materials, mechanical, metallurgical, nuclear, and petroleum), social science (economics, organizational psychology, political science, and sociology), and science (biological sciences, computer science, geology, information technology, mathematics, microbiology, and physics). They must be willing to participate in co-ops with the DOE. Along with their application, they must submit a 2-page essay on why a career in public service interests them, how their academic major connects with their stated DOE career goal, why the DOE should invest in them through this program, and how they believe the DOE will benefit from this investment. Selection is based on academic achievement, financial need, demonstrated commitment to public service, and interest in federal employment with the DOE.

Financial data The stipend is $3,000 per year.

Duration 1 year; may be renewed up to 2 additional years if the recipient maintains full-time enrollment and a GPA of 2.8 or higher.

Additional information This program, sponsored by DOE's Office of Economic Impact and Diversity, is administered by the Hispanic Scholarship Fund Institute as part of its effort to increase Hispanic participation in federal service.

Number awarded Varies each year.

Deadline February of each year.

[256]
NMJGSA SCHOLARSHIPS

National Minority Junior Golf Scholarship Association
Attn: Scholarship Committee
120 West Osborn Road
Phoenix, AZ 85013
(602) 258-7851   Fax: (602) 258-3412
Web: www.nmjgsa.org

Purpose To provide financial assistance to minority high school seniors and undergraduate students who excel at golf.

Eligibility This program is open to minority high school seniors and undergraduate students already enrolled in college. Applicants are asked to write a 500-word essay on this question: "One of the principal goals of education and golf is fostering ways for people to respect and get along with individuals who think, dress, look, and act differently. How might you make this goal a reality?" Selection is based on academic achievement, entrance examination scores, financial need, references, community service, and golfing ability.

Financial data Stipends range from 1-time awards of $1,000 to 4-year awards of $6,000 per year. Funds are paid directly to the recipient's college.

Duration 1 year or longer.

Additional information This program was established in 1984. Support is provided by the Jackie Robinson Foundation, PGA of America, Anheuser-Busch, the Tiger Woods Foundation, and other cooperating organizations.

Number awarded Varies; generally 80 or more each year.

Deadline May of each year.

[257]
NORTH DAKOTA SPACE GRANT PROGRAM SCHOLARSHIPS

North Dakota Space Grant Program
c/o University of North Dakota
Department of Space Studies
Clifford Hall, Fifth Floor
P.O. Box 9008
University Avenue and Tulane
Grand Forks, ND 58202-9008
(701) 777-4856   (800) 828-4274
Fax: (701) 777-3711   E-mail: bieri@space.edu
Web: www.space.edu/spacegrant/fellowinfo.html

Purpose To provide financial assistance for space-related study to undergraduates at associate member institutions of the North Dakota Space Grant Program (NDSGP).

Eligibility This program is open to undergraduate students at NDSGP associate colleges and universities who are studying in fields related to space. U.S. citizenship is required. Other qualifying criteria are set by each participating institution. The NDSGP is a component of the U.S. National Aeronautics and Space Administration (NASA) Space Grant program, which encourages the participation of women, underrepresented minorities, and persons with disabilities.

Financial data Stipends are $500 at 2-year public and tribal colleges or $750 at 4-year public state universities.

Additional information Associate NDSCP members are Bismarck State College, Cankdeska Cikana Community (Little Hoop Community College), Dickinson State University, Fort Berthold Community College, Lake Region State College, Mayville State University, Minot State University, Minot State University-Bottineau Campus, North Dakota State College of Science, Sitting Bull College, Turtle Mountain Community College, Valley City State University, and Williston State College. This program is funded by NASA.

Number awarded 39 each year: 3 at each participating college and university.

[258]
NORTHROP GRUMMAN/HENAAC SCHOLARS PROGRAM

Hispanic Engineer National Achievement Awards Conference
3900 Whiteside Street
Los Angeles, CA 90063
(323) 262-0997   Fax: (323) 262-0946
E-mail: info@henaac.org
Web: www.henaac.org/scholarships.htm

Purpose To provide financial assistance to Hispanic undergraduate students majoring in engineering and related fields.

Eligibility This program is open to Hispanic undergraduate students who are majoring in the following engineering fields: aerospace, chemical, civil, computer, electrical, industrial, manufacturing, marine, mechanical, ocean, or structural. Students majoring in computer science, information science, mathematics, naval architecture, and physics are also eligible. Applicants must have a GPA of 3.0 or higher.

Financial data The stipend is $5,000.

Duration 1 year.

Additional information This program is sponsored by Northrop Grumman as part of its effort to support the mission of the Hispanic Engineer National Achievement Awards Conference (HENAAC) to promote technical excellence and leadership in the Hispanic community.

Number awarded 5 each year.

Deadline April of each year.

[259]
NORTHWEST JOURNALISTS OF COLOR SCHOLARSHIP AWARDS

Northwest Journalists of Color
c/o Asian American Journalists Association-Seattle Chapter
c/o Lori Matsukawa
KING-TV5
333 Dexter Avenue North
Seattle, WA 98109
(206) 448-3853   E-mail: lmatsukawa@king5.com
Web: www,aajaseattle.org

Purpose To provide financial assistance to minority students from Washington state who are interested in careers in journalism.

Eligibility These scholarships are open to minority (Asian American, African American, Native American, and Latino) students from Washington state who are planning a career in broadcast, photo, or print journalism. Applicants may be high school seniors or college undergraduates who are residents of Washington state, although they may attend college anywhere in the country. Students are not required to major in journalism, but they should have a strong interest in the subject.

Financial data Stipends range from $500 to $1,000.

Duration 1 year; may be renewed.

Additional information This program, established in 1986, is sponsored by the Seattle chapters of the Asian American Journalists Association, the Native American Journalists Association, the

National Association of Black Journalists, and the Latino Media Association. It includes the Walt and Milly Woodward Memorial Scholarship donated by the Western Washington Chapter of the Society of Professional Journalists. Other funding is provided by KING/5 Television, the *Seattle Post-Intelligencer,* and the *Seattle Times.*

Number awarded Varies each year. Recently, 6 of these scholarships were awarded: 2 at $1,000 and 4 at $500.

Deadline May of each year.

[260]
NOSOTROS SCHOLARSHIP PROGRAM

Nosotros
Attn: Office of the President
650 North Bronson Avenue, Suite 102
Los Angeles, CA 90004
(323) 466-8566   Fax: (323) 466-8540
E-mail: nosotrosnews@nosotros.org
Web: www.nosotros.org

Purpose To help adult Hispanic students in California pursue postsecondary education in the performing arts.

Eligibility Applicants must be working on a degree in film, television, theater, comedy, acting, directing, producing, script writing, stage production, film production, music choreography, or related fields. They must be at least 25 years of age, California residents, and of Latino/Hispanic descent.

Financial data A stipend is awarded (amount not specified).

Duration 1 year.

Additional information Recipients must attend school on a full-time basis. Telephone inquiries are prohibited and may result in disqualification.

Deadline March of each year.

[261]
NSCA WOMEN AND MINORITY SCHOLARSHIP

National Strength and Conditioning Association
Attn: Foundation
1955 North Union Boulevard
P.O. Box 9908
Colorado Springs, CO 80932-0908
(719) 632-6722   (800) 815-6826
Fax: (719) 632-6367   E-mail: nsca@nsca-lift.org
Web: www.nsca-lift.org/foundation

Purpose To provide financial assistance to women and minorities interested in preparing for a career in strength training and conditioning.

Eligibility This program is open to women and minorities who are 17 years of age and older. Applicants must demonstrate they have been accepted into an accredited postsecondary institution, their intention to graduate with a degree in the strength and conditioning field, their goals beyond college, and their record of community service.

Financial data A stipend is awarded (amount not specified).

Duration 1 year; nonrenewable.

Additional information The NSCA is a nonprofit organization of strength and conditioning professionals, including coaches, athletic trainers, physical therapists, educators, researchers, and physicians. This program was first offered in 2003.

Number awarded 1 or more each year.

[262]
OHIO NEWSPAPERS FOUNDATION MINORITY SCHOLARSHIPS

Ohio Newspapers Foundation
1335 Dublin Road, Suite 216-B
Columbus, OH 43215-7038
(614) 486-6677   Fax: (614) 486-4940
E-mail: kpouliot@ohionews.org
Web: www.ohionews.org/scholarships.html

Purpose To provide financial assistance for college to minority high school seniors in Ohio planning to prepare for a career in journalism.

Eligibility This program is open to high school seniors in Ohio who are members of minority groups (African American, Hispanic, Asian American, or American Indian) and planning to pursue careers in newspaper journalism. Applicants must have a high school GPA of 2.5 or higher and demonstrate writing ability in an autobiography of 750 to 1,000 words that describes their academic and career interests, awards, extracurricular activities, and journalism-related activities.

Financial data The award is $1,500.

Duration 1 year; nonrenewable.

Number awarded 3 each year.

Deadline March of each year.

[263]
OHIO SPACE GRANT CONSORTIUM JUNIOR SCHOLARSHIP

Ohio Space Grant Consortium
c/o Ohio Aerospace Institute
22800 Cedar Point Road
Cleveland, OH 44142
(440) 962-3032   (800) 828-OSGC
Fax: (440) 962-3120   E-mail: osgc@oai.org
Web: www.osgc.org

Purpose To provide financial assistance to American citizens who wish to work on a baccalaureate degree in an aerospace-related discipline at major universities in Ohio.

Eligibility These scholarships are available to U.S. citizens who expect to complete within 2 years the requirements for a bachelor of science degree in an aerospace-related discipline (aeronautical engineering, aerospace engineering, astronomy, biology, chemical engineering, chemistry, civil engineering, computer engineering and science, control engineering, electrical engineering, engineering mechanics, geography, geology, industrial engineering, manufacturing engineering, materials science and engineering, mathematics, mechanical engineering, petroleum engineering, physics, and systems engineering). They must be attending 1 of the participating universities in Ohio. Women, underrepresented minorities, and physically challenged persons are particularly encouraged to apply. Selection is based on academic record, recommendations, and a personal statement of career goals and anticipated benefits from the Space Grant program; the statement should also discuss plans for a research laboratory experience.

Financial data The stipend is $2,000.

Duration 1 year.

Additional information These scholarships are funded through the National Space Grant College and Fellowship Program administered by the National Aeronautics and Space Administration (NASA), with matching funds provided by the member universities, the Ohio Aerospace Institute, and private industry. The participating institutions include the University of Akron, Case Western Reserve University, Cedarville College, Central State University, University of Cincinnati, Cleveland State University, University of Dayton, Marietta College (petroleum engineering), Miami University (manufacturing engineering), Ohio Northern University, Ohio State University, Ohio University, University of Toledo, Wilberforce University, Wright State University, and Youngstown State University.

Deadline February of each year.

[264]
ORANGE COUNTY HISPANIC EDUCATION ENDOWMENT FUND ARCHITECTURE AND ENGINEERING SCHOLARSHIPS

Orange County Community Foundation
Attn: Scholarship Coordinator
2081 Business Center Drive, Suite 100
Irvine, CA 92612-1115
(949) 553-4202, ext. 22   Fax: (949) 553-4211
E-mail: occf@oc-communityfoundation.org
Web: www.oc-communityfoundation.org/grantsscholar

Purpose To provide financial assistance to Hispanic students from Orange County, California who are interested in studying engineering or architecture in college.

Eligibility This program is open to Hispanic students in Orange County, California who are 1) graduating high school seniors with a GPA of 3.5 or higher, or 2) second-year community college transfer students with a GPA of 3.2 or higher. All applicants must have been accepted into an accredited 4-year program in architecture or engineering. Selection is based on financial need, extracurricular activities, academic ability, and community service.

Financial data Stipends range from $2,000 to $2,500 per year.

Duration 1 year.

Number awarded 2 each year.

Deadline February of each year.

[265]
ORANGE COUNTY HISPANIC EDUCATION ENDOWMENT FUND ARTS SCHOLARSHIPS

Orange County Community Foundation
Attn: Scholarship Coordinator
2081 Business Center Drive, Suite 100
Irvine, CA 92612-1115
(949) 553-4202, ext. 22   Fax: (949) 553-4211
E-mail: occf@oc-communityfoundation.org
Web: www.oc-communityfoundation.org/grantsscholar

Purpose To provide financial assistance to Hispanic students from Orange County, California who are interested in studying the arts in college.

Eligibility This program is open to Hispanic students in Orange County, California who are graduating high school seniors. Applicants must be interested in working on a college degree in a field of the arts, including 1) the performance of music, drama, and dance; and 2) visual arts, such as fine art and graphic design. Selection is based on financial need, extracurricular activities, academic ability, and community service.

Financial data The stipend is $1,000 per year.

Duration 1 year.

Number awarded 1 each year.

Deadline February of each year.

[266]
OREGON SPACE GRANT UNDERGRADUATE SCHOLAR PROGRAM

Oregon Space Grant
c/o Oregon State University
Department of Nuclear Engineering
130 Radiation Center
Corvallis, OR 97331-5902
(541) 737-2414   Fax: (541) 737-0480
E-mail: kleina@ne.orst.edu
Web: www.ne.orst.edu

Purpose To provide financial assistance for study in space-related fields to undergraduate students at colleges and universities that are members of Oregon Space Grant (OSG).

Eligibility This program is open to undergraduate students at member institutions who are enrolled full time in science and engineering fields related to the mission of the U.S. National Aeronautics and Space Administration (NASA). U.S. citizenship is required. Selection is based on scholastic achievement, career goals, a 500-word essay on a space-related topic, and 2 letters of recommendation. Applications are especially encouraged from women, underrepresented minorities, and people with disabilities.

Financial data The stipend is $1,000.

Duration 1 year.

Additional information Institutions that are members of OSG include Oregon State University, Portland State University, the University of Oregon, Southern Oregon University, Eastern Oregon University, and Oregon Institute of Technology. This program is funded by NASA.

Number awarded 10 each year.

Deadline October of each year.

[267]
OSGC EDUCATION PROGRAM

Oklahoma NASA Space Grant Consortium
c/o University of Oklahoma
College of Geosciences
710 Asp Avenue, Suite 5
Norman, Oklahoma 73069
(405) 447-8483   Fax: (405) 447-8455
E-mail: vduca@ou.edu
Web: www.okspacegrant.ou.edu

Purpose To provide financial assistance to students in Oklahoma who are enrolled in aerospace-related studies at the undergraduate and graduate level.

Eligibility This program is open to undergraduate and graduate students at member and affiliate institutions of the Oklahoma Space Grant Consortium (OSGC). U.S. citizenship is required. The OSGC is a component of the U.S. National Aeronautics and Space Administration (NASA) Space Grant program, which encourages participation by women, underrepresented minorities, and persons with disabilities.

Financial data Financing depends on the availability of funds.

Additional information Members of OSGC are Oklahoma State University, the University of Oklahoma, Cameron University, and Langston University. Write to the sponsor for information on the program at each participating university. This program is funded by NASA.

[268]
PADRINO SCHOLARSHIPS

Society of Mexican American Engineers and Scientists
Attn: National Office Director
13337 South Street, Suite 349
Cerritos, CA 90703
E-mail: maes@tamu.edu
Web: www.maes-natl.org

Purpose To provide financial assistance to undergraduate and graduate student members of the Society of Mexican American Engineers and Scientists (MAES).

Eligibility This program is open to MAES student members who are full-time undergraduate or graduate students at a college or university in the United States. Community college students must be enrolled in majors that can transfer to a 4-year institution offering a baccalaureate degree. All applicants must be majoring in a field of science or engineering. U.S. citizenship or permanent resident status is required. Selection is based on financial need; academic achievement; personal qualities, strengths, and leadership abilities; and timeliness and completeness of the application.

Financial data The stipend is $3,000.

Duration 1 year.

Additional information Information is also available from José M. Hernández, Chair, MAES Scholarship Committee, 4015 North Water Iris Cort, Houston, TX 77059. Recipients must attend the MAES International Symposium's Medalla de Oro Banquet in October.

Number awarded 1 or more each year.

Deadline October of each year.

[269]
PAGE EDUCATION FOUNDATION GRANTS

Page Education Foundation
P.O. Box 581254
Minneapolis, MN 55458-1254
(612) 332-0406   E-mail: pagemail@mtn.org
Web: www.page-ed.org

Purpose To provide funding for college to students of color in Minnesota.

Eligibility This program is open to students of color who are graduating from high school in Minnesota and planning to attend a postsecondary school in the state. Applicants must submit an essay of 400 to 500 words that deals with why they believe education is important, their plans for the future, and the service-to-children project they would like to complete in the coming school year. Selection is based on the essay, 3 letters of recommendation, and financial need.

Financial data Stipends range from $900 to $2,500 per year.

Duration 1 year; may be renewed up to 3 additional years.

Additional information This program was founded in 1988 by Alan Page, a former football player for the Minnesota Vikings. While attending college, the Page Scholars fulfill a service-to-children contract that brings them into contact with K-8 grade school students of color.

Number awarded Nearly 125 each year; recently, 49% of the scholars were African American, 42% Asian American, 6% Hispanic, and 3% Native American.

Deadline April of each year.

[270]
PALH SCHOLARSHIPS

American Academy of Physician Assistants
Attn: Physician Assistants of Latino Heritage
950 North Washington Street
Alexandria, VA 22314-1552
(800) 596-7494   Fax: (703) 684-1924
E-mail: palh@aapa.org
Web: www.aapa.org/spec/scholar.htm

Purpose To provide financial assistance to student members of the Physician Assistants of Latino Heritage (PALH) within the American Academy of Physician Assistants (AAPA).

Eligibility Applicants for these scholarships must be members of both the AAPA and its PALH caucus enrolled in a physician assistant program. Their application must include a statement on their personal background, pertinent experiences working with underserved Latino communities, future goals and expectations upon completing their physician assistant program, and why they should be considered for a PALH scholarship. Financial need is not considered in the selection process.

Financial data The stipend is $500 per year.

Duration 1 year.

Number awarded 3 each year.

Deadline March of each year.

[271]
PATRICIA ASIP SCHOLARSHIP FOR MARKETING AND PROMOTION

Hispanic Designers, Inc.
Attn: National Hispanic Education and Communications
    Projects
1101 30th Street, N.W., Suite 500
Washington, DC 20007
(202) 337-9636   Fax: (202) 337-9635
E-mail: HispDesign@aol.com
Web: www.hispanicdesigners.org

Purpose To provide financial assistance to Hispanic students enrolled in fashion design schools.

Eligibility Applicants must be Hispanic or of Hispanic descent, be able to demonstrate financial need, be U.S. citizens or residents, have participated in an internship or work training program in the field of fashion, and have a GPA of 3.0 or higher. They must be enrolled in an accredited postsecondary institution studying for a degree or in certified programs in fashion design or a related field. Selection is based on the presentation of a merchandising strategy for a ready-to-wear collection targeting the U.S. Hispanic market; the presentation must include samples of advertising in English and Spanish, description of the target customer, price range, type of store and department in which the collection would be carried, a press kit on the designer and the collection, a design hang tag for garments in the collection, and a design label or logo for the collection.

Financial data The stipend is $5,000 per year; awards are paid directly to the recipient's institution.

Duration 1 year.

Additional information This program was established in 1998 to honor Patricia V. Asip, who coordinated the Hispanic Designers Model Search for her employer, JCPenney Company, Inc. No telephone inquiries are accepted.

Number awarded 1 each year.

Deadline August of each year.

[272]
PENNSYLVANIA SPACE GRANT CONSORTIUM SCHOLARSHIPS

Pennsylvania Space Grant Consortium
c/o Pennsylvania State University
2217 Earth-Engineering Sciences Building
University Park, PA 16802
(814) 863-7687   Fax: (814) 863-8286
E-mail: spacegrant@psu.edu
Web: www.psu.edu/spacegrant/highered/scholar.html

Purpose To provide financial assistance for space-related study to undergraduate students at universities affiliated with the Pennsylvania Space Grant Consortium.

Eligibility This program is open to full-time undergraduate students at participating universities. Applicants must be studying a field that does, or can, promote the understanding, assessment, and utilization of space, including aerospace, earth science, or space science. U.S. citizenship is required. Students from underrepresented groups (women, minorities, rural populations, and those with disabilities) are especially encouraged to apply.

Financial data The stipend is set by each participating university. At Pennsylvania State University, for instance, it is $4,000 per year.

Duration 1 year.

Additional information Participating institutions include Carnegie Mellon University, Clarion University, Pennsylvania State University, University of Pittsburgh, Susquehanna University, Lincoln University, Temple University, West Chester University, and Pennsylvania State University at Abington. At Pennsylvania State University, the award is designated as the Sylvia Stein Memorial Space Grant Scholarship. This program is sponsored by the U.S. National Aeronautics and Space Administration (NASA).

Number awarded Varies each year.

Deadline Each participating university sets its own deadline.

[273]
PFIZER/UNCF CORPORATE SCHOLARS PROGRAM

United Negro College Fund
Attn: Corporate Scholars Program
P.O. Box 1435
Alexandria, VA 22313-9998
(866) 671-7237   E-mail: internship@uncf.org
Web: www.uncf.org/Scholarship/CorporateScholars.asp

Purpose To provide financial assistance and work experience to minority undergraduate and graduate students majoring in designated fields and interested in an internship at a Pfizer facility.

Eligibility This program is open to sophomores, juniors, graduate students, and first-year law students who are African American, Hispanic American, Asian/Pacific Islander American, or American Indian/Alaskan Native. Applicants must have a GPA of 3.0 or higher and be enrolled at an institution that is a member of the United Negro College Fund (UNCF) or at another targeted college or university. They must be pursuing 1) a bachelor's degree in animal science, business, chemistry (organic or analytical), human resources, logistics, microbiology, organizational development, operations management, pre-veterinary medicine, or supply chain management; 2) a master's degree in chemistry (organic or analytical), finance, human resources, or organizational development; or 3) a law degree. Eligibility is limited to U.S. citizens, permanent residents, asylees, refugees, and lawful temporary residents. Along with their application, they must submit a 1-page essay about themselves and their career goals, including information about their interest in Pfizer (the program's sponsor), their personal background, and any particular challenges they have faced.

Financial data The program provides an internship stipend of up to $5,000, housing accommodations near Pfizer Corporate facilities, and (based on successful internship performance) a $15,000 scholarship.

Duration 8 to 10 weeks for the internship; 1 year for the scholarship.

Additional information Opportunities for first-year law students include the summer internship only.

Number awarded Varies each year.

Deadline December of each year.

[274]
PLANNING & THE BLACK COMMUNITY DIVISION SCHOLARSHIP

American Planning Association
Attn: Member Services Department
122 South Michigan Avenue, Suite 1600
Chicago, IL 60603-6107
(312) 431-9100   Fax: (312) 431-9985
E-mail: Fellowships@planning.org
Web: www.planning.org

Purpose To provide financial assistance to underrepresented minority undergraduate students interested in majoring in planning or a related field.

Eligibility This program is open to African American, Hispanic, and Native American undergraduate students in their second, third, or fourth year of study. Applicants must be majoring in planning or a related field (e.g., community development, environmental sciences, public administration, transportation, or urban studies). U.S. citizenship is required.

Financial data The stipend is $2,500.

Duration 1 year.

Number awarded 1 each year.

Deadline May of each year.

[275]
PNI KNIGHT RIDDER MINORITY SCHOLARS PROGRAM

Philadelphia Inquirer
Attn: Ivan Sample
400 North Broad Street
P.O. Box 8263
Philadelphia, PA 19101
(215) 854-2429   Fax: (215) 854-2578
E-mail: isample@phillynews.com
Web: www.philly.com/mld/philly

Purpose To provide financial assistance to minority high school seniors from the circulation area of Philadelphia Newspapers Inc. (PNI) who are interested in careers in journalism.

Eligibility This program is open to minority seniors graduating from high schools in the service area of the PNI newspapers (the *Philadelphia Inquirer* and the *Philadelphia Daily News*) in Delaware, New Jersey, and Pennsylvania. Applicants must be interested in majoring in journalism in college.

Financial data The stipend is $500.

Duration 1 year; nonrenewable.

Additional information The recipients of these scholarships are automatically entered into competition for the Knight Ridder Minority Scholarship Program of $10,000 per year for 4 years.

Number awarded 4 each year.

Deadline January of each year.

[276]
PORTLAND PRESS HERALD/MAINE SUNDAY TELEGRAM SCHOLARSHIP FUND

Maine Community Foundation
Attn: Program Director
245 Main Street
Ellsworth, ME 04605
(207) 667-9735   (877) 700-6800
Fax: (207) 667-0447   E-mail: info@mainecf.org
Web: www.mainecf.org/scholar.html

Purpose To provide financial assistance to students of color who are interested in studying journalism at a college or university in Maine.

Eligibility This program is open to students of color from anywhere in the United States who are interested in majoring in journalism, media studies, or related majors. First priority is given to students at the University of Southern Maine, but if no qualifying candidates apply from that school, students attending other 4-year postsecondary educational institutions in Maine are considered. Preference is given to applicants entering or currently enrolled as full-time students pursuing a career in print journalism. Selection is based on academic potential, financial need, and a demonstrated interest in and aptitude for print journalism.

Financial data A stipend is paid (amount not specified).

Duration 1 year; may be renewed.

Additional information This program was established in 2000.

Number awarded 1 or more each year.

Deadline May of each year.

[277]
PPG SCHOLARSHIPS PLUS PROGRAM

American Chemical Society
Attn: Department of Diversity Programs
1155 16th Street, N.W.
Washington, DC 20036
(202) 872-6250   (800) 227-5558, ext. 6250
Fax: (202) 776-8003   E-mail: scholars@acs.org
Web: www.acs.org/scholars

Purpose To provide financial assistance and summer work experience to underrepresented minority high school seniors from designated communities who wish to pursue a career in a chemically-related science.

Eligibility This program is open to high school seniors in the following communities: Natrium and New Martinsville, West Virginia; Lake Charles, Louisiana; Pittsburgh, Pennsylvania; Shelby and Lexington, North Carolina; Oak Creek, Wisconsin; Cleveland, Ohio; and Houston, Texas. Applicants must be African American, Hispanic/Latino, or American Indian. They must plan to be full-time students pursuing a 4-year degree in either chemistry or chemical engineering. Students planning careers in medicine or pharmacy are not eligible. U.S. citizenship or permanent resident status is required. Selection is based on academic merit (GPA of 3.0 or higher) and financial need.

Financial data The maximum stipend is $2,500 per year.

Duration Up to 4 years.

Additional information In addition to scholarship support, recipients are eligible for summer research assignments at plant sites of PPG Industries (which sponsors this program) near their permanent residences. This program was first offered in 1997.

Number awarded Approximately 10 each year.

Deadline February of each year.

[278]
PRIVATE COLLEGES & UNIVERSITIES MAGAZINE COMMUNITY SERVICE SCHOLARSHIP PROGRAM FOR MINORITY STUDENTS

Private Colleges & Universities
Attn: *PC&U* Scholarship Program
239 Littleton Road
P.O. Box 349
Westford, MA 01886
(978) 692-2313

Purpose To provide financial assistance to high school seniors and graduates of color who are planning to enroll as a freshman in a private college or university.

Eligibility All students of color who are currently residents of the United States or its territories and who plan to enroll in a baccalaureate degree program at a participating private college or university (for a list, write to the sponsor) are eligible to apply. To apply, students must complete the application form, write a 1,000-word statement about their community service activities, submit a high school transcript, and include a recommendation by someone in their community (not a family member). Selection is based on academic merit (transcripts, class rank, and GPA) and on service to the community.

Financial data The stipend is $1,000.

Duration 1 year; nonrenewable.

Number awarded Up to 20 each year.

Deadline December of each year.

[279]
PROCTER & GAMBLE ORAL CARE–HDA FOUNDATION SCHOLARSHIPS

Hispanic Dental Association
Attn: HDA Foundation
188 West Randolph Street, Suite 415
Chicago, IL 60601
(312) 577-4013   (800) 852-7921
Fax: (312) 577-0052   E-mail: hdassoc1@qwest.net
Web: www.hdassoc.org

Purpose To provide financial assistance to Hispanic students interested in preparing for a career in a dental profession.

Eligibility This program is open to Hispanics who have been accepted into an accredited dental, dental hygiene, dental assisting, or dental technician program. Selection is based on scholastic achievement, community service, leadership skill, and commitment to improving health in the Hispanic community.

Financial data Stipends are $1,000 or $500.

Duration 1 year.

Additional information This program is sponsored by Procter & Gamble Company.

Number awarded Numerous scholarships are awarded each year.

Deadline June of each year.

[280]
PROJECT SEED SCHOLARSHIPS

American Chemical Society
Attn: Education Division
1155 16th Street, N.W.
Washington, DC 20036
(202) 872-4380   (800) 227-5558, ext. 4380
E-mail: r_rasheed@acs.org
Web: www.acs.org/education/SEED.html

Purpose To provide financial assistance for college to high school students who participated in the American Chemical Society's Project SEED: Summer Education Experience for the Disadvantaged.

Eligibility Applicants for Project SEED must have completed the junior or senior year in high school, live within commuting distance of a sponsoring institution, have completed a course in high school chemistry, and come from an economically disadvantaged family. The standards for economic disadvantage follow federal poverty guidelines for family size, but the maximum family income is $27,000 except in cases where other factors are present that may deter a student from considering a career in science; family income may be up to $34,000 if the student is a member of an ethnic group underrepresented in the sciences (African American, Hispanic, American Indian), if the parents have not attended college, or if the family is single-parent or very large. Participants in the Project SEED program are eligible to apply for these scholarships during their senior year in high school if they plan to major in college in a chemical science or engineering field, such as chemistry, chemical engineering, biochemistry, materials science, or another closely-related field.

Financial data Stipends up to $5,000 per year are available.

Duration 1 year; nonrenewable.

Additional information This program includes the following named scholarships: Bayer Corporation Scholars, Mettler-Toledo, Inc. Scholars, Eli Lilly and Company Scholars, and Bader Scholars.

Number awarded Varies each year; recently, 35 of these scholarships were awarded.

Deadline February of each year.

[281]
PUBLIC RELATIONS STUDENT SOCIETY OF AMERICA MULTICULTURAL AFFAIRS SCHOLARSHIPS

Public Relations Student Society of America
Attn: Director of Education
33 Irving Place, Third Floor
New York, NY 10003-2376
(212) 460-1474   Fax: (212) 995-0757
E-mail: hq@prsa.org
Web: www.prssa.org

Purpose To provide financial assistance to minority college students who are interested in preparing for a career in public relations.

Eligibility This program is open to minority (African American/Black, Hispanic/Latino, Asian, Native American, Alaskan Native, or Pacific Islander) students who are at least juniors at an accredited 4-year college or university. Applicants must be attending full time, be able to demonstrate financial need, and have earned a GPA of 3.0 or higher. Membership in the Public Relations Student Society of America is preferred but not required. A major or minor in public relations is preferred; students who attend a school that does not offer a public relations degree or program must be enrolled in a communications degree program.

Financial data The stipend is $1,500.

Duration 1 year.

Number awarded 2 each year.

Deadline April of each year.

[282]
PUERTO RICAN CHAMBER OF COMMERCE RAUL JULIA MEMORIAL SCHOLARSHIP FUND

Dade Community Foundation
Attn: Director of Development
200 South Biscayne Boulevard, Suite 2780
Miami, FL 33131-2343
(305) 371-2711   Fax: (305) 371-5342
E-mail: Dadecomfnd@aol.com

Purpose To provide financial assistance for college to Puerto Rican high school seniors in south Florida.

Eligibility This program is open to high school seniors born in Puerto Rico or of Puerto Rican descent who are no older than 19 years of age, graduating from a Dade or Broward County, Florida public or private high school (or earning a GED) with a minimum GPA of 3.0, and in financial need. Applicants must plan to continue their education at the university level.

Financial data The stipend is $1,000.

Duration 1 year.

Number awarded 3 each year: 1 in the arts and humanities, 1 in science, and 1 in business.

Deadline March of each year.

[283]
PUERTO RICO NATIONAL GUARD TUITION ASSISTANCE FUND

Puerto Rico National Guard
Attn: Education Services Officer
P.O. Box 9023786
Juana Diaz, PR 00902-3786
(787) 289-1502   E-mail: ortegaj@pr.ngb.army.mil

Purpose To provide financial assistance for college to National Guard members in Puerto Rico and their families.

Eligibility This program is open to 1) active members of the Puerto Rico National Guard who are interested in pursuing studies on the undergraduate or graduate level (up to the Ph.D. degree); 2) spouses of members interested in pursuing studies on the undergraduate or graduate level (up to a master's degree); and 3) children of members interested in pursuing undergraduate or vocational study. Guard members may not receive support at the same time as a spouse and/or child.

Financial data For Guard members, the program pays $50 per credit to a maximum of $900 per year for undergraduate or vocational study, $75 per credit to a maximum of $1,350 per year for graduate study, or a maximum of $1,000 per year for study for an M.D. degree. For spouses, the program pays $75 per credit to a maximum of $1,350 per semester for graduate study. For spouses and children, the program pays $50 per credit to a maximum of $900 per semester for undergraduate or vocational study.

Duration 1 year; may be renewed. Guard members are limited to 18 credits of study per year; spouses and children are limited to 18 credits per semester.

Number awarded Varies each year.

[284]
PWC MINORITY SCHOLARS PROGRAM

PricewaterhouseCoopers LLP
Attn: Ellen Jackson
1900 K Street, N.W., Suite 900
Washington, DC 20006-1100
(202) 822-4091   Fax: (202) 861-7959
Web: www.pwcglobal.com/ocp

Purpose To provide financial assistance to underrepresented minority undergraduate students interested in preparing for a career in the professional services industry.

Eligibility This program is open to African American, Native American, and Hispanic American students entering their sophomore or junior year of college. Applicants must have a GPA of 3.3 or higher, be able to demonstrate interpersonal skills and leadership ability, and intend to pursue a career in the professional services industry. They must be attending 1 of the 31 colleges and universities that are part of the PricewaterhouseCoopers' Priority School Network and must be legally authorized to work in the United States.

Financial data The stipend is $5,000 per year.

Duration 1 year; may be renewed if the recipient maintains a GPA of 3.3 or higher.

Additional information Recipients also participate in the annual Minorities in Business Leadership Conference (held in New York City), are considered for an internship position with the sponsor, and engage in a mentoring program.

Number awarded 40 new and 4 renewal scholarships are offered each year.

[285]
RACE RELATIONS MULTIRACIAL STUDENT SCHOLARSHIP

Christian Reformed Church
Attn: Ministry of Race Relations
10356 Artesia Boulevard
Bellflower, CA 90706
(562) 925-2852
E-mail: norbertowolf@CRMinistryCenter.net
Web: www.crcna.org

Purpose To provide financial assistance to undergraduate and graduate minority students interested in attending colleges related to the Christian Reformed Church in North America (CRCNA).

Eligibility Students of various ethnicities both in the United States and Canada are eligible to apply. Normally, applicants are expected to be members of CRCNA congregations who plan to pursue their educational goals at Calvin Theological Seminary or any of the colleges affiliated with the CRCNA. Students who have no prior history with the CRCNA must attend a CRCNA-related college or seminary for a full academic year before they are eligible to apply for this program. Students entering their sophomore year must have earned a GPA of 2.0 or higher as freshmen; students entering their junior year must have earned a GPA of 2.3 or higher as sophomores; students entering their senior year must have earned a GPA of 2.6 or higher as juniors.

Financial data First-year students receive $500 per semester. Other levels of students may receive up to $2,000 per academic year.

Duration 1 year.

Additional information This program was first established in 1971 and revised in 1991. Recipients are expected to train to engage actively in the ministry of racial reconciliation in church and in society. They must be able to work in the United States or Canada upon graduating and must consider working for 1 of the agencies of the CRCNA.

Deadline March of each year.

[286]
RACIAL ETHNIC EDUCATIONAL SCHOLARSHIPS

Synod of the Trinity
Attn: Scholarships
3040 Market Street
Camp Hill, PA 17011-4599
(717) 737-0421   (800) 242-0534
Fax: (717) 737-8211   E-mail: Scholarships@syntrin.org
Web: www.syntrin.org/program/funding.htm

Purpose To provide financial assistance to ethnic minority students in Pennsylvania, West Virginia, and designated counties in Ohio who are in financial need.

Eligibility Persons applying for aid must be members of a racial minority group (Asian, African American, Hispanic, or Native Americans); residents of Pennsylvania, West Virginia, or the Ohio counties of Belmont, Harrison, Jefferson, Monroe, or Columbiana; and accepted or enrolled as a full-time student at an accredited undergraduate or vocational school. Financial aid is given only after the synod has determined that an applicant is eligible and that family resources are insufficient to meet college costs. Recipients may be of any religious persuasion.

Financial data Awards range from $100 to $1,000 per year, depending on the need of the recipient.

Duration 1 year; may be renewed. Students may not apply for this program and the Synod of the Trinity Educational Scholarship Program.

Number awarded Varies each year.

Deadline March of each year.

[287]
RALPH BUNCHE SUMMER INSTITUTE

American Political Science Association
Attn: Ralph Bunch Summer Institute
1527 New Hampshire Avenue, N.W.
Washington, DC 20036-1206
(202) 483-2512   Fax: (202) 483-2657
E-mail: minority@apsanet.org
Web: www.apsanet.org/about/minority/rbsi.cfm

Purpose To introduce underrepresented minority undergraduate students to the world of graduate study and to encourage their eventual application to a Ph.D. program in political science.

Eligibility Applications are invited from African American, Latino(a), and Native American students completing their junior year. They must be interested in attending graduate school and working on a degree in a field related to political science. U.S. citizenship is required.

Financial data Participants receive a stipend of $200 per week plus full support of tuition, transportation, room, board, books, and instructional materials.

Duration 5 weeks, during the summer.

Additional information The institute includes 2 transferable credit courses (1 in quantitative analysis and the other on race

and American politics). In addition, guest lecturers and recruiters from Ph.D. programs visit the students. Classes are held on the campus of Duke University. Most students who attend the institute excel in their senior year and go on to graduate school, many with full graduate fellowships and teaching assistantships.

Number awarded 20 each year.

Deadline February of each year.

[288]
RAYMOND H. TROTT SCHOLARSHIP FOR BANKING

Rhode Island Foundation
Attn: Scholarship Coordinator
One Union Station
Providence, RI 02903
(401) 274-4564   Fax: (401) 331-8085
E-mail: libbym@rifoundation.org
Web: www.rifoundation.org

Purpose To provide financial assistance to Rhode Island undergraduates of color interested in preparing for a career in banking.

Eligibility This program is open to minority residents of Rhode Island who are entering their senior year in college. Applicants must plan to pursue a career in banking and be able to demonstrate financial need. Along with their application, they must submit an essay (up to 300 words) on the impact they would like to have on the banking industry.

Financial data The stipend is $1,000.

Duration 1 year; nonrenewable.

Number awarded 1 each year.

Deadline June of each year.

[289]
RCA ETHNIC SCHOLARSHIP FUND

Reformed Church in America
Attn: Policy, Planning, and Administration Services
475 Riverside Drive, Room 1814
New York, NY 10115
(212) 870-3243   (800) 722-9977, ext. 3243
Fax: (212) 870-2499   E-mail: kbradsell@rca.org
Web: www.rca.org/aboutus/councils/scholarships.php

Purpose To provide assistance to minority student members of the Reformed Church in America (RCA) who are interested in working on an undergraduate degree.

Eligibility Applicants must be a member of a minority group (American Indian, African American, Hispanic, or Pacific or Asian American), be admitted to a college or other institution of higher learning, and be a member of an RCA congregation or be admitted to an RCA college. Priority is given to applicants who will enter undergraduate colleges or universities and students enrolled in undergraduate occupational training programs. Selection is based primarily on financial need.

Financial data The stipend depends on the need of the recipient, but is at least $500.

Duration 1 academic year; may be renewed until completion of an academic program.

Number awarded Several each year.

Deadline April of each year.

[290]
RDW GROUP, INC. MINORITY SCHOLARSHIP FOR COMMUNICATIONS

Rhode Island Foundation
Attn: Scholarship Coordinator
One Union Station
Providence, RI 02903
(401) 274-4564　　　　　Fax: (401) 331-8085
E-mail: libbym@rifoundation.org
Web: www.rifoundation.org

Purpose To provide financial assistance to Rhode Island students of color interested in preparing for a career in communications.

Eligibility This program is open to minority undergraduate and graduate students who are Rhode Island residents. Applicants must intend to pursue a course of study in communications. They must be able to demonstrate their commitment to a career in communications and financial need. Along with their application, they must submit an essay (up to 300 words) on the impact they would like to have on the communications field.

Financial data The stipend is $2,000.

Duration 1 year; nonrenewable.

Additional information This program is sponsored by the RDW Group, Inc.

Number awarded 1 each year.

Deadline June of each year.

[291]
RECORD-JOURNAL MINORITY INTERNSHIP/SCHOLARSHIP

Record-Journal
Attn: Executive Editor
11 Crown Street
Meriden, CT 06450
(203) 317-2370　　　　　E-mail: jsmith@record-journal.com
Web: www.record-journal.com

Purpose To provide financial assistance and summer work experience to minority residents of Connecticut interested in a career in journalism.

Eligibility This program is open to minority residents of Connecticut who live within the circulation area of the *Record-Journal*. Applicants must be high school seniors or college students majoring in journalism or a related field and planning to pursue a career in the field. They must submit a completed application, transcripts, an essay, and documentation of financial need.

Financial data The scholarship stipend is $1,500 per year. The program includes an internship at the *Record-Journal,* usually during the summer, that pays up to $3,500.

Duration 1 year; may be renewed up to 3 additional years.

Additional information Recipients are urged to work at the *Record-Journal* after graduation.

Number awarded 1 each year.

Deadline January of each year.

[292]
RENE MATOS SCHOLARSHIP

National Hispanic Coalition of Federal Aviation Employees
Attn: Scholarship Selection Committee
Cambridge Park
C-3 Chestnut Hill Avenue
San Juan, PR 00926
Web: www.nhcfae.com

Purpose To provide financial assistance to minority and women students who are working on an undergraduate or graduate degree.

Eligibility This program is open to minority and women students who are accepted to or attending an accredited college, university, or vocational/trade school. Applicants may be graduating high school seniors, current undergraduates, or graduate students. Selection is based on academic achievement, community involvement, financial need, honors and awards, leadership, personal qualities and strengths, and student activities.

Financial data A stipend is awarded (amount not specified).

Duration 1 year; may be renewed.

Additional information The National Hispanic Coalition of Federal Aviation Employees, established in 1978, is a nonprofit organization comprised mainly of Hispanics who are employed at the Federal Aviation Administration. Requests for applications must be accompanied by a self-addressed stamped envelope. Phone calls and faxed applications are not accepted.

Number awarded 1 or more each year.

Deadline April of each year.

[293]
RHODE ISLAND SPACE GRANT UNDERGRADUATE SCHOLARSHIP PROGRAM

Rhode Island Space Grant
c/o Brown University
Lincoln Field Building
Box 1846
Providence, RI 02912-1846
(401) 863-2889　　　　　Fax: (401) 863-1292
E-mail: RISpaceGrant@brown.edu
Web: www.planetary.brown.edu/RI_Space_Grant

Purpose To provide financial assistance to undergraduate students at institutions that are members of the Rhode Island Space Grant Consortium (RISGC) who are interested in a career in a space-related field of science, mathematics, or engineering.

Eligibility This program is open to undergraduate students at RISGC-member universities. Applicants must be studying in science, mathematics, or engineering fields of interest to the National Aeronautics and Space Administration (NASA). U.S. citizenship is required. The sponsor is a component of NASA's Space Grant program, which encourages participation by women, underrepresented minorities, and persons with disabilities.

Financial data A stipend is provided (amount not specified).

Duration 1 year.

Additional information Members of the RISGC are Bryant College, Community College of Rhode Island, Providence College, Roger Williams University, Rhode Island College, Rhode Island School of Design, Salve Regina University, University of Rhode Island, and Wheaton College. This program is funded by NASA. Scholars are required to devote 75% of their time to their studies and 25% of their time to science education outreach activities organized and coordinated by Rhode Island Space Grant.

Number awarded Varies each year; recently, 9 of these scholarships were awarded.

[294]
RICHARD S. SMITH SCHOLARSHIP

United Methodist Youth Organization
P.O. Box 340003
Nashville, TN 37203-0003
(615) 340-7184   (877) 899-2780, ext. 7184
Fax: (615) 340-1764   E-mail: umyouthorg@gbod.org
Web: www.umyouth.org/scholarships.html

Purpose To provide financial assistance to minority high school seniors or graduates who wish to prepare for a Methodist church-related career.

Eligibility Minority students who are beginning college are eligible to apply if they are members of the United Methodist Church, have been active in their local church for at least 1 year, can demonstrate financial need, have maintained a "C" average throughout high school, and are interested in pursuing a church-related career after graduation.

Financial data The stipend is up to $1,000.

Duration 1 year; nonrenewable. Recipients must enroll full time in their first year of undergraduate study.

Deadline May of each year.

[295]
RMHC/HACER SCHOLARSHIP PROGRAM

McDonald's Corporation
Attn: Public and Community Affairs
Kroc Drive
Oak Brook, IL 60523
(800) 736-5219
Web: www.rmhc.org

Purpose To provide financial assistance for college to Hispanic students in specified geographic areas.

Eligibility This program is open to high school seniors in designated McDonald's market areas. Applicants must be U.S. citizens or permanent residents with at least 1 parent of Hispanic heritage. Selection is based on high school academic achievement, financial need, community involvement, and personal qualities and strengths.

Financial data Individual awards range from $1,000 to $5,000 per year.

Duration 1 year; nonrenewable.

Additional information This program, the Hispanic American Commitment to Educational Resources (HACER), was established in 1985; it is funded by Ronald House Charities (RMHC) and local McDonald's operators. Applications are available from high school counselors and McDonald's in participating market areas. Some of those market areas are extensive, extending over whole regions and including locations in more than 1 state. The market areas that were participating in the program recently were the following: Albuquerque, New Mexico (including all the state); Amarillo, Texas (including portions of New Mexico); Atlanta, Georgia: Austin, Texas; Bakersfield (Kern County), California; Billings, Montana (including all of Montana and all of Wyoming except Converse, Hot Springs, Laramie, and Washakie counties); Chattanooga, Tennessee; Chicago, Illinois (including northwestern Indiana); Colorado Springs, Colorado; Dallas/Fort Worth, Texas; Den-

ver, Colorado (including portions of Wyoming and Nebraska); Des Moines, Iowa; El Paso, Texas (including Doña Ana County in New Mexico); Fargo, North Dakota (including portions of Minnesota and South Dakota); Fresno, California; Hartford, Connecticut (including portions of Massachusetts); Hershey, Pennsylvania; Houston, Texas; Laredo, Texas; Las Vegas, Nevada; Lawton, Oklahoma/Wichita Falls, Texas; Los Angeles, California; Lubbock, Texas; Miami, Florida; Midland/Odessa, Texas; Milwaukee, Wisconsin; the tri-state area of New York; Norfolk, Virginia (including portions of North Carolina); Oklahoma City, Oklahoma; Orlando, Florida; Philadelphia, Pennsylvania (including portions of Delaware and New Jersey); Phoenix, Arizona; Puerto Rico; Raleigh, North Carolina (including 77 counties in North Carolina and 6 in South Carolina); Reno, Nevada; Sacramento, California; Salt Lake City, Utah (including adjoining areas of Nevada); San Antonio, Texas; San Francisco, California; Sioux City, Iowa (including portions of Nebraska and South Dakota); Spokane, Washington (limited to students at Washington State University); Tampa, Florida; Temple/Waco, Texas; Victoria, Texas; and Washington, D.C. (including portions of Maryland, Virginia, and West Virginia).

Number awarded Varies each year; recently, the program awarded more than $1.5 million in scholarships.

Deadline January of each year.

[296]
ROCKWELL CORPORATION SCHOLARSHIPS

Society of Women Engineers
230 East Ohio Street, Suite 400
Chicago, IL 60611-3265
(312) 596-5223   Fax: (312) 644-8557
E-mail: hq@swe.org
Web: www.swe.org

Purpose To provide financial assistance to undergraduate women majoring in engineering, especially those underrepresented in the field.

Eligibility Applicants must be women majoring in engineering and entering their junior year at an ABET-accredited or SWE-approved college or university. Applicants must have a GPA of 3.5 or higher and have demonstrated leadership ability. Preference is given to members of groups underrepresented in the field (e.g., minorities). Selection is based on merit.

Financial data The stipend is $3,000.

Duration 1 year.

Additional information This program was established in 1991.

Number awarded 2 each year.

Deadline January of each year.

[297]
ROCKY MOUNTAIN NASA SPACE GRANT
CONSORTIUM UNDERGRADUATE SCHOLARSHIPS

Rocky Mountain NASA Space Grant Consortium
c/o Utah State University
EL Building, Room 302
Logan, UT 84322-4140
(435) 797-4042   Fax: (435) 797-4044
E-mail: rmc@sdl.usu.edu
Web: www.rmc.sdl.usu.edu

Purpose To provide financial support to undergraduate students at designated universities in Utah or Colorado who are working on a degree in fields of interest to the National Aeronautics and Space Administration (NASA).

Eligibility This program is open to undergraduate students at member institutions of the Rocky Mountain NASA Space Grant Consortium who are studying engineering, science, medicine, or technology. U.S. citizenship is required. Selection is based on academic performance to date and potential for the future, with emphasis on space-related research interests. This program is part of the NASA Space Grant program, which encourages participation by women, underrepresented minorities, and persons with disabilities.

Financial data The amount of the awards depends on the availability of funds.

Additional information Members of the consortium are Utah State University, the University of Utah, Brigham Young University, University of Denver, Weber State University, Snow College, and Southern Utah University. This program is funded by NASA.

Number awarded Varies each year.

[298]
RONALD H. BROWN MEMORIAL SCHOLARSHIP

Travel Industry Association of America
Attn: TIA Foundation
1100 New York Avenue, N.W., Suite 450
Washington, DC 20005-3934
(202) 408-8422   Fax: (202) 408-1255
Web: www.tia.org

Purpose To provide financial assistance to minority undergraduate students interested in studying travel and tourism.

Eligibility This program is open to minorities who are interested in pursuing an undergraduate degree in the travel and tourism field. Candidates must first be nominated by a department head at a 4-year college or university that has a travel and tourism program. Nominees are then contacted by the foundation and invited to complete an application, including an essay on what segment of the tourism industry interests them and why.

Financial data The stipend is $3,000 per year.

Duration 1 year.

Number awarded 1 each year.

[299]
RONALD MCDONALD HOUSE CHARITIES/HISPANIC AMERICAN COMMITMENT TO EDUCATIONAL RESOURCES SCHOLARSHIPS

Ronald McDonald House Charities of San Diego
3615 Kearny Villa Road, Suite 104
San Diego, CA 92123-1968
(858) 467-4750, ext. 22
Web: www.sdmcdonalds.com/rmhc_scholarships.lasso

Purpose To provide financial assistance for college to Hispanic high school seniors in San Diego County, California.

Eligibility This program is open to graduating high school seniors who have at least 1 parent of Hispanic origin and are residents of San Diego County (California). U.S. citizenship or permanent resident status is required. Applicants must submit a statement that provides information about their Hispanic background, current community involvement, and potential future contributions to the Hispanic community based on their career goals. Selection is based on that statement, a letter of recommendation, academic achievement in high school, and financial need.

Financial data The stipend is $1,000.

Duration 1 year; nonrenewable.

Additional information The national counterpart of this program was established in 1985. The local program began in 1990.

Number awarded 50 each year.

Deadline March of each year.

[300]
SACNAS–IBM UNDERGRADUATE RESEARCH SCHOLARSHIP

Society for Advancement of Chicanos and Native Americans in Science
333 Front Street, Suite 104
P.O. Box 8526
Santa Cruz, CA 95061-8526
(831) 459-0170   Fax: (831) 459-0194
E-mail: info@sacnas.org
Web: www.sacnas.org

Purpose To provide financial assistance and summer work experience to Native American and Chicano/Latino students majoring in physical science, computer science, or engineering.

Eligibility This program is open to Chicano/Latino and Native American undergraduate students who are currently completing their sophomore or junior years. Applicants must be majoring in chemistry, physics, material science, computer science, or a related engineering field. They must be able to participate in a summer research institute at IBM's Almaden Research Center in San Jose, California.

Financial data The award is $2,500. During the internship period, a stipend is paid.

Duration 1 year, plus a 10-week internship.

Number awarded 1 each year.

Deadline July of each year.

[301]
SACRAMENTO BEE MINORITY JOURNALISM SCHOLARSHIPS

Sacramento Bee
Attn: Community Relations Department
2100 Q Street
P.O. Box 15779
Sacramento, CA 95852
(916) 321-1794   Fax: (916) 321-1783
Web: www.sacbee.com/scholarships

Purpose To provide financial assistance to minority students from the circulation area of the *Sacramento Bee* who are interested in preparing for a career in the newspaper business.

Eligibility This program is open to minorities residing in Sacramento, Placer, Yolo, or western El Dorado counties (California) who are high school seniors or full-time college students. Applicants must have demonstrated an interest in pursuing a career in the newspaper business, including journalism, photography, arts and graphics, online, advertising, or marketing. They must submit an essay of 1,000 to 1,500 words on why they are interested in a career in either newspaper or online media, up to 6 samples of their published work (class assignments and essays are accepted for high school students), a transcript, a resume, and 2 letters of recommendation. High school seniors must have a GPA of 3.0 or higher, current college students 2.5 or higher. Selection is based on the essay (40 points), published work (30 points), transcript (10 points), resume (10 points), and letters of recommendation (10 points). Financial need may also be considered.

Financial data Stipends range from $1,500 to $2,500.
Duration 1 year.
Number awarded Up to 8 each year.
Deadline January of each year.

[302]
SALEF HEALTH SCHOLARSHIP PROGRAM

Salvadoran American Leadership and Educational Fund
Attn: Education and Youth Programs Manager
1625 West Olympic Boulevard, Suite 718
Los Angeles, CA 90015
(213) 480-1052   Fax: (213) 487-2530
E-mail: info@salef.org
Web: www.salef.org

Purpose To provide financial assistance to undergraduate and graduate students of Central American ancestry interested in a health-related career.

Eligibility This program is open to high school seniors and graduates who have been accepted at a 4-year university, undergraduates in 2- and 4-year colleges and universities, and graduate students. Applicants do not need to provide proof of documented immigrant status, but they must be of Central American ancestry and interested in a health-related career (physician, nurse, psychologist, or other professional). Along with their application, they must submit a 750-word statement on their goals, aspirations, and ambitions; ways to give back to the community; leadership involvement; why they chose their field of study; and short- and long-term goals and how they plan to contribute to the community after graduation. They must be able to demonstrate financial need, have a GPA of at least 2.5, and have a history of community service and involvement. An interview may be required.

Financial data Stipends range from $1,000 to $2,500.
Duration 1 year.
Additional information This program began in 2002. Funding is provided by the California Wellness Foundation.
Number awarded 15 each year.
Deadline June of each year.

[303]
SAN DIEGO COUNTY HISPANIC CHAMBER OF COMMERCE SCHOLARSHIP

San Diego County Hispanic Chamber of Commerce
1250 Sixth Avenue, Suite 904
San Diego, CA 92101
(619) 702-0790   Fax: (619) 696-3282
Web: www.sdchcc.com

Purpose To provide financial assistance for college to high school seniors of Hispanic heritage in San Diego County, California.

Eligibility Eligible to apply for these scholarships are high school seniors who reside in San Diego County, California, have a GPA of 3.0 or higher, are U.S. citizens or permanent residents, and have at least 1 parent of Hispanic origin. To apply, students must submit a completed application, an official transcript, a 2-page narrative, proof of citizenship or residency status, and 3 letters of reference. Financial need is not considered in the selection process.

Financial data The maximum stipend is $1,000. Funds are paid directly to the recipient's school.
Duration 1 year.

Deadline May of each year.

[304]
SAN DIEGO GAS & ELECTRIC SCHOLARSHIP FUND

United States Naval Sea Cadet Corps
Attn: Executive Director
2300 Wilson Boulevard
Arlington, VA 22201-3308
(703) 243-6910   Fax: (703) 243-3985

Purpose To provide financial assistance to minority Naval Sea Cadet Corps cadets and former cadets from the San Diego area who are interested in continuing their education at an accredited 4-year college/university.

Eligibility This program is open to cadets and former cadets who are interested in continuing their education at an accredited 4-year college or university. Applicants must be members of a minority group who reside in the area served by San Diego Gas & Electric and are studying, or will study, engineering. They must have been a member of the corps for at least 2 years, have attained a minimum rating of NSCC E-3, be recommended by their commanding officer or other official, have earned a GPA of 3.0 or higher, and have been accepted by an accredited college or university. Applicants may submit financial need statements. All other factors being equal, these statements may be considered in determining award recipients. Applicants who have received full scholarships from other sources (e.g., ROTC) will be considered for this award only if there are no other qualified applicants.

Financial data The stipend is $1,000.
Duration 1 year.
Additional information Cadets are also eligible to apply for scholarships sponsored by the Navy League of the United States.
Number awarded 1 each year.
Deadline May of each year.

[305]
SAN JOSE GI FORUM SCHOLARSHIPS

American GI Forum of San Jose
Attn: San Jose GI Forum Scholarship Foundation
756 Story Road
San Jose, CA 95122
(408) 288-9470   Fax: (408) 923-4356
E-mail: message@sjgif.org
Web: www.sjgif.org/scholarship.htm

Purpose To provide financial assistance for college to Hispanic high school seniors in Santa Clara County, California.

Eligibility Applicants must 1) be graduating from a high school in Santa Clara County, California, 2) have at least 50% Hispanic heritage, and 3) be enrolled or plan to be enrolled in an accredited college or university in a course of study leading to an associate or bachelor's degree. All applicants must participate in a 15-minute oral interview, which focuses on school and extracurricular activities, general leadership qualities, and career aspirations. Selection is based on academic achievements and financial need.

Financial data Stipends are generally at least $1,000 per year. More than $40,000 is distributed annually. Since the program began, more than $1.3 million in scholarships has been awarded.
Duration 1 year or longer.

[306]
SBC L.C. AND DAISY BATES MEMORIAL SCHOLARSHIP

Arkansas Community Foundation
700 South Rock Street
Little Rock, AR 72202
(501) 372-1116 (800) 220-ARCF
Fax: (501) 372-1166 E-mail: acf@arcf.org
Web: www.arcf.org/grantsscholarships/scholarships.html

Purpose To provide financial assistance for college to minorities graduating from high schools in Arkansas.

Eligibility Applicants must be minority high school seniors, U.S. citizens, and residents of Arkansas. They must be planning to attend an accredited 4-year college in Arkansas on a full-time basis. Along with their application, they must submit an essay, up to 500 words, on their plans as they relate to their educational and career objectives and long-term goals. Selection is based on such factors as academics, school activities, community service, future goals, faculty and advisor recommendations, and financial need.

Financial data The stipend is $2,500 per year. Funds are paid directly to the recipient's school and may be used for any legitimate educational expense, such as tuition, fees, books, room, and board.

Duration 1 year.

Additional information This program, which began in 1987, is funded by the SBC Foundation. Neither faxed nor e-mailed applications are accepted.

Number awarded 9 each year.

Deadline March of each year.

[307]
SCHOLARSHIPS FOR MINORITY ACCOUNTING STUDENTS

American Institute of Certified Public Accountants
Attn: Academic and Career Development Division
1211 Avenue of the Americas
New York, NY 10036-8775
(212) 596-6223 Fax: (212) 596-6292
E-mail: educat@aicpa.org
Web: www.aicpa.org/members/div/career/mini/smas.htm

Purpose To provide financial assistance to underrepresented minorities interested in studying accounting at the undergraduate or graduate school level.

Eligibility Undergraduate applicants must be minority students who are enrolled full time, have completed at least 30 semester hours of college work (including at least 6 semester hours in accounting), are majoring in accounting with an overall GPA of 3.3 or higher, and are U.S. citizens or permanent residents. Minority students who are interested in a graduate degree must be 1) in the final year of a 5-year accounting program; 2) an undergraduate accounting major currently accepted or enrolled in a master's-level accounting, business administration, finance, or taxation program; or 3) any undergraduate major currently accepted in a master's-level accounting program. Selection is based primarily on merit (academic and personal achievement); financial need is evaluated as a secondary criteria. For purposes of this program, the American Institute of Certified Public Accountants (AICPA) considers minority students to be those of Black, Native American/Alaskan Native, Pacific Island, or Hispanic ethnic origin.

Financial data The maximum stipend is $5,000 per year.

Duration 1 year; may be renewed, if recipients are making satisfactory progress toward graduation.

Additional information These scholarships are granted by the institute's Minority Educational Initiatives Committee.

Number awarded Varies each year; recently, 187 students received funding through this program.

Deadline June of each year.

[308]
SCIENCE TEACHER PREPARATION PROGRAM

Alabama Alliance for Science, Engineering, Mathematics, and Science Education
Attn: Project Director
University of Alabama at Birmingham
Campbell Hall, Room 401
1300 University Boulevard
Birmingham, AL 35294-1170
(205) 934-8762 Fax: (205) 934-1650
E-mail: LDale@uab.edu
Web: www.uab.edu/istp/alabama.html

Purpose To provide financial assistance to underrepresented minority students at designated institutions in Alabama who are interested in preparing for a career as a science teacher.

Eligibility This program is open to members of underrepresented minority groups who have been unconditionally admitted to a participating Alabama college or university. Applicants may 1) be entering freshmen or junior college transfer students who intend to major in science education and become certified to teach in elementary, middle, or high school; 2) have earned a degree in mathematics, science, or education and now are seeking to become certified to teach; or 3) have earned a degree in mathematics, science, or education and now are enrolled in a fifth-year education program leading to a master's degree and certification.

Financial data The stipend is $1,000 per year.

Duration 1 year; may be renewed.

Additional information Support for this program is provided by the National Science Foundation. The participating institutions are Alabama A&M University, Alabama State University, Auburn University, Miles College, Stillman College, Talladega College, Tuskegee University, University of Alabama at Birmingham, and University of Alabama in Huntsville.

Number awarded Varies each year.

[309]
SCOTTS COMPANY SCHOLARS PROGRAM

Golf Course Superintendents Association of America
Attn: Scholarship Coordinator
1421 Research Park Drive
Lawrence, KS 66049-3859
(785) 832-3678 (800) 472-7878, ext. 678
E-mail: psmith@gcsaa.org
Web: www.gcsaa.org

Purpose To provide financial assistance and summer work experience to high school seniors and college students, particularly those from diverse backgrounds, who are preparing for a career in golf management.

Eligibility This program is open to high school seniors and college students (freshmen, sophomores, and juniors) who are interested in preparing for a career in golf management (the "green industry"). Women and candidates from diverse ethnic, cultural, and socio-economic backgrounds are particularly considered. Selection is based on cultural diversity, academic achievement, extracurricular activities, leadership, employment potential, essay responses, and letters of recommendation. Financial need is not considered. Finalists are selected for summer internships and then compete for scholarships.

Financial data Each intern receives a $500 award. Scholarship stipends are $2,500.

Duration 1 year.

Additional information The program is funded by a permanent endowment established by Scotts Company. Finalists are responsible for securing their own internships.

Number awarded 5 interns and 2 scholarship winners are selected each year.

Deadline February of each year.

[310]
SHARON D. BANKS MEMORIAL UNDERGRADUATE SCHOLARSHIP

Women's Transportation Seminar
Attn: National Headquarters
1666 K Street, N.W., Suite 1100
Washington, DC 20006
(202) 496-4340   Fax: (202) 496-4349
E-mail: wts@wtsnational.org
Web: www.wtsnational.org/scholarship_undergrad.asp

Purpose To provide financial assistance to undergraduate women interested in a career in transportation.

Eligibility This program is open to women who are pursuing an undergraduate degree in transportation or a transportation-related field (e.g., transportation engineering, planning, finance, or logistics). Applicants must have at least a 3.0 GPA and be interested in a career in transportation. They must submit a 500-word statement about their career goals after graduation and why they think they should receive the scholarship award. Applications must be submitted first to a local chapter; the chapters forward selected applications for consideration on the national level. Minority candidates are encouraged to apply. Selection is based on transportation involvement and goals, job skills, and academic record; financial need is not considered.

Financial data The stipend is $2,000.

Duration 1 year.

Additional information The Women's Transportation Seminar (WTS) was founded in 1977 and now has more than 3,000 members, both female and male, in chapters throughout the United States. This scholarship program was established in 1992.

Number awarded 1 each year.

Deadline Applications must be submitted by the end of September to a local WTS chapter.

[311]
SHELL CHEMICAL COMPANY ACS SCHOLARS PROGRAM

American Chemical Society
Attn: Department of Diversity Programs
1155 16th Street, N.W.
Washington, DC 20036
(202) 872-6250   (800) 227-5558, ext. 6250
Fax: (202) 776-8003   E-mail: scholars@acs.org
Web: www.acs.org/scholars

Purpose To provide financial assistance to underrepresented minority high school seniors in selected parts of Texas who have a strong interest in chemistry and a desire to pursue a career in a chemically-related science.

Eligibility This program is open to high school seniors planning to enroll in a 2-year chemical technology program at a school in or near Houston, Texas or in southeastern or southern Texas extending to the Harlingen and Brownsville areas. Applicants must be African American, Hispanic/Latino, or American Indian. Students planning careers in medicine or pharmacy are not eligible. U.S. citizenship or permanent resident status is required. Selection is based on academic merit (GPA of 3.0 or higher) and financial need.

Financial data The maximum stipend is $2,500 per year.

Duration 1 year; may be renewed.

Additional information This program is supported by Shell Chemical Company.

Number awarded Varies each year.

Deadline February of each year.

[312]
SOCIETY OF ACTUARIES SCHOLARSHIPS FOR MINORITY STUDENTS

Society of Actuaries
Attn: Minority Scholarship Coordinator
475 North Martingale Road, Suite 800
Schaumburg, IL 60173-2226
(847) 706-3509   Fax: (847) 706-3599
E-mail: snelson@soa.org
Web: www.beanactuary.org/minority/scholarships.htm

Purpose To provide financial assistance to underrepresented minority undergraduate students who are interested in preparing for an actuarial career.

Eligibility This program is open to African Americans, Hispanics, and Native North Americans who are U.S. citizens or have a permanent resident visa. Before applying for this program, students should have taken either the SAT or the ACT. Applicants must be admitted to a college or university offering either a program in actuarial science or courses that will prepare them for an actuarial career. Scholarships are awarded on the basis of individual merit and financial need.

Financial data The amount of the award depends on the need and merit of the recipient. There is no limit to the size of the scholarship.

Duration 1 year; may be renewed.

Additional information This program is jointly sponsored by the Society of Actuaries and the Casualty Actuarial Society.

Number awarded There is no limit to the number of scholarships awarded.

Deadline April of each year.

[313]
SOCIETY OF HISPANIC PROFESSIONAL ENGINEERS SCHOLARSHIPS

Society of Hispanic Professional Engineers Foundation
Attn: Kathy Borunda
5400 East Olympic Boulevard, Suite 210
Los Angeles, CA 90022
(323) 888-2080   Fax: (323) 888-2089
E-mail: kathy@shpefoundation.org
Web: www.shpefoundation.org/scholarship-program.html

Purpose To provide undergraduate or graduate scholarships to deserving Hispanic American students preparing for a career in engineering or science.

Eligibility Applicants must be enrolled or planning to enroll in an undergraduate or graduate engineering/science program in a college or university. They must be planning to pursue a career in 1 of those areas. Selection is based on an essay on long-range goals (25 points), membership in the Society of Hispanic Professional Engineers (15 points), GPA (15 points), counselor's comments (10 points), school and community activities (10 points), financial need (10 points), educational desire (5 points), and a resume (5 points).

Financial data The stipends range from $500 to $7,000 per year.

Duration 1 academic year; renewal is possible.

Number awarded Varies each year. Recently, 375 of these scholarships, worth $275,000, were awarded.

Deadline April of each year.

[314]
SOUTH CAROLINA SPACE GRANT CONSORTIUM UNDERGRADUATE SCHOLARSHIP PROGRAM

South Carolina Space Grant Consortium
c/o College of Charleston
Department of Geology
58 Coming Street
Charleston, SC 29424
(843) 953-5463   Fax: (843) 953-5446
E-mail: baughmant@cofc.edu
Web: www.cofc.edu/~scsgrant

Purpose To provide financial assistance for space-related study to undergraduate students in South Carolina.

Eligibility This program is open to undergraduate students at member institutions of the South Carolina Space Grant Consortium. Applicants should be rising juniors or seniors majoring in space-related studies, although students from the basic sciences, astronomy, science education, planetary science, environmental studies, engineering, fine arts, and journalism are also eligible to apply. U.S. citizenship is required. Selection is based on academic qualifications of the applicant; 2 letters of recommendation; a description of past activities, current interests, and future plans concerning an aerospace-related field; and faculty sponsorship. The South Carolina Space Grant Consortium is a component of the U.S. National Aeronautics and Space Administration (NASA) Space Grant program, which encourages the participation of women, underrepresented minorities, and persons with disabilities.

Financial data The stipend is $1,500 per year.

Duration 1 year.

Additional information Members of the consortium are Benedict College, The Citadel, College of Charleston, Clemson University, Coastal Carolina University, Furman University, University of

South Carolina, Wofford College, South Carolina State University, The Medical University of South Carolina, and University of the Virgin Islands. This program is funded by NASA.

Number awarded Varies each year.

Deadline January of each year.

[315]
SPACE STATION ENGINEERING SCHOLARS PROGRAM

National Action Council for Minorities in Engineering
350 Fifth Avenue, Suite 2212
New York, NY 10118-2299
(212) 279-2626   Fax: (212) 629-5178
E-mail: awalter@nacme.org
Web: www.nacme.org/univ/scol/nasa.html

Purpose To provide financial assistance to students at designated minority institutions who are majoring in engineering fields relevant to the Human Exploration and Development of Space (HEDS) strategic enterprise of the U.S. National Aeronautics and Space Administration (NASA).

Eligibility This program is open to students majoring in engineering fields relevant to the HEDS strategic enterprise at 5 designated minority institutions. Applicants must have a GPA of 3.0 or higher, be enrolled full time, have earned no more than 39 credit hours, be able to demonstrate financial need, and be U.S. citizens. They must be nominated by the NASA liaison at their university.

Financial data Awards provide support for tuition during the academic year.

Duration 1 year; may be renewed up to 3 additional years if the recipient maintains a GPA of 3.0 or higher and satisfactory academic progress.

Additional information Students submit applications through participating universities; currently, those are California State University at Los Angeles, City College of New York, North Carolina A&T University (Greensboro, North Carolina), Prairie View A&M University (Prairie View, Texas), and the University of Texas at El Paso. The National Action Council for Minorities in Engineering (NACME), in consultation with NASA, selects the recipients. This program began in 2000.

Number awarded Varies each year.

Deadline Nominations are usually made between the months of March and May.

[316]
SPORTS JOURNALISM INSTITUTE

National Association of Black Journalists
Attn: Student Education Enrichment and Development
    Program
8701-A Adelphi Road
Adelphi, MD 20783-1716
(301) 445-7100, ext. 108   Fax: (301) 445-7101
E-mail: warren@nabj.org
Web: www.nabj.org

Purpose To provide student journalists (especially those of color) with an opportunity to learn more about sports journalism during the summer.

Eligibility This program is open to college juniors and sophomores, especially members of ethnic and racial minority groups. Applicants must be interested in participating in a summer program that includes a crash course in sports journalism followed by an internship in the sports department of a daily newspaper. They must submit a current college transcript, 2 letters of recommendation, up to 7 writing samples or clips, and an essay of up to 500 words stating why they should be chosen to participate in the program. Selection is based on academic achievement, demonstrated interest in sports journalism as a career, and the essay. Eligibility is not limited to journalism majors.

Financial data All expenses are paid during the crash course segment. A salary is paid during the internship portion. At the conclusion of the program, participants receive a $500 scholarship for the following year of college.

Duration 10 days for the crash course (at the end of June); 7 weeks for the internship (July through mid-August).

Additional information The crash course takes place during the annual convention of the Associated Press Sports Editors (ASPE), which sponsors this program.

Number awarded 10 each year.

Deadline December of each year.

[317]
SPRINT SCHOLARSHIP PROGRAM

North Carolina Community College System
Attn: Student Support Services
200 West Jones Street
Raleigh, NC 27603-1379
(919) 733-7051   Fax: (919) 733-0680
Web: www.ncccs.cc.nc.us

Purpose To provide financial assistance to North Carolina residents studying at publicly-supported technical or vocational schools in the state.

Eligibility This program is open to North Carolina residents enrolled full time in community colleges in Sprint's local service areas in the state. Applicants must be enrolled or planning to enroll in a course of study leading to an associate of applied science degree or vocational diploma. Priority is given to "displaced workers" and minorities (defined by Sprint as African Americans, Spanish Surname Americans, American Indians/Native Alaskans, and Asians). Selection is based on scholastic achievements, individual financial need, participation in outside activities, and demonstrated interest in a technical or vocational career.

Financial data The stipend is $550 per year.

Duration 1 year; may be renewed 1 additional year if the recipient maintains a GPA at or above the level required for graduation

Additional information Recipients are encouraged to seek employment with Sprint (the program's sponsor) after graduation. There are no special application forms for the scholarship. Students apply to their local community college, not to the system office. Each eligible school selects its own recipients from applicants meeting the above criteria.

Number awarded 70 each year.

[318]
SRI MULTICULTURAL SCHOLARSHIP

Scholarship Research Institute
Attn: Scholarship Selection Committee
P.O. Box 1146
Winona, MN 55987-7146
(507) 453-3675   Fax: (507) 453-3675
E-mail: sri@srifunding.zzn.com
Web: www.angelfire.com/biz/funding

Purpose To provide financial assistance for college to students of color.

Eligibility Applicants for this program must be persons of color attending or planning to attend an institution of higher education, including 2-year colleges and technical schools. Applicants must submit a personal statement on their understanding of cultural diversity and why it is needed. Selection is based only on the statement; GPA, class rank, ACT/SAT scores, and family income are not considered.

Financial data The stipend is $600 per year.

Duration 1 year.

Number awarded Varies each year; recently, 2 of these scholarships were awarded.

Deadline Applications may be submitted at any time.

[319]
STAN BECK FELLOWSHIP

Entomological Society of America
Attn: Entomological Foundation
9301 Annapolis Road, Suite 210
Lanham, MD 20706-3115
(301) 459-9082   Fax: (301) 459-9084
E-mail: melodie@entfdn.org
Web: www.entfdn.org/beck.html

Purpose To assist "needy" students pursuing an undergraduate or graduate degree in science who are nominated by members of the Entomological Society of America (ESA).

Eligibility Candidates for this fellowship must be nominated by members of the society. Nominees may be studying science on any level. However, they must be "needy" students. For the purposes of this program, need may be based on physical limitations, or economic, minority, or environmental conditions.

Financial data The stipend varies each year.

Duration 1 year; may be renewed up to 3 additional years. Recipients are expected to be present at the society's annual meeting, where the award will be presented.

Number awarded 1 or more each year.

Deadline August of each year.

[320]
STANLEY E. JACKSON SCHOLARSHIP AWARD FOR ETHNIC MINORITY GIFTED/TALENTED STUDENTS WITH DISABILITIES

Council for Exceptional Children
Attn: Yes I Can! Foundation for Exceptional Children
1110 North Glebe Road, Suite 300
Arlington, VA 22201-5704
(703) 620-3660   (800) 224-6830, ext. 462
Fax: (703) 264-9494   TTY: (703) 264-9446
E-mail: yesican@cec.sped.org
Web: yesican.sped.org/scholarship/index.html

Purpose To provide financial assistance for college to gifted minority students with disabilities.

Eligibility Applicants must be gifted or talented in 1 or more of the following categories: general intellectual ability, specific academic aptitude, creativity, leadership, or visual or performing arts. They must be disabled, financially needy, ready to begin college, and a member of an ethnic minority group (e.g., Asian, African American, Hispanic, or Native American). Candidates must submit a 250-word statement of philosophical, educational, and occupational goals as part of the application process. Selection is based on academic achievement, ability, promise, and financial need. U.S. citizenship is required.

Financial data The stipend is $500.

Duration 1 year; nonrenewable.

Additional information Scholarships may be used for 2- or 4-year college programs or for vocational, technical, or fine arts training programs. Recipients must enroll full time.

Number awarded 1 or more each year.

Deadline January of each year.

[321]
STANLEY E. JACKSON SCHOLARSHIP AWARD FOR ETHNIC MINORITY STUDENTS WITH DISABILITIES

Council for Exceptional Children
Attn: Yes I Can! Foundation for Exceptional Children
1110 North Glebe Road, Suite 300
Arlington, VA 22201-5704
(703) 620-3660   (800) 224-6830, ext. 462
Fax: (703) 264-9494   TTY: (703) 264-9446
E-mail: yesican@cec.sped.org
Web: yesican.sped.org/scholarship/index.html

Purpose To provide financial assistance for college to minority students with disabilities.

Eligibility Applicants must be students with disabilities who intend to enroll for the first time on a full-time basis in a college, university, vocational/technical school, or fine arts institute and are able to document financial need. Only minority (African American, Asian, Native American, or Hispanic) students are eligible for the award. Candidates must submit a 250-word statement of philosophical, educational, and occupational goals as part of the application process. Selection is based on academic achievement, ability, promise, and financial need. U.S. citizenship is required.

Financial data The stipend is $500.

Duration 1 year; nonrenewable.

Additional information Scholarships may be used for 2- or 4-year college programs or for vocational, technical, or fine arts training programs. Recipients must enroll full time.

Number awarded 1 or more each year.

Deadline January of each year.

[322]
STRATTON/TIPTON SCHOLARSHIP FOR ADULT RETURNING STUDENTS

Kentucky Association of Vocational Education Special Needs Personnel
c/o Donna Ledden
Boone County High School
7056 Burlington Pike
Florence, KY 41042
(859) 282-5655   E-mail: dledden1@boone.k12.ky.us
Web: www.kavesnp.org/scholar.htm

Purpose To provide financial assistance to students with special needs enrolled at a college or university in Kentucky.

Eligibility This program is open to residents of Kentucky who are studying for 1) an associate degree or certificate/diploma through the Kentucky Community and Technical College System (KCTCS), or 2) an associate or bachelor's degree from a Kentucky college or university. Applicants must meet the definition of a special needs student: persons with disabilities, educationally and economically disadvantaged people, foster children, individuals preparing for nontraditional employment, single parents (including single pregnant women), displaced homemakers, individuals of limited English language proficiency, individuals in a correctional institution, and individuals with other barriers to educational achievement. They must have a GPA of 2.5 or higher from the most recently completed semester of course work at a KCTCS institution or a Kentucky college or university. Selection is based on academic achievement, letters of reference, and career potential.

Financial data The stipend is $500.

Duration 1 year; nonrenewable.

Number awarded 1 each year.

Deadline March of each year.

[323]
STRATTON/TIPTON SCHOLARSHIP FOR HIGH SCHOOL SENIORS

Kentucky Association of Vocational Education Special Needs Personnel
c/o Donna Ledden
Boone County High School
7056 Burlington Pike
Florence, KY 41042
(859) 282-5655   E-mail: dledden1@boone.k12.ky.us
Web: www.kavesnp.org/scholar.htm

Purpose To provide financial assistance for college to high school seniors with special needs in Kentucky.

Eligibility This program is open to seniors at high schools in Kentucky who are planning to 1) enroll in a certificate/diploma program or associate degree program at an institution that is part of the Kentucky Community and Technical College System (KCTCS), or 2) work on an associate or bachelor's degree at a college or university. Applicants must meet the definition of a special needs student: persons with disabilities, educationally and economically disadvantaged people, foster children, individuals preparing for nontraditional employment, single parents (including single pregnant women), displaced homemakers, individuals of limited English language proficiency, individuals in a correctional institution, and individuals with other barriers to educational achievement. They must have a cumulative GPA of 2.5 or higher for grades 9-12. Selection is based on academic achievement, letters of reference, and career potential.

Financial data The stipend is $500.

Duration 1 year; nonrenewable.

Number awarded 1 each year.

Deadline March of each year.

[324]
STUDENT CEC ETHNIC DIVERSITY SCHOLARSHIP

Council for Exceptional Children
Attn: Coordinator of Student Activities
1110 North Glebe Road, Suite 300
Arlington, VA 22201-5704
(703) 264-9412   (888) CEC-SPED
Fax: (703) 264-9494   TTY: (703) 264-9446
E-mail: charlesr@cec.sped.org
Web: www.cec.sped.org/ab/awards.html

Purpose To provide financial assistance to ethnic minority student members of the Council for Exceptional Children (CEC).

Eligibility Eligible are student members of the council who are citizens of the United States or Canada, members of an ethnically diverse group (African American or Black, American Indian, Alaska Native, Native Canadian, Hispanic, Asian, or Pacific Islander), and juniors, seniors, or graduate students enrolled in an accredited college or university. They must be majoring in special education and have a GPA of 2.5 or higher. Applicants must provide 2 letters of recommendation, a summary of Student CEC and/or other activities relating to individuals with disabilities, and a brief biography explaining why they chose special education as a career, how they view the role of special educators, and what they hope to accomplish as a special educator. Financial need is not considered.

Financial data The stipend is $500.

Duration 1 year; nonrenewable.

Number awarded 1 each year.

Deadline November of each year.

[325]
STUDENT OPPORTUNITY SCHOLARSHIPS FOR ETHNIC MINORITY GROUPS

Presbyterian Church (USA)
Attn: Office of Financial Aid for Studies
100 Witherspoon Street, Room M042
Louisville, KY 40202-1396
(502) 569-5745   (877) 728-7228, ext. 5745
Fax: (502) 569-8766   E-mail: KSmith@ctr.pcusa.org
Web: www.pcusa.org/highered

Purpose To provide financial assistance for college to high school seniors of racial/ethnic minority heritage who are Presbyterians.

Eligibility This program is open to members of the Presbyterian Church (USA) who are from racial/ethnic minority groups (Asian American, African American, Hispanic American, Native American, Alaska Native). Applicants must be able to demonstrate financial need, be high school seniors entering college as full-time students, and be U.S. citizens or permanent residents. They must submit a recommendation from their high school guidance counselor, a high school transcript, and an essay (up to 500 words in length) on their career goals and how they plan to achieve them.

Financial data Stipends range from $100 to $1,000 per year, depending upon the financial need of the recipient.

Duration 1 year; may be renewed for up to 3 additional years if the recipient continues to need financial assistance and demonstrates satisfactory academic progress.

Number awarded Varies each year.

Deadline March of each year.

[326]
SYNOD OF LIVING WATERS RACIAL ETHNIC COLLEGE SCHOLARSHIP

Synod of Living Waters
318 Seaboard Lane, Suite 205
Franklin, TN 37067-8242
(615) 261-4008   Fax: (615) 261-4010
E-mail: info@synodoflivingwaters.com
Web: www.synodoflivingwaters.com

Purpose To provide financial assistance to minority college students who reside within the boundaries of the Presbyterian Synod of Living Waters.

Eligibility This program is open to members of racial ethnic minorities (African American, Asian American, Hispanic American, or Native American) who reside within the Synod of Living Waters (Alabama, Kentucky, Mississippi, and Tennessee). Applicants must be full-time students attending a synod Presbyterian college. They must have a GPA of 3.0 or higher, be able to demonstrate participation in the spiritual life of their school, and have financial need.

Financial data The stipend is $1,000.

Duration 1 year.

Number awarded 10 each year.

[327]
SYNOD OF THE COVENANT ETHNIC FULL-TIME SCHOLARSHIPS

Synod of the Covenant
Attn: CECA Ethnic Scholarship Committee
6172 Busch Boulevard, Suite 3000
Columbus, OH 43229
(614) 436-3310   (800) 848-1030
E-mail: larrye@unidial.com
Web: www.synodofcovenant.org/ceca/scholarship.html

Purpose To provide financial assistance to ethnic students working full time on an undergraduate degree (with priority given to Presbyterian applicants from Ohio and Michigan).

Eligibility This funding is available for full-time study toward a baccalaureate degree or certification at a college, university, or vocational school. The program is open to ethnic students. Priority is given to Presbyterian applicants from the states of Michigan and Ohio. Financial need is considered in the selection process.

Financial data The maximum amount allowed within a calendar year is between $600 (for first-time applicants) and $800 (for renewals). Funds are made payable to the session for distribution.

Duration Students are eligible to receive scholarships 1 time per year, up to a maximum of 5 years. Renewals are granted provided 1) the completed application is received before the deadline date, 2) the recipient earned at least a 3.0 GPA last year, and 3) the application contains evidence of Presbyterian church participation and continued spiritual development.

Number awarded Varies each year.

Deadline Applications must be submitted by the end of January for the spring semester and by mid-August for the fall semester.

[328]
TALLAHASSEE DEMOCRAT/KNIGHT RIDDER MINORITY SCHOLARSHIPS

Tallahassee Democrat
Attn: Community Relations
277 North Magnolia Drive
P.O. Box 990
Tallahassee, FL 32302
(850) 599-2181   E-mail: avalencic@taldem.com
Web: www.tallahaseee.com/mld/democrat

Purpose To provide financial assistance for college to minority high school seniors from the circulation area of the *Tallahassee Democrat* who are interested in preparing for a career in journalism or the communications business.

Eligibility This program is open to minority seniors at high schools in the Big Bend area of Florida who plan to enter journalism or the communications business. Along with their application, they must submit 2 letters of recommendation; transcripts; SAT or ACT scores; up to 5 samples of their work with bylines or other examples; and an essay covering why they want to pursue a career in newspapers, what they know about Knight Ridder, and how they see themselves working at Knight Ridder. Selection is based primarily on academic performance and participation in school activities.

Financial data The stipend is $500.

Duration 1 year.

Additional information The recipients of these scholarships are automatically entered into competition for the Knight Ridder Minority Scholarship Program of $10,000 per year for 4 years.

Number awarded 1 or more each year.

Deadline January of each year.

[329]
TAYLOR MICHAELS SCHOLARSHIP PROGRAM

Magic Johnson Foundation
600 Corporate Pointe, Suite 1080
Culver City, CA 90230
(888) MAGIC-05
Web: www.magicjohnson.org/aboutmjf/taylorm.html

Purpose To provide financial assistance to high school seniors from designated inner-city areas who are interested in attending a 4-year university.

Eligibility This program is open to seniors at high schools in inner-city areas of Atlanta, Cleveland, Houston, Los Angeles, and New York. Applicants must have a GPA of 2.5 or higher and be planning to attend a 4-year university in the following fall. They must agree to participate in various activities of the sponsor, including a mentoring program, life and practical skills classes conducted by the foundation staff and guest presenters, and "A Midsummer Night's Magic" scholarship award ceremony.

Financial data A stipend is provided (amount not specified).

Duration 4 years.

Additional information This program was established in 1998. During their 4 years in college, scholars continue to participate in activities arranged by the sponsor: mentorship for incoming scholarship recipients, community service, support of sponsor events as volunteers, seminars that assist students applying for graduate school, and seminars that assist students in making the transition from college to the workplace.

Number awarded Varies each year. Since its establishment, 83 students have received support.

[330]
TEACHER EDUCATION SCHOLARSHIP PROGRAM OF THE ALABAMA SPACE GRANT CONSORTIUM

Alabama Space Grant Consortium
c/o University of Alabama in Huntsville
Materials Science Building, Room 205
Huntsville, AL 35899
(256) 890-6800   Fax: (256) 890-6061
E-mail: jfreasoner@matsci.uah.edu
Web: www.uah.edu/ASGC

Purpose To provide financial assistance to undergraduate students at universities participating in the Alabama Space Grant Consortium who wish to prepare for a career as a teacher of science or mathematics.

Eligibility This program is open to students enrolled in or accepted for enrollment as full-time undergraduates at universities in Alabama participating in the consortium. Applicants must intend to enter the teacher certification program and teach in a pre-college setting. Priority is given to those majoring in science, mathematics, or earth/space/environmental science. Applicants should have a GPA of 3.0 or higher and must be U.S. citizens. Individuals from underrepresented groups (African Americans, Hispanic Americans, American Indians, Pacific Islanders, and women of all races) are encouraged to apply.

Financial data The stipend is $1,000 per year.

Duration 1 year; nonrenewable.

Additional information The member universities are University of Alabama in Huntsville, Alabama A&M University, University of Alabama, University of Alabama at Birmingham, University of South Alabama, Tuskegee University, and Auburn University. Funding for this program is provided by NASA.

Number awarded Varies each year; recently, 4 of these scholarships were awarded.

Deadline February of each year.

[331]
TEACHERS FOR TOMORROW SCHOLARSHIP PROGRAM

Edison International
Attn: Educational Relations
P.O. Box 800
Rosemead, CA 91770
(626) 302-3382   Fax: (626) 302-3007
Web: www.edison.com

Purpose To provide financial assistance to students at designated campuses of the California State University (CSU) system who are working on their teaching credential.

Eligibility This program is open to students enrolled as a full-time CSU student in a teacher preparation program (single subject, multiple subject, or special education credential) at designated campuses in southern California. Applicants must have a cumulative GPA of 3.0 or higher and be able to demonstrate financial need. Preference is given to applicants who are economically and educationally disadvantaged (particularly minorities). Selection is based on 2 letters of reference, a 2-page essay describing reasons for entering the teaching profession, and a

1-page statement that reflects a commitment to education and service to the community.

Financial data The stipend is $5,000 per year.

Duration 1 year.

Additional information The eligible CSU campuses are those at Dominguez Hills, Fullerton, Long Beach, Los Angeles, Northridge, Pomona, and San Bernardino. This program was established in 1999.

Number awarded 25 each year.

Deadline Students must apply to the financial aid office of their university by January of each year; each financial aid officer must submit the nominations from that institution by February of each year.

[332]
TECH FORCE/3M PRE-ENGINEERING PRIZES

National Action Council for Minorities in Engineering
350 Fifth Avenue, Suite 2212
New York, NY 10118-2299
(212) 279-2626   Fax: (212) 629-5178
E-mail: awalter@nacme.org
Web: www.nacme.org/prec/scol/techforce.html

Purpose To provide financial assistance to underrepresented minority high school seniors who are planning a career in chemical or mechanical engineering.

Eligibility This program is open to African American, Latino, and American Indian high school seniors who have demonstrated outstanding academic achievement, community involvement, and participation in precollege math and science programs. Students must be nominated by directors of pre-college or high school programs focused on mathematics, science, and engineering that are recognized by the National Association of Pre-college Directors. They must have been admitted as full-time students at a 4-year accredited program in chemical or mechanical engineering. U.S. citizenship or permanent resident status is required.

Financial data The stipend is $2,500 per year.

Duration 4 years.

Additional information This program is supported by the 3M Company.

Number awarded 2 each year.

Deadline December of each year.

[333]
TELACU ARTS AWARD

TELACU Education Foundation
5400 East Olympic Boulevard, Suite 300
Los Angeles, CA 90022
(323) 721-1655   Fax: (323) 724-3372
E-mail: info@telacu.com
Web: www.telacu.com

Purpose To provide financial assistance to Latino students in the Los Angeles area who are interested in studying the arts in college.

Eligibility This program is open to Latino high school seniors and continuing undergraduate students residing in unincorporated areas of east Los Angeles, as well as the cities of Bell Gardens, Commerce, Huntington Park, Los Angeles, Montebello, Monterey Park, Pico Rivera, Santa Ana, and South Gate. Applicants may attend any postsecondary institution as long as they major in fine arts, music, dance, drama, or theater. Continuing college students must maintain a GPA of 2.5 or higher. Selection

is based on an interview and 2 essays: 1 that addresses their goals and ambitions, reasons for pursuing a degree in the field they have chosen, commitment to their community, and how they plan to help their community after graduation, and 1 that describes why they should be considered for this special award.

Financial data The stipend is $1,000.

Duration 1 year; renewable.

Number awarded 1 each year.

Deadline April of each year.

[334]
TELACU ENGINEERING AWARD

TELACU Education Foundation
5400 East Olympic Boulevard, Suite 300
Los Angeles, CA 90022
(323) 721-1655   Fax: (323) 724-3372
E-mail: info@telacu.com
Web: www.telacu.com

Purpose To provide financial assistance to Latino college students from the Los Angeles area of California who are interested in majoring in selected science or business fields.

Eligibility This program is open to Latino residents of unincorporated portions of east Los Angeles and the cities of Bell Gardens, Commerce, Huntington Park, Los Angeles, Montebello, Monterey Park, Pico Rivera, Santa Ana, and South Gate. Applicants must 1) be majoring in computer science, quantitative business, chemistry, or engineering at 1 of 23 designated colleges or universities; 2) have completed at least 12 college credits with a GPA of 3.0 or higher; 3) be a first-generation college student; 4) be from a low-income family, and 5) be a U.S. citizen, national, or permanent resident. Selection is based on an interview and 2 essays: 1 that addresses their goals and ambitions, reasons for pursuing a degree in the field they have chosen, commitment to their community, and how they plan to help their community after graduation, and 1 that describes why they should be considered for this special award.

Financial data The stipend is $10,000 per year.

Duration 1 year.

Number awarded 1 each year.

Deadline April of each year.

[335]
TELACU SCHOLARSHIPS

TELACU Education Foundation
5400 East Olympic Boulevard, Suite 300
Los Angeles, CA 90022
(323) 721-1655   Fax: (323) 724-3372
E-mail: info@telacu.com
Web: www.telacu.com

Purpose To provide financial assistance to Latino students in the Los Angeles area who are interested in furthering their formal education at the undergraduate level.

Eligibility This program is open to Latino students residing in unincorporated areas of east Los Angeles, as well as the cities of Bell Gardens, Commerce, Huntington Park, Los Angeles, Montebello, Monterey Park, Pico Rivera, Santa Ana, and South Gate. Applicants must 1) be a first-generation college student; 2) be from a low-income family; 3) have a GPA of 2.5 or higher; and 4) be a U.S. citizen, national, or permanent resident. They must be attending or planning to attend 1 of 23 participating institutions in southern California. Full-time enrollment is required.

Selection is based on an interview and a 200-word narrative that addresses their goals and ambitions, reasons for pursuing a degree in the field they have chosen, commitment to their community, and how they plan to help their community after graduation.

Financial data Stipends range from $500 to $1,500 per year.

Duration Up to 4 years.

Number awarded Varies each year.

Deadline April of each year.

[336]
TEXAS BROADCAST EDUCATION FOUNDATION SCHOLARSHIPS

Texas Broadcast Education Foundation
c/o Texas Association of Broadcasters
502 East 11th Street, Suite 200
Austin, TX 78701-2619
(512) 322-9944   Fax: (512) 322-0522
E-mail: tab@tab.org
Web: www.tab.org/scholarships.html

Purpose To provide financial assistance to undergraduates in Texas who are interested in preparing for a career in broadcasting.

Eligibility This program is open to students enrolled in a fully-accredited program of instruction that emphasizes radio or television broadcasting or communications at a college that is a member of Texas Association of Broadcast Educators. Applicants must have a GPA of 2.5 or higher and submit a letter from the department head certifying that they have a reasonable chance of successfully completing the course of instruction. Selection is based on depth of thought, clarity of expression, commitment to broadcasting, extracurricular activities, community involvement, and financial need. All students are encouraged to apply; special consideration is given to students from disadvantaged ethnic or economic backgrounds.

Financial data The stipend is $2,000.

Duration 1 year.

Additional information Awards include the Belo Corporation Scholarship for a junior or senior at a 4-year college, the Bonner McLane Scholarship for a junior or senior at a 4-year college, the Tom Reiff Scholarship for a rising junior or senior at a 4-year college, the Lady Bird Johnson Scholarship for a University of Texas at Austin student, the Vann Kennedy Scholarship for a student at any college or university, the Wendell Mayes, Jr. Scholarship for a student at any college or university, an unnamed scholarship for a freshman or sophomore at a 4-year college, and another unnamed scholarship for a student at a 2-year college or technical school.

Number awarded 8 each year.

Deadline May of each year.

[337]
TEXAS SPACE GRANT CONSORTIUM UNDERGRADUATE SCHOLARSHIPS

Texas Space Grant Consortium
Attn: Administrative Assistant
3925 West Braker Lane, Suite 200
Austin, TX 78759
(512) 471-3583   (800) 248-8742
Fax: (512) 471-3585   E-mail: jurgens@tsgc.utexas.edu
Web: www.tsgc.utexas.edu/grants

Purpose To provide financial assistance for undergraduate study at Texas universities in the fields of space science and engineering.

Eligibility Applicants must be U.S. citizens, eligible for financial assistance, and registered for full-time study as juniors or seniors in an undergraduate program at 1 of the participating universities. Students apply to their university representative; each representative then submits up to 3 candidates into the statewide selection process. The program encourages participation by members of groups underrepresented in science and engineering (persons with disabilities, women, African Americans, Hispanic Americans, Native Americans, and Pacific Islanders). Scholarships are awarded competitively, on the basis of above-average performance in academics, participation in space education projects, participation in research projects, and exhibited leadership qualities.

Financial data The stipend is $1,000.

Duration 1 year; nonrenewable.

Additional information The participating universities are Baylor University, Lamar University, Prairie View A&M University, Rice University, Southern Methodist University, Sul Ross State University, Texas A&M University at Kingsville, Texas A&M University, Texas Christian University, Texas Southern University, Texas Tech University, University of Houston, University of Houston/Clear Lake, University of Houston/Downtown, University of Texas at Arlington, University of Texas at Austin, University of Texas at Dallas, University of Texas at El Paso, University of Texas at San Antonio, University of Texas–Pan American, and West Texas A&M University. This program is funded by the National Aeronautics and Space Administration (NASA).

Number awarded Approximately 20 to 25 each year.

Deadline April of each year.

[338]
TEXAS YES! SCHOLARSHIPS

Texas Engineering Foundation
Attn: Programs Director
3501 Manor Road
P.O. Box 2145
Austin, TX 78768
(512) 472-9286   (800) 580-8973 (within TX)
Fax: (512) 472-2934   E-mail: scholarships@tspe.org
Web: www.tspe.org

Purpose To provide financial assistance to high school seniors in Texas who are women or minorities or have participated in designated educational programs and are interested in majoring in engineering in college.

Eligibility This program is open to high school seniors in Texas who have a GPA of 3.0 or higher, have minimum scores of 600 in math and 550 in verbal on the SAT or 29 in math and 25 in English on the ACT, are planning to major in engineering in college, are U.S. citizens, and are planning to attend a Texas college or university with an ABET-accredited engineering program. Applicants must be women or minorities or have participated in 1 or more of the following educational programs offered by the Texas Society of Professional Engineers (TSPE): JETS or Texas YES! chapters in junior or senior high school; MATHCOUNTS for students in the seventh and eighth grades; National Engineering Design Challenge or the Texas Engineering Challenge for high school students; TEAMS competitions for high school students; or the Texas Engineering Skills Competitions for high school students. They must submit an essay of up to 750 words on the people and/or events in their lives that led them to choose to study engineering, accomplishments that illustrate their aptitude for and interest in engineering, and the aspects of engineering that influenced their decision to select it as a profession. Selection is based on academic record, achievement, leadership, and career goals. Financial need is not considered in the selection process.

Financial data The stipend is $1,000.

Duration 1 year.

Additional information These scholarships are sponsored by TSPE and the Texas Engineering Foundation.

Number awarded 3 each year.

Deadline January of each year.

[339]
TILLIE GOLUB-SCHWARTZ MEMORIAL SCHOLARSHIP FOR MINORITIES

Golub Foundation
c/o Price Chopper Scholarship Office, Mailbox 60
P.O. Box 1074
Schenectady, NY 12301
(518) 356-9450   (877) 877-0870
Web: www.pricechopper.com

Purpose To provide financial assistance for college to minority high school seniors in selected areas of Connecticut, Massachusetts, New Hampshire, New York, Pennsylvania, and Vermont.

Eligibility This program is open to high school seniors in areas of Connecticut, Massachusetts, New Hampshire, New York, Pennsylvania, and Vermont served by Price Chopper Supermarkets who plan to attend an accredited 2-year or 4-year college or university in those states. Applicants must be Alaskan Native, American Indian, Asian, Pacific Islander, Black (not of Hispanic origin), Puerto Rican, Mexican American, or other Hispanic. Along with their application, they must submit information on their educational history, including grades, Regents marks (if applicable), rank in class, and SAT and/or ACT scores; honors and awards; participation in school, extracurricular, civic, and/or leadership activities; 3 reference letters; and a 1,000-word essay on how they have demonstrated a commitment to humanity through their involvement in community, church, and/or school activities.

Financial data The stipend is $2,000 per year.

Duration 4 years.

Additional information The Golub Corporation is the parent company of Price Chopper Supermarkets, which operates in the following counties: in Connecticut, Litchfield, New Haven, and Windham; in Massachusetts, Berkshire, Hampden, Hampshire, Middlesex, and Worcester; in New Hampshire, Cheshire, Grafton, and Sullivan; in New York, Albany, Broome, Cayuga, Chenango, Clinton, Columbia, Cortland, Delaware, Dutchess, Essex, Franklin, Fulton, Greene, Hamilton, Herkimer, Jefferson, Lewis, Madison, Montgomery, Oneida, Onondaga, Orange, Oswego, Otsego, Rensselaer, St. Lawrence, Saratoga, Schenectady, Sullivan, Schoharie, Tioga, Tompkins, Ulster, Warren, and Washington; in

Pennsylvania, Lackawanna, Luzerne, Susquehanna, Wayne, and Wyoming; in Vermont, Addison, Bennington, Caledonia, Chittenden, Essex, Franklin, Grand Isle, Lamoille, Orange, Orleans, Rutland, Washington, Windham, and Windsor.

Number awarded 1 each year.

Deadline March of each year.

[340]
TRANSFER ENGINEERING STUDENT AWARD

National Association of Minority Engineering Program
    Administrators, Inc.
1133 West Morse Boulevard, Suite 201
Winter Park, FL 32789
(407) 647-8839   Fax: (407) 629-2502
E-mail: namepa@namepa.org
Web: www.namepa.org/pages/awards.htm

Purpose To provide financial assistance to underrepresented minority college transfer students who are planning to major in engineering.

Eligibility This program is open to African American, Hispanic, and American Indian college transfer students who are coming from a junior college, community college, or 3/2 dual-degree program. Applicants must be transferring to an engineering program at an institution affiliated with the National Association of Minority Engineering Program Administrators (NAMEPA). For a list of affiliated schools, write to the sponsor. They must have a GPA of 3.0 or higher. Along with their application, they must submit a copy of their college transcript, a letter of recommendation, and a 1-page essay on why they have chosen engineering as a profession, why they think they should be selected, and an overview of their future aspirations as an engineer. Financial need is not considered in the selection process.

Financial data The stipend is $1,000, paid in 2 equal installments.

Duration 1 year; nonrenewable.

Deadline March of each year.

[341]
TYLER WARD MINORITY JOURNALISM SCHOLARSHIP

Society of Professional Journalists-Mid-Florida Chapter
c/o Randy Miller
University of South Florida
School of Mass Communications
4202 East Fowler Avenue, CIS 1040
Tampa, FL 33620-7800
(813) 974-6791   Fax: (813) 974-2592
E-mail: rmiller@chuma.cas.usf.edu

Purpose To provide financial assistance to minority students in mid-Florida who are interested in preparing for a career in journalism.

Eligibility This program is open to minority college students who are from the mid-Florida (Tampa Bay and Orlando areas) region or who attend colleges or universities there. Applicants must submit an essay on why they want to become a journalist and a reference letter from a journalism professor or a campus media adviser.

Financial data The stipend is $1,000.

Duration 1 year.

Number awarded 1 each year.

Deadline November of each year.

[342]
UNCF/HOUSEHOLD CORPORATE SCHOLARS PROGRAM

United Negro College Fund
Attn: Program Services Department
8260 Willow Oaks Corporate Drive
P.O. Box 10444
Fairfax, VA 22031-8044
(703) 205-3490   (866) 671-7237
Fax: (703) 205-3550   E-mail: internship@uncf.org
Web: www.uncf.org/Scholarship/CorporateScholars.asp

Purpose To provide financial assistance and work experience to minority and other students majoring in fields related to business.

Eligibility This program is open to rising juniors majoring in accounting, business, computer science, finance, human resources, or marketing with a GPA of 3.0 or higher. Applicants must be interested in an internship with Household, the program's sponsor, at 1 of the following sites: Bridgewater, New Jersey; Charlotte, North Carolina; Chesapeake, Virginia; Chicago, Illinois; Dallas, Texas; Indianapolis, Indiana; Jacksonville, Florida; Monterey, California; New Castle, Delaware; San Diego, California; and Tampa, Florida. Preference is given to applicants who reside in those areas, but students who live in other areas are also considered. African Americans, Hispanics, Native Americans, and Asian Americans are encouraged to apply. Along with their application, students must submit a 1-page personal statement, a letter of recommendation, and a current undergraduate transcript.

Financial data The students selected for this program receive paid internships and need-based scholarships that range from $5,000 to $10,000 per year.

Duration 8 to 10 weeks for the internships; 1 year for the scholarships, which may be renewed.

Number awarded Varies each year.

Deadline February of each year.

[343]
UNCF/SPRINT SCHOLARS PROGRAM

United Negro College Fund
Attn: Program Services Department
8260 Willow Oaks Corporate Drive
P.O. Box 10444
Fairfax, VA 22031-8044
(703) 205-3490   (866) 671-7237
Fax: (703) 205-3550   E-mail: internship@uncf.org
Web: www.uncf.org/Scholarship/CorporateScholars.asp

Purpose To provide financial assistance and work experience to minority students who are interested in preparing for a career in telecommunications.

Eligibility This program is open to members of minority groups who are enrolled full time as seniors at a 4-year college or university in the United States. Applicants must have a GPA of 3.0 or higher and be majoring in accounting, communications, computer engineering, computer science, economics, electrical engineering, finance, industrial engineering, information systems, journalism, logistics, marketing, management information systems, public relations, or statistics. They must be interested in a summer internship at Sprint. Along with their application, they must submit a 500-word personal statement describing their career interests and goals. Selection is based on GPA, demonstrated skills and abilities, and interest in pursuing a career in telecommunications. Preference is given to students at the 39 member institutions of the United Negro College Fund (UNCF), other Historically Black Colleges and Universities (HBCUs), and the following schools: Central Missouri State University, DeVry Institutes, Georgia Institute of Technology, Iowa State University, Kansas State University, Northwest Missouri State University, North Carolina State University, Oklahoma State University, Pittsburg State University, Rockhurst University, Southwest Missouri State University, Truman State University, University of Florida, University of Kansas, University of Missouri at Columbia, University of Missouri at Kansas City, University of Missouri at Rolla, University of Nebraska at Lincoln, Virginia Tech, Washburn University, and Wichita State University.

Financial data Each student receives $2,500 as well as additional compensation for the internship, a need-based scholarship up to $7,500, and a travel allowance of $500.

Duration 1 year.

Additional information The corporate sponsor of this program, Sprint, also provides mentorships to the participating students.

Number awarded Varies each year.

Deadline November of each year.

[344]
UNDERGRADUATE SCHOLARSHIP PROGRAM OF THE ALABAMA SPACE GRANT CONSORTIUM

Alabama Space Grant Consortium
c/o University of Alabama in Huntsville
Materials Science Building, Room 205
Huntsville, AL 35899
(256) 890-6800   Fax: (256) 890-6061
E-mail: jfreasoner@matsci.uah.edu
Web: www.uah.edu/ASGC

Purpose To provide financial assistance to undergraduates who are studying the space sciences at universities participating in the Alabama Space Grant Consortium.

Eligibility This program is open to full-time students entering their junior or senior year at the universities participating in the Alabama Space Grant Consortium. Applicants must be studying in a field related to space, including the physical, natural, and biological sciences; engineering, education; economics; business; sociology; behavioral sciences; computer science; communications; law; international affairs; and public administration. They must be U.S. citizens and have a GPA of 3.0 or higher. Individuals from underrepresented groups (African Americans, Hispanic Americans, American Indians, Pacific Islanders, Asian Americans, and women of all races) are encouraged to apply. Interested students should submit a completed application with a career goal statement, personal references, a brief resume, and transcripts. Selection is based on 1) academic qualifications, 2) quality of the career goal statement, and 3) an assessment of the applicant's motivation for a career in aerospace.

Financial data The stipend is $1,000 per year.

Duration 1 year; may be renewed 1 additional year.

Additional information The member universities are University of Alabama in Huntsville, Alabama A&M University, University of Alabama, University of Alabama at Birmingham, University of South Alabama, Tuskegee University, and Auburn University. Funding for this program is provided by NASA.

Number awarded Varies each year; recently, 37 of these scholarships were awarded.

Deadline February of each year.

[345]

UNITED CHURCH OF CHRIST SPECIAL HIGHER EDUCATION PROGRAM

United Church of Christ
Attn: Justice and Witness Ministries
Higher Education Program
700 Prospect Avenue East
Cleveland, OH 44115-1100
(216) 736-2169   Fax: (216) 736-2171
E-mail: whited@ucc.org
Web: www.ucc.org

Purpose To provide financial assistance for college to minority undergraduate students who are members of the United Church of Christ.

Eligibility Undergraduate students are eligible to apply for this support if they are African Americans, Native Americans, Asian Americans, or Hispanics and have financial need. Members of the United Church of Christ (UCC), especially those participating in the UCC Matching Program, receive priority, as do students at UCC-related colleges. Applicants who do not have large financial assistance packages, and who are not outstanding athletes or scholars, also receive priority.

Financial data Awards range from $150 to $250 per semester (maximum: $500/year).

Duration 1 semester; may be renewed.

Additional information The United Church of Christ's Justice and Witness Ministries offers recipients assistance in locating other sources of financial aid, tutorials, and other special services beneficial to them while in college. It also counsels students on adjusting to college life and parents on the dynamics of higher education, including the availability and acquisition of financial aid and the procedures for filing applications.

Number awarded Up to 200 each year.

Deadline June of each year for fall; December of each year for spring.

[346]

UNITED METHODIST SCHOLARSHIP PROGRAM

United Methodist Church
Attn: Office of Loans and Scholarships
1001 19th Avenue South
P.O. Box 871
Nashville, TN 37202-0871
(615) 340-7344   Fax: (615) 340-7367
E-mail: umscholar@gbhem.org
Web: www.gbhem.org

Purpose To provide financial assistance to undergraduate and graduate students attending schools affiliated with the United Methodist Church.

Eligibility This program is open to U.S. citizens and permanent residents who have been active, full members of a United Methodist Church for at least 1 year prior to applying; members of the A.M.E., A.M.E. Zion, and other "Methodist" denominations are not eligible. Undergraduates must have been admitted to a full-time degree program at a United Methodist-related college or university and have earned a GPA of 2.5 or above. Most graduate scholarships are designated for persons pursuing a degree in theological studies (M.Div., D.Min., Ph.D.) or higher education administration, or for older adults changing their careers. Some scholarships are designated for racial ethnic undergraduate or graduate students. Applications are available from the financial aid office of the United Methodist school the applicant attends

or from the chair of their annual conference Board of Higher Education and Campus Ministry.

Financial data The funding is intended to supplement the students' own resources.

Duration 1 year; renewal policies are set by participating universities.

Number awarded Varies each year.

[347]

UNITED PARCEL SERVICE SCHOLARSHIP FOR MINORITY STUDENTS

Institute of Industrial Engineers
Attn: Chapter Operations Board
25 Technology Park/Atlanta
Norcross, GA 30092-2988
(770) 449-0460   (800) 494-0460
Fax: (770) 441-3295
Web: www.iienet.org

Purpose To provide financial assistance to minority undergraduates who are studying industrial engineering at a school in the United States, Canada, or Mexico.

Eligibility Eligible to be nominated are minority undergraduate students enrolled in any school in the United States and its territories, Canada, or Mexico, provided the school's engineering program is accredited by an agency recognized by the Institute of Industrial Engineers (IIE) and the student is pursuing a full-time course of study in industrial engineering with a GPA of at least 3.4. They must have at least 5 full quarters or 3 full semesters remaining until graduation. Students may not apply directly for these awards; they must be nominated by the head of their industrial engineering department. Nominees must be IIE members. Selection is based on scholastic ability, character, leadership, potential service to the industrial engineering profession, and need for financial assistance.

Financial data The stipend is $4,000.

Duration 1 year.

Additional information Funding for this program is provided by the UPS Foundation.

Number awarded 1 each year.

Deadline November of each year.

[348]

UNITY FOUNDERS SCHOLARSHIP

Unity: Journalists of Color, Inc.
1601 North Kent Street, Suite 1003
Arlington, VA 22209
(703) 469-2100   E-mail: jbruce@unityjournalists.org
Web: www.unityjournalists.org

Purpose To provide financial assistance to journalism undergraduates who demonstrate experience and interest in multicultural issues.

Eligibility This program is open to college juniors and seniors majoring in journalism or mass communications at an accredited college or university. Applicants must have a GPA of 3.0 or higher, demonstrated experience and potential in the field of journalism, and an informed interest in and commitment to understanding multicultural issues. They must be a member of 1 of the following organizations: the Asian American Journalists Association (AAJA), the National Association of Black Journalists (NABJ), the National Association of Hispanic Journalists (NAHJ), or the Native American Journalists Association (NAJA). Selection is based on 1) print, photographic, audio, or video examples of past journalistic work focused on racial, ethnic, or diversity issues; 2) a 1- to 2-page essay that clearly expresses a cognitive understanding of a multicultural issue related to journalism and/or the mass media; 3) 3 letters of recommendation; 4) a resume of work experience with an emphasis on experience that demonstrates an interest in and commitment to multicultural issues; and 5) a university transcript.

Financial data The stipend is $2,500. Funds are sent directly to the college or university.

Duration 1 year; nonrenewable.

Additional information This scholarship is dedicated to the members of AAJA, NABJ, NAHJ, and NAJA who founded Unity: Journalists of Color, Inc.

Number awarded 1 or more each year.

Deadline April of each year.

[349]
UPS DIVERSITY SCHOLARSHIPS

American Society of Safety Engineers
Attn: ASSE Foundation
1800 East Oakton Street
Des Plaines, IL 60018
(847) 768-3441   Fax: (847) 296-9220
E-mail: mrosario@asse.org
Web: www.asse.org

Purpose To provide financial assistance to minority undergraduate student members of the American Society of Safety Engineers (ASSE).

Eligibility This program is open to ASSE student members who are enrolled in a 4-year degree program in occupational safety and health or a closely-related field (e.g., safety engineering, safety management, systems safety, environmental science, industrial hygiene, ergonomics, fire science). Applicants must be U.S. citizens and members of a minority ethnic or racial group. They must be full-time students who have completed at least 60 semester hours with a GPA of 3.2 or higher. As part of the selection process, they must submit 2 essays of 300 words or less: 1) why they are seeking a degree in safety, a brief description of their current activities, and how those relate to their career goals and objectives; and 2) why they should be awarded this scholarship (including career goals and financial need).

Financial data Stipends range from $3,000 to $4,000 per year.

Duration 1 year; nonrenewable.

Additional information Funding for this program is provided by the UPS Foundation.

Number awarded Varies each year.

Deadline November of each year.

[350]
USA FUNDS ACCESS TO EDUCATION SCHOLARSHIPS

Scholarship America
Attn: Scholarship Management Services
1505 Riverview Road
P.O. Box 297
St. Peter, MN 56082
(507) 931-1682   (800) 537-4180
Fax: (507) 931-9168   E-mail: scholarship@usafunds.org
Web: www.usafunds.org

Purpose To provide financial assistance to undergraduate and graduate students, especially those who are members of ethnic minority groups or have physical disabilities.

Eligibility This program is open to high school seniors and graduates who plan to enroll or are already enrolled in full-time undergraduate or graduate course work at an accredited 2- or 4-year college, university, or vocational/technical school. Half-time undergraduate students are also eligible. Up to 50% of the awards are targeted at students who have a documented physical disability or are a member of an ethnic minority group, including but not limited to Native Hawaiian, Alaskan Native, Black/African American, Asian, Pacific Islander, American Indian, or Hispanic/Latino. Residents of all 50 states, the District of Columbia, Puerto Rico, Guam, the U.S. Virgin Islands, and all U.S. territories and commonwealths are eligible. Preference is given to applicants from the following areas: Arizona, Hawaii and the Pacific Islands, Indiana, Kansas, Maryland, Mississippi, Nevada, and Wyoming. Applicants must also be U.S. citizens or eligible non-citizens and come from a family with an annual adjusted gross income of $35,000 or less. In addition to financial need, selection is based on past academic performance and future potential, leadership and participation in school and community, work experience, career and educational aspirations and goals, and references.

Financial data The stipend is $1,500 per year for full-time undergraduate or graduate students or $750 per year for half-time undergraduate students. Funds are paid jointly to the student and the school.

Duration 1 year; may be renewed until the student receives a final degree or certificate or until the total award to a student reaches $6,000, whichever comes first. Renewal requires the recipient to maintain a GPA of 2.5 or higher.

Additional information This program, established in 2000, is sponsored by USA Funds which serves as the education loan guarantor and administrator in the 8 states and the Pacific Islands where the program gives preference.

Number awarded Varies each year; recently, 2,519 of these scholarships were awarded.

Deadline April of each year.

[351]
UTAH JAZZ "TEACHERS FOR ALL" SCHOLARSHIP

Utah Education Association
Attn: Children at Risk Foundation
875 East 5180 South
Murray, UT 84107
(801) 266-4461, ext. 154   (800) 594-8996
Fax: (801) 265-2249
Web: www.utea.org

Purpose To provide financial assistance to residents of Utah who wish to become teachers in minority communities.

Eligibility There is no age requirement to apply. Applicants may be high school seniors, current college students, or adults not in college but who have completed a high school diploma. All applicants must be Utah residents interested in becoming teachers in minority communities. Applicants who are not minorities themselves must have experience, skills, and demonstrated commitment to working with minority communities. Foreign language ability is helpful but not required. Recipients are selected on the basis of academic achievement, participation in minority communities (e.g., civic, church, educational, or club activities), public service to minority communities, and recommendations by those familiar with their work.

Financial data The stipend is $1,000. Upon attainment of their teaching certificate, recipients are awarded an additional $500 stipend.

Duration 1 year.

Number awarded 10 each year.

Deadline February of each year.

[352]
VERIZON SCHOLARSHIP PROGRAM

Hispanic Scholarship Fund
Attn: Selection Committee
55 Second Street, Suite 1500
San Francisco, CA 94105
(877) HSF-INFO   Fax: (415) 808-2302
E-mail: info@hsf.net
Web: www.hsf.net

Purpose To provide financial assistance to Hispanic American high school seniors in selected communities who are interested in attending college.

Eligibility This program is open to U.S. citizens, permanent residents, and visitors with a passport stamped I-551 residing in selected communities (see below). Applicants must be of Hispanic heritage (each parent half Hispanic or 1 parent fully Hispanic) and seniors in high schools in selected communities. They must have a high school GPA of 3.0 or higher and plan to enroll full time at an accredited college or university for the following fall. As part of the application process, they must submit a 2-page essay that addresses the following topics: their Hispanic heritage and family background, personal and academic achievements, academic plans and career goals, efforts toward making a difference in the community, and financial need.

Financial data The stipend is $1,500.

Duration 1 year.

Additional information The participating communities currently include Boston, Massachusetts; Dallas, Texas; Los Angeles, California; New York, New York; Philadelphia, Pennsylvania; Tampa, Florida; and Washington, D.C. Funding for this program is provided by the Verizon Foundation. Requests for applications must be accompanied by a self-addressed stamped envelope.

Number awarded Varies each year.

Deadline February of each year.

[353]
VERMONT SPACE GRANT UNDERGRADUATE SCHOLARSHIPS

Vermont Space Grant Consortium
c/o University of Vermont
College of Engineering and Mathematics
Votey Building, Room 209
12 Colchester Avenue
Burlington, VT 05405-0156
(802) 656-1429   Fax: (802) 656-8802
E-mail: zeno@emba.uvm.edu
Web: www.emba.uvm.edu/VSGC/awards.html

Purpose To provide financial assistance for undergraduate study in space-related fields to students in Vermont.

Eligibility This program is open to Vermont residents who are 1) enrolled in an undergraduate degree program at a Vermont institution of higher education with a GPA of 3.0 or higher or 2) seniors graduating from a high school in Vermont. Applicants must be planning to pursue a professional career that has direct relevance to the U.S. aerospace industry and the goal of the National Aeronautics and Space Administration (NASA), such as astronomy, biology, engineering, mathematics, physics, and other basic sciences (including earth sciences and medicine). They must submit an essay, up to 3 pages in length, on their career plans and the relationship of those plans to areas of interest to NASA. U.S. citizenship is required. Selection is based on academic standing, letters of recommendation, and the essay. The Vermont Space Grant Consortium (VSGC) is a component of the NASA Space Grant program, which encourages participation by women, underrepresented minorities, and persons with disabilities.

Financial data The stipend is $1,500 per year.

Duration 1 year; may be renewed upon reapplication.

Additional information This program is funded by NASA. Participating institutions are the College of Engineering and Mathematics at the University of Vermont, St. Michael's College, Norwich University, Vermont Technical College, the Vermont State Mathematics Coalition, and Aviation Technology School/Burlington Technical Center.

Number awarded Up to 10 each year.

Deadline February of each year.

[354]
VETERANS OF FOREIGN WARS OF MEXICAN ANCESTRY SCHOLARSHIP PROGRAM

Veterans of Foreign Wars of the United States of Mexican Ancestry
Central California Committee
c/o Emilio Olguin
651 Harrison Road
Monterey Park, CA 91755-6732
(626) 288-0498

Purpose To provide financial assistance for college to Mexican American high school students in California.

Eligibility This program is open to high school seniors of Mexican descent who reside in California. They must have earned a GPA of 3.5 or higher and need financial assistance to attend college. Preference is given to the children of veterans.

Financial data Stipends range from $500 to $1,000.

Duration 1 year.

Additional information Students who live in the central portion of California (from Los Angeles to Fresno) should write to the

Central California Committee to obtain an application; students who live north of there should contact Robert Gonzalez, 3210 Santa Maria Avenue, Santa Clara, CA 95051-1622, (408) 248-1677; students who live south of there should contact Gilbert Castorena, 3981 Coleman Avenue, San Diego, CA 92154-2516, (619) 690-0907.

Number awarded Varies; a total of $9,000 is available for these scholarships each year: $3,000 in each of the 3 districts.

Deadline March of each year.

[355]
VIKKI CARR SCHOLARSHIP AWARDS

Vikki Carr Scholarship Foundation
P.O. Box 780968
San Antonio, TX 78278
(210) 699-0205   Fax: (210) 699-0611
E-mail: info@vcsf.net
Web: www.vcsf.net

Purpose To provide financial assistance for college to Latino residents of Texas.

Eligibility This program is open to students of Latino heritage who are between 17 and 22 years of age, legal U.S. residents, and residents of Texas. Applicants must submit a short autobiography (up to 500 words) on their special interests, career goals, and reasons for pursuing a higher education. Selection is based on the essay, academic achievement, financial need, and community involvement.

Financial data The stipend ranges from $500 to $3,000.

Duration 1 year; renewable.

Additional information This program was established in 1971.

Number awarded Varies each year.

Deadline March of each year.

[356]
VIRGINIA HIGHER EDUCATION TEACHER ASSISTANCE PROGRAM

State Council of Higher Education for Virginia
Attn: Financial Aid Office
James Monroe Building
101 North 14th Street, Ninth Floor
Richmond, VA 23219-3659
(804) 225-2600   (877) 515-0138
Fax: (804) 225-2604   TDD: (804) 371-8017
E-mail: fainfo@schev.edu
Web: www.schev.edu

Purpose To provide financial assistance to residents of Virginia who are enrolled or interested in enrolling in a K-12 teacher preparation program in college.

Eligibility This program is open to residents of Virginia who are enrolled, or intend to enroll, full time in an eligible K-12 teacher preparation program at a public or private Virginia college or university. Applicants must 1) be U.S. citizens or eligible noncitizens; 2) demonstrate financial need; 3) have a cumulative college GPA of 2.5 or higher; and 4) be nominated by a faculty member. Preference is given to applicants enrolled in a teacher shortage content area, minorities, and males

Financial data Stipends are $2,000 per year for students at 4-year institutions or $1,000 per year for students at 2-year institutions.

Duration 1 year; may be renewed if funds are available and the recipient maintains satisfactory academic progress.

Additional information Applications and further information are available at the financial aid office of colleges and universities in Virginia. This program, established in 2000, is funded in part with federal funds from the Special Leveraging Educational Assistance Partnership (SLEAP) program. Recently, the teacher shortage areas included special education, mathematics, chemistry, physics, earth and space science, foreign languages, and technology education. Priority was also given to minority students enrolled in any content area for teacher preparation and male students enrolled in any approved elementary or middle school teacher preparation program.

Number awarded Varies each year.

[357]
VIRGINIA SOCIETY OF CERTIFIED PUBLIC ACCOUNTANTS MINORITY UNDERGRADUATE SCHOLARSHIP

Virginia Society of Certified Public Accountants Education
    Foundation
P.O. Box 4620
Glen Allen, VA 23058-4620
(804) 270-5344   (800) 733-8272
Fax: (804) 273-1741   E-mail: vscpa@vscpa.com
Web: www.vscpa.com

Purpose To provide financial assistance to minority students enrolled in an undergraduate accounting program in Virginia.

Eligibility Applicants must be minority students (African Americans, Hispanic Americans, Native Americans, American Indians, or Asian Pacific Americans) currently enrolled in a Virginia college or university undergraduate accounting program. They must be U.S. citizens, be majoring in accounting, have completed at least 6 hours of accounting, be currently registered for 3 more credit hours of accounting, and have a GPA of 3.0 or higher. Selection is based on their most recent official transcript (15%), a current resume (25%), a faculty letter of recommendation (10%), and an essay on how they plan to finance their education (50%).

Financial data A stipend is awarded (amount not specified).

Duration 1 year.

Number awarded Varies each year; a total of $10,000 is available for this program.

Deadline July of each year.

[358]
VIRGINIA SPACE GRANT COMMUNITY COLLEGE SCHOLARSHIP PROGRAM

Virginia Space Grant Consortium
Attn: Fellowship Coordinator
Old Dominion University Peninsula Center
600 Butler Farm Road
Hampton, VA 23666
(757) 766-5210   Fax: (757) 766-5205
E-mail: vsgc@pen.k12.va.us
Web: www.vsgc.odu.edu/html/fellowships.htm

Purpose To provide financial assistance to students who are interested in pursuing space-related studies at community colleges in Virginia.

Eligibility This program is open to students currently enrolled in a Virginia community college who are U.S. citizens and have completed at least the first semester of their program with a GPA of 3.0 or higher. Awards are generally made to full-time students, but part-time students demonstrating academic merit are also eligible. Applicants can be enrolled in any program that includes course work related to an understanding of or interest in technological fields supporting aerospace. A particular goal of the program is to increase the participation of underrepresented minorities, women, and persons with disabilities in aerospace-related, high technology careers.

Financial data   The maximum stipend is $1,500.

Duration   1 year; nonrenewable.

Additional information   This program is funded by the U.S. National Aeronautics and Space Administration (NASA).

Number awarded   Approximately 10 each year.

Deadline   February of each year.

[359]
VIRGINIA SPACE GRANT TEACHER EDUCATION SCHOLARSHIP PROGRAM

Virginia Space Grant Consortium
Attn: Fellowship Coordinator
Old Dominion University Peninsula Center
600 Butler Farm Road
Hampton, VA 23666
(757) 766-5210   Fax: (757) 766-5205
E-mail: vsgc@pen.k12.va.us
Web: www.vsgc.odu.edu/html/fellowships.htm

Purpose   To provide financial assistance for college to students in Virginia planning a career as science, mathematics, or technology educators.

Eligibility   This program is open to full-time undergraduate students at 1 of the Virginia Space Grant Consortium (VSGC) Colleges in a track that will qualify them to teach in a pre-college setting. Priority is given to those majoring in technology education, mathematics, or science, particularly earth/space/environmental science. Applicants may apply while seniors in high school or sophomores in a community college, with the award contingent on their matriculation at a VSGC college and entrance into a teacher certification program. They must submit a statement of academic goals and plan of study, explaining their reasons for desiring to enter the teaching profession, specifically the fields of science, mathematics, or technology education. Students currently enrolled in a VSGC college can apply when they declare their intent to enter the teacher certification program. Students enrolled in a career transition program leading to a degree in education are also eligible to apply. Applicants must be U.S. citizens with a GPA of 3.0 or higher. Since an important purpose of this program is to increase the participation of underrepresented minorities, women, and persons with disabilities in science, mathematics, and technology education, the VSGC especially encourages applications from those students.

Financial data   The maximum stipend is $1,000.

Duration   1 year; nonrenewable.

Additional information   The VSGC colleges are College of William and Mary, Hampton University, Old Dominion University, the University of Virginia, and Virginia Polytechnic Institute and State University. This program is funded by the U.S. National Aeronautics and Space Administration (NASA).

Number awarded   Approximately 10 each year.

Deadline   February of each year.

[360]
VIRGINIA UNDERGRADUATE STUDENT FINANCIAL ASSISTANCE (LAST DOLLAR) PROGRAM

State Council of Higher Education for Virginia
Attn: Financial Aid Office
James Monroe Building
101 North 14th Street, Ninth Floor
Richmond, VA 23219-3659
(804) 225-2600   (877) 515-0138
Fax: (804) 225-2604   TDD: (804) 371-8017
E-mail: fainfo@schev.edu
Web: www.schev.edu

Purpose   To provide financial assistance to minority undergraduate students enrolled in Virginia colleges or universities.

Eligibility   Eligible to apply for this program are minority undergraduate students who are enrolled at least half time for the first time (as freshmen) in state-supported 2-year or 4-year colleges or universities in Virginia. They must be enrolled in an eligible baccalaureate program. The program is intended to assist students who 1) receive financial aid packages that do not fully meet their need or include excessive self-help (loan or work) as determined by the institution; 2) apply and are accepted for admission after an institution has awarded all available grant resources; and 3) are accepted for admission and do not originally apply for financial aid but later determine that aid is needed to attend and apply after other financial aid resources are depleted.

Financial data   The stipends range from $200 per term to the total cost of attendance (tuition, required fees, room, board, supplies, and personal expenses).

Duration   1 year; nonrenewable.

Additional information   Applications and further information are available at the financial aid office of colleges and universities in Virginia. This program was established in 1988.

Number awarded   Varies each year.

Deadline   Deadline dates vary by school.

[361]
WAL-MART ACHIEVERS AWARD

Hispanic Association of Colleges and Universities
Attn: Scholarship Programs
8415 Datapoint Drive, Suite 400
San Antonio, TX 78229
(210) 692-3805   Fax: (210) 692-0823
E-mail: hacu@hacu.net
Web: www.hacu.net/student_resources/index.shtml

Purpose   To provide financial assistance to undergraduate business students at institutions that are members of the Hispanic Association of Colleges and Universities (HACU).

Eligibility   This program is open to full-time undergraduate students at HACU member and partner colleges and universities who are enrolled in at least their sophomore year with a major in business administration, general management, or retail management. Applicants must submit an essay of 200 to 250 words that describes their academic and/or career goals, where they expect to be and what they expect to be doing 10 years from now, and what skills they can bring to an employer. They must be able to demonstrate financial need and a GPA of 3.0 or higher. Preference is given to applicants who are working while attending school and have an interest in retail management.

Financial data   The stipend is $1,000 per year.

Duration   1 year; nonrenewable.

Additional information This program is sponsored by Wal-Mart and administered by HACU.
Number awarded 1 or more each year.
Deadline June of each year.

[362]
WARNER NORCROSS & JUDD PARALEGAL ASSISTANT STUDIES SCHOLARSHIP

Grand Rapids Community Foundation
Attn: Scholarship Coordinator
209-C Waters Building
161 Ottawa Avenue N.W.
Grand Rapids, MI 49503-2757
(616) 454-1751, ext. 103   Fax: (616) 454-6455
E-mail: rbishop@grfoundation.org
Web: www.grfoundation.org

Purpose To provide financial assistance to minority residents of Michigan who are interested in studying in a paralegal studies program at an institution in the state.
Eligibility This program is open to minority students currently residing in Michigan. Applicants must be accepted at or enrolled in an accredited public or private 2- or 4-year college or university with a declared major in paralegal/legal assistant studies. The institution must also be in Michigan.
Financial data The stipend is $2,000.
Duration 1 year.
Additional information Funding for this program is provided by the law firm Warner Norcross & Judd LLP.
Number awarded 1 each year.
Deadline April of each year.

[363]
WARNER NORCROSS & JUDD SECRETARIAL STUDIES SCHOLARSHIP

Grand Rapids Community Foundation
Attn: Scholarship Coordinator
209-C Waters Building
161 Ottawa Avenue N.W.
Grand Rapids, MI 49503-2757
(616) 454-1751, ext. 103   Fax: (616) 454-6455
E-mail: rbishop@grfoundation.org
Web: www.grfoundation.org

Purpose To provide financial assistance to minority residents of Michigan who are interested in studying in a legal assistant/secretarial program at an institution in the state.
Eligibility This program is open to minority students currently residing in Michigan. Applicants must be accepted at or enrolled in an accredited public or private 2- or 4-year college, university, vocational school, or business school with a declared major in legal assistant/legal secretarial studies. The institution must also be in Michigan.
Financial data The stipend is $1,000.
Duration 1 year.
Additional information Funding for this program is provided by the law firm Warner Norcross & Judd LLP.
Number awarded 1 each year.
Deadline April of each year.

[364]
WASA/PEMCO 21ST CENTURY EDUCATOR SCHOLARSHIP

Washington Association of School Administrators
825 Fifth Avenue, S.E.
Olympia, WA 98501
(360) 943-5717

Purpose To provide financial assistance to minority and other high school seniors in the state of Washington who are interested in majoring in education in college.
Eligibility This program is open to high school seniors who are enrolled in a Washington public or accredited private school, have a GPA of 3.0 or higher, and intend to major and pursue a career in K-12 education. To apply, students must submit a completed application form, a criteria essay, a goals essay, 3 reference letters, and an official grades transcript. Selection is based on leadership, community service, honors and awards, student activities, and educational goals. Each year, 1 of the scholarships is awarded to a minority applicant.
Financial data The stipend is $1,000 per year.
Duration 4 years.
Additional information This program is sponsored jointly by the Washington Association of School Administrators (WASA) and PEMCO Financial Services. Faxed applications will not be accepted.
Number awarded 3 each year: 1 to a minority student, 1 to a student from eastern Washington, and 1 to a student from western Washington.
Deadline March of each year.

[365]
WASHINGTON NASA SPACE GRANT CONSORTIUM UNDERGRADUATE SCHOLARSHIPS

Washington NASA Space Grant Consortium
c/o University of Washington
401A Johnson Hall
Box 351310
Seattle, WA 98195-1310
(206) 543-1943   (800) 659-1943
Fax: (206) 543-0179   E-mail: nasa@u.washington.edu
Web: www.waspacegrant.org

Purpose To provide financial assistance for college to students in Washington who wish to study science, engineering, or mathematics with an emphasis on space.
Eligibility This program is open to residents of Washington who are attending or planning to attend institutions that are members of the Washington NASA Space Grant Consortium. Applicants must be interested in majoring in space-related aspects of science, engineering, or mathematics. U.S. citizenship is required. The program values diversity and strongly encourages women and minorities to apply.
Financial data Each participating college or university determines its awards.
Duration 1 year; may be renewed.
Additional information This program is funded by the U.S. National Aeronautics and Space Administration (NASA). Members of the consortium include Northwest Indian College, Seattle Central Community College, the University of Washington, and Washington State University.
Number awarded Varies each year.

Deadline Each participating college or university establishes its own deadline.

[366]
WASHINGTON SOCIETY OF CPAS SCHOLARSHIP FOR MINORITY ACCOUNTING MAJORS

Washington Society of Certified Public Accountants
Attn: Scholarship Committee
902 140th Avenue N.E.
Bellevue, WA 98005-3480
(425) 644-4800   (800) 272-8273 (within WA)
Fax: (425) 562-8853   E-mail: memberservices@wscpa.org
Web: www.wscpa.org

Purpose To provide financial assistance to minority undergraduates in Washington who are majoring in accounting.

Eligibility This program is open to accounting majors who have completed their sophomore year at an accredited 4-year institution in Washington by fall of the year they are applying. Applicants must be members of a minority group (African American, Asian American, Hispanic, or Native American). U.S. citizenship is required. Selection is based on academic achievement (GPA of 3.0 or higher), campus and/or community activities, work history, a personal statement that includes their career goals and interests and how they anticipate that the accounting curriculum will enhance their career objectives, and 2 letters of recommendation.

Financial data The stipend is $3,500 per year. Funds may be used to pay for tuition only.

Duration 1 year; nonrenewable.

Number awarded 1 each year.

Deadline March of each year.

[367]
WASHINGTON STATE GEAR UP SCHOLARSHIP PROGRAM

Washington Higher Education Coordinating Board
917 Lakeridge Way
P.O. Box 43430
Olympia, WA 98504-3430
(360) 753-7833   Fax: (360) 753-7808
TDD: (360) 753-7809   E-mail: johnmcl@hecb.wa.gov
Web: www.hecb.wa.gov/CollegePrep/gu/guindex.asp

Purpose To provide financial and other assistance for college to low-income, disadvantaged middle and high school students (including minorities) in designated areas of Washington.

Eligibility This program is open to students in grades 7-12 in designated Washington communities who are low income and at risk (particularly minorities). Participants receive tutoring and academic and career counseling, visit college campuses, perform community service, meet regularly with mentors, and attend informational seminars on such topics as financial aid, admissions, career planning, and student success strategies. During their junior and senior years, they get help preparing for college entrance examinations and completing admissions and financial aid applications.

Financial data Participants receive stipends and scholarships for postsecondary study.

Duration Up to 4 years, provided the recipient remains drug-, crime-, and alcohol-free; maintains a GPA of 2.0 or higher; and participates in community service projects.

Additional information The communities currently participating in this program are Aberdeen, Elma, Hoquiam, Inchelium,

Quincy, Seattle, Spokane, Tacoma, Taholah, Wapato, White Swan, and Yakima. GEAR UP is a federal program that stands for Gaining Early Awareness and Readiness for Undergraduate Programs. In Washington, it operates as a partnership among the Higher Education Coordinating Board, the Office of the Governor, and the University of Washington. It began operating in 1999 as the successor to the National Early Intervention Scholarship and Partnership Program.

Number awarded Currently, 1,200 students in grades 7-12 are participating.

[368]
WASHINGTON STATE NEED GRANT

Washington Higher Education Coordinating Board
917 Lakeridge Way
P.O. Box 43430
Olympia, WA 98504-3430
(360) 753-7851   Fax: (360) 753-7808
TDD: (360) 753-7809   E-mail: info@hecb.wa.gov
Web: www.hecb.wa.gov/financialaid/sng/sngindex.asp

Purpose To provide financial assistance for undergraduate study to Washington residents who come from a low-income or disadvantaged family (including minorities).

Eligibility This program is open to residents of Washington (particularly minorities) whose family income is equal to or less than 55% of the state median (currently defined as $18,000 for a family of 1 ranging to $48,000 for a family of 8) or who are disadvantaged (defined to mean a student who by reasons of adverse cultural, educational, environmental, experiential, or familial circumstance is unlikely to aspire to, or enroll in, higher education. Applicants must be enrolled or planning to enroll at least half time in an eligible certificate, bachelor's degree, or first associate degree program. They may not be pursuing a degree in theology.

Financial data The stipend depends on the type of institution the recipient attends. Recently, it was $1,908 per year at community, technical, and private career colleges; $3,026 at public comprehensive universities (Central Washington University, Eastern Washington University, The Evergreen State College, and Western Washington University); $3,798 at public research universities (University of Washington and Washington State University); or $4,032 at independent universities.

Duration 1 academic year; renewal is possible for up to 3 additional years.

Additional information Consideration is automatic with the institution's receipt of the student's completed financial aid application. This program began in 1969.

Number awarded Varies each year; recently, more than 49,000 students received about $106 million in benefits from this program.

Deadline Varies according to the participating institution; generally in October of each year.

[369]

WEST VIRGINIA SPACE GRANT CONSORTIUM UNDERGRADUATE NASA SPACE GRANT FELLOWSHIPS

West Virginia Space Grant Consortium
c/o West Virginia University
College of Engineering and Mineral Resources
G-68 Engineering Sciences Building
P.O. Box 6070
Morgantown, WV 26506-6070
(304) 293-4099   Fax: (304) 293-4970
E-mail: nasa@cemr.wvu.edu
Web: www.cemr.wvu.edu/~wwwnasa

Purpose To provide financial assistance to high school seniors who wish to attend institutions affiliated with the West Virginia Space Grant Consortium to prepare for a career in space-related science or engineering.

Eligibility This program is open to high school seniors in West Virginia who are planning to attend a college or university that is a member of the West Virginia Space Grant Consortium. U.S. citizenship is required. Selection is based on academic record and desire to pursue a career in science or engineering. The consortium is a component of the Space Grant program of the U.S. National Aeronautics and Space Administration (NASA), which encourages participation by women, underrepresented minorities, and persons with disabilities.

Financial data The program provides payment of full tuition, fees, room, and board.

Duration 4 years.

Additional information Funding for this program is provided by NASA. During the summers, some recipients work at a NASA center on a project under the supervision of a NASA advisor; others work with researchers at their respective colleges. The consortium includes Bethany College, Fairmont State College, Marshall University, Salem International University, Shepherd College, West Liberty State College, West Virginia Institute of Technology, West Virginia State College, West Virginia University, West Virginia Wesleyan College, and Wheeling-Jesuit University.

Number awarded Varies each year.

Deadline Each participating college or university establishes its own deadline.

[370]

WEST VIRGINIA SPACE GRANT CONSORTIUM UNDERGRADUATE SCHOLARSHIP PROGRAM

West Virginia Space Grant Consortium
c/o West Virginia University
College of Engineering and Mineral Resources
G-68 Engineering Sciences Building
P.O. Box 6070
Morgantown, WV 26506-6070
(304) 293-4099   Fax: (304) 293-4970
E-mail: nasa@cemr.wvu.edu
Web: www.cemr.wvu.edu/~wwwnasa

Purpose To provide financial assistance to undergraduates at member institutions of the West Virginia Space Grant Consortium who wish to prepare for a career in space-related science or engineering.

Eligibility This program is open to undergraduates at member institutions of the consortium. Applicants must be U.S. citizens and West Virginia residents. Selection is based on academic record and desire to pursue a career in science or engineering.

The consortium is a component of the Space Grant program of the U.S. National Aeronautics and Space Administration (NASA), which encourages participation by women, underrepresented minorities, and persons with disabilities.

Financial data Stipends are either $2,000 or $1,000.

Duration 1 year.

Additional information Funding for this program is provided by NASA. In addition to their class work, recipients either work with faculty members in their major department on a research project or participate in the Consortium Challenge Program by working with elementary students on their science projects. The consortium members are Bethany College, Fairmont State College, Marshall University, Salem International University, Shepherd College, West Liberty State College, West Virginia Institute of Technology, West Virginia State College, West Virginia University, West Virginia Wesleyan College, and Wheeling-Jesuit University.

Number awarded Varies each year.

Deadline Each participating college or university establishes its own deadline.

[371]

WESTERN REGION SCHOLARSHIPS

Society of Mexican American Engineers and Scientists-
    Western Region
c/o Phillip Diaz
Northrop Grumman-Mission Systems
DH4-2936
1815 Glenn Curtiss Street
Carson, CA 90746
(310) 764-3157
Web: www.maeslongbeach.org/conference

Purpose To provide financial assistance for college to undergraduate members of the Society of Mexican American Engineers and Scientists (MAES) enrolled at colleges and universities in selected western states.

Eligibility This program is open to Hispanic Americans who have completed at least 1 semester as a full-time undergraduate at a college or university in Arizona, California, Idaho, Montana, Nevada, Oregon, Utah, Washington, or Wyoming. Applicants must be U.S. citizens or permanent residents, members of MAES, and majoring in science or engineering. Community college applicants must be enrolled in majors that can transfer to a 4-year institution offering a baccalaureate degree. Along with their application, they must submit a 1- to 2-page personal statement covering their family background, involvement in school and community activities, leadership roles and activities, achievements, current higher education status, career goals, and financial need.

Financial data Stipends range from $200 to $1,000.

Duration 1 year.

Additional information Recipients are required to attend the scholarship awards banquet.

Number awarded 1 or more each year.

Deadline February of each year.

[372]
WHITNEY M. YOUNG, JR. MEMORIAL SCHOLARSHIP AND INCENTIVE AWARDS

New York Urban League
Attn: Education Department
204 West 136th Street
New York, NY 10030-2696
(212) 926-8000
Web: www.nyul.org/scholwhi.htm

Purpose To provide financial assistance for college to minority students graduating from high schools in New York City.

Eligibility This program is open to residents of New York City who are of African American, Latino, Asian, or Native American heritage. Applicants must be high school graduates or recipients of a GED certificate who have been accepted as freshmen at an accredited college or university in pursuit of a baccalaureate or associate degree at the time the award is presented. Selection is based on GPA (10%); test scores (10%); extracurricular activities (10%); 2 letters of recommendation regarding the applicant's character and participation in school, community, and extracurricular activities (10%); awards and honors (10%); a scholarly essay of at least 500 words on current events in New York City and the steps the applicant would take to promote racial harmony (30%); and an interview (20%). Financial need is considered only if 2 or more candidates have equal qualifications.

Financial data Stipends are either $2,500 (for scholarships) or $1,000 (for incentive awards).

Duration 1 year; nonrenewable.

Additional information This program, which began in 1973, is funded by revenue from the annual Whitney M. Young, Jr. Football Classic.

Number awarded 10 each year.

[373]
WILLIAM E. MCKNIGHT SCHOLARSHIP

Rochester Area Community Foundation
Attn: Scholarship Manager
500 East Avenue
Rochester, NY 14607-1912
(585) 271-4100, ext. 4306   Fax: (585) 271-4292
E-mail: brainey@racf.org
Web: www.racf.org/scholarships

Purpose To provide financial assistance for college to minority high school seniors in upstate New York.

Eligibility This program is open to high school seniors of color who are interested in going to college and are residents of Genesee, Livingston, Monroe, Ontario, Orleans, or Wayne counties (New York). Selection is based on academic achievement (GPA of 3.0 or higher) and financial need.

Financial data The stipend is $1,250 per year.

Duration 1 year; renewable.

Additional information Information on this program, established in 1986, is also available from the Urban League of Rochester, NY, Inc., 265 North Clinton Avenue, Rochester, NY 14605, (585) 325-6530.

Number awarded 1 each year.

Deadline March of each year.

[374]
WILLIAM RUCKER GREENWOOD SCHOLARSHIP

Association for Women Geoscientists
Attn: AWG Foundation
P.O. Box 30645
Lincoln, NE 68503-0645
E-mail: office@awg.org
Web: www.awg.org/eas/scholarships.html

Purpose To provide financial assistance to minority women working on an undergraduate or graduate degree in the geosciences in the Potomac Bay region.

Eligibility This program is open to minority women who are currently enrolled as full-time undergraduate or graduate geoscience majors in an accredited, degree-granting college or university in Delaware, the District of Columbia, Maryland, Virginia, or West Virginia. Selection is based on the applicant's 1) awareness of the importance of community outreach by participation in geoscience or earth science educational activities, and 2) potential for leadership as a future geoscience professional.

Financial data The stipend is $1,000. The recipient also is granted a 1-year membership in the Association for Women Geoscientists (AWG).

Duration 1 year.

Additional information This program is sponsored by the AWG Potomac Area Chapter. Information is also available from Laurel M. Bybell, U.S. Geological Survey, 926 National Center, Reston, VA 20192.

Number awarded 1 each year.

Deadline April of each year.

[375]
WISCONSIN INSTITUTE OF CERTIFIED PUBLIC ACCOUNTANTS FOUR-YEAR SCHOLARSHIPS

Wisconsin Institute of Certified Public Accountants
Attn: WICPA Educational Foundation
235 North Executive Drive, Suite 200
P.O. Box 1010
Brookfield, WI 53008-1010
(414) 785-0445   (800) 772-6939 (within WI and MN)
Fax: (414) 785-0838   E-mail: Tammy@wicpa.org
Web: www.wicpa.org/Student_Teacher/scholarships.htm

Purpose To provide financial assistance to minority high school seniors in Wisconsin who are interested in majoring in accounting.

Eligibility This program is open to high school seniors who are residents of Wisconsin and African American, Hispanic, Native American, Indian, or Asian. Applicants must have earned a GPA of 3.0 or higher, be planning to attend a Wisconsin college or university, and be planning to begin academic work leading to an accounting major and a bachelor's degree.

Financial data The stipend is $375 per academic semester for the first 2 years, $500 per semester during the third year, and $750 per semester during the fourth year. The total award is $4,000 over 4 years. Funds may be used only for tuition and books.

Duration 4 years.

Number awarded Varies each year; recently, 2 of these scholarships were awarded.

Deadline February of each year.

[376]

WISCONSIN MINORITY UNDERGRADUATE RETENTION GRANTS

Wisconsin Higher Educational Aids Board
131 West Wilson Street, Room 902
P.O. Box 7885
Madison, WI 53707-7885
(608) 267-2212   Fax: (608) 267-2808
E-mail: mary.kuzdas@heab.state.wi.us
Web: heab.state.wi.us/programs.html

Purpose To provide financial assistance to minorities in Wisconsin who are currently enrolled in college.

Eligibility African Americans, Hispanic Americans, and American Indians in Wisconsin are eligible to apply if they are enrolled as sophomores, juniors, seniors, or fifth-year undergraduates in a 4-year nonprofit institution or as second-year students in a 2-year program at a public vocational institution in the state. The grant also includes students who were admitted to the United States after December 31, 1975 and who are a former citizen of Laos, Vietnam, or Cambodia or whose ancestor was a citizen of 1 of those countries. They must be nominated by their institution and be able to demonstrate financial need.

Financial data Stipends range from $250 to $2,500 per year.

Duration Up to 4 years.

Additional information The Wisconsin Higher Educational Aids Board administers this program for students in private nonprofit institutions and public vocational institutions. The University of Wisconsin has a similar program for students attending any of the branches of that system. Eligible students should apply through their school's financial aid office.

Number awarded Varies each year.

Deadline Deadline dates vary by institution; check with your school's financial aid office.

[377]

WISCONSIN SPACE GRANT CONSORTIUM UNDERGRADUATE SCHOLARSHIPS

Wisconsin Space Grant Consortium
c/o University of Wisconsin at Green Bay
Natural and Applied Sciences
2420 Nicolet Drive
Green Bay, WI 54311-7001
(920) 465-2941   Fax: (920) 465-2376
E-mail: brandts@uwgb.edu
Web: www.uwgb.edu/wsgc

Purpose To provide financial support to undergraduate students at universities participating in the Wisconsin Space Grant Consortium (WSGC).

Eligibility This program is open to undergraduate students enrolled at 1 of the universities participating in the WSGC. Applicants must be U.S. citizens; be working full time on a bachelor's degree in space science, aerospace, or interdisciplinary space studies (including, but not limited to, engineering, the sciences, architecture, law, business, and medicine); and have a GPA of 3.0 or higher. The consortium especially encourages applications from underrepresented minorities, women, and students with disabilities. Selection is based on academic performance and potential for success.

Financial data Stipends up to $1,500 per year are available.

Duration 1 academic year.

Additional information Funding for this program is provided by the U.S. National Aeronautics and Space Administration. The schools participating in the consortium include the University of Wisconsin campuses at Green Bay, La Crosse, Madison, Milwaukee, Oshkosh, Parkside, and Whitewater; College of the Menominee Nation; Marquette University; Carroll College; Lawrence University; Milwaukee School of Engineering; Ripon College; and Medical College of Wisconsin.

Number awarded Varies each year; recently, 21 of these scholarships were awarded.

Deadline February of each year.

[378]

WISCONSIN TALENT INCENTIVE PROGRAM (TIP) GRANTS

Wisconsin Higher Educational Aids Board
131 West Wilson Street, Room 902
P.O. Box 7885
Madison, WI 53707-7885
(608) 266-1665   Fax: (608) 267-2808
E-mail: john.whitt@heab.state.wi.us
Web: heab.state.wi.us/programs.html

Purpose To provide supplemental grants to the most needy and educationally disadvantaged students in Wisconsin during their postsecondary schooling.

Eligibility To be eligible for a grant, a student must be a Wisconsin resident, be a first-year (freshman) college student, and possess at least 2 of the following characteristics: 1) be a member of a minority group (Hispanic, Native American, Indian, Black, or Asian American); 2) be a student with a disability, be a first-generation postsecondary student, or be currently or formerly incarcerated in a correctional institution; 3) be a dependent student whose expected parents' contribution is $2,000 or less; 4) be a student who is or will be enrolled in a special academic support program due to insufficient preparation; 5) be a member of a family receiving welfare benefits; 6) be a member of a family whose parent is ineligible for unemployment compensation and has no current income from employment.

Financial data Grants range up to $1,800 per year for first-year students and up to $1,250 per year for continuing students.

Duration Up to 10 semesters.

Additional information Additional information is available from the Wisconsin Educational Opportunity Program, 101 West Pleasant Street, Bottlehouse Atrium, Milwaukee, WI 53212.

Number awarded Varies each year.

[379]

WORLDSTUDIO FOUNDATION SCHOLARSHIPS

Worldstudio Foundation
225 Varick Street, Ninth Floor
New York, NY 10014
(212) 366-1317, ext. 18   Fax: (212) 807-0024
E-mail: scholarships@worldstudio.org
Web: www.worldstudio.org/scholar/intro.html

Purpose To provide financial assistance to disadvantaged and ethnic minority undergraduate and graduate students who wish to study fine or commercial arts, design, or architecture.

Eligibility This program is open to disadvantaged or minority college students who are currently enrolled (must attend an accredited school) and majoring in the 1 of the following areas: advertising, architecture, crafts, environmental graphics, fashion design, film/video, film/theater design (including set and costume design), fine arts, furniture design, graphic design, industrial/product design, interior architecture, interior design, landscape architecture, new media, photography, surface/textile design, or urban planning. Both graduate and undergraduate students are eligible. International students may apply if they are enrolled at a U.S. college or university. Applicants must have a GPA of 2.0 or higher. Selection is based on the quality of submitted work, a 600-word written statement of purpose, financial need, and academic record.

Financial data Basic scholarships range from $1,000 to $2,000, but awards between $3,000 and $5,000 are also presented at the discretion of the jury. Honorable mentions are $100. Funds are paid directly to the recipient's school.

Duration 1 academic year. Recipients may reapply.

Additional information The foundation encourages the scholarship recipients to focus on ways that their work can address issues of social and environmental responsibility. This program includes the following named awards: the Gaggenau Award for Design, the New York Design Center Awards, the ALU Awards for Design, the Color Wheel Award, the Honda Award for Environmental Design, the Rado Watch Scholarship for Design, the Janou Pakter Award, the Impac Group Award, the Color Optics Award. the AIGA Award, the Lonn Beaudry Memorial Award, and the Robert J. Hurst Award.

Number awarded Varies each year; recently, 20 scholarships and 10 honorable mentions were awarded.

Deadline April of each year.

[380]
WORLDSTUDIO FOUNDATION SPECIAL ANIMATION AND ILLUSTRATION SCHOLARSHIPS

Worldstudio Foundation
225 Varick Street, Ninth Floor
New York, NY 10014
(212) 366-1317, ext. 18   Fax: (212) 807-0024
E-mail: scholarships@worldstudio.org
Web: www.worldstudio.org/scholar/intro.html

Purpose To provide financial assistance to members of disadvantaged and ethnic minority groups who wish to study illustration, animation, or cartooning in college.

Eligibility This program is open to members of disadvantaged or minority groups who are currently enrolled or planning to enroll in an accredited college or university in the United States. Applicants must be majoring or planning to major in illustration, animation, or cartooning. They must submit their most recent college or high school transcripts, documentation of financial need, a portfolio of their work, and a 600-word statement of purpose that includes a brief autobiography and how they plan to contribute to the community. International students are also eligible. Selection is based on the quality of submitted work, the strength of the written statement of purpose, financial need, and academic record.

Financial data This stipend is $1,500. Funds are paid directly to the recipient's school.

Duration 1 academic year. Recipients may reapply.

Additional information This program was established in 2002 with funding from the W.K. Kellogg Foundation.

Number awarded 25 each year.

Deadline April of each year.

[381]
WYOMING HISPANIC ORGANIZATION SCHOLARSHIP

Wyoming Hispanic Organization
P.O. Box 1027
Green River, WY 82935
E-mail: rufarnsw@wyoming.com

Purpose To provide financial assistance for college to Hispanic American students in selected counties in Wyoming.

Eligibility Applicants must be U.S. citizens or permanent residents who are of Hispanic ancestry and a resident of 1 of the following counties in Wyoming: Sweetwater, Sublette, Lincoln, or Uinta. Applicants may be high school seniors or currently-enrolled college students. They must have at least a 2.5 GPA. In addition to a completed application form and an official transcript, applicants must submit a personal letter of intent detailing their career goals and educational plans and 2 letters of recommendation. Selection is based on academic achievement.

Financial data The stipend is $500, paid in 2 equal installments.

Duration 1 year. Recipients may not apply for a second consecutive year, but they may reapply after waiting 1 full year.

Additional information Information is also available from Ruth Farnsworth, 305 North Wagonwheel Drive, Green River, WY 82935, (307) 875-4393. Recipients must attend school on a full-time basis.

Deadline August of each year.

[382]
XEROX TECHNICAL MINORITY SCHOLARSHIP PROGRAM

Xerox Corporation
Attn: Technical Minority Scholarship Program
907 Culver Road
Rochester, NY 14609-7192
(585) 422-7689   E-mail: xtmsp@imcouncil.com
Web: www.xerox.com

Purpose To provide financial assistance to minorities interested in undergraduate or graduate education in the sciences and/or engineering.

Eligibility This program is open to minorities (people of African American, Asian, Pacific Islander, American Indian, Native Alaskan, or Hispanic descent) enrolled full time in the following science and engineering degree programs at the baccalaureate level or above: chemistry, engineering (chemical, computer, electrical, imaging, mechanical, optical, software), information management, material science, or physics. Applicants must be U.S. citizens or permanent residents with a GPA of 3.0 or higher.

Financial data The maximum stipend is $1,000 per year.

Duration 1 year.

Deadline September of each year.

[383]
YALE NEW HAVEN HOSPITAL MINORITY NURSING AND ALLIED HEALTH SCHOLARSHIPS

Yale New Haven Hospital
Attn: Human Resources
20 York Street
New Haven, CT 06504
(203) 688-2414   Fax: (203) 688-6670
E-mail: lacamera@ynhh.org
Web: www.ynhh.org

Purpose To provide financial assistance to minority high school seniors in Connecticut interested in studying nursing or allied health fields in college.

Eligibility This program is open to graduating seniors at high schools in Connecticut who are members of minority groups. Applicants must be interested in attending a 4-year college or university with an accredited program in nursing, respiratory therapy, medical technology, pharmacy, or radiation therapy. Selection is based on academic record, teacher evaluations, a personal essay, and extracurricular activities.

Financial data The stipend is $1,500 per year.

Duration 1 year.

Number awarded 4 each year.

Deadline February of each year.

[384]
YOF SCHOLARSHIPS

Youth Opportunities Foundation
8820 South Sepulveda Boulevard, Suite 208
P.O. Box 45762
Los Angeles, CA 90045
(310) 670-7664   Fax: (310) 670-5238

Purpose To provide financial assistance for college to Hispanic American high school seniors in California.

Eligibility Financial assistance is available to graduating high school seniors in California if they have at least 1 parent of Latin American origin, rank in the top 10% of their class, have SAT scores of 1000 or higher, and have a demonstrated record of leadership activities.

Financial data Stipends range from $100 to $1,000.

Duration These are 1-time grants.

Number awarded Varies each year.

Deadline February of each year.

Fellowships

Described here are 254 funding programs open to Hispanic Americans that are to be used to fund studies on the graduate level (for a master's degree, doctorate, professional degree, or specialist's certificate) in the United States. Usually no return of service or repayment is required. Note: other funding opportunities for Hispanic Americans on the graduate school level are also described in the Loans, Grants, Awards, and Internships sections. So, if you are looking for a particular program and don't find it in this section, be sure to check the Program Title Index to see if it is covered elsewhere in the directory.

[385]
AAAA MULTICULTURAL SCHOLARSHIPS

American Association of Advertising Agencies
Attn: Manager of Diversity Programs
405 Lexington Avenue, 18th Floor
New York, NY 10174-1801
(212) 682-2500   (800) 676-9333
Fax: (212) 682-8391   E-mail: tiffany@aaaa.org
Web: www.aaaa.org

Purpose To provide financial assistance to racial minority students interested in working on a graduate degree in advertising.

Eligibility This program is open to African Americans, Asian Americans, Hispanic Americans, and Native Americans who are interested in studying the advertising creative arts at designated institutions. Applicants must have already received an undergraduate degree and be able to demonstrate financial need. As part of the selection process, they must submit 10 samples of creative work in their respective field of expertise.

Financial data Stipends are $10,000 or $5,000.

Duration Most awards are for 2 years.

Additional information This program began in 1997 and currently provides scholarships to students at the Adcenter at Virginia Commonwealth University, the Creative Circus and the Portfolio Center in Atlanta, the Miami Ad School, and the University of Texas at Austin.

Number awarded Varies each year; recently, 17 students received scholarships worth $165,000.

[386]
ABA LEGAL OPPORTUNITY SCHOLARSHIP

American Bar Association
Attn: Fund for Justice and Education
750 North Lake Shore Drive
Chicago, IL 60611
(312) 988-5415   E-mail: fje@staff.abanet.org
Web: www.abanet.org/fje

Purpose To provide financial assistance to racial and ethnic minority students who are interested in attending law school.

Eligibility This program is open to racial and ethnic minority college graduates who are interested in attending an ABA-accredited law school. Only students beginning law school may apply; law students who have completed 1 or more semesters of law school are not eligible. Applicants must have a cumulative GPA of 2.5 or higher and be citizens or permanent residents of the United States. Financial need must be demonstrated.

Financial data The stipend is $5,000 per year.

Duration 1 year; may be renewed for 2 additional years if satisfactory performance in law school has been achieved.

Additional information This program began in the 2000-01 academic year.

Number awarded Approximately 20 each year.

Deadline February of each year.

[387]
ABC HISPANIC SCHOLARSHIP FUNDS

American Baptist Churches USA
Attn: Educational Ministries
P.O. Box 851
Valley Forge, PA 19482-0851
(610) 768-2067   (800) ABC-3USA, ext. 2067
Fax: (610) 768-2056   E-mail: paula.weiss@abc-usa.org
Web: www.abc-em.org

Purpose To provide financial assistance to Hispanic Americans who are interested in preparing for or furthering a church career in the American Baptist Church (ABC).

Eligibility This program is open to Hispanic American members of the church or its recognized institutions who demonstrate financial need. They must be enrolled on at least a two-thirds basis in an accredited institution, working on an undergraduate degree or first professional degree in a seminary. Applicants must be currently serving or planning to serve in a vocation with the church or with its recognized institutions. They must be U.S. citizens who have been a member of an American Baptist Church for at least 1 year.

Financial data The stipend is $500 per year.

Duration 1 year; may be renewed.

Deadline May of each year.

[388]
ADRIENNE M. AND CHARLES SHELBY ROOKS FELLOWSHIP FOR RACIAL AND ETHNIC THEOLOGICAL STUDENTS

United Church of Christ
Local Church Ministries
Attn: Coordinator of Grants, Scholarships, and Resources
700 Prospect Avenue East
Cleveland, OH 44115-1100
(216) 736-3839   Fax: (216) 736-3783
E-mail: jeffersv@ucc.org
Web: www.ucc.org/education/scholarships

Purpose To provide financial assistance to minority students who are either enrolled at an accredited seminary preparing for a career of service in the United Church of Christ or working on a doctoral degree in the field of religion.

Eligibility This program is open to members of a congregation of the United Church of Christ who are from a minority ethnic group (African American, Hispanic American, Asian American, Native American Indian, or Pacific Islander). Applicants must be either 1) enrolled in an accredited school of theology in the United States or Canada with the intent to become a pastor or teacher within the United Church of Christ, or 2) doctoral (Ph.D., Th.D., or Ed.D.) students within a field related to religious studies. Seminary students must have a GPA in all postsecondary work of 3.0 or higher and must have begun the in-care process; preference is given to students who have demonstrated leadership through a history of service to the church and scholarship through exceptional academic performance. For doctoral students, preference is given to applicants who have demonstrated academic excellence, teaching effectiveness, and commitment to the United Church of Christ and who intend to become professors in colleges, seminaries, or graduate schools.

Financial data Grants range from $500 to $5,000 per year.

Duration 1 year; may be renewed.

Number awarded Varies each year.

Deadline February of each year.

[389]
AICPA FELLOWSHIPS FOR MINORITY DOCTORAL STUDENTS

American Institute of Certified Public Accountants
Attn: Academic and Career Development Division
1211 Avenue of the Americas
New York, NY 10036-8775
(212) 596-6270   Fax: (212) 596-6292
E-mail: educat@aicpa.org
Web: www.aicpa.org/members/div/career/mini/fmds.htm

Purpose   To provide financial assistance to minorities who wish to prepare for a career teaching accounting at the college level.

Eligibility   This program is open to minority students who have applied to and/or been accepted into a doctoral program with a concentration in accounting; have earned a master's degree or completed a minimum of 3 years of full-time work in accounting, are attending or planning to attend school full time; and agree not to work full time in a paid position, teach more than 1 course as a teaching assistant, or work more than 25% as a research assistant. U.S. citizenship is required. Preference is given to applicants who have attained a CPA designation. For purposes of this program, the American Institute of Certified Public Accountants (AICPA) considers minority students as those of Black, Native American, or Pacific Island races, or of Hispanic ethnic origin.

Financial data   The stipend is $12,000 per year.

Duration   1 year; may be renewed up to 4 additional years.

Number awarded   Varies each year; recently, 22 of these fellowships were awarded.

Deadline   March of each year.

[390]
ALABAMA SPACE GRANT CONSORTIUM GRADUATE FELLOWSHIP PROGRAM

Alabama Space Grant Consortium
c/o University of Alabama in Huntsville
Materials Science Building, Room 205
Huntsville, AL 35899
(256) 890-6800   Fax: (256) 890-6061
E-mail: jfreasoner@matsci.uah.edu
Web: www.uah.edu/ASGC

Purpose   To provide financial assistance for graduate study or research related to the space sciences at universities participating in the Alabama Space Grant Consortium.

Eligibility   This program is open to full-time graduate students enrolled at the universities participating in the consortium. Applicants must be studying in a field related to space, including the physical, natural, and biological sciences; engineering; education; economics; business; sociology; behavioral sciences; computer science; communications; law; international affairs; and public administration. They must 1) present a proposed research plan related to space that includes an extramural experience at a field center of the National Aeronautics and Space Administration (NASA); 2) propose a multidisciplinary plan and course of study; 3) plan to be involved in consortium outreach activities; and 4) intend to pursue a career in line with NASA's aerospace, science, and technology programs. U.S. citizenship is required. Individuals from underrepresented groups (African Americans, Hispanics, American Indians, Pacific Islanders, and women of all races) are encouraged to apply. Interested students should submit a completed application form, a description of the proposed research, a schedule, a budget, a list of references, a vitae, and undergraduate and graduate transcripts. Selection is based on 1) academic

qualifications, 2) quality of the proposed research program or plan of study and its relevance to the aerospace science and technology program of NASA, 3) quality of the proposed interdisciplinary approach, 4) merit of the proposed utilization of a NASA center to carry out the objectives of the program, 5) prospects for completing the project within the allotted time, and 6) applicant's motivation for a career in aerospace.

Financial data   The award for 12 months includes $16,000 for a student stipend and up to $6,000 for a tuition/student research allowance.

Duration   Up to 36 months.

Additional information   The member universities are University of Alabama in Huntsville, Alabama A&M University, University of Alabama, University of Alabama at Birmingham, University of South Alabama, Tuskegee University, and Auburn University. Funding for this program is provided by NASA.

Number awarded   Varies each year; recently, 11 of these fellowships were awarded.

Deadline   February of each year.

[391]
ALBERT W. DENT STUDENT SCHOLARSHIP

American College of Healthcare Executives
One North Franklin Street, Suite 1700
Chicago, IL 60606-3491
(312) 424-2800   Fax: (312) 424-0023
E-mail: ache@ache.org
Web: www.ache.org

Purpose   To provide financial assistance to minority graduate student members of the American College of Healthcare Executives.

Eligibility   This program is open to student associates of the organization in good standing. Applicants must be minority students enrolled full time in a health care management graduate program, able to demonstrate financial need, and a U.S. or Canadian citizen.

Financial data   The stipend is $3,500.

Duration   1 year.

Additional information   The program was established and named in honor of Dr. Albert W. Dent, the foundation's first Black fellow and president emeritus of Dillard University.

Number awarded   Varies each year.

Deadline   March of each year.

[392]
AMELIA KEMP MEMORIAL SCHOLARSHIP

Women of the Evangelical Lutheran Church in America
Attn: Scholarships
8765 West Higgins Road
Chicago, IL 60631-4189
(773) 380-2730   (800) 638-3522, ext. 2730
Fax: (773) 380-2419   E-mail: womenelca@elca.org
Web: www.elca.org/wo/index.html

Purpose   To provide financial assistance to lay women of color who are members of Evangelical Lutheran Church of America (ELCA) congregations and who wish to study on the undergraduate, graduate, professional, or vocational school level.

Eligibility   These scholarships are available to ELCA lay women of color who are at least 21 years of age and have experienced an interruption of at least 2 years in their education since high school. Applicants must have been admitted to an educational institution to prepare for a career in other than a church-certified profession. U.S. citizenship is required.

Financial data The amount of the award varies, depending on the availability of funds.

Duration Up to 2 years.

Number awarded Varies each year, depending upon the funds available.

Deadline February of each year.

[393]
AMERICAN COLLEGE OF SPORTS MEDICINE GRADUATE SCHOLARSHIPS FOR MINORITIES AND WOMEN

American College of Sports Medicine
Attn: Research Review Committee
401 West Michigan Street
P.O. Box 1440
Indianapolis, IN 46206-1440
(317) 637-9200   Fax: (317) 637-7817
E-mail: jreed@acsm.org
Web: www.acsm.org/GRANTS/scholarships.htm

Purpose To provide financial assistance to minority and women graduate students who are interested in preparing for a career in sports medicine or exercise science.

Eligibility This program is open to minorities and women who have been accepted into a full-time master's, Ph.D., M.D., or equivalent degree program in sports medicine, exercise science, or other related field. Minorities include American Indians, Alaskan Natives, Asians, Pacific Islanders, Blacks, and Hispanics. Applicants must submit 3 letters of professional recommendation (including at least 1 from a current member of the American College of Sports Medicine), evidence of participation in sports medicine or exercise science (including documentation of research and scholarly activities), transcripts, GRE or MCAT scores, and a 300-word description of short- and long-term career goals.

Financial data The stipend is $1,500 per year. Funds are to be used to cover tuition and/or fees.

Duration 1 year; may be renewed for up to 3 additional years.

Additional information Recipients are given a 1 year's free membership in the American College of Sports Medicine.

Deadline April of each year.

[394]
AMERICAN DIETETIC ASSOCIATION GRADUATE SCHOLARSHIPS

American Dietetic Association
Attn: Accreditation, Education Programs, and Student
    Operations
216 West Jackson Boulevard, Suite 800
Chicago, IL 60606-6995
(312) 899-0040   (800) 877-1600, ext. 5400
Fax: (312) 899-4817   E-mail: education@eatright.org
Web: www.eatright.org

Purpose To provide financial assistance to students interested in working on a graduate degree in dietetics.

Eligibility Planned or current enrollment in a graduate degree program in dietetics is required. Applicants who are currently completing a dietetic internship or preprofessional practice program that is combined with a graduate program may also apply. The graduate scholarships are available only to U.S. citizens and permanent residents. Applicants should intend to practice in the field of dietetics. Some scholarships require specific areas of study (e.g., public health nutrition, food service administration) and status as a registered dietitian. Others may require membership in the association, specific dietetic practice group membership, residency in a specific state, or underrepresented minority group status. The same application form can be used for all categories.

Financial data Awards range from $500 to $5,000.

Duration 1 year.

Number awarded Varies each year, depending upon the funds available. Recently, the sponsoring organization awarded 209 scholarships for all its programs.

Deadline February of each year.

[395]
AMERICAN POLITICAL SCIENCE ASSOCIATION MINORITY FELLOWS PROGRAM

American Political Science Association
Attn: APSA Minority Fellows Program
1527 New Hampshire Avenue, N.W.
Washington, DC 20036-1206
(202) 483-2512   Fax: (202) 483-2657
E-mail: apsa@apsanet.org
Web: www.apsanet.org/about/minority/fellows.cfm

Purpose To provide financial assistance to underrepresented minorities interested in working on a doctoral degree in political science.

Eligibility This program is open to African Americans, Latino-(a)s, and Native Americans who are in their senior year at a college or university or currently enrolled in a master's degree program. Applicants must be planning to enroll in a doctoral program in the following academic year for the first time. They must be U.S. citizens and able to demonstrate financial need.

Financial data The stipend is $2,000 per year.

Duration 2 years.

Additional information In addition to the fellows who receive stipends from this program, fellows without stipend are recommended for admission and financial support to every doctoral political science program in the country. This program was established in 1969.

Number awarded 6 each year.

Deadline October of each year.

[396]
AMERICAN SOCIETY OF CRIMINOLOGY FELLOWSHIPS FOR ETHNIC MINORITIES

American Society of Criminology
Attn: Awards Committee
1314 Kinnear Road, Suite 212
Columbus, OH 43212-1156
(614) 292-9207   Fax: (614) 292-6767
E-mail: asc41@infinet.com
Web: www.asc41.com/minorfel.htm

Purpose To provide financial assistance to ethnic minority doctoral students in criminology and criminal justice.

Eligibility This program is open to African American, Asian American, Latino, and Native American doctoral students planning to enter the field of criminology and criminal justice. Applicants must submit an up-to-date curriculum vitae; an indication of race or ethnicity; copies of undergraduate and graduate transcripts; a statement of need and prospects for other financial assistance; a letter describing career plans, salient experiences, and nature of interest in criminology and criminal justice; and 3 letters of reference.

Financial data Stipends up to $6,000 are available.

Duration 1 year.

Additional information This fellowship was first awarded in 1989.

Number awarded 3 each year.

Deadline February of each year.

[397]
AMERICAN SPEECH-LANGUAGE-HEARING FOUNDATION YOUNG SCHOLARS AWARD FOR MINORITY STUDENTS

American Speech-Language-Hearing Foundation
Attn: Director of Programs and Corporate Development
10801 Rockville Pike
Rockville, MD 20852-3279
(301) 897-5700　　　　　　　　(800) 498-2071
Fax: (301) 571-0457　　　　　　TTY: (301) 897-0157
Web: www.ashfoundation.org

Purpose To provide financial assistance to minority graduate students in communication sciences and disorders programs.

Eligibility This program is open to full-time graduate students who are enrolled in communication sciences and disorders programs, with preference given to a student who is a racial/ethnic minority and a U.S. citizen. Selection is based on academic promise and outstanding academic achievement. Master's (but not doctoral) candidates must be enrolled in an ASHA Educational Standards Board (ESB) accredited program.

Financial data The stipend is $4,000.

Duration 1 year.

Number awarded 1 each year.

Deadline June of each year.

[398]
APA PLANNING FELLOWSHIPS

American Planning Association
Attn: Member Services Department
122 South Michigan Avenue, Suite 1600
Chicago, IL 60603-6107
(312) 431-9100　　　　　　　　Fax: (312) 431-9985
E-mail: Fellowships@planning.org
Web: www.planning.org

Purpose To support underrepresented minority students enrolled in master's degree programs at recognized planning schools.

Eligibility Candidates must be nominated by a planning school or department that is approved by the Planning Accreditation Board. Students are eligible to be nominated if they are or will be enrolled in full-time programs in urban or transportation planning and are members of the following minority groups: African American, Hispanic, or Native American. They must be citizens of the United States and able to document financial need. Each school may nominate no more than 1 candidate for the fellowship. The application must include a 1-page statement written by the student describing the reasons for interest in city or regional planning, a letter of recommendation from the planning faculty, copies of all transcripts or previous academic work, copies of GRE scores or similar data, a complete statement documenting the student's financial need, and written verification from the uni-

versity's financial officer or copies of a school publication indicating the average cost for 8 months of graduate school.

Financial data Awards range from $2,000 to $4,000 per year. The money may be applied to tuition and living expenses only. Payment is made to the recipient's university and divided by terms in the school year.

Duration 1 year; recipients may reapply.

Additional information The fellowship program started in 1970 as a Ford Foundation Minority Fellowship Program.

Number awarded 10 each year.

Deadline May of each year.

[399]
ARL INITIATIVE TO RECRUIT A DIVERSE WORKFORCE

Association of Research Libraries
Attn: Director, Organizational Learning Services
21 Dupont Circle, N.W., Suite 800
Washington, DC 20036
(202) 296-2296　　　　　　　　Fax: (202) 872-0884
E-mail: arlhq@arl.org
Web: www.arl.org/diversity/init

Purpose To provide financial assistance to members of racial and ethnic groups who are interested in preparing for a career as an academic or research librarian.

Eligibility This program is open to members of racial and ethnic minority groups that are underrepresented as professionals in academic and research libraries. Applicants must be interested in working on an M.L.S. degree in an ALA-accredited program. Along with their application, they must submit a 350-word essay on what attracts them to a career in a research library. The essays are judged on clarity and content of form, clear goals and benefits, enthusiasm, potential growth perceived, and professional goals.

Financial data The stipend is $2,500 per year.

Duration 2 years.

Additional information This program began in 2000. Recipients must agree to work for at least 2 years in a library that is a member of the Association of Research Libraries (ARL) after completing their degree.

Number awarded The program's goal is to award up to 15 of these scholarships each year.

Deadline May of each year.

[400]
ASME GRADUATE TEACHING FELLOWSHIP

ASME International
Attn: Education Department
Three Park Avenue
New York, NY 10016-5990
(212) 591-8131　　　　　　　　(800) THE-ASME
Fax: (212) 591-7143　　　　　E-mail: oluwanifiset@asme.org
Web: www.asme.org/educate/aid/fellow.htm

Purpose To encourage members of the American Society of Mechanical Engineers (ASME) to work on a doctorate in mechanical engineering and to select engineering education as a profession.

Eligibility This program is open to U.S. citizens or permanent residents who hold an undergraduate degree from an ABET-accredited program, belong to the society as a student member, are currently employed as a teaching assistant, and are working on a doctorate in mechanical engineering. Applications from women and minorities are particularly encouraged.

Financial data Fellowship stipends are $5,000 per year.

Duration Up to 2 years. Recipients must teach at least 1 lecture course.

Number awarded Up to 4 each year.

Deadline October of each year.

[401]
ASSOCIATION OF CUBAN ENGINEERS SCHOLARSHIPS

Association of Cuban Engineers
Attn: President
P.O. Box 557575
Miami, FL 33255-7575
(305) 649-7429

Purpose To provide financial assistance to undergraduate and graduate students of Cuban American heritage and others who are interested in preparing for a career in engineering.

Eligibility This program is open to U.S. citizens and legal residents who have completed at least 50 units of college work in the United States and are majoring or planning to major in some aspect of engineering. Applicants must be attending an ABET-accredited college or university within the United States or Puerto Rico as a full-time student. They must be of Cuban American heritage. If an insufficient number of qualified Cuban American students apply, scholarships may be made available to other Hispanic, African American, and women applicants. Selection is based on GPA (up to 35 points, 3.0 or higher), financial need (up to 25 points for an applicant needing $5,470), participation in extracurricular activities (up to 25 points), and student class standing (3.75 points for sophomores, 7.5 points for juniors, 11.25 points for seniors, and 15 points for graduate students).

Financial data Stipends range from $500 to $1,000 per year.

Duration 1 year.

Additional information This program includes the Luciano Goicochea Award (for the top-rated Cuban American student at Florida International University) and the Noel Betancourt Award (for the top-rated Cuban American student at the University of Miami).

Number awarded Up to 20 each year.

Deadline October of each year.

[402]
ASSOCIATION OF LATINO PROFESSIONALS IN FINANCE AND ACCOUNTING SCHOLARSHIPS

Association of Latino Professionals in Finance and
  Accounting
Attn: National Executive Director
510 West Sixth Street, Suite 400
Los Angeles, CA 90017
(213) 243-0004   Fax: (213) 243-0006
E-mail: scholarships.national@alpfa.org
Web: www.alpfa.org

Purpose To provide financial assistance to undergraduate and graduate students of Hispanic descent who are preparing for a career in a field related to finance or accounting.

Eligibility This program is open to full-time undergraduate and graduate students who have completed at least 15 undergraduate units at a college or university in the United States or Puerto Rico with a GPA of 3.0 or higher. Applicants must be of Hispanic

heritage, defined as having 1 parent fully Hispanic or both parents half Hispanic. They must be pursuing a degree in accounting, finance, or a related field. Along with their application, they must submit a 2-page personal statement that addresses their Hispanic heritage and family background, personal and academic achievements, academic plans and career goals, efforts and plans for making a difference in their community, and financial need. U.S. citizenship or permanent resident status is required.

Financial data The stipend is at least $1,250 per year.

Duration 1 year.

Additional information The sponsoring organization was formerly named the American Association of Hispanic Certified Public Accountants. This program is administered by the Hispanic Scholarship Fund, 55 Second Street, Suite 1500, San Francisco, CA 94105, (877) HSF-INFO, E-mail: specialprograms@hsf.net.

Number awarded Varies each year; recently, 78 of these scholarships, worth $195,000, were awarded.

Deadline May of each year.

[403]
AT&T LABORATORIES FELLOWSHIP PROGRAM FELLOWSHIPS

AT&T Laboratories
Attn: Fellowship Administrator
180 Park Avenue, Room C103
P.O. Box 971
Florham Park, NJ 07932-0971
(973) 360-8109   Fax: (973) 360-8881
Web: www.research.att.com/academic

Purpose To provide financial assistance and work experience to underrepresented minority and women students who are pursuing doctoral studies in computer and communications-related fields.

Eligibility This program is open to minorities underrepresented in the sciences (Blacks, Hispanics, and Native Americans) and to women. Applicants must be U.S. citizens or permanent residents beginning full-time Ph.D. study in a discipline relevant to the business of AT&T; currently, those include communications, computer science, electrical engineering, human computer interaction, industrial engineering, information science, mathematics, operations research, and statistics. Along with their application, they must submit a statement describing their technical interests and accomplishments, official transcripts, 3 academic references, and GRE scores. Selection is based on potential for success in scientific research. Fellowships are offered to students who receive no other support for graduate study.

Financial data This program covers all educational expenses during the school year, including tuition, books, fees, and approved travel expenses; education expenses for summer study or university research; a stipend for living expenses of $1,400 per month (paid for 12 months the first 2 years and for 10 months in the following years); and support for attending approved scientific conferences.

Duration 1 year; may be renewed for up to 5 additional years, as long as the fellow continues making satisfactory progress toward the Ph.D.

Additional information The AT&T Laboratories Fellowship Program (ALFP) provides a mentor who is a staff member at AT&T Labs as well as a summer research internship within AT&T Laboratories during the first summer. The ALFP replaces the Graduate Research Program for Women (GRPW) and the Cooperative Research Fellowship Program (CRFP) run by the former AT&T Bell

Laboratories. If students receive other fellowship support, the tuition support and stipend provided as part of the ALFP Fellowship will cease, but the other provisions will remain in force and the student will remain eligible for an ALFP Grant.

Number awarded   Varies each year.

Deadline   January of each year.

[404]
AT&T LABORATORIES FELLOWSHIP PROGRAM GRANTS

AT&T Laboratories
Attn: Fellowship Administrator
180 Park Avenue, Room C103
P.O. Box 971
Florham Park, NJ 07932-0971
(973) 360-8109   Fax: (973) 360-8881
Web: www.research.att.com/academic

Purpose   To provide financial assistance and work experience to underrepresented minority and women students who are pursuing doctoral studies in computer and communications-related fields.

Eligibility   This program is open to minorities underrepresented in the sciences (Blacks, Hispanics, and Native Americans) and to women. Applicants must be U.S. citizens or permanent residents beginning full-time Ph.D. study in a discipline relevant to the business of AT&T; currently, those include communications, computer science, electrical engineering, human computer interaction, industrial engineering, information science, mathematics, operations research, and statistics. Along with their application, they must submit a statement describing their technical interests and accomplishments, official transcripts, 3 academic references, and GRE scores. Selection is based on potential for success in scientific research. Grants are offered to students who receive other support for graduate study.

Financial data   This program provides an annual stipend of $2,000 and conference travel support.

Duration   1 year; may be renewed for up to 5 additional years, as long as the fellow continues making satisfactory progress toward the Ph.D.

Additional information   The AT&T Laboratories Fellowship Program (ALFP) provides a mentor who is a staff member at AT&T Laboratories as well as a summer research internship within AT&T Laboratories during the first summer. The ALFP replaces the Graduate Research Program for Women (GRPW) and the Cooperative Research Fellowship Program (CRFP) run by the former AT&T Bell Laboratories.

Number awarded   Varies each year.

Deadline   January of each year.

[405]
BALFOUR PHI DELTA PHI MINORITY SCHOLARSHIP PROGRAM

Phi Delta Phi International Legal Fraternity
1750 N Street, N.W.
Washington, DC 20036-2998
(202) 628-0148   (800) 368-5606
Fax: (202) 296-7619   E-mail: phideltaphi@worldnet.att.net
Web: www.phideltaphi.org

Purpose   To provide financial assistance to minorities who are members of Phi Delta Phi International Legal Fraternity.

Eligibility   All ethnic minority members of the legal fraternity are eligible to apply for this scholarship. Selection is based on participation, ethics, and scholastics.

Financial data   The stipend is $3,000 per year.

Duration   1 year.

Additional information   This scholarship was established in 1997. Funding for this scholarship comes from the Lloyd G. Balfour Foundation.

Number awarded   1 each year.

[406]
BARBARA JORDAN MEMORIAL SCHOLARSHIP

Association of Texas Professional Educators
Attn: Scholarships
305 East Huntland Drive, Suite 300
Austin, TX 78752-3792
(512) 467-0071   (800) 777-ATPE
Fax: (512) 467-2203
Web: www.atpe.org/AboutATPE/bjordaninfo.htm

Purpose   To provide financial assistance to undergraduate and graduate students enrolled in educator preparation programs at predominantly ethnic minority institutions in Texas.

Eligibility   This program is open to juniors, seniors, and graduate students enrolled in educator preparation programs at predominantly ethnic minority institutions in Texas. Applicants must submit a 2-page essay on their personal philosophy toward education, why they want to become an educator, who influenced them the most in making their career decision, and why they are applying for the scholarship. Financial need is not considered in the selection process.

Financial data   The stipend is $1,500 per year.

Duration   1 year.

Additional information   The qualifying institutions are Huston-Tillotson College, Jarvis Christian College, Our Lady of the Lake University, Paul Quinn College, Prairie View A&M University, St. Mary's University of San Antonio, Sul Ross State University, Sul Ross State University Rio Grande College, Texas A&M International University, Texas A&M-Kingsville, Texas Southern University, University of Houston, University of Houston-Downtown, University of St. Thomas, University of Texas at Brownsville and Texas Southmost College, University of Texas at El Paso, University of Texas at San Antonio, University of Texas-Pan American, University of the Incarnate Word, and Wiley College.

Number awarded   Up to 4 each year.

Deadline   November of each year.

[407]
BAY AREA MINORITY LAW STUDENT SCHOLARSHIPS

Bar Association of San Francisco
Attn: Coordinator of Diversity Programs
465 California Street, Suite 1100
San Francisco, CA 94104-1826
(415) 782-8975   (888) 741-4949
Fax: (415) 477-2388   E-mail: etam@sfbar.org
Web: www.sfbar.org

Purpose   To provide financial assistance to students of color interested in attending law school in northern California.

Eligibility   This program is open to students of color (African Americans, Native Americans, Latinos/Chicanos, and southeast Asians) who accept offers of admission from designated law schools in northern California. Financial need is considered in the selection process.

Financial data The stipend is $5,000 per year.

Duration 3 years.

Additional information This program was established in 1998. The applicable law schools are Boalt, Davis, Golden Gate University, Hastings, McGeorge, Santa Clara University, Stanford, and University of San Francisco.

Number awarded Varies each year; recently, 3 of these fellowships were awarded.

Deadline May of each year.

[408]
BOARD OF GOVERNORS MEDICAL SCHOLARSHIP PROGRAM

North Carolina State Education Assistance Authority
Attn: Scholarship and Grant Services
10 T.W. Alexander Drive
P.O. Box 14103
Research Triangle Park, NC 27709-4103
(919) 549-8614   (800) 700-1775
Fax: (919) 549-8481   E-mail: information@ncseaa.edu
Web: www.ncseaa.edu

Purpose To provide financial assistance to residents of North Carolina who have been admitted to a medical school in the state.

Eligibility Students must be nominated for this program. Nominees must be residents of North Carolina, be able to demonstrate financial need, express an intent to practice medicine in North Carolina, and have been accepted for admission to 1 of the 4 medical schools in North Carolina: Bowman Gray School of Medicine at Wake Forest University, Duke University School of Medicine, East Carolina University School of Medicine, and the University of North Carolina at Chapel Hill School of Medicine. Minorities are especially encouraged to apply.

Financial data Each scholarship provides a stipend of $5,000 a year, plus tuition and mandatory fees.

Duration 1 year; renewable up to 3 additional years, provided the recipient makes satisfactory academic progress, continues to have financial need, and remains interested in medical practice in North Carolina.

Number awarded 20 new awards are granted each year. Recently, a total of 75 students were receiving $1,321,592 in support through this program

Deadline April of each year.

[409]
BRISTOL-MYERS SQUIBB PRLDEF CORPORATE LEGAL FELLOWSHIP

Puerto Rican Legal Defense and Education Fund
Attn: Education Division Director
99 Hudson Street, 14th Floor
New York, NY 10013-2815
(212) 219-3360, ext. 223   (800) 328-2322, ext. 223
Fax: (212) 431-4276   E-mail: education@prldef.org
Web: www.prldef.org/education.htm

Purpose To provide summer work experience and financial assistance to minority law students interested in a career in corporate legal departments.

Eligibility This program is open to first- and second-year law students of color who are interested in preparing for a career in corporate legal departments. Students who complete the intern-

ship successfully and demonstrate academic excellence are eligible for a scholarship.

Financial data The stipend for the internship is $9,000. The scholarship, for those who complete the internship, is $1,000.

Duration 10 weeks in the summer for the internship; 1 year for the scholarship.

Additional information Interns are matched with mentors within Bristol-Myers Squibb (the program's sponsor) who provide ongoing guidance on professional development throughout their academic career and subsequent graduation.

Number awarded Varies each year.

Deadline November of each year.

[410]
C. CLYDE FERGUSON LAW SCHOLARSHIP

New Jersey Commission on Higher Education
Attn: Educational Opportunity Fund
20 West State Street, Seventh Floor
P.O. Box 542
Trenton, NJ 08625-0542
(609) 984-2709   Fax: (609) 292-7225
E-mail: nj_che@che.state.nj.us
Web: www.state.nj.us/highereducation

Purpose To provide financial assistance to disadvantaged and minority students who want to study law in New Jersey.

Eligibility Applicants must be disadvantaged students or members of an ethnic minority group that has been historically underrepresented in the legal profession. They must have been New Jersey residents for at least 12 months before receiving the award. They must plan to enroll full time in the Minority Student Program at law schools in New Jersey. Applicants may be former or current undergraduate recipients of the New Jersey Educational Opportunity Fund (EOF) grant or students who would have met the undergraduate EOF grant eligibility requirements. Financial need must be demonstrated.

Financial data Awards are based on financial need. In no case, however, can awards exceed the maximum amount of tuition, fees, room, and board charged at Rutgers University School of Law at Newark.

Duration 1 year; may be renewed.

[411]
CALIFORNIA SPACE GRANT GRADUATE STUDENT PROGRAM

California Space Grant Consortium
c/o University of California at San Diego
California Space Institute
9500 Gilman Drive, Department 0524
La Jolla, CA 92093
(858) 822-1597   Fax: (858) 534-7840
E-mail: spacegrant@ucsd.edu
Web: calspace.ucsd.edu/spacegrant/california/index.html

Purpose To provide financial assistance for graduate study and research in space-related science, engineering, or technology at the 8 branches of the University of California.

Eligibility This program is open to graduate students in space-related science, engineering, and technology at the 8 campuses of the UC system. Most programs include research components. U.S. citizenship is required. As the California element of the Space Grant program of the U.S. National Aeronautics and Space Administration (NASA), this program encourages applications from underrepresented ethnic or gender groups and by persons with disabilities.

Financial data Each campus sets its own stipend.

Duration 1 year.

Additional information This program is funded by NASA.

Number awarded Varies each year.

Deadline Each of the participating UC campuses sets its own deadline.

[412]
CALIFORNIA STATE PSYCHOLOGICAL ASSOCIATION FOUNDATION MINORITY SCHOLARSHIP PROGRAM

California State Psychological Association Foundation
Attn: Scholarship Coordinator
1022 G Street, Suite 202
Sacramento, CA 95814-0817
(916) 325-9786, ext. 124   Fax: (916) 325-9790
E-mail: bgomez@calpsychlink.org
Web: www.calpsychlink.org

Purpose To provide financial assistance to minority students interested in working on a doctoral degree in psychology in California.

Eligibility Applicants must be full-time graduate students who are enrolled or accepted in a doctoral-level psychology program at an accredited California school. Applicants must belong to 1 of the following ethnic groups: Black/African American, Hispanic/Latino, Asian/Asian American, American Indian/Alaskan Native, or Pacific Islander. Along with their application, they must submit 3 to 5 letters of recommendation, an official transcript, and documentation of financial need. Selection is based on potential for pursuing doctoral level work in psychology. No distinction or preference is made for practitioner versus academic programs. Priority is given to applicants with demonstrated community involvement or leadership, whose graduate program focuses on ethnic minority cultural issues, and who plan to work with direct delivery of services to a culturally diverse population in either private or public settings.

Financial data The stipend is $2,500.

Duration 1 year; nonrenewable.

Additional information This program was established in 1991.

Number awarded 3 each year: 1 each to a first-, second-, and third-year doctoral student.

Deadline October of each year.

[413]
CANFIT PROGRAM SCHOLARSHIPS

California Adolescent Nutrition and Fitness Program
2140 Shattuck Avenue, Suite 610
Berkeley, CA 94704
(510) 644-1533   (800) 200-3131
Fax: (510) 644-1535   E-mail: info@canfit.org
Web: www.canfit.org

Purpose To provide financial assistance to minority undergraduate and graduate students who are studying nutrition or physical education in California.

Eligibility Eligible to apply are American Indians/Alaska Natives, African Americans, Asians/Pacific Islanders, and Latinos/Hispanics who are enrolled in either: 1) an approved master's or doctoral graduate program in nutrition, public health nutrition, or physical education or in a preprofessional practice pro-

gram approved by the American Dietetic Association at an accredited university in California; or, 2) an approved bachelor's or professional certificate program in culinary arts, nutrition, or physical education at an accredited university or college in California. Graduate student applicants must have completed at least 12 units of graduate course work and have a cumulative GPA of 3.0 or higher; undergraduate applicants must have completed 50 semester units or the equivalent of college credits and have a cumulative GPA of 2.5 or higher. Selection is based on financial need, academic goals, and community nutrition or physical education activities.

Financial data Graduate stipends are $1,000 each and undergraduate stipends are $500 per year.

Additional information A goal of the California Adolescent Nutrition and Fitness (CANFit) program is to improve the nutritional status and physical fitness of California's low-income multiethnic youth aged 10 to 14. By offering these scholarships, the program hopes to encourage more students to consider careers in adolescent nutrition and fitness.

Number awarded 5 graduate scholarships and 10 undergraduate scholarships are available each year.

Deadline March of each year.

[414]
CARL A. SCOTT BOOK FELLOWSHIPS

Council on Social Work Education
Attn: Chair, Carl A. Scott Memorial Fund
1725 Duke Street, Suite 500
Alexandria, VA 22314-3457
(703) 683-8080   Fax: (703) 683-8099
E-mail: eafrancis@cswe.org
Web: www.cswe.org

Purpose To provide financial assistance to ethnic minority social work students in their last year of study for a baccalaureate or master's degree.

Eligibility This program is open to students from ethnic groups of color (African American, Asian American, Mexican American, Puerto Rican, and American Indian) who are in the last year of study for a social work degree in an accredited baccalaureate or master's degree program. Applicants must have a cumulative GPA of 3.0 or higher and be enrolled full time. They must demonstrate a commitment to work for equity and social justice in social work.

Financial data The award is $500.

Duration This is a 1-time award.

Number awarded 2 each year.

Deadline May of each year.

[415]
CATHY L. BROCK MEMORIAL SCHOLARSHIP

Institute for Diversity in Health Management
Attn: Education Program Coordinator
One North Franklin Street, 30th Floor
Chicago, IL 60606
(800) 233-0996   Fax: (312) 422-4566
E-mail: clopez@aha.org
Web: www.diversityconnection.com

Purpose To provide financial assistance to minority upper-division and graduate students in health care management or business management.

Eligibility This program is open to members of ethnic minority groups who are college juniors, seniors, or graduate students. Applicants must be accepted or enrolled in an accredited program in health care management or business management and have a GPA of 3.0 or higher. They must demonstrate commitment to a career in health services administration, financial need, solid extracurricular and community service activities, and a strong interest and experience in finance. U.S. citizenship or permanent resident status is required.

Financial data The stipend is $1,000.

Duration 1 year.

Number awarded 1 or more each year, depending on the availability of funds.

Deadline June of each year.

[416]
CHEERIOS BRAND HEALTH INITIATIVE SCHOLARSHIP

Congressional Black Caucus Foundation, Inc.
Attn: Director, Educational Programs
1004 Pennsylvania Avenue, S.E.
Washington, DC 20003
(202) 675-6739   (800) 784-2577
Fax: (202) 547-3806   E-mail: spouses@cbcfonline.org
Web: www.cbcfonline.org/cbcspouses/scholarship.html

Purpose To provide financial assistance to minority and other undergraduate and graduate students who reside in a congressional district represented by an African American and are interested in preparing for a health-related career.

Eligibility This program is open to 1) minority and other graduating high school seniors planning to attend an accredited institution of higher education and 2) currently-enrolled full-time undergraduate, graduate, and doctoral students in good academic standing with a GPA of 2.5 or higher. Applicants must reside, attend school, or have attended high school in a congressional district represented by an African American member of Congress. They must be interested in pursuing a career in a health-related field, including pre-medicine, nursing, chemistry, biology, physical education, and engineering. As part of the application process, they must include a 250-word personal statement describing how this scholarship will assist them in their educational career.

Financial data The program provides tuition assistance.

Duration 1 year.

Additional information The program was established in 1998 with support from General Mills, Inc.

Number awarded Varies each year.

Deadline May or September of each year.

[417]
CHICANA/LATINA FOUNDATION SCHOLARSHIP COMPETITION

Chicana/Latina Foundation
Attn: Scholarship Program
P.O. Box 1941
El Cerrito, CA 94530-4941
(510) 526-5861   E-mail: info@chicanalatina.org
Web: www.chicanalatina.org/scholarship.html

Purpose To provide financial assistance for college or graduate school to Latina women in the San Francisco Bay area.

Eligibility This program is open to Latina women who either have resided for at least 2 years in or are currently enrolled in accredited colleges, universities, or community colleges in the following California counties: Alameda, Contra Costa, Marin, Monterey, Napa, San Francisco, San Mateo, Santa Clara, Santa Cruz, Solano, or Sonoma. Undergraduate students must have completed at least 15 college units, must be enrolled as full-time students, must have a GPA of 2.5 or higher, and must complete 3 essays (on their family background, their community activities, and their career goals). Graduate students must verify acceptance to a graduate school and complete a supplementary application that requires 3 essays: on an issue affecting the Latina community in the Bay area, on their personal background, and on their leadership of their younger Chicana/Latina sisters so they stay in school and graduate. Selection is based on commitment to Latina women's progress and development, demonstrated leadership qualities, involvement within the Latino community, clarity of direction and goals, academic achievement, and letters of recommendation. Students who received a scholarship from the foundation within the past 4 years are not eligible.

Financial data The stipend is $1,000 per year.

Duration 1 year.

Additional information The foundation was formerly known as the Chicana Foundation of Northern California. Requests for applications must be accompanied by a self-addressed stamped envelope.

Number awarded Varies each year; recently, 18 of these scholarships were awarded.

Deadline March of each year.

[418]
CLA SCHOLARSHIP FOR MINORITY STUDENTS IN MEMORY OF EDNA YELLAND

California Library Association
717 20th Street, Suite 200
Sacramento, CA 95814
(916) 447-8541   Fax: (916) 447-8394
E-mail: info@cla-net.org
Web: www.cla-net.org

Purpose To provide financial assistance to students of ethnic minority origin in California who are interested in preparing for a career in library or information science.

Eligibility This program is open to California residents who are members of ethnic minority groups (American Indian, African American/Black, Mexican American/Chicano, Latino/Hispanic, Asian American, Pacific Islander, or Filipino). Applicants must be enrolled or accepted for enrollment in a master's program at an accredited graduate library school in California. Evidence of financial need and U.S. citizenship or permanent resident status must be submitted. Finalists are interviewed.

Financial data The amount of the award depends on the availability of funds and the need of the recipient. Recently, awards were $2,500.

Duration 1 academic year.

Additional information This fellowship is named for the executive secretary of the California Library Association from 1947 to 1963 who worked to promote the goals of the California Library Association and the profession. Until 1985, it was named the Edna Yelland Memorial Scholarship.

Number awarded Varies each year; recently, 3 of these scholarships were awarded.

Deadline May of each year.

[419]
COLLEGE SCHOLARSHIP PROGRAM OF THE HISPANIC SCHOLARSHIP FUND

Hispanic Scholarship Fund
Attn: Selection Committee
55 Second Street, Suite 1500
San Francisco, CA 94105
(877) HSF-INFO   Fax: (415) 808-2302
E-mail: info@hsf.net
Web: www.hsf.net

Purpose To provide financial assistance for college or graduate school to Hispanic American students.

Eligibility This program is open to U.S. citizens, permanent residents, and visitors with a passport stamped I-551. Applicants must be of Hispanic heritage (each parent half Hispanic or 1 parent fully Hispanic) and enrolled full time in a degree-seeking program at an accredited college or university in the United States or Puerto Rico. They may be undergraduate or graduate students, but they must have completed at least 12 undergraduate units with a GPA of 2.7 or higher. Along with their application, they must submit a 2-page essay that addresses the following topics: their Hispanic heritage and family background, personal and academic achievements, academic plans and career goals, efforts toward making a difference in the community, and financial need.

Financial data Stipends normally range from $1,000 to $3,000 per year.

Duration 1 year; recipients may reapply.

Additional information Since this program began in 1975, more than $47 million has been awarded to more than 40,000 Hispanic students. Requests for applications must be accompanied by a self-addressed stamped envelope.

Number awarded More than 4,000 each year.

Deadline October of each year.

[420]
COLORADO SOCIETY OF CPAS ETHNIC DIVERSITY SCHOLARSHIPS FOR COLLEGE STUDENTS

Colorado Society of Certified Public Accountants
Attn: Educational Foundation
7979 East Tufts Avenue, Suite 500
Denver, CO 80237-2843
(303) 741-8613   (800) 523-9082 (within CO)
Fax: (303) 773-6344
E-mail: cpa-staff@cscpa.denver.co.us
Web: www.cocpa.org

Purpose To provide financial assistance to minority undergraduate or graduate students in Colorado who are studying accounting.

Eligibility This program is open to African American, Hispanic, Asian American, American Indian, and Pacific Islander students studying at a college or university in Colorado at the associate, baccalaureate, or graduate level. Applicants must have completed at least 1 intermediate accounting class, be declared accounting majors, have completed at least 8 semester hours of accounting classes, and have a GPA of at least 3.0. Selection is based first on scholastic achievement and second on financial need.

Financial data The stipend is $1,000.

Duration 1 year; recipients may reapply.

Number awarded 2 each year.

Deadline November of each year.

[421]
COMISION FEMENIL DE LOS ANGELES SCHOLARSHIP

Comisión Femenil de Los Angeles
Attn: Scholarship Committee
P.O. Box 86013
Los Angeles, CA 90086
(818) 549-9530

Purpose To provide financial assistance to Latinas in southern California interested in working on an undergraduate or graduate degree.

Eligibility This program is open to Latinas who reside in the Los Angeles County area. Applicants must be interested in attending a 2-year or 4-year college, university, trade school, or professional school (e.g., law school, medical school) in southern California. They must submit a 1-page biographical essay and a 1-page essay on topics relating to their goals and aspirations. Finalists are interviewed. Selection is based on academic achievement (at least a 3.0 GPA), evidence of character and promise, demonstration of leadership, the essays, letters of recommendation, the interview, and financial need.

Financial data The amount awarded depends upon the needs of the recipient. Funds are paid in 2 installments: the first half is issued when verification of enrollment is received; the second is issued upon satisfactory completion of the first term.

Duration 1 year.

Number awarded Varies each year.

Deadline July of each year.

[422]
CONGRESSIONAL BLACK CAUCUS SPOUSES SCHOLARSHIP FUND PROGRAM

Congressional Black Caucus Foundation, Inc.
Attn: Director, Educational Programs
1004 Pennsylvania Avenue, S.E.
Washington, DC 20003
(202) 675-6739   (800) 784-2577
Fax: (202) 547-3806   E-mail: spouses@cbcfonline.org
Web: www.cbcfonline.org/cbcspouses/scholarship.html

Purpose To provide financial assistance to minority and other undergraduate and graduate students who reside in a congressional district represented by an African American.

Eligibility This program is open to 1) minority and other graduating high school seniors planning to attend an accredited institution of higher education and 2) currently-enrolled full-time undergraduate, graduate, and doctoral students in good academic standing with a GPA of 2.5 or higher. Applicants must reside, attend school, or have attended high school in a congressional district represented by an African American member of Congress. Relatives of caucus members, spouses, and staff are not eligible.

Financial data The program provides tuition assistance.

Duration 1 year.

Additional information The program was established in 1988.

Number awarded Varies each year.

Deadline May or September of each year.

[423]
CONGRESSIONAL HISPANIC CAUCUS INSTITUTE SCHOLARSHIP AWARDS

Congressional Hispanic Caucus Institute, Inc.
504 C Street, N.E.
Washington, DC 20002
(202) 543-1771   (800) EXCEL-DC
Fax: (202) 546-2143   E-mail: chci@chci.org
Web: www.chci.org

Purpose To provide financial assistance for college or graduate school to students of Hispanic descent.

Eligibility This program is open to U.S. citizens and permanent residents who are Hispanic as defined by the U.S. Census Bureau (individuals of Mexican, Puerto Rican, Cuban, Central and South American, and other Spanish and Latin American descent). Applicants must be attending or planning to attend an accredited community college, 4-year university, or professional or graduate program. They must submit evidence of financial need, consistent and active participation in public service activities, and 3 1-page essays on 1) how effective the public education system has been in addressing the needs of the Latino community and what policy recommendations they suggest to improve the system; 2) the field of study they plan to pursue and how the Latino community will benefit; and 3) their definition of leadership and which Latino leader best exemplifies their definition of leadership.

Financial data The stipend is $5,000 at 4-year and graduate institutions or $1,500 at 2-year community colleges.

Duration 1 year.

Number awarded Varies each year; recently, 40 undergraduates and 15 graduate students received these scholarships.

Deadline April of each year.

[424]
CONSORTIUM FOR GRADUATE STUDY IN MANAGEMENT FELLOWSHIPS

Consortium for Graduate Study in Management
5585 Pershing Avenue, Suite 240
St. Louis, MO 63112
(314) 877-5500   (888) 658-6814
Fax: (314) 877-5505   E-mail: frontdesk@cgsm.org
Web: www.cgsm.org

Purpose To provide financial assistance and work experience to underrepresented racial minorities in graduate school who are interested in preparing for managerial positions in business.

Eligibility Eligible to apply are African Americans, Hispanic Americans (Chicanos, Cubans, Dominicans, and Puerto Ricans), and Native Americans who have graduated from college and are interested in a career in business. An undergraduate degree in business or economics is not required. Applicants must be U.S. citizens and planning to pursue a Master's of Business Administration degree at 1 of the consortium's 14 schools. Preference is given to applicants under 31 years of age.

Financial data The fellowship pays full tuition and required fees. Summer internships with the consortium's cooperative sponsors, providing paid practical experience, are also offered.

Duration Up to 4 semesters. The participating schools are University of California at Berkeley, Carnegie Mellon University, Dartmouth College, Emory University, Indiana University, University of Michigan, New York University, University of North Carolina at Chapel Hill, University of Rochester, University of Southern California, University of Texas at Austin, University of Virginia, Wash-

ington University, and University of Wisconsin at Madison. Fellowships are tenable at member schools only.

Number awarded Varies; up to 400 each year.

Deadline The early deadline is the end of November of each year. The final deadline is in January of each year.

[425]
CONSUELO W. GOSNELL MEMORIAL SCHOLARSHIPS

National Association of Social Workers
Attn: NASW Foundation
750 First Street, N.E., Suite 700
Washington, DC 20002-4241
(202) 336-8298   Fax: (202) 336-8313
E-mail: naswfoundation@naswdc.org
Web: www.naswfoundation.org/gosnell.html

Purpose To provide financial assistance to Native American, Hispanic American, and other students interested in working on a master's degree in social work.

Eligibility This program is open to students who have applied to or been accepted into an accredited M.S.W. program. Applicants must have demonstrated a commitment to working with, or have a special affinity with, American Indian, Alaska Native, or Hispanic/Latino populations in the United States. They must have the potential for completing an M.S.W. program and have a GPA of 3.0 or higher. Applicants who have demonstrated a commitment to working with public or voluntary nonprofit agencies or with local grassroots groups in the United States are also eligible.

Financial data The stipends range from $1,000 to $4,000 per year.

Duration Up to 1 year; may be renewed for 1 additional year.

Number awarded Up to 10 each year.

Deadline February of each year.

[426]
COORS LIGHT ACADEMIC SUCCESS IN EDUCATION (CLASE) SCHOLARSHIP AWARD

Hispanic Association of Colleges and Universities
Attn: Scholarship Programs
8415 Datapoint Drive, Suite 400
San Antonio, TX 78229
(210) 692-3805   Fax: (210) 692-0823
E-mail: hacu@hacu.net
Web: www.hacu.net/student_resources/index.shtml

Purpose To provide financial assistance to undergraduate and graduate students at institutions in the United States, Puerto Rico, and Mexico that are members of the Hispanic Association of Colleges and Universities (HACU).

Eligibility This program is open to full-time undergraduate and graduate students at HACU member and partner colleges. Students in the United States and Puerto Rico may study at their home institution or at an HACU-member institution in Mexico. Students in Mexico may study at a U.S. HACU-member institution. All academic majors are eligible. Applicants must submit an essay of 200 to 250 words that describes their academic and/or career goals, where they expect to be and what they expect to be doing 10 years from now, and what skills they can bring to an employer. They must be able to demonstrate financial need and a GPA of 3.2 or higher.

Financial data The stipend is $1,000 per year.

Duration 1 year; nonrenewable.

Additional information This program is sponsored by the Coors Brewing Company and administered by HACU. Recently, the sponsor provided additional funding in conjunction with the concert tour of the musical group *Maná Revolución de Amor*. For every concert ticket sold, the group donated $0.50 and Coors matched with an additional $0.50, to a combined maximum contribution of $200,000.

Number awarded Up to 200 each year.

Deadline June of each year.

[427]
D. AUGUSTUS STRAKER SCHOLARSHIP

D. Augustus Straker Bar Association
Attn: Foundation Board
P.O. Box 1898
Troy, MI 48099-1898
Web: www.michbar.org

Purpose To provide financial assistance to minority students at law schools in Michigan.

Eligibility This program is open to minority students enrolled in a certified law school program within the state of Michigan. Applicants must demonstrate scholarly dedication, involvement in school and community activities, and the ability to articulate a vision that indicates prospects for long-term success in the practice of law, especially as it relates to representing minority viewpoints within the system of jurisprudence.

Financial data The stipend is $2,500.

Duration 1 year.

Additional information The D. Augustus Straker Bar Association was founded in 1990 as a proactive organization for African American attorneys. It was named in honor of the first African American attorney to argue a case before the Michigan Supreme Court in 1890.

Number awarded 2 each year.

Deadline March of each year.

[428]
DAVID C. LIZARRAGA GRADUATE FELLOWSHIPS

TELACU Education Foundation
5400 East Olympic Boulevard, Suite 300
Los Angeles, CA 90022
(323) 721-1655　　　　　　Fax: (323) 724-3372
E-mail: info@telacu.com
Web: www.telacu.com

Purpose To provide financial assistance to Latino students in the Los Angeles area who are interested in furthering their formal education at the graduate level.

Eligibility This program is open to Latino students residing in unincorporated areas of east Los Angeles, as well as the cities of Bell Gardens, Commerce, Huntington Park, Los Angeles, Montebello, Monterey Park, Pico Rivera, Santa Ana, and South Gate. Applicants must have exhibited an interest and ability in helping to improve their community through education and economic empowerment.

Financial data A stipend is awarded (amount not specified).

Duration 1 year.

Number awarded 1 or more each year.

Deadline April of each year.

[429]
DELL/UNCF CORPORATE SCHOLARS PROGRAM

United Negro College Fund
Attn: Corporate Scholars Program
P.O. Box 1435
Alexandria, VA 22313-9998
(866) 671-7237　　　　　　E-mail: internship@uncf.org
Web: www.uncf.org/Scholarship/CorporateScholars.asp

Purpose To provide financial assistance and work experience to undergraduate and graduate students, especially minorities, majoring in designated fields and interested in an internship at Dell Computer Corporation's corporate headquarters near Austin, Texas.

Eligibility This program is open to rising juniors and graduate students who are African Americans, Hispanics, Asian/Pacific Islanders, Caucasians, and Native Americans. Applicants must be enrolled full time at institutions that are members of the United Negro College Fund (UNCF) or at other targeted colleges and universities. They must be majoring in business administration, computer science, engineering (computer, electrical, or mechanical), finance, human resources, management information systems, marketing, or supply chain management with a GPA of 3.0 or higher. Along with their application, they must submit a 1-page essay about themselves and their career goals, including information about their personal background and any particular challenges they have faced. Finalists are interviewed by a team of representatives from Dell, the program's sponsor.

Financial data The program provides a paid summer internship, housing accommodations in Austin, round-trip transportation to and from Austin, and (based on financial need and successful internship performance) a $10,000 scholarship.

Duration 8 to 10 weeks for the internship; 1 year for the scholarship.

Number awarded Varies each year.

Deadline February of each year.

[430]
DELORES A. AUZENNE FELLOWSHIP FOR GRADUATE STUDY

State University System of Florida
Attn: Office of Academic and Student Services
325 West Gaines Street, Suite 1501
Tallahassee, FL 32399-1950
(850) 201-7216　　　　　　Fax: (850) 201-7185
E-mail: lpage@borfl.org
Web: www.borfl.org

Purpose To provide financial assistance to minority students in Florida working on a graduate degree in an underrepresented discipline.

Eligibility Eligible to be nominated are minority students working on a graduate degree at a public university in Florida. Nominees must be enrolled in full-time studies in a discipline in which there is an underrepresentation of the minority group to which the applicant belongs. A GPA of 3.0 or higher is required. Only U.S. citizens are eligible.

Financial data The stipend is $5,000 per year.

Duration 1 year; may be renewed if the recipient maintains full-time enrollment and at least a 3.0 GPA.

Additional information This program is administered by the equal opportunity program at each of the 10 public 4-year institutions in Florida. Contact that office for further information.

Number awarded 5 each year.

[431]
DISTRICT OF COLUMBIA SPACE GRANT CONSORTIUM AWARDS

District of Columbia Space Grant Consortium
c/o American University
Department of Physics
McKinley Building, Suite 106
4400 Massachusetts Avenue, N.W.
Washington, DC 20016-8058
(202) 885-2780   Fax: (202) 885-2723
E-mail: SpaceGrant@aol.com
Web: www.DCSpaceGrant.org

Purpose To provide financial assistance to undergraduate and graduate students studying space-related fields at member institutions of the District of Columbia Space Grant Consortium.

Eligibility This program is open to students at member institutions of the consortium. Each participating university conducts its own program. The consortium is a component of the Space Grant program of the U.S. National Aeronautics and Space Administration (NASA), which encourages participation by women, underrepresented minorities, and persons with disabilities.

Financial data Each university determines the amount of the awards.

Additional information Institutions participating in the consortium include American University, Gallaudet University, George Washington University, Howard University, and the University of the District of Columbia. Funding for this program is provided by NASA.

Number awarded Varies each year.

[432]
DR. JUAN D. VILLARREAL–HDA FOUNDATION SCHOLARSHIPS

Hispanic Dental Association
Attn: HDA Foundation
188 West Randolph Street, Suite 415
Chicago, IL 60601
(312) 577-4013   (800) 852-7921
Fax: (312) 577-0052   E-mail: hdassoc1@qwest.net
Web: www.hdassoc.org

Purpose To provide financial assistance to Hispanic dental hygiene and dental students at institutions in Texas.

Eligibility This program is open to Hispanic dental hygiene and dental students. Applicants must have been accepted or be currently enrolled at an accredited dental school in Texas.

Financial data Stipends are $1,000 or $500.

Duration 1 year.

Number awarded 1 or more each year.

Deadline June of each year.

[433]
DR. NANCY FOSTER SCHOLARSHIP PROGRAM

National Oceanic and Atmospheric Administration
Attn: National Ocean Service
Office of the Assistant Administrator
1305 East-West Highway, 13th Floor
Silver Spring, MD 20910-3281
(301) 713-3074   E-mail: fosterscholars@noaa.gov
Web: fosterscholars.noaa.gov

Purpose To provide financial assistance to graduate students, especially minorities and women, who are interested in working on a degree in fields related to marine sciences.

Eligibility This program is open to U.S. citizens, particularly women and members of minority groups, currently pursuing or intending to pursue a master's or doctoral degree in oceanography, marine biology, or maritime archaeology, including the curation, preservation, and display of maritime artifacts. Selection is based on academic record, recommendations, financial need, career goals and objectives, and the applicant's potential for success in a graduate study program.

Financial data The stipend is $16,800 per year, paid directly to the recipient. Those funds are not intended to be used as a research grant. In addition, the recipient's school receives an annual cost-of-education allowance of up to $12,000.

Duration Up to 2 years for master's degree students or up to 4 years for doctoral students.

Additional information These scholarships were first awarded in 2001.

Number awarded Approximately 5 each year.

Deadline April of each year.

[434]
EAST EUROPEAN INDIVIDUAL LANGUAGE TRAINING GRANTS

American Council of Learned Societies
Attn: Office of Fellowships and Grants
633 Third Avenue, 8C
New York, NY 10017-6795
(212) 697-1505   Fax: (212) 949-8058
E-mail: grants@acls.org
Web: www.acls.org/eeguide.htm

Purpose To provide financial support to graduate students and others interested in studying eastern European languages during the summer.

Eligibility Applicants must have completed at least a 4-year college degree. They must be interested in a program of training, primarily in intensive courses offered by institutions of higher education in the United States, in the languages of eastern Europe (except those of the successor states of the Soviet Union), including Albanian, Bosnian-Croatian-Serbian, Bulgarian, Czech, Hungarian, Macedonian, Polish, Romanian, Slovak, or Slovene. The language course may be at the beginning, intermediate, or advanced level. The awards are intended for people who will use east European languages in academic research or teaching. Applications are particularly encouraged from women and members of minority groups.

Financial data Grants up to $2,500 are available.

Duration Summer months.

Additional information This program was reinstituted in 2002.

Number awarded Approximately 12 each year.

Deadline February of each year.

[435]
EAST OHIO CONFERENCE BOARD OF ORDAINED MINISTRY ETHNIC MINORITY GRANTS

East Ohio Conference Board of Ordained Ministry
c/o Preston Forbes, Grant/Scholarship Secretary
9071 Inverrary Drive
Warren, OH 44484
(330) 856-2631   E-mail: forbes@onecom.com

Purpose To provide financial assistance to ethnic minority undergraduate and graduate students who are preparing for ordained ministry in the East Ohio Conference.

Eligibility This program is open to ethnic minority college and graduate students who are preparing for ordained ministry in the East Ohio Conference. Students must be recommended to receive this aid either by their District Superintendent or by the District Committee on Ordained Ministry where they hold their relationship. Applicants must attend a college or seminary that is fully accredited by the University Senate. They do not need to be certified candidates. Ethnic minority undergraduate pre-theological students are also eligible.

Financial data The stipend is $500 per year.

Duration 1 year.

Number awarded 1 or more each year.

Deadline September of each year.

[436]
EDWARD S. ROTH MANUFACTURING ENGINEERING SCHOLARSHIP

Society of Manufacturing Engineers
Attn: SME Education Foundation
One SME Drive
P.O. Box 930
Dearborn, MI 48121-0930
(313) 271-1500, ext. 1707   (800) 733-4763
Fax: (313) 271-2861   E-mail: monzcyn@sme.org
Web: www.sme.org

Purpose To provide financial assistance to students enrolled or planning to enroll in a degree program in manufacturing engineering at selected universities.

Eligibility This program is open to U.S. citizens who are graduating high school seniors or currently-enrolled undergraduate or graduate students. Applicants must be enrolled or planning to enroll as a full-time student at 1 of 13 selected 4-year universities to pursue a bachelor's or master's degree in manufacturing engineering. They must have a GPA of 3.0 or higher. Preference is given to 1) students demonstrating financial need, 2) minority students, and 3) students participating in a co-op program.

Financial data The stipend is $2,500.

Duration 1 year; may be renewed.

Additional information The eligible institutions are California Polytechnic State University at San Luis Obispo, California State Polytechnic State University at Pomona, University of Miami (Florida), Bradley University, Central State University (Ohio), Miami University (Ohio), Boston University, Worcester Polytechnic Institute, University of Massachusetts, St. Cloud State University, University of Texas-Pan American, Brigham Young University, and Utah State University.

Number awarded 1 each year.

Deadline January of each year.

[437]
ELI LILLY GRADUATE SCHOLARSHIPS

Society for Advancement of Chicanos and Native Americans in Science
333 Front Street, Suite 104
P.O. Box 8526
Santa Cruz, CA 95061-8526
(831) 459-0170   Fax: (831) 459-0194
E-mail: info@sacnas.org
Web: www.sacnas.org

Purpose To provide financial assistance for graduate study in biology or organic chemistry to Chicano or Native American students.

Eligibility This program is open to Chicano/Latino and Native American senior undergraduate students who have accepted an offer to enter graduate school or demonstrate a commitment to enter graduate school. Applicants must be planning to pursue a research degree (M.S. or Ph.D.) in biology or organic chemistry.

Financial data The stipend is $1,250.

Duration 1 year; nonrenewable.

Additional information Funding for these scholarships is provided by Eli Lilly and Company.

Number awarded 2 each year.

Deadline July of each year.

[438]
ELLIOTT C. ROBERTS, SR. SCHOLARSHIP

Institute for Diversity in Health Management
Attn: Education Program Coordinator
One North Franklin Street, 30th Floor
Chicago, IL 60606
(800) 233-0996   Fax: (312) 422-4566
E-mail: clopez@aha.org
Web: www.diversityconnection.com

Purpose To provide financial assistance to minority graduate students in health care management or business management.

Eligibility This program is open to members of ethnic minority groups who are second-year graduate students. Applicants must be accepted or enrolled in an accredited program in health care management or business management and have a GPA of 3.0 or higher. They must demonstrate commitment to a career in health services administration, financial need, solid extracurricular activities, and a commitment to community service. U.S. citizenship or permanent resident status is required.

Financial data The stipend is $1,000.

Duration 1 year.

Number awarded 1 or more each year, depending on the availability of funds.

Deadline June of each year.

[439]
EMAF FELLOWSHIP PROGRAM

Society for Human Resource Management
Attn: Employment Management Association Foundation
1800 Duke Street
Alexandria, VA 22314-3499
(703) 548-3440   Fax: (703) 535-6490
E-mail: wflowers@shrm.org
Web: www.shrm.org

Purpose To provide financial assistance to students enrolled or planning to enroll in a graduate program in the human resources field.

Eligibility Students are eligible to apply if they are 1) full-time college seniors who intend to pursue a career in human resources in a generalist or employment/staffing capacity and have been accepted into an accredited graduate program; 2) full-time graduate students currently working on a degree that will lead them to a career in human resources in a generalist or employment/staffing capacity who have a GPA of 3.0 or higher; or 3) experienced degree holders who are returning to school for the purpose of re-careering or career advancement and have been accepted in an accredited graduate program related to the human resources generalist or employment/staffing field. Selection is based on demonstrated scholastic achievement, leadership ability, work experience, and commitment to a career in a human resources field. At least 1 of the awards is designated for a qualified applicant from an ethnic or racial group underrepresented in the profession.

Financial data The stipend is $5,000, payable in 2 equal installments. Funds are made payable jointly to the recipient and the recipient's school.

Additional information This program includes 1 fellowship designated as the Richard Gast Fellowship. Funding for this program is provided by the Employment Management Association Foundation; the program is administered by Scholarship America, 1505 Riverview Road, P.O. Box 297, St. Peter, MN 56082, (507) 931-1682, (800) 537-4180, Fax: (507) 931-9168, E-mail: smsinfo@csfa.org.

Duration 1 year; recipients may reapply but may receive only 1 additional award.

Number awarded Up to 6 each year.

Deadline January of each year.

[440]
ENVIRONMENTAL EDUCATIONAL SCHOLARSHIP PROGRAM

Missouri Department of Natural Resources
P.O. Box 176
Jefferson City, MO 65102
(573) 751-2518   (800) 334-6946
TDD: (800) 379-2419
Web: dnr.state.mo.us/eesp

Purpose To provide financial assistance to underrepresented and minority students from Missouri who are studying an environmental field in college or graduate school.

Eligibility This program is open to minority and underrepresented residents of Missouri who have graduated from an accredited high school with a GPA of 3.0 or higher. Students who are already enrolled in college must have a GPA of 2.5 or higher and must be full-time students. Applicants may be 1) engineering students pursuing undergraduate and graduate degrees in civil, chemical, mechanical, or agricultural engineering; 2) environmen-

tal students pursuing undergraduate or graduate degrees in geology, biology, wildlife management, planning, natural resources, or a closely-related course of study; 3) chemistry students pursuing undergraduate or graduate degrees in the field of environmental chemistry; or 4) law enforcement students pursuing undergraduate or graduate degrees in environmental law enforcement. Selection is based on GPA and test scores, school and community activities, leadership and character, and a 1-page essay.

Financial data A stipend is awarded (amount not specified).

Duration 1 year; may be renewed if the recipient maintains a GPA of 2.5 or higher and full-time enrollment.

Number awarded Varies each year.

Deadline November of each year.

[441]
ETHNIC MINORITY MASTER'S SCHOLARSHIPS IN ONCOLOGY NURSING

Oncology Nursing Society
Attn: ONS Foundation
501 Holiday Drive
Pittsburgh, PA 15220-2749
(412) 921-7373, ext. 231   Fax: (412) 921-6565
E-mail: foundation@ons.org
Web: www.ons.org

Purpose To provide financial assistance to ethnic minorities interested in working on a master's degree in oncology nursing.

Eligibility The candidate must 1) demonstrate an interest in and commitment to cancer nursing; 2) be enrolled in a graduate nursing degree program at an NLN- or CCNE-accredited school of nursing (the program must have application to oncology nursing); 3) not have previously received a master's scholarship from this sponsor; 4) have a current license to practice as a registered nurse; and 5) be a member of an ethnic minority group (Native American, African American, Asian American, Pacific Islander, Hispanic/Latino, or other ethnic minority background).

Financial data The stipend is $3,000.

Duration 1 year.

Additional information Recipients may attend school on a part-time or full-time basis. This program includes a mentoring component with an individual in the applicant's area of clinical interest. When appropriate, efforts are made to match the applicant and mentor by ethnicity. At the end of each year of scholarship participation, recipients must submit a summary describing their educational activities.

Number awarded 2 each year.

Deadline January of each year.

[442]
FATHER JOSEPH P. FITZPATRICK SCHOLARSHIPS

Puerto Rican Legal Defense and Education Fund
Attn: Education Division Director
99 Hudson Street, 14th Floor
New York, NY 10013-2815
(212) 219-3360, ext. 223   (800) 328-2322, ext. 223
Fax: (212) 431-4276   E-mail: education@prldef.org
Web: www.prldef.org/education.htm

Purpose To provide economic support to Puerto Rican and other Latino students who need financial assistance to attend law school.

Eligibility Applicants must be Puerto Rican or other Latino students who are currently enrolled in law school (first- and second-year students). Selection is based on academic standing, financial need, and demonstrated interest and involvement in the Latino community.

Financial data The stipend is $1,500.

Duration 1 year.

Number awarded 4 each year.

Deadline January of each year.

[443]
FELLOWSHIPS IN APPLIED ECONOMICS

Social Science Research Council
810 Seventh Avenue
New York, NY 10019
(212) 377-2700   Fax: (212) 377-2727
E-mail: pae@ssrc.org
Web: www.ssrc.org

Purpose To provide funding to doctoral students in economics interested in predissertation research and training.

Eligibility This program is open to full-time graduate students enrolled in economics and related Ph.D. programs (e.g., public policy or agricultural economics) at U.S. universities. There are no citizenship, residency, or nationality requirements. Applicants must have completed required course work and qualifying examinations, but not necessarily an approved dissertation prospectus; normally they should be entering their third year of graduate work, although more advanced students may also apply. Fellowship support is not provided solely for dissertation research and write-up. Instead, applicants must develop a plan for intellectual development outside the normal course of training in the home department. Plans may include, for example, acquiring expertise for formulating and conducting research in areas of interest, developing specialized skills not taught at the home institution, or training in the approaches and methodologies of related disciplines. The program also encourages students to take on short-term internships in government or international agencies or at policy institutes. Minorities and women are particularly encouraged to apply.

Financial data The stipend is $15,000. A modest contribution to tuition, health insurance, and research expenses is also provided.

Duration 1 year.

Additional information This program, established in 1997, is administered by the Social Science Research Council with funds provided by the John D. and Catherine T. MacArthur Foundation.

Number awarded Varies each year.

Deadline January of each year.

[444]
FERMILAB DOCTORAL FELLOWSHIP PROGRAM FOR MINORITY STUDENTS IN PHYSICS

Fermi National Accelerator Laboratory
Attn: Manager, Equal Opportunity Office
MS 117
P.O. Box 500
Batavia, IL 60510
(630) 840-3415   Fax: (630) 840-5207
E-mail: engram@fnal.gov
Web: www.fnal.gov

Purpose To provide financial assistance for doctoral study in physics to underrepresented minority students at universities that are members of the Universities Research Association, Inc. (URA).

Eligibility This program is open to doctoral students who are members of minority groups historically underrepresented in physics (Hispanics, African Americans, and Native Americans). Applicants must be enrolled at any of the 81 universities in the United States that are URA members. They must be U.S. citizens or permanent residents. Along with their application, they must submit a statement on why they want to participate in this program, why they are considering physics as their course of study in graduate school, how they intend to use their physics training after they complete their education, and whether they plan to work or do postdoctoral study after completing their education. Selection is based on that statement, financial need, university transcripts, and a progress letter from the thesis advisor.

Financial data The stipend depends on the availability of funds and the needs of the student.

Duration 1 year; may be renewed up to 6 additional years.

Additional information Fermilab scientists are assigned to all recipients as advisors to aid their progress in graduate school. In addition, students are encouraged to work summers at Fermilab under the supervision of a staff physicist. Funding support for this program is provided by the U.S. Department of Energy.

Number awarded Varies each year.

Deadline July of each year.

[445]
FINNEGAN HENDERSON DIVERSITY SCHOLARSHIP

Finnegan, Henderson, Farabow, Garrett & Dunner, LLP
Attn: Director of Professional Recruitment and Development
1300 I Street, N.W.
Washington, D.C. 20005-3315
(202) 408-4034   Fax: (202) 408-4400
E-mail: suzanne.gentes@finnegan.com
Web: www.finnegan.com

Purpose To provide financial assistance and work experience to minority law students interested in a career in intellectual property law.

Eligibility This program is open to law students from underrepresented minority groups who have demonstrated a commitment to a career in intellectual property law and are currently enrolled either as a first-year full-time student or second-year part-time student. The sponsor defines underrepresented minorities to include American Indians/Alaskan Natives, Blacks/African Americans, Asian Americans/Pacific Islanders, and Hispanics/Latinos. Applicants must have earned an undergraduate degree in life sciences, engineering, or computer science, or have substantial prior trademark experience. Selection is based on academic performance at the undergraduate, graduate (if applicable), and law school level; relevant work experience; community service; leadership skills; and special accomplishments.

Financial data The stipend is $12,000 per year.

Duration 1 year; may be renewed 1 additional year as long as the recipient completes a summer associateship with the sponsor and maintains of GPA of 3.0 or higher.

Additional information The sponsor, the world's largest intellectual property law firm, established this scholarship in 2003. Summer associateships are available at its offices in Washington, D.C.; Atlanta, Georgia; Cambridge, Massachusetts; Palo Alto, California; or Reston, Virginia.

Number awarded 1 each year.

Deadline May of each year.

[446]
FLEMMIE D. KITTRELL FELLOWSHIP

American Association of Family and Consumer Sciences
Attn: Manager of Awards and Grants
1555 King Street
Alexandria, VA 22314-2752
(703) 706-4600   (800) 424-8080, ext. 119
Fax: (703) 706-4663   E-mail: staff@aafcs.org
Web: www.aafcs.org/fellowships/brochure.html

Purpose To provide financial assistance to minority graduate students in the field of family and consumer sciences.

Eligibility This program is open to minority students pursuing a full-time graduate degree in an area of family and consumer sciences. Selection is based on scholarship and special aptitudes for advanced study and research, educational and/or professional experiences, professional contributions to family and consumer sciences, and the significance of the proposed research problem to the public well-being and the advancement of family and consumer sciences. Applicants are encouraged to complete at least 1 year of professional family and consumer sciences experience, serving in such positions as a graduate/undergraduate assistant, trainee, or intern.

Financial data The stipend is $3,500.

Duration 1 year.

Additional information The fellowship, initiated in 1973, honors Flemmie D. Kittrell, who served for 27 years as the chair of the Home Economics Department (now the School of Human Ecology) at Howard University and pioneered in the development of international cooperation in home economics in Africa and India. The fellowship has been supported by annual gifts from the JCPenney Company, Inc. The application fee is $40. The association reserves the right to reconsider an award in the event the student receives a similar award for the same academic year.

Number awarded 1 each year.

Deadline January of each year.

[447]
FLORIDA LIBRARY ASSOCIATION MINORITY SCHOLARSHIPS

Florida Library Association
Attn: Chair, Scholarship Committee
1133 West Morse Boulevard, Suite 201
Winter Park, FL 32789-3788
(407) 647-8839   Fax: (407) 629-2502
Web: www.flalib.org/library/fla/schol.htm

Purpose To provide financial assistance to minority students working on a graduate degree in library and information science in Florida.

Eligibility This program is open to residents of Florida who are working on a degree in library and information science in the state. Applicants must be members of a minority group: Black/African American, American Indian/Alaska Native, Asian/Pacific Islander, or Hispanic/Latino. They must have some experience in a Florida library and must commit to working in a Florida library for at least 1 year after graduation. Along with their application, they must submit an essay detailing why they want to become a librarian, a brief summary of their previous library work experience, and information on their financial need.

Financial data The stipend is $2,000 per year.

Duration 1 year.

Number awarded 1 each year.

Deadline February of each year.

[448]
FLORIDA NICARAGUAN AND HAITIAN SCHOLARSHIPS

Florida Department of Education
Attn: Office of Student Financial Assistance
1940 North Monroe Street, Suite 70
Tallahassee, FL 32303-4759
(850) 410-5185   (888) 827-2004
Fax: (850) 488-3612   E-mail: osfa@mail.doe.state.fl.us
Web: www.firn.edu/doe/osfa

Purpose To provide financial assistance for undergraduate and graduate studies to residents of Florida who were born in Nicaragua or Haiti.

Eligibility This program is open to residents of Florida who are citizens of, or were born in, Nicaragua or Haiti. Applicants must be enrolled or planning to enroll in an undergraduate or graduate level program of study at a state university in Florida. They must have at least a 3.0 cumulative GPA either in high school (if a graduating senior) or in college (if currently enrolled). Selection is based on academic achievement and community service.

Financial data The stipend ranges from $4,000 to $5,000 per year.

Duration 1 year; nonrenewable, although recipients may reapply in subsequent years.

Number awarded 2 each year: 1 to a Nicaraguan and 1 to a Haitian.

Deadline June of each year.

[449]
FLORIDA SPACE GRANT CONSORTIUM FELLOWSHIP PROGRAM

Florida Space Grant Consortium
c/o Center for Space Education
Building M6-306, Room 7010
Mail Stop: FSGC
Kennedy Space Center, FL 32899
(321) 452-4301   Fax: (321) 449-0739
E-mail: fsgc@mail.ufl.edu
Web: fsgc.engr.ucf.edu

Purpose To provide financial assistance and summer work experience to doctoral students in space studies at universities participating in the Florida Space Grant Consortium (FSGC).

Eligibility Eligible to be nominated for this program are U.S. citizens who are enrolled full time in doctoral programs at universities participating in the consortium. Nominees must be enrolled in a space-related field of study, broadly defined to include aeronautics, astronautics, remote sensing, atmospheric sciences, and other fundamental sciences and technologies relying on and/or directly impacting space technological resources. Included within that definition are space science; earth observing science; space life sciences; space medicine; space policy, law, and engineering; astronomy and astrophysics; space facilities and applications; and space education. Their undergraduate GPA should be at least 3.5. The program particularly solicits nominations of women, underrepresented minorities, and students with disabilities.

Financial data Each fellow receives a $12,000 stipend and a supplementary summer traineeship stipend from a participating industry, government, or private laboratory.

Duration Up to 3 years.

Additional information Fellows work during the summer in a government, industry, or private laboratory. This program is funded by the U.S. National Aeronautics and Space Administration (NASA). The consortium member universities are Bethune-Cookman College, Eckerd College, Embry-Riddle Aeronautical University, Florida A&M University, Florida Atlantic University, Florida Community Colleges, Florida Gulf Coast University, Florida Institute of Technology, Florida International University, Florida Southern College, Florida State University, University of Central Florida, University of Florida, University of Miami, University of North Florida, University of South Florida, and University of West Florida.

Number awarded 3 each year.

Deadline Notices of intent must be submitted by February of each year. Completed proposals are due in March.

[450]
FLOYD H. SKINNER LAW SCHOLARSHIPS

Floyd H. Skinner Bar Association
c/o President, Angela T. Ross
Smith Haughley Rice and Roegge
200 Calder Plaza Building
250 Monroe Avenue, N.W.
Grand Rapids, MI 49503-2251
(616) 774-8000   Fax: (616) 774-2461
E-mail: atross@shrr.com

Purpose To provide financial assistance for law school to minorities with a tie to western Michigan.

Eligibility This program is open to minority law students who 1) are residents of western Michigan; 2) attend a Michigan law school; or 3) have previously participated in the Grand Rapids Minority Clerkship program. Applicants must be admitted to or currently attending law school full time. Selection is based on academic achievement, demonstrated leadership ability, community activism, and financial need.

Financial data The stipend is $1,000.

Duration 1 year.

Additional information Most members of the Floyd H. Skinner Bar Association are African American attorneys. Information is also available from the Scholarship Committee Chair, James L. Hopewell, Meijer, Inc., Fredrick Meijer Building 985/4, 2929 Walker Avenue, N.W., Grand Rapids, MI 49544, (616) 453-6711.

Number awarded 1 or more each year, depending on the number of qualified applicants and availability of funds.

Deadline October of each year.

[451]
FOLEY & LARDNER MINORITY SCHOLARSHIP

Foley & Lardner, Attorneys at Law
Firstar Center
777 East Wisconsin Avenue
Milwaukee, WI 53202-5367
Fax: (414) 297-4900
Web: www.foleylardner.com

Purpose To provide scholarships to first-year minority students attending selected law schools.

Eligibility Minority students in the first year of law school are eligible to apply if they are attending the following schools: Duke, Florida, Georgetown, Michigan, Northwestern, Stanford, UCLA, or Wisconsin. First-year law students include both summer starters and fall starters. Selection is based on interest in or ties to

a city in which the sponsor practices, involvement in community activities or minority student organizations, undergraduate record, and work or personal achievements.

Financial data The stipend is $5,000; funds are paid at the beginning of the recipient's second semester in law school.

Duration 1 semester (the second semester of the first year in law school).

Additional information The U.S. cities in which the sponsor has offices are Chicago, Detroit, Denver, Los Angeles, Sacramento, San Diego, San Francisco, Jacksonville, Orlando, Tallahassee, Tampa, West Palm Beach, Madison, Milwaukee, and Washington, D.C.

Number awarded 8 each year (1 at each of the participating schools).

Deadline September of each year.

[452]
FORD FOUNDATION PREDOCTORAL FELLOWSHIP PROGRAM FOR MINORITIES

National Research Council
Attn: Fellowship Office
500 Fifth Street, N.W.
Washington, DC 20001
(202) 334-2872   Fax: (202) 334-3419
E-mail: infofell@nas.edu
Web: www7.national-academies.org

Purpose To provide financial assistance to underrepresented minority students who are beginning graduate study.

Eligibility This program is open to underrepresented minority students, defined as Black/African Americans, Puerto Ricans, Mexican Americans/Chicanos/Chicanas, Alaska Natives (Eskimos and Aleuts), Native Pacific Islanders (Polynesians and Micronesians), and Native American Indians, who are enrolled in or planning to enroll in a research-based Ph.D. or Sc.D. program. Applicants must be U.S. citizens or nationals interested in a teaching and research career. They may not already have earned a doctorate in any field. All applicants must take the GRE General Test. Awards are made for study in the physical and life sciences, behavioral and social sciences, humanities, engineering, mathematics, or interdisciplinary programs comprised of 2 or more eligible disciplines. Awards are not made in such areas as audiology, business, education, fine arts, guidance, health sciences, home economics, library and information science, management and administration, nursing, performing arts, personnel, social welfare, social work, or speech pathology. In addition, awards are not made for work leading to terminal master's degrees, doctorates in education, Doctor of Fine Arts degrees, joint degrees such as M.D./Ph.D. or M.F.A./Ph.D., or professional degrees in such areas as medicine, law, or public health. The fellowships are tenable at any accredited nonprofit institution of higher education in the United States that offers Ph.D.s or Sc.D.s in the fields eligible for support.

Financial data The program provides a stipend to the student of $16,000 per year and an award to the host institution of $7,500 per year in lieu of tuition and fees.

Duration 3 years of support is provided, to be used within a 5-year period.

Additional information The competition for this program is conducted by the National Research Council on behalf of the Ford Foundation. Applicants who merit receiving the fellowship but to whom awards cannot be made because of insufficient funds are given Honorable Mentions; this recognition does not carry with it a monetary award but honors applicants who have demonstrated substantial academic achievement. The National Research Council publishes a list of those Honorable Mentions who wish their names publicized. Fellows may not accept remuneration from another fellowship or similar external award while on this program; however, supplementation from institutional funds, educational benefits from the Department of Veterans Affairs, or educational incentive funds may be received concurrently with Ford Foundation support. Predoctoral fellows are required to submit an interim progress report 6 months after the start of the fellowship and a final report at the end of the 12 month tenure.

Number awarded Approximately 60 each year.

Deadline November of each year.

[453]
FOUNDERS SCHOLARSHIP

Society of Mexican American Engineers and Scientists
Attn: National Office Director
13337 South Street, Suite 349
Cerritos, CA 90703
E-mail: maes@tamu.edu
Web: www.maes-natl.org

Purpose To provide financial assistance to undergraduate and graduate student members of the Society of Mexican American Engineers and Scientists (MAES).

Eligibility This program is open to MAES student members who are full-time undergraduate or graduate students at a college or university in the United States. Community college students must be enrolled in majors that can transfer to a 4-year institution offering a baccalaureate degree. All applicants must be majoring in a field of science or engineering. U.S. citizenship or permanent resident status is required. Selection is based on financial need; academic achievement; personal qualities, strengths, and leadership abilities; and timeliness and completeness of the application.

Financial data The stipend is $2,000.

Duration 1 year.

Additional information Information is also available from José M. Hernández, Chair, MAES Scholarship Committee, 4015 North Water Iris Cort, Houston, TX 77059. Recipients must attend the MAES International Symposium's Medalla de Oro Banquet in October.

Number awarded 1 each year.

Deadline October of each year.

[454]
FREDRIKSON & BYRON FOUNDATION MINORITY SCHOLARSHIPS

Fredrikson & Byron Foundation
4000 Pillsbury Center
200 South Sixth Street
Minneapolis, MN 55402-1425
(612) 492-7117 Fax: (612) 492-7077
Web: www.fredlaw.com/firm/scholarship.htm

Purpose To provide financial assistance and summer work experience to minority law students who will be practicing in the Twin Cities area of Minnesota.

Eligibility This program is open to African American, Asian American, Pacific Islander, Hispanic, Native American, and Alaska Native students enrolled in their first year of law school. Applicants must be interested in practicing law in the Minneapolis-St.

Paul area. Along with their application, they must submit 2 recommendations, a writing sample from their first-year legal writing course, transcripts from undergraduate and law school, and a resume. Financial need is not considered.

Financial data The fellowship stipend is $5,000. The internship portion of the program provides a $1,000 weekly stipend.

Duration 1 year.

Additional information Fellows are also eligible to participate in an internship at the firm's offices in Minneapolis.

Number awarded Up to 2 each year.

Deadline March of each year.

[455]
FULFILLING OUR DREAMS SCHOLARSHIP PROGRAM

Salvadoran American Leadership and Educational Fund
Attn: Education and Youth Programs Manager
1625 West Olympic Boulevard, Suite 718
Los Angeles, CA 90015
(213) 480-1052 Fax: (213) 487-2530
E-mail: info@salef.org
Web: www.salef.org

Purpose To provide financial assistance for college and graduate school to Salvadoran Americans and other Americans of Hispanic descent.

Eligibility This program is open to high school seniors and graduates who have been accepted at a 4-year university, undergraduates in 2- and 4-year colleges and universities, and graduate students. Applicants do not need to provide proof of documented immigrant status, but they must be of Salvadoran, Central American, or other Latino background. Along with their application, they must submit a 750-word statement on their goals, aspirations, and ambitions; ways to give back to the community; leadership involvement; why they chose their field of study; and short- and long-term goals and how they plan to contribute to the community after graduation. They must be able to demonstrate financial need, have a GPA of at least 2.5, and have a history of community service and involvement. An interview may be required.

Financial data Stipends range from $500 to $2,500.

Duration 1 year.

Additional information This program began in 1998. Recipients are paired with a professional in their field of study who serves as a mentor, providing moral support and direction. Funding for this program comes from the Bank of America Foundation and the Los Angeles Department of Water and Power.

Number awarded 50 each year.

Deadline June of each year.

[456]
GATES MILLENNIUM GRADUATE SCHOLARS PROGRAM

Bill and Melinda Gates Foundation
P.O. Box 10500
Fairfax, VA 22031-8044
(877) 690-GMSP
Web: www.gmsp.org

Purpose To provide financial assistance for graduate studies in selected areas to outstanding low-income minority students.

Eligibility This program is open to low-income African Americans, Native Alaskans, American Indians, Hispanic Americans, and Asian Pacific Islander Americans who need money to attend graduate school. Eligible to be nominated are U.S. citizens who are enrolled or about to enroll in graduate school. They must pursue a graduate degree in engineering, mathematics, science, education, or library science. In addition, applicants must have at least a 3.3 GPA, be able to demonstrate significant financial need, and have demonstrated leadership commitment through participation in community service (i.e., mentoring/tutoring, volunteer work in social service organizations, and involvement in church initiatives), extracurricular activities (student government and athletics), or other activities that reflect leadership abilities.

Financial data The program covers the full cost of graduate study: tuition, fees, books, and living expenses not paid for by grants and scholarships already committed as part of the recipient's financial aid package.

Duration Up to 4 years (up to and including the doctorate), if the recipient maintains at least a 3.0 GPA.

Additional information This program, established in 1999, is funded by the Bill and Melinda Gates Foundation and administered by the United Negro College Fund with support from the American Indian Graduate Center, the Hispanic Scholarship Fund, and the Organization of Chinese Americans.

Number awarded Under the Gates Millennium Scholars Program, a total of 4,000 students receive support each year.

Deadline January of each year.

[457]
GEM M.S. ENGINEERING FELLOWSHIP PROGRAM

National Consortium for Graduate Degrees for Minorities in
    Engineering and Science (GEM)
P.O. Box 537
Notre Dame, IN 46556
(574) 631-7771   Fax: (574) 287-1486
E-mail: gem.1@nd.edu
Web: www.gemfellowship.org

Purpose To provide financial assistance and summer work experience to underrepresented minority graduate students in engineering.

Eligibility This program is open to U.S. citizens who are members of ethnic groups underrepresented in engineering: American Indians, African Americans, Mexican Americans, Puerto Ricans, and other Hispanic Americans. Applicants must be enrolled as at least a junior in an accredited engineering discipline with an academic record that indicates the ability to pursue graduate studies in engineering (including a GPA of 2.8 or higher). Recipients must attend 1 of the 88 GEM member universities that offer a master's degree.

Financial data The fellowship pays tuition, fees, and a stipend of $10,000 over its lifetime. In addition, each participant receives a salary during the summer work assignment as a GEM Summer Intern, making the value of the total award between $20,000 and $60,000. Employer members reimburse GEM participants for travel expenses to and from the summer work site.

Duration Up to 3 semesters or 4 quarters, plus a summer work internship lasting 10 to 14 weeks for up to 3 summers, depending on whether the student applies as a junior, senior, or college graduate; recipients begin their internship upon acceptance into the program and work each summer until completion of their master's degree.

Additional information During the summer internship, each fellow is assigned an engineering project in a research setting. Each project is based on the fellow's interest and background

and is carried out under the supervision of an experienced engineer. At the conclusion of the internship, each fellow writes a project report. Recipients must seek the master's degree in the same engineering discipline as their baccalaureate degree.

Number awarded Varies each year; recently, 327 of these fellowships were awarded.

Deadline November of each year.

[458]
GEM PH.D. ENGINEERING FELLOWSHIP PROGRAM

National Consortium for Graduate Degrees for Minorities in
    Engineering and Science (GEM)
P.O. Box 537
Notre Dame, IN 46556
(574) 631-7771   Fax: (574) 287-1486
E-mail: gem.1@nd.edu
Web: www.gemfellowship.org

Purpose To provide financial assistance and summer work experience to underrepresented minority students interested in obtaining a Ph.D. degree in engineering.

Eligibility This program is open to U.S. citizens who are members of ethnic groups underrepresented in engineering: American Indians, African Americans, Mexican Americans, Puerto Ricans, and other Hispanic Americans. Applicants must have attained or be in the process of attaining a master's degree in engineering with an academic record that indicates the ability to pursue doctoral studies in engineering (including a GPA of 3.0 or higher).

Financial data The stipend is $14,000 per year, plus tuition and fees; the total value of the award is between $60,000 and $100,000.

Duration 3 to 5 years for the fellowship; 12 weeks during at least 1 summer for the internship.

Additional information This program is valid only at 1 of 88 participating GEM member universities; write to GEM for a list. The fellowship award is designed to support the student in the first year of the doctoral program without working. Subsequent years are subsidized by the respective university and will usually include either a teaching or research assistantship. Recipients must participate in the GEM summer internship; failure to agree to accept the internship cancels the fellowship.

Number awarded Varies each year; recently, 49 of these fellowships were awarded.

Deadline November of each year.

[459]
GEM PH.D. SCIENCE FELLOWSHIP PROGRAM

National Consortium for Graduate Degrees for Minorities in
    Engineering and Science (GEM)
P.O. Box 537
Notre Dame, IN 46556
(574) 631-7771   Fax: (574) 287-1486
E-mail: gem.1@nd.edu
Web: www.gemfellowship.org

Purpose To provide financial assistance and summer work experience to underrepresented minority students interested in obtaining a Ph.D. degree in the natural sciences.

Eligibility This program is open to U.S. citizens who are members of ethnic groups underrepresented in the natural sciences: American Indians, African Americans, Mexican Americans, Puerto Ricans, and other Hispanic Americans. Applicants must be juniors, seniors, or recent baccalaureate graduates in the natural sciences (biological sciences, chemistry, computer science, earth sciences, mathematics, and physics) with an academic record that indicates the ability to pursue doctoral studies in the natural sciences (including a GPA of 3.0 or higher).

Financial data The stipend is $14,000 per year, plus tuition and fees. In addition, there is a summer internship program that provides a salary and reimbursement for travel expenses to and from the summer work site. The total value of the award is between $60,000 and $100,000, depending upon academic status at the time of application, summer employer, and graduate school attended.

Duration 3 to 5 years for the fellowship; 12 weeks during at least 1 summer for the internship. Fellows selected as juniors or seniors intern each summer until entrance to graduate school; fellows selected after college graduation intern at least 1 summer.

Additional information This program is valid only at 1 of 88 participating GEM member universities; write to GEM for a list. The fellowship award is designed to support the student in the first year of the doctoral program without working. Subsequent years are subsidized by the respective university and will usually include either a teaching or research assistantship. Recipients must participate in the GEM summer internship; failure to agree to accept the internship cancels the fellowship. Recipients must enroll in the same scientific discipline as their undergraduate major.

Number awarded Varies each year; recently, 40 of these fellowships were awarded.

Deadline November of each year.

[460]
GENERAL MOTORS ENGINEERING EXCELLENCE AWARD

Hispanic Association of Colleges and Universities
Attn: Scholarship Programs
8415 Datapoint Drive, Suite 400
San Antonio, TX 78229
(210) 692-3805   Fax: (210) 692-0823
E-mail: hacu@hacu.net
Web: www.hacu.net/student_resources/index.shtml

Purpose To provide financial assistance to undergraduate and graduate engineering students at institutions that are members of the Hispanic Association of Colleges and Universities (HACU).

Eligibility This program is open to full-time undergraduate and graduate students at 4-year HACU member and partner colleges and universities who are working on an engineering degree. Applicants must submit an essay of 200 to 250 words that describes their academic and/or career goals, where they expect to be and what they expect to be doing 10 years from now, and what skills they can bring to an employer. They must be able to demonstrate financial need and a GPA of 3.2 or higher.

Financial data The stipend is $2,000 per year.

Duration 1 year; may be renewed.

Additional information This program is sponsored by General Motors and administered by HACU.

Number awarded 1 or more each year.

Deadline June of each year.

[461]
GEORGE A. STRAIT MINORITY STIPEND

American Association of Law Libraries
Attn: Membership Coordinator
53 West Jackson Boulevard, Suite 940
Chicago, IL 60604
(312) 939-4770, ext. 24   Fax: (312) 431-1097
E-mail: membership@aall.org
Web: www.aallnet.org

Purpose To provide financial assistance to minority college seniors or college graduates who are interested in becoming law librarians.

Eligibility Applicants must be members of a minority group; college seniors, college graduates, or matriculated graduate library school students with an interest in law librarianship; citizens of the United States or Canada (or able to submit evidence of becoming naturalized at the beginning of the award period); interested in and able to demonstrate an aptitude for law library work; and able to show financial need. Preference is given to applicants with previous service to, or interest in, law librarianship.

Financial data The stipend is $3,500.

Duration 1 year.

Number awarded 1 each year.

Deadline March of each year.

[462]
GEORGE M. BROOKER COLLEGIATE SCHOLARSHIP FOR MINORITIES

Institute of Real Estate Management Foundation
Attn: Foundation Coordinator
430 North Michigan Avenue
Chicago, IL 60611-4090
(312) 329-6008   Fax: (312) 410-7908
E-mail: kholmes@irem.org
Web: www.irem.org

Purpose To provide financial assistance to minorities interested in preparing (on the undergraduate or graduate level) for a career in the real estate management industry.

Eligibility This program is open to junior, senior, and graduate minority (non-Caucasian) students majoring in real estate, preferably with an emphasis on management, asset management, or related fields. Applicants must be interested in entering a career in real estate management upon graduation. They must have earned a GPA of 3.0 or higher in their major, have completed at least 2 college courses in real estate, and write an essay (up to 500 words) on why they want to follow a career in real estate management. U.S. citizenship is required. Selection is based on academic success and a demonstrated commitment to a career in real estate management.

Financial data The stipend for undergraduates is $1,000; the stipend for graduate students is $2,500. Funds are disbursed to the institution the student attends to be used only for tuition expenses.

Duration 1 year; nonrenewable.

Number awarded 3 each year: 2 undergraduate awards and 1 graduate award.

Deadline February of each year.

[463]
GERALDINE R. DODGE FOUNDATION FELLOWSHIP

College Art Association of America
Attn: Fellowship Program
275 Seventh Avenue
New York, NY 10001-6798
(212) 691-1051, ext. 206   Fax: (212) 627-2381
E-mail: fellowship@collegeart.org
Web: www.collegeart.org/caa/career/fellowship.html

Purpose To provide financial assistance and work experience to artists or art historians from culturally diverse backgrounds who are completing graduate degrees and are interested in working in New Jersey.

Eligibility This program is open to artists or art historians who have been underrepresented in the field because of their race, religion, gender, age, national origin, sexual orientation, disability, or history of economic disadvantage. Applicants must be U.S. citizens or permanent residents and able to demonstrate financial need. They must expect to receive the M.F.A., terminal M.A., or Ph.D. degree in the year following application and then be interested in working at a cultural institution in New Jersey.

Financial data The stipend is $5,000 per year.

Duration 2 years: the final year of their degree program and the first year following completion of their degree.

Additional information In addition to receiving a stipend for the terminal year of their degree program, fellows participate in an internship in New Jersey during the year following graduation. The College Art Association helps fellows secure an internship at a cultural institution, with collections in American art, pre-Columbian art, Tibetan art, Native American art, textiles, or numismatics. The Geraldine R. Dodge Foundation subsidizes a portion of the fellow's salary during their first professional year. Salaries and terms of employment are determined in consultation with each fellow and potential host institution.

Number awarded 1 each year.

Deadline January of each year.

[464]
G.R.A.D. SCHOLARSHIPS

Pueblo Hispanic Education Foundation
Administration Building, Room 325
2200 Bonforte Boulevard
Pueblo, CO 81001
(719) 546-2563   Fax: (719) 546-0504
E-mail: pphef@aol.com
Web: www.phef.net

Purpose To provide financial assistance to Hispanic graduate students from Colorado.

Eligibility This program is open to full-time Hispanic graduate students who are residents of Colorado. Applicants must submit an essay on their career and educational goals, school activities and awards, interests, community service and volunteer work, and work experience. Selection is based on financial need, proven ability, GPA, community and volunteer service, and educational desire. Preference is given to students of low to moderate income, continuing students, and single parents.

Financial data Stipends are generally $1,000 per year.

Duration 1 year. Recipients may reapply if they maintain a cumulative GPA of 2.5 or higher.

Additional information The title of this program stands for "Grooming Role Models for Advanced Degrees." It was estab-

lished in 1993 and is sponsored by the Temple Buell Foundation and the Pueblo Hispanic Education Foundation.

Number awarded Varies each year; recently, 4 of these scholarships were awarded.

Deadline February of each year.

[465]
HACE NATIONAL SCHOLARSHIP PROGRAM

Hispanic Alliance for Career Enhancement
Attn: Student Development Program
14 East Jackson Avenue, Suite 1310
Chicago, IL 60604
(312) 435-0498, ext. 21   Fax: (312) 435-1494
E-mail: haceorg@enteract.com
Web: www.hace-usa.org/programs/scholar.htm

Purpose To provide financial assistance to Hispanic students working on an undergraduate or graduate degree.

Eligibility Applicants may be undergraduate or graduate students who are enrolled full time in an institution of higher education in the United States. They must be working on a bachelor's degree or higher. Undergraduates must have completed at least 12 credit hours of college course work before applying. All applicants must have a GPA of 2.5 or higher. Selection is based on academic achievement, letters of recommendation, community involvement, leadership skills, and financial need.

Financial data A stipend is awarded (amount not specified).

Duration 1 year; nonrenewable.

Number awarded Several each year.

Deadline August of each year.

[466]
HARRIETT G. JENKINS PREDOCTORAL FELLOWSHIP PROGRAM

United Negro College Fund Special Programs Corporation
2750 Prosperity Avenue, Suite 600
Fairfax, VA 22031
(703) 205-7656   (800) 231-9155
Fax: (703) 205-7645   E-mail: hgjfellows@uncfsp.org
Web: www.uncfsp.org/nasa.asp

Purpose To provide financial assistance to women, minorities, and people with disabilities working on a graduate degree in a field of interest to the National Aeronautics and Space Administration (NASA).

Eligibility This program is open to members of groups underrepresented in mathematics, science, technology, and engineering—women, minorities, and people with disabilities. Applicants must be full-time graduate students in a program leading to a master's or doctoral degree in a NASA-related discipline (aeronautics, aerospace, astronomy, bioengineering, biology, chemistry, computer science, earth sciences, engineering, environmental sciences, life sciences, materials sciences, mathematics, meteorology, physical sciences, physics/health physics, and science education). They must be U.S. citizens with a GPA of 3.0 or higher. Priority is given to 1) applicants who have previously participated in NASA undergraduate programs; 2) applicants who have received their undergraduate degree from minority institutions; and 3) undergraduate minority, women, and disabled applicants from majority institutions.

Financial data The stipend is $22,000 per year for doctoral fellows or $16,000 for master's degree students. Fellows who are also awarded a research mini-grant at a NASA Center or the Jet

Propulsion Laboratory receive an additional $6,000 stipend, $700 housing allowance, and $700 travel allowance.

Duration 3 years.

Additional information This program, established in 2001, is funded by NASA and administered by the United Negro College Fund Special Programs Corporation. Fellows may also compete for a research mini-grant to engage in a NASA research experience that is closely aligned with the research conducted at the fellow's institution. The participating NASA facilities are Ames Research Center (Moffett Field, California), Jet Propulsion Laboratory (Pasadena, California), Dryden Flight Research Center (Edwards, California), Johnson Space Center (Houston, Texas), Stennis Space Center (Stennis Space Center, Mississippi), Marshall Space Flight Center (Marshall Space Flight Center, Alabama), Glenn Research Center (Cleveland, Ohio), Kennedy Space Center (Kennedy Space Center, Florida), Langley Research Center (Hampton, Virginia), and Goddard Space Flight Center (Greenbelt, Maryland).

Number awarded Up to 20 each year.

Deadline January of each year.

[467]
HELENE M. OVERLY MEMORIAL GRADUATE SCHOLARSHIP

Women's Transportation Seminar
Attn: National Headquarters
1666 K Street, N.W., Suite 1100
Washington, DC 20006
(202) 496-4340   Fax: (202) 496-4349
E-mail: wts@wtsnational.org
Web: www.wtsnational.org/scholarship_grad.asp

Purpose To provide financial assistance to women graduate students interested in preparing for a career in transportation.

Eligibility This program is open to women who are enrolled in a graduate degree program in a transportation-related field (e.g., transportation engineering, planning, finance, or logistics). Applicants must have at least a 3.0 GPA and be interested in a career in transportation. They must submit a 500-word statement about their career goals after graduation and why they think they should receive the scholarship award. Applications must be submitted first to a local chapter; the chapters forward selected applications for consideration on the national level. Minority women are particularly encouraged to apply. Selection is based on transportation involvement and goals, job skills, and academic record.

Financial data The stipend is $3,000.

Duration 1 year.

Additional information The Women's Transportation Seminar (WTS) was founded in 1977 and now has more than 3,000 members, both female and male, in chapters throughout the United States. This scholarship program was established in 1981.

Number awarded 1 each year.

Deadline Applications must be submitted by the end of September to a local WTS chapter.

[468]
HENAAC STUDENT LEADERSHIP AWARDS

Hispanic Engineer National Achievement Awards Conference
3900 Whiteside Street
Los Angeles, CA 90063
(323) 262-0997   Fax: (323) 262-0946
E-mail: info@henaac.org
Web: www.henaac.org/scholarships.htm

Purpose To provide financial assistance to Hispanic undergraduate and graduate students majoring in engineering and related fields.

Eligibility This program is open to Hispanic undergraduate and graduate students who are majoring in computer science, engineering, material science, or mathematics. Applicants must have a GPA of 3.0 or higher. Academic achievement and campus community activities are considered in the selection process.

Financial data The stipend is $5,000.

Duration 1 year.

Additional information This program is sponsored by the Hispanic Engineer National Achievement Awards Conference (HENAAC) to promote technical excellence and leadership in the Hispanic community.

Number awarded 2 each year: 1 undergraduate and 1 graduate student.

Deadline April of each year.

[469]
HERBERT W. NICKENS, M.D. MINORITY MEDICAL STUDENT SCHOLARSHIPS

Association of American Medical Colleges
Attn: Division of Community and Minority Programs
2450 N Street, N.W.
Washington, DC 20037-1127
(202) 828-0570   Fax: (202) 828-1125
E-mail: dallen@aamc.org
Web: www.aamc.org/about/awards/hwnstud.htm

Purpose To provide financial assistance to underrepresented minority medical students.

Eligibility This program is open to Black Americans, Mexican Americans, Mainland Puerto Ricans, and Native Americans (Native Hawaiians, Alaska Natives, and American Indians) who are entering their third year of medical school. Each medical school may nominate 1 student for these awards. The letter of nomination must describe the candidate's academic progress through the first and second year, including special awards and honors, clerkships or special research projects, and extracurricular activities in which the student exemplified leadership abilities. In addition, the nomination letter should highlight the candidate's demonstrated efforts in addressing the educational, societal, and health care needs of minorities. Candidates must submit a 250-word essay that discusses their motivation to pursue a medical career and their future plans. U.S. citizenship is required.

Financial data The stipend is $5,000.

Duration 1 year.

Number awarded Varies each year; recently, 5 of these scholarships were awarded.

Deadline June of each year.

[470]
HISPANIC CHURCH MULTIPLICATION TEAM SCHOLARSHIPS

Southern Baptist Convention
Attn: North American Mission Board
4200 North Point Parkway
Alpharetta, GA 30022-4176
(770) 410-6227   Fax: (770) 410-6012
E-mail: mrodriguez@namb.net
Web: www.namb.net

Purpose   To provide financial assistance to Hispanic American Baptists interested in religious vocations.

Eligibility   This program is open to Hispanic Americans who are U.S. citizens involved in some type of approved Baptist ministry. Applicants must be able to demonstrate financial need. Only students in accredited institutions working toward a basic college (bachelor's) or seminary (M.Div.) degree are eligible. As part of the selection process, applicants must submit an essay describing their interest in and commitment to a Christian vocation.

Financial data   The maximum grants are $500 per year for students attending accredited colleges, $600 per year for students in non-Southern Baptist Convention seminaries, and $850 per year for students at 1 of the 6 Southern Baptist Convention seminaries.

Duration   1 year; renewable.

Additional information   The 6 Southern Baptist seminaries are Golden Gate Baptist Theological Seminary (Mill Valley, California), Midwestern Baptist Theological Seminary (Kansas City, Missouri), New Orleans Baptist Theological Seminary (New Orleans, Louisiana), Southeastern Baptist Theological Seminary (Wake Forest, North Carolina), Southern Baptist Theological Seminary (Louisville, Kentucky), and Southwestern Baptist Theological Seminary (Fort Worth, Texas).

Number awarded   Varies each year.

Deadline   Applications may be submitted at any time, but they must be received at least 1 month (preferably sooner) before the student enrolls in a school.

[471]
HISPANIC LAWYERS SCHOLARSHIP FUND

Hispanic Lawyers Association of Illinois
c/o Jesse H. Ruiz
Gardner, Carton & Douglas LLC
191 North Wacker Drive, Suite 3700
Chicago, IL 60606-1698
(312) 569-1135   Fax: (312) 569-3135
E-mail: jruiz@gcd.com
Web: www.hnba.com/HLSF_First_Year_Scholarship.htm

Purpose   To provide financial assistance to first-year Latino law students in Illinois.

Eligibility   This program is open to first-year Latino law students who either attend an Illinois law school or are Illinois residents attending law school in another state. Applicants must submit a 2-page statement on why their background and experience illustrate a commitment to the legal and social needs of the Latino community. Selection is based on academic achievement, financial need, and contributions to the Latino community.

Financial data   The stipend is $2,500 per year.

Duration   1 year; nonrenewable.

Number awarded   4 or 5 each year.

Deadline   March of each year.

[472]
HISPANIC SCHOLARSHIP FUND/SOUTH TEXAS SCHOLARSHIP PROGRAM

L&F Distributors
3900 North McColl Road
McAllen, TX 78501
(956) 687-7751   E-mail: specialprograms@hsf.net
Web: www.hsf.net/scholarship/Special.htm

Purpose   To provide financial assistance to Hispanic undergraduate and graduate students from designated counties in south Texas.

Eligibility   This program is open to community college, undergraduate, and graduate students who are residents of south Texas. Applicants must be U.S. citizens or permanent residents of Hispanic heritage (each parent half Hispanic or 1 parent fully Hispanic). They must have earned at least 12 undergraduate units, have a GPA of 2.7 or higher, and be enrolled full time in a degree program at an accredited U.S. college or university. As part of the application process, they must submit a 2-page essay that addresses the following topics: their Hispanic heritage and family background, personal and academic achievements, academic plans and career goals, efforts toward making a difference in their community, and financial need.

Financial data   Stipends range from $1,000 to $2,500.

Duration   1 year.

Additional information   South Texas is defined to include the following counties: Aransas, Bee, Brooks, Cameron, Duval, Goliad, Hidalgo, Jim Hogg, Jim Wells, Karnes, Kenedy, Kleberg, La Salle, Live Oak, McMullen, Nueces, Refugio, San Patricio, Starr, Webb, Willacy, and Zapata. This program is administered by the Hispanic Scholarship Fund (HSF), 55 Second Street, Suite 1500, San Francisco, CA 94105, (877) HSF-INFO, Fax: (415) 808-2302.

Number awarded   Varies each year.

Deadline   September of each year

[473]
HISPANIC THEOLOGICAL INITIATIVE DOCTORAL GRANTS

Hispanic Theological Initiative
12 Library Place
Princeton, NJ 08540
(609) 252-1721   (800) 575-5522
Fax: (609) 252-1738   E-mail: hti@ptsem.edu
Web: www.htiprogram.org

Purpose   To provide financial assistance to Latino/a doctoral students who are interested in a career of scholarly service to a faith community.

Eligibility   This program is open to full-time doctoral students (Ph.D., Ed.D., or equivalent only) who are Latinos/as from the United States, Puerto Rico, or Canada. Applicants must be committed to serving the Latino faith community in their home country. Candidates who are teaching or planning to teach in Latin America or Europe are not eligible. Selection is based on the scholarly promise of the applicant as indicated by GPA and GRE scores, academic quality of written work submitted by the applicant, recommendations by professors giving witness to the applicant's potential to contribute to the academic community as a scholar, and recommendations by Latino church/community leaders giving witness to the applicant's commitment to and leadership in the Latino community.

Financial data Recipients are awarded a grant of $13,000 per year. The program requires that their institution provide them with a tuition scholarship.

Duration Up to 2 years. Scholars who apply during the first year of doctoral course work receive support for 1 year only. The award may not be used during the year the students undergo their doctoral examinations and are not taking courses.

Additional information The program, funded by Pew Charitable Trusts, also provides the awardees with 1) a Latino/a faculty member to serve as a mentor to monitor and encourage their progress; 2) participation in an annual 3-day summer workshop to assist them in developing research, writing, and teaching skills; 3) a subscription to *Apuntes* and to *The Journal of Hispanic/Latino Theology;* 4) membership in either the Asociación para la educación teológica hispana (AETH) or the Academy of Catholic Hispanic Theologians in the U.S. (ACHTUS); and 5) participation in smaller regional meetings that will continue to foster community building, networking, and collegial support.

Number awarded 9 each year.

Deadline December of each year.

[474]
HIV/AIDS RESEARCH FELLOWSHIPS

American Psychological Association
Attn: Minority Fellowship Program
750 First Street, N.E.
Washington, DC 20002-4242
(202) 336-6027   Fax: (202) 336-6012
TDD: (202) 336-6123   E-mail: mfp@apa.org
Web: www.apa.org/mfp

Purpose To provide financial assistance to minority doctoral students who are preparing for a career involving research on HIV/AIDS issues and ethnic minority populations.

Eligibility This program is open to full-time doctoral students who are specializing in such research areas as HIV prevention, AIDS treatment adherence, provider education, and psychoneuroimmunology, although students of any specialty in psychology will be considered if they plan careers in HIV/AIDS research. Applicants must be U.S. citizens or permanent residents, a member of an ethnic minority group (African American, Alaskan Native, American Indian, Asian American, Hispanic, or Pacific Islander), and/or committed to a career in psychology with a specialty in HIV/AIDS research related to ethnic minority populations. Selection is based on professional commitment to ethnic minority HIV/AIDS research, knowledge of ethnic minority psychology or HIV/AIDS issues, potential as demonstrated through accomplishments and productivity, scholarship and grades, and letters of recommendation. Students enrolled in a master's only graduate program are not eligible.

Financial data The stipend varies from year to year, depending on federal guidelines.

Duration 1 year; may be renewed for up to 2 additional years.

Additional information Funding is provided by the U.S. National Institute of Mental Health. Students who receive a federally-funded grant from another source may not also accept funds from this program.

Number awarded 1 or more each year.

Deadline March of each year.

[475]
HOLLY A. CORNELL SCHOLARSHIP

American Water Works Association
Attn: Scholarship Coordinator
6666 West Quincy Avenue
Denver, CO 80235-3098
(303) 347-6206   Fax: (303) 794-6303
E-mail: acarabetta@awwa.org
Web: www.awwa.org

Purpose To provide financial assistance to outstanding minority and female students interested in pursuing advanced training in the field of water supply and treatment.

Eligibility Minority and female students who anticipate completing the requirements for a master's degree in engineering no sooner than December of the following year are eligible. Students who have been accepted into graduate school but have not yet begun graduate study are encouraged to apply. Recipients of the Larson Aquatic Research Support (LARS) MS Scholarship are not considered for this program. Selection is based on the quality of the applicant's academic record and the potential to provide leadership in the field of water supply and treatment.

Financial data The stipend is $5,000.

Duration 1 year.

Additional information Funding for this program comes from the consulting firm CH2M Hill. The association reserves the right not to make an award for any year in which an outstanding candidate is not identified.

Number awarded 1 each year.

Deadline January of each year.

[476]
HOWARD HUGHES MEDICAL INSTITUTE PREDOCTORAL FELLOWSHIPS IN BIOLOGICAL SCIENCES

National Research Council
Attn: Fellowship Office
500 Fifth Street, N.W.
Washington, DC 20001
(202) 334-2872   Fax: (202) 334-3419
E-mail: infofell@nas.edu
Web: www7.national-academies.org/fellowships/hhmiprogram.html

Purpose To provide funding to students (particularly minorities and women) interested in working on a graduate degree in the biological sciences.

Eligibility This is an international program: both American citizens and foreign nationals may apply. Foreign nationals must study at a U.S. institution, but U.S. citizens may study in the United States or abroad. Applicants must be able to demonstrate superior scholarship, be able to show great promise for future achievement, and be interested in working full time toward a Ph.D. or Sc.D. degree in the biological sciences (biochemistry, bioinformatics, biomedical engineering, biophysics, biostatistics, cell biology, developmental biology, epidemiology, genetics, immunology, mathematical and computational biology, microbiology, molecular biology, neuroscience, pharmacology, physiology, structural biology, or virology). Study in chemistry, mathematics, computer science, engineering, physics, or other related departments is allowed if the department provides ample opportunity for formal study in the biological sciences. Individuals pursuing or who hold a medical or dental degree are also eligible to apply if they have not completed 1 academic year or more of graduate study in biological sciences since receipt of their medical or dental degree. The program is aimed at students who are at or near the beginning of their graduate program; those eligible at the time of application are college seniors, college graduates with no or limited postbaccalaureate graduate study in the biological sciences, and first-year graduate students. Minorities underrepresented in the sciences (Blacks, Hispanics, Alaska Natives, American Indians, and Native Pacific Islanders) and women are particularly encouraged to apply.

Financial data The stipends are $21,000 per year. In addition, the program provides an annual fellow's allowance of $2,500, which can be used for health insurance, health care expenses, books and supplies, journal subscriptions, a computer and computer-related expenses, travel to scientific meetings, professional fees or dues, tuition for special summer courses, secretarial or clerical services relevant to the program of study, or other purposes relevant to a fellow's study. It also provides an annual institutional allowance of $13,500 in lieu of tuition and assessed fees.

Duration Up to 5 years, provided the recipient maintains satisfactory academic progress.

Additional information This program is administered by the National Research Council; the Howard Hughes Medical Institute selects the recipients.

Number awarded Approximately 80 each year.

Deadline November of each year.

[477]
HOWARD MAYER BROWN FELLOWSHIP

American Musicological Society
201 South 34th Street
Philadelphia, PA 19104-6313
(215) 898-8698   (888) 611-4AMS
Fax: (215) 573-3673   E-mail: ams@sas.upenn.edu
Web: www.ams-net.org/hmb.html

Purpose To provide financial assistance to minority students who are working on a doctoral degree in the field of musicology.

Eligibility This program is open to members of minority groups historically underrepresented in the field of musicology. In the United States, that includes African Americans, Native Americans, Hispanic Americans, and Asian Americans. In Canada, it refers to visible minorities. Applicants must have completed at least 1 year of academic work at an institution with a graduate program in musicology and be planning to complete a Ph.D. degree in the field. There are no restrictions on research area, age, or sex. Candidates must submit a personal statement summarizing their musical and academic background and stating why they wish to pursue an advanced degree in musicology, letters of support from 3 faculty members, a curriculum vitae, and samples of their work (such as term papers or published material). U.S. or Canadian citizenship is required.

Financial data The stipend is $14,000 per year.

Duration 1 year; nonrenewable.

Additional information Information is also available from Ellen T. Harris, Massachusetts Institute of Technology, 4-246, 77 Massachusetts Avenue, Cambridge, MA 02139-4301, E-mail: eharris@mit.edu.

Number awarded 1 each year.

Deadline January of each year.

[478]
HUGH J. ANDERSEN MEMORIAL SCHOLARSHIPS

National Medical Fellowships, Inc.
Attn: Scholarship Program
5 Hanover Square, 15th Floor
New York, NY 10004
(212) 483-8880   Fax: (212) 483-8897
E-mail: info@nmfonline.org
Web: www.nmf-online.org

Purpose To provide financial assistance to underrepresented minority medical students who reside or attend school in Minnesota.

Eligibility This program is open to African Americans, Mexican Americans, Native Hawaiians, Alaska Natives, American Indians, and mainland Puerto Ricans who have completed at least 1 year of medical school. Applicants must be Minnesota residents enrolled in an accredited U.S. medical school or students from any state attending Minnesota medical schools. Selection is based on leadership, community service, and financial need. Direct applications are not accepted; candidates must be nominated by medical school deans.

Financial data The award is $2,500.

Duration 1 year.

Additional information This award was established in 1982.

Number awarded 2 each year.

Deadline Nominations must be submitted by September of each year.

[479]
IBM COOPERATIVE FELLOWSHIP PROGRAM

IBM Corporation
Attn: University Relations
P.O. Box 218
Yorktown Heights, NY 10598
E-mail: CFellow@us.ibm.com
Web: www-4.ibm.com

Purpose To provide financial assistance and work experience to students pursuing a Ph.D. in a technical area of broad interest to IBM.

Eligibility Students nominated for this fellowship should be enrolled full time in an accredited U.S. or Canadian college or university and should have completed at least 1 year of graduate study in the following fields: chemistry, computer science, electrical engineering, material sciences, mathematics, mechanical engineering, physics, or related disciplines. They should be planning a career in advanced technology and product development as well as related research areas. Nominations must be made by a faculty member and endorsed by the department head. IBM values diversity and encourages nominations of women, minorities, and others who contribute to that diversity. Selection is based on the nominee's technical excellence and the strong interest of a participating IBM development laboratory in the nominee's desired research areas.

Financial data The fellowship covers tuition and fees as well as providing the recipient a stipend of $15,000. In addition, a small number of Distinguished Fellowships (for recipients who show "exceptional promise") are awarded, with a stipend of $20,000.

Duration 1 year; may be renewed, provided the recipient is renominated and demonstrates continued progress and achievement.

Additional information Recipients are offered an internship at 1 of the IBM's development laboratories as well as the opportunity to interact with IBM technical staff in a variety of settings. As interns, they are given an IBM ThinkPad.

Number awarded 25 each year.

Deadline November of each year.

[480]
IBM RESEARCH FELLOWSHIP PROGRAM

IBM Corporation
Attn: University Relations
P.O. Box 218
Yorktown Heights, NY 10598
E-mail: RFellow@us.ibm.com
Web: www-4.ibm.com

Purpose To provide financial assistance and work experience to students working on a Ph.D. in a research area of broad interest to IBM.

Eligibility Students nominated for this fellowship should be enrolled full time in an accredited U.S. or Canadian college or university and should have completed at least 1 year of graduate study in the following fields: chemistry, computer science, electrical engineering, material sciences, mathematics, mechanical engineering, physics, or related disciplines. They should be planning a career in research. Nominations must be made by a faculty member and endorsed by the department head. IBM values diversity and encourages nominations of women, minorities, and others who contribute to that diversity. Selection is based on research excellence and the student's overall potential for a research career.

Financial data The fellowship covers tuition and fees as well as providing the recipient a stipend of $15,000. In addition, up to 4 Distinguished Fellowships (for recipients who show "exceptional promise") are awarded, with a stipend of $20,000.

Duration 1 year; may be renewed, provided the recipient is renominated and demonstrates continued progress and achievement.

Additional information Recipients are offered an internship at 1 of the IBM Research Division laboratories and are given an IBM ThinkPad.

Number awarded 25 each year.

Deadline November of each year.

[481]
ILLINOIS MINORITY GRADUATE INCENTIVE PROGRAM

Southern Illinois University at Carbondale
Attn: IMGIP/ICEOP Administrator
Woody Hall C-224
Carbondale, IL 62901-4723
(618) 453-4558   E-mail: fellows@siu.edu
Web: www.imgip.sie.edu

Purpose To provide financial assistance to underrepresented minority students working on a doctoral degrees in science, mathematics, or engineering at graduate schools in Illinois.

Eligibility This program is open to U.S. citizens and permanent residents who are members of underrepresented minority groups (African American, Hispanic American, Native American). Applicants must 1) have an earned baccalaureate degree from an accredited institution of higher learning; 2) have a GPA of 2.75 or higher in the last 60 hours of undergraduate work or 3.2 or

higher in at least 9 hours of graduate work; and 3) unconditional acceptance to a doctoral program in a field with a severe underrepresentation (currently, the life sciences, physical sciences, mathematics, and engineering) at a participating school in Illinois.

Financial data In addition to full tuition and fees, each fellow receives an annual stipend of $17,500 plus an annual $1,500 allowance for books, supplies, and travel. Upon completion of the degree and acceptance of appropriate employment, fellows are eligible to receive a $15,000 placement incentive.

Duration 1 year; may be renewed for up to 2 additional years.

Additional information This program was established in 1985 and is funded by a Higher Education Cooperation Act grant from the Illinois State Board of Higher Education. The participating schools are Illinois Institute of Technology, Illinois State University, Loyola University of Chicago, Northern Illinois University, Northwestern University, University of Chicago, Rush University, University of Illinois at Chicago, University of Illinois at Urbana-Champaign, and Southern Illinois University at Carbondale. Each fellow must sign a letter of intent agreeing to seek and accept appropriate employment at an Illinois college or university upon completion of the doctoral degree.

Number awarded Varies; generally, about 5 each year.

Deadline February of each year.

[482]
ILLINOIS MINORITY REAL ESTATE SCHOLARSHIP

Illinois Association of Realtors
Attn: Illinois Real Estate Educational Foundation
3180 Adloff Lane, Suite 400
P.O. Box 19451
Springfield, IL 62794-9451
(217) 529-2600   E-mail: IARaccess@iar.org
Web: www.illinoisrelator.org/iar/about/scholarships.htm

Purpose To provide financial assistance to Illinois residents who are members of minority groups and preparing for a career in real estate.

Eligibility This program is open to residents of Illinois who are African American, Hispanic or Latino, Native American, or Asian. Applicants must be interested in preparing for a career in real estate by pursuing: 1) courses to meet Illinois salesperson license requirement; 2) course work to meet Illinois broker license requirement; 3) course work required for Illinois appraisal licensing/certification; 4) professional development unrelated to obtaining license/certification; or 5) undergraduate or graduate studies. Along with their application, they must submit information on their employment history, transcripts, evidence of financial need, and an essay that describes their career goals and explains why they believe they should receive scholarship assistance through this program.

Financial data A stipend is awarded (amount not specified); checks are made payable to the school, not to the recipient.

Duration Funds must be used within 24 months of the award date.

Deadline Applications may be submitted at any time, but they must be received at least 12 weeks prior to the beginning of the school term for which financial assistance is requested.

[483]
IMA DIVERSITY SCHOLARSHIP PROGRAM

Institute of Management Accountants
Attn: Committee on Students
10 Paragon Drive
Montvale, NJ 07645-1760
(201) 573-9000　　　　　　　　(800) 638-4427, ext. 1543
Fax: (201) 573-8438　　　　　　E-mail: students@imanet.org
Web: www.imanet.org

Purpose To provide financial assistance to minority and disabled student members of the Institute of Management Accountants (IMA) who are interested in working on an undergraduate or graduate degree in management accounting or financial management.

Eligibility This program is open to undergraduate and graduate students of American Indian/Alaska Native, Asian/Pacific Islander, Black, or Hispanic heritage and students with physical disabilities (defined as hearing impairment, vision impairment, missing extremities, partial paralysis, complete paralysis, or severe distortion of limbs and/or spine). Applicants must be in their sophomore, junior, or senior year or in a graduate program with a major in management accounting, financial management, or information technology. Selection is based on 1) academic merit; 2) quality of their application presentation; 3) demonstrated community leadership; 4) potential for success in expressed career goals in a financial management position; 5) a written statement from applicants expressing their short-term and long-term career goals and objectives, including their participation in the IMA; and 6) letters of recommendation.

Financial data Stipends are $3,000 per year.

Duration 1 year.

Additional information Up to 15 finalists in each category (including the scholarship winners) receive a scholarship to take 5 parts of the CMA and/or CFM examination within a year of graduation.

Number awarded At least 13 each year.

Deadline February of each year.

[484]
INDIVIDUAL PREDOCTORAL NATIONAL RESEARCH SERVICE AWARDS FOR M.D./PH.D. FELLOWS

National Institute on Alcohol Abuse and Alcoholism
Attn: Division of Basic Research
6000 Executive Boulevard, Suite 402
Bethesda, MD 20892-7003
(301) 443-1273　　　　　　　　Fax: (301) 594-0673
E-mail: tv9f@nih.gov
Web: www.niaaa.nih.gov

Purpose To provide financial assistance to students enrolled in an M.D./Ph.D. program who plan careers in mental health, drug abuse and addiction, and alcohol abuse research.

Eligibility Applicants must be 1) U.S. citizens or permanent residents of the United States; 2) enrolled in an M.D./Ph.D. program at an approved medical school; 3) accepted in a related scientific Ph.D. program; and 4) supervised by a mentor in that scientific discipline when the application is submitted. Normally, students apply during the first year of medical school, but applications may be submitted at any stage of medical study. Applicants must be proposing a course of study to prepare themselves to conduct research in areas of demonstrable mental health, drug abuse and addiction, or alcohol abuse relevance. They must be able to document that the proposed graduate program offers

them an opportunity to develop expert research skills and knowledge. Racial/ethnic minority individuals, women, and persons with disabilities are especially encouraged to apply.

Financial data The annual stipend is $18,156; fellows may also request funds for tuition and fees. The institution may receive an allowance of $2,000 per fellow per 12-month period to help cover such expenses as research supplies, equipment, travel to scientific meetings, and related items.

Duration Up to 6 years.

Additional information This award is offered by 3 of the institutes within the National Institutes of Health (NIH): the National Institute on Alcohol Abuse and Alcoholism (NIAAA), the National Institute on Drug Abuse (NIDA), and the National Institute of Mental Health (NIMH). Information is available from various components of those 3 institutes.

Number awarded Varies each year.

Deadline April, August, or December of each year.

[485]
INDUSTRY/GOVERNMENT GRADUATE FELLOWSHIPS

American Meteorological Society
Attn: Fellowship/Scholarship Coordinator
45 Beacon Street
Boston, MA 02108-3693
(617) 227-2426, ext. 246　　　　　Fax: (617) 742-8718
E-mail: amsinfo@ametsoc.org
Web: www.ametsoc.org

Purpose To encourage students entering their first year of graduate school to work on an advanced degree in the atmospheric and related oceanic and hydrologic sciences.

Eligibility This program is open to students entering their first year of graduate study who wish to pursue advanced degrees in the atmospheric or related oceanic or hydrologic sciences. Students currently studying chemistry, computer sciences, engineering, environmental sciences, mathematics, or physics who intend to prepare for a career in the atmospheric or related oceanic or hydrologic sciences are also eligible to apply. Applicants must be U.S. citizens or permanent residents and have a GPA of 3.0 or higher. Along with their application, they must submit 2 essays of 100 words or less: 1 on their career goals in the atmospheric or related oceanographic or hydrologic fields and 1 on their most important achievements that qualify them for this scholarship. The sponsor specifically encourages applications from women, minorities, and students with disabilities who are traditionally underrepresented in the atmospheric and related oceanic sciences. Selection is based on academic performance as an undergraduate and plans to pursue a career in the atmospheric or related oceanic and hydrologic sciences.

Financial data The stipend is $15,000 per academic year.

Duration 9 months.

Additional information This program was initiated in 1991. It is funded by high-technology firms and government agencies. Requests for an application must be accompanied by a self-addressed stamped envelope.

Number awarded Varies each year; recently, 16 of these scholarships were awarded.

Deadline February of each year.

[486]
INSTITUTE FOR INTERNATIONAL PUBLIC POLICY FELLOWSHIPS

United Negro College Fund Special Programs Corporation
2750 Prosperity Avenue, Suite 600
Fairfax, VA 22031
(703) 205-7624   (800) 530-6232
Fax: (703) 205-7645   E-mail: iipp@uncfsp.org
Web: www.uncfsp.org/iipp

Purpose To provide financial assistance and work experience to minority students who are interested in preparing for a career in international affairs.

Eligibility This program is open to full-time sophomores at 4-year institutions who have a GPA of 3.2 or higher and are nominated by the president of their institution. Applicants must be African American, Hispanic/Latino American, Asian American, American Indian, Alaskan Native, Native Hawaiian, or Pacific Islander. They must be interested in participating in policy institutes, study abroad, language training, internships, and graduate education that will prepare them for a career in international service. U.S. citizenship or permanent resident status is required. Preference is given to students interested in pursuing advanced language and area studies in targeted world areas who are supported by Title VI fellowships. Targeted languages include Arabic, Azeri, Armenian, Dari, Hindi, Kazakh, Kyrgyz, Persian, Pashto, Tajik, Turkish, Turkmen, Uzbek, Urdu, and other languages spoken in central and south Asia, the Middle East, and Russia/eastern Europe.

Financial data For the sophomore summer policy institute, fellows receive student housing and meals in a university facility, books and materials, all field trips and excursions, and a $1,050 stipend. For the junior year study abroad component, half the expenses for 1 semester are provided. For the junior summer policy institute, fellows receive student housing and meals in a university facility, books and materials, travel to and from the institute, and a $1,000 stipend. For the summer language institute, fellows receive tuition and fees, books and materials, room and board, travel to and from the institute, and a $1,000 stipend. During the internship, a stipend of up to $3,500 is paid. During the graduate school period, fellowships are funded jointly by this program and the participating graduate school. The program provides $15,000 toward a master's degree in international affairs with the expectation that the graduate school will provide $15,000 in matching funds.

Duration 2 years of undergraduate work and 2 years of graduate work, as well as the intervening summers.

Additional information This program consists of 6 components: 1) a sophomore year summer policy institute based at Clark Atlanta University's Department of International Affairs and Development, comprised of lectures, discussions, and group assignments, complemented by guest speakers and local site visits to international agencies and organizations in Washington, D.C. and New York; the program of study includes international politics, research methods, U.S. foreign policy, international business, economics, and selected area studies; 2) a junior year study abroad program at an accredited overseas institution; 3) a junior year summer institute of intensive academic preparation for graduate school, with course work in economics, mathematics, communication skills, and policy analysis; 4) for students without established foreign language competency, a summer language institute following the senior year; 5) fellows with previously established foreign language competence participate in a post-baccalaureate internship to provide the practical experience

needed for successful graduate studies in international affairs; and 6) a master's degree in international affairs (for students who are admitted to such a program). This program is administered by the United Negro College Fund Special Programs Corporation in partnership with the Hispanic Scholarship Fund Institute and the Association of Professional Schools of International Affairs; funding is provided by a grant from the U.S. Department of Education.

Number awarded 20 each year.

Deadline February of each year.

[487]
IOWA ANNUAL CONFERENCE ETHNIC MINORITY SCHOLARSHIP

United Methodist Church-Iowa Annual Conference
c/o Melvin W. Ammon
838 North 25th Street
Fort Dodge, IA 50501
(515) 573-3514

Purpose To provide financial assistance to minority students preparing for ordained ministry under the Iowa Annual Conference of the United Methodist Church.

Eligibility This program is open to African American, Asian American, Hispanic American, or Native American applicants who are either 1) a diaconal ministry candidate under the care of the Iowa Annual Conference Board of Diaconal Ministry or 2) a United Methodist Postulant or Certified Candidate for ordained ministry under the care of an Iowa Annual Conference District Committee on Ordained Ministry.

Financial data The stipend is $500.

Duration 1 year; may be renewed for up to 2 additional years.

Deadline Applications may be submitted in September or December.

[488]
JAMES CARLSON MEMORIAL SCHOLARSHIP

Oregon Student Assistance Commission
Attn: Private Awards Grant Department
1500 Valley River Drive, Suite 100
Eugene, OR 97401-2146
(541) 687-7395   (800) 452-8807, ext. 7395
Fax: (541) 687-7419
E-mail: awardinfo@mercury.osac.state.or.us
Web: www.osac.state.or.us

Purpose To provide financial assistance to Oregon residents majoring in education on the undergraduate or graduate school level.

Eligibility This program is open to residents of Oregon who are U.S. citizens or permanent residents. Applicants must be college seniors or fifth-year students majoring in elementary or secondary education, or graduate students pursuing an elementary or secondary certificate. Full-time enrollment and financial need are required. Priority is given to 1) members of African American, Asian American, Hispanic, or Native American ethnic groups; 2) dependents of members of the Oregon Education Association; and 3) applicants committed to teaching autistic children.

Financial data Scholarship amounts vary, depending upon the needs of the recipient.

Duration 1 year.

Number awarded Varies each year.

Deadline February of each year.

[489]
JAMES ECHOLS SCHOLARSHIP

California Association for Health, Physical Education,
   Recreation and Dance
Attn: Chair, Scholarship Committee
1501 El Camino Avenue, Suite 3
Sacramento, CA 95815-2748
(916) 922-3596   (800) 499-3596 (within CA)
Fax: (916) 922-0133   E-mail: cahperd@aol.com
Web: www.cahperd.org

Purpose To provide financial assistance to minority student members of the California Association for Health, Physical Education, Recreation and Dance.

Eligibility This program is open to California residents who have been members of the association for at least 60 days and are attending a 2-year or 4-year college or university in California. Applicants must be undergraduate or graduate students majoring in health, physical education, recreation, or dance and have completed at least 60 semester hours of college work. Selection is based on scholastic proficiency (a GPA of 3.0 or higher); leadership ability in school, community, and professional activities; and personal qualities of enthusiasm, cooperativeness, responsibility, initiative, and ability to work with others. This scholarship is awarded to the highest-ranked minority (Asian, African American, Latino, or Native American) applicant.

Financial data The stipend is $750.

Duration 1 year.

Number awarded 1 each year.

Deadline January of each year.

[490]
JOHN AND MURIEL LANDIS SCHOLARSHIPS

American Nuclear Society
Attn: Scholarship Program
555 North Kensington Avenue
La Grange Park, IL 60526-5592
(708) 352-6611   Fax: (708) 352-0499
E-mail: outreach@ans.org
Web: www.ans.org/honors/scholarships

Purpose To provide financial assistance to undergraduate or graduate students (particularly minorities) who are interested in pursuing a career in nuclear-related fields.

Eligibility This program is open to undergraduate and graduate students at colleges or universities located in the United States who are pursuing, or planning to pursue, a career in nuclear science, nuclear engineering, or a nuclear-related field. Qualified high school seniors are also eligible. Applicants must have greater than average financial need and "have experienced circumstances that render them disadvantaged." U.S. citizenship is not required. Selection is primarily based on financial need and potential for academic and professional success. Applicants must be sponsored by an organization within the American Nuclear Society (ANS). If the student does not know of a sponsoring organization, the society will help to establish contact. Augmentation of this scholarship program with matching or supplemental funds by the sponsoring organization is encouraged (though not required).

Financial data The stipend is $3,000, to be used to cover tuition, books, fees, room, and board.

Duration 1 year. Requests for an application must be accompanied by a self-addressed stamped envelope.

Number awarded Up to 8 each year.

Deadline January of each year.

[491]
JOHN MCLENDON MEMORIAL MINORITY POSTGRADUATE SCHOLARSHIP AWARD

NACDA Foundation
Attn: Membership Coordinator
24651 Detroit Road
Westlake, Oh 44145
(440) 892-4000   Fax: (440) 892-4007
E-mail: bhorning@nacda.com
Web: nacda.fansonly.com/foundation/found-mclendon.html

Purpose To provide financial assistance to minority college seniors who are interested in working on a graduate degree in athletics administration.

Eligibility This program is open to minority college students who are seniors, are attending school on a full-time basis, have earned a GPA of 3.0 or higher, intend to attend graduate school to earn a degree in athletics administration, and are involved on the college or community level. Candidates are not required to be student athletes.

Financial data The stipend is $5,000. In addition, 1 recipient each year is offered the opportunity to serve a 9-month internship in the NACDA office.

Duration 1 year. Recipients must maintain full-time status during the senior year to retain their eligibility. They must attend NACDA member institutions.

Number awarded 10 each year.

Deadline January of each year.

[492]
JOHN STANFORD MEMORIAL WLMA SCHOLARSHIP

Washington Library Media Association
P.O. Box 50194
Bellevue, WA 98015-0194
E-mail: wlma@wlma.org
Web: www.wlma.org

Purpose To provide financial assistance to ethnic minorities in Washington who are interested in preparing for a library media career.

Eligibility This program is open to residents of Washington who are working toward a library media endorsement or graduate degree in the field. Applicants must be members of an ethnic minority group. Selection is based on academic record, work experience, financial need, and recommendations.

Financial data The stipend is $1,000.

Duration 1 year.

Additional information Information is also available from the WLMA Scholarship Chair, Camille Hefty, (253) 589-3223, E-mail: Camille_Hefty@fp.k12.wa.us.

Number awarded 1 each year.

Deadline April of each year.

[493]
JOSE MARTI SCHOLARSHIP CHALLENGE GRANT FUND

Florida Department of Education
Attn: Office of Student Financial Assistance
1940 North Monroe Street, Suite 70
Tallahassee, FL 32303-4759
(850) 410-5185   (888) 827-2004
Fax: (850) 488-3612   E-mail: osfa@mail.doe.state.fl.us
Web: www.firn.edu/doe/osfa

Purpose To provide financial assistance to Hispanic American high school seniors and graduate students in Florida.

Eligibility This program is open to Florida residents of Spanish culture who were born in, or whose natural parent was born in, Mexico, Spain, or a Hispanic country of the Caribbean, Central America, or South America. Applicants must be citizens or eligible noncitizens of the United States, be enrolled or planning to enroll as full-time undergraduate or graduate students at an eligible postsecondary school in Florida, be able to demonstrate financial need as determined by a nationally-recognized needs analysis service, and have earned a cumulative GPA of 3.0 or higher in high school or, if a graduate school applicant, in undergraduate course work.

Financial data The grant is $2,000 per academic year. Available funds are contingent upon matching contributions from private sources.

Duration 1 year; may be renewed if the student maintains full-time enrollment and a GPA of 3.0 or higher and continues to demonstrate financial need.

Number awarded Varies each year; recently, this program presented 98 awards.

Deadline March of each year.

[494]
JUANITA ROBLES-LOPEZ/PAMPERS PARENTING INSTITUTE AND PROCTER & GAMBLE SCHOLARSHIP

National Association of Hispanic Nurses
Attn: National Awards and Scholarship Committee Chair
1501 16th Street, N.W.
Washington, DC 20036
(202) 387-2477   Fax: (202) 483-7183
E-mail: thehispanicnurses@earthlink.net
Web: www.thehispanicnurses.org

Purpose To provide financial assistance to members of the National Association of Hispanic Nurses (NAHN) interested in a master's degree in maternal-child nursing.

Eligibility Eligible are members of the association enrolled in a master's degree program in a maternal-child nursing program. Applicants must submit an statement outlining the maternal child needs affecting Hispanic communities and their potential leadership in that area. Selection is based on academic excellence (preferably a GPA of 3.0 or higher), potential for leadership in nursing, and financial need.

Financial data The stipend is $2,000.

Duration 1 year.

Additional information Funding for this scholarship is provided by Procter & Gamble Company and Pampers Parenting Institute.

Number awarded 1 each year.

Deadline April of each year.

[495]
KALA SINGH MEMORIAL SCHOLARSHIP

American Speech-Language-Hearing Foundation
Attn: Director of Programs and Corporate Development
10801 Rockville Pike
Rockville, MD 20852-3279
(301) 897-5700   (800) 498-2071
Fax: (301) 571-0457   TTY: (301) 897-0157
Web: www.ashfoundation.org

Purpose To provide financial assistance to international or minority students who are interested in working on a graduate degree in communication sciences and disorders.

Eligibility Applicants must be college graduates who are accepted for graduate study in the United States in a communication sciences and disorders program or enrolled as a full-time graduate student. The fund gives priority to foreign or minority (American Indian, Alaskan Native, Asian, Pacific Islander, Black, Hispanic) students. Students who previously received a scholarship from the American Speech-Language-Hearing Foundation are not eligible.

Financial data The award is $4,000.

Duration The award is granted annually.

Number awarded 1 each year.

Deadline June of each year.

[496]
KANSAS CITY HISPANIC SCHOLARSHIP FUND

Greater Kansas City Community Foundation
Attn: Scholarship Coordinator
1055 Broadway, Suite 130
Kansas City, MO 64105-1595
(816) 842-0944   Fax: (816) 842-8079
E-mail: scholars@gkccf.org
Web: www.gkccf.org

Purpose To provide financial assistance for college or graduate school to Hispanic students from the greater Kansas City area.

Eligibility This program is open to Hispanic students who are permanent residents of the greater Kansas City area (including Cass, Clay, Jackson, and Platte counties in Missouri and Johnson and Wyandotte counties in Kansas). Applicants must be or plan to be full-time undergraduate or graduate students.

Financial data The stipends range from $250 to $1,200 per year.

Duration 1 year.

Additional information Further information is available from the LULAC Educational Center, 301 East Armour Boulevard, Suite 460, Kansas City, MO 64111, (816) 561-0227, Fax: (816) 561-8319, E-mail: lnesc@latino-net.org.

Number awarded 1 or more each year, depending on the availability of funds.

Deadline February of each year.

[497]
KANSAS SPACE GRANT CONSORTIUM PROGRAM

Kansas Space Grant Consortium
c/o University of Kansas
135 Nichols Hall
2335 Irving Hill Road
Lawrence, KS 66045-7612
(785) 864-7401　　　　　　　　　Fax: (785) 864-3361
E-mail: ksgc@ukans.edu
Web: www.ksgc.org

Purpose To provide funding for space-related activities to students and faculty at member institutions of the Kansas Space Grant Consortium.

Eligibility This program is open to faculty and students at member institutions. Support is provided for undergraduate research scholarships, graduate research assistantships, undergraduate and graduate student participation in activities sponsored by the U.S. National Aeronautics and Space Administration (NASA), faculty participation in NASA research projects, and other activities in fields of interest to NASA. The consortium is a component of NASA's Space Grant program, which encourages participation by women, underrepresented minorities, and persons with disabilities.

Financial data Each participating institution determines the amounts of its awards.

Additional information The member institutions of the consortium are Emporia State University, Fort Hayes State University, Haskell Indian Nations University, Kansas State University, Pittsburgh State University, University of Kansas, and Wichita State University. Funding for this program is provided by NASA.

Number awarded Varies each year.

Deadline Each participating institution establishes its own deadlines.

[498]
KEN INOUYE SCHOLARSHIP

Society of Professional Journalists-Greater Los Angeles
　　Professional Chapter
c/o Christopher Burnett, Scholarship Chair
California State University at Long Beach
Department of Journalism
1250 Bellflower Boulevard
Long Beach, CA 90840-4601
(562) 985-5779　　　　　　E-mail: cburnett@csulb.edu
Web: www.spj.org/losangeles

Purpose To provide financial assistance to minority undergraduate and graduate students in southern California who are interested in pursuing careers in journalism.

Eligibility Minority college juniors, seniors, or graduate students who are interested in careers in journalism (but not public relations, advertising, publicity, law, or a related field) are eligible to apply if they are residents of or attending school in Los Angeles, Ventura, or Orange counties, California. Applicants should be enrolled as journalism majors, but if their university does not offer such a major they may present other evidence of intent to pursue a career in the field. Selection is based on evidence of unusual accomplishment and potential to advance in a news career; financial need is considered only if 2 applicants are equally qualified.

Financial data The stipend is $1,000 per year.

Duration 1 year; may be renewed. The sponsor reserves the right to split the scholarship equally if 2 or more applicants appear

equally qualified or to make no award if there are no promising applicants.

Number awarded 1 each year.

Deadline March of each year.

[499]
KENTUCKY SPACE GRANT CONSORTIUM GRADUATE FELLOWSHIPS

Kentucky Space Grant Consortium
c/o Western Kentucky University
Department of Physics and Astronomy, TCCW 246
Hardin Planetarium and Astrophysical Observatory
One Big Red Way
Bowling Green, KY 42101-3576
(270) 745-4156　　　　　　　Fax: (270) 745-4255
E-mail: Richard.Hackney@wku.edu
Web: www.wku.edu/KSGC

Purpose To provide financial assistance for study and research in space-related fields to graduate students in Kentucky.

Eligibility This program is open to graduate students at member institutions of the Kentucky Space Grant Consortium (KSGC). Applicants must be enrolled in a graduate degree program in a space-related field or teaching specialization. As part of the program, a faculty member must agree to serve as a mentor on a research project. U.S. citizenship is required. Selection is based on academic qualifications of the applicant, quality of the proposed research program and its relevance to space-related science and technology, and applicant's motivation for a space-related career as expressed in an essay on interests and goals. Applications are encouraged from women, underrepresented minorities, and students involved in projects of the U.S. National Aeronautics and Space Administration (NASA) such as NASA EPSCoR and SHARP.

Financial data The stipend is $16,000 per year, with an additional $2,000 for use in support of the student's mentored research project. Matching grants of at least $12,000 are required. Preference is given to applicants from schools that agree to waive tuition for the fellow as part of the program.

Duration 1 year; may be renewed, depending on the quality of the student's research and satisfactory grades, presentation of research results, and evaluation of progress by the mentor.

Additional information This program is funded by NASA. The KSGC member institutions are Centre College, Eastern Kentucky University, Kentucky State University, Morehead State University, Murray State University, Northern Kentucky University, Transylvania University, University of Kentucky, University of Louisville, and Western Kentucky University.

Number awarded Varies each year.

Deadline April of each year.

[500]
KPMG MINORITY ACCOUNTING DOCTORAL SCHOLARSHIPS

KPMG Foundation
Attn: Scholarship Administrator
Three Chestnut Ridge Road
Montvale, NJ 07645-0435
(201) 307-7628   Fax: (201) 307-7093
E-mail: fionarose@kpmg.com
Web: www.kpmgfoundation.org/graduate.html

Purpose To provide funding to underrepresented minority students working on a doctoral degree in accounting.

Eligibility Applicants must be African Americans, Hispanic Americans, or Native Americans. They must be U.S. citizens or permanent residents and accepted or enrolled in a full-time accounting doctoral program.

Financial data The stipend is $10,000 per year.

Duration Up to 5 years.

Additional information These funds are not intended to replace funds normally made available by the recipient's institution. The foundation recommends that the recipient's institution also award, to the recipient, a $5,000 annual stipend, a teaching or research assistantship, and a waiver of tuition and fees.

Number awarded Varies each year; recently, 21 of these scholarships were awarded.

Deadline April of each year.

[501]
LASPACE FELLOWSHIPS

Louisiana Space Consortium
c/o Louisiana State University
Physics and Astronomy
371 Nicholson Hall
Baton Rouge, LA 70803-4001
(225) 578-8697   Fax: (225) 578-1222
E-mail: wefel@phunds.phys.lsu.edu
Web: phacts.phys.lsu.edu

Purpose To provide financial assistance to students working on a graduate degree in an aerospace-related discipline at a college or university belonging to the Louisiana Space Consortium (LaSPACE).

Eligibility This program is open to U.S. citizens working on a master's or doctoral degree in a space- or aerospace-related field as a full-time student at 1 of the LaSPACE member schools. LaSPACE is a component of the U.S. National Aeronautics and Space Administration (NASA) Space Grant program, which encourages participation by members of groups underrepresented in science, mathematics, and engineering (women, minorities, and persons with disabilities).

Financial data The stipend is $17,500 per year for students working on a master's degree or $20,000 per year for students working on a doctorate.

Duration 1 year; renewable for up to 2 additional years for master's degree students and up to 4 additional years for Ph.D. students.

Additional information Fellows work with an established aerospace researcher at 1 of the LaSPACE member institutions: Dillard University, Grambling State University, L.S.U. Agricultural Center, Louisiana State University and A&M College, Louisiana Tech University, Loyola University, McNeese State University, Nicholls State University, Northwestern State University of Louisiana, Southeastern Louisiana University, Southern University and A&M College, Southern University at New Orleans, Southern University at Shreveport-Bossier City, Tulane University, University of New Orleans, University of Louisiana at Lafayette, University of Louisiana at Monroe, and Xavier University of Louisiana. Funding for this program is provided by NASA. Fellows are expected to describe the work in a yearly written report and in seminars presented to various audiences.

Number awarded 1 to 3 each year.

Deadline October of each year.

[502]
LAWRENCE WADE JOURNALISM FELLOWSHIP

Heritage Foundation
Attn: Selection Committee
214 Massachusetts Avenue, N.E.
Washington, DC 20002-4999
(202) 546-4400   Fax: (202) 546-8328
E-mail: info@heritage.org
Web: www.heritage.org

Purpose To provide financial assistance and work experience to undergraduate or graduate students who are interested in a career in journalism.

Eligibility This program is open to undergraduate or graduate students who are currently enrolled full time and are interested in a career as a journalist upon graduation. Applicants need not be majoring in journalism, but they must submit writing samples of published news stories, editorial commentaries, or broadcast scripts. Preference is given to candidates who are Asian Americans, African Americans, Hispanic Americans, or Native Americans.

Financial data The winner receives a $1,000 scholarship and participates in a 10-week salaried internship at the Heritage Foundation.

Duration 1 year.

Additional information This program was established in 1991.

Number awarded 1 each year.

Deadline February of each year.

[503]
LEADERSHIP FOR DIVERSITY SCHOLARSHIP

California School Library Association
717 K Street, Suite 515
Sacramento, CA 95814
(916) 447-2684   Fax: (916) 447-2695
E-mail: csla@pacbell.net
Web: www.schoollibrary.org

Purpose To encourage underrepresented minority students to get a credential as a library media teacher in California.

Eligibility This program is open to students who are members of a traditionally underrepresented group enrolled in a college or university library media teacher credential program in California. Applicants must intend to work as a library media teacher in a California school library media center for a minimum of 3 years. Financial need is considered in awarding the scholarship.

Financial data The stipend is $1,000.

Duration 1 year.

Number awarded 1 each year.

Deadline May of each year.

[504]
LIBRARY AND INFORMATION TECHNOLOGY ASSOCIATION/OCLC MINORITY SCHOLARSHIP

American Library Association
Attn: Library and Information Technology Association
50 East Huron Street
Chicago, IL 60611-2795
(312) 280-4269   (800) 545-2433, ext. 4269
Fax: (312) 280-3257   TDD: (312) 944-7298
TDD: (888) 814-7692   E-mail: lita@ala.org
Web: www.lita.org/a&s/awards.htm

Purpose To provide financial assistance to minority graduate students interested in preparing for a career in library automation.
Eligibility Applicants must be American or Canadian citizens, interested in pursuing a master's degree in library/information science (with a focus on library automation), and a member of 1 of the following ethnic groups: American Indian, Alaskan Native, Asian, Pacific Islander, African American, or Hispanic. The award is based on academic excellence, leadership potential, evidence of a commitment to a career in library automation and information technology, and prior activity and experience in those fields. Economic need is considered when all other criteria are equal.
Financial data The stipend is $3,000.
Duration 1 year.
Additional information This scholarship, first awarded in 1991, is funded by Online Computer Library Center (OCLC) and administered by the Library and Information Technology Association (LITA) of the American Library Association.
Number awarded 1 each year.
Deadline February of each year.

[505]
LIONEL C. BARROWS MINORITY DOCTORAL STUDENT SCHOLARSHIP

Association for Education in Journalism and Mass
   Communication
Attn: Communication Theory and Methodology Division
234 Outlet Pointe Boulevard, Suite A
Columbia, SC 29210-5667
(803) 798-0271   Fax: (803) 772-3509
E-mail: aejmchq@vm.sc.edu
Web: www.aejmc.org

Purpose To provide financial assistance to minorities who are interested in working on a doctorate in mass communication.
Eligibility This program is open to minority students enrolled in a Ph.D. program in journalism and mass communication. Applicants must submit 2 letters of recommendation, a resume, and a brief letter outlining their research interests and career plans. Membership in the association is not required, but applicants must be U.S. citizens or permanent residents.
Financial data The stipend is $1,200.
Duration 1 year.
Additional information Information is also available from Craig W. Trumbo, University of Wisconsin, Department of Life Sciences Communication, 440 Henry Mall, Madison, WI 53706, (608) 262-4902, Fax: (608) 265-3042, E-mail: cwtrumbo@facstaff.wisc.edu.
Number awarded 1 or more each year.
Deadline May of each year.

[506]
LITA/LSSI MINORITY SCHOLARSHIP

American Library Association
Attn: Library and Information Technology Association
50 East Huron Street
Chicago, IL 60611-2795
(312) 280-4269   (800) 545-2433, ext. 4269
Fax: (312) 280-3257   TDD: (312) 944-7298
TDD: (888) 814-7692   E-mail: lita@ala.org
Web: www.lita.org/a&s/awards.htm

Purpose To provide financial assistance to minority graduate students interested in preparing for a career in library automation.
Eligibility Applicants must be American or Canadian citizens, interested in pursuing a master's degree in library/information science (with a focus on library automation), and a member of 1 of the following ethnic groups: American Indian, Alaskan Native, Asian, Pacific Islander, African American, or Hispanic. The award is based on academic excellence, leadership potential, evidence of a commitment to a career in library automation and information technology, and prior activity and experience in those fields. Economic need is considered when all other criteria are equal.
Financial data The stipend is $2,500.
Duration 1 year.
Additional information This scholarship, first awarded in 1995, is funded by Library Systems & Services, Inc. (LSSI) and administered by the Library and Information Technology Association (LITA) of the American Library Association.
Number awarded 1 each year.
Deadline February of each year.

[507]
LUCENT TECHNOLOGIES COOPERATIVE RESEARCH FELLOWSHIP PROGRAM

Lucent Technologies
Attn: Fellowship Programs Manager
283 King George Road, Room B1-D26
Warren, NJ 07059
(732) 559-6971   E-mail: fellowships@lucent.com
Web: www.bell-labs.com/fellowships/CRFP

Purpose To provide financial assistance and summer internships at Bell Laboratories to members of minority groups underrepresented in scientific and technological fields who wish to pursue doctoral studies in designated science and engineering fields.
Eligibility This program is open to U.S. citizens or permanent residents who are members of a minority group currently underrepresented in the sciences (Blacks, Native American Indians, and Hispanics). Applicants must be college seniors who plan to pursue full-time doctoral study in the following fall in chemical engineering, chemistry, communications science, computer science and engineering, electrical engineering, information science, materials science, mathematics, mechanical engineering, operations research, physics, or statistics. U.S. citizenship or permanent resident status is required. Selection is based on scholastic attainment, evidence of ability, and potential as research scientists.
Financial data Fellowships provide full tuition and university fees, a book allowance, an annual stipend of $17,000, and related travel expenses. During their summer internships, fellows receive salaries commensurate with their level of experience and training.
Duration 1 year; may be renewed for up to 3 additional years if the fellow makes satisfactory progress toward the doctoral degree.

Additional information This program is sponsored by Lucent Technologies Foundation and Bell Laboratories. During the summers, fellows conduct research at Bell Laboratories under the mentorship of staff scientists and engineers.

Number awarded 6 each year.

Deadline December of each year.

[508]
LULAC GENERAL AWARDS

League of United Latin American Citizens
Attn: LULAC National Education Service Centers
2000 L Street, N.W., Suite 610
Washington, DC 20036
(202) 833-6130   Fax: (202) 833-6135
E-mail: LNESCAward@aol.com
Web: www.lulac.org/Programs/Scholar.html

Purpose To provide financial assistance to Hispanic American undergraduate and graduate students.

Eligibility This program is open to Hispanic Americans who are U.S. citizens or permanent residents currently enrolled or planning to enroll at an accredited college or university as a graduate or undergraduate student. Although grades are considered in the selection process, emphasis is placed on the applicant's motivation, sincerity, and integrity, as revealed through a personal interview and in an essay. Need, community involvement, and leadership activities are also considered. Candidates must live near a participating local council of the League of United Latin American Citizens (LULAC) and must apply directly to that council.

Financial data The stipend ranges from $250 to $1,000 per year, depending on the need of the recipient.

Duration 1 year.

Additional information This program represents an attempt to forge a partnership between the corporate world and the community. Under its fundsharing concept, LULAC's National Education Service Center gathers contributions nationally from corporations, while LULAC councils raise money locally. The total corporate donations are then apportioned back to the councils according to effort. Applications must be obtained directly from participating LULAC councils; for a list, send a self-addressed stamped envelope to the sponsor.

Number awarded Varies; approximately 500 each year.

Deadline March of each year.

[509]
LULAC HONORS AWARDS

League of United Latin American Citizens
Attn: LULAC National Education Service Centers
2000 L Street, N.W., Suite 610
Washington, DC 20036
(202) 833-6130   Fax: (202) 833-6135
E-mail: LNESCAward@aol.com
Web: www.lulac.org/Programs/Scholar.html

Purpose To provide financial assistance to Hispanic American undergraduate and graduate students.

Eligibility This program is open to Hispanic Americans who are U.S. citizens or permanent residents currently enrolled or planning to enroll at an accredited college or university as a graduate or undergraduate student. Applicants who are already in college must have a GPA of 3.25 or higher. Entering freshmen must have ACT scores of 20 or higher or SAT scores of 840 or higher. In addition, applicants must demonstrate motivation, sincerity, and

integrity through a personal interview and in an essay. Need, community involvement, and leadership activities are also considered. Candidates must live near a participating local council of the League of United Latin American Citizens (LULAC) and must apply directly to that council.

Financial data The stipend ranges from $250 to $1,000 per year, depending on the need of the recipient.

Duration 1 year.

Additional information This program represents an attempt to forge a partnership between the corporate world and the community. Under its fundsharing concept, LULAC's National Education Service Center gathers contributions nationally from corporations, while LULAC councils raise money locally. The total corporate donations are then apportioned back to the councils according to effort. Applications must be obtained directly from participating LULAC councils; for a list, send a self-addressed stamped envelope to the sponsor.

Number awarded Varies each year.

Deadline March of each year.

[510]
LULAC NATIONAL SCHOLASTIC ACHIEVEMENT AWARDS

League of United Latin American Citizens
Attn: LULAC National Education Service Centers
2000 L Street, N.W., Suite 610
Washington, DC 20036
(202) 833-6130   Fax: (202) 833-6135
E-mail: LNESCAward@aol.com
Web: www.lulac.org/Programs/Scholar.html

Purpose To provide financial assistance to Hispanic American undergraduate and graduate students.

Eligibility This program is open to Hispanic Americans who are U.S. citizens or permanent residents currently enrolled or planning to enroll at an accredited college or university as a graduate or undergraduate student. Applicants who are already in college must have a GPA of 3.5 or higher. Entering freshmen must have ACT scores of 23 or higher or SAT scores of 970 or higher. In addition, applicants must demonstrate motivation, sincerity, and integrity through a personal interview and in an essay. Need, community involvement, and leadership activities are also considered. Candidates must live near a participating local council of the League of United Latin American Citizens (LULAC) and must apply directly to that council.

Financial data Stipends are at least $1,000 per year.

Duration 1 year.

Additional information This program represents an attempt to forge a partnership between the corporate world and the community. Under its fundsharing concept, LULAC's National Education Service Center gathers contributions nationally from corporations, while LULAC councils raise money locally. The total corporate donations are then apportioned back to the councils according to effort. Applications must be obtained directly from participating LULAC councils; for a list, send a self-addressed stamped envelope to the sponsor.

Number awarded Varies each year.

Deadline March of each year.

[511]
MAES GENERAL SCHOLARSHIPS

Society of Mexican American Engineers and Scientists
Attn: National Office Director
13337 South Street, Suite 349
Cerritos, CA 90703
E-mail: maes@tamu.edu
Web: www.maes-natl.org

Purpose To provide financial assistance to undergraduate and graduate student members of the Society of Mexican American Engineers and Scientists (MAES).

Eligibility This program is open to MAES student members who are full-time undergraduate or graduate students at a college or university in the United States. Community college students must be enrolled in majors that can transfer to a 4-year institution offering a baccalaureate degree. All applicants must be majoring in a field of science or engineering. U.S. citizenship or permanent resident status is required. Selection is based on financial need; academic achievement; personal qualities, strengths, and leadership abilities; and timeliness and completeness of the application.

Financial data The stipend is $1,000.

Duration 1 year.

Additional information Information is also available from José M. Hernández, Chair, MAES Scholarship Committee, 4015 North Water Iris Cort, Houston, TX 77059.

Number awarded 1 or more each year.

Deadline October of each year.

[512]
MALDEF LAW SCHOOL SCHOLARSHIP PROGRAM

Mexican American Legal Defense and Educational Fund
634 South Spring Street, 11th Floor
Los Angeles, CA 90014-1974
(213) 629-2512   Fax: (213) 629-0266
Web: www.maldef.org/education/scholarships.htm

Purpose To provide financial assistance to Latino students who are attending or interested in attending law school.

Eligibility Any person of Latino descent who is presently enrolled or will be enrolled during the year of application as a full-time law student is eligible to apply. Selection is based upon academic achievement, demonstrated involvement in and commitment to serve the Latino community through the legal profession, potential for successful completion of a graduate or law degree, and financial need.

Financial data Stipends range from $2,000 to $6,000 per year.

Duration 1 year.

Number awarded Varies each year; recently, 8 of these scholarships were awarded.

Deadline June of each year.

[513]
MARRIAGE AND FAMILY THERAPY MINORITY FELLOWSHIP PROGRAM

American Association for Marriage and Family Therapy
Attn: Awards Program
1133 15th Street, N.W., Suite 300
Washington, DC 20005-2710
(202) 452-0109   Fax: (202) 223-2329
Web: www.aamft.org

Purpose To provide financial assistance to minority students enrolled in graduate and post-degree training programs in marital and family therapy.

Eligibility Eligible to apply are minority students (including African Americans, Hispanics, Native Americans, Asian Americans, and Pacific Islanders) enrolled in university graduate education programs or post-degree institutes that provide training in marital and family therapy. They must be citizens of the United States or Canada and show promise in and commitment to a career in marital and family therapy education, research, or practice.

Financial data The stipend is up to $2,500. Awardees also receive reimbursement of up to $1,000 for travel to the association's annual conference and waiver of conference registration fee.

Duration 1 year.

Additional information This program began in 1986.

Number awarded Up to 3 each year.

Deadline March of each year.

[514]
MARTIN LUTHER KING, JR. MEMORIAL SCHOLARSHIP FUND

California Teachers Association
Attn: Human Rights Department
P.O. Box 921
Burlingame, CA 94011-0921
(650) 697-1400   E-mail: scholarships@cta.org
Web: www.cta.org

Purpose To provide financial assistance to racial and ethnic minority group members in California needing a year to prepare for leadership roles in education.

Eligibility Applicants must be members of a racial or ethnic minority group; U.S. citizens and California residents; graduating high seniors, current college undergraduate students, or current graduate students; pursuing a degree or credential for a teaching-related career in public education at an accredited institution of higher education; and active members of the California Teachers Association (CTA), members of the Student CTA, or dependents of active, retired, or deceased CTA members.

Financial data Stipends vary each year, depending upon the amount of contributions received and the financial need of individual recipients.

Duration The fellowship is awarded annually.

Number awarded Varies; up to 7 each year.

Deadline March of each year.

[515]
MAS FAMILY SCHOLARSHIP PROGRAM

Jorge Mas Canosa Freedom Foundation
P.O. Box 440069
Miami, FL 33144-9926
(305) 592-7768

Purpose To provide financial assistance to students of Cuban descent who are working on an undergraduate or graduate degree in selected subject areas.

Eligibility This program is open to students who are direct descendants of those who left Cuba or were born in Cuba themselves. Applicants must be or have been in the top 10% of their high school graduating class and have a college GPA of 3.5 or higher. They must be able to meet federal standards of financial need. At least 1 parent or 2 grandparents must have been born in Cuba. Both undergraduate and graduate students may apply, provided they are majoring in 1 of the following subjects: engineering, business, international relations, economics, communications, or journalism. Selection is based on academic performance, leadership qualities, financial need, potential to contribute to the advancement of a free society, and the likelihood of succeeding in their chosen field. Finalists may be interviewed.

Financial data The amount of the award depends on the cost of tuition at the recipient's selected institution, on the family's situation, and on the amount of funds received from other sources. The amount of the yearly award cannot exceed $10,000. Full scholarships are not awarded to students who will be receiving full tuition scholarships and/or stipendiary support from other sources.

Duration 1 year; recipients may reapply and are given preference over other candidates.

Additional information This program was previously offered by the Cuban American National Foundation.

Deadline March of each year.

[516]
MASSACHUSETTS SPACE GRANT CONSORTIUM GRADUATE FELLOWSHIPS

Massachusetts Space Grant Consortium
c/o Massachusetts Institute of Technology
Building 33, Room 208
77 Massachusetts Avenue
Cambridge, MA 02139
(617) 258-5546   Fax: (617) 253-0823
E-mail: halaris@mit.edu
Web: www.mit.edu

Purpose To provide funding to first-year graduate students for space-related research or study at institutions in Massachusetts.

Eligibility This program is open to first-year graduate students at institutions that are members of the Massachusetts Space Grant Consortium (MASGC). Applicants must be pursuing research or study in space-related science or engineering fields. U.S. citizenship is required. Selection is based on academic achievement and interest in space science or space engineering. MASGC is a component of the U.S. National Aeronautics and Space Administration (NASA) Space Grant program, which encourages participation by women, underrepresented minorities, and persons with disabilities.

Financial data The fellowships provide full tuition plus a stipend.

Duration 1 academic year.

Additional information Graduate member institutions of the MASGC are Boston University, the Five College Astronomy Department, Harvard University, Massachusetts Institute of Technology, Tufts University, University of Massachusetts, Wellesley College, and Worcester Polytechnic Institute. This program is funded by NASA.

Number awarded Varies each year.

Deadline February of each year.

[517]
MEDICAL INFORMATICS RESEARCH TRAINING AWARDS

National Library of Medicine
Attn: Division of Extramural Programs
6705 Rockledge Drive, Suite 301
Bethesda, MD 20892
(301) 594-4882   Fax: (301) 402-2952
E-mail: pc49n@nih.gov
Web: www.nlm.nih.gov

Purpose To provide financial assistance to pre- and postdoctoral students who wish to pursue research training on the use of computers and telecommunications to manage health information.

Eligibility This program is open to students at both the predoctoral and postdoctoral level who wish to pursue a program of research training in medical informatics, the interaction of computers and telecommunications with biomedicine. Candidates may apply either to selected institutions that have received grants from the National Library of Medicine (NLM) of the National Institutes of Health (NIH) to operate such programs or directly to the NLM to pursue a program of research training with a mentor and institution of their own choice. All applicants must be U.S. citizens, nationals, or permanent residents. Applications from minorities and women are strongly encouraged.

Financial data Annual stipends for predoctoral fellows are $18,156; for postdoctoral fellows, the annual stipend ranges from $31,092 to $48,852 per year, depending on the years of postdoctoral experience.

Duration 1 to 3 years.

Additional information Currently, the funded sites are at Baylor/Rice, Columbia, Harvard/MIT/Tufts, North Carolina/Duke, Minnesota, Missouri, Oregon, Pittsburgh, Stanford, Yale, Utah, and the Regenstrief Institute; for the name and address of the program director at each of the institutions, contact the address above.

Number awarded Varies each year.

Deadline Each of the funded institutions sets its own application deadlines. For students applying directly to the NLM, applications must be submitted by April, August, or December of each year.

[518]
MELLON FELLOWSHIPS IN HUMANISTIC STUDIES

Woodrow Wilson National Fellowship Foundation
Attn: Director
5 Vaughn Drive, Suite 300
CN 5329
Princeton, NJ 08543-5329
(609) 452-7007   (800) 899-9963
Fax: (609) 452-0066   E-mail: mellon@woodrow.org
Web: www.woodrow.org/mellon

Purpose To provide financial assistance for the first year of graduate study in the humanities.

Eligibility Any college senior or recent graduate who has not yet begun graduate study and is applying to a graduate program in Canada or the United States leading to a Ph.D. in a humanistic field is encouraged to compete. Eligible fields of study are: art history, classics, comparative literature, creative writing, critical theory, cultural anthropology, cultural studies (including all area studies), English literature, ethnic studies, ethnomusicology, foreign language and literature, history, history of architecture, history and philosophy of mathematics, history and philosophy of science, interdisciplinary studies, linguistics, music history and theory, philosophy, political philosophy, political theory, religion, and religious studies, rhetoric, and women's studies. Ineligible programs include archaeology (except within art history), education (or any studies leading to the Ed.D.), fine arts, performing arts, international studies, law, political science, psychology, public policy, science and medicine, and sociology. Holders of master's degrees are not eligible unless the program was terminal (no Ph.D. offered) or in a field substantially different from the proposed Ph.D. field. GPA and scores on the Graduate Record Examination (GRE) are considered strongly in the selection process, but future promise and academic honors and awards are also considered. Applicants must also submit a 1,000-word statement explaining their interest in their chosen field and a 5- to 7-page sample of their academic writing. Members of underrepresented groups are particularly encouraged to apply.

Financial data The fellowship provides for payment of tuition and required fees plus a stipend of $17,500. Payment is made to the recipient in 2 equal installments, in September and in January.

Duration 1 academic year.

Additional information This program, which began in 1982, is funded by the Andrew W. Mellon Foundation and administered by the Woodrow Wilson National Fellowship Foundation. Fellows are expected to carry a full course load. They may not accept supplementary institutional awards or hold teaching assistantships during the period of the fellowship.

Number awarded 85 each year.

Deadline December of each year.

[519]
MENTAL HEALTH AND SUBSTANCE ABUSE SERVICES FELLOWSHIP

American Psychological Association
Attn: Minority Fellowship Program
750 First Street, N.E.
Washington, DC 20002-4242
(202) 336-6027   Fax: (202) 336-6012
TDD: (202) 336-6123   E-mail: mfp@apa.org
Web: www.apa.org/mfp

Purpose To provide financial assistance to doctoral students committed to providing mental health and substance abuse services to ethnic minority populations.

Eligibility Applicants must be U.S. citizens or permanent residents, enrolled full time in an accredited doctoral program, and committed to a career in psychology related to ethnic minority mental health and substance abuse services. Members of ethnic minority groups (African Americans, Hispanics/Latinos, American Indians, Alaskan Natives, Asian Americans, Native Hawaiians, and other Pacific Islanders) are especially encouraged to apply. Preference is given to students specializing in clinical, school, and counseling psychology. Students of any other specialty will be considered if they plan careers in which their training will lead to delivery of mental health or substance abuse services to ethnic minority populations. Selection is based on professional commitment to ethnic minority health and substance abuse services, knowledge of ethnic minority psychology or mental health services issues, potential as demonstrated through accomplishments and productivity, scholarship and grades, and letters of recommendation.

Financial data The stipend varies from year to year, depending on federal guidelines.

Duration 1 academic or calendar year; may be renewed for up to 2 additional years.

Additional information Funding is provided by the U.S. Substance Abuse and Mental Health Services Administration. Recipients are obligated to provide clinical services to underserved populations within 24 months after the completion of their training and for a period equal to the length of the award. This obligation may not be fulfilled in private clinical practice.

Deadline January of each year.

[520]
MENTAL HEALTH RESEARCH FELLOWSHIP

American Psychological Association
Attn: Minority Fellowship Program
750 First Street, N.E.
Washington, DC 20002-4242
(202) 336-6027   Fax: (202) 336-6012
TDD: (202) 336-6123   E-mail: mfp@apa.org
Web: www.apa.org/mfp

Purpose To provide financial assistance to doctoral students interested in preparing for a career in mental health or psychological research as it relates to ethnic minority populations.

Eligibility Applicants must be U.S. citizens or permanent residents, enrolled full time in an accredited doctoral program, and committed to a career as a researcher specializing in mental health issues of concern to ethnic minority populations. African American Hispanic/Latino, American Indian, Asian American, Alaskan Native, Native Hawaiian, and other Pacific Islander students are especially encouraged to apply. Preference is given to students specializing in psychopathology, community, social, developmental, educational, health, aging, and cognitive psychology (or other related areas). Selection is based on professional commitment to ethnic minority mental health research, knowledge of ethnic minority psychology or mental health issues, potential as demonstrated through accomplishments and productivity, scholarship and grades, and letters of recommendation.

Financial data The stipend varies from year to year, depending on federal guidelines.

Duration 1 academic or calendar year; may be renewed for up to 2 additional years.

Additional information Funding is provided by the U.S. National Institute of Mental Health, a component of the National Institutes of Health.

Deadline January of each year.

[521]
METROPOLITAN LIFE FOUNDATION AWARDS PROGRAM FOR ACADEMIC EXCELLENCE IN MEDICINE

National Medical Fellowships, Inc.
Attn: Scholarship Program
5 Hanover Square, 15th Floor
New York, NY 10004
(212) 483-8880 Fax: (212) 483-8897
E-mail: info@nmfonline.org
Web: www.nmf-online.org/Programs/MeritAwards/MetLife/Overview.htm

Purpose To provide financial assistance to underrepresented minority medical students who reside or attend school in designated cities.

Eligibility This program is open to African American, mainland Puerto Rican, Mexican American, Native Hawaiian, Alaska Native, or American Indian medical students in their second through fourth year who are nominated by their dean. Nominees must be enrolled in medical schools located in (or residents of) the following cities: Phoenix, Arizona; San Francisco/Oakland/Bay area, California; Los Angeles, California; Denver, Colorado; Miami, Florida; Tampa/St. Petersburg, Florida; Atlanta, Georgia; Aurora/Chicago, Illinois; Boston, Massachusetts; St. Louis, Missouri; Albany, New York; metropolitan New York area (including New York City, southern New York, Long Island, central and northern New Jersey, and southern Connecticut); Rensselaer, New York; Utica, New York; Dayton, Ohio; Tulsa, Oklahoma; Philadelphia, Pennsylvania; Pittsburgh, Pennsylvania; Scranton, Pennsylvania; Warwick/Providence, Rhode Island; Greenville, South Carolina; Austin, Texas; Dallas/Fort Worth, Texas; or Houston, Texas. Selection is based on demonstrated financial need, outstanding academic achievement, leadership, and potential for distinguished contributions to medicine.

Financial data The stipend is $4,000.

Duration 1 year; nonrenewable.

Additional information Funding for this program, established in 1987, is provided by the Metropolitan Life Foundation of New York, New York.

Number awarded 17 each year.

Deadline November of each year.

[522]
MEXICAN AMERICAN ENGINEERS AND SCIENTISTS PRESIDENTIAL SCHOLARSHIP

Society of Mexican American Engineers and Scientists
Attn: National Office Director
13337 South Street, Suite 349
Cerritos, CA 90703
E-mail: maes@tamu.edu
Web: www.maes-natl.org

Purpose To provide financial assistance to undergraduate and graduate student members of the Society of Mexican American Engineers and Scientists (MAES).

Eligibility This program is open to MAES student members who are full-time undergraduate or graduate students at a college or university in the United States. Community college students must be enrolled in majors that can transfer to a 4-year institution offering a baccalaureate degree. All applicants must be majoring in a field of science or engineering. U.S. citizenship or permanent resident status is required. Selection is based on financial need; academic achievement; personal qualities, strengths, and leadership abilities; and timeliness and completeness of the application.

Financial data The stipend is $2,000.

Duration 1 year.

Additional information Information is also available from José M. Hernández, Chair, MAES Scholarship Committee, 4015 North Water Iris Cort, Houston, TX 77059. Recipients must attend the MAES International Symposium's Medalla de Oro Banquet in October.

Number awarded 1 each year.

Deadline October of each year.

[523]
MEXICAN FIESTA SCHOLARSHIPS

Wisconsin Hispanic Scholarship Foundation, Inc.
1220 West Windlake Avenue
Milwaukee, WI 53215
(414) 383-7066 Fax: (414) 383-6677
E-mail: mexicanf@aol.com
Web: www.mexicanfiesta.org

Purpose To provide financial assistance to Hispanic American students in Wisconsin who are interested in attending college or graduate school.

Eligibility Applicants must be at least 50% Hispanic, be high school seniors or full-time undergraduate or graduate students, have earned a GPA of 2.75 or higher, be Wisconsin residents, and be bilingual in Spanish and English.

Financial data The amount of the stipend depends on the number of students selected.

Duration 1 year; recipients may reapply.

Additional information Recipients can attend college in any state. Funds for this program are raised each year at the Mexican Fiesta, held in Milwaukee for 3 days each August. Recipients must perform 20 hours of volunteer work in the Hispanic community.

Number awarded Varies; a total of $20,000 is awarded in scholarships each year.

Deadline May of each year.

[524]
MFT MINORITY SUPERVISION STIPEND PROGRAM

American Association for Marriage and Family Therapy
Attn: Awards Program
1133 15th Street, N.W., Suite 300
Washington, DC 20005-2710
(202) 452-0109   Fax: (202) 223-2329
Web: www.aamft.org

Purpose To support the recruitment, training, and retention of minorities as supervisors in the field of marriage and family therapy.

Eligibility Eligible to apply are minority individuals (including African Americans, Hispanics, Native Americans, Asian Americans, and Pacific Islanders) enrolled in a program to become marriage and family therapy supervisors approved by the American Association for Marriage and Family Therapy (AAMFT). Applicants must be U.S. or Canadian citizens or permanent visa residents and hold a graduate degree in marriage and family therapy or a related discipline. Information on financial need is not required but is a significant factor considered in the review process.

Financial data Awardees receive up to $1,000 and waiver of the processing fee.

Duration 1 year.

Additional information This program began in 1990.

Number awarded Up to 2 each year.

Deadline March of each year.

[525]
MILDRED COLODNY SCHOLARSHIP FOR STUDY OF HISTORIC PRESERVATION

National Trust for Historic Preservation
Attn: Scholarship Coordinator
1785 Massachusetts Avenue, N.W.
Washington, DC 20036-2117
(202) 588-6124   (800) 944-NTHP, ext. 6124
Fax: (202) 588-6059   E-mail: david_field@nthp.org
Web: www.nthp.org/help/colodny.html

Purpose To provide financial assistance and summer work experience to graduate students interested in working on a degree in a field related to historic preservation.

Eligibility Eligible to apply are students in their final year of undergraduate study intending to enroll in a graduate program in historic preservation and graduate students enrolled in or intending to enroll in historic preservation programs; these programs may be in a department of history, architecture, American studies, urban planning, museum studies, or a related field with a primary emphasis on historic preservation. Applicants must submit an essay in which they discuss their career goals and how their pursuit of a graduate preservation degree relates to those goals, including evidence of their interest in, commitment to, and/or potential for leadership in the field of preservation. Selection is based on the essay, a resume, 2 letters of recommendation, academic transcripts, and financial need. Applications are especially encouraged from people of diverse racial, ethnic, cultural, and economic backgrounds.

Financial data The program provides a stipend of up to $15,000 towards graduate school tuition, a stipend of $5,000 for a summer internship with the sponsor following the student's first year of study, and up to $1,500 towards the student's attendance at a National Preservation Conference.

Duration 1 year.

Additional information Internships may be completed at 1) the sponsor's Washington, D.C. office; 2) a regional office or historic museum site; or 3) the offices of 1 of the sponsor's partner organizations.

Number awarded 1 each year.

Deadline February of each year.

[526]
MINNESOTA SPACE GRANT CONSORTIUM SCHOLARSHIPS AND FELLOWSHIPS

Minnesota Space Grant Consortium
c/o University of Minnesota
Department of Aerospace Engineering and Mechanics
107 Akerman Hall
110 Union Street S.E.
Minneapolis, MN 55455
(612) 625-8000   Fax: (612) 626-1558
E-mail: mnsgc@aem.umn.edu
Web: www.aem.umn.edu/msgc/awards

Purpose To provide financial assistance for space-related science and engineering studies to undergraduate and graduate students in Minnesota.

Eligibility This program is open to graduate and undergraduate students at institutions that are affiliates of the Minnesota Space Grant Consortium. U.S. citizenship and a GPA of 3.2 or higher are required. The Minnesota Space Grant Consortium is a component of the U.S. National Aeronautics and Space Administration (NASA) Space Grant program, which encourages participation by women, underrepresented minorities, and persons with disabilities.

Financial data More than $50,000 is available from this program each year for scholarships and fellowships. The amounts of the awards are set by each of the participating institutions, which augment funding from this program with institutional resources.

Duration 1 year; renewable.

Additional information This program is funded by NASA. The member institutions are: Augsburg College, Bethel College, Bemidji State University, College of St. Catherine, Carleton College, Fond du Lac Tribal and Community College, Leech Lake Tribal College, Macalaster College, Normandale Community College, Southwest State University, University of Minnesota at Duluth, University of Minnesota at Twin Cities, and University of St. Thomas.

Number awarded 8 to 12 undergraduate scholarships and 2 to 3 graduate fellowships are awarded each year.

Deadline February of each year.

[527]
MINORITIES IN GOVERNMENT FINANCE SCHOLARSHIP

Government Finance Officers Association
Attn: Scholarship Committee
180 North Michigan Avenue, Suite 800
Chicago, IL 60601-7476
(312) 977-9700   Fax: (312) 977-4806
Web: www.gfoa.org

Purpose To provide financial assistance to minority undergraduate and graduate students who are preparing for a career in state and local government finance.

Eligibility This program is open to upper-division undergraduate and graduate students who are enrolled in a full-time program and preparing for a career in public finance. Applicants must be members of a minority group, citizens or permanent residents of the United States or Canada, and able to provide a letter of recommendation from the dean of their school. Selection is based on career plans, academic record, plan of study, letters of recommendation, and GPA. Financial need is not considered.

Financial data The stipend is $5,000.

Duration 1 year.

Additional information Funding for this program is provided by Fidelity Investments Tax-Exempt Services Company.

Number awarded 1 or more each year.

Deadline February of each year.

[528]
MINORITY ACADEMIC INSTITUTIONS FELLOWSHIPS FOR GRADUATE ENVIRONMENTAL STUDY

Environmental Protection Agency
Attn: National Center for Environmental Research
Ariel Rios Building - 8723R
1200 Pennsylvania Avenue, N.W.
Washington, DC 20460
(202) 564-6923   E-mail: broadway.virginia@epa.gov
Web: es.epa.gov/ncer/rfa

Purpose To provide financial assistance to graduate students in minority academic institutions (MAIs) who are interested in studying and conducting research in fields related to the environment.

Eligibility Applicants for this program must be U.S. citizens or permanent residents who are enrolled or accepted for enrollment in a master's or doctoral program in an academic discipline related to environmental research, including physical, biological, and social sciences and engineering. Students who have completed more than 1 year in a master's program or 4 years in a doctoral program are not eligible. As part of their graduate degree program, applicants may conduct research outside the United States, but they must attend an MAI in this country, defined as Historically Black Colleges and Universities (HBCUs), Hispanic Serving Institutions (HSIs), Tribal Colleges (TCs), Native Hawaiian Serving Institutions (NHSIs), and Alaska Native Serving Institutions (ANSIs).

Financial data The maximum award is $34,000 per year, including a stipend of $17,000, an allowance of $5,000 for authorized expenses (including any foreign travel to conduct research), and up to $12,000 for tuition and fees.

Duration Up to 2 years for master's degree students; up to 3 years for doctoral students.

Additional information These fellowships were formerly known as Culturally Diverse Academic Institutions Fellowships for Graduate Environmental Study.

Number awarded Approximately 25 each year.

Deadline November of each year.

[529]
MINORITY ACCESS TO RESEARCH CAREERS (MARC) FACULTY PREDOCTORAL FELLOWSHIPS

National Institute of General Medical Sciences
Attn: Division of Minority Opportunities in Research
45 Center Drive, Suite 2AS37
Bethesda, MD 20892-6200
(301) 594-3900   Fax: (301) 480-2753
E-mail: at21z@nih.gov
Web: www.nih.gov/nigms

Purpose To enable faculty at minority institutions to complete a Ph.D. degree in the biomedical sciences.

Eligibility Institutions with student enrollments drawn substantially from minorities may nominate faculty who lack a Ph.D. degree for these awards. Nominees must have been full-time faculty members in biomedically-related sciences or mathematics for at least 3 years at the institution, which may be a university, 4-year college, or health professional school. Fellows may train at any nonprofit private or public institution in the United States with suitable facilities, but they are expected to return to their sponsoring institutions after completion of their fellowships.

Financial data The fellowships provide payment of tuition and fees, a stipend that is based on the applicant's current salary but that may not exceed $31,092 per year, and an allowance of $2,000 to help cover the cost of supplies and limited travel.

Duration Up to 5 years.

Deadline April or December of each year.

[530]
MINORITY DENTAL STUDENT SCHOLARSHIP

American Dental Association
Attn: ADA Endowment and Assistance Fund
211 East Chicago Avenue, Suite 820
Chicago, IL 60611-2678
(312) 440-2567   Fax: (312) 440-2822
Web: www.ada.org/ada/charitable/endow/scholarship.html

Purpose To provide financial assistance to underrepresented minorities who wish to enter the field of dentistry.

Eligibility Applicants must be U.S. citizens from a minority group that is currently underrepresented in the dental profession: Native American Indians, Black/African Americans, or Hispanics; they must have a GPA of 3.0 or higher and be entering second-year students at a dental school in the United States accredited by the Commission on Dental Accreditation. Selection is based upon academic achievement, a written summary of personal and professional goals, letters of reference, and demonstrated financial need.

Financial data The maximum amount of the stipend is $2,500; it is sent directly to the student's financial aid office to be used to cover tuition, fees, books, supplies, and living expenses.

Duration 1 year.

Additional information This program, established in 1991, is jointly supported by the ADA Endowment and Assistance Fund and the ADA Health Foundation. Additional funding is provided by the Harry J. Bosworth Company, John O. Butler Company, Eastman Kodak Company, Colgate-Palmolive, Oral-B Laboratories, and Procter & Gamble Company. Students receiving a full scholarship from any other source are ineligible to receive this scholarship.

Number awarded Varies each year.

Deadline July of each year.

[531]
MINORITY FELLOWSHIP PROGRAM IN MENTAL HEALTH

American Sociological Association
Attn: Minority Affairs Program
1307 New York Avenue, N.W., Suite 700
Washington, DC 20005-4701
(202) 383-9005, ext. 322   Fax: (202) 638-0882
TDD: (202) 872-0486   E-mail: minority.affairs@asanet.org
Web: www.asanet.org/student/mfp.html

Purpose To provide financial assistance to minority doctoral candidates in sociology who are interested in preparing to conduct research on mental health issues relating to minority groups.

Eligibility These fellowships are available to U.S. citizens or permanent residents who are Blacks/African Americans, Latinos (e.g., Chicanos, Puerto Ricans, Cubans), American Indians or Alaskan Natives, Asian Americans (e.g., southeast Asian, Japanese, Chinese, Korean), or Pacific Islanders (e.g., Filipino, Samoan, Hawaiian, Guamanian). The competition is open to students beginning or continuing study in sociology at the doctoral level. Selection is based on commitment to research in mental health and mental illness, scholarship, writing ability, research potential, and financial need.

Financial data The stipend is $15,060 per year.

Duration 1 year; renewable for 2 additional years.

Additional information This program is funded by a grant from the U.S. National Institute of Mental Health, a component of the National Institutes of Health. Upon completion of their studies, recipients are expected to engage in mental health and mental illness research and/or teaching for a period equal to the period of support beyond 12 months.

Number awarded 10 to 12 each year.

Deadline December of each year.

[532]
MINORITY GEOSCIENCE GRADUATE SCHOLARSHIPS

American Geological Institute
Attn: Minority Participation Program
4220 King Street
Alexandria, VA 22302-1502
(703) 379-2480   Fax: (703) 379-7563
Web: www.agiweb.org/education/mpp/gradmpp.html

Purpose To provide financial assistance to underrepresented minority graduate students interested in working on a degree in the geosciences.

Eligibility This program is open to members of ethnic minority groups underrepresented in the geosciences (Blacks, Hispanics, American Indians, Eskimos, Hawaiians, and Samoans). U.S. citizenship is required. Applicants must be full-time graduate students enrolled in an accredited institution with a major in the geosciences, including geology, geophysics, hydrology, meteorology, physical oceanography, planetary geology, and earth science education; students in other natural sciences, mathematics, or engineering are not eligible. Selection is based on a 250-word essay on career goals and why the applicant has chosen a geoscience as a major, work experience, recommendations, honors and awards, extracurricular activities, and financial need.

Financial data Up to $4,000 per year.

Duration 1 academic year; renewable if the recipient maintains satisfactory performance.

Additional information Funding for this program comes from geoscience corporations and professional societies.

Number awarded Varies each year; recently, 17 of these scholarships were awarded.

Deadline February of each year.

[533]
MINORITY NEUROSCIENCE PREDOCTORAL FELLOWSHIP PROGRAM

Society for Neuroscience
Attn: Education Department
11 Dupont Circle, N.W., Suite 500
Washington, DC 20036
(202) 462-6688   Fax: (202) 462-9740
E-mail: info@sfn.org
Web: www.sfn.org

Purpose To provide funding to minority graduate students participating in mental health related neuroscience research and training programs.

Eligibility This program is open to doctoral students in neuroscience who are members of traditionally underrepresented racial and ethnic minority groups (African Americans, Hispanics, Native Americans, Alaskan Natives, Asians, and Pacific Islanders). Applicants must be U.S. citizens or permanent residents enrolled in a program of research and training to prepare for a career in neuroscience research laboratories. Along with their application, they must submit 2 academic letters of recommendation, a 1- to 2-page essay describing their area of interest and future goals in neuroscience, undergraduate and graduate transcripts, a current resume or curriculum vitae, copies of papers and abstracts they have authored or co-authored, and a biosketch of the home institution advisor (if available).

Financial data Fellows receive a stipend in accordance with standard National Research Service Award guidelines (currently, $18,156 per year). Other benefits include travel assistance and registration to attend the annual meeting of the Society for Neuroscience (SFN), enrichment programs that include funds to participate in activities outside the fellow's home laboratory, and mentoring opportunities with a mentor chosen from the SFN membership.

Duration 3 years, contingent upon adequate research progress and academic standing.

Additional information This program, established in 1991, is sponsored largely by the National Institute of Mental Health with additional support from the National Institute of Neurological Disorders and Stroke. Information is also available from Joanne Berger-Sweeney, Wellesley College, Department of Biological Sciences, 106 Central Street, Wellesley, MA 02481-8203, (781) 283-3503, Fax: (781) 283-3704, E-mail: mnfp@wellesley.edu.

Number awarded 8 each year.

Deadline February or August of each year.

[534]
MISSISSIPPI SPACE GRANT CONSORTIUM CAMPUS ACTIVITIES

Mississippi Space Grant Consortium
c/o University of Mississippi
217 Vardaman Hall
P.O. Box 1848
University, MS 38677-1848
(662) 915-1187   Fax: (662) 915-3927
E-mail: arandle@olemiss.edu
Web: www.olemiss.edu/programs/nasa/spacegrant.html

Purpose To provide funding to undergraduate and graduate students for space-related activities at colleges and universities that are members of the Mississippi Space Grant Consortium.

Eligibility This program is open to undergraduate and graduate students at member institutions of the Mississippi consortium. Each participating college or university establishes its own program and criteria for admission, but all activities are in engineering, mathematics, and science fields of interest to the U.S. National Aeronautics and Space Administration (NASA). U.S. citizenship is required. The consortium is a component of NASA's Space Grant program, which encourages participation by women, underrepresented minorities, and persons with disabilities.

Financial data Each participating institution establishes the amounts of the awards. Recently, the average undergraduate award was $1,308 and the average graduate award was $2,975. A total of $96,350 was awarded.

Additional information Consortium members include Alcorn State University, Coahoma Community College, Delta State University, Hinds Community College (Utica Campus), Itawamba Community College, Jackson State University, Meridian Community College, Mississippi Delta Community College, Mississippi Gulf Coast Community College (Jackson County Campus), Mississippi State University, Mississippi University for Women, Mississippi Valley State University, Northeast Mississippi Community College, Pearl River Community College, the University of Mississippi, and the University of Southern Mississippi. This program is funded by NASA.

Number awarded Varies each year; recently, a total of 66 students received support through this program.

[535]
MISSOURI SPACE GRANT CONSORTIUM GRADUATE FELLOWSHIPS

Missouri Space Grant Consortium
c/o University of Missouri at Rolla
229 Mechanical Engineering Building
1870 Miner Circle
Rolla, MO 65409-0050
(573) 341-4887   Fax: (573) 341-6899
E-mail: kchrist@umr.edu
Web: www.umr.edu/~spaceg

Purpose To provide financial assistance to graduate students in Missouri who are working on a degree in an aerospace field.

Eligibility This program is open to graduate students pursuing a degree in an aerospace field at member institutions of the Missouri Space Grant Consortium. Selection is based on academic records, recommendation letters from sponsoring faculty, student publications and academic achievements, and a statement of interest. U.S. citizenship is required. The Missouri Space Grant Consortium is a component of the U.S. National Aeronautics and Space Administration (NASA), which encourages participation by women, underrepresented minorities, and persons with disabilities.

Financial data The maximum stipend is $13,000 per year.

Duration 1 year.

Additional information The consortium members are Southwest Missouri State University, University of Missouri at Columbia, University of Missouri at Rolla, University of Missouri at St. Louis, and Washington University. This program is funded by NASA.

Number awarded 5 each year.

[536]
MLA SCHOLARSHIP FOR MINORITY STUDENTS

Medical Library Association
Attn: Professional Development Department
65 East Wacker Place, Suite 1900
Chicago, IL 60601-7298
(312) 419-9094, ext. 28   Fax: (312) 419-8950
E-mail: mlapd2@mlahq.org
Web: www.mlanet.org/awards/grants/minstud.html

Purpose To assist minority students interested in preparing for a career in medical librarianship.

Eligibility This program is open to racial minority students (Asians, African Americans, Hispanics, Native Americans, or Pacific Islander Americans) who are entering a graduate program in librarianship or who have completed less than half of their academic requirements for the master's degree in library science. They must be interested in pursuing a career in medical librarianship. Selection is based on academic record, letters of reference, professional potential, and the applicant's statement of career objectives. U.S. or Canadian citizenship or permanent resident status is required.

Financial data The stipend is $5,000.

Duration 1 year.

Additional information This scholarship was first awarded in 1973.

Number awarded 1 each year.

Deadline November of each year.

[537]
MONTANA SPACE GRANT CONSORTIUM GRADUATE FELLOWSHIPS

Montana Space Grant Consortium
c/o Montana State University
261 EPS Building
P.O. Box 173835
Bozeman, MT 59717-3835
(406) 994-4223   Fax: (406) 994-4452
E-mail: msgc@montana.edu
Web: www.montana.edu

Purpose To provide financial assistance to students in Montana who are interested in working on a graduate degree in the space sciences and/or engineering.

Eligibility This program is open to full-time graduate students in Montana working on degrees in fields related to space sciences and engineering; those fields include, but are not limited to, astronomy, biological and life sciences, chemical engineering, chemistry, civil engineering, computer sciences, electrical engineering, geological sciences, mechanical engineering, and physics. Priority is given to students who have been involved in aerospace-related research. U.S. citizenship is required. The Montana Space Grant Consortium is a component of the U.S. National Aeronautics and Space Administration (NASA) Space Grant program, which encourages participation by women, underrepresented minorities, and persons with disabilities. Financial need is not considered in the selection process.

Financial data The fellowships provide payment of tuition and fees plus a stipend of $15,000 per year.

Duration 1 year; may be renewed.

Additional information Funding for this program is provided by NASA.

Number awarded Varies each year; recently, 5 of these fellowships were awarded.

Deadline March of each year.

[538]
MORRIS SCHOLARSHIP

Morris Scholarship Fund
Attn: Scholarship Selection Committee
525 S.W. Fifth Street, Suite A
Des Moines, IA 50309-4501
(515) 282-8192   Fax: (515) 282-9117
E-mail: morris@assoc-mgmt.com
Web: www.morrisscholarship.org

Purpose To provide financial assistance to minority undergraduate and graduate students in Iowa.

Eligibility This program is open to minority students (African Americans, Asian/Pacific Islanders, Hispanics, or Native Americans) who are interested in studying at a college, graduate school, or law school. Applicants must be either Iowa residents and high school graduates who are attending a college or university anywhere in the United States or non-Iowa residents who are attending a college or university in Iowa; preference is given to native Iowans who are attending an Iowa college or university. Selection is based on academic achievement (GPA of 2.5 or higher), a statement of educational and career goals, community service, and financial need.

Financial data The stipend is $1,500 per year.

Duration 1 year; may be renewed.

Additional information This fund was established in 1977 in honor of the J.B. Morris family, who founded the Iowa branches of the National Association for the Advancement of Colored People and published the *Iowa Bystander* newspaper.

Number awarded 30 each year.

Deadline February of each year.

[539]
NAHJ SCHOLARSHIPS

National Association of Hispanic Journalists
Attn: Scholarship Committee
1000 National Press Building
529 14th Street, N.W.
Washington, DC 20045-2001
(202) 662-7145   (888) 346-NAHJ
Fax: (202) 662-7144   E-mail: nahj@nahj.org
Web: www.nahj.org/scholarship.html

Purpose To provide financial assistance to Hispanic American undergraduate and graduate students interested in preparing for careers in the media.

Eligibility Hispanic American high school seniors, undergraduates, and graduate students are eligible to apply for this support.

They must be interested in majoring in print, broadcast (radio or television), or photojournalism (broadcast or print); students majoring in other fields must be able to demonstrate a strong interest in preparing for a career in journalism. Applicants must submit an official transcript; a 1-page resume with their educational background, work history, awards, internships, other scholarships, language proficiency, and any work done for their school newspaper, radio, and/or television station; samples of their work; 2 reference letters; a 500-word autobiography in third person in the form of a news story; and documentation of financial need.

Financial data Stipends range from $1,000 to $2,000.

Duration 1 year.

Additional information This program is administered by the National Association of Hispanic Journalists (NAHJ) as a component of its Rubén Salazar Scholarship Fund.

Number awarded Varies each year; recently 35 scholarships were awarded through this program, including 4 for radio broadcasting, 10 for television broadcasting, 33 for print journalism, and 2 for photography.

Deadline January of each year.

[540]
NASA EARTH SYSTEM SCIENCE FELLOWSHIP PROGRAM

National Aeronautics and Space Administration
Attn: NASA Peer Review Services, Code Y
500 E Street, S.W., Suite 200
Washington, DC 20024-2760
(202) 358-0855   E-mail: acrouch@hq.nasa.gov
Web: research.hq.nasa.gov/research.cfm

Purpose To provide financial assistance to graduate students in earth system science.

Eligibility This program is open to students accepted or enrolled in a full-time M.Sc. and/or Ph.D. program at accredited U.S. universities. Applicants must be interested in conducting interdisciplinary research involving the study of the earth as a system. Both basic science and applied research are supported. Basic science topics fall into 5 categories: 1) how is the global earth system changing? 2) what are the primary forcings of the earth system? 3) how does the earth system respond to natural and human-induced changes? 4) what are the consequences of change in the earth system for human civilization? and 5) how well can we predict future changes in the earth system? Applied research themes are organized around the following: biology and biogeochemistry of ecosystems and the global carbon cycle; atmospheric chemistry, aerosols, and solar radiation; global water and energy cycle; oceans and ice in the earth system; and solid earth science. Applications are accepted for research in atmospheric chemistry and physics, ocean biology and physics, ecosystem dynamics, hydrology, cryospheric processes, geology, geophysics, or information science and engineering; research in paleo-climate, paleo-ecology, and paleo-hydrology is discouraged. U.S. citizens and permanent residents are given preference, although the program is not restricted to them. Students with disabilities and from underrepresented minority groups (African Americans, Native Americans, Alaskan Natives, Mexican Americans, Puerto Ricans, and Native Pacific Islanders) are especially urged to apply.

Financial data The award is $24,000 per year, to be used to cover the recipient's stipend ($18,000); travel expenses to scientific conferences and seminars, health insurance, books, and other items ($3,000); and tuition and fees, payable as a university allowance ($3,000).

Duration 1 year; may be renewed for up to 2 additional years.

Additional information This program was established in 1990. Beginning in 1996, the National Aeronautics and Space Administration (NASA) combined the earth science portion of its Graduate Student Researchers Program (GSRP), supported by the NASA Education Division, and the Graduate Student Fellowship in Global Change Research, supported by the Office of Earth Science, to establish this program.

Number awarded Up to 50 each year.

Deadline March of each year for new applications; May of each year for renewal applications.

[541]
NASA/DVSGC GRADUATE STUDENT FELLOWSHIPS

Delaware Valley Space Grant College Consortium
c/o University of Delaware
Bartol Research Institute
104 Center Mall, #217
Newark, DE 19716-4793
(302) 831-1094   Fax: (302) 831-1843
E-mail: nfness@bartol.udel.edu
Web: www.delspace.org

Purpose To provide financial support to graduate students in Delaware and Pennsylvania involved in space-related studies.

Eligibility This program is open to graduate students at member institutions of the Delaware Valley Space Grant College (DVSGC) Consortium embarking on or involved in aerospace-related research, technology, or design. U.S. citizenship is required. The DVSGC is a component of the U.S. National Aeronautics and Space Administration (NASA) Space Grant program, which encourages applications from women, minorities, and persons with disabilities.

Financial data This program provides tuition and stipends.

Duration 1 year; may be renewed.

Additional information This program is funded by NASA. Members of the consortium include Delaware State University (Dover, Delaware), Delaware Technical and Community College (Dover, Delaware), Franklin and Marshall College (Lancaster, Pennsylvania), Gettysburg College (Gettysburg, Pennsylvania), Lehigh University (Bethlehem, Pennsylvania), Lincoln University (Lincoln University, Pennsylvania), Swarthmore College (Swarthmore, Pennsylvania), University of Delaware–Bartol Research Institute (Newark, Delaware), University of Pennsylvania (Philadelphia, Pennsylvania), Villanova University (Villanova, Pennsylvania), and Wilmington College (New Castle, Delaware).

Number awarded Varies each year; recently, 3 students received these fellowships.

Deadline February of each year.

[542]
NASP MINORITY SCHOLARSHIP

National Association of School Psychologists
Attn: Education and Research Trust
4340 East West Highway, Suite 402
Bethesda, MD 20814
(301) 657-0270, ext. 234   Fax: (301) 657-0275
E-mail: kbritton@naspweb.org
Web: www.nasponline.org/about_nasp/minority.html

Purpose To provide financial assistance to minority graduate students enrolled in a school psychology program.

Eligibility This program is open to minority students who are U.S. citizens enrolled in a regionally-accredited school psychology program in the United States. Applicants must have a GPA of 3.0 or higher. Doctoral candidates are not eligible. Applications must be accompanied by 1) a resume that includes undergraduate and/or graduate schools attended, awards and honors, student and professional activities, work and volunteer experiences, research and publications, workshops or other presentations, and any special skills, training, or experience, such as bilingualism, teaching experience, or mental health experience; 2) a statement, up to 1,000 words, of professional goals; 3) at least 2 letters of recommendation, including at least 1 from a faculty member from their undergraduate or graduate studies (if a first-year student) or at least 1 from a faculty member of their school psychology program (if a second- or third-year student); 4) a completed financial statement; 5) an official transcript of all graduate course work (first-year students may submit an official undergraduate transcript); 6) other personal accomplishments that the applicant wishes to be considered; and 7) a letter of acceptance from a school psychology program for first-year applicants.

Financial data The stipend is $5,000.

Duration 1 year; may be renewed up to 2 additional years.

Number awarded 1 each year.

Deadline January of each year.

[543]
NATIONAL ASSOCIATION OF HISPANIC NURSES SCHOLARSHIPS

National Association of Hispanic Nurses
Attn: National Awards and Scholarship Committee Chair
1501 16th Street, N.W.
Washington, DC 20036
(202) 387-2477   Fax: (202) 483-7183
E-mail: thehispanicnurses@earthlink.net
Web: www.thehispanicnurses.org

Purpose To provide financial assistance for nursing education to members of the National Association of Hispanic Nurses (NAHN).

Eligibility Eligible are members of the association enrolled in associate, diploma, baccalaureate, graduate, or practical/vocational nursing programs at NLN-accredited schools of nursing. Applicants must submit a 1-page essay that reflects their qualifications and potential for leadership in nursing for the Hispanic community. Selection is based on academic excellence (preferably a GPA of 3.0 or higher), potential for leadership in nursing, and financial need.

Financial data The stipend is $1,000.

Duration 1 year.

Number awarded Varies each year, depending on the availability of funds.

Deadline April of each year.

[544]
NATIONAL ASSOCIATION OF UNIVERSITY WOMEN FELLOWSHIP

National Association of University Women
Attn: Fellowship Chair
1001 E Street, S.E.
Washington, DC 20003
(202) 547-3967   Fax: (202) 783-8094
Web: www.nauw.org

Purpose To provide financial assistance to minority and other women who are working on a doctoral degree.

Eligibility This program is open to women who already hold a master's degree and are enrolled in a program leading to a doctoral degree. They should be close to completing their degree. Preference is given to applications from minority women.

Financial data A stipend is awarded (amount not specified).

Duration 1 year.

Number awarded 1 or more each year.

Deadline May of each year.

[545]
NATIONAL DEFENSE SCIENCE AND ENGINEERING GRADUATE FELLOWSHIP PROGRAM

American Society for Engineering Education
Attn: NDSEG Fellowship Program
1818 N Street, N.W., Suite 600
Washington, DC 20036-2479
(202) 331-3516   Fax: (202) 265-8504
E-mail: ndseg@asee.org
Web: www.asee.org/ndseg

Purpose To provide financial assistance to doctoral students in areas of science and engineering that are of military importance.

Eligibility Graduate students in the following specialties are eligible: aeronautical and astronautical engineering; biosciences, including toxicology; chemical engineering; chemistry; cognitive, neural, and behavioral sciences; computer science; electrical engineering; geosciences, including terrain, water, and air; materials science and engineering; mathematics; mechanical engineering; naval architecture and ocean engineering; oceanography; and physics, including optics. Applicants must be U.S. citizens or nationals at or near the beginning of their graduate study planning to pursue a doctoral degree in 1 of the indicated specialties. Applications are particularly encouraged from women, underrepresented minorities (American Indians, African Americans, Hispanics, Native Alaskans, and Pacific Islanders), and persons with disabilities. Selection is based on all available evidence of ability, including academic records, letters of recommendation, and GRE scores.

Financial data The annual stipend is $23,500 for the first year, $24,500 for the second year; and $25,500 for the third year; the program also pays the recipient's institution full tuition and required fees (not to include room and board). An additional allowance may be considered for a student with a disability.

Duration 3 years, as long as satisfactory academic progress is maintained.

Additional information This program is sponsored by the Army Research Office, the Air Force Office of Scientific Research, and the Office of Naval Research. Recipients do not incur any military or other service obligation.

Number awarded Varies each year; recently, 170 of these fellowships were awarded. Recipients must attend school on a full-time basis.

Deadline January of each year.

[546]
NATIONAL LIBRARY OF MEDICINE FELLOWSHIP IN APPLIED INFORMATICS

National Library of Medicine
Attn: Division of Extramural Programs
6705 Rockledge Drive, Suite 301
Bethesda, MD 20892
(301) 594-4882   Fax: (301) 402-2952
E-mail: pc49n@nih.gov
Web: www.nlm.nih.gov

Purpose To provide financial assistance to health professionals and students who wish to pursue additional training in the use of computers and telecommunications to manage health information.

Eligibility Physicians, nurses, health science librarians, researchers, administrators, and others involved in health care activities are eligible. They must be nominated by domestic, non-profit, public or private organizations, such as universities, colleges, hospitals, laboratories, units of state and local government, and eligible agencies of the federal government. Candidates must hold a baccalaureate, master's, or doctoral degree in a field related to health care, or be enrolled in a program leading to such a degree. They may, but need not, utilize the training for credit leading to a degree or certification in an educational program. Both mid-career professionals and junior applicants are eligible. Applications from minority individuals and women are strongly encouraged.

Financial data Stipends are based on the salary or remuneration that the individual would have been paid by the home institution, to a maximum of $58,000 per year. The applicant's institution may request an institutional allowance up to $4,000 per year for supplies, equipment, travel, tuition, fees, insurance, and other training-related costs.

Duration 1 or 2 years.

Additional information These awards are intended for health science professionals whose primary interest is not in research but in learning how to put informatics into practice, develop modern information systems in traditional organizations, use the new information techniques in a specific field, and help disseminate promising programs and systems. The National Library of Medicine (NLM) is a component of the National Institutes of Health.

Number awarded Varies each year.

Deadline April, August, or December of each year.

[547]
NATIONAL OCEANIC AND ATMOSPHERIC ADMINISTRATION EDUCATIONAL PARTNERSHIP PROGRAM WITH MINORITY SERVING INSTITUTIONS GRADUATE SCIENCES PROGRAM

Oak Ridge Institute for Science and Education
Attn: Education and Training Division
P.O. Box 117
Oak Ridge, TN 37831-0117
(865) 576-9272   Fax: (865) 241-5220
E-mail: babcockc@orau.gov
Web: www.orau.gov/orise.htm

Purpose To provide financial assistance and summer research experience to graduate students at minority serving institutions who are majoring in scientific fields of interest to the National Oceanic and Atmospheric Administration (NOAA).

Eligibility This program is open to graduate students pursuing master's or doctoral degrees at minority serving institutions, including Hispanic Serving Institutions (HSIs), Historically Black Colleges and Universities (HBCUs), and Tribal Colleges and Universities (TCUs). Applicants must be majoring in biology, chemistry, computer science, economics, engineering, geography, geology, mathematics, physical science, physics, social science, or other fields specific to NOAA such as cartography, environmental planning, fishery biology, hydrology, meteorology, or oceanography. They must also be interested in pursuing a training program during the summer at a NOAA research facility.

Financial data During the school year, the program provides payment of tuition and fees, books, housing, meals, and travel expenses. During the summer, students receive a salary and benefits.

Duration 2 years of study plus 16 weeks of research training during the summer.

Additional information This program is funded by NOAA and administered by the Education and Training Division (ETD) of Oak Ridge Institute for Science and Education (ORISE).

Number awarded 5 each year.

Deadline January of each year.

[548]
NATIONAL PHYSICAL SCIENCE CONSORTIUM GRADUATE FELLOWSHIPS

National Physical Science Consortium
University Village
3375 South Hoover Street, Suite E 200
Los Angeles, CA 90007
(213) 821-2409   (800) 854-NPSC
Fax: (213) 821-2410   E-mail: npschq@npsc.org
Web: www.npsc.org

Purpose To provide financial assistance and summer work experience to underrepresented minorities and women interested in working on a Ph.D. in designated science and engineering fields.

Eligibility This program is open to U.S. citizens who are seniors graduating from college with a GPA of 3.0 or higher, enrolled in the first year of a doctoral program, completing a terminal master's degree, or returning from the work force and holding no more than a master's degree. Applicants must be interested in pursuing a Ph.D. in astronomy, chemistry, computer science, geology, materials science, mathematical sciences, physics, chemical engineering, computer engineering, electrical engineering, environmental engineering, or mechanical engineering. The program welcomes applications from all qualified students and continues to emphasize the recruitment of underrepresented minority (African American, Hispanic, Native American Indian, Eskimo, Aleut, and Pacific Islander) and women physical science and engineering students. Fellowships are provided to students at the 113 universities that are members of the consortium. Selection is based on academic standing (GPA), course work taken in preparation for graduate school, university and/or industry research experience, letters of recommendation, and GRE scores.

Financial data The fellowship pays tuition and fees plus an annual stipend of $16,000. It also provides on-site paid summer employment to enhance technical experience. The exact value of the fellowship depends on academic standing, summer employment, and graduate school attended, but exceeds $200,000.

Duration Up to 6 years.

Additional information Tuition and fees are provided by the participating universities. Stipends and summer internships are provided by 11 private corporations and governmental research facilities.

Number awarded Varies each year.

Deadline November of each year.

[549]
NATIONAL RESEARCH SERVICE AWARDS FOR INDIVIDUAL PREDOCTORAL FELLOWS

National Institute on Alcohol Abuse and Alcoholism
Attn: Division of Basic Research
6000 Executive Boulevard, Suite 402
Bethesda, MD 20892-7003
(301) 443-1273   Fax: (301) 594-0673
E-mail: tv9f@nih.gov
Web: www.niaaa.nih.gov

Purpose To provide funding to doctoral candidates interested in pursuing research training in areas of behavioral, biomedical, or social science that deal with alcohol, drug abuse, and mental health.

Eligibility Applicants must be U.S. citizens or permanent residents enrolled in a program leading to a research doctorate (e.g., Ph.D. or D.Sc.) at a domestic or foreign nonprofit private or public institution, including a federal laboratory. This program is not available for study leading to the M.D., D.O., D.D.S., Psy.D., or similar professional degrees. Women, minorities, and individuals with disabilities are especially encouraged to apply.

Financial data The annual stipend is $18,156; fellows may also request funds for tuition and fees, which are normally reimbursed at a rate of 100% up to $2,000 and 60% for all costs above $2,000. The institution may receive an allowance of $3,000 per fellow per 12-month period to help cover such expenses as research supplies, equipment, travel to scientific meetings, and related items.

Duration Up to 5 years.

Additional information This award is offered by 3 of the institutes within the National Institutes of Health (NIH): the National Institute on Alcohol Abuse and Alcoholism (NIAAA), the National Institute on Drug Abuse (NIDA), and the National Institute of Mental Health (NIMH). Information is available not only from the address above, but from other components of those 3 institutes as well.

Number awarded Varies each year.

Deadline April, August, or December of each year.

[550]
NATIONAL SOCIETY OF HISPANIC MBAS SCHOLARSHIP PROGRAM

National Society of Hispanic MBAs
Attn: Education Specialist
1303 Walnut Hill Lane, Suite 300
Irving, TX 75038
(214) 596-9338, ext. 228   (877) 467-4622
Fax: (214) 596-9325   E-mail: xguerra@nshmba.org
Web: www.nshmba.org

Purpose To provide financial assistance to Hispanic American graduate students interested in working on a master's degree in business administration.

Eligibility Eligible to apply are full-time or part-time graduate students who are interested in working on a master's degree in management or business. Applicants may be currently enrolled in graduate school or planning to attend. They must be U.S. citizens or permanent residents and be of Hispanic background (1 parent must be fully Hispanic or both parents must be half Hispanic). Selection is based on academic achievement (GPA of 3.0 or higher), participation in community development or service, letters of recommendation, financial need, and a 1-page essay on issues affecting Hispanics in the United States (recently, applicants were asked to assume that they were the admissions director of a university and to describe how they would increase Hispanic representation in the graduate management and business program).

Financial data Stipends generally range from $2,500 to $15,000,

Duration 1 year.

Additional information This program is offered in cooperation with the Hispanic Scholarship Fund, 55 Second Street, Suite 1500, San Francisco, CA 94105, (877) HSF-INFO.

Number awarded Varies each year. Recently, this program awarded $617,000 in scholarships, including 3 at $15,000, 15 at $10,000, and many others ranging from $2,500 to $7,500.

Deadline May of each year.

[551]
NCAA ETHNIC MINORITY POSTGRADUATE SCHOLARSHIP PROGRAM

National Collegiate Athletic Association
Attn: NCAA Foundation
700 West Washington Avenue
P.O. Box 6222
Indianapolis, IN 46206-6222
(317) 917-6222   Fax: (317) 917-6888
Web: www.ncaa.org/ncaa_foundation/programs.html

Purpose To provide funding to minority graduate students who are interested in preparing for a career in intercollegiate athletics.

Eligibility This program is open to members of minority groups who have been accepted into a program at a National Collegiate Athletic Association (NCAA) member institution that will prepare them for a career in intercollegiate athletics (athletics administrator, coach, athletic trainer, or other career that provides a direct service to intercollegiate athletics). Applicants must be U.S. citizens, have performed with distinction as a student body member at their respective undergraduate institution, and be entering the first semester or term of their postgraduate studies. Selection is based on the applicant's involvement in extracurricular activities, course work, commitment to pursuing a career in intercollegiate

athletics, and promise for success in such a career. Financial need is not considered.

Financial data The stipend is $6,000; funds are paid to the college or university of the recipient's choice.

Duration 1 year; nonrenewable.

Number awarded 15 each year; 3 of the scholarships are reserved for applicants who completed undergraduate study at an NCAA Division III institution.

Deadline February of each year.

[552]
NEBHE DOCTORAL SCHOLARS PROGRAM IN SCIENCE, ENGINEERING AND MATHEMATICS

New England Board of Higher Education
45 Temple Place
Boston, MA 02111
(617) 357-9620   Fax: (617) 338-1577
E-mail: pubinfo@nebhe.org
Web: www.nebhe.org/doctoral.html

Purpose To provide financial assistance to African American, Hispanic American, and Native American doctoral students in science, mathematics, and engineering at universities in New England.

Eligibility This program is open to African American, Hispanic American, and Native American students who wish to begin doctoral study in order to pursue a career in college teaching. Applicants must be interested in studying biological sciences, chemistry, engineering, geological sciences, mathematics, or physics at designated universities in New England.

Financial data The program provides tuition and fee forgiveness in all years, a stipend in the first year, guaranteed research or teaching assistantships for the second year and beyond, and travel funds so scholars can attend a national teaching institute and professional conferences.

Duration Up to 5 years.

Additional information Other benefits of this program include faculty mentoring within the doctoral department, peer support by clustering 4 to 6 participating scholars within each graduate department, and networking events where scholars can build community with other graduate students and faculty of color in New England. This program is part of the national Compact for Faculty Diversity, established in 1994 by the New England Board for Higher Education (NEBHE), the Western Interstate Commission for Higher Education (WICHE), and the Southern Regional Education Board (SREB) with assistance from the Pew Charitable Trusts, the Ford Foundation, participating states, and doctoral universities. Recently, the participating programs included molecular and cell biology at the University of Connecticut; biological sciences at the University of Rhode Island; pathobiology at Brown University; ecology and evolutionary biology at the University of Connecticut; biotechnology at Brown University; neuroscience at Brown University; chemistry at the University of Connecticut, the University of New Hampshire, and Wesleyan University; electrical engineering and computer science at the University of Rhode Island; geological sciences at Brown University; mathematics and applied mathematics at Dartmouth College, the University of Connecticut, and Brown University; and oceanography at the University of Rhode Island. Candidates should contact the participating doctoral department for applications and further information.

Number awarded Varies each year.

[553]
NEBRASKA SPACE GRANT STATEWIDE SCHOLARSHIP COMPETITION

Nebraska Space Grant Consortium
c/o University of Nebraska at Omaha
Allwine Hall 422
6001 Dodge Street
Omaha, NE 68182-0406
(402) 554-3772   (800) 858-8648, ext. 4-3772 (within NE)
Fax: (402) 554-3781   E-mail: nasa@unomaha.edu
Web: www.unomaha.edu/~nasa/funding/ssc.html

Purpose To provide financial assistance to undergraduate and graduate students in Nebraska interested in aerospace-related study or research.

Eligibility This program is open to undergraduate and graduate students at schools that are members of the Nebraska Space Grant Consortium. Applicants must be U.S. citizens participating in approved aviation or aerospace-related research or course work. Selection is based primarily on past academic performance in the classroom. Special attention is given to applications submitted by women, underrepresented minorities, and persons with disabilities.

Financial data Maximum awards are $500 per semester for undergraduate or graduate course work, $750 per semester for undergraduate research, or $2,500 per semester for graduate research.

Duration 1 semester; may be renewed if the recipient maintains a GPA of 3.0 or higher.

Additional information The following schools are members of the Nebraska Space Grant Consortium: University of Nebraska at Omaha, University of Nebraska at Lincoln, University of Nebraska at Kearney, University of Nebraska Medical Center, Creighton University, Western Nebraska Community College, Chadron State College, College of St. Mary, Metropolitan Community College, Grace University, Hastings College, Little Priest Tribal College, and Nebraska Indian Community College. Funding for this program is provided by the National Aeronautics and Space Administration.

Deadline April of each year.

[554]
NEVADA SPACE GRANT CONSORTIUM GRADUATE FELLOWSHIP PROGRAM

Nevada Space Grant Consortium
c/o University of Nevada at Reno
1664 North Virginia Street
MS/172
Reno, NV 89557-0138
(775) 784-6261   Fax: (775) 327-2235
E-mail: nvsg@mines.unr.edu
Web: www.unr.edu/spacegrant

Purpose To provide financial assistance for space-related study to graduate students at institutions that are members of the Nevada Space Grant Consortium (NSGC).

Eligibility This program is open to graduate students at NSGC member institutions. Applicants must be working on a degree in an aerospace-related field (including the behavioral sciences, biological sciences, business, communications, computer science, economics, education, engineering, international affairs, law, natural sciences, physical sciences, public administration, and sociology) that is concerned with or likely to improve the understanding, assessment, development, and utilization of space. They

must be U.S. citizens, be enrolled full time (or accepted for full-time study), present a proposed research or activity plan related to space, include in the research or activity plan an extramural experience at a field center of the U.S. National Aeronautics and Space Administration (NASA), plan to be involved in NSGC outreach activities, not receive other federal funds, and intend to pursue a career in a field of interest to NASA. Members of underrepresented groups (African Americans, Hispanics, American Indians, Pacific Islanders, physically disabled people, and women of all races) who have an interested in aerospace fields are encouraged to apply.

Financial data The grant is $22,500, including $16,000 as a stipend for the student and $6,500 for tuition and a student research and travel allowance.

Duration 12 months; may be renewed up to 24 additional months.

Additional information Members of the NSGC include all state institutes of higher learned in Nevada: 2 Ph.D.-granting universities (the University of Nevada at Las Vegas and the University of Nevada at Reno), 4 community colleges (Southern Nevada, Great Basin, Truckee Meadows, and Western Nevada), and the system's research organization, the Desert Research Institute. Funding for this program is provided by NASA.

Number awarded Varies each year; recently, 13 of these awards were granted.

Deadline March of each year.

[555]
NEW MEXICO GRADUATE SCHOLARSHIP PROGRAM

New Mexico Commission on Higher Education
Attn: Financial Aid and Student Services
1068 Cerrillos Road
P.O. Box 15910
Santa Fe, NM 87506-5910
(505) 827-7383   (800) 279-9777
Fax: (505) 827-7392   E-mail: highered@che.state.nm.us
Web: www.nmche.org

Purpose To provide financial assistance for graduate education to underrepresented groups in New Mexico.

Eligibility Applicants for this program must be New Mexico residents who are members of underrepresented groups, particularly minorities and women. Preference is given to 1) students enrolled in business, engineering, computer science, mathematics, or agriculture and 2) American Indian students enrolled in any graduate program. All applicants must be U.S. citizens or permanent residents enrolled in graduate programs at public institutions of higher education in New Mexico.

Financial data The maximum stipend is $7,500 per year.

Duration 1 year; may be renewed.

Additional information Information is available from the dean of graduate studies at the participating New Mexico public institution. Recipients must serve 10 hours per week in an unpaid internship or assistantship.

Number awarded Varies each year, depending on the availability of funds.

[556]
NEW YORK SPACE GRANT CONSORTIUM GRADUATE FELLOWSHIPS

New York Space Grant Consortium
c/o Cornell University
Astronomy Department
517 Space Sciences Building
Ithaca, NY 14853-6801
(607) 255-2710   Fax: (607) 255-1767
E-mail: sfc1@cornell.edu
Web: astro.cornell.edu/SpaceGrant/grad.html

Purpose To provide financial assistance for graduate study in space-related fields at designated universities in New York.

Eligibility This program is open to graduate students at selected universities that belong to the New York Space Grant Consortium. Applicants must be studying space-related fields, including aerospace engineering, astronomy, electrical engineering, geological sciences, and mechanical engineering. U.S. citizenship is required. The New York Space Grant Consortium is a component of the U.S. National Aeronautics and Space Administration (NASA) Space Grant program, which encourages participation by women, underrepresented minorities, and persons with disabilities.

Financial data The stipends paid depend on the availability of funding.

Duration 1 year.

Additional information The participating universities are Cornell University, City College of the City University of New York, Clarkson University, Columbia University, SUNY Buffalo, Polytechnic University, and Rensselaer Polytechnic Institute. This program is funded by NASA.

Number awarded Varies each year.

[557]
NHFA ENTERTAINMENT INDUSTRY SCHOLARSHIPS

National Hispanic Foundation for the Arts
1010 Wisconsin Avenue, N.W., Suite 210
Washington, D.C. 20007
(202) 293-8330   Fax: (202) 965-5252
Web: www.hispanicarts.org/application.html

Purpose To provide financial assistance to Hispanic American graduate students at selected universities who are interested in preparing for a career in the entertainment arts and industry.

Eligibility This program is open to full-time graduate students at 5 designated universities who are enrolled in disciplines leading to careers in the entertainment arts and industry. Those disciplines include, but are not limited to, acting, costume design, film, lighting design, motion picture production, music, playwriting, radio and television, set design, and theater. Also eligible are students working on a graduate degree in law and/or business who either 1) are seeking joint degrees, certificates, or concentrations in entertainment-related fields, or 2) already possess undergraduate degrees in the disciplines listed above and who plan to pursue careers in the entertainment arts and industry. Applicants must be U.S. citizens of Hispanic origin residing in any of the 50 states or U.S. territories and have a cumulative GPA of 3.0 or better. They must be able to demonstrate financial need, defined as family income at or below 60% of the area's median family income, based on family size. Preference is given to students who can demonstrate special talent in areas related to the entertainment arts and industry; they may submit portfolios and/or video/audio tapes of their work.

Financial data Stipends are based on the need of the recipient and the availability of funds.

Additional information The designated universities are New York University, Columbia University, Yale University, the University of California at Los Angeles, and the University of Southern California.

Number awarded Varies each year. Recently, 45 of these scholarships were awarded: 10 at NYU, 11 at Columbia, 5 at Yale, 16 at UCLA, and 3 at USC.

[558]
NINR NATIONAL RESEARCH SERVICE AWARD INDIVIDUAL PREDOCTORAL FELLOWSHIPS

National Institute of Nursing Research
Attn: Division of Extramural Research
45 Center Drive, Room 3AN-12
Bethesda, MD 20892-6300
(301) 594-6906   Fax: (301) 480-8260
E-mail: jl84p@nih.gov
Web: www.nih.gov/ninr

Purpose To provide financial aid to registered nurses who are pursuing doctoral study in a field relevant to the work of the National Institute of Nursing Research (NINR).

Eligibility This program is open to registered nurses who are enrolled or accepted for enrollment full time in a doctoral degree program (but not a health professional degree such as M.D., D.O., D.D.S., or D.V.M.). Applicants must be U.S. citizens, nationals, or permanent residents. Women, minorities, and individuals with disabilities are especially encouraged to apply.

Financial data The award provides an annual stipend of $18,156, a tuition and fee allowance, and an annual institutional allowance of $2,000.

Duration Up to 5 years.

Number awarded Varies each year, depending on the availability of funds.

Deadline April, August, or December of each year.

[559]
NLN NURSE EDUCATOR SCHOLARSHIP PROGRAM

National League for Nursing
Attn: NLN Foundation for Nursing Education
61 Broadway, 33rd Floor
New York, NY 10006
(212) 363-5555, ext. 289   (800) 669-9656
Fax: (613) 591-4240   E-mail: crogers@nln.org
Web: www.nlnfoundation.org/scholarships.htm

Purpose To provide financial assistance to graduate students interested in becoming nursing faculty.

Eligibility This program is open to students admitted or enrolled in a master's or post-master's program that prepares nurses to teach in an academic setting. Both full-time (enrolled in at least 21 semester hours or equivalent during the academic year) and part-time (enrolled in at least 12 semester hours or equivalent during the academic year) students are eligible. Applicants must submit a personal statement (500 words or less) about their career goals and the contributions they expect to make to nursing education. Priority is given to applicants who will complete their master's or post-master's program during the scholarship award period. Underrepresented minorities and men are encouraged to apply.

Financial data The stipend is $5,000 for part-time study or $10,000 for full-time study.

Duration 1 year.

Additional information This program, established in 2002, is supported by Johnson & Johnson.

Number awarded 12 each year.

Deadline May of each year.

[560]
NMF NEED-BASED SCHOLARSHIP PROGRAM

National Medical Fellowships, Inc.
Attn: Scholarship Program
5 Hanover Square, 15th Floor
New York, NY 10004
(212) 483-8880   Fax: (212) 483-8897
E-mail: info@nmfonline.org
Web: www.nmf-online.org

Purpose To provide financial assistance to underrepresented minority medical students.

Eligibility Applicants must be U.S. citizens enrolled in the first or second year of an accredited M.D. or D.O. degree-granting program in the United States. They must be African American, Mexican American, Native Hawaiian, Alaska Native, American Indian, or mainland Puerto Rican. A personal interview is required of all applicants. Selection is based on academic achievement, leadership, and community service. Financial need must be demonstrated.

Financial data The amount of the award depends on the student's total resources (including parental and spousal support), cost of education, and receipt of additional scholarships; recently, individual awards ranged from $500 to $10,000 per year.

Duration 1 year for first-year students; may be renewed for the second year only.

Number awarded Varies each year; recently, more than 300 students received support from this program.

Deadline June of each year.

[561]
NORTH AMERICAN DOCTORAL FELLOWSHIPS

The Fund for Theological Education, Inc.
825 Houston Mill Road, Suite 250
Atlanta, GA 30329
(404) 727-1450   Fax: (404) 727-1490
E-mail: fte@thefund.org
Web: www.thefund.org

Purpose To provide financial assistance to underrepresented racial and ethnic minority students enrolled in a doctoral program in religious or theological studies.

Eligibility This program is open to continuing students enrolled full time in a Ph.D. or Th.D. program in religious or theological studies. Applicants must be citizens or permanent residents of the United States or Canada who are racial or ethnic minority students traditionally underrepresented in graduate education. D.Min. students are ineligible. Preference is given to students nearing completion of their degree. Selection is based on commitment to teaching and scholarship, academic achievement, capacity for leadership in theological scholarship, and financial need.

Financial data Fellows receive a stipend of up to $7,500 per year, depending on financial need.

Duration 1 year; may be renewed up to 2 additional years.

Additional information Funding for this program is provided by the National Council of Churches, proceeds from the book *Stony the Road We Trod: African American Biblical Interpretation,* an endowment from the Hearst Foundation, and the previously established FTE Black Doctoral Program supported by Lilly Endowment, Inc.

Number awarded Varies each year; recently, 8 of these scholarships were awarded.

Deadline February of each year.

[562]
NSF GRADUATE RESEARCH FELLOWSHIPS

Oak Ridge Associated Universities
Attn: NSF Graduate Research Fellowship Program
P.O. Box 3010
Oak Ridge, TN 37831-3010
(865) 241-4300   Fax: (865) 241-4513
E-mail: nsfgrfp@orau.gov
Web: www.orau.org/nsf/nsffel.htm

Purpose To provide financial assistance to women, minorities, persons with disabilities, and others interested in working on a master's or doctoral degree in fields supported by the National Science Foundation (NSF).

Eligibility The program is open to U.S. citizens, nationals, and permanent residents who wish to pursue graduate study leading to research-based master's or doctoral degrees in science, mathematics, and engineering. Awards are also made for work toward a research-based Ph.D. in science education that requires a science competence comparable to that for Ph.D. candidates in scientific disciplines. Research in bioengineering is also eligible if it involves 1) diagnosis or treatment-related goals that apply engineering principles to problems in biology and medicine while advancing engineering knowledge, or 2) aiding persons with disabilities. Other work in medical, dental, law, public health, or practice-oriented professional degree programs, or in joint science-professional degree programs such as M.D./Ph.D. and J.D./Ph.D. programs, is not eligible. Other categories of ineligible support include 1) clinical, counseling, business, or management fields; 2) other education programs; 3) history (except in history of science) or social work; 4) clinical research or research with disease-related goals, including work on the etiology, diagnosis, or treatment of physical or mental disease, abnormality, or malfunction in human beings or animals; 5) research involving animal models of research with disease-related goals; and 6) testing of drugs or other procedures for disease-related goals. Applications normally should be submitted during the senior year in college or in the first year of graduate study; eligibility is limited to those who have completed no more than 20 semester hours, 30 quarter hours, or the equivalent of graduate study since completion of a baccalaureate degree. Applicants who have already earned an advanced degree in science, engineering, or medicine (including an M.D., D.D.S., or D.V.M.) are ineligible. Selection is based on intellectual merit and broader impacts. Intellectual merit includes intellectual ability and other accepted requisites for scholarly scientific study, such as the ability to work as a member of a team as well as independently, to communicate, and to plan and conduct research. The broader impacts criterion includes contributions to community, both social and scholarly; in their written statements, applicants should address the issue of diversity and the goal of broadening opportunities and enabling the participation of all citizens—women and men, underrepresented minorities, and persons with disabilities—in science and engineering.

Financial data The stipend is $20,500 per year, plus a $10,500 cost-of-education allowance given to the recipient's institution. In addition, there is a $1,000 Special International Research Travel Allowance for 3 months or more of research in countries outside of the United States.

Duration Up to 3 years, usable over a 5-year period. Fellows may not reserve the first year in order to use an alternative means of support for graduate study in the United States, but they may do so for the first year or 2 years to accept a competitive international fellowship or for study or research abroad and then take up this fellowship for the next 3 years.

Additional information Fellows may choose as their fellowship institution any appropriate nonprofit U.S. or foreign institution of higher education. Oak Ridge Associated Universities administers the program for the National Science Foundation.

Number awarded Approximately 900 each year.

Deadline November of each year.

[563]
OHIO SPACE GRANT CONSORTIUM DOCTORAL FELLOWSHIP

Ohio Space Grant Consortium
c/o Ohio Aerospace Institute
22800 Cedar Point Road
Cleveland, OH 44142
(440) 962-3032   (800) 828-OSGC
Fax: (440) 962-3120   E-mail: osgc@oai.org
Web: www.osgc.org

Purpose To provide financial assistance to American citizens who wish to work on a doctorate in an aerospace-related discipline at major universities in Ohio.

Eligibility These fellowships are available to U.S. citizens enrolled in a doctoral program in an aerospace-related discipline (aeronautical engineering, aerospace engineering, astronomy, biology, chemical engineering, chemistry, civil engineering, computer engineering and science, control engineering, electrical engineering, engineering mechanics, geology, industrial engineering, manufacturing engineering, materials science and engineering, mathematics, mechanical engineering, petroleum engineering, physics, and systems engineering) at 1 of the participating universities in Ohio. Women, underrepresented minorities, and physically challenged persons are particularly encouraged to apply. Selection is based on academic achievement, recommendations, academic background, and the relevance of the applicant's research interests and experience.

Financial data The stipend is $18,000 per year plus tuition at the university attended.

Duration Up to 3 years.

Additional information These fellowships are funded through the National Space Grant College and Fellowship Program administered by the National Aeronautics and Space Administration (NASA), with matching funds provided by the member universities, the Ohio Aerospace Institute, and private industry. The participating universities include: Air Force Institute of Technology, University of Akron, Case Western Reserve University, University of Cincinnati, Cleveland State University, University of Dayton, Ohio State University, Ohio University, University of Toledo, Wright State University, and Youngstown State University. Recipients are required to conduct a significant portion of their doctoral research in residence at NASA Glenn Research Center/Ohio Aerospace Institute or at another approved NASA center.

Number awarded 2 each year.

Deadline February of each year.

[564]
OHIO SPACE GRANT CONSORTIUM MASTER'S FELLOWSHIP

Ohio Space Grant Consortium
c/o Ohio Aerospace Institute
22800 Cedar Point Road
Cleveland, OH 44142
(440) 962-3032   (800) 828-OSGC
Fax: (440) 962-3120   E-mail: osgc@oai.org
Web: www.osgc.org

Purpose To provide financial assistance to American citizens who wish to work on a master's degree in an aerospace-related discipline at major universities in Ohio.

Eligibility These fellowships are available to U.S. citizens enrolled in a master's degree program in an aerospace-related discipline (aeronautical engineering, aerospace engineering, astronomy, biology, chemical engineering, chemistry, civil engineering, computer engineering and science, control engineering, electrical engineering, engineering mechanics, geology, industrial engineering, manufacturing engineering, materials science and engineering, mathematics, mechanical engineering, petroleum engineering, physics, and systems engineering) at 1 of the participating universities in Ohio. Women, underrepresented minorities, and physically challenged persons are particularly encouraged to apply. Selection is based on academic achievement, recommendations, academic background, and the relevance of the applicant's research interests and experience.

Financial data The stipend is $14,000 per academic year plus tuition at the university attended.

Duration Up to 18 months; may be renewed for an additional 12 months.

Additional information These fellowships are funded through the National Space Grant College and Fellowship Program administered by the National Aeronautics and Space Administration (NASA), with matching funds provided by the member universities, the Ohio Aerospace Institute, and private industry. The participating universities include: Air Force Institute of Technology, University of Akron, Case Western Reserve University, University of Cincinnati, Cleveland State University, University of Dayton, Ohio State University, Ohio University, University of Toledo, Wright State University, and Youngstown State University.

Number awarded 4 each year.

Deadline February of each year.

[565]
ONE-YEAR-ON-CAMPUS PROGRAM

Sandia National Laboratories
Attn: Staffing Department 3535
MS1023
P.O. Box 5800
Albuquerque, NM 87185-1023
(505) 844-3441   Fax: (505) 844-6636
E-mail: pacover@sandia.gov
Web: www.sandia.gov

Purpose To enable minority students to obtain a master's degree in engineering or computer science and also work at Sandia National Laboratories.

Eligibility This program is open to minority students with a bachelor's degree in engineering or computer science and a GPA of 3.2 or higher. Participants must apply to 3 schools jointly selected by the program and themselves. They must be prepared to obtain a master's degree within 1 year. The fields of study (not all fields are available at all participating universities) include computer science, electrical engineering, mechanical engineering, civil engineering, chemical engineering, nuclear engineering, materials sciences, and petroleum engineering. Applicants must be interested in working at the sponsor's laboratories during the summer between graduation from college and the beginning of their graduate program, and then following completion of their master's degree.

Financial data Participants receive a competitive salary while working at the laboratories on a full-time basis and a stipend while attending school.

Duration 1 year.

Additional information During their summer assignment, participants work at the laboratories, either in Albuquerque, New Mexico or in Livermore, California. Upon successful completion of the program, they return to Sandia's hiring organization as a full-time member of the technical staff. This program began in 1968. Application to schools where students received their undergraduate degree is not recommended. After the schools accept an applicant, the choice of a school is made jointly by the laboratories and the participant.

Number awarded Varies each year; since the program began, more than 350 engineers and computer scientists have gone to work at Sandia with master's degrees.

[566]
OSB SCHOLARSHIPS

Oregon State Bar
Attn: Affirmative Action Program
5200 S.W. Meadows Road
P.O. Box 1689
Lake Oswego, OR 97035-0889
(503) 620-0222, ext. 337   (800) 452-8260 (within OR)
Fax: (503) 684-1366   E-mail: smanabe@osbar.org
Web: www.osbar.org

Purpose To provide financial assistance to minority students in Oregon who are currently attending law school.

Eligibility This program is open to minority (African American, Asian, Hispanic, Native American) students who are entering or attending an Oregon law school and planning to practice law in Oregon upon graduation. Selection is based on financial need and participation in community activities.

Financial data The stipend is $1,000 per semester. Funds are credited to the recipient's law school tuition account.

Duration 1 year; recipients may reapply.

Additional information Recipients are encouraged to contribute monetarily to the Oregon State Bar's affirmative action program once they become employed.

Number awarded 18 each year.

Deadline March of each year.

[567]
OSGC EDUCATION PROGRAM

Oklahoma NASA Space Grant Consortium
c/o University of Oklahoma
College of Geosciences
710 Asp Avenue, Suite 5
Norman, Oklahoma 73069
(405) 447-8483   Fax: (405) 447-8455
E-mail: vduca@ou.edu
Web: www.okspacegrant.ou.edu

Purpose To provide financial assistance to students in Oklahoma who are enrolled in aerospace-related studies at the undergraduate and graduate level.

Eligibility This program is open to undergraduate and graduate students at member and affiliate institutions of the Oklahoma Space Grant Consortium (OSGC). U.S. citizenship is required. The OSGC is a component of the U.S. National Aeronautics and Space Administration (NASA) Space Grant program, which encourages participation by women, underrepresented minorities, and persons with disabilities.

Financial data Financing depends on the availability of funds.

Additional information Members of OSGC are Oklahoma State University, the University of Oklahoma, Cameron University, and Langston University. Write to the sponsor for information on the program at each participating university. This program is funded by NASA.

[568]
PADRINO SCHOLARSHIPS

Society of Mexican American Engineers and Scientists
Attn: National Office Director
13337 South Street, Suite 349
Cerritos, CA 90703
E-mail: maes@tamu.edu
Web: www.maes-natl.org

Purpose To provide financial assistance to undergraduate and graduate student members of the Society of Mexican American Engineers and Scientists (MAES).

Eligibility This program is open to MAES student members who are full-time undergraduate or graduate students at a college or university in the United States. Community college students must be enrolled in majors that can transfer to a 4-year institution offering a baccalaureate degree. All applicants must be majoring in a field of science or engineering. U.S. citizenship or permanent resident status is required. Selection is based on financial need; academic achievement; personal qualities, strengths, and leadership abilities; and timeliness and completeness of the application.

Financial data The stipend is $3,000.

Duration 1 year.

Additional information Information is also available from José M. Hernández, Chair, MAES Scholarship Committee, 4015 North Water Iris Cort, Houston, TX 77059. Recipients must attend the MAES International Symposium's Medalla de Oro Banquet in October.

Number awarded 1 or more each year.

Deadline October of each year.

[569]
PENNSYLVANIA SPACE GRANT CONSORTIUM FELLOWSHIPS

Pennsylvania Space Grant Consortium
c/o Pennsylvania State University
2217 Earth-Engineering Sciences Building
University Park, PA 16802
(814) 863-7687   Fax: (814) 863-8286
E-mail: spacegrant@psu.edu
Web: www.psu.edu/spacegrant/highered/scholar.html

Purpose To provide financial assistance for space-related study to graduate students at universities affiliated with the Pennsylvania Space Grant Consortium.

Eligibility This program is open to graduate students at participating universities. Applicants must be studying a field that does, or can, promote the understanding, assessment, and utilization of space, including aerospace, earth science, or space science. U.S. citizenship is required. Students from underrepresented groups (women, minorities, rural populations, and those with disabilities) are especially encouraged to apply.

Financial data The stipend is $5,000 per year.

Duration 2 years.

Additional information Participating institutions include Pennsylvania State University, Carnegie-Mellon University, Temple University, and the University of Pittsburgh. This program is sponsored by the U.S. National Aeronautics and Space Administration (NASA).

Number awarded Varies each year.

Deadline February of each year.

[570]
PFIZER/UNCF CORPORATE SCHOLARS PROGRAM

United Negro College Fund
Attn: Corporate Scholars Program
P.O. Box 1435
Alexandria, VA 22313-9998
(866) 671-7237   E-mail: internship@uncf.org
Web: www.uncf.org/Scholarship/CorporateScholars.asp

Purpose To provide financial assistance and work experience to minority undergraduate and graduate students majoring in designated fields and interested in an internship at a Pfizer facility.

Eligibility This program is open to sophomores, juniors, graduate students, and first-year law students who are African American, Hispanic American, Asian/Pacific Islander American, or American Indian/Alaskan Native. Applicants must have a GPA of 3.0 or higher and be enrolled at an institution that is a member of the United Negro College Fund (UNCF) or at another targeted college or university. They must be pursuing 1) a bachelor's degree in animal science, business, chemistry (organic or analytical), human resources, logistics, microbiology, organizational development, operations management, pre-veterinary medicine, or supply chain management; 2) a master's degree in chemistry (organic or analytical), finance, human resources, or organizational development; or 3) a law degree. Eligibility is limited to U.S. citizens, permanent residents, asylees, refugees, and lawful temporary residents. Along with their application, they must submit a 1-page essay about themselves and their career goals, including information about their interest in Pfizer (the program's sponsor), their personal background, and any particular challenges they have faced.

Financial data The program provides an internship stipend of up to $5,000, housing accommodations near Pfizer Corporate facilities, and (based on successful internship performance) a $15,000 scholarship.

Duration 8 to 10 weeks for the internship; 1 year for the scholarship.

Additional information Opportunities for first-year law students include the summer internship only.

Number awarded Varies each year.

Deadline December of each year.

[571]
PORTER PHYSIOLOGY FELLOWSHIPS FOR MINORITIES

American Physiological Society
Attn: Education Office
9650 Rockville Pike
Bethesda, MD 20814-3991
(301) 530-7132   Fax: (301) 530-7098
E-mail: educatio@the-aps.org
Web: www.the-aps.org

Purpose To provide financial assistance to underrepresented minorities for doctoral study in physiology.

Eligibility This program is open to U.S. citizens and permanent residents who are members of underrepresented ethnic minority groups (African Americans, Hispanics, Native Americans, Native Alaskans, and Native Pacific Islanders). Applicants must be currently enrolled in or accepted to a doctoral program in physiology at a North American university as full-time students. Selection is based on academic records, proposed study and training goals, research plans, letters of recommendation, and progress in training if already engaged.

Financial data The stipend is $18,000. No provision is made for a dependency allowance or tuition and fees.

Duration 1 year; may be renewed for 1 additional year and, in exceptional cases, for a third year.

Additional information This program is supported by the William Townsend Porter Foundation (formerly the Harvard Apparatus Foundation). The first Porter Fellowship was awarded in 1920. In 1966 and 1967, the American Physiological Society established the Porter Physiology Development Committee to award fellowships to minority students engaged in graduate study in physiology.

Number awarded Varies each year; recently, 9 of these fellowships were awarded.

Deadline January or June of each year.

[572]
PREDOCTORAL FELLOWSHIP AWARDS FOR MINORITY STUDENTS

National Institutes of Health
Division of Extramural Outreach and Information Resources
Attn: GrantsInfo
6701 Rockledge Drive, Suite 6095
Bethesda, MD 20892-7910
(301) 435-0714   Fax: (301) 480-8443
E-mail: GrantsInfo@nih.gov
Web: www.nih.gov

Purpose To provide financial assistance to students from underrepresented minority groups who are pursuing or planning to pursue advanced degrees in the biomedical and behavioral sciences.

Eligibility Applicants must be citizens, nationals, or permanent residents of the United States who are working on a Ph.D. or equivalent research degree, a combined M.D./Ph.D. degree, or other combined professional doctorate/research Ph.D. degrees in the biomedical or behavioral sciences. Support is not available for individuals enrolled in medical or other professional schools unless they are enrolled in a combined professional doctorate/Ph.D. degree program in biomedical or behavioral research. Applicants must be underrepresented minority students, defined as individuals belonging to a particular ethnic or racial group that has been determined by the applicant's graduate institution to be underrepresented in biomedical or behavioral research in the United States; the program gives priority consideration to applications from African Americans, Hispanics, Native Americans, Alaskan Natives, and Pacific Islanders.

Financial data The fellowship provides an annual stipend of $18,156, a tuition and fee allowance of 100% of all costs up to $3,000 and 60% of costs above $3,000, and an institutional allowance of $2,500 for travel to scientific meetings and for laboratory and other training expenses. Additional funds may be requested to make changes or adjustments in the academic or research environment to make it possible for the individual to perform the work necessary to meet the requirements of the degree program.

Duration Up to 5 years.

Additional information These fellowships are offered by most components of the National Institutes of Health (NIH). For a list of names and telephone numbers of responsible officers at each component, contact the Division of Extramural Outreach and Information Resources.

Number awarded Varies each year.

Deadline April or November of each year.

[573]
PREDOCTORAL FELLOWSHIP IN BEHAVIORAL NEUROSCIENCE

Texas Consortium in Behavioral Neuroscience
c/o University of Texas
Department of Psychology
1 University Station A8000
Austin, TX 78712
(512) 471-1068   Fax: (512) 471-1073
E-mail: gonzalez-lima@psy.utexas.edu

Purpose To provide an opportunity for underrepresented minority doctoral candidates to obtain research training at selected universities in Texas.

Eligibility This program is open to members of underrepresented minority groups who hold a bachelor's degree and plan to work on a doctoral degree in neuroscience. Applicants must be interested in a program of research training at the University of Texas at Austin, the University of Texas at San Antonio, the University of Texas Health Science Center at San Antonio, Texas A&M University, or Texas A&M University System Health Science Center. U.S. citizenship or permanent resident status is required.

Financial data The program provides a total of $25,705 each year, including $6,349 for tuition, fees, and health insurance, $1,200 in travel funds, and a stipend of $18,156.

Duration 3 years.

Additional information This program is sponsored by 3 components of the National Institutes of Health: the National Institute of Mental Health, the National Institute on Drug Abuse, and the National Institute of Neurological Disorders and Stroke. The train-

ing program covers brain metabolic mapping of behavioral functions, neuropharmacology, electrophysiology, and molecular neurobiology. Trainees are required to complete courses covering the brain and behavior, scientific ethics, experimental design, and statistical analysis.

Number awarded 10 each year.

Deadline Applications may be submitted at any time.

[574]
PREDOCTORAL FELLOWSHIPS IN THE NEUROSCIENCES

American Psychological Association
Attn: Minority Fellowship Program
750 First Street, N.E.
Washington, DC 20002-4242
(202) 336-6027   Fax: (202) 336-6012
TDD: (202) 336-6123   E-mail: mfp@apa.org
Web: www.apa.org/mfp

Purpose To provide financial assistance to minority and other students who are interested in completing a doctorate in neuroscience.

Eligibility This program is intended to increase representation of African Americans, Alaskan Natives, Hispanics/Latinos, American Indians, Pacific Islanders, and Asian Americans in neuroscience, but all students who are pursuing a Ph.D. in neuroscience are eligible. Applicants may be seeking training in behavioral neurobiology, cellular neurobiology, developmental neurobiology, membrane biophysics, molecular neurobiology, neuroanatomy, neurobiology of aging, neuroimmunology, neuropathology, neuropharmacology, neurophysiology, or neurotoxicology. U.S. citizenship or permanent resident status is required. Selection is based on scholarship, research experience, suitability of laboratory and mentor, research potential and proposal, commitment to a research career in neuroscience, and writing ability.

Financial data The stipend depends on the number of years of research experience; recently, the average annual award was $12,532 per year. The fellowship also provides travel funds to visit universities being considered for graduate training, travel funds to attend the annual meeting of the Society for Neuroscience, and a program of summer training at the Marine Biological Laboratory in Woods Hole, Massachusetts.

Duration 1 year; may be renewed for up to 2 additional years.

Additional information The program was established in 1987. It is funded by the U.S. National Institute of Mental Health of the National Institutes of Health and administered by the American Psychological Association.

Number awarded 1 or more each year.

Deadline January of each year.

[575]
PREPROFESSIONAL PRACTICE PROGRAM SCHOLARSHIPS

American Dietetic Association
Attn: Accreditation, Education Programs, and Student Operations
216 West Jackson Boulevard, Suite 800
Chicago, IL 60606-6995
(312) 899-0040   (800) 877-1600, ext. 5400
Fax: (312) 899-4817   E-mail: education@eatright.org
Web: www.eatright.org

Purpose To provide financial assistance to students who have applied to a dietetic preprofessional practice program.

Eligibility This program is open to students who have applied or plan to apply to a CADE-approved dietetic preprofessional practice program (AP4). Students who are currently completing the experience component of an AP4 that is combined with a graduate program should apply for the American Dietetic Association's Graduate Scholarship. All applicants for this program must be participating in the computer-matching process, be U.S. citizens or permanent residents, and show promise of being a valuable, contributing member of the profession. Some scholarships require membership in the association, specific dietetic practice group membership, residency in a specific state, or underrepresented minority group status. The same application form can be used for all categories.

Financial data Awards range from $500 to $5,000.

Duration 1 year.

Number awarded Varies each year, depending upon the funds available. Recently, the sponsoring organization awarded 209 scholarships for all its programs.

Deadline February of each year.

[576]
PRESBYTERIAN CHURCH CONTINUING EDUCATION GRANT AND LOAN PROGRAM

Presbyterian Church (USA)
Attn: Office of Financial Aid for Studies
100 Witherspoon Street, Room M042
Louisville, KY 40202-1396
(502) 569-5735   (877) 728-7228, ext. 5735
Fax: (502) 569-8766   E-mail: LBryan@ctr.pcusa.org
Web: www.pcusa.org/highered

Purpose To provide financial assistance for continuing education, in the form of educational grants and loans, to professional church workers of the Presbyterian Church (USA) who are employed by small congregations, women, and racial/ethnic minorities.

Eligibility This program provides grants and loans for postgraduate study and professional development to professional church staff members employed by Presbyterian Church (USA) congregations with 150 members or less. Continuing education loans (but not grants) for postgraduate study and professional development are also available for professional church staff members employed by congregations larger than 150 members. Applicants must be 1) enrolled at least part time at an accredited institution or attending a PCUSA sponsored training event, and 2) endorsed by their session or the moderator of their committee on ministry. The program also provides continuing education grants and loans for postgraduate religious studies to women and racial ethnic minorities. Applicants must be enrolled at least part time, members of a Presbyterian Church (USA) congregation, and

endorsed by their session or the moderator of their committee on ministry.

Financial data Grants for degree students range from $500 to $1,000 per year and for non-degree students from $100 to $500 per year. The maximum loan is $2,000 per year.

Duration 1 year. Professionals at small churches are eligible for unlimited renewal of grants. Women and racial ethnic minorities are eligible for a total of 4 grants. Loans may be renewed to a maximum of $6,000.

Number awarded Varies each year.

[577]
PRESBYTERIANS FOR RENEWAL SCHOLARS AWARD

Presbyterians for Renewal
Attn: Director of Seminary Ministry
8134 New LaGrange Road, Suite 227
Louisville, KY 40222-4679
(502) 425-4630
Web: www.pfrseminary.edu

Purpose To provide financial assistance to members of the Presbyterian Church (U.S.A.) with pastoral experience who are interested in working on a doctoral degree.

Eligibility This program is open to students with 4 or 5 years of Presbyterian pastoral experience who are interested in working on a Ph.D. degree to prepare for a career in theological education. Applicants must have above average academic records and a commitment to the goals of Presbyterians for Renewal. Along with their application, they must submit essays on Christian faith and life, Christian and theological influences and projections as to field of study, understanding of Reformed distinctives, and involvement in and vision for the theological and missional goals of the Presbyterian Church (U.S.A.). The selection process includes "sensitivity to the gender and ethnic diversity of the church."

Financial data The stipend is $16,000 per year.

Duration 4 years.

Deadline January of each year.

[578]
PROCTER & GAMBLE ORAL CARE–HDA FOUNDATION SCHOLARSHIPS

Hispanic Dental Association
Attn: HDA Foundation
188 West Randolph Street, Suite 415
Chicago, IL 60601
(312) 577-4013   (800) 852-7921
Fax: (312) 577-0052   E-mail: hdassoc1@qwest.net
Web: www.hdassoc.org

Purpose To provide financial assistance to Hispanic students interested in preparing for a career in a dental profession.

Eligibility This program is open to Hispanics who have been accepted into an accredited dental, dental hygiene, dental assisting, or dental technician program. Selection is based on scholastic achievement, community service, leadership skill, and commitment to improving health in the Hispanic community.

Financial data Stipends are $1,000 or $500.

Duration 1 year.

Additional information This program is sponsored by Procter & Gamble Company.

Number awarded Numerous scholarships are awarded each year.

Deadline June of each year.

[579]
PROFESSIONAL DEVELOPMENT FELLOWSHIPS FOR ARTISTS AND ART HISTORIANS

College Art Association of America
Attn: Fellowship Program
275 Seventh Avenue
New York, NY 10001-6798
(212) 691-1051, ext. 206   Fax: (212) 627-2381
E-mail: fellowship@collegeart.org
Web: www.collegeart.org/caa/career/fellowship.html

Purpose To provide financial assistance and work experience to artists or art historians from culturally diverse backgrounds who are completing graduate degrees.

Eligibility This program is open to artists or art historians who have been underrepresented in the field because of their race, religion, gender, age, national origin, sexual orientation, disability, or history of economic disadvantage. Applicants must be U.S. citizens or permanent residents and able to demonstrate financial need. They must expect to receive the M.F.A., terminal M.A., or Ph.D. degree in the year following application.

Financial data The stipend is $5,000 per year.

Duration 2 years: the final year of their degree program and the first year following completion of their degree.

Additional information In addition to receiving a stipend for the terminal year of their degree program, fellows participate in an internship during the year following graduation. The College Art Association helps fellows secure internships at museums, art centers, colleges, or universities and subsidizes part of their salaries. In addition to administrative and/or teaching responsibilities, all fellows' positions must include a curatorial component. Salaries and terms of employment are determined in consultation with each fellow and potential host institution.

Number awarded Varies each year.

Deadline January of each year.

[580]
PROGRAM FOR MINORITY RESEARCH TRAINING IN PSYCHIATRY

American Psychiatric Association
Attn: American Psychiatric Institute for Research and
   Education
1400 K Street, N.W.
Washington, DC 20005
(202) 682-6225   (800) 852-1390
Fax: (202) 682-6850   E-mail: eguerra@psych.org
Web: www.psych.org/res_res/pmrtp5302.cfm

Purpose To provide financial assistance to underrepresented minority medical students and residents interested in psychiatric research training.

Eligibility This program is open to underrepresented minorities (American Indians, Blacks/African Americans, Hispanics, and Pacific Islanders) at 3 levels: medical students, residents, and graduates of residency programs. All candidates must be interested in training at research-intensive departments of psychiatry in major U.S. medical schools. Training sites with excellence as demonstrated by research facilities and resources, funded research, research faculty (including minority researchers), and successful training history are preferred.

Financial data Annual stipends are $18,156 for medical students, from $42,648 to $44,616 for residents, and up to $48,852 for post-residency fellows. Other benefits include travel funds to attend the annual meeting of the American Psychiatric Association (APA) or the American College of Neuropsychopharmacology and limited tuition assistance for full-time trainees to attend specific courses that are required as part of their training.

Duration For medical students and residents, 2 months to 1 year. For post-residency fellows, generally 2 years, although a third year is possible if appropriate to a trainee's career development.

Additional information This program is funded by the National Institute of Mental Health and administered by the APA's American Psychiatric Institute for Research and Education.

Number awarded Varies each year.

Deadline Medical students and residents seeking less than 1 year of training may apply at any time, but applications must be received at least 3 months before the proposed training is to begin; medical students seeking summer training should apply by March of each year; residents seeking a year or more of training and post-residency fellows should apply by November of each year.

[581]
PUBLIC POLICY AND INTERNATIONAL AFFAIRS FELLOWSHIPS

Public Policy and International Affairs Fellowship Program
c/o Association for Public Policy Analysis and Management
2100 M Street, N.W., Suite 610
P.O. Box 18766
Washington, DC 20036-8766
(202) 496-0130   Fax: (202) 496-0134
E-mail: ppia@ppiaprogram.org
Web: www.ppiaprogram.org

Purpose To provide financial assistance to minority undergraduate students who are interested in preparing for graduate study in the fields of public policy and/or international affairs.

Eligibility This program is open to people of color historically underrepresented in public policy and international affairs, including African Americans, Asian Americans, Pacific Islanders, Hispanic Americans, Alaska Natives, and Native Americans. In most cases, most persons enter the program when they apply to participate in a summer institute following the junior year of college. Currently, persons who are beyond the junior year of college are also invited to apply. Applicants must be U.S. citizens or permanent residents interested in a summer institute in public policy and international affairs. They must first apply directly to the summer institute. Following participation in that institute, they apply for graduate study in fields of their choice at more than 30 designated universities. For a list of participating institutions, contact the sponsor.

Financial data During the summer institute portion of the program, participants receive transportation to and from the institute site, room and board, and a $1,000 stipend. More than 30 graduate programs in public policy and/or international affairs have agreed to waive application fees and grant fellowships of at least $5,000 to students who have participated in the summer institutes.

Duration 1 summer and 1 academic year.

Additional information This program was established in 1981 when the Alfred P. Sloan Foundation provided a grant to the Association for Public Policy Analysis and Management (APPAM). From 1981 through 1988, participants were known as Sloan Fellows. From 1889 through 1995, the program was supported by the Ford Foundation and administered by the Woodrow Wilson National Fellowship Administration, so participants were known as Woodrow Wilson Fellows in Public Policy and International Affairs. Beginning in 1995, the program's name was shortened to the Public Policy and International Affairs Fellowship Program (PPIA) and its administration was moved to the Academy for Educational Development. To complement APPAM's role, the Association of Professional Schools of International Affairs (APSIA) also became an institutional sponsor. In 1999, the Ford Foundation ended its support for PPIA effective with the student cohort that participated in summer institutes in 1999. The APPAM and APSIA incorporated PPIA as an independent organization and operated the summer institutes in 2000. In 2001, the National Association of Schools of Public Affairs and Administration (NASPAA) also became a sponsor of PPIA. Beginning in summer of that year, summer institutes have been held at 4 universities: the Summer Program in Public Policy and International Affairs at the Gerald R. Ford School of Public Policy at the University of Michigan, the Maryland Leadership Institute at the School of Public Affairs at the University of Maryland, the UCPPIA Summer Institute at the Richard & Rhoda Goldman School of Public Policy at the University of California at Berkeley, and the Junior Summer Institute at the Woodrow Wilson School of Public and International Affairs at Princeton University. For information on those institutes, contact the respective school. Additional support is currently provided by the Foundation for Child Development and the William T. Grant Foundation.

Number awarded Varies each year.

[582]
PUERTO RICAN BAR ASSOCIATION SCHOLARSHIP AWARD

Puerto Rican Legal Defense and Education Fund
Attn: Education Division Director
99 Hudson Street, 14th Floor
New York, NY 10013-2815
(212) 219-3360, ext. 223   (800) 328-2322, ext. 223
Fax: (212) 431-4276   E-mail: education@prldef.org
Web: www.prldef.org/education.htm

Purpose To provide financial assistance to Latino law students.

Eligibility Puerto Rican and other Latino students planning to enroll or currently enrolled in law school are eligible to apply. Selection is based on financial need and academic promise, as well as a commitment to the Latino community.

Financial data The stipend is $2,000 per year.

Duration 1 year.

Additional information The Puerto Rican Legal Defense and Education Fund provides the candidates for selection by the Puerto Rican Bar Association, located in New York City.

Number awarded 1 or more each year.

Deadline November of each year.

[583]
PUERTO RICO NATIONAL GUARD TUITION ASSISTANCE FUND

Puerto Rico National Guard
Attn: Education Services Officer
P.O. Box 9023786
Juana Diaz, PR 00902-3786
(787) 289-1502   E-mail: ortegaj@pr.ngb.army.mil

Purpose To provide financial assistance for college to National Guard members in Puerto Rico and their families.

Eligibility This program is open to 1) active members of the Puerto Rico National Guard who are interested in pursuing studies on the undergraduate or graduate level (up to the Ph.D. degree); 2) spouses of members interested in pursuing studies on the undergraduate or graduate level (up to a master's degree); and 3) children of members interested in pursuing undergraduate or vocational study. Guard members may not receive support at the same time as a spouse and/or child.

Financial data For Guard members, the program pays $50 per credit to a maximum of $900 per year for undergraduate or vocational study, $75 per credit to a maximum of $1,350 per year for graduate study, or a maximum of $1,000 per year for study for an M.D. degree. For spouses, the program pays $75 per credit to a maximum of $1,350 per semester for graduate study. For spouses and children, the program pays $50 per credit to a maximum of $900 per semester for undergraduate or vocational study.

Duration 1 year; may be renewed. Guard members are limited to 18 credits of study per year; spouses and children are limited to 18 credits per semester.

Number awarded Varies each year.

[584]
RACE RELATIONS MULTIRACIAL STUDENT SCHOLARSHIP

Christian Reformed Church
Attn: Ministry of Race Relations
10356 Artesia Boulevard
Bellflower, CA 90706
(562) 925-2852
E-mail: norbertowolf@CRMinistryCenter.net
Web: www.crcna.org

Purpose To provide financial assistance to undergraduate and graduate minority students interested in attending colleges related to the Christian Reformed Church in North America (CRCNA).

Eligibility Students of various ethnicities both in the United States and Canada are eligible to apply. Normally, applicants are expected to be members of CRCNA congregations who plan to pursue their educational goals at Calvin Theological Seminary or any of the colleges affiliated with the CRCNA. Students who have no prior history with the CRCNA must attend a CRCNA-related college or seminary for a full academic year before they are eligible to apply for this program. Students entering their sophomore year must have earned a GPA of 2.0 or higher as freshmen; students entering their junior year must have earned a GPA of 2.3 or higher as sophomores; students entering their senior year must have earned a GPA of 2.6 or higher as juniors.

Financial data First-year students receive $500 per semester. Other levels of students may receive up to $2,000 per academic year.

Duration 1 year.

Additional information This program was first established in 1971 and revised in 1991. Recipients are expected to train to engage actively in the ministry of racial reconciliation in church and in society. They must be able to work in the United States or Canada upon graduating and must consider working for 1 of the agencies of the CRCNA.

Deadline March of each year.

[585]
RACIAL ETHNIC LEADERSHIP SUPPLEMENTAL GRANTS

Presbyterian Church (USA)
Attn: Office of Financial Aid for Studies
100 Witherspoon Street, Room M042
Louisville, KY 40202-1396
(502) 569-5760   (877) 728-7228, ext. 5760
Fax: (502) 569-8766   E-mail: MariaA@ctr.pcusa.org
Web: www.pcusa.org/highered

Purpose To provide financial assistance to minority graduate students who are Presbyterian Church members interested in preparing for church occupations.

Eligibility This program is open to racial/ethnic graduate students (Asian American, African American, Hispanic American, Native American, or Alaska Native) who are members of the Presbyterian Church (USA). Applicants must be studying for the first professional degree, enrolled as an inquirer or candidate by a presbytery for a church occupation or planning to take a position within the Presbyterian Church (USA) or an ecumenical agency in which it participates, a U.S. citizen or permanent resident, enrolled full time in a prescribed program of study approved by the presbytery, recommended by the financial aid officer at their theological institution, and able to demonstrate financial need.

Financial data The awards are intended to be supplementary and range from $500 to $1,500 per year.

Duration 1 year; may be renewed.

Number awarded Varies each year.

Deadline Applications may be submitted at any time.

[586]
RALPH W. SHRADER SCHOLARSHIPS

Armed Forces Communications and Electronics Association
Attn: Educational Foundation
4400 Fair Lakes Court
Fairfax, VA 22033-3899
(703) 631-6149   (800) 336-4583, ext. 6149
Fax: (703) 631-4693   E-mail: scholarship@afcea.org
Web: www.afcea.org

Purpose To provide financial assistance to master's degree students in fields related to communications and electronics.

Eligibility This program is open to any student working on a master's degree who is a U.S. citizen attending an accredited college or university in the United States. Applicants must be enrolled full time and studying engineering (electrical, electronic, or communications), physics, mathematics, computer science, or information management systems. At least 1 of these scholarships is set aside for a woman or a minority.

Financial data The stipend is $3,000. Funds are paid directly to the recipient.

Duration 1 year. Requests for applications must be accompanied by a self-addressed stamped envelope.

Number awarded 3 each year, at least 1 of which is for a women or minority candidate.

Deadline January of each year.

[587]
RDW GROUP, INC. MINORITY SCHOLARSHIP FOR COMMUNICATIONS

Rhode Island Foundation
Attn: Scholarship Coordinator
One Union Station
Providence, RI 02903
(401) 274-4564   Fax: (401) 331-8085
E-mail: libbym@rifoundation.org
Web: www.rifoundation.org

Purpose To provide financial assistance to Rhode Island students of color interested in preparing for a career in communications.

Eligibility This program is open to minority undergraduate and graduate students who are Rhode Island residents. Applicants must intend to pursue a course of study in communications. They must be able to demonstrate their commitment to a career in communications and financial need. Along with their application, they must submit an essay (up to 300 words) on the impact they would like to have on the communications field.

Financial data The stipend is $2,000.

Duration 1 year; nonrenewable.

Additional information This program is sponsored by the RDW Group, Inc.

Number awarded 1 each year.

Deadline June of each year.

[588]
REFORMA SCHOLARSHIP

REFORMA (National Association to Promote Library Services to the Spanish Speaking)
P.O. Box 832
Anaheim, CA 92815-0832
Web: www.reforma.org/schinfo.html

Purpose To encourage and enable qualified Spanish-speaking students to pursue a career in library or information science.

Eligibility The program is open to citizens and permanent residents of the United States who are Spanish-speaking college seniors. While eligibility is not restricted by age, sex, creed, national origin, or minority group/association membership, it is required that those who apply have a definite interest in service to the Spanish-speaking. Applicants must show evidence of commitment to a career in librarianship and the potential for high academic achievement. They should be able to demonstrate an understanding of, aptitude for, and desire to serve the Spanish-speaking community. Applicants are also judged on the basis of character and leadership potential.

Financial data The stipend is at least $2,000.

Duration 1 year.

Additional information Information is also available from the REFORMA Scholarship Committee Chair, Armando Ramírez, Biblioteca Lationoamericana, 921 South First Street, San Jose, CA 95110, (408) 294-1237, ramirezarma@hotmail.com. The scholarship must be used within the academic year following notification of the award. The recipient must enter an accredited M.L.S. or Ph.D. degree program.

Number awarded Varies each year.

Deadline March of each year.

[589]
RENE MATOS SCHOLARSHIP

National Hispanic Coalition of Federal Aviation Employees
Attn: Scholarship Selection Committee
Cambridge Park
C-3 Chestnut Hill Avenue
San Juan, PR 00926
Web: www.nhcfae.com

Purpose To provide financial assistance to minority and women students who are working on an undergraduate or graduate degree.

Eligibility This program is open to minority and women students who are accepted to or attending an accredited college, university, or vocational/trade school. Applicants may be graduating high school seniors, current undergraduates, or graduate students. Selection is based on academic achievement, community involvement, financial need, honors and awards, leadership, personal qualities and strengths, and student activities.

Financial data A stipend is awarded (amount not specified).

Duration 1 year; may be renewed.

Additional information The National Hispanic Coalition of Federal Aviation Employees, established in 1978, is a nonprofit organization comprised mainly of Hispanics who are employed at the Federal Aviation Administration. Requests for applications must be accompanied by a self-addressed stamped envelope. Phone calls and faxed applications are not accepted.

Number awarded 1 or more each year.

Deadline April of each year.

[590]
RHODE ISLAND SPACE GRANT GRADUATE FELLOWSHIP PROGRAM

Rhode Island Space Grant
c/o Brown University
Lincoln Field Building
Box 1846
Providence, RI 02912-1846
(401) 863-2889   Fax: (401) 863-1292
E-mail: RISpaceGrant@brown.edu
Web: www.planetary.brown.edu/RI_Space_Grant

Purpose To provide financial assistance to graduate students at institutions that are members of the Rhode Island Space Grant Consortium (RISGC) who wish to pursue studies and space-related research in science, mathematics, or engineering.

Eligibility This program is open to graduate students at RISGC-member universities. Applicants must be studying in science, mathematics, or engineering fields of interest to the National Aeronautics and Space Administration (NASA). U.S. citizenship is required. The sponsor is a component of NASA's Space Grant program, which encourages participation by women, underrepresented minorities, and persons with disabilities.

Financial data A stipend is provided (amount not specified).

Duration 1 year.

Additional information Members of the RISGC are Bryant College, Community College of Rhode Island, Providence College, Roger Williams University, Rhode Island College, Rhode Island School of Design, Salve Regina University, University of Rhode Island, and Wheaton College. This program is funded by NASA. Fellows are required to devote 75% of their time to their studies and research and 25% of their time to science education outreach activities organized and coordinated by Rhode Island Space Grant.

Number awarded Varies each year; recently, 4 of these fellowships were awarded.

[591]
RICHARD AND HELEN BROWN COREM SCHOLARSHIPS

United Church of Christ
Local Church Ministries
Attn: Coordinator of Grants, Scholarships, and Resources
700 Prospect Avenue East
Cleveland, OH 44115-1100
(216) 736-3839   Fax: (216) 736-3783
E-mail: jeffersv@ucc.org
Web: www.ucc.org/education/scholarships

Purpose To provide financial assistance to minority seminary students who are interested in becoming a pastor in the United Church of Christ (UCC).

Eligibility This program is open to students at accredited seminaries who have been members of a UCC congregation for at least 1 year. Applicants must work through 1 of the member bodies of the Council for Racial and Ethnic Ministries (COREM): United Black Christians (UBC), Council of Hispanic Ministries (CHM), Pacific Islander and Asian American Ministries (PAAM), or Council for American Indian Ministries (CAIM). They must 1) have a GPA of 3.0 or higher, 2) be enrolled in a course of study leading to ordained ministry, 3) be in care of an association or conference at the time of application, and 4) demonstrate leadership ability through participation in their local church, association, conference, or academic environment.

Financial data Stipends are approximately $10,000 per year.

Duration 1 year.

Additional information Information on the UBC is available from the Minister for African American Relations, (216) 736-2189. Information on the CHM is available from the Minister for Hispanic Relations, (216) 736-2193. Information on the PAAM is available from the Minister for Pacific Islander and Asian American Relations, (216) 736-2195. Information on the CAIM is available from the Minister for Native American Relations, (216) 736-2194.

Number awarded Varies each year.

[592]
RICHARD D. HAILEY LAW STUDENT SCHOLARSHIPS

Association of Trial Lawyers of America
Attn: Minority Caucus
1050 31st Street, N.W.
Washington, DC 20007
(202) 944-2827   (800) 424-2725
Fax: (202) 298-6849   E-mail: info@astlahq.org
Web: www.atla.org

Purpose To provide financial assistance for law school to minority student members of the Association of Trial Lawyers of America (ATLA).

Eligibility This program is open to African American, Hispanic, Asian American, Native American, and biracial members of the association who are enrolled in the second or third year of law school. Selection is based on commitment to the association and dedication to its mission through involvement in student chapter activities, desire to represent victims, interest and proficiency of skills in trial advocacy, and financial need. Applicants must submit a 500-word essay on how they meet those criteria and 3 letters of recommendation.

Financial data The stipend is $1,000.

Duration 1 year.

Number awarded Up to 6 each year.

Deadline April of each year.

[593]
ROBERT AND MARTHA ATHERTON SCHOLARSHIP

Unitarian Universalist Association
Attn: Office of Ministerial Education
25 Beacon Street
Boston, MA 02108-2800
(617) 948-6403   Fax: (617) 742-2875
E-mail: cmay@uua.org
Web: www.uua.org/info/scholarships.html

Purpose To provide financial assistance to seminary students preparing for the Unitarian Universalist (UU) ministry.

Eligibility This program is open to second- or third-year seminary students currently enrolled full time in a UU ministerial training program with Candidate status. First priority is given to Meadville-Lombard students. Preference is also given to 1) African American, Hispanic, and Native American students, and 2) foreign students who intend to spread the faith in their native countries. Applicants must have proven their ability and dedication to the UU faith and to helping mankind.

Financial data The stipend is at least $2,500 per year.

Duration 1 year.

Number awarded 2 each year.

Deadline April of each year.

[594]
ROCKY MOUNTAIN NASA SPACE GRANT CONSORTIUM GRADUATE RESEARCH FELLOWSHIPS

Rocky Mountain NASA Space Grant Consortium
c/o Utah State University
EL Building, Room 302
Logan, UT 84322-4140
(435) 797-4042   Fax: (435) 797-4044
E-mail: rmc@sdl.usu.edu
Web: www.rmc.sdl.usu.edu

Purpose To provide financial support for research and study to graduate students at designated universities in Utah or Colorado who are working on a degree in fields of interest to the National Aeronautics and Space Administration (NASA).

Eligibility This program is open to graduate students at member institutions of the Rocky Mountain NASA Space Grant Consortium who are studying engineering, science, medicine, or technology. U.S. citizenship is required. Selection is based on academic performance to date and potential for the future, with emphasis on space-related research interests. This program is part of the NASA Space Grant program, which encourages participation by women, underrepresented minorities, and persons with disabilities.

Financial data The amount of the awards depends on the availability of funds.

Additional information Members of the consortium are Utah State University, the University of Utah, Brigham Young University, and the University of Denver. This program is funded by NASA.

Number awarded Varies each year.

[595]
SALEF HEALTH SCHOLARSHIP PROGRAM

Salvadoran American Leadership and Educational Fund
Attn: Education and Youth Programs Manager
1625 West Olympic Boulevard, Suite 718
Los Angeles, CA 90015
(213) 480-1052   Fax: (213) 487-2530
E-mail: info@salef.org
Web: www.salef.org

Purpose To provide financial assistance to undergraduate and graduate students of Central American ancestry interested in a health-related career.

Eligibility This program is open to high school seniors and graduates who have been accepted at a 4-year university, undergraduates in 2- and 4-year colleges and universities, and graduate students. Applicants do not need to provide proof of documented immigrant status, but they must be of Central American ancestry and interested in a health-related career (physician, nurse, psychologist, or other professional). Along with their application, they must submit a 750-word statement on their goals, aspirations, and ambitions; ways to give back to the community; leadership involvement; why they chose their field of study; and short- and long-term goals and how they plan to contribute to the community after graduation. They must be able to demonstrate financial need, have a GPA of at least 2.5, and have a history of community service and involvement. An interview may be required.

Financial data Stipends range from $1,000 to $2,500.

Duration 1 year.

Additional information This program began in 2002. Funding is provided by the California Wellness Foundation.

Number awarded 15 each year.

Deadline June of each year.

[596]
SANTA CLARA LA RAZA LAWYERS SCHOLARSHIP

La Raza Lawyers Association of Santa Clara County
c/o Richard Alvarez
P.O. Box 30
San Jose, CA 95103
E-mail: larazalawyers@yahoo.com
Web: www.larazalawyers-santaclara.com

Purpose To provide financial assistance to Hispanic law students who are from the San Francisco Bay area or attend law school there.

Eligibility This program is open to Hispanic students currently enrolled in law school. Applicants must either be residents of the San Francisco Bay area (as defined by the sponsor on a case-by-case basis) or attending 1 of the following law schools: Santa Clara University, Lincoln, University of California at Berkeley, University of San Francisco, UC Hastings, Stanford, Golden Gate University, University of California at Davis, or McGeorge. Selection is based on community activities, academic accomplishment, and financial need.

Financial data The stipend is at least $1,000 and may be as high as $5,000. Funds may be used for living expenses, tuition, books, bar examination course expenses, or anything else needed to further legal education.

Duration 1 year.

Additional information Information is also available from Chris Arriola, (408) 792-2978.

Number awarded Varies each year; recently, 3 of these scholarships were awarded (1 at $5,000, 1 at $2,500, and 1 at $1,500).

Deadline July of each year.

[597]
SCHOLARSHIPS FOR MINORITY ACCOUNTING STUDENTS

American Institute of Certified Public Accountants
Attn: Academic and Career Development Division
1211 Avenue of the Americas
New York, NY 10036-8775
(212) 596-6223   Fax: (212) 596-6292
E-mail: educat@aicpa.org
Web: www.aicpa.org/members/div/career/mini/smas.htm

Purpose To provide financial assistance to underrepresented minorities interested in studying accounting at the undergraduate or graduate school level.

Eligibility Undergraduate applicants must be minority students who are enrolled full time, have completed at least 30 semester hours of college work (including at least 6 semester hours in accounting), are majoring in accounting with an overall GPA of 3.3 or higher, and are U.S. citizens or permanent residents. Minority students who are interested in a graduate degree must be 1) in the final year of a 5-year accounting program; 2) an undergraduate accounting major currently accepted or enrolled in a master's-level accounting, business administration, finance, or taxation program; or 3) any undergraduate major currently accepted in a master's-level accounting program. Selection is based primarily on merit (academic and personal achievement); financial need is evaluated as a secondary criteria. For purposes of this program, the American Institute of Certified Public Accountants (AICPA) considers minority students to be those of Black, Native American/Alaskan Native, Pacific Island, or Hispanic ethnic origin.

Financial data The maximum stipend is $5,000 per year.

Duration 1 year; may be renewed, if recipients are making satisfactory progress toward graduation.

Additional information These scholarships are granted by the institute's Minority Educational Initiatives Committee.

Number awarded Varies each year; recently, 187 students received funding through this program.

Deadline June of each year.

[598]
SCIENCE TEACHER PREPARATION PROGRAM

Alabama Alliance for Science, Engineering, Mathematics,
  and Science Education
Attn: Project Director
University of Alabama at Birmingham
Campbell Hall, Room 401
1300 University Boulevard
Birmingham, AL 35294-1170
(205) 934-8762   Fax: (205) 934-1650
E-mail: LDale@uab.edu
Web: www.uab.edu/istp/alabama.html

Purpose To provide financial assistance to underrepresented minority students at designated institutions in Alabama who are interested in preparing for a career as a science teacher.

Eligibility This program is open to members of underrepresented minority groups who have been unconditionally admitted to a participating Alabama college or university. Applicants may 1) be entering freshmen or junior college transfer students who intend to major in science education and become certified to teach in elementary, middle, or high school; 2) have earned a degree in mathematics, science, or education and now are seeking to become certified to teach; or 3) have earned a degree in mathematics, science, or education and now are enrolled in a fifth-year education program leading to a master's degree and certification.

Financial data The stipend is $1,000 per year.

Duration 1 year; may be renewed.

Additional information Support for this program is provided by the National Science Foundation. The participating institutions are Alabama A&M University, Alabama State University, Auburn University, Miles College, Stillman College, Talladega College, Tuskegee University, University of Alabama at Birmingham, and University of Alabama in Huntsville.

Number awarded Varies each year.

[599]
SELECTED PROFESSIONS FELLOWSHIPS FOR WOMEN OF COLOR

American Association of University Women
Attn: AAUW Educational Foundation
2201 North Dodge Street
P.O. Box 4030
Iowa City, IA 52243-4030
(319) 337-1716   Fax: (319) 337-1204
E-mail: aauw@act.org
Web: www.aauw.org

Purpose To aid women of color who are in their final year of graduate training in the fields of business administration, law, or medicine.

Eligibility This program is open to women of color who are entering their final year of graduate study in these historically underrepresented fields: business administration (M.B.A., E.M.B.A.), law (J.D.), and medicine (M.D., D.O.). Women in medical programs may apply for either their third or final year of study. U.S. citizenship or permanent resident status is required. Special consideration is given to applicants who demonstrate professional promise in innovative or neglected areas of research and/or practice in public interest concerns.

Financial data Stipends range from $5,000 to $12,000 for the academic year.

Duration 1 academic year, beginning in September.

Deadline January of each year.

[600]
SEMICONDUCTOR RESEARCH CORPORATION MASTER'S SCHOLARSHIP PROGRAM

Semiconductor Research Corporation
Attn: Graduate Fellowship Program
Brighton Hall, Suite 120
1101 Slater Road
P.O. Box 12053
Research Triangle Park, NC 27709-2053
(919) 941-9400   Fax: (919) 941-9450
E-mail: students@src.org
Web: www.src.org

Purpose To provide financial assistance to minorities and women interested in working on a master's degree in a field of microelectronics relevant to the interests of the Semiconductor Research Corporation (SRC).

Eligibility This program is open to women and members of underrepresented minority groups (African Americans, Hispanics, and Native Americans). Applicants must be U.S. or Canadian citizens or permanent residents admitted to an SRC participating university to pursue a master's degree in a field relevant to microelectronics under the guidance of an SRC-sponsored faculty member and under an SRC-funded contract.

Financial data The fellowship provides full tuition and fee support, a monthly stipend of $1,880, an annual grant of $2,000 to the university department with which the student recipient is associated, and travel expenses to the Graduate Fellowship Program Annual Conference.

Duration Up to 2 years.

Additional information This program was established in 1997 for underrepresented minorities and expanded to include women in 1999.

Number awarded Varies each year; recently 10 new scholars were appointed to this program.

Deadline January of each year.

[601]
SHERRY R. ARNSTEIN MINORITY STUDENT SCHOLARSHIP

American Association of Colleges of Osteopathic Medicine
Attn: Communications and Member Services
5550 Friendship Boulevard, Suite 310
Chevy Chase, MD 20815-7231
(301) 968-4100   Fax: (301) 968-4101
Web: www.aacom.org

Purpose To provide financial assistance to underrepresented minority students enrolled in osteopathic medical school.

Eligibility This program is open to Black, Hispanic, and Native American students currently enrolled in good standing in their first, second, or third year of osteopathic medical school. Applicants must submit a 750-word essay on what osteopathic medical schools can do to recruit and retain more underrepresented minority students, what they personally plan to do as a student and as a future D.O. to help increase minority student enrollment at a college of osteopathic medicine, and how and why they were drawn to osteopathic medicine.

Financial data The stipend is $2,000.

Duration 1 year; nonrenewable.

Deadline April of each year.

[602]
SHERRY R. ARNSTEIN NEW STUDENT MINORITY STUDENT SCHOLARSHIP

American Association of Colleges of Osteopathic Medicine
Attn: Communications and Member Services
5550 Friendship Boulevard, Suite 310
Chevy Chase, MD 20815-7231
(301) 968-4100   Fax: (301) 968-4101
Web: www.aacom.org

Purpose To provide financial assistance to underrepresented minority students planning to enroll at an osteopathic medical school.

Eligibility This program is open to Black, Hispanic, and Native American students who have been accepted and are planning to enroll at any of the 19 colleges of osteopathic medicine that are members of the American Association of Colleges of Osteopathic Medicine (AACOM). Applicants must submit a 750-word essay on what osteopathic medical schools can and should do to recruit and retain more underrepresented minority students and how and why they were drawn to osteopathic medicine.

Financial data The stipend is $2,000.

Duration 1 year; nonrenewable.

Deadline May of each year.

[603]
SIDNEY B. WILLIAMS, JR. INTELLECTUAL PROPERTY LAW SCHOOL SCHOLARSHIPS

Thurgood Marshall Scholarship Fund
60 East 42nd Street, Suite 833
New York, NY 10165
(212) 573-8888   Fax: (917) 573-8497
E-mail: hrios@tmsf.org
Web: www.thurgoodmarshallfund.org

Purpose To provide financial assistance to underrepresented minority law school students who are interested in preparing for a career in intellectual property law.

Eligibility This program is open to members of minority groups currently enrolled in or accepted to an ABA-accredited law school. Applicants must be U.S. citizens with a demonstrated intent to engage in the full-time practice of intellectual property law. Along with their application, they must submit a 250-word essay on how this scholarship will help make a difference to them in meeting their goal of engaging in the full-time practice of intellectual property law and why they intend to do so. Selection is based on 1) demonstrated commitment to developing a career in intellectual property law; 2) academic performance at the undergraduate, graduate, and law school levels (as applicable); 3) general factors, such as leadership skills, community activities, or special accomplishments; and 4) financial need.

Financial data The stipend is $10,000 per year. Funds may be used for tuition, fees, books, supplies, room, board, and a patent bar review course.

Duration 1 year; may be renewed if the recipient maintains a GPA of 2.0 or higher.

Additional information This program, which began in 2002, is sponsored by the American Intellectual Property Law Education Foundation, 11911 Freedom Drive, Suite 730, Reston, VA 20190, (800) 324-2639. Additional funding is provided by the American Intellectual Property Law Association, the American Bar Association's Section of Intellectual Property Law, the Minority Corporate Counsel Association, and the National Council of Intellectual Property Law Associations. The first class of recipients included a Chinese American, an Asian Pacific American, Mexican Americans, and African Americans. Recipients are required to join and maintain membership in the American Intellectual Property Law Association.

Number awarded Varies each year; recently, 9 of these scholarships were awarded.

Deadline February

[604]
SLA AFFIRMATIVE ACTION SCHOLARSHIP

Special Libraries Association
Attn: SLA Membership Department
1700 18th Street, N.W.
Washington, DC 20009-2514
(202) 234-4700   Fax: (202) 265-9317
E-mail: sla@sla.org
Web: www.sla.org

Purpose To provide financial assistance to minority group members who are interested in preparing for a career in the fields of library or information science in the United States or Canada.

Eligibility To be eligible, applicants must be members of a racial minority group (Black, Hispanic, Asian, Pacific Islander, American Indian, or Alaskan Native); enrolled or accepted for enrollment in a recognized school of library or information science; and in financial need. Preference is given to members of the Special Libraries Association and to persons who have worked in and for special libraries.

Financial data The stipend is $6,000.

Duration 3 quarters or 2 semesters.

Number awarded 1 each year.

Deadline October of each year.

[605]
SLA BOSTON CHAPTER MINORITY SCHOLARSHIP

Special Libraries Association-Boston Chapter
Attn: Danielle Green Barney, Co-Chair, Affirmative Action
    Committee
6 Warren Road
Framingham, MA 01702
(617) 495-8306   Fax: (617) 496-3811
E-mail: dbarney@hbs.edu
Web: www.sla.org/chapter/cbos

Purpose To provide financial assistance for library education to minority students from New England.

Eligibility This program is open to members of underrepresented minority groups (African Americans, Hispanics, Asian Americans, Pacific Islanders, Native Hawaiians, American Indians, and Alaskan Natives) who are enrolled or planning to enroll in an accredited graduate library science program. Applicants must be residents of New England or attending school in the region. They must submit an essay (500 to 750 words) on their interest and experience in special libraries. Financial need is not considered in the selection process.

Financial data The stipend is $2,000.

Duration 1 year.

Number awarded 1 each year.

Deadline April of each year.

[606]
SLOAN SCHOLARSHIPS

National Action Council for Minorities in Engineering
350 Fifth Avenue, Suite 2212
New York, NY 10118-2299
(212) 279-2626   Fax: (212) 629-5178
E-mail: dwalden_sloanphd@nacme.org
Web: sloanphds.org

Purpose To provide financial assistance to underrepresented minority students interested in working on a Ph.D. in mathematics, science, or engineering.

Eligibility This program is open to African Americans, Hispanic Americans, and Native Americans who are U.S. citizens or permanent residents. Applicants must be interested in pursuing a Ph.D. degree in 1 of the following fields: aeronautics and astronautics engineering, animal sciences, applied mathematics, biochemistry, bioengineering, biological sciences, chemical engineering, chemistry, civil engineering, computer engineering, computer science, electrical engineering, engineering management, environmental engineering, environmental science, industrial engineering, geoscience, materials engineering, materials science, mechanical engineering, meteorology, natural resources science, neurosciences, nuclear engineering, oceanography, optical sciences, pharmacology, physics and applied physics, plant physiology, statistics, and systems and operational engineering. Students must apply to and be accepted at a university that is participating in this program. Once they have been accepted, the faculty member with whom they will be working recommends them for support as a Sloan Scholar. Selection of Sloan Scholars is based on their application, faculty recommendation, appropriate field of study, and financial need.

Financial data Each Sloan Scholar receives a scholarship grant of up to $30,000. Scholars may draw on that money at any time during their tenure in the Ph.D. program to cover the cost of tuition, stipend, books, summer support while working toward the Ph.D., travel to professional meetings, or other approved purposes. Scholars are encouraged to discuss with their faculty and others involved with their financial support when and for what purposes they should draw upon their scholarship grant.

Duration The scholarship is a 1-time grant which scholars may utilize throughout their doctoral program.

Additional information This program, which was established in 1995, is administered by the National Action Council for Minorities in Education (NACME) and funded by the Alfred P. Sloan Foundation, 630 Fifth Avenue, Suite 2550, New York, NY 10111-0242, (212) 649-1645, Fax: (212) 757-5117, E-mail: greenwood@sloan.org. Currently, selected faculty at 38 universities are participating. For a list of those faculty members, and the fields of study that are available at each university, contact NACME.

Number awarded Varies each year. Since the program was established, it has supported more than 200 students.

Deadline Applications are accepted on a rolling basis.

[607]
SOCIETY OF HISPANIC PROFESSIONAL ENGINEERS SCHOLARSHIPS

Society of Hispanic Professional Engineers Foundation
Attn: Kathy Borunda
5400 East Olympic Boulevard, Suite 210
Los Angeles, CA 90022
(323) 888-2080   Fax: (323) 888-2089
E-mail: kathy@shpefoundation.org
Web: www.shpefoundation.org/scholarship-program.html

Purpose To provide undergraduate or graduate scholarships to deserving Hispanic American students preparing for a career in engineering or science.

Eligibility Applicants must be enrolled or planning to enroll in an undergraduate or graduate engineering/science program in a college or university. They must be planning to pursue a career in 1 of those areas. Selection is based on an essay on long-range goals (25 points), membership in the Society of Hispanic Professional Engineers (15 points), GPA (15 points), counselor's comments (10 points), school and community activities (10 points), financial need (10 points), educational desire (5 points), and a resume (5 points).

Financial data The stipends range from $500 to $7,000 per year.

Duration 1 academic year; renewal is possible.

Number awarded Varies each year. Recently, 375 of these scholarships, worth $275,000, were awarded.

Deadline April of each year.

[608]
SOCIETY OF MEXICAN AMERICAN ENGINEERS AND SCIENTISTS GRADUATE STUDENT SCHOLARSHIPS

Society of Mexican American Engineers and Scientists
Attn: National Office Director
13337 South Street, Suite 349
Cerritos, CA 90703
E-mail: maes@tamu.edu
Web: www.maes-natl.org

Purpose To provide financial assistance to graduate student members of the Society of Mexican American Engineers and Scientists (MAES).

Eligibility This program is open to MAES student members who are full-time graduate students at a college or university in the United States majoring in a field of science or engineering. U.S. citizenship or permanent resident status is required. Selection is based on financial need; academic achievement; personal qualities, strengths, and leadership abilities; and timeliness and completeness of the application.

Financial data The stipend is $2,000.

Duration 1 year.

Additional information Information is also available from José M. Hernández, Chair, MAES Scholarship Committee, 4015 North Water Iris Cort, Houston, TX 77059.

Number awarded 1 or more each year.

Deadline October of each year.

[609]
SOUTH CAROLINA SPACE GRANT CONSORTIUM GRADUATE FELLOWSHIPS

South Carolina Space Grant Consortium
c/o College of Charleston
Department of Geology
58 Coming Street
Charleston, SC 29424
(843) 953-5463   Fax: (843) 953-5446
E-mail: baughmant@cofc.edu
Web: www.cofc.edu/~scsgrant

Purpose To provide financial assistance for space-related study to graduate students in South Carolina.

Eligibility This program is open to graduate students at member institutions of the South Carolina Space Grant Consortium. Applicants must be interested in space-related studies, although the program has accepted students with interests ranging from remote sensing and engineering to astrophysics. U.S. citizenship is required. Selection is based on academic qualifications of the applicant; 2 letters of recommendation; a description of past activities, current interests, and future plans concerning an aerospace-related field; and faculty sponsorship. The South Carolina Space Grant Consortium is a component of the U.S. National Aeronautics and Space Administration (NASA) Space Grant program, which encourages the participation of women, underrepresented minorities, and persons with disabilities.

Financial data The stipend is $3,000 per year.

Duration 1 year.

Additional information Members of the consortium are Benedict College, The Citadel, College of Charleston, Clemson University, Coastal Carolina University, Furman University, University of South Carolina, Wofford College, South Carolina State University, The Medical University of South Carolina, and University of the Virgin Islands. This program is funded by NASA.

Number awarded Varies each year.

Deadline February of each year.

[610]
SPECTRUM INITIATIVE SCHOLARSHIPS

American Library Association
Attn: Office for Diversity
50 East Huron Street
Chicago, IL 60611-2795
(312) 280-4276   (800) 545-2433, ext. 4276
Fax: (312) 280-3256   TDD: (312) 944-7298
TDD: (888) 814-7692   E-mail: spectrum@ala.org
Web: www.ala.org/spectrum

Purpose To provide financial assistance to minority students planning to work on a degree in librarianship.

Eligibility This program is open to ethnic minority students (African American or African Canadian, Asian or Pacific Islander, Latino or Hispanic, and Native People of the United States or Canada). Applicants must be U.S. or Canadian citizens or permanent residents who are planning to attend an accredited school of library science. Selection is based on academic leadership, outstanding service, commitment to a career in librarianship, statements indicating the nature of the applicant's library and other work experience, letters of reference, and personal presentation.

Financial data The stipend is $5,000 per year.

Duration 1 year.

Additional information This program began in 1998. It is administered by a joint committee of the American Library Association (ALA), with representatives from the Office for Library Personnel Resources, the Office for Literacy and Outreach Services, and the Council Committee on Minority Concerns and Cultural Diversity. Funding is provided by outside contributions and returns from the ALA Future Fund and the Giles and Leo Albert Funds.

Number awarded 50 each year.

Deadline February of each year.

[611]
SREB DOCTORAL SCHOLARS PROGRAM

Southern Regional Education Board
592 10th Street N.W.
Atlanta, GA 30318-5790
(404) 875-9211, ext. 273   Fax: (404) 872-1477
E-mail: doctoral.scholars@sreb.org
Web: www.sreb.org

Purpose To provide financial assistance to minority students who wish to work on a doctoral degree at designated universities in the southern states.

Eligibility This program is open to U.S. citizens who are members of racial/ethnic minority groups (Native Americans, Hispanic Americans, Asian Americans, and African Americans) and hold or will receive a bachelor's degree from an accredited college or university. Applicants must intend to work on a Ph.D. in science, mathematics, engineering, or science or mathematics education at a participating institution. They must indicate an interest in becoming a college professor at an institution in the South. Students who are already enrolled in a doctoral program are not eligible. Study for professional degrees, such as the M.D., D.D.S., J.D., or D.V.M., as well as graduate study in education leading to an Ed.D., does not qualify.

Financial data Scholars receive waiver of tuition and fees (in or out of state) for up to 5 years, an annual stipend of $12,000 for 3 years, an annual allowance for books and materials of $500, and reimbursement of travel expenses to attend the Doctoral Scholars annual meeting.

Duration Up to 5 years.

Additional information This program is part of the national Compact for Faculty Diversity, established in 1994 by the New England Board for Higher Education (NEBHE), the Western Interstate Commission for Higher Education (WICHE), and the Southern Regional Education Board (SREB) with assistance from the Pew Charitable Trusts, the Ford Foundation, participating states, and doctoral universities.

Number awarded Varies each year; recently, the program was supporting 208 scholars at 54 institutions in 22 states.

Deadline Applications received by March of each year receive first consideration.

[612]
STAN BECK FELLOWSHIP

Entomological Society of America
Attn: Entomological Foundation
9301 Annapolis Road, Suite 210
Lanham, MD 20706-3115
(301) 459-9082   Fax: (301) 459-9084
E-mail: melodie@entfdn.org
Web: www.entfdn.org/beck.html

Purpose To assist "needy" students pursuing an undergraduate or graduate degree in science who are nominated by members of the Entomological Society of America (ESA).

Eligibility Candidates for this fellowship must be nominated by members of the society. Nominees may be studying science on any level. However, they must be "needy" students. For the purposes of this program, need may be based on physical limitations, or economic, minority, or environmental conditions.

Financial data The stipend varies each year.

Duration 1 year; may be renewed up to 3 additional years. Recipients are expected to be present at the society's annual meeting, where the award will be presented.

Number awarded 1 or more each year.

Deadline August of each year.

[613]
STUDENT CEC ETHNIC DIVERSITY SCHOLARSHIP

Council for Exceptional Children
Attn: Coordinator of Student Activities
1110 North Glebe Road, Suite 300
Arlington, VA 22201-5704
(703) 264-9412   (888) CEC-SPED
Fax: (703) 264-9494   TTY: (703) 264-9446
E-mail: charlesr@cec.sped.org
Web: www.cec.sped.org/ab/awards.html

Purpose To provide financial assistance to ethnic minority student members of the Council for Exceptional Children (CEC).

Eligibility Eligible are student members of the council who are citizens of the United States or Canada, members of an ethnically diverse group (African American or Black, American Indian, Alaska Native, Native Canadian, Hispanic, Asian, or Pacific Islander), and juniors, seniors, or graduate students enrolled in an accredited college or university. They must be majoring in special education and have a GPA of 2.5 or higher. Applicants must provide 2 letters of recommendation, a summary of Student CEC and/or other activities relating to individuals with disabilities, and a brief biography explaining why they chose special education as a career, how they view the role of special educators, and what they hope to accomplish as a special educator. Financial need is not considered.

Financial data The stipend is $500.

Duration 1 year; nonrenewable.

Number awarded 1 each year.

Deadline November of each year.

[614]
SUBSTANCE ABUSE TRAINING PROGRAM FOR MINORITY NURSES

American Nurses Association
Attn: Ethnic/Racial Minority Fellowship Programs
600 Maryland Avenue, S.W., Suite 100 West
Washington, DC 20024-2571
(202) 651-7245   Fax: (202) 651-7007
E-mail: cporter@ana.org
Web: www.nursingworld.org

Purpose To provide financial assistance for predoctoral research training to minority nurses pursuing careers in substance abuse prevention, intervention, or comorbidity in minority communities.

Eligibility Applications are accepted from registered nurses who 1) are members of an ethnic or racial minority group, including but not limited to African Americans, Hispanics, American Indians, Asian Americans, Pacific Islanders; 2) U.S. citizens or permanent residents; 3) members of the American Nurses Association (ANA); 4) holders of master's degrees; and 5) able to demonstrate a commitment to a research career related to ethnic/racial, underserved, and underrepresented minority populations. The proposed research training program must relate to substance abuse prevention, intervention, and comorbidity within the parameters of ethnic/minority and psychiatric/mental health issues.

Financial data The maximum stipend is $11,748 per year.

Duration Up to 3 years.

Additional information Funds for this program are provided by the Substance Abuse and Mental Health Services Administration.

Deadline January of each year.

[615]
SUNY UNDERREPRESENTED GRADUATE FELLOWSHIP PROGRAM

State University of New York
Attn: Assistant Vice Chancellor
Diversity and Affirmative Action
SUNY Plaza
Albany, NY 12246
(518) 443-5676   Fax: (518) 443-5103

Purpose To provide financial assistance for graduate study at any of the campuses of the State University of New York (SUNY) to underrepresented minority students.

Eligibility This program is open to African Americans, Hispanic Americans, and Native Americans who are U.S. citizens or permanent residents and full-time graduate or professional students at any of the participating SUNY colleges.

Financial data Awards range from $7,500 to $10,000.

Duration 1 year; renewable.

Additional information The participating institutions include the University Centers at Albany, Binghampton, Buffalo, and Stony Brook; the Health Science Centers at Brooklyn and Syracuse; the University Colleges of Arts and Sciences at Brockport, Buffalo, Cortland, Fredonia, Geneseo, New Paltz, Oneonta, Oswego, Plattsburgh, Potsdam, and Purchase; Empire State College; the College of Ceramics at Alfred University; the Institute of Technology at Utica/Rome; the College of Optometry; the Maritime College; the College of Environmental Science and Forestry; and the College of Agriculture and Life Sciences, the College of

Human Ecology, the School of Industrial and Labor Relations, and the College of Veterinary Medicine at Cornell University.

Number awarded 500 each year.

[616]
SWS MINORITY SCHOLAR FUND

Sociologists for Women in Society
Attn: Executive Officer
University of Akron
Department of Sociology
Olin Hall 247
Akron, OH 44325-1905
(330) 972-7918   Fax: (330) 972-5377
E-mail: sws@uakron.edu
Web: www.socwomen.org

Purpose To provide financial assistance for graduate studies in sociology to minority women.

Eligibility Women minority graduate students are eligible to apply if they are interested in preparing for a career in sociology.

Financial data The stipend is $2,500.

Duration 1 year.

Additional information This program was established in 1986-87.

Number awarded 1 each year.

[617]
SYNOD OF LIVING WATERS RACIAL ETHNIC SEMINARY SCHOLARSHIP

Synod of Living Waters
318 Seaboard Lane, Suite 205
Franklin, TN 37067-8242
(615) 261-4008   Fax: (615) 261-4010
E-mail: info@synodoflivingwaters.com
Web: www.synodoflivingwaters.com

Purpose To provide financial assistance to minority seminary students who reside within the boundaries of the Presbyterian Synod of Living Waters.

Eligibility This program is open to members of racial ethnic minorities (African American, Asian American, Hispanic American, or Native American) who reside within the Synod of Living Waters (Alabama, Kentucky, Mississippi, and Tennessee). Applicants must be full-time students attending a Presbyterian seminary with a GPA of 3.0 or higher. They must be able to demonstrate participation in the spiritual life of their school and financial need.

Financial data The stipend is $1,000.

Duration 1 year.

Number awarded 2 each year.

[618]
SYNOD OF THE COVENANT ETHNIC THEOLOGICAL SCHOLARSHIPS

Synod of the Covenant
Attn: CECA Ethnic Scholarship Committee
6172 Busch Boulevard, Suite 3000
Columbus, OH 43229
(614) 436-3310   (800) 848-1030
E-mail: larrye@unidial.com
Web: www.synodofcovenant.org/ceca/scholarship.html

Purpose To provide financial assistance to ethnic students working on a degree at an approved Presbyterian theological institution (with priority given to Presbyterian applicants from Ohio and Michigan).

Eligibility This program is open to ethnic individuals enrolled in church vocations at approved Presbyterian theological institutions. Priority is given to Presbyterian applicants from the states of Michigan and Ohio. Financial need is considered in the selection process.

Financial data Students may be awarded a maximum of $1,500 on initial application. They may receive up to $2,000 on subsequent applications with evidence of continuing progress. Funds are made payable to the session for distribution.

Duration Students are eligible to receive scholarships 1 time per year, up to a maximum of 5 years.

Number awarded Varies each year.

Number awarded Varies each year.

Deadline Applications must be submitted by the end of January for the spring semester and by mid-August for the fall semester.

[619]
TEXAS ASSOCIATION OF CHICANOS IN HIGHER EDUCATION GRADUATE FELLOWSHIP AWARDS

Texas Association of Chicanos in Higher Education
P.O. Box 986
Austin, TX 78767-0986
Web: www.tache.org

Purpose To provide financial assistance to Hispanic residents of Texas who are enrolled in a graduate program to prepare for a career in higher education.

Eligibility This program is open to residents of Texas who are of Chicano/Latino heritage (1 parent fully Hispanic or both parents half Hispanic). Applicants must be enrolled full time in a Texas graduate or professional school in a degree program to prepare for a career in higher education or administration. They must have a cumulative GPA of 3.0 or higher. Along with their application, they must submit a personal statement of 500 to 600 words that describes their Hispanic heritage and family background; past, current, and future efforts toward making a difference in the Hispanic community; personal and academic achievements, including honors and awards; educational and career goals; and financial need.

Financial data The stipend is $2,000 per year.

Duration 1 year.

Additional information Information is also available from Julio Llanas, Fellowship Selection Committee Chair, Texas Tech University, Box 41073, Lubbock, TX 79424, (806) 742-3627, Fax: (806) 742-2592, E-mail: Julio.llanas@ttu.edu. Recipients are required to become members of the Texas Association of Chicanos in Higher Education.

Number awarded 4 each year.

Deadline November of each year.

[620]
TEXAS MEDICAL ASSOCIATION MINORITY SCHOLARSHIP PROGRAM

Texas Medical Association
Attn: Minority Scholarship Program
401 West 15th Street
Austin, TX 78701-1680
(512) 370-1375   (800) 880-2828, ext. 1375
Fax: (512) 370-1635   E-mail: marcia.collins@texmed.org
Web: www.texmed.org

Purpose To provide financial assistance to members of underrepresented minority groups who are interested in attending medical school in Texas.

Eligibility This program is open to members of minority groups that are underrepresented in the medical profession. Applicants must have been accepted to a medical school in Texas.

Financial data The stipend is $5,000.

Duration 1 year; renewable.

Additional information This program began in 1999.

Number awarded 1 each year.

[621]
TEXAS SPACE GRANT CONSORTIUM GRADUATE FELLOWSHIPS

Texas Space Grant Consortium
Attn: Administrative Assistant
3925 West Braker Lane, Suite 200
Austin, TX 78759
(512) 471-3583   (800) 248-8742
Fax: (512) 471-3585   E-mail: jurgens@tsgc.utexas.edu
Web: www.tsgc.utexas.edu/grants

Purpose To provide financial assistance for graduate study at Texas universities in the fields of space science and engineering.

Eligibility Applicants must be U.S. citizens, eligible for financial assistance, and registered for full-time study in a graduate program at 1 of the participating universities. Students apply to their respective university representative; each representative then submits up to 3 candidates into the statewide selection process. Applications from women and underrepresented students (persons with disabilities, African Americans, Hispanic Americans, Native Americans, and Pacific Islanders) are encouraged. Fellowships are awarded competitively, on the basis of GPA, Graduate Record Examination scores, interest in space, and recommendations from the applicant's university.

Financial data The stipend is $5,000 per year, to be used to supplement half-time graduate support (or a fellowship) offered by the home institution.

Duration 1 year; may be renewed for up to a maximum of 3 years, provided the recipient spends no more than 2 of those years as a master's degree candidate.

Additional information The participating universities are Baylor University, Lamar University, Prairie View A&M University, Rice University, Southern Methodist University, Sul Ross State University, Texas A&M University at Kingsville, Texas A&M University, Texas Christian University, Texas Southern University, Texas Tech University, University of Houston, University of Houston/Clear Lake, University of Houston/Downtown, University of Texas at Arlington, University of Texas at Austin, University of Texas at Dallas, University of Texas at El Paso, University of Texas at San Antonio, University of Texas Health Science Center at Houston, University of Texas Health Science Center at San Antonio, University of Texas Medical Branch at Galveston, University of Texas/Pan American, University of Texas Southwestern Medical Center, and West Texas A&M University. This program is funded by the National Aeronautics and Space Administration (NASA).

Number awarded 20 to 25 each year.

Deadline February of each year.

[622]
UNDERREPRESENTED MENTAL HEALTH MINORITY RESEARCH FELLOWSHIP PROGRAM

Council on Social Work Education
Attn: Minority Fellowship Program
1725 Duke Street, Suite 500
Alexandria, VA 22314-3457
(703) 683-8080, ext. 217   Fax: (703) 683-8099
E-mail: mfp@cswe.org
Web: www.cswe.org

Purpose To provide funding to racial minority members interested in preparing for a career in mental health research.

Eligibility This program is open to U.S. citizens and permanent residents who have been underrepresented in the field of social work. These include but are not limited to the following groups: American Indians/Alaskan Natives, Asian/Pacific Islanders (e.g., Chinese, East Indians, South Asians, Filipinos, Hawaiians, Japanese, Koreans, and Samoans), Blacks, and Hispanics (e.g., Mexicans/Chicanos, Puerto Ricans, Cubans, Central or South Americans). Applicants must be interested in enrolling in a doctoral-level social work program that provides strong research courses and research training in mental health. They must be interested in working on a doctoral degree as a full-time student.

Financial data Awards provide a stipend of $16,500 per year and tuition support at the rate of 100% of the first $3,000 and 60% of the remaining tuition.

Duration 1 academic year; renewable for 2 additional years if funds are available and the recipient makes satisfactory progress toward the degree objectives.

Additional information This program has been funded since 1974 by the National Institute of Mental Health of the National Institutes of Health.

Deadline February of each year.

[623]
UNITED CHURCH OF CHRIST FELLOWSHIP PROGRAM IN HEALTH AND HUMAN SERVICE MANAGEMENT

United Church of Christ
Attn: Council for Health and Human Service Ministries
700 Prospect Avenue East
Cleveland, OH 44115-1100
(216) 736-2250   Fax: (216) 736-2251
E-mail: nehringa@ucc.org
Web: www.ucc.org

Purpose To provide financial assistance to clergy and lay members who wish to work on a graduate degree in health and human service management.

Eligibility This program is open to clergy persons with ecclesiastical standing and active lay members of a community of faith who possess at least a baccalaureate degree. Candidates must be able to articulate their faith motivation for entering a ministry of health and human service management. They must qualify for admission and successfully complete any accredited academic

program in theology and/or management as full-time students; successfully complete any state or federal examinations and obtain licensure as required by their administrative discipline; complete all residency, mentoring, and special project assignments at sponsoring institutions; and accept full-time employment, if offered, in an organization of the United Church of Christ (UCC) for a period of 5 years following completion of the fellowship. Fields of study include: long-term care and retirement housing; hospital and community health services; services to children, youth, and families; and services to persons with developmental disabilities. Applications from women and persons of color are especially encouraged.

Financial data The amount of the award is negotiable, based on the costs of the program.

Duration Varies, depending on the background of the fellow and the training required.

Number awarded 1 each year.

[624]
UNITED METHODIST CHURCH CRUSADE SCHOLARSHIP PROGRAM

United Methodist Church
Attn: General Board of Global Ministries
475 Riverside Drive, Room 1338
New York, NY 10115
(212) 870-3787   (800) 654-5929
E-mail: EGoldste@gbgm-umc.org
Web: www.gbgm-umc.org

Purpose To provide financial assistance to minority and foreign students who are interested in attending graduate school to prepare for leadership within the United Methodist Church.

Eligibility This program is open to 1) U.S. citizens and permanent residents who are ethnic and racial minority graduate students (African Americans, Hispanic Americans, Pacific/Asian Americans, and Native Americans) and 2) international students who are still resident in their home country and have the recommendation of the United Methodist home scholarship committee. Applicants must be seeking their first graduate degree (M.Div., M.A., Ph.D., D.D.S., M.D., M.Ed., M.B.A., or other graduate degree). Preference is given to members of the United Methodist Church and to persons entering Christian vocations. All applicants should be committed to preparing themselves for leadership in mission to church and society. Financial need must be demonstrated.

Financial data The amount awarded varies, depending upon the availability of funds.

Duration Up to 3 years.

Additional information These awards are funded by the World Communion Offering received in United Methodist churches on the first Sunday in October.

Number awarded Varies each year.

Deadline January of each year.

[625]
UNITED METHODIST SCHOLARSHIP PROGRAM

United Methodist Church
Attn: Office of Loans and Scholarships
1001 19th Avenue South
P.O. Box 871
Nashville, TN 37202-0871
(615) 340-7344   Fax: (615) 340-7367
E-mail: umscholar@gbhem.org
Web: www.gbhem.org

Purpose To provide financial assistance to undergraduate and graduate students attending schools affiliated with the United Methodist Church.

Eligibility This program is open to U.S. citizens and permanent residents who have been active, full members of a United Methodist Church for at least 1 year prior to applying; members of the A.M.E., A.M.E. Zion, and other "Methodist" denominations are not eligible. Undergraduates must have been admitted to a full-time degree program at a United Methodist-related college or university and have earned a GPA of 2.5 or above. Most graduate scholarships are designated for persons pursuing a degree in theological studies (M.Div., D.Min., Ph.D.) or higher education administration, or for older adults changing their careers. Some scholarships are designated for racial ethnic undergraduate or graduate students. Applications are available from the financial aid office of the United Methodist school the applicant attends or from the chair of their annual conference Board of Higher Education and Campus Ministry.

Financial data The funding is intended to supplement the students' own resources.

Duration 1 year; renewal policies are set by participating universities.

Number awarded Varies each year.

[626]
URBAN FELLOWSHIP PROGRAM

North Central Texas Council of Governments
Attn: Transportation Department
616 Six Flags Drive, Centerpoint Two
P.O. Box 5888
Arlington, TX 76005-5888
(817) 608-2325   Fax: (817) 640-7806
E-mail: lucile@dwinfo.com
Web: www.dfwinfo.com/trans/fellowship

Purpose To provide financial assistance and work experience to ethnic minorities, women, and economically disadvantaged persons who are interested in obtaining a master's degree in public management and/or planning at a university in Texas.

Eligibility This program is open to ethnic minorities (African Americans, Hispanics, American Indians, Alaskan Natives, Asians, and Pacific Islanders), women, and those who are economically disadvantaged. Only U.S. citizens or permanent residents may apply. Applicants must be interested in obtaining a master's degree at a university in Texas as preparation for a career in public management and/or planning. Full-time enrollment is required. Selection is based on 1) financial need; 2) interest in, and commitment to, a professional career in urban management and/or planning; and 3) the applicant's ability to complete the academic and work placement responsibilities of the program.

Financial data The academic portion of this program pays the cost of tuition and books. The work experience portion of the program pays a salary of $8.50 per hour for 20 hours per week.

Duration 1 year; may be renewed if the recipient maintains a GPA of 3.0 or higher.

Additional information These fellowships are financed by the U.S. Department of Housing and Urban Development in conjunction with local governments in north central Texas (the Dallas/Fort Worth metropolitan area). Fellows are assigned to an internship in a local government in that area. Universities currently participating in the program are the University of North Texas, the University of Texas at Arlington, and the University of Texas at Dallas. Fellows are required to agree to make a good-faith effort to obtain employment in community-building fields for at least 2 consecutive years after graduation.

Deadline July of each year.

[627]
USA FUNDS ACCESS TO EDUCATION SCHOLARSHIPS

Scholarship America
Attn: Scholarship Management Services
1505 Riverview Road
P.O. Box 297
St. Peter, MN 56082
(507) 931-1682   (800) 537-4180
Fax: (507) 931-9168   E-mail: scholarship@usafunds.org
Web: www.usafunds.org

Purpose To provide financial assistance to undergraduate and graduate students, especially those who are members of ethnic minority groups or have physical disabilities.

Eligibility This program is open to high school seniors and graduates who plan to enroll or are already enrolled in full-time undergraduate or graduate course work at an accredited 2- or 4-year college, university, or vocational/technical school. Half-time undergraduate students are also eligible. Up to 50% of the awards are targeted at students who have a documented physical disability or are a member of an ethnic minority group, including but not limited to Native Hawaiian, Alaskan Native, Black/African American, Asian, Pacific Islander, American Indian, or Hispanic/Latino. Residents of all 50 states, the District of Columbia, Puerto Rico, Guam, the U.S. Virgin Islands, and all U.S. territories and commonwealths are eligible. Preference is given to applicants from the following areas: Arizona, Hawaii and the Pacific Islands, Indiana, Kansas, Maryland, Mississippi, Nevada, and Wyoming. Applicants must also be U.S. citizens or eligible non-citizens and come from a family with an annual adjusted gross income of $35,000 or less. In addition to financial need, selection is based on past academic performance and future potential, leadership and participation in school and community, work experience, career and educational aspirations and goals, and references.

Financial data The stipend is $1,500 per year for full-time undergraduate or graduate students or $750 per year for half-time undergraduate students. Funds are paid jointly to the student and the school.

Duration 1 year; may be renewed until the student receives a final degree or certificate or until the total award to a student reaches $6,000, whichever comes first. Renewal requires the recipient to maintain a GPA of 2.5 or higher.

Additional information This program, established in 2000, is sponsored by USA Funds which serves as the education loan guarantor and administrator in the 8 states and the Pacific Islands where the program gives preference.

Number awarded Varies each year; recently, 2,519 of these scholarships were awarded.

Deadline April of each year.

[628]
VIRGIL HAWKINS FELLOWSHIP PROGRAM

State University System of Florida
Attn: Office of Academic and Student Services
325 West Gaines Street, Suite 1501
Tallahassee, FL 32399-1950
(850) 201-7216   Fax: (850) 201-7185
E-mail: lpage@borfl.org
Web: www.borfl.org

Purpose To provide financial assistance to minorities in Florida who are interested in legal careers.

Eligibility First-year minority students who are attending law schools at accredited state universities in Florida are eligible to apply.

Financial data The stipend is $5,000 per year.

Duration 1 year; renewable up to 2 additional years.

Additional information This program is administered by the equal opportunity program at each of the 10 public 4-year institutions in Florida. Contact that office for further information.

Number awarded 10 each year.

[629]
VIRGINIA F. CUTLER FELLOWSHIP IN CONSUMER STUDIES

American Association of Family and Consumer Sciences
Attn: Manager of Awards and Grants
1555 King Street
Alexandria, VA 22314-2752
(703) 706-4600   (800) 424-8080, ext. 119
Fax: (703) 706-4663   E-mail: staff@aafcs.org
Web: www.aafcs.org/fellowships/brochure.html

Purpose To provide financial assistance to minority and international students interested in graduate study in consumer affairs.

Eligibility This program is open to members of U.S. minority groups and international students interested in pursuing consumer studies on a full-time basis at the graduate level. Selection is based on scholarship and special aptitudes for advanced study and research, educational and/or professional experiences, professional contributions to family and consumer sciences, and the significance of the proposed research problem to the public well-being and the advancement of family and consumer sciences. Applicants are encouraged to complete at least 1 year of professional family and consumer sciences experience, serving in such positions as a graduate/undergraduate assistant, trainee, or intern.

Financial data The stipend is $3,500.

Duration 1 year.

Additional information This fellowship was first awarded for the 1976-77 academic year. The application fee is $40. The association reserves the right to reconsider an award in the event the student receives a similar award for the same academic year.

Number awarded 1 each year.

Deadline January of each year.

[630]
WALLY DAVIS LEGAL MEMORIAL SCHOLARSHIPS

Orange County Community Foundation
Attn: Scholarship Coordinator
2081 Business Center Drive, Suite 100
Irvine, CA 92612-1115
(949) 553-4202, ext. 22   Fax: (949) 553-4211
E-mail: occf@oc-communityfoundation.org
Web: www.oc-communityfoundation.org/grantsscholar

Purpose To provide financial assistance for law school to Hispanic students who reside or attend school in Orange County, California.

Eligibility This program is open to Hispanic law students who either reside in or attend (or plan to attend) school in Orange County, California. Selection is based on financial need and involvement in the Latino community and law school.

Financial data The stipend is $1,000 per year.

Duration 1 year.

Additional information This program is supported by the Hispanic Bar Association of Orange County.

Number awarded 3 each year.

Deadline February of each year.

[631]
WARNER NORCROSS & JUDD LAW SCHOOL STUDIES SCHOLARSHIP

Grand Rapids Community Foundation
Attn: Scholarship Coordinator
209-C Waters Building
161 Ottawa Avenue N.W.
Grand Rapids, MI 49503-2757
(616) 454-1751, ext. 103   Fax: (616) 454-6455
E-mail: rbishop@grfoundation.org
Web: www.grfoundation.org

Purpose To provide financial assistance for law school to minorities with a residential connection to Michigan.

Eligibility This program is open to minority students entering, accepted at, or currently attending an accredited law school within the United States. Applicants must be residents of Michigan or have a connection to the state (e.g., family members reside in the state, student previously resided in the state, student attended a school in the state).

Financial data The stipend is $5,000.

Duration 1 year.

Additional information Funding for this program is provided by the law firm Warner Norcross & Judd LLP.

Number awarded 1 each year.

Deadline April of each year.

[632]
WES MCJULIEN MINORITY GRADUATE SCHOLARSHIP

Association for Educational Communications and
　Technology
Attn: ECT Foundation
1800 North Stonelake Drive, Suite 2
Bloomington, IN 47408
(812) 335-7675　　　　　　　　(877) 677-AECT
Web: slm.usu.edu/AECT/Minority.htm

Purpose To provide financial assistance to minority members
of the Association for Educational Communications and Technology (AECT) working on a doctorate in the field of educational
communications and technology.

Eligibility This program is open to AECT members who are
members of minority groups. Applicants must be full-time graduate students enrolled in a degree-granting program in educational
technology at the masters (M.S.), specialist (Ed.S.), or doctoral
(Ph.D., Ed.D.) levels with a GPA of 3.0 or higher. Along with their
application, they must submit an essay on what they believe to
be an important issue confronting minorities in the field of media
and 3 letters of recommendation.

Financial data The stipend is $500.

Duration 1 year.

Additional information Information is also available from
Hans-Erik Wennberg, Elizabethtown College, Communications
Department, One Alpha Drive, Elizabethtown, PA, 17022-2298,
(717) 361-1259, (717) 361-1180, E-mail: wenn-
berg@acad.etown.edu.

Number awarded 1 each year.

Deadline October of each year.

[633]
WILLIAM G. ANDERSON, D.O. SCHOLARSHIP FOR MINORITY STUDENTS

American Osteopathic Foundation
Attn: Program Manager
142 East Ontario Street
Chicago, IL 60611-2864
(312) 202-8232　　　　　　　　(800) 621-1773
Fax: (312) 202-8216　　　　E-mail: vheck@aoa-net.org
Web: www.osteopathic.org

Purpose To provide financial assistance to minority students
enrolled in colleges of osteopathic medicine.

Eligibility This program is open to minority (African American,
Native American, Asian American, or Hispanic) students entering
their second, third, or fourth year at an accredited college of
osteopathic medicine. Applicants must demonstrate academic
achievement and outstanding leadership qualities.

Financial data The stipend is $5,000.

Duration 1 year.

Additional information This program was established in 1998.

Number awarded 1 each year.

[634]
WILLIAM RUCKER GREENWOOD SCHOLARSHIP

Association for Women Geoscientists
Attn: AWG Foundation
P.O. Box 30645
Lincoln, NE 68503-0645
E-mail: office@awg.org
Web: www.awg.org/eas/scholarships.html

Purpose To provide financial assistance to minority women
working on an undergraduate or graduate degree in the geosciences in the Potomac Bay region.

Eligibility This program is open to minority women who are
currently enrolled as full-time undergraduate or graduate geoscience majors in an accredited, degree-granting college or university in Delaware, the District of Columbia, Maryland, Virginia, or
West Virginia. Selection is based on the applicant's 1) awareness
of the importance of community outreach by participation in geoscience or earth science educational activities, and 2) potential
for leadership as a future geoscience professional.

Financial data The stipend is $1,000. The recipient also is
granted a 1-year membership in the Association for Women
Geoscientists (AWG).

Duration 1 year.

Additional information This program is sponsored by the
AWG Potomac Area Chapter. Information is also available from
Laurel M. Bybell, U.S. Geological Survey, 926 National Center,
Reston, VA 20192.

Number awarded 1 each year.

Deadline April of each year.

[635]
W.K. KELLOGG FOUNDATION FELLOWSHIP PROGRAM IN HEALTH RESEARCH

National Medical Fellowships, Inc.
Attn: Scholarship Program
5 Hanover Square, 15th Floor
New York, NY 10004
(212) 483-8880　　　　　　　　Fax: (212) 483-8897
E-mail: info@nmfonline.org
Web: www.nmf-online.org

Purpose To provide financial assistance to minorities enrolled
in a doctoral program in health policy research who are committed to working with underserved populations.

Eligibility This program is open to members of minority groups
(African Americans, Native Americans, Asians, and Hispanics)
enrolled in graduate programs in public health, social policy, or
health policy leading to a doctorate (Ph.D., Dr.P.H., or Sc.D.).
Applicants must demonstrate a willingness to complete relevant
dissertation research and a commitment to work with underserved populations upon completion of the doctorate. They must
include an essay of 500 to 1,000 words discussing their reasons
for applying for a fellowship, their qualifications, how it will support their career plans, and which of 4 areas of focus (health policy, men's health, mental health, substance abuse) most interests
them and why.

Financial data Fellowships cover tuition, fees, and a partial living stipend.

Duration Up to 5 years: 2 years to do the necessary course
work and 3 years to complete the dissertation.

Additional information The program was created in 1998 with
grant support from the W.K. Kellogg Foundation. Recently, it
operated at 8 institutions: the RAND Graduate School, the Heller

Graduate School at Brandeis University, the Joseph L. Mailman School of Public Health at Columbia University, the Harvard School of Public Health, the Johns Hopkins School of Hygiene and Public Health, the UCLA School of Public Health, the University of Michigan School of Public Health, and the University of Pennsylvania. Information is also available from the sponsor's Washington office at 1627 K Street, N.W., Suite 1200, Washington, DC 20006-1702, (202) 296-4431, Fax: (202) 293-1990.

Number awarded 5 each year.

Deadline June of each year.

[636]
WOLVERINE BAR FOUNDATION SCHOLARSHIP

Wolverine Bar Association
Attn: Wolverine Bar Foundation
645 Griswold, Suite 961
Detroit, MI 48226
(313) 962-0250   Fax: (313) 962-5906
Web: www.michbar.org

Purpose To provide financial assistance for law school to Michigan minority students.

Eligibility This program is open to minority law students who are either currently enrolled in a Michigan law school or are Michigan residents enrolled in an out-of-state law school. Applicants must be in at least their second year of law school. Selection is based on financial need, merit, and an interview.

Financial data The stipend is at least $1,000.

Duration 1 year; nonrenewable.

Additional information The Wolverine Bar Association was established by a number of African American attorneys during the 1930s. It was the successor to the Harlan Law Club, founded in 1919 by attorneys in the Detroit area who were excluded from other local bar associations in Michigan. Information is also available from the Scholarship Committee co-chairs, Kimberly D. Stevens, (313) 235-7711, E-mail: kds0183@hotmail.com, or Vanessa Peterson Williams, (313) 877-7000, E-mail: vpwilliams@mbpia.com.

Number awarded 1 or more each year.

Deadline January of each year.

[637]
WORLDSTUDIO FOUNDATION SCHOLARSHIPS

Worldstudio Foundation
225 Varick Street, Ninth Floor
New York, NY 10014
(212) 366-1317, ext. 18   Fax: (212) 807-0024
E-mail: scholarships@worldstudio.org
Web: www.worldstudio.org/scholar/intro.html

Purpose To provide financial assistance to disadvantaged and ethnic minority undergraduate and graduate students who wish to study fine or commercial arts, design, or architecture.

Eligibility This program is open to disadvantaged or minority college students who are currently enrolled (must attend an accredited school) and majoring in the 1 of the following areas: advertising, architecture, crafts, environmental graphics, fashion design, film/video, film/theater design (including set and costume design), fine arts, furniture design, graphic design, industrial/product design, interior architecture, interior design, landscape architecture, new media, photography, surface/textile design, or urban planning. Both graduate and undergraduate students are eligible. International students may apply if they are enrolled at a U.S. college or university. Applicants must have a GPA of 2.0 or higher. Selection is based on the quality of submitted work, a 600-word written statement of purpose, financial need, and academic record.

Financial data Basic scholarships range from $1,000 to $2,000, but awards between $3,000 and $5,000 are also presented at the discretion of the jury. Honorable mentions are $100. Funds are paid directly to the recipient's school.

Duration 1 academic year. Recipients may reapply.

Additional information The foundation encourages the scholarship recipients to focus on ways that their work can address issues of social and environmental responsibility. This program includes the following named awards: the Gaggenau Award for Design, the New York Design Center Awards, the ALU Awards for Design, the Color Wheel Award, the Honda Award for Environmental Design, the Rado Watch Scholarship for Design, the Janou Pakter Award, the Impac Group Award, the Color Optics Award. the AIGA Award, the Lonn Beaudry Memorial Award, and the Robert J. Hurst Award.

Number awarded Varies each year; recently, 20 scholarships and 10 honorable mentions were awarded.

Deadline April of each year.

[638]
XEROX TECHNICAL MINORITY SCHOLARSHIP PROGRAM

Xerox Corporation
Attn: Technical Minority Scholarship Program
907 Culver Road
Rochester, NY 14609-7192
(585) 422-7689   E-mail: xtmsp@imcouncil.com
Web: www.xerox.com

Purpose To provide financial assistance to minorities interested in undergraduate or graduate education in the sciences and/or engineering.

Eligibility This program is open to minorities (people of African American, Asian, Pacific Islander, American Indian, Native Alaskan, or Hispanic descent) enrolled full time in the following science and engineering degree programs at the baccalaureate level or above: chemistry, engineering (chemical, computer, electrical, imaging, mechanical, optical, software), information management, material science, or physics. Applicants must be U.S. citizens or permanent residents with a GPA of 3.0 or higher.

Financial data The maximum stipend is $1,000 per year.

Duration 1 year.

Deadline September of each year.

Loans

Described here are 39 programs open to Hispanic Americans that provide money which must eventually be repaid—in cash or in service and with or without interest. If you are looking for a particular program and don't find it in this section, be sure to check the Program Title Index to see if it is covered elsewhere in the directory.

[639]
ARKANSAS MINORITY MASTERS FELLOWS PROGRAM

Arkansas Department of Higher Education
Attn: Financial Aid Division
114 East Capitol Avenue
Little Rock, AR 72201-3818
(501) 371-2050 (800) 54-STUDY
Fax: (501) 371-2001 E-mail: finaid@adhe.arknet.edu
Web: www.arscholarships.com/mmasters.html

Purpose To provide fellowship/loans to minority graduate students in Arkansas who want to become teachers in selected subject areas.

Eligibility Applicants must be minority (African American, Hispanic, or Asian American) residents of Arkansas who are U.S. citizens and enrolled as full-time master's degree students in mathematics, the sciences, or foreign languages at an Arkansas public or independent institution with a minimum cumulative GPA of 2.75. Also eligible are minority students in the fifth year of a 5-year teacher certification program. Recipients must be willing to teach in an Arkansas public school or public institution of higher education for at least 2 years after completion of their education. Preference is given to applicants who completed their baccalaureate degrees within the previous 2 years.

Financial data The stipend is up to $7,500 per year for full-time students (or up to $2,500 per summer for part-time summer students). This is a fellowship/loan program. The loan will be forgiven at the rate of 50% for each year the recipient teaches full time in an Arkansas public school or public institution of higher education. If the recipient does not attend college on a full-time basis, withdraws from an approved teacher education program, or does not fulfill the required teaching obligation, the loan must be repaid in full with interest at a rate up to 5 percentage points above the Federal Reserve discount rate.

Duration 1 year; may be renewed if the recipient remains a full-time student with a GPA of 3.0 or higher.

Number awarded Varies each year; recently, 25 of these fellowship/loans were approved.

Deadline May of each year.

[640]
ARKANSAS MINORITY TEACHER SCHOLARS PROGRAM

Arkansas Department of Higher Education
Attn: Financial Aid Division
114 East Capitol Avenue
Little Rock, AR 72201-3818
(501) 371-2050 (800) 54-STUDY
Fax: (501) 371-2001 E-mail: finaid@adhe.arknet.edu
Web: www.arscholarships.com/mteachers.html

Purpose To provide scholarship/loans to minority undergraduates in Arkansas who want to become teachers.

Eligibility Applicants must be minority (African American, Native American, Hispanic, or Asian American) residents of Arkansas who are U.S. citizens and enrolled as full-time juniors or seniors in an approved teacher certification program at an Arkansas public or independent 4-year institution. They must have a minimum cumulative GPA of 2.5 and be willing to teach in an Arkansas public school for at least 5 years after completion of their teaching certificate (3 years if the teaching is in 1 of the 42 counties of Arkansas designated as the Delta Region; or if the teaching is in mathematics, science, or foreign language; or if the

recipient is an African American male and teaches at the elementary level; or if the service is as a guidance counselor).

Financial data Awards up to $5,000 per year are available. This is a scholarship/loan program. The loan will be forgiven at the rate of 20% for each year the recipient teaches full time in an Arkansas public school (or 33% per year if the obligation is fulfilled in 3 years as described above). If the loan is not forgiven by service, it must be repaid with interest at a rate up to 5% points above the Federal Reserve discount rate.

Duration 1 year; may be renewed for 1 additional year if the recipient remains a full-time student with a GPA of 2.5 or higher.

Deadline May of each year.

Number awarded Varies each year; recently, 97 of these scholarship/loans were approved.

[641]
CALIFORNIA STATE UNIVERSITY FORGIVABLE LOAN/DOCTORAL INCENTIVE PROGRAM

California State University
Office of the Chancellor
Attn: Human Resources
401 Golden Shore, Fourth Floor
Long Beach, CA 90802-4210
(562) 951-4426 Fax: (562) 951-4954
E-mail: lfaure@calstate.edu
Web: www.calstate.edu

Purpose To provide forgivable loans to graduate students who can help increase the diversity of persons qualified to compete for instructional faculty positions at campuses of the California State University (CSU) system.

Eligibility This program is open to new and continuing full-time students enrolled in a doctoral program anywhere in the United States, whether affiliated with a CSU campus or not. Applicants must present a plan of support from a full-time CSU faculty sponsor who will agree to advise and support the candidate throughout doctoral study. Selection is based on the applicant's academic record, professional qualifications, and motivation to educate a diverse student body in the CSU system. The elements considered include actual acceptance into a specific doctoral program, the quality of the proposed doctoral program, and other experiences or skills that enhance the potential of the candidate to educate a diverse student body; those experiences and characteristics may include experience working with persons with a wide range of backgrounds and perspectives, research interests related to educating an increasingly diverse student body, a history of successfully overcoming economic disadvantage and adversity, experience in a variety of cultural environments, and being a first generation college student. Special consideration is given to candidates whose proposed area of study falls where CSU campuses anticipate the greatest difficulty in filling instructional faculty positions; currently, those disciplines include computer science, electrical engineering, and nursing.

Financial data Participants receive up to $10,000 per year or a maximum of $30,000 over 5 years. The loans are converted to fellowships at the rate of 20% of the total loan amount for each postdoctoral year that the program participant teaches, for up to 5 years. Thus, the entire loan will be forgiven after the recipient has taught full time for 5 years on a CSU campus. Recipients who do not teach on a CSU campus or who discontinue full-time studies will be required to repay the total loan amount within a 15-year period at the rate established for other student loans. The minimum repayment required for a $30,000 loan is approximately

$287 per month to amortize the 8% per annum loan over a 15-year period. Waiver of loan obligations can be made in those exceptional cases where graduate work was discontinued for valid reasons and where repayment of the loan would cause an unnecessary or undue hardship.

Duration Up to 5 years.

Additional information This program began in 1987. It has loaned $29 million to 1,323 doctoral students enrolled in universities throughout the nation and abroad.

Number awarded Varies each year.

Deadline The deadline varies at different CSU campuses but typically falls in February of each year.

[642]
DAVID A. DEBOLT TEACHER SHORTAGE SCHOLARSHIP PROGRAM

Illinois Student Assistance Commission
Attn: Scholarship and Grant Services
1755 Lake Cook Road
Deerfield, IL 60015-5209
(847) 948-8550   (800) 899-ISAC
Fax: (847) 831-8549   TDD: (847) 831-8326, ext. 2822
E-mail: cssupport@isac.org
Web: www.isac1.org/ilaid/DeBolt.html

Purpose To provide scholarship/loans to college students in Illinois who are interested in training or retraining for a teaching career in academic shortage areas.

Eligibility Eligible for support under this program are Illinois residents who are enrolled at the sophomore level or higher in an Illinois institution of higher education. Applicants must be planning to pursue a career as a preschool, elementary, or secondary school teacher in designated teacher shortage disciplines. Priority is given to minority students.

Financial data This program pays tuition and fees, room and board, or a commuter allowance at academic institutions in Illinois, to a maximum of $5,000. Funds are paid directly to the school. This is a scholarship/loan program. Recipients must agree to teach in an Illinois public, private, or parochial preschool, elementary school, or secondary school for 1 year for each full year of assistance received. The teaching obligation must be completed within 5 years of completion of the degree or certificate program for which the scholarship was awarded. That time period may be extended if the recipient serves in the U.S. armed forces, enrolls full time in a graduate program related to teaching, becomes temporarily disabled, is unable to find employment as a teacher, or takes additional courses on at least a half-time basis to teach in a specialized teacher shortage discipline. Recipients who fail to honor this work obligation must repay the award with interest.

Duration 1 year; may be renewed.

Number awarded Varies each year, depending on the availability of funds.

Deadline February of each year.

[643]
DEFENSE INTELLIGENCE AGENCY UNDERGRADUATE TRAINING ASSISTANCE PROGRAM

Defense Intelligence Agency
Attn: DAH-2
Bolling Air Force Base
200 MacDill Boulevard
Washington, DC 20340-5100
(202) 231-4713   Fax: (202) 231-4889
TTY: (202) 231-5002
Web: www.dia.mil/Careers/Programs/utap.html

Purpose To provide loans-for-service to high school seniors interested in majoring in specified fields and working for the U.S. Defense Intelligence Agency (DIA).

Eligibility This competitive program is open to graduating high school seniors who are interested in majoring in 1 of the following fields in college: computer science, geography, foreign area studies, international relations, or political science. Applicants must have a high school GPA of 3.0 or higher, have an SAT score of 1000 or higher or an ACT score of 21 or higher, be able to demonstrate financial need (household income ceiling of $60,000 for a family of 4 or $75,000 for a family of 5 or more), be U.S. citizens and from a family of U.S. citizens, and demonstrate leadership abilities through extracurricular activities, civic involvement, volunteer work, or part-time employment. Minorities, women, and people with disabilities are strongly encouraged to apply.

Financial data Students accepted into this program receive tuition (up to $17,000 per year) at an accredited college or university selected by the student and endorsed by the sponsor; an annual salary for summer employment; and a position at the sponsoring agency after graduation. Recipients must work for DIA after college graduation for at least 1 and a half times the length of study. For participants who leave DIA earlier than scheduled, the agency arranges for payments to reimburse DIA for the total cost of education (including the employee's pay and allowances).

Duration 4 years.

Additional information Recipients are provided challenging summer work and guaranteed a job at the agency in their field of study upon graduation. Recipients must attend school on a full-time basis.

Number awarded Only a few are awarded each year.

Deadline November of each year.

[644]
DIRECT FARM LOANS FOR SOCIALLY DISADVANTAGED PERSONS

Department of Agriculture
Farm Service Agency
Attn: Office of Minority and Socially Disadvantaged Farmers
    Assistance
1400 Independence Avenue, S.W.
Washington, DC 20250-0568
(202) 720-1584   (866) 538-2610
Fax: (202) 690-3432   Fax: (888) 211-7286
E-mail: msda@wdc.usda.gov
Web: www.fsa.usda.gov

Purpose To lend money to eligible members of socially disadvantaged groups for the purchase or operation of family-size farms or ranches.

Eligibility For the purposes of this program, a "socially disadvantaged group" is 1 whose members "have been subjected to racial, ethnic, or gender prejudice because of their identity as members of a group without regard to their individual qualities." Those groups are women, African Americans, American Indians, Alaskan Natives, Hispanics, Asian Americans, and Pacific Islanders. Applicants may be seeking either farm ownership loans (to purchase or enlarge a farm or ranch, purchase easements or rights of way needed in the farm's operation, erect or improve buildings such as a dwelling or barn, promote soil and water conservation, or pay closing costs) or farm operating loans (to purchase livestock, poultry, farm and home equipment, feed, seed, fertilizer, chemicals, hail and other crop insurance, food, clothing, medical care, and hired labor). Loans are made to individuals, partnerships, joint operations, corporations, and cooperatives primarily and directly engaged in farming and ranching on family-size operations; a family-size farm is defined as a farm that a family can operate and manage itself. In addition to belonging to a "socially disadvantaged group," borrowers must have a satisfactory history of meeting credit obligations, have 3 years of experience in operating a farm or ranch for an ownership loan or 1 year's experience within the last 5 years for an operating loan, be a U.S. citizen or legal resident, possess the legal capacity to incur the obligations of a loan or credit sale, and be unable to obtain sufficient credit elsewhere at reasonable rates.

Financial data The maximum loan is $200,000. Interest rates are set periodically according to the federal government's cost of borrowing.

Duration Repayment terms are generally up to 40 years for ownership loans or 1 to 7 years for operating loans.

Deadline Applications may be submitted at any time.

[645]
GUARANTEED FARM LOANS FOR SOCIALLY DISADVANTAGED PERSONS

Department of Agriculture
Farm Service Agency
Attn: Office of Minority and Socially Disadvantaged Farmers Assistance
1400 Independence Avenue, S.W.
Washington, DC 20250-0568
(202) 720-1584   (866) 538-2610
Fax: (202) 690-3432   Fax: (888) 211-7286
E-mail: msda@wdc.usda.gov
Web: www.fsa.usda.gov

Purpose To guarantee loans to eligible members of socially disadvantaged groups for the purchase or operation of family-size farms or ranches.

Eligibility For the purposes of this program, a "socially disadvantaged group" is 1 whose members "have been subjected to racial, ethnic, or gender prejudice because of their identity as members of a group without regard to their individual qualities." Those groups are women, African Americans, American Indians, Alaskan Natives, Hispanic Americans, Asian Americans, and Pacific Islanders. Applicants may be seeking guarantees of loans either for farm ownership (to purchase or enlarge a farm or ranch, purchase easements or rights of way needed in the farm's operation, erect or improve buildings such as a dwelling or barn, promote soil and water conservation, or pay closing costs) or farm operation (to purchase livestock, poultry, farm and home equipment, feed, seed, fertilizer, chemicals, hail and other crop insurance, food, clothing, medical care, and hired labor). Guarantees are provided on loans by lending institutions subject to federal or state supervision. Loans are made to individuals, partnerships, joint operations, corporations, and cooperatives primarily and directly engaged in farming and ranching on family-size operations; a family-size farm is defined as a farm that a family can operate and manage itself. In addition to belonging to a "socially disadvantaged group," borrowers must have a satisfactory history of meeting credit obligations, have 3 years of experience in operating a farm or ranch for an ownership loan or 1 year's experience within the last 5 years for an operating loan, be a U.S. citizen or legal resident, possess the legal capacity to incur the obligations of a loan or credit sale, and be unable to obtain sufficient credit elsewhere at reasonable rates.

Financial data The size of the loan is agreed upon by the borrower and the lender, but the maximum indebtedness in guaranteed loans of the Farm Service Agency (FSA) may not exceed $762,000. Interest rates can be fixed or variable, as agreed upon by the borrower and the lender, but may not exceed the rate the lender charges its average farm customer. FSA guarantees up to 95% of the loan principal and interest against loss.

Duration Repayment terms are generally up to 40 years for ownership loans or 1 to 7 years for operating loans.

Deadline Applications may be submitted at any time.

[646]
ILLINOIS CONSORTIUM FOR EDUCATIONAL OPPORTUNITY PROGRAM

Southern Illinois University at Carbondale
Attn: IMGIP/ICEOP Administrator
Woody Hall C-224
Carbondale, IL 62901-4723
(618) 453-4558   E-mail: fellows@siu.edu
Web: www.imgip.sie.edu

Purpose To provide fellowship/loans that will increase the participation of minority students in graduate school programs in Illinois.

Eligibility To be eligible for this award, an applicant must be a resident of Illinois, a U.S. citizen or permanent resident, a recipient of an earned baccalaureate degree, of above-average academic ability (GPA of 2.75 or higher in the last 60 hours of undergraduate work or 3.2 or higher in at least 9 hours of graduate study), admitted to a graduate or first professional degree program at a participating institution in Illinois, in financial need, and a member of an underrepresented minority group—African Americans, Hispanics, Native Americans, and Asian Americans (but only in those disciplines where they are underrepresented). Financial need must be demonstrated.

Financial data The stipend is $10,000 per year for full-time study or $5,000 per year for part-time study. This is a fellowship/loan program. Award recipients must agree to accept a position, in teaching or administration, in an Illinois postsecondary educational institution, on an Illinois higher education governing or coordinating board staff, or as an employee in Illinois in an education-related capacity, for a period equal to the number of years of the award. Recipients failing to fulfill the conditions of the award are required to repay 20% of the total award.

Duration Up to 2 years for master's and professional degree students; up to 4 years for doctoral students.

Additional information The intent of this program is to increase the number of minorities employed in faculty and administrative positions in postsecondary institutions and in state agencies and governing boards in Illinois. It was established by the Illinois General Assembly in 1985 and may be utilized at any of the 34 participating institutions in Illinois.

Deadline February of each year.

[647]
INDIANA MINORITY TEACHER SCHOLARSHIP

State Student Assistance Commission of Indiana
ISTA Center Building
150 West Market Street, Suite 500
Indianapolis, IN 46204-2811
(317) 232-2350   (888) 528-4719 (within IN)
Fax: (317) 232-3260   E-mail: special@ssaci.state.in.us
Web: www.in.gov/ssaci/programs/m-teach.html

Purpose To provide scholarship/loans to Black and Hispanic undergraduate students in Indiana interested in preparing for a teaching career.

Eligibility This program is open to Black and Hispanic students who reside in Indiana and are enrolled or accepted for enrollment as full-time students in an academic institution in Indiana. Students who are already enrolled in college must have at least a 2.0 GPA. Applicants must be preparing to teach in an accredited elementary or secondary school in Indiana. U.S. citizenship is required. Financial need may be considered, but it is not a requirement. Preference is given to students enrolling in college for the first time.

Financial data Up to $1,000 annually; if students demonstrate financial need, they may receive up to $4,000 annually. Following graduation and teacher certification, recipients must teach full time in an elementary or secondary school in Indiana for 3 out of the next 5 years. If they fail to meet the teaching requirement, they are required to reimburse the state of Indiana for all funds received.

Duration 1 year; may be renewed up to 3 additional years if recipients maintain a 2.0 GPA. They may, however, take up to 6 years to complete the program from the start of receiving the first scholarship.

Additional information This program was established in 1988. Participating colleges in Indiana select the recipients. Students must submit their application to the financial aid office of the college they plan to attend (not to the State Student Assistance Commission of Indiana).

Number awarded Varies each year.

Deadline Each participating college or university establishes its filing deadline for this program.

[648]
INDIANA SPECIAL EDUCATION SERVICES SCHOLARSHIP

State Student Assistance Commission of Indiana
ISTA Center Building
150 West Market Street, Suite 500
Indianapolis, IN 46204-2811
(317) 232-2350   (888) 528-4719 (within IN)
Fax: (317) 232-3260   E-mail: special@ssaci.state.in.us
Web: www.in.gov/ssaci/programs/m-teach.html

Purpose To provide scholarship/loans to students in Indiana interested in preparing for a teaching career in the shortage area of special education and in the fields of occupational and physical therapy.

Eligibility This program is open to students seeking a special education teaching certification and students seeking an occupa-

tional or physical therapy certification. Applicants must be Indiana residents (residency is defined by the college the student plans to attend), be admitted to an eligible institution as a full-time student (or already attending as a full-time student), be planning to teach special education in an accredited elementary or secondary school in Indiana or practice occupational or physical therapy in the state, and—if already enrolled in college—have at least a 2.0 GPA. Individual colleges in Indiana are responsible for making the actual award. They may not base selection solely on merit. Financial need may be considered, but it is not a requirement. Preference is given to Black and Hispanic students and students enrolling in college for the first time.

Financial data The maximum scholarship is $1,000 per year; minority recipients who demonstrate financial need may receive up to $4,000 per year. Recipients must agree to enroll in a program leading to an Indiana teacher, occupational, or physical therapy certification and teach on a full-time basis in an accredited Indiana elementary or secondary school, or practice in the field of occupational or physical therapy in an accredited school, vocational rehabilitation center, or community mental retardation or other developmental disabilities center for 3 out of the first 5 years following certification. If they fail to meet that service requirement, they are required to reimburse the state of Indiana for all funds received.

Duration 1 year; may be renewed up to 3 additional years if recipients maintain a 2.0 GPA. They may, however, take up to 6 years to complete the program from the start of receiving the first scholarship.

Additional information This program's origins began in 1988 when the Indiana General Assembly moved to address the critical shortage of Black and Hispanic teachers in Indiana by establishing the Indiana Minority Teacher Scholarship program. In 1990 that program was amended to include special education and in 1991 the fields of occupational and physical therapy were added to make this a separate program not limited to minority students. Students must submit their application to the financial aid office of the college they plan to attend (not to the State Student Assistance Commission of Indiana).

Number awarded Varies each year.

Deadline Each participating college or university establishes its filing deadline for this program.

[649]
KANSAS TEACHER SERVICE SCHOLARSHIP

Kansas Board of Regents
Attn: Student Financial Aid
1000 S.W. Jackson Street, Suite 520
Topeka, KS 66612-1368
(785) 296-3518   Fax: (785) 296-0983
E-mail: dlindeman@ksbor.org
Web: www.kansasregents.com

Purpose To provide scholarship/loans to high school seniors, high school graduates, and selected undergraduates who are interested in preparing for a career as a teacher in Kansas.

Eligibility This program is open to Kansas residents who plan to enter the teaching profession in specific curriculum areas; recently, those included special education, mathematics, science, and secondary level foreign language. Applicants must submit evidence of completion of the Regents Scholars Curriculum (4 years of English, 3 years of mathematics, 3 years of science, 3 years of social studies, and 2 years of foreign language), ACT or SAT scores, high school GPA, high school class rank, and (if relevant) college transcripts and letters of recommendation from a college or university official. Special consideration is given to minority applicants, because minorities continue to be underrepresented in the teaching profession in Kansas schools. Second priority goes to students who have completed the Regents Recommended Curriculum and have competitive GPAs, ACT scores, and class rank.

Financial data Participants receive $5,000 per year. This is a scholarship/loan program. Recipients must teach in Kansas 1 year for every year of funding received, or they must repay the amount received with interest.

Duration 1 year; may be renewed for up to 3 additional years or up to 4 additional years for designated 5-year courses of study requiring graduate work. There is a $10 application fee.

Number awarded Approximately 100 each year.

Deadline March of each year.

[650]
KENTUCKY MINORITY EDUCATOR RECRUITMENT AND RETENTION SCHOLARSHIPS

Kentucky Department of Education
Attn: Division of Minority Educator Recruitment and
   Retention
500 Mero Street, 17th Floor
Frankfort, KY 40601
(502) 564-1479   Fax: (502) 564-6952
E-mail: dlhocken@kde.state.ky.us
Web: www.kde.state.ky.us

Purpose To provide forgivable loans to minority undergraduate and graduate students enrolled in Kentucky public institutions who want to become teachers.

Eligibility This program is open to residents of Kentucky who are undergraduate or graduate students pursuing initial teacher certification at a public institution in the state. Applicants must have a GPA of 2.5 or higher and either maintain full-time enrollment or be a part-time student within 18 semester hours of receiving a teacher education degree. U.S. citizenship is required.

Financial data Awards up to $5,000 per year are available. This is a scholarship/loan program. Recipients are required to teach 1 semester in Kentucky for each semester or summer term the scholarship is received. If they fail to fulfill that requirement, the scholarship converts to a loan at 12% interest.

Duration 1 year; may be renewed.

Additional information The Kentucky General Assembly established this program in 1992.

Number awarded Varies each year.

Deadline Each state college of teacher education sets its own deadline.

[651]
MENTAL HEALTH AND SUBSTANCE ABUSE CLINICAL FELLOWSHIP PROGRAM

Council on Social Work Education
Attn: Minority Fellowship Program
1725 Duke Street, Suite 500
Alexandria, VA 22314-3457
(703) 683-8080, ext. 217   Fax: (703) 683-8099
E-mail: mfp@cswe.org
Web: www.cswe.org

Purpose To provide forgivable loans to racial minority members

interested in preparing for a clinical career in the mental health fields.

Eligibility This program is open to U.S. citizens and permanent residents who have been underrepresented in the field of social work. These include but are not limited to the following groups: American Indians/Alaskan Natives, Asian/Pacific Islanders (e.g., Chinese, East Indians, South Asians, Filipinos, Hawaiians, Japanese, Koreans, and Samoans), Blacks, and Hispanics (e.g., Mexicans/Chicanos, Puerto Ricans, Cubans, Central or South Americans). Applicants must be interested in and committed to a career in mental health and/or substance abuse with specialization in the delivery of services of ethnic and racial minority groups. They must hold a master's degree in social work and be accepted to or enrolled in a full-time doctoral degree program.

Financial data Awards provide a stipend of $16,500 per year and tuition support to a maximum of $3,000.

Duration 1 academic year; renewable for 2 additional years if funds are available and the recipient makes satisfactory progress toward the degree objectives.

Additional information This program has been funded since 1978 by the Center for Mental Health Services of the Substance Abuse and Mental Health Services Administration.

Deadline February of each year.

[652]
MINORITY TEACHERS OF ILLINOIS SCHOLARSHIP PROGRAM

Illinois Student Assistance Commission
Attn: Scholarship and Grant Services
1755 Lake Cook Road
Deerfield, IL 60015-5209
(847) 948-8550   (800) 899-ISAC
Fax: (847) 831-8549   TDD: (847) 831-8326, ext. 2822
E-mail: cssupport@isac.org
Web: www.isac1.org/ilaid/mti.html

Purpose To provide scholarship/loans to minority students in Illinois who plan to become teachers at the preschool, elementary, or secondary level.

Eligibility Applicants must be Illinois residents, U.S. citizens or eligible noncitizens, members of a minority group (African American/Black, Hispanic American, Asian American, or Native American), and high school graduates or holders of a General Educational Development (GED) certificate. They must be enrolled in college full time at the sophomore level or above, have at least a 2.5 GPA, not be in default on any student loan, and be enrolled or accepted for enrollment in a teacher education program.

Financial data Grants up to $5,000 per year are awarded. This is a scholarship/loan program. Recipients must agree to teach full time 1 year for each year of support received. The teaching agreement may be fulfilled at a public, private, or parochial preschool, elementary school, or secondary school in Illinois; at least 30% of the student body at those schools must be minority. It must be fulfilled within the 5-year period following the completion of the undergraduate program for which the scholarship was awarded. The time period may be extended if the recipient serves in the U.S. armed forces, enrolls full time in a graduate program related to teaching, becomes temporarily disabled, is unable to find employment as a teacher at a qualifying school, or takes additional courses on at least a half-time basis to obtain certification as a teacher in Illinois. Recipients who fail to honor this work obligation must repay the award with 5% interest.

Duration 1 year.

Number awarded   Varies each year.

Deadline   April of each year.

[653]
MISSOURI MINORITY TEACHER EDUCATION SCHOLARSHIP PROGRAM

Missouri Department of Elementary and Secondary
   Education
P.O. Box 480
Jefferson City, MO 65102-0480
(573) 751-1668   E-mail: lharriso@mail.dese.state.mo.us
Web: www.dese.state.mo.us

Purpose   To provide scholarship/loans to minority high school seniors, high school graduates, and college students in Missouri who are interested in preparing for a teaching career in mathematics or science.

Eligibility   This program is open to Missouri residents who are African American, Asian American, Hispanic American, or Native American. Applicants must be 1) high school seniors, college students, or returning adults (without a degree) who ranked in the top 25% of their high school class and scored at or above the 75th percentile on the ACT or SAT examination; 2) individuals who have completed 30 college hours with a cumulative GPA of 3.0 or better; or 3) baccalaureate degree-holders who are returning to an approved mathematics or science program. All applicants must attend an approved teacher education program at a community college, 4-year college, or university in Missouri. Selection is based on high school class rank, ACT/SAT scores, school and community activities, interests, leadership skills, employment experience, desire to enter the field of education, and recommendations.

Financial data   The stipend is $3,000 per year. This is a scholarship/loan program. The amount of the recipient's potential obligation is reduced by 20% for each year of teaching science or mathematics in the state. Recipients who fail to honor part or all of the 5-year teaching requirement must repay the balance.

Duration   Up to 4 years.

Number awarded   100 each year.

Deadline   February of each year.

[654]
NATIONAL RESEARCH SERVICE AWARD SENIOR FELLOWSHIPS

National Institutes of Health
Division of Extramural Outreach and Information Resources
Attn: GrantsInfo
6701 Rockledge Drive, Suite 6095
Bethesda, MD 20892-7910
(301) 435-0714   Fax: (301) 480-8443
E-mail: GrantsInfo@nih.gov
Web: www.nih.gov

Purpose   To provide forgivable loans for mentored research training to experienced scientists who wish to make major changes in the direction of their research careers.

Eligibility   Applications for this program may be submitted on behalf of the candidates by a sponsoring institution, which may be private (profit or nonprofit) or public, including a federal laboratory. Individuals requesting foreign-site training must justify the particular suitability of the foreign site, based on the nature of the facilities and/or training opportunity, rather than a domestic institution. Only in cases where there are clear scientific advantages will foreign training be supported. Candidates must have received a Ph.D., D.D.S., D.M.D., or equivalent degree from an accredited domestic or foreign institution and must have had at least 7 subsequent years of relevant research experience. Applications from minorities and women are particularly encouraged.

Financial data   Salaries are determined individually, based on the salary or remuneration which the individual would have received from the home institution, but may not exceed $48,852 per year. Institutional allowances for tuition, fees, individual health insurance, research supplies, equipment, travel to scientific meetings, and related items are up to $5,500 for fellows at nonfederal, nonprofit, and foreign sponsoring institutions and $4,400 for fellows at for-profit institutions or federal laboratories. The initial 12 months of postdoctoral support carries a service payback requirement, which can be fulfilled by continued training under the award or by engaging in other health-related research training, health-related research, or health-related teaching. Fellows who fail to fulfill the payback requirement of 1 month of acceptable service for each month of the initial 12 months of support received must repay all funds received with interest.

Duration   5 years; nonrenewable.

Additional information   This program is offered by 8 components of the National Institutes of Health: the National Institute on Aging, the National Institute on Alcohol Abuse and Alcoholism, the National Institute of Allergy and Infectious Diseases, the National Institute of Arthritis and Musculoskeletal and Skin Diseases, the National Cancer Institute, the National Institute of Child Health and Human Development, the National Institute on Deafness and Other Communication Disorders, and the National Institute of Dental and Craniofacial Research.

Number awarded   Varies each year.

Deadline   April, August, or December of each year.

[655]
NATIONAL RESEARCH SERVICE AWARDS FOR INDIVIDUAL POSTDOCTORAL FELLOWS

National Institutes of Health
Division of Extramural Outreach and Information Resources
Attn: GrantsInfo
6701 Rockledge Drive, Suite 6095
Bethesda, MD 20892-7910
(301) 435-0714   Fax: (301) 480-8443
E-mail: GrantsInfo@nih.gov
Web: www.nih.gov

Purpose   To provide forgivable loans to postdoctoral scholars interested in pursuing research training in the biomedical or behavioral sciences.

Eligibility   Applicants must 1) be U.S. citizens or permanent residents; 2) have received a Ph.D., M.D., D.O., D.D.S., D.V.M., or equivalent doctoral degree from an accredited domestic or foreign institution; 3) be interested in conducting biomedical or behavioral research; and 4) have arranged for appointment to an appropriate institution and acceptance by a sponsor who will supervise the training and research experience. The institution may be private (nonprofit or for-profit) or public, including a federal laboratory. If a foreign institution is selected as the research training site, applicants must explain the reasons for the choice. Applications are especially encouraged from women, minorities, individuals with disabilities, and clinicians who wish to become researchers.

Financial data   The award provides an annual stipend based on the number of years of postdoctoral experience, ranging from

$31,092 for less than 1 year to $48,852 for 7 or more years. For fellows sponsored by domestic nonfederal institutions, the stipend is paid through the sponsoring institution; for fellows sponsored by federal or foreign institutions, the monthly stipend is paid directly to the fellow. Institutions also receive an allowance to help defray such awardee expenses as self-only health insurance, research supplies, equipment, travel to scientific meetings, and related items; the allowance is $5,500 per 12-month period for fellows at nonfederal, nonprofit, and foreign institutions and $4,400 per 12-month period at federal laboratories and for-profit institutions. In addition, tuition and fees are reimbursed at a rate of 100% up to $2,000 and 60% for costs above $2,000. Awards for training at a foreign site include economy or coach round-trip airfare for the fellow only; no allowance is provided for dependents. The initial 12 months of National Research Service Award postdoctoral support carries a service payback requirement, which can be fulfilled by continued training under the award or by engaging in other health-related research training, health-related research, or health-related teaching. Fellows who fail to fulfill the payback requirement of 1 month of acceptable service for each month of the initial 12 months of support received must repay all funds received with interest.

Duration Up to 3 years.

Additional information This award is offered by all funding Institutes and Centers of the National Institutes of Health (NIH) as part of the National Research Service Award (NRSA) program, originally established in 1974.

Number awarded Varies each year; recently, 793 awards were made through this program.

Deadline April, August, or December of each year.

[656]
NATIONAL SECURITY AGENCY UNDERGRADUATE TRAINING PROGRAM

National Security Agency
Manager, Undergraduate Training Program
Attn: S232R (UTP)
9800 Savage Road, Suite 6840
Fort Meade, MD 20755-6840
(410) 854-4725   (800) 669-0703
Web: www.nsa.gov

Purpose To provide minority and other high school seniors with scholarship/loans and work experience at the National Security Agency (NSA).

Eligibility This program is open to graduating high school seniors, particularly minorities, who are planning a college major in electrical or computer engineering, computer science, mathematics, or foreign languages (the particular languages vary; consult the agency to determine which languages it accepts at the time you apply). Minimum scores of 1100 on the SAT or 25 on the ACT are required. Applicants and immediate family members must be U.S. citizens and be eligible for a high-level security clearance.

Financial data Participants receive college tuition for 4 years, reimbursement for books and certain fees, a year-round salary, and a housing allowance and travel reimbursement during summer employment if the distance between the agency and school exceeds 75 miles. Following graduation, participants must work for the agency for 1 and a half times their length of study, usually 5 years. Students who leave agency employment earlier must repay the tuition cost.

Duration 4 years, followed by employment at the agency for 5 years.

Additional information Participants must attend classes full time and work at the agency during the summer in jobs tailored to their course of study. They must maintain at least a 3.0 GPA.

Number awarded Varies each year.

Deadline November of each year.

[657]
NEW MEXICO MINORITY DOCTORAL ASSISTANCE LOAN-FOR-SERVICE PROGRAM

New Mexico Commission on Higher Education
Attn: Financial Aid and Student Services
1068 Cerrillos Road
P.O. Box 15910
Santa Fe, NM 87506-5910
(505) 827-7383   (800) 279-9777
Fax: (505) 827-7392   E-mail: highered@che.state.nm.us
Web: www.nmche.org

Purpose To provide loans-for-service to underrepresented minorities and women who reside in New Mexico and are interested in working on a graduate degree in selected fields.

Eligibility Eligible to apply for this program are ethnic minorities and women who have received a baccalaureate and/or master's degree from a state-supported 4-year higher education institution in New Mexico; wish to pursue a doctoral degree at an eligible sponsoring New Mexico institution in mathematics, engineering, the physical or life sciences, or any other academic discipline in which ethnic minorities and women are demonstrably underrepresented in New Mexico colleges and universities; and are willing after obtaining their degree to teach at an institution of higher education in the state. Applicants must be U.S. citizens and New Mexico residents.

Financial data This is a loan-for-service program in which the amount of the loan (up to $25,000 per year) may be wholly or partially forgiven upon completion of service as a college instructor in New Mexico.

Duration 1 year; may be renewed for up to 2 additional years for students who enter with a master's degree or up to 3 additional years for students who begin with a baccalaureate degree.

Additional information Sponsoring institutions nominate candidates to the Commission on Higher Education for these awards. Recipients must agree to teach at the college/university level in New Mexico upon completion of their doctoral degree. If the sponsoring institution where the recipient completes the degree is unable to provide a tenure-track position, it must arrange placement at another alternate and mutually-acceptable New Mexico public postsecondary institution.

Number awarded Up to 12 each year.

Deadline March of each year.

[658]
NEW YORK STATE REGENTS HEALTH CARE SCHOLARSHIPS

New York State Education Department
Office of K-16 Initiatives and Access Programs
Attn: Scholarship Unit
Education Building Addition, Room 1078
Albany, NY 12234
(518) 486-1319   E-mail: kiap@mail.nysed.gov
Web: www.highered.nysed.gov/kiap/scholarships/rhc.htm

Purpose To provide fellowship/loans to minority or educationally disadvantaged students in New York who are entering or already enrolled in an approved program in medicine or dentistry.

Eligibility This program is open to U.S. citizens or permanent residents who are residents of New York. Applicants must be interested in studying full time at an approved New York State medical or dental school. The law requires that awards be made to eligible candidates in the following order: first priority is given to candidates who are economically disadvantaged and a minority group member historically underrepresented in the professions; second priority is given to candidates who are a minority group member historically underrepresented in the professions; and third priority is given to any candidate who is enrolled in or a graduate of 1 of these state-supported opportunity programs: Search for Education, Elevation and Knowledge (SEEK) or College Discovery at City University; Educational Opportunity Program (EOP) in the State University system; or Higher Education Opportunity Program (HEOP) at an independent college. For purposes of this program, underrepresented minorities include African Americans, Hispanics, Native Americans, and Alaskan Natives. Students are considered economically disadvantaged if they are a member of 1) a household supported by 1 parent if dependent, by the student or by a spouse if independent, whose total annual income is less than specified levels that range from $10,750 for a family of 1 to $40,150 for a family of 7; 2) a household supported by more than 1 worker (parent if dependent, student and spouse if independent) in which the total annual income does not exceed the specified levels by more than $2,700; or 3) a household supported by 1 worker (parent if dependent, student if independent) who is the sole support of a 1-parent family in which the total annual income does not exceed the specified levels by more than $2,700.

Financial data Scholarship holders receive from $1,000 to $10,000 per year, depending on income. No award can exceed the actual cost of attendance. After completion of their professional studies, scholarship holders are required to practice 12 months for each annual payment received, including at least 24 months in a designated physician-shortage area in New York. If they fail to comply with the service commitment requirements, they must repay the full amount of the scholarship plus interest within 5 years.

Duration Up to 4 years.

Additional information Information is also available from the New York State Higher Education Services Corporation, 99 Washington Avenue, Albany, NY 12255, (518) 473-1574, (888) NYS-HESC, Fax: (518) 473-3749, TDD: (800) 445-5234, E-mail: webmail@hesc.com.

Number awarded Varies each year; recently, more than 90 students received more than $893,000 in assistance through this program.

Deadline April of each year.

[659]
NEW YORK STATE REGENTS PROFESSIONAL OPPORTUNITY SCHOLARSHIPS

New York State Education Department
Office of K-16 Initiatives and Access Programs
Attn: Scholarship Unit
Education Building Addition, Room 1078
Albany, NY 12234
(518) 486-1319   E-mail: kiap@mail.nysed.gov
Web: www.highered.nysed.gov/kiap/scholarships/pos.htm

Purpose To provide forgivable loans to underrepresented minority and economically disadvantaged students in New York who are interested in preparing for selected professional careers.

Eligibility Candidates must be U.S. citizens or permanent residents and legal residents of New York for 1 year prior to application. The law requires that awards be made to eligible candidates in the following order: first priority is given to candidates who are economically disadvantaged and a minority group member historically underrepresented in the professions; second priority is given to candidates who are a minority group member historically underrepresented in the professions; and third priority is given to candidates who are enrolled in or a graduate of 1 of these state-supported opportunity programs: Search for Education, Elevation and Knowledge (SEEK) or College Discovery at City University; Educational Opportunity Program (EOP) in the State University system; or Higher Education Opportunity Program (HEOP) at an independent college. Scholarships are available for study in the following areas: accounting (bachelor's level), acupuncture (master's), architecture (bachelor's or master's), athletic trainer (bachelor's), audiology (master's), chiropractic medicine (doctoral), dental hygiene (associate), dietetics/nutrition (associate or bachelor's), engineering (bachelor's), interior design (bachelor's), landscape architecture (bachelor's or master's), law (juris doctoral), massage therapy (associate), midwifery (master's), nurse practitioner (master's), nursing (bachelor's), occupational therapy assistant (associate), occupational therapy (bachelor's or master's), ophthalmic dispensing (associate), optometry (doctoral), pharmacy (bachelor's or doctoral), physical therapy assistant (associate), physical therapy (bachelor's or master's), registered physician assistant (associate, bachelor's, or master's), podiatry (doctoral), psychology (doctoral), social work (master's), speech language pathology (masters), veterinary medicine (doctoral), and veterinary technology (associate or bachelor's). For purposes of this program, underrepresented minorities include African Americans, Hispanics, Native Americans, and Alaskan Natives. Students are considered economically disadvantaged if they are a member of 1) a household supported by 1 parent if dependent, by the student or by a spouse if independent, whose total annual income is less than specified levels that range from $10,750 for a family of 1 to $40,150 for a family of 7; 2) a household supported by more than 1 worker (parent if dependent, student and spouse if independent) in which the total annual income does not exceed the specified levels by more than $2,700; or 3) a household supported by 1 worker (parent if dependent, student if independent) who is the sole support of a 1-parent family in which the total annual income does not exceed the specified levels by more than $2,700.

Financial data The stipends range from $1,000 to $5,000 per year, depending on income. No award can exceed the actual cost of attendance. After completion of their professional studies, scholarship holders are required to practice in New York for 12 months for each annual payment received. If they do not comply with the service commitment requirements, they must repay the full amount of the scholarship monies plus penalty and interest within 5 years.

Duration Up to 4 years (or 5 years for certain programs), within a 7-year period.

Additional information Information is also available from the New York State Higher Education Services Corporation, 99 Washington Avenue, Albany, NY 12255, (518) 473-1574, (888) NYS-HESC, Fax: (518) 473-3749, TDD: (800) 445-5234, E-mail: webmail@hesc.com.

Number awarded Varies each year; recently, nearly 600 students received more than $2.3 million in assistance through this program.

Deadline April of each year.

[660]
NORTH CAROLINA TEACHING FELLOWS SCHOLARSHIP PROGRAM

North Carolina Teaching Fellows Commission
Koger Center, Cumberland Building
3739 National Drive, Suite 210
Raleigh, NC 27612
(919) 781-6833   Fax: (919) 781-6527
E-mail: tfellows@ncforum.org
Web: www.teachingfellows.org

Purpose To provide scholarship/loans to high school seniors in North Carolina who wish to prepare for a career in teaching.

Eligibility This program is open to seniors at high schools in North Carolina who are interested in preparing for a career as a teacher and have been accepted for enrollment at a participating school in the state. Applicants must demonstrate superior achievement on the basis of high school grades, class standing, SAT scores, a writing sample, community service, extracurricular activities, and references from teachers and members of the community. U.S. citizenship is required. A particular goal of the program is to recruit and retain greater numbers of male and minority teacher education candidates in North Carolina.

Financial data The maximum stipend is $6,500 per year. This is a scholarship/loan program; recipients must teach in a North Carolina public school 1 year for each year of support received. If they cannot fulfill the service requirement, they must repay the loan with 10% interest.

Duration 1 year; renewable for up to 3 additional years if the recipient maintains full-time enrollment and a GPA of 2.25 or higher for the freshman year and 2.50 or higher in the sophomore year.

Additional information The participating schools are Appalachian State University, East Carolina University, Elon College, Meredith College, North Carolina A&T State University, University of North Carolina at Asheville, North Carolina Central University, North Carolina State University, University of North Carolina at Pembroke, University of North Carolina at Chapel Hill, University of North Carolina at Charlotte, University of North Carolina at Greensboro, University of North Carolina at Wilmington, and Western Carolina University. This program was established in 1986 and the first fellows were named in 1987.

Number awarded Up to 400 each year. Approximately 20% of the program's recipients are minority and 30% are male.

Deadline October of each year.

[661]
NORTH CAROLINA UNDERGRADUATE NURSE SCHOLARS PROGRAM

North Carolina State Education Assistance Authority
Attn: Scholarship and Grant Services
10 T.W. Alexander Drive
P.O. Box 14103
Research Triangle Park, NC 27709-4103
(919) 549-8614   (800) 700-1775
Fax: (919) 549-8481   E-mail: information@ncseaa.edu
Web: www.ncseaa.edu

Purpose To provide scholarship/loans to students in North Carolina who wish to prepare for a career in nursing.

Eligibility Applicants must be high school seniors, high school graduates, or currently-enrolled college students who are U.S. citizens, North Carolina residents, and interested in becoming a nurse. Students must plan to enter a North Carolina college, university, or hospital that prepares students for licensure as a registered nurse. Applications are encouraged from nontraditional students, including older individuals, ethnic minorities, males, and individuals with previous careers and/or degrees who are pursuing nurse education. U.S. citizenship and full-time enrollment are required. Selection is based on academic achievement, leadership potential, and the promise of service as a registered nurse in North Carolina; financial need is not considered.

Financial data Annual stipends are $3,000 for candidates for an associate degree, $3,000 for registered nurses completing a B.S.N. degree, $3,000 for community college transfer students and juniors in a B.S.N. program, or $5,000 for freshmen and nontraditional students in a B.S.N. program. This is a scholarship/loan program; 1 year of full-time work as a nurse in North Carolina cancels 1 year of support under this program. Recipients who fail to honor the work obligation must repay the balance plus 10% interest.

Duration 1 year; may be renewed 1 additional year by candidates for an associate degree, registered nurses completing a B.S.N. degree, and community college transfer students and juniors in a B.S.N. program, or for 3 additional years by freshmen and nontraditional students in a B.S.N. program.

Additional information The North Carolina General Assembly created this program in 1989; the first recipients were funded for the 1990-91 academic year.

Number awarded Varies; generally, up to 600 new undergraduate degree awards are made each year. Recently, a total of 795 students were receiving $3,141,939 through this program.

Deadline February of each year for B.S.N. programs; May of each year for A.D.N. and diploma students and for R.N.s entering a B.S.N. completion program.

[662]
NORTH DAKOTA DEPARTMENT OF TRANSPORTATION EDUCATIONAL GRANTS

North Dakota Department of Transportation
503 38th Street South
Fargo, ND 58103-1198
(701) 239-8900   Fax: (701) 239-8915
TTY: (701) 328-4156
Web: www.discovernd.com/dot

Purpose To provide forgivable loans to undergraduates in North Dakota colleges and universities who are majoring in fields related to the needs and missions of the North Dakota Department of Transportation.

Eligibility This program is open to students who are attending an institution of higher learning in North Dakota, have completed 1 year of study, and are majoring in civil engineering, survey technology, construction engineering, or other field that meets the needs and missions of the department. Current department employees are also eligible for aid if they have completed 1 year of study or have worked for the department as a classified employee for at least 2 years. All applicants must be attending a college or university in North Dakota. Priority is given to students who are available for summer employment with the department. Women and minorities are particularly encouraged to apply. Selection is based on: potential to contribute to the department's program, financial need, academic achievement, and relevant experience.

Financial data The maximum stipend is $2,000 per year. These are forgivable loans. Recipients who fail to honor their work obligation must repay the grant on a prorated basis at 6% interest. Funds must be used only for educational expenses, including tuition, required fees, books, materials, and necessary personal expenses while attending college.

Duration 1 year; may be renewed up to 2 additional years. Upon graduation, recipients must agree to work for the department for a period of time at least equal to the grant study period.

Number awarded Varies each year.

[663]
OLD DOMINION UNIVERSITY PRESIDENT'S GRADUATE FELLOWSHIP

Old Dominion University
Attn: Office of Research and Graduate Studies
New Administration Building, Room 210
Norfolk, VA 23529-0013
(757) 683-3460   Fax: (757) 683-3004
Web: www.odu.edu/ao/research/pres.htm

Purpose To provide forgivable loans to minorities and women working toward their terminal degree who are willing to serve in a tenure-track faculty position at Old Dominion University.

Eligibility This program is open to women and minorities who show strong potential for success in advanced graduate study and whose academic disciplines correspond to the programmatic needs of Old Dominion University. Candidates may be undergraduate or master's-level students. They must be enrolled in or accepted into a graduate program leading to a terminal degree (generally at a university other than Old Dominion). All applicants must be U.S. citizens. Fellowships are awarded on the basis of their potential to contribute to their chosen discipline as a faculty member at Old Dominion.

Financial data Participants are given a non-tenure track faculty appointment with the appropriate academic department at Old Dominion University. Financial support includes payment of tuition and fees plus a stipend, normally $20,000 per year. The combined annual award for stipend and educational expenses cannot exceed $30,000. Every recipient is required to sign a program agreement with Old Dominion University that contains, among other items, an interest-bearing promissory note that will be cancelled upon successful completion of 3 years of employment with the university in a tenure-track faculty position. If a fellow fails to complete the degree within the program terms, or serves the university for fewer than 3 years because of unsatisfactory performance resulting in either involuntary or voluntary termination of employment, the portion of the note and interest which remains unfilled must be repaid.

Duration Up to 3 years. An extension of up to 2 years before joining the faculty may be granted but without financial support.

Additional information Upon completion of the terminal degree, fellows must assume a tenure-track position in the designated department at Old Dominion University.

Deadline January of each year.

[664]
PAT AND DICK HAZEL MINORITY SCHOLARSHIP AWARD

Community Foundation of the Eastern Shore, Inc.
200 West Main Street
P.O. Box 156
Salisbury, MD 21803-0152
(410) 742-9911   Fax: (410) 742-6638

Purpose To provide scholarship/loans to minority high school seniors who are preparing for a teaching career in selected counties of Maryland.

Eligibility This program is open to minority residents of Wicomico, Somerset, and Worcester counties, in Maryland. Applicants must be high school seniors who have been admitted as a full-time student by a college or university in Maryland or Delaware. They must be planning for a career as a teacher and must indicate a willingness to teach for 2 years in the 3 counties following graduation. The application package must include a completed application form, a 1-page essay on why they want to teach, official high school transcripts, the letter of acceptance from their college or university, a summary of financial assistance from their college or university's financial aid office, a copy of their parents' or guardian's most recent income tax return, and 2 letters of recommendation. Selection is based on financial need, community involvement, academic achievement, and extracurricular activities.

Financial data Generally, annual stipends not do exceed $2,000. Funds are paid to the recipient's school and must be used for tuition, fees, and books.

Duration 1 year; may be renewed if the recipient continues to meet eligibility requirements and maintains a GPA of 2.5 or higher.

Deadline April of each year.

[665]
PRESBYTERIAN CHURCH CONTINUING EDUCATION GRANT AND LOAN PROGRAM

Presbyterian Church (USA)
Attn: Office of Financial Aid for Studies
100 Witherspoon Street, Room M042
Louisville, KY 40202-1396
(502) 569-5735   (877) 728-7228, ext. 5735
Fax: (502) 569-8766   E-mail: LBryan@ctr.pcusa.org
Web: www.pcusa.org/highered

Purpose To provide financial assistance for continuing education, in the form of educational grants and loans, to professional church workers of the Presbyterian Church (USA) who are employed by small congregations, women, and racial/ethnic minorities.

Eligibility This program provides grants and loans for postgraduate study and professional development to professional church staff members employed by Presbyterian Church (USA) congregations with 150 members or less. Continuing education loans (but not grants) for postgraduate study and professional development are also available for professional church staff members employed by congregations larger than 150 members. Applicants must be 1) enrolled at least part time at an accredited institution or attending a PCUSA sponsored training event, and 2) endorsed by their session or the moderator of their committee on ministry. The program also provides continuing education grants and loans for postgraduate religious studies to women and racial ethnic minorities. Applicants must be enrolled at least part time, members of a Presbyterian Church (USA) congregation, and endorsed by their session or the moderator of their committee on ministry.

Financial data Grants for degree students range from $500 to $1,000 per year and for non-degree students from $100 to $500 per year. The maximum loan is $2,000 per year.

Duration 1 year. Professionals at small churches are eligible for unlimited renewal of grants. Women and racial ethnic minorities are eligible for a total of 4 grants. Loans may be renewed to a maximum of $6,000.

Number awarded Varies each year.

[666]
PRIMARY CARE RESOURCE INITIATIVE FOR MISSOURI

Missouri Department of Health
Attn: Health Systems Development Unit
P.O. Box 570
Jefferson City, MO 65102-0570
(573) 751-6400   (800) 891-7415
Fax: (573) 751-6010
Web: www.health.state.mo.us

Purpose To provide scholarship/loans to residents of Missouri who are interested in working as a health care professional in an underserved area of the state following graduation.

Eligibility This program is open to residents of Missouri who have lived for 1 or more years in the state for purposes other than attending an educational institution. Applicants must have been accepted by or currently be attending a school offering a course of study leading to a degree as a doctor of allopathic (M.D.) or osteopathic (D.O.) medicine; a bachelor of science (B.S.) degree in a field leading to acceptance into a school of medicine; or a bachelor of master of science (B.S.N. or M.S.N.) degree leading to certification as a primary care advanced practice nurse as a pediatric, family, adult, or geriatric practitioner. Physicians in primary care residency programs are also eligible. Priority is given to residents of medically underserved areas in Missouri, minority group members, and previous recipients.

Financial data For undergraduate (B.S. or B.S.N.) and master's (M.S.N.) students, the maximum loan is $5,000 per year for full-time enrollment or $3,000 per year for part-time enrollment. Master's in nursing students are also eligible for a 1-time loan of $5,000 to cover the expenses of a preceptorship for the nurse practitioner. Medical (M.D. or D.O.) students are eligible for loans in the amount of tuition, to a maximum of $20,000 per year. Physicians in primary care residency programs are eligible for loans of $10,000 per year. This is a scholarship/loan program. Loans of 5 years or more are forgiven at the rate of 20% per year for qualifying employment in an area of defined need (a geographic area or a population that is experiencing a shortage of primary health care providers in Missouri). Loans for less than 5 years are forgiven on a year-for-year basis. If the loan is not forgiven by service, it must be repaid within 48 months at 9.5% interest.

Duration Full-time undergraduate students may receive up to 4 loans; part-time undergraduates may receive up to 6 loans. Full-time M.S.N. students may receive up to 2 loans; part-time M.S.N. students may receive up to 4 loans. Medical students may receive loans for up to 4 years. Physicians in primary care residency programs may receive up to 3 years of loans.

Additional information This program is also known as the PRIMO Loan Program.

Number awarded Varies each year.

Deadline July of each year.

[667]
SOUTHEASTERN NEW MEXICO TEACHERS' LOAN-FOR-SERVICE PROGRAM

New Mexico Commission on Higher Education
Attn: Financial Aid and Student Services
1068 Cerrillos Road
P.O. Box 15910
Santa Fe, NM 87506-5910
(505) 827-7383   (800) 279-9777
Fax: (505) 827-7392   E-mail: highered@che.state.nm.us
Web: www.nmche.org

Purpose To provide scholarship/loans to underrepresented minority and disabled residents of designated counties in southeastern New Mexico who are interested in becoming teachers in that area.

Eligibility Eligible to apply for this program are underrepresented minorities and people with disabilities who are current or former residents of Lea, Otero, Eddy, Chaves, or Roosevelt counties in New Mexico. Applicants must intend to provide service at public schools in 1 of those counties and must be U.S. citizens or permanent residents.

Financial data This is a scholarship/loan program in which the amount of the loan (up to $4,000 per year, depending on financial need) may be wholly or partially forgiven upon completion of service as an educator in the designated New Mexico counties as follows: for the first year served, all interest then accrued plus 15% of the principal; for the second year served, all interest then accrued plus 20% of the original principal; for the third year served, all interest then accrued plus 30% of the original principal; for the fourth year served, all interest then accrued plus the remaining principal balance. Recipients who complete their professional education and do not serve in a designated county are assessed a penalty of 18% interest.

Duration 1 year; may be renewed.

Number awarded Varies each year.

Deadline June of each year.

[668]
TENNESSEE MINORITY TEACHING FELLOWS PROGRAM

Tennessee Student Assistance Corporation
Parkway Towers
404 James Robertson Parkway, Suite 1950
Nashville, TN 37243-0820
(615) 741-1346   (800) 342-1663
Fax: (615) 741-6101   E-mail: tsac@mail.state.tn.us
Web: www.state.tn.us/tsac

Purpose To provide scholarship/loans to minority Tennesseans who wish to enter the teaching field.

Eligibility This program is open to minority residents of Tennessee who are either 1) entering freshmen with a high school GPA of 2.75 or higher or 2) continuing college students with a college GPA of 2.5 or higher. All applicants must have been in the top 25% of their high school class and have scored at least 850 on the SAT or 18 on the ACT. They must be attending a college or university in Tennessee and agree to teach at the K-12 level in a Tennessee public school following graduation from college.

Financial data The scholarship/loan is $5,000 per year. Recipients incur an obligation to teach at the K-12 level in a Tennessee public school 1 year for each year the award is received.

Duration 1 year; may be renewed for up to 3 additional years.

Additional information This program was established in 1989.

Number awarded Varies each year.

Deadline April of each year.

[669]
TEXAS DEPARTMENT OF TRANSPORTATION CONDITIONAL GRANT PROGRAM

Texas Department of Transportation
Attn: Employment Opportunities Section
125 East 11th Street
Austin, TX 78701-2483
(512) 416-4976
Web: www.dot.state.tx.us

Purpose To provide scholarship/loans to minorities and women in Texas who are interested in majoring in designated areas and then working for the Texas Department of Transportation.

Eligibility This program is open to minorities (Black, Hispanic, American Indian, Asian, Pacific Islander) and women who are residents of Texas. High school applicants must have a GPA of 3.0 or higher or at least 850 on the SAT or 21 on the ACT; plan to attend an accredited 4-year public college or university in Texas as a full-time student; plan to major in civil engineering; be willing to work for the Texas Department of Transportation for at least 2 years after graduation; and not be more than 30 days delinquent on any child support obligation. College or university applicants must have a GPA of 2.5 or higher; be attending a 4-year public college or university in Texas; be taking at least 12 hours per semester; have declared a major in civil engineering; be willing to work for the Texas Department of Transportation for at least 2 years after graduation; not be in repayment status for a previously-awarded Conditional Grant; and be no more than 30 days delinquent on any child support obligation.

Financial data The grant covers tuition, fees and a stipend, up to a maximum of $3,000 per semester or $6,000 per year. The exact amount awarded is based on the recipient's documented financial need. This is a scholarship/loan program. Recipients must repay the full amount of the grant if they fail to graduate, or maintain a cumulative GPA of 2.5 or higher, or stay in school, or stay in an approved major, or work for the Texas Department of Transportation for the required period of time.

Duration 1 year; may be renewed.

Additional information Recipients must attend school on a full-time basis (at least 12 hours per semester), maintain a GPA of 2.5 or higher, graduate in an approved major, and work for the Texas Department of Transportation for at least 2 years.

Number awarded Varies each year.

Deadline February of each year.

[670]
THOMAS R. PICKERING FOREIGN AFFAIRS FELLOWSHIPS

Woodrow Wilson National Fellowship Foundation
Attn: Foreign Affairs Fellowship Program
5 Vaughn Drive, Suite 300
P.O. Box 2437
Princeton, NJ 08543-2437
(609) 452-7007 Fax: (609) 452-0066
E-mail: pickeringfaf@woodrow.org
Web: www.woodrow.org/public-policy

Purpose To provide forgivable loans for study and work experience to undergraduate students interested in preparing for a career with the Department of State's Foreign Service.

Eligibility Applicants must be U.S. citizens in the sophomore year of undergraduate study at an accredited college or university with a cumulative GPA of 3.2 or higher. They must plan to pursue graduate study in the field of international affairs and a career in the Foreign Service. Selection is based on strength of undergraduate course work, financial need, college honors and awards, and participation and leadership in extracurricular and community activities. Women and members of minority groups historically underrepresented in the Foreign Service are especially encouraged to apply.

Financial data The award includes tuition, room, board, and mandatory fees during the final 2 years of undergraduate study and the first year of graduate work. The cost of books and 1 round trip are reimbursed. The graduate institution provides similar support during the second year of graduate study, depending upon financial need. For the summer institute and the internships, travel expenses and stipends are paid. The overseas internship includes medical insurance. Married fellows receive additional funding for university room and board, but they are responsible for travel and accommodations for their spouse and family during the institute and the internships.

Duration 4 years: the final 2 years of undergraduate study and the first 2 years of graduate work (provided the student maintains at least a 3.2 GPA).

Additional information During the summer between their junior and senior years, fellows attend a 7-week summer institute at 1 of 5 participating graduate schools of public policy and international affairs. They take courses in economics, calculus, and policy analysis, along with exercises to develop oral and written communication skills. During summers of the graduate portion of the program, fellows participate in 1 overseas and 1 domestic internship within the U.S. Department of State. This program is funded by the State Department and administered by the Woodrow Wilson National Fellowship Foundation. It was formerly known as the U.S. Department of State Foreign Affairs Fellowship Program Fellows must commit to a minimum of 4 and a half years of service in an appointment as a Foreign Service Officer following the second year of graduate study. Candidates who do not successfully complete the program and Foreign Service entry requirements may be subject to a reimbursement obligation to the Department of State.

Number awarded Approximately 10 each year.

Deadline February of each year.

[671]
THOMAS R. PICKERING GRADUATE FOREIGN AFFAIRS FELLOWSHIPS

Woodrow Wilson National Fellowship Foundation
Attn: Foreign Affairs Fellowship Program
5 Vaughn Drive, Suite 300
P.O. Box 2437
Princeton, NJ 08543-2437
(609) 452-7007   Fax: (609) 452-0066
E-mail: pickeringfaf@woodrow.org
Web: www.woodrow.org/public-policy

Purpose To provide forgivable loans for study and work experience to graduate students interested in pursuing a career with the Department of State's Foreign Service.

Eligibility This program is open to U.S. citizens who are applying to a 2-year full-time master's degree program, such as public policy, international affairs, public administration, or such academic fields as business, economics, foreign languages, political science, or sociology. Applicants must have a minimum undergraduate cumulative GPA of at least 3.2. They must plan to pursue a career in the Foreign Service. Selection is based on leadership skills, academic achievement, and financial need. Women, members of minority groups historically underrepresented in the Foreign Service, and students with financial need are especially encouraged to apply.

Financial data Tuition, room, board, and mandatory fees are paid, along with reimbursement for books and 1 round trip. Fellows also receive stipends for participation in the internships.

Duration 2 years (provided the student maintains a GPA of 3.2 or higher).

Additional information Graduate fellows participate in 1 domestic summer internship between the first and second year of graduate school and 1 summer overseas internship following the second year of graduate school. This program is funded by the State Department and administered by the Woodrow Wilson National Fellowship Foundation. Fellows must commit to a minimum of 3 years of service in an appointment as a Foreign Service Officer following the second year of graduate study. Candidates who do not successfully complete the program and Foreign Service entry requirements may be subject to a reimbursement obligation to the Department of State.

Number awarded Varies each year, depending on the availability of funding.

Deadline February of each year.

[672]
UNDERGRADUATE SCHOLARSHIP PROGRAM FOR INDIVIDUALS FROM DISADVANTAGED BACKGROUNDS

National Institutes of Health
Attn: Loan Repayment and Scholarship Programs
7550 Wisconsin Avenue, Room 604
Bethesda, MD 20892-9121
(800) 528-7689   Fax: (301) 480-5481
TTY: (888) 352-3001   E-mail: kk10b@nih.gov
Web: www.nih.gov

Purpose To provide loans-for-service for undergraduate education in the life sciences to students from disadvantaged backgrounds.

Eligibility Eligible are U.S. citizens, nationals, and permanent residents who are enrolled or accepted for enrollment as full-time students at accredited institutions of higher education and planning to pursue a career in biomedical research. To qualify as disadvantaged, applicants must come from either 1) an environment that inhibited (but did not prevent) them from obtaining the knowledge, skills, and ability required to enroll in an undergraduate institution; or 2) a family with an annual income below $10,900 for a 1-person family, ranging to below $28,500 for families of 6 or more. Students who do not meet the family income requirement may provide a personal statement explaining why they still qualify as disadvantaged (e.g., underrepresented minority, person with a disability). All applicants must have a GPA of 3.5 or higher or be in the top 5% of their class. They are ranked according to the following priorities: first, juniors and seniors who have completed 2 years of undergraduate course work; second, other undergraduates who have completed 4 core science courses in biology, chemistry, physics, and calculus; third, freshmen and sophomores at accredited undergraduate institutions; and fourth, high school seniors who have been accepted for enrollment as full-time students at accredited undergraduate institutions.

Financial data Stipends are available up to $20,000 per year, to be used for tuition, educational expenses (such as books and lab fees), and qualified living expenses while attending a college or university. Recipients incur a service obligation to work as an employee of the National Institutes of Health (NIH) in Bethesda, Maryland for 10 consecutive weeks (during the summer) during the sponsored year and, upon graduation, for 12 months for each academic year of scholarship support. The NIH 12-month employment obligation may be deferred if the recipient goes to graduate or medical school.

Duration 1 year; may be renewed for up to 3 additional years.

Number awarded 15 each year.

Deadline March of each year.

[673]
VIRGINIA MEDICAL SCHOLARSHIP PROGRAM

Virginia Department of Health
Attn: Center for Primary Care and Rural Health
1500 East Main Street, Suite 227
Richmond, VA 23219
(804) 786-4891   Fax: (804) 371-0116
Web: www.vdh.state.va.us

Purpose To provide loans-for-service to medical students who are willing to practice as primary care physicians in Virginia.

Eligibility This program is open to medical students pursuing primary care medical education at designated schools in Virginia and Tennessee. Graduate medical students in the first year of a primary care residency are also eligible. Primary care specialties include family practice, general internal medicine, pediatrics, and obstetrics/gynecology. Applicants must intend to practice in underserved areas within Virginia. Preference is given to residents of Virginia, residents from rural and medically underserved areas, and minority students.

Financial data The maximum assistance is $10,000 per year. Repayment begins after completion of a 3-year residency (or 4 years for obstetrics/gynecology). Repayment is made through practice as a primary care physician in Virginia Medically Underserved Areas (VMUAs) designated by the Board of Health.

Duration 1 year; may be renewed for up to 4 additional years, for a total loan of $50,000.

Additional information The designated schools are Eastern Virginia Medical School of the Medical College of Hampton Roads (Norfolk, Virginia), the University of Virginia School of Medicine (Charlottesville, Virginia), the Medical College of Virginia of the Virginia Commonwealth University (Richmond, Virginia), James H. Quillen College of Medicine of East Tennessee State University (Johnson City, Tennessee), and Pikeville College School of Osteopathic Medicine (Pikeville, Kentucky).

Number awarded Varies each year; 4 scholarships are set aside for East Tennessee State University and the number assigned to the 3 Virginia schools is determined by the funding provided by the Virginia General Assembly.

Deadline Deadlines are established by the directors of financial aid at the participating medical schools.

[674]
VIRGINIA NURSE PRACTITIONER/NURSE MIDWIFE SCHOLARSHIP PROGRAM

Virginia Department of Health
Attn: Center for Primary Care and Rural Health
1500 East Main Street, Suite 227
P.O. Box 2448
Richmond, VA 23218
(804) 371-4090   Fax: (804) 371-0116
Web: www.vdh.state.va.us

Purpose To provide forgivable loans to nursing students in Virginia who are willing to work as nurse practitioners and/or midwives in the state following graduation.

Eligibility This program is open to residents of Virginia who are enrolled or accepted for enrollment full time at a nurse practitioner program in the state or a nurse midwifery program in a nearby state. Applicants must have a cumulative GPA of at least 3.0 in undergraduate and/or graduate courses. Preference is given to 1) residents of designated medically underserved areas of Virginia; 2) students enrolled in family practice, obstetrics and gynecology, pediatric, adult health, and geriatric nurse practitioner programs; and 3) minority students. Selection is based on scholastic achievement, character, and state commitment to postgraduate employment in a medically underserved area of Virginia.

Financial data The amount of the award depends on the availability of funds. Recipients must agree to serve in a designated medically underserved area of Virginia for a period of years equal to the number of years of scholarship support received. The required service must begin within 2 years of the recipient's graduation and must be in a facility that provides services to persons who are unable to pay for the service and that participates in all government-sponsored insurance programs designed to assure full access to medical care service for covered persons. If the recipient fails to complete the course of study, or pass the licensing examination, or provide the required service, all scholarship funds received must be repaid with interest.

Duration 1 year; may be renewed for 1 additional year.

Number awarded Varies each year.

Deadline June of each year.

[675]
VIRGINIA TEACHER SCHOLARSHIP LOAN PROGRAM

Virginia Department of Education
101 North 14th Street
P.O. Box 2120
Richmond, VA 23218-2120
(804) 371-2522   (800) 292-3820
Fax: (804) 786-6759
Web: www.pen.k12.va.us/VDOE/newvdoe/vtslp.htm

Purpose To provide scholarship/loans to students in Virginia who are interested in a career in teaching.

Eligibility Full-time students who are Virginia residents and juniors or seniors in a state-approved teacher preparation program in Virginia with a minimum GPA of 2.7 are eligible for this program. Males interested in teaching at the elementary and middle school levels and minorities in all teaching areas also qualify. Recipients must agree to engage in full-time teaching in designated teacher shortage areas within Virginia following graduation.

Financial data The scholarship/loan is $3,720 per year. Loans are forgiven at the rate of $2,000 for each year the recipient teaches in designated teacher shortage areas. If the recipient fails to fulfill the teaching service requirement, the loan must be repaid with interest.

Duration 1 year; may be renewed 1 additional year.

Additional information Critical shortage teaching areas in Virginia are currently identified as foreign languages (Italian, Latin, Russian, Chinese, and other Asian languages), science (chemistry, earth science, space science, and physics), all areas of special education (emotionally disturbed, hearing impaired, learning disabled, mental retardation, severely/profoundly disabled, visually impaired, early childhood special education, and speech-language pathology), technology education, and mathematics.

Number awarded 100 each year. Recently, that included 38 in special education, 20 males in elementary education, 17 minorities, 10 in mathematics, 6 in science, 7 in foreign languages, and 2 in technology education.

[676]
WELLS FARGO LATINO BUSINESS LOAN PROGRAM

Wells Fargo Bank
Attn: National Business Banking Center
P.O. Box 340214
Sacramento, CA 95834-0214
(800) 35-WELLS, ext. 350
Web: www.wellsfargo.com

Purpose To loan money to Latinos who own businesses.

Eligibility To qualify for a loan, Latino business owners must have a satisfactory personal and business credit history, have been in business for at least 3 years, have a profitable business with sufficient cash flow to meet their new and current financial obligations, and have not declared bankruptcy in the past 10 years. Applicants may be interested in 1) an unsecured, revolving line of credit; 2) financing for new and used machinery, equipment, and vehicles; or 3) equity loans or lines of credit secured by commercial real estate.

Financial data This program offers unsecured, revolving lines of credit up to $100,000, equipment loans up to $50,000, and equity loans from $25,000 to $250,000. Interest rates are variable.

Number awarded Varies each year. This program, established in 1997 in conjunction with the United States Hispanic Chamber of Commerce, has a goal of lending $3 billion over 10 years to Latino small business owners.

Deadline Applications may be requested at any time.

[677]
WISCONSIN MINORITY TEACHER LOANS

Wisconsin Higher Educational Aids Board
131 West Wilson Street, Room 902
P.O. Box 7885
Madison, WI 53707-7885
(608) 267-2212   Fax: (608) 267-2808
E-mail: mary.kuzdas@heab.state.wi.us
Web: heab.state.wi.us/programs.html

Purpose To provide scholarship/loans to minorities in Wisconsin who are interested in teaching in Wisconsin school districts with large minority enrollments.

Eligibility African Americans, Hispanic Americans, and American Indians in Wisconsin are eligible to apply if they are enrolled full time as juniors or seniors in an independent or public institution in the state. The program also includes students who were admitted to the United States after December 31, 1975 and who are a former citizen of Laos, Vietnam, or Cambodia or whose ancestor was a citizen of 1 of those countries. Applicants must be enrolled in a program leading to teaching licensure and must agree to teach in a Wisconsin school district in which minority students constitute at least 29% of total enrollment or in a school district participating in the inter-district pupil transfer program.

Financial data Scholarship/loans are provided up to $2,500 per year. For each year the student teaches in an eligible school district, 25% of the loan is forgiven; if the student does not teach in an eligible district, the loan must be repaid at an interest rate of 5%.

Duration 1 year; may be renewed 1 additional year.

Additional information Eligible students should apply through their school's financial aid office.

Number awarded Varies each year.

Deadline Deadline dates vary by institution; check with your school's financial aid office.

Grants

Described here are 356 programs that provide funds to Hispanic Americans for innovative efforts, travel, projects, creative activities, or research on any level (from undergraduate to postdoctorate and professional). In some cases, proposals may be submitted by institutions or organizations only; in others, individual Hispanic Americans may submit proposals directly. If you are looking for a particular program and don't find it in this section, be sure to check the Program Title Index to see if it is covered elsewhere in the directory.

[678]
AAAS/EPA ENVIRONMENTAL FELLOWSHIPS

American Association for the Advancement of Science
Attn: Science and Technology Policy Fellowship Programs
1200 New York Avenue, N.W.
Washington, DC 20005-3920
(202) 326-6700   Fax: (202) 289-4950
E-mail: science_policy@aaas.org
Web: fellowships.aaas.org/environmental/index.html

Purpose To provide postdoctoral and mid-career scientists and engineers with an opportunity to work with the U.S. Environmental Protection Agency (EPA) or U.S. Department of Energy (DOE) on projects relating to science, policy, and the environment.

Eligibility Prospective fellows must have a Ph.D. at the time of application and must show exceptional competence in some area of science or engineering related to environmental science; have a good scientific and technical background; have a strong interest and some experience in applying scientific or other professional knowledge toward the identification and assessment of future environmental problems; and be interested in working at the EPA or DOE. Applications are invited from individuals in a physical, biological, or social science, any field of engineering, or any relevant interdisciplinary field. Persons with a master's degree in engineering and at least 3 years of post-degree experience are also eligible. U.S. citizenship is required; federal employees are not eligible. Underrepresented minorities and persons with disabilities are especially encouraged to apply.

Financial data The stipend is $55,000, plus allowances for health insurance, relocation, and professional travel.

Duration 1 year, beginning in September. May be renewed 1 additional year.

Additional information At EPA, fellows work on ecosystem health; pollution prevention; sustainability; community-based solutions; human and environmental risk assessment; environmental socioeconomic concerns; hazardous air pollutants; global environmental hazards; pesticides, including biologicals; municipal waste water; drinking water; management and control of hazardous substances; chemical testing and assessment; radiation; and innovative technologies, such as green technologies. At DOE, fellows work in the Office of Science on a wide range of policy issues related to basic research.

Number awarded Approximately 10 each year.

Deadline January of each year.

[679]
AAAS/NIH SCIENCE POLICY FELLOWSHIPS

American Association for the Advancement of Science
Attn: Science and Technology Policy Fellowship Programs
1200 New York Avenue, N.W.
Washington, DC 20005-3920
(202) 326-6700   Fax: (202) 289-4950
E-mail: science_policy@aaas.org
Web: fellowships.aaas.org/nih/index.html

Purpose To provide postdoctoral and mid-career scientists and engineers with an opportunity to work at the National Institutes of Health (NIH) in Bethesda, Maryland.

Eligibility Applicants must have a Ph.D., M.D. or equivalent doctoral level degree at the time of application in a physical, biological, or behavioral science or any field of engineering. They must 1) be critical thinkers who are articulate, adaptable, and able to work with a variety of people with different professional backgrounds; 2) demonstrate exceptional competence in a specific area of science; 3) be cognizant of and demonstrate sensitivity toward policy issues; and 4) have a strong interest in applying their professional knowledge toward the development of health policy. U.S. citizenship is required; federal employees are not eligible. Underrepresented minorities and persons with disabilities are encouraged to apply.

Financial data The stipend ranges from $55,000 to $71,000, plus allowances for health insurance, relocation, and professional travel.

Duration 1 year, beginning in September. May be renewed 1 additional year.

Additional information Fellows work at 1 of the NIH institutes or centers, the Office of Science Policy, or the Office of the Director. Responsibilities may include the following: collect and analyze scientific and technical information pertinent to the preparation of reports and other documents regarding a broad range of NIH research policy and planning issues; participate in the evaluation of scientific opportunities, funding implications, and impact of federal policies on the conduct of biomedical research; initiate scholarly activities and coordinate analytic approaches to evaluate and interpret the economic impact of biomedical research on public health and society; participate in activities that consider and advance safeguards of research on human subjects; coordinate and organize planning and policy activities in response to Congressional actions and recommendations of external advisors and the NIH leadership; promote policies and planning that enhance the interactions among public and private research sectors with the goals of fostering collaboration and improved efficiency in the transfer of scientific knowledge and technologies to benefit the health of the nation; and advise on the development of policies to promote and advance the public awareness of, and interest in, biomedical research and health benefits to society.

Number awarded Up to 2 each year.

Deadline January of each year.

[680]
AAAS/NSF FELLOWSHIP PROGRAM

American Association for the Advancement of Science
Attn: Science and Technology Policy Fellowship Programs
1200 New York Avenue, N.W.
Washington, DC 20005-3920
(202) 326-6700   Fax: (202) 289-4950
E-mail: science_policy@aaas.org
Web: fellowships.aaas.org/research/index.html

Purpose To provide postdoctoral and mid-career scientists and engineers with an opportunity to work at the National Science Foundation (NSF) in Arlington, Virginia.

Eligibility Applicants must have a Ph.D. or equivalent doctoral level degree at the time of application in a physical, biological, or social science or any field of engineering; persons with a master's degree in engineering and at least 3 years of post-degree experience are also eligible. They must be interested in working at the NSF. Candidates must demonstrate exceptional competence in some area of science or engineering directly related to the focus of the program; they should be critical thinkers who are articulate, adaptable, and adept at working with a variety of people from differing professional backgrounds, including decision makers and others outside of the scientific and engineering community. U.S. citizenship is required; federal employees are not eligible. Underrepresented minorities and persons with disabilities are especially encouraged to apply.

Financial data The stipend is $55,000, plus allowances for health insurance, relocation, and professional travel.

Duration 1 year, beginning in September. May be renewed 1 additional year.

Additional information Fellows work at the NSF, learning how it funds science and providing scientific, engineering, and educational input on issues relating to its mission. They are placed in offices throughout the NSF, working on projects of mutual interest to the fellows and the host directorate or office. Fellows work with staff involved in planning, development, and oversight of agency programs in all fields of fundamental scientific and engineering research as well as technology, education, and public, legal, and legislative affairs.

Number awarded Up to 3 each year.

Deadline January of each year.

[681]
AAAS/NTI FELLOWSHIPS IN GLOBAL SECURITY

American Association for the Advancement of Science
Attn: Science and Technology Policy Fellowship Programs
1200 New York Avenue, N.W.
Washington, DC 20005-3920
(202) 326-6700   Fax: (202) 289-4950
E-mail: science_policy@aaas.org
Web: fellowships.aaas.org/NTI/index.html

Purpose To provide postdoctoral and mid-career biomedical and public health experts with an opportunity to work in Congressional offices in the area of biological threats.

Eligibility Applicants must have a D.V.M., M.D., or Ph.D. in the biological sciences, public health, or a related field at the time of the application. They must be able to write clearly; be able to articulate scientific concepts for non-scientific audiences; have the ability to work productively in an interdisciplinary setting with policy-makers and others outside the public health and medical/bioscience communities; have an interest in applying public health, medical, and scientific knowledge to national security and foreign policy issues; have an appreciation of political, social, and economic issues; and have a strong desire to reduce the global threat of bioweapon use. International experience is desirable but not required. U.S. citizenship is required; federal employees are not eligible. Underrepresented minorities and persons with disabilities are encouraged to apply.

Financial data The stipend is $55,000, plus allowances for health insurance, relocation, and professional travel.

Duration 1 year, beginning in September. May be renewed 1 additional year.

Additional information Fellows work in collaboration with the Nuclear Threat Initiative (NTI), established in 2001 by Ted Turner and former U.S. Senator Sam Nunn, to reduce global threats from nuclear, biological, and chemical weapons. Fellows work to bring public health and medical expertise to bear on issues related to biological weapons, bioterrorism nonproliferation, and federal-response planning efforts. Information is also available from NTI, 1747 Pennsylvania Avenue, N.W., Seventh Floor, Washington, D.C. 20006, (202) 296-4810, (202) 296-4811.

Number awarded At least 1 each year.

Deadline January of each year.

[682]
ABE FELLOWSHIP PROGRAM

Social Science Research Council
810 Seventh Avenue
New York, NY 10019
(212) 377-2700   Fax: (212) 377-2727
E-mail: abe@ssrc.org
Web: www.ssrc.org

Purpose To support postdoctoral research on contemporary policy-relevant affairs in Japan.

Eligibility This program is open to American and Japanese research professionals who have doctorate-equivalent or professional experience (other nationals affiliated with an American or Japanese institution are also eligible to apply). Applicants should be interested in policy-relevant topics of long-range importance; they must be willing and able to become key members of a bilateral and global research network built around such topics. Previous language training is not a prerequisite for this fellowship. Minorities and women are particularly encouraged to apply.

Financial data The terms of the fellowship include a base award and funds to pay supplementary research and travel expenses as necessary for completion of the research project.

Duration 3 to 12 months (although fellowship tenure need not be continuous).

Additional information Fellows are expected to affiliate with an American or Japanese institution appropriate to their research aims. In addition to receiving fellowship awards, fellows attend annual Abe Fellows Conferences, which promote the development of an international network of scholars concerned with research on contemporary policy issues. Funds are provided by the Japan Foundation's Center for Global Partnership. Fellows should plan to spend at least one third of their tenure abroad in Japan or the United States.

Deadline August of each year.

[683]
ABF POSTDOCTORAL FELLOWSHIPS IN LAW AND SOCIAL SCIENCE

American Bar Foundation
Attn: Assistant Director
750 North Lake Shore Drive
Chicago, IL 60611
(312) 988-6580   Fax: (312) 988-6579
E-mail: fellowships@abfn.org
Web: www.abf-sociolegal.org

Purpose To provide funding to postdoctoral scholars who wish to conduct research on law, the legal profession, and legal institutions.

Eligibility Applications are invited from junior scholars who completed all requirements for their Ph.D. within the past 2 years; in exceptional circumstances, candidates with a J.D. who have substantial social science training may also be considered. Proposed research must be in the general area of sociolegal studies or in social scientific approaches to law, the legal profession, or legal institutions and legal processes. Applications must include 1) a sample of written work; 2) 2 letters of recommendation; 3) a curriculum vitae; and 4) a statement describing research interests and achievements to date and plans for the fellowship period. Minority candidates are especially encouraged to apply.

Financial data The stipend is $30,000 per year; fringe benefits are also provided. Fellows may request up to $3,500 each fellowship year for research support. Relocation expenses of up to $1,000 may be reimbursed on application.

Duration 1 year; may be renewed for 1 additional year.

Additional information Fellows are offered access to the computing and word processing facilities of the American Bar Foundation and the libraries of Northwestern University and the University of Chicago. This program was established in 1996. Fellowships must be held in residence at the American Bar Foundation. Appointments to the fellowship are full time; fellows are not permitted to undertake other work.

Number awarded 2 each year.

Deadline January of each year.

[684]
ACADEMY OF NATURAL SCIENCES RESEARCH EXPERIENCES FOR UNDERGRADUATES FELLOWSHIPS

Academy of Natural Sciences of Philadelphia
Attn: REU Coordinator
1900 Benjamin Franklin Parkway
Philadelphia, PA 19103-1195
(215) 299-1000   Fax: (215) 299-1028
E-mail: reucoordinator@acnatsci.org
Web: www.acnatsci.org/research/reu.html

Purpose To provide undergraduate students with an opportunity to conduct summer research in botany, entomology, ichthyology, malacology, ornithology, or paleontology at the Academy of Natural Sciences of Philadelphia.

Eligibility This program is open to U.S. citizens and permanent residents who are entering their sophomore, junior, or senior year at a college or university. Applicants must be interested in working on a research project under the mentorship of an academy scientist in systematics, natural history, evolutionary biology, and ecology. Their proposals should draw upon the academy's collections in botany, entomology, ichthyology, malacology, ornithology, and paleontology, as well as the library and archives. Applications are encouraged from women, minorities, and students with disabilities.

Financial data The program provides travel to and from Philadelphia; housing; expenses for supplies, field trips, and research; and a stipend of $300 per week.

Duration 10 weeks, beginning in June.

Number awarded Varies each year.

Deadline February of each year.

[685]
ACE FELLOWS PROGRAM

American Council on Education
Attn: ACE Fellows Program
One Dupont Circle, N.W., Suite 800
Washington, DC 20036-1193
(202) 939-9420   Fax: (202) 785-8056
E-mail: fellows@ace.nche.edu
Web: www.acenet.edu

Purpose To provide an opportunity for college faculty and administrators, especially minorities, to pursue leadership training in higher education.

Eligibility Faculty members and junior administrators may be nominated by the president/senior officer of an American academic institution. Nominees must have at least 5 years of teaching or administrative experience and demonstrate an ability for

academic administration. They must be interested in pursuing a program of leadership development, either by visiting a host institution or by remaining at their sponsoring institution and making periodic visits to other institutions. Minorities and community college candidates are strongly urged to apply.

Financial data Fellows receive their regular salary and benefits from their sponsoring institution plus a professional development budget of up to $12,000. Funds from that budget must be used to participate in seminars, leadership team events, and national conferences arranged by the American Council on Education (ACE).

Duration 1 academic year or 1 semester.

Additional information Fellows and their sponsoring institutions may select from 1 of 3 options: 1) year-long fellowship at another campus (the host institution pays the professional development budget and provides the fellow with the mentorship of senior administrators); 2) semester placement at another campus (the host institution and the sponsoring institution each pay half the professional development budget and the fellow participates in an internship at another campus but remains under the mentorship of senior administrators at the home institution); 3) periodic visits to other campuses (the host institution pays the professional development budget and permits the fellow to make several month-long visits during the year). The first 2 options require the sponsoring institution to release the fellow from all responsibilities at the home campus. The third option requires the sponsoring institution to provide the fellow with sufficient release time from regular responsibilities to visit other campuses. The program requires the payment of a $5,000 fee to the ACE. For year-long fellowships at another campus, the host institution pays the fee. For semester placements at another campus, the host and sponsoring institutions each pay half the fee. For periodic visits, the sponsoring institution pays the fee.

Number awarded Approximately 35 each year.

Deadline October of each year.

[686]
ACLS FELLOWSHIPS

American Council of Learned Societies
Attn: Office of Fellowships and Grants
633 Third Avenue, 8C
New York, NY 10017-6795
(212) 697-1505   Fax: (212) 949-8058
E-mail: grants@acls.org
Web: www.acls.org/felguide.htm

Purpose To provide research funding to scholars in all disciplines of the humanities and the humanities-related social sciences.

Eligibility This program is open to scholars at all stages of their careers. Independent scholars are encouraged to apply, as are those scholars, both tenured and non-tenured, whose teaching responsibilities restrict the time available for research, and whose normal places of work are remote from depositories of research materials. Applicants must be U.S. citizens or permanent residents who hold a Ph.D. degree and have not held supported leave time for at least 3 years prior to the start of the proposed research. Appropriate fields of specialization include, but are not limited to, anthropology, archaeology, art history, economics, geography, history, languages and literatures, law, linguistics, musicology, philosophy, political science, psychology, religion, and sociology. Proposals in those fields of the social sciences are eligible only if they employ predominantly humanistic approaches (e.g., economic history, law and literature, political philosophy). Proposals in interdisciplinary and cross-disciplinary studies are welcome, as are proposals focused on any geographic region or on any cultural or linguistic group. Awards are available at 3 academic levels: full professor, associate professor, and assistant professor. Applications are particularly invited from women and members of minority groups.

Financial data The maximum grant is $50,000 for full professors and equivalent, $40,000 for associate professors and equivalent, or $30,000 for assistant professors and equivalent. Normally, fellowships are intended as salary replacement and may be held concurrently with other fellowships, grants, and sabbatical pay, up to an amount equal to the candidate's current academic year salary.

Duration 6 to 12 months.

Additional information This program is supported in part by funding from the Ford Foundation, the Andrew W. Mellon Foundation, the National Endowment for the Humanities, the William and Flora Hewlett Foundation, and the Rockefeller Foundation.

Number awarded Approximately 60 each year: 20 at each academic level. In addition, the Andrew W. Mellon Foundation has provided funding for an additional 22 fellowships for assistant professors or equivalent who have at least 2 years of teaching experience.

Deadline September of each year.

[687]
ACLS/SSRC/NEH INTERNATIONAL AND AREA STUDIES FELLOWSHIPS

American Council of Learned Societies
Attn: Office of Fellowships and Grants
633 Third Avenue, 8C
New York, NY 10017-6795
(212) 697-1505   Fax: (212) 949-8058
E-mail: grants@acls.org
Web: www.acls.org/felguide.htm

Purpose To provide funding to postdoctoral scholars for research on the societies and cultures of Asia, Africa, the Near and Middle East, Latin America and the Caribbean, eastern Europe, and the former Soviet Union.

Eligibility This program is open to U.S. citizens and residents who have lived in the United States for at least 3 years. Applicants must have a Ph.D. degree and not have received supported research leave time for at least 3 years prior to the start of the proposed research. They must be interested in conducting humanities and humanities-related social science research on the societies and cultures of Asia, Africa, the Near and Middle East, Latin America and the Caribbean, east Europe, or the former Soviet Union. Selection is based on the intellectual merit of the proposed research and the likelihood that it will produce significant and innovative scholarship. Applications are particularly invited from women and members of minority groups.

Financial data The maximum grant is $50,000 for full professors and equivalent, $40,000 for associate professors and equivalent, or $30,000 for assistant professors and equivalent. These fellowships may not be held concurrently with another major fellowship.

Duration 6 to 12 months.

Additional information This program is jointly supported by the American Council of Learned Societies (ACLS) and the Social Science Research Council (SSRC), with funding provided by the National Endowment for the Humanities (NEH).

Number awarded Approximately 10 each year.
Deadline September of each year.

[688]
ADVANCE FELLOWS AWARDS

National Science Foundation
Attn: ADVANCE Program
4201 Wilson Boulevard
Arlington, VA 22230
(703) 292-5111   TDD: (703) 292-5090
E-mail: ahogan@nsf.gov
Web: www.nsf.gov/home/crssprgm/advance

Purpose To provide funding to women scholars who are entering or reentering an academic career and wish to undertake research and other projects in science and engineering fields supported by the National Science Foundation (NSF).

Eligibility This program is open to women who are affiliated or plan to affiliate with an institution of higher learning in the United States, its territories or possessions, or the Commonwealth of Puerto Rico. Applicants must hold a Ph.D. in a field of science or engineering supported by NSF; be a U.S. citizen, national, or permanent resident; and be establishing a full-time independent academic research and education career. They must 1) have received their first doctoral degree in science or engineering from 1 to 4 years previously, be in a postdoctoral or equivalent status, have never held a tenure-track or tenured position, and have not served as a principal investigator on any NSF award with the exception of doctoral dissertation, postdoctoral fellowship, or research-planning grants; or 2) be out of the full-time science and engineering workforce and have been out of that workforce for 2 to 8 years to attend to family responsibilities; or 3) either have resigned from a full-time academic science or engineering appointment because of relocation of a spouse in the preceding 24 months and not hold a tenure-track or tenured position or be planning to leave a full-time academic science or engineering appointment because of relocation of a spouse to occur in the 12 months following the proposal due date. All applications must include a career development component that describes plans for career-enhancing research and education activities. Applicants who already hold an academic affiliation must describe the facilities at their institution that are available for them to carry out their career development plan; applicants who are not currently affiliated must identify the institutional resources necessary for the proposed activities and describe plans for affiliating with a host institution. Members of underrepresented minority groups and individuals with disabilities are especially encouraged to apply.

Financial data Awards provide annual salary support of up to $60,000 plus applicable fringe benefits and a career development allotment of up to $25,000 per year (to be used for activities directly related to the proposed research and education activities in the fellow's career development plan, such as computing, travel to professional workshops, materials and supplies, publication charges, technical support, student support, and related needs). Indirect costs may be included at the host or home institution's standard rate.

Duration Up to 3 years.

Additional information Information is available from coordinators in each of the NSF directorates; for a list of their names and telephone numbers, contact the sponsor. If the recipient does not currently hold an academic appointment, the award will commence only when she affiliates with a host institution that agrees to provide resources necessary to support the proposed career-development plan.

Number awarded 20 to 40 each year.

Deadline June of each year.

[689]
ADVANCED FOSSIL RESOURCE UTILIZATION RESEARCH BY HISTORICALLY BLACK COLLEGES AND UNIVERSITIES AND OTHER MINORITY INSTITUTIONS

Department of Energy
Attn: National Energy Technology Laboratory
626 Cochrans Mill Road
P.O. Box 10940 (MS 921-107)
Pittsburgh, PA 15236-0940
(412) 386-4862   (800) 553-7681
Fax: (412) 386-6137   E-mail: mitchell@netl.doe.gov
Web: www.netl.doe.gov

Purpose To provide support to researchers at Historically Black Colleges and Universities (HBCUs) and other minority institutions for research projects on advanced coal, oil, and natural gas concepts.

Eligibility Applications are solicited from federally-recognized HBCUs and other minority institutions to conduct research projects on fossil energy. Proposals must involve collaboration with an industrial partner, and each research team must include a teaching professor and at least 30% of personnel time must be to pay for student assistance. The proposed research must relate to 1 of the following technical topics: 1) advanced environmental control technologies for coal; 2) advanced coal utilization; 3) clean fuels technology; 4) heavy oil upgrading and processing; 5) advanced recovery, completion/stimulation, and geoscience technologies for oil; 6) natural gas supply, storage, and processing; 7) infrastructure reliability for natural gas; and 8) fuel cells. A ninth category is faculty/student exploratory research training grants.

Financial data For the 8 technical topics, maximum grants are $85,000 for 1 year, $150,000 for 2 years, or $200,000 for 3 years. Maximum funding for faculty/student exploratory research training grants is $20,000 per year. Total annual funding for this program is approximately $900,000.

Duration Up to 3 years for technical topic grants; 1 year for faculty/student exploratory research training grants.

Number awarded Approximately 4 to 6 grants on technical topics and 4 to 8 faculty/student exploratory research training grants are awarded each year.

Deadline March of each year.

[690]
ADVANCED POSTDOCTORAL FELLOWSHIPS IN DIABETES RESEARCH

Juvenile Diabetes Research Foundation
Attn: Grant Administrator
120 Wall Street, 19th Floor
New York, NY 10005-4001
(212) 479-7519   (800) 533-CURE
Fax: (212) 785-9595   E-mail: cstone@jdrf.org
Web: www.jdrf.org/research/advanced.php

Purpose To provide advanced research training to scientists who are beginning their professional careers and are interested in conducting research on the causes, treatment, prevention, or cure of diabetes or its complications.

Eligibility This program is open to postdoctorates who show extraordinary promise for a career in diabetes research. Applicants must have received their first doctoral (M.D., Ph.D., or M.D./Ph.D.) degree within the past 5 years and should have completed 1 or 2 years of postdoctoral training. They may not have a faculty appointment. There are no citizenship requirements. Applications are encouraged from women and members of minority groups underrepresented in the sciences. The proposed research training may be conducted at foreign and domestic, for-profit and nonprofit, and public and private institutions, including universities, colleges, hospitals, laboratories, units of state and local government, and eligible agencies of the federal government. Selection is based on the applicant's ability and potential for a research career, the caliber of the proposed research, and the quality of the training to be provided.

Financial data The total award is $90,000 per year, of which up to $50,000 may be requested for research allowance (supplies, equipment, and travel). Salary requests must be consistent with the established salary structure of the applicant's institution. Equipment requests in years other than the first must be strongly justified. Indirect costs are not allowed.

Duration 3 years.

Deadline January or August of each year.

[691]
AERA/IES DISSERTATION GRANTS PROGRAM

American Educational Research Association
1230 17th Street, N.W.
Washington, DC 20036-3078
(202) 223-9485   Fax: (202) 775-1824
Web: www.aera.net/programs/ies/index.htm

Purpose To provide funding to doctoral students writing their dissertation on educational policy.

Eligibility This program is open to advanced graduate students writing their dissertation on an education-related issue. Priority is given to research that addresses mathematics and literacy education and the education of poor, urban, or minority students. Additional topics may include cultural and linguistic diversity; alternative forms of educational assessment; school persistence; early childhood education; contextual factors (individual, curricular, and school-related) in education; materials (curriculum) development; school reform; and the quality of educational institutions. Preference is given to research that intersects theory and practice. Underrepresented and underserved researchers in the area of education are strongly encouraged to apply. Selection is based on the relevance of the proposal to program goals, the potential contribution of the work to both theory and practice, the strength and appropriateness of the methods for the work proposed, and the feasibility of the work.

Financial data The maximum grant is $15,000 for a 1-year project or $25,000 for a 2-year project. Institutions may not charge indirect costs on these awards. Each year, grantees receive one third of the total award at the beginning of the grant period, one third upon acceptance of the progress report, and one third upon acceptance of the final report. In most cases, grantees may choose whether to have funds sent directly to them or to have the funds channeled through their institutions.

Duration 1 or 2 years.

Additional information Funding for this program is provided by the U.S. Department of Education's Institute of Education Sciences (IES). Grantees must submit a brief (3 to 6 pages) progress report midway through the grant period. A final report must be submitted at the end of the grant period. The final report may be either an article suitable for publication in a scholarly journal or a copy of the dissertation.

Number awarded 4 each year.

Deadline April or October of each year.

[692]
AERA/IES POSTDOCTORAL FELLOWSHIP PROGRAM

American Educational Research Association
1230 17th Street, N.W.
Washington, DC 20036-3078
(202) 223-9485   Fax: (202) 775-1824
Web: www.aera.net/programs/ies/index.htm

Purpose To provide funding to recent postdoctorates interested in pursuing additional research training in an area of educational policy.

Eligibility This program is open to researchers within 10 years of receiving a higher degree (Ph.D., Ed.D., or equivalent) who show potential or demonstrated capacity to perform educational research. Applicants must have established a relationship with an established member of the education research community who has agreed to serve as a mentor. The host institution may not be the applicant's doctoral degree-granting institution. Research topics may cover a wide range of education-related issues. Priority is given to research that addresses mathematics and literacy education and the education of poor, urban, or minority students. Additional topics may include cultural and linguistic diversity; alternative forms of educational assessment; school persistence; early childhood education; contextual factors (individual, curricular, and school-related) in education; materials (curriculum) development; school reform; and the quality of educational institutions. Preference is given to research that intersects theory and practice. Applications are strongly encouraged from the following 1) researchers from underrepresented and underserved populations in education research and candidates whose research will provide information about the needs of underrepresented and underserved groups; 2) candidates seeking to expand their research competencies either by moving into new areas or by obtaining preparation not offered in their doctoral programs; and 3) candidates working in institutions that do not presently have large concentrations of well-recognized educational researchers. Applicants from fields other than education can propose research and study that will develop their capability for research relevant to education. All applicants must be U.S. citizens or permanent residents.

Financial data Grants provide an annual stipend for the fellow of $40,000, up to $3,000 per year for the fellow's relocation and professional travel, up to $4,000 for equipment (during the term of the award) for support of the fellow's research, tuition or fees that are required by the institution for all such research fellows, up to $5,000 per year for research expenses for the mentor's research program related to the fellow's work, and an 8% administrative fee to the institution on direct costs related to the fellow's support.

Duration 2 to 3 years.

Additional information Funding for this program is provided by the U.S. Department of Education's Institute of Education Sciences (IES). Fellows must submit a final report on their research.

Number awarded Up to 12 each year.

Deadline April or October of each year.

[693]
AERA/IES RESEARCH GRANTS PROGRAM

American Educational Research Association
1230 17th Street, N.W.
Washington, DC 20036-3078
(202) 223-9485   Fax: (202) 775-1824
Web: www.aera.net/programs/ies/index.htm

Purpose To provide funding to faculty members and other postdoctorates interested in conducting research on educational policy.

Eligibility This program is open to scholars interested in conducting research on an education-related issue. Priority is given to research that addresses mathematics and literacy education and the education of poor, urban, or minority students. Additional topics may include cultural and linguistic diversity; alternative forms of educational assessment; school persistence; early childhood education; contextual factors (individual, curricular, and school-related) in education; materials (curriculum) development; school reform; and the quality of educational institutions. Preference is given to research that intersects theory and practice. Underrepresented and underserved researchers in the area of education are strongly encouraged to apply. Selection is based on the relevance on the proposal to program goals, the potential contribution of the work to both theory and practice, the strength and appropriateness of the methods for the work proposed, and the relevant experience and research record of the applicant.

Financial data The maximum grant is $15,000 for a 1-year project or $25,000 for a 2-year project. Institutions may not charge indirect costs on these awards. Each year, grantees receive one third of the total award at the beginning of the grant period, one third upon acceptance of the progress report, and one third upon acceptance of the final report. In most cases, grantees may choose whether to have funds sent directly to them or have the funds channeled through their institutions.

Duration 1 or 2 years.

Additional information Funding for this program is provided by the U.S. Department of Education's Institute of Education Sciences (IES). Grantees must submit a brief (3 to 6 pages) progress report midway through the grant period. A final report must be submitted at the end of the grant period. The final report should be of a quality and in a format suitable for publication in a scholarly journal.

Number awarded Up to 10 each year.

Deadline April or October of each year.

[694]
AGA RESEARCH SCHOLAR AWARDS

Foundation for Digestive Health and Nutrition
Attn: Research Awards Coordinator
7910 Woodmont Avenue, Suite 700
Bethesda, MD 20814-3015
(301) 222-4005   Fax: (301) 222-4010
E-mail: info@fdhn.org
Web: www.fdhn.org

Purpose To provide salary support for young investigators developing an independent career in an area of gastroenterology, hepatology, or related fields.

Eligibility Applicants must hold full-time faculty positions at North American universities or professional institutes at the time of application. They should be early in their careers (fellows and established investigators are not appropriate candidates). Those who have been at the assistant professor level for more than 5 years are not eligible. Membership in the American Gastroenterological Association (AGA) is required. The primary intent of this award is to support physician-investigators who have the potential to develop independent, productive research careers in gastroenterology and hepatology. However, nonphysician candidates with a Ph.D. are also considered. Selection is based on novelty, feasibility and significance of the proposal, attributes of the candidate, evidence of institutional commitment, and the laboratory environment. Special consideration is given to applications with a focus in nutrition or geriatrics. Women and minority investigators are strongly encouraged to apply. To increase the number of underrepresented minority scientists participating in gastroenterology research, the association has reserved 1 of these awards specifically for an applicant who is African American, Mexican American, Mainland Puerto Rican, or Native American (Alaska Native, American Indian, or Native Hawaiian).

Financial data The award consists of $65,000 per year. Funds are to be used for project costs, including salary, supplies, and equipment but excluding travel. Indirect costs are not allowed.

Duration 3 years.

Additional information This award is administered by the ADHF and sponsored by the American Gastroenterological Association (AGA). Funding is provided by TAP Pharmaceuticals, Inc., AstraZeneca Pharmaceuticals, L.P., Janssen Pharmaceutica Products, L.P., Johnson & Johnson/Merck Consumer Pharmaceuticals, and Wyeth-Ayerst Laboratories. At least 70% of the recipient's research effort should relate to the gastrointestinal tract or liver. Recipients cannot hold or have held a R01, R29, K121, K08, VA Research Award, or any award with similar objectives from nonfederal sources.

Number awarded Up to 6 each year; 1 of the awards is specifically set aside for an underrepresented minority scholar.

Deadline September of each year.

[695]
AGA STUDENT RESEARCH FELLOWSHIP AWARDS

Foundation for Digestive Health and Nutrition
Attn: Research Awards Coordinator
7910 Woodmont Avenue, Suite 700
Bethesda, MD 20814-3015
(301) 222-4005   Fax: (301) 222-4010
E-mail: info@fdhn.org
Web: www.fdhn.org

Purpose To provide funding for research on digestive diseases or nutrition to students at any level.

Eligibility This program is open to high school, undergraduate, graduate, or medical students at accredited universities in North America who are not yet engaged in thesis research. They must be interested in conducting research on digestive diseases or nutrition. Candidates must not hold similar salary support awards from other agencies (e.g., American Liver Foundation, Crohn's and Colitis Foundation). Women and underrepresented minority students are strongly encouraged to apply. Research must be conducted under the supervision of a preceptor who is a full-time faculty member at a North American institution, directing a research project in a gastroenterology-related area, and an individual member of any of the partner organizations. Selection is based on novelty, feasibility and significance of the proposal, attributes of the candidate, record of the preceptor, institutional commitment, and laboratory environment. Applicants are grouped and evaluated according to educational level.

Financial data Grants range from $1,500 to $2,500. No indirect costs are allowed. The award is paid directly to the student and is to be used as a stipend or for thesis research.

Duration 10 to 12 weeks. The work may take place at any time during the year.

Additional information In an effort to attract and encourage minorities, 7 of the awards are set aside specifically for underrepresented minority students, defined as African Americans, Mexican Americans, Mainland Puerto Ricans, and Native Americans (Alaskan Natives, American Indians, and American Indians). This award is administered by the American Digestive Health Foundation (ADHF) and sponsored by the American Gastroenterological Association (AGA). Funds may not be used to support thesis research.

Number awarded Up to 30 each year. Of those, 7 are set aside specifically for underrepresented minorities (African Americans, American Indians, Alaska and Hawaiian Natives, Mexican Americans, and Mainland Puerto Ricans).

Deadline March of each year.

[696]
AGI CONGRESSIONAL SCIENCE FELLOWSHIP

American Geological Institute
Attn: Government Affairs Program
4220 King Street
Alexandria, VA 22302-1502
(703) 379-2480   Fax: (703) 379-7563
E-mail: govt@agiweb.org
Web: www.agiweb.org/gapac/csf.html

Purpose To provide members of an American Geological Institute (AGI) component society with an opportunity to gain professional experience in the office of a member of Congress or a congressional committee.

Eligibility This program is open to members of 1 of AGI's 35 member societies who have a master's degree and at least 3 years of post-degree work experience or a Ph.D. Applicants should have a broad geoscience background and excellent written and oral communications skills. They must be interested in working with Congress. Although prior experience in public policy is not required, a demonstrated interest in applying science to the solution of public problems is desirable. Applications from women and minorities are especially encouraged. Preference is given to U.S. citizens and permanent residents.

Financial data Fellows receive a stipend of up to $42,000 plus allowances for health insurance, relocation, and travel.

Duration 12 to 16 months, beginning in September.

Additional information This program is 1 of more than 20 Congressional Science Fellowships that operate in affiliation with the American Association for the Advancement of Science (AAAS), which provides a 2-week orientation on congressional and executive branch operations.

Number awarded 1 each year.

Deadline January of each year.

[697]
AIR FORCE OFFICE OF SCIENTIFIC RESEARCH BROAD AGENCY ANNOUNCEMENT

Air Force Office of Scientific Research
Attn: Directorate of Academic and International Affairs
4015 Wilson Boulevard, Room 713
Arlington, VA 22203-1954
(703) 696-5994   Fax: (703) 696-9733
E-mail: harry.haraldsen@afosr.af.mil
Web: www.afosr.af.mil

Purpose To provide funding to investigators interested in conducting scientific research of interest to the U.S. Air Force.

Eligibility This program is open to investigators qualified to perform research in designated scientific and technical areas. The general fields of interest include aerospace and materials sciences, physics and electronics, chemistry and life sciences, and mathematics and space sciences. Assistance includes grants to university scientists, support for academic institutions, contracts for industry research, cooperative agreements, and support for basic research in Air Force laboratories. Because the Air Force encourages the sharing and transfer of technology, it welcomes proposals that envision cooperation among 2 or more partners from academia, industry, and Air Force organizations. It particularly encourages proposals from Historically Black Colleges and Universities (HBCUs), other Minority Institutions (MIs), and minority researchers.

Financial data The amounts of the awards depend on the nature of the proposals and the availability of funds. Recently, a total of $226 million per year has been available for this program; the average award has been approximately $150,000. Each year, a percentage of total funding is set aside for HBCUs and MIs.

Duration Grants are normally for up to 5 years.

Additional information Contact the Air Force Office of Scientific Research for details on particular program areas of interest. Outstanding principal investigators on grants issued through this program are nominated to receive Presidential Early Career Awards for Scientists and Engineers.

Number awarded Varies each year; recently, this program awarded 1,393 grants and contracts to 372 academic institutions and industrial firms.

Deadline Each program area specifies deadline dates.

[698]
ALABAMA SPACE GRANT CONSORTIUM GRADUATE FELLOWSHIP PROGRAM

Alabama Space Grant Consortium
c/o University of Alabama in Huntsville
Materials Science Building, Room 205
Huntsville, AL 35899
(256) 890-6800   Fax: (256) 890-6061
E-mail: jfreasoner@matsci.uah.edu
Web: www.uah.edu/ASGC

Purpose To provide financial assistance for graduate study or research related to the space sciences at universities participating in the Alabama Space Grant Consortium.

Eligibility This program is open to full-time graduate students enrolled at the universities participating in the consortium. Applicants must be studying in a field related to space, including the physical, natural, and biological sciences; engineering; education; economics; business; sociology; behavioral sciences; computer science; communications; law; international affairs; and public administration. They must 1) present a proposed research plan

related to space that includes an extramural experience at a field center of the National Aeronautics and Space Administration (NASA); 2) propose a multidisciplinary plan and course of study; 3) plan to be involved in consortium outreach activities; and 4) intend to pursue a career in line with NASA's aerospace, science, and technology programs. U.S. citizenship is required. Individuals from underrepresented groups (African Americans, Hispanics, American Indians, Pacific Islanders, and women of all races) are encouraged to apply. Interested students should submit a completed application form, a description of the proposed research, a schedule, a budget, a list of references, a vitae, and undergraduate and graduate transcripts. Selection is based on 1) academic qualifications, 2) quality of the proposed research program or plan of study and its relevance to the aerospace science and technology program of NASA, 3) quality of the proposed interdisciplinary approach, 4) merit of the proposed utilization of a NASA center to carry out the objectives of the program, 5) prospects for completing the project within the allotted time, and 6) applicant's motivation for a career in aerospace.

Financial data The award for 12 months includes $16,000 for a student stipend and up to $6,000 for a tuition/student research allowance.

Duration Up to 36 months.

Additional information The member universities are University of Alabama in Huntsville, Alabama A&M University, University of Alabama, University of Alabama at Birmingham, University of South Alabama, Tuskegee University, and Auburn University. Funding for this program is provided by NASA.

Number awarded Varies each year; recently, 11 of these fellowships were awarded.

Deadline February of each year.

[699]
AMERICAN ANTHROPOLOGICAL ASSOCIATION MINORITY DISSERTATION FELLOWSHIP PROGRAM

American Anthropological Association
Attn: Minority Dissertation Fellowship Program
4350 North Fairfax Drive, Suite 640
Arlington, VA 22203
(703) 528-1902   Fax: (703) 528-3546
E-mail: ksharp@aaanet.org
Web: www.aaanet.org/committees/minoirty/minordis.htm

Purpose To provide funding to minorities who are working on a Ph.D. dissertation in anthropology.

Eligibility Native American, African American, Latino(a), and Asian American doctoral students who have been admitted to degree candidacy in anthropology are invited to apply. Applicants must be U.S. citizens, enrolled in a full-time academic program leading to a doctoral degree in anthropology, and a member of the American Anthropological Association. They must have a record of outstanding academic success, have had their dissertation proposal approved by their dissertation committee prior to application, be writing a dissertation in an area of anthropological research, and need funding to complete the dissertation. To apply, students must submit an application form, a cover letter, a research plan summary, a curriculum vitae, a statement regarding employment, a disclosure statement providing information about other sources of available and pending financial support, 3 letters of recommendation, and an official transcript from their doctoral program. Selection is based on the quality of the submitted information and the judged likelihood that the applicant will have a good chance at completing the dissertation. Consideration is also given to the implications of the applicant's research to issues and concerns of the U.S. historically disadvantaged populations, relevant service to the community, and future plans.

Financial data The stipend is $10,000. Funds are sent in 2 installments (in September and in January) to the recipient's institution.

Duration 1 year; nonrenewable.

Number awarded 1 each year.

Deadline February of each year.

[700]
AMERICAN ASSOCIATION OF UNIVERSITY WOMEN POSTDOCTORAL RESEARCH LEAVE FELLOWSHIPS

American Association of University Women
Attn: AAUW Educational Foundation
2201 North Dodge Street
P.O. Box 4030
Iowa City, IA 52243-4030
(319) 337-1716   Fax: (319) 337-1204
E-mail: aauw@act.org
Web: www.aauw.org

Purpose To enable American women scholars who have achieved distinction or promise of distinction in their fields of scholarly work to engage in additional research.

Eligibility Women of outstanding scholarly achievement who are working on postdoctoral research in any field and are U.S. citizens or permanent residents are eligible to apply; 1 award is set aside specifically for an underrepresented minority woman. Applicants must have earned the doctorate by the time the application is submitted. Selection is based on scholarly excellence, experience in teaching or mentoring female students, and active commitment to helping women and girls through service in community, profession, or field of research.

Financial data The stipend is $30,000.

Duration 1 year, beginning in July.

Additional information Postdoctoral fellowships normally will not be awarded to women who have received the doctorate within the past 3 years or for revision of the dissertation. Recipients are expected to spend the fellowship year in full-time research. The award may be not be used to cover the costs of research equipment, research assistants, publication, travel to professional meetings or seminars, tuition for additional course work, or repayment of loans or other personal obligations. Applications should be made 1 year in advance of the academic year for which funding is sought.

Number awarded 20 each year in 3 fields: the arts and humanities, the social sciences, and the natural sciences. The fellowship reserved for an underrepresented minority woman is available to an applicant in any field.

Deadline November of each year.

[701]
AMERICAN EDUCATIONAL RESEARCH ASSOCIATION DISSERTATION GRANTS PROGRAM

American Educational Research Association
1230 17th Street, N.W.
Washington, DC 20036-3078
(202) 223-9485   Fax: (202) 775-1824
Web: www.aera.net/grantsprogram/subweb/DGFly.html

Purpose To provide funding to doctoral students writing their dissertation on educational policy.

Eligibility This program is open to advanced graduate students who are writing their dissertations. Minority researchers are strongly encouraged to apply. Dissertation topics may cover a wide range of policy-related issues including but not limited to: school persistence and career entry; teachers and teaching, including supply, quality, and demand; policies and practices related to student achievement and assessment; policies and practices that influence student and parental attitudes; contextual factors (individual, curricular, and school related) in education; education in middle schools; educational participation and persistence (kindergarten through graduate school); at-risk students; early childhood education; U.S. education in an international context; school finance; materials (curriculum) development; research and informal science education; undergraduate science, engineering, and mathematics education; the supply (pipeline) of students taking mathematics and science courses from K-12; research career development; the quality of educational institutions; and methodological studies. Applicants must be interested in utilizing at least 1 National Science Foundation (NSF) or National Center for Education Statistics (NCES) data set in the dissertation. They must submit a proposal (up to 4 pages in length) describing their research study and a budget. Selection is based on the importance of the proposed policy issue, the strength of the methodological model and proposed statistical analysis of the study, and relevant experience or research record of the applicant.

Financial data The maximum grant is $15,000 per year. No support is provided for indirect costs to institutions. Funding is linked to approval of the recipient's progress report and final report. Grantees receive one third of the total award at the beginning of the grant period, one third upon acceptance of the progress report, and one third upon acceptance of the final report. Funds can be sent either to the recipients or to their institutions.

Duration 1 year.

Additional information Funding for this program is provided by the NSF, the NCES, and the U.S. Department of Education's Institute of Education Sciences (IES). Information is also available from Jeanie Murdock, Executive Director, AERA Grants Program, 5662 Calle Real, Number 254, Goleta, CA 93117-2317, (805) 964-5264, Fax: (805) 964-5054, E-mail: jmurdock@aera.net. Grantees must submit a brief (3 to 6 pages) progress report midway through the grant period. A final report must be submitted at the end of the grant period. The final report may be either an article suitable for publication in a scholarly journal or a copy of the dissertation.

Number awarded Several each year.

Deadline January, March, or September of each year.

[702]
AMERICAN EDUCATIONAL RESEARCH ASSOCIATION FELLOWS PROGRAM

American Educational Research Association
1230 17th Street, N.W.
Washington, DC 20036-3078
(202) 223-9485   Fax: (202) 775-1824
Web: www.aera.net/grantsprogram/subweb/AFFly.html

Purpose To provide an opportunity for senior researchers to focus on education policy-related research while in residence at either the National Science Foundation (NSF) or the National Center for Education Statistics (NCES).

Eligibility This program is open to senior researchers at various professional levels (tenured or at least 7 years past the doctorate).

They must be interested in conducting independent research at NSF or NCES. Important areas of research include but are not limited to: teacher education, early childhood education, state education research and statistics, adult assessment, and international comparisons of educational systems and performance. Minority researchers are strongly encouraged to apply. U.S. citizenship or permanent resident status is required. Selection is based on quality of the proposed research project, ability to work collaboratively, and ability to produce in a timely fashion.

Financial data The amount awarded depends upon the recipient's experience and academic background.

Duration Scholars may be placed for up to 1 year, but most assignments extend 4 to 9 months.

Additional information Funding for this program is provided by the NSF and the NCES. Fellows placed at NSF are referred to as Leigh Burstein Fellows. Fellows placed at NCES are referred to as Jeanne Griffith Fellows. Information is also available from Jeanie Murdock, Executive Director, AERA Grants Program, 5662 Calle Real, Number 254, Goleta, CA 93117-2317, (805) 964-5264, Fax: (805) 964-5054, E-mail: jmurdock@aera.net. Fellows must submit a final report on their research.

Number awarded Several each year.

Deadline January, March, or September of each year.

[703]
AMERICAN EDUCATIONAL RESEARCH ASSOCIATION MINORITY FELLOWSHIP PROGRAM

American Educational Research Association
1230 17th Street, N.W.
Washington, DC 20036-3078
(202) 223-9485   Fax: (202) 775-1824
Web: www.aera.net/programs/minority

Purpose To provide funding to minority doctoral students writing their dissertation on educational research.

Eligibility This program is open to U.S. citizens and native residents of a U.S. possession who have advanced to candidacy and successfully defended their Ph.D./Ed.D. dissertation research proposal. Applicants must plan to work full time on their dissertation in educational research. This program is targeted for members of groups historically underrepresented in higher education (African Americans, American Indians, Alaskan Natives, Filipino Americans, Native Pacific Islanders, Mexican Americans, and Puerto Ricans). Selection is based on scholarly achievements and publications, letters of recommendation, quality and significance of the proposed research, and commitment of the applicant's faculty mentor to the goals of the program.

Financial data The grant is $10,000 per year.

Duration 1 year; may be renewed for 1 additional year upon demonstration of satisfactory progress.

Number awarded 2 each year.

Deadline February of each year.

[704]
AMERICAN EDUCATIONAL RESEARCH ASSOCIATION POSTDOCTORAL FELLOWS PROGRAM

American Educational Research Association
1230 17th Street, N.W.
Washington, DC 20036-3078
(202) 223-9485   Fax: (202) 775-1824
Web: www.aera.net/grantsprogram/subweb/PDFly.html

Purpose To provide funding to postdoctorates interested in pursuing research training in a field related to educational policy.

Eligibility This program is open to postdoctorates interested in conducting independent research under the guidance of a qualified mentor, preferably within a school of education at a host institution of higher education. Applicants must have completed a doctoral degree in education, science, mathematics, statistics, sociology, economics, psychology, or a related field within the past 7 years. They must be interested in conducting research on a topic that may cover a wide range of policy-related issues, including but not limited to: school persistence and career entry; teachers and teaching, including supply, quality, and demand; policies and practices related to student achievement and assessment; policies and practices that influence student and parental attitudes; contextual factors (individual, curricular, and school related) in education; education in middle schools; educational participation and persistence (kindergarten through graduate school); at-risk students; early childhood education; U.S. education in an international context; school finance; materials (curriculum) development; research and informal science education; undergraduate science, engineering, and mathematics education; the supply (pipeline) of students taking mathematics and science courses from K-12; research career development; the quality of educational institutions; and methodological studies. Interdisciplinary research is encouraged. The research must be quantitative in nature, using large-scale nationally or internationally representative data sets for education policy, including at least 1 from the National Science Foundation (NSF) or National Center for Education Statistics (NCES). Applicants must submit a proposal (up to 4 pages in length) describing their research study and a budget. Minority researchers are strongly encouraged to apply. U.S. citizenship or permanent resident status is required. Selection is based on the relevant experience, research record, and professional potential of the applicant; the strength of the proposed research project (the importance of the policy issue, the strength of the methodology, and the originality of the research; and the match between the applicant and the mentor/institution.

Financial data The stipend is $40,000 per year. Fellows also receive up to $2,500 for relocation expenses and $2,500 for travel to professional meetings. The institution is entitled to 8% for overhead expenses.

Duration 1 year; nonrenewable.

Additional information Funding for this program is provided by the NSF, NCES, and the U.S. Department of Education's Institute of Education Sciences (IES). Information is also available from Jeanie Murdock, Executive Director, AERA Grants Program, 5662 Calle Real, Number 254, Goleta, CA 93117-2317, (805) 964-5264, Fax: (805) 964-5054, E-mail: jmurdock@aera.net.

Number awarded Several each year.

Deadline January of each year.

[705]

AMERICAN EDUCATIONAL RESEARCH ASSOCIATION RESEARCH FELLOWS PROGRAM

American Educational Research Association
1230 17th Street, N.W.
Washington, DC 20036-3078
(202) 223-9485   Fax: (202) 775-1824
Web: www.aera.net/grantsprogram/subweb/RFFly.html

Purpose To provide funding to beginning researchers (including advanced graduate students) interested in conducting research on educational policy while in residence at either the National Science Foundation (NSF) or the National Center for Education Statistics (NCES).

Eligibility This program is open to beginning researchers, including advanced graduate students, postdoctoral researchers, assistant professors, and those who have received their doctorate within the past 7 years. Applicants must be interested in conducting an independent research project at NSF or NCES. Minority researchers are strongly encouraged to apply. Selection is based on quality of the proposed research project, ability to work collaboratively, and ability to produce in a timely fashion.

Financial data Stipends are based on experience and academic background but are equivalent to a beginning assistant professor's salary, plus $1,000 in travel funds.

Duration At least 9 months.

Additional information Funding for this program is provided by the NSF and NCES. Information is also available from Jeanie Murdock, Executive Director, AERA Grants Program, 5662 Calle Real, Number 254, Goleta, CA 93117-2317, (805) 964-5264, Fax: (805) 964-5054, E-mail: jmurdock@aera.net. Fellows must submit a final report on their research.

Number awarded Several each year.

Deadline January, March, or September of each year.

[706]

AMERICAN EDUCATIONAL RESEARCH ASSOCIATION RESEARCH GRANTS PROGRAM

American Educational Research Association
1230 17th Street, N.W.
Washington, DC 20036-3078
(202) 223-9485   Fax: (202) 775-1824
Web: www.aera.net/grantsprogram/subweb/RGFly.html

Purpose To provide funding to faculty members and other postdoctorates interested in conducting research on educational policy.

Eligibility This program is open to faculty at institutions of higher education, postdoctoral researchers, and other doctoral-level researchers. Applicants must be interested in conducting research on a topic that may cover a wide range of policy-related issues, including but not limited to: school persistence and career entry; teachers and teaching, including supply, quality, and demand; policies and practices related to student achievement and assessment; policies and practices that influence student and parental attitudes; contextual factors (individual, curricular, and school related) in education; education in middle schools; educational participation and persistence (kindergarten through graduate school); at-risk students; early childhood education; U.S. education in an international context; school finance; materials (curriculum) development; research and informal science education; undergraduate science, engineering, and mathematics education; the supply (pipeline) of students taking mathematics and science courses from K-12; research career development;

the quality of educational institutions; and methodological studies. Applicants must be interested in utilizing at least 1 National Science Foundation (NSF) or National Center for Education Statistics (NCES) data set in their research. They must submit a proposal (up to 7 pages in length) describing their research study and a budget. Minority researchers are strongly encouraged to apply. Selection is based on the importance of the proposed policy issue, the strength of the methodological model and proposed statistical analysis of the study, and relevant experience or research record.

Financial data Grants up to $20,000 for 1 year or $35,000 for 2 years are available. Funding is linked to the approval of the recipient's progress report and final report. Grantees receive one third of the total award at the beginning of the grant period, one third upon acceptance of the progress report, and one third upon acceptance of the final report.

Duration 1 or 2 years.

Additional information Funding for this program is provided by the NSF, NCES, and the U.S. Department of Education's Institute of Education Sciences (IES). Information is also available from Jeanie Murdock, Executive Director, AERA Grants Program, 5662 Calle Real, Number 254, Goleta, CA 93117-2317, (805) 964-5264, Fax: (805) 964-5054, E-mail: jmurdock@aera.net. Grantees must submit a brief (3 to 6 pages) progress report midway through the grant period. A final report must be submitted at the end of the grant period.

Number awarded Several each year.

Deadline January, March, or September of each year.

[707]

AMERICAN HEART ASSOCIATION ESTABLISHED INVESTIGATOR GRANT

American Heart Association
Attn: Division of Research Administration
7272 Greenville Avenue
Dallas, TX 75231-4596
(214) 706-1457   Fax: (214) 706-1341
E-mail: ncrp@heart.org
Web: www.americanheart.org

Purpose To provide research funding to clinician-scientists who have recently acquired independent status as cardiovascular investigators.

Eligibility Applicants must be U.S. citizens or permanent residents who hold an M.D., Ph.D., D.O., or equivalent degree at the time of application. They must be full-time members of a department or unit within an academic or research institution, usually with the rank of assistant professor; customarily, they should be 4 to 9 years past their first faculty appointment. The proposed research project must have received no previous financial support from other granting agencies. For research to be conducted outside the United States, the applicant must be a U.S. citizen. At least 6% of all funds for this program is set aside for awards to underrepresented minority scientists.

Financial data The annual award of $75,000 includes salary, fringe benefits, 10% indirect costs, and project costs (up to $35,000 for salary and at least $40,000 for project support).

Duration 4 years; nonrenewable.

Deadline June of each year.

Number awarded 50 each year.

[708]

AMERICAN HEART ASSOCIATION GRANT-IN-AID

American Heart Association
Attn: Division of Research Administration
7272 Greenville Avenue
Dallas, TX 75231-4596
(214) 706-1457   Fax: (214) 706-1341
E-mail: ncrp@heart.org
Web: www.americanheart.org

Purpose To encourage development of well-defined research proposals by independent beginning investigators and by established investigators pursuing new areas of research broadly related to cardiovascular function and disease, stroke, basic science, clinical, or public health problems.

Eligibility Proposals may be submitted by junior independent investigators or established investigators pursuing new areas of research. Applicants must have earned a doctoral degree (M.D., Ph.D., D.O., or equivalent), be on the staff of nonprofit institutions, and be U.S. citizens, permanent residents, or foreign nationals holding H1, H1B, O1, TC, TN, or J1 immigrant status (only U.S. citizens may apply to conduct research outside the United States). The proposed research must be clearly distinct from ongoing research activities and must relate to cardiovascular function and disease, stroke, basic science, clinical, or public health problems. At least 6% of all funds for this program is set aside for awards to underrepresented minority scientists.

Financial data The annual award of $71,500 includes salary, fringe benefits, 10% indirect costs, and project costs. Up to $32,500 per year may be requested for principal investigator salary and fringe benefits.

Duration Up to 3 years.

Number awarded 100 each year.

Deadline June of each year.

[709]

AMERICAN HEART ASSOCIATION SCIENTIST DEVELOPMENT GRANT

American Heart Association
Attn: Division of Research Administration
7272 Greenville Avenue
Dallas, TX 75231-4596
(214) 706-1457   Fax: (214) 706-1341
E-mail: ncrp@heart.org
Web: www.americanheart.org

Purpose To assist promising beginning scientists to develop independent research programs by supporting a program that bridges the gap between completion of research training and readiness to apply for funding as an independent investigator.

Eligibility This program is open to citizens or permanent residents of the United States who hold an M.D., Ph.D., D.O., or equivalent degree and who are in the final year of a postdoctoral research fellowship or in the initial 4 years of their first faculty appointment. Applicants cannot hold or have held any other national award. They must need to bridge the gap between completion of research training and readiness to apply for funding as an independent investigator. Applications for research to be conducted outside the United States are limited to U.S. citizens. At least 6% of all funds for this program is set aside for awards to underrepresented minority scientists.

Financial data The award includes $65,000 annually for salary, fringe benefits, 10% indirect costs, and project costs (including up to $30,000 for salary and at least $35,000 for project support).

Duration 4 years; nonrenewable.

Number awarded 70 each year.

Deadline June of each year.

[710]

AMERICAN METEOROLOGICAL SOCIETY GRADUATE FELLOWSHIP IN THE HISTORY OF SCIENCE

American Meteorological Society
Attn: Fellowship/Scholarship Coordinator
45 Beacon Street
Boston, MA 02108-3693
(617) 227-2426, ext. 246   Fax: (617) 742-8718
E-mail: amsinfo@ametsoc.org
Web: www.ametsoc.org

Purpose To provide financial assistance to graduate students interested in conducting dissertation research on the history of meteorology.

Eligibility This program is open to graduate students who are planning to complete a dissertation on the history of the atmospheric or related oceanic or hydrologic sciences. Fellowships may be used to support research at a location away from the student's institution, provided the plan is approved by the student's thesis advisor. In such an instance, an effort is made to place the student into a mentoring relationship with a member of the society at an appropriate institution. The sponsor specifically encourages applications from women, minorities, and students with disabilities who are traditionally underrepresented in the atmospheric and related oceanic sciences.

Financial data The stipend is $15,000 per year.

Duration 1 year.

Number awarded 1 each year.

Deadline February of each year.

[711]

AMERICAN NURSES FOUNDATION SCHOLAR AWARDS PROGRAM

American Nurses Foundation
600 Maryland Avenue, S.W., Suite 100 West
Washington, DC 20024-2571
(202) 651-7298   Fax: (202) 651-7354
E-mail: anf@ana.org
Web: www.ana.org/anf

Purpose To provide funding to nurses interested in conducting research.

Eligibility This program is open to registered nurses who have earned a baccalaureate or higher degree. Applicants may be either beginning researchers (who have had no more than 3 research-based publications in refereed journals and have received, as a principal investigator, no more than $5,000 in extramural funding in any 1 research area) or experienced researchers (who may apply only if their proposals are in a new field of research for them). Proposed research may be for a master's thesis or doctoral dissertation only if the project has been approved by the principal investigator's thesis or dissertation committee. This program includes 1 grant restricted to a minority nurse to conduct research on a topic related to a minority issue and 1 grant restricted to research that addresses a core issue of the sponsoring organization (workplace rights, appropriate staffing, workplace health and safety, continuing competence, and patient safety/advocacy). The other grants are unrestricted but are limited to beginning researchers.

Financial data Grants are $5,000 or $3,500. Funds may not be used as a salary for the principal investigator.

Duration 1 year. There is a $50 application fee.

Number awarded 5 each year: 4 at $5,000 (including 2 with restrictions on use) and 1 at $3,500.

Deadline April of each year.

[712]
AMERICAN SOCIETY FOR CELL BIOLOGY MINORITIES AFFAIRS COMMITTEE VISITING PROFESSOR AWARDS

American Society for Cell Biology
8120 Woodmont Avenue, Suite 750
Bethesda, MD 20814-2755
(301) 530-7153   Fax: (301) 530-7139
E-mail: ascbinfo@ascb.org
Web: www.ascb.org/committees/mac/vp.htm

Purpose To provide funding for research to faculty members at primarily teaching institutions that serve minority students and scientists.

Eligibility Eligible to apply for this support are professors at primarily teaching institutions. They must be interested in working in the laboratories of members of the American Society for Cell Biology during the summer. Hosts and visitor scientists are asked to submit their applications together as a proposed team. Minority professors and professors in colleges and universities with a high minority enrollment are especially encouraged to apply for this award. Minorities are defined as U.S. citizens of Black, Native American, Chicano/Hispanic, or Pacific Islands background.

Financial data The stipend for the summer is $12,000, plus $700 for travel expenses and $2,000 to the host institution for supplies.

Duration From 8 to 10 weeks during the summer.

Additional information Funds for this program, established in 1997, are provided by the Minorities Access to Research Careers (MARC) program of the National Institutes of Health.

Number awarded Varies each year; recently, 5 of these grants were awarded.

Deadline March of each year.

[713]
ANDREW W. MELLON FOUNDATION EARLY CAREER FELLOWSHIP IN ECONOMIC STUDIES

Brookings Institution
Attn: Mellon Fellows Program
1775 Massachusetts Avenue, N.W.
Washington, DC 20036-2188
(202) 797-6127   Fax: (202) 797-6181
E-mail: Erobinson@brookings.edu
Web: www.brook.edu

Purpose To provide funding to economists interested in conducting an independent research project in residence at the Brookings Institution.

Eligibility This program is open to economists, especially junior faculty members who have between 2 and 6 years of teaching experience. Applicants should have a Ph.D. or equivalent and an expressed interest in analyzing applied and policy issues and empirical research. They must submit a curriculum vitae, a 500-word research proposal, 2 letters of recommendation, and copies

of up to 5 significant publications and working papers. The institution particularly encourages applications from women and members of minority groups.

Financial data Fellows receive a salary and partial support for staff and research assistance.

Duration 1 year.

Additional information Fellows participate in workshops and conferences at the institution. Funding for this program is provided by the Andrew W. Mellon Foundation. Fellows are expected to pursue their research at the Brookings Institution.

Number awarded 1 or more each year.

Deadline November of each year.

[714]
ANDREW W. MELLON POSTDOCTORAL FELLOWSHIPS AT BRYN MAWR COLLEGE

Bryn Mawr College
Attn: Office of the Provost
101 North Merion Avenue
Bryn Mawr, PA 19010-2899
(610) 526-5074   E-mail: lkolonay@brynmawr.edu
Web: www.brynmawr.edu

Purpose To provide funding to postdoctorates interested in conducting research at Bryn Mawr College.

Eligibility This program is open to postdoctorates interested in conducting research at Bryn Mawr College. The specialties supported change annually but recently included 1) history of science, and 2) Asian American or Latina performance studies, dance, or theater. Applicants must have earned their doctorate prior to the commencement of the fellowship. Women and members of underrepresented groups (e.g., minorities) are particularly encouraged to apply.

Financial data The stipend is $31,000.

Duration 1 year.

Number awarded 2 each year.

Deadline February of each year.

[715]
ANDREW W. MELLON POSTDOCTORAL RESEARCH FELLOWSHIP AT OMOHUNDRO INSTITUTE

Omohundro Institute of Early American History and Culture
P.O. Box 8781
Williamsburg, VA 23187-8781
(757) 221-1115   Fax: (757) 221-1047
E-mail: ieahc1@wm.edu
Web: www.wm.edu/oieach/fello.html

Purpose To provide funding to scholars in American studies who wish to revise their first book manuscript in residence at the Omohundro Institute of Early American History and Culture in Williamsburg, Virginia.

Eligibility Applicants must have received a Ph.D. at least 12 months previously in a field that encompasses an aspect of the lives of North America's indigenous and immigrant peoples during the colonial, Revolutionary, and early national periods of the United States and the related histories of Canada, the Caribbean, Latin American, the British Isles, Europe, and Africa, from the 16th century to approximately 1815. They must submit a completed book-length manuscript that they wish to revise for publication while in residence at the institute. The manuscript must not be under contract to another publisher, because the institute will hold the rights to publishing the revised study. Applicants may not have previously published a book or have a book under contract. Members of underrepresented groups (including people of color, persons with disabilities, Vietnam veterans, and women) are encouraged to apply.

Financial data The fellowship includes a stipend of $45,000, a comprehensive benefits package, funds for travel to conferences and research centers, and access to office, research, and computer facilities at the institute.

Duration 1 year.

Additional information Funding for this program is provided by the Andrew W. Mellon Foundation.

Number awarded 1 each year.

Deadline October of each year.

[716]
ARKANSAS SPACE GRANT CONSORTIUM RESEARCH INFRASTRUCTURE GRANTS

Arkansas Space Grant Consortium
c/o University of Arkansas at Little Rock
Graduate Institute of Technology
2801 South University Avenue
Little Rock, AR 72204
(501) 569-8212   Fax: (501) 569-8039
E-mail: asgc@ualr.edu
Web: asgc.ualr.edu/spacegrant

Purpose To provide research funding to faculty at member universities of the Arkansas Space Grant Consortium (ASGC).

Eligibility This program is open to faculty at institutions that are members of the ASGC. Applicants must be seeking research starter grants for projects that seem likely to receive support from the U.S. National Aeronautics and Space Administration (NASA) and be willing to mentor student scholarship and fellowship research. Fields of study include astronomy, biochemistry, biology, chemistry, computer science, earth science, engineering, engineering technology, instrumentation, materials science, mathematics, physics, psychology, and space medicine. The consortium is a component of NASA's Space Grant program, which encourages participation by underrepresented minorities, women, and persons with disabilities.

Financial data The funding depends on the nature of the proposal.

Duration Up to 3 years.

Additional information ASGC member institutions are Arkansas State University, University, Arkansas Tech University, Harding University, Henderson State University, Hendrix College, Lyon College, Ouachita Baptist University, University of Central Arkansas, University of Arkansas at Fayetteville, University of Arkansas at Little Rock, University of Arkansas at Montecito, University of Arkansas at Pine Bluff, University of Arkansas for Medical Sciences, and University of the Ozarks. This program is funded by NASA.

Number awarded Varies each year; since this program began in 1990, it has awarded approximately 300 of these grants.

[717]
ARKANSAS SPACE GRANT CONSORTIUM SCHOLARSHIPS AND FELLOWSHIPS

Arkansas Space Grant Consortium
c/o University of Arkansas at Little Rock
Graduate Institute of Technology
2801 South University Avenue
Little Rock, AR 72204
(501) 569-8212   Fax: (501) 569-8039
E-mail: asgc@ualr.edu
Web: asgc.ualr.edu/spacegrant

Purpose To provide funding to students at designated universities in Arkansas who are interested in working on a space-related research project.

Eligibility This program is open to undergraduate and graduate students at colleges and universities that participate in the Arkansas Space Grant Consortium (ASGC). Applicants must be interested in working with a faculty mentor on a specific research project. Fields of study include astronomy, biochemistry, biology, chemistry, computer science, earth science, engineering, engineering technology, instrumentation, materials science, mathematics, physics, psychology, and space medicine. Students must be U.S. citizens. The consortium is a component of NASA's Space Grant program, which encourages participation by underrepresented minorities, women, and persons with disabilities.

Financial data The funding depends on the nature of the proposal.

Additional information ASGC member institutions are Arkansas State University, Arkansas Tech University, Harding University, Henderson State University, Hendrix College, Lyon College, Ouachita Baptist University, University of Central Arkansas, University of Arkansas at Fayetteville, University of Arkansas at Little Rock, University of Arkansas at Montecito, University of Arkansas at Pine Bluff, University of Arkansas for Medical Sciences, and University of the Ozarks. This program is funded by NASA.

Number awarded Varies each year; since this program began in 1990, it has awarded nearly 400 undergraduate scholarships and 100 graduate fellowships.

[718]
ARMY RESEARCH LABORATORY BROAD AGENCY ANNOUNCEMENT

Army Research Office
Attn: AMSRL-RO-RI
4300 South Miami Boulevard
P.O. Box 12211
Research Triangle Park, NC 27709-2211
(919) 549-4375   Fax: (919) 549-4388
E-mail: haire@arl.aro.army.mil
Web: www.aro.army.mil/research/index.htm

Purpose To provide funding to investigators interested in conducting scientific research of interest to the U.S. Army.

Eligibility This program is open to investigators qualified to perform research in designated scientific and technical areas. Included within the program are several sites within the Army Research Laboratory (ARL): 1) the Army Research Office (ARO), which supports research in the areas of chemistry, electronics, environmental sciences, life sciences, materials sciences, mathematical and computer sciences, mechanical sciences, and physics; 2) the Computational and Information Sciences Directorate; 3) the Human Research and Engineering Directorate; 4) the Sensors and Electronic Devices Directorate; 5) the Survivability/Lethality Analysis Directorate; 6) the Vehicle Technology Directorate; and 7) the Weapons and Materials Research Directorate. Applications are especially encouraged from Historically Black Colleges and Universities (HBCUs) and Minority Institutions (MIs).

Financial data The amounts of the awards depend on the nature of the proposal and the availability of funds.

Duration 3 years. Although the Army Research Office intends to award a fair proportion of its acquisitions to HBCUs and MIs, it does not set aside a specified percentage.

Number awarded Varies each year.

Deadline Applications may be submitted at any time.

[719]
ARTISTS' BOOK PRODUCTION GRANTS

Women's Studio Workshop
P.O. Box 489
Rosendale, NY 12472
(845) 658-9133   Fax: (845) 658-9031
E-mail: wsw@ulster.net
Web: www.wsworkshop.org

Purpose To assist women artists working on the publication of smaller scale books.

Eligibility This program is open to female artists working in their own studios on the publication of smaller scale projects. Applications should include a 1-page description of the proposed project; specify the medium to be used to print the book, number of pages, page size, and edition size; and provide a structural dummy, a materials budget, a resume, and 6 to 10 slides of recent work. These grants are not intended for re-issuing already published material or as partial funding for a larger project. Applications are especially encouraged from women of color.

Financial data Up to $750 to cover the production costs of new book works.

Duration From 1 to 2 months.

Number awarded Varies each year.

Deadline November of each year.

[720]
ARTISTS' BOOK RESIDENCY GRANTS

Women's Studio Workshop
P.O. Box 489
Rosendale, NY 12472
(845) 658-9133   Fax: (845) 658-9031
E-mail: wsw@ulster.net
Web: www.wsworkshop.org

Purpose To provide financial assistance and a residency to women book artists.

Eligibility Female artists should submit proposals for new books that are in a press run of at least 100 copies. Applications should include a 1-page description of the proposed project; specify the medium used to print the book, number of pages, page size, and edition number; and provide a dummy, a materials budget, and a resume. Women of color are particularly encouraged to apply.

Financial data The program provides a stipend of $1,800, a $450 materials grant, and housing while in residence.

Duration 4 to 6 weeks.

Additional information This program provides an opportunity for book artists to come and work in residency at the studio in Rosendale, New York. Selected artists are involved in all aspects of the design and production of their new books. The studio pro-

vides technical advice and, when possible, help with editing. Assistance with marketing is also available. No residencies are available during the summer.

Number awarded Varies each year.

Deadline November of each year.

[721]
ASM MINORITY UNDERGRADUATE RESEARCH FELLOWSHIP

American Society for Microbiology
Attn: Education Board
1752 N Street, N.W.
Washington, DC 20036-2904
(202) 942-9283   Fax: (202) 942-9329
E-mail: fellowships-careerinformation@asmusa.org
Web: www.asmusa.org/edusrc/edu23b.htm

Purpose To provide underrepresented minority college students with the opportunity to work on a summer research project in microbiology under the mentorship of a member of the American Society for Microbiology (ASM).

Eligibility This program is open to African Americans, Hispanic Americans, Native Americans, Alaskan Native Americans, and Native Pacific Islanders who 1) are enrolled as full-time undergraduate students; 2) have taken introductory courses in biology, chemistry, and (preferably) microbiology prior to applying; 3 have a strong interest in obtaining a Ph.D. or M.D./Ph.D. in the microbiological sciences; 4) have laboratory research experience; and 5) are U.S. citizens or permanent residents. Applicants must be interested in conducting basic science research at a host institution during the summer under an ASM mentor. Selection is based on academic achievement, achievement in previous research experiences or independent projects, career goals as a research scientist, commitment to research, personal motivation to participate in the project, willingness to conduct summer research with an ASM member located at an institution other than their own, and leadership skills.

Financial data Students receive $2,500 as a stipend, up to $850 for student lodging, up to $650 for round-trip travel to the host institution, up to $500 for research supplies and/or miscellaneous administrative costs, 1-year student membership in the ASM, and travel support if they present the results of the research project at the ASM general meeting the following year.

Duration 8 to 12 weeks, during the summer.

Additional information Recently, placements were available at Albert Einstein College of Medicine (Bronx, New York) and Tufts University School of Medicine (Boston, Massachusetts). In addition to their research activities, fellows participate in a weekly seminar series, journal club, GRE preparatory course, graduate admission counseling, and career counseling.

Number awarded 5 to 8 students are placed at each institution.

Deadline January of each year.

[722]
ASNE/APME FELLOWS PROGRAM

Freedom Forum
Attn: Partnerships and Initiatives
1101 Wilson Boulevard
Arlington, VA 22209
(703) 284-3508   Fax: (703) 284-3543
E-mail: cstiff@freedomforum.org
Web: www.freedomforum.org

Purpose To provide an opportunity for journalists of color to work at smaller newspapers.

Eligibility This program is open to journalists of color interested in working at daily newspapers with circulation less than 75,000. Applicants must agree to 1) accept a newsroom opportunity at a participating newspaper for at least 2 years; 2) write a report every 6 months on what they are learning about newspaper journalism and how effectively they are carrying out their assignment; 3) attend, with a key editor from their newspaper, 1 professional convention each of the first 2 years at the newspaper and to share knowledge gained there with colleagues at the newspaper; 4) work with the newspaper's high school projects targeted at interesting young people in newspaper newsroom careers; 5) participate fully in any news-budget meetings, committee, or project opportunities offered at the newspaper; 6) take advantage of work with both the mentor and colleague partners offered by the newspaper; and 7) work with the career coach provided by the program. The sponsoring newspaper must agree to 1) participate in the annual newsroom survey conducted by the American Society of Newspaper Editors (ASNE); 2) verify that a fellow hired by the newspaper increases staff diversity by race, in both percentage and number of newsroom professionals; 3) provide both a mentor and a partnering colleague to the fellow; 4) enable the fellow to attend 1 professional convention in each of the first 2 years; 5) have a key editor accompany the fellow to that convention; 6) involve the fellow in news-budget meetings and other committee or project work in the newsroom and, if possible, in other departments at the newspaper; 7) involve the fellow in the newspaper's local efforts to encourage high school students toward journalism careers; 8) have quarterly career conversations between a key editor and the fellow; and 9) work with the career coach provided by the program for the fellow's professional development.

Financial data Fellowships provide a stipend of $20,000, with the first $5,000 paid within the first month of employment at a newspaper and 3 other payments at 6-month intervals. The program also pays expenses for attendance at a professional convention each year.

Duration 2 years.

Additional information This program was established in 2000. Funding is provided by the Freedom Forum, which works with the other 2 sponsors, the ASNE and Associated Press Managing Editors (APME) to develop a pool of candidates from such sources as metro-newspaper interns, Dow Jones Newspaper Fund interns, and Chips Quinn Scholars who have completed their college degrees. Participating newspapers may also suggest candidates and interested journalists can apply directly.

Number awarded Up to 50 of these fellows will be selected.

[723]
ASPEN INSTITUTE NONPROFIT SECTOR RESEARCH FUND

Aspen Institute
Attn: Director, Nonprofit Sector Research Fund
One Dupont Circle, N.W., Suite 700
Washington, DC 20036
(202) 736-5838   Fax: (202) 293-0525
E-mail: nsrf@aspeninstitute.org
Web: www.aspeninstitute.org

Purpose To support research by scholars and practitioners on nonprofit activities, including philanthropy and its underlying values.

Eligibility Grants are awarded to institutions and individuals. In addition to supporting scholars who are already working in the nonprofit sector field, the fund encourages applications from scholars new to the field, researchers and practitioners working in nonprofit organizations, doctoral candidates, women, and minorities. For-profit consulting firms are not eligible. The fund is particularly interested in research in the following areas: cross-sector comparisons; market-oriented activity of nonprofits; impact of welfare reform and other public policy changes on nonprofits and the people they serve; nonprofit advocacy and civic participation; and performance and accountability of nonprofits and philanthropy.

Financial data Grants are awarded in 2 categories: 1) up to $20,000 to support doctoral dissertation research; and 2) from $5,000 to $50,000 to support research by any eligible applicant.

Duration 1 year.

Additional information This program was established in 1991.

Number awarded Varies each year.

Deadline September of each year.

[724]
ASTRAZENECA FELLOWSHIP/FACULTY TRANSITION AWARDS

Foundation for Digestive Health and Nutrition
Attn: Research Awards Coordinator
7910 Woodmont Avenue, Suite 700
Bethesda, MD 20814-3015
(301) 222-4005   Fax: (301) 222-4010
E-mail: info@fdhn.org
Web: www.fdhn.org

Purpose To provide funding to physicians for research training in an area of gastrointestinal or liver function.

Eligibility Applicants must be M.D.s currently holding a gastroenterology-related fellowship at an accredited North American institution. They must be committed to an academic career; have completed 2 years of research at the time they use this award; be sponsored by a member of the American Gastroenterological Association (AGA) who directs a gastroenterology-related unit that is engaged in research training in a North American medical school, affiliated teaching hospital, or research institute; and be cosponsored by the director of a basic research laboratory (or other comparable laboratory) who is committed to the training and development of the applicant. Individuals who hold a Ph.D. degree are not eligible. Minorities and women investigators are strongly encouraged to apply. Selection is based on novelty, feasibility, and significance of the proposal; attributes of the candidate; record and commitment of the sponsors; and the institutional and laboratory environment. Special consideration is given to applications with a focus in nutrition or geriatrics.

Financial data The stipend is $36,000 per year. Funds are to be used as salary support for the recipient. Indirect costs are not allowed.

Duration 2 years.

Additional information This training can be considered the equivalent of the practical training ordinarily provided in a Ph.D. program. This award is administered by the Foundation for Digestive Health and Nutrition (FDHN) and sponsored by the American Gastroenterological Association (AGA) with support from Astra-Zeneca Pharmaceuticals, L.P. Finalists for the award are interviewed. Although the host institution may supplement the award, the applicant may not concurrently hold a similar training award or grant from another organization. All publications coming from work funded by this program must acknowledge the support of the award.

Number awarded Up to 4 each year.

Deadline September of each year.

[725]
ASTRONOMY AND ASTROPHYSICS POSTDOCTORAL FELLOWSHIPS

National Science Foundation
Directorate for Mathematical and Physical Sciences
Attn: Division of Astronomical Sciences
4201 Wilson Boulevard, Room 1045
Arlington, VA 22230
(703) 292-4895   TDD: (703) 292-5090
E-mail: efriel@nsf.gov
Web: www.nsf.gov/mps.general.htm

Purpose To provide funding to recent doctoral recipients in astronomy or astrophysics who are interested in pursuing a program of research and education.

Eligibility This program is open to U.S. citizens, nationals, and permanent residents who completed a Ph.D. in astronomy or astrophysics during the previous 3 years. Applicants must be interested in a program of research of an observational, instrumental, or theoretical nature, especially research that is particularly facilitated or enabled by new ground-based capability in radio, optical/IR, or solar astrophysics. The proposal must include a coherent program of educational activities, such as teaching a course each year at the host institution or an academic institution with ties to the host institution, or engaging in a significant, coordinated program of outreach or general education. Women, underrepresented minorities, and persons with disabilities are strongly encouraged to apply.

Financial data Grants up to $60,000 per year are available, including stipends of $45,000 per year, a research allowance of $10,000 per year, and an institutional allowance of $5,000 per year.

Duration Up to 3 years.

Number awarded Up to 10 each year.

Deadline October of each year.

[726]
BEHAVIORAL SCIENCES POSTDOCTORAL FELLOWSHIPS IN EPILEPSY

Epilepsy Foundation
Attn: Department of Research and Professional Education
4351 Garden City Drive
Landover, MD 20785-7223
(301) 459-3700   (800) EFA-1000
Fax: (301) 577-2684   TDD: (800) 332-2070
E-mail: grants@efa.org
Web: www.epilepsyfoundation.org/research/grants.html

Purpose To provide funding to postdoctorates in the behavioral sciences who wish to pursue research training in an area related to epilepsy.

Eligibility Individuals who have received their doctoral degree in a behavioral science field by the time the fellowship begins and desire additional postdoctoral research experience in epilepsy may apply. Academic faculty holding the rank of instructor or above are not eligible, nor are graduate or medical students, medical residents, permanent government employees, or employees of private industry. Appropriate fields of study in the behavioral sciences include sociology, social work, anthropology, nursing, economics, and others relevant to epilepsy research and practice. Because these fellowships are designed as training opportunities, the quality of the training plans and environment are considered in the selection process. Other selection criteria include the scientific quality of the proposed research, a statement regarding the relevance of the research to epilepsy, the applicant's qualifications, and the preceptor's qualifications. Applications from women, members of minority groups, and people with disabilities are especially encouraged. U.S. citizenship is not required, but the research must be conducted in the United States.

Financial data Grants up to $30,000 per year are available.

Duration 1 year.

Number awarded 1 each year.

Deadline February of each year.

[727]
BEHAVIORAL SCIENCES STUDENT FELLOWSHIPS IN EPILEPSY

Epilepsy Foundation
Attn: Department of Research and Professional Education
4351 Garden City Drive
Landover, MD 20785-7223
(301) 459-3700   (800) EFA-1000
Fax: (301) 577-2684   TDD: (800) 332-2070
E-mail: grants@efa.org
Web: www.epilepsyfoundation.org/research/grants.html

Purpose To provide funding to undergraduate and graduate students interested in working on a summer research training project in a field relevant to epilepsy.

Eligibility This program is open to undergraduate and graduate students in a behavioral science program relevant to epilepsy research or clinical care, including, but not limited to, sociology, social work, psychology, anthropology, nursing, economics, vocational rehabilitation, counseling, and political science. Applicants must be interested in pursuing an epilepsy research project under the supervision of a qualified mentor. Because the program is designed as a training opportunity, the quality of the training plans and environment are considered in the selection process. Other selection criteria include the quality of the proposed project, the relevance of the proposed work to epilepsy, the applicant's interest in the field of epilepsy, the applicant's qualifications, and the mentor's qualifications, including his or her commitment to the student and the project. U.S. citizenship is not required, but the project must be conducted in the United States. Applications from women, members of minority groups, and people with disabilities are especially encouraged.

Financial data   The grant is $3,000.

Duration   3 months, during the summer.

Additional information   This program is supported by the American Epilepsy Society, Abbott Laboratories, Ortho-McNeil Pharmaceutical Corporation, and Pfizer Inc.

Number awarded   Varies each year, depending on the availability of funds.

Deadline   February of each year.

[728]
BEHREND MINORITY DISSERTATION FELLOWSHIPS

Penn State Erie, The Behrend College
Attn: Office of the Provost and Dean
5091 Station Road
Erie, PA 16563-0101
(814) 898-6160   Fax: (814) 898-6461
E-mail: twortman@psu.edu
Web: www.pserie.psu.edu

Purpose   To provide an opportunity for doctoral candidates, especially members of underrepresented minority groups, to work on their dissertation in residence at Penn State Erie, The Behrend College.

Eligibility   This program is open to dissertation-stage doctoral degree candidates at accredited institutions in the United States studying in a field taught at the college. Candidates from underrepresented groups are encouraged to apply. Applicants should be in their final year of writing their dissertation and intend to pursue a career that includes teaching at the college or university level. Preference is given to candidates who have participated in teaching, research, mentoring, or outreach programs in a diverse educational environment and who are prepared to enhance the curriculum and program goals of the college's diversity initiatives. Only citizens and nationals of the United States are eligible.

Financial data   The salary is $30,000 plus benefits. Additional funds are available for travel and research-related expenses.

Duration   1 academic year.

Additional information   Fellows teach 1 course per semester, work with a faculty mentor, and support co-curricular activities.

Number awarded   1 or 2 each year.

Deadline   March of each year.

[729]
BERNARD MAJEWSKI FELLOWSHIP

University of Wyoming
Attn: American Heritage Center
P.O. Box 3924
Laramie, WY 82071-3924
(307) 766-4114   Fax: (307) 766-5511
E-mail: ahc@uwyo.edu
Web: uwadmnweb.uwyo.edu/AHC/majewski/default.htm

Purpose   To provide funding to scholars who are interested in using the resources at the University of Wyoming's American Heritage Center to conduct research in economic geology.

Eligibility   This program is open to scholars who are interested in conducting research at the center in the history of economic geology. For purposes of the fellowship, economic geology is defined as the activities of exploration and development of petroleum and base, precious, and industrial minerals, including basic geological research. Acceptable related fields include history; oral history; historical archaeology pertaining to economic geology, environmental, and natural resources history; and business or economic history related to economic geology. Applicants must be recognized scholars in 1 of those fields of research. They should have a record of publication in the field or show significant potential for publication. Young scholars, minorities, and multi-disciplinary researchers are encouraged to apply.

Financial data   The grant is $2,500.

Duration   1 calendar year.

Number awarded   1 each year.

Deadline   February of each year.

[730]
BERRIEN FRAGOS THORN ARTS SCHOLARSHIPS FOR MIGRANT FARMWORKERS

BOCES Geneseo Migrant Center
27 Lackawanna Avenue
Mount Morris, NY 14510-1096
(585) 658-7960   (800) 245-5681
Fax: (585) 658-7969   E-mail: info@migrant.net
Web: www.migrant.net/sch_thorn.htm

Purpose   To provide financial assistance to migrant farmworkers who are interested in developing their talents in the arts.

Eligibility   This program is open to students with a "history of migration to obtain work in agriculture." Applicants must be at least 16 years of age, but they do not need to be enrolled in school. They must be interested in pursuing further development of their talents in 1 of the following disciplines: visual arts (e.g., painting, sculpture, photography); performing arts (e.g., dance, theater, music); media (e.g., film, video, animation, computer graphics); literature (e.g., poetry, short stories); or crafts (e.g., traditional folk arts, furniture, weaving, pottery). Students may submit either a complete application that includes a budget and portfolio or samples of work, or only a partial form providing basic personal information and letters of recommendation.

Financial data   The maximum grant is $2,500 for students who utilize the complete application or $500 for those who submit only partial forms.

Duration   These are 1-time grants.

Number awarded   Varies each year.

Deadline   Complete applications must be submitted by May or October of each year. Partial forms may be submitted at any time.

[731]
BYRD FELLOWSHIP PROGRAM

Ohio State University
Byrd Polar Research Center
Attn: Fellowship Committee
Scott Hall Room 108
1090 Carmack Road
Columbus, OH 43210-1002
(614) 292-6531   Fax: (614) 292-4697
Web: www-bprc.mps.ohio-state.edu

Purpose   To provide funding for postdoctorates interested in conducting research on the Arctic or Antarctic areas at Ohio State University.

Eligibility This program is open to postdoctorates of superior academic background who are interested in pursuing advanced research on either Arctic or Antarctic problems at the Byrd Polar Research Center at Ohio State University. Applicants must have received their doctorates within the past 5 years. Each application should include a statement of general research interest, a description of the specific research to be conducting during the fellowship, and a curriculum vitae. Women, minorities, Vietnam-era veterans, disabled veterans, and individuals with disabilities are particularly encouraged to apply.

Financial data The stipend is $35,000 per year, plus an allowance of $3,000 for research and travel.

Duration 18 months.

Additional information This program was established by a major gift from the Byrd Foundation in memory of Rear Admiral Richard Evelyn Byrd and Marie Ames Byrd, his wife. Except for field work or other research activities requiring absence from campus, fellows are expected to be in residence at the university for the duration of the program.

Deadline April of each year.

[732]
BYRON HANKE FELLOWSHIP FOR GRADUATE RESEARCH ON COMMUNITY ASSOCIATIONS

Community Association Institute Research Foundation
Attn: Coordinator, Special Projects
225 Reinekers Lane, Suite 300
Alexandria, VA 22314-2875
(703) 548-8600, ext. 340   Fax: (703) 684-1581
E-mail: jgold@caionline.org
Web: www.cairf.org

Purpose To provide funding to graduate students interested in working on research related to community associations.

Eligibility Applicants must be enrolled in an accredited master's, doctoral, or law program. They may be working in any subject area, but their proposed research must relate to community associations (organizations that govern common-interest communities of any kind—condominiums, cooperatives, townhouse developments, planned unit developments, and other developments where homeowners support an association with mandatory financial assessments and are subject to use and aesthetic restrictions). Academic disciplines include law, economics, sociology, and urban planning. The foundation is especially interested in substantive papers from the social sciences which place community association housing within political or economic organizational models. Minority applicants are particularly encouraged to apply. Selection is based on academic achievement, faculty recommendations, demonstrated research and writing ability, and the nature of the proposed topic and its benefit to the study and understanding of community associations.

Financial data The grant is $2,000. Funds are paid in 2 equal installments and may be used for tuition, books, or other educational expenses.

Duration 1 year.

Additional information The foundation may publish the final project. Recipients must provide the foundation with a copy of their final project.

Deadline Applications may be submitted at any time.

[733]
CALDER SUMMER UNDERGRADUATE RESEARCH PROGRAM

Fordham University
Attn: Louis Calder Center Biological Field Station
53 Whippoorwill Road
P.O. Box 887
Armonk, NY 10504
(914) 273-3078, ext. 10   Fax: (914) 273-2167
E-mail: wehr@fordham.edu
Web: www.fordham.edu

Purpose To provide an opportunity for undergraduates to pursue summer research activities in biology at Fordham University's Louis Calder Center Biological Field Station.

Eligibility This program is open to undergraduates interested in conducting a summer research project of their own design at the center. Fields of interest must relate to the activities of staff who will serve as mentors on the projects; those include forest ecology, limnology, wildlife ecology, microbial ecology, Lyme disease, insect-plant interactions, evolutionary ecology, and the effects of urbanization on ecosystem processes. Applications from underrepresented minorities and women are especially encouraged.

Financial data The program provides a stipend of $3,600, housing on the site, and support for research supplies and local travel.

Duration 12 weeks, during the summer.

Additional information This program has operated since 1967,

Number awarded Up to 8 each year.

Deadline February of each year.

[734]
CALIFORNIA DENTAL GRADUATE LOAN REDUCTION PROGRAM

California Dental Association
Attn: CDA Foundation
1201 K Street Mall, Eighth Floor
Sacramento, CA 95814
(916) 443-3382, ext. 8051   (800) 736-7071, ext. 8051
Fax: (916) 498-6182   E-mail: foundationinfo@cda.org
Web: www.cdafoundation.org

Purpose To help repay the educational loans of dentists willing to practice in underserved areas of California.

Eligibility This program is open to dental school graduates who 1) come from a disadvantaged background (as documented by their academic institution); 2) lived in a rural, highly minority, or Health Professional Shortage Area (HPSA) community for an extended period of time, particularly from birth to 18 years of age; and 3) demonstrate an initiative to develop cultural and linguistic competencies reflecting 1 or more diverse socioeconomic or ethnic communities in California. Applicants must be citizens or nationals of the United States, be current residents of California, have successfully graduated (or be within 3 months from graduation) from an accredited dental school with a D.D.S. or D.M.D. degree, be eligible to practice dentistry in California, and have received student loans from governmental and/or commercial lending institutions. They must be willing and able to sign a contract to serve at least 3 years in a California Dental HSPA (as defined by federal law), an area of the state where unmet priority needs for dentists exist as determined by the California Health

Manpower Policy Commission, or an underserved work site as determined by the CDA Foundation board of directors.

Financial data Grants provide repayment of educational loans up to $35,000 per year for loans that total $105,000 or more. If loans are less than $105,000, the maximum repayment is the total of the qualified educational loan amount.

Duration 3 years. Recipients may apply for additional 1-year contracts. Extensions are competitive and not automatic. Preference is given to recipients who have successfully completed an initial 3-year contract and are willing to continue working in an underserved site. Recipients must agree to provide 30 hours or more per week of hands-on clinical practice in a California underserved work site.

Number awarded Varies each year.

[735]
CALIFORNIA SPACE GRANT GRADUATE STUDENT PROGRAM

California Space Grant Consortium
c/o University of California at San Diego
California Space Institute
9500 Gilman Drive, Department 0524
La Jolla, CA 92093
(858) 822-1597   Fax: (858) 534-7840
E-mail: spacegrant@ucsd.edu
Web: calspace.ucsd.edu/spacegrant/california/index.html

Purpose To provide financial assistance for graduate study and research in space-related science, engineering, or technology at the 8 branches of the University of California.

Eligibility This program is open to graduate students in space-related science, engineering, and technology at the 8 campuses of the UC system. Most programs include research components. U.S. citizenship is required. As the California element of the Space Grant program of the U.S. National Aeronautics and Space Administration (NASA), this program encourages applications from underrepresented ethnic or gender groups and by persons with disabilities.

Financial data Each campus sets its own stipend.

Duration 1 year.

Additional information This program is funded by NASA.

Number awarded Varies each year.

Deadline Each of the participating UC campuses sets its own deadline.

[736]
CANCER EDUCATION AND CAREER DEVELOPMENT PROGRAM

National Cancer Institute
Attn: Office of Centers, Training and Resources
6130 Executive Boulevard, Room 520
Bethesda, MD 20892-7390
(301) 496-8580   Fax: (301) 402-4472
E-mail: lb200w@nih.gov
Web: www.nci.nih.gov

Purpose To provide funding to principal investigators for the development and implementation of curriculum-dependent programs to train predoctoral and postdoctoral candidates in cancer research.

Eligibility This program is open to principal investigators at domestic, nonfederal organizations, public or private, such as medical, dental, or nursing schools or other institutions of higher education. Applicants must be interested in managing, coordinating, and evaluating a training program at their institution for predoctoral and postdoctoral scholars in cancer research. This program is particularly applicable to cancer prevention and control, epidemiology, nutrition, and the behavioral and population sciences, but it is also relevant to other highly interdisciplinary areas of research. Racial/ethnic minority individuals, women, and persons with disabilities are encouraged to apply as principal investigators.

Financial data Grants up to $500,000 per year in direct costs are available. Funds may be used for salary of the principal investigator (up to $125,900 per year), predoctoral stipends (up to $20,000 per year), postdoctoral stipends (up to $75,000 per year), and other research expenses (up to $20,000 per year). Facilities and administrative costs may be reimbursed at the rate of 8% of total direct costs.

Duration Up to 5 years; may be renewed.

Number awarded Varies each year.

Deadline January, May, or September of each year.

[737]
CAREER ADVANCEMENT AWARDS FOR MINORITY SCIENTISTS AND ENGINEERS

National Science Foundation
Directorate for Education and Human Resources
Attn: Senior Staff Associate for Cross Directorate Programs
4201 Wilson Boulevard, Room 805
Arlington, VA 22230
(703) 292-8600   TDD: (703) 292-5090
Web: www.nsf.gov

Purpose To enable minority researchers whose science/engineering careers are still evolving (or who are changing research direction, or who have had a significant research career interruption) to progress in their research activities.

Eligibility The applicant should have had some prior experience as a principal investigator or research project leader, hold a faculty or research-related position at a U.S. institution, be an underrepresented minority (Native American, African American, Hispanic, Native Alaskan, or Native Pacific Islander), and be a U.S. citizen or national. Normally, candidates should be at least 5 years beyond any postdoctoral appointment and applying for funding to: 1) help acquire expertise in new areas to enhance research capability; 2) support the development of innovative research methods in collaboration with investigators at the applicant's home institution or at another appropriate institution (including 1 in a foreign country); 3) assist the conduct of exploratory or pilot work to determine the feasibility of a new line of inquiry; or 4) make it possible for those who have had a significant career interruption to acquire updating for reentry into their respective fields.

Financial data Awards of up to $50,000 are available; an additional amount of up to $10,000 may be requested for equipment. Funds are provided for salary, professional travel, consultant fees, research assistants, and other research-related expenses.

Duration 1 year; these are 1-time, nonrenewable awards.

Additional information This program is offered through the various disciplinary divisions of the National Science Foundation (NSF); for the telephone numbers of the participating divisions, contact the address above. These awards are not substitutes for regular research grants, and they are not intended to provide start-up funds to establish a laboratory.

Deadline Each of the participating NSF disciplinary divisions sets its own deadline.

[738]
CAREER AWARDS AT THE SCIENTIFIC INTERFACE

Burroughs Wellcome Fund
21 T.W. Alexander Drive, Suite 100
P.O. Box 13901
Research Triangle Park, NC 27709-3901
(919) 991-5100   Fax: (919) 991-5160
E-mail: info@bwfund.org
Web: www.bwfund.org

Purpose To provide funding to postdoctorates in the physical and computational sciences who are interested in pursuing research training in the biomedical sciences.

Eligibility Applicants must hold a Ph.D. degree in the fields of mathematics, physics, chemistry (physical, theoretical, or computational), computer science, statistics, or engineering. They must have completed at least 6 but not more than 48 months of postdoctoral training and must not hold or have accepted a faculty appointment as an assistant professor at the time of application. Degree-granting institutions in the United States and Canada, including their medical schools, graduate schools, and all affiliated hospitals and research institutes, may nominate up to 2 candidates for the award. Institutions are encouraged to nominate women and members of underrepresented minority groups. The research proposal must address questions in an area of biomedical science, including any combination of experiment, computation, mathematical modeling, statistical analysis, or computer simulation. Nominees must be citizens or permanent residents of the United States or Canada. Selection is based on the depth and rigor of training in a scientific discipline other than biology, importance of biological questions identified in the proposal and innovation in the approaches chosen to answer them, interdisciplinary nature of the research plan, potential of the candidate to establish a successful independent research career, and quality of proposed collaborations.

Financial data In the first year of postdoctoral support, the salary is $44,000, the research allowance is $35,000, and the administrative fee is $5,000; in the second year of postdoctoral support, the salary is $47,000, the research allowance is $12,000, and the administrative fee is $5,000; in the first year of faculty support, the maximum salary support is $45,000, the research allowance is $73,000, and the administrative fee is $12,000; in the second year of faculty support, the maximum salary support is $49,000, the research allowance is $69,000, and the administrative fee is $12,000; in the third year of faculty support, the maximum salary support is $54,000, the research allowance is $64,000, and the administrative fee is $12,000. The maximum total grant is $538,000. During the first year of the faculty period, at least 50% of the starting salary must be provided by the institution. If an institution's salary scale for either the postdoctoral or faculty position exceeds the amounts provided by the award, then the institution must supplement the awardee's salary. For awardees in the United States, the administrative fee is intended to cover the cost of medical insurance and other benefits. For awardees in Canada, the fee is to be used as a contribution to the employer's benefit plan.

Duration The awards provide 1 to 2 years of postdoctoral support and up to 3 years of support during the faculty appointment. Awardees are required to devote at least 80% of their time to research-related activities.

Number awarded 1 or more each year.

Deadline April of each year.

[739]
CAREER AWARDS IN THE BIOMEDICAL SCIENCES

Burroughs Wellcome Fund
21 T.W. Alexander Drive, Suite 100
P.O. Box 13901
Research Triangle Park, NC 27709-3901
(919) 991-5100   Fax: (919) 991-5160
E-mail: info@bwfund.org
Web: www.bwfund.org

Purpose To provide funding to biomedical scientists in the United States and Canada who require assistance to make the transition from postdoctoral training to faculty appointment.

Eligibility This program is open to U.S. and Canadian researchers in the biomedical sciences who have completed at least 1 but not more than 4 years of postdoctoral training and require support for bridging research to faculty status. Individuals who hold a tenure-track faculty appointment are not eligible. The biomedical sciences are defined to include reproductive science. Applicants must be U.S. or Canadian citizens pursuing postdoctoral training at an accredited degree-granting institution in the United States, Canada, or the United Kingdom. Each U.S. and Canadian institution may nominate up to 6 candidates; institutions that nominate at least 1 candidate in the reproductive sciences may nominate a total of 7 candidates; institutions that nominate at least 1 candidate from an underrepresented minority group (African American, Hispanic, or Native American) may nominate an additional candidate. A U.K. institution, including its medical school, graduate schools, and all affiliated hospitals and research institutes, may nominate up to 2 candidates. Following their postdoctoral training, awardees may accept a faculty position at a U.S. or Canadian institution. The sponsor encourages applications from women and members of underrepresented minority groups.

Financial data In the first year of postdoctoral support, the stipend is $38,000, the research allowance is $15,360, and the administrative fee is $4,640; in the second year of postdoctoral support, the stipend is $41,000, the research allowance is $12,360, and the administrative fee is $4,640; in the first year of faculty support, the stipend is $54,000, the research allowance is $63,600, and the administrative fee is $10,400; in the second year of faculty support, the stipend is $59,000, the research allowance is $58,600, and the administrative fee is $10,400; in the third year of faculty support, the stipend is $65,000, the research allowance is $52,600, and the administrative fee is $10,400. The maximum portion of the award that can be used during the postdoctoral period is $116,000 or $58,000 per year. The faculty portion of the award is $500,000 minus the portion used during the postdoctoral years. The maximum support per year in the faculty portion of the award is $128,000.

Duration The awards provide 1 to 2 years of postdoctoral support and up to 3 years of support during the faculty appointment.

Additional information Since this program began in 1995, more than $70 million in support has been provided to 149 U.S. and Canadian scientists. Awardees are required to devote at least 80% of their time to research-related activities.

Number awarded At least 21 each year: approximately half of the awards go to researchers with a Ph.D. degree in a biomedical science and half go to researchers with an M.D. or M.D./Ph.D. degree.

Deadline September of each year.

[740]
CAREER DEVELOPMENT AWARDS IN DIABETES RESEARCH

Juvenile Diabetes Research Foundation
Attn: Grant Administrator
120 Wall Street, 19th Floor
New York, NY 10005-4001
(212) 479-7519 (800) 533-CURE
Fax: (212) 785-9595 E-mail: cstone@jdrf.org
Web: www.jdrf.org/research/career.php

Purpose To assist young scientists of any nationality to develop into independent investigators in diabetes-related research.

Eligibility This program is open to postdoctorates early in their faculty careers who show promise as diabetes researchers. Applicants must have received their first doctoral (M.D., Ph.D., D.M.D., D.V.M., or equivalent) degree at least 3 but not more than 7 years previously. They may not hold an academic position at the associate professor, professor, or equivalent level, but they must be a faculty member (instructor or assistant professor) in a university, health science center, or comparable institution with strong, well-established research and training programs. There are no citizenship requirements. Applications are encouraged from women and members of minority groups underrepresented in the sciences. The proposed research may be conducted at foreign and domestic, for-profit and nonprofit, and public and private institutions, including universities, colleges, hospitals, laboratories, units of state and local government, and eligible agencies of the federal government. Selection is based on the applicant's perceived ability and potential for a research career, the caliber of the proposed research, and the quality of the host institution.

Financial data The total award may be up to $125,000 each year, up to $65,000 of which may be requested for research allowance. The salary request must be consistent with the established salary structure of the applicant's institution. Indirect costs cannot exceed 10%.

Duration Up to 5 years. Fellows must spend up to 75% of their time in research.

Deadline January or August of each year.

[741]
CARNEGIE INSTITUTION OF WASHINGTON POSTDOCTORAL FELLOWSHIPS

Carnegie Institution of Washington
1530 P Street, N.W.
Washington, DC 20005-1910
(202) 387-6400 Fax: (202) 387-8092
Web: www.carnegieinstitution.org

Purpose To encourage the development of researchers in the fields of astronomy, geophysics, physics and related subjects, plant biology, and embryology.

Eligibility Qualified scientists who have obtained the doctoral degree are eligible. Candidates are evaluated on the basis of academic record, recommendations of professors and associates, and growth potential. Special efforts are made to recruit qualified minorities and women.

Financial data Stipends average approximately $15,000 each year; in addition to financial support, fellows receive the use of the institution's laboratory and observational facilities, including special equipment when needed. Some travel funds are provided.

Duration 1 to 2 years.

Additional information Facilities of the Carnegie Institution include the Department of Embryology in Baltimore, Maryland, the Department of Plant Biology in Stanford, California, the Geophysical Laboratory and the Department of Terrestrial Magnetism in Washington, D.C., and the Observatories in Pasadena, California and Las Campanas, Chile. Fellowships are tenable at the institution's facilities only.

Number awarded More than 70 each year.

Deadline Applications should be submitted at least 1 year in advance.

[742]
CARNEGIE INSTITUTION OF WASHINGTON PREDOCTORAL FELLOWSHIPS

Carnegie Institution of Washington
1530 P Street, N.W.
Washington, DC 20005-1910
(202) 387-6400 Fax: (202) 387-8092
Web: www.carnegieinstitution.org

Purpose To fund doctoral thesis research in the sciences.

Eligibility Doctoral students from universities situated near Carnegie departments or other major universities may apply for funding to carry out their thesis research using Carnegie Institution facilities if they are working in the following areas: embryology, plant biology, or astronomy. Special consideration is given to applications submitted by women and minorities.

Financial data The amount awarded varies, depending upon the scope of the funded research.

Duration 1 academic year, generally starting in July.

Additional information The relevant Carnegie facilities are the Department of Embryology on the grounds of The Johns Hopkins University (Baltimore, Maryland), the Department of Plant Biology on the Stanford University campus (Stanford, California), and the Observatories situated near the California Institute of Technology (Pasadena, California).

Number awarded Varies each year.

Deadline December of each year.

[743]
CAROLINA POSTDOCTORAL PROGRAM FOR FACULTY DIVERSITY

University of North Carolina at Chapel Hill
Attn: Office of the Vice Chancellor for Graduate Studies and Research
312 South Building
CB#4000
Chapel Hill, NC 27599-4000
(919) 962-1319 Fax: (919) 962-1476
E-mail: joann_gustafson@unc.edu
Web: resarch.unc.edu/gsr/postdoc.html

Purpose To support minority scholars who are interested in teaching and conducting research at the University of North Carolina (UNC).

Eligibility This program is open to scholars from underrepresented groups who have completed their doctoral degree within the past 4 years. Applicants must be interested in teaching and conducting research at UNC. Preference is given to U.S. citizens and permanent residents. Selection is based on the evidence of scholarship potential and ability to compete for tenure tract appointments at UNC and other research universities.

Financial data Fellows receive $34,000 per year, plus an allowance for research and travel.

Duration Up to 2 years.

Additional information Fellows must be in residence at the Chapel Hill campus for the duration of the program. They teach 1 course per year and spend the rest of the time in research. This program began in 1983.

Number awarded 5 or 6 each year.

Deadline January of each year.

[744]
CBBF OI TREATMENT CHALLENGE

Children's Brittle Bone Foundation
Scientific Advisory Board
c/o Vanderbilt University Medical School
Division of Nephrology
S-3223 MCN
Nashville, TN 37232
(615) 343-9867   Fax: (615) 343-4704
E-mail: Matthew.Breyer@mcmail.vanderbilt.edu
Web: www.oif.org/tier2/cbbfinfo.htm

Purpose To provide funding to investigators interested in conducting research related to osteogenesis imperfecta (OI).

Eligibility This program is open to senior investigators at domestic and foreign, nonprofit and for-profit, public and private organizations, including universities, colleges, hospitals, laboratories, units of state and local governments, and eligible agencies of the federal government. Applicants should hold an M.D. and/or Ph.D. They must be interested in conducting basic or clinical research to develop novel strategies for treatment of OI or areas of research that may provide new insights into its biology. Minorities and women are encouraged to apply.

Financial data Grants up to $100,000 per year in direct costs are available. Funds may be used for salaries for the principal investigator, postdoctoral fellows, doctoral students, research assistants, or clinical coordinators. The requested budget may also include funds for laboratory supplies, equipment, and animal expenses. Indirect costs may not exceed 10% of direct costs.

Duration Up to 3 years.

Additional information The Children's Brittle Bone Foundation (CBBF) was established in 1991. It added this program in 1999.

Number awarded 1 or more each year.

Deadline October of each year.

[745]
CENTER FOR REGIONAL STUDIES POSTDOCTORAL FELLOWSHIPS

University of New Mexico
Attn: Center for Regional Studies
MSC05 3020
Albuquerque, NM 87131-0001
(505) 277-2857   Fax: (505) 277-2693
E-mail: crsinf@unm.edu
Web: www.unm.edu/~cswrref/engcrs.html

Purpose To provide funding to recent postdoctorates interested in conducting research on topics of interest to the University of New Mexico's Center for Regional Studies (CRS).

Eligibility Applicants must have completed their Ph.D. requirements within the past 7 years and be interested in conducting research related to the following topics: 19th- and 20th-century Southwest social history, political problems, public policy issues, women in New Mexico politics, leadership questions, comparative studies (United States, the Americas, Spain, Quebec), community documentation, histories of institutions, theoretical discourse, and family histories. Candidates qualified and interested in developing Chicano Studies curriculum are strongly encouraged to apply. Preference is given to applicants with the potential of becoming full-time permanent faculty at the University of New Mexico.

Financial data The stipend is $32,000 per year.

Duration 1 year. Work must be conducted at the University of New Mexico.

Number awarded 1 or more each year.

Deadline Applications may be submitted at any time.

[746]
CESAR E. CHAVEZ DISSERTATION FELLOWSHIP FOR U.S. LATINA/O SCHOLARS

Dartmouth College
Attn: Assistant Dean of Graduate Studies
6062 Wentworth, Room 304
Hanover, NH 03755-3526
(603) 646-2107
Web: www.dartmouth.edu/artsci/gradstdy/fellows.html

Purpose To provide funding to Hispanic American doctoral students who are interested in working on their dissertation at Dartmouth College.

Eligibility This program is open to U.S. citizens of Latina/o descent who are planning a career in college or university teaching. They must have completed all other Ph.D. requirements and be interested in working on their dissertation at Dartmouth College.

Financial data The stipend is $25,000. In addition, fellows receive office space, library privileges, and a $2,500 research allowance.

Duration 1 year, beginning in September.

Additional information The fellows are affiliated with a department or program at Dartmouth College. Fellows are expected to be in residence at Dartmouth College for the duration of the program and to complete their dissertation during that time. They are also expected to teach a course, either as the primary instructor or as part of a team.

Number awarded 1 each year.

Deadline February of each year.

[747]
CHANCELLOR'S POSTDOCTORAL FELLOWSHIPS FOR ACADEMIC DIVERSITY

University of California at Berkeley
Attn: Office of the Chancellor
200 California Hall
Berkeley, CA 94720-1500
(510) 642-1935   E-mail: bridget3@uclink4.berkeley.edu
Web: www.chance.berkeley.edu/fea

Purpose To increase the number of ethnic minority faculty members at the University of California at Berkeley.

Eligibility Applicants must be U.S. citizens or permanent residents and must have received a doctorate within 4 years of the start of the fellowship. The program particularly solicits applications from individuals who are members of ethnic minority groups that are underrepresented in American universities. Special consideration is given to applicants committed to careers in university research and teaching and whose life experience, research, or employment background will contribute significantly to academic diversity and excellence at the Berkeley campus. An application form is not required. Interested applicants should submit a curriculum vitae, a statement of proposed research (up to 5 pages), sample publications, and 1 dissertation chapter. In addition, 3 letters of recommendation are required (1 must be from the dissertation advisor).

Financial data The stipend is $31,000 per year (11 months, plus 1 month vacation). Costs associated with 1-way transportation to Berkeley for the fellow and immediate family members and removal expenses are reimbursable, up to $2,000. In addition, up to $500 is available each year for supplies and related expenses, $1,000 for research-related expenses, and $1,000 for health insurance.

Duration 2 years.

Additional information Research opportunities, mentoring, and guidance are provided as part of the program.

Deadline November of each year.

[748]
CHARLES A. RYSKAMP RESEARCH FELLOWSHIPS

American Council of Learned Societies
Attn: Office of Fellowships and Grants
633 Third Avenue, 8C
New York, NY 10017-6795
(212) 697-1505   Fax: (212) 949-8058
E-mail: grants@acls.org
Web: www.acls.org/rysguide.htm

Purpose To provide financial assistance to advanced assistant professors in all disciplines of the humanities and the humanities-related social sciences.

Eligibility This program is open to tenure-track faculty members at the assistant professor level who have successfully completed their institution's review for reappointment (or equivalent) but have not yet been reviewed for tenure. Applicants must be employed at institutions in the United States and must remain so for the duration of the fellowship. Appropriate fields of specialization include, but are not limited to, anthropology, archaeology, art history, economic history, geography, history, languages and literatures, law, linguistics, musicology, philosophy, political science, religion, and historical sociology. Proposals in the social sciences are eligible only if they employ predominantly humanistic approaches (e.g., law and literature, political philosophy). Proposals in interdisciplinary and cross-disciplinary studies are welcome, as are proposals focused on any geographic region or on any cultural or linguistic group. Applicants are encouraged to spend substantial periods of their leaves in residential interdisciplinary centers, research libraries, or other scholarly archives in the United States or abroad. Applications are particularly invited from women and members of minority groups.

Financial data Fellows receive a stipend of $60,000, a fund of $2,500 for research and travel, and an additional 2/9 of the stipend ($13,333) for 1 summer's support, if justified by a persuasive case.

Duration 1 academic year (9 months) plus an additional summer's research (2 months) if justified.

Additional information This program, first available for the 2002-03 academic year, is supported by funding from the Andrew W. Mellon Foundation.

Number awarded Up to 15 each year.

Deadline October of each year.

[749]
CHICANA DISSERTATION FELLOWSHIP

University of California at Santa Barbara
Department of Chicano Studies
Attn: Administrative Adviser
Phelps 1315
Santa Barbara, CA 93106-4120
(805) 893-5546   Fax: (805) 893-4076
Web: www.chicst.ucsb.edu

Purpose To assist promising Chicana scholars in completing their dissertations, preparing for university teaching and/or research, and achieving increased professional recognition.

Eligibility Candidates must be Ph.D. candidates working on a dissertation in the humanities, social sciences, or interdisciplinary studies whose research focuses on Chicana studies. Interested women should submit a letter of application describing progress toward the Ph.D., a dissertation proposal, a curriculum vitae, and a writing sample. They must be interested in completing their dissertation while in residence at the University of California at Santa Barbara.

Financial data The value of the award is $20,000 plus benefits.

Duration 9 months.

Additional information Fellows are expected to work on their dissertation and teach an undergraduate course during the fellowship period. Recipients must be in residence at the University of California at Santa Barbara for the entire fellowship period.

Number awarded 2 each year.

Deadline March of each year.

[750]
CHICANA/LATINA DISSERTATION FELLOWSHIP

University of California at Davis
Attn: Chicana/Latina Research Center
2223 Social Sciences and Humanities
One Shields Avenue
Davis, CA 95616
(530) 752-8882   Fax: (530) 754-8622
E-mail: clrc@ucdavis.edu
Web: cougar.ucdavis.edu/chi/clrc/index.html

Purpose To provide funding to women interested in conducting dissertation research in Chicana/Latina studies in residence at the University of California at Davis (UCD).

Eligibility This program is open to women who are engaged in dissertation research on issues of concern to Chicanas/Latinas at universities other than UCD. Comparative studies of Chicanas/Latinas and indigenous women are also eligible. Applicants must have been advanced to candidacy by the fellowship period, have completed their dissertation prospectus, and have made substantial progress on their dissertation.

Financial data The fellowship provides a stipend of $18,000 plus an allowance of $1,500 for research and conference travel.

Duration 1 academic year.

Additional information In addition to conducting research, fellows are given the opportunity to deliver 1 public lecture and participate in the activities of the Chicana/Latina Research Center. Fellows must be in residence on the Davis campus.

Number awarded 1 each year.

Deadline March of each year.

[751]
CHICANO STUDIES POSTDOCTORAL AND VISITING SCHOLARS FELLOWSHIP PROGRAM

University of California at Los Angeles
Chicano Studies Research Center
Attn: Fellowship Coordinator
193 Haines Hall
Box 951544
Los Angeles, CA 90095-1544
(310) 825-2363
Web: www.gdnet.ucla.edu/iacweb/iachome.htm

Purpose To provide funding to scholars interested in conducting research in Chicano studies at UCLA's Chicano Studies Research Center.

Eligibility Applicants must have completed a doctoral degree in Chicano or related studies. They must be interested in teaching or conducting research at UCLA's Chicano Studies Research Center. UCLA faculty, students, and staff are not eligible. U.S. citizenship or permanent resident status is required.

Financial data Amounts vary, depending upon scholarly background and experience. In general, fellows receive $27,000 to $32,000 for the academic year, health benefits, and up to $4,000 in research support.

Duration 1 academic year; may be renewed.

Additional information Fellows must teach or do research in the programs of the center. The award is offered in conjunction with UCLA's Institute of American Cultures.

Number awarded 1 each year.

Deadline December of each year.

[752]
CHILDREN'S BRITTLE BONE FOUNDATION FELLOWSHIPS

Children's Brittle Bone Foundation
Scientific Advisory Board
c/o Vanderbilt University Medical School
Division of Nephrology
S-3223 MCN
Nashville, TN 37232
(615) 343-9867   Fax: (615) 343-4704
E-mail: Matthew.Breyer@mcmail.vanderbilt.edu
Web: www.oif.org/tier2/cbbfinfo.htm

Purpose To provide funding to recent postdoctorates and junior faculty interested in a program of research training related to osteogenesis imperfecta (OI).

Eligibility This program is open to recent postdoctorates who do not yet hold a faculty appointment and to junior faculty. All applicants must be interested in conducting research into the pathophysiology and treatment of OI. Appropriate research areas should relate specifically to OI and include, but are not limited to, therapeutic approaches to OI (e.g., gene therapy, drug therapy, hormonal therapy), regulation of collagen-synthesis, and bone growth and differentiation factors. Postdoctoral applicants must have a faculty sponsor who will provide a research environment and training to the fellow; they must devote 100% of their effort to the proposed research. Junior faculty must devote at least 25% of their effort to the proposed work. Applicants not working in their native country must submit a notarized statement of immigration status. Minorities and women are encouraged to apply.

Financial data Grants up to $50,000 per year are available. Funding includes approximately $35,000 in salary plus benefits and a research allowance. The remainder of the award may be used for other research-related expenses (e.g., supplies, equipment, travel). Indirect costs are not provided.

Duration 2 years.

Additional information The Children's Brittle Bone Foundation (CBBF) was established in 1991 to support biomedical research to find the causes, prevention, diagnosis, and treatment of OI.

Number awarded 1 or more each year.

Deadline October of each year.

[753]
CINTAS FOUNDATION FELLOWSHIPS

Institute of International Education
Attn: Student Programs Division
809 United Nations Plaza
New York, NY 10017-3580
(212) 984-5565   Fax: (212) 984-5325
E-mail: cintas@iie.org
Web: www.iie.org/fulbright/cintas

Purpose To enable creative artists of Cuban birth or lineage to pursue their artistic endeavors anywhere outside of Cuba.

Eligibility Eligible are creative artists of Cuban citizenship or lineage living outside of Cuba who desire to pursue their artistic activities in the United States or other countries. Applications are accepted, on a rotational basis, in the fields of literature (in 2004), architecture (in 2005), and the visual arts, photography, film, and music composition (in 2006). Only professionals who have completed their training may apply.

Financial data Grants are $10,000.

Duration 1 year.

Additional information These fellowships are funded by the Cintas Foundation, established in memory of Oscar B. Cintas, former Cuban Ambassador to the United States. Fellowships are not awarded for academic study, research, or writing; performing artists are not eligible.

Number awarded Up to 10 each year.

Deadline March of each year.

[754]
CIRES VISITING FACULTY AND POSTDOCTORAL FELLOWSHIPS

University of Colorado at Boulder
Attn: Cooperative Institute for Research in Environmental
   Sciences
Campus Box 216
Boulder, CO 80309-0216
(303) 492-8773   Fax: (303) 492-1149
E-mail: cires@cires.colorado.edu
Web: cires.colorado.edu/cires.vf.html

Purpose To provide an opportunity for scholars to conduct research in the sciences at the Cooperative Institute for Research in Environmental Sciences (CIRES) at the University of Colorado.

Eligibility This program is open to Ph.D. scientists at all levels and to faculty planning sabbatical leave. Recent Ph.D. recipients and those affiliated with minority institutions are especially encouraged to apply. Scientists from all countries are eligible. Applicants must be interested in conducting research at CIRES in the following areas: advanced observing and modeling systems, climate system variability, geodynamics, planetary metabolism, and regional processes. Selection is based on the likelihood of interactions between the visiting fellows and the scientists at

CIRES and the degree to which both parties will benefit from the exchange of new ideas.

Financial data The salary is commensurate with qualifications, current salary, and cost of living considerations.

Duration 1 year; the program may begin at anytime during the year.

Additional information This program is sponsored jointly by the University of Colorado and the National Oceanic and Atmospheric Administration (with support from other public and private sources).

Number awarded Up to 6 each year.

Deadline December of each year.

[755]
CLINICAL ASSOCIATE PHYSICIAN PROGRAM

National Center for Research Resources
Attn: Research Infrastructure Area
6705 Rockledge Drive, Suite 6030
Bethesda, MD 20892-7965
(301) 435-0790   Fax: (301) 480-3661
E-mail: dw171w@nih.gov
Web: www.ncrr.nih.gov

Purpose To provide funding for research training at General Clinical Research Centers (GCRCs) to physicians who wish to focus on patient-oriented research.

Eligibility Candidates must have a clinical degree (M.D., D.D.S., or equivalent) and must have completed their clinical training, including specialty and, if applicable, subspecialty (non-research) training. They must identify a mentor with extensive clinical research experience and must be willing to spend a minimum of 75% of full-time professional effort conducting clinical research. Applications should be submitted, on behalf of candidates, by the principal investigator of the GCRC at the parent institution. The proposed training must be in the area of patient-oriented research, defined as research conducted with human subjects (or on material of human origin such as tissues, specimens, and cognitive phenomena) for which an investigator directly interacts with human subjects. The area of research includes mechanisms of human disease, therapeutic interventions, clinical trials, and the development of new technologies. Minorities, women, and individuals with disabilities are encouraged to apply as candidates. If feasible, women, minority individuals, and persons with disabilities should be involved as mentors and role models. Candidates must be U.S. citizens, nationals, or permanent residents.

Financial data This program provides: salary of up to $75,000 per year plus fringe benefits; research development support (tuition, fees, books, supplies, equipment, technical personnel, travel to research meetings or training, and statistical services) of up to $25,000 per year; and reimbursement of facilities and administrative costs at up to 8% of total direct costs.

Duration Up to 5 years; nonrenewable.

Additional information This program was restructured in April 1998 to incorporate the former Minority Clinical Associate Physician Program and the Clinical Research Scholars Program.

Number awarded Varies each year.

Deadline January, May, or September of each year.

[756]
CLINICAL RESEARCH LOAN REPAYMENT PROGRAM

National Institutes of Health
Attn: Loan Repayment and Scholarship Programs
7550 Wisconsin Avenue, Room 604
Bethesda, MD 20892-9121
(301) 402-5666   (800) 528-7689
Fax: (301) 480-5481   TTY: (888) 352-3001
E-mail: mh18h@nih.gov
Web: www.nih.gov

Purpose To recruit health professionals from disadvantaged backgrounds who are interested in receiving loan repayment benefits in exchange for service at the National Institutes of Health (NIH).

Eligibility Eligible are U.S. citizens, nationals, and permanent residents who hold an M.D., D.O., D.D.S., D.M.D., A.D.N./B.S.N., or equivalent degree, are willing to become NIH employees, and have qualifying educational debt in excess of 20% of their annual salary. Applicants must meet this definition of disadvantaged: they either 1) come from an environment that inhibited (but did not prevent) them from obtaining the knowledge, skills, and ability required to enroll in a medical or graduate institution; or 2) come from a family with an annual income below $10,500 for a 1-person family, ranging to below $27,600 for families of 6 or more. First priority is given to applicants who have demonstrated good academic performance, state a career goal of pursuing biomedical or biobehavioral research, and have characteristics that support the likelihood they will complete their service obligations. Second priority is given to individuals who are underrepresented in biomedical and biobehavioral research, including women, individuals from minority groups, and persons with disabilities.

Financial data The program pays a maximum of $35,000 per year directly to the recipients' lenders for qualifying educational debt. Actual loan repayments are based on funding availability and the proportion of the participants' qualifying debt relative to their NIH salary.

Duration At least 2 years.

Additional information During their service tenure at the NIH facilities in Bethesda, Maryland, recipients engage in biomedical and behavioral studies of etiology, epidemiology, prevention (and prevention strategies), diagnosis, or treatment of diseases, disorders, or conditions, including but not limited to clinical trials.

Number awarded Varies each year.

[757]
CLINICAL RESEARCH TRAINING FELLOWSHIPS IN EPILEPSY

Epilepsy Foundation
Attn: Department of Research and Professional Education
4351 Garden City Drive
Landover, MD 20785-7223
(301) 459-3700   (800) EFA-1000
Fax: (301) 577-2684   TDD: (800) 332-2070
E-mail: grants@efa.org
Web: www.epilepsyfoundation.org/research/grants.html

Purpose To offer qualified individuals the opportunity to develop expertise in clinical epilepsy and epilepsy research through training and involvement in an epilepsy research project.

Eligibility Applicants must hold a doctoral degree and be a resident or postdoctoral fellow at a university, medical school, research institution, or medical center. They must be interested in participating in a training experience and research project that has potential significance for understanding the causes, treatment, or consequences of epilepsy. The program is intended to develop academic clinicians who will advance knowledge about epilepsy through research and teach patient care of people with epilepsy. Academic faculty holding the rank of instructor or higher are not eligible, nor are graduate or medical students, medical residents, permanent government employees, or employees of private industry. Applications from women, members of minority groups, and people with disabilities are especially encouraged. Because these fellowships are designed as training opportunities, the quality of the training plans and environment are considered in the selection process. Other selection criteria include the scientific quality of the proposed research, quality of the clinical training plan, relevance of the research to epilepsy, applicant's qualifications, and mentor's qualifications.

Financial data The grant is $40,000.

Duration 1 year.

Additional information This program includes 4 named fellowships: the Merritt-Putnam Research Clinical Training Fellowship, the Dixon Woodbury Research Clinical Training Fellowship, the William Gowers Research Clinical Training Fellowship, and the Victor Horsley Research Clinical Training Fellowship. Support is provided by the American Epilepsy Society (for research in the United States or Canada) and by the Epilepsy Foundation (for activities only in the United States or its territories).

Number awarded Approximately 7 each year.

Deadline September of each year.

[758]
CLINICAL SCHOLAR AWARD IN DIABETES RESEARCH

Juvenile Diabetes Research Foundation
Attn: Grant Administrator
120 Wall Street, 19th Floor
New York, NY 10005-4001
(212) 479-7519 (800) 533-CURE
Fax: (212) 785-9595 E-mail: cstone@jdrf.org
Web: www.jdrf.org/research/clinical.php

Purpose To provide funding to established independent physician scientists interested in conducting translational diabetes-related research.

Eligibility This program is open to established investigators in diabetes-related research who hold an M.D. or M.D./Ph.D. degree and a faculty appointment at the later assistant professor or associate professor level. Individuals holding the rank of professor are ineligible. There are no citizenship requirements. Applications are encouraged from women and members of minority groups under-represented in the sciences. Examples of translational research appropriate for this award include the following: mechanisms of disease, including etiology and pathogenesis; clinical knowledge, diagnosis (including development of new diagnostic methods or devices), and natural history of disease; disease management, including gene therapy, molecular therapeutics, molecular epidemiology, and limited small-scale clinical trials involving novel approaches or interventions; large-scale clinical trials, epidemiological studies, and other studies relevant to the sponsor's mission. The proposed research may be conducted at foreign and domestic, for-profit and nonprofit, and public and private institutions, including universities, colleges, hospitals, laboratories, units of state and local government, and eligible agencies of the federal government.

Financial data The total award may be up to $150,000 each year, up to $75,000 of which may be requested for research allowance (including a technician, supplies, equipment, and travel). The salary request must be consistent with the established salary structure of the applicant's institution. Equipment purchases in years other than the first must be strongly justified. Indirect costs may not exceed 10%.

Duration Up to 5 years.

Deadline January or August of each year.

[759]
CLINICAL SCIENTIST AWARDS IN TRANSLATIONAL RESEARCH

Burroughs Wellcome Fund
21 T.W. Alexander Drive, Suite 100
P.O. Box 13901
Research Triangle Park, NC 27709-3901
(919) 991-5100 Fax: (919) 991-5160
E-mail: info@bwfund.org
Web: www.bwfund.org/translational_clinical_awards.htm

Purpose To provide funding to physician/scientists in the United States and Canada who wish to conduct translational research on the 2-way transfer between basic research and patient care.

Eligibility This program is open to established independent physician/scientists who are citizens or permanent residents of the United States or Canada affiliated with accredited degree-granting U.S. or Canadian medical schools. Applicants must be interested in conducting translational research, defined to involve studies in the following areas: etiology, pathogenesis, and mechanisms of disease (particularly studies with potential application to disease prevention and treatment); clinical knowledge, improved diagnosis (including development of new diagnostic methods or devices), and natural history of disease; and disease management (including therapeutics aimed at molecular targets), molecular epidemiology, and limited small-scale trials involving novel approaches or interventions that provide evidence for effectiveness of therapy. Large-scale clinical trials, epidemiological studies, and health services research are not eligible. Applicants must hold an M.D. or M.D./Ph.D. degree and be tenure-track investigators at the late assistant professor or associate professor level; individuals holding the rank of professor are ineligible. Nominations may come from a wide range of departments, including pharmacology, pediatrics, obstetrics and gynecology, surgery, medicine, neurology, pathology, and psychiatry; applications are especially encouraged in the area of reproductive science. The sponsor encourages applications from women and members of underrepresented minority groups. Selection is based on qualifications of the candidate and potential to conduct innovative translational research; demonstration of track record and commitment to mentoring physician-scientist trainees; quality and originality of the proposed research and its potential to advance clinical care; and clear-cut plans for translating results into the clinical setting.

Financial data The grant provides $150,000 per year. No more than $100,000 of the award may be used for the awardee's salary support. At least $50,000 of the award must be allocated annually to research expense.

Duration 5 years. Awardees are required to devote at least 75% of their time to research-related activities.

Number awarded Up to 10 each year.

Deadline August of each year.

[760]
COLIN L. POWELL MINORITY POSTDOCTORAL FELLOWSHIP IN TROPICAL DISEASE RESEARCH

National Foundation for Infectious Diseases
Attn: Grants Manager
4733 Bethesda Avenue, Suite 750
Bethesda, MD 20814-5278
(301) 656-0003   Fax: (301) 907-0878
E-mail: info@nfid.org
Web: www.nfid.org

Purpose To provide funding to underrepresented minorities who wish to become specialists and researchers in the field of tropical diseases.

Eligibility This program is open to members of minority groups underrepresented in the biomedical sciences who hold a doctorate from a recognized university and are citizens or permanent residents of the United States (or the spouse of a U.S. citizen or permanent resident). Applicants must have arranged with an American or foreign laboratory where they can conduct their research. The laboratory should be supervised by a recognized leader in tropical disease research. Researchers who have received a fellowship, research grant, or traineeship in excess of the amount of this award from the federal government or another foundation are ineligible.

Financial data The grant is $30,000, of which $3,000 may be used for travel and supplies (at the discretion of the fellow).

Duration 1 year.

Additional information This program is sponsored by the National Foundation for Infectious Diseases and GlaxoSmithKline.

Number awarded 1 each year.

Deadline January of each year.

[761]
COLLABORATIVE NEUROLOGICAL SCIENCES AWARD

National Institute of Neurological Disorders and Stroke
Attn: Division of Extramural Activities
7550 Wisconsin Avenue, Room 9C10
Bethesda, MD 20892-9190
(301) 496-9223   Fax: (301) 402-0182
E-mail: ag38x@nih.gov
Web: www.ninds.nih.gov

Purpose To provide funding for neurological science research to scientists at predominantly minority institutions.

Eligibility This program is open to an applicant investigator, who holds a doctoral degree in a basic or clinical science area and is a full-time employee of a predominantly minority institution in the United States, and a collaborating investigator, who is a grantee from a research-intensive institution and who has current support from the National Institutes of Health (NIH) to conduct neurological science research. The applicant investigator must document the potential for excellence in research and teaching and provide evidence of the intent to develop a career in neurological science research. The collaborating investigator must be an individual holding a senior academic position, such as an associate or full professor, and must have demonstrated research competency by competing successfully for current NIH research grant support. The applicant investigator must also be a U.S. citizen, national, or permanent resident. The proposal must involve joint research efforts, specialized training in research techniques, and participation in research seminars.

Financial data Awards range from $150,000 to $200,000 per year in direct costs.

Duration Up to 5 years.

Number awarded Varies each year.

[762]
CONGRESSIONAL FELLOWSHIPS

American Association for the Advancement of Science
Attn: Science and Technology Policy Fellowship Programs
1200 New York Avenue, N.W.
Washington, DC 20005-3920
(202) 326-6700   Fax: (202) 289-4950
E-mail: science_policy@aaas.org
Web: fellowships.aaas.org/congressional/index.html

Purpose To provide postdoctoral and mid-career scientists and engineers with an opportunity to work as special legislative assistants on the staffs of members of Congress or congressional committees.

Eligibility Applicants must have a Ph.D. or equivalent doctoral level degree at the time of application in a physical, biological, or social science or any field of engineering; persons with a master's degree in engineering and at least 3 years of post-degree experience are also eligible. Candidates must demonstrate exceptional competence in some area of science or engineering; have a good scientific and technical background; be cognizant of many matters in nonscientific areas; demonstrate sensitivity toward political and social issues; have a strong interest and some experience in applying personal knowledge toward the solution of societal problems; and be interested in working as special legislative assistants for Congress. U.S. citizenship is required; federal employees are not eligible. Underrepresented minorities and persons with disabilities are especially encouraged to apply.

Financial data The stipend is $55,000, plus allowances for health insurance and relocation

Duration 1 year, beginning in September.

Additional information The program includes an orientation on congressional and executive branch operations and a year-long seminar program on issues involving science and public policy. Approximately 30 other national science and engineering societies sponsor fellows in collaboration with this program; for a list of all of those, contact the sponsor.

Number awarded 2 each year.

Deadline January of each year.

[763]
CONNECTICUT SPACE GRANT COLLEGE CONSORTIUM GRADUATE FELLOWSHIP IN EDUCATION

Connecticut Space Grant College Consortium
c/o University of Hartford
UT 219
200 Bloomfield Avenue
West Hartford, CT 06117-1599
(860) 768-4813   Fax: (860) 768-5220
E-mail: ctspgrant@mail.hartford.edu
Web: uhaweb.hartford.edu/ctspgrant

Purpose To enable graduate students in education at member institutions of the Connecticut Space Grant College Consortium to work on a space-related research project.

Eligibility This program is open to full-time graduate students at member institutions of the Connecticut Space Grant College Consortium. Applicants must be interested in conducting a research project involving the 167 Connecticut school districts and the needs of their K-12 teachers in science and mathematics for professional development and/or curriculum. U.S. citizenship is required. The program actively encourages women, underrepresented minorities, and those with disabilities to apply.

Financial data The grant is $6,250.

Duration 1 year.

Additional information Member institutions are the University of Connecticut, University of Hartford, University of New Haven, and Trinity College. This program is funded by the U.S. National Aeronautics and Space Administration (NASA).

Number awarded 1 each year.

Deadline March of each year.

[764]
CONNECTICUT SPACE GRANT COLLEGE CONSORTIUM GRADUATE STUDENT FELLOWSHIPS

Connecticut Space Grant College Consortium
c/o University of Hartford
UT 219
200 Bloomfield Avenue
West Hartford, CT 06117-1599
(860) 768-4813   Fax: (860) 768-5220
E-mail: ctspgrant@mail.hartford.edu
Web: uhaweb.hartford.edu/ctspgrant

Purpose To enable graduate students at member institutions of the Connecticut Space Grant College Consortium to work on space-related projects under the guidance of a faculty member.

Eligibility This program is open to full-time graduate students at member institutions of the Connecticut Space Grant College Consortium. Applicants must be proposing to conduct research in aerospace science and engineering in areas normally funded by the U.S. National Aeronautics and Space Administration (NASA). U.S. citizenship is required. The program actively encourages women, underrepresented minorities, and those with disabilities to apply.

Financial data The grant is $6,250.

Duration 1 semester or 1 year.

Additional information Member institutions are the University of Connecticut, University of Hartford, University of New Haven, and Trinity College. This program is funded by NASA.

Number awarded 4 each year.

Deadline March of each year.

[765]
CONNECTICUT SPACE GRANT COLLEGE CONSORTIUM STUDENT PROJECT GRANTS

Connecticut Space Grant College Consortium
c/o University of Hartford
UT 219
200 Bloomfield Avenue
West Hartford, CT 06117-1599
(860) 768-4813   Fax: (860) 768-5220
E-mail: ctspgrant@mail.hartford.edu
Web: uhaweb.hartford.edu/ctspgrant

Purpose To provide funding to undergraduate students at member institutions of the Connecticut Space Grant College

Consortium who need to purchase supplies or equipment for space-related projects.

Eligibility This program is open to undergraduate students at member institutions of the Connecticut Space Grant College Consortium. Applicants must be proposing to conduct a project in aerospace science and engineering in areas normally funded by the U.S. National Aeronautics and Space Administration (NASA). U.S. citizenship is required. A faculty member must agree to serve as project advisor. The program actively encourages women, underrepresented minorities, and those with disabilities to apply.

Financial data The maximum grant is $500. Funds may be used for supplies and materials, such as electronic components and chemicals. No permanent equipment, computer access charges, salaries, fringe benefits, or indirect costs may be charged.

Duration 1 semester or 1 year.

Additional information Member institutions are the University of Connecticut, University of Hartford, University of New Haven, and Trinity College. This program is funded by NASA.

Number awarded 1 or more each year.

Deadline March of each year.

[766]
CONNECTICUT SPACE GRANT COLLEGE CONSORTIUM UNDERGRADUATE STUDENT FELLOWSHIPS

Connecticut Space Grant College Consortium
c/o University of Hartford
UT 219
200 Bloomfield Avenue
West Hartford, CT 06117-1599
(860) 768-4813   Fax: (860) 768-5220
E-mail: ctspgrant@mail.hartford.edu
Web: uhaweb.hartford.edu/ctspgrant

Purpose To enable undergraduate students at member institutions of the Connecticut Space Grant College Consortium to work on space-related projects under the guidance of a faculty member.

Eligibility This program is open to full-time undergraduate students at member institutions of the Connecticut Space Grant College Consortium. Applicants must be proposing to conduct a senior project, honors research, or other educational project in aerospace science and engineering in areas normally funded by the U.S. National Aeronautics and Space Administration (NASA). U.S. citizenship is required. The program actively encourages women, underrepresented minorities, and those with disabilities to apply.

Financial data Grants are $2,500.

Duration 1 semester or 1 year.

Additional information Member institutions are the University of Connecticut, University of Hartford, University of New Haven, and Trinity College. This program is funded by NASA.

Number awarded 10 each year.

Deadline March of each year.

[767]
CORNELL UNIVERSITY LIBRARY FELLOWSHIP PROGRAM

Cornell University
Attn: Director of Library Human Resources
201 Olin Library
Ithaca, NY 14853-5301
(607) 255-5181   E-mail: sem2@cornell.edu
Web: www.library.cornell.edu/Adminops/minority.html

Purpose To increase the number of underrepresented minority staff members at Cornell University's academic libraries.

Eligibility Eligible to apply for this fellowship are African Americans, Latinos, and Native Americans who recently completed their M.L.S. degree and want the opportunity to learn about academic libraries. Applicants must be energetic, self-directed, and interested in a fellowship assignment at Cornell. They must have earned their graduate degree from an ALA-accredited program, be able to demonstrate critical thinking skills, and have excellent oral and written communication skills. Experience and interest in emerging library technologies are strongly desired. To apply, applicants must submit a cover letter indicating their specific areas of interest, program expectations, and short-term professional goals; a resume; and the names of 3 references.

Financial data The appointment will be at the Assistant Librarian level, with full benefits, including 23 vacation days, 11 paid holidays, health insurance, life insurance, and university retirement contributions.

Duration 2 years.

Additional information The program allows fellows to work in at least 2 department or functional areas, to explore new information technologies, to work on a variety of grant-funded projects, and to participate in a challenging work environment. In addition, the program provides conference travel funding, a mentoring program, specialized training, continuing education, library committee assignments, and administrative assignments. Fellows will be considered for regular continuing appointments that might arise during their tenure.

Number awarded 1 or more each year.

[768]
CULTURAL ANTHROPOLOGY GRANTS FOR HIGH RISK EXPLORATORY RESEARCH

National Science Foundation
Directorate for Social, Behavioral, and Economic Sciences
Attn: Division of Behavioral and Cognitive Sciences
4201 Wilson Boulevard, Room 995
Arlington, VA 22230
(703) 292-8758   TDD: (703) 292-9068
E-mail: splattne@nsf.gov
Web: www.nsf.gov/sbe/bcs/anthro/highrisk.htm

Purpose To provide funding to scholars interested in conducting high-risk research in cultural anthropology.

Eligibility This program is open to scholars interested in conducting research projects in anthropology that might be considered too risky for normal review procedures. A project is considered risky if the data may not be obtainable in spite of all reasonable preparation on the researcher's part. Proposals for extremely urgent research where access to the data may not be available in the normal review schedule, even with all reasonable preparation by the researcher, are also appropriate for this program. Graduate students are not eligible to apply. Women, minorities,

and persons with disabilities are strongly encouraged to participate in this program.

Financial data Grants up to $25,000, including indirect costs, are available.

Number awarded Varies each year, depending on the availability of funds.

Deadline Applications may be submitted at any time.

[769]
CULTURAL ANTHROPOLOGY RESEARCH EXPERIENCE FOR GRADUATES SUPPLEMENTS

National Science Foundation
Directorate for Social, Behavioral, and Economic Sciences
Attn: Division of Behavioral and Cognitive Sciences
4201 Wilson Boulevard, Room 995
Arlington, VA 22230
(703) 292-8758   TDD: (703) 292-9068
E-mail: splattne@nsf.gov
Web: www.nsf.gov/sbe/sber/anthro

Purpose To provide funding to graduate students interested in conducting dissertation research in cultural anthropology.

Eligibility Applications may be submitted through regular university channels by dissertation advisors on behalf of graduate students in cultural anthropology. The faculty member must currently be a principal investigator on a research award from the National Science Foundation. The application must be for supplemental funds for a doctoral student's closely mentored but independent research experience. The student's research should be a creative project, not a clerk or assistant's task. Selection is based on the appropriateness and value of the educational experience for the student participant, particularly the independence and theoretical significance of the student's activities and the quality of the supervision. Each principal investigator normally may seek funding for only 1 graduate student; exceptions are considered for training additional qualified students who are members of underrepresented groups. Women, minorities, and persons with disabilities are strongly encouraged to participate in this program.

Financial data Supplemental grants up to $5,000 are available. Institutions are encouraged to treat these supplements like dissertation research grants (which incur no indirect costs).

Duration 1 year.

Number awarded Varies each year, depending on the availability of funds.

Deadline January of each year.

[770]
DEFENSE POLICY FELLOWSHIPS

American Association for the Advancement of Science
Attn: Science and Technology Policy Fellowship Programs
1200 New York Avenue, N.W.
Washington, DC 20005-3920
(202) 326-6700   Fax: (202) 289-4950
E-mail: science_policy@aaas.org
Web: fellowships.aaas.org/defense/index.html

Purpose To provide postdoctoral and mid-career scientists and engineers with an opportunity to supply current technical knowledge to U.S. Department of Defense (DoD) programs.

Eligibility Prospective fellows must have a Ph.D. or equivalent doctoral level degree in a physical, biological, or social science, any field of engineering, or any relevant interdisciplinary field; persons with a master's degree in engineering and at least 3 years of post-degree experience are also eligible. Candidates must demonstrate exceptional competence in some area of science or engineering; communicate and work effectively with decision makers and others outside of the scientific and engineering community; exhibit willingness and flexibility to tackle problems in a number of non-scientific areas; demonstrate sensitivity toward political, economic, and technological issues; and have some experience and/or strong interest in integrating modern science, technology, and business practices in the area of defense. Applicants must be U.S. citizens and must obtain a security clearance; federal employees are not eligible. Underrepresented minorities and persons with disabilities are especially encouraged to apply.

Financial data The stipend is $55,000, plus allowances for health insurance and professional travel.

Duration 1 year, beginning in September; may be renewed for 1 additional year.

Additional information Fellows work in 1 of the following offices: the Office of the Under Secretary of Defense for Acquisition, Technology and Logistics; the U.S. Army's Research Office; or the Defense Threat Reduction Agency. Assignments may involve significant interagency, congressional, or international activity. The program includes a 2-week orientation on international affairs and executive branch and congressional operations.

Number awarded 3 or more each year.

Deadline January of each year.

[771]
DEFENSE UNIVERSITY RESEARCH INSTRUMENTATION PROGRAM

Army Research Office
Attn: AMSRL-RO-RI
4300 South Miami Boulevard
P.O. Box 12211
Research Triangle Park, NC 27709-2211
(919) 549-4207   Fax: (919) 549-4248
E-mail: seitz@arl.aro.army.mil
Web: www.aro.army.mil/research/index.htm

Purpose To provide funding to researchers at colleges and universities in designated states, especially those at Historically Black Colleges and Universities (HBCUs) and other Minority Institutions (MIs), for the purchase of equipment.

Eligibility This program is open to researchers at colleges and universities in the United States with degree-granting programs in science, mathematics, and/or engineering. Applicants must be seeking funding for the acquisition of major equipment to augment current or to develop new research capabilities to support research in technical areas of interest to the Department of Defense. Proposals are encouraged from researchers at HBCUs and MIs.

Financial data Grants range from $50,000 to $1,000,000; recently, grants averaged $213,000.

Duration Grants are typically 1 year in length.

Additional information Information about this program is also available from the Air Force Office of Scientific Research, 4015 Wilson Boulevard, Room 713, Arlington, VA 22203-1954, (703) 696-7315, Fax: (703) 696-7320, E-mail: spencer.wu@afosr.af.mil; Office of Naval Research, 800 North Quincy Street, Room 804, Arlington, VA 22217-5660, (703) 696-4111, Fax: (703) 588-1013, E-mail: bardenp@onr.navy.mil; and the Missile Defense Agency, 7100 Defense Pentagon, Washington, DC 20301-7100, (703) 697-3577, Fax: (703) 695-5694.

Number awarded Varies; a total of approximately $45 million in new awards is available through the participating Department of Defense agencies each year.

Deadline August of each year.

[772]
DEPARTMENT OF DEFENSE EXPERIMENTAL PROGRAM TO STIMULATE COMPETITIVE RESEARCH

Army Research Office
Attn: AMSRL-RO-RI
4300 South Miami Boulevard
P.O. Box 12211
Research Triangle Park, NC 27709-2211
(919) 549-4207   Fax: (919) 549-4248
E-mail: seitz@arl.aro.army.mil
Web: www.aro.army.mil/research/index.htm

Purpose To provide funding to researchers at colleges and universities in designated states, especially those at Historically Black Colleges and Universities (HBCUs) and other Minority Institutions (MIs).

Eligibility This program is open to researchers at colleges and universities in states and territories that have traditionally not received a large number of research awards (Alabama, Alaska, Arkansas, Hawaii, Idaho, Kansas, Kentucky, Maine, Montana, Nebraska, Nevada, North Dakota, Oklahoma, Puerto Rico, South Carolina, South Dakota, Vermont, U.S. Virgin Islands, West Virginia, and Wyoming). Special consideration is given to applications from scholars at HBCUs and MIs. All applying institutions must have an accredited, degree-granting program in science, engineering, or mathematics and a history of graduating students in those fields. Applicants must be proposing a program of research in a science, engineering, or mathematics field of interest to the Department of Defense.

Financial data Grants range up to $100,000.

Additional information Information about this program is also available from the Air Force Office of Scientific Research, 4015 Wilson Boulevard, Room 713, Arlington, VA 22203-1954, (703) 696-7312, Fax: (703) 696-7320, E-mail: thomas.kim@afosr.af.mil; Office of Naval Research, 800 North Quincy Street, Room 804, Arlington, VA 22217-5660, (703) 696-4111, E-mail: 363_DEPS-COR@onr.navy.mil; and the Missile Defense Agency, 7100 Defense Pentagon, Washington, DC 20301-7100, (703) 697-8015.

Number awarded Varies; a total of approximately $10 million in new awards is available through the participating Department of Defense agencies each year.

Deadline October of each year.

[773]
DEVELOPMENTAL GRANTS FOR MINORITY COLLABORATIVE PROJECTS

National Institute on Alcohol Abuse and Alcoholism
Attn: Division of Basic Research
6000 Executive Boulevard, Suite 402
Bethesda, MD 20892-7003
(301) 443-1273   Fax: (301) 594-0673
E-mail: tv9f@nih.gov
Web: www.niaaa.nih.gov

Purpose To provide financial assistance for collaborative research projects between established alcohol research scientists and scientists in minority and/or predominantly minority institutions.

Eligibility This program is open to investigators at domestic nonprofit and for-profit public and private minority and/or predominantly minority institutions, such as universities, colleges, hospitals, and laboratories. The principal investigator must apply with a colleague from a laboratory or research site in the collaborating institution. The proposal should encourage exploratory/developmental studies that complement and enhance existing alcohol research efforts. Racial/ethnic minority individuals, women, and persons with disabilities are encouraged to apply as principal investigators.

Financial data Awards may be up to $70,000 in direct costs per year, but most are expected to be smaller.

Duration Up to 2 years.

Number awarded Up to 4 each year, depending on the availability of funds.

Deadline January, April, or August of each year.

[774]
DIPLOMACY FELLOWSHIPS

American Association for the Advancement of Science
Attn: Science and Technology Policy Fellowship Programs
1200 New York Avenue, N.W.
Washington, DC 20005-3920
(202) 326-6700   Fax: (202) 289-4950
E-mail: science_policy@aaas.org
Web: fellowships.aaas.org/diplomacy/index.html

Purpose To provide postdoctoral and mid-career scientists and engineers with an opportunity to work with various federal agencies in areas that involve international affairs, foreign policy, or international development.

Eligibility Prospective fellows must have a Ph.D. or equivalent doctoral level degree in a physical, biological, or social science, any field of engineering, or any relevant interdisciplinary field; persons with a master's degree in engineering and at least 3 years of post-degree experience are also eligible. Candidates must demonstrate exceptional competence in some area of science or engineering; be cognizant of the ways in which science and technology affect a broad range of international development and foreign policy issues; communicate and work effectively with decision makers and others outside of the scientific and engineering communities; exhibit willingness and flexibility to tackle problems in a number of nonscientific areas; demonstrate sensitivity toward political, economic, and social issues; and have some experience and/or strong interest in applying knowledge toward the solution of problems in the area of foreign affairs or international development. Applicants must be U.S. citizens and must obtain a security clearance; federal employees are not eligible. Underrepresented minorities and persons with disabilities are especially encouraged to apply.

Financial data The stipend ranges from $55,000 to $71,000, plus allowances for health insurance and professional travel.

Duration 1 year, beginning in September; may be renewed for 1 additional year.

Additional information Assignments are available at: 1) the U.S. Agency for International Development (USAID), where fellows work on matters related to sustainable development, especially in economic growth, the environment, population and health, democratization, humanitarian assistance, and education; 2) the Department of State's Bureau of Oceans and International Scientific Affairs, where they assist in foreign policy development

and implementation in the areas of biodiversity, biosafety, conservation, and transboundary environmental issues; 3) the Fogarty International Center of the National Institutes of Health (NIH) where they work with a community of researchers, administrators, and policymakers to advance medical research through international cooperation; or 4) the Cooperative State Research, Education, and Extension Service of the U.S. Department of Agriculture (USDA), where they work with program specialists and national program leaders to help develop activities that support international project objectives in Armenia. All fellowship assignments provide international travel opportunities. At the State Department, that program is known as the Parker-Gentry Fellowship. At NIH, the program is designated the Sheldon M. Wolff, M.D. Fellowship on International Health. to USAID receive stipends from the American Association for the Advancement of Science.

Number awarded 15 or more each year: 10 or more at USAID, 1 or more at the State Department, 1 at NIH, and 1 at USDA.

Deadline January of each year.

[775]
DISSERTATION FELLOWSHIPS FOR THE STUDY OF INTERNATIONAL MIGRATION TO THE UNITED STATES

Social Science Research Council
810 Seventh Avenue
New York, NY 10019
(212) 377-2700, ext. 604   Fax: (212) 377-2727
E-mail: migration@ssrc.org
Web: www.ssrc.org

Purpose To provide financial assistance for doctoral dissertation research that advances a theoretical understanding of immigration to the United States, the processes of settlement, and the outcomes for both immigrants and Americans.

Eligibility Eligible are U.S. citizens, permanent residents, and foreign students matriculated in social science doctoral programs (including history) at U.S. institutions. Applicants must have their proposals approved by their dissertation committees and must complete all course work and exams before the fellowship begins. The proposed research should focus on international migration to the United States and its economic, sociocultural, and political contexts. Applications from women and from members of minority racial, ethnic, and nationality groups are especially encouraged.

Financial data The fellowships provide a stipend of $15,000 and up to $3,000 in research expenses.

Duration 1 academic year; applicants who do not intend to finish their research by the end of the 1-year fellowship must explain how they plan to complete the unfunded portion of their research.

Additional information Funding for this program is provided by the Andrew W. Mellon Foundation.

Number awarded Approximately 8 each year.

Deadline January of each year.

[776]
DISSERTATION FELLOWSHIPS IN EAST EUROPEAN STUDIES

American Council of Learned Societies
Attn: Office of Fellowships and Grants
633 Third Avenue, 8C
New York, NY 10017-6795
(212) 697-1505   Fax: (212) 949-8058
E-mail: grants@acls.org
Web: www.acls.org/eeguide.htm

Purpose To provide funding to doctoral candidates interested in conducting dissertation research in the social sciences and humanities relating to eastern Europe.

Eligibility Applicants must be U.S. citizens or permanent residents who have completed all requirements for the doctorate except the dissertation. Their field of study must be in the social sciences or humanities relating to Albania, Bulgaria, the Czech Republic, Estonia, Hungary, Latvia, Lithuania, Poland, Romania, Slovakia, or the successor states of Yugoslavia. Comparative projects are also welcomed. The fellowships are to be used for work outside east Europe, although short visits to the area may be proposed as part of a coherent program primarily based elsewhere. Selection is based on the scholarly potential, accomplishments, and financial need of the applicant; the quality and scholarly importance of the proposed work; and its importance to the development of east European studies. Applications are particularly invited from women and members of minority groups.

Financial data The maximum stipend is $15,000. Recipients' home universities are required (consistent with their policies and regulations) to provide or to waive normal academic year tuition payments or to provide alternative cost-sharing support.

Duration 1 year.

Additional information This program is sponsored jointly by the American Council of Learned Societies, (ACLS) and the Social Science Research Council, funded by the U.S. Department of State under the Research and Training for Eastern Europe and the Independent States of the Former Soviet Union Act of 1983 (Title VIII) but administered by ACLS.

Number awarded Approximately 10 to 12 each year.

Deadline October of each year.

[777]
DISSERTATION FELLOWSHIPS OF THE MINORITY SCHOLAR-IN-RESIDENCE PROGRAM

Consortium for a Strong Minority Presence at Liberal Arts Colleges
c/o Administrative Assistant, President's Office
Grinnell College
1121 Park Street
Grinnell, IA 50112-1690
(515) 269-3000   E-mail: Cousins@grinnell.edu
Web: www.grinnell.edu/dean/csmp/csmpindex.html

Purpose To make available the facilities of liberal arts colleges to minority scholars who are working on their dissertation.

Eligibility This program is open to African American, Asian American, Hispanic American, and Native American doctoral candidates who have completed all the requirements for the Ph.D. or M.F.A. except the dissertation. Applicants must be interested in a residency at a member institution of the Consortium for a Strong Minority Presence at Liberal Arts Colleges during which they will complete their dissertation.

Financial data Dissertation fellows receive a stipend based on the average salary paid to instructors at the participating college. Modest funds are made available to finance the fellow's proposed research, subject to the usual institutional procedures.

Duration 1 year.

Additional information The following schools are participating in the program: Bowdoin College, Bryn Mawr College, Carleton College, Coe College, Colorado College, DePauw University, Gettysburg College, Grinnell College, Hamilton College, Haverford College, Juniata College, Luther College, Macalester College, Mount Holyoke College, Oberlin College, Occidental College, Pomona College, Rhodes College, Southwestern University, Swarthmore College, Union College, University of the South, Vassar College, Wellesley College, and Wheaton College. Fellows are expected to teach at least 1 semester course, participate in departmental seminars, and interact with students.

Number awarded Varies each year.

Deadline November of each year.

[778]
DISSERTATION YEAR FELLOWSHIPS FOR GRADUATE STUDENTS OF COLOR IN HUMANITIES AND SOCIAL SCIENCES

Northeast Consortium for Dissertation Scholars-in-Residence
Attn: Dean Donnie Perkins
Northeastern University
360 Huntington Avenue
Boston, MA 02115
(617) 373-2133   E-mail: d.perkins@neu.edu

Purpose To provide an opportunity for doctoral candidates from underrepresented minority groups to complete their dissertation while in residence at participating colleges and universities in the Northeast.

Eligibility This program is open to members of underrepresented minority groups who are at the dissertation writing stage of their doctoral program in the humanities or social sciences. Applicants may be working at a university anywhere in the country but must be interested in completing their dissertation at a college or university in the Northeast. They must be able to demonstrate that they can complete the dissertation while at the host campus. Along with their application, they must submit a curriculum vitae, a statement of scholarship and teaching goals, 3 letters of recommendation (including 1 from the dissertation advisor at their home campus), a copy of the dissertation prospectus, and a graduate school transcript.

Financial data The stipend is $22,000. The host campus will provide computer and library privileges as well as office space for each of its scholars.

Duration 12 months.

Additional information This program began in 2001. Recently, the host campuses were Northeastern University, Boston College, Middlebury College, and the University of Vermont. Although the scholars have no formal teaching assignment, they are expected to present their work-in-progress at 2 or 3 campuswide or department-wide forums during the year and to meet with undergraduates to discuss succeeding in graduate school.

Number awarded Varies each year. Each participating college or university hosts 1 or more dissertation scholars.

Deadline February of each year.

[779]
DISSERTATION YEAR/POSTDOCTORAL FELLOWSHIP FOR ACADEMIC DIVERSITY

Virginia Polytechnic Institute and State University
Graduate School
Attn: Director of Graduate Student Services
213 Sandy Hall
Blacksburg, VA 24061-0325
(540) 231-9561   Fax: (540) 231-3714
E-mail: fellows@vt.edu
Web: www.grads.vt.edu/ABD/ABDdocument.html

Purpose To provide a teaching and research experience in a department at Virginia Polytechnic Institute and State University for doctoral students and recent postdoctorates who are from underrepresented groups and plan a career in academia.

Eligibility This program is open to 1) doctoral students who have completed all degree requirements except the dissertation (ABD), and 2) postdoctorates who have graduated within the last year. The university seeks individuals who have been or who are currently underrepresented in their disciplines (e.g., minorities). Applicants should be preparing for a career in academia. They must be able to demonstrate the potential for success as a faculty member. U.S. citizenship is required.

Financial data Fellows receive up to $500 for travel and expenses related to relocating to Blacksburg. Upon arrival, they receive a 1-time grant of $1,000 to cover relocation costs. The salary is $25,000 and full benefits for the academic year.

Duration 1 academic year. Fellows must be in residence at Virginia Tech for the entire fellowship period. They are expected to teach but to emphasize research and make significant progress toward completing their degree.

Number awarded 2 or 3 each year.

Deadline January of each year.

[780]
DOCTORAL DISSERTATION FELLOWSHIPS IN LAW AND SOCIAL SCIENCE

American Bar Foundation
Attn: Assistant Director
750 North Lake Shore Drive
Chicago, IL 60611
(312) 988-6580   Fax: (312) 988-6579
E-mail: fellowships@abfn.org
Web: www.abf-sociolegal.org

Purpose To provide funding to doctoral candidates who wish to conduct research on law, the legal profession, and legal institutions.

Eligibility Applications are invited from outstanding students who are candidates for the Ph.D. degree in the social sciences. They must have completed all doctoral requirements except the dissertation. Proposed research must be in the general area of sociolegal studies or in social scientific approaches to law, the legal profession, or legal institutions. The dissertation must address critical issues in the field and show promise of making a major contribution to social scientific understanding of law and legal processes. Applications must include 1) transcripts of graduate work; 2) 2 letters of recommendation; 3) a curriculum vitae; and 4) a dissertation prospectus or proposal with an outline of the substance and methodology of the intended research. Minority students are especially encouraged to apply.

Financial data The stipend is $15,000 per year. Fellows also may request up to $1,000 each fellowship year to reimburse

expenses associated with dissertation research, travel to meet with dissertation advisors, and travel to conferences at which papers are presented. Moving expenses of up to $1,000 may be reimbursed on application.

Duration 1 year; may be renewed for 1 additional year.

Additional information Fellows are offered access to the computing and word processing facilities of the American Bar Foundation and the libraries of Northwestern University and the University of Chicago. This program was established in 1987. Fellowships must be held in residence at the American Bar Foundation. Appointments to the fellowship are full time; fellows are not permitted to undertake other work.

Number awarded 2 each year.

Deadline January of each year.

[781]
DOCTORAL DISSERTATION IMPROVEMENT GRANTS IN THE DIRECTORATE FOR BIOLOGICAL SCIENCES

National Science Foundation
Directorate for Biological Sciences
Attn: Division of Environmental Biology
4201 Wilson Boulevard
Arlington, VA 22230
(703) 292-8480   TDD: (703) 292-5090
E-mail: ddig-deb@nsf.gov
Web: www.nsf.gov/bio

Purpose To provide partial support for dissertation research in selected areas supported by the National Science Foundation (NSF) Directorate for Biological Sciences (DBS).

Eligibility Applications may be submitted through regular university channels by dissertation advisors on behalf of graduate students who have advanced to candidacy and have begun or are about to begin dissertation research. Students must be enrolled at U.S. institutions but need not be U.S. citizens. Proposals should focus on the ecology, ecosystems, systematics, or population biology programs in the DBS Division of Environmental Biology, or the animal behavior or ecological and evolutionary physiology programs in the DBS Division of Integrative Biology and Neuroscience. Women, minorities, and persons with disabilities are strongly encouraged to apply.

Financial data Grants range up to $12,000; funds may be used for travel to specialized facilities or field research locations, specialized research equipment, purchase of supplies and services not otherwise available, fees for computerized or other forms of data, and rental of environmental chambers or other research facilities. Funding is not provided for stipends, tuition, textbooks, journals, allowances for dependents, travel to scientific meetings, publication costs, dissertation preparation or reproduction, or indirect costs.

Duration Normally 2 years.

Additional information Information on programs in the Division of Environmental Biology is available at the address and telephone number above; information from the Division of Integrative Biology and Neuroscience is available at (703) 292-7875, E-mail: ddig-ibm@nsf.gov.

Number awarded 90 each year; approximately $900,000 is available for this program each year.

Deadline November of each year.

[782]
DOCTORAL DISSERTATION RESEARCH IMPROVEMENT GRANTS IN THE DIRECTORATE FOR SOCIAL, BEHAVIORAL, AND ECONOMIC SCIENCES

National Science Foundation
Directorate for Social, Behavioral, and Economic Sciences
Attn: Division of Social and Economic Sciences
4201 Wilson Boulevard
Arlington, VA 22230
(703) 292-8670   TDD: (703) 292-5090
E-mail: sesfl@nsf.gov
Web: www.nsf.gov/sbe/docdiss

Purpose To provide partial support to doctoral candidates conducting dissertation research in selected areas of the social, behavioral, and economic sciences.

Eligibility Applications may be submitted through regular university channels by dissertation advisors on behalf of graduate students who have advanced to candidacy and have begun or are about to begin dissertation research. Students must be enrolled at U.S. institutions but need not be U.S. citizens. Programs that have been most active in supporting dissertation research include archaeology; cognitive neuroscience; cultural anthropology; decision, risk, and management science; geography and regional science; law and social science; linguistics; physical anthropology; political science; science and technology studies; sociology; and societal dimensions of engineering, science, and technology. Other disciplines that receive support if appropriate include economics; human cognition and perception; and methodology, measurement, and statistics. Budget requests may be submitted for such dissertation research-related expenses as data collection and sample survey costs, microfilms and other forms of specialized data, payments to subjects or informants, specialized research equipment, analysis and services not otherwise available, supplies and travel to specialized facilities or field research locations, and partial living expenses for conducting necessary research away from the student's university. Women, minorities, and persons with disabilities are strongly encouraged to apply.

Financial data Grants have the limited purpose of providing funds to enhance the quality of dissertation research. They are to be used exclusively for necessary expenses incurred in the actual conduct of the dissertation research. Funding is not provided for stipends, tuition, textbooks, journals, allowances for dependents, travel to scientific meetings, publication costs, dissertation preparation or reproduction, or indirect costs.

Duration Up to 2 years.

Additional information Information is also available from the Division of Behavioral and Cognitive Sciences, (703) 292-8740.

Number awarded 200 to 300 each year. Approximately $2.5 million is available for this program annually.

Deadline Deadline dates for the submission of dissertation improvement grant proposals differ by program within the Division of Social and Economic Science and the Division of Behavioral and Cognitive Sciences; applicants should obtain information regarding target dates for proposals from the relevant program.

[783]
EARLY CAREER PATIENT-ORIENTED DIABETES RESEARCH AWARD

Juvenile Diabetes Research Foundation
Attn: Grant Administrator
120 Wall Street, 19th Floor
New York, NY 10005-4001
(212) 479-7519   (800) 533-CURE
Fax: (212) 785-9595   E-mail: cstone@jdrf.org
Web: www.jdrf.org/research/early.php

Purpose To provide funding to physician scientists interested in pursuing a program of clinical diabetes-related research training.

Eligibility This program is open to investigators in diabetes-related research who hold an M.D. or M.D./Ph.D. degree and a faculty appointment at the late training or assistant professor level. Applicants must be sponsored by an investigator who is affiliated full time with an accredited institution, who pursues patient-oriented clinical research, and who agrees to supervise the applicant's training. There are no citizenship requirements. Applications are encouraged from women and members of minority groups underrepresented in the sciences. Areas of relevant research can include: mechanisms of human disease, therapeutic interventions, clinical trials, and the development of new technologies. The proposed research may be conducted at foreign and domestic, for-profit and nonprofit, and public and private institutions, including universities, colleges, hospitals, laboratories, units of state and local government, and eligible agencies of the federal government.

Financial data The total award may be up to $150,000 each year, up to $75,000 of which may be requested for research (including a technician, supplies, equipment, and travel). The salary request must be consistent with the established salary structure of the applicant's institution. Equipment purchases in years other than the first must be strongly justified. Indirect costs may not exceed 10%. Awardees may also be eligible for repayment of up to $100,000 in educational loans.

Duration The award is for 5 years and may be renewed for an additional 2 years.

Deadline January or August of each year.

[784]
EDUCATIONAL TESTING SERVICE POSTDOCTORAL FELLOWSHIP AWARD PROGRAM

Educational Testing Service
MS 09-R
Princeton, NJ 08541-0001
(609) 734-1806   E-mail: ldelauro@ets.org
Web: www.ets.org

Purpose To provide financial assistance to postdoctorates who wish to conduct independent research at the Educational Testing Service (ETS).

Eligibility Applicants must hold a doctorate in a relevant discipline and be able to provide evidence of prior research. They must be interested in conducting research at ETS in 1 of the following areas: computer science, education, learning, literacy, minority issues, policy research, psychology, statistics, teaching, educational technology, or testing issues (including alternate forms of assessment for special populations and new forms of assessment). Selection is based on the scholarship and importance of the proposed research. An explicit goal of the program is to increase the number of women and minority professionals in educational measurement and related fields.

Financial data The stipend is $38,000; fellows and their families also receive limited reimbursement for relocation expenses.

Duration 1 year, normally beginning in September.

Additional information Fellows work with senior staff at the Educational Testing Service in Princeton, New Jersey.

Number awarded Up to 3 each year.

Deadline January of each year.

[785]
EISENHOWER GRANTS FOR RESEARCH FELLOWSHIPS

Department of Transportation
Federal Highway Administration
Attn: National Highway Institute
4600 North Fairfax Drive, Suite 800
Arlington, VA 22203-1553
(703) 235-0538   Fax: (703) 235-0593
E-mail: ilene.payne@fhwa.dov.gov
Web: www.nhi.fhwa.dot.gov/fellowships.html

Purpose To enable students to participate in research activities at facilities of the U.S. Department of Transportation (DOT) Federal Highway Administration in the Washington, D.C. area.

Eligibility This program is open to 1) students in their junior year of a baccalaureate program who will complete their junior year before being awarded a fellowship; 2) students in their senior year of a baccalaureate program; and 3) students who have completed their baccalaureate degree and are enrolled in a program leading to a master's, Ph.D., or equivalent degree. Applicants must be U.S. citizens enrolled in an accredited U.S. institution of higher education pursuing a degree full time and planning to enter the transportation profession after completing their higher education. They select 1 or more projects from a current list of research projects underway at various DOT facilities. They conduct research with academic supervision provided by a faculty advisor from their home university (which grants academic credit for the research project) and with technical direction provided by the DOT staff. Specific requirements for the target projects vary; most require engineering backgrounds, but others involve transportation planning, information management, public administration, physics, materials science, statistical analysis, operations research, chemistry, economics, technology transfer, urban studies, geography, and urban and regional planning. The DOT encourages students at Historically Black Colleges and Universities (HBCUs) and Hispanic Serving Institutions (HSIs) to apply for these grants. Selection is based on match of the student's qualifications with the proposed research project (including the student's ability to accomplish the project in the available time), recommendation letters regarding the nominee's qualifications to conduct the research, academic records (including class standing, GPA, and transcripts), and transportation work experience (if any) including the employer's endorsement.

Financial data Fellows receive full tuition and fees that relate to the academic credits for the approved research project and a monthly stipend of $1,450 for college seniors, $1,700 for master's students, or $2,000 for doctoral students. An allowance for travel to and from the DOT facility where the research is conducted is also provided, but selectees are responsible for their own housing accommodations. Faculty advisors are allowed 1 site review on projects over 6 months and 2 site reviews on projects over 9 months; travel and per diem are provided for those site reviews.

Duration Tenure is normally 3, 6, 9, or 12 months.

Number awarded Varies each year; recently, 9 students participated in this program.

Deadline February of each year.

[786]
ELEANOR ROOSEVELT PROFESSIONAL DEVELOPMENT FELLOWSHIPS

American Association of University Women
Attn: AAUW Educational Foundation
2201 North Dodge Street
P.O. Box 4030
Iowa City, IA 52243-4030
(319) 337-1716   Fax: (319) 337-1204
E-mail: aauw@act.org
Web: www.aauw.org

Purpose To provide financial assistance to women public school teachers interested in participating in professional development activities.

Eligibility This program is open to women public school teachers in grades K-12 who have taught for at least 3 years. Applicants must be interested in attending a professional development workshop or conference, including the Eleanor Roosevelt Teaching Institute in Washington, D.C. Activities should help improve girls' learning opportunities (especially in mathematics, science, and technology) and promote equity and long-term change in classrooms, schools, and school systems. U.S. citizenship or permanent resident status is required. Applications are especially encouraged from women of color and others from underrepresented groups as well as those who teach underserved students.

Financial data Grants up to $5,000 are available. Additional support is available to colleagues interested in attending the Eleanor Roosevelt Teaching Institute.

Duration These are 1-time grants. The Eleanor Roosevelt Teaching Institute lasts 5 days.

Additional information This program was established in 1990. Colleagues attending the Eleanor Roosevelt Teaching Institute may include male and female teachers and administrators.

Number awarded Varies each year.

Deadline January of each year.

[787]
ELEANOR ROOSEVELT PROJECT IMPLEMENTATION GRANTS

American Association of University Women
Attn: AAUW Educational Foundation
2201 North Dodge Street
P.O. Box 4030
Iowa City, IA 52243-4030
(319) 337-1716   Fax: (319) 337-1204
E-mail: aauw@act.org
Web: www.aauw.org

Purpose To provide funding to women public school teachers interested in developing classroom programs to advance gender equity.

Eligibility This program is open to women public school teachers in grades K-12 who have taught for at least 3 years. Applicants must be interested in developing a classroom or school program to advance gender equity. U.S. citizenship or permanent resident status is required. Applications are especially encouraged from women of color and others from underrepresented groups as well as those who teach underserved students. Preference is given to prior recipients of Eleanor Roosevelt Professional Development Fellowships.

Financial data Grants up to $10,000 are available.

Duration These are 1-time grants.

Additional information This program was established in 1990.

Number awarded Varies each year.

Deadline January of each year.

[788]
ELSEVIER RESEARCH INITIATIVE AWARDS

Foundation for Digestive Health and Nutrition
Attn: Research Awards Coordinator
7910 Woodmont Avenue, Suite 700
Bethesda, MD 20814-3015
(301) 222-4005   Fax: (301) 222-4010
E-mail: info@fdhn.org
Web: www.fdhn.org

Purpose To provide funding to new or established investigators for pilot research projects in areas related to gastroenterology or hepatology.

Eligibility Applicants must hold an M.D. or Ph.D. degree (or the equivalent) and a faculty position at an accredited North American institution. They may not hold awards on a similar topic from other agencies. Individual membership in the American Gastroenterology Association (AGA) is required. Women and minority investigators are strongly encouraged to apply. Selection is based on novelty, importance, feasibility, environment, commitment of the institution, and overall likelihood that the projects will lead to more substantial grant applications.

Financial data The grant is $25,000 per year. Funds may be used for salary, supplies, or equipment. Indirect costs are not allowed.

Duration 1 year.

Additional information This award is administered by the Foundation for Digestive Health and Nutrition and sponsored by the AGA and Elsevier Science Publishing Company.

Number awarded 1 each year.

Deadline January of each year.

[789]
EMERGING MINORITY SCHOLARS IN AGING PROGRAM

Gerontological Society of America
Attn: Minority Student Research Center
1030 15th Street, N.W., Suite 250
Washington, DC 20005-1503
(202) 842-1275   Fax: (202) 842-1150
E-mail: geron@geron.org
Web: www.geron.org

Purpose To provide various forms of assistance to minority master's degree students who are interested in a research career in gerontology.

Eligibility This program is open to minority (African American, Asian, Pacific Islander, American Indian, Alaskan Native, Hispanic) students pursuing a master's degree in gerontology. Applicants must have a GPA of 3.0 or higher, a demonstrated commitment to minority aging concerns, excellence in writing and analytic skills, and 2 letters of recommendation from faculty members or mentors. U.S. citizenship or permanent resident status is required.

Financial data Benefits of the program include a $2,500 travel stipend each year to attend national scientific meetings, seminars, and workshops relevant to research on aging; workshops that complement and enrich the recipient's graduate study; mentors to assist students put together a personalized plan for developing research skills; career guidance and assistance; and a professional and peer support network.

Duration 2 years.

Additional information Funding support for this program is provided by the National Institute on Aging.

Number awarded 5 each year.

Deadline February of each year.

[790]
EPILEPSY FOUNDATION HEALTH SCIENCES STUDENT FELLOWSHIPS

Epilepsy Foundation
Attn: Department of Research and Professional Education
4351 Garden City Drive
Landover, MD 20785-7223
(301) 459-3700   (800) EFA-1000
Fax: (301) 577-2684   TDD: (800) 332-2070
E-mail: grants@efa.org
Web: www.epilepsyfoundation.org/research/grants.html

Purpose To provide financial assistance to medical and health science graduate students interested in working on an epilepsy project during the summer.

Eligibility This program is open to students enrolled, or accepted for enrollment, in a medical school, a doctoral program, or other graduate program. Applicants must have a defined epilepsy-related study or research plan to be carried out under the supervision of a qualified mentor. Because the program is designed as a training opportunity, the quality of the training plans and environment are considered in the selection process. Other selection criteria include the quality of the proposed project, the relevance of the proposed work to epilepsy, the applicant's interest in the field of epilepsy, the applicant's qualifications, and the mentor's qualifications, including his or her commitment to the student and the project. U.S. citizenship is not required, but the project must be conducted in the United States. Applications from women, members of minority groups, and people with disabilities are especially encouraged.

Financial data Stipends are $3,000.

Duration 3 months, during the summer.

Additional information This program is supported by the American Epilepsy Society, Abbott Laboratories, Ortho-McNeil Pharmaceutical Corporation, and Pfizer Inc.

Number awarded Varies each year.

Deadline February of each year.

[791]
EPILEPSY RESEARCH AWARDS PROGRAM

American Epilepsy Society
342 North Main Street
West Hartford, CT 06117-2507
(860) 586-7505   Fax: (860) 586-7550
Web: asenet.org/awards/research.htm

Purpose To provide funding to investigators anywhere in the world interested in conducting research related to epilepsy.

Eligibility This program is open to active scientists and clinicians working in all aspects of epilepsy. Candidates must be nominated by their home institution. There are no geographic restrictions; nominations from outside the United States and North America are welcome. Nominations of women and members of minority groups are especially encouraged.

Financial data The grant is $50,000. No institutional overhead is allowed.

Additional information This program, established in 1991, is funded by the Milken Family Foundation.

Number awarded 2 each year.

Deadline August of each year.

[792]
EURASIA DISSERTATION WRITE-UP FELLOWSHIPS

Social Science Research Council
810 Seventh Avenue
New York, NY 10019
(212) 377-2700   Fax: (212) 377-2727
E-mail: eurasia@ssrc.org
Web: www.ssrc.org

Purpose To provide funding to graduate students working on a dissertation dealing with Eurasia.

Eligibility This program is open to students who have completed research for their doctoral dissertation and who expect to complete the writing of their dissertation during the next academic year. Applicants must be U.S. citizens and specializing in a discipline of the social sciences or humanities that deals with the Soviet Union and its successor states. Research is especially encouraged in the following areas: social welfare structures or set processes of economic exchange, organization, or property relations in historical, cultural, or social contexts; the conditionality or construction of regional identity or state sovereignty; the emergent role of non-state actors and international structures; or the organization, ideologies, or significance of science and technology. Minorities and women are particularly encouraged to apply.

Financial data Grants up to $15,000 are available.

Duration Up to 1 year.

Additional information Funding for this program is provided by the U.S. Department of State under the Program for Research and Training on Eastern Europe and the Independent States of the Former Soviet Union (Title VIII).

Number awarded Varies each year; recently, 7 of these fellowships were awarded.

Deadline October of each year.

[793]
EURASIA GRADUATE TRAINING FELLOWSHIPS

Social Science Research Council
810 Seventh Avenue
New York, NY 10019
(212) 377-2700   Fax: (212) 377-2727
E-mail: eurasia@ssrc.org
Web: www.ssrc.org

Purpose To provide funding to graduate students interested in conducting research related to Eurasia area studies.

Eligibility This program is open to U.S. citizens and permanent residents enrolled in accredited graduate programs in a discipline of the social sciences or humanities that deals with the Soviet Union and its successor states. Applicants must be seeking to enhance their disciplinary, methodological, or language training in relation to research. The awards are not intended to support dissertation field research; applicants should not yet have submit-

ted a dissertation prospectus or proposal to their department. Minorities and women particularly encouraged to apply.

Financial data Grants up to $10,000 are available.

Duration 3 to 9 months.

Additional information Funding for this program is provided by the U.S. Department of State under the Program for Research and Training on Eastern Europe and the Independent States of the Former Soviet Union (Title VIII).

Number awarded Varies each year; recently, 5 of these fellowships were awarded.

Deadline October of each year.

[794]
EURASIA POSTDOCTORAL FELLOWSHIPS

Social Science Research Council
810 Seventh Avenue
New York, NY 10019
(212) 377-2700   Fax: (212) 377-2727
E-mail: eurasia@ssrc.org
Web: www.ssrc.org

Purpose To improve the academic employment and tenure opportunities of scholars who recently received a Ph.D. in the study of Eurasia.

Eligibility This program is open to U.S. citizens and permanent residents who have received a Ph.D. within the last 6 years but who are still untenured. Applicants may propose research in any discipline of the social sciences and humanities as long as it relates to the Soviet Union and its successor states. They must indicate the anticipated location of their research. Women and members of minority groups are especially encouraged to apply.

Financial data The maximum grant is $24,000.

Duration The grant may be spent flexibly over a 2-year period.

Additional information Funding for this program is provided by the U.S. Department of State under the Program for Research and Training on Eastern Europe and the Independent States of the Former Soviet Union (Title VIII).

Number awarded Varies each year; recently, 3 of these fellowships were awarded.

Deadline October of each year.

[795]
FACULTY AWARDS FOR RESEARCH

National Aeronautics and Space Administration
Office of Equal Opportunity Programs
Attn: Minority University Research and Education Division
500 E Street, S.W., Suite 200
Washington, DC 20024-2760
(202) 358-0948   Fax: (202) 358-3745
E-mail: muredsupport@mail.nasaprs.com
Web: research@hq.nasa.gov

Purpose To provide funding for space-related research to faculty at recognized minority colleges and universities.

Eligibility This program is open to tenured and tenure-track faculty holding Ph.D.s in relevant engineering, mathematics, or science disciplines and employed at institutions recognized as a Hispanic-Serving Institution (HSI) or Historically Black College or University (HBCU) and to full-time faculty at a recognized Tribal College or University (TCU). The university must offer degrees in engineering, mathematics, science, or technology. Applicants must be proposing to conduct research at their university or at any institution or facility engaged in substantial research for the

National Aeronautics and Space Administration (NASA). U.S. citizenship is required. Awards are offered at levels of senior career (received Ph.D. degree more than 13 years previously), mid-career (received Ph.D. degree between 3 and 13 years previously), and early career (received Ph.D. degree within the past 3 years). Senior and mid-career level faculty may not have received more than $250,000 in NASA research grants during the last 5 years. Early career level faculty may never have received a NASA research award.

Financial data Senior and mid-career level faculty may receive grants up to $100,000 per year. Research funding may include support of research assistants, undergraduate student researchers, professional travel, research supplies and equipment, principal investigator summer salary, and release time for conducting research. For early career level faculty, the maximum grant is $10,000 per year.

Duration Up to 3 years for senior and mid-career level grants; 1 year for early career level grants.

Additional information The program strongly encourages participation of persons with disabilities. To facilitate the participation of such individuals, the program provides up to $5,000 in supplemental funding for special assistance and/or equipment necessary to enable the principal investigator to perform the work under the award.

Number awarded Approximately 40 each year: 20 for senior and mid-career level faculty and 20 for early career level faculty.

Deadline The deadline dates differ each year the program is offered; recently, notices of intent were due in May.

[796]
FACULTY EARLY CAREER DEVELOPMENT PROGRAM

National Science Foundation
Directorate for Education and Human Resources
Attn: Senior Staff Associate for Cross Directorate Programs
4201 Wilson Boulevard, Room 805
Arlington, VA 22230
(703) 292-8600   TDD: (703) 292-5090
Web: www.nsf.gov/career

Purpose To provide support for science and engineering research to outstanding new faculty who intend to develop academic careers involving both research and education.

Eligibility This program, identified as the CAREER program, is open to faculty members who meet all of the following requirements: 1) be employed in a tenure-track (or equivalent) position at an institution in the United States, its territories or possessions, or the Commonwealth of Puerto Rico which awards a baccalaureate or advanced degree in a field supported by the National Science Foundation (NSF); 2) hold a doctoral degree in a field of science or engineering supported by NSF: 3) not have competed more than 2 times in this program; 4) be untenured; and 5) not be a current or former recipient of a Presidential Early Career Award for Scientists and Engineers (PECASE) or CAREER award. Applicants must be U.S. citizens, nationals, or permanent residents. They must submit a career development plan that indicates 1) the objectives and significance of the proposed integrated research and education activities; 2) the relationship of the research to the current state of knowledge in the field, and of the education activities to the current state of knowledge on effective teaching and learning in the field of study; 3) an outline of the plan of work, describing the methods and procedures to be used, including evaluation of the education activities; 4) the relation of

the plan to the applicants' career goals and job responsibilities, and to the goals of their department or organization; and 5) a summary of prior research and educational accomplishments. Proposals from women, underrepresented minorities, and persons with disabilities are especially encouraged.

Financial data The total grant is $400,000 (or $500,000 for the Directorate of Biological Sciences) over the full period of the award.

Duration 5 years.

Additional information This program is operated by various disciplinary divisions within the NSF; for a list of the participating divisions and their telephone numbers, contact the sponsor. Outstanding recipients of these grants are nominated for the NSF component of the PECASE awards, which are awarded to 20 recipients of these grants as an honorary award.

Number awarded 300 to 350 each year. Approximately $60 million is budgeted to support this program annually.

Deadline July of each year.

[797]
FACULTY LOAN REPAYMENT PROGRAM

Health Resources and Services Administration
Bureau of Health Professions
Parklawn Building, Room 8-34
5600 Fishers Lane
Rockville, MD 20857
(301) 443-1700   (888) 275-4772
Fax: (301) 443-0846   E-mail: flrpinfo@hrsa.gov
Web: www.hrsa.gov

Purpose To repay the educational loans of faculty from disadvantaged backgrounds in health professions schools.

Eligibility Applicants for this assistance must be from a disadvantaged background, defined as individuals who either 1) come from an environment that has inhibited them from obtaining the knowledge, skill, and abilities required to enroll in and graduate from a health professions school (e.g., minorities) or from a program providing education or training in an allied health profession; or 2) come from a low-income family, with an income ranging from less than $10,700 for a family with 1 dependent to $28,100 for a family with 6 or more dependents. They must 1) have a degree from a school of medicine, osteopathic medicine, dentistry, nursing, or another health profession; 2) be enrolled in an approved graduate training program in those health professions; or 3) be enrolled as a full-time student in the final year of training, leading to a degree from an eligible school.

Financial data This program repays, for each year of service, as much as $20,000 of the outstanding principal and interest on the recipient's educational loans. The employing school must agree to pay a sum (in addition to faculty salary) equal to that paid by this program.

Duration Service must be for a minimum of 2 years. Recipients must agree to serve as a faculty member at a school of medicine, osteopathic medicine, dentistry, veterinary medicine, optometry, podiatric medicine, pharmacy, public health, allied health (including baccalaureate or graduate degree programs in dental hygiene, medical laboratory technology, occupational therapy, physical therapy, radiologic technology, speech pathology, audiology, and medical nutrition therapy), nursing, or graduate program in behavioral and mental health (including clinical psychology, clinical social work, professional counseling, and marriage and family therapy).

Number awarded Approximately 25 each year.

Deadline May of each year.

[798]
FACULTY RESEARCH AWARDS FOR HISTORICALLY BLACK, HISPANIC-SERVING, AND TRIBAL COLLEGES AND UNIVERSITIES

National Endowment for the Humanities
Attn: Division of Research Programs
1100 Pennsylvania Avenue, N.W., Room 318
Washington, DC 20506
(202) 606-8466   Fax: (202) 606-8204
TDD: (866) 372-2930   E-mail: er-faculty@neh.gov
Web: www.neh.gov/grants/guidelines/facultyresearch.html

Purpose To provide funding to faculty members at Historically Black Colleges and Universities (HBCUs), Hispanic Serving Institutions (HSIs), and Tribal Colleges and Universities (TCUs) who are interested in working on a research project in the humanities.

Eligibility This program is open to faculty members at HBCUs, HSIs, and TCUs who hold a full-time tenured, tenure track, or annual contract position. Applicants must be U.S. citizens or foreign nationals who have resided in the United States or its jurisdictions for at least 3 years. The proposed project should contribute to scholarly knowledge or to the public's understanding of the humanities in the form of publications, presentations, and classroom teaching. Grants may be awarded to individual faculty or 2 faculty collaborating on a single project. Support is not provided for graduate course work, but the proposed project may contribute to the completion of a doctoral dissertation. Grants are not provided for studying teaching methods or theories; surveying courses and programs; preparing institutional curricula; works in the creative or performing arts; projects that seek to promote a particular political, philosophical, religious, or ideological point of view; or projects that advocate a particular program of social action. Selection is based on: 1) the intellectual significance of the project, including its potential contribution to research and teaching in the humanities; 2) the quality or promise of quality of the applicant's work as an interpreter of the humanities; 3) the conception, definition, organization, and description of the proposed project, including, in the case of dual projects, the quality of the contributions to be made by each participant and arrangements for coordinating the project as a whole; 4) the feasibility of the work plan and likelihood that the applicant will complete the project; and 5) the quality of plans for dissemination, including publications, professional and public presentations, and teaching.

Financial data Maximum grants are $24,000 for projects up to 8 months or $40,000 for projects up to 12 months.

Duration Recipients may devote to their project either 6 to 8 months of full-time tenure (or equivalent) or 9 to 12 months of full-time tenure (or equivalent). They must complete their grant tenure within 2 years of the beginning of their award.

Number awarded Varies each year.

Deadline April of each year.

[799]
FACULTY RESEARCH ENHANCEMENT SUPPORT PROGRAM

National Institutes of Health
Attn: Extramural Associates Program
6701 Rockledge Drive, Room 6178A
Bethesda, MD 20892-7910
(301) 435-2736   Fax: (301) 480-0393
E-mail: mk51q@nih.gov
Web: www.nih.gov

Purpose To improve opportunities for minorities and women to participate in and contribute to biomedical research by enabling faculty or administrators to participate in a program at the National Institutes of Health (NIH) in Bethesda, Maryland.

Eligibility Academic institutions that have a significant enrollment of underrepresented minorities, or are women's colleges, may nominate 1 scientific faculty member or academic administrator. In addition to the qualifications and interests of the nominee, selection is based on the demonstrated contribution of the institution to the advancement of ethnic minorities and/or women, its readiness to improve health research or research training, and its plan to utilize the associate's expertise after participating in the program. This program is intended for nominees from institutions that do not award degrees in health-related sciences higher than the baccalaureate and have little or no research funding. Community colleges with recognized science programs or those which have established a bridge with a 4-year institution are also eligible.

Financial data Salaries are comparable to those being received by the associate at the time of selection. Cost-sharing is required, depending on the institution's resources. Travel, housing, and subsistence expenses while at NIH, and any costs incurred that are directly related to the training, are reimbursed by the NIH. The maximum award to sponsoring institutions is $25,000 in direct costs for the first year and $30,000 annually for subsequent years; facilities and administrative costs are fixed at 8% of total direct costs.

Duration 10 weeks, during the summer. Awards to institutions are up to 3 years.

Additional information During their tenure at the NIH, associates acquire a thorough knowledge of the NIH, the support mechanisms through which research is being accomplished, and the policies and procedures which govern the awarding of grants and contracts. Associates also obtain information about other federal health-related programs; grant and contract activities; legislative, budgetary and similar processes; and administrative procedures, including participation in staff meetings, review meetings, site visits, workshops, and conferences. Following completion of the program, associates return to their institutions with an Extramural Associates Research Development Award (EARDA) which provides developmental funds to the associate's institution for a period of 3 years, with a possible extension to 6 years.

Number awarded Varies each year; recently, 3 to 5 awards have been available through this program.

Deadline Letters of intent must be submitted by December of each year; completed applications are due the following February.

[800]
FELLOWSHIPS FOR POSTDOCTORAL RESEARCH IN EAST EUROPEAN STUDIES

American Council of Learned Societies
Attn: Office of Fellowships and Grants
633 Third Avenue, 8C
New York, NY 10017-6795
(212) 697-1505   Fax: (212) 949-8058
E-mail: grants@acls.org
Web: www.acls.org/eeguide.htm

Purpose To provide funding to postdoctorates interested in conducting original research in the social sciences and humanities relating to eastern Europe.

Eligibility Applicants must be U.S. citizens or permanent residents who hold a Ph.D. degree or equivalent as demonstrated by professional experience and publications. Their field of study must be in the social sciences or humanities relating to Albania, Bulgaria, the Czech Republic, Estonia, Hungary, Latvia, Lithuania, Poland, Romania, Slovakia, or the successor states of Yugoslavia. Proposals dealing with Albania, Bulgaria, Romania, or the former Yugoslavia are especially encouraged. Comparative work considering more than 1 country of east Europe or relating east European societies to those of other parts of the world are also supported. All proposals should be for scholarly work, the product of which is to be disseminated in English. The fellowships are to be used for work outside east Europe, although short visits to the area may be proposed as part of a coherent program primarily based elsewhere. Selection is based on the scholarly merit of the proposal, its importance to the development of eastern European studies, and the scholarly potential, accomplishments, and financial need of the applicant. Applications are particularly invited from women and members of minority groups.

Financial data Up to $25,000 is provided as a stipend. Funds are intended primarily as salary replacement, but they may be used to supplement sabbatical salaries or awards from other sources.

Duration 6 to 12 consecutive months.

Additional information This program is sponsored jointly by the American Council of Learned Societies, (ACLS) and the Social Science Research Council, funded by the U.S. Department of State under the Research and Training for Eastern Europe and the Independent States of the Former Soviet Union Act of 1983 (Title VIII) but administered by ACLS.

Number awarded Approximately 4 to 6 each year.

Deadline October of each year.

[801]
FELLOWSHIPS IN APPLIED ECONOMICS

Social Science Research Council
810 Seventh Avenue
New York, NY 10019
(212) 377-2700   Fax: (212) 377-2727
E-mail: pae@ssrc.org
Web: www.ssrc.org

Purpose To provide funding to doctoral students in economics interested in predissertation research and training.

Eligibility This program is open to full-time graduate students enrolled in economics and related Ph.D. programs (e.g., public policy or agricultural economics) at U.S. universities. There are no citizenship, residency, or nationality requirements. Applicants must have completed required course work and qualifying examinations, but not necessarily an approved dissertation prospectus;

normally they should be entering their third year of graduate work, although more advanced students may also apply. Fellowship support is not provided solely for dissertation research and write-up. Instead, applicants must develop a plan for intellectual development outside the normal course of training in the home department. Plans may include, for example, acquiring expertise for formulating and conducting research in areas of interest, developing specialized skills not taught at the home institution, or training in the approaches and methodologies of related disciplines. The program also encourages students to take on short-term internships in government or international agencies or at policy institutes. Minorities and women are particularly encouraged to apply.

Financial data The stipend is $15,000. A modest contribution to tuition, health insurance, and research expenses is also provided.

Duration 1 year.

Additional information This program, established in 1997, is administered by the Social Science Research Council with funds provided by the John D. and Catherine T. MacArthur Foundation.

Number awarded Varies each year.

Deadline January of each year.

[802]
FELLOWSHIPS IN SCIENCE AND INTERNATIONAL AFFAIRS

Harvard University
John F. Kennedy School of Government
Belfer Center for Science and International Affairs
Attn: Fellowship Coordinator
79 John F. Kennedy Street
Cambridge, MA 02138
(617) 495-3745   E-mail: kathleen_siddell@harvard.edu
Web: ksgnotes1.harvard.edu

Purpose To provide funding for research (by professionals, postdoctorates, or graduate students) in areas of interest to the Belfer Center for Science and International Affairs at Harvard University in Cambridge, Massachusetts.

Eligibility This program is open to recent recipients of the Ph.D. or equivalent degree, university faculty members, and employees of government, military, international, humanitarian, and private research institutions who have appropriate professional experience. Applicants for predoctoral fellowships must have passed general examinations. Lawyers, economists, physical scientists, and others of diverse disciplinary backgrounds are also welcome to apply. The program especially encourages applications from women, minorities, and citizens of all countries. All applicants must be seeking to conduct research in 1 of the 4 major program areas of the center: the international security program; the science, technology, and public policy program; the World Peace Foundation program on intrastate conflict, conflict prevention, and conflict resolution; and the strengthening democratic institutions project. Fellowships may also be available in other specialized programs, such as domestic preparedness for terrorism; research and assessment systems for sustainability; the Harvard information infrastructure project; legal, political, and cultural studies of science and technology; the managing the atom project; the energy technology innovation project; deepening democracy in Russia; and the Caspian studies project.

Financial data The stipend is $31,000 for postdoctoral research fellows or $18,000 for predoctoral research fellows. Health insurance is also provided.

Duration 10 months.
Number awarded A limited number each year.
Deadline January of each year.

[803]
FIRST BOOK GRANT PROGRAM FOR MINORITY SCHOLARS

Louisville Institute
Attn: Executive Director
1044 Alta Vista Road
Louisville, KY 40205-1798
(502) 895-3411, ext. 487   Fax: (502) 894-2286
E-mail: info@louisville-institute.org
Web: www.louisville-institute.org/firstbook.html

Purpose To provide funding to scholars of color interested in completing a major research and book project that focuses on an aspect of Christianity in North America.

Eligibility This program is open to members of a racial/ethnic minority group (African Americans, Hispanics, Native Americans, Asian Americans, and Pacific Islanders) who have an earned doctoral degree (normally the Ph.D. or Th.D.). Applicants must be a pre-tenured faculty member in a full-time, tenure-track position at an accredited institution of higher education (college, university, or seminary) in North America. They must be able to negotiate a full academic year free from teaching and committee responsibilities in order to engage in a scholarly research project leading to the publication of their first (or second) book focusing on an aspect of Christianity in North America. Selection is based on the intellectual quality of the research and writing project, its potential to contribute to scholarship in religion, and the potential contribution of the research to the vitality of North American Christianity.

Financial data The grant is $45,000. Awards are intended to make possible a full academic year of sabbatical research and writing by providing up to half of the grantee's salary and benefits for that year. Funds are paid directly to the grantee's institution, but no indirect costs are allowed.

Duration 1 academic year; nonrenewable.

Additional information The Louisville Institute is located at Louisville Presbyterian Theological Seminary and is supported by the Lilly Endowment. Grantees may not accept other awards that provide a stipend during the tenure of this award and must be released from all teaching and committee responsibilities during the award year.

Number awarded Up to 2 each year.
Deadline January of each year.

[804]
FIVE COLLEGE FELLOWSHIP PROGRAM FOR MINORITY SCHOLARS

Five Colleges, Incorporated
Attn: Five Colleges Fellowship Program Committee
97 Spring Street
Amherst, MA 01002-2324
(413) 256-8316   Fax: (413) 256-0249
E-mail: neckert@fivecolleges.edu
Web: www.fivecolleges.edu

Purpose To provide funding to minority graduate students who have completed all the requirements for the Ph.D. except the dissertation and are interested in teaching at selected colleges in Massachusetts.

Eligibility Fellows are chosen by the host department in each of the 5 participating campuses (Amherst, Hampshire, Mount Holyoke, Smith, and the University of Massachusetts). Applicants must be minority graduate students who have completed all doctoral requirements except the dissertation and are interested in devoting full time to the completion of the dissertation.

Financial data The stipend is $25,000, plus office space, library privileges, and housing assistance.

Duration 9 months, beginning in September.

Additional information Although the primary goal is completion of the dissertation, each fellow also has many opportunities to experience working with students and faculty colleagues on the host campus as well as with those at the other colleges. The fellows are also given an opportunity to teach (generally as a team teacher, in a section of a core course, or in a component within a course). Fellows meet monthly with each other to share their experiences. At Smith College, this program is named Mendenhall Fellowships for Minority Scholars.

Number awarded Approximately 4 to 6 each year.
Deadline January of each year.

[805]
FORD FOUNDATION DISSERTATION FELLOWSHIP PROGRAM FOR MINORITIES

National Research Council
Attn: Fellowship Office
500 Fifth Street, N.W.
Washington, DC 20001
(202) 334-2872   Fax: (202) 334-3419
E-mail: infofell@nas.edu
Web: www7.national-academies.org

Purpose To provide funding to underrepresented minority graduate students who need assistance in completing their dissertations.

Eligibility This program is open to Black/African American, Puerto Rican, Mexican American/Chicano/Chicana, Native American Indian, Alaska Native (Eskimo or Aleut), and Native Pacific Islander (Micronesian or Polynesian) graduate students who have completed all the requirements for the doctorate except the dissertation. Applicants must be citizens or nationals of the United States at the time of application. Awards are made for the final year of full-time dissertation work in research-based Ph.D. or Sc.D. programs in the behavioral and social sciences, humanities, education, engineering, life sciences, mathematics, physical sciences, and interdisciplinary programs comprised of 2 or more eligible disciplines. Awards are not made in such areas as administration and management, audiology, business, educational administration and leadership, fine arts, guidance, health sciences, home economics, law, library and information science, medicine, nursing, performing arts, personnel, physical education, public health, social welfare, social work, or speech pathology. The fellowships are tenable at any accredited nonprofit institution of higher education in the United States that offers Ph.D.s or Sc.D.s in the fields eligible for support. Selection is based on achievement and ability as demonstrated by academic records, letters of recommendation, the time table and proposed plan for completion of the doctoral degree, and the applicant's ability to present a well-written, thoughtfully-prepared application.

Financial data The stipend is $21,000 per year; stipend payments are made through fellowship institutions.

Duration 9 to 12 months.

Additional information The competition for this program is conducted by the National Research Council on behalf of the Ford Foundation. Applicants who merit receiving the fellowship but to whom awards cannot be made because of insufficient funds will be given Honorable Mentions; this recognition does not carry with it a monetary award but honors applicants who have demonstrated substantial academic achievement. The National Research Council will publish a list of those Honorable Mentions who wish their names publicized. Fellows may not accept remuneration from another fellowship or similar external award while on this program; however, supplementation from institutional funds, educational benefits from the Department of Veterans Affairs, or educational incentive funds may be received concurrently with Ford Foundation support. Dissertation fellows are required to submit an interim progress report 6 months after the start of the fellowship and a final report at the end of the 12 month tenure.

Number awarded Approximately 35 each year.

Deadline November of each year.

[806]
FORD FOUNDATION POSTDOCTORAL FELLOWSHIPS FOR MINORITIES

National Research Council
Attn: Fellowship Office
500 Fifth Street, N.W.
Washington, DC 20001
(202) 334-2860   Fax: (202) 334-3419
E-mail: infofell@nas.edu
Web: www7.national-academies.org

Purpose To provide funding to members of underrepresented minority groups already engaged in college or university teaching who are interested in conducting additional research.

Eligibility This program is open to U.S. citizens and nationals who are members of 1 of the following ethnic minority groups: Black/African Americans, Mexican Americans/Chicanos or Chicanas, Native Pacific Islanders (Micronesians or Polynesians), Puerto Ricans, Alaska Natives (Eskimo or Aleut), or Native American Indians. Within the past 7 years, applicants must have earned a Ph.D. or Sc.D. degree in 1 of the eligible fields (behavioral and social sciences, humanities, education, engineering, mathematics, physical sciences, life sciences, and interdisciplinary programs). Awards are not made to candidates in professional fields, including medicine, law, social welfare, social work, library and information science, public health, nursing, administration and management, business, fine arts, performing arts, speech pathology, audiology, health sciences, home economics, personnel, guidance, physical education, and educational administration and leadership. Fellowships are normally tenable at nonprofit institutions of higher education in the United States, including universities, museums, libraries, government or national laboratories, privately-sponsored institutes, government chartered research organizations, and centers for advanced study. Applicants who wish to affiliate with institutions outside the United States must provide evidence of the particular benefits that would accrue from affiliation with a foreign center. Selection is based on achievement and ability as evidenced by academic records and quality of the proposed plan of study or research.

Financial data The stipend is $34,000; in addition, fellows receive a travel and relocation allowance up to $3,000. Most institutions receive a $2,000 cost-of-research allowance to provide partial support for the fellow's study and research program. The allowance is prorated for tenure less than 12 months. Finally, each fellow's employing institution is given a $2,500 grant-in-aid for the fellow's use once the fellowship tenure is completed. The employing institution is expected to match the grant. These funds are designated to be used for the fellow's research expenditures.

Duration 9 or 12 months. Fellows may not accept another major fellowship while they are being supported by this program.

Number awarded Varies; approximately 24 each year.

Deadline February of each year.

[807]
FOREIGN POLICY STUDIES PREDOCTORAL FELLOWSHIPS

Brookings Institution
Attn: Foreign Policy Studies
1775 Massachusetts Avenue, N.W.
Washington, DC 20036-2188
(202) 797-6016   Fax: (202) 797-6003
E-mail: fpcomment@brook.edu
Web: www.brook.edu

Purpose To support predoctoral policy-oriented research in U.S. foreign policy and international relations at the Brookings Institution.

Eligibility Candidates cannot apply to conduct research at the institution; they must be nominated by their graduate department. Nominees must be doctoral students who have completed their preliminary examinations and have selected a dissertation topic that directly relates to public policy issues and the major research issues of the Brookings Institution. Selection is based on 1) relevance of the topic to contemporary U.S. foreign policy and/or post-Cold War international relations, and 2) evidence that the research will be facilitated by access to the institution's resources or to Washington-based organizations. The institution particularly encourages the nomination of women and minority candidates.

Financial data Fellows receive a stipend of $19,500 for the academic year, supplementary assistance for copying and other essential research requirements up to $750, reimbursement for transportation, health insurance, reimbursement for research-related travel up to $750, and access to computer/library facilities.

Duration 1 year, beginning in September.

Additional information Fellows participate in seminars, conferences, and meetings at the institution. Outstanding dissertations may be published by the institution. Fellows are expected to pursue their research at the Brookings Institution.

Number awarded A limited number are awarded each year.

Deadline Nominations must be submitted by mid-December and applications by mid-February.

[808]
FREDERICK BURKHARDT RESIDENTIAL FELLOWSHIPS FOR RECENTLY TENURED SCHOLARS

American Council of Learned Societies
Attn: Office of Fellowships and Grants
633 Third Avenue, 8C
New York, NY 10017-6795
(212) 697-1505   Fax: (212) 949-8058
E-mail: grants@acls.org
Web: www.acls.org/burkguid.htm

Purpose To provide funding to scholars in all disciplines of the humanities and the humanities-related social sciences who are interested in conducting research at designated residential centers.

Eligibility This program is open to citizens and permanent residents of the United States and Canada who achieved tenure in a humanities or humanities-related social science discipline at a U.S. or Canadian institution within the past 4 years. Applicants must be interested in conducting research at 1 of 9 participating residential centers in the United States or abroad. Appropriate fields of specialization include, but are not limited to, anthropology, archaeology, art history, economics, geography, history, languages and literatures, law, linguistics, musicology, philosophy, political science, psychology, religion, and sociology. Proposals in those fields of the social sciences are eligible only if they employ predominantly humanistic approaches (e.g., economic history, law and literature, political philosophy). Proposals in interdisciplinary and cross-disciplinary studies are welcome, as are proposals focused on any geographic region or on any cultural or linguistic group. Applications are particularly invited from women and members of minority groups.

Financial data The stipend is $65,000. If that stipend exceeds the fellow's normal academic year salary, the excess is available for research and travel expenses.

Duration 1 academic year.

Additional information This program, which began in 1999, is supported by funding from the Andrew W. Mellon Foundation with additional support from the Rockefeller Foundation. The participating residential research centers are the National Humanities Center (Research Triangle Park, North Carolina), the Center for Advanced Study in the Behavioral Sciences (Stanford, California), the Institute for Advanced Study, Schools of Historical Studies and Social Science (Princeton, New Jersey), the American Antiquarian Society (Worcester, Massachusetts), the Folger Shakespeare Library (Washington, D.C.), the Newberry Library (Chicago, Illinois), the Huntington Library, Art Collections, and Botanical Gardens (San Marino, California), the American Academy in Rome, and Villa I Tatti (Florence, Italy).

Number awarded Up to 11 each year.

Deadline September of each year.

[809]
FURNISS FOUNDATION/AMERICAN ORCHID SOCIETY GRADUATE FELLOWSHIPS

American Orchid Society
16700 AOS Lane
Delray Beach, FL 33446-4351
(561) 404-2000   Fax: (561) 404-2045
E-mail: TheAOS@aos.org
Web: www.theaos.org

Purpose To provide funding to doctoral candidates who are conducting dissertation research related to orchids.

Eligibility This program is open to graduate students whose doctoral dissertation relates to orchids within the disciplines of physiology, molecular biology, structure, systematics, cytology, ecology, and/or evolution. Women, minorities, and persons with disabilities are especially encouraged to apply.

Financial data The grant is $9,000 per year.

Duration Up to a maximum of 3 years.

Number awarded Varies each year.

Deadline March of each year.

[810]
GAIUS CHARLES BOLIN FELLOWSHIPS FOR MINORITY GRADUATE STUDENTS

Williams College
Attn: Dean of the Faculty
Hopkins Hall
P.O. Box 141
Williamstown, MA 01267
(413) 597-4351   E-mail: gburda@williams.edu
Web: www.williams.edu/admin-depts/deanfac

Purpose To provide financial assistance to minority doctoral students who are interested in preparing for a career in college teaching.

Eligibility Applicants must be minority graduate students, have completed all doctoral work except for the dissertation, be U.S. citizens, be working on degrees in the humanities or the natural, social, or behavioral sciences, and be willing to teach a course at Williams College. They must submit a full curriculum vitae, a graduate school transcript, 3 letters of recommendation, a copy of their dissertation prospectus, and a description of their teaching interests.

Financial data Fellows receive $27,500 for the academic year, plus housing assistance, office space, computer and library privileges, and a research allowance of up to $4,000.

Duration 1 academic year, beginning in September.

Additional information Bolin fellows are assigned a faculty advisor in the appropriate department. This program was established in 1985. Fellows are expected to teach a 1-semester course. They must be in residence at Williams College for the duration of the fellowship.

Number awarded 2 each year.

Deadline December of each year.

[811]
GEOLOGICAL SOCIETY OF AMERICA GENERAL RESEARCH GRANTS PROGRAM

Geological Society of America
Attn: Program Officer Grants, Awards and Medals
3300 Penrose Place
P.O. Box 9140
Boulder, CO 80301-9140
(303) 357-1037   Fax: (303) 447-1133
E-mail: lcarter@geosociety.org
Web: www.geosociety.org

Purpose To provide support to graduate student members of the Geological Society of America (GSA) interested in conducting research at universities in the United States, Canada, Mexico, or Central America.

Eligibility This program is open to GSA members working on a master's or doctoral degree at a university in the United States, Canada, Mexico, or Central America. Applicants must be interested in conducting research on geology. Applications from minorities, women, and persons with disabilities are strongly encouraged.

Financial data The budget may include the cost of travel, room and board in the field, materials and supplies, and other expenses directly related to the fulfillment of the research contract. Expenses requested for equipment or rental of equipment, film, some supplies, computer time, software, thin sections, and in-house charges for analytical instruments usually provided by a university must be fully justified. Funds cannot be used for the purchase of ordinary field equipment, for maintenance of the families of the grantees and their assistants, as reimbursement for work already accomplished, to attend professional meetings, for thesis preparation, to defray the costs of tuition, or for the employment of persons to conduct research.

Duration 1 year.

Additional information In addition to general grants, GSA awards a number of specialized grants: the Gretchen L. Blechschmidt Award for women (especially in the fields of biostratigraphy and/or paleooceanography); the John T. Dillon Alaska Research Award for earth science problems particular to Alaska; the Robert K. Fahnestock Memorial Award for the field of sediment transport or related aspects of fluvial geomorphology; the Lipman Research Award for volcanology and petrology; the Bruce L. "Biff" Reed Award for studies in the tectonic and magmatic evolution of Alaska; the Alexander Sisson Award for studies in Alaska and the Caribbean; the Harold T. Stearns Fellowship Award for work on the geology of the Pacific Islands and the circum-Pacific region; and the John Montagne Fund Award for research in the field of quaternary geomorphology. Furthermore, 9 of the 14 GSA divisions (geophysics, hydrogeology, sedimentary geology, structural geology and tectonics, archaeological geology, coal geology, planetary geology, quaternary geology and geomorphology, and engineering geology) also offer divisional grants. Some of those awards are named: the Allan V. Cox Award of the Geophysics Division, the Claude C. Albritton, Jr. Scholarship of the Archaeological Geology Division, the Antoinette Lierman Medlin Scholarships of the Coal Geology Division, the J. Hoover Mackin Research Grants and the Arthur D. Howard Research Grants of the Quaternary Geology and Geomorphology Division, and the Roy J. Shlemon Scholarship Awards of the Engineering Geology Division. In addition, 4 of the 6 geographic sections (south-central, north-central, southeastern, and northeastern) offer grants to graduate students at universities within their section.

Number awarded Varies each year; recently, the society awarded 224 grants worth more than $400,000 through this and all of its specialized programs.

Deadline January of each year.

[812]
GEOLOGICAL SOCIETY OF AMERICA
UNDERGRADUATE STUDENT RESEARCH GRANTS

Geological Society of America
Attn: Program Officer Grants, Awards and Medals
3300 Penrose Place
P.O. Box 9140
Boulder, CO 80301-9140
(303) 357-1037   Fax: (303) 447-1133
E-mail: lcarter@geosociety.org
Web: www.geosociety.org

Purpose To provide support to undergraduate student members of the Geological Society of America (GSA) interested in conducting research at universities in designated sections of the United States.

Eligibility This program is open to undergraduate students who are majoring in geology at universities in 4 GSA sections: north-central, northeastern, south-central, and southeastern. Applicants must be Student Associates of the GSA. Applications from women, minorities, and persons with disabilities are strongly encouraged.

Financial data Grant amounts vary.

Duration 1 year.

Additional information Within the 4 participating sections, information is available from the secretary. For the name and address of the 4 section secretaries, contact the sponsor.

Number awarded 1 or more each year in each of the 4 sections.

Deadline January of each year.

[813]
GEORGE WASHINGTON WILLIAMS FELLOWSHIPS

Independent Press Association
Attn: Executive Editor
2729 Mission Street, Suite 201
San Francisco, CA 94110
(415) 643-4401, ext. 116   Fax: (415) 643-4402
E-mail: diversity@indypress.org
Web: www.indypress.org/programs/gwwfellow.html

Purpose To provide journalists of color with an opportunity to devote a period of time to engage in public interest and socially responsible journalism.

Eligibility This program is open to journalists of color who have at least 3 years of professional reporting and writing experience. College journalism or internship experience does not qualify as professional experience. Preference is given to applicants with backgrounds in investigative or enterprise reporting. Previous reporting or other experience in the chosen subject area is desirable. The program is open only to U.S. citizens or to foreign journalists who have established relationships with U.S. publications. Applicants must be seeking support for either an individual story or investigative depth reporting. The preferred topics change periodically, but recently included environmental justice, health care and health care policy, new Americans, welfare reform, and gay and lesbian people of color.

Financial data Investigative depth reporting fellows receive $1,500 per month plus expenses to produce 1 or more stories. Individual story fellows are paid a rate equivalent to the going national commercial rate for comparable stories and assisted in placing the story.

Duration 3 to 12 months.

Additional information This program is named in honor of the African American journalist who first exposed conditions in the former Belgian Congo when he published an open letter to King Leopold II in 1890. Fellows are required to complete either a story or series of stories for publication. They may also be expected to attend special events and conferences sponsored by the program to present reports on their work to date and to discuss their own journalistic experiences with interns in the sponsor's student journalism program.

Number awarded 1 or more each year.

Deadline April or November of each year.

[814]
GERALD OSHITA MEMORIAL FELLOWSHIP

Djerassi Resident Artists Program
Attn: Judy Freeland, Program Assistant
2325 Bear Gulch Road
Woodside, CA 94062-4405
(650) 747-1250   Fax: (650) 747-0105
E-mail: drap@djerassi.org
Web: www.djerassi.org

Purpose To provide an opportunity for composers of color to participate in the Djerassi Resident Artists Program.

Eligibility This program is open to composers of color interested in utilizing a residency to compose, study, rehearse, and otherwise advance their own creative projects.

Financial data The fellow is offered housing, meals, studio space, and a stipend of $2,500.

Duration 4 to 5 weeks, from late March through mid-November.

Additional information This fellowship was established in 1994. The program is located in northern California, 45 miles south of San Francisco, on 600 acres of rangeland, redwood forests, and hiking trails.

Number awarded 1 each year.

Deadline February of each year.

[815]
GERBER FELLOWSHIP IN PEDIATRIC NUTRITION

National Medical Fellowships, Inc.
Attn: Scholarship Program
5 Hanover Square, 15th Floor
New York, NY 10004
(212) 483-8880   Fax: (212) 483-8897
E-mail: info@nmfonline.org
Web: www.nmf-online.org

Purpose To provide funding to underrepresented minority medical students and residents who are interested in conducting research on pediatric nutrition.

Eligibility This program is open to African Americans, Native Hawaiians, Alaska Natives, American Indians, Mexican Americans, and mainland Puerto Ricans who are 1) students enrolled in accredited U.S. medical schools, 2) students enrolled in U.S. colleges of osteopathic medicine, or 3) medical residents in U.S. programs. Candidates must be nominated by their deans or graduate education directors. They must be participating in ongoing research in the area of pediatric nutrition. U.S. citizenship is required. Selection is based on academic achievement and motivation to pursue a career in pediatric nutrition research.

Financial data The grant is $3,000.

Duration 1 year; nonrenewable.

Additional information This award was established in 1997 with grant support from the Gerber Companies Foundation.

Number awarded 1 each year.

Deadline October of each year.

[816]
GERTRUDE AND MAURICE GOLDHABER DISTINGUISHED FELLOWSHIPS

Brookhaven National Laboratory
Attn: Dr. Leonard Newman
Building 815E
P.O. Box 5000
Upton, NY 11973-5000
E-mail: newman@bnl.gov
Web: www.bnl.gov/bnlweb/pubaf/goldhaber.htm

Purpose To provide funding to postdoctoral scientists interested in conducting research at Brookhaven National Laboratory (BNL).

Eligibility This program is open to scholars who are no more than 3 years past receipt of the Ph.D. and are interested in working at BNL. Candidates must be interested in working in close collaboration with a member of the BNL scientific staff and qualifying for a scientific staff position at BNL upon completion of the

appointment. The sponsoring scientist must have an opening and be able to support the candidate at the standard starting salary for postdoctoral research associates. The program especially encourages applications from minorities and women.

Financial data The program provides additional funds to bring the salary to $70,000 per year.

Duration 3 years.

Additional information This program is funded by Battelle Memorial Institute and the State University of New York at Stony Brook.

Number awarded 1 or 2 each year.

[817]
GILBERT F. WHITE POSTDOCTORAL FELLOWSHIP PROGRAM

Resources for the Future
Attn: Coordinator for Academic Programs
1616 P Street, N.W.
Washington, DC 20036-1400
(202) 328-5060   Fax: (202) 939-3460
E-mail: mankin@rff.org
Web: www.rff.org/about_rff/white.htm

Purpose To provide funding to postdoctoral researchers who wish to devote a year to scholarly work at Resources for the Future (RFF) in Washington, D.C.

Eligibility This program is open to individuals in any discipline who have completed their doctoral requirements and are interested in conducting scholarly research at RFF in the social or policy sciences in areas related to natural resources, energy, or the environment. Teaching and/or research experience at the postdoctoral level is preferred though not essential. Individuals holding positions in government as well as at academic institutions are eligible. Women and minority candidates are strongly encouraged to apply.

Financial data Fellows receive an annual stipend (based on their academic salary) plus research support, office facilities at RFF, and an allowance of up to $1,000 for moving or living expenses. Fellowships do not provide medical insurance or other RFF fringe benefits.

Duration 11 months.

Additional information Fellows reside in an RFF research division—the Energy and Natural Resources Division, the Quality of the Environment Division, or the Center for Risk Management. Fellows are expected to be in residence at Resources for the Future for the duration of the program.

Number awarded 2 each year.

Deadline February of each year.

[818]
GLOBAL CHANGE GRADUATE RESEARCH ENVIRONMENTAL FELLOWSHIPS (GREF)

Oak Ridge Institute for Science and Education
Attn: Global Change Education Program
120 Badger Avenue, M.S. 36
P.O. Box 117
Oak Ridge, TN 37831-0117
(865) 576-9655   E-mail: kinneym@orau.gov
Web: www.orau.gov/gcep

Purpose To provide doctoral students with an opportunity to conduct research on global change.

Eligibility This program is open to students who have completed their first year of graduate school, unless they previously participated in the Global Change Summer Undergraduate Research Experience (SURE) or the Significant Opportunities in Atmospheric Research and Science (SOARS) program. Applicants must be proposing to conduct research at a national laboratory in a program area within the Department of Energy's Office of Biological and Environmental Research (DOE-OBER): atmospheric chemistry program, atmospheric radiation measurement program, terrestrial carbon program, etc. They must provide 1) a 5-page description of their proposed research; 2) undergraduate and graduate transcripts; and 3) letters of recommendation from their 2 mentors (a university thesis advisor and a national laboratory researcher who will guide the thesis research activities) and from an outside individual. Minority and female students are particularly encouraged to apply. U.S. citizenship is preferred.

Financial data Participants receive an annual support stipend, tuition at the college or university they attend, and transportation and housing for summer activities.

Duration Up to 5 years.

Additional information This program began in 1999. Fellows are encouraged to participate in the Summer Undergraduate Research Experience (SURE) orientation and focus sessions at a participating university.

Number awarded 10 to 15 each year.

Deadline January of each year.

[819]
GLOBAL CHANGE SUMMER UNDERGRADUATE RESEARCH EXPERIENCE (SURE)

Oak Ridge Institute for Science and Education
Attn: Global Change Education Program
120 Badger Avenue, M.S. 36
P.O. Box 117
Oak Ridge, TN 37831-0117
(865) 576-9655   E-mail: kinneym@orau.gov
Web: www.orau.gov/gcep

Purpose To provide undergraduate students with an opportunity to conduct research during the summer on global change.

Eligibility This program is open to undergraduates in their sophomore and junior years, although outstanding freshman applicants are also considered. Applicants must be proposing to conduct research in a program area within the Department of Energy's Office of Biological and Environmental Research (DOE-OBER): atmospheric chemistry program, atmospheric radiation measurement program, terrestrial carbon program, etc. Minority and female students are particularly encouraged to apply. U.S. citizenship is preferred.

Financial data Participants receive a weekly stipend and support for travel and housing.

Duration 10 weeks, during the summer. Successful participants are expected to reapply for a second year of research with their mentors.

Additional information This program began in summer 1999. The first 2 weeks are spent in an orientation and focus session at a participating university. For the remaining 10 weeks, students conduct mentored research at 1 of the national laboratories or universities conducting OBER-supported global change research.

Number awarded 20 to 30 each year.

Deadline January of each year.

[820]
GOALI FACULTY IN INDUSTRY AWARDS

National Science Foundation
Attn: Directorate for Engineering GOALI Coordinator
4201 Wilson Boulevard
Arlington, VA 22230
(703) 292-8300   TDD: (703) 292-5090
E-mail: lejohnso@nsf.gov
Web: www.eng.nsf.gov

Purpose To provide funding to science and engineering faculty who wish to conduct research as part of the Grant Opportunities for Academic Liaison with Industry (GOALI) program of the National Science Foundation (NSF).

Eligibility This program is open to full-time faculty members at U.S. colleges and universities in science and engineering fields of interest to NSF. Applicants must present a plan for collaboration between their institution and industry, with a description of the facilities and resources that will be available at the industrial site to support the proposed research. The program encourages participation by women and underrepresented minority engineers and scientists and those with disabilities.

Financial data Awards range from $25,000 to $50,000, including 50% of the faculty member's salary and fringe benefits during the industrial residency period. Up to 20% of the total requested amount may be used for travel and research expenses for the faculty and his/her students, including materials but excluding equipment; up to 10% of the total direct cost may be allocated for administrative expenses in lieu of indirect costs. The industrial partner must commit to support the other 50% of the faculty salary and fringe benefits.

Duration 1 year.

Number awarded Varies each year.

[821]
GOALI POSTDOCTORAL INDUSTRIAL FELLOWSHIPS

National Science Foundation
Attn: Directorate for Engineering GOALI Coordinator
4201 Wilson Boulevard
Arlington, VA 22230
(703) 292-8300   TDD: (703) 292-5090
E-mail: lejohnso@nsf.gov
Web: www.eng.nsf.gov

Purpose To provide an opportunity for recent postdoctorates to work in industry as part of the Grant Opportunities for Academic Liaison with Industry (GOALI) program of the National Science Foundation (NSF).

Eligibility Applicants for these fellowships must have held a Ph.D. degree in a science or engineering field of interest to NSF for no more than 3 years. They must submit a plan for full-time work in industry under the guidance of an academic adviser and an industrial mentor. The program encourages participation by women and underrepresented minority engineers and scientists and those with disabilities.

Financial data Awards range up to $42,000, including 67% of the stipend for the fellow and transportation and moving expenses up to $3,000. Up to 10% of the total budget allowance may be used by the faculty adviser for research-related expenses. Up to 10% of the total direct cost may be allocated for administrative expenses in lieu of indirect costs. The industrial partner must commit to support the other 33% of the fellow's stipend.

Duration 1 or 2 years.

Number awarded Varies each year.

[822]
GOVERNMENTAL STUDIES PREDOCTORAL FELLOWSHIPS

Brookings Institution
Attn: Governmental Studies
1775 Massachusetts Avenue, N.W.
Washington, DC 20036-2188
(202) 797-6054   Fax: (202) 797-6144
E-mail: Kweaver@brook.edu
Web: www.brook.edu

Purpose To support predoctoral policy-oriented research in governmental studies at the Brookings Institution.

Eligibility Candidates cannot apply to conduct research at the institution; they must be nominated by their graduate department. Nominees must be doctoral students who have completed their preliminary examinations and have selected a dissertation topic that directly relates to public policy issues and the major research issues of the Brookings Institution. The proposed research should benefit from access to the data, opportunities for interviewing, and consultation with senior staff members afforded by the institution and by residence in Washington, D.C. The institution particularly encourages the nomination of women and minority candidates.

Financial data Fellows receive a stipend of $19,500 for the academic year, supplementary assistance for copying and other essential research requirements up to $750, reimbursement for research-related travel up to $750, health insurance, reimbursement for transportation, and access to computer/library facilities.

Duration 1 year.

Additional information Fellows participate in seminars, conferences, and meetings at the institution. Outstanding dissertations may be published by the institution. Of the fellowships awarded, 1 is designated the Robert W. Hartley Memorial Fellowship. Fellows are expected to pursue their research at the Brookings Institution.

Number awarded A limited number are awarded each year.

Deadline Nominations must be submitted by mid-December and applications by mid-February.

[823]
HAMBURG FELLOWSHIP PROGRAM

Stanford University
Center for International Security and Cooperation
Attn: Director of Fellowship Programs
Encina Hall, Room E210
616 Serra Street
Stanford, CA 94305-6165
(650) 723-9626   Fax: (650) 723-0089
E-mail: barbara.platt@stanford.edu
Web: www.cisac.stanford.edu

Purpose To provide funding to doctoral students who are interested in writing a dissertation at Stanford University's Center for International Security and Cooperation on issues related to preventing deadly conflict.

Eligibility This program is open to advanced doctoral students who have completed all of the curricular and residency requirements at their own institutions and who are engaged in the research and write-up stage of their dissertations in a field related to the prevention of deadly conflict. Applicants may be studying a broad range of disciplines, including anthropology, economics, history, law, medicine, the natural and physical sciences, political science, sociology, and other related fields. They must be interested in writing their dissertation at Stanford University's Center for International Security and Cooperation. Applications from women and minorities are encouraged.

Financial data The stipend is $20,000. Reimbursement for some travel and health insurance expenses may be available for fellows and their immediate dependents.

Duration 9 months.

Additional information This program began in 1997. It honors Dr. David Hamburg, the retiring president of the Carnegie Corporation of New York, whose gift to the center made the program possible. Fellows join faculty, research staff, and other fellows at the center, where they have an office to ensure their integration into the full spectrum of research activities.

Number awarded Varies each year.

Deadline January of each year.

[824]
HARVARD SCHOOL OF PUBLIC HEALTH MINORITY POSTDOCTORAL FELLOWSHIP PROGRAM

Harvard School of Public Health
Division of Public Health Practice
Attn: Program Coordinator
1552 Tremont Street
Boston, MA 02120
(617) 495-4000   Fax: (617) 495-8543
Web: www.hsph.harvard.edu/php/programs

Purpose To provide minority postdoctorates with an opportunity to pursue a program of research training at Harvard School of Public Health.

Eligibility This program is open to members of underrepresented ethnic groups (African Americans, Hispanics, Native Americans, and Pacific Islanders) who are U.S. citizens or permanent residents. Applicants must have a doctoral degree, but their degree may be in any of a number of fields as long as they are interested in pursuing a career in public health. They must submit 3 letters of recommendation, a curriculum vitae, a proposal for research to be undertaken during the fellowship, a statement of career goals in public health, a list of publications, and a sample publication.

Financial data The stipend is $40,000.

Duration 1 year.

Additional information Fellows are associated with a faculty mentor who assists in the transition to an academic career. With the help of the faculty mentor, fellows establish their own research agenda, present their research in school and national settings, gain experience in publishing papers in peer-reviewed journals and in obtaining grant support, participate in teaching related to their field, and learn to develop their own courses.

Number awarded 1 each year.

Deadline January of each year.

[825]
HENRY LUCE FOUNDATION/ACLS DISSERTATION FELLOWSHIPS IN AMERICAN ART

American Council of Learned Societies
Attn: Office of Fellowships and Grants
633 Third Avenue, 8C
New York, NY 10017-6795
(212) 697-1505   Fax: (212) 949-8058
E-mail: grants@acls.org
Web: www.acls.org/luceguid.htm

Purpose To provide financial assistance to doctoral students interested in conducting dissertation research on the history of American art.

Eligibility Eligible to apply are Ph.D. candidates in departments of art history whose dissertations are focused on the history of the visual arts in the United States. Interdisciplinary and interdepartmental projects are eligible only if the degree is to be granted in art history. U.S. citizenship is required. Students preparing theses for a Master of Fine Arts degree are not eligible. Applications are particularly invited from women and members of minority groups.

Financial data The grant is $20,000. Fellowship funds may not be used to pay tuition costs.

Duration 1 year; nonrenewable.

Additional information This program is funded by the Henry Luce Foundation and administered by the American Council of Learned Societies (ACLS).

Number awarded 10 each year.

Deadline November of each year.

[826]
HERBERT W. NICKENS, M.D. MINORITY FACULTY FELLOWSHIP

Association of American Medical Colleges
Attn: Division of Community and Minority Programs
2450 N Street, N.W.
Washington, DC 20037-1127
(202) 828-0570   Fax: (202) 828-1125
E-mail: dallen@aamc.org
Web: www.aamc.org/about/awards/hwnfell.htm

Purpose To provide funding to underrepresented minority faculty members who are committed to careers in academic medicine.

Eligibility This program is open to Black Americans, Mexican Americans, Mainland Puerto Ricans, and Native Americans (Native Hawaiians, Alaska Natives, and American Indians) who hold the rank of assistant professor or instructor in a medical school department. Candidates must be nominated by the dean of their school. They must be seeking funding for academic and professional activities, have an M.D. or Ph.D., and have held their faculty appointment for no more than 3 years. The letter of nomination must discuss the nominee's potential for a career in academic medicine and must be accompanied by a current curriculum vitae of the nominee, 2 letters of recommendation, and a personal statement from the nominee describing career objectives, research interests, and how the funds will be used.

Financial data The grant is $15,000.

Duration Funds can be spent over a 2-year period.

Number awarded 1 each year.

Deadline June of each year.

[827]
HHMI-NIH RESEARCH SCHOLARS PROGRAM

Howard Hughes Medical Institute
One Cloister Court
Bethesda, MD 20814-1460
(301) 951-6770   (800) 424-9924
Fax: (301) 951-6776   E-mail: gpub@hhmi.org
Web: www.hhmi.org/cloister

Purpose To give outstanding students at U.S. medical or dental schools the opportunity to receive educational funding and research training at the National Institutes of Health (NIH), in Bethesda, Maryland.

Eligibility To apply, students must be in good standing at a medical or dental school in the United States or Puerto Rico. There are no citizenship requirements, but applicants must be authorized to work in the United States. Those who are enrolled in an M.D./Ph.D. program or who already have an M.D. or a Ph.D. in a natural science are not eligible. After the conclusion of the program year, a small number of outstanding Research Scholars are selected to receive continued support for up to 2 years while completing studies toward the M.D. degree. To be eligible for this support, Research Scholars must be returning directly to medical school at the conclusion of their participation in the Research Scholars Program, and they may not be enrolled in an M.D./Ph.D., Ph.D., or Sc.D. degree program. These awards are based on demonstrated research abilities, potential for future achievement in biomedical research, and career intentions (including any plans for additional research training upon completion of medical school). Students' financial indebtedness resulting from school loans may also be considered as a secondary factor. Women and members of underrepresented minority groups are encouraged to apply.

Financial data Research Scholars receive an annual salary of $17,800 for rent, food, and other living expenses. Scholars are also eligible for medical, life, and accidental death and dismemberment insurance. Students are reimbursed for round-trip moving expenses for personal belongings (not furniture) for themselves and their dependents from and back to medical school. In addition, tuition is paid for Research Scholars who wish to take courses from the Foundation for Advanced Education in the Sciences (FAES). They also receive allowances for the purchase of textbooks and scientific journals related to their area of research and for travel to scientific meetings. Research Scholars who are chosen to receive support to complete their studies toward the M.D. degree are given an annual stipend of $16,000 and a $15,000 annual allowance toward tuition and other education-related expenses.

Duration 1 year, beginning in July or August; may be extended for 2 additional years.

Additional information Research Scholars work as part of a research team in a laboratory at the NIH's main campus in Bethesda, conducting basic research under the mentorship of an NIH senior investigator or preceptor. They learn the latest laboratory techniques and experience the creative thinking involved in at least 1 of the following biomedical areas: biochemistry, biophysics, biostatistics, cell biology, developmental biology, epidemiology, genetics, immunology, mathematical and computational biology, microbiology, molecular biology, neuroscience, pharmacology, physiology, structural biology, and virology. This program is unique in that it does not require students to propose a research project or select a laboratory at the NIH as part of the application process. Instead, Research Scholars are encouraged to take their first couple of weeks in the program to interview investigators and explore different laboratories at the NIH before making a selection. This program is jointly sponsored by the Howard Hughes Medical Institute and the National Institutes of Health—the largest private and public biomedical research institutions in the United States. It complements the HHMI Research Training Fellowships for Medical Students Program; students may not apply to both programs in the same year.

Number awarded   40 each year.

Deadline   January of each year.

[828]
HISPANIC THEOLOGICAL INITIATIVE DISSERTATION YEAR GRANTS

Hispanic Theological Initiative
12 Library Place
Princeton, NJ 08540
(609) 252-1721   (800) 575-5522
Fax: (609) 252-1738   E-mail: hti@ptsem.edu
Web: www.htiprogram.org

Purpose   To provide financial assistance to Latino/a doctoral candidates who are completing a dissertation as part of their preparation for a career of scholarly service to a faith community.

Eligibility   This program is open to Latinos/as who have completed all requirements for a Ph.D. or Ed.D. except the dissertation and plan to complete the dissertation at the end of the award year. Applicants must be committed to serving the Latino faith community in the United States, Puerto Rico, or Canada. Candidates who plan to study in Latin America or Europe are not eligible. Selection is based on recommendations by professors giving witness to the applicant's potential to contribute to the academic community as a scholar, recommendations by Latino church or community leaders giving witness to the applicant's commitment and leadership to the Latino community, the potential of the applicant to contribute to the academic community as demonstrated by the dissertation proposal, and the ability of the applicant to articulate the relevance of the research to the Latino community.

Financial data   The grant is $16,000.

Duration   1 year; nonrenewable.

Additional information   The program, funded by Pew Charitable Trusts, also provides the awardees with 1) skilled editorial support to facilitate a timely completion of the dissertation; 2) a mid-year workshop to monitor and encourage the writing process, to provide a time for discussion of the dissertation, and to provide collegial support; 3) participation in an annual 3-day summer workshop; 4) a subscription to *Apuntes* and to *The Journal of Hispanic/Latino Theology;* 5) membership in either the Asociación para la educación teológica hispana (AETH) or the Academy of Catholic Hispanic Theologians in the U.S. (ACHTUS); and 6) participation in smaller regional meetings that will foster community building, networking, and collegial support.

Number awarded   9 each year.

Deadline   January of each year.

[829]
HORIZONS/FRAMELINE FILM AND VIDEO COMPLETION FUND

Frameline
Attn: Film and Video Completion Fund
145 Ninth Street, Suite 300
San Francisco, CA 94103
(415) 703-8650   Fax: (415) 861-1404
E-mail: info@frameline.org
Web: www.frameline.org/fund

Purpose   To provide funding to lesbian and gay film/video artists.

Eligibility   This program is open to lesbian and gay artists who are in the last stages of the production of documentary, educational, animated, or experimental projects about or of interest to lesbians, gay men, bisexuals, and transgender people and their communities. Applicants must be interested in completion or post-production work, including subtitling or conversion from video to film (or vice versa). In particular, women and people of color are encouraged to apply. Selection is based on financial need, the contribution the grant will make to completing the project, assurances that the project will be completed, and the statement the project makes about lesbian, gay, bisexual, and transgender people and/or issues of concern to them and their communities. Grants are not awarded for script development, research, or pre-production work.

Financial data   Grants range from $2,000 to $3,000.

Number awarded   Varies each year; recently, 4 of these grants were awarded.

Deadline   October of each year.

[830]
HOWARD HUGHES MEDICAL INSTITUTE RESEARCH TRAINING FELLOWSHIPS FOR MEDICAL STUDENTS

Howard Hughes Medical Institute
Attn: Office of Grants and Special Programs
4000 Jones Bridge Road
Chevy Chase, MD 20815-6789
(301) 215-8883   Fax: (301) 215-8888
E-mail: fellows@hhmi.org
Web: www.hhmi.org/fellowships

Purpose   To provide financial assistance to medical students interested in pursuing research training.

Eligibility   Applicants must be enrolled in a medical school in the United States, although they may be citizens of any country. They must describe a proposed research project to be conducted at an academic or nonprofit research institution in the United States, other than a facility of the National Institutes of Health in Bethesda, Maryland. Research proposals should reflect the interests of the Howard Hughes Medical Institute (HHMI), especially in biochemistry, bioinformatics, biophysics, biostatistics, cell biology, developmental biology, epidemiology, genetics, immunology, mathematical and computational biology, microbiology, molecular biology, neuroscience, pharmacology, physiology, structural biology, and virology. Applications from women and minorities underrepresented in the sciences (Blacks, Hispanics, Native Americans, Native Alaskans, and Native Pacific Islanders) are especially encouraged. Students enrolled in M.D./Ph.D., Ph.D., or Sc.D. programs and those who have completed a Ph.D. or Sc.D. in a laboratory-based science are not eligible. Selection is based on letters of reference, the research plan, and a mentor's plans for training the student.

Financial data Fellows receive a stipend of $21,000 per year; their institution receives an institutional allowance of $5,500 and a research allowance of $5,500. Research Training Fellows who are chosen to receive support to complete their studies toward the M.D. degree are given an annual stipend of $21,000 and a $16,000 annual allowance toward tuition and other education-related expenses.

Duration 1 year; may be renewed for a second year of research. A small number of fellows may be allowed to return to medical school and continue receiving support for 2 additional years.

Additional information This program complements the HHMI-NIH Research Scholars Program; students may not apply to both programs in the same year. Fellows may not be enrolled in an M.D./Ph.D. program.

Number awarded Up to 60 each year.

Deadline November of each year for initial awards; March of each year for continued awards.

[831]
HUD DOCTORAL DISSERTATION RESEARCH GRANT PROGRAM

Department of Housing and Urban Development
Attn: Office of University Partnerships
451 Seventh Street, S.W., Room 8106
Washington, DC 20410
(202) 708-3061, est. 3852   Fax: (202) 708-0309
E-mail: Susan_S_Brunson@hud.gov
Web: www.oup.org/about/aboutddrg

Purpose To provide funding to doctoral candidates interested in conducting dissertation research related to housing and urban development issues.

Eligibility This program is open to currently-enrolled doctoral candidates in an academic discipline that provides policy-relevant insight on issues in housing and urban development. Applicants must have fully-developed and approved dissertation proposals that can be completed within 2 years and must have completed all written and oral Ph.D. requirements. Funded fields of study have included anthropology, architecture, economics, history, planning, political science, public policy, social work, and sociology. Research must relate to the empowerment principles of the Department of Housing and Urban Development (HUD): a commitment to 1) socially and economically viable communities, 2) stable and supportive families, 3) economic growth, 4) reciprocity and balancing individual rights and responsibilities, and 5) reducing the separation of communities by race and income in American life. Women and minority candidates are encouraged to apply.

Financial data The stipend is $25,000 per year. The program expects that the recipients' universities will support their research by contributing a substantial waiver of tuition and fees, office space, equipment, computer time, or similar items needed to complete the dissertation.

Duration These are 1-time grants.

Additional information This program was established in 1994. Information is also available from University Partnerships Clearinghouse,, P.O. Box 6091, Rockville, MD 20849-6091, (800) 245-2691, Fax: (301) 519-5767, TDD: (800) 483-2209, E-mail: oup@oup.org

Number awarded Up to 16 each year.

Deadline June of each year.

[832]
IDAHO SPACE GRANT CONSORTIUM GRADUATE FELLOWSHIPS

Idaho Space Grant Consortium
c/o University of Idaho
College of Engineering
P.O. Box 441011
Moscow, ID 83844-1011
(208) 885-6438   Fax: (208) 885-6645
E-mail: isgc@uidaho.edu
Web: ivc.uidaho.edu/isgc/fellow.html

Purpose To provide funding for research in space-related fields to graduate students at institutions belonging to the Idaho Space Grant Consortium (ISGC).

Eligibility This program is open to graduate students at ISGC member institutions. Applicants may be majoring in engineering, mathematics, science, or science/math education, but they must be interested in conducting research in an area of focus of the National Aeronautics and Space Administration (NASA). An undergraduate and current GPA of 3.0 or higher and U.S. citizenship are required. As a component of the NASA Space Grant program, ISGC encourages participation by women, underrepresented minorities, and persons with disabilities.

Financial data The stipend is $6,000 per year.

Duration 1 year; may be renewed.

Additional information Members of the consortium include Albertson College of Idaho, Boise State University, College of Southern Idaho, Idaho State University, Lewis Clark State College, North Idaho College, Northwest Nazarene College, Brigham Young University of Idaho, and the University of Idaho. This program is funded by NASA.

Number awarded Varies each year.

Deadline February of each year.

[833]
IDAHO SPACE GRANT CONSORTIUM RESEARCH INITIATION GRANTS

Idaho Space Grant Consortium
c/o University of Idaho
College of Engineering
P.O. Box 441011
Moscow, ID 83844-1011
(208) 885-7303   Fax: (208) 885-6645
E-mail: isgc@uidaho.edu
Web: ivc.uidaho.edu/isgc

Purpose To provide funding for research in space-related fields to faculty members at institutions belonging to the Idaho Space Grant Consortium (ISGC).

Eligibility This program is open to faculty members in aeronautics, space, and related fields at institutions affiliated with ISGC. Applicants must be seeking funding for research programs that will result in proposals to the U.S. National Aeronautics and Space Administration (NASA) and other federal, state, and private organizations for further funding and continued program development. Travel to a NASA center or enterprise is strongly encouraged. U.S. citizenship is required. As a component of the NASA Space Grant program, ISGC encourages participation by women, underrepresented minorities, and persons with disabilities. Selection is based on the relevance of the proposal to ISGC and NASA goals, relevance to aerospace and space sciences, collaboration plan with a NASA center or enterprise, involvement of undergraduate students in the research, technical merit, potential for continued external funding, and the proposed budget.

Financial data Grants up to $10,000 are provided but require an equal matching amount from the recipient's university, college, or department. Salaries may be used as a source of the required match.

Duration Projects must be completed within 1 year.

Additional information Members of the consortium include Albertson College of Idaho, Boise State University, College of Southern Idaho, Idaho State University, Lewis Clark State College, North Idaho College, Northwest Nazarene College, Brigham Young University of Idaho, and the University of Idaho. This program is funded by NASA.

Number awarded Varies each year.

Deadline January of each year.

[834]
ILLINOIS ARTS COUNCIL ETHNIC AND FOLK ARTS MASTER/APPRENTICE PROGRAM

Illinois Arts Council
100 West Randolph, Suite 10-500
Chicago, IL 60601
(312) 814-6750   (800) 237-6994 (within IL)
Fax: (312) 814-1471   TTY: (312) 814-4831
E-mail: info@arts.state.il.us
Web: www.state.il.us/agency/iac

Purpose To provide funding to master ethnic and folk artists in Illinois and their apprentices for a program of training in traditional art forms.

Eligibility This program is open to teams of 2 Illinois residents, 1 of whom qualifies as a master artist (an individual who is recognized within his or her community as a person who has achieved the highest possible level of a traditional or classical ethnic art form) and 1 of whom qualifies as an apprentice (an individual with some experience in a traditional or classical ethnic art form who wishes to attain mastery of that art). Ethnic and folk arts are defined as those artistic practices that have a community or family base, express that community's aesthetic heritage and tradition, and have endured through several generations; they should reflect the particular culture of the ethnic, language, regional, tribal, or nationality group from which they spring. The art form may involve traditional crafts, music, dance, or storytelling. Both the master artist and the apprentice must be U.S. citizens or permanent residents who have resided in Illinois for at least 12 months. Selection is based on the artistic quality of both master artist and apprentice as determined by community standards, traditionality of art form and master artist, evidence of apprentice's commitment to the traditional art form, content and feasibility of work planned for the period of the apprenticeship, and quality and appropriateness of the documentation submitted. Priority is given to apprenticeships that take place outside of institutional settings.

Financial data The honoraria are $2,000 for the master and $1,000 for the apprentice.

Duration Most apprenticeships should include between 80 and 120 hours of instruction.

Number awarded Varies each year.

Deadline August of each year.

[835]
INDEPENDENT SCIENTIST AWARDS

National Institutes of Health
Division of Extramural Outreach and Information Resources
Attn: GrantsInfo
6701 Rockledge Drive, Suite 6095
Bethesda, MD 20892-7910
(301) 435-0714   Fax: (301) 480-8443
E-mail: GrantsInfo@nih.gov
Web: www.nih.gov

Purpose To provide financial support to scientists in health-related fields who have recently become independent investigators and are seeking funding for research.

Eligibility This program is open to candidates who have a doctoral degree and peer-reviewed, independent research support at the time the award is made. They must be willing to spend a minimum of 75% of full-time professional effort conducting research and research career development activities for the period of the award. Candidates must demonstrate that the requested period of research focus will foster their career as highly productive scientists in the indicated field of research. Applications may be submitted on behalf of candidates by domestic, nonfederal public or private organizations, such as medical, dental, or nursing schools or other institutions of higher education. Minorities and women are particularly encouraged to apply. Candidates must be U.S. citizens or permanent residents.

Financial data This program provides salary and fringe benefits for the candidate only; each component establishes its own salary limits on career awards. Facilities and administrative costs are reimbursed at 8% of modified total direct costs, or at the actual indirect cost rate, whichever is less.

Duration 5 consecutive 12-month appointments.

Additional information Awards under this program are available from 12 agencies of the National Institutes of Health (NIH): the National Institute on Aging, the National Institute on Alcohol Abuse and Alcoholism, the National Institute of Allergy and Infectious Diseases, the National Institute of Arthritis and Musculoskeletal and Skin Diseases, the National Institute of Child Health and Human Development, the National Institute on Deafness and Other Communication Disorders, the National Institute of Dental and Craniofacial Research, the National Institute of Diabetes and Digestive and Kidney Diseases, the National Institute on Drug Abuse, the National Institute of Environmental Health Sciences, the National Heart, Lung, and Blood Institute, and the National Institute of Mental Health. The names and addresses of staff people at each agency are available from the address above.

Number awarded Varies each year.

Deadline January, May, or September of each year.

[836]
INDIANA SPACE GRANT CONSORTIUM GRADUATE FELLOWSHIPS

Indiana Space Grant Consortium
c/o Purdue University
School of Industrial Engineering
1287 Grissom Hall
West Lafayette, IN 47907-1287
(765) 494-5873   Fax: (765) 496-3449
E-mail: bcaldwel@ecn.purdue.edu
Web: www.insgc.org

Purpose To provide funding to graduate students at member institutions of the Indiana Space Grant Consortium (INSGC) interested in conducting research related to space.

Eligibility This program is open to graduate students enrolled full time at institutions that are members of the INSGC. Applicants must be interested in conducting research related to 1 of the strategic enterprise areas of the U.S. National Aeronautics and Space Administration (NASA): space science, earth science, biological and physical research, human exploration and development of space, and aerospace technology. U.S. citizenship is required. The program encourages representation of women, underrepresented minorities, and persons with disabilities.

Financial data The maximum grant is $5,000 per year for master's degree students or $10,000 for doctoral students.

Duration 1 year; students may not receive an award in consecutive years.

Additional information This program is funded by NASA. The academic member institutions of the INSGC are Purdue University, Ball State University, Indiana University, Indiana University-Purdue University at Indianapolis, Purdue University at Calumet, Taylor University, University of Evansville, University of Notre Dame, and Valparaiso University.

Number awarded Varies each year. Approximately $60,000 is available for undergraduate scholarships and graduate fellowships.

Deadline February of each year.

[837]
INDIANA SPACE GRANT CONSORTIUM UNDERGRADUATE SCHOLARSHIPS

Indiana Space Grant Consortium
c/o Purdue University
School of Industrial Engineering
1287 Grissom Hall
West Lafayette, IN 47907-1287
(765) 494-5873   Fax: (765) 496-3449
E-mail: bcaldwel@ecn.purdue.edu
Web: www.insgc.org

Purpose To provide funding to undergraduate students at member institutions of the Indiana Space Grant Consortium (INSGC) interested in conducting research related to space.

Eligibility This program is open to undergraduate students enrolled full time at institutions that are members of the INSGC. Applicants must be interested in conducting research related to 1 of the strategic enterprise areas of the U.S. National Aeronautics and Space Administration (NASA): space science, earth science, biological and physical research, human exploration and development of space, and aerospace technology. U.S. citizenship is required. The program encourages representation of women, underrepresented minorities, and persons with disabilities.

Financial data The maximum grant is $1,500 per year.

Duration 1 year; may be renewed.

Additional information This program is funded by NASA. The academic member institutions of the INSGC are Purdue University, Ball State University, Indiana University, Indiana University-Purdue University at Indianapolis, Purdue University at Calumet, Taylor University, University of Evansville, University of Notre Dame, and Valparaiso University.

Number awarded Varies each year. Approximately $60,000 is available for undergraduate scholarships and graduate fellowships.

Deadline February of each year.

[838]
INDUSTRY-BASED GRADUATE RESEARCH ASSISTANTSHIPS AND COOPERATIVE FELLOWSHIPS IN THE MATHEMATICAL SCIENCES

National Science Foundation
Directorate for Mathematical and Physical Sciences
Attn: Division of Mathematical Sciences
4201 Wilson Boulevard, Room 1025
Arlington, VA 22230
(703) 292-4862   TDD: (703) 292-5090
E-mail: ldouglas@nsf.gov
Web: www.nsf.gov/mps/general.htm

Purpose To provide financial assistance to graduate students in mathematics who want to gain experience in industrial settings.

Eligibility This program is open to graduate students in mathematics who are U.S. citizens, nationals, or permanent residents. Applicants may propose either 1) a research assistantship, in which they conduct research for a master's thesis or doctoral dissertation under the joint supervision of a university faculty member and an industrial scientist, spending part time at the industrial site on a regular basis and the remainder in the classroom or in other campus-based activities; or 2) a cooperative fellowship, in which they work full time as an intern in an industrial setting. Applications are especially encouraged from women, underrepresented minorities, and persons with disabilities.

Financial data The program provides up to 50% (with an upper limit of $20,000) of the total support for each student. The university faculty member involved in the joint supervision of these students may request up to $6,000 as a faculty research allowance.

Duration Up to 1 year.

Number awarded Varies each year.

Deadline November of each year.

[839]
INFORMATION TECHNOLOGY RESEARCH GRANTS

National Science Foundation
Attn: Information Technology Research Program
4201 Wilson Boulevard
Arlington, VA 22230
(703) 292-5111   TDD: (703) 292-5090
E-mail: itr@nsf.gov
Web: www.itr.nsf.gov

Purpose To provide funding to investigators interested in conducting research related to information technology.

Eligibility This program is open to investigators at U.S. academic institutions and nonprofit research institutions. Collaborations with international researchers, for-profit corporations, and national laboratories are encouraged, but the proposal must be submitted through a U.S. institution. Applicants must be interested in conducting research on computers and computation; networking and communication; information and data storage, manipulation, and presentation; new applications of information technology in all science and engineering disciplines; new science and engineering research that is facilitated by information technology and by collaboration with computer scientists; and uses of this knowledge and technology to advance social, educational, scientific, and engineering goals. Fundamental research that contributes to national security, including new models for information and network security, new information technology for emergency response, and new information technology for prevention, detection, remediation, and attribution of terrorist attacks, is especially encouraged. Proposals may be for small projects, medium projects, or large projects. Proposals from women, underrepresented minorities, and persons with disabilities are especially encouraged.

Financial data Small project grants may have a total budget up to $500,000, not to exceed $180,000 in each year; medium project grants may have a total budget from $500,000 to $4 million, not to exceed $1 million in each year; large project grants may have a total budget from $4 million to $15 million, not to exceed $3 million in each year.

Duration 3 years for small projects; 5 years for medium and large projects.

Additional information This program, which began in 2000, is operated by various disciplinary divisions within the NSF; for a list of the participating divisions and their telephone numbers, contact the sponsor.

Number awarded Varies each year, depending on the availability of funds. Recently, the program expected to award 60 to 90 small project grants, 40 to 50 medium project grants, and 3 to 4 large project grants. The total allocated to this program recently was $145 million. Normally, 30% of total funding is spent on small projects, 40 to 60% on medium projects, and 10 to 20% to large projects.

Deadline For small project, pre-proposals are not required and full proposals are due in December of each year. For medium projects, pre-proposals are not required and full proposals are due in February of each year. For large projects, pre-proposals must be submitted in November and full proposals are due the following March.

[840]
INSTITUTE FOR RESEARCH ON POVERTY MINORITY SCHOLARS PROGRAM

University of Wisconsin at Madison
Attn: Institute for Research on Poverty
3412 Social Science Building
1180 Observatory Drive
Madison, WI 53706-1393
(608) 262-6358   Fax: (608) 265-3119
E-mail: evanson@ssc.wisc.edu
Web: www.ssc.wisc.edu/irp

Purpose To provide minority scholars with an opportunity to visit the Institute for Research on Poverty (IRP) at the University of Wisconsin at Madison.

Eligibility This program is open to minority scholars, especially those in the beginning years of their academic careers. Applicants should submit a letter describing their poverty research interests and experience, the proposed dates for a visit, a current curriculum vitae, and 2 examples of written material.

Financial data Limited support is provided.

Duration 1 to 2 weeks.

Additional information During their visit, scholars are invited to give a seminar, to work on their own projects, and to confer with an IRP adviser who will arrange for an interchange with other IRP affiliates.

Number awarded Up to 3 each year.

Deadline September of each year.

[841]
INSTITUTE OF ECOSYSTEM STUDIES RESEARCH EXPERIENCES FOR UNDERGRADUATES PROGRAM

Institute of Ecosystem Studies
Attn: Undergraduate Research Program
181 Sharon Turnpike
P.O. Box R
Millbrook, NY 12545
(845) 677-7600, ext. 326   Fax: (845) 677-6455
E-mail: dahlh@ecostudies.org
Web: www.ecostudies.org/education/reu/reu1.html

Purpose To provide undergraduate students with an opportunity to conduct research during the summer at the Institute of Ecosystem Studies (IES) at Millbrook, New York.

Eligibility This program is open to undergraduate freshmen, sophomores, juniors, and first semester seniors. Applicants must be interested in conducting an independent research project of their own design under the guidance of a mentor scientist. They must identify their interest in ecological research, their current career plans, and how participating in this program could help them in their degree program and their future pursuits. Each year, a variety of research topics underway at IES are open to undergraduate participation; some recent topics included microbial processes in urban ecosystems, segregation of tree species along soil nutrient gradients, effects of air pollutants on the forests of the Catskill Mountains, and groundwater ecology. Preference is given to students from underrepresented groups and from colleges that do not provide undergraduate research opportunities.

Financial data The stipend is $3,000. Some assistance for travel is available.

Duration 12 weeks, during the summer.

Additional information This program is supported by the National Science Foundation and the Andrew W. Mellon Foundation

Deadline February of each year.

[842]
INTERNATIONAL SECURITY AND COOPERATION POSTDOCTORAL FELLOWSHIPS

Stanford University
Center for International Security and Cooperation
Attn: Director of Fellowship Programs
Encina Hall, Room E210
616 Serra Street
Stanford, CA 94305-6165
(650) 723-9626   Fax: (650) 723-0089
E-mail: barbara.platt@stanford.edu
Web: www.cisac.stanford.edu

Purpose To provide funding for postdoctorates who are interested in conducting research on arms control and international security at Stanford University's Center for International Security and Cooperation.

Eligibility Postdoctorates interested in researching international security and arms control issues at the center are eligible to apply. Topics suitable for support might include security relationships around the world; U.S.-Russian strategic relations; peacekeeping; prevention of deadly conflicts; U.S. defense and arms control policies; proliferation of nuclear, chemical, and biological weapons; security in south and east Asia; the commercialization of national defense technologies; and ethnic and civil conflict. Applications are welcome from military officers or civilian members of the U.S. government, members of military or diplomatic services from other countries, and journalists interested in arms control and international security issues. The center is especially interested in applications from minorities and women.

Financial data The stipend is at least $33,000, depending on experience. Additional funds may be available for dependents and travel.

Duration 9 months.

Number awarded Varies; generally, 2 each year.

Deadline January of each year.

[843]
INTERNATIONAL SECURITY AND COOPERATION PREDOCTORAL FELLOWSHIPS

Stanford University
Center for International Security and Cooperation
Attn: Director of Fellowship Programs
Encina Hall, Room E210
616 Serra Street
Stanford, CA 94305-6165
(650) 723-9626   Fax: (650) 723-0089
E-mail: barbara.platt@stanford.edu
Web: www.cisac.stanford.edu

Purpose To provide funding to doctoral students who are interested in writing a dissertation on the problems of arms control and international security at Stanford University's Center for International Security and Cooperation.

Eligibility Students currently enrolled in doctoral programs (particularly those that involve U.S.-Soviet security relations and east Asian security issues) at academic institutions in the United States who would benefit from access to the facilities offered by the center are eligible to apply. Topics suitable for support might include security relationships around the world; U.S.-Russian strategic relations; peacekeeping; prevention of deadly conflicts; U.S. defense and arms control policies; proliferation of nuclear, chemical, and biological weapons; security in south and east Asia; the commercialization of national defense technologies; and ethnic and civil conflict. The center is especially interested in receiving applications from minorities and women.

Financial data The stipend is $20,000. Additional funds may be available for dependents and travel.

Duration 9 months.

Number awarded Varies; generally, 4 each year.

Deadline January of each year.

[844]
INVESTIGATOR AWARDS IN HEALTH POLICY RESEARCH

Robert Wood Johnson Foundation
College Road East and U.S. Route 1
P.O. Box 2316
Princeton, NJ 08543-2316
(609) 452-8701   E-mail: mail@rwjf.org
Web: www.rwjf.org

Purpose To provide funding to investigators from diverse fields interested in conducting research on health policy.

Eligibility This program is open to investigators from such fields as allied health, anthropology, business, economics, education, ethics, genetics, history, health and social policy, journalism, law, management, medicine, nursing, philosophy, political science, public health, psychology, science policy, social work, and

sociology. Members of minority groups and individuals in non-academic settings, such as research firms and policy organizations, are specifically encouraged to apply. The proposed research should help develop, interpret, or substantially advance ideas or knowledge that can improve health or health care policy in the United States. Selection is based on the potential for the work to inform and influence the development or implementation of health policy; the contribution and potential significance of the project to the theoretical underpinnings and knowledge base of health care, health policy, or other disciplines; the extent to which the work represents an innovative perspective on health, health care, or health policy; the soundness of the project's conceptual framework and methodology; the feasibility of the work; the likelihood that the findings can be useful to a variety of key decision makers, based on the applicant's identification of potential audiences for the proposed work; and the capability of the investigator to undertake and complete the project on schedule.

Financial data Grants up to $275,000 are provided. Funds are to be used primarily for project salary support for the principal investigator(s).

Duration 24 to 36 months.

Additional information Further information is available from the program's Deputy Director, Rutgers, the State University of New Jersey, Institute for Health, Health Care Policy, and Aging Research, 317 George Street, Suite 400, New Brunswick, NJ 08901-2008, (732) 932-3817, ext. 256, E-mail: depdir@ihhcpar.rutgers.edu.

Number awarded Approximately 10 each year.

Deadline October of each year.

[845]
INVESTIGATORS IN PATHOGENESIS OF INFECTIOUS DISEASE

Burroughs Wellcome Fund
21 T.W. Alexander Drive, Suite 100
P.O. Box 13901
Research Triangle Park, NC 27709-3901
(919) 991-5100   Fax: (919) 991-5160
E-mail: info@bwfund.org
Web: www.bwfund.org/infectious_pathogenesis.htm

Purpose To provide funding to physician/scientists in the United States and Canada who wish to conduct research on pathogenesis, with a focus on the intersection of human and pathogen biology.

Eligibility This program is open to established independent physician/scientists who are citizens or permanent residents of the United States or Canada affiliated with accredited degree-granting U.S. or Canadian medical schools. Applicants must be interested in conducting research projects that hold potential for advancing significantly the biochemical, pharmacological, immunological, and molecular biological understanding of how infectious agents and the human body interact. Although work on AIDS, malaria, and tuberculosis is not excluded, preference is given to research shedding new light on unexplored pathogenesis. Research on understudied infectious diseases, including pathogenic fungi, metazoan parasites, and emerging viral diseases, is of especial interest. Applicants must hold an M.D. or M.D./Ph.D. degree and be tenure-track investigators as an assistant professor or equivalent at a degree-granting institution. The sponsor encourages applications from women and members of underrepresented minority groups. Selection is based on qualifications of the candidate and potential to conduct innovative research; demonstration of an established record of independent research; and quality and originality of the proposed research and its potential to advance understanding of fundamental issues of how infectious agents and human hosts interact.

Financial data The grant provides $80,000 per year.

Duration 5 years.

Additional information This program was established in 2001 as a replacement for several former programs: New Investigator and Scholar Awards in Molecular Pathogenic Mycology, New Investigator and Scholar Awards in Molecular Parasitology, and New Initiatives in Malaria Awards. Awardees are required to devote at least 75% of their time to research-related activities.

Number awarded 16 each year.

Deadline October of each year.

[846]
IRVINE MINORITY SCHOLARS PROGRAM

University of San Francisco
College of Arts and Sciences
Attn: Gerardo Marin
2130 Fulton Street
San Francisco, CA 94117-1080
(415) 422-5555   E-mail: nobles@usfca.edu
Web: www.usfca.edu

Purpose To offer ethnic minorities an opportunity to teach and conduct dissertation research at the University of San Francisco (USF).

Eligibility This program is open to U.S. citizens or permanent residents who have finished all course work leading to the Ph.D., are interested in considering a career in teaching, and are members of 1 of the following ethnic/racial groups: African American, Asian American, Hispanic/Latino, or American Indian. Applicants must be interested in teaching at USF while they complete their dissertation. Recently, appointments have been available in the following programs: 1) College of Arts and Sciences: communication studies, dance, English, international and development economics, Latin American studies, politics, clinical neuropsychology, and theology and religious studies; 2) College of Professional Studies: ethics, organizational development; and 3) School of Education: organization and educational leadership. Selection is based on university teaching experience, evidence of scholarly promise, and an understanding of and commitment to support the mission of the university.

Financial data The stipend is $30,000. Scholars also receive allowances for research costs, housing, and relocation expenses.

Duration 1 academic year.

Additional information Scholars teach 1 course per semester in their discipline, serve as resources to students and faculty, and contribute to the university's multicultural living/learning environment through activities that celebrate ethnic diversity and cultural pluralism. This program is sponsored by the James Irvine Foundation.

Number awarded 1 or more each year.

Deadline January of each year.

[847]
JANINE GONZALEZ MCAT SCHOLARSHIP FUND

Latino Medical Student Association
c/o Amanda Perez
3741 Westwood Boulevard, Number 5
Los Angeles, CA 90034
Web: latino.ucsf.edu/cmsa/scholarship/SchoInfo.html

Purpose To provide funding to Latino students who require assistance to prepare for or take the MCAT examination.

Eligibility This program is open to Latino undergraduate students who have completed at least 2 and a half years at a 4-year institution, including a year of chemistry, physics, and biology and at least 1 semester of a course in compositional writing or its equivalent. Applicants should be able to demonstrate a desire to advance the state of health care and education in Latino communities through extracurricular activities and/or membership in civic organizations. They must be committed to pursuing a professional career in medicine and dedicated to serving the Latino community. Selection is based on personal qualities, academic achievement, and financial need.

Financial data Funds are provided for MCAT registration fees or payment for a MCAT preparation course. The amount of the assistance depends on the need of the recipient but normally is approximately 50% of the cost of test preparation courses. Funds may be used as reimbursement for a previously paid MCAT or preparation course or for an anticipated test.

Duration These are 1-time grants.

Additional information Until 2002, this organization was known as the Chicano/Latino Medical Student Association of California. It established this program in 1995.

Number awarded Varies each year.

Deadline February of each year.

[848]
JAPAN ADVANCED RESEARCH GRANTS

Social Science Research Council
810 Seventh Avenue
New York, NY 10019
(212) 377-2700   Fax: (212) 377-2727
E-mail: japan@ssrc.org
Web: www.ssrc.org

Purpose To provide funding for advanced research on Japan in all areas of the social sciences and humanities.

Eligibility Eligible to apply are scholars who are U.S. citizens (or have been resident in the United States for at least 3 consecutive years) and have either a Ph.D. or equivalent research or analytical experience. The program encourages innovative research in the social sciences that is comparative and contemporary in nature, and has long-range applied policy implications, or that engages Japan in wide regional and global debates. Special attention is given to Japan specialists who are interested in broadening their skills and expertise through additional training or comparative work in an additional geographic area. Minorities and women are particularly encouraged to apply.

Financial data The maximum award is $25,000.

Duration 2 months to 1 year.

Additional information Depending on the nature of the proposed project, the research may be carried out in Japan, the United States, and/or other countries. Scholars may apply for support to conduct research in collaboration with Japanese scholars who have other support. Funding for this program is provided by the Japan-United States Friendship Commission. These grants are not for training and candidates for academic degrees are not eligible. If travel is planned, applicants must try to arrange for affiliation with an American or foreign university or research institute.

Number awarded Varies each year.

Deadline November of each year.

[849]
JEFFREY CAMPBELL GRADUATE FELLOWS PROGRAM

St. Lawrence University
Attn: Human Resources/Office of Equity Programs
Jeffrey Campbell Graduate Fellowship Program
Canton, NY 13617
(315) 229-5509
Web: www.stlawu.edu

Purpose To provide funding to minority graduate students who have completed their course work and are interested in conducting research at St. Lawrence University in New York.

Eligibility This program is open to graduate students who are members of racial or ethnic groups historically underrepresented at the university and in American higher education. Applicants must have completed their course work and preliminary examinations for the Ph.D. or M.F.A. They must be interested in working on their dissertations or terminal degree projects while in residence at the University.

Financial data The stipend is $25,000 per academic year. Additional funds may be available to support travel to conferences and professional meetings. Office space and a personal computer are provided.

Duration 1 academic year.

Additional information This program is named for 1 of the university's early African American graduates. Recipients must teach 1 course a semester in a department or program at St. Lawrence University related to their research interests. In addition, they must present a research-based paper in the fellows' lecture series each semester.

Deadline February of each year.

[850]
JOHN AND ELIZABETH PHILLIPS FELLOWSHIP

Phillips Exeter Academy
Attn: Dean of Faculty
20 Main Street
Exeter, NH 03833-2460
(603) 772-3405   Fax: (603) 772-4393
E-mail: faculty@exeter.edu
Web: www.exeter.edu/dean_faculty/phillips_fellows.html

Purpose To provide funding to underrepresented teachers interested in a residency at Phillips Exeter Academy in Exeter, New Hampshire.

Eligibility This program is open to scholars and teachers from groups traditionally underrepresented in the secondary school environment (e.g., minorities) who might not otherwise consider teaching in a residential secondary school. Candidates may come from other educational institutions, direct from college or graduate school, or from non-academic settings.

Financial data Fellows receive a competitive salary.

Duration 1 to 3 academic years.

Additional information Fellows live in residence at Phillips Exeter Academy, where they affiliate with a specific academic department and coordinate their teaching responsibilities with a faculty mentor. They serve on important faculty committees and engage in oversight of dormitories, athletics, and extracurricular activities. This fellowship was first offered for the 1998-99 academic year.

Number awarded Up to 4 each year.

[851]
JOHN M. OLIN POSTDOCTORAL FELLOWSHIPS IN MILITARY HISTORY AND STRATEGY

Yale University
Attn: International Security Studies
34 Hillhouse Avenue
P.O. Box 208353
New Haven, CT 06520-8353
(203) 432-6246   Fax: (203) 432-6250
E-mail: iss@yale.edu
Web: www.yale.edu/iss

Purpose To provide funding to postdoctorates interested in conducting research in the fields of U.S. military history and strategic studies at Yale University.

Eligibility This program is open to younger scholars whose research interests focus on how military and international security issues (and their histories) bear upon the United States. Applicants should have received their doctorate by the time they would begin this program. Candidates who are interested in conducting their research at Yale should submit their vitae, a research proposal, their transcripts, a short (up to 50 pages) writing sample, and 3 references. Females, minorities, and candidates with disabilities, as well as veterans, are encouraged to apply.

Financial data The stipend is $30,000 per year.

Duration 2 years. This is a residential fellowship; fellows are expected to be in residence at Yale University for the duration of the program.

Number awarded 1 or 2 each year.

Deadline January of each year.

[852]
JOSE L. NAZAR GRANTS FOR LATINO PROJECTS AND/OR LATINO FILMMAKERS

Women in Film Foundation
Attn: WIF Foundation Administrator
8857 West Olympic Boulevard, Suite 201
Beverly Hills, CA 90211
(310) 657-5144, ext. 16   E-mail: membersvcs@wif.org
Web: wif.org/home/wiff/index.hmtl

Purpose To provide funding to women for the completion of films about Latinos.

Eligibility Independent producers and nonprofit corporations are eligible to submit proposals for completion funding on an existing film or video. Projects of any length and in any film or video format are considered. This program is restricted to Latino projects and/or Latino filmmakers. Submissions must relate to the goals of the sponsor: increase employment and promote equal opportunities for women, encourage individual creative projects by women, enhance media images of women, further the professional development of women, and influence prevailing attitudes and practices regarding and on behalf of women. Projects in development or pre-production are not considered, nor are student projects.

Financial data Grants up to $5,000 are available.

Additional information A $20 application fee is charged for processing and mailing.

Number awarded Varies each year.

Deadline November of each year.

[853]
JOSEPH L. FISHER DOCTORAL DISSERTATION FELLOWSHIPS

Resources for the Future
Attn: Coordinator for Academic Programs
1616 P Street, N.W.
Washington, DC 20036-1400
(202) 328-5060   Fax: (202) 939-3460
E-mail: mankin@rff.org
Web: www.rff.org/about_rff/fisher.htm

Purpose To support doctoral dissertation research in economics on issues related to the environment, natural resources, or energy.

Eligibility This fellowship is intended to support graduate students in the final year of their dissertation research. The sponsor particularly encourages women and minority group members to apply. Applicants must submit the following: a brief letter of application and a curriculum vitae, a graduate transcript, a 1-page abstract of the dissertation, a technical summary of the dissertation (up to 2,500 words), a letter from the student's department chair, and 2 letters of recommendation from faculty members on the student's dissertation committee. The technical summary should describe clearly the aim of the dissertation, its significance in relation to the existing literature, and the research methods to be used.

Financial data The stipend is $12,000 per year.

Duration 1 academic year.

Additional information It is expected that recipients will not hold other employment during the fellowship period. Recipients must notify Resources for the Future of any financial assistance they receive from any other source for support of doctoral work.

Number awarded 5 each year.

Deadline February of each year.

[854]
JUNIOR INVESTIGATOR RESEARCH GRANTS IN EPILEPSY

Epilepsy Foundation
Attn: Department of Research and Professional Education
4351 Garden City Drive
Landover, MD 20785-7223
(301) 459-3700   (800) EFA-1000
Fax: (301) 577-2684   TDD: (800) 332-2070
E-mail: grants@efa.org
Web: www.epilepsyfoundation.org/research/grants.html

Purpose To support basic and clinical research in the biological, behavioral, and social sciences that will advance the understanding, treatment, and prevention of epilepsy.

Eligibility Applicants must have a doctoral degree and an academic appointment at the level of assistant professor in a university or medical school (or equivalent standing at a research institution or medical center). They must be interested in conducting research into the causes of epilepsy. Applications from women, members of minority groups, and people with disabilities are especially encouraged. U.S. citizenship is not required, but the research must be conducted in the United States. Selection is

based on the scientific quality of the research plan, the relevance of the proposed research to epilepsy, the applicant's qualifications, and the adequacy of the institution and facility where research will be conducted.

Financial data Support is limited to $40,000.

Duration 1 year. An additional year of support may be requested through re-application.

Number awarded Varies each year.

Deadline September of each year.

[855]
KANSAS SPACE GRANT CONSORTIUM PROGRAM

Kansas Space Grant Consortium
c/o University of Kansas
135 Nichols Hall
2335 Irving Hill Road
Lawrence, KS 66045-7612
(785) 864-7401   Fax: (785) 864-3361
E-mail: ksgc@ukans.edu
Web: www.ksgc.org

Purpose To provide funding for space-related activities to students and faculty at member institutions of the Kansas Space Grant Consortium.

Eligibility This program is open to faculty and students at member institutions. Support is provided for undergraduate research scholarships, graduate research assistantships, undergraduate and graduate student participation in activities sponsored by the U.S. National Aeronautics and Space Administration (NASA), faculty participation in NASA research projects, and other activities in fields of interest to NASA. The consortium is a component of NASA's Space Grant program, which encourages participation by women, underrepresented minorities, and persons with disabilities.

Financial data Each participating institution determines the amounts of its awards.

Additional information The member institutions of the consortium are Emporia State University, Fort Hayes State University, Haskell Indian Nations University, Kansas State University, Pittsburgh State University, University of Kansas, and Wichita State University. Funding for this program is provided by NASA.

Number awarded Varies each year.

Deadline Each participating institution establishes its own deadlines.

[856]
KENTUCKY SPACE GRANT CONSORTIUM GRADUATE FELLOWSHIPS

Kentucky Space Grant Consortium
c/o Western Kentucky University
Department of Physics and Astronomy, TCCW 246
Hardin Planetarium and Astrophysical Observatory
One Big Red Way
Bowling Green, KY 42101-3576
(270) 745-4156   Fax: (270) 745-4255
E-mail: Richard.Hackney@wku.edu
Web: www.wku.edu/KSGC

Purpose To provide financial assistance for study and research in space-related fields to graduate students in Kentucky.

Eligibility This program is open to graduate students at member institutions of the Kentucky Space Grant Consortium (KSGC). Applicants must be enrolled in a graduate degree program in a space-related field or teaching specialization. As part of the program, a faculty member must agree to serve as a mentor on a research project. U.S. citizenship is required. Selection is based on academic qualifications of the applicant, quality of the proposed research program and its relevance to space-related science and technology, and applicant's motivation for a space-related career as expressed in an essay on interests and goals. Applications are encouraged from women, underrepresented minorities, and students involved in projects of the U.S. National Aeronautics and Space Administration (NASA) such as NASA EPSCoR and SHARP.

Financial data The stipend is $16,000 per year, with an additional $2,000 for use in support of the student's mentored research project. Matching grants of at least $12,000 are required. Preference is given to applicants from schools that agree to waive tuition for the fellow as part of the program.

Duration 1 year; may be renewed, depending on the quality of the student's research and satisfactory grades, presentation of research results, and evaluation of progress by the mentor.

Additional information This program is funded by NASA. The KSGC member institutions are Centre College, Eastern Kentucky University, Kentucky State University, Morehead State University, Murray State University, Northern Kentucky University, Transylvania University, University of Kentucky, University of Louisville, and Western Kentucky University.

Number awarded Varies each year.

Deadline April of each year.

[857]
KENTUCKY SPACE GRANT CONSORTIUM RESEARCH GRANTS

Kentucky Space Grant Consortium
c/o Western Kentucky University
Department of Physics and Astronomy, TCCW 246
Hardin Planetarium and Astrophysical Observatory
One Big Red Way
Bowling Green, KY 42101-3576
(270) 745-4156   Fax: (270) 745-4255
E-mail: Richard.Hackney@wku.edu
Web: www.wku.edu/KSGC

Purpose To provide financial assistance to faculty members at designated institutions in Kentucky who are interested in conducting space-related research.

Eligibility This program is open to faculty members at member institutions of the Kentucky Space Grant Consortium. Applicants must be interested in conducting research that will enhance their competitiveness for future funding. Preference is given to proposals that involve students in the research. Investigators are encouraged to develop projects related to strategic enterprises of the U.S. National Aeronautics and Space Administration (NASA), to collaborate with NASA field centers, or to utilize NASA data. The Kentucky Space Grant Consortium is a component of the NASA Space Grant program, which encourages participation by women, underrepresented minorities, and persons with disabilities.

Financial data Awards up to $5,000 require a 1:1 institutional match; awards up to $10,000 require a 2:1 match.

Duration 1 year; may be renewed.

Additional information This program is funded by NASA. The KSGC member institutions are Centre College, Eastern Kentucky University, Kentucky State University, Morehead State University, Murray State University, Northern Kentucky University, Transylva-

nia University, University of Kentucky, University of Louisville, and Western Kentucky University. The institution must provide adequate faculty time and any indirect costs.

Number awarded Varies each year.

Deadline April of each year.

[858]
KENTUCKY SPACE GRANT CONSORTIUM UNDERGRADUATE SCHOLARSHIPS

Kentucky Space Grant Consortium
c/o Western Kentucky University
Department of Physics and Astronomy, TCCW 246
Hardin Planetarium and Astrophysical Observatory
One Big Red Way
Bowling Green, KY 42101-3576
(270) 745-4156   Fax: (270) 745-4255
E-mail: Richard.Hackney@wku.edu
Web: www.wku.edu/KSGC

Purpose To provide financial assistance to undergraduate students at member institutions of the Kentucky Space Grant Consortium (KSGC) interested in pursuing education and research in space-related fields.

Eligibility This program is open to undergraduate students at member institutions of the KSGC. Applicants must be enrolled in a baccalaureate degree program in a space-related field or teaching specialization. As part of the program, a faculty member must agree to serve as a mentor on a research project. U.S. citizenship is required. Selection is based on academic qualifications of the applicant, quality of the proposed research program and its relevance to space-related science and technology, and applicant's motivation for a space-related career as expressed in an essay on interests and goals. Applications are encouraged from women, underrepresented minorities, and students involved in projects of the U.S. National Aeronautics and Space Administration (NASA) such as NASA EPSCoR and SHARP.

Financial data The stipend is $3,000 per year, with an additional $500 to support the student's mentored research project. Matching grants of at least $3,000 are required. Preference is given to applicants from schools that agree to waive tuition for the scholar as part of the program.

Duration 1 year; may be renewed depending on the quality of the student's research and satisfactory performance in the program of study as evidenced by grades, presentation of research results, and evaluation of progress by the mentor.

Additional information This program is funded by NASA. The KSGC member institutions are Centre College, Eastern Kentucky University, Kentucky State University, Morehead State University, Murray State University, Northern Kentucky University, Transylvania University, University of Kentucky, University of Louisville, and Western Kentucky University.

Number awarded Varies each year.

Deadline April of each year.

[859]
LATINO POSTDOCTORAL FELLOWSHIPS AT THE SMITHSONIAN INSTITUTION

Smithsonian Institution
Attn: Office of Fellowships
Victor Building, Suite 9300, MRC 902
P.O. Box 37012
Washington, DC 20013-7012
(202) 275-0655   Fax: (202) 275-0489
E-mail: siofg@si.edu
Web: www.si.edu/ofg/fell.htm

Purpose To provide funding to Latino postdoctoral scholars interested in conducting research at the Smithsonian Institution.

Eligibility This program is open Latino/a scholars who have completed a doctoral degree less than 7 years before the application deadline. Applicants must intend to conduct research in U.S. Latino history, art, or culture at the Smithsonian Institution. Selection is based on the proposal's merit, including the significance of the study to the discipline in general and to Latino research in particular, the methodology to be used, the applicant's ability to carry out the proposed research and study, the likelihood that the research could be completed in the requested time, and the extent to which the Smithsonian, through its various resources, could contribute to the proposed research.

Financial data The stipend is $30,000 per year; also provided are a travel allowance and a research allowance of up to $4,000.

Duration From 3 to 12 months. Fellows are expected to spend most of their tenure in residence at the Smithsonian, although up to one third of the fellowship tenure may be spent away from the Smithsonian conducting research at another institution or in the field (but not at the applicant's home institution).

Number awarded Varies each year, depending on the availability of funds.

Deadline January of each year.

[860]
LATINO PREDOCTORAL FELLOWSHIPS AT THE SMITHSONIAN INSTITUTION

Smithsonian Institution
Attn: Office of Fellowships
Victor Building, Suite 9300, MRC 902
P.O. Box 37012
Washington, DC 20013-7012
(202) 275-0655   Fax: (202) 275-0489
E-mail: siofg@si.edu
Web: www.si.edu/ofg/fell.htm

Purpose To provide funding to Latino doctoral students interested in conducting research at the Smithsonian Institution.

Eligibility This program is open to Latinos/as who have completed preliminary course work and examinations for the doctoral degree and are engaged in dissertation research in U.S. Latino history, art, or culture. Applicants must have the approval of their university to conduct their doctoral research at the Smithsonian Institution. Selection is based on the proposal's merit, including the significance of the study to the discipline in general and to Latino research in particular, the methodology to be used, the applicant's ability to carry out the proposed research and study, the likelihood that the research could be completed in the requested time, and the extent to which the Smithsonian, through its various resources, could contribute to the proposed research.

Financial data The stipend is $17,000 per year; also provided are a travel allowance and a research allowance of up to $4,000.

Duration From 3 to 12 months. Fellows are expected to spend most of their tenure in residence at the Smithsonian, although up to one third of the fellowship tenure may be spent away from the Smithsonian conducting research at another institution or in the field (but not at the applicant's home institution).

Number awarded Varies each year, depending on the availability of funds.

Deadline January of each year.

[861]
LATINO PUBLIC BROADCASTING GRANTS

Latino Public Broadcasting
6777 Hollywood Boulevard, Suite 500
Los Angeles, CA 90028
(323) 466-7110   Fax: (323) 466-7521
E-mail: latinopublicbroadcasting@yahoo.com
Web: www.lpbp.org

Purpose To provide funding to film and video producers interested in developing projects for broadcast on public television that relate to the Latino experience in America.

Eligibility This program is open to independent producers and production entities that are creating programs on the Latino experience. The programs must be independent of the support of a film studio or commercial broadcast entity. The producer or production entity must retain the copyright and have artistic, budgetary, and editorial control over the proposed project. Applicants must be at least 18 years of age, be citizens or legal residents of the United States or its territories, and have previous film or television experience that can be documented by detailed personnel resumes and by sample tapes upon request. Projects that are ineligible include thesis projects and student films; producers or production entities that are foreign based, owned, or controlled; industrial or promotional projects; projects for which the exclusive domestic television rights are not available; projects with a primarily commercial interest; and current recipients of these grants who have not completed delivery. The project genres may include drama, comedy, animation, documentary, or mixed genre. The project may be at any stage of production. Applications must be accompanied by a budget summary, project description, detailed project budget, list of key personnel, and samples of prior work.

Financial data Grants average between $5,000 and $100,000.

Additional information Funding for these grants is provided by the Corporation for Public Broadcasting. Producers must agree to complete the program according to the proposed schedule, project description, and budget, and to certain oversight rights and accountability obligations to the sponsor. The producer also agrees to royalty participation by the sponsor in a percentage of net revenues from ancillary distribution.

Number awarded Varies each year.

Deadline May of each year.

[862]
LATINO SENIOR FELLOWSHIPS AT THE SMITHSONIAN INSTITUTION

Smithsonian Institution
Attn: Office of Fellowships
Victor Building, Suite 9300, MRC 902
P.O. Box 37012
Washington, DC 20013-7012
(202) 275-0655   Fax: (202) 275-0489
E-mail: siofg@si.edu
Web: www.si.edu/ofg/fell.htm

Purpose To provide funding to senior Latino scholars interested in conducting research at the Smithsonian Institution.

Eligibility This program is open to Latinos/as who have completed a doctoral degree more than 7 years before the application deadline. Applicants must intend to conduct research in U.S. Latino history, art, or culture at the Smithsonian Institution. Selection is based on the proposal's merit, including the significance of the study to the discipline in general and to Latino research in particular, the methodology to be used, the applicant's ability to carry out the proposed research and study, the likelihood that the research could be completed in the requested time, and the extent to which the Smithsonian, through its various resources, could contribute to the proposed research.

Financial data The stipend is $30,000 per year; also provided are a travel allowance and a research allowance of up to $4,000.

Duration From 3 to 12 months. Fellows are expected to spend most of their tenure in residence at the Smithsonian, although up to one third of the fellowship tenure may be spent away from the Smithsonian conducting research at another institution or in the field (but not at the applicant's home institution).

Number awarded Varies each year, depending on the availability of funds.

Deadline January of each year.

[863]
LAWRENCE UNIVERSITY PRE-DOCTORAL MINORITY FELLOWSHIP

Lawrence University
Office of the Dean of the Faculty
Appleton, WI 54912-0599
(920) 833-6528   Fax: (920) 832-6978
Web: www.lawrence.edu/dept/faculty_dean

Purpose To provide an opportunity for minority doctoral students to teach and conduct research at Lawrence University in Appleton, Wisconsin.

Eligibility This program is open to minority students who have completed all requirements for a Ph.D. in the liberal arts except for the dissertation. Preference is given to minorities with U.S. citizenship (e.g., African Americans, Asian Americans, Hispanic Americans, and Native Americans). To apply, students should send a curriculum vitae, a cover letter, 3 letters of recommendation (1 of which must be from their dissertation advisor), official graduate school transcripts, and an outline of their dissertation.

Financial data The stipend is $27,500, plus $1,500 for research and travel.

Duration 1 year.

Additional information Recipients must teach 1 course each semester. They must be in residence for the complete academic year.

Number awarded 2 each year.

Deadline November of each year.

[864]
LEROY C. MERRITT HUMANITARIAN FUND AWARD

LeRoy C. Merritt Humanitarian Fund
Attn: Secretary
50 East Huron Street
Chicago, IL 60611
(312) 280-4226   (800) 545-2433, ext. 4226
Fax: (312) 280-4227   E-mail: merrittfund@ala.org
Web: www.merrittfund.org

Purpose To provide financial support to librarians facing discrimination on the basis of race, sex, or other factors.

Eligibility The fund was established in 1970 to provide direct financial aid for the support, maintenance, medical care, legal fees, and welfare of librarians who are or have been "threatened with loss of employment or discharged because of their stand for the cause of intellectual freedom." In 1975, the scope of the fund was broadened to include librarians who had been discriminated against on the basis of gender, age, race, color, creed, sexual orientation, place of national origin, or defense of intellectual freedom. Applicants should describe their situation, including a brief explanation of its financial ramifications and of the amount of aid requested.

Financial data The amount awarded varies, depending upon the needs of the recipient.

Duration The award is granted annually.

Number awarded Varies each year.

Deadline Applications may be submitted at any time.

[865]
LIBRARY OF CONGRESS FELLOWSHIPS IN INTERNATIONAL STUDIES

American Council of Learned Societies
Attn: Office of Fellowships and Grants
633 Third Avenue, 8C
New York, NY 10017-6795
(212) 697-1505   Fax: (212) 949-8058
E-mail: grants@acls.org
Web: www.acls.org/locguide.htm

Purpose To provide financial assistance to scholars in all disciplines of the humanities and the social sciences who are interested in using the foreign language collections of the Library of Congress.

Eligibility This program is open to U.S. citizens and permanent residents who hold a Ph.D. in a discipline of the humanities or social sciences. Proposals in multidisciplinary and cross-disciplinary studies are also welcome, as are proposals focused on single or multiple geographical areas. Research must require use of the foreign language collections of the Library of Congress. Preference is given to scholars at an early stage of their career (within 7 years of completing their doctorate). Applicants may be affiliated with any academic institution, although independent scholars are also eligible. Applications are particularly invited from women and members of minority groups.

Financial data The stipend is $3,500 per month.

Duration 4 to 9 months; fellowships may be combined with sabbatical and other fellowship funds to extend the research period up to a total of 12 months.

Additional information This program is supported by funding from the Andrew W. Mellon Foundation, the Association of American Universities, and the Library of Congress. Additional support for research concerning east or southeast Asia is provided by the Henry Luce Foundation.

Number awarded Up to 10 each year.

Deadline October of each year.

[866]
LILLA JEWEL AWARD FOR WOMEN ARTISTS

McKenzie River Gathering Foundation
Attn: Office Manager
2705 East Burnside, Suite 210
Portland, OR 97214
(503) 289-1517   Fax: (503) 232-1731
E-mail: info@mrgfoundation.org
Web: www.mrgfoundation.org

Purpose To provide funding to women artists in Oregon.

Eligibility Eligible to apply for this funding are women artists in Oregon. The artistic category rotates on a triennial cycle among music and dance, media and multi-arts, and visual arts. Preference is given to members of other traditionally underfunded groups, such as lesbians, women of color, and artists whose work challenges the status quo. Selection is based on the artistic impact of the work presented for consideration, the artist's history, how well the application narrative articulates the ideas embodied in the work itself, whether or not the work is reflective of the sponsor's progressive grantmaking philosophy, and the potential impact of the award on an artist at the particular point in her career.

Financial data The maximum grant is $4,000.

Duration 1 year.

Additional information This is the only funding available to individuals through the McKenzie River Gathering Foundation.

Number awarded 1 each year.

Deadline April of each year.

[867]
LLNL RESEARCH COLLABORATIONS PROGRAM FOR HISTORICALLY BLACK UNIVERSITIES AND COLLEGES AND OTHER MINORITY INSTITUTIONS

Lawrence Livermore National Laboratory
Attn: University Relations Program
P.O. Box 808, L-041
Livermore, CA 94551
(925) 423-1112   E-mail: reed5@llnl.gov
Web: www.llnl.gov/urp/HBCU/homepage.html

Purpose To provide opportunities for research collaborations at Lawrence Livermore National Laboratory (LLNL) to students, postdoctoral researchers, and faculty of Historically Black Colleges and Universities (HBCUs) and other Minority Institutions (MIs).

Eligibility This program is open to undergraduate students, graduate students, postdoctoral researchers, and faculty at HBCUs and other MIs. Applicants must be proposing to conduct research with principal investigators at LLNL in areas of LLNL core competencies, including nonlinear optics, atomic physics, materials science, spectroscopy, plasma diagnostics, and massively parallel computing.

Financial data Students receive stipends based on their discipline, education, and experience; faculty members receive release time from their home institutions.

Duration Most opportunities are in the summer, although some fall and spring assignments may be available.

Additional information Funding for this program is provided from a variety of sources, principally from the Office of Defense Programs of the U.S. Department of Energy.

Number awarded Varies each year.

Deadline Applications may be submitted at any time.

[868]
LONG-TERM MINORITY INVESTIGATOR RESEARCH SUPPLEMENT

National Institutes of Health
Division of Extramural Outreach and Information Resources
Attn: GrantsInfo
6701 Rockledge Drive, Suite 6095
Bethesda, MD 20892-7910
(301) 435-0714   Fax: (301) 480-8443
E-mail: GrantsInfo@nih.gov
Web: www.nih.gov

Purpose To supply long-term research support to underrepresented minority faculty members who are seeking to enhance their research skills in areas of interest to the National Institutes of Health (NIH).

Eligibility The minority investigator may be affiliated with either the applicant institution or any other institution. The investigator must have a doctoral degree, be beyond the level of a research trainee, and be a member of the faculty with at least 1 year of postdoctoral experience. Individuals who have received previous funding from a component institute or center as an independent principal investigator on regular research grants, program project grants, or research career program awards are not eligible. The sponsor considers African Americans, Hispanic Americans, Native Americans, Alaskan Natives, and Pacific Islanders as underrepresented minority investigators.

Financial data The requested salary and fringe benefits must be in accordance with the salary structure of the grantee institution, consistent with the level of effort. Additional funds up to $10,000 may be requested for supplies and travel. Equipment may not be purchased except in unusual circumstances.

Duration At least 30% time during each 12-month period, for up to 4 years.

Number awarded Varies each year.

Deadline Requests for supplements may be submitted at any time.

[869]
LS-LAMP SMET TRAVEL/SMALL RESEARCH GRANTS

Louis Stokes-Louisiana Alliance for Minority Participation
Southern University and A&M College
P.O. Box 9274 Owens Hall
Baton Rouge, LA 70813
(225) 771-2777   Fax: (225) 771-2311
Web: www.ls-lamp.org

Purpose To provide funding for travel or research to 1) minority students majoring in the sciences or 2) science faculty at Louis Stokes-Louisiana Alliance for Minority Participation (LS-LAMP) institutions.

Eligibility Eligible to apply for travel or research support are minority students majoring in the sciences (including mathematics, engineering, and technology) at LS-LAMP institutions or their faculty members. They must need funding to attend relevant conferences, present papers, visit a graduate program, participate in GRE preparation workshops, or conduct a research project. Eligible faculty and students must submit an application form, a recommendation letter, and a proposal.

Financial data Grants range up to $1,000.

Duration These are 1-time grants. Recipients must submit a report on their travel or research grant activities. All original itemized receipts for travel must be submitted as well.

Number awarded Several each year.

Deadline Applications may be submitted any time but must be received at least 3 weeks before the funding is needed.

[870]
LYMAN T. JOHNSON POSTDOCTORAL FELLOWSHIP

University of Kentucky
Attn: Vice President for Research
201 Gillis Building
Lexington, KY 40506-0033
(859) 257-5294   Fax: (859) 323-2800
E-mail: jfink@pap.uky.edu
Web: www.rgs.uky.edu/vpresearch/lyman.htm

Purpose To provide an opportunity for recent minority postdoctorates to conduct research at the University of Kentucky (UK).

Eligibility This program is open to minorities who have completed a doctoral degree within the past 2 years in a graduate or professional area in which minorities are underrepresented. Applicants must demonstrate evidence of scholarship with competitive potential for a tenure-track faculty appointment at a research university and compatibility of specific research interests with those in doctorate-granting units at the UK. They should submit a letter of application, a curriculum vitae, sample publications or dissertation chapters, a research proposal, 3 letters of recommendation, and a letter from a potential mentor at the university outlining the general research program. U.S. citizenship or permanent resident status is required.

Financial data The fellowship provides a stipend of $30,000 plus $5,000 for support of research activities.

Duration Up to 2 years.

Additional information In addition to conducting an individualized research program under the mentorship of 1 or more UK professors, fellows actively participate in research and teaching as well as service to the university, their profession, and the community. This program began in 1992.

Number awarded 1 each year.

Deadline January or July of each year.

[871]
MAINE SPACE GRANT CONSORTIUM GRADUATE RESEARCH FELLOWSHIPS

Maine Space Grant Consortium
Attn: Executive Director
87 Winthrop Street, Suite 200
Augusta, ME 04330
(207) 621-6350   (877) 397-7223, ext. 173
Fax: (207) 622-4548   E-mail: shehata@msgc.org
Web: www.msgc.org/eduation_students.asp

Purpose To provide funding to graduate students in Maine interested in working on research projects related to space.

Eligibility This program is open to U.S. citizens who are enrolled on a full-time basis in an approved graduate program at a Maine educational institution. Applicants must be proposing to conduct a research project in earth science or space science and engineering either under the mentorship of a faculty member at their home institution and/or at a flight center of the U.S. National Aeronautics and Space Administration (NASA). Selection is based on the relevance of the proposed research project to NASA's mission. Applications are especially encouraged from women and minorities.

Financial data Stipends vary at participating institutions, ranging from $5,000 to $15,000 per year.

Duration 1 year; may be renewed.

Additional information The member institutions are the University of Maine, the University of Southern Maine, the University of New England, and Maine Maritime Academy. This program is funded by NASA.

Number awarded Varies each year.

Deadline Each participating institution sets its own deadline.

[872]
MAINE SPACE GRANT CONSORTIUM UNDERGRADUATE RESEARCH SCHOLARSHIPS

Maine Space Grant Consortium
Attn: Executive Director
87 Winthrop Street, Suite 200
Augusta, ME 04330
(207) 621-6350   (877) 397-7223, ext. 173
Fax: (207) 622-4548   E-mail: shehata@msgc.org
Web: www.msgc.org/eduation_students.asp

Purpose To provide funding to undergraduate students in Maine interested in conducting research projects related to space.

Eligibility This program is open to U.S. citizens who are enrolled or planning to enroll as an undergraduate on a full-time basis at Maine educational institutions that are members of the Maine Space Grant Consortium. Applicants must be interested in working on a research project in earth and space science or technology transfer under the mentorship of a faculty member and/or at a flight center of the U.S. National Aeronautics and Space Administration (NASA). Women and minorities are especially encouraged to apply.

Financial data Stipends are established by each participating institution and range from $2,500 to $4,500 per year.

Duration Up to 2 years.

Additional information The member institutions are the University of Maine, the University of Southern Maine, the University of New England, and Maine Maritime Academy. This program is funded by NASA.

Number awarded Varies each year.

[873]
MALICE DOMESTIC GRANTS FOR UNPUBLISHED WRITERS

Malice Domestic, Ltd.
Attn: Grants Chair
P.O. Box 31137
Bethesda, MD 20824-1137
E-mail: grants@malicedomestic.org
Web: www.malicedomestic.org/grants.htm

Purpose To provide funding to unpublished writers in the malice domestic genre.

Eligibility This program is open to writers who have a demonstrated commitment to the malice domestic genre. Characteristics of the genre include an amateur detective, characters who know each other, and no gore, gratuitous violence, or explicit sex. Applicants must not have published a book, short story, or dramatic work in the mystery field, either in print, electronic, or audio form. Minority candidates are especially encouraged to apply.

Financial data The grants are $1,000. Funds may be used to offset registration, travel, or other expenses related to attendance at a writer's conference or similar event. In the case of nonfiction, the grant may be used to offset research expenses.

Duration Funds must be used within 1 year of the date of the award.

Number awarded 2 each year.

Deadline December of each year.

[874]
MANY VOICES MULTICULTURAL COLLABORATION GRANTS

Playwrights' Center
2301 Franklin Avenue East
Minneapolis, MN 55406-1099
(612) 332-7481   Fax: (612) 332-6037
E-mail: info@pwcenter.org
Web: www.pwcenter.org/fellowships_MV.htm

Purpose To provide funding for culturally diverse teams to collaborate on the creation and development of new plays for production in Minnesota.

Eligibility This program is open to teams of 2 or more artists collaborating on the creation and development of new theater pieces. The primary artistic leader of the team must be a Minnesota playwright of color; other team members need not be from Minnesota and may be from any cultural background or artistic discipline. Applicants must have a commitment from a Minnesota theater or organization to publicly present, sponsor, or produce the work. Along with the application, they must submit a 30-page play script by the principal Minnesota playwright, a 1-page narrative describing the proposed collaboration, artistic resumes for each member of the team, a letter of intent from a Minnesota organization to produce the work, and a budget. Selection is based on the artistic merit of the proposed project and the artistic excellence demonstrated by the team members.

Financial data Grants range up to $2,000. Funds are intended to support artistic development of work prior to presentation and/or production. Up to 10% of the grant funds may be paid to the presenting organization. Funds may not be used for marketing, publicity, or equipment purchase.

Duration Grants are awarded annually.

Number awarded 3 each year.

Deadline July of each year.

[875]
MANY VOICES RESIDENCIES

Playwrights' Center
2301 Franklin Avenue East
Minneapolis, MN 55406-1099
(612) 332-7481   Fax: (612) 332-6037
E-mail: info@pwcenter.org
Web: www.pwcenter.org/fellowships_MV.htm

Purpose To provide funding for Minnesota playwrights of color so they can spend a year in residence at the Playwrights' Center in Minneapolis.

Eligibility This program is open to playwrights of color who have been citizens or permanent residents of the United States and residents of Minnesota for at least 1 year. Applicants must be interested in playwriting and creating theater in a supportive artists' community at the Playwrights' Center. Selection is based on the applicant's commitment, proven talent, and artistic potential.

Financial data The program provides a stipend of $1,250; a mentorship with an established playwright or theater artist of their choosing; a full scholarship to a center class; a private script workshop with professional actors, directors, and dramaturgs; a public reading with professional actors and an audience discussion; and a 1-year membership in the Playwrights' Center.

Duration 9 months, beginning in October.

Additional information Fellows must be in residence at the Playwrights' Center for the duration of the program.

Number awarded 8 each year.

Deadline July of each year.

[876]
MARTIN LUTHER KING, JR., CESAR CHAVEZ, ROSA PARKS VISITING PROFESSORS PROGRAM

University of Michigan
Attn: Office of the Associate Provost—Academic Affairs
503 Thompson Street
3084 Fleming Administration Building 1340
Ann Arbor, MI 48109-1340
(734) 763-8123   Fax: (734) 764-4546
E-mail: provost@umich.edu
Web: www.umich.edu/~provost

Purpose To provide funds for minority scholars to visit and lecture/teach at the University of Michigan.

Eligibility Outstanding minority (African American, Asian American, Latino/a (Hispanic) American, and Native American) postdoctorates or scholars/practitioners are eligible to be nominated by University of Michigan department chairs or deans to visit and lecture there. Nominations that include collaborations with other universities are of high priority.

Financial data Visiting Professors receive round-trip transportation and an appropriate honorarium.

Duration Visits range from 1 to 5 days.

Additional information This program was established in 1986. Visiting Professors are expected to lecture or teach at the university, offer at least 1 event open to the general public, and meet with minority campus/community groups, including local K-12 schools.

Number awarded Varies each year.

Deadline January for the summer term; March for the fall term; August for the winter term; and November for the spring term.

[877]
MASSACHUSETTS SPACE GRANT CONSORTIUM UNDERGRADUATE RESEARCH OPPORTUNITY PROGRAM

Massachusetts Space Grant Consortium
c/o Massachusetts Institute of Technology
Building 33, Room 208
77 Massachusetts Avenue
Cambridge, MA 02139
(617) 258-5546   Fax: (617) 253-0823
E-mail: halaris@mit.edu
Web: www.mit.edu

Purpose To provide funding to undergraduates in Massachusetts who are interested in conducting research in space science or engineering.

Eligibility This program is open to undergraduate students at institutions that are members of the Massachusetts Space Grant Consortium (MASGC). Applicants must be proposing to conduct research related to space science and/or space engineering with faculty or at nearby laboratories. U.S. citizenship is required. MASGC is a component of the U.S. National Aeronautics and Space Administration (NASA) Space Grant program, which encourages participation by women, underrepresented minorities, and persons with disabilities.

Financial data The amount of the award depends on the availability of funding and the nature of the proposal.

Duration 1 semester.

Additional information Undergraduate member institutions of the MASGC are Boston University, College of the Holy Cross, the Five College Astronomy Department, Harvard University, Massachusetts Institute of Technology, Northeastern University, Tufts University, University of Massachusetts, Williams College, Wellesley College, and Worcester Polytechnic Institute. This program is funded by NASA.

Number awarded Varies each year.

Deadline December of each year.

[878]
MATHEMATICAL SCIENCES POSTDOCTORAL RESEARCH FELLOWSHIPS

National Science Foundation
Directorate for Mathematical and Physical Sciences
Attn: Division of Mathematical Sciences
4201 Wilson Boulevard, Room 1025
Arlington, VA 22230
(703) 292-4862   TDD: (703) 292-5090
E-mail: msprf@nsf.gov
Web: www.nsf.gov/mps.general.htm

Purpose To provide financial assistance to postdoctorates interested in pursuing research training in mathematics.

Eligibility Applicants for these fellowships must 1) be U.S. citizens, nationals, or permanent residents; 2) have earned a Ph.D. in a mathematical science or have had equivalent research training and experience; 3) have held the Ph.D. for no more than 2 years; and 4) have not previously held any other postdoctoral fellowship from the National Science Foundation (NSF). They must be proposing to conduct a program of postdoctoral research training at an appropriate nonprofit U.S. institution, including government laboratories, national laboratories, and privately sponsored nonprofit institutes, as well as institutions of higher education. Occasionally, research may be conducted at a foreign institution. A senior scientist at the institution must indicate availability for consultation and agreement to work with the fellow. Women, underrepresented minorities, and persons with disabilities are strongly encouraged to apply.

Financial data The total award is $108,000, consisting of 3 components: 1) a monthly stipend of $4,000 for full-time support or $2,000 for half-time support, paid directly to the fellow; 2) a research allowance of $7,500, also paid directly to the fellow; and 3) an institutional allowance of $4,500, paid to the host institution for fringe benefits (including health insurance payments for the fellow) and expenses incurred in support of the fellow, such as space, equipment, and general purpose supplies.

Duration The program provides ongoing support for 2 9-month academic years and 6 summer months, for a total of 24 months of support, within a 48-month period. Fellows have 2 options for the academic years' stipend: 1) full-time support for any 18 academic-year months in a 3-year period, in intervals not shorter than 3 consecutive months, or 2) a combination of full-time and half-time support over a period of 3 academic years, usually 1 academic year full-time and 2 academic years half-time. Not more than 2 summer months' support may be received in any calendar year.

Additional information Under certain circumstances, it may be desirable for portions of the work to be done at foreign institutions. Approval to do so must be obtained in advance from both the sponsoring senior scientist and the NSF. Information is also available from the American Mathematical Society, 210 Charles Street, P.O. Box 6248, Providence, RI 02940, (401) 455-4105, Fax: (401) 455-4004, E-mail: nsfpostdocs@ams.org.

Number awarded 30 to 35 each year.

Deadline October of each year.

[879]
MATHEMATICAL SCIENCES UNIVERSITY–INDUSTRY POSTDOCTORAL RESEARCH FELLOWSHIPS

National Science Foundation
Directorate for Mathematical and Physical Sciences
Attn: Division of Mathematical Sciences
4201 Wilson Boulevard, Room 1025
Arlington, VA 22230
(703) 292-4862   TDD: (703) 292-5090
E-mail: ldouglas@nsf.gov
Web: www.nsf.gov/mps/general.htm

Purpose To provide financial assistance to recent doctoral recipients in mathematics who wish to broaden their knowledge, experience, and research perspectives in an industrial environment.

Eligibility To become fellows, candidates must 1) be U.S. citizens, nationals, or permanent residents; 2) be eligible to be appointed as a research associate or assistant professor at the institution submitting the proposal; 3) have earned a Ph.D. in a mathematical science or have had equivalent research training and experience; 4) have held the Ph.D. for no more than 7 years; 5) have not held tenured position at any academic institution; and 6) have not previously held any other postdoctoral fellowship from the National Science Foundation (NSF). Applications must be submitted by a university principal investigator who will serve as scientific mentor to a fellow with an industrial sponsor. The proposal may either identify the prospective postdoctoral fellow or present a plan for recruiting the fellows. Principal investigators are encouraged to submit proposals that include women, underrepresented minorities, and persons with disabilities as postdoctoral fellows. Selection is based on the quality of the proposed research to be conducted at both the academic and industrial sites, the qualifications of and commitment by both the faculty mentor and the industrial sponsor, the appropriateness of the academic/industrial interaction, and the impact of the proposed training on the professional development of the postdoctoral fellow.

Financial data The total award is $111,000, of which $71,000 is provided by the National Science Foundation and $40,000 by the industrial sponsor. The award includes a stipend allowance for the fellow of $80,000 ($40,000 per year) plus a fringe benefit allowance of $16,000 ($8,000 per year), an allowance of $4,500 for the sponsoring institution in lieu of indirect costs, a research allowance of $4,500 for the fellow to be used for travel, publication costs, and other research-related expenses, and an allowance of $6,000 for the faculty mentor for research expenses related to the industrial partnership.

Duration 2 years.

Number awarded Varies each year.

Deadline November of each year.

[880]
MATHEMATICAL SCIENCES UNIVERSITY–INDUSTRY SENIOR RESEARCH FELLOWSHIPS

National Science Foundation
Directorate for Mathematical and Physical Sciences
Attn: Division of Mathematical Sciences
4201 Wilson Boulevard, Room 1025
Arlington, VA 22230
(703) 292-4862   TDD: (703) 292-5090
E-mail: ldouglas@nsf.gov
Web: www.nsf.gov/mps/general.htm

Purpose To provide financial assistance to senior scholars in mathematics who wish to broaden their knowledge, experience, and research perspectives by exposure to industrial environments, and to industrial researchers who wish to experience and participate in the full range of university research environments.

Eligibility This program is open to faculty members and industrial scientists who are U.S. citizens, nationals, or permanent residents and who have earned a Ph.D. in a mathematical science or have had research training and experience equivalent to that represented by such a degree. Faculty members must be proposing to conduct research in an industrial setting, and industrial scientists must be proposing to conduct research in a university environment. All applicants must make a commitment to return to the home institution for a minimum of 1 year following the fellowship tenure. Applications are especially encouraged from women, underrepresented minorities, and persons with disabilities.

Financial data The program provides a salary equivalent to the fellow's regular 6-month full-time salary (to a maximum of $50,000, or $60,000 including fringe benefits), a research allowance of $10,000, and an institutional allowance, in lieu of indirect costs, of $10,000.

Duration Normally 12 months.

Additional information Faculty fellows are usually expected to participate in this program during a sabbatical leave.

Number awarded Varies each year.

Deadline November of each year.

[881]
MEDICAL INFORMATICS RESEARCH TRAINING AWARDS

National Library of Medicine
Attn: Division of Extramural Programs
6705 Rockledge Drive, Suite 301
Bethesda, MD 20892
(301) 594-4882   Fax: (301) 402-2952
E-mail: pc49n@nih.gov
Web: www.nlm.nih.gov

Purpose To provide financial assistance to pre- and postdoctoral students who wish to pursue research training on the use of computers and telecommunications to manage health information.

Eligibility This program is open to students at both the predoctoral and postdoctoral level who wish to pursue a program of research training in medical informatics, the interaction of computers and telecommunications with biomedicine. Candidates may apply either to selected institutions that have received grants from the National Library of Medicine (NLM) of the National Institutes of Health (NIH) to operate such programs or directly to the NLM to pursue a program of research training with a mentor and institution of their own choice. All applicants must be U.S. citizens, nationals, or permanent residents. Applications from minorities and women are strongly encouraged.

Financial data Annual stipends for predoctoral fellows are $18,156; for postdoctoral fellows, the annual stipend ranges from $31,092 to $48,852 per year, depending on the years of postdoctoral experience.

Duration 1 to 3 years.

Additional information Currently, the funded sites are at Baylor/Rice, Columbia, Harvard/MIT/Tufts, North Carolina/Duke, Minnesota, Missouri, Oregon, Pittsburgh, Stanford, Yale, Utah, and the Regenstrief Institute; for the name and address of the program director at each of the institutions, contact the address above.

Number awarded Varies each year.

Deadline Each of the funded institutions sets its own application deadlines. For students applying directly to the NLM, applications must be submitted by April, August, or December of each year.

[882]
MENTORED CLINICAL SCIENTIST DEVELOPMENT AWARDS

National Institutes of Health
Division of Extramural Outreach and Information Resources
Attn: GrantsInfo
6701 Rockledge Drive, Suite 6095
Bethesda, MD 20892-7910
(301) 435-0714   Fax: (301) 480-8443
E-mail: GrantsInfo@nih.gov
Web: www.nih.gov

Purpose To provide financial support for specialized study to clinically trained professionals who are committed to a career in research and have the potential to develop into independent investigators.

Eligibility This program is open to candidates who 1) have a clinical degree or its equivalent; 2) can identify a mentor with extensive research experience; and 3) are willing to spend a minimum of 75% of full-time professional effort conducting research and research career development activities for the period of the award. Applications may be submitted on behalf of candidates by domestic, nonfederal organizations, public or private, such as medical, dental, or nursing schools or other institutions of higher education. Minorities and women are particularly encouraged to apply. Candidates must be U.S. citizens or permanent residents.

Financial data This program provides salary and fringe benefits for the candidate only; each component establishes its own salary limits on career awards. Each appointee is allowed up to $20,000 per year for tuition, fees, and books related to career development; research expenses, such as supplies, equipment, and technical personnel; travel to research meetings or training; and statistical services, including personnel and computer time. Facilities and administrative costs are reimbursed at 8% of modified total direct costs.

Duration 3 to 5 years.

Additional information Awards under this program are available from 15 agencies of the National Institutes of Health (NIH): the National Institute on Aging, the National Institute on Alcohol Abuse and Alcoholism, the National Institute of Allergy and Infectious Diseases, the National Institute of Arthritis and Musculoskeletal and Skin Diseases, the National Cancer Institute, the National Institute of Child Health and Human Development, the National Institute on Deafness and Other Communication Disorders, the National Institute of Dental and Craniofacial Research, the National Institute of Diabetes and Digestive and Kidney Diseases, the National Institute on Drug Abuse, the National Institute of Environmental Health Sciences, the National Eye Institute, the National Heart, Lung, and Blood Institute, the National Institute of Mental Health, and the National Institute of Neurological Disorders and Stroke. The names and addresses of staff people at each agency are available from the address above.

Number awarded Varies each year.

Deadline January, May, or September of each year.

[883]
MENTORED CLINICAL SCIENTIST DEVELOPMENT PROGRAM AWARDS

National Institutes of Health
Division of Extramural Outreach and Information Resources
Attn: GrantsInfo
6701 Rockledge Drive, Suite 6095
Bethesda, MD 20892-7910
(301) 435-0714   Fax: (301) 480-8443
E-mail: GrantsInfo@nih.gov
Web: www.nih.gov

Purpose To provide financial support to clinicians who wish to become independent researchers.

Eligibility Individuals participating in this program must be recruited and selected by departments or divisions from domestic, nonfederal organizations, such as medical, dental, or nursing schools, or from comparable institutions of higher education that have strong, well-established research and training programs. Candidates must be U.S. citizens or permanent residents who have a clinical degree or its equivalent, have initiated internship and residency training (or its equivalent), and are provided with a mentor who has extensive research experience and a record of providing the type of training required. The candidate must also be willing to spend a minimum of 75% of full-time professional effort conducting research, career development, and/or research-related activities. Minorities and women are particularly encouraged to apply.

Financial data This program provides salary and fringe benefits for the candidate only; each component establishes its own salary limits on career awards. Each appointee is allowed up to $20,000 per year for tuition, fees, and books related to career development; research expenses, such as supplies, equipment, and technical personnel; travel to research meetings or training; and statistical services, including personnel and computer time. Facilities and administrative costs are reimbursed at 8% of modified total direct costs.

Duration 3 to 5 years.

Additional information Awards under this program are available from 2 agencies of the National Institutes of Health (NIH): the National Institute on Aging and the National Institute of Dental and Craniofacial Research. The names and addresses of staff people at each agency are available from the address above.

Number awarded Varies each year.

Deadline January, May, or September of each year.

[884]
MENTORED PATIENT-ORIENTED RESEARCH CAREER DEVELOPMENT AWARD

National Institutes of Health
Division of Extramural Outreach and Information Resources
Attn: GrantsInfo
6701 Rockledge Drive, Suite 6095
Bethesda, MD 20892-7910
(301) 435-0714   Fax: (301) 480-8443
E-mail: GrantsInfo@nih.gov
Web: www.nih.gov

Purpose To support the career development of biomedical science investigators who have made a commitment to focus their research endeavors on patient-oriented research.

Eligibility Applicants must have a clinical degree or its equivalent: M.D., D.D.S., D.M.D., D.O., D.C., O.D., and D.S.N.; individuals holding the Ph.D. degree may apply if they have been certified to perform clinical duties (clinical psychologist, clinical geneticist, etc.). For purposes of this program, patient-oriented research is defined as research conducted with human subjects (or on material of human origin such as tissues, specimens, and cognitive phenomena) for which an investigator directly interacts with human subjects; research includes mechanisms of human disease, therapeutic interventions, clinical trials, and the development of new technologies. Applicants must identify a mentor at a medical, dental, or nursing school or other institution of higher education where they propose to conduct the research training and which must sponsor their application. Minorities, women, and individuals with disabilities are particularly encouraged to apply. U.S. citizenship or permanent resident status is required.

Financial data Awards provide: salary of up to $75,000 per year plus fringe benefits; research development support of up to $25,000 per year, to cover tuition and fees related to career development, research expenses (supplies, equipment, and technical personnel), travel to research meetings or training, and statistical services (including personnel and computer time); and facilities and administrative costs at 8% of modified total direct costs.

Duration 3 to 5 years.

Additional information This program is offered by most components of the National Institutes of Health (NIH); for the name and address of the responsible officer at each institute, contact the address above.

Number awarded Approximately 80 each year.

Deadline   January, May, or September of each year.

[885]
MENTORED RESEARCH SCIENTIST DEVELOPMENT AWARDS

National Institutes of Health
Division of Extramural Outreach and Information Resources
Attn: GrantsInfo
6701 Rockledge Drive, Suite 6095
Bethesda, MD 20892-7910
(301) 435-0714   Fax: (301) 480-8443
E-mail: GrantsInfo@nih.gov
Web: www.nih.gov

Purpose   To provide financial support to research scientists who need an additional period of sponsored research training as a way to gain expertise in a research area new to them or in an area that would demonstrably enhance their scientific career.

Eligibility   This program is open to candidates who have a research or a health-professional doctorate or its equivalent and who have demonstrated the capacity or potential for highly productive independent research in the period after the doctorate. The candidate must identify a mentor with extensive research experience and must be willing to spend a minimum of 75% of full-time professional effort conducting research and research career development activities for the period of the award. Applications may be submitted on behalf of candidates by domestic, nonfederal organizations, public or private, such as medical, dental, or nursing schools or other institutions of higher education. Minorities and women are particularly encouraged to apply. Candidates must be U.S. citizens or permanent residents.

Financial data   This program provides salary and fringe benefits for the candidate only; each component establishes its own salary limits on career awards. Each appointee is allowed up to $20,000 per year for tuition, fees, and books related to career development; research expenses, such as supplies, equipment, and technical personnel; travel to research meetings or training; and statistical services, including personnel and computer time. Facilities and administrative costs are reimbursed at 8% of modified total direct costs.

Duration   3 to 5 years.

Additional information   Awards under this program are available from 10 agencies of the National Institutes of Health (NIH): the National Institute on Aging, the National Institute on Alcohol Abuse and Alcoholism, the National Institute of Arthritis and Musculoskeletal and Skin Diseases, the National Cancer Institute, the National Institute on Drug Abuse, the National Institute of Environmental Health Sciences, the National Institute of Mental Health, the National Institute of Neurological Disorders and Stroke, the National Institute of Nursing Research, the National Human Genome Research Institute, and the National Center for Research Resources. The names and addresses of staff people at each agency are available from the address above.

Number awarded   Varies each year.

Deadline   January, May, or September of each year.

[886]
MENTORED SCIENTIST DEVELOPMENT AWARD FOR NEW MINORITY FACULTY

National Institute of Mental Health
Attn: Office for Special Populations
5600 Fishers Lane, Room 17C-14
Rockville, MD 20857-8030
(301) 443-3641   Fax: (301) 443-8552
E-mail: rc30x@nih.gov
Web: www.nimh.nih.gov

Purpose   To provide financial support to new minority faculty members to initiate a program of research and to help them to become outstanding independent investigators in the mental health field.

Eligibility   This program is open to non-tenured faculty members at domestic, nonprofit, public and private universities, colleges, and professional schools engaged in mental health research who are U.S. citizens and members of minority groups (American Indians, Alaskan Natives, Asian/Pacific Islanders, Blacks, and Hispanics). Applicants must have earned a doctorate (Ph.D., M.D., D.Sc., etc.) by the time the award is made and must be proposing to devote at least 75% of professional time to career development activities, research, or other research-related activities relevant to their career goals.

Financial data   Salary support depends on the established structure for full-time, 12-month staff appointments at the grantee institution. The awards through this program are 100% of base for salaries up to $45,000, $45,000 for base salaries of $45,001 to $60,000, or 75% of base for salaries over $60,001, to a maximum of $75,000.

Duration   5 years; nonrenewable.

Additional information   Applications must designate a mentor to work with the candidate. The proposed mentor must be a recognized, well-established, active investigator in the candidate's proposed research area who has not served in this role during the candidate's pre- or postdoctoral training.

Deadline   January, May, or September of each year.

[887]
MICHELE CLARK FELLOWSHIP

Radio and Television News Directors Foundation
1000 Connecticut Avenue, N.W., Suite 615
Washington, DC 20036-5302
(202) 467-5218   Fax: (202) 223-4007
E-mail: karenb@rtndf.org
Web: www.rtndf.org/asfi/fellowships/minority.html

Purpose   To provide financial assistance for professional development to minority journalists employed in electronic news.

Eligibility   This program is open to minority journalists employed in television or radio news who have 10 years or less of full-time experience. Applications must include samples of the journalist's work done as the member of a news staff, with a script and tape (audio or video) up to 15 minutes.

Financial data   The grant is $1,000, plus an expense-paid trip to the international convention of the Radio-Television News Directors Association held that year.

Duration   The grant is presented annually.

Additional information   The grant, named for CBS journalist Michele Clark, may be used in any way to improve the craft and enhance the excellence of the recipient's news operation.

Number awarded   1 each year.

Deadline April of each year.

[888]
MICHIGAN NONPROFIT RESEARCH PROGRAM

Aspen Institute
Attn: Director, Nonprofit Sector Research Fund
One Dupont Circle, N.W., Suite 700
Washington, DC 20036
(202) 736-5838   Fax: (202) 467-0790
E-mail: nsrf@aspeninstitute.org
Web: www.aspeninstitute.org

Purpose To support research by scholars and practitioners on the activities of nonprofit organizations in Michigan.

Eligibility Grants are awarded to institutions and individuals interested in nonprofit activities in Michigan. Proposals are welcome from academic researchers, independent scholars, nonprofit practitioners, and policy analysts. Applications are especially encouraged from minorities and women, nonprofit practitioners, scholars new to the field (including graduate students), and scholars from disciplines (such as psychology, political science, and anthropology) that are not well represented in nonprofit research. Both Michigan residents and persons living outside Michigan may apply, but proposed studies must relate to the Michigan nonprofit sector. Areas of interest include: 1) the societal role of Michigan nonprofits and philanthropy; 2) the impact of public policy on Michigan nonprofits and the people they serve; and 3) nonprofit accountability, governance, and management in Michigan.

Financial data Grants are usually made in 2 categories: 1) up to $15,000 to support doctoral dissertation research, and 2) up to $25,000 to support research by any eligible applicant.

Duration 1 year; requests for renewal for 1 additional year may be considered.

Additional information Funding for this program has been provided by the Carnegie Corporation of New York, James Irvine Foundation, David and Lucile Packard Foundation, Charles Steward Mott Foundation, William Randolph Hearst Foundation, Ford Foundation, W.K. Kellogg Foundation, and the McGregor Fund.

Number awarded Varies each year.

Deadline August of each year.

[889]
MICHIGAN SPACE GRANT CONSORTIUM FELLOWSHIPS

Michigan Space Grant Consortium
c/o University of Michigan
2106 Space Physics Research Laboratory
2455 Hayward Avenue
Ann Arbor, MI 48109-2143
(734) 764-9508   Fax: (734) 764-4585
E-mail: blbryant@umich.edu
Web: www.umich.edu/~msgc

Purpose To provide funding to students at member institutions of the Michigan Space Grant Consortium who wish to conduct space-related research.

Eligibility This program is open to undergraduate and graduate students at affiliates of the Michigan consortium who are proposing to conduct research in aerospace, space science, earth system science, and other related fields in science, engineering, or mathematics; students working on educational research topics in mathematics, science, or technology are also eligible. Applicants

must identify a mentor in the faculty research, education, or public service communities with whom they intend to work and who is available to write a letter of recommendation for the student. U.S. citizenship is required. Women, underrepresented minorities, and persons with disabilities are especially encouraged to apply.

Financial data The maximum grant is $2,500 for undergraduates or $5,000 for graduate students.

Additional information The consortium consists of Eastern Michigan University, Grand Valley State University, Hope College, Michigan State University, Michigan Technological University, Oakland University, Saginaw Valley State University, University of Michigan, Wayne State University, and Western Michigan University. This program is supported by the U.S. National Aeronautics and Space Administration (NASA).

Number awarded Varies; a total of $125,000 is available for these fellowships each year.

Deadline November of each year.

[890]
MICHIGAN SPACE GRANT CONSORTIUM RESEARCH SEED GRANTS

Michigan Space Grant Consortium
c/o University of Michigan
2106 Space Physics Research Laboratory
2455 Hayward Avenue
Ann Arbor, MI 48109-2143
(734) 764-9508   Fax: (734) 764-4585
E-mail: blbryant@umich.edu
Web: www.umich.edu/~msgc

Purpose To provide funding to faculty at member institutions of the Michigan Space Grant Consortium (MSGC) who are interested in conducting space-related research.

Eligibility This program is open to faculty (research and professorial) at affiliates of the MSGC. Applicants must be interested in conducting a research project in engineering, science, mathematics, life sciences, or related educational areas. Preference is given to projects focusing on aerospace, space, or earth system science, although awards are not strictly limited to those topics. Initiation of a new area of research is preferred over efforts to continue an existing project or study. Women, underrepresented minorities, and persons with disabilities are encouraged to apply.

Financial data Grants up to $5,000 are available. At least 1:1 cost matching (cash contributions or in-kind support) with nonfederal funds is required.

Additional information The consortium consists of Eastern Michigan University, Grand Valley State University, Hope College, Michigan State University, Michigan Technological University, Oakland University, Saginaw Valley State University, University of Michigan, Wayne State University, and Western Michigan University. This program is supported by the U.S. National Aeronautics and Space Administration (NASA).

Number awarded Varies each year.

Deadline November of each year.

[891]
MID-CAREER INVESTIGATOR AWARD IN PATIENT-ORIENTED RESEARCH

National Institutes of Health
Division of Extramural Outreach and Information Resources
Attn: GrantsInfo
6701 Rockledge Drive, Suite 6095
Bethesda, MD 20892-7910
(301) 435-0714   Fax: (301) 480-8443
E-mail: GrantsInfo@nih.gov
Web: www.nih.gov

Purpose To provide funding to clinicians who are interested in conducting patient-oriented research and acting as mentors for beginning clinical investigators.

Eligibility Applicants must have a clinical degree or its equivalent: M.D., D.D.S., D.M.D., D.O., D.C., O.D., and D.S.N.; individuals holding the Ph.D. degree may apply if they have been certified to perform clinical duties (clinical psychologist, clinical geneticist, etc.). They must have completed their specialty training within 15 years of applying, but there is no age limit. Candidates must be working in a research environment, conducting patient-oriented research, and have independent research support. For purposes of this program, patient-oriented research is defined as research conducted with human subjects (or on material of human origin, such as tissues, specimens, and cognitive phenomena) for which an investigator directly interacts with human subjects; research includes mechanisms of human disease, therapeutic interventions, clinical trials, and the development of new technologies. Applications must be submitted through a medical, dental or nursing school or other institution of higher education where the proposed research will take place and where the candidates will serve as mentors for beginning clinicians in training; they must devote at least 25% effort to the proposed activities. Minorities, women, and individuals with disabilities are encouraged to apply. U.S. citizenship or permanent resident status is required.

Financial data Awards provide: salary of up to $62,500 per year plus fringe benefits for 50% effort; research development support of up to $25,000 per year, to cover tuition and fees related to career development, research expenses (supplies, equipment, and technical personnel), travel to research meetings or training, and statistical services (including personnel and computer time); and facilities and administrative costs at 8% of modified total direct costs.

Duration 3 to 5 years.

Additional information This program is offered by most components of the National Institutes of Health (NIH); for the name and address of the responsible officer at each institute, contact the address above.

Number awarded 60 to 80 each year.

Deadline January, May, or September of each year.

[892]
MILLENDER FELLOWSHIP

Wayne State University
Attn: Associate Provost for Academic Programs
656 West Kirby
4116 Faculty/Administration Building
Detroit, MI 48202
(313) 577-2023   Fax: (313) 577-5666

Purpose To provide work experience in Detroit to minorities who recently earned a master's degree and are interested in preparing for a public service-oriented career.

Eligibility Prior affiliation with Wayne State University is not required. Eligibility is open to minorities who have a commitment to public service and can demonstrate a record of successful accomplishment in some graduate educational program and/or through equivalent experience. Applicants must have completed a master's degree (or have equivalent professional experience) by the start of the fellowship. Writing, research, computer, and Internet skills are important.

Financial data The stipend is $30,000, plus fringe benefits. Some funds may be available to assist with moving.

Duration 9 months; nonrenewable.

Additional information Funds for this program come from the Robert L. Millender Sr. Memorial Fund. Fellows work directly with top executives of major public or private nonprofit organizations in Detroit. Previous fellows have served in the office of the mayor of Detroit, Detroit Economic Growth Corporation, New Detroit Inc., Southeastern Michigan Council of Governments, and similar agencies. This program is modeled after the White House and Congressional Fellowship programs. Fellows must devote full time to their assignments. They must live in the Detroit metropolitan area for the duration of the program. A mid-year and a final report are required.

Number awarded 1 each year.

Deadline March of each year.

[893]
MINORITIES IN MEDICAL ONCOLOGY PROGRAM GRANTS

National Cancer Institute
Attn: Comprehensive Minority Biomedical Program
6130 Executive Boulevard, Room 620
Bethesda, MD 20892-7405
(301) 496-7344   Fax: (301) 402-4551
E-mail: ss165i@nih.gov
Web: www.nci.nih.gov

Purpose To provide funding to underrepresented minority physicians for research in medical oncology.

Eligibility This program is open to individuals with an M.D. or D.O. degree who are members of an ethnic or racial group that is underrepresented in biomedical and behavioral research, i.e., African Americans, Latinos (Mexican Americans, Cubans, Puerto Ricans, and Central Americans), Native Americans, and non-Asian Pacific Islanders. Applicants must be proposing a program of intensive, supervised research in medical oncology, including such subjects as the development and application of biomarkers for assessing cancer risk in minority populations, cancer treatment or prevention clinical trials targeting minority populations, or psychosocial aspects of cancer prevention and control in defined populations. Candidates must be nominated by domestic nonprofit and for-profit, public and private organizations, such as universities, colleges, hospitals, laboratories, units of state or local government, and eligible agencies of the federal government. Women and persons with disabilities are encouraged to apply as principal investigators.

Financial data The amount of the award depends on the candidate's training, experience, and accomplishments, to a maximum of $50,000 per year for salary and a total of $15,000 per year for supplies, travel, equipment, fringe benefits, and other allowable expenses.

Duration Up to 4 years.

Number awarded Varies each year, depending on the availability of funds.

Deadline January, May, or September of each year.

[894]
MINORITY ACADEMIC INSTITUTIONS FELLOWSHIPS FOR GRADUATE ENVIRONMENTAL STUDY

Environmental Protection Agency
Attn: National Center for Environmental Research
Ariel Rios Building - 8723R
1200 Pennsylvania Avenue, N.W.
Washington, DC 20460
(202) 564-6923   E-mail: broadway.virginia@epa.gov
Web: es.epa.gov/ncer/rfa

Purpose To provide financial assistance to graduate students in minority academic institutions (MAIs) who are interested in studying and conducting research in fields related to the environment.

Eligibility Applicants for this program must be U.S. citizens or permanent residents who are enrolled or accepted for enrollment in a master's or doctoral program in an academic discipline related to environmental research, including physical, biological, and social sciences and engineering. Students who have completed more than 1 year in a master's program or 4 years in a doctoral program are not eligible. As part of their graduate degree program, applicants may conduct research outside the United States, but they must attend an MAI in this country, defined as Historically Black Colleges and Universities (HBCUs), Hispanic Serving Institutions (HSIs), Tribal Colleges (TCs), Native Hawaiian Serving Institutions (NHSIs), and Alaska Native Serving Institutions (ANSIs).

Financial data The maximum award is $34,000 per year, including a stipend of $17,000, an allowance of $5,000 for authorized expenses (including any foreign travel to conduct research), and up to $12,000 for tuition and fees.

Duration Up to 2 years for master's degree students; up to 3 years for doctoral students.

Additional information These fellowships were formerly known as Culturally Diverse Academic Institutions Fellowships for Graduate Environmental Study.

Number awarded Approximately 25 each year.

Deadline November of each year.

[895]
MINORITY ACCESS TO RESEARCH CAREERS (MARC) SENIOR FACULTY FELLOWSHIPS

National Institute of General Medical Sciences
Attn: Division of Minority Opportunities in Research
45 Center Drive, Suite 2AS37
Bethesda, MD 20892-6200
(301) 594-3900   Fax: (301) 480-2753
E-mail: at21z@nih.gov
Web: www.nih.gov/nigms

Purpose To provide opportunities for advanced research training for selected faculty members at 4-year academic institutions serving predominantly minority students.

Eligibility Colleges, universities, and health professional schools with substantial enrollments of underrepresented minorities may nominate for these fellowships full-time, permanent faculty members in biomedically-related science or mathematics who have held that position for at least 3 years and who received the Ph.D. or equivalent at least 7 years before the date of the

application. Underrepresented minorities include African Americans, Hispanic Americans, Native Americans, and Pacific Islanders. The candidate must demonstrate a commitment to research and teaching in a minority institution and be a U.S. citizen, national, or permanent resident. Fellows must pursue a program of postdoctoral studies and research training in the biomedical sciences, and are expected to return to their home institutions after completion of their fellowships.

Financial data Annual stipends up to $48,852 are provided. An institutional allowance of up to $3,000 may also be requested to help defray costs directly related to the candidate's training.

Duration 1 to 2 years. Fellows may train at any nonprofit private or public institution in the United States with suitable facilities.

Number awarded Varies each year.

Deadline April or December of each year.

[896]
MINORITY DISSERTATION RESEARCH GRANTS IN AGING

National Institute on Aging
Attn: Office of Extramural Affairs
7201 Wisconsin Avenue, Room 2C-218
Bethesda, MD 20892-9205
(301) 496-9322   Fax: (301) 402-2945
E-mail: rb42h@nih.gov
Web: www.nih.gov/nia

Purpose To provide financial assistance to minority doctoral students who wish to conduct research on aging.

Eligibility This program is open to minority graduate students enrolled in an accredited doctoral program in the biomedical, social, or behavioral sciences. The National Institute on Aging (NIA) defines underrepresented minorities as African Americans, Hispanics, Native Americans, Alaskan Natives, and Pacific Islanders. Applicants must have completed all requirements for the doctoral degree except the dissertation and have had their dissertation proposal approved. Their research must deal with some aspect of aging. Grants are administered by the applicant's institution, which must be within the United States, although the performance site may be foreign or domestic.

Financial data Direct costs may not exceed $30,000 in total or $25,000 in any 1 year. The institution may receive up to 8% of direct costs as facilities and administrative costs in any 1 year. Salary for the investigator, included in direct costs, may not exceed $12,000 for 12 months.

Duration Up to 2 years.

Number awarded 5 or 6 each year.

Deadline March or November of each year.

[897]
MINORITY DISSERTATION RESEARCH GRANTS IN MENTAL HEALTH

National Institute of Mental Health
Attn: Division of Epidemiology and Services Research
5600 Fishers Lane, Room 10C-06
Rockville, MD 20857
(301) 443-4235   Fax: (301) 443-4045
E-mail: ah21k.nih.gov
Web: www.nimh.nih.gov

Purpose To provide financial support to minority doctoral candidates planning to pursue research careers in any area relevant to mental health and/or mental disorders.

Eligibility Applicants must be African Americans, Hispanic Americans, American Indians, Alaskan Natives, or Asian and Pacific Islanders enrolled in an accredited doctoral degree program in the behavioral, biomedical, or social sciences. Their dissertation topic, which must have been approved by their academic committee, must focus on a significant problem in mental health/mental disorders.

Financial data The maximum award is $25,000 per year; that includes the investigator's salary (up to $14,000 per 12 months of full-time effort) and direct research project expenses, such as data processing, payments to subjects, supplies, and printing and binding of the dissertation. Travel funds up to $750 may be requested to attend 1 scientific meeting. No funding is provided for tuition, alterations/renovations, contracting costs, or space rental.

Duration 1 year; may be renewed 1 additional year.

Additional information Inquiries on programs of prevention, clinical services and service systems research, epidemiology, psychopathology, violence and traumatic stress, assessment, classification, law and mental health, and health and behavior, with special attention to minority and other populations, should be directed to the Division of Epidemiology and Services Research, (301) 443-3373; questions involving behavioral and social sciences, cognitive sciences, and neurosciences, including neuroimaging, neurophysiology, neuropsychopharmacology, and cellular and molecular neurobiology, with special attention to minority and other special populations, should be addressed to the Division of Neuroscience and Behavioral Science, (301) 443-4347; for further information on psychopathology, classification, assessment, etiology, genetics, clinical course, outcome, and treatment of mental disorders with emphasis on schizophrenic disorders, affective and anxiety disorders, and mental disorders of children and adolescents, the elderly, minorities, and other special populations, contact the Division of Clinical and Treatment Research, (301) 443-3264; for research that focuses on mental health issues for persons with AIDS, persons who are HIV positive, or persons who are at risk of contracting the virus, contact the Office on Aids, (301) 443-6100.

Number awarded Up to 25 each year.

Deadline April, August, or December of each year.

[898]
MINORITY FACULTY FELLOWSHIP PROGRAM

Indiana University
Attn: Minority Faculty Fellowship Program
Memorial Hall West, Room 108
1021 East Third Street
Bloomington, IN 47405-7005
(812) 855-0542   Fax: (812) 856-5477
E-mail: mffp@indiana.edu
Web: www.indiana.edu/~mffp

Purpose To aid in recruiting outstanding underrepresented minority faculty to the Indiana University campus and to identify minority scholars who might be available for longer-term positions.

Eligibility African American, U.S. Latino(a), and Native American scholars who either are nearing completion of the doctorate or have completed the doctorate within the last 4 years are encouraged to apply for this appointment at Indiana University. The program seeks candidates who have demonstrated a strong

commitment to scholarly research and creative teaching. U.S. citizenship or permanent resident status is required.

Financial data The fellowship package includes a salary equivalent to that ordinarily paid to an Indiana University faculty member of the same rank, plus a $4,000 stipend for research and living expenses.

Duration Summer months or academic year.

Number awarded Up to 10 each year.

Additional information The program was established in 1986. Summer fellows teach 1 or 2 courses. Academic-year fellows teach in the fall and spring terms.

Deadline October of each year.

[899]
MINORITY MEDICAL FACULTY DEVELOPMENT PROGRAM

Robert Wood Johnson Foundation
College Road East and U.S. Route 1
P.O. Box 2316
Princeton, NJ 08543-2316
(609) 627-5776   Fax: (609) 514-5532
E-mail: mail@rwjf.org
Web: www.mmfdp.org

Purpose To provide financial support and research training to minority physicians who are interested in academic careers in biomedical research, clinical investigation, or health services research.

Eligibility African American, Mexican American, Native American, and mainland Puerto Rican physicians residing in the United States are eligible to apply if they have completed or will have completed formal clinical training. Applicants must be U.S. citizens or permanent residents with outstanding academic backgrounds and a commitment to academic medicine. Preference is given to physicians who have recently completed their clinical training and are seeking advanced research training. An interview is required.

Financial data The stipend is $65,000 per year; an additional $26,350 per year is provided as a research allowance.

Duration 2 years; renewable for an additional 2 years.

Additional information Fellows study and conduct research under the supervision of a senior faculty member located at any academic center in the United States that is noted for the training of young faculty and that offers research opportunities of interest to the fellow. Further information on this program is available from James R. Gavin III, Program Director, Minority Medical Faculty Development Program, 8701 Georgia Avenue, Suite 411, Silver Spring, MD 20910-3713, (301) 565-4080, Fax: (301) 565-4088, E-mail: mmfdp@msm.edu.

Number awarded Up to 12 each year.

Deadline March of each year.

[900]
MINORITY NEUROSCIENCE POSTDOCTORAL FELLOWSHIP PROGRAM

Society for Neuroscience
Attn: Education Department
11 Dupont Circle, N.W., Suite 500
Washington, DC 20036
(202) 462-6688   Fax: (202) 462-9740
E-mail: info@sfn.org
Web: www.sfn.org

Purpose To provide funding to minority postdoctoral fellows participating in mental health related neuroscience research and training programs.

Eligibility This program is open to postdoctoral fellows in neuroscience who are members of traditionally underrepresented racial and ethnic minority groups (African Americans, Hispanics, Native Americans, Alaskan Natives, Asians, and Pacific Islanders). Applicants must be U.S. citizens or permanent residents enrolled in a program of research and training to prepare for a career in neuroscience research laboratories. Along with their application, they must submit 2 academic letters of recommendation, a 1- to 2-page essay describing their area of interest and future goals in neuroscience, undergraduate and graduate transcripts, a current resume or curriculum vitae, copies of papers and abstracts they have authored or co-authored, a 1-page summary of their dissertation, and a biosketch of the home institution advisor (if available).

Financial data Fellows receive a stipend that is based on number of years of postdoctoral experience, in accordance with standard National Research Service Award guidelines (currently, ranging from $18,156 per year for no experience to $48,852 for 7 or more years). Other benefits include travel assistance and registration to attend the annual meeting of the Society for Neuroscience (SFN), enrichment programs that include funds to participate in activities outside the fellow's home laboratory, and mentoring opportunities with a mentor chosen from the SFN membership.

Duration 2 years, contingent upon adequate research progress and academic standing.

Additional information This program, established in 1991, is sponsored largely by the National Institute of Mental Health with additional support from the National Institute of Neurological Disorders and Stroke. Information is also available from Joanne Berger-Sweeney, Wellesley College, Department of Biological Sciences, 106 Central Street, Wellesley, MA 02481-8203, (781) 283-3503, Fax: (781) 283-3704, E-mail: mnfp@wellesley.edu.

Number awarded 3 each year.

Deadline February or August of each year.

[901]
MINORITY NEUROSCIENCE PREDOCTORAL FELLOWSHIP PROGRAM

Society for Neuroscience
Attn: Education Department
11 Dupont Circle, N.W., Suite 500
Washington, DC 20036
(202) 462-6688   Fax: (202) 462-9740
E-mail: info@sfn.org
Web: www.sfn.org

Purpose To provide funding to minority graduate students participating in mental health related neuroscience research and training programs.

Eligibility This program is open to doctoral students in neuroscience who are members of traditionally underrepresented racial and ethnic minority groups (African Americans, Hispanics, Native Americans, Alaskan Natives, Asians, and Pacific Islanders). Applicants must be U.S. citizens or permanent residents enrolled in a program of research and training to prepare for a career in neuroscience research laboratories. Along with their application, they must submit 2 academic letters of recommendation, a 1- to 2-page essay describing their area of interest and future goals in neuroscience, undergraduate and graduate transcripts, a current resume or curriculum vitae, copies of papers and abstracts they have authored or co-authored, and a biosketch of the home institution advisor (if available).

Financial data Fellows receive a stipend in accordance with standard National Research Service Award guidelines (currently, $18,156 per year). Other benefits include travel assistance and registration to attend the annual meeting of the Society for Neuroscience (SFN), enrichment programs that include funds to participate in activities outside the fellow's home laboratory, and mentoring opportunities with a mentor chosen from the SFN membership.

Duration 3 years, contingent upon adequate research progress and academic standing.

Additional information This program, established in 1991, is sponsored largely by the National Institute of Mental Health with additional support from the National Institute of Neurological Disorders and Stroke. Information is also available from Joanne Berger-Sweeney, Wellesley College, Department of Biological Sciences, 106 Central Street, Wellesley, MA 02481-8203, (781) 283-3503, Fax: (781) 283-3704, E-mail: mnfp@wellesley.edu.

Number awarded 8 each year.

Deadline February or August of each year.

[902]
MINORITY ONCOLOGY ACADEMIC LEADERSHIP AWARD

National Cancer Institute
Attn: Comprehensive Minority Biomedical Program
6130 Executive Boulevard, Room 620
Bethesda, MD 20892-7405
(301) 496-7344   Fax: (301) 402-4551
E-mail: ss165i@nih.gov
Web: www.nci.nih.gov

Purpose To provide funding to faculty members at minority health professional schools for research and development activities in medical oncology.

Eligibility Nominations for this program may be submitted by minority health professional schools, defined as medical, dental, pharmacy, public health, or equivalent schools in which students of minority ethnic groups (African Americans, Hispanics, American Indians, and Asians or Pacific Islanders) comprise a significant proportion of the enrollment and that have a commitment to the special encouragement of minority faculty, students, and investigators. Nominees must 1) have an appropriate clinical academic appointment at the school; 2) be a U.S. citizen, national, or permanent resident; 3) have appropriate documented research experience and background in a clinical oncology specialty and/or cancer research; 4) present a program for developing or improving clinical cancer research and training capabilities at the grantee institution; and 5) commit a minimum of 60% total time and effort to the research and development aspects of the program.

Financial data The awards provide: 1) a portion of the salary of the faculty leader up to a maximum of $50,000 per year and related fringe benefits; 2) costs for further optional preparation of the faculty leader in additional clinical or basic research methodologies; 3) domestic travel expenses for the awardee to attend professional meetings, training courses, and an annual 2-day awardee meeting in Bethesda, Maryland; 4) partial salary support up to $40,000 per year for an additional faculty or staff researcher as a direct participant in research-related activities or services; 5) up to $10,000 per year in supplies for research activities; and 6) facilities and administrative costs up to 8% of direct costs. The total award may not exceed $100,000 in direct costs per year.
Duration 3 to 5 years.
Number awarded Varies each year, depending on the availability of funds.
Deadline January, May, or September of each year.

[903]
MINORITY POSTDOCTORAL RESEARCH FELLOWSHIPS

National Science Foundation
Directorate for Biological Sciences
Attn: Division of Biological Infrastructure
4201 Wilson Boulevard, Room 615
Arlington, VA 22230
(703) 292-8470   TDD: (703) 292-5090
E-mail: ckimsey@nsf.gov
Web: www.nsf.gov/bio

Purpose To provide financial assistance for postdoctoral research training to underrepresented minority scientists in the biological, social, economic, and behavioral sciences.
Eligibility Eligible to apply are underrepresented minorities (African Americans, Hispanics, Native Pacific Islanders, and Native Americans) who are American citizens or permanent residents and will complete their doctorate within a year or have completed it within the previous 4 years but have not completed more than 2 years of postdoctoral support. They must be proposing research training that falls within the program areas of the National Science Foundation (NSF) Directorate for Biological Sciences or the Directorate for Social, Behavioral, and Economic Sciences to be conducted at any appropriate nonprofit U.S. or foreign institution (government laboratory, institution of higher education, national laboratory, or public or private research institute), but not at the same institution where the doctorate was obtained.
Financial data The program provides a stipend of $36,000 per year, an institutional allowance of $5,000 for partial reimbursement of indirect research costs (space, equipment, general purpose supplies, and fringe benefits), and a special allowance of $9,000 for direct research costs (scientific supplies, research-related travel, publication expenses, and other research-related costs).
Duration 2 years; applicants who propose to spend their 2-year tenure at a foreign institution may apply for a third year of support at an appropriate U.S. institution.
Additional information Information on the programs from the Directorate for Social, Behavioral, and Economic Sciences is available at (703) 292-8763, E-mail: jperhoni@nsf.gov.
Number awarded Approximately 12 each year.
Deadline November of each year.

[904]
MISSILE DEFENSE AGENCY PILOT PROGRAM FOR SCIENCE AND TECHNOLOGY RESEARCH AT HISTORICALLY BLACK COLLEGES AND UNIVERSITIES AND MINORITY INSTITUTIONS

Missile Defense Agency
Attn: Office of the Advanced Systems (MDA/AS)
FOB 2, Navy Annex, Room 3704A
7100 Defense Pentagon
Washington, DC 20301-7100
(703) 697-3579   E-mail: external.affairs@mda.osd.mil
Web: www.acq.osd.mil/bmdo/barbb/barbb.htm

Purpose To provide funding to investigators at Historically Black Colleges and Universities (HBCUs) and Minority Institutions (MIs) interested in conducting research related to the mission of the Missile Defense Agency (MDA).
Eligibility This program is open to investigators at HBCUs and MIs interested in conducting research in the following general areas: 1) sensing, imaging, ranging, and discrimination; 2) phenomenology studies for ballistic missile defense; 3) electronic and photonic materials and devices; 4) information processing and computing technologies; 5) directed energy and non-linear optical devices and processes; 6) miniature interceptor technology, propulsion, and kill enhancement; and 7) power generation and conditioning. Selection is based on anticipated benefits of the research effort to the MDA mission; scientific/technical quality of the research proposal and its relevance to the topic description; qualifications of the principal investigator, other key staff, and consultants; and adequacy of management planning and controls.
Financial data The maximum grant is $150,000 per year.
Duration 12 to 24 months.
Number awarded Varies each year.
Deadline December of each year.

[905]
MISSOURI SPACE GRANT CONSORTIUM UNDERGRADUATE RESEARCH INTERNSHIPS

Missouri Space Grant Consortium
c/o University of Missouri at Rolla
229 Mechanical Engineering Building
1870 Miner Circle
Rolla, MO 65409-0050
(573) 341-4887   Fax: (573) 341-6899
E-mail: kchrist@umr.edu
Web: www.umr.edu/~spaceg

Purpose To provide research experience to undergraduate students in Missouri working on a degree in an aerospace field.
Eligibility This program is open to undergraduate students studying engineering, physics, astronomy, or planetary sciences at member institutions of the Missouri Space Grant Consortium. Applicants must be proposing a specific research or education project in a research laboratory, a computing facility, or the galleries of the St. Louis Science Center. U.S. citizenship is required. The Missouri Space Grant Consortium is a component of the U.S. National Aeronautics and Space Administration (NASA), which encourages participation by women, underrepresented minorities, and persons with disabilities.
Financial data Awards are approximately $2,000 for the summer or $3,000 for the academic year.
Duration Both summer and academic year appointments are available.

Additional information The consortium members are Southwest Missouri State University, University of Missouri at Columbia, University of Missouri at Rolla, University of Missouri at St. Louis, and Washington University. This program is funded by NASA.

Number awarded Varies each year; recently, 25 students received approximately $60,000 in support.

[906]
MONTANA SPACE GRANT CONSORTIUM RESEARCH INITIATION GRANTS

Montana Space Grant Consortium
c/o Montana State University
261 EPS Building
P.O. Box 173835
Bozeman, MT 59717-3835
(406) 994-4223   Fax: (406) 994-4452
E-mail: msgc@montana.edu
Web: www.montana.edu/~wwwmsgc

Purpose To provide seed money for research related to space sciences and engineering.

Eligibility This program is open to individuals in Montana (most of the awards go to full-time graduate students) who need support to conduct research related to space sciences and/or engineering. This program is part of the U.S. National Aeronautics and Space Administration (NASA) Space Grant program, which encourages participation by women, underrepresented minorities, and persons with disabilities.

Financial data These grants provide "seed money" only.

Duration 1 year; generally nonrenewable. Awardees are required to submit a follow-on proposal to NASA for regular research funding during the year of the grant.

Number awarded Varies each year; recently, 4 of these grants were awarded.

[907]
MORE FACULTY DEVELOPMENT AWARDS

National Institute of General Medical Sciences
Attn: Division of Minority Opportunities in Research
45 Center Drive, Suite 2AS37
Bethesda, MD 20892-6200
(301) 594-3900   Fax: (301) 480-2753
E-mail: at21z@nih.gov
Web: www.nih.gov/nigms

Purpose To enable faculty at minority institutions to sharpen their research skills by spending intervals conducting full-time research in a research-intensive laboratory.

Eligibility Candidates for this program must have been full-time permanent faculty in a biomedically-related science, including behavioral science, or mathematics at the home institution for at least 3 years; have received the Ph.D. or equivalent at least 5 years before the date of the application; intend to remain at the home institution at the end of the training period; demonstrate a commitment to research and teaching in a minority institution; plan to conduct research in a science (including mathematics) related to biomedical or behavioral research; and be a citizen or permanent resident of the United States. The home institution must be a domestic private or public educational institution with a significant enrollment of underrepresented minorities, defined as African Americans, Hispanic Americans, Native Americans, and Pacific Islanders, that offers at least the baccalaureate

degree in the biomedical or behavioral sciences or mathematics. The research institution is the university or other institution at which the candidate conducts full-time research and takes courses; the research institution may not be the same as the home institution.

Financial data Candidates may request a salary equal to their actual annual salary and appropriate fringe benefits prorated for the time during which they are engaged in full-time research (salary support is not provided for the time candidates are enrolled in academic courses); up to $3,000 per year for supplies, equipment, travel, and other costs directly related to their full-time research experience; and funds to pay tuition and fees for 1 course per academic term to be taken at the research institution. Any expected concurrent sabbatical or any other salary support for the proposed period in residence is taken into account. A travel allowance equivalent to round-trip coach airfare between the visiting scientist's home institution and the sponsoring institution is provided. The sponsoring institution may receive up to $3,000 as an allowance for costs of supplies, supporting services, and demonstration costs related to activities proposed for the visiting scientist.

Duration Research may be conducted at intervals over a period of 2 to 5 years.

Additional information The National Institute of General Medical Sciences, a component of the National Institutes of Health (NIH), operates this program as part of its Minority Opportunities for Research (MORE) Division.

Number awarded Varies each year.

Deadline January, May, or September of each year.

[908]
MULTIDISCIPLINARY RESEARCH PROGRAM OF THE UNIVERSITY RESEARCH INITIATIVE

Office of Naval Research
Attn: Code 363
800 North Quincy Street, Room 304
Arlington, VA 22217-5660
(703) 696-0431   E-mail: 363_MURI@onr.navy.mil
Web: www.onr.navy.mil/sci_tech/industrial/muri.htm

Purpose To provide funding for research on subjects of interest to the Department of Defense (DoD) that intersect several traditional science and engineering disciplines.

Eligibility This program is open to research teams at U.S. institutions of higher education with degree-granting programs in science and/or engineering or by consortia led by such institutions. Applications must be for research on topics specified by the participating defense agencies that may change annually. Recent topics have included 1) minimal organotypic cell systems; 2) self-assembling multifunctional ceramic composites; 3) fundamental theoretical/experimental molecular science underpinning fuel cell systems; 4) integrated artificial muscle, high-lift bio-hydrodynamic and neuro-control for biorobotic autonomous undersea vehicles; 5) direct thermal to electric energy conversion; 6) image processing sensors for autonomous vehicles, robotics, and remote sensing; 7) hybrid inferencing from fused information; 8) biologically enabled synthesis of ceramic microdevices; 9) active-vision for control of agile maneuvering aerial vehicles in complex 3-D environments; 10) direct nanoscale conversion of biomolecular signals into electronic information; 11) synthesis of long-chained sequence-controlled heteropolymers; and 12) laboratory instrumentation design research. DoD encourages proposals from researchers at Historically Black Colleges and Universities and at minority institutions, either individually or as members of a team.

Financial data Grants normally range from $500,000 to $1,000,000 per year, depending on the topic, technical goals, and availability of funds.

Duration Varies; recent grants have been for 3 years with 2 additional years possible as options.

Additional information This is an inter-agency DoD program. Information is available from the Office of Naval Research (ONR) at the address above; the Air Force Office of Scientific Research (AFOSR), 4015 Wilson Boulevard, Room 713, Arlington, VA 22203, (703) 696-7315; the Army Research Office (ARO), 4300 South Miami Boulevard, P.O. Box 12211, Research Triangle Park, NC 27709-2211, (919) 549-4211; the Defense Advanced Research Projects Agency (DARPA), 3701 North Fairfax Drive, Arlington, VA 22203-1714, (703) 696-0048; and the Office of the Under Secretary of Defense for Laboratories and Basic Science (ODUSD-LABS), 4015 Wilson Boulevard, Suite 209, Arlington, VA 22203, (703) 696-0363. Research topics 1-3 were sponsored by ARO, 4-6 by ONR, 7-9 by AFOSR, 10 by DARPA, and 11-12 by ODUSD-LABS.

Number awarded Varies each year; recently, 17 grants worth $25.5 million over 3 years were awarded.

Deadline September of each year.

[909]
NASA ADMINISTRATOR'S FELLOWSHIP PROGRAM

United Negro College Fund Special Programs Corporation
2750 Prosperity Avenue, Suite 600
Fairfax, VA 22031
(703) 205-7656   (800) 231-9155
Fax: (703) 205-7645   E-mail: nafp@uncfsp.org
Web: www.uncfsp.org/nasa/nafp

Purpose To provide financial assistance to faculty members at Minority-Serving Institutions (MSIs) who wish to conduct research in a field of interest to the National Aeronautics and Space Administration (NASA).

Eligibility This program is open to full-time, tenure-tack faculty members at MSIs (Historically Black Colleges and Universities, Hispanic Serving Institutions, and Tribal Colleges and Universities) who have a Ph.D., Sc.D., or equivalent in science, engineering, technology, or mathematics with expertise in NASA-related fields (aerospace, biology, chemistry, computer science, electrical engineering, mathematics, mechanical engineering, physics, physiology, and structural engineering). Applicants must be proposing to conduct research at a NASA center, another government agency, a research university, or a private sector organization. U.S. citizenship is required.

Financial data Fellows remain on the payroll of the institution where they are employed and the fellowship provides the institution with their current salary and benefits. Fellows also receive an additional 55% of the host site per diem rate if it is necessary to relocate for participation in the program.

Duration 12 months.

Additional information This program is funded by NASA and administered by the United Negro College Fund Special Programs Corporation. In addition to faculty at MSIs, the program is open to NASA employees who spend 18 to 22 months teaching and/or conducting research at an MSI. Fellows must agree to return to their home institution for at least 2 years after conclusion of the program.

Number awarded 12 each year: 6 MSI faculty members and 6 NASA employees.

Deadline February of each year.

[910]
NASA GRADUATE STUDENT RESEARCHERS PROGRAM

National Aeronautics and Space Administration
Attn: Office of Human Resources and Education
Code FE
Washington, DC 20546-0001
(202) 358-0402   Fax: (202) 358-3032
E-mail: kblanding@mail.hq.nasa.gov
Web: fellowships.hq.nasa.gov/gsrp

Purpose To provide funding to graduate students interested in conducting research in fields of interest to the U.S. National Aeronautics and Space Administration (NASA).

Eligibility This program is open to full-time students enrolled or planning to enroll in an accredited graduate program at a U.S. college or university. Applicants must be citizens of the United States, sponsored by a faculty advisor or department chair, and interested in conducting research in space sciences at their home university or at NASA field centers. Selection is based on academic qualifications, quality of the proposed research and its relevance to NASA's program, the student's proposed utilization of center research facilities (except for NASA headquarters), and ability of the student to accomplish the defined research. African Americans, Native Americans, Alaskan Natives, Mexican Americans, Puerto Ricans, Native Pacific Islanders, women, and persons with disabilities are strongly urged to apply.

Financial data The program provides a $18,000 student stipend, a $3,000 student expense allowance, and a $3,000 university allowance.

Duration 1 year; may be renewed for up to 2 additional years.

Additional information This program was established in 1980. Awards for NASA Headquarters are sponsored by the Office of Space Science (OSS), the Office of Biological and Physical Research (OBPR), and the Office of Earth Science (OES). The areas of interest include structure/evolution of the universe, origins/planetary systems, solar system exploration, sun-earth connection, information systems, microgravity science and applications, life sciences, and earth sciences. Fellows selected by NASA Headquarters conduct research at their respective universities. Other awards are distributed through NASA field centers, each of which has its own research agenda and facilities. These centers include Ames Research Center (Moffett Field, California), Dryden Flight Research Facility (Edwards, California), Goddard Space Flight Center (Greenbelt, Maryland), Jet Propulsion Laboratory (Pasadena, California), Johnson Space Center (Houston, Texas), Kennedy Space Center (Kennedy Space Center, Florida), Langley Research Center (Hampton, Virginia), Glenn Research Center (Cleveland, Ohio), Marshall Space Flight Center (Huntsville, Alabama), and Stennis Space Center (Stennis Space Center, Mississippi). Fellows spend some period of time in residence at the center, taking advantage of the unique research facilities of the installation and working with center personnel. Travel outside the United States is allowed if it is essential to the research effort and charged to a grant.

Number awarded This program supports approximately 300 graduate students each year.

Deadline January of each year.

[911]
NASA/DVSGC UNDERGRADUATE SUMMER SCHOLARSHIPS

Delaware Valley Space Grant College Consortium
c/o University of Delaware
Bartol Research Institute
104 Center Mall, #217
Newark, DE 19716-4793
(302) 831-1094   Fax: (302) 831-1843
E-mail: nfness@bartol.udel.edu
Web: www.delspace.org

Purpose To provide funding to undergraduate students in Delaware and Pennsylvania for summer research on space-related subjects.

Eligibility This program is open to undergraduate students at member or affiliate colleges and universities of the Delaware Valley Space Grant College (DVSGC) Consortium. Applicants must have a proven interest and aptitude for space-related studies and be proposing a summer research project. U.S. citizenship is required. The DVSGC is a component of the U.S. National Aeronautics and Space Administration (NASA) Space Grant program, which encourages applications from women, minorities, and persons with disabilities.

Financial data A stipend is provided (amount not specified).

Duration Summer months.

Additional information This program is funded by NASA. Members of the consortium include Delaware State University (Dover, Delaware), Delaware Technical and Community College (Dover, Delaware), Franklin and Marshall College (Lancaster, Pennsylvania), Gettysburg College (Gettysburg, Pennsylvania), Lehigh University (Bethlehem, Pennsylvania), Lincoln University (Lincoln University, Pennsylvania), Swarthmore College (Swarthmore, Pennsylvania), University of Delaware–Bartol Research Institute (Newark, Delaware), University of Pennsylvania (Philadelphia, Pennsylvania), and Villanova University (Villanova, Pennsylvania), and Wilmington College (New Castle, Delaware).

Number awarded Varies each year; recently, 9 of these scholarships were awarded.

Deadline February of each year.

[912]
NATIONAL ASSESSMENT OF EDUCATIONAL PROGRESS (NAEP) VISITING SCHOLAR PROGRAM

Educational Testing Service
MS 09-R
Princeton, NJ 08541-0001
(609) 734-1806   E-mail: ldelauro@ets.org
Web: www.ets.org

Purpose To provide funding to postdoctoral scholars who wish to conduct research on education for minorities at the Educational Testing Service (ETS).

Eligibility Applicants must have earned a doctorate in a relevant discipline. They must be prepared to conduct independent research at ETS on some aspect of education using the database of the National Assessment of Educational Progress (NAEP). Studies focused on issues concerning the education of minority students are especially encouraged. Selection is based on scholarship, importance of the research, and relevance to NAEP. An explicit goal of the program is to increase the number of minority professionals in educational measurement and related fields.

Financial data The stipend is set in relation to compensation at the home institution. Scholars and their families also receive reimbursement for relocation expenses.

Duration 10 months, from September through June of the following year.

Additional information Fellows work with senior staff at the Educational Testing Service in Princeton, New Jersey and have access to senior NAEP research staff.

Number awarded 1 each year.

Deadline January of each year.

[913]
NATIONAL CANCER INSTITUTE MENTORED CAREER DEVELOPMENT AWARD

National Cancer Institute
Attn: Comprehensive Minority Biomedical Program
6130 Executive Boulevard, Room 620
Bethesda, MD 20892-7405
(301) 496-7344   Fax: (301) 402-4551
E-mail: ss165i@nih.gov
Web: www.nci.nih.gov

Purpose To provide funding to underrepresented minority scientists who are transitioning from a mentored research environment to an independent research and academic career.

Eligibility This program is open to members of an ethnic or racial group that is underrepresented in biomedical and behavioral research who 1) have a research or a health professional doctorate or its equivalent; 2) have demonstrated the potential for a productive research career; 3) received an underrepresented minority supplement award at the postdoctoral or junior faculty level, funded by the National Cancer Institute (NCI); and 4) demonstrate the potential for establishing an independent research program highly relevant to the understanding of human biology and human disease as it relates to the etiology, pathogenesis, prevention, diagnosis, and treatment of cancer. Candidates must be sponsored by a domestic, nonprofit or for-profit organization, public or private, such as a university, college, hospital, laboratory, unit of state or local government, or eligible agency of the federal government. The sponsor must provide a mentor to work with the candidate; the mentor must be a senior or mid-level faculty member with research competence and a major interest in the training of underrepresented minority investigators in cancer research. If feasible, women and underrepresented minority mentors should be involved as role models. Candidates must be U.S. citizens, nationals, or permanent residents.

Financial data The award provides salary up to $75,000 per year plus related fringe benefits. During the mentored phase, up to $25,000 per year is provided for the following types of expenses: research expenses; statistical services, including personnel and computer time; tuition, fees, and books related to career development; travel to research meetings; and travel to an annual 2-day NCI awardee meeting and/or peer review related and training expenses. During the independent research phase, that supplemental award increases to $50,000 per year.

Duration Up to 5 years. During the first phase, the recipient participates in research activities at the mentored institution. In the second phase, the recipient secures a junior faculty position either at the same institution as the mentored experience or a different institution.

Number awarded Varies each year, depending on the availability of funds.

Deadline January, May, or September of each year.

[914]
NATIONAL CENTER FOR ATMOSPHERIC RESEARCH POSTDOCTORAL APPOINTMENTS

National Center for Atmospheric Research
Attn: Advanced Study Program
1850 Table Mesa Drive
P.O. Box 3000
Boulder, CO 80307-3000
(303) 497-1601   Fax: (303) 497-1646
E-mail: barbm@ucar.edu
Web: www.asp.ucar.edu/asp/pdann.html

Purpose   To provide funding to recent Ph.D.s who wish to conduct research at the National Center for Atmospheric Research (NCAR) in Boulder, Colorado.

Eligibility   This program is open to recent Ph.D.s and Sc.D.s in applied mathematics, chemistry, engineering, and physics as well as specialists in atmospheric sciences from such disciplines as biology, economics, geography, geology, and science education. Applicants must be interested in conducting research at the center in atmospheric sciences and global change. Selection is based on the applicant's scientific capability and potential, originality and independence, and ability to take advantage of the research opportunities at center. Applications from women and minorities are encouraged.

Financial data   The stipend is $38,500 in the first year and $40,500 in the second year. Fellows also receive life and health insurance, a relocation allowance (up to $800 for travel within the United States or up to $2,500 for travel from abroad), and scientific travel reimbursement up to $1,200 per year.

Duration   2 years.

Additional information   NCAR is operated by the University Corporation for Atmospheric Research (a consortium of 61 universities) and sponsored by the National Science Foundation.

Number awarded   Varies; currently, 8 to 10 each year.

Deadline   January of each year.

[915]
NATIONAL CONSORTIUM ON VIOLENCE RESEARCH CAREER DEVELOPMENT PROGRAM

National Consortium on Violence Research
c/o Carnegie Mellon University
H. John Heinz III School of Public Policy and Management
Hamburg Hall, Room 2505
5000 Forbes Avenue
Pittsburgh, PA 15213-3890
(412) 268-8010   E-mail: cmiller2@andrew.cmu.edu
Web: www.ncovr.heinz.cmu.edu

Purpose   To provide funding to new faculty members who are interested in conducting research related to violence.

Eligibility   Applicants for these fellowships must have received, within the past 4 years, a doctorate in a field relevant to violence research and be on the faculty of a college or university for less than 4 years. They must be interested in a program of research related to violence in cooperation with a mentor who is a member of the National Consortium on Violence Research (NCOVR). Their proposal may involve developing a research proposal or paper, collecting data, engaging in analysis, investigating relevant literature, attending meetings or conferences on the topic, or preparing papers for publication. Selection is based on the applicant's determination to acquire technical and analytical skills necessary for carrying out research on violence, willingness to collaborate with NCOVR members from different disciplines, and presenta-

tion of research interests to the selection committee in a telephone interview. Women and minorities are strongly encouraged to apply.

Financial data   A stipend is awarded (amount not specified). Funds may be used to attend professional meetings, to meet the mentor, to cover out-of-pocket research costs, or to attend the Inter-University Consortium for Political and Social Research summer program.

Duration   Up to 3 years. Fellows must attend the NCOVR summer workshop and the November meeting of the American Society of Criminology. Funds to participate in the workshop, the meeting, and other designated activities are included as part of the fellowship.

Number awarded   Varies each year; recently, 1 of these grants was awarded.

Deadline   January of each year.

[916]
NATIONAL CONSORTIUM ON VIOLENCE RESEARCH POSTDOCTORAL FELLOWSHIP PROGRAM

National Consortium on Violence Research
c/o Carnegie Mellon University
H. John Heinz III School of Public Policy and Management
Hamburg Hall, Room 2505
5000 Forbes Avenue
Pittsburgh, PA 15213-3890
(412) 268-8010   E-mail: cmiller2@andrew.cmu.edu
Web: www.ncovr.heinz.cmu.edu

Purpose   To provide funding to recent postdoctorates interested in participating in a program of research training related to violence.

Eligibility   Applicants for these fellowships must hold a doctorate in a field related to violence research. They must be affiliated with an institution that is a member of the National Consortium on Violence Research (NCOVR) and be interested in working under the mentorship of 2 consortium members, each from a different discipline. Excellent communication and analytical skills are required. Applicants must be strongly motivated, committed to pursuing advanced training in an aspect of violence research, and willing to relocate to the institution of their primary NCOVR mentor. Selection is based on compatibility of research interests with NCOVR objectives, demonstrated scholarly and research abilities, commitment to violence research, letters of reference, and presentation of research interests to the selection committee in a telephone interview. Women and minorities are strongly encouraged to apply.

Financial data   Recipients are granted $5,000 per year. Funds may be used to attend professional meetings, to meet the mentor, to cover out-of-pocket research costs, or to attend the Inter-University Consortium for Political and Social Research summer program.

Duration   Up to 2 years. Fellows must attend the NCOVR summer workshop and the November meeting of the American Society of Criminology. Funds to participate in the workshop, the meeting, and other designated activities are included as part of the fellowship.

Number awarded   Varies each year; recently, 3 of these grants were awarded.

Deadline   January of each year.

[917]
NATIONAL CONSORTIUM ON VIOLENCE RESEARCH PREDOCTORAL FELLOWSHIP PROGRAM

National Consortium on Violence Research
c/o Carnegie Mellon University
H. John Heinz III School of Public Policy and Management
Hamburg Hall, Room 2505
5000 Forbes Avenue
Pittsburgh, PA 15213-3890
(412) 268-8010   E-mail: cmiller2@andrew.cmu.edu
Web: www.ncovr.heinz.cmu.edu

Purpose To provide funding to doctoral students interested in conducting dissertation research related to violence.

Eligibility This program is open to students who are attending (or will attend) a university that includes a faculty member associated with the National Consortium on Violence Research (NCOVR). The application should provide an endorsement from the consortium member that includes a commitment to supply appropriate institutional resources to support the fellow. Selection is based on the reasonableness and soundness of the research objectives, the quality of the fit between the candidate's research objectives and the NCOVR member's research agenda, and the presentation of research interests to the selection committee during a telephone interview. Women and minorities are strongly encouraged to apply.

Financial data The grant is $2,000 per year. Funds may be used to attend professional meetings, to meet the mentor, to cover out-of-pocket research costs, or to attend the Inter-University Consortium for Political and Social Research summer program.

Duration 1 to 3 years. Fellows must attend the NCOVR summer workshop and the November meeting of the American Society of Criminology. Funds to participate in the workshop, the meeting, and other designated activities are included as part of the fellowship.

Number awarded Varies each year; recently, 9 of these grants were awarded.

Deadline January of each year.

[918]
NATIONAL EDUCATIONAL ENRICHMENT PROGRAM FOR MINORITY GRADUATE STUDENTS FELLOWSHIP IN GERONTOLOGY

National Hispanic Council on Aging
2713 Ontario Road, N.W.
Washington, DC 20009
(202) 745-2521   Fax: (202) 745-2222
E-mail: nhcoa@nhcoa.org
Web: www.nhcoa.org/andrus_foundation.htm

Purpose To provide funding to graduate students from underrepresented minority groups interested in conducting research and attending a seminar about current developments related to minority elderly people.

Eligibility This program is open to Latino, African American, and Native American graduate students. Applicants must be interested in participating in a program that includes 1) research activities at their home academic institutions or another campus, and 2) a seminar at the sponsoring organization.

Financial data Fellows receive a $2,000 stipend, travel and per diem for the seminar, and reimbursement for books and other approved expenses.

Duration 2 months, including 1 week for the seminar in Washington, D.C.

Additional information The seminar includes study of the policy-making process, the resource allocation process in relation to minority aging, review of research being conducted presently that addresses issues of minority elderly, the research topic of each fellow, and examination of leadership roles that future minority gerontologists must assume to improve the quality of life for minority elderly. This program is jointly sponsored by the National Caucus and Center on Black Aged, the National Hispanic Council on Aging, and the National Indian Council on Aging. Funding is provided by the Andrus Foundation of the American Association of Retired Persons

Number awarded 9 each year: 3 selected by each sponsoring organization.

[919]
NATIONAL ESTUARINE RESEARCH RESERVE SYSTEM GRADUATE FELLOWSHIPS

National Oceanic and Atmospheric Administration
Office of Ocean and Coastal Resource Management
Attn: Estuarine Reserves Division
Silver Spring Metro Center Building 4, 11th Floor
1305 East-West Highway
Silver Spring, MD 20910
(301) 713-3155, ext. 172   Fax: (301) 713-4363
E-mail: erica.seiden@noaa.gov
Web: www.ocrm.nos.noaa.gov/nerr/fellow.html

Purpose To provide funding to graduate students interested in conducting research within National Estuarine Research Reserves.

Eligibility This program is open to students admitted to or enrolled in a full-time master's or doctoral program at U.S. accredited universities. Applicants should have completed a majority of their course work at the beginning of their fellowship and have an approved thesis research program focused on improving coastal zone management while providing hands-on training in conducting ecological monitoring. Proposed research topics must address 1 of the following topics: 1) eutrophiation, effects of non-point source pollution and/or nutrient dynamics; 2) habitat conservation and/or restoration; 3) biodiversity and/or the effects of invasive species on estuarine ecosystems; 4) mechanisms for sustaining resources within estuarine ecosystems; or 5) economic, sociological, and/or anthropological research applicable to estuarine ecosystem management. They must be willing to conduct their research within the National Estuarine Research Reserves. Minority students are encouraged to apply.

Financial data The amount of the fellowship is $17,500; at least 30% of total project cost match is required by the applicant (i.e., $7,500 match for a total project cost of $25,000). Requested overhead costs are limited to 10% of the federal amount. Waived overhead costs may be used as match. Funds may be used for any combination of research support, salary, tuition, supplies, or other costs as needed, including overhead.

Duration 1 to 3 years.

Additional information For a list of the National Estuarine Research Reserves, with the name and address of a contact person at each, write to the sponsor. Fellows are required to work with the research coordinator or manager at the host reserve to develop a plan to participate in the reserve's research and/or monitoring program for up to 15 hours per week.

Number awarded Approximately 27 each year.

Deadline October of each year.

[920]
NATIONAL HEART, LUNG, AND BLOOD INSTITUTE MENTORED RESEARCH SCIENTIST DEVELOPMENT AWARD FOR MINORITY FACULTY

National Heart, Lung, and Blood Institute
Attn: Division of Lung Diseases
6701 Rockledge Drive, Room 10112
Bethesda, MD 20892-7952
(301) 435-0222   Fax: (301) 480-3557
E-mail: mr50w@nih.gov
Web: www.nhlbi.nih.gov

Purpose To develop the research capabilities of underrepresented minority faculty investigators in areas relevant to cardiovascular, pulmonary, and hematologic diseases and resources, and to increase the number of minority individuals involved in research endeavors.

Eligibility Awards in this program are made to domestic institutions or organizations on behalf of awardees. Individuals must possess a doctoral degree (M.D., Ph.D., D.V.M., D.O., or equivalent), have a faculty appointment at an accredited college or university, be U.S. citizens, noncitizen nationals, or permanent residents at the time of application, and be members of a minority ethnic group that is underrepresented in biomedical or behavioral research (Blacks, Hispanics, Native Americans, and Pacific Islanders). Candidates must identify a sponsor who is an accomplished investigator in the proposed research area and has experience in developing independent investigators.

Financial data The awardee receives salary support of up to $50,000 per year plus fringe benefits. Support for up to 5% of the sponsor's salary may also be requested. In addition, up to $30,000 per year will be provided for research support. These research funds may be used for equipment, supplies, travel, tuition and fees, and other related costs (e.g., personnel, publication costs, computer costs).

Duration 3 to 5 years.

Additional information Support is also available through the Division of Heart and Vascular Diseases, the Division of Blood Diseases and Resources, and the Division of Epidemiology and Clinical Applications.

Number awarded Varies each year; recently, 12 awards were available through this program with total funding of $1,300,000.

Deadline August of each year.

[921]
NATIONAL HEART, LUNG, AND BLOOD INSTITUTE MINORITY INSTITUTION FACULTY MENTORED RESEARCH SCIENTIST DEVELOPMENT AWARD

National Heart, Lung, and Blood Institute
Attn: Division of Lung Diseases
6701 Rockledge Drive, Room 10112
Bethesda, MD 20892-7952
(301) 435-0222   Fax: (301) 480-3557
E-mail: mr50w@nih.gov
Web: www.nhlbi.nih.gov

Purpose To encourage the development of faculty investigators at minority schools in areas relevant to cardiovascular, pulmonary, and hematologic diseases.

Eligibility Candidates for this award must be faculty members who are U.S. citizens, noncitizen nationals, or permanent resi-

dents at the time of application; have a doctoral degree or equivalent in a biomedical science; wish to receive specialized training in cardiovascular, pulmonary, or hematologic, or sleep disorders research; and have the background and potential to benefit from the training. They must be teaching at an institution in which minority ethnic students (including Blacks, Hispanics, American Indians, and Asian or Pacific Islanders) comprise more than 50% of the school's enrollment. Each candidate must identify and complete arrangements with a nearby mentor (within approximately 100 miles) who is recognized as an accomplished investigator in the research area proposed and who will provide guidance for the awardee's development and research plans. For the purposes of this program, "minority school" is defined as a medical or nonmedical college, university, or equivalent school in which 1) students of minority ethnic groups (including but not limited to African Americans, Hispanics, Native Americans, and Asian or Pacific Islanders) comprise a majority or significant proportion of the school's enrollment; 2) there is a commitment to the special encouragement of minority faculty, students, and investigators; and 3) few or no members of its faculty are actively engaged in biomedical research.

Financial data The awardee receives salary support of up to $50,000 per year plus fringe benefits for 5 years. The actual amount of support awarded is based on the recipient's current salary and must be consistent with the established salary structure of the minority institution for persons of equivalent qualifications, experience, and rank. Support for up to 5% of the mentor's salary during the summer experience may also be awarded. In addition, up to $36,000 per year will be provided for research support. These research funds may be used for equipment, supplies, travel, tuition and fees, and other related costs (e.g., personnel, publication costs, computer costs).

Duration 2 to 3 months during the summer and quarter time during the academic year for up to 5 years.

Additional information Support is also available through the Division of Heart and Vascular Diseases, the Division of Blood Diseases and Resources, the Division of Epidemiology and Clinical Applications, and the National Center for Sleep Disorders Research.

Number awarded Varies each year; recently, 4 awards were available through this program with total funding of $895,000.

Deadline Letters of intent must be submitted by August of each year; final applications are due in September.

[922]
NATIONAL INSTITUTES OF HEALTH INDIVIDUAL RESEARCH PROJECT GRANTS

National Institutes of Health
Division of Extramural Outreach and Information Resources
Attn: GrantsInfo
6701 Rockledge Drive, Suite 6095
Bethesda, MD 20892-7910
(301) 435-0714   Fax: (301) 480-8443
E-mail: GrantsInfo@nih.gov
Web: www.nih.gov

Purpose To support biomedical and behavioral research that will improve human health in areas of interest to the National Institutes of Health (NIH).

Eligibility Investigators at nonprofit and for-profit public and private organizations, such as universities, colleges, hospitals, laboratories, units of state and local governments, and eligible agencies of the federal government may apply for these research grants. Applications are accepted for health-related research and development in all areas within the scope of the institutes' mission and by all component institutes and centers. Specific subjects of research are announced periodically either as Program Announcements (PAs) for ongoing research or as Requests for Applications (RFAs) for specific 1-time research projects. Usually, the research is to be conducted within the United States, but research projects conducted at foreign sites may be proposed if they meet the following conditions: 1) have specific relevance to the institutes and have the potential for significantly advancing the health sciences in the United States; 2) present special opportunities for further research through the use of unusual talents, resources, populations, or environmental conditions; and 3) have a rating that falls within the normally established payline. For all projects, racial/ethnic minority individuals, women, and persons with disabilities are particularly encouraged to apply as principal investigators.

Financial data The level of funding depends on the scope of the proposed research. Funds may be used for supplies, equipment, personnel, and travel. Foreign institutions do not receive support for administrative costs associated with the research.

Duration 1 year or longer.

Additional information These grants are offered by 21 of NIH's component institutes. The most meritorious first-time recipients of these awards who are new investigators (with no more than five years of research experience since completion of postdoctoral training) are also nominated to receive Presidential Early Career Awards for Scientists and Engineers.

Deadline January, May, or September of each year.

[923]
NATIONAL INSTITUTES OF HEALTH SMALL GRANT PROGRAM

National Institutes of Health
Division of Extramural Outreach and Information Resources
Attn: GrantsInfo
6701 Rockledge Drive, Suite 6095
Bethesda, MD 20892-7910
(301) 435-0714   Fax: (301) 480-8443
E-mail: GrantsInfo@nih.gov
Web: www.nih.gov

Purpose To support pilot projects conducted by new and established investigators, and other scientists, who would benefit from assistance to position themselves to compete successfully for research project grant support.

Eligibility This program is open to investigators changing areas of research, investigators whose research careers were interrupted and are intended to be resumed, established investigators needing quick support for a pilot project, minority and women investigators, people with disabilities, those located at institutions not traditionally associated with health research, and recently trained or less experienced investigators. The awards are available to applicants at both nonprofit and for-profit organizations. The research may deal with relevant biomedical or behavioral science.

Financial data Applicants may request up to $50,000 (direct costs) for supplies, travel, small items of equipment, and salary for technical personnel; no more than $35,000 may be awarded for any 1 year.

Duration Up to 24 months.

Additional information These grants are offered by all component institutes and centers within the National Institutes of Health (NIH).

Number awarded Varies each year.

Deadline April, August, or December of each year.

[924]
NATIONAL KIDNEY FOUNDATION OF MASSACHUSETTS, RHODE ISLAND, NEW HAMPSHIRE, AND VERMONT RESEARCH GRANTS

National Kidney Foundation of Massachusetts, Rhode Island, New Hampshire, and Vermont, Inc.
Attn: Medical Advisory Board
129 Morgan Drive
Norwood, MA 02062
(781) 278-0222   (800) 542-4001
Fax: (781) 278-0333   E-mail: sdean@kidneyhealth.org
Web: www.kidneyhealth.org

Purpose To encourage research in the northeast that will have significant impact on the understanding and treatment of adult kidney and urological diseases.

Eligibility This program is open to scientists in Massachusetts, Rhode Island, New Hampshire, and Vermont who are interested in conducting research related to all areas of adult kidney and urological diseases, including hypertension and transplantation. Both clinical and basic research proposals are considered. Applicants should have a serious commitment to a career in research. They may not currently hold a grant from NIH. There is no age limitation, and applications from women and members of underrepresented minority groups are encouraged.

Financial data The grant is $35,000.

Duration 1 year.

Additional information This program includes the following named awards: the Joseph E. Murray Award, the Joseph Shankman Award, the Theodore I. Steinman Clinical Research Award, and the Volunteer/Donor Research Award.

Number awarded 4 each year.

Deadline January of each year.

[925]
NATIONAL SCIENCE FOUNDATION RESEARCH OPPORTUNITY AWARDS

National Science Foundation
Directorate for Education and Human Resources
Attn: Senior Staff Associate for Cross Directorate Programs
4201 Wilson Boulevard, Room 805
Arlington, VA 22230
(703) 292-8600   TDD: (703) 292-5090
Web: www.ehr.nsf.gov/crssprgm/rui/start.shtm

Purpose To enable faculty members at predominantly undergraduate institutions to pursue research as visiting scientists on projects of investigators who are supported by the National Science Foundation (NSF).

Eligibility Participants must be citizens or nationals of the United States teaching at predominantly undergraduate institutions, defined as U.S. 2-year, 4-year, master's-level, and small doctoral colleges and universities that 1) grant baccalaureate degrees in NSF-supported fields or provide programs of instruction for students pursuing such degrees after transferring; 2) have undergraduate enrollment exceeding graduate enrollment; and 3) award no more than an average of 10 Ph.D. and/or D.Sc. degrees per year in all disciplines that NSF supports. Applicants must be teaching in a department that offers courses that qualify for bachelor's degree credit in NSF-supportable fields and may offer master's degrees but may not award a doctorate or offer doctoral courses and supervise doctoral research. Applications must be submitted by an NSF-supported investigator at another institution who wishes to employ the proposed visiting researcher under a Research Opportunity Award (ROA) collaboration. Individuals interested in becoming visiting researchers make their own contacts with investigators who currently have or are applying for NSF research grants. A principal investigator may also initiate the collaboration. Applications may be submitted as part of a new NSF proposal, as a supplement to an ongoing NSF award, or by rearranging the project budget in an ongoing award without requesting supplemental funding from NSF. Selection is based on the capability of the investigators, the technical soundness of the proposed effort, the contribution of the ROA activity to the ongoing research project, and its potential impact upon the ROA visitor and the visitor's institution. The NSF strongly encourages women, minorities, and persons with disabilities to participate in this program.

Financial data Funding is usually provided as a supplement to an ongoing NSF research grant. It may be covered by rebudgeting funds already awarded or by inclusion in the original proposal to NSF. Most NSF programs limit support to moderate amounts, frequently including only the direct costs of participation (e.g., salary and fringe benefits for the visitor, travel costs, and essential supplies).

Duration Support generally ranges from 2 to 12 months. Most ROA activities are summer experiences, although partial support of sabbaticals is occasionally provided.

Additional information This program operates through the various disciplinary divisions within the NSF; for a list of the respective telephone numbers, contact the Senior Staff Associate for Cross Directorate Programs.

Number awarded Depends on the number of grant applications that seek the use of a visiting researcher.

Deadline Applications for supplemental funding may be submitted at any time, but they must be received at least 3 months before the funds are needed.

[926]
NATIONAL URBAN/RURAL FELLOWS PROGRAM

National Urban Fellows, Inc.
Attn: Director of Programs
59 John Street, Suite 310
New York, NY 10038
(212) 349-6200   Fax: (212) 349-7478
E-mail: edacevedo@nuf.org
Web: www.nuf.org

Purpose To provide mid-career minority and women public sector professionals with an opportunity to strengthen leadership skills through an academic program coupled with a mentorship.

Eligibility Eligible to apply are minorities and women who are U.S. citizens, have a bachelor's degree, have 3 to 5 years of full-time work experience in an administrative or managerial capacity, have demonstrated exceptional ability and leadership potential, meet academic admission requirements, have a high standard of integrity and work ethic, and are willing to relocate for the duration of the fellowship year.

Financial data The maximum stipend is $20,000. The program also provides full payment of tuition fees, a relocation allowance

of $500, a book allowance of $500, and reimbursement for program-related travel.

Duration 14 months.

Additional information The program begins with a semester of study at Bernard M. Baruch College of the City University of New York. Following this, fellows spend 9 months in mentorship assignments as special assistants to governors, mayors, city managers, or county administrators of urban and rural organizations. Fellows who successfully complete all requirements are granted a master's of public administration from Bernard M. Baruch College.

Number awarded Varies; approximately 20 each year.

Deadline February of each year.

[927]
NAVAL RESEARCH LABORATORY BROAD AGENCY ANNOUNCEMENT

Naval Research Laboratory
Attn: Deputy for Small Business
4555 Overlook Avenue, S.W.
Washington, DC 20375-5320
(202) 767-6263   Fax: (202) 767-0494
E-mail: nicholl@contracts.nrl.navy.mil
Web: www.nrl.navy.mil

Purpose To provide funding to investigators interested in conducting scientific research of interest to the U.S. Navy.

Eligibility This program is open to investigators qualified to perform research in designated scientific and technical areas. Topics cover a wide range of technical and scientific areas; recent programs included radar technology, artificial intelligence technologies, software engineering, surface chemistry sciences, ceramic materials, structural acoustics, and seafloor sciences. The Naval Research Laboratory (NRL) encourages industry, educational institutions, small businesses, small disadvantaged business concerns, women-owned small businesses, veteran-owned small businesses, Historically Black Colleges and Universities, and Minority Institutions to submit proposals. Selection is based on the degree to which new and creative solutions to technical issues important to NRL programs are proposed and the offeror's understanding of the proposed approach and technical objectives; the offeror's ability to implement the proposed approach; the degree to which technical data and/or computer software developed under the proposed contract are to be delivered to the NRL with rights compatible with NRL research and development objectives; proposed cost and cost realism; and the extent to which offerors identify and commit to small business, small disadvantaged business, veteran-owned small business, women-owned small business, Historically Black College and University, or Minority Institution participation in the proposed effort, whether as a joint venture, teaming arrangement, or subcontractor.

Financial data The typical range of funding is from $100,000 to $2,000,000.

Duration 1 year.

Additional information The Naval Research Laboratory conducts most of its research in its own facilities in Washington, D.C., Stennis Space Center, Mississippi, and Monterey, California, but also funds some related research.

Number awarded Varies each year.

Deadline Each program establishes its own application deadline; for a complete list of all the programs, including their deadlines, contact the address above.

[928]
NEW HAMPSHIRE SPACE GRANT CONSORTIUM PROJECT SUPPORT

New Hampshire Space Grant Consortium
c/o University of New Hampshire
Institute for the Study of Earth, Oceans, and Space
Morse Hall
39 College Road
Durham, NH 03824-3525
(603) 862-0094   Fax: (603) 862-1915
E-mail: nhspacegrant@unh.edu
Web: www.nhsgc.sr.unh.edu

Purpose To provide financial assistance to students at member institutions of the New Hampshire Space Grant Consortium (NHSGC) who are interested in participating in space-related activities.

Eligibility This program is open to students at member institutions of the NHSGC. Applicants must be studying space physics, astrophysics, astronomy, or aspects of computer science, engineering, earth sciences, ocean sciences, atmospheric sciences, or life sciences that utilize space technology and/or adopt a planetary view of the global environment. U.S. citizenship is required. The New Hampshire Space Grant Consortium is a component of the U.S. National Aeronautics and Space Administration (NASA) Space Grant program, which encourages participation by women, underrepresented minorities, and persons with disabilities.

Financial data The amount of the award depends on the nature of the project.

Duration From 1 quarter to 1 year.

Additional information This program is funded by NASA. Currently, projects operating through this program include space grant fellowships at the University of New Hampshire, Agnes M. Lindsay Trust/NASA Challenge Scholars Initiative at the New Hampshire Community Technical College System, Presidential Scholars Research Assistantships at Dartmouth College, and Women in Science Internships at Dartmouth.

Number awarded Varies each year.

Deadline Each participating college or university sets its own deadline.

[929]
NEW JERSEY SPACE GRANT CONSORTIUM INDUSTRY/UNIVERSITY COOPERATIVE RESEARCH GRANTS

New Jersey Space Grant Consortium
c/o Stevens Institute of Technology
Edward A. Stevens Hall, Room 130-B
Hoboken, NJ 07030
(201) 216-8964   Fax: (201) 216-8929
E-mail: sthangam@stevens-tech.edu
Web: attila.stevens-tech.edu/njsgc

Purpose To provide funding for space-related faculty research at institutions in New Jersey.

Eligibility This program is open to full-time tenure-track faculty members at member institutions of the New Jersey Space Grant Consortium (NJSGC). Applicants must be proposing a program of research in collaboration with industrial partners and with the involvement of graduate students. U.S. citizenship is required. The project must be relevant to aerospace and fit into a strategic enterprise of the U.S. National Aeronautics and Space Administration (NASA) on aerospace technology, human exploration and

development of space, earth science, and space science. Preference is given to proposals intended to seed new work rather than to augment established programs. The highest priority is given to proposals from junior faculty members. The NJSGC is a component of the NASA Space Grant program, which encourages participation by women, minorities, and people with disabilities.

Financial data Grants up to $25,000 are available, with a matching requirement for the industrial partner.

Duration Varies.

Additional information Members of the NJSGC include New Jersey Institute of Technology, Princeton University, Rutgers University, Stevens Institute of Technology, and the University of Medicine and Dentistry of New Jersey. This program is funded by NASA.

Number awarded 4 or 5 each year.

Deadline June of each year.

[930]
NEW YORK PUBLIC LIBRARY FELLOWSHIPS

American Council of Learned Societies
Attn: Office of Fellowships and Grants
633 Third Avenue, 8C
New York, NY 10017-6795
(212) 697-1505   Fax: (212) 949-8058
E-mail: grants@acls.org
Web: www.acls.org/felguide.htm

Purpose To provide funding to postdoctorates interested in conducting research at the New York Public Library's Center for Scholars and Writers.

Eligibility Applicants must be U.S. citizens or permanent residents who hold a Ph.D. degree and have not held supported research leave time for at least 3 years prior to the start of the proposed research. Applicants must be interested in conducting research in the humanities and humanities-related social sciences at the New York Public Library's Center for Scholars and Writers. Applications are particularly invited from women and members of minority groups.

Financial data Fellowships provide a maximum stipend of $50,000 and, if necessary, a housing allowance to enable the fellow to live in New York during the fellowship term.

Duration 9 months, beginning in September

Additional information This program was first offered for 1999-2000, the inaugural year of the center. Candidates must also submit a separate application that is available from the New York Public Library, Humanities and Social Sciences Library, Center for Scholars and Writers, Fifth Avenue and 42nd Street, New York, NY 10018-2788, E-mail: csw@nypl.org. Fellows are required to be in continuous residence at the center and participate actively in its activities and programs.

Number awarded Up to 15 each year.

Deadline September of each year.

[931]
NEW YORK SEA GRANT AND HUDSON RIVER NATIONAL ESTUARINE RESEARCH RESERVE COOPERATIVE RESEARCH FELLOWSHIP

New York Sea Grant
Attn: Nordica Holochuck, Extension Specialist
74 John Street
Kingston, NY 12401-3824
(914) 340-3983   E-mail: nch8@cornell.edu
Web: flounder/seagrant/sunysb.edu

Purpose To provide funding for master's and doctoral candidates who are working on a thesis related to the Hudson River.

Eligibility This program is open to master's and doctoral candidates who are seeking funding for thesis research related to the Hudson River. Although they are preferred, the fellowship is not limited to students in New York state. Minority and female students are especially encouraged to submit applications. Although research in other areas relevant to the missions of the sponsors may be submitted, proposals that emphasize 1 or more of the following 4 areas are given priority: 1) develop evaluation techniques to measure restoration success and/or remediation techniques to restore disturbed coastal environments and habitat; 2) determine functional impacts/importance of introduced and native species on estuarine wetland ecosystem functioning and develop effective detection and control mechanisms; 3) identify and/or evaluate anthropogenic effects on estuarine wetland ecosystem functions; and 4) identify and/or evaluate relationships between wetland ecosystems and the drainage basin.

Financial data The stipend is $14,000, plus $2,000 to cover operational costs (e.g., travel costs and supplies).

Duration 1 year, beginning between June 1 and September 1.

Additional information This program is jointly sponsored by the New York Sea Grant and the Hudson River National Estuarine Research Reserve. Information is also available from Charles Nieder, Research Coordinator, Hudson River National Estuarine Research Reserve, New York State Department of Environmental Conservation, c/o Bard College Field Station, Annandale, NY 12504, (914) 758-7013, E-mail: wcnieder@gw.dec.state.ny.us. Recipients must submit a 6-month progress report and a final report. They must also make a final oral presentation and/or a poster of research results.

Number awarded 1 each year.

Deadline March of each year.

[932]
NEXT GENERATION FELLOWSHIP PROGRAM

Council on Foreign Relations
Attn: Membership and Fellowship Affairs
58 East 68th Street
New York, NY 10021
(212) 434-9489   Fax: (212) 434-9801
E-mail: fellowships@cfr.org
Web: www.cfr.org/public/fp.html

Purpose To provide scholars and practitioners in international affairs with an opportunity to conduct research in residence at the Council on Foreign Relations in New York or Washington.

Eligibility This program is open to individuals between 27 and 40 years of age who have earned a doctorate or other advanced degree and/or have equivalent experience in government or elsewhere. Applicants are welcomed from any field within international relations, but preference is given to those whose work seeks to join regional or functional expertise with economics. Uni-

versity deans and professors as well as other experts in the field are invited to nominate candidates, but individuals are also encouraged to apply on their own. All candidates are invited to submit samples of recent written work and to provide a proposal for a potential research project at the council. The program actively seeks candidates from diverse backgrounds (e.g., minorities).

Financial data The stipend is determined according to individual budget statements; in general, the program attempts to meet the major portion of the fellow's current income.

Duration 2 to 3 years.

Number awarded Approximately 12 fellows are in residence at any time.

Deadline Applications and nominations are accepted at any time.

[933]
NMSGC RESEARCH OPPORTUNITIES AWARDS PROGRAM

New Mexico Space Grant Consortium
c/o New Mexico State University
Wells Hall, Bay 4
Box 30001, Department SG
Las Cruces, NM 88003-0001
(505) 646-6414   Fax: (505) 646-7791
E-mail: nmsgc@pathfinder.nmsu.edu
Web: spacegrant.nmsu.edu

Purpose To provide funding for space-related research to faculty members at institutions that are members of the New Mexico Space Grant Consortium (NMSGC).

Eligibility This program is open to faculty at NMSGC institutions who do not currently have research support. Proposals may include, but are not limited to, pre-proposal visits to a field center of the U.S. National Aeronautics and Space Administration (NASA), support for an undergraduate or graduate student to join a faculty member at a field center for part of a summer term, support to develop a new research project among scientists at several consortium campuses, and/or faculty summer support at facilities not covered by existing programs. All research must be space, aerospace, aeronautics, or launch related. All faculty, students, or staff who receive support for this program must be U.S. citizens. The NMSGC is a component of the NASA Space Grant program, which encourages participation by women, underrepresented minorities, and persons with disabilities.

Financial data Grants up to $20,000 are available.

Duration Up to 1 year.

Additional information The NMSGC institutional members are: New Mexico State University, New Mexico Institute of Mining and Technology, University of New Mexico, Doña Ana Branch Community College, and San Juan Community College. This program is funded by NASA.

Number awarded Varies each year.

Deadline October of each year.

[934]
NMSGC UNDERGRADUATE EDUCATION ENHANCEMENT PROGRAM

New Mexico Space Grant Consortium
c/o New Mexico State University
Wells Hall, Bay 4
Box 30001, Department SG
Las Cruces, NM 88003-0001
(505) 646-6414   Fax: (505) 646-7791
E-mail: nmsgc@pathfinder.nmsu.edu
Web: spacegrant.nmsu.edu

Purpose To provide support for development of space-related academic programs to faculty at institutions that are members of the New Mexico Space Grant Consortium (NMSGC).

Eligibility This program is open to faculty at NMSGC institutions who are seeking funding for project-based course development, capstone courses, curriculum or course re-design, course re-design for web-based courses or distance education, and student retention and achievement programs in the undergraduate science, engineering, and technology areas. Courses must be part of the regular academic program in space, aerospace, aeronautics, and launch-related areas. They should focus on involving women, underrepresented groups, and persons with disabilities in all aspects of education, including fellowship awards, curriculum development, and degree programs in scientific, engineering, and technical fields. All faculty, staff, and students who receive support for this program must be U.S. citizens. The NMSGC is a component of the U.S. National Aeronautics and Space Administration (NASA) Space Grant program, which encourages participation by women, underrepresented minorities, and persons with disabilities.

Financial data Grants range from $1,000 to $20,000. Institutions must provide 120% nonfederal matching funds. Grants may be used to support faculty or staff release time, graduate and undergraduate student support, or travel related to the course. Funds may not be used to support tuition.

Duration Up to 1 year.

Additional information The NMSGC institutional members are: New Mexico State University, New Mexico Institute of Mining and Technology, University of New Mexico, Doña Ana Branch Community College, and San Juan Community College. This program is funded by NASA.

Number awarded Varies each year.

Deadline October of each year.

[935]
NORTH CAROLINA SPACE GRANT CONSORTIUM GRADUATE FELLOWSHIPS

North Carolina Space Grant Consortium
c/o North Carolina State University
Mechanical and Aerospace Engineering
1009 Capability Drive, Room 216E
Box 7515
Raleigh, NC 27695-7515
(919) 515-4240   Fax: (919) 515-5934
E-mail: space_grant@eos.ncsu.edu
Web: www.mae.ncsu.edu/spacegrant

Purpose To provide funding for space-related research by graduate students at institutions affiliated with the North Carolina Space Grant Consortium (NCSGC).

Eligibility This program is open to graduate students at institutions affiliated with the NCSGC. Applicants must be pursuing

degrees in engineering or science disciplines of interest to the U.S. National Aeronautics and Space Administration (NASA) and have a GPA of 3.0 or greater. Selection is based on the quality of the research proposal, relevance to space, and academic achievement. U.S. citizenship and full-time enrollment are required. A primary goal of this program is the recruitment and retention of underrepresented minorities, women, and the physically challenged into space-related fields.

Financial data The grant is $5,000.

Additional information The affiliated institutions are North Carolina State University, North Carolina A&T State University, Duke University, North Carolina Central University, the University of North Carolina at Charlotte, the University of North Carolina at Chapel Hill, the University of North Carolina at Pembroke, and Winston-Salem State University. This program is funded by NASA.

Number awarded At least 5 each year.

Deadline January of each year.

[936]
NORTH CAROLINA SPACE GRANT CONSORTIUM UNDERGRADUATE SCHOLARSHIPS

North Carolina Space Grant Consortium
c/o North Carolina State University
Mechanical and Aerospace Engineering
1009 Capability Drive, Room 216E
Box 7515
Raleigh, NC 27695-7515
(919) 515-4240   Fax: (919) 515-5934
E-mail: space_grant@eos.ncsu.edu
Web: www.mae.ncsu.edu/spacegrant

Purpose To provide funding for space-related research by undergraduate students at institutions affiliated with the North Carolina Space Grant Consortium (NCSGC).

Eligibility This program is open to undergraduate students at institutions affiliated with the NCSGC. Applicants must be pursuing degrees in engineering or science disciplines of interest to the U.S. National Aeronautics and Space Administration (NASA) and have a GPA of 3.0 or greater. Selection is based on the quality of the research proposal, relevance to space, and academic achievement. U.S. citizenship and full-time enrollment are required. A primary goal of this program is the recruitment and retention of underrepresented minorities, women, and the physically challenged into space-related fields.

Financial data The grant is $4,000.

Additional information The affiliated institutions are North Carolina State University, North Carolina A&T State University, Duke University, North Carolina Central University, the University of North Carolina at Charlotte, the University of North Carolina at Chapel Hill, the University of North Carolina at Pembroke, and Winston-Salem State University. This program is funded by NASA.

Number awarded At least 10 each year.

Deadline January of each year.

[937]
NORTH DAKOTA SPACE GRANT PROGRAM FELLOWSHIPS

North Dakota Space Grant Program
c/o University of North Dakota
Department of Space Studies
Clifford Hall, Fifth Floor
P.O. Box 9008
University Avenue and Tulane
Grand Forks, ND 58202-9008
(701) 777-4856   (800) 828-4274
Fax: (701) 777-3711   E-mail: bieri@space.edu
Web: www.space.edu/spacegrant/fellowinfo.html

Purpose To provide funding for space-related research to undergraduate and graduate students at academic institutions affiliated with the North Dakota Space Grant Program (NDSGP).

Eligibility This program is open to undergraduate and graduate students at specified NDSGP universities who are studying in fields related to space and are paired with an advisor for a research project. U.S. citizenship is required. Other qualifying criteria are set by each participating institution. The NDSGP is a component of the U.S. National Aeronautics and Space Administration (NASA) Space Grant program, which encourages the participation of women, underrepresented minorities, and persons with disabilities.

Financial data The stipend is $2,000.

Additional information Participating NDSCP members are the University of North Dakota and North Dakota State University. This program is funded by NASA.

Number awarded Varies each year.

[938]
N.S. BIENSTOCK FELLOWSHIP

Radio and Television News Directors Foundation
1000 Connecticut Avenue, N.W., Suite 615
Washington, DC 20036-5302
(202) 467-5218   Fax: (202) 223-4007
E-mail: karenb@rtndf.org
Web: www.rtndf.org
Web: www.rtndf.org/asfi/fellowships/minority.html

Purpose To provide professional development grants to minority journalists employed in electronic news.

Eligibility This program is open to minority journalists employed in electronic news who have 10 years or less of full-time experience. Applications must include samples of the journalist's work done as the member of a news staff, with a script and tape (audio or video) up to 15 minutes.

Financial data The grant is $2,500, plus an expense-paid trip to the international convention of the Radio-Television News Directors Association held that year.

Duration The grant is presented annually.

Additional information The grant, established in 1999, may be used in any way to improve the craft and enhance the excellence of the recipient's news operation.

Number awarded 1 each year.

Deadline April of each year.

[939]
NSF SCHOLAR-IN-RESIDENCE AT NIH PROGRAM

National Science Foundation
Directorate for Engineering
4201 Wilson Boulevard
Arlington, VA 22230
(703) 292-8300   TDD: (703) 292-5090
E-mail: rkhosla@nsf.gov
Web: www.eng.nsf.gov

Purpose To provide an opportunity for science and engineering faculty to conduct research in laboratories of the National Institutes of Health (NIH).

Eligibility This program is open to full-time faculty members at U.S. colleges and universities in mathematics, physical science, and engineering fields of interest to the National Science Foundation (NSF). Applicants must be proposing to conduct research at the intramural laboratories of the NIH that focuses on the interaction between their field and the medical and biological sciences and biomedical engineering. Women, minorities, and persons with disabilities are strongly encouraged to apply.

Financial data The NSF provides summer salary, travel, and per diem costs for the visiting scholar while on the NIH campus, as well as travel costs associated with short-term visits to the NIH campus by students working with the scholar at his/her home institution. The home institution of the scholar is expected to provide cost sharing through sabbatical salary or other resources. NIH provides office space, research facilities, research costs in the form of expendable and minor equipment purchases to the host laboratory, and the time of its research staff.

Duration 6 months to 1 year, either consecutively or staggered within an 18-month time frame.

Additional information This program is offered through 2 NSF directorates: engineering (see above for contact information) and mathematical and physical sciences, (703) 292-8800, E-mail: dcaldwel@nsf.gov.

Number awarded Up to 10 each year.

Deadline Applications may be submitted at any time.

[940]
NSF STANDARD AND CONTINUING GRANTS

National Science Foundation
4201 Wilson Boulevard
Arlington, VA 22230
(703) 292-5111   TDD: (703) 292-5090
E-mail: info@nsf.gov
Web: www.nsf.gov

Purpose To provide financial support for research in broad areas of science and engineering.

Eligibility The National Science Foundation (NSF) supports research through its Directorates of Biological Sciences; Computer and Information Science and Engineering; Education and Human Resources; Engineering; Geosciences; Mathematical and Physical Sciences; and Social, Behavioral, and Economic Sciences. Within those general areas of science and engineering, NSF awards 2 types of grants: 1) standard grants, in which NSF agrees to provide a specific level of support for a specified period of time with no statement of NSF intent to provide additional future support without submission of another proposal; and 2) continuing grants, in which NSF agrees to provide a specific level of support for an initial specified period of time with a statement of intent to provide additional support of the project for additional periods, provided funds are available and the results achieved warrant further support. Although NSF often solicits proposals for support of targeted areas through issuance of specific program solicitations, it also accepts unsolicited proposals. Scientists, engineers, and educators usually act as the principal investigator and initiate proposals that are officially submitted by their employing organization. Most employing organizations are universities, colleges, and nonprofit nonacademic organizations (such as museums, observatories, research laboratories, and professional societies). Certain programs are open to for-profit organizations, state and local governments, or unaffiliated individuals. Principal investigators usually must be U.S. citizens, nationals, or permanent residents. NSF particularly encourages members of racial and ethnic minority groups, women, and persons with disabilities to apply as principal investigators.

Financial data Funding levels vary, depending on the nature of the project and the availability of funds. Awards resulting from unsolicited research proposals are subject to statutory cost-sharing.

Duration Standard grants specify the period of time, usually up to 1 year; continuing grants normally specify 1 year as the initial period of time, with support to continue for additional periods.

Additional information Researchers interested in support from NSF should contact the address above to obtain further information on areas of support and programs operating within the respective directorates. They should consult with a program officer before submitting an application. Information on programs is available on the NSF home page. NSF does not normally support technical assistance, pilot plant efforts, research requiring security classification, the development of products for commercial marketing, or market research for a particular project or invention. Bioscience research with disease-related goals, including work on the etiology, diagnosis, or treatment of physical or mental disease, abnormality, or malfunction in human beings or animals, is normally not supported.

Number awarded Approximately 10,000 new awards are issued each year.

Deadline Many programs accept proposals at any time. Other programs establish target dates or deadlines; those target dates and deadlines are published in the *NSF Bulletin* and in specific program announcements/solicitations.

[941]
NUTRITION ACTION FELLOWSHIP

Center for Science in the Public Interest
Attn: Executive Director
1875 Connecticut Avenue, N.W., Suite 300
Washington, DC 20009-5728
(202) 332-9110   Fax: (202) 265-4954
E-mail: cspi@cspinet.org
Web: www.cspinet.org/job/nutrition_fellow.html

Purpose To provide funding to postdoctorates interested in serving as a nutrition advocate at the Center for Science in the Public Interest.

Eligibility This program is open to recent graduates with a Ph.D. or M.D. who are interested in serving as a nutrition advocate at the center. Applicants should have demonstrated interest in public interest advocacy and nutrition science, food safety, or health policy. They should also be able to document academic achievement and writing ability. Minorities, women, and persons with disabilities are particularly encouraged to apply.

Financial data The stipend is $35,000. A generous and comprehensive benefits package is also provided.

Duration 1 year, preferably starting in summer.

Additional information Fellows work in the center's Washington office on nutrition science policy and/or food safety issues.

Number awarded 1 each year.

Deadline Applications may be submitted at any time.

[942]
OFFICE OF NAVAL RESEARCH BROAD AGENCY ANNOUNCEMENT

Office of Naval Research
800 North Quincy Street
Arlington, VA 22217-5660
(703) 696-4111
Web: www.onr.navy.mil/02/baa

Purpose To provide financial support to investigators interested in long-range science and technology research on topics of interest to the U.S. Navy.

Eligibility This program is open to researchers at all levels in academia and industry who are interested in conducting long-range science and technical research projects that offer potential for advancement and improvement of Navy and Marine Corps operations. The proposed research may cover a range of science and engineering disciplines, as described in specific program announcements issued periodically. Researchers at Historically Black Colleges and Universities (HBCUs) and Minority Institutions (MIs) are encouraged to submit proposals and join others in submitting proposals. Selection is based on 1) overall scientific and technical merits of the proposal; 2) potential naval relevance and contributions of the effort to the sponsor's specific mission; 3) the applicant's capabilities, related experience, facilities, techniques, or unique combinations of those that are integral factors for achieving the proposal objectives; 4) the qualifications, capabilities, and experience of the proposed principal investigator, team leader, and key personnel; and 5) the realism of the proposed cost and availability of funds.

Financial data The amounts of the grants depend on the research area and the technical approach to be pursued by the awardee.

Additional information Potential applicants are strongly encouraged to contact the program officer whose program best matches the applicant's field of interest. Programs are offered through the following 6 departments: information, electronics, and surveillance; ocean, atmosphere, and space; engineering, materials, and physical science; human systems; naval expeditionary warfare; and industrial and corporate programs.

Number awarded Varies each year.

Deadline Applications may be submitted at any time.

[943]
OFFICE OF NAVAL RESEARCH SABBATICAL LEAVE PROGRAM

American Society for Engineering Education
Attn: Projects Department
1818 N Street, N.W., Suite 600
Washington, DC 20036-2479
(202) 331-3525   Fax: (202) 265-8504
E-mail: projects@asee.org
Web: www.asee.org

Purpose To provide support to faculty members in engineering and science who wish to conduct research at selected Navy facilities while on sabbatical leave.

Eligibility This program is open to U.S. citizens with teaching or research appointments in engineering and science at U.S. universities or colleges. Applicants must intend to conduct research while in residence at selected facilities of the U.S. Navy. Faculty from Historically Black Colleges and Universities, Hispanic Serving Institutions, and Tribal Colleges and Universities are especially encouraged to apply.

Financial data Fellows receive a stipend equivalent to the difference between their regular salary and the sabbatical leave pay from their home institution. Fellows who must relocate their residence receive a relocation allowance and all fellows receive a travel allowance.

Duration Appointments are for a minimum of 1 semester and a maximum of 1 year.

Additional information Participating facilities include the Naval Air Warfare Center, Aircraft Division (Patuxent River, Maryland); Naval Air Warfare Center, Naval Training Systems Division (Orlando, Florida); Naval Air Warfare Center, Weapons Division (China Lake, California); Space and Naval Warfare Systems Center (San Diego, California); Naval Facilities Engineering Service Center (Port Hueneme, California); Naval Research Laboratories (Washington, D.C.; Stennis Space Center, Mississippi; and Monterey, California); Naval Surface Warfare Centers (Bethesda, Maryland; Indian Head, Maryland; Dahlgren, Virginia; and Panama City, Florida); Naval Undersea Warfare Center (Newport, Rhode Island and New London, Connecticut); Defense Equal Opportunity Management Institute (Cocoa Beach, Florida); Navy Personnel Research, Studies & Technology Department (Millington, Tennessee); Naval Dental Research Institute (Great Lakes, Illinois); Naval Aerospace Medical Research Laboratory (Pensacola, Florida); Naval Health Research Center (San Diego, California); Naval Medical Research Center (Silver Spring, Maryland); Naval Medical Research Center Detachment (Lima and Iquitos, Peru); Naval Medical Research Unit 2 (Jakarta, Indonesia); Naval Medical Research Unit 3 (Cairo, Egypt); Naval Medical Research Institute Toxicology Detachment (Wright Patterson Air Force Base, Dayton, Ohio); and Naval Submarine Medical Research Laboratory (Groton, Connecticut); This program is funded by the U.S. Navy's Office of Naval Research but administered by the American Society for Engineering Education.

Number awarded Varies each year.

Deadline Applications may be submitted at any time, but they must be received at least 6 months prior to the proposed sabbatical leave starting date.

[944]
OFFICE OF NAVAL RESEARCH SUMMER FACULTY RESEARCH PROGRAM

American Society for Engineering Education
Attn: Projects Department
1818 N Street, N.W., Suite 600
Washington, DC 20036-2479
(202) 331-3525   Fax: (202) 265-8504
E-mail: projects@asee.org
Web: www.asee.org

Purpose To provide support to faculty members in engineering and science who wish to conduct summer research at selected Navy facilities.

Eligibility This program is open to U.S. citizens with teaching or research appointments in engineering and science at U.S. universities or colleges. In addition to appointments as Summer Faculty Fellows, positions as Senior Summer Faculty Fellows are available to applicants who have at least 6 years of research experience in their field of expertise since earning a Ph.D. or equivalent degree and a substantial, significant record of research accomplishments and publications. A limited number of appointments are also available as Distinguished Summer Faculty Fellows to faculty members who are pre-eminent in their field of research, with a senior appointment at a leading research university and international recognition for their research accomplishments. Faculty from Historically Black Colleges and Universities, Hispanic Serving Institutions, and Tribal Colleges and Universities are especially encouraged to apply.

Financial data The weekly stipend is $1,400 at the Summer Faculty Fellow level, $1,650 at the Senior Summer Faculty Fellow level, and $1,900 at the Distinguished Summer Faculty Fellow level. Fellows who must relocate their residence receive a relocation allowance and all fellows receive a travel allowance.

Duration 10 weeks, during the summer; fellows may reapply in subsequent years.

Additional information Participating facilities include the Naval Air Warfare Center, Aircraft Division (Patuxent River, Maryland); Naval Air Warfare Center, Naval Training Systems Division (Orlando, Florida); Naval Air Warfare Center, Weapons Division (China Lake, California); Space and Naval Warfare Systems Center (San Diego, California); Naval Facilities Engineering Service Center (Port Hueneme, California); Naval Research Laboratories (Washington, D.C.; Stennis Space Center, Mississippi; and Monterey, California); Naval Surface Warfare Centers (Bethesda, Maryland; Indian Head, Maryland; Dahlgren, Virginia; and Panama City, Florida); Naval Undersea Warfare Center (Newport, Rhode Island and New London, Connecticut); Defense Equal Opportunity Management Institute (Cocoa Beach, Florida); Navy Personnel Research, Studies & Technology Department (Millington, Tennessee); Naval Dental Research Institute (Great Lakes, Illinois); Naval Aerospace Medical Research Laboratory (Pensacola, Florida); Naval Health Research Center (San Diego, California); Naval Medical Research Center (Silver Spring, Maryland); Naval Medical Research Center Detachment (Lima and Iquitos, Peru); Naval Medical Research Unit 2 (Jakarta, Indonesia); Naval Medical Research Unit 3 (Cairo, Egypt); Naval Medical Research Institute Toxicology Detachment (Wright Patterson Air Force Base, Dayton, Ohio); and Naval Submarine Medical Research Laboratory (Groton, Connecticut); This program is funded by the U.S. Navy's Office of Naval Research but administered by the American Society for Engineering Education.

Number awarded Varies each year.

Deadline November of each year.

[945]
OHIO SPACE GRANT CONSORTIUM SENIOR SCHOLARSHIP

Ohio Space Grant Consortium
c/o Ohio Aerospace Institute
22800 Cedar Point Road
Cleveland, OH 44142
(440) 962-3032   (800) 828-OSGC
Fax: (440) 962-3120   E-mail: osgc@oai.org
Web: www.osgc.org

Purpose To provide financial assistance to American citizens who wish to conduct research while working on a baccalaureate degree in an aerospace-related discipline at major universities in Ohio.

Eligibility These scholarships are available to U.S. citizens who expect to complete the requirements for a bachelor of science degree in an aerospace-related discipline (aeronautical engineering, aerospace engineering, astronomy, biology, chemical engineering, chemistry, civil engineering, computer engineering and science, control engineering, electrical engineering, engineering mechanics, geography, geology, industrial engineering, manufacturing engineering, materials science and engineering, mathematics, mechanical engineering, petroleum engineering, physics, and systems engineering) within 1 year. They must be attending 1 of the participating universities in Ohio. Women, underrepresented minorities, and physically challenged persons are particularly encouraged to apply. Applicants must propose a research project to be conducted during the scholarship period in a campus laboratory. Selection is based on academic record, recommendations, the proposed research project, and a personal statement of career goals and anticipated benefits from the Space Grant program.

Financial data The grant is $3,000.

Duration 1 year.

Additional information These scholarships are funded through the National Space Grant College and Fellowship Program administered by the National Aeronautics and Space Administration (NASA), with matching funds provided by the member universities, the Ohio Aerospace Institute, and private industry. The participating institutions are the University of Akron, Case Western Reserve University, Cedarville College, Central State University, University of Cincinnati, Cleveland State University, University of Dayton, Marietta College (petroleum engineering), Miami University (manufacturing engineering), Ohio Northern University, Ohio State University, Ohio University, University of Toledo, Wilberforce University, Wright State University, and Youngstown State University. Scholars are required to describe their research at an annual spring research symposium sponsored by the consortium.

Deadline February of each year.

[946]
OMOHUNDRO INSTITUTE POSTDOCTORAL NEH FELLOWSHIP

Omohundro Institute of Early American History and Culture
P.O. Box 8781
Williamsburg, VA 23187-8781
(757) 221-1110   Fax: (757) 221-1047
E-mail: ieahc1@wm.edu
Web: www.wm.edu/oieach/fello.html

Purpose To provide funding to scholars in American studies who wish to revise their dissertation or other manuscript in residence at the Omohundro Institute of Early American History and Culture in Williamsburg, Virginia.

Eligibility Applicants must have completed a Ph.D. in a field that encompasses all aspects of the lives of North America's indigenous and immigrant peoples during the colonial, Revolutionary, and early national periods of the United States and the related histories of Canada, the Caribbean, Latin America, the British Isles, Europe, and Africa, from the 16th century to approximately 1815. They must be U.S. citizens or have lived in the United States for the 3 previous years. The proposed fellowship project must not be under contract to another publisher. The revisions must be made at the Omohundro Institute. Applicants may not have previously published a book or have entered into a contract for the publication of a scholarly monograph. Members of

underrepresented groups (including people of color, persons with disabilities, Vietnam veterans, and women) are encouraged to apply. Selection is based on the potential of the candidate's dissertation or other manuscript to make a distinguished, book-length contribution to scholarship.

Financial data The fellowship includes a stipend of $40,000 per year in the first year, funds for travel to conferences and research centers, and access to office, research, and computer facilities at the institute.

Duration 2 years.

Additional information Funding for this program is provided by the National Endowment for the Humanities (NEH). Fellows hold concurrent appointment as assistant professor in the appropriate department at the College of William and Mary and teach a total of 6 semester hours during the 2-year term.

Number awarded 1 each year.

Deadline October of each year.

[947]
ONS FOUNDATION ETHNIC MINORITY RESEARCHER AND MENTORSHIP GRANTS

Oncology Nursing Society
Attn: Research Team
501 Holiday Drive
Pittsburgh, PA 15220-2749
(412) 921-7373, ext. 250   Fax: (412) 921-1762
E-mail: research@ons.org
Web: www.ons.org

Purpose To provide funding to members of ethnic minority groups interested in conducting oncology nursing research.

Eligibility Principal investigators must be ethnic minority researchers (Native American, African American, Asian American, Pacific Islander, Hispanic/Latino, or other ethnic minority background). Beginning or novice researchers must utilize a research mentor for consultive services in research design and statistical analyses. Preference is given to projects that involve nurses in the design and conduct of the research activity and that promote theoretically based oncology practice. Graduate students are encouraged to apply for funding that supports work that is considered preliminary in nature or related to their thesis or dissertation.

Financial data The grant is $5,000 ($4,000 for the conduct of the research project and $1,000 for the research mentor or consultant). Funding is not provided for projects that are already completed or nearing completion, payment of tuition, or institutional indirect costs.

Duration Up to 2 years.

Additional information Every effort is made to find an ethnic minority mentor; however, the primary criteria for matching the investigator and mentor is the substantive area of the research and the expertise of the mentor.

Number awarded 2 each year.

Deadline October of each year.

[948]
OPEN SOCIETY INSTITUTE COMMUNITY FELLOWSHIPS

Open Society Institute
Attn: Community Fellowship Program
400 West 59th Street
New York, NY 10019
(212) 548-0152   Fax: (212) 548-4679
E-mail: sharris@sorosny.org
Web: www.soros.org/fellow/community.html

Purpose To provide funding to scholars and professionals who are interested in serving disadvantaged communities.

Eligibility Applicants may be in any field, including but not limited to architecture, business, education, engineering, law, management, or medicine. Individuals from disadvantaged communities as well as minorities are strongly encouraged to apply. They must be interested in working in either New York City or Baltimore at a nonprofit community service organization that serves as a sponsor, but applicants need not be from New York or Baltimore. Individuals at later stages in their professional careers, as well as more recent graduates, are encouraged to apply. Current employees of sponsoring organizations are not eligible.

Financial data The stipend is $48,750. Stipends may be augmented by support from other sources, including the sponsoring organization. Limited relief for graduate school debt payments may be provided on a case-by-case basis. Sponsoring organizations are asked to provide medical benefits and overhead costs as necessary.

Duration 18 months; may be renewed for an additional 18 months.

Additional information Information is also available from the Baltimore office of the Open Society Institute at P.O. Box 529, Brooklandville, MD 21022-0529, (410) 234-1091, Fax: (410) 234-2816.

Number awarded 20 each year: 10 in New York and 10 in Baltimore.

Deadline March of each year.

[949]
OPEN SOCIETY INSTITUTE PROJECT ON DEATH IN AMERICA FACULTY SCHOLARS PROGRAM

Open Society Institute
Attn: Project on Death in America
400 West 59th Street
New York, NY 10019
(212) 548-0150   Fax: (212) 548-4613
E-mail: pdiagrants@sorosny.org
Web: www.soros.org/death/fs_announcement.htm

Purpose To provide funding to university faculty members and clinicians who wish to develop projects related to death and dying.

Eligibility This program is open to physicians in all relevant disciplines and doctorate-level faculty members from accredited health professions educational institutions in the United States who hold a rank of instructor, assistant professor, or associate professor (full professors are not eligible). Nurses, lawyers, and social scientists who hold appointments through health professions educational institutions are encouraged to apply, as are women and minorities. Applicants must be interested in disseminating existing models of good care for those near the end of life, developing new models for improving the care of the dying, and developing new approaches to the education of health pro-

fessionals about the care of dying patients and their families. Their programs must consist of 3 components: 1) a clinical, research, educational, or advocacy project carried out at the individual's institution; 2) an individualized professional development plan to enhance the scholar's effectiveness as a leader in caring for the dying and their families; and 3) a faculty development program in which all of the scholars work together on professional development activities.

Financial data The maximum grant is $70,000 per year, of which up to $65,000 may be used to support 60% of the scholar's salary and benefits and $5,000 may be used for travel to national meetings, research assistance, summer stipends, and other costs related to work on the scholar's project. Another $6,500 (or 10% of the scholar's salary and benefits) is granted to the scholar's institution for overhead costs.

Duration 2 years.

Additional information Further information is also available from the Faculty Scholars Program Director, Dana Farber Cancer Institute, Adult Psychosocial Oncology Program, 44 Binney Street, Boston, MA 02115, (617) 632-6182, E-mail: jerry_garcia@dfci.harvard.edu.

Number awarded Approximately 5 to 8 each year.

Deadline January of each year.

[950]
OSGC RESEARCH PROGRAM

Oklahoma NASA Space Grant Consortium
c/o University of Oklahoma
College of Geosciences
710 Asp Avenue, Suite 5
Norman, Oklahoma 73069
(405) 447-8483   Fax: (405) 447-8455
E-mail: vduca@ou.edu
Web: www.okspacegrant.ou.edu

Purpose To provide funding to faculty and staff at member institutions of the Oklahoma Space Grant Consortium (OSGC) who are interested in conducting research related to the mission of the U.S. National Aeronautics and Space Administration (NASA).

Eligibility This program provides support for space-related research activities at member and affiliate institutions of the OSGC. Proposals may be submitted by faculty and staff of those institutions 1) to foster multi-disciplinary and multi-university research through special conferences, programs, and correspondence; and 2) to enhance the support infrastructure for faculty to facilitate the pursuit of NASA-related research, including both administrative support and marginal funds for travel and critical equipment or supplies. The OSGC is a component of the NASA Space Grant program, which encourages participation by women, minorities, and persons with disabilities.

Financial data Financing depends on the availability of funds.

Additional information Members of OSGC are Oklahoma State University, the University of Oklahoma, Cameron University, and Langston University. This program is funded by NASA.

[951]
PAUL P. VOURAS DISSERTATION RESEARCH GRANT

Association of American Geographers
Attn: Executive Assistant
1710 16th Street, N.W.
Washington, DC 20009-3198
(202) 234-1450   Fax: (202) 234-2744
E-mail: ekhater@aag.org
Web: www.aag.org

Purpose To provide financial assistance to members of the Association of American Geographers who are working on dissertations in geography.

Eligibility Graduate students currently working on a Ph.D. in geography are eligible to apply if they have completed all of the requirements except the dissertation and have been members of the association for at least 1 year prior to submitting an application. Preference is given to minority applicants.

Financial data The amount awarded varies, up to a maximum of $500.

Duration 1 year. Funds must be used for direct research expenses only and may not be used to cover overhead costs.

Number awarded 1 each year.

Deadline December of each year.

[952]
PEACE SCHOLAR DISSERTATION FELLOWSHIPS

United States Institute of Peace
Attn: Jennings Randolph Program for International Peace
1200 17th Street, N.W., Suite 200
Washington, DC 20036-3011
(202) 457-1700   Fax: (202) 429-6063
TDD: (202) 457-1719   E-mail: jrprogram@usip.org
Web: www.usip.org/fellows.html

Purpose To support the research and writing of doctoral dissertations that address the nature of international conflict and ways to prevent or end conflict and to sustain peace.

Eligibility Dissertation projects from a broad range of disciplines (those have been political science, history, sociology, economics, anthropology, psychology, conflict resolution, and other fields within the humanities and social sciences, including interdisciplinary programs) are welcome. Priority is given to projects that promise to make a contribution to theory and practice in international affairs. Proposals may be submitted by citizens of any country who are doctoral candidates at a university in the United States and who have completed all requirements for the doctorate except the dissertation. Women and members of minority groups are especially encouraged to apply. Selection is based on the candidate's record of achievement and/or leadership potential; the significance and potential of the project for making an important contribution to knowledge, practice, or public understanding; and the quality of the project design and its feasibility within the timetable proposed.

Financial data The stipend is $17,000 per year.

Duration 12 months, beginning in September.

Additional information Fellowships are tenable at the recipient's university or any other appropriate research site. This program is offered as part of the Jennings Randolph Program for International Peace at the United States Institute of Peace. These awards are not made for projects that constitute policymaking for a government agency or private organization; focus to any sub-

stantial degree on conflicts within U.S. domestic society, or adopt a partisan, advocacy, or activist stance.

Number awarded Varies each year; recently, 10 of these fellowships were awarded.

Deadline October of each year.

[953]
PEDIATRIC RENAL RESEARCH AWARD

National Kidney Foundation of Massachusetts, Rhode Island, New Hampshire, and Vermont, Inc.
Attn: Medical Advisory Board
129 Morgan Drive
Norwood, MA 02062
(781) 278-0222   (800) 542-4001
Fax: (781) 278-0333   E-mail: sdean@kidneyhealth.org
Web: www.kidneyhealth.org

Purpose To encourage research in the northeast that will have significant impact on the understanding and treatment of pediatric kidney and urological diseases.

Eligibility This program is open to scientists in Massachusetts, Rhode Island, New Hampshire, and Vermont who are interested in conducting research related to all areas of pediatric kidney and urological diseases, including developmental abnormalities of the kidney and focal sclerosis. Preference is given to research addressing the pathophysiology and treatment of Nephrotic Syndrome in children. Both clinical and basic research proposals are considered. Applicants should have a serious commitment to a career in research. They may not currently hold a grant from NIH. There is no age limitation, and applications from women and members of underrepresented minority groups are encouraged.

Financial data The grant is $35,000.

Duration 1 year.

Number awarded 1 each year.

Deadline January of each year.

[954]
PEMBROKE CENTER POSTDOCTORAL FELLOWSHIPS

Brown University
Attn: Pembroke Center for Teaching and Research on Women
Box 1958
Providence, RI 02912
(401) 863-2643   Fax: (401) 863-1298
E-mail: Elizabeth_Barboza@Brown.edu
Web: www.brown.edu

Purpose To provide research support for scholars interested in conducting research on the cross-cultural study of gender.

Eligibility Fellowships are open to anyone in the humanities, social sciences, or life sciences who does not hold a tenured position at an American college or university. Applicants must be willing to spend a year in residence at the Pembroke Center for Teaching and Research on Women and participate in a research project related to gender on a theme that changes annually. A recent theme was "Shame." The center encourages minority and Third World scholars to apply.

Financial data The stipend is $30,000.

Duration 1 academic year.

Additional information Postdoctoral fellows in residence participate in weekly seminars and present at least 2 public papers during the year, as well as pursue an individual research project.

Supplementary funds are available for assistance with travel expenses from abroad.

Number awarded 3 or 4 each year.

Deadline December of each year.

[955]
PHARMACIA AND UPJOHN MINORITY SUMMER FELLOW PROGRAM

American College of Neuropsychopharmacology
Attn: Secretariat
2014 Broadway, Suite 320
Nashville, TN 37203
(615) 322-2075   Fax: (615) 343-0662
E-mail: acnp@acnp.org
Web: www.acnp.org

Purpose To provide funding for summer research to minority graduate students and residents who are interested in preparing for a career in psychopharmacology and the neurosciences.

Eligibility Minority graduate students and residents interested in preparing for a career in psychopharmacology or the neurosciences and conducting research at a selected laboratory are eligible to apply. Selection is based on academic record and research/laboratory experience.

Financial data The total grant is $7,000, which is distributed to cover room and board, transportation to and from the laboratory site, and attendance at the American College of Neuropsychopharmacology's (ACNP) annual conference. Just how the funds are distributed to each recipient is somewhat negotiable and depends in part on the trainee's projected costs for living and travel.

Duration 6 to 8 weeks during the summer.

Additional information Recipients carry out a research project in the laboratory of ACNP's immediate past president. Funding for this program is provided by Pharmacia and Upjohn, Inc.

Number awarded 1 each year.

Deadline March of each year.

[956]
POSTDOCTORAL FELLOWSHIP IN BEHAVIORAL NEUROSCIENCE

Texas Consortium in Behavioral Neuroscience
c/o University of Texas
Department of Psychology
1 University Station A8000
Austin, TX 78712
(512) 471-1068   Fax: (512) 471-1073
E-mail: gonzalez-lima@psy.utexas.edu

Purpose To provide an opportunity for underrepresented minority postdoctorates to obtain research training at selected universities in Texas.

Eligibility This program is open to members of underrepresented minority groups who hold a doctoral degree in neuroscience, psychology, biomedical or natural sciences, or engineering. Applicants must be interested in a program of research training at the University of Texas at Austin, the University of Texas at San Antonio, the University of Texas Health Science Center at San Antonio, Texas A&M University, or Texas A&M University System Health Science Center. U.S. citizenship or permanent resident status is required.

Financial data The program provides $3,090 for health insurance, $1,200 in travel funds, and a stipend of $31,092 in the first year and $32,820 in the second year.

Duration 2 years.

Additional information This program is sponsored by 3 components of the National Institutes of Health: the National Institute of Mental Health, the National Institute on Drug Abuse, and the National Institute of Neurological Disorders and Stroke. The training program covers brain metabolic mapping of behavioral functions, neuropharmacology, electrophysiology, and molecular neurobiology.

Number awarded 5 each year.

Deadline Applications may be submitted at any time.

[957]
POSTDOCTORAL FELLOWSHIPS FOR THE STUDY OF INTERNATIONAL MIGRATION TO THE UNITED STATES

Social Science Research Council
810 Seventh Avenue
New York, NY 10019
(212) 377-2700, ext. 604   Fax: (212) 377-2727
E-mail: migration@ssrc.org
Web: www.ssrc.org

Purpose To provide financial assistance for original research that advances theoretical understanding of immigration to the United States, the processes of settlement, and the outcomes for both immigrants and Americans.

Eligibility Applicants must be U.S. citizens or permanent residents who have earned a Ph.D. or equivalent within the past 7 years in any of the social sciences (including history) or in a related professional field. Foreign scholars are eligible if they are affiliated with a U.S. academic or research institution during the time of the award. The proposed research should focus on international migration to the United States and its economic, sociocultural, and political contexts. Applications from women and from members of minority racial, ethnic, and nationality groups are especially encouraged.

Financial data The maximum stipend is $23,000. Funds can be used for research expenses and salary.

Duration 1 academic year; applicants who do not intend to finish their research by the end of the 1-year fellowship must explain how they plan to complete the unfunded portion of their research.

Additional information Funding for this program is provided by the Andrew W. Mellon Foundation.

Number awarded Approximately 5 each year.

Deadline January of each year.

[958]
POSTDOCTORAL FELLOWSHIPS IN DIABETES RESEARCH

Juvenile Diabetes Research Foundation
Attn: Grant Administrator
120 Wall Street, 19th Floor
New York, NY 10005-4001
(212) 479-7519   (800) 533-CURE
Fax: (212) 785-9595   E-mail: cstone@jdrf.org
Web: www.jdrf.org/research/postdoc.php

Purpose To provide research training to scientists who are beginning their professional careers and are interested in participating in research training on the causes, treatment, prevention, or cure of diabetes or its complications.

Eligibility This program is open to postdoctorates who are interested in a career in Type 1 diabetes-relevant research. Applicants must have received their first doctoral (M.D., Ph.D., D.M.D., or D.V.M.) degree within the past 5 years and should not have a faculty appointment. There are no citizenship requirements. Applications are encouraged from women and members of minority groups underrepresented in the sciences. The proposed research training may be conducted at foreign and domestic, for-profit and nonprofit, and public and private institutions, including universities, colleges, hospitals, laboratories, units of state and local government, and eligible agencies of the federal government. Applicants must be sponsored by an investigator who is affiliated full time with an accredited institution and who agrees to supervise the applicant's training. Selection is based on the applicant's ability and potential for a research career, the caliber of the proposed research, and the quality of the training to be provided.

Financial data Stipends range from $28,260 to $40,560 (depending upon years of experience). In any case, the award may not exceed the salary the recipient is currently earning. Fellows also receive a research allowance of $5,000.

Duration 1 year; may be renewed for up to 1 additional year. Fellows must devote at least 80% of their effort to the fellowship project.

Deadline January or August of each year.

[959]
POSTDOCTORAL FELLOWSHIPS IN THE NEUROSCIENCES

American Psychological Association
Attn: Minority Fellowship Program
750 First Street, N.E.
Washington, DC 20002-4242
(202) 336-6027
TDD: (202) 336-6123
Fax: (202) 336-6012
E-mail: mfp@apa.org
Web: www.apa.org/mfp

Purpose To provide funding to minority postdoctorates who are interested in pursuing research training in neuroscience.

Eligibility This program is open to all U.S. citizens and permanent residents who hold a Ph.D. or M.D. degree and prior graduate training in neuroscience or in other basic sciences (e.g. cell or molecular biology or immunology). The program, however, is designed to increase representation of African American, Alaskan Native, Hispanic/Latino, American Indian, Pacific Islander, and Asian American students within neuroscience. Applicants must be interested in pursuing a program of postdoctoral research training in behavioral neuroscience, cellular neurobiology, cognitive neuroscience, computational neuroscience, developmental neurobiology, membrane biophysics, molecular neurobiology, neuroanatomy, neurobiology of aging, neurobiology of disease, neurochemistry, neurogenetics, neuroimmunology, neuropathology, neuropharmacology, neurophysiology, neurotoxicology, or systems neuroscience. Selection is based on scholarship, research experience and potential, a research proposal, the suitability of the proposed laboratory and mentor, commitment to a research career in neuroscience, writing ability, and appropriateness to program goal.

Financial data The stipend depends on the number of years of research experience and is equivalent to the standard postdoctoral stipend level of the National Institutes of Health. The fellowship also provides travel funds to visit universities being considered for postdoctoral training, travel funds to attend the annual meeting of the Society for Neuroscience, and participation in the Summer Program in Neuroscience, Ethics, and Survival (SPINES) at the Marine Biological Laboratory in Woods Hole, Massachusetts.

Duration 1 year; may be renewed for up to 1 additional year.

Additional information The program was established in 1987. It is funded by the U.S. National Institute of Mental Health of the National Institutes of Health and administered by the American Psychological Association.

Number awarded 1 or more each year.

Deadline January of each year.

[960]
POSTDOCTORAL FELLOWSHIPS OF THE MINORITY SCHOLAR-IN-RESIDENCE PROGRAM

Consortium for a Strong Minority Presence at Liberal Arts Colleges
c/o Administrative Assistant, President's Office
Grinnell College
1121 Park Street
Grinnell, IA 50112-1690
(515) 269-3000
E-mail: Cousins@grinnell.edu
Web: www.grinnell.edu/dean/csmp/csmpindex.html

Purpose To make available the facilities of liberal arts colleges to minority scholars who recently received their doctoral/advanced degree.

Eligibility This program is open to African American, Asian American, Hispanic American, and Native American scholars in the liberal arts and engineering who received the Ph.D. or M.F.A. degree within the past 5 years. Applicants must be interested in a residency at a participating institution that is part of the Consortium for a Strong Minority Presence at Liberal Arts Colleges.

Financial data Fellows receive a stipend equivalent to the average salary paid by the host college to beginning assistant professors. Modest funds are made available to finance the fellow's proposed research, subject to the usual institutional procedures.

Duration 1 year.

Additional information The following schools are participating in the program: Bowdoin College, Bryn Mawr College, Carleton College, Coe College, Colorado College, DePauw University, Gettysburg College, Grinnell College, Hamilton College, Haverford College, Juniata College, Luther College, Macalester College, Mount Holyoke College, Oberlin College, Occidental College, Pomona College, Rhodes College, Southwestern University, Swarthmore College, Union College, University of the South, Vassar College, Wellesley College, and Wheaton College. Fellows are expected to teach at least 1 course in each academic term of residency, participate in departmental seminars, and interact with students.

Number awarded Varies each year.

Deadline November of each year.

[961]
POSTDOCTORAL RESEARCH FELLOWSHIPS IN BIOLOGICAL INFORMATICS

National Science Foundation
Directorate for Biological Sciences
Attn: Division of Biological Infrastructure
4201 Wilson Boulevard, Room 615
Arlington, VA 22230
(703) 292-8470   TDD: (703) 292-5090
E-mail: ckimsey@nsf.gov
Web: www.nsf.gov/bio

Purpose To provide opportunities for junior doctoral-level scientists to conduct research and acquire training either in the United States or abroad in biological fields that overlap with the informational, computational, mathematical, and statistical sciences.

Eligibility This program is open to persons who are citizens, nationals, or permanent residents of the United States at the time of application. Applicants must have earned a Ph.D. no earlier than 2 years preceding the deadline date and have not been a principal investigator or co-principal investigator on a federal research grant of more than $20,000. Applicants must be proposing a research and training plan in biological informatics at an appropriate nonprofit U.S. or foreign host institution (colleges and universities, government and national laboratories and facilities, and privately-sponsored nonprofit institutes and museums). Preference is given to applicants who choose foreign locations or those moving to new institutions and research environments with which they have not had prior affiliation. The fellowship may not be held at the same institution as where the doctorate was earned. Applications are strongly encouraged from women, minorities, and persons with disabilities.

Financial data The grant is $50,000 per year; that includes an annual stipend of $36,000; a research allowance of $9,000 per year paid to the fellow for materials and supplies, subscription fees, and recovery costs for databases, travel, and publication expenses; and an institutional allowance of $5,000 per year for fringe benefits and expenses incurred in support of the fellow.

Duration 2 years; may be renewed for 1 additional year at a U.S. institution if the first 2 years are at a foreign institution.

Number awarded Approximately 20 each year.

Deadline November of each year.

[962]
POSTDOCTORAL RESEARCH FELLOWSHIPS IN MICROBIAL BIOLOGY

National Science Foundation
Directorate for Biological Sciences
Attn: Division of Biological Infrastructure
4201 Wilson Boulevard, Room 615
Arlington, VA 22230
(703) 292-8470   TDD: (703) 292-5090
E-mail: ckimsey@nsf.gov
Web: www.nsf.gov/bio

Purpose To provide opportunities for junior doctoral-level scientists to conduct research and acquire training either in the United States or abroad in microbial biology.

Eligibility This program is open to persons who are citizens, nationals, or permanent residents of the United States at the time of application. Applicants must have earned a Ph.D. no earlier than 18 months preceding the deadline date and have not received a federal research grant previously. They must be proposing a research and training plan in microbial biology (including systematics, ecology, physiology, biochemistry, and genetics) at an appropriate nonprofit U.S. or foreign host institution (colleges and universities, government and national laboratories and facilities, and privately-sponsored nonprofit institutes and museums). Preference is given to applicants who choose foreign locations or those moving to new institutions and research environments with which they have not had prior affiliation. The fellowship may not be held at the same institution as where the doctorate was earned. Applications are strongly encouraged from women, minorities, and persons with disabilities.

Financial data The grant is $50,000 per year; that includes an annual stipend of $36,000; a research allowance of $9,000 per year paid to the fellow for materials and supplies, subscription fees, and recovery costs for databases, travel, and publication expenses; and an institutional allowance of $5,000 per year for fringe benefits and expenses incurred in support of the fellow.

Duration 2 or 3 years. Fellows are encouraged to spend at least part of that time at a foreign host institution.

Number awarded 20 each year. Approximately $2 million is available for this program each year.

Deadline September of each year.

[963]
POSTDOCTORAL SCIENTIST PROGRAM AT THE INTERNATIONAL RESEARCH INSTITUTE FOR CLIMATE PREDICTION

University Corporation for Atmospheric Research
Attn: Visiting Scientist Programs
3300 Mitchell Lane, Suite 2200
P.O. Box 3000
Boulder, CO 80307-3000
(303) 497-8649   Fax: (303) 497-8668
E-mail: vsp@ucar.edu
Web: www.vsp.ucar.edu

Purpose To provide funding to recent postdoctorates who wish to conduct research at the International Research Institute for Climate Prediction (IRI) in Palisades, New York.

Eligibility This program is open to postdoctorates (preferably those who received their Ph.D. within the preceding 5 years) who wish to conduct research with experienced scientists at the IRI on the campus of the Lamont-Doherty Earth Observatory. Applicants must be proposing to conduct research related to the program of the IRI that 1) develops global climate forecasts of temperature and rainfall variations; 2) assesses the regional consequences of those variations; and 3) applies that information to support practical decision making in critical sectors impacted by climate fluctuations, such as emergency preparedness, public health and safety, energy, fisheries, agriculture, and water resources. Applications are especially encouraged from women and minorities.

Financial data Fellows receive a fixed annual salary. Benefits include health and dental insurance, sick and annual leave, paid holidays, participation in a retirement fund, and life insurance. Allowances are provided for relocation, scientific travel, and other support costs.

Duration 2 years.

Additional information This program is administered by the Lamont-Doherty Earth Observatory of Columbia University with funding provided by the Office of Global Programs of the National Oceanic and Atmospheric Administration (NOAA).

Number awarded Approximately 4 each year.

Deadline January of each year.

[964]
PRE-DOCTORAL RESEARCH TRAINING FELLOWSHIPS IN EPILEPSY

Epilepsy Foundation
Attn: Department of Research and Professional Education
4351 Garden City Drive
Landover, MD 20785-7223
(301) 459-3700   (800) EFA-1000
Fax: (301) 577-2684   TDD: (800) 332-2070
E-mail: grants@efa.org
Web: www.epilepsyfoundation.org/research/grants.html

Purpose To provide funding to doctoral candidates in designated fields for dissertation research on a topic related to epilepsy.

Eligibility This program is open to graduate students pursuing a Ph.D. in biochemistry, genetics, neuroscience, nursing, pharmacology, pharmacy, physiology, or psychology. Applicants must be conducting dissertation research on a topic relevant to epilepsy under the guidance of a mentor with expertise in the area of epilepsy investigation. Applications from women, members of minority groups, and people with disabilities are especially encouraged. Selection is based on the relevance of the proposed work to epilepsy, the applicant's qualifications, the mentor's qualifications, the scientific quality of the proposed dissertation research, the quality of the training environment for research related to epilepsy, and the adequacy of the facility.

Financial data The grant is $16,000, consisting of $15,000 for a stipend and $1,000 to support travel to attend the annual meeting of the American Epilepsy Society.

Duration 1 year.

Additional information This program began in 1998.

Number awarded Varies each year, depending on the availability of funds.

Deadline September of each year.

[965]
PROGRAM FOR MINORITY RESEARCH TRAINING IN PSYCHIATRY

American Psychiatric Association
Attn: American Psychiatric Institute for Research and
   Education
1400 K Street, N.W.
Washington, DC 20005
(202) 682-6225   (800) 852-1390
Fax: (202) 682-6850   E-mail: eguerra@psych.org
Web: www.psych.org/res_res/pmrtp5302.cfm

Purpose To provide financial assistance to underrepresented minority medical students and residents interested in psychiatric research training.

Eligibility This program is open to underrepresented minorities (American Indians, Blacks/African Americans, Hispanics, and Pacific Islanders) at 3 levels: medical students, residents, and graduates of residency programs. All candidates must be interested in training at research-intensive departments of psychiatry in major U.S. medical schools. Training sites with excellence as demonstrated by research facilities and resources, funded research, research faculty (including minority researchers), and successful training history are preferred.

Financial data Annual stipends are $18,156 for medical students, from $42,648 to $44,616 for residents, and up to $48,852 for post-residency fellows. Other benefits include travel funds to attend the annual meeting of the American Psychiatric Association (APA) or the American College of Neuropsychopharmacology and limited tuition assistance for full-time trainees to attend specific courses that are required as part of their training.

Duration For medical students and residents, 2 months to 1 year. For post-residency fellows, generally 2 years, although a third year is possible if appropriate to a trainee's career development.

Additional information This program is funded by the National Institute of Mental Health and administered by the APA's American Psychiatric Institute for Research and Education.

Number awarded Varies each year.

Deadline Medical students and residents seeking less than 1 year of training may apply at any time, but applications must be received at least 3 months before the proposed training is to begin; medical students seeking summer training should apply by March of each year; residents seeking a year or more of training and post-residency fellows should apply by November of each year.

[966]
PROGRAM ON THE ARTS DISSERTATION FELLOWSHIPS

Social Science Research Council
810 Seventh Avenue
New York, NY 10019
(212) 377-2700   Fax: (212) 377-2727
E-mail: arts@ssrc.org
Web: www.ssrc.org

Purpose To provide financial support for dissertation research on the social dimension of art.

Eligibility This program is open to full-time students in the social sciences and other relevant fields who are enrolled in doctoral programs in the United States. There are no citizenship requirements or limitations on where the research is conducted. Applications from women and persons of color are especially encouraged. Applicants must have completed all requirements for the Ph.D. except their dissertation research. The proposed research should deal with the social dimension of art in relation to a number of key issues, including globalization, multiculturalism, and new technologies. The program encourages projects that explore diverse aspects of the artistic experience, including its production, distribution, and consumption, as well as projects that address the construction of artistic "value" and the place of art in contemporary society. Preference is given to proposals that show promise of strengthening social science research in the arts. All applicants should have a strong record of achievement in their respective disciplines and show evidence of a thorough knowledge of the major concepts and methods appropriate to their research. The rationale, feasibility, theoretical concerns, and contribution of the project to existing knowledge should be clearly presented.

Financial data The stipend is $16,500.

Duration 9 to 12 months.

Additional information Funding for this program is provided by the Rockefeller Foundation.

Number awarded Up to 14 each year.

Deadline February of each year.

[967]
PROGRAM ON THE CORPORATION AS A SOCIAL INSTITUTION GRANTS

Social Science Research Council
810 Seventh Avenue
New York, NY 10019
(212) 377-2700　　　　　　　　　Fax: (212) 377-2727
E-mail: corporation@ssrc.org
Web: www.ssrc.org

Purpose To support graduate students interested in participating in a program that is part of a larger initiative on the study of business institutions in society.

Eligibility This program is open to graduate students in sociology, economics, law, and business. Applicants should be interested in participating in a series of workshops and conferences that bring graduate students together with scholars working on an initiative to develop a stronger, conceptually richer and potentially more interdisciplinary approach to the study of the nature of firms and other business institutions. Specific themes that are of interest to the initiative include, but are not limited to: What role does power play within corporations and for corporations in society? To what extent do institutional culture and cultural environments play a role in organization structure and action? To what extent do conceptions of the corporation vary within and across organizations, across societies, and across time? What role do social networks play in business relations and negotiations? How are the internal structures of the firm shaped by the social relations within and outside the firm? How do political interventions and laws shape corporate behavior? What does law mean for corporations and other types of organizations? Doctoral students who have been advanced to candidacy and are interested in those types of questions are invited to apply to participate in the workshops. A selected number of workshop participants will receive additional funding for their dissertation research. There are no citizenship or nationality restrictions for this program. Women and members of minority groups are encouraged to apply.

Financial data Funding of up to $10,000 is available for dissertation research.

Duration Workshops are held 4 times over the course of 2 years.

Additional information Funding for this program is provided by the Alfred P. Sloan Foundation. Workshops take place at the Center for Culture, Organizations, and Politics at the Institute for Industrial Relations of the University of California at Berkeley.

Number awarded A limited number of dissertation support grants are awarded each year.

Deadline January of each year.

[968]
PSYCHIATRIC CLINICAL TRAINING PROGRAM FOR MINORITY NURSES

American Nurses Association
Attn: Ethnic/Racial Minority Fellowship Programs
600 Maryland Avenue, S.W., Suite 100 West
Washington, DC 20024-2571
(202) 651-7245　　　　　　　　　Fax: (202) 651-7007
E-mail: cporter@ana.org
Web: www.nursingworld.org

Purpose To provide financial assistance to minority nurses preparing for careers as psychiatric/mental health nurses who serve a minority population.

Eligibility Applications are accepted from registered nurses who 1) are members of an ethnic or racial minority group, including but not limited to African Americans, Hispanics, American Indians, Asian Americans, and Pacific Islanders; 2) U.S. citizens or permanent residents; 3) members of the American Nurses Association (ANA); 4) holders of master's degrees; and 5) able to demonstrate a commitment to a research career related to ethnic/racial, underserved, and underrepresented minority populations. The proposed research training must relate to the clinical practice of psychiatric/mental health nursing and mental health service delivery to ethnic/minority communities.

Financial data The maximum stipend is $11,748 per year.

Duration Up to 3 years.

Additional information Funds for this program are provided by the Substance Abuse and Mental Health Services Administration.

Deadline January of each year.

[969]
R. ROBERT & SALLY D. FUNDERBURG RESEARCH SCHOLAR AWARD IN GASTRIC BIOLOGY RELATED TO CANCER

Foundation for Digestive Health and Nutrition
Attn: Research Awards Coordinator
7910 Woodmont Avenue, Suite 700
Bethesda, MD 20814-3015
(301) 222-4005　　　　　　　　　Fax: (301) 222-4010
E-mail: info@fdhn.org
Web: www.fdhn.org

Purpose To provide funding to established investigators who are working on research that enhances fundamental understanding of gastric cancer pathobiology.

Eligibility This program is open to faculty at accredited North American institutions who have established themselves as independent investigators in the field of gastric biology, pursuing novel approaches to gastric mucosal cell biology, regeneration and regulation of cell growth, inflammation as precancerous lesions, genetics of gastric carcinoma, oncogenes in gastric epithelial malignancies, epidemiology of gastric cancer, etiology of gastric epithelial malignancies, or clinical research in diagnosis or treatment of gastric carcinoma. Applicants must be individual members of the American Gastroenterological Association (AGA). Women and minority investigators are strongly encouraged to apply. Selection is based on the feasibility and significance of the proposal; attributes of the candidate; and the likelihood that support will lead the applicant toward a research career in the field of gastric cancer biology. Preference is given to novel approaches, especially for initiation of projects by young investigators or established investigators new to the field.

Financial data The award is $25,000 per year. Funds are to be used for the salary of the investigator. Indirect costs are not allowed.

Duration 2 years.

Additional information This program is administered by the Foundation for Digestive Health and Nutrition (FDHN) and sponsored by the AGA.

Number awarded 1 each year.

Deadline September of each year.

[970]
RAND GRADUATE STUDENT SUMMER ASSOCIATE PROGRAM

RAND
Attn: Director, Graduate Student Summer Associate Program
1700 Main Street
P.O. Box 2138
Santa Monica, CA 90407-2138
(310) 393-0411, ext. 6546
E-mail: Edward_Keating@rand.org
Web: www.rand.org/edu_op/fellowships/gsap

Purpose To provide graduate students with an opportunity to conduct research at RAND during the summer.

Eligibility This program is open to students who have completed at least 2 years of graduate work leading to a doctorate or professional degree. Applicants must be interested in conducting summer research on topics that RAND is currently investigating. Research at RAND focuses on a wide range of national security problems and domestic and international social policy issues. Most RAND research projects are interdisciplinary. Recently, 62% of RAND's research activity involved national security research (included 10% on strategic geopolitics, 18% on force modernization and employment, 16% on technology application, and 18% on research allocation and management) and 38% involved other domestic and international research (including 16% on health, 6% on education, 5% on labor and population, 3% on technology policy, 3% on civil justice, 2% on criminal justice, and 3% on other areas). Applications are welcomed from qualified women, minorities, and individuals with disabilities.

Financial data A stipend is paid (amount not specified).

Duration 3 months, during the summer.

Additional information Each associate is assigned to a research project and is mentored by a senior research staff member. Students may work in the headquarters office in Santa Monica, California, or in the Washington or Pittsburgh offices, depending on where the research staff members sponsoring them are housed. They have full access to all of RAND's research facilities. Students are required to prepare a paper and to present a seminar at the conclusion of the associateship.

Number awarded Approximately 25 each year.

Deadline January of each year.

[971]
REGINALD F. LEWIS AND CHARLES HAMILTON HOUSTON FELLOWSHIPS FOR LAW TEACHING

Harvard Law School
Attn: Lewis/Houston Committee
Griswold 220
Cambridge, MA 02138
(617) 495-3100
Web: www.law.harvard.edu

Purpose To provide an opportunity for lawyers, especially minorities, to prepare for a career in law school by pursuing a research project at Harvard Law School.

Eligibility This program is open to law graduates who will enhance the diversity of the profession; applications from minority candidates are especially encouraged. Applicants must be interested in preparing for a career as a law professor by conducting a research project in the field in which they expect to teach. They must submit a detailed description (3 to 4 pages) of the project, a statement of their interests in teaching, a statement of the fields in which they expect to teach and pursue research, a resume, a copy of their undergraduate and law school transcripts, and 2 letters of reference.

Financial data The stipend is $25,000 per year.

Duration 1 year.

Additional information The Lewis Fellowship is named for a prominent African American graduate of the Harvard Law School; the Houston Fellowship is named for a distinguished lawyer and teacher who was the first African American to serve on the *Harvard Law Review*. Fellows must prepare a major article for publication during the fellowship period; a schedule of research and work must be established with a faculty supervisor. Although fellows may audit courses, they may not be degree candidates.

Number awarded 2 each year.

Deadline February of each year.

[972]
RESEARCH AND TRAINING PROGRAM ON POVERTY AND PUBLIC POLICY POSTDOCTORAL FELLOWSHIPS

University of Michigan
Gerald R. Ford School of Public Policy
Attn: Program on Poverty and Public Policy
1015 East Huron Street
Ann Arbor, MI 48104-1689
(734) 615-4326   Fax: (734) 615-8047
E-mail: fordschoolinfo@umich.edu
Web: www.fordschool.umich.edu/poverty/fellowship.htm

Purpose To provide funding to minority postdoctorates interested in conducting research and pursuing intensive training on poverty-related public policy issues at the University of Michigan.

Eligibility This program is open to U.S. citizens who are members of a minority group that is underrepresented in the social sciences. Applicants must have received the Ph.D. degree within the past 5 years and be engaged in research on poverty and public policy. Preference is given to proposals that would benefit from resources available at the University of Michigan and from interactions with affiliated faculty.

Financial data The stipend is $44,000 per calendar year.

Duration 1 or 2 years.

Additional information This program is funded by the Ford Foundation. Fellows spend the year participating in a seminar on poverty and public policy and conducting their own research. Topics currently pursued include welfare reform and the well-being of families and children, the effects of economic conditions on minority and majority poverty rates and family well-being, the intergenerational transmission of poverty and welfare dependency, poverty and mental health, minority women in the labor market, adolescent motherhood and teen pregnancy, and qualitative research on barriers to self-sufficiency. Fellows must be in residence at the University of Michigan for the duration of the program.

Deadline January of each year.

[973]
RESEARCH AND WRITING GRANTS COMPETITION IN GLOBAL SECURITY AND SUSTAINABILITY

John D. and Catherine T. MacArthur Foundation
Attn: Program on Global Security and Sustainability
140 South Dearborn Street
Chicago, IL 60603-5285
(312) 726-8000   Fax: (312) 917-0200
TDD: (312) 920-6285   E-mail: 4answers@macfound.org
Web: www.macfound.org

Purpose To provide funding to investigators interested in conducting research on global security and sustainability.

Eligibility This program is open to individual scholars and 2-person teams of any age or citizenship. Applications from women, minorities, non-U.S. citizens, and younger scholars are particularly encouraged. Applicants must be proposing to conduct research on either 1) migration and refugees or 2) technological change and global security and sustainability. For either of those themes, proposals that deal with exclusively U.S.-based topics are not considered, unless the topic has significant international dimensions. Grants may not be used for research or writing of doctoral dissertations. Also ineligible are projects that include requests to hold workshops or conferences; to produce textbooks, manuals, films, works of photojournalism or works of fiction; to edit volumes; or to develop curricular materials. Projects that include development of an Internet site are considered only if the site is in addition to a substantial written product intended for hard-copy publication. Studies that are predominantly technical or clinical in nature are not eligible. Proposals may be for research conducted independently or in an appropriate institutional setting.

Financial data The maximum grant is $75,000 for individuals or $100,000 for 2-person teams.

Duration 18 months or less.

Number awarded 1 or more each year.

Deadline January of each year.

[974]
RESEARCH PLANNING GRANTS FOR MINORITY SCIENTISTS AND ENGINEERS

National Science Foundation
Directorate for Education and Human Resources
Attn: Senior Staff Associate for Cross Directorate Programs
4201 Wilson Boulevard, Room 805
Arlington, VA 22230
(703) 292-8600   TDD: (703) 292-5090
Web: www.nsf.gov

Purpose To enable minority scientists to conduct preliminary studies and other activities to facilitate the development of more competitive National Science Foundation (NSF) research proposals.

Eligibility This program is open to members of certain ethnic groups (African Americans, Native Americans, Hispanics, Alaskan Natives, and Native Pacific Islanders) who are U.S. citizens or nationals; hold faculty or research-related positions in U.S. colleges, universities, or other nonprofit institutions; and have not previously served as principal investigators on independent federal awards for scientific or engineering research. Tenure or tenure-track status is not an eligibility factor. A co-investigator is not appropriate for this program, although use of senior researchers is encouraged.

Financial data Grants up to $18,000 are available.

Duration Up to 18 months; not renewable.

Additional information This program is offered through the various disciplinary divisions of the National Science Foundation (NSF); for the telephone numbers of the participating divisions, contact the sponsor. Recipients are expected to submit a research proposal to the NSF regular research program after completion of the planning grant.

Deadline Each of the participating NSF disciplinary divisions sets its own deadline.

[975]
RESEARCH TRAINING FELLOWSHIPS IN EPILEPSY

Epilepsy Foundation
Attn: Department of Research and Professional Education
4351 Garden City Drive
Landover, MD 20785-7223
(301) 459-3700   (800) EFA-1000
Fax: (301) 577-2684   TDD: (800) 332-2070
E-mail: grants@efa.org
Web: www.epilepsyfoundation.org/research/grants.html

Purpose To offer qualified individuals the opportunity to develop expertise in epilepsy research through training and involvement in an epilepsy research project.

Eligibility Applicants must hold a doctoral degree and be a resident or postdoctoral fellow at a university, medical school, research institution, or medical center. They must be interested in participating in a training experience and research project that has potential significance for understanding the causes, treatment, or consequences of epilepsy. The program is geared toward applicants who will be trained in research in epilepsy rather than those who use epilepsy as a tool for research in other fields. Equal consideration is given to applicants interested in acquiring experience either in basic laboratory research or in the conduct of human clinical studies. Academic faculty holding the rank of instructor or higher are not eligible, nor are graduate or medical students, medical residents, permanent government employees, or employees of private industry. Applications from women, members of minority groups, and people with disabilities are especially encouraged. Because these fellowships are designed as training opportunities, the quality of the training plans and environment are considered in the selection process. Other selection criteria include the scientific quality of the proposed research, relevance of the research to epilepsy, the applicant's qualifications, and the mentor's qualifications.

Financial data The grant is $40,000.

Duration 1 year. The fellowship must be carried out at a facility where there is an ongoing epilepsy research program in the United States.

Number awarded Varies each year.

Deadline September of each year.

[976]
RHODE ISLAND SPACE GRANT GRADUATE FELLOWSHIP PROGRAM

Rhode Island Space Grant
c/o Brown University
Lincoln Field Building
Box 1846
Providence, RI 02912-1846
(401) 863-2889   Fax: (401) 863-1292
E-mail: RISpaceGrant@brown.edu
Web: www.planetary.brown.edu/RI_Space_Grant

Purpose To provide financial assistance to graduate students at institutions that are members of the Rhode Island Space Grant Consortium (RISGC) who wish to pursue studies and space-related research in science, mathematics, or engineering.

Eligibility This program is open to graduate students at RISGC-member universities. Applicants must be studying in science, mathematics, or engineering fields of interest to the National Aeronautics and Space Administration (NASA). U.S. citizenship is required. The sponsor is a component of NASA's Space Grant program, which encourages participation by women, underrepresented minorities, and persons with disabilities.

Financial data A stipend is provided (amount not specified).

Duration 1 year.

Additional information Members of the RISGC are Bryant College, Community College of Rhode Island, Providence College, Roger Williams University, Rhode Island College, Rhode Island School of Design, Salve Regina University, University of Rhode Island, and Wheaton College. This program is funded by NASA. Fellows are required to devote 75% of their time to their studies and research and 25% of their time to science education outreach activities organized and coordinated by Rhode Island Space Grant.

Number awarded Varies each year; recently, 4 of these fellowships were awarded.

[977]
RHODE ISLAND SPACE GRANT UNDERGRADUATE SUMMER SCHOLAR PROGRAM

Rhode Island Space Grant
c/o Brown University
Lincoln Field Building
Box 1846
Providence, RI 02912-1846
(401) 863-2889   Fax: (401) 863-1292
E-mail: RISpaceGrant@brown.edu
Web: www.planetary.brown.edu/RI_Space_Grant

Purpose To provide funding for summer research activities to undergraduate students at institutions that are members of the Rhode Island Space Grant Consortium (RISGC) who are interested in a career in a space-related field of science, mathematics, or engineering.

Eligibility This program is open to undergraduate students at RISGC-member universities. Applicants must be studying in science, mathematics, or engineering fields of interest to the National Aeronautics and Space Administration (NASA). They must be interested in participating in a research project during the summer with an advisor in their own department. U.S. citizenship is required. The sponsor is a component of NASA's Space Grant program, which encourages participation by women, underrepresented minorities, and persons with disabilities.

Financial data A research stipend is provided (amount not specified).

Duration 1 summer.

Additional information Members of the RISGC are Bryant College, Community College of Rhode Island, Providence College, Roger Williams University, Rhode Island College, Rhode Island School of Design, Salve Regina University, University of Rhode Island, and Wheaton College. This program is funded by NASA. Scholars are required to devote 75% of their time to their research and 25% of their time to science education outreach activities organized and coordinated by Rhode Island Space Grant.

Number awarded Varies each year; recently, 8 of these scholarships were awarded.

[978]
RISK POLICY FELLOWSHIPS

American Association for the Advancement of Science
Attn: Science and Technology Policy Fellowship Programs
1200 New York Avenue, N.W.
Washington, DC 20005-3920
(202) 326-6700   Fax: (202) 289-4950
E-mail: science_policy@aaas.org
Web: fellowships.aaas.org/risk/index.html

Purpose To provide postdoctoral and mid-career scientists and engineers with an opportunity to offer scientific and technical input on issues of human health, economic, and environmental aspects of risk assessment or risk management.

Eligibility Applicants must have a Ph.D. or equivalent doctoral degree in a physical, biological, or social science, any field of engineering, or any relevant interdisciplinary field; holders of a D.V.M., M.D., or Ph.D. in the natural sciences or economics are especially encouraged to apply. Applicants with a master's degree in engineering and at least 3 years of post-degree professional experience are eligible. Candidates must demonstrate exceptional competence in some area of science or engineering and an interest in applying their expertise to the economic and technical assessment of problems related to human health or the environment. U.S. citizenship is required; federal employees are not eligible. Underrepresented minorities and persons with disabilities are especially encouraged to apply.

Financial data The stipend is $55,000, plus allowances for health insurance, relocation, and professional travel.

Duration 1 year, beginning in September.

Additional information Fellows provide scientific and technical input on issues relating to human health, economic, and environmental aspects of risk assessment or risk management in areas of relevance to the U.S. Food and Drug Administration (FDA), the U.S. Department of Agriculture (USDA), or the Joint Institute for Food Safety Research (JIFSR). Fellows working with the FDA are assigned to its Center for Food Safety and Applied Nutrition, which focuses on risk assessment to ensure that balanced scientific conclusions are drawn regarding adverse human health effects resulting from exposure to foodborne chemical and microbiological hazards. Fellows assigned to USDA work in the Office of Risk Assessment and Cost-Benefit Analysis or the Food Safety and Inspection Service; assignments involve providing additional scientific and technical input on food safety, environmental human health, and economic issues relating to risk assessment. The JIFSR, supported by the Departments of Agriculture and Health and Human Services, coordinates information management and decision processes across federal food safety agencies engaged in food safety research.

Number awarded Up to 5 each year.

Deadline January of each year.

[979]
ROBERT D. WATKINS MINORITY GRADUATE FELLOWSHIP

American Society for Microbiology
Attn: Education Board
1752 N Street, N.W.
Washington, DC 20036-2904
(202) 942-9283   Fax: (202) 942-9329
E-mail: fellowships-careerinformation@asmusa.org
Web: www.asmusa.org/edusrc/edu23c.htm

Purpose To provide funding for research in microbiology to underrepresented minority doctoral students who are members of the American Society for Microbiology (ASM).

Eligibility This program is open to African Americans, Hispanic Americans, Native Americans, Alaskan Native Americans, and Native Pacific Islanders enrolled as full-time graduate students who have completed their first year of doctoral study and who are members of the society. Applicants must propose a joint research plan in collaboration with a society member scientist. They must have completed all graduate course work requirements for the doctoral degree by the date of the activation of the fellowship. U.S. citizenship or permanent resident status is required. Selection is based on academic achievement, evidence of a successful research plan developed in collaboration with a research advisor/mentor, and relevant career goals in the microbiological sciences.

Financial data Students receive $15,000 per year as a stipend; funds may not be used for tuition or fees.

Duration 3 years.

Number awarded Varies each year.

Deadline April of each year.

[980]
ROBERT M. COVER FELLOWSHIP IN PUBLIC INTEREST LAW

Jerome N. Frank Legal Services Organization
Attn: Office Manager
Yale Law School
133 Wall Street
P.O. Box 209090
New Haven, CT 06520-9090
(203) 432-1334   Fax: (203) 432-1426
E-mail: kathryn.stoddard@yale.edu

Purpose To offer postgraduate fellowships at Yale Law School to experienced attorneys interested in teaching clinical law.

Eligibility This program is open to lawyers with at least 4 years of practice (or equivalent experience) who are interested in a long-term career as a law school clinical teacher. Candidates must be able to work both independently and as part of a team, and they must possess strong written and oral communication skills. Spanish-speaking applicants are preferred. Yale University is an affirmative action, equal opportunity employer.

Financial data The stipend is $37,000 per year, plus health benefits and access to university facilities.

Duration 2 years.

Additional information This fellowship was established in 1992 with a grant from Legal Services Corporation; initially, the program provided for 1-year internships for recent law school graduates and focused on offering legal services to people infected with HIV. The fellowship provides time for research and writing as well as representing clients, community outreach, training and classes, and supervising students. Fellows are encouraged to audit courses within the academic curriculum.

Number awarded 1 or more each year.

Deadline December of each year.

[981]
ROBERT R. MCCORMICK TRIBUNE MINORITY FELLOWSHIP IN URBAN JOURNALISM AT THE CHICAGO REPORTER

Chicago Reporter
Attn: Editor and Publisher
332 South Michigan Avenue, Suite 500
Chicago, IL 60604
(312) 427-4830   Fax: (312) 427-6130
Web: www.chicagoreporter.com

Purpose To provide opportunities for minority journalists to work on projects at the *Chicago Reporter.*

Eligibility Experienced minority journalists with a baccalaureate degree and at least 3 years of print reporting experience are eligible to apply for this fellowship at the *Chicago Reporter.* Fluency in Spanish is a plus. Interested candidates must submit a resume and 5 clips.

Financial data The position pays a competitive salary and benefits.

Duration 1 year.

Additional information Fellows work at the *Chicago Reporter,* a monthly newspaper known for its coverage of the role minorities play in newspapers. Recipients may take courses at Northwestern University's Medill School of Journalism.

Number awarded 1 each year.

Deadline June of each year.

[982]
ROCKEFELLER FOUNDATION HUMANITIES FELLOWSHIPS

Rockefeller Foundation
420 Fifth Avenue
New York, NY 10018-2702
(212) 852-8486   Fax: (212) 852-8436
Web: www.rockfound.org

Purpose To provide funding to scholars and writers who wish to conduct research at designated humanities-oriented institutions.

Eligibility This program is open to scholars in the humanities who wish to conduct research at 29 designated host institutions (primarily minority and women related) that focus on transnational issues, non-Western cultures, and the diverse cultural heritage of the United States. Host institutions, each of which is usually funded for a 3-year period, include academic departments, interdisciplinary programs, museums, research libraries, and community cultural centers. Scholars submit applications directly to the institutions; for a list of current programs, contact the Rockefeller Foundation.

Financial data The amounts of the stipends and other terms of the award are established by the host institutions. Generally, fellowships provide a stipend of $35,000 and an allowance of $2,000 for travel, benefits, and relocation costs.

Duration Most fellowships are for 8 to 10 months.

Additional information The current host institutions include the CUNY Dominican Studies Institute at the Graduate School and University Center of the City College of the City University of New York; the Center for Black Music Research at Columbia College in Chicago; the Program for the Study of Sexuality, Gender, Health and Human Rights at the Columbia University School of Public Health; the Guadalupe Cultural Arts Center in San Antonio, Texas; the Center for Lesbian and Gay Studies at the Graduate School and University Center of the City College of the City University of New York; the African Humanities Institute at Harvard University; the Instituto de Estudos Religiao in Rio de Janeiro, Brazil; the Native Philosophy Project at Lakehead University, Canada; the Center for the Study of Ethnicity and Gender in Appalachia at Marshall University; the Inter University Program for Latino Research and the Smithsonian Institution; the Indigenous Research Center of the Americas at the University of California at Davis; the Institute for the Study of Gender in Africa at the University of California at Los Angeles; the Womanist Studies Consortium at the University of Georgia; and the Project for Critical Asian Studies at the University of Washington.

Number awarded Varies; usually each participating institution is authorized to award 2 grants per year.

[983]
ROCKY MOUNTAIN NASA SPACE GRANT CONSORTIUM GRADUATE RESEARCH FELLOWSHIPS

Rocky Mountain NASA Space Grant Consortium
c/o Utah State University
EL Building, Room 302
Logan, UT 84322-4140
(435) 797-4042   Fax: (435) 797-4044
E-mail: rmc@sdl.usu.edu
Web: www.rmc.sdl.usu.edu

Purpose To provide financial support for research and study to graduate students at designated universities in Utah or Colorado who are working on a degree in fields of interest to the National Aeronautics and Space Administration (NASA).

Eligibility This program is open to graduate students at member institutions of the Rocky Mountain NASA Space Grant Consortium who are studying engineering, science, medicine, or technology. U.S. citizenship is required. Selection is based on academic performance to date and potential for the future, with emphasis on space-related research interests. This program is part of the NASA Space Grant program, which encourages participation by women, underrepresented minorities, and persons with disabilities.

Financial data The amount of the awards depends on the availability of funds.

Additional information Members of the consortium are Utah State University, the University of Utah, Brigham Young University, and the University of Denver. This program is funded by NASA.

Number awarded Varies each year.

[984]
ROGER REVELLE FELLOWSHIP IN GLOBAL STEWARDSHIP

American Association for the Advancement of Science
Attn: Science and Technology Policy Fellowship Programs
1200 New York Avenue, N.W.
Washington, DC 20005-3920
(202) 326-6700   Fax: (202) 289-4950
E-mail: science_policy@aaas.org
Web: fellowships.aaas.org/revelle/index.html

Purpose To provide postdoctoral and mid-career scientists and engineers with an opportunity to work in the Washington, D.C. policy community on domestic or international environmental issues.

Eligibility Prospective fellows must have a Ph.D. or equivalent doctoral level degree and at least 3 years of post-degree experience; persons with a master's degree in engineering and at least 6 years of post-degree experience are also eligible. Candidates must be interested in an assignment in the Washington, D.C. policy community; demonstrate exceptional competence in some area of science or engineering; have a good scientific and technical background; be cognizant of many matters in nonscientific areas; demonstrate sensitivity toward political and social issues; and have a strong interest and some experience applying personal knowledge toward the solution of societal problems. They must be interested in a program that focuses on human interaction with ecosystems, including population, sustainable development, food, oceans, global climate change, and related environmental concerns. U.S. citizenship is required; federal employees are not eligible. Underrepresented minorities and persons with disabilities are especially encouraged to apply.

Financial data The stipend is $55,000, plus allowances for health insurance, relocation, and professional travel.

Duration 1 year, beginning in September.

Additional information Fellows work in Congress, an executive branch agency, or a non-governmental organization within the environmental policy community. The program includes an orientation on executive branch and congressional operations.

Number awarded 1 each year.

Deadline January of each year.

[985]
RUI FACULTY RESEARCH PROJECTS

National Science Foundation
Directorate for Education and Human Resources
Attn: Senior Staff Associate for Cross Directorate Programs
4201 Wilson Boulevard, Room 805
Arlington, VA 22230
(703) 292-8600   TDD: (703) 292-5090
Web: www.ehr.nsf.gov/crssprgm/rui/start.shtm

Purpose To provide support to faculty at predominantly undergraduate institutions who are interested in conducting science or engineering research.

Eligibility This program is open to faculty members in all fields of science and engineering supported by the National Science Foundation (NSF) who are teaching at predominantly undergraduate institutions, defined as U.S. 2-year, 4-year, masters-level, and small doctoral colleges and universities that 1) grant baccalaureate degrees in NSF-supported fields or provide programs of instruction for students pursuing such degrees after transferring; 2) have undergraduate enrollment exceeding graduate enrollment; and 3) award no more than an average of 10 Ph.D. and/or

D.Sc. degrees per year in all disciplines that NSF supports. Applicants must be teaching in a department that offers courses that qualify for bachelor's degree credit in NSF-supportable fields and may offer master's degrees but may not award a doctorate or offer doctoral courses and supervise doctoral research. Proposals may be for research at the home institution (including work in the field) and/or away from the home institution at a research university or a government or industrial laboratory. Applications are especially encouraged from women, minorities, and persons with disabilities.

Financial data Awards range from $10,000 to more than $100,000. Funding may cover salaries and wages, research assistantships (focused upon undergraduate students), fringe benefits, travel, materials and supplies, publication costs and page charges, consultant services, equipment needed for individual research projects with a single research focus, field work, research at other institutions, and indirect costs.

Duration 1 to 3 years.

Additional information This program is part of the NSF Research in Undergraduate Institutions (RUI) program; it is operated by various disciplinary divisions within the NSF; for a list of the participating divisions and their telephone numbers, contact the Senior Staff Associate for Cross Directorate Programs.

Deadline Deadlines are established by the respective participating NSF disciplinary divisions.

[986]
RUI RESEARCH INSTRUMENTATION GRANTS

National Science Foundation
Directorate for Education and Human Resources
Attn: Senior Staff Associate for Cross Directorate Programs
4201 Wilson Boulevard, Room 805
Arlington, VA 22230
(703) 292-8600   TDD: (703) 292-5090
Web: www.ehr.nsf.gov/crssprgm/rui/start.shtm

Purpose To provide funding for the acquisition of research equipment to multi-investigator/user teams at predominantly undergraduate institutions.

Eligibility This program is open to teams of 2 or more co-investigators who are faculty members in all fields of science and engineering supported by the National Science Foundation (NSF) teaching at predominantly undergraduate institutions, defined as U.S. 2-year, 4-year, masters-level, and small doctoral colleges and universities that 1) grant baccalaureate degrees in NSF-supported fields or provide programs of instruction for students pursuing such degrees after transferring; 2) have undergraduate enrollment exceeding graduate enrollment; and 3) award no more than an average of 10 Ph.D. and/or D.Sc. degrees per year in all disciplines that NSF supports. Applicants must be teaching in a department that offers courses that qualify for bachelor's degree credit in NSF-supportable fields and may offer master's degrees but may not award a doctorate or offer doctoral courses and supervise doctoral research. Proposals may be for 1) purchasing or upgrading instrumentation or equipment needed for conducting the proposed faculty research, or 2) developing new instrumentation that will extend current capability in terms of sensitivity or resolution, or that will provide new or alternative techniques for detection and observation. Requests may be for single items or multi-component systems. Applications are especially encouraged from women, minorities, and persons with disabilities.

Financial data Awards range from $10,000 to more than $100,000. This program requires cost-sharing; matching require-

ments differ by program, but may range up to half of the total cost.

Additional information This program is part of the NSF Research in Undergraduate Institutions (RUI) program; it is operated by various disciplinary divisions within the NSF; for a list of the participating divisions and their telephone numbers, contact the Senior Staff Associate for Cross Directorate Programs.

Deadline Deadlines are established by the respective participating NSF disciplinary divisions.

[987]
SABBATICALS FOR LONG-TIME ACTIVISTS OF COLOR

Alston/Bannerman Fellowship Program
1627 Lancaster Street
Baltimore, MD 21231
(410) 327-6220   Fax: (501) 421-5862
E-mail: info@AlstonBannerman.org
Web: www.AlstonBannerman.org

Purpose To finance a sabbatical for people of color who have been community activists for at least 10 years.

Eligibility This program is open to persons of color (people of African, Latino, Asian, Pacific Islander, Native American, or Arab descent) who are U.S. residents and have at least 10 years of experience as community activists. Applicants must be committed to continuing to work for social change. Preference is given to applicants whose work attacks root causes of injustice by organizing those affected to take collective action; challenges the systems that perpetrate injustice and effects institutional change; builds their community's capacity for self-determination and develops grassroots leadership; acknowledges the cultural values of the community; creates accountable participatory structures in which community members have decision-making power; and contributes to building a movement for social change by making connections between issues, developing alliances with other constituencies, and collaborating with other organizations. Individuals are ineligible if they only provide services (such as substance abuse counseling, after-school programs, HIV-AIDS outreach, or shelter for the homeless) or if they advocate on behalf of a community without directly involving the members of that community in asserting their own interests and choosing their own leadership. An equal number of men and women are selected.

Financial data The stipend is $15,000.

Duration The sabbaticals are to be 3 months or longer.

Additional information Fellows are encouraged to use their sabbaticals to engage in activities that are substantially different from their normal routine. Activities during the sabbatical must strengthen the recipient's ability to contribute to social change in the future. This program was established in 1987 as the Bannerman Fellowship Program. Its name was changed in 2002. Sabbaticals must be taken within 1 year of receipt of the award. Fellows must submit a report on their sabbatical.

Number awarded At least 10 each year. Since 1988, more than 140 fellowships have been awarded.

Deadline November of each year.

[988]
SALTONSTALL-KENNEDY GRANT PROGRAM

National Oceanic and Atmospheric Administration
Attn: National Marine Fisheries Service
1315 East-West Highway
SSMC3
Silver Spring, MD 20910
(301) 713-2358   E-mail: Alicia.Jarboe@noaa.gov
Web: www.nmfs.noaa.gov/sfweb/skhome.html

Purpose To provide funding to scholars and others interested in conducting projects that promote the development and growth of the fishing industry in the United States.

Eligibility Universities, state and local governments, fisheries development foundations, industry associations, private firms, and individuals are eligible to submit proposals. Projects must address 1 of the following current priorities: 1) promote the continued development of the Atlantic salmon aquaculture industry; 2) promote the reduction of excess harvesting capacity in appropriate fisheries; 3) reduce or eliminate adverse interactions between fishing operations and nontargeted, protected, or prohibited species; 4) reduce or eliminate factors such as diseases, human health hazards, and quality problems that limit the utilization of fish and their products; 5) advance the implementation of marine aquaculture; or 6) improve the understanding of the socio-economic impacts of fisheries. Women and minorities are particularly encouraged to apply as principal investigators.

Financial data The amount of the grant depends on the nature of the proposal and the availability of funds. Recently, $10.3 million was available for this program, of which $5 million was designated for Atlantic salmon aquaculture development and $5 million was available for other funding priorities.

Duration Grants up to 18 months are available, but most are for 1 year.

Number awarded Varies each year.

Deadline July of each year.

[989]
SCIENCE, JUSTICE, AND PUBLIC POLICY FELLOWSHIPS

American Association for the Advancement of Science
Attn: Science and Technology Policy Fellowship Programs
1200 New York Avenue, N.W.
Washington, DC 20005-3920
(202) 326-6700   Fax: (202) 289-4950
E-mail: science_policy@aaas.org
Web: fellowships.aaas.org/doj/index.html

Purpose To provide postdoctoral and mid-career scientists and engineers with an opportunity to work on scientific and engineering issues within the U.S. Department of Justice.

Eligibility Prospective fellows must have a Ph.D. or equivalent doctoral level degree in a physical, biological, or social science or engineering at the time of application; persons with a master's degree in engineering and at least 3 years of post-degree experience are also eligible. Applicants must demonstrate exceptional competence in some area of science or engineering directly related to the focus of the program. They are also expected to be critical thinkers who are articulate, adaptable, and adept at working with a variety of people from differing professional backgrounds, including decision makers and others outside of the scientific and engineering community. U.S. citizenship is required; federal employees are not eligible. Underrepresented minorities and persons with disabilities are especially encouraged to apply.

Financial data The stipend is $55,000, plus allowances for health insurance, relocation, and professional travel.

Duration 1 year, beginning in September; may be renewed for 1 additional year.

Additional information Various agencies of the Department of Justice participate in this program. In the Environmental and Natural Resources Division, fellows help attorneys draft environmental regulations, provide technical support to attorneys involved in environmental litigation, and provide general technical advice and interpretation on environmental issues. In the Federal Bureau of Investigation, fellows work in the Laboratory Division, analyzing broad, long-term issues affecting the mission and function of the laboratory and its role within the forensic science community and the criminal justice system. In the Justice Management Division, fellows work on policy evaluation related to information systems or technical and financial management and provide advice on design and implementation of multiple technology projects. In the Office of Policy Development, fellows provide scientific and technical expertise on different projects, serve as the office's point of contact with the department's chief science and technology advisor, and participate in and observe policy development. In the Office of Justice Programs, fellows assist in the office's goals to identify, define, and promote the understanding of critical crime, delinquency, and justice issues. In the Senior Management Offices, fellows support the department's Chief Science and Technology Advisor on wide-ranging technology issues from the uses of DNA in forensics to cyber crime.

Number awarded Up to 3 each year.

Deadline January of each year.

[990]
SCIENCE POLICY AND INTERNATIONAL SECURITY FELLOWSHIP PROGRAM

Stanford University
Center for International Security and Cooperation
Attn: Director of Fellowship Programs
Encina Hall, Room E210
616 Serra Street
Stanford, CA 94305-6165
(650) 723-9626   Fax: (650) 723-0089
E-mail: barbara.platt@stanford.edu
Web: www.cisac.stanford.edu

Purpose To provide funding to mid-career scholars who are interested in conducting research on international security or arms control issues at Stanford University's Center for International Security and Cooperation.

Eligibility This program is open to scientists and engineers who have demonstrated excellence in their specialties. Applicants should be interested in conducting interdisciplinary research at the center on such topics as policy issues regarding nuclear, biological, and chemical weapons and delivery systems; prospects for international control of weapons of mass destruction; nuclear weapons safety and security; global diffusion of information technology; assessing antiballistic missile defenses; export controls on high technology; defense conversion; environmental security; and security issues associated with energy development. Fellowships are available for both postdoctoral fellows and mid-career professionals. Scientists in academic and research institutions, government, and industry from both the United States and abroad may apply. The center is particularly interested in receiving applications from minorities or women.

Financial data Stipends are determined on a case-by-case basis commensurate with experience and availability of other funds. Health insurance is provided, and funds are available for travel and other research-related expenses.

Duration 11 months.

Additional information Science fellows pursue research, audit courses, and work with the center's faculty and research staff. They have the opportunity to interact with specialists in arms control, politics, and military affairs.

Number awarded 3 each year.

Deadline February of each year.

[991]
SCMRE POSTGRADUATE ARCHIVAL CONSERVATION FELLOWSHIP

Smithsonian Center for Materials Research and Education
Attn: Archives Fellowship and Internship Program
Museum Support Center
4210 Silver Hill Road
Suitland, MD 20746-2863
(301) 238-3700, ext. 147　　　　Fax: (301) 238-3709
E-mail: vanderreyden@scmre.si.edu
Web: www.si.edu/scmre/educationoutreach/internship.htm

Purpose To provide training at the Smithsonian Center for Materials Research and Education (SCMRE) and other Smithsonian facilities to recent graduates interested in preservation of archival materials.

Eligibility This program is open to recent graduates of recognized conservation training programs with an emphasis on preservation of archival materials. Applicants must be interested in working at SCMRE and with collections in the Smithsonian Institution, undertaking surveys, designing and carrying out rehousing projects, participating in and learning to organize training workshops, initiating training projects for collections managers, and carrying out research. Along with their application, they must submit a statement of their interests and intent in applying for the fellowship; copies of pertinent publications, lectures, or other written material; transcripts of both undergraduate and graduate academic work; 2 supporting letters; and a curriculum vitae including references. Minorities are particularly encouraged to apply.

Financial data The stipend is $22,000. An additional $2,000 for travel and research is available. Health insurance can be provided for those without personal coverage.

Duration 1 year.

Number awarded 1 each year.

Deadline February of each year.

[992]
SENIOR SCIENTIST AWARDS

National Institutes of Health
Division of Extramural Outreach and Information Resources
Attn: GrantsInfo
6701 Rockledge Drive, Suite 6095
Bethesda, MD 20892-7910
(301) 435-0714　　　　Fax: (301) 480-8443
E-mail: GrantsInfo@nih.gov
Web: www.nih.gov

Purpose To provide funding to outstanding scientists who have already demonstrated a sustained, high level of productivity in research.

Eligibility This program is open to senior scientists who have a distinguished record of original research contributions, long-term support from a funding institute or center, and peer-reviewed grant support at the time of the award. Applications may be submitted on behalf of candidates by domestic, nonfederal organizations, public or private, such as medical, dental, or nursing schools or other institutions of higher education. Minorities and women are particularly encouraged to apply. Candidates must be U.S. citizens or permanent residents.

Financial data This program provides salary and fringe benefits for the candidate only; each component establishes its own salary limits on career awards. Facilities and administrative costs are reimbursed at 8% of modified total direct costs.

Duration 5 years.

Additional information Awards under this program are available from 3 agencies of the National Institutes of Health (NIH): the National Institute on Alcohol Abuse and Alcoholism, the National Institute on Drug Abuse, and the National Institute of Mental Health. The names and addresses of staff people at each agency are available from the address above.

Number awarded Varies each year.

Deadline January, May, or September of each year.

[993]
SEXUALITY RESEARCH PROGRAM DISSERTATION FELLOWSHIPS

Social Science Research Council
810 Seventh Avenue
New York, NY 10019
(212) 377-2700　　　　Fax: (212) 377-2727
E-mail: srfp@ssrc.org
Web: www.ssrc.org

Purpose To provide financial support for dissertation research on sexuality topics.

Eligibility Students should have completed all requirements for the Ph.D. except the dissertation and be matriculating in a full-time graduate program in the United States leading to the Ph.D. in a social or behavioral science. Students enrolled in a public health department or division of an accredited U.S. college or university are also eligible. Applications are invited from a wide range of disciplines, including but not limited to anthropology, demography, economics, education, ethics, history, cultural and women's studies, political science, psychology, and sociology; applications from other fields, such as the nursing, law, and clinical/social work, are welcome as long as they are grounded in social science theory and methodology. The research proposals should seek to investigate a wide range of sexuality topics as conceptualized by the respective disciplines and conducted within the United States, including but not limited to: sexual/gender role socialization within the context of society and culture; historical, comparative, and/or cross-cultural analyses of sexuality; social construction analysis of sexuality; the diversity and distribution of sexual values, beliefs, and behaviors within different populations and their meanings for individuals; the link between sexuality and gender relations; sexual orientation; sexual coercion; the impact of economic change or of other institutional influences, such as religion or the media, on sexuality; and the formation of social policy based on cultural norms regarding sexuality. Women and members of minority groups are especially encouraged to apply. There are no citizenship, residency, or nationality requirements.

Financial data The stipend of $28,000 covers direct research costs, matriculation fees, and living expenses. An additional

$3,000 is awarded to the fellow's host institution and $3,000 to the fellow's research advisor or associate to defray expenses associated with the fellow's training, including direct research.
Duration Up to 12 months.
Additional information Funding for this program is provided by the Ford Foundation.
Number awarded Approximately 10 each year.
Deadline December of each year.

[994]
SEXUALITY RESEARCH PROGRAM POSTDOCTORAL FELLOWSHIPS

Social Science Research Council
810 Seventh Avenue
New York, NY 10019
(212) 377-2700   Fax: (212) 377-2727
E-mail: srfp@ssrc.org
Web: www.ssrc.org

Purpose To provide financial support for postdoctoral research on sexuality topics.
Eligibility Applicants must hold the Ph.D. or its equivalent in a social or behavioral science from an accredited university in the United States, or an equivalent Ph.D. degree from an accredited foreign university. Applications are invited from a wide range of disciplines, including but not limited to anthropology, demography, economics, education, ethics, history, cultural and women's studies, political science, psychology, and sociology; applications from other fields, such as the nursing, law, and clinical/social work, are welcome as long as they are grounded in social science theory and methodology. The applicant may be a recent recipient of the doctorate or well advanced in the postdoctoral research process. Fellows may have conducted research in the field of human sexuality or may be newly committing themselves to using their more general training to address sexuality issues. Postdoctoral candidates who have conducted research on sexuality for more than 8 years are not considered. The research proposals should seek to investigate a wide range of sexuality topics as conceptualized by the respective disciplines and conducted within the United States, including but not limited to: sexual/gender role socialization within the context of society and culture; historical, comparative, and/or cross-cultural analyses of sexuality; social construction analysis of sexuality; the diversity and distribution of sexual values, beliefs, and behaviors within different populations and their meanings for individuals; the link between sexuality and gender relations; sexual orientation; sexual coercion; the impact of economic change or of other institutional influences, such as religion or the media, on sexuality; and the formation of social policy based on cultural norms regarding sexuality. Women and members of minority groups are especially encouraged to apply. There are no citizenship, residency, or nationality requirements.
Financial data The stipend is $38,000 per year, to cover research costs and living expenses.
Duration Up to 2 years; continuation of the grant for more than 12 months requires submission and satisfactory review of a progress report to the fellowship program.
Additional information Funding for this program is provided by the Ford Foundation. This program does not support curriculum development or evaluation, direct service provision, public/community education, or the creation and maintenance of organizations.
Number awarded Approximately 4 each year.

Deadline December of each year.

[995]
SHORT-TERM TRAINING FOR MINORITY AND WOMEN DENTAL STUDENTS

National Institute of Dental and Craniofacial Research
Attn: Division of Extramural Research
45 Center Drive, Room 4AN-18J
Bethesda, MD 20892-6402
(301) 594-2618   Fax: (301) 480-8318
E-mail: jl46d@nih.gov
Web: www.nidr.nih.gov

Purpose To provide underrepresented minority and women dental students with an opportunity to receive research training in the dental sciences.
Eligibility Applicants for this program must be women or members of an ethnic or racial group underrepresented in biomedical or behavioral research nationally (Blacks, Hispanics, Native Americans, or Pacific Islanders). They must be U.S. citizens or nationals who have successfully completed at least 1 semester in a dental school in the United States or Puerto Rico.
Financial data Grants provide a stipend of $1,224 per month.
Duration 2 months during the summer.
Additional information At their dental school, recipients engage in a program to prepare for a career in basic and clinical oral health research. For a list of the participating institutions, contact the address above.
Number awarded Varies each year.
Deadline Application deadlines are established by each dental school participating in the program but are usually in the spring of each year.

[996]
SLOAN SCHOLARSHIP FACULTY GRANTS

Alfred P. Sloan Foundation
630 Fifth Avenue, Suite 2550
New York, NY 10111-0242
(212) 649-1645   Fax: (212) 757-5117
E-mail: greenwood@sloan.org
Web: www.sloan.org

Purpose To provide funding to faculty interested in recruiting underrepresented minority students to work on a Ph.D. in mathematics, natural science, or engineering.
Eligibility This program is open to mathematics, natural science, and engineering faculty who are interested in recruiting, mentoring, and graduating African Americans, Hispanic Americans, and Native Americans with Ph.D.s. Preference is given to faculty with a record of success in graduating minority students with Ph.D.s, but for faculty who have not had an opportunity to work with minority Ph.D. students, other factors are considered. Young minority faculty applicants are usually preferred. Interested faculty should submit a table with the following data for each African American, Hispanic American, and Native American student who has entered the Ph.D. program during the last 10 years: name, citizenship status, where they earned their undergraduate or master's degree, date of entry into the Ph.D. program, name of the faculty advisor, current status of the student (still enrolled, graduated with Ph.D., left program without Ph.D.), and place of initial employment for those who have graduated. Once faculty are selected to participate in this program, they are encouraged to recruit new Ph.D. students from underrepresented minority

groups. For each candidate they recruit who is designated as a Sloan Scholar, they receive this funding.

Financial data Each Sloan Scholarship grant that is awarded triggers a recruiting grant of $2,000 to the faculty or designated university office. Funds may be used for any purpose related to further recruitment of minority Ph.D. students, but not to provide direct benefits to minority students that are not available to other students.

Number awarded Varies each year.

Deadline Proposals may be submitted at any time.

[997]
SOUTH CAROLINA ARTS COMMISSION ETHNIC ARTIST GRANTS

South Carolina Arts Commission
Attn: Executive Director
1800 Gervais Street
Columbia, SC 29201-3585
(803) 734-8696   Fax: (803) 734-8526
TDD: (803) 734-8983   E-mail: burnecla@arts.state.sc.us
Web: www.state.sc.us/arts

Purpose To provide assistance to ethnic artists in South Carolina.

Eligibility Ethnic (African American, Asian American, Hispanic, and American Indian) dance, literary, media, music, theater, and visual artists are eligible for these grants. Applicants may be proposing career advancement projects or professional development activities. Examples of acceptable proposals include the creation of art that reflects the culture of an ethnic or tribal community; professional development opportunities; development of marketing, promotion, and documentation; and performances, exhibitions, or readings. Applicants must be at least 18 years of age and have maintained a permanent residence address in South Carolina for at least 6 months prior to the date of application and throughout the grant period. Degree-seeking, full-time undergraduate students and students who will earn academic credit as a result of the proposed project are ineligible. Selection is based on appropriateness and feasibility of the proposed culturally diverse project, extent to which the project will contribute to the professional development or career advancement of the applicant, artistic quality of the work samples submitted, qualifications of the applicant to undertake the proposed project, and appropriateness and feasibility of the proposed budget. Artists may receive no more than 2 of these grants per fiscal year; they may not be funded currently or previously by an annual or quarterly project grant from the commission.

Financial data The maximum award is $1,000; most grants are funded for less. Matching of 50% by the recipient is required, although up to half of the cash match may be accounted for by the cash value of the artist's time.

Duration 3 months. Recipients are only eligible to receive project support for 2 consecutive years.

Number awarded Varies each year; within the guidelines, funds are distributed on a first-come, first-served basis.

Deadline For projects starting from July through September, May of each year; for projects starting from October through December, August of each year; for projects starting from January through March, November of each year; for projects starting from April through June, February of each year.

[998]
SOUTH CAROLINA SPACE GRANT CONSORTIUM RESEARCH GRANTS

South Carolina Space Grant Consortium
c/o College of Charleston
Department of Geology
58 Coming Street
Charleston, SC 29424
(843) 953-5463   Fax: (843) 953-5446
E-mail: baughmant@cofc.edu
Web: www.cofc.edu/~scsgrant

Purpose To provide funding for space-related research to faculty at institutional members of the South Carolina Space Grant Consortium.

Eligibility This program is open to tenured or tenure-track faculty at member institutions of the South Carolina Space Grant Consortium. Applicants must be proposing to conduct research in earth science, space science, aeronautics, or the human exploration and development of space. Priority is given to researchers who wish to conduct research at a center of the U.S. National Aeronautics and Space Administration (NASA). Selection is based on scientific merit of the proposed project, relevancy to NASA strategic plans, project personnel, and reasonableness of budget. The South Carolina Space Grant Consortium is a component of the NASA Space Grant program, which encourages the participation of women, underrepresented minorities, and persons with disabilities.

Financial data Grants range up to $25,000. Grants must be matched on a 1:1 basis with nonfederal funds.

Duration 1 year.

Additional information Members of the consortium are Benedict College, The Citadel, College of Charleston, Clemson University, Coastal Carolina University, Furman University, University of South Carolina, Wofford College, South Carolina State University, The Medical University of South Carolina, and University of the Virgin Islands. This program is funded by NASA.

Number awarded Varies each year; a total of $100,000 is available for this program each year.

Deadline Letters of intent must be submitted by May of each year. Final proposals are due in June.

[999]
SOUTH CAROLINA SPACE GRANT CONSORTIUM UNDERGRADUATE RESEARCH PROGRAM

South Carolina Space Grant Consortium
c/o College of Charleston
Department of Geology
58 Coming Street
Charleston, SC 29424
(843) 953-5463   Fax: (843) 953-5446
E-mail: baughmant@cofc.edu
Web: www.cofc.edu/~scsgrant

Purpose To provide financial assistance for space-related research to undergraduate students in South Carolina.

Eligibility This program is open to undergraduate students at member institutions of the South Carolina Space Grant Consortium. Applicants should be rising juniors or seniors interested in aerospace and space-related studies, including the basic sciences, astronomy, science education, planetary science, environmental studies, engineering, fine arts, and journalism. U.S. citizenship is required. Selection is based on academic qualifications of the applicant; 2 letters of recommendation; a description of past activities, current interests, and future plans concerning a space science or aerospace-related field; and faculty sponsorship. Women and minorities are encouraged to apply.

Financial data The grant is $3,000. Up to $500 of the grant is available for research-related expenses, not including application fees.

Duration 1 academic year or 10 weeks during the summer.

Additional information Members of the consortium are Benedict College, The Citadel, College of Charleston, Clemson University, Coastal Carolina University, Furman University, University of South Carolina, Wofford College, South Carolina State University, The Medical University of South Carolina, and University of the Virgin Islands. This program is funded by the U.S. National Aeronautics and Space Administration

Number awarded Varies each year.

Deadline January of each year.

[1000]
SOUTHERN REGIONAL EDUCATION BOARD DISSERTATION-YEAR FELLOWSHIP

Southern Regional Education Board
592 10th Street N.W.
Atlanta, GA 30318-5790
(404) 875-9211, ext. 269   Fax: (404) 872-1477
E-mail: doctoral.scholars@sreb.org
Web: www.sreb.org

Purpose To provide financial assistance to minority students who wish to complete a doctoral dissertation while in residence at a university in the southern states.

Eligibility This program is open to U.S. citizens who are members of racial/ethnic minority groups (Native Americans, Hispanic Americans, Asian Americans, and African Americans) and have completed all requirements for a Ph.D. except the dissertation. Applicants must be in a position to write full time and must expect to complete the dissertation within the year of the fellowship. Eligibility is limited to individuals who plan to become full-time faculty members at a southern institution upon completion of their doctoral degree.

Financial data Fellows receive waiver of tuition and fees (in or out of state) and a stipend of $12,000.

Duration 1 year; nonrenewable.

Additional information This program is part of the national Compact for Faculty Diversity, established in 1994 by the New England Board for Higher Education (NEBHE), the Western Interstate Commission for Higher Education (WICHE), and the Southern Regional Education Board (SREB) with assistance from the Pew Charitable Trusts, the Ford Foundation, participating states, and doctoral universities.

Number awarded Varies each year.

Deadline Applications received by March of each year receive first consideration.

[1001]
SPONSORED RESEARCH INFRASTRUCTURE PROGRAM

National Institutes of Health
Attn: Extramural Associates Program
6701 Rockledge Drive, Room 6187A
Bethesda, MD 20892-7910
(301) 435-2736   Fax: (301) 480-0393
E-mail: mk51q@nih.gov
Web: www.nih.gov

Purpose To provide opportunities for minority and women faculty or administrators to contribute to biomedical research by participating in a program at the National Institutes of Health (NIH) in Bethesda, Maryland.

Eligibility Academic institutions that have a significant enrollment of minorities, or are women's colleges, may nominate 1 scientific faculty member or academic administrator. In addition to the qualifications and interests of the nominee, selection is based on the demonstrated contribution of the institution to the advancement of ethnic minorities and/or women, its readiness to improve health research or research training, and its plan to utilize the associate's expertise after participating in the program at NIH. This program is intended for nominees from institutions that award master's, Ph.D.s, and professional degrees, such as the M.D., D.D.S., D.V.M., and Pharm.D.

Financial data Salaries are comparable to those being received by the associate at the time of selection. Cost-sharing is required, depending on the institution's resources. Travel, housing, and subsistence expenses while at NIH, and any costs incurred that are directly related to the training, are reimbursed by the NIH. The maximum award to sponsoring institutions is $35,000 for the first year and $50,000 annually thereafter; institutions may also request up to $35,000 annually in the second and third years for pilot research projects, seminars, and student participation in research projects. Facilities and administrative costs are fixed at 8% of total direct costs.

Duration 5 months. Awards to institutions are up to 3 years.

Additional information During their tenure at the NIH, associates acquire a thorough knowledge of the NIH, the support mechanisms through which research is being accomplished, and the policies and procedures which govern the awarding of grants and contracts. Associates also obtain information about other federal health-related programs; grant and contract activities; legislative, budgetary and similar processes; and administrative procedures, including participation in staff meetings, review meetings, site visits, workshops, and conferences. Following completion of the program, associates return to their institutions with an Extramural Associates Research Development Award (EARDA) which provides developmental funds to the associate's institution for a period of 3 years, with a possible extension to 6 years.

Number awarded Varies each year; recently, 3 to 5 awards have been available through this program.

[1002]
STANFORD HUMANITIES CENTER EXTERNAL FACULTY FELLOWSHIPS

Stanford Humanities Center
424 Santa Teresa Street
Stanford, CA 94305-4015
(650) 723-3052   Fax: (650) 723-1895
Web: shc.stanford.edu

Purpose To offer scholars in the humanities an opportunity to conduct research and teach at Stanford University.

Eligibility External fellowships at Stanford University fall into 2 categories: 1) senior fellowships for well-established scholars, and 2) junior fellowships for scholars who at the time of application are at least 3 but normally no more than 10 years beyond receipt of the Ph.D. The fields of study should be the humanities as defined in the act that established the National Foundation for the Arts and Humanities. Scholars who are members of traditionally underrepresented groups (e.g., minorities) are encouraged to apply. Applications are judged on 1) the promise of the specific research project being proposed; 2) the originality and intellectual distinction of the candidate's previous work; 3) the research project's potential interest to scholars in different fields of the humanities; and 4) the applicant's ability to engage in collegial interaction.

Financial data The annual stipend is up to $35,000 for junior fellows and up to $50,000 for senior fellows. In addition, a housing/travel subsidy of up to $10,000, depending on size of family, is offered.

Duration 1 academic year.

Additional information In addition to these External Fellowships, the Humanities Center offers 6 Internal Fellowships to Stanford faculty each year. All fellows are expected to make an intellectual contribution not only within the center but to humanistic studies in general at Stanford. Normally, this requirement is fulfilled by teaching an undergraduate or graduate course or seminar for 1 quarter within a particular department or program. Fellows should live within the immediate area of Stanford University. Regular attendance at center events is expected and fellows are expected to be present during the fall, winter, and spring quarters and to attend weekday lunches on a regular basis.

Number awarded 6 to 8 each year.

Deadline October of each year.

[1003]
STANFORD SUMMER RESEARCH PROGRAM IN BIOMEDICAL SCIENCES

Stanford University
School of Medicine
Attn: Office of Graduate Affairs
M.S.O.B. Room 341
251 Campus Drive
Stanford, CA 94305-5404
(650) 723-6861   Fax: (650) 725-7855
E-mail: SSRPBS@list.stanford.edu
Web:
www.med.stanford.edu/school/biosciences/ssrpbs.html

Purpose To provide underrepresented minority undergraduate students with a summer research experience at Stanford University in biological and biomedical sciences.

Eligibility Eligible are undergraduates who, by reason of their culture, class, race, ethnicity, background, work and life experiences, skills, and interests would bring diversity to graduate study in the biological and biomedical sciences (biochemistry, biophysics, cancer biology, cell biology, developmental biology, ecology, epidemiology, evolutionary biology, genetics, immunology, marine biology, microbiology, medical information sciences, neurosciences, molecular pharmacology, physiology, plant biology, and population biology). The program especially encourages applications from Black/African Americans, Hispanic Americans, Native Americans, Pacific Islanders, and others whose backgrounds and experience would bring such diversity. Applicants must have at least 1 year of undergraduate education remaining before graduation and should be planning to prepare for and enter Ph.D. programs in the biological and biomedical sciences. U.S. citizenship or permanent resident status is required.

Financial data The program provides a stipend of $1,500, room and board, and transportation to and from the San Francisco Bay area.

Duration 8 weeks, during the summer.

Additional information The program provides a rigorous research experience with comprehensive mentoring and advising.

Deadline February of each year.

[1004]
STARTER RESEARCH GRANTS

National Science Foundation
Directorate for Biological Sciences
Attn: Division of Biological Infrastructure
4201 Wilson Boulevard, Room 615
Arlington, VA 22230
(703) 292-8470   TDD: (703) 292-5090
E-mail: ckimsey@nsf.gov
Web: www.nsf.gov/bio

Purpose To assist underrepresented minority scientists interested in establishing an independent research program in the biological, social, economic, and behavioral sciences.

Eligibility Eligible to apply are underrepresented minorities (African Americans, Hispanics, Native Pacific Islanders, and Native Americans) who received a Minority Postdoctoral Research Fellowship from the National Science Foundation (NSF) and have accepted a tenure-track position at a U.S. institution. Their field of study must fall within the program areas of the NSF Directorate for Biological Sciences or Directorate for Social, Behavioral, and Economic Sciences.

Financial data Grants up to $50,000 are available; the recipient's institution must provide matching funds on a 2:1 basis.

Duration 1 year; nonrenewable.

Additional information Information on the programs from the Directorate for Social, Behavioral, and Economic Sciences is available at (703) 292-8763, E-mail: jperhoni@nsf.gov.

Number awarded 6 each year.

Deadline Applications may be submitted at any time.

[1005]
SUMMER INSTITUTE IN MATHEMATICS FOR UNDERGRADUATES

University of Puerto Rico at Humacao
Attn: Department of Mathematics
Estacion C.U.H.
100 Route 908
Humacao, PR 00791-4300
(787) 850-0000, ext. 9036   Fax: (787) 850-9355
E-mail: simu@cuhwww.upr.clu.edu
Web: cuhwww.upr.clu.edu/~simu

Purpose To enable Chicano/Latino and Native American undergraduate students to participate in a mathematics institute at the University of Puerto Rico at Humacao.

Eligibility This program is open to students at universities in the United States and Puerto Rico who are interested in a research and educational experience in an area of modern mathematics not normally available in an undergraduate mathematics curriculum. Applicants must be Chicano/Latino or Native American undergraduates who have completed at least 2 years of university-level mathematics courses, want to conduct undergraduate research in the mathematical sciences, and are interested in pursuing a graduate degree in mathematics. Selection is based on an essay of 300 to 800 words on why the applicant is interested in mathematics and wishes to participate in the institute.

Financial data Participants receive round-trip travel to Puerto Rico, room and board, and a stipend of $2,200.

Duration 6 weeks, during the summer.

Additional information This institute, first offered in 1998, is jointly sponsored by the University of Puerto Rico at Humacao and the Society for Advancement of Chicanos and Native Americans in Science. Funding is provided by the National Science Foundation (NSF) through its Research Experiences for Undergraduates (REC) program. Participants take 1 of the 2 seminars and engage in team research in 1 of the mathematical areas. The topics of the seminars change annually; recently, the 2 seminars were on "Computational Mathematics Applied to Fluid Motion," and "Integrals: An Introduction to Research in Mathematics."

Number awarded 24 each year: 12 in each of the seminars.

Deadline February of each year.

[1006]
SUMMER RESEARCH PROGRAM FOR UNDERGRADUATES AT CORNELL UNIVERSITY

Cornell University
Mathematical and Theoretical Biology Institute
Attn: Biometrics Department
435 Warren Hall
Ithaca, NY 14853-7801
(607) 255-8103   Fax: (607) 255-4698
E-mail: mtbi@cornell.edu
Web: www.biom.cornell.edu/MTBI/index.html

Purpose To enable underrepresented minority undergraduates to participate in a summer institute on mathematical biology at Cornell University.

Purpose This program is open to undergraduate students who will complete their sophomore or junior year during the current academic year, who are majoring in mathematics, biology, or related fields, and who have had at least 1 year of calculus. Chicano, Latino, Native American, and African American students are strongly encouraged to apply. U.S. citizenship or permanent resident status is required. Applicants must be interested in studying the mathematical theory of population dynamics and its applications to demography, ecology, epidemiology, and evolutionary biology at Cornell University.

Financial data Participants receive a stipend of $2,000, round-trip transportation to Ithaca, New York, and room and board.

Duration 8 weeks, during the summer.

Additional information This program began in 1996. It is sponsored by the Society for Advancement of Chicanos and Native Americans in Science (SACNAS), 333 Front Street, Suite 104, P.O. Box 8526, Santa Cruz, CA 95061-8526, (831) 459-0170, Fax: (831) 459-0194, E-mail: info@sacnas.org. Funding is provided by the National Security Agency, the National Science Foundation, and, at Cornell University, the Office of the Provost, the College of Agriculture and Life Sciences, and the Biometrics Department. Participants work in an independent group setting to establish a relevant research question. They develop mathematical models and conduct analyses and numerical simulations for the projects on their own, but approved and guided by the faculty. The students' research focuses on problems at the interface of biology and mathematics. Each group writes a research technical report and presents their findings in an open colloquia at Cornel. Research topics address such topics at the evolution of virulence, coexistence of species, medical physiology, and the dynamics of communicable, sexually-transmitted, and vector born topical diseases.

Number awarded 30 each year.

Deadline March of each year.

[1007]
SUPPORT OF CONTINUOUS RESEARCH EXCELLENCE

National Institute of General Medical Sciences
Attn: Division of Minority Opportunities in Research
45 Center Drive, Suite 2AS37
Bethesda, MD 20892-6200
(301) 594-3900   Fax: (301) 480-2753
E-mail: em18v@nih.gov
Web: www.nih.gov/nigms

Purpose To provide funding for biomedical research to faculty at minority-serving educational institutions.

Eligibility To be eligible for a grant under this program, an applicant must be affiliated with 1) a public or private nonprofit university, 4-year college, or other institution offering undergraduate, graduate, or health professional degrees, with a traditionally high (more than 50%) minority student enrollment; or 2) a public or private nonprofit 2-year college, with a traditionally high (more than 50%) minority student enrollment; or 3) a public or private nonprofit university, 4-year college, or other institution offering undergraduate, graduate, or health professional degrees where a significant proportion of the student enrollment (but not necessarily more than 50%) is derived from ethnic minorities, provided the institution has a demonstrated commitment to the special encouragement of and assistance to ethnic minority faculty, students, and investigators; or 4) an American Indian tribe that has a recognized governing body and that performs substantial governmental functions, or an Alaska Regional Corporation as defined in the Alaska Native Claims Settlement Act. Applicants must be located in the United States or its territories. They must be proposing to conduct either individual research projects or faculty pilot projects in a biomedical field.

Financial data Direct costs for individual research projects may range up to $40,000 per year; for faculty pilot projects, the maximum annual grant is $25,000.

Duration 3 to 5 years.

Additional information This program is offered as part of the Minority Biomedical Research Support (MBRS) Program.

Number awarded Varies each year.

Deadline January, May, or September of each year.

[1008]
SYLVIA TAYLOR JOHNSON MINORITY FELLOWSHIP IN EDUCATIONAL MEASUREMENT

Educational Testing Service
MS 09-R
Princeton, NJ 08541-0001
(609) 734-1806   E-mail: ldelauro@ets.org
Web: www.ets.org

Purpose To provide funding to minority scholars who are interested in conducting independent research under the mentorship of senior researchers at the Educational Testing Service (ETS).

Eligibility This program is open to minority scholars who have earned a doctorate within the past 10 years and are U.S. citizens or permanent residents. Applicants must be prepared to conduct independent research at ETS under the mentorship of a senior researcher. They should have a commitment to education and an independent body of scholarship that signals the promise of continuing contributions to educational measurement. Studies focused on issues concerning the education of minority students are especially encouraged. Selection is based on the scholar's record of accomplishment and proposed topic of research.

Financial data The stipend is set in relation to compensation at the home institution. Scholars and their families also receive reimbursement for relocation expenses.

Duration 1 year.

Number awarded 1 each year.

Deadline January of each year.

[1009]
TED SCRIPPS FELLOWSHIPS IN ENVIRONMENTAL JOURNALISM

University of Colorado at Boulder
Attn: Center for Environmental Journalism
1511 University Avenue
Campus Box 478
Boulder, CO 80309-0478
(303) 492-4114   E-mail: cej@colorado.edu
Web: www.colorado.edu/journalism/cej

Purpose To provide journalists with an opportunity to gain more knowledge about environmental issues at the University of Colorado at Boulder.

Eligibility This program is open to full-time U.S. print and broadcast journalists who have at least 5 years' professional experience and have completed an undergraduate degree. Applicants may be general assignment reporters, editors, producers, environmental reporters, or full-time freelancers. Prior experience in covering the environment is not required. Professionals in such related fields as teaching, public relations, or advertising are not eligible. Applicants must be interested in a program at the university that includes classes, weekly seminars, and field trips. They also must engage in independent study expected to lead to a significant piece of journalistic work. Applications are especially

encouraged from women, ethnic minorities, disabled persons, and veterans (particularly veterans of the Vietnam era).

Financial data The program covers tuition and fees and pays a $34,000 stipend. Employers are strongly encouraged to continue benefits, including health insurance.

Duration 9 months.

Additional information This is a non-degree program. Fellows must obtain a leave of absence from their regular employment and must return to their job following the fellowship.

Number awarded 5 each year.

Deadline February of each year.

[1010]
TRAINEESHIPS IN AIDS PREVENTION STUDIES (TAPS) PROGRAM POSTDOCTORAL FELLOWSHIPS

University of California at San Francisco
Attn: Center for AIDS Prevention Studies
74 New Montgomery Street, Suite 510
San Francisco, CA 94105
(415) 597-9260   Fax: (415) 597-9125
E-mail: RHartwig@psg.ucsf.edu
Web: www.caps.ucsf.edu/tapsindex.html

Purpose To provide funding to scientists doing HIV prevention research with minority communities.

Eligibility This program is open to U.S. citizens, nationals, and permanent residents who have a Ph.D., M.D., or equivalent degree. Applicants must be interested in a program of research training at CAPS in the following areas of special emphasis in AIDS research: behavioral medicine and interventions, health policy analysis, minority populations, substance abuse, epidemiology, and other public health and clinical aspects of AIDS. Recent postdoctorates who have just completed their training as well as those who are already faculty members of academic or clinical departments are eligible. Members of minority ethnic groups are strongly encouraged to apply.

Financial data Stipends range from $28,260 for fellows with no relevant postdoctoral experience to $44,412 to those with 7 or more years of experience. Other benefits include a computer, travel to at least 1 annual professional meeting, health insurance, and other required support. The costs of the M.P.H. degree, if required, are covered.

Duration 2 or 3 years.

Additional information The TAPS program is designed to ensure that at the end of the training each fellow will have: 1) developed a strong affiliation with a research project and worked closely with a mentor who is a senior scientist at UCSF or CAPS; 2) completed the M.P.H. degree or its equivalent; 3) taken advanced courses in research methods, statistics, and other topics relevant to a major field of interest; 4) participated in and led numerous seminars on research topics within CAPS, as well as in the formal teaching programs of the university; 5) designed several research protocols and completed at least 1 significant research project under the direction of a faculty mentor; and 6) made presentations at national or international meetings and submitted several papers for publication.

Number awarded Varies each year.

Deadline December of each year.

[1011]
TRAVEL AWARDS FOR MINORITY GRADUATE STUDENTS

National Science Foundation
Directorate for Biological Sciences
Attn: Division of Biological Infrastructure
4201 Wilson Boulevard, Room 615
Arlington, VA 22230
(703) 292-8470   TDD: (703) 292-5090
E-mail: ckimsey@nsf.gov
Web: www.nsf.gov/bio

Purpose To assist underrepresented minority graduate students with the travel necessary to select a postdoctoral mentor and to apply for postdoctoral fellowships.

Eligibility Eligible to apply are underrepresented minorities (African Americans, Hispanics, Native Pacific Islanders, and Native Americans) who are American citizens or permanent residents and are within 18 months of earning their Ph.D. degrees. Their field of study must fall within the program areas of the Directorate for Biological Sciences or the Directorate for Social, Behavioral, and Economic Sciences of the National Science Foundation (NSF). Awards are intended to allow them to travel within the United States or abroad to select a postdoctoral mentor or to develop an application for an NSF Minority Postdoctoral Research Fellowship.

Financial data Awards up to $4,000 are provided for airfare and living expenses while visiting the host scientist's institution.

Duration Up to 3 visits may be supported.

Additional information Information on the programs from the Directorate for Social, Behavioral, and Economic Sciences is available at (703) 292-8763, E-mail: jperhoni@nsf.gov.

Number awarded 7 each year.

Deadline Applications may be submitted at any time, but they must be received at least 3 months prior to the planned travel.

[1012]
UCSB LIBRARY FELLOWSHIP PROGRAM

University of California at Santa Barbara
Attn: Associate University Librarian, Human Resources
Davidson Library
Santa Barbara, CA 93106
(805) 893-2478   E-mail: gorrindo@library.ucsb.edu
Web: www.library.ucsb.edu

Purpose To provide an opportunity for recent library school graduates, especially underrepresented minorities, to serve in the library system at the University of California at Santa Barbara (UCSB).

Eligibility This program is open to students who are about to graduate or who recently graduated from a library school accredited by the American Library Association. Applicants must be interested in a postgraduate appointment at UCSB. They must have a knowledge of and interest in academic librarianship and a strong desire for professional growth. Members of underrepresented groups are encouraged to apply.

Financial data Fellows are regular (but temporary) employees of the university and receive the same salary and benefits as other librarians at the assistant librarian level ($37,920 to $42,996 per year).

Duration 2 years.

Additional information The program began in 1985. Fellows spend time in at least 2 different departments in the library, serve on library committees, attend professional meetings, receive travel support for 2 major conferences, and participate in the Librarians' Association of the University of California.

Number awarded 1 each year.

Deadline May of each year.

[1013]
UNCF/PFIZER POSTDOCTORAL FELLOWSHIPS

United Negro College Fund
Attn: Pfizer Biomedical Research Initiative
8260 Willow Oaks Corporate Drive
P.O. Box 10444
Fairfax, VA 22031-4511
(703) 205-3503   Fax: (703) 205-3574
E-mail: uncfpfizer@uncf.org
Web: www.uncf.org/pfizer/textpage.htm

Purpose To provide financial assistance to underrepresented minority postdoctoral fellows who are interested in conducting biomedical research.

Eligibility This program is open to members of minority groups that are underrepresented in the biomedical science research fields and who have been appointed as postdoctoral fellows at an academic or non-academic research institution (private industrial laboratories are excluded). Applicants must be U.S. citizens or permanent residents interested in pursuing a career in biomedical science education and research. They must hold a Ph.D. in a life or physical science.

Financial data The total award is $53,500, including up to $44,500 as a stipend for the fellow (the maximum stipend is $35,000 for any 12-month period), up to $4,000 for fringe benefits, and up to $5,000 for supplies, equipment, and travel. Funds may not be used to support institutional indirect costs or faculty and staff salaries.

Duration 12 to 24 months.

Additional information This program is funded by Pfizer Inc.

Number awarded At least 4 each year.

Deadline April of each year.

[1014]
UNITED STATES INSTITUTE OF PEACE SENIOR FELLOWSHIPS

United States Institute of Peace
Attn: Jennings Randolph Program for International Peace
1200 17th Street, N.W., Suite 200
Washington, DC 20036-3011
(202) 457-1700   Fax: (202) 429-6063
TDD: (202) 457-1719   E-mail: jrprogram@usip.org
Web: www.usip.org/fellows.html

Purpose To provide funding to a wide range of professionals who wish to conduct research at the United States Institute of Peace in Washington, D.C.

Eligibility This program is open to candidates from a broad range of professional backgrounds, including college and university faculty, journalists, diplomats, writers, educators, military officers, international negotiators, and lawyers. Fellows may be at any stage of their careers and have any educational background. They should be proposing a research project related to preventive diplomacy, ethnic and regional conflicts, peacekeeping and peace operations, peace settlements, post-conflict reconstruction and reconciliation, democratization and the rule of law, cross-cultural negotiations, U.S. foreign policy in the 21st century, and related topics. Preference is given to projects that demonstrate relevance to current policy debates. Candidates must be proposing to produce 1 or more products, such as books or monographs, articles for professional or academic journals, op-eds and articles for newspapers or magazines, radio or TV media projects, demonstrations or simulations, teaching curricula, lectures or other public speaking, or workshops, seminars, or symposia, while at the institute. Applicants may be citizens of any country. Women and members of minority groups are especially encouraged to apply. Selection is based on the candidate's record of achievement and/or leadership potential; the significance and potential of the project for making an important contribution to knowledge, practice, or public understanding; and the quality of the project design and its feasibility within the timetable proposed.

Financial data The stipend is based on the fellow's earned income for the preceding year, up to a maximum of $80,000. In the case of candidates from countries with salaries greatly different from the United States, seniority is the basis for calculation. Also provided are transportation to and from Washington, D.C. for the fellow and eligible family members.

Duration Up to 10 months.

Additional information Fellowships are tenable at the United States Institute of Peace in Washington, D.C., where fellows interact with other fellows and Institute staff by presenting their work and participating in workshops, conferences, and other events. These awards are not made for projects that constitute policymaking for a government agency or private organization; focus to any substantial degree on conflicts within U.S. domestic society, or adopt a partisan, advocacy, or activist stance.

Number awarded Varies each year; recently, 14 of these fellowships were awarded.

Deadline September of each year.

[1015]
UNIVERSITY OF WISCONSIN VISITING MINORITY SCHOLAR LECTURE PROGRAM

University of Wisconsin at Madison
Attn: Wisconsin Center for Education Research
1025 West Johnson Street
Madison, WI 53706-1796
(608) 263-4200   Fax: (608) 263-6448
Web: www.wcer.wisc.edu

Purpose To make minority scholars and their work in education more visible on the University of Wisconsin campus.

Eligibility Minority scholars on the faculty of other universities are invited to present lectures on topics related to minorities and education at the University of Wisconsin. Candidates are nominated through a solicitation process within the university's school of education.

Financial data Lecturers receive travel expenses and an honorarium.

Duration Each visit lasts 2 days.

Additional information The visiting scholar makes a general presentation open to the University of Wisconsin's community and meets with a group of minority students at the university to discuss the scholar's work. This program is cosponsored by the University of Wisconsin's School of Education and the Wisconsin Center for Education Research.

Number awarded 6 each year.

[1016]
UNIVERSITY POSTDOCTORAL FELLOWSHIP PROGRAM

Ohio State University
Attn: Dean of the Graduate School
250E University Hall
230 North Oval Mall
Columbus, OH 43210-1366
(614) 292-6031   Fax: (614) 292-3656
E-mail: clark.31@osu.edu
Web: www.gradsch.ohio-state.edu/html/fw_03.html

Purpose To provide an opportunity for recent postdoctorates to conduct research at Ohio State University (OSU).

Eligibility Nominations may be submitted by OSU graduate faculty members who would like to coordinate a fellow's research. Faculty sponsors can host only 1 University Postdoctoral Fellow at a time. Eligible to be nominated are individuals who have held a doctorate or M.F.A. for 5 years or less. Nomination of minority and women candidates is particularly encouraged. Certain categories of persons are ineligible to be nominated: persons with doctoral or M.F.A. degrees from OSU, persons currently on appointment at OSU (or who have held a postdoctoral appointment there), senior faculty (associate or full professors) from other institutions, individuals who received a Ph.D. or M.F.A. more than 5 years ago, and international scholars who would not qualify for a J1 visa. Selection is based on the credentials of the postdoctoral candidates, the reputation of the faculty sponsors and the quality of their research program, the project proposed by the postdoctoral candidates with the guidance of their faculty sponsors, and the extent to which the candidates will enhance the research environment at the university through interactions with faculty, researchers, and graduate students.

Financial data The monthly stipend is $2,000, plus a $500 moving allowance and a $500 travel allowance (to attend professional meetings).

Duration From 9 to 12 months; nonrenewable.

Additional information Fellows are not OSU employees so they may not conduct research required by a grant and may not be asked to teach a course.

Number awarded Approximately 10 each year.

Deadline January of each year.

[1017]
VIRGINIA SPACE GRANT AEROSPACE GRADUATE RESEARCH FELLOWSHIPS

Virginia Space Grant Consortium
Attn: Fellowship Coordinator
Old Dominion University Peninsula Center
600 Butler Farm Road
Hampton, VA 23666
(757) 766-5210   Fax: (757) 766-5205
E-mail: vsgc@pen.k12.va.us
Web: www.vsgc.odu.edu/html/fellowships.htm

Purpose To provide financial assistance for research in space-related fields to graduate students in Virginia.

Eligibility This program is open to graduate students who will be enrolled in a program of full-time study in an aerospace-related discipline at 1 of the Virginia Space Grant Consortium (VSGC) Colleges. Applicants must be U.S. citizens with a GPA of 3.0 or higher. They must submit a proposed research and plan of study that includes its key elements, what the applicant intends to accomplish, and the aerospace application of the proposed research activity. Selection is based on the applicants' academic qualifications, the quality of their proposed research plan, and its relevance to this program. Since an important purpose of this program is to increase the participation of underrepresented minorities, females, and persons with disabilities in aerospace-related careers, the VSGC especially encourages applications from those students.

Financial data The grant is $5,000. Funds are add-on awards, designed to supplement and enhance such basic graduate research support as research assistantships, teaching assistantships, and nonfederal scholarships and fellowships.

Duration 1 year; may be renewed up to 2 additional years.

Additional information The VSGC colleges are College of William and Mary, Hampton University, Old Dominion University, the University of Virginia, and Virginia Polytechnic Institute and State University. This program is funded by the U.S. National Aeronautics and Space Administration (NASA). Awardees are required to certify through their academic department that basic research support of at least $5,000 is being provided before receipt of Space Grant funds.

Number awarded At least 5 each year.

Deadline February of each year.

[1018]
VIRGINIA SPACE GRANT AEROSPACE UNDERGRADUATE RESEARCH SCHOLARSHIPS

Virginia Space Grant Consortium
Attn: Fellowship Coordinator
Old Dominion University Peninsula Center
600 Butler Farm Road
Hampton, VA 23666
(757) 766-5210   Fax: (757) 766-5205
E-mail: vsgc@pen.k12.va.us
Web: www.vsgc.odu.edu/html/fellowships.htm

Purpose To provide financial assistance for research in space-related fields to undergraduate students in Virginia.

Eligibility This program is open to undergraduate students who will be enrolled in a program of full-time study in an aerospace-related discipline at 1 of the Virginia Space Grant Consortium (VSGC) Colleges. Applicants must be U.S. citizens who have completed at least 2 years of an undergraduate program with a GPA of 3.0 or higher. They must be proposing to participate in an active, identified research activity that has aerospace applications. The research must be supervised by a faculty mentor and may be conducted on the home campus or at an industrial or government facility. It should be continuous and may be conducted any time during the academic year, summer, or both. Since an important purpose of this program is to increase the participation of underrepresented minorities, females, and persons with disabilities in aerospace-related careers, the VSGC especially encourages applications from those students.

Financial data Grants provide a student stipend of $3,000 during the academic year and a $3,500 stipend during the summer (either before or after the academic year). Recipients may request an additional $1,000 research allocation for materials and travel to support research activities conducted during the academic year and/or a $1,000 research allocation during the summer. The maximum award per year cannot exceed $8,500.

Duration 1 year; renewable.

Additional information The VSGC colleges are College of William and Mary, Hampton University, Old Dominion University, the University of Virginia, and Virginia Polytechnic Institute and State

University. This program is funded by the U.S. National Aeronautics and Space Administration (NASA). Awardees are required to participate in the VSGC annual student research conference in late March or early April.

Number awarded Varies each year.

Deadline February of each year.

[1019]
WASHINGTON NASA SPACE GRANT CONSORTIUM SEED GRANTS FOR FACULTY

Washington NASA Space Grant Consortium
c/o University of Washington
401A Johnson Hall
Box 351310
Seattle, WA 98195-1310
(206) 543-1943   (800) 659-1943
Fax: (206) 543-0179   E-mail: nasa@u.washington.edu
Web: www.waspacegrant.org/minigrnt.html

Purpose To provide funding to faculty at member institutions of the Washington NASA Space Grant Consortium who are interested in conducting space-related research.

Eligibility This program is open to faculty members at institutions that are members of the consortium. Applicants must be interested in initiating research efforts in disciplines relevant to the missions of the U.S. National Aeronautics and Space Administration (NASA) on earth and in space. The program values diversity and strongly encourages women and minorities to apply.

Financial data Grants range from $10,000 to $20,000. Matching funds must be provided.

Duration 1 year.

Additional information This program is funded by NASA. Members of the consortium include Northwest Indian College, Seattle Central Community College, the University of Washington, and Washington State University.

Number awarded 1 each year.

[1020]
WASHINGTON STATE UNIVERSITY SUMMER DOCTORAL FELLOWS PROGRAM

Washington State University
Attn: Graduate School
P.O. Box 641030
Pullman, WA 99164-1030
(509) 335-6412   E-mail: bonnie@wsu.edu
Web: www.wsu.edu/~gradsch

Purpose To provide financial assistance to students from diverse backgrounds (e.g., minorities) who are completing their doctoral program at any school and are interested in working closely with faculty members at Washington State University during the summer to prepare for their academic careers.

Eligibility This summer program is open to U.S. citizens from diverse backgrounds (e.g., minorities) who have completed all requirements other than the dissertation for their doctorate. They must be interested in a career in higher education and working on their degree in 1 of these areas: agriculture and home economics, business and economics, education, engineering, architecture, liberal arts, nursing, pharmacy, sciences, or veterinary medicine. Interested candidates should submit a curriculum vitae, graduate school transcripts, 3 letters of recommendation, and a 3- to 5-page statement of career goals and research interests.

Financial data The stipend is $3,000, plus university housing.

Duration 5 weeks during the summer, beginning in June.

Additional information This program was established in 1993 and initially involved only the College of Education at Washington State University. In 1998, the program was expanded to additional colleges at the university; it is coordinated by the Graduate School. During the program, fellows are actively engaged in seminars on the changing roles and expectations of faculty, the future of academia, the changing nature of higher education, and issues facing faculty of color and women in higher education. Fellows are expected to design individualized programs for enhancing their ability to teach, conduct research, and other scholarly activities.

Deadline March of each year.

[1021]
W.E.B. DUBOIS FELLOWSHIP PROGRAM

Department of Justice
National Institute of Justice
Attn: W.E.B. DuBois Fellowship Program
810 Seventh Street, N.W.
Washington, DC 20531
(202) 616-3233
Web: www.ojp.usdoj.gov/nij/funding.htm

Purpose To provide funding to junior investigators interested in conducting research on the "confluence of crime, justice, and culture in various societal contexts."

Eligibility This program is open to investigators who hold a Ph.D. or other doctoral-level degree or a legal degree of J.D. or higher. Applicants should be early in their careers. They must be interested in conducting research that relates to the following high-priority topics: law enforcement/policing; justice systems (sentencing, courts, prosecution, defense); corrections; investigative and forensic sciences, including DNA; counterterrorism and critical incidents; crime prevention and causes of crime; violence and victimization, including violent crimes; drugs, alcohol, and crime; interoperability, spatial information, and automated systems; and program evaluation. The research should emphasize crime, violence, and the administration of justice in diverse cultural contexts. Because of that focus, the sponsor strongly encourages applications from diverse racial and ethnic backgrounds.

Financial data The grant is approximately $75,000. Funds may be used for salary, fringe benefits, reasonable costs of relocation, travel essential to the project, and office expenses not provided by the sponsor. Indirect costs are limited to 20%.

Duration 6 to 12 months; fellows are required to be in residence at the National Institute of Justice (NIJ) for the first 2 months and may elect to spend all or part of the remainder of the fellowship period either in residence at NIJ or at their home institution.

Number awarded 1 each year.

Deadline January of each year.

[1022]
WEST VIRGINIA SPACE GRANT CONSORTIUM GRADUATE FELLOWSHIP PROGRAM

West Virginia Space Grant Consortium
c/o West Virginia University
College of Engineering and Mineral Resources
G-68 Engineering Sciences Building
P.O. Box 6070
Morgantown, WV 26506-6070
(304) 293-4099   Fax: (304) 293-4970
E-mail: nasa@cemr.wvu.edu
Web: www.cemr.wvu.edu/~wwwnasa

Purpose To provide financial assistance to graduate students at designated institutions affiliated with the West Virginia Space Grant Consortium who wish to conduct research on space-related science or engineering topics.

Eligibility This program is open to graduate students at participating member institutions of the consortium. Applicants must be interested in working on a research project with a faculty member who has received a West Virginia Space Grant Consortium Research Initiation Grant. U.S. citizenship is required. The consortium is a component of the Space Grant program of the U.S. National Aeronautics and Space Administration (NASA), which encourages participation by women, underrepresented minorities, and persons with disabilities.

Financial data The amount of the award for the graduate student depends on the amount of the research grant that the faculty member has received.

Duration 1 year.

Additional information Funding for this program is provided by NASA. The participating consortium members are Marshall University, West Virginia Institute of Technology, West Virginia University, and Wheeling-Jesuit University.

Number awarded Varies each year.

[1023]
WEST VIRGINIA SPACE GRANT CONSORTIUM RESEARCH CAPABILITY ENHANCEMENT MINIGRANTS

West Virginia Space Grant Consortium
c/o West Virginia University
College of Engineering and Mineral Resources
G-68 Engineering Sciences Building
P.O. Box 6070
Morgantown, WV 26506-6070
(304) 293-4099   Fax: (304) 293-4970
E-mail: nasa@cemr.wvu.edu
Web: www.cemr.wvu.edu/~wwwnasa

Purpose To provide funding to faculty at institutions affiliated with the West Virginia Space Grant Consortium for support of space-related activities.

Eligibility This program is open to faculty members at colleges and universities that are members of the West Virginia Space Grant Consortium. Applicants must be seeking funding for such activities as trips to centers of the U.S. National Aeronautics and Space Administration (NASA) to develop research collaborations or attendance at conferences to present research findings. The consortium is a component of NASA's Space Grant program, which encourages participation by women, underrepresented minorities, and persons with disabilities.

Financial data Grants range up to $1,000.

Additional information Funding for this program is provided by NASA. The consortium includes Bethany College, Fairmont State College, Marshall University, Salem International University, Shepherd College, West Liberty State College, West Virginia Institute of Technology, West Virginia State College, West Virginia University, West Virginia Wesleyan College, and Wheeling-Jesuit University.

Number awarded 15 to 20 each year.

[1024]
WEST VIRGINIA SPACE GRANT CONSORTIUM RESEARCH INITIATION GRANTS

West Virginia Space Grant Consortium
c/o West Virginia University
College of Engineering and Mineral Resources
G-68 Engineering Sciences Building
P.O. Box 6070
Morgantown, WV 26506-6070
(304) 293-4099   Fax: (304) 293-4970
E-mail: nasa@cemr.wvu.edu
Web: www.cemr.wvu.edu/~wwwnasa

Purpose To provide funding for space-related research to faculty at institutions affiliated with the West Virginia Space Grant Consortium.

Eligibility This program is open to junior faculty members at colleges and universities that are members of the West Virginia Space Grant Consortium. Applicants must be seeking to pursue research in areas of interest to the U.S. National Aeronautics and Space Administration (NASA) and to establish long-term relationships with NASA researchers. U.S. citizenship is required. The consortium is a component of NASA's Space Grant program, which encourages participation by women, underrepresented minorities, and persons with disabilities.

Financial data Grants range from $5,000 to $20,000. At least 35% of the award must be allocated for a graduate student research assistant.

Duration 1 year.

Additional information Funding for this program is provided by NASA. The consortium includes Bethany College, Fairmont State College, Marshall University, Salem International University, Shepherd College, West Liberty State College, West Virginia Institute of Technology, West Virginia State College, West Virginia University, West Virginia Wesleyan College, and Wheeling-Jesuit University.

Number awarded 4 to 6 each year.

[1025]
WILLIAM TOWNSEND PORTER FELLOWSHIP FOR MINORITY INVESTIGATORS

Woods Hole Marine Biological Laboratory
Attn: Fellowship Coordinator
7 MBL Street
Woods Hole, MA 02543-1015
(508) 289-7441   Fax: (508) 457-1924
E-mail: skaufman@mbl.edu
Web: www.mbl.edu/research/fellowships.html

Purpose To support underrepresented minority physiologists who wish to conduct research during the summer at the Woods Hole Marine Biological Laboratory (MBL).

Eligibility This program is open to young scientists (undergraduates, senior graduate students, and postdoctoral trainees) who are from an underrepresented minority group (African American, Hispanic American, or Native American), are U.S. citizens or permanent residents, and are interested in conducting research in the field of physiology with senior investigators at MBL.

Financial data Participants receive a stipend and a travel allowance.

Duration Summer months.

Additional information This fellowship was first awarded in 1921. Funding is provided by the Harvard Apparatus Foundation.

Number awarded Varies each year.

Deadline January of each year.

[1026]
WISCONSIN SPACE GRANT CONSORTIUM GRADUATE FELLOWSHIPS

Wisconsin Space Grant Consortium
c/o University of Wisconsin at Green Bay
Natural and Applied Sciences
2420 Nicolet Drive
Green Bay, WI 54311-7001
(920) 465-2941   Fax: (920) 465-2376
E-mail: brandts@uwgb.edu
Web: www.uwgb.edu/wsgc

Purpose To provide financial assistance to graduate students at member institutions of the Wisconsin Space Grant Consortium (WSGC) who are interested in conducting aerospace, space science, or other interdisciplinary aerospace-related research.

Eligibility This program is open to graduate students enrolled at the universities participating in the WSGC. Applicants must be U.S. citizens; be enrolled full time in a master's or Ph.D. program related to space science, aerospace, or interdisciplinary aerospace studies (including, but not limited to, engineering, the sciences, architecture, law, business, and medicine); have a GPA of 3.0 or higher; and be interested in conducting space-related research. The consortium especially encourages applications from underrepresented minorities, women, persons with disabilities, and those pursuing interdisciplinary aerospace studies. Selection is based on academic performance and space-related promise.

Financial data Grants up to $5,000 per year are provided.

Duration 1 academic year.

Additional information Funding for this program is provided by the U.S. National Aeronautics and Space Administration. The schools participating in the consortium include the University of Wisconsin campuses at Green Bay, La Crosse, Madison, Milwaukee, Oshkosh, Parkside, and Whitewater; College of the Menominee Nation; Marquette University; Carroll College; Lawrence University; Milwaukee School of Engineering; Ripon College; and Medical College of Wisconsin.

Number awarded Varies each year; recently, 7 of these fellowships were awarded.

Deadline February of each year.

[1027]
WISCONSIN SPACE GRANT CONSORTIUM RESEARCH INFRASTRUCTURE PROGRAM

Wisconsin Space Grant Consortium
c/o University of Wisconsin at Madison
Space Science and Engineering Center
1225 West Dayton Street, Room 251
Madison, WI 53706-1280
(608) 263-4206   Fax: (608) 263-5974
E-mail: toma@ssec.wisc.edu
Web: www.uwgb.edu/wsgc

Purpose To provide funding to staff at academic and industrial affiliates of the Wisconsin Space Grant Consortium (WSGC) who are interested in developing space-related research infrastructure.

Eligibility This program is open to faculty and research staff at the WSGC universities and colleges and staff at WSGC industrial affiliates. Applicants must be interested in establishing a space-related research program. Faculty and staff on university/industry teams in all areas of research are considered, but research initiatives must focus on activities related to the mission of the U.S. National Aeronautics and Space Administration (NASA). Those activities include earth and atmospheric sciences, astronautics, aeronautics, space sciences, and other space-related fields (e.g., agriculture, business, law, medicine, nursing, social and behavioral sciences, and space architecture). Grants are made in 2 categories: 1) faculty research seed grants and/or faculty proposal writing grants; and 2) other research initiatives, such as seminars, workshops, and/or travel to NASA centers. Preference is given to applications that emphasize new lines of space-related research, establishing collaborations among faculty from liberal arts colleges with faculty from research-intensive doctoral universities, linking academic and industrial affiliates, coordinated efforts with other NASA programs, increasing research capability, building research infrastructure, establishing research collaborations, and initiating research opportunities in line with the NASA Strategic Enterprises, especially by women, underrepresented minorities, and persons with disabilities. Selection is based on the proposal topic, quality, credentials of the investigator(s), and probability of success in developing space-related research infrastructure.

Financial data For faculty research seed grants and proposal writing grants, most awards range up to $5,000, although 1 grant of $10,000 is available. For other research initiatives, the maximum grant is $1,000.

Duration 1 year. Proposals for 2-year projects may be considered if they include a 2-year budget and justification of why the project requires a 2-year effort.

Additional information Funding for this program is provided by NASA. Academic members of WSGC include the University of Wisconsin campuses at Green Bay, La Crosse, Madison, Milwaukee, Oshkosh, Parkside, and Whitewater; College of the Menominee Nation; Marquette University; Carroll College; Lawrence University; Milwaukee School of Engineering; Ripon College; and Medical College of Wisconsin. Industrial affiliates include Astronautics Corporation of America, Orbital Technologies Corporation, Space Explorers, Inc., Wisconsin Association of CESA Administrators, Wisconsin Department of Public Instruction, Wisconsin Department of Transportation, and Wisconsin Space Business Roundtable.

Number awarded Varies each year; recently, 4 of these grants were awarded.

Deadline February of each year.

[1028]
WISCONSIN SPACE GRANT CONSORTIUM UNDERGRADUATE RESEARCH AWARDS

Wisconsin Space Grant Consortium
c/o University of Wisconsin at Madison
Space Science and Engineering Center
1225 West Dayton Street, Room 251
Madison, WI 53706-1280
(608) 263-4206   Fax: (608) 263-5974
E-mail: toma@ssec.wisc.edu
Web: www.uwgb.edu/wsgc

Purpose To provide funding to undergraduate students at colleges and universities participating in the Wisconsin Space Grant Consortium (WSGC) who are interested in conducting space-related research.

Eligibility This program is open to undergraduate students enrolled at 1 of the institutions participating in the WSGC. Applicants must be U.S. citizens; be enrolled full time in an undergraduate program related to space science, aerospace, or interdisciplinary space studies; and have a GPA of 3.0 or higher. They must be proposing to create and implement a small research project of their own design as academic year, summer, or part-time employment that is directly related to their interests and career objectives in space science, aerospace, or space-related studies. Students must request a faculty or research staff member on their campus to act as an advisor; the consortium locates a scientist or engineer from 1 of the research-intensive universities to serve as a second mentor for successful applicants. The consortium especially encourages applications from students pursuing interdisciplinary space studies (e.g., engineering, the sciences, architecture, law, business, and medicine), underrepresented minorities, women, and persons with disabilities. Selection is based on academic performance and space-related promise.

Financial data Stipends up to $3,500 per year or summer session are available. An additional $500 may be awarded for exceptional expenses, such as high travel costs.

Duration 1 academic year or summer.

Additional information Funding for this program is provided by the U.S. National Aeronautics and Space Administration. The schools participating in the consortium include the University of Wisconsin campuses at Green Bay, La Crosse, Madison, Milwaukee, Oshkosh, Parkside, and Whitewater; College of the Menominee Nation; Marquette University; Carroll College; Lawrence University; Milwaukee School of Engineering; Ripon College; and Medical College of Wisconsin.

Number awarded Varies each year; recently, 9 of these grants were awarded.

Deadline February of each year.

[1029]
W.K. KELLOGG FOUNDATION FELLOWSHIP PROGRAM IN HEALTH RESEARCH

National Medical Fellowships, Inc.
Attn: Scholarship Program
5 Hanover Square, 15th Floor
New York, NY 10004
(212) 483-8880   Fax: (212) 483-8897
E-mail: info@nmfonline.org
Web: www.nmf-online.org

Purpose To provide financial assistance to minorities enrolled in a doctoral program in health policy research who are committed to working with underserved populations.

Eligibility This program is open to members of minority groups (African Americans, Native Americans, Asians, and Hispanics) enrolled in graduate programs in public health, social policy, or health policy leading to a doctorate (Ph.D., Dr.P.H., or Sc.D.). Applicants must demonstrate a willingness to complete relevant dissertation research and a commitment to work with underserved populations upon completion of the doctorate. They must include an essay of 500 to 1,000 words discussing their reasons for applying for a fellowship, their qualifications, how it will support their career plans, and which of 4 areas of focus (health policy, men's health, mental health, substance abuse) most interests them and why.

Financial data Fellowships cover tuition, fees, and a partial living stipend.

Duration Up to 5 years: 2 years to do the necessary course work and 3 years to complete the dissertation.

Additional information The program was created in 1998 with grant support from the W.K. Kellogg Foundation. Recently, it operated at 8 institutions: the RAND Graduate School, the Heller Graduate School at Brandeis University, the Joseph L. Mailman School of Public Health at Columbia University, the Harvard School of Public Health, the Johns Hopkins School of Hygiene and Public Health, the UCLA School of Public Health, the University of Michigan School of Public Health, and the University of Pennsylvania. Information is also available from the sponsor's Washington office at 1627 K Street, N.W., Suite 1200, Washington, DC 20006-1702, (202) 296-4431, Fax: (202) 293-1990.

Number awarded 5 each year.

Deadline June of each year.

[1030]
W.K. KELLOGG NONPROFIT RESEARCH FELLOWSHIP

Aspen Institute
Attn: Director, Nonprofit Sector Research Fund
One Dupont Circle, N.W., Suite 700
Washington, DC 20036
(202) 736-5838   Fax: (202) 467-0790
E-mail: nsrf@aspeninstitute.org
Web: www.aspeninstitute.org

Purpose To support research by doctoral candidates on the activities of nonprofit organizations in Michigan.

Eligibility This program is open to doctoral students in any discipline who wish to conduct research of practical value to nonprofit organizations in Michigan. Applications are especially encouraged from minorities and students who have had practical experience in the nonprofit sector. Preference is given to students at Michigan universities, but students at institutions located outside Michigan are also eligible if they plan to do research on the Michigan nonprofit sector. Fellows, however, must reside in Michigan and must be sponsored by a Michigan nonprofit organization that will house them during their fellowship. The proposed project does not need to be the same as the applicant's doctoral dissertation; it may take a variety of forms, including original research, synthesis of existing research, or development of a resource manual for use by practitioners and/or policymakers.

Financial data Grants include awards ranging up to $20,000 to the fellow for living and other personal expenses and up to $5,000 for research expenses to the nonprofit organization that agrees to house the fellow and collaborate on the project.

Duration 1 year; may be extended.

Additional information Funding for this program is provided by the W.K. Kellogg Foundation.

Number awarded Varies each year.

Deadline August of each year.

[1031]
WOMEN'S STUDIES PROGRAMS DISSERTATION SCHOLARS

University of California at Santa Barbara
Attn: Women's Studies Program
4704 South Hall
Santa Barbara, CA 93106
(805) 893-8246   Fax: (805) 893-8676
E-mail: lockwood@womst.ucsb.edu

Purpose To provide funding to doctoral candidates working on dissertations in women's studies.

Eligibility This program is open to graduate students at any university in the United States who are U.S. citizens, have advanced to candidacy in the humanities or social sciences, demonstrate strong research and teaching interests, expect completion of their dissertation within a year. and would benefit from a residency at the University of California at Santa Barbara. Applicants should be working on a dissertation in women's studies that reflects the intersections of race, class, gender, sexuality, and cultural difference. They should send a curriculum vitae, a brief description of the dissertation project, a writing sample (up to 25 pages), and 3 letters of reference. Applications are particularly encouraged from members of traditionally underrepresented groups (e.g., minorities).

Financial data The stipend is approximately $20,000.

Duration 9 months.

Additional information Recipients teach 1 undergraduate course and present 1 colloquium while in residence. Recipients are expected to be in residence during the residency and complete their dissertation.

Number awarded 2 each year.

Deadline February of each year.

[1032]
W.T. GRANT SCHOLARS PROGRAM

William T. Grant Foundation
Attn: Faculty Scholars Program
570 Lexington Avenue, 18th Floor
New York, NY 10022-6837
(212) 752-0071   Fax: (212) 752-1398
E-mail: info@wtgrantfdn.org
Web: www.wtgrantfdn.org

Purpose To provide funding to young scholars interested in conducting research on youth development.

Eligibility This program is open to faculty at colleges and universities in the United States and abroad who are in their first level or rank of appointment (normally, the assistant professor level in a tenure-track faculty appointment). Applicants must be interested in conducting research in 1 of the following areas: 1) original research on youth development; 2) evaluations and analyses of programs, policies, laws, and systems affecting young people; or 3) original research on adult attitudes about and perceptions of young people, and on the consequences of those attitudes and perceptions. Proposals should focus on young people between 8 and 25 years of age. The sponsor is particularly interested in research that is interdisciplinary; examines young people in social, institutional, community, and cultural contexts; and addresses issues that are relevant to youth-related programs and policies. Preference is given to applicants from diverse disciplines and those who are underrepresented (e.g., minority scholars) in research on adolescence and youth. Awards are not intended for established investigators. Candidates must be nominated by their home institution.

Financial data Awards are made to the applicant's institution to provide support for up to $60,000 per year, including an indirect cost allowance of 7.5%. The money may be used only for the research efforts of the investigator, with no more than half of the faculty member's salary met by the grant, which must not replace current university support.

Duration Up to 5 years.

Additional information This program began in 1981. Fellows must spend at least 50% of their time in research on areas of interest to the foundation.

Number awarded 4 to 6 each year.

Deadline June of each year.

[1033]
WYOMING SPACE GRANT UNDERGRADUATE FELLOWSHIPS

Wyoming Space Grant Consortium
c/o University of Wyoming
Physical Sciences Building, Room 210
P.O. Box 3905
Laramie, WY 82071-3905
(307) 766-2862   Fax: (307) 766-2652
E-mail: wy.spacegrant@uwyo.edu
Web: wyoskies.uwyo.edu/spacegrant

Purpose To provide funding for space-related research to undergraduate students in Wyoming.

Eligibility This program is currently open to undergraduate students at the University of Wyoming and all community colleges in Wyoming. Applicants must be U.S. citizens who are interested in conducting a space-related research project under the mentorship of a faculty member. A major in science or engineering is not required, because the program assumes that even non-science majors broaden their educations with a research experience. Selection is based on the scientific merit of the proposed project, the pedagogical benefits to the student as a result of the overall research experience, and the probability that the recipient will develop a successful research program resulting in publications. Wyoming Space Grant is a component of the Space Grant program of the U.S. National Aeronautics and Space Administration (NASA), which encourages participation by women, underrepresented minorities, and persons with disabilities.

Financial data Awards range from $3,000 to $5,000. Funds may be used only for undergraduate salary support, at the rate of $7.19 per hour. Tuition is not provided for the student's home institution, special institutes, or off-campus programs. Other expenditures not usually supported include travel, page charges, equipment, and supplies; applicants are encouraged to seek matching funds to cover those expenditures, and proposals that include matching by nonfederal funds are given priority.

Duration Research may be conducted during the academic year or summer.

Additional information This program is funded by NASA. Recipients are expected to keep the program informed of their progress, submit a final report in a timely manner, participate in publications of research results, and present a colloquium on their research.

Number awarded 4 to 6 each year.

Deadline February of each year.

Awards

Described in this section are 44 competitions, prizes, and honoraria open to Hispanic Americans in recognition or support of creative work, personal accomplishments, professional contributions, or public service. Excluded are prizes received solely as the result of entering contests. If you are looking for a particular program and don't find it in this section, be sure to check the Program Title Index to see if it is covered elsewhere in the directory.

[1034]
ANISFIELD-WOLF BOOK AWARDS

Cleveland Foundation
1422 Euclid Avenue, Suite 1300
Cleveland, OH 44115-2001
(216) 861-3810   Fax: (216) 861-1729
E-mail: asktcf@clevefdn.org
Web: www.anisfield-wolf.org

Purpose To recognize and reward recent books that have contributed to an understanding of racism or appreciation of the rich diversity of human cultures.

Eligibility Works published in English during the preceding year that "expose racism or explore literary diversity" are eligible to be considered. Entries may be either scholarly or imaginative (fiction, poetry, memoir). Plays and screenplays are not eligible, nor are works in progress. Manuscripts and self-published works are not eligible, and no grants are made for completing or publishing manuscripts.

Financial data The prize is $10,000. If more than 1 author is chosen in a given year, the prize is divided equally among the winning books.

Duration The award is presented annually.

Additional information These awards were first presented in 1936.

Number awarded 3 each year: 1 for fiction, 1 for nonfiction, and 1 for lifetime achievement.

Deadline January of each year.

[1035]
BORDER PLAYWRIGHT'S PROJECT

Borderlands Theater
P.O. Box 2791
Tucson, AZ 85702-2791
(520) 882-8607   Fax: (520) 882-7406
E-mail: bltheater@aol.com

Purpose To recognize and reward unproduced, full-length scripts by playwrights whose work reflects the cultural diversity of the Border region and the Border as a metaphor.

Eligibility Eligible plays must be unproduced (except in workshops or as readings) and unpublished. English, Spanish, or bilingual scripts are acceptable. Although the program emphasizes plays that explore the U.S./Mexico border and border culture, it also considers plays that explore the concept of other borders, including immigration and issues of class, race, and gender.

Financial data The winning playwrights receive an honorarium, plus travel to and lodging in Tucson.

Duration The competition is held annually.

Additional information Borderlands Theater is a multicultural arts organization in Tucson, Arizona. Winning plays are produced by Borderlands.

Number awarded 1 or more each year.

[1036]
CAREY MCWILLIAMS AWARD

MultiCultural Review
Attn: Managing Editor
Greenwood Publishing Group
88 Post Road West
P.O. Box 5007
Westport, CT 06881-5007
(203) 226-3571   Fax: (203) 226-6009
E-mail: mcreview@aol.com
Web: www.mcreview.com

Purpose To recognize and reward scholarly and literary writings on multiculturalism in the United States.

Eligibility English language book-length adult fiction or nonfiction reviewed in *MultiCultural Review* and published during the preceding year may be submitted for consideration (2 copies of each book must be submitted). The submissions must deal with historical, cultural, or other aspects of ethnic and minority relations in the United States.

Financial data The winning author receives a certificate and a $500 prize; the publisher of the winning book receives a complimentary full-page advertisement for the book in *MultiCultural Review*. Winners are announced at the annual American Library Association conference.

Duration The competition is held annually.

Additional information This award was established in 1992 and is named for an author who devoted much of his life to examining the minority experience and seeking ways to make democracy work better in the United States. Information is also available from Lyn Miller-Lachmann, *MultiCultural Review*, 6 Birch Hill Road, Ballston Lake, NY 12019.

Number awarded 1 each year.

Deadline April of each year.

[1037]
CHICANO/LATINO LITERARY CONTEST

University of California at Irvine
Department of Spanish and Portuguese
Attn: Prize Coordinator
322 Humanities Hall
Irvine, CA 92715-5275
(949) 824-5443   E-mail: cllp@uci.edu
Web: www.hnet.uci.edu

Purpose To recognize and reward the outstanding writing of Chicanos/Latinos in the United States.

Eligibility Chicano/Latino writers who identify strongly with the Hispanic community are eligible to submit unpublished manuscripts of at least 90 typed pages. Applicants must be U.S. citizens or permanent residents. Each year, a different genre of unpublished writing is rewarded, rotating among short story collections (2004), poetry collections (2005), drama (2006), and novels (in 2007). Submissions may be in Spanish or English.

Financial data The first-prize winner receives $1,000, plus transportation to Irvine, California and publication of the award-winning manuscript. The second-place winner receives $500 and the third-place winner receives $250.

Duration The competition is held annually.

Additional information The manuscripts may be in English, Spanish, or both languages.

Number awarded 3 each year.

Deadline May of each year.

[1038]
C.S. KILNER LEADERSHIP AWARD

A Better Chance, Inc.
Attn: College Preparatory Schools Program
88 Black Falcon Avenue, Suite 250
Boston, MA 02210-2414
(617) 421-0950   (800) 562-7865
Fax: (617) 421-0965
Web: www.abetterchance.org

Purpose To recognize and reward outstanding minority high school students.

Eligibility This award is presented to the ABC (A Better Chance) senior who has best displayed leadership qualities throughout his or her secondary school career. Only nominations are accepted.

Financial data The award is $1,000.

Duration The award is presented annually.

Additional information A Better Chance, Inc. (ABC) is a national, nonprofit organization that selects, recruits, and places students of color in participating schools, including 99 independent boarding schools, 100 independent day schools, and 26 public boarding schools in suburban communities. Approximately 325 students are selected to participate each year. The independent boarding and day schools contribute scholarships for participating students; the communities in which the public high schools are located provide housing and other support.

Number awarded 1 each year.

Deadline March of each year.

[1039]
EDWARD A. BOUCHET AWARD

American Physical Society
Attn: Honors Program
One Physics Ellipse
College Park, MD 20740-3844
(301) 209-3268   Fax: (301) 209-0865
E-mail: honors@aps.org
Web: www.aps.org/praw/bouchet/index.html

Purpose To recognize and reward outstanding research in physics by a member of an underrepresented minority group.

Eligibility Nominees for this award must be Blacks, Hispanics, or Native Americans who have made significant contributions to physics research.

Financial data The award consists of a grant of $3,500 to the recipient, a travel allowance for the recipient to visit 3 academic institutions to deliver lectures, and an allowance for travel expenses to the meeting of the American Physical Society (APS) at which the prize is presented.

Duration The award is presented annually.

Additional information This award was established in 1994 and is currently funded by a grant from the Research Corporation. As part of the award, the recipient visits 3 academic institutions where the impact of the visit on minority students will be significant. The purpose of those visits is to deliver technical lectures on the recipient's field of specialization, to visit classrooms where appropriate, to assist the institution with precollege outreach efforts where appropriate, and to talk informally with faculty and students about research and teaching careers in physics.

Number awarded 1 each year.

Deadline June of each year.

[1040]
EL ANDAR PRIZE FOR LITERARY EXCELLENCE

el ANDAR Publications
Attn: Literary Award
P.O. Box 7745
Santa Cruz, CA 95061
(831) 457-8353   Fax: (831) 457-8354
E-mail: info@elandar.com
Web: www.elandar.com/award/index.html

Purpose To recognize and reward outstanding literary work on themes relevant to Latino youth.

Eligibility Writers are invited to submit poetry, fiction, and creative nonfiction. Entries may be in Spanish, English, or a mix of both languages and should relate to Latino life and experiences. Stories and creative nonfiction should not exceed 4,000 words. Poems may be any length. Only unpublished work is eligible.

Financial data First prize is $1,000 and a 3-year subscription to el ANDAR. Second prize is $250 and a 2-year subscription to el ANDAR. Honorable mentions receive a 1-year subscription to el ANDAR.

Duration The competition is held annually.

Additional information el ANDAR is a literary magazine directed to Latino youth. It established this competition in 2000. The reading fee is $15 for each story, creative nonfiction work, or 3 poems.

Number awarded In each of the 3 categories, 1 first prize, 1 second prize, and up to 10 honorable mentions are selected each year.

Deadline September of each year.

[1041]
FOUNDERS DISTINGUISHED SENIOR SCHOLAR AWARD

American Association of University Women
Attn: AAUW Educational Foundation
1111 16th Street, N.W.
Washington, DC 20036-4873
(202) 785-7609   (800) 326-AAUW
Fax: (202) 463-7169   TDD: (202) 785-7777
E-mail: foundation@aauw.org
Web: www.aauw.org

Purpose To recognize and reward American women for a lifetime of scholarly excellence.

Eligibility Eligible for nomination are women scholars who can demonstrate a lifetime of outstanding research, college or university teaching, publications, and positive impact upon women in their profession and community. U.S. citizenship or permanent resident status is required. Selection is based on lifetime commitment to women's issues in the profession or in the community, significance and impact of the nominee's scholarship upon her field, demonstrated excellence in and commitment to teaching and mentoring female college students, and total impact upon her profession and the community. The sponsor strongly encourages nomination of women of color and other underrepresented groups.

Financial data The award is $1,000.

Duration The award is presented annually.

Additional information The award includes a trip to the annual AAUW convention (where the award is presented).

Number awarded 1 each year.

Deadline February of each year.

[1042]
FRANKLIN C. MCLEAN AWARD

National Medical Fellowships, Inc.
Attn: Scholarship Program
5 Hanover Square, 15th Floor
New York, NY 10004
(212) 483-8880   Fax: (212) 483-8897
E-mail: info@nmfonline.org
Web: www.nmf-online.org

Purpose To recognize and reward the outstanding academic achievement, leadership, and community service of senior medical school minority students.

Eligibility This competition is open to African American, Native Hawaiian, Alaska Native, American Indian, Mexican American, and mainland Puerto Rican students enrolled in accredited U.S. medical schools or osteopathic colleges. Candidates must be nominated by their schools during the summer preceding their senior year. Selection is based on academic achievement, leadership, and community service.

Financial data This honor includes a certificate of merit and a $3,000 award.

Duration 1 year; nonrenewable.

Additional information This award, the first award offered by the National Medical Fellowship, was established in 1968 in memory of the Chicago bone physiologist who founded the organization.

Number awarded 1 each year.

Deadline Nominations must be submitted by July of each year.

[1043]
GREAT PLAINS FILM FESTIVAL AWARDS

Great Plains Film Festival
Mary Riepma Ross Film Theater
University of Nebraska
College of Fine and Performing Arts
P.O. Box 880302
Lincoln, NE 68588-0302
(402) 472-9100   Fax: (402) 472-2576
E-mail: dladely1@unl.edu
Web: www.rossfilmtheater.org

Purpose To recognize and reward outstanding films and videotapes, particularly those that deal with the Great Plains.

Eligibility This program is open to film and videomakers from the Great Plains and to those whose film/video relates in content or in narrative to the Great Plains: Colorado, Iowa, Kansas, Minnesota, Missouri, Montana, Nebraska, New Mexico, North Dakota, Oklahoma, South Dakota, Texas, Wyoming, Alberta, Manitoba, and Saskatchewan. The festival encourages film/video that accentuates and enhances the region's multicultural diversity. Entries must be submitted on 1/2 inch VHS videotape. Feature length (45 minutes and longer) and short (under 45 minutes) entries are judged in the following categories: narrative feature, documentary feature, narrative short, documentary short, made for public television, and young media artists (open to high school age or younger). All entries are also eligible for the Rainbow Award, presented to the best Latino entry.

Financial data Prizes range from $500 to the Grand Prize of $3,000. The Rainbow Award is $2,500.

Duration The competition is held annually.

Number awarded A total of $15,000 in prizes is awarded each year.

Deadline May of each year.

[1044]
GREGORY KOLOVAKOS AWARD

PEN American Center
Attn: Literary Awards Manager
568 Broadway, Suite 401
New York, NY 10012-3225
(212) 334-1660, ext. 108   Fax: (212) 334-2181
E-mail: pen@pen.org
Web: www.pen.org/translation/gkaward.html

Purpose To recognize and reward outstanding contributions made by translators, editors, or critics to Hispanic literature in English translation.

Eligibility Writers, critics, and translators whose work has aided the cause of Latin American literature in English may be nominated for this award. Letters of nomination must be received from the candidate's editor or colleague, accompanied by a copy of the nominee's vitae. Self nominations are not accepted. The award focuses on works from Spanish, but distinguished contributions from other languages of the Hispanic world are also considered.

Financial data The award is $2,000.

Duration The award is given triennially (2004, 2007, etc.).

Additional information This award was established in 1992.

Number awarded 1 every third year.

Deadline October prior to the year of the award.

[1045]
GUILLERMO MARTINEZ-MARQUEZ JOURNALISM AWARD

National Association of Hispanic Journalists
Attn: Educational Programs Manager
1000 National Press Building
529 14th Street, N.W.
Washington, DC 20045-2001
(202) 662-7145   (888) 346-NAHJ
Fax: (202) 662-7144   E-mail: nahj@nahj.org
Web: www.nahj.org

Purpose To recognize and reward outstanding journalism by members of the National Association of Hispanic Journalists (NAHJ) that benefits the Hispanic community in the United States.

Eligibility This competition is open to any Hispanic journalist who contributes to either English language or Spanish language media (including newspapers, magazines, television, and radio) and is a member of the association. Awards are granted in 3 categories: print, television, and radio. Print entries may be no longer than 3 parts, including sidebars; television and radio entries may be no longer than 5 parts, with the total not to exceed 30 minutes; documentaries and public service announcements are not eligible. From among the 3 award winners, an overall winner is selected to receive this cash prize.

Financial data The cash prize is $1,000.

Duration The competition is held annually.

Additional information This program is named for a prominent journalist in his native Cuba, where he was an editor and publisher; he became a Miami-based nationally-syndicated Spanish language columnist and a strong proponent of freedom of the press in America. All applicants must submit a contest fee of $35 per entry. Nonmembers must also include a membership fee of $50.

Number awarded 1 overall winner each year.

Deadline March of each year.

[1046]
HIGH SCHOOL WORKSHOPS FOR MINORITY STUDENTS IN JOURNALISM SCHOLARSHIPS

Dow Jones Newspaper Fund
P.O. Box 300
Princeton, NJ 08543-0300
(609) 452-2820   Fax: (609) 520-5804
E-mail: newsfund@wsf.dowjones.com
Web: DJNewspaperFund.dowjones.com

Purpose   To recognize and reward outstanding participants in journalism workshops for minority high school students.

Eligibility   Each summer, workshops on college campuses around the country allow minority high school students to experience work on a professional-quality publication. Students are taught to write, report, design, and layout a newspaper on topics relevant to youth. The director of each workshop nominates 1 student who submits an article from the workshop newspaper and an essay on why he/she wants to pursue journalism as a career. The students whose articles and essay are judged most outstanding receive these college scholarships.

Financial data   The stipend is $1,000.

Duration   Workshops normally last 10 days during the summer. Scholarships are for 1 year and may be renewed for 1 additional year if the recipient maintains a GPA of 2.5 or higher and an interest in journalism.

Additional information   Recently, workshops were held on college campuses in Alabama, Arizona, California, the District of Columbia, Florida, Georgia, Illinois, Kentucky, Massachusetts, Minnesota, Mississippi, Missouri, New Jersey, New York, Ohio, Oregon, Pennsylvania, Texas, Virginia, Washington, and Wisconsin. For the name and address of the director of each workshop, contact the Newspaper Fund.

Number awarded   8 each year.

[1047]
HISPANIC HERITAGE YOUTH AWARDS

Hispanic Heritage Awards Foundation
2600 Virginia Avenue, N.W., Suite 406
Washington, DC 20037
(202) 861-9797   Fax: (202) 861-9799
E-mail: info@HispanicAwards.org
Web: www.HispanicAwards.org

Purpose   To recognize and reward Hispanic high school seniors from designated cities who have excelled in various areas of activity.

Eligibility   This program is open to high school seniors in the following cities: Chicago, Dallas, Houston, Los Angeles, Miami, New York City, Philadelphia, Phoenix, San Antonio, San Diego, San Jose, and Washington, D.C. Applicants must be U.S. citizens or permanent residents and of Hispanic heritage (at least 1 parent must be of able to trace family origins to Spain, Latin America, or the Spanish-speaking Caribbean). They may compete for awards in the following categories: the Youth Award for Leadership/Community Service, the Youth Award for Sports, the Youth Award for Literature/Journalism, the Youth Award for Academic Excellence, the Youth Award for Science and Technology, and the Youth Award for Mathematics. Selection criteria include, but are not limited to, the following: meritorious achievements in the applicant's chosen category, contribution to the community, ability to overcome adversity or disadvantage, dedication to self-improvement, and overall character as a role model.

Financial data   Regional winners receive $2,000 to use for their education and a state-of-the-art personal computer. The sponsor also makes a $1,000 donation to a community service organization designated by each regional winner. National winners receive an additional $5,000 educational grant plus an all-expense paid trip to Washington, D.C. for the winner and a parent or guardian to attend the awards ceremony at the John F. Kennedy Center for the Performing Arts.

Duration   The awards are presented annually.

Additional information   This program began in 1998 with sponsorship by the Fannie Mae Foundation for 5 cities and 1 category. More sponsors have resulted in the additional categories as more cities have also been added. Currently, Dr Pepper sponsors the awards for leadership and community service, NBC Television Stations Division for literature and journalism, Chase Manhattan Bank and MasterCard for academic excellence, Microsoft Corporation for science and technology, and ExxonMobil Corporation for mathematics.

Number awarded   72 regional winners are selected each year: 1 in each of the 6 categories from each of the 12 cities. From those, 6 national winners are chosen: 1 in each of the categories.

Deadline   February of each year.

[1048]
JAMES A. RAWLEY PRIZE

Organization of American Historians
Attn: Award and Prize Committee Coordinator
112 North Bryan Street
Bloomington, IN 47408-4199
(812) 855-9852   Fax: (812) 855-0696
E-mail: awards@oah.org
Web: www.oah.org/activities/awards/rawley/index.html

Purpose   To recognize and reward outstanding books dealing with race relations in the United States.

Eligibility   This award is presented to the author of the outstanding book on the history of race relations in America. Entries must have been published during the current calendar year.

Financial data   The award is $1,000 and a certificate.

Duration   The award is presented annually.

Additional information   The award was established in 1990.

Number awarded   1 each year.

Deadline   September of each year.

[1049]
JAMES H. ROBINSON MEMORIAL PRIZE IN SURGERY

National Medical Fellowships, Inc.
Attn: Scholarship Program
5 Hanover Square, 15th Floor
New York, NY 10004
(212) 483-8880   Fax: (212) 483-8897
E-mail: info@nmfonline.org
Web: www.nmf-online.org

Purpose   To recognize and reward outstanding surgical performance by underrepresented minority medical students enrolled in their senior year at accredited medical schools.

Eligibility   Only nominations are accepted; students may not apply directly. Nominees must be underrepresented minority students (African American, Native Hawaiian, Alaska Native, American Indian, Mexican American, or mainland Puerto Rican) attending accredited medical schools in the United States who are graduating during the academic year in which the awards are available. Awards are given for outstanding performance in the surgical disciplines and for overall good academic standing.

Financial data The honor includes a certificate of merit and a $500 stipend.

Duration The awards are presented annually; they are nonrenewable.

Additional information These awards were established in 1986 to honor the memory of James H. Robinson, who was clinical professor of surgery and associate dean of student affairs at Jefferson Medical College of Thomas Jefferson University in Philadelphia.

Number awarded 1 each year.

Deadline Nominations must be submitted by February of each year.

[1050]
JOANNE KATHERINE JOHNSON AWARD FOR UNUSUAL ACHIEVEMENT IN MATHEMATICS OR SCIENCE

A Better Chance, Inc.
Attn: College Preparatory Schools Program
88 Black Falcon Avenue, Suite 250
Boston, MA 02210-2414
(617) 421-0950   (800) 562-7865
Fax: (617) 421-0965
Web: www.abetterchance.org

Purpose To recognize and reward minority high school students who have excelled in mathematics or science.

Eligibility This award is presented to the ABC (A Better Chance) high school junior who has best demonstrated his or her accomplishment in mathematics or sciences. Only nominations are accepted.

Financial data The award is $500.

Duration The award is presented annually.

Additional information A Better Chance, Inc. (ABC) is a national, nonprofit organization that selects, recruits, and places students of color in participating schools, including 99 independent boarding schools, 100 independent day schools, and 26 public boarding schools in suburban communities. Approximately 325 students are selected to participate each year. The independent boarding and day schools contribute scholarships for participating students; the communities in which the public high schools are located provide housing and other support.

Number awarded 1 each year.

Deadline March of each year.

[1051]
LEE & LOW BOOKS NEW VOICES AWARD

Lee & Low Books
95 Madison Avenue, Suite 606
New York, NY 10016
(212) 779-4400   Fax: (212) 683-1894
E-mail: info@leeandlow.com
Web: www.leeandlow.com/editorial/voices.html

Purpose To recognize and reward outstanding unpublished children's picture books by writers of color.

Eligibility The contest is open to writers of color who are residents of the United States and who have not previously published a children's picture book. Writers who have published in other venues, (e.g., children's magazines, young adult fiction and non-

fiction, books for adults) are eligible. Manuscripts previously submitted to the sponsor are not eligible. Submissions should be no more than 1,500 words and must address the needs of children of color by providing stories with which they can identify and relate. Of special interest are stories in contemporary settings. Submission may be realistic fiction or nonfiction for children between the ages of 2 and 10. Folklore and animal stories will not be considered. Up to 2 submissions may be submitted per entrant.

Financial data The award is a $1,000 advance against royalties and a publication contract. The Honor Award winner receives a cash grant of $500.

Duration The competition is held annually. Manuscripts may not be sent to any other publishers while under consideration for this award.

Number awarded 2 each year.

Deadline September of each year.

[1052]
LEONARD WERTHEIMER MULTILINGUAL AWARD

American Library Association
Attn: Public Library Association
50 East Huron Street
Chicago, IL 60611-2795
(312) 280-5023   (800) 545-2433, ext. 5023
Fax: (312) 280-5029   TDD: (312) 944-7298
TDD: (888) 814-7692   E-mail: pla@ala.org
Web: www.pla.org

Purpose To recognize and reward work that enhances, improves, and promotes multilingual public library service.

Eligibility Persons, groups, or organizations may be nominated for this award. The nominee's achievements should represent an outstanding contribution in the area of publications, lectures, programs, or other projects that have been presented in a public library setting and have encouraged the development of multilingual service on a national or international scale.

Financial data The award consists of $1,000 and a plaque.

Duration The award is presented annually.

Additional information Funding for this award, established in 1988, is provided by the NTC Publishing Group.

Number awarded 1 each year.

Deadline November of each year.

[1053]
MARIE F. PETERS ETHNIC MINORITIES OUTSTANDING ACHIEVEMENT AWARD

National Council on Family Relations
3989 Central Avenue, N.E., Suite 550
Minneapolis, MN 55421
(763) 781-9331   (888) 781-9331
Fax: (763) 781-9348   E-mail: ncfr3989@ncfr.org
Web: www.ncfr.org

Purpose To recognize and reward minorities who have made significant contributions to the area of ethnic minority families.

Eligibility Members of the National Council on Family Relations (NCFR) who have demonstrated excellence in the area of ethnic minority families are eligible for this award. Selection is based on leadership and/or mentoring, scholarship and/or service, research, publication, teaching, community service, contribution to the ethnic minorities section, and contribution to the NCFR.

Financial data The award is $1,000 and a plaque.

Duration The award is granted biennially, in even-numbered years.

Additional information This award, which was established in 1983, is named after a prominent Black researcher and family sociologist who served in many leadership roles in NCFR. It is sponsored by the Ethnic Minorities Section of NCFR.

Number awarded 1 every other year.

Deadline April of even-numbered years.

[1054]
MINORITY AFFAIRS COMMITTEE AWARD FOR OUTSTANDING SCHOLASTIC ACHIEVEMENT

American Institute of Chemical Engineers
Attn: Awards Administrator
Three Park Avenue
New York, NY 10016-5991
(212) 591-7478   Fax: (212) 591-8882
E-mail: awards@aiche.org
Web: www.aiche.org/awards

Purpose To recognize and reward chemical engineering minority students who serve as role models for other minority students.

Eligibility Members of the American Institute of Chemical Engineers (AIChE) may nominate any chemical engineering student who serves as a role model for minority students in that field. Nominees must be members of a minority group that is underrepresented in chemical engineering (i.e., African American, Hispanic, Native American, Alaskan Native). Selection is based on the nominee's academic and scholarship achievements, including a GPA of 3.0 or higher, scholastic awards, research contributions, and technical presentations; the nominee's exemplary outreach activities that directly benefit or encourage minority youth in their academic pursuits; a letter from the nominee describing his or her outreach activities; and extraordinary circumstances, such as job or family matters, that impose additional responsibility.

Financial data The award consists of a plaque and a $1,500 honorarium.

Duration The award is presented annually.

Additional information This award was first presented in 1996.

Number awarded 1 each year.

Deadline Nominations must be submitted by April of each year.

[1055]
MODELO MUNDIAL-WORLD MODEL COMPETITION

JCPenney Company, Inc.
Attn: Modelo Mundial
P.O. Box 100001
Dallas, TX 75301-8112
(972) 431-4655   E-mail: cbsmith@jcpenney.com
Web: www.jcpenneymodelomundial.com

Purpose To recognize and reward outstanding Hispanic models.

Eligibility This program is open to men and women of Hispanic descent who are between the ages of 16 and 21, reside in the vicinity of a participating JCPenney store, are currently enrolled in high school or an accredited institution of higher education, and have a GPA of 3.0 or higher. Applicants may not be professional models or currently affiliated with a modeling agency. They must submit a 1-page essay describing their academic achievements, extracurricular achievements, and community involvement. Essays are judged on writing skills, flair for self-expression,

and leadership skills. Men and women compete separately at the regional level, and the winners advance to the national competition in Miami, Florida in June.

Financial data Regional winners receive round-trip airfare to Miami and hotel accommodations for 5 days. National winners receive a $10,000 scholarship and a $1,000 JCPenney gift card. National runners-up receive a $5,000 scholarship and a $500 JCPenney gift care.

Duration The competition is held annually.

Additional information This competition has been sponsored by JCPenney since 1990. Through 2002, it was known as the Hispanic Designers Model Search. Its current sponsors include the Havanera Company, Mudd, Reebok, and The Original Arizona Jean Company. Scholarships are provided by Univision, a Spanish language television network in the United States. The participating JCPenney stores operate in Albuquerque, Chicago, Dallas/Fort Worth, Denver, El Paso, Houston, Las Vegas, Los Angeles/San Diego, Miami, McAllen/Harlingen/Brownsville (Texas), New Jersey/New York, Orlando, Phoenix/Tucson, Sacramento/Fresno, Salt Lake City, San Antonio, San Francisco/San Jose, Tampa, Washington, D.C., Puerto Rico, and (in Mexico) Monterrey, Mexico City, and Leon.

Number awarded 46 regional winners (1 man and 1 woman from each of the 23 markets), 2 national grand winners (1 man and 1 woman), and 2 runners-up (also 1 man and 1 woman).

Deadline May of each year.

[1056]
MS. LATINA USA

Dawn Ramos Productions
P.O. Box 1515
Denison, TX 75021
(903) 891-9761   E-mail: info@misslatina.com
Web: www.misslatina.com

Purpose To recognize and reward young Latina women who compete in a national beauty pageant.

Eligibility This program is open to women between 18 and 29 years of age who are at least 25% Hispanic. Applicants may be single, married, or divorced, and they may have children. They appear in a nationally-televised pageant where selection is based one third on an interview, one third on swimsuit appearances, and one third on evening gown appearances. Height and weight are not factors, but contestants should be proportionate. Pageant experience and fluency in Spanish are not required.

Financial data Each year, prizes include scholarships, gifts, a cruise to the Bahamas, a trip to Las Vegas, a modeling contract, and use of an apartment in Miami. The total value is more than $100,000.

Duration The pageant is held annually

Number awarded 1 winner and 4 runners-up are selected each year.

[1057]
NAHJ PHOTOJOURNALISM COMPETITION

National Association of Hispanic Journalists
Attn: Educational Programs Manager
1000 National Press Building
529 14th Street, N.W.
Washington, DC 20045-2001
(202) 662-7145   (888) 346-NAHJ
Fax: (202) 662-7144   E-mail: nahj@nahj.org
Web: www.nahj.org

Purpose To recognize excellence in photography by photojournalists who are members of the National Association of Hispanic Journalists (NAHJ).

Eligibility The competition is open to photojournalists in either English language or Spanish language media (including newspapers and magazines). Photos must be published during the year preceding the competition. Judging is conducted in 6 categories: news, features, portrait/personality, illustration, picture story, and sports. Winners in each category compete for selection as "Best of Show."

Financial data The prize for "Best of Show" is $500.

Duration The competition is held annually.

Additional information There is an entry fee of $20 for members of the Association; nonmembers must also pay a membership fee of $50.00.

Number awarded 1 cash prize each year.

Deadline March of each year.

[1058]
NATIONAL OPERA ASSOCIATION LEGACY AWARDS

National Opera Association
Attn: Executive Secretary
P.O. Box 60869
Canyon, TX 79016-0869
(806) 651-2857   Fax: (806) 651-2958
E-mail: rhansen@mail.wtamu.edu
Web: www.noa.org

Purpose To provide career development assistance to outstanding minority opera singers.

Eligibility Opera singers who are minorities and between the ages of 25 and 40 may enter this audition and competition that is designed to promote racial and ethnic diversity in opera. Membership in the National Opera Association is required. Applicants submit a cassette tape with 2 arias; judges select the finalists on the basis of those recordings. Finalists are then invited to auditions where they identify 4 arias with appropriate recitatives and present 2 of them, 1 chosen by the singer and 1 by the judges.

Financial data The prize is $500.

Duration The competition is held annually. Contestants must enclose a $30 nonrefundable entry fee.

Number awarded 2 each year.

Deadline October of each year.

[1059]
PAULA AWARD FOR YOUNG WRITERS

el ANDAR Publications
Attn: Literary Award
P.O. Box 7745
Santa Cruz, CA 95061
(831) 457-8353   Fax: (831) 457-8354
E-mail: info@elandar.com
Web: www.elandar.com/award/index.html

Purpose To recognize and reward outstanding literary work on themes relevant to Latino youth.

Eligibility Writers 18 years of age and younger are invited to submit poetry, fiction, and creative nonfiction. Entries may be in Spanish, English, or a mix of both languages and should relate to Latino life and experiences. Stories and creative nonfiction should not exceed 4,000 words. Poems may be any length. Only unpublished work is eligible.

Financial data First prize is $1,000 and a 3-year subscription to el ANDAR. Second prize is $250 and a 2-year subscription to el ANDAR. Honorable mentions receive a 1-year subscription to el ANDAR.

Duration The competition is held annually.

Additional information el ANDAR is a literary magazine directed to Latino youth. It established this competition in 2000. The reading fee is $15 for each story, creative nonfiction work, or 3 poems.

Number awarded 1 first prize, 1 second prize, and up to 10 honorable mentions are selected each year.

Deadline September of each year.

[1060]
PAVESNP LIFE/WORK CHALLENGE AWARDS

Pennsylvania Association of Vocational Education Special
    Needs Personnel
c/o Vocational Education Services in Pennsylvania
Penn State McKeesport
4000 University Drive
101 Ostermayer
McKeesport, PA 15132
(412) 675-9065
Web: www.pavesnp.org

Purpose To recognize and reward outstanding vocational education students in Pennsylvania who have special needs.

Eligibility Nominations for these awards may be submitted by professionals or paraprofessionals who are members of the Pennsylvania Association of Vocational Education Special Needs Personnel (PAVESNP). Nominees must be enrolled in an approved career and technical program in the current or previous school year and be receiving services from a special needs program (disabled, disadvantaged, or limited-English proficient). They must demonstrate evidence of a personal commitment to maximizing individual potential, social skills that enhance employability, strong personal work ethic, and occupational competence.

Financial data Awards are $500 for first place, $300 for second, and $100 for third.

Duration Awards are presented annually.

Additional information Information is also available from Marjorie Eckman, Pittsburgh Public Schools, 1398 Page Street, Pittsburgh, PA 15233.

Number awarded 3 each year.

Deadline February of each year.

[1061]
PRESIDENTIAL AWARDS FOR EXCELLENCE IN MATHEMATICS AND SCIENCE TEACHING

National Science Foundation
Directorate for Education and Human Resources
Attn: Division of Elementary, Secondary and Informal
    Education
4201 Wilson Boulevard, Room 885
Arlington, VA 22230
(703) 292-5131   TDD: (703) 292-5090
Web: www.ehr.nsf.gov/pres_awards/info.htm

Purpose To recognize and reward outstanding K-12 teachers of science and mathematics.

Eligibility This program is open to teachers of science or mathematics in a public or private school in the United States or its territories. Teachers must be nominated. Anyone (e.g., principals, teachers, students, and other members of the general public) may nominate a teacher, but self nominations are not accepted. Nominees must be full-time employees of their school districts and anticipate a classroom teaching assignment for the following year. They must have at least 5 years of K-12 teaching experience in science and/or mathematics. Awards are presented in 4 categories: elementary mathematics, elementary science, secondary mathematics, and secondary science. Applications are especially encouraged from underrepresented minority groups (American Indians, African Americans, Hispanics, Native Alaskans, Native Pacific Islanders). Candidates are first selected in 54 regional jurisdictions (1 for each state, the District of Columbia, Puerto Rico, U.S. territories, and schools outside the United States maintained by the federal government for dependents of its employees). Committees in each state and the other 4 jurisdictions select 12 finalists (3 in each category) for the national competition. Selection is based on teaching performance, background, and experience.

Financial data National winners receive a grant of $10,000 for their school, to be spent at their direction to improve the school's mathematics and science programs. They also receive an expense-paid trip to Washington, D.C. to receive their awards.

Duration Awards are presented annually: teachers in grades K-6 are honored in even-numbered years and teachers in grades 7-12 are honored in odd-numbered years.

Additional information This program was established in 1983.

Number awarded 200 each year.

Deadline February of each year.

[1062]
PRESIDIO LA BAHIA AWARD

Sons of the Republic of Texas
Attn: Administrative Assistant
1717 Eighth Street
Bay City, TX 77414
(979) 245-6644   E-mail: srttexas@srttexas.org
Web: www.srttexas.org/labahia.html

Purpose To recognize and reward the most outstanding works that demonstrate the impact and influence of the Spanish colonial heritage on the laws, customs, language, religion, architecture, and art of Texas.

Eligibility The competition is open to any person interested in Spanish colonial influence on Texas culture. Eligible to be consid-

ered are books, published papers, articles published in periodicals, and non-literary projects (such as art, architecture, and archaeological discovery).

Financial data A total of $2,000 is available annually as awards. The prize for the best book is at least $1,200; the organization may award a second-place book prize. The amounts of prizes for best published paper, article published in a periodical, and non-literary project vary each year.

Duration The competition is held annually.

Additional information This award was established in 1968.

Number awarded From 1 to 5 each year.

Deadline September of each year.

[1063]
PURA BELPRE BOOK AWARD

American Library Association
Attn: Association for Library Service to Children
50 East Huron Street
Chicago, IL 60611-2795
(312) 280-1398   (800) 545-2433, ext. 1398
Fax: (312) 280-3255   TDD: (312) 944-7298
TDD: (888) 814-7692   E-mail: alsc@ala.org
Web: www.ala.org/alsc

Purpose To recognize and reward Latino/a authors and illustrators of outstanding books for children.

Eligibility Eligible to be nominated for this award are Latino/a authors and illustrators of outstanding original children's books that portray, affirm, and celebrate the Latino/a cultural experience. The book must have been published in, and nominees must be citizens or residents of, the United States or Puerto Rico. Fiction and nonfiction books for children published in Spanish, English, or bilingual format are eligible.

Financial data The award is $1,000 and a medal.

Duration The award is presented biennially.

Additional information This program, established in 1996, is sponsored by REFORMA (National Association to Promote Library Services to the Spanish Speaking) and the Association for Library Service to Children of the American Library Association.

Number awarded 2 each even-numbered year: 1 to an author and 1 to an illustrator.

Deadline December of odd-numbered years.

[1064]
RALPH J. BUNCHE AWARD

American Political Science Association
1527 New Hampshire Avenue, N.W.
Washington, DC 20036-1206
(202) 483-2512   Fax: (202) 483-2657
E-mail: apsa@apsanet.org
Web: www.apsanet.org/about/awards/bunche.cm

Purpose To recognize and reward outstanding scholarly books on ethnic/cultural pluralism.

Eligibility Eligible to be nominated (by publishers or individuals) are scholarly political science books issued the previous year that explore issues of ethnic and/or cultural pluralism.

Financial data The award is $500.

Duration The competition is held annually.

Number awarded 1 each year.

Deadline February of each year.

[1065]
RALPH W. ELLISON MEMORIAL PRIZE

National Medical Fellowships, Inc.
Attn: Scholarship Program
5 Hanover Square, 15th Floor
New York, NY 10004
(212) 483-8880 Fax: (212) 483-8897
E-mail: info@nmfonline.org
Web: www.nmf-online.org

Purpose To recognize and reward outstanding underrepresented minorities who are graduating from medical school.

Eligibility This award is open to African American, Native Hawaiian, Alaska Native, American Indian, Mexican American, and mainland Puerto Rican students enrolled in accredited U.S. medical schools. Candidates must be nominated by their medical schools during their senior year. Selection is based on academic achievement, leadership, community service, and potential to make significant contributions to medicine.

Financial data This honor includes a certificate of merit and a $500 award.

Duration 1 year; nonrenewable.

Additional information This award was established in 1994 to honor Ralph W. Ellison, the novelist and author of *The Invisible Man* who co-chaired a fund-raising effort of National Medical Fellowships, Inc.

Number awarded 1 each year.

Deadline Nominations must be submitted by February of each year.

[1066]
RECOGNITION AWARD FOR EMERGING SCHOLARS

American Association of University Women
Attn: AAUW Educational Foundation
1111 16th Street, N.W.
Washington, DC 20036-4873
(202) 785-7609 (800) 326-AAUW
Fax: (202) 463-7169 TDD: (202) 785-7777
E-mail: emergingscholar@aauw.org
Web: www.aauw.org

Purpose To recognize and reward young American women who show promise of future academic distinction.

Eligibility Eligible for nomination are nontenured American women faculty members who earned a Ph.D. or equivalent within the past 5 years. Selection is based on demonstrated excellence in teaching, a documented and active research record, and evidence of potentially significant contributions to the awardee's field of study. The sponsor strongly encourages nomination of women of color and other underrepresented groups.

Financial data The award is $5,000.

Duration The award is presented annually.

Additional information The award includes a trip to the annual AAUW convention (where the award is presented).

Number awarded 1 each year.

Deadline Nominations must be submitted by February of each year.

[1067]
SI TV PLAYWRITING AWARD

John F. Kennedy Center for the Performing Arts
Education Department
Attn: Kennedy Center American College Theater Festival
2700 F Street, N.W.
Washington, DC 20566
(202) 416-8857 Fax: (202) 416-8802
E-mail: skshaffer@kennedy-center.org
Web: kennedy-center.org/education/actf/actfsitv.html

Purpose To recognize and reward outstanding plays by Latino playwrights.

Eligibility Latino students at any accredited junior or senior college in the United States are eligible to compete, provided their college agrees to participate in the Kennedy Center American College Theater Festival (KCACTF). Undergraduate students must be carrying at least 6 semester hours, graduate students must be enrolled in at least 3 semester hours, and continuing part-time students must be enrolled in a regular degree or certificate program. This award is presented to the best student-written play by a Latino.

Financial data The prize is $2,500. The winner also receives an internship to a prestigious playwriting retreat program. Dramatic Publishing Company presents the winning playwright with an offer of a contract to publish, license, and market the winning play. A grant of $500 is made to the theater department of the college or university producing the award-winning play.

Duration The award is presented annually.

Additional information This award, first presented in 2000, is supported by Sí TV, the nation's first television programming service designed specifically for English dominant/bilingual Latino viewers. It is part of the Michael Kanin Playwriting Awards Program. The sponsoring college or university must pay a registration fee of $250 for each production.

Number awarded 1 each year.

Deadline November of each year.

[1068]
SIMON BOLIVAR LECTURE AWARD

American Psychiatric Association
Attn: Council on Minority Mental Health and Health Disparities
1400 K Street, N.W.
Washington, DC 20005
(202) 682-6000 Fax: (202) 682-6850
E-mail: apa@psych.org
Web: www.psych.org

Purpose To recognize and reward Hispanic statesmen who have helped to publicize the problems and goals of Hispanics in the United States and to sensitize the American Psychiatric Association (APA) membership to these problems and goals.

Eligibility Prominent Hispanic statesmen who have focused attention on the problems and goals of Hispanics in the United States and Puerto Rico are considered for this award.

Financial data The award provides a $500 honorarium and a plaque. The recipient delivers a lecture at the APA annual meeting. Nonmember winners also receive travel expenses.

Duration The award is presented annually.

Additional information The winner is selected by the Committee of Hispanic Psychiatrists. This program was established in 1975.

Number awarded 1 each year.

[1069]
SPHINX COMPETITION AWARDS

Sphinx Organization
Attn: Artistic Director
3319 Greenfield Road, Suite 705
Dearborn, MI 48120-1212
(313) 336-9809   Fax: (313) 336-9033
E-mail: info@sphinxmusic.org
Web: www.sphinxmusic.org

Purpose To recognize and reward outstanding junior high, high school, and college-age Black and Latino string instrumentalists.

Eligibility This competition is open to Black and Latino instrumentalists in 2 divisions: junior, for participants who are younger than 18 years of age, and senior, for participants who are at least 18 but younger than 27 years of age. All entrants must be current U.S. residents who can compete in the instrumental categories of violin, viola, cello, and double bass. Along with their applications, they must submit a preliminary audition tape that includes all of the required preliminary repertoire for their instrument category. Based on those tapes, qualifiers are invited to participate in the semifinals and finals competitions, held at sites in Detroit and Ann Arbor, Michigan.

Financial data In the senior division, the first-place winner receives a $10,000 cash prize, solo appearances with major orchestras, and a performance with the Sphinx Symphony; the second-place winner receives a $5,000 cash prize and a performance with the Sphinx Symphony; the third-place winner receives a $3,500 cash prize and a performance with the Sphinx Symphony. In the junior division, the first-place winner receives a $5,000 cash prize and 2 performances with the Sphinx Symphony; the second-place winner receives a $3,500 cash prize and a performance with the Sphinx Symphony; the third-place winner receives a $2,000 cash prize and a performance with the Sphinx Symphony. All semifinalists receive scholarships to attend a summer program at Aspen, Blossom, BU Tanglewood, Chautauqua, DSO Summer Institute, ENCORE, Interlochen, Mark O'Connor Fiddle Conference, Musicorda, National Symphony Summer Institute, National Orchestral Institute, Orchestra of the Americas, Sewanee, or Walnut Hill School. They also receive modest stipends to augment their instrumental studies from the Music Assistance Fund (MAF) of the American Symphony Orchestra League.

Duration The competition is held annually.

Additional information The sponsoring organization was incorporated in 1996 to hold this competition, first conducted in 1998. The Sphinx Symphony is an all African American and Latino orchestra that performs at Orchestra Hall in Detroit. The MAF program was established by the New York Philharmonic in 1965 and transferred to the American Symphony Orchestra League in 1994. In 2002, it partnered with the Sphinx Organization to provide scholarships to all 18 semifinalists. Additional support for MAF is provided by ABC, Inc., Foundation, the Brown Foundation, Inc. (Houston, Texas), the International Conference of Symphony and Opera Musicians and Anheuser-Busch. The MAF program also provides full tuition scholarships to Sphinx semifinalists who attend the Indiana University School of Music, Julliard School, Manhattan School of Music, and the University of Michigan School of Music. Applications must be accompanied by a $35 fee. That fee may be waived if demonstrable need is shown.

Number awarded 18 semifinalists (from both divisions and all instrumental categories) are selected each year. Of those, 3 junior and 3 senior competitors win cash prizes.

Deadline November of each year.

[1070]
STEPHEN H. COLTRIN AWARD FOR EXCELLENCE IN COMMUNICATION EDUCATION

International Radio and Television Society Foundation
Attn: Director, Special Projects
420 Lexington Avenue, Suite 1601
New York, NY 10170-0101
(212) 867-6650, ext. 306   (888) 627-1266
Fax: (212) 867-6653   E-mail: apply@irts.org
Web: www.irts.org/coltrinteam.htm

Purpose To recognize and reward college faculty members who teach electronic communications and participate in a case study competition.

Eligibility Each year, the sponsoring organization conducts a faculty/industry seminar for 75 faculty members who teach in fields relevant to electronic communications at schools nationwide. At the seminar, teams of participants engage in a case study competition on methods of teaching in the field. The winning team receives this award. Minority faculty are given priority.

Financial data The prize is $2,500 to be divided among team members.

Duration The prize is awarded annually. The registration fee to attend the seminar is $150. That covers hotel accommodations and most meals, but participants are responsible for their own transportation and incidental expenses.

Number awarded 1 each year.

Deadline December of each year.

[1071]
TACHE DISTINGUISHED COMMUNITY COLLEGE FACULTY AWARD

Texas Association of Chicanos in Higher Education
P.O. Box 986
Austin, TX 78767-0986
Web: www.tache.org

Purpose To recognize and reward outstanding community college faculty members in Texas who are members of the Texas Association of Chicanos in Higher Education (TACHE).

Eligibility Eligible to be nominated for this award are active TACHE members who have taught for at least the last 5 years at a Texas community college. Nominees must have demonstrated a consistent pattern of teaching excellence, innovation in teaching, contributions to discipline-specific scholarship, a consistent pattern of service to the community, a consistent pattern of support of Chicano/Latino programs and students, support for and promotion of postsecondary education, and a consistent pattern of mentoring other faculty and/or students. Self nominations are accepted.

Financial data The award is $1,000.

Duration The award is presented annually.

Additional information Information is also available from Rudy Duarte, Distinguished Community College Faculty Award Chair, Del Mar College, 101 Baldwin, Corpus Christi, TX 78404.

Number awarded 1 each year.

Deadline November of each year.

[1072]
TACHE DISTINGUISHED UNIVERSITY FACULTY AWARD

Texas Association of Chicanos in Higher Education
P.O. Box 986
Austin, TX 78767-0986
Web: www.tache.org

Purpose To recognize and reward outstanding university faculty members in Texas who are members of the Texas Association of Chicanos in Higher Education (TACHE).

Eligibility Eligible to be nominated for this award are active TACHE members who have taught for at least the last 5 years at a Texas university. Nominees must have demonstrated a consistent pattern of excellence in teaching, innovation in teaching, a record of scholarly publications or other contributions to the profession or academic discipline, a consistent pattern of service to the community, a consistent pattern of support of Chicano/Latino programs and students, support for and promotion of postsecondary and graduate education, and a consistent pattern of mentoring other faculty and/or students. Self nominations are accepted.

Financial data The award is $1,000.

Duration The award is presented annually.

Additional information Information is also available from Gloria B. Bahamón, Distinguished University Faculty Award Chair, University of North Texas, P.O. Box 310937, Denton, TX 76203-0937.

Number awarded 1 each year.

Deadline November of each year.

[1073]
TEEN LATINA USA

Dawn Ramos Productions
P.O. Box 1515
Denison, TX 75021
(903) 891-9761   E-mail: info@misslatina.com
Web: www.misslatina.com

Purpose To recognize and reward teen-aged Latina women who compete in a national beauty pageant.

Eligibility This program is open to women between 13 and 17 years of age who are at least 25% Hispanic. Applicants must be single and they may not have children. They appear in a nationally-televised pageant where selection is based one third on an interview, one third on swimsuit appearances, and one third on evening gown appearances. Height and weight are not factors, but contestants should be proportionate. Pageant experience and fluency in Spanish are not required.

Financial data Each year, prizes include scholarships, gifts, a cruise to the Bahamas, a trip to Las Vegas, a modeling contract, and use of an apartment in Miami. The total value is more than $25,000.

Duration The pageant is held annually

Number awarded 1 winner and 4 runners-up are selected each year.

[1074]
TOMAS RIVERA MEXICAN AMERICAN CHILDREN'S BOOK AWARD

Southwest Texas State University
Attn: Department of Curriculum and Instruction
601 University Drive
San Marcos, TX 78666-4616
(512) 245-2157
Web: www.education.swt.edu/rivera/mainpage.html

Purpose To recognize and reward outstanding children's books that reflect the culture of Mexican Americans in the United States.

Eligibility Eligible to be nominated for this award are children's books that authentically reflect Mexican American culture in the Untied States.

Financial data The award is $3,000.

Duration The award is presented annually, during Hispanic Heritage month at Southwest Texas State University.

Additional information The award was first presented in 1995.

Number awarded 1 each year.

Deadline January of each year.

[1075]
VIGIL POSTER PRESENTATION AWARDS

Society for Advancement of Chicanos and Native Americans in Science
333 Front Street, Suite 104
P.O. Box 8526
Santa Cruz, CA 95061-8526
(831) 459-0170   Fax: (831) 459-0194
E-mail: info@sacnas.org
Web: www.sacnas.org

Purpose To recognize and reward outstanding undergraduate research posters presented at the annual conference of the Society for Advancement of Chicanos and Native Americans in Science (SACNAS).

Eligibility Chicano and Native American undergraduate students who present research posters in biological and physical sciences at the society's annual conference are eligible for these awards.

Financial data The award consists of a certificate and a $1,000 scholarship.

Duration The competition is held annually.

Number awarded 4 each year.

Deadline July of each year.

[1076]
WILLIAM AND CHARLOTTE CADBURY AWARD

National Medical Fellowships, Inc.
Attn: Scholarship Program
5 Hanover Square, 15th Floor
New York, NY 10004
(212) 483-8880   Fax: (212) 483-8897
E-mail: info@nmfonline.org
Web: www.nmf-online.org

Purpose To recognize and reward underrepresented minority medical school students' outstanding academic achievement, leadership, and community service.

Eligibility This award is open to minority students enrolled in their senior year at an accredited U.S. medical school. For the purposes of this program, "minority" is defined as African American, Native Hawaiian, Alaska Native, American Indian, Mexican American, and mainland Puerto Rican. Candidates must be nominated by their medical school during the summer preceding their senior year. Selection is based on academic achievement, leadership, and community service.

Financial data This honor includes a certificate of merit and a $2,000 stipend.

Duration The award is presented annually.

Additional information This award was established in 1977.

Number awarded 1 each year.

Deadline Nominations must be submitted by July of each year.

[1077]
WYETH-AYERST LABORATORIES PRIZE IN WOMEN'S HEALTH

National Medical Fellowships, Inc.
Attn: Scholarship Program
5 Hanover Square, 15th Floor
New York, NY 10004
(212) 483-8880   Fax: (212) 483-8897
E-mail: info@nmfonline.org
Web: www.nmf-online.org

Purpose To recognize and reward outstanding underrepresented minority women medical students.

Eligibility This program is open to underrepresented minority (African American, Native Hawaiian, Alaska Native, American Indian, Mexican American, and mainland Puerto Rican) women medical students in their fourth year of study. Candidates must demonstrate exceptional academic achievement, leadership, and the potential to make significant contributions in the field of women's health. Direct applications are not accepted; candidates must be nominated by their medical school dean.

Financial data This honor includes a certificate of merit and a $5,000 stipend.

Duration The award is presented annually.

Additional information Funding for this program is provided by Wyeth-Ayerst Laboratories.

Number awarded 2 each year.

Deadline Nominations must be submitted by February of each year.

Internships

Described here are 236 work experience programs open to undergraduate, graduate, or postgraduate Hispanic Americans. Only salaried positions are covered. If you are looking for a particular program and don't find it in this section, be sure to check the Program Title Index to see if it is covered elsewhere in the directory.

[1078]
ACT SUMMER INTERNSHIP PROGRAM

American College Testing
Attn: Human Resources Department
2201 North Dodge Street
P.O. Box 168
Iowa City, IA 52243-0168
(319) 337-1006   E-mail: employment@act.org
Web: www.act.org

Purpose To provide work experience during the summer to graduate students (particularly women and minorities) interested in careers in testing and measurement.

Eligibility This program is open to graduate students enrolled in such fields as educational psychology, measurement, program evaluation, counseling psychology, educational policy, mathematical and applied statistics, industrial or organizational psychology, and counselor education. Selection is based on technical skills, previous practical or work experience, interest in careers in testing, general academic qualifications, and the match of course work and research interests with those of sponsoring mentors. The program is also intended to assist in increasing the number of women and minority professionals in measurement and related fields.

Financial data Interns receive a stipend of $3,500 and round-trip transportation between their graduate institution and Iowa City. A supplemental living allowance of $400 is provided if a spouse and/or children accompany the intern.

Duration 8 weeks, during the summer.

Additional information Assignments are available in 4 categories: 1) policy research, program evaluation, and institutional services; 2) industrial and organizational psychology; 3) psychometric and statistical analysis; and 4) vocational psychology. Interns work with assigned mentors and participate in weekly seminars led by the professional staff of American College Testing (ACT).

Number awarded Varies each year.

Deadline February of each year.

[1079]
¡ADELANTE! FUND SCHOLARSHIP PROGRAM

¡Adelante! U.S. Education Leadership Fund
8415 Datapoint Drive, Suite 400
San Antonio, TX 78229
(210) 692-1971   Fax: (210) 692-1951
E-mail: rubeng@dcci.com

Purpose To provide financial aid, internships, and leadership training to upper-division Hispanic students enrolled in Hispanic Serving Institutions (HSIs).

Eligibility This program is open to Hispanic students currently enrolled in HSIs. Applicants must have a GPA of 3.0 or higher, be eligible to receive financial aid, be juniors or seniors in college, agree to attend the Adelante Leadership Institute, be eligible to participate in a summer internship, exhibit leadership, and provide 2 letters of recommendation. Most recipients are the first in their families to complete a college education.

Financial data The maximum stipend is $3,000 per year.

Duration 1 year.

Additional information This fund was established by the Hispanic Association of Colleges and Universities in 1997 and became a separate organization in 1999. Recipients must participate in a summer internship and the Adelante Leadership Institute.

Number awarded Varies each year; recently, 22 students received scholarships.

[1080]
ADVANCED SIMULATION AND COMPUTING PIPELINE PROGRAM

Lawrence Livermore National Laboratory
Attn: Science & Technology Education Program
P.O. Box 808, L-428
Livermore, CA 94551
(925) 422-5460   Fax: (925) 422-5761
E-mail: education@llnl.gov
Web: education.llnl.gov/asci_interns

Purpose To provide an opportunity for undergraduate students to work on a high-performance, computer-based modeling and simulation project at Lawrence Livermore National Laboratory.

Eligibility This program is open to advanced undergraduate students who are U.S. citizens with a GPA of 3.0 (preferably 3.4) or higher. Applicants should be majoring in computer science and interested in working on a project at the laboratory in the discipline of high-performance, computer-based modeling and simulation. A particular goal of this program is "to increase the students majoring in computer science who represent America's ethnic diversity." Selection is based on academic achievement, prior experience, technical interest, and number of positions available.

Financial data Participants receive a competitive salary. Travel expenses may be reimbursed.

Duration Approximately 12 weeks, during the summer or semester.

Additional information This program began in 2000 as a pilot program for students at Northern Arizona University, California State University at Hayward, and San Jose State University. Currently, all undergraduate students who meet the eligibility requirements are considered.

Number awarded Varies each year.

Deadline February of each year.

[1081]
ALASKA SPACE GRANT PROGRAM FELLOWSHIPS

Alaska Space Grant Program
c/o University of Alaska at Fairbanks
Duckering Hall, Room 225
P.O. Box 755919
Fairbanks, AK 99775-5919
(907) 474-6833   Fax: (907) 474-5135
E-mail: fyspace@uaf.edu
Web: www.uaf.edu/asgp

Purpose To provide undergraduate and graduate students at member institutions of the Alaska Space Grant Program (ASGP) with an opportunity to work on aerospace-related projects.

Eligibility This program is open to undergraduate and graduate students at the lead institution and academic affiliates of the ASGP. Applicants must be interested in assisting on projects that provide a professional development opportunity for the student but also develop aerospace capabilities within Alaska. The ASGP is a component of the Space Grant program of the U.S. National Aeronautics and Space Administration (NASA), which encourages participation by women, underrepresented minorities, and persons with disabilities.

Financial data The amount of each award depends on the scope of the project and the level of responsibility assumed by the recipient. Most awards are less than $5,000.

Additional information The ASGP lead institution is the University of Alaska at Fairbanks; academic affiliates include the University of Alaska Southeast, the University of Alaska at Anchorage, and Alaska Pacific University. Funding for this program is provided by NASA.

Number awarded Varies each year.

[1082]
AMERICAN HEART ASSOCIATION UNDERGRADUATE STUDENT RESEARCH PROGRAM

American Heart Association-Western States Affiliate
Attn: Research Department
1710 Gilbreth Road
Burlingame, CA 94010-1317
(650) 259-6725   Fax: (650) 259-6891
E-mail: research@heart.org
Web: www.heartsource.org

Purpose To provide gifted students from all disciplines with an opportunity to work on a cardiovascular and cerebrovascular research project.

Eligibility This program is open to college students who are enrolled full time at an accredited academic institution at the junior or senior level. They must be 1) interested in interning at a laboratory concerned with cardiovascular and cerebrovascular research and 2) residents of California, Nevada, or Utah, or attending a college or university in 1 of those states. Applicants must have completed the following (or equivalent) courses: 4 semesters (or 6 quarters) of biological sciences, physics, or chemistry; and 1 quarter of calculus, statistics, computational methods, or computer science. Selection is based on an assessment of the student's application, academic record (preference is given to students with superior academic standing), and faculty recommendations. Women and minorities are particularly encouraged to apply.

Financial data Participants receive a $4,000 stipend.

Duration 10 weeks, during the summer.

Additional information Participants are assigned to laboratories in California, Nevada, or Utah to work under the direction and supervision of experienced scientists.

Deadline Applications must be requested by December of each year and submitted by January of each year.

[1083]
ANCHORAGE DAILY NEWS INTERNSHIPS

Anchorage Daily News
Attn: Human Resources
1001 Northway Drive
P.O. Box 149001
Anchorage, AK 99514-9001
(907) 257-4402   (800) 478-4200
Fax: (907) 257-4472   E-mail: kmacknicki@adn.com
Web: www.adn.com/adn/intern/intern.html

Purpose To provide work experience at the *Anchorage Daily News* during the summer to college students and graduates interested in journalism as a career.

Eligibility Applicants must have completed at least 2 years of journalism education, including graduate students and career changers. They must have published work in school or other publications and have been trained in the basics of journalism. Internships are available in reporting and photography. Members of minority groups and women are encouraged to apply.

Financial data The salary is approximately $9.50 per hour for 40 hours per week.

Duration 12 weeks in the summer.

Number awarded 3 each year: 2 in reporting (1 in news and 1 in feature writing) and 1 in photography.

Deadline December of each year for reporters; January of each year for photographers.

[1084]
ANUARIO HISPANO HISPANIC DIVISION FELLOWSHIP

Library of Congress
Attn: Hispanic Division
101 Independence Avenue, S.E.
Washington, DC 20540-4850
(202) 707-5400   Fax: (202) 707-2005
E-mail: akur@loc.gov

Purpose To provide work experience in the Hispanic Division of the Library of Congress to students or recent graduates.

Eligibility Applicants must either be enrolled in an ongoing academic program at the junior, senior, or graduate level, or have just completed their degree at an accredited college or university. Thorough knowledge of Spanish is required. Applications from women, minorities, and persons with disabilities are particularly encouraged.

Financial data The stipend is $1,200 per month.

Duration Approximately 8 weeks, during the summer.

Additional information The Hispanic Division of the Library of Congress determines the scope of the assignment, but it involves doing bibliographical research, producing finding aids and bibliographic records, assisting Hispanic Division patrons, and working closely with primary source materials and publications dealing with Hispanics. Funding for this program is provided by the Anuario Hispano/Hispanic Yearbook.

Number awarded Varies each year.

Deadline April of each year.

[1085]
ARIZONA SPACE GRANT CONSORTIUM UNDERGRADUATE RESEARCH INTERNSHIPS

Arizona Space Grant Consortium
c/o University of Arizona
Gerard P. Kuiper Space Sciences Building, Room 345
1629 East University Boulevard
Tucson, AZ 85721
(520) 621-8556   Fax: (520) 621-4933
E-mail: sbrew@lpl.arizona.edu
Web: spacegrant.arizona.edu/undergrad_internships

Purpose To provide an opportunity for undergraduate students at member and affiliate institutions of the Arizona Space Grant Consortium to participate as interns in scientific research activities on campus.

Eligibility This program is open to full-time undergraduate students at member institutions (University of Arizona, Northern Arizona University, and Arizona State University) and affiliate institutions (Eastern Arizona College) of the consortium. Applicants must be at least sophomores and U.S. citizens, but they do not need to be science or engineering majors. Applications are especially encouraged from members of underrepresented minority groups and women.

Financial data Interns are paid at the rate of $7 per hour.

Duration 1 academic year.

Additional information Interns work with faculty members and graduate students on space-related science projects. Funding for this program is provided by the U.S. National Aeronautics and Space Administration (NASA).

Number awarded Varies; recently, the program provided for 55 interns at the University of Arizona, 9 at Northern Arizona University, 24 at Arizona State University, and 4 at Eastern Arizona College.

Deadline June of each year.

[1086]
ARMY JUDGE ADVOCATE GENERAL'S CORPS SUMMER INTERN PROGRAM

U.S. Army
Attn: Judge Advocate Recruiting Office
901 North Stuart Street, Suite 700
Arlington, VA 22203-1837
(703) 696-2822   (866) ARMY-JAG
Web: www.jagcnet.army.mil

Purpose To provide law students with an opportunity to gain work experience during the summer in Army legal offices throughout the United States and overseas.

Eligibility This program is open to full-time students enrolled in law schools accredited by the American Bar Association. Applications are accepted both from students who are completing the first year of law school and those completing the second year. Students must be interested in a summer internship with the Army Judge Advocate General's Corps (JAGC). U.S. citizenship is required. The program actively seeks applications from women and minority group members. Selection is based on academic ability and demonstrated leadership potential.

Financial data Interns who have completed the first year of law school are paid at the GS-5 scale, or approximately $525 per week. Interns who have completed the second year of law school are paid at the GS-7 scale, or approximately $605 per week.

Duration Approximately 60 days, beginning in May or June.

Additional information Interns work under the supervision of an attorney and perform legal research, write briefs and opinions, conduct investigations, interview witnesses, and otherwise assist in preparing civil or criminal cases. Positions are available at Department of the Army legal offices in Washington, D.C. and at Army installations throughout the United States and overseas. These are not military positions. No military obligation is incurred by participating in the summer intern program.

Number awarded 100 per year: 25 first-year students and 75 second-year students.

Deadline February of each year for first-year students; October of each year for second-year students.

[1087]
ART PETERS PROGRAM

Philadelphia Inquirer
Attn: Oscar Miller, Director of Recruiting
400 North Broad Street
P.O. Box 8263
Philadelphia, PA 19101
(215) 854-5102   Fax: (215) 854-2578
E-mail: inkyjobs@phillynews.com
Web: www.philly.com/mld/philly

Purpose To provide copy editing experience during the summer at the *Philadelphia Inquirer* to minority college students interested in careers in journalism.

Eligibility Minority college students entering their sophomore, junior, or senior year in college are eligible to apply if they are interested in the practical work of copy editing. The internship is at the *Philadelphia Inquirer*. Selection is based on experience, potential, academic record, and extracurricular activities.

Financial data The salary is $573 per week.

Duration 10 weeks beginning in June.

Additional information After 1 week of orientation, interns are given their assignments at the *Philadelphia Inquirer:* reporters cover and write stories for the city, business, sports, or features desks; copy editors write headlines and edit articles for those desks or the national/foreign copy desk.

Number awarded 7 each year: 4 in copy-editing and 3 in reporting.

Deadline November of each year.

[1088]
ARTS EDUCATION INTERNSHIPS

Very Special Arts
Attn: Director of Human Resources
1300 Connecticut Avenue, N.W., Suite 700
Washington, DC 20036
(202) 628-2800   (800) 933-8721
Fax: (202) 737-0725   TTY: (202) 737-0645
E-mail: hr@vsarts.org
Web: www.vsarts.org/info/interns/arteducation.html

Purpose To provide work experience in arts education at the Very Special Arts program of the John F. Kennedy Center for the Performing Arts.

Eligibility This program is open to students in arts education or arts administration who are interested in active participation to gain experience and knowledge in the areas of service delivery to an affiliate-based constituency, arts in education research, program and services evaluation, conference and meeting planning, and the overall implementation of arts in education. Applicants must demonstrate excellent oral and written communication skills, basic knowledge of arts education programming, ability to work cooperatively as a team member towards specific goals, motivation to excel in a fast-paced environment, orientation to detail, and willingness to be mentored. Minorities and persons with disabilities are encouraged to apply.

Financial data A stipend is paid (amount not specified).

Duration 1 semester.

Number awarded 1 or more each year.

[1089]
ASA S. BUSHNELL INTERNSHIP PROGRAM
Eastern College Athletic Conference
Attn: Kyle Kravchuk
1311 Craigville Beach Road
Centerville, MA 02632
(508) 771-5060 Fax: (508) 771-9481
Web: www.ecac.com

Purpose To provide work experience to recent college graduates interested in college sports.

Eligibility This program is open to recent graduates of a member institution of the Eastern College Athletic Conference (ECAC) with an undergraduate degree. Applicants must submit the following: a cover letter describing their experience in athletics administration, public relations, sports information or sports writing, event management, marketing, fund-raising, and computer literacy; a current resume detailing academic achievement, intercollegiate athletics participation, extracurricular activities and honors, and employment history; 2 writing samples or publications, if available; and 2 written recommendations and 1 additional reference. They must have demonstrated an interest in pursuing a career in athletics administration and should have proficient working knowledge of Microsoft Office, Quark X-Press, and desktop publishing. Women and minorities are encouraged to apply.

Financial data The stipend is $1,000 per month. Medical, dental, and long-term disability insurance are also provided.

Duration 9 months, from September through May.

Additional information The ECAC is comprised of 309 colleges and universities located in New England and the Middle Atlantic states. Most schools hold dual membership with the Ivy, Northeast, or Patriot Leagues or the America East, Atlantic 10, Big East, Colonial Athletic, or Metro Atlantic conferences. Interns work at the ECAC offices in Centerville, Massachusetts. Recently, the internship concentrations included public relations, championships, marketing, and ice hockey league administration.

Number awarded 2 or 3 each year.

Deadline March of each year.

[1090]
ASPET INDIVIDUAL SUMMER UNDERGRADUATE RESEARCH FELLOWSHIPS
American Society for Pharmacology and Experimental
  Therapeutics
9650 Rockville Pike
Bethesda, MD 20814-3995
(301) 530-7060 Fax: (301) 530-7061
E-mail: info@aspet.org
Web: www.aspet.org

Purpose To provide funding to undergraduate students who are interested in participating in a summer research project at a laboratory affiliated with the American Society for Pharmacology and Experimental Therapeutics (ASPET).

Eligibility This program is open to undergraduate students interested in working during the summer in the laboratory of a society member who must agree to act as a sponsor. Applications must be submitted jointly by the student and the sponsor, and they must include 1) a letter from the sponsor with a brief description of the proposed research, a statement of the qualifications of the student, the degree of independence the student will have, a description of complementary activities available to the student, and a description of how the student will report on

the research results; 2) a letter from the student indicating the nature of his or her interest in the project and a description of future plans; 3) a copy of the sponsor's updated curriculum vitae; and 4) copies of all the student's undergraduate transcripts. Selection is based on the nature of the research opportunities provided, student and sponsor qualifications, and the likelihood the student will pursue a career in pharmacology. Applications from underrepresented minorities and women are particularly encouraged.

Financial data The stipend is $2,500. Funds are paid directly to the institution but may be used only for student stipends.

Duration 10 weeks, during the summer.

Additional information This program is funded through the Glenn E. Ullyot Fund; the recipients are designated as the Ullyot Fellows.

Number awarded Varies each year; recently, 16 of these fellowships were awarded.

Deadline February of each year.

[1091]
ATLAS SCHOLARS PROGRAM
Johns Hopkins University
Applied Physics Laboratory
Attn: College Relations Office
11100 Johns Hopkins Road
Laurel, MD 20723-6099
(443) 778-6031 Fax: (443) 778-5274
Web: www.jhuapl.edu

Purpose To provide an opportunity for undergraduate students from Historically Black Colleges and Universities (HBCUs) and other minority institutions (MIs) to obtain research experience during the summer at Johns Hopkins University's Applied Physics Laboratory (APL).

Eligibility This program is open to students at selected HBCUs and MIs who are in their junior year. Applicants must be majoring in electrical engineering or computer sciences and have a GPA of 3.5 or higher. They must be interested in working at the laboratory on a research project under the mentorship of a staff scientist or engineer.

Financial data Scholars receive a stipend (amount not specified) and round-trip travel expenses.

Duration 12 weeks, during the summer.

Additional information This program was established in 1997 as the APL Technology Leaders Summer Internship Program.

Number awarded Varies each year.

Deadline January of each year.

[1092]
AT&T LABORATORIES FELLOWSHIP PROGRAM FELLOWSHIPS
AT&T Laboratories
Attn: Fellowship Administrator
180 Park Avenue, Room C103
P.O. Box 971
Florham Park, NJ 07932-0971
(973) 360-8109 Fax: (973) 360-8881
Web: www.research.att.com/academic

Purpose To provide financial assistance and work experience to underrepresented minority and women students who are pursuing doctoral studies in computer and communications-related fields.

Eligibility This program is open to minorities underrepresented in the sciences (Blacks, Hispanics, and Native Americans) and to women. Applicants must be U.S. citizens or permanent residents beginning full-time Ph.D. study in a discipline relevant to the business of AT&T; currently, those include communications, computer science, electrical engineering, human computer interaction, industrial engineering, information science, mathematics, operations research, and statistics. Along with their application, they must submit a statement describing their technical interests and accomplishments, official transcripts, 3 academic references, and GRE scores. Selection is based on potential for success in scientific research. Fellowships are offered to students who receive no other support for graduate study.

Financial data This program covers all educational expenses during the school year, including tuition, books, fees, and approved travel expenses; education expenses for summer study or university research; a stipend for living expenses of $1,400 per month (paid for 12 months the first 2 years and for 10 months in the following years); and support for attending approved scientific conferences.

Duration 1 year; may be renewed for up to 5 additional years, as long as the fellow continues making satisfactory progress toward the Ph.D.

Additional information The AT&T Laboratories Fellowship Program (ALFP) provides a mentor who is a staff member at AT&T Labs as well as a summer research internship within AT&T Laboratories during the first summer. The ALFP replaces the Graduate Research Program for Women (GRPW) and the Cooperative Research Fellowship Program (CRFP) run by the former AT&T Bell Laboratories. If students receive other fellowship support, the tuition support and stipend provided as part of the ALFP Fellowship will cease, but the other provisions will remain in force and the student will remain eligible for an ALFP Grant.

Number awarded Varies each year.

Deadline January of each year.

[1093]
AT&T LABORATORIES FELLOWSHIP PROGRAM GRANTS

AT&T Laboratories
Attn: Fellowship Administrator
180 Park Avenue, Room C103
P.O. Box 971
Florham Park, NJ 07932-0971
(973) 360-8109   Fax: (973) 360-8881
Web: www.research.att.com/academic

Purpose To provide financial assistance and work experience to underrepresented minority and women students who are pursuing doctoral studies in computer and communications-related fields.

Eligibility This program is open to minorities underrepresented in the sciences (Blacks, Hispanics, and Native Americans) and to women. Applicants must be U.S. citizens or permanent residents beginning full-time Ph.D. study in a discipline relevant to the business of AT&T; currently, those include communications, computer science, electrical engineering, human computer interaction, industrial engineering, information science, mathematics, operations research, and statistics. Along with their application, they must submit a statement describing their technical interests and accomplishments, official transcripts, 3 academic references, and GRE scores. Selection is based on potential for success in

scientific research. Grants are offered to students who receive other support for graduate study.

Financial data This program provides an annual stipend of $2,000 and conference travel support.

Duration 1 year; may be renewed for up to 5 additional years, as long as the fellow continues making satisfactory progress toward the Ph.D.

Additional information The AT&T Laboratories Fellowship Program (ALFP) provides a mentor who is a staff member at AT&T Laboratories as well as a summer research internship within AT&T Laboratories during the first summer. The ALFP replaces the Graduate Research Program for Women (GRPW) and the Cooperative Research Fellowship Program (CRFP) run by the former AT&T Bell Laboratories.

Number awarded Varies each year.

Deadline January of each year.

[1094]
AT&T UNDERGRADUATE RESEARCH PROGRAM

AT&T Laboratories
Attn: Undergraduate Research Program
180 Park Avenue, Room C103
P.O. Box 971
Florham Park, NJ 07932-0971
(973) 360-8109   Fax: (973) 360-8881
Web: www.research.att.com/academic

Purpose To provide work experience at AT&T Laboratories during the summer to women or members of underrepresented minority groups interested in technical employment.

Eligibility This program is open to U.S. citizens and permanent residents who are undergraduate students in at least their third year but who are not graduating prior to the summer. Applicants must be women or members of a minority group that is underrepresented in the sciences (Blacks, Hispanics, or Native Americans). They must be studying communications, computer science, electrical engineering, human computer interaction, industrial engineering, information science, mathematics, operations research, or statistics. Selection is based on academic achievement, personal motivation, and compatibility of student interests with current AT&T Laboratories activities.

Financial data Salaries are commensurate with those of regular AT&T Laboratories employees who have comparable education and work experience (approximately $500 per week). Trainees are reimbursed for their travel to and from New Jersey. Assistance in locating housing is offered.

Duration The minimum traineeship is 10 weeks during the summer.

Additional information Trainees work at AT&T Laboratories located in Crawford Hill, Holmdel, Murray Hill, Shippany, South Plainfield, Short Hills, or West Long Branch, New Jersey. This program replaces the Summer Research Program of the former AT&T Bell Laboratories. Information is also available from the AT&T Labs Undergraduate Research Program, 200 Laurel Avenue South, Room D32A04, Middletown, NJ 07748.

Number awarded 60 to 100 each year.

Deadline November of each year.

[1095]
BANK ONE/UNCF CORPORATE SCHOLARS PROGRAM

United Negro College Fund
Attn: Program Services Department
8260 Willow Oaks Corporate Drive
P.O. Box 10444
Fairfax, VA 22031-8044
(703) 205-3490 (866) 671-7237
Fax: (703) 205-3550 E-mail: internship@uncf.org
Web: www.uncf.org/Scholarship/CorporateScholars.asp

Purpose To provide financial assistance and work experience to minority undergraduates who are interested in preparing for a career in banking.

Eligibility This program is open to African American, Asian/Pacific Islander, Hispanic, and Native American/Alaskan Native students at targeted colleges and universities and those that are members of the United Negro College Fund (UNCF). Applicants must be sophomores or juniors with a GPA of 3.0 or higher. All majors are welcome; degrees in accounting, business administration, finance, and retail management are preferred. Along with their application, students must submit an official school transcript, a letter of recommendation from a faculty member, a resume, a personal statement of career interest, and a financial need statement. Finalists are interviewed by representatives of Bank One, the program's sponsor.

Financial data Recipients are assigned paid internships at a Bank One location in the areas of accounting, business administration, and finance. Following successful completion of the internship, they receive a scholarship up to $10,000 to cover school expenses.

Duration 8 weeks for the internship; 1 academic year for the scholarship.

Number awarded 12 each year.

Deadline January of each year.

[1096]
BARBARA JORDAN HEALTH POLICY SCHOLARS PROGRAM

Henry J. Kaiser Family Foundation
c/o Celia J. Maxwell, Assistant Vice President for Health
   Affairs
Howard University
2041 Georgia Avenue, N.W., Suite 6000
Washington, DC 20060
(202) 865-4827 Fax: (202) 667-5694
Web: www.kff.org/docs/topics/jordanscholars.html

Purpose To provide minority college seniors and recent graduates with an opportunity to work during the summer in a Congressional office with major health policy responsibilities.

Eligibility This program is open to members of minority groups who are entering or currently enrolled in their senior year of college or who have graduated within the last 12 months from an accredited U.S. college or university. Current law, medical, and graduate students are not eligible. Applicants must demonstrate an active interest in health policy, strong leadership skills, and community commitment. Along with their applications, they must submit 400-word essays on 1) their personal background and how it led them to be interested in health policy, and 2) their views on a current health policy issue. Selection is based on the essays, academic performance, letters of recommendation, and extracurricular activities.

Financial data Scholars receive lodging at Howard University in Washington, D.C., round-trip transportation to Washington, D.C., a daily expense allowance for meals and local transportation, and a stipend of $1,500 upon completion of the program.

Duration 9 weeks, during the summer.

Additional information Scholars are first provided with an orientation to the program by its sponsors: Howard University and the Henry J. Kaiser Family Foundation. They are then assigned to work for a Congressional office or committee with significant health policy involvement. This program began in 2000.

Number awarded 13 each year.

Deadline January of each year.

[1097]
BEAUFORT GAZETTE INTERNSHIP FOR MINORITIES

Beaufort Gazette
Attn: Editor
P.O. Box 399
Beaufort, SC 29901
(843) 524-3183

Purpose To provide summer work experience at the *Beaufort Gazette* in South Carolina to minorities interested in careers in journalism.

Eligibility This program is open to minorities who are interested in working during the summer in news, editorial, or photography positions at the *Beaufort Gazette* in Beaufort, South Carolina. Applicants must be college students (seniors preferred) and may reside in any state.

Financial data The stipend is $300 per week.

Duration 10 weeks during the summer.

Number awarded 2 each year: 1 in news/editorial and 1 in photography.

Deadline March of each year.

[1098]
BILOXI SUN HERALD INTERNSHIP FOR MINORITIES

Biloxi Sun Herald
Attn: Managing Editor
P.O. Box 4567
Biloxi, MS 39535
(228) 896-2345

Purpose To provide summer work experience at the *Biloxi Sun Herald* in Mississippi to minorities interested in careers in journalism.

Eligibility This program is open to minorities who are interested in working during the summer in news or editorial positions at the *Biloxi Sun Herald* in Biloxi, Mississippi. Applicants must be college students (any level) and may reside in any state.

Financial data This is a paid internship.

Duration 10 to 12 weeks during the summer.

Number awarded Up to 2 each summer.

Deadline March of each year.

[1099]
BIOMEDICAL RESEARCH TRAINING PROGRAM FOR UNDERREPRESENTED MINORITIES

National Heart, Lung, and Blood Institute
Attn: Office of Special Concerns
31 Center Drive, Room 4A28
Bethesda, MD 20892-2490
(301) 496-1763   Fax: (301) 402-2322
Web: www.nhlbi.nih.gov

Purpose To provide training in fundamental biomedical sciences and clinical research disciplines to underrepresented minority undergraduate and graduate students.

Eligibility This program is open to students who are members of ethnic groups underrepresented in the biomedical and behavioral research fields nationally. Applicants must 1) be juniors or seniors enrolled full time in an accredited undergraduate institution or graduate students enrolled full time in an accredited academic institution; 2) have a major in biological, physical, behavioral, mathematical, engineering, or statistical sciences; 3) have completed a minimum of 18 hours of academic training in science-related course work relevant to biomedical, behavioral, or statistical research; 4) have a cumulative GPA of 3.3 or better; and 5) be U.S. citizens, nationals, or permanent residents who will be eligible for U.S. citizenship within 4 years. Research experiences available include clinical research on the normal and abnormal pathophysiologic functioning of the cardiac, pulmonary, circulatory, and endocrine systems; basic research on normal and abnormal cellular behavior at the molecular level as well as in some areas of genetic studies; and training in epidemiology, clinical trials, and biostatistics relating to the prevalence, etiology, prevention, and treatment of heart, vascular, pulmonary, and blood diseases.

Financial data Stipends are paid at the annual rate of $16,900 for juniors, $17,400 for seniors, $17,950 for first-year graduate students, $18,400 for second-year graduate students, $18,900 for third-year graduate students, or $19,400 for postgraduate students.

Duration 12 to 24 months over a 2-year period; training must be completed in increments during consecutive academic years.

Additional information Training is conducted in the laboratories of the National Heart, Lung, and Blood Institute in Bethesda, Maryland.

Number awarded Varies each year.

Deadline December of each year.

[1100]
BRISTOL-MYERS SQUIBB PRLDEF CORPORATE LEGAL FELLOWSHIP

Puerto Rican Legal Defense and Education Fund
Attn: Education Division Director
99 Hudson Street, 14th Floor
New York, NY 10013-2815
(212) 219-3360, ext. 223   (800) 328-2322, ext. 223
Fax: (212) 431-4276   E-mail: education@prldef.org
Web: www.prldef.org/education.htm

Purpose To provide summer work experience and financial assistance to minority law students interested in a career in corporate legal departments.

Eligibility This program is open to first- and second-year law students of color who are interested in preparing for a career in corporate legal departments. Students who complete the intern-

ship successfully and demonstrate academic excellence are eligible for a scholarship.

Financial data The stipend for the internship is $9,000. The scholarship, for those who complete the internship, is $1,000.

Duration 10 weeks in the summer for the internship; 1 year for the scholarship.

Additional information Interns are matched with mentors within Bristol-Myers Squibb (the program's sponsor) who provide ongoing guidance on professional development throughout their academic career and subsequent graduation.

Number awarded Varies each year.

Deadline November of each year.

[1101]
BROOKHAVEN NATIONAL LABORATORY MINORITY HIGH SCHOOL APPRENTICESHIP PROGRAM

Brookhaven National Laboratory
Attn: Science Education Center
Building 438
P.O. Box 5000
Upton, New York 11973-5000
(631) 344-3316   Fax: (631) 344-5832
E-mail: flack@bnl.gov
Web: www.bnl.gov/scied/programs/mhsap/index.html

Purpose To provide summer research experience in scientific areas at Brookhaven National Laboratory (BNL) to underrepresented minority high school students.

Eligibility This program at BNL is open to underrepresented minority (African American/Black, Hispanic, Native American, or Pacific Islander) students who have demonstrated ability and/or potential in science-oriented studies and activities. High schools in Suffolk County, New York and Inner City Outreach schools are invited to submit nominations of freshmen and sophomores.

Financial data Stipends and supplies are provided.

Duration 4 weeks, during the summer.

Additional information Students work with members of the scientific, technical, and professional staff of BNL in an educational training program developed to give research experience and classroom instruction in biology and hydroponics, chemistry, environmental science, and physics.

Number awarded 45 each year.

Deadline March of each year.

[1102]
BROOKHAVEN NATIONAL LABORATORY SCIENCE AND ENGINEERING OPPORTUNITIES PROGRAM FOR MINORITIES AND WOMEN

Brookhaven National Laboratory
Attn: Diversity Office, Human Resources Division
Building 185A
P.O. Box 5000
Upton, New York 11973-5000
(631) 344-2703   Fax: (631) 344-5305
E-mail: taylor5@bnl.gov
Web: www.bnl.gov

Purpose To provide on-the-job training in scientific areas at Brookhaven National Laboratory (BNL) during the summer to underrepresented minority and women students.

Eligibility This program at BNL is open to women and underrepresented minority (African American/Black, Hispanic, Native

American, or Pacific Islander) students who have completed their freshman, sophomore, or junior year of college. Applicants must be U.S. citizens or permanent residents, at least 18 years of age, and majoring in applied mathematics, engineering, physical and life sciences, or scientific journalism. Since no transportation or housing allowance is provided, preference is given to students who reside in the BNL area.

Financial data Participants receive a competitive stipend.

Duration 10 to 12 weeks, during the summer.

Additional information Students work with members of the scientific, technical, and professional staff of BNL in an educational training program developed to give research experience in areas of applied mathematics, biology, chemistry, engineering, high and low energy particle accelerators, nuclear medicine, physics, and science writing.

Number awarded Approximately 9 each year.

Deadline March of each year.

[1103]
BUSINESS REPORTING INTERN PROGRAM FOR MINORITY COLLEGE SOPHOMORES AND JUNIORS

Dow Jones Newspaper Fund
P.O. Box 300
Princeton, NJ 08543-0300
(609) 452-2820   Fax: (609) 520-5804
E-mail: newsfund@wsj.dowjones.com
Web: DJNewspaperFund.dowjones.com

Purpose To provide work experience and financial assistance to minority college students who are interested in careers in journalism.

Eligibility This program is open to college sophomores and juniors who are U.S. citizens interested in careers in journalism and participating in a summer internship at a daily newspaper as a business reporter. Applicants must be members of a minority group (African American, Hispanic, Asian American, Pacific Islander, American Indian or Alaskan Native) enrolled as full-time students.

Financial data Interns receive a salary of $325 per week during the summer and a $1,000 scholarship at the successful completion of the program.

Duration 10 weeks for the summer internship; 1 year for the scholarship.

Number awarded Up to 12 each year.

Deadline October of each year.

[1104]
CAHSEE YOUNG EDUCATORS PROGRAM

The Center for the Advancement of Hispanics in Science
    and Engineering Education
Attn: Director of Fellowships and Internships
1444 Eye Street, N.W., Suite 800
P.O. Box 34102
Washington, DC 20043-4102
(202) 835-3600, ext. 120   E-mail: mbarboza@cahsee.org
Web: www.cahsee.org/programs/yep.html

Purpose To provide an opportunity for undergraduate and graduate students to work as instructors or teaching assistants during the summer at the Science, Technology, Engineering, and Mathematics (STEM) Institute of The Center for the Advancement of Hispanics in Science and Engineering Education (CAHSEE).

Eligibility This program is open to undergraduate and graduate students interested in working at a STEM Institute, teaching science, technology, engineering, and mathematics to Latino pre-college students. Applicants must identify all mathematics, science, and engineering courses they have taken and the grades they received; any leadership positions they have held while in college; any tutoring, teaching, or mentoring experiences they have had; and any summer internships and/or research experiences.

Financial data Fellows receive housing, air travel, and a stipend of $2,750 to $3,000 (depending on assignment and educational level).

Duration The program runs for 8 weeks in the summer, beginning with 2 weeks of seminars in Washington, D.C. on teaching, leadership, the theory of knowledge, and the educational system, followed by 5 weeks of teaching college-level courses to Latino high school students at a STEM Institute, concluding with 1 week preparing a report on the experience.

Additional information STEM Institutes meet at George Washington University, the City University of New York, the University of Illinois at Chicago, Merrimack College, and yet-to-be-determined schools in Santa Clara and Los Angeles. Graduate students and advanced seniors serve as instructors, working with undergraduates who serve as teaching assistants. Funding for this program is provided by the U.S. National Aeronautics and Space Administration.

Number awarded Approximately 30 each year.

[1105]
CALIFORNIA COMMUNITY SERVICE SCHOLARSHIPS

National Medical Fellowships, Inc.
Attn: Scholarship Program
5 Hanover Square, 15th Floor
New York, NY 10004
(212) 483-8880   Fax: (212) 483-8897
E-mail: info@nmfonline.org
Web: www.nmf-online.org/Programs/Scholarships/CaliforniaCSSP/Overview.htm

Purpose To provide financial assistance to underrepresented minority medical students at schools in California.

Eligibility This program is open to third- or fourth-year medical students who are African Americans, mainland Puerto Ricans, Mexican Americans, Native Hawaiians, Alaska Natives, and American Indians. Applicants must be attending an M.D.-granting institution or college of osteopathic medicine in California. They must be interested in a clinical rotation at an approved community health center in California dedicated to medically underserved populations. Selection is based on demonstrated commitment to practice in California, interest in community-based primary care or research, academic performance, financial need, and leadership.

Financial data The stipend is $7,500.

Duration 6 weeks.

Additional information This program was established in 2002 with support from the California Endowment. Information is also available from the administrator's California Regional Office, The Chancery Building, 564 Market Street, Suite 209, San Francisco, CA 94104, (415) 397-2526, Fax: (415) 397-2556.

Number awarded 10 each year.

Deadline December of each year.

[1106]
CALIFORNIA SPACE GRANT UNDERGRADUATE PROGRAM

California Space Grant Consortium
c/o University of California at San Diego
California Space Institute
9500 Gilman Drive, Department 0524
La Jolla, CA 92093
(858) 822-1597 Fax: (858) 534-7840
E-mail: spacegrant@ucsd.edu
Web: calspace.ucsd.edu/spacegrant/california/index.html

Purpose To provide assistance to undergraduate students at member institutions of the California Space Grant Consortium who are interested in interning on space-related projects.

Eligibility This program is open to undergraduate students at member institutions in California who are interested in earth and space sciences projects. The nature and availability of projects varies from time to time and institution to institution but typically involves work as a research intern on an ongoing activity by faculty at a member institution and/or industry affiliate. The California Space Grant Consortium is a component of the U.S. National Aeronautics and Space Administration (NASA) Space Grant program, which encourages participation by underrepresented minorities, women, and persons with disabilities.

Financial data Each campus sets its own stipend.

Duration 1 semester, summer, or year.

Additional information The participating institutions include the 8 campuses of the University of California (at Berkeley, Davis, Irvine, Los Angeles, Riverside, San Diego, Santa Barbara, and Santa Cruz), California State Polytechnic University at Pomona, California State University at Long Beach, Palomar Community College, Pomona College, San Diego State University, San Francisco Art Institute, San Jose State University, Santa Clara University, Stanford University, and the University of San Diego. This program is funded by NASA.

Number awarded Varies each year.

Deadline Each of the participating institutions sets its own deadline.

[1107]
CAPITOL HILL NEWS INTERNSHIPS

Radio and Television News Directors Foundation
1000 Connecticut Avenue, N.W., Suite 615
Washington, DC 20036-5302
(202) 467-5218 Fax: (202) 223-4007
E-mail: karenb@rtndf.org
Web: www.rtndf.org/asfi/internships/internships.html

Purpose To provide work experience to recent graduates (especially minorities) in electronic journalism who are interested in covering congressional activities in Washington, D.C.

Eligibility Eligible are recent (within 2 years) college graduates who majored in electronic journalism; preference is given to minority students. Applicants must include an essay explaining why they are interested in this program and how it will help meet their career goals. Excellent writing skills are essential. The sponsor recognizes African Americans, Asian Americans, Hispanic Americans, and Native Americans as minorities.

Financial data The stipend is $1,000 per month. Interns are responsible for their own housing, travel, and living expenses.

Duration 3 months; the spring program begins in March and the summer program begins in June.

Additional information Interns cover newsworthy congressional activities and help coordinate broadcast coverage of those activities; they obtain hands-on experience in the House and Senate radio-TV galleries, working side by side with the Washington press and congressional staff to cover the political process. The sponsor defines electronic journalism to include radio, television, cable, and online news.

Number awarded 4 each year: 2 in the spring and 2 in the summer.

Deadline January of each year for the spring program; March of each year for the summer program.

[1108]
CENTER FOR LAW AND SOCIAL POLICY RESEARCH FELLOWSHIPS

Center for Law and Social Policy
Attn: Executive Director
1616 P Street, N.W., Suite 150
Washington, DC 20036-1434
(202) 528-5140 Fax: (202) 528-5129
E-mail: ahouse@clasp.org
Web: www.clasp.org

Purpose To enable recent college graduates to obtain work experience at the Center for Law and Social Policy (CLASP).

Eligibility This program is generally open to recent college graduates who are contemplating law school or graduate education in areas related to public policy for low-income families. Applicants must hold a bachelor's degree in government, psychology, sociology, or a related field; have at least a 3.0 GPA; demonstrate excellent writing and research skills; and have an interest in a career in public policy or public interest law. They must be interested in interning at CLASP. Women, people of color, and disabled persons are encouraged to apply.

Financial data The salary is $25,000 per year; health and dental care benefits are provided.

Duration 1 year, beginning in September.

Additional information CLASP is a public policy organization that does policy research, produces reports, advocates before state and federal legislative and administrative bodies, and provides support to state advocacy organizations. It does not litigate or represent individual clients.

Number awarded 2 or 3 each year.

Deadline January of each year.

[1109]
CENTER ON BUDGET AND POLICY PRIORITIES INTERNSHIPS

Center on Budget and Policy Priorities
Attn: Internship Coordinator
820 First Street, N.E., Suite 510
Washington, DC 20002
(202) 408-1095, ext. 386 Fax: (202) 408-1056
E-mail: internship@center.cbpp.org
Web: www.cbpp.org/internship.html

Purpose To provide work experience at the Center on Budget and Policy Priorities (CBPP) in Washington, D.C. to undergraduates, graduate students, and recent college graduates.

Eligibility This program is open to undergraduates, graduate students, and recent college graduates who are interested in public policy issues affecting low-income families and individuals. Applicants must be interested in working at CBPP in the following areas: media, federal legislation, health policy, housing policy, income security policy, international budget project, national budget and tax policy, outreach campaigns, state budget and tax policy, state low-income initiatives, and food stamps. They should have research, fact-gathering, writing, analytic, and computer skills and a willingness to do administrative as well as substantive tasks. Women and minorities are encouraged to apply.

Financial data Undergraduate students receive $7.50 per hour for a first internship and up to $8.00 per hour subsequently. Graduate students receive $9.00 per hour for a first internship and up to $9.50 per hour subsequently. Students with a master's degree receive $10.00 per hour. Recent college graduates receive $8.00 per hour for a first internship and up to $8.50 per hour subsequently.

Duration 1 semester; may be renewed.

Additional information The center specializes in research and analysis oriented toward practical policy decisions and produces analytic reports that are accessible to public officials at national, state, and local levels, to nonprofit organizations, and to the media.

Number awarded Varies each semester.

Deadline March of each year for summer internships; July of each year for fall internships; November of each year for spring internships.

[1110]
CENTRAL INTELLIGENCE AGENCY INTERNSHIP PROGRAM

Central Intelligence Agency
Attn: Recruitment Center
P.O. Box 4090
Reston, VA 20195
(800) JOBS CIA
Web: www.cia.gov/cia/employment

Purpose To give promising undergraduate students (particularly minorities and persons with disabilities) an opportunity to gain practical summer work experience at the Central Intelligence Agency (CIA).

Eligibility To qualify for this program, students must have completed their sophomore year, be U.S. citizens, have and maintain a GPA of 3.0 or higher, and meet the same employment standards at the CIA as permanent employees. Applicants should be studying business, cartography, computer science, economics, engineering, foreign area studies, geography, graphic design, history, human resources, non-Romance languages, mathematics, or the sciences. Particularly encouraged to apply are minorities and people with disabilities.

Financial data Salaries range from GS-05 to GS-07, depending upon the number of credit hours completed. Interns receive many of the same benefits as permanent employees and are eligible to apply for the agency's tuition assistance program.

Duration Interns normally work at least 2 summers or a summer and a semester.

Number awarded Several each year.

Deadline Applications may be submitted at any time, but the must be received 6 to 9 months prior to availability for work.

[1111]
CHICAGO SUN-TIMES MINORITY SCHOLARSHIP AND INTERNSHIP PROGRAM

Chicago Sun-Times
Attn: Director of Editorial Administration
401 North Wabash Avenue
Chicago, IL 60611
(312) 321-3000

Purpose To provide financial assistance and work experience to minority college students in the Chicago area who are interested in preparing for a career in print journalism.

Eligibility This program is open to minority college students and recent graduates who graduated from a Chicago-area high school or have lived in the Chicago metropolitan area for the past 5 years. Applicants must have demonstrated an interest in print journalism, including reporting, editing, graphics, or photography. They must submit a 500-word essay about themselves, explaining why they want to become a newspaper reporter, editor, or photographer.

Financial data Students selected for this program receive a $1,500 scholarship plus a paid internship at the *Chicago Sun-Times*.

Duration 1 year for the scholarship; 12 weeks during the summer for the internship.

Additional information The Chicago metropolitan area includes Cook, DuPage, Kane, Lake, McHenry, and Will counties in Illinois and Lake and Porter counties in Indiana. Recipients may use the scholarship at any school of their choosing. For the summer internships, assignments are available in reporting, editing, graphics, or photography.

Number awarded 1 or more each year.

Deadline December of each year.

[1112]
CHIPS QUINN SCHOLARS PROGRAM

Freedom Forum
Attn: Chips Quinn Scholars Program
1101 Wilson Boulevard
Arlington, VA 22209
(703) 284-2863   Fax: (703) 284-3543
E-mail: chipsquinnscholars@freedomforum.org
Web: www.chipsquinn.org

Purpose To provide work experience, career mentoring, and scholarship support to minority college students and recent graduates who are majoring in journalism.

Eligibility This program is open to students enrolled at an historically Black college or university or a college or university that has significant numbers of students who are members of ethnic or racial minority groups. Deans of the journalism schools at those colleges and universities are invited to nominate up to 4 juniors, seniors, or recent graduates who are majoring or minoring in journalism or have clearly demonstrated an interest in journalism as a career. Nominees must also apply for an internship. Scholars who subsequently work for at least 3 years in newspaper newsrooms are eligible to apply for additional funding to participate in journalism seminars, such as those at the American Press Institute, Poynter Institute, Northwestern University Media Management Center, or Maynard Institute for Journalism Education.

Financial data Students chosen for this program receive a travel stipend to attend a workshop at the Freedom Forum in Arlington, Virginia and, upon completion of the internship, a

$1,000 scholarship. Scholars selected to participate in a journalism seminar receive an additional $2,500 in funding.

Duration 1 year, including the internship.

Additional information Students are invited to the workshop at the Freedom Forum and then work as an intern during the summer at a newspaper where they are linked with a mentor editor. This program was established in 1991 in memory of the late John D. Quinn Jr., managing editor of the *Poughkeepsie Journal.* Funding is provided by the Freedom Forum, formerly the Gannett Foundation.

Number awarded Approximately 150 each year. From all participants in the program, 12 are selected each year to attend a journalism seminar.

Deadline March of each year for programs to begin in fall or spring; October of each year for programs to begin in summer.

[1113]
THE CLOISTERS SUMMER INTERNSHIP PROGRAM FOR COLLEGE STUDENTS

Metropolitan Museum of Art
Attn: Internship Programs
1000 Fifth Avenue
New York, NY 10028-0198
(212) 570-3710   Fax: (212) 570-3782
Web: www.metmuseum.org/education/er_internship.asp

Purpose To provide art museum work experience during the summer to college students.

Eligibility This program is open to undergraduate college students, especially freshmen and sophomores, who are interested in art and museum careers. They must enjoy working with children and be willing to intern at the Metropolitan Museum of Art. Applicants of diverse backgrounds (e.g., minorities) are particularly encouraged to apply.

Financial data The internship stipend is $2,500.

Duration 9 weeks, beginning in June.

Additional information Interns are assigned to the education department of The Cloisters, the branch museum of the Metropolitan Museum of Art devoted to the art of medieval Europe. They conduct gallery workshops for New York City day campers. This program is funded in part by the Norman and Rosita Winston Foundation, Inc.

Number awarded Varies each year.

Deadline January of each year.

[1114]
COLLEGE FUND/COCA-COLA CORPORATE INTERN PROGRAM

United Negro College Fund
Attn: Corporate Scholars Program
P.O. Box 1435
Alexandria, VA 22313-9998
(866) 671-7237   E-mail: internship@uncf.org
Web: www.uncf.org/Scholarship/CorporateScholars.asp

Purpose To provide financial assistance and work experience to students of color majoring in designated fields and interested in an internship at Coca-Cola Company's corporate headquarters in Atlanta, Georgia.

Eligibility This program is open to students of color, including African Americans, Hispanic Americans, Asian/Pacific Islander Americans, and American Indians/Alaskan Natives, who attend member institutions of the United Negro College Fund (UNCF),

the Hispanic Association of Colleges and Universities (HACU), other targeted Historically Black Colleges and Universities (HBCUs), and designated majority institutions. Applicants must be sophomores majoring in business (sales interest), chemistry, communications, engineering, finance, human resources, information technology, or marketing with a GPA of 3.0 or higher. They must be a U.S. citizen, permanent resident, asylee, refugee, or lawful temporary resident under amnesty programs. Along with their application, they must submit a 1-page essay about themselves and their career goals, including information about their personal background and any particular challenges they have faced. Interviews are required.

Financial data The program provides a stipend of $2,500 per month during the internship, housing accommodations in Atlanta, round-trip transportation to and from Atlanta, local transportation to and from the internship site, and (based on successful internship performance) a $10,000 scholarship.

Duration 8 to 10 weeks for the internship; 1 year for the scholarship.

Number awarded Approximately 50 each year.

Deadline December of each year.

[1115]
COLORADO SPACE GRANT RESEARCH SUPPORT

Colorado Space Grant Consortium
c/o University of Colorado at Boulder
Engineering and Applied Science Department
Engineering Center, Room 1B-76
Campus Box 520
Boulder, CO 80309-0520
(303) 492-3141   Fax: (303) 492-5456
E-mail: elaine.hansen@colorado.edu
Web: spacegrant.colorado.edu

Purpose To provide an opportunity to participate in space-related research to undergraduate and graduate students at member institutions of the Colorado Space Grant Consortium (CSGC).

Eligibility This program is open to undergraduate and graduate students at the 14 colleges and universities affiliated with the consortium. Applicants must be interested in participating in designing, flying, building, operating, and analyzing real space engineering and science experiments. The sponsored research activities are part of the Space Grant program of the U.S. National Aeronautics and Space Administration (NASA), which encourages participation by women, underrepresented minorities, and people with disabilities.

Financial data Stipends are provided.

Additional information The members of CSGC include the University of Colorado at Boulder, the University of Colorado at Colorado Springs, Colorado State University, the United States Air Force Academy, Pikes Peak Community College, the University of Southern Colorado, Mesa State College, the University of Northern Colorado, Western State College, Adams State College, Colorado School of Mines, Fort Lewis College, Metro State College, and Front Range Community College. This program is funded by NASA.

Number awarded Varies each year.

[1116]
CONGRESSIONAL HISPANIC CAUCUS INSTITUTE CORPORATE FELLOWSHIP

Congressional Hispanic Caucus Institute, Inc.
504 C Street, N.E.
Washington, DC 20002
(202) 543-1771　　　　　　　　(800) EXCEL-DC
Fax: (202) 546-2143　　　　　　E-mail: chci@chci.org
Web: www.chci.org

Purpose To provide Latino graduate students and recent college graduates with the opportunity to apply their academic expertise in the area of public-private partnerships during a work experience program in Washington, D.C.

Eligibility This program is open to U.S. citizens and permanent residents of Latino background who graduated from a college or university (with a bachelor's or graduate degree) within the past year or are currently-enrolled graduate students. Applicants must be interested in gaining experience in the area of public-private partnerships. Preference is given to applicants with a GPA of 3.0 or higher. Selection is based on evidence of leadership potential as demonstrated through goal setting, initiative, and responsibility; active interest in community affairs, balanced with academics; and analytical and communication skills (oral and written).

Financial data This program provides transportation to and from Washington, D.C., a monthly stipend of $2,061 (or $2,500 for fellows who already hold a graduate degree), and health insurance.

Duration 9 months, beginning in September.

Additional information Fellows are placed in the public affairs office of a corporation.

Number awarded 1 or more each year.

Deadline February of each year.

[1117]
CONGRESSIONAL HISPANIC CAUCUS INSTITUTE GENERAL PUBLIC POLICY FELLOWSHIP PROGRAM

Congressional Hispanic Caucus Institute, Inc.
504 C Street, N.E.
Washington, DC 20002
(202) 543-1771　　　　　　　　(800) EXCEL-DC
Fax: (202) 546-2143　　　　　　E-mail: chci@chci.org
Web: www.chci.org

Purpose To provide Latino graduate students and recent college graduates with the opportunity to apply their academic expertise in the area of public policy during a work experience program in Washington, D.C.

Eligibility This program is open to U.S. citizens and permanent residents of Latino background who graduated from a college or university (with a bachelor's or graduate degree) within the past year or are currently-enrolled graduate students. Applicants must be interested in gaining experience in the area of public policy. Preference is given to applicants with a GPA of 3.0 or higher. Selection is based on evidence of leadership potential as demonstrated through goal setting, initiative, and responsibility; active interest in community affairs, balanced with academics; and analytical and communication skills (oral and written).

Financial data This program provides transportation to and from Washington, D.C., a monthly stipend of $2,061 (or $2,500 for fellows who already hold a graduate degree), and health insurance.

Duration 9 months, beginning in September.

Additional information Placements are available in congressional offices and federal agencies, advocacy groups, the media, and a broad range of policy-related organizations. Fellows select the placement that best matches their interests.

Number awarded Approximately 20 each year.

Deadline February of each year.

[1118]
CONGRESSIONAL HISPANIC CAUCUS INSTITUTE SUMMER INTERNSHIP PROGRAM

Congressional Hispanic Caucus Institute, Inc.
504 C Street, N.E.
Washington, DC 20002
(202) 543-1771　　　　　　　　(800) EXCEL-DC
Fax: (202) 546-2143　　　　　　E-mail: chci@chci.org
Web: www.chci.org

Purpose To provide Hispanic Americans with an opportunity during the summer to work directly with members of Congress on their committees or as personal staff.

Eligibility This program is open to undergraduate students who have completed at least 1 year of college and are interested in an internship on Capitol Hill. College seniors graduating before the program begins are ineligible. Applicants must be U.S. citizens, permanent residents, or students with a work visa; have a GPA of 3.0 or higher; demonstrate leadership potential through initiative, responsibility, and maturity; have a record of consistent and active participation in public service-oriented activities; and have strong writing and communication skills.

Financial data The internship provides a stipend of $2,000, transportation to and from Washington, and housing in university dormitories.

Duration 8 weeks, during the summer. The internship begins in June.

Additional information In addition to their internship, participants attend seminars and lectures that offer exposure to critical components of policy making.

Number awarded Approximately 30 each year.

Deadline January of each year.

[1119]
CONNECTICUT COMMUNITY COLLEGE MINORITY FELLOWSHIPS

Community-Technical Colleges of Connecticut
Attn: Affirmative Action Officer
61 Woodland Street
Hartford, CT 06105-9949
(860) 566-8760　　　　　　　　(800) 33-CLASS
Fax: (860) 566-6624
Web: www.commnet.edu

Purpose To provide work experience to selected minority and disabled graduate students in Connecticut who are interested in preparing for a career in community college teaching or administration.

Eligibility Applicants must have completed at least 6 credits of graduate work and have indicated an interest in a career in community colleges. They must be willing to commit to at least 1 year of employment in the Connecticut Community College System. Although all qualified graduate students are eligible, the program is intended to diversify the professional workforce of the Connecticut Community Colleges with respect to Asians, Blacks, Hispanics, and persons with disabilities. Special efforts are made to recruit candidates from those historically underrepresented groups.

Financial data Fellows receive $3,000 per semester; that includes the usual compensation for part-time work plus a stipend for a period of orientation.

Duration 1 year; may be renewed.

Additional information Fellows spend 6 hours per week in community college classroom-related or administrative-related activities. They are invited to faculty and staff meetings and a minority fellowship orientation.

[1120]
CONSORTIUM FOR GRADUATE STUDY IN MANAGEMENT FELLOWSHIPS

Consortium for Graduate Study in Management
5585 Pershing Avenue, Suite 240
St. Louis, MO 63112
(314) 877-5500   (888) 658-6814
Fax: (314) 877-5505   E-mail: frontdesk@cgsm.org
Web: www.cgsm.org

Purpose To provide financial assistance and work experience to underrepresented racial minorities in graduate school who are interested in preparing for managerial positions in business.

Eligibility Eligible to apply are African Americans, Hispanic Americans (Chicanos, Cubans, Dominicans, and Puerto Ricans), and Native Americans who have graduated from college and are interested in a career in business. An undergraduate degree in business or economics is not required. Applicants must be U.S. citizens and planning to pursue a Master's of Business Administration degree at 1 of the consortium's 14 schools. Preference is given to applicants under 31 years of age.

Financial data The fellowship pays full tuition and required fees. Summer internships with the consortium's cooperative sponsors, providing paid practical experience, are also offered.

Duration Up to 4 semesters. The participating schools are University of California at Berkeley, Carnegie Mellon University, Dartmouth College, Emory University, Indiana University, University of Michigan, New York University, University of North Carolina at Chapel Hill, University of Rochester, University of Southern California, University of Texas at Austin, University of Virginia, Washington University, and University of Wisconsin at Madison. Fellowships are tenable at member schools only.

Number awarded Varies; up to 400 each year.

Deadline The early deadline is the end of November of each year. The final deadline is in January of each year.

[1121]
CRISTINA SARALEGUI SCHOLARSHIP PROGRAM

National Association of Hispanic Journalists
Attn: Scholarship Committee
1000 National Press Building
529 14th Street, N.W.
Washington, DC 20045-2001
(202) 662-7145   (888) 346-NAHJ
Fax: (202) 662-7144   E-mail: nahj@nahj.org
Web: www.nahj.org/scholarship.html

Purpose To provide financial assistance and work experience to Hispanic American undergraduate students interested in preparing for careers in the media.

Eligibility College sophomores are eligible to apply if they are of Hispanic descent, fluent in Spanish, and planning to pursue a

career in broadcast journalism. Applicants must submit an official transcript of grades; a 1-page resume with their educational background, work history, awards, internships, other scholarships, language proficiency, and any work done for their school newspaper, radio, and/or television station; samples of their work; 2 reference letters; a 500-word autobiography in third person in the form of a news story; and documentation of financial need.

Financial data The stipend is $5,000 per year; the program also provides funding to attend the association's convention and an internship during the summer following the junior year.

Duration 2 years.

Additional information This program, which began in 2000, is sponsored by the Spanish language talk show host Cristina Saralegüi and administered by the National Association of Hispanic Journalists (NAHJ) as part of its Rubén Salazar Scholarship Fund. The recipient participates in a summer internship on the Cristina Saralegüi show.

Number awarded 1 each year.

Deadline January of each year.

[1122]
C.T. LANG JOURNALISM MINORITY SCHOLARSHIP AND INTERNSHIP

Albuquerque Journal
Attn: Scholarship Committee
7777 Jefferson Street, N.E.
P.O. Drawer J
Albuquerque, NM 87103
(505) 823-7777

Purpose To provide financial assistance and work experience to minority undergraduates in journalism programs at universities in New Mexico.

Eligibility This program is open to minority students majoring or minoring in journalism at a New Mexico university in their junior year with a GPA of 2.5 or higher. Applicants must be enrolled full time. They must be planning a career in newswriting, photography, design, copy editing, or online. Selection is based on clips of published stories, a short autobiography that explains the applicant's interest in the field, a grade transcript, and a letter of recommendation.

Financial data The scholarship is $1,000 per semester; the recipient also receives a paid internship and moving expenses.

Duration The scholarship is for 2 semesters (fall and spring). The internship is for 1 semester.

Additional information This program is funded by the *Albuquerque Journal,* where the internship takes place.

Number awarded 1 each year.

Deadline February of each year.

[1123]
CULTURAL RESOURCES DIVERSITY INTERN PROGRAM

Student Conservation Association, Inc.
Attn: College Diversity Program
1800 North Kent Street, Suite 102
Arlington, VA 22209
(703) 524-2441   Fax: (703) 524-2451
E-mail: internships@sca-inc.org
Web: www.sca-inc.org/vol/ccdc/ccdccrdip.htm

Purpose To provide work experience to ethnically diverse college students and students with disabilities at facilities of the U.S. National Park Service (NPS).

Eligibility This program is open to currently-enrolled students at the sophomore or higher level. Applicants must be U.S. citizens or permanent residents with a GPA of 3.0 or higher. Although all students may apply, the program is designed to give ethnically diverse students and students with disabilities the opportunity to experience the diversity of careers in the federal sector. Applicants are assigned to a position within the NPS. Possible placements include archaeology and anthropology; historic building preservation; journalism and graphic design; civil and environmental engineering; project management and research; costumed interpretation and living history; landscape architecture; museum studies and library relations; web site design; public relations and outreach; and Native American studies.

Financial data The weekly stipend ranges from $390 to $510, depending on the intern's academic level. Other benefits include a pre-term orientation, transportation to the orientation and the work site, worker's compensation, and accident insurance.

Duration 10 weeks in the summer (beginning in June) or 15 weeks in the fall (beginning in August).

Additional information While participating in the internship, students engage in tri-weekly evening career and professional development events, ongoing career counseling, mentoring, and personal and career development services.

Number awarded Varies each year; recently, 12 summer and 6 fall internships were available.

Deadline March of each year for summer; June of each year for fall.

[1124]
DALMAS A. TAYLOR MEMORIAL SUMMER MINORITY POLICY FELLOWSHIP

Society for the Psychological Study of Social Issues
343 South Main Street, Suite 200
P.O. Box 1248
Ann Arbor, MI 48106-1248
(734) 662-9130   Fax: (734) 662-5607
TTY: (734) 662-9130   E-mail: spssi@spssi.org
Web: www.spssi.org/taylor.html

Purpose To enable graduate students of color to be involved in the public policy activities of the American Psychological Association (APA) during the summer.

Eligibility This program is open to graduate students who are members of an ethnic minority group (including, but not limited to, African American, Alaskan Native, American Indian, Asian American, Hispanic, and Pacific Islander) and/or have demonstrated a commitment to a career in psychology or a related field with a focus on ethnic minority issues. Applicants must be interested in spending a summer in Washington, D.C. to work on public policy issues in conjunction with the Minority Fellowship Program of the APA. Their application must indicate why they are interested in the fellowship, their previous research experience and current interest, their interest and involvement in ethnic minority psychological issues, and how the fellowship would contribute to their career goals.

Financial data The stipend is $3,000. Housing and travel funds are also provided.

Duration Summer months.

Additional information This program was established in 2000.

Number awarded 1 each year.

Deadline March of each year.

[1125]
DELL/UNCF CORPORATE SCHOLARS PROGRAM

United Negro College Fund
Attn: Corporate Scholars Program
P.O. Box 1435
Alexandria, VA 22313-9998
(866) 671-7237   E-mail: internship@uncf.org
Web: www.uncf.org/Scholarship/CorporateScholars.asp

Purpose To provide financial assistance and work experience to undergraduate and graduate students, especially minorities, majoring in designated fields and interested in an internship at Dell Computer Corporation's corporate headquarters near Austin, Texas.

Eligibility This program is open to rising juniors and graduate students who are African Americans, Hispanics, Asian/Pacific Islanders, Caucasians, and Native Americans. Applicants must be enrolled full time at institutions that are members of the United Negro College Fund (UNCF) or at other targeted colleges and universities. They must be majoring in business administration, computer science, engineering (computer, electrical, or mechanical), finance, human resources, management information systems, marketing, or supply chain management with a GPA of 3.0 or higher. Along with their application, they must submit a 1-page essay about themselves and their career goals, including information about their personal background and any particular challenges they have faced. Finalists are interviewed by a team of representatives from Dell, the program's sponsor.

Financial data The program provides a paid summer internship, housing accommodations in Austin, round-trip transportation to and from Austin, and (based on financial need and successful internship performance) a $10,000 scholarship.

Duration 8 to 10 weeks for the internship; 1 year for the scholarship.

Number awarded Varies each year.

Deadline February of each year.

[1126]
DEPARTMENT OF STATE STUDENT INTERN PROGRAM

Department of State
Attn: Recruitment Division, SA-1
Intern Coordinator
2401 E Street, N.W., Room H518
Washington, DC 20522-0151
(202) 261-8888   (800) JOB-OVERSEAS
Fax: (202) 261-8841
Web: www.state.gov/www/careers/rinterndetails.html

Purpose To provide a work/study opportunity to undergraduate and graduate students interested in foreign service.

Eligibility This program is open to full- and part-time continuing college and university juniors, seniors, and graduate students. Applications are encouraged from students with a broad range of majors, such as business or public administration, social work, economics, information management, journalism, and the biological and physical sciences, as well as those majors more traditionally identified with international affairs. U.S. citizenship is required. The State Department particularly encourages eligible women and minority students with an interest in foreign affairs to apply.

Financial data Most internships are unpaid. A few paid internships are granted to applicants who can demonstrate financial need. If they qualify for a paid internship, college juniors are placed at the GS-4 level with an annual salary of $20,322; college seniors and first-year graduate students are placed at the GS-5 level with an annual salary of $22,737; second-year graduate students are placed at the GS-7 level with an annual salary of $28,164. Interns placed abroad may also receive housing, medical insurance, a travel allowance, and a dependents' allowance.

Duration Paid internships are available only for 10 weeks during the summer. Unpaid internships are available for 1 semester or quarter during the academic year, or for 10 weeks during the summer.

Additional information About half of all internships are in Washington, D.C., or occasionally in other large cities in the United States. The remaining internships are at embassies and consulates abroad. Depending upon the needs of the department, interns are assigned junior-level professional duties, which may include research, preparing reports, drafting replies to correspondence, working in computer science, analyzing international issues, financial management, intelligence, security, or assisting in cases related to domestic and international law. Interns must agree to return to their schooling immediately upon completion of their internship.

Number awarded Approximately 800 internships are offered each year, but only about 5% of those are paid positions.

Deadline February of each year for a fall internship; June of each year for a spring internship; October of each year for a summer internship.

[1127]
DIETETIC INTERNSHIP SCHOLARSHIPS

American Dietetic Association
Attn: Accreditation, Education Programs, and Student
   Operations
216 West Jackson Boulevard, Suite 800
Chicago, IL 60606-6995
(312) 899-0040   (800) 877-1600, ext. 5400
Fax: (312) 899-4817   E-mail: education@eatright.org
Web: www.eatright.org

Purpose To provide financial assistance to students who have applied for a dietetic internship.

Eligibility This program is open to students who have applied for a CADE-accredited dietetic internship. Applicants must be participating in the computer-matching process, be U.S. citizens or permanent residents, and show promise of being a valuable, contributing member of the profession. Some scholarships require membership in the association, specific dietetic practice group membership, residency in a specific state, or underrepresented minority group status. The same application form can be used for all categories. Students who are currently completing the internship component of a combined graduate/dietetic internship should apply for the American Dietetic Association's Graduate Scholarship.

Financial data Awards range from $500 to $5,000.

Duration 1 year.

Number awarded Varies each year, depending upon the funds available. Recently, the sponsoring organization awarded 209 scholarships for all its programs.

Deadline February of each year.

[1128]
DOI DIVERSITY INTERN PROGRAM

Student Conservation Association, Inc.
Attn: College Diversity Program
1800 North Kent Street, Suite 102
Arlington, VA 22209
(703) 524-2441   Fax: (703) 524-2451
E-mail: internships@sca-inc.org
Web: www.sca-inc.org/vol/ccdc/ccdcdip.htm

Purpose To provide work experience to ethnically diverse college students and students with disabilities at federal agencies involved with natural and cultural resources.

Eligibility This program is open to currently-enrolled students at the sophomore or higher level. Applicants must be U.S. citizens or permanent residents with a GPA of 3.0 or higher. Although all students may apply, the program is designed to give ethnically diverse students and students with disabilities the opportunity to experience the diversity of careers in the federal sector. Applicants are assigned to a position within the U.S. Department of the Interior (DOI). Possible placements include archaeology and anthropology; wildlife and fisheries biology; business administration, accounting, and finance; civil and environmental engineering; computer science, especially GIS applications; human resources; mining and petroleum engineering; communications and public relations; web site and database design; environmental and realty law; geology, hydrology, and geography; Native American studies; interpretation and environmental education; natural resource and range management; public policy and administration; and surveying and mapping.

Financial data The weekly stipend ranges from $420 to $520, depending on the intern's academic level. Other benefits include a pre-term orientation, transportation to the orientation and the work site, worker's compensation, and accident insurance.

Duration 10 weeks in the summer (beginning in June) or 15 weeks in the fall (beginning in August) or spring (beginning in January).

Additional information While participating in the internship, students engage in tri-weekly evening career and professional development events, ongoing career counseling, mentoring, and personal and career development services.

Number awarded Varies each year.

Deadline February of each year for summer; June of each year for fall; November of each year for spring.

[1129]
EATON MULTICULTURAL ENGINEERING SCHOLARS PROGRAM

Eaton Corporation
c/o INROADS
The Lorenzo Carter Building
1360 West Ninth Street, Suite 260
Cleveland, OH 44113
(216) 623-1010
Web: www.eaton.com

Purpose To provide financial assistance and work experience to minority college students interested in a career as an engineer.

Eligibility This program is open to full-time minority engineering students who are U.S. citizens or permanent residents. Applicants must have completed 1 year in an accredited engineering program and have 3 remaining years of course work before completing a bachelor's degree. They must have a GPA of 2.8 or higher and an expressed interest in at least 1 of the following areas of engineering as a major: computer, electrical, electronic, industrial, manufacturing, materials, mechanical, or software. Selection is based on academic performance, the student's school recommendation, and an expressed interest in pursuing challenging and rewarding internship assignments.

Financial data Stipends up to $2,500 per year are provided. Funds are paid directly to the recipient's university to cover the cost of tuition, books, supplies, equipment, and fees.

Duration 3 years.

Additional information In addition to the scholarships, recipients are offered paid summer internships at company headquarters in Cleveland. The target schools participating in this program are Cornell, Detroit-Mercy, Florida A&M, Georgia Tech, Illinois at Chicago, Illinois at Urbana-Champaign, Lawrence Technological, Marquette, Massachusetts Institute of Technology, Michigan at Ann Arbor, Michigan at Dearborn, Michigan State, Milwaukee School of Engineering, Minnesota, Morehouse College, North Carolina A&T State, North Carolina State, Northwestern, Notre Dame, Ohio State, Purdue, Southern, Tennessee, Western Michigan, and Wisconsin at Madison. This program was established in 1994. Until 2002, it was known as the Eaton Minority Engineering Scholars Program.

Number awarded Varies each year.

Deadline January of each year.

[1130]
EDUCATIONAL TESTING SERVICE SUMMER PROGRAM IN RESEARCH FOR GRADUATE STUDENTS

Educational Testing Service
MS 09-R
Princeton, NJ 08541-0001
(609) 734-1806   E-mail: ldelauro@ets.org
Web: www.ets.org/research/fellowship.html

Purpose To provide work experience at the Educational Testing Service (ETS) during the summer to minority, women, and other graduate students in educational measurement and related fields.

Eligibility This internship at ETS is open to graduate students who are currently enrolled in a doctoral program and have completed at least 1 year of full-time study. Applicants must be pursuing a doctoral degree in a discipline relevant to the following areas: computer science, education, learning, linguistics, literacy, minority issues, policy research, psychology, psycholinguistics, psychometrics, statistics, teaching, educational technology, or testing issues (including alternate forms of assessment for special populations and new forms of assessment). Selection is based on academic record and the match of applicant interests with participating ETS researchers. An explicit goal of the program is to attract women and minority graduate students to the field of educational measurement and related disciplines.

Financial data The stipend is $4,000. In addition, participants and their families are reimbursed for travel expenses from their universities to ETS (in Princeton) and back.

Duration 8 weeks, beginning in June.

Additional information Participants work under the supervision of ETS staff members.

Number awarded Up to 12 each year.

Deadline February of each year.

[1131]
EDWARD R. ROYBAL PUBLIC HEALTH FELLOWSHIP

Congressional Hispanic Caucus Institute, Inc.
504 C Street, N.E.
Washington, DC 20002
(202) 543-1771   (800) EXCEL-DC
Fax: (202) 546-2143   E-mail: chci@chci.org
Web: www.chci.org

Purpose To provide Latino graduate students and recent college graduates with the opportunity to apply their academic expertise in the area of public health policy during a work experience program in Washington, D.C.

Eligibility This program is open to U.S. citizens and permanent residents of Latino background who graduated from a college or university (with a bachelor's or graduate degree) within the past year or are currently-enrolled graduate students. Applicants must be interested in gaining experience in the area of public health policy. Preference is given to applicants with a GPA of 3.0 or higher. Selection is based on evidence of leadership potential as demonstrated through goal setting, initiative, and responsibility; active interest in community affairs, balanced with academics; and analytical and communication skills (oral and written).

Financial data This program provides transportation to and from Washington, D.C., a monthly stipend of $2,061 (or $2,500 for fellows who already hold a graduate degree), and health insurance.

Duration 9 months, beginning in September.

Additional information Placements are available in congressional offices and federal agencies, advocacy groups, the media, and a broad range of policy-related organizations, but must focus on health issues.

Number awarded 1 each year.

Deadline February of each year.

[1132]
EISENHOWER GRANTS FOR RESEARCH FELLOWSHIPS

Department of Transportation
Federal Highway Administration
Attn: National Highway Institute
4600 North Fairfax Drive, Suite 800
Arlington, VA 22203-1553
(703) 235-0538   Fax: (703) 235-0593
E-mail: ilene.payne@fhwa.dov.gov
Web: www.nhi.fhwa.dot.gov/fellowships.html

Purpose To enable students to participate in research activities at facilities of the U.S. Department of Transportation (DOT) Federal Highway Administration in the Washington, D.C. area.

Eligibility This program is open to 1) students in their junior year of a baccalaureate program who will complete their junior year before being awarded a fellowship; 2) students in their senior year of a baccalaureate program; and 3) students who have completed their baccalaureate degree and are enrolled in a program leading to a master's, Ph.D., or equivalent degree. Applicants must be U.S. citizens enrolled in an accredited U.S. institution of higher education pursuing a degree full time and planning to enter the transportation profession after completing their higher education. They select 1 or more projects from a current list of research projects underway at various DOT facilities. They conduct research with academic supervision provided by a faculty advisor from their home university (which grants academic credit for the research project) and with technical direction provided by the DOT staff. Specific requirements for the target projects vary; most require engineering backgrounds, but others involve transportation planning, information management, public administration, physics, materials science, statistical analysis, operations research, chemistry, economics, technology transfer, urban studies, geography, and urban and regional planning. The DOT encourages students at Historically Black Colleges and Universities (HBCUs) and Hispanic Serving Institutions (HSIs) to apply for these grants. Selection is based on match of the student's qualifications with the proposed research project (including the student's ability to accomplish the project in the available time), recommendation letters regarding the nominee's qualifications to conduct the research, academic records (including class standing, GPA, and transcripts), and transportation work experience (if any) including the employer's endorsement.

Financial data Fellows receive full tuition and fees that relate to the academic credits for the approved research project and a monthly stipend of $1,450 for college seniors, $1,700 for master's students, or $2,000 for doctoral students. An allowance for travel to and from the DOT facility where the research is conducted is also provided, but selectees are responsible for their own housing accommodations. Faculty advisors are allowed 1 site review on projects over 6 months and 2 site reviews on projects over 9 months; travel and per diem are provided for those site reviews.

Duration Tenure is normally 3, 6, 9, or 12 months.

Number awarded Varies each year; recently, 9 students participated in this program.

Deadline February of each year.

[1133]
EMMA L. BOWEN FOUNDATION INTERNSHIPS

Emma L. Bowen Foundation
1299 Pennsylvania Avenue, N.W., 11th Floor
Washington, DC 20004
(202) 637-4494   Fax: (202) 637-4495
E-mail: phyllis.eagle-oldson@corporate.ge.com
Web: www.emmabowenfoundation.com

Purpose To provide minority students with an opportunity to gain work experience during the summer at participating media companies.

Eligibility This program is open to minority students who apply as early as their junior year in high school. Applicants must be interested in working at a media company during the summer and school breaks until they graduate from college.

Financial data Interns receive an hourly wage and matching compensation to help pay for college tuition and other expenses.

Duration 1 summer; may be renewed until the intern graduates from college if he or she maintains a GPA of 3.0 or higher.

Additional information Many sponsoring companies also assign mentors to work with the student interns.

Number awarded Varies each year; recently, 32 new interns were selected, including 1 to work at ABC, Inc., 1 at A&E Network, 1 at AT&T, 1 at AT&T National Digital Media Center, 1 at BMI, 1 at CBS Corporation, 1 at C-SPAN, 1 at Discovery Networks, 2 at Fox Television Stations, Inc., 14 at NBC, 1 at Tribune Foundation, 5 at Turner Entertainment Networks, 1 at Procter & Gamble, and 1 at The Weather Channel.

[1134]
EQUAL RIGHTS ADVOCATES LAW CLERKSHIPS

Equal Rights Advocates, Inc.
1663 Mission Street, Suite 250
San Francisco, CA 94103
(415) 621-0672   Fax: (415) 621-6744
E-mail: info@equalrights.org
Web: www.equalrights.org

Purpose To provide work experience to law students who are interested in working for the equal rights of women.

Eligibility Applicants should be entering second- or third-year law students who are committed to public interest law and women's issues. Selection criteria include demonstrated involvement in issues of public concern, legal skills, public speaking skills, ability to work with diverse communities, critical thinking, ability to write well, and a sense of humor; the ability to speak Spanish is a plus. Applications are encouraged from people of diverse ethnic, racial, religious, and economic backgrounds, and from people who are lesbian, gay, bisexual, transgender, and/or disabled.

Financial data These are paid internships.

Duration 1 semester or summer. The position requires at least 16 hours per week of service.

Additional information Equal Rights Advocates (ERA) is a nonprofit, public interest law firm that specializes in sex discrimination issues. The responsibilities of the clerks include staffing the advice and counseling line, assisting with impact litigation, assisting with legislative advocacy, offering community education training, and participating as a member of program staff.

Number awarded 3 each semester or summer.

Deadline January of each year for summer; November of each year for spring.

[1135]
FAYETTEVILLE OBSERVER INTERNSHIPS

Fayetteville Observer
Attn: Managing Editor
458 Whitfield Street
P.O. Box 849
Fayetteville, NC 28302
(910) 486-3558   (800) 682-3476
Web: www.fayettevillenc.com

Purpose To provide work experience during the summer at the *Fayetteville Observer* in North Carolina to college students interested in careers in journalism.

Eligibility This program at the *Observer* is open to students from any state, with a preference for sophomores, juniors, and seniors. Applicants must be planning to pursue careers in news reporting, sports reporting, feature reporting, or photography. Minorities are especially encouraged to apply.

Financial data The salary is $300 per week. No other benefits are provided. Interns must provide their own lodging and transportation.

Duration 12 weeks, during the summer.

Number awarded 9 each year: 6 in news, 1 in features, 1 in sports, and 1 in photo.

Deadline January of each year.

[1136]
FELLOWSHIP PROGRAM IN ACADEMIC MEDICINE FOR MINORITY STUDENTS

National Medical Fellowships, Inc.
Attn: Scholarship Program
5 Hanover Square, 15th Floor
New York, NY 10004
(212) 483-8880   Fax: (212) 483-8897
E-mail: info@nmfonline.org
Web: www.nmf-online.org

Purpose To provide work experience to underrepresented minority medical school students interested in a career in biomedical research and academic medicine.

Eligibility This program is open to U.S. citizens who are members of 1 of the following underrepresented minority groups: African American, Alaska Native, American Indian, Native Hawaiian, Mexican American, or mainland Puerto Rican. Applicants must be first- through third-year students attending accredited medical schools or osteopathic colleges in the United States. M.D./Ph.D. candidates are eligible but do not receive first consideration. Applicants must submit a statement discussing their career goals over the next 10 years and how the fellowship would be instrumental in reaching those goals. Selection is based on academic achievement, potential for playing a responsible role in academic medicine, leadership ability, the clarity of the project description, the definition of the project objectives, a clear demonstration of the student's grasp of the project objectives, and evidence of a clear relationship between the student and a mentor.

Financial data The grant is $6,000, up to $2,000 of which is available to the mentor to offset expenses during the research period.

Duration 8 to 12 weeks, either during the summer or as an elective rotation during the academic year.

Additional information Interns work in a major research laboratory under the tutelage of a well-known biomedical scientist. The program was created in 1983 with grant support from The Commonwealth Fund of New York to foster mentor relationships between students and prominent scientists. The Bristol-Myers Squibb Foundation joined as a cosponsor in 1990 and assumed sole sponsorship in 1993.

Number awarded Up to 35 each year.

Deadline November of each year.

[1137]
FEMINIST MAJORITY FOUNDATION INTERNSHIP PROGRAM

Feminist Majority
Attn: Internship Coordinator
1600 Wilson Boulevard, Suite 801
Arlington, VA 22209
(703) 522-2214   Fax: (703) 522-2219
E-mail: femmaj@feminist.org
Web: www.feminist.org

Purpose To provide work experience at the Feminist Majority to students who aspire to become leaders in the feminist movement.

Eligibility This program is open to feminist undergraduate students of any major. Preference is given to applicants who have prior experience working on women's issues on campus, in their communities, or through a previous internship. Applications are especially encouraged from people of color, people with disabilities, and mathematics and science majors.

Financial data Interns may perform up to 10 hours a week of administrative work at $8 per hour.

Duration 2 months or longer. Full-time internships are available during the summer and full- or part-time internships are offered during the spring and fall.

Additional information Assignments at the Feminist Majority are available in the following project areas: Campaign to Help Afghan Women and Girls, Campus Program, Feminist Majority Foundation Online, Million4Roe Campaign, *Ms.* Magazine, National Center for Women and Policing, National Clinic Access Project, Press Team, and Rock for Choice. Interns work in the Washington, D.C. area (see the contact address) or in the Los Angeles office (433 South Beverly Drive, Beverly Hills, CA 90212, (310) 556-2500, Fax: (310) 556-2509), E-mail: mlwood@feminist.org.

Number awarded Varies each year.

Deadline Applications may be submitted at any time; internships begin in September, January, and June of each year.

[1138]
FERMILAB SUMMER INTERNSHIPS IN SCIENCE AND TECHNOLOGY FOR MINORITY STUDENTS

Fermi National Accelerator Laboratory
Attn: Manager, Equal Opportunity Office
MS 117
P.O. Box 500
Batavia, IL 60510
(630) 840-3415   Fax: (630) 840-5207
E-mail: sist@fnal.gov
Web: sist.fnal.gov

Purpose To provide summer research experience at Fermi National Accelerator Laboratory (Fermilab) to college students, especially underrepresented minorities.

Eligibility This program is open to students who have completed at least 1 year at a 4-year college in the United States with a GPA of 3.0 or higher. Strong preference is given to members of minority groups that have historically been underrepresented in science and technology (Hispanics, African Americans, and Native Americans). As part of the application process, they must submit an essay on the technical courses and projects that have interested them, the technical project that gave them the most enjoyment and why, and how this relates to what they want to do.

Financial data Weekly stipends are $540 for freshmen, $572 for sophomores, $605 for juniors, or $637 for seniors. In addition, the program provides round-trip airfare to the laboratory, housing at partial cost to the interns, and transportation between housing and the laboratory.

Duration 12 weeks, beginning in late May.

Additional information Interns join selected staff members on research projects, attend academic lectures, and prepare a final report. This program began in 1971.

Number awarded Approximately 20 each year.

Deadline February of each year.

[1139]
FINANCIAL SERVICES FELLOWSHIPS

Congressional Hispanic Caucus Institute, Inc.
504 C Street, N.E.
Washington, DC 20002
(202) 543-1771 (800) EXCEL-DC
Fax: (202) 546-2143 E-mail: chci@chci.org
Web: www.chci.org

Purpose To provide Latino graduate students and recent college graduates with the opportunity to apply their academic expertise in the area of the financial services industry during a work experience program in Washington, D.C.

Eligibility This program is open to U.S. citizens and permanent residents of Latino background who graduated from a college or university (with a bachelor's or graduate degree) within the past year or are currently-enrolled graduate students. Applicants must be interested in gaining experience in an area related to the financial services industry. Preference is given to applicants with a GPA of 3.0 or higher. Selection is based on evidence of leadership potential as demonstrated through goal setting, initiative, and responsibility; active interest in community affairs, balanced with academics; and analytical and communication skills (oral and written).

Financial data This program provides transportation to and from Washington, D.C., a monthly stipend of $2,061 (or $2,500 for fellows who already hold a graduate degree), and health insurance.

Duration 15 months, beginning in September.

Additional information Placements are available in congressional offices and federal agencies, advocacy groups, the media, and a broad range of policy-related organizations, but must focus on the financial services industry.

Number awarded 1 or more each year.

Deadline February of each year.

[1140]
FINNEGAN HENDERSON DIVERSITY SCHOLARSHIP

Finnegan, Henderson, Farabow, Garrett & Dunner, LLP
Attn: Director of Professional Recruitment and Development
1300 I Street, N.W.
Washington, D.C. 20005-3315
(202) 408-4034 Fax: (202) 408-4400
E-mail: suzanne.gentes@finnegan.com
Web: www.finnegan.com

Purpose To provide financial assistance and work experience to minority law students interested in a career in intellectual property law.

Eligibility This program is open to law students from underrepresented minority groups who have demonstrated a commitment to a career in intellectual property law and are currently enrolled either as a first-year full-time student or second-year part-time student. The sponsor defines underrepresented minorities to include American Indians/Alaskan Natives, Blacks/African Americans, Asian Americans/Pacific Islanders, and Hispanics/Latinos. Applicants must have earned an undergraduate degree in life sciences, engineering, or computer science, or have substantial prior trademark experience. Selection is based on academic performance at the undergraduate, graduate (if applicable), and law school level; relevant work experience; community service; leadership skills; and special accomplishments.

Financial data The stipend is $12,000 per year.

Duration 1 year; may be renewed 1 additional year as long as the recipient completes a summer associateship with the sponsor and maintains of GPA of 3.0 or higher.

Additional information The sponsor, the world's largest intellectual property law firm, established this scholarship in 2003. Summer associateships are available at its offices in Washington, D.C.; Atlanta, Georgia; Cambridge, Massachusetts; Palo Alto, California; or Reston, Virginia.

Number awarded 1 each year.

Deadline May of each year.

[1141]
FLORIDA SOCIETY OF NEWSPAPER EDITORS MINORITY SCHOLARSHIP PROGRAM

Florida Society of Newspaper Editors
c/o Kevin Walsh, Scholarship Committee
Florida Press Association
122 South Calhoun Street
Tallahassee, FL 32301-1554
(850) 222-5790 Fax: (850) 224-6012
E-mail: info@fsne.org
Web: www.fsne.org/minorityscholar.html

Purpose To provide financial assistance and summer work experience to minority upper-division students majoring in journalism at a college or university in Florida.

Eligibility This program is open to minority students in accredited journalism or mass communication programs at Florida 4-year colleges and universities. Applicants must be full-time students in their junior year, have at least a 3.0 GPA, and be willing to participate in a paid summer internship at a Florida newspaper. As part of the application process, they must write a 300-word autobiographical essay explaining why they want to pursue a career in print journalism and provide a standard resume, references, and clips or examples of relevant classroom work.

Financial data Winners are given a paid summer internship at a participating newspaper between their junior and senior year. Upon successfully completing the internship, the students are awarded a $3,600 scholarship (paid in 2 equal installments) to be used during their senior year.

Duration 1 summer for the internship; 1 academic year for the scholarship.

Deadline December of each year.

[1142]
FLORIDA SPACE GRANT CONSORTIUM FELLOWSHIP PROGRAM

Florida Space Grant Consortium
c/o Center for Space Education
Building M6-306, Room 7010
Mail Stop: FSGC
Kennedy Space Center, FL 32899
(321) 452-4301 Fax: (321) 449-0739
E-mail: fsgc@mail.ufl.edu
Web: fsgc.engr.ucf.edu

Purpose To provide financial assistance and summer work experience to doctoral students in space studies at universities participating in the Florida Space Grant Consortium (FSGC).

Eligibility Eligible to be nominated for this program are U.S. citizens who are enrolled full time in doctoral programs at universities participating in the consortium. Nominees must be enrolled in a space-related field of study, broadly defined to include aeronautics, astronautics, remote sensing, atmospheric sciences, and other fundamental sciences and technologies relying on and/or directly impacting space technological resources. Included within that definition are space science; earth observing science; space life sciences; space medicine; space policy, law, and engineering; astronomy and astrophysics; space facilities and applications; and space education. Their undergraduate GPA should be at least 3.5. The program particularly solicits nominations of women, underrepresented minorities, and students with disabilities.

Financial data Each fellow receives a $12,000 stipend and a supplementary summer traineeship stipend from a participating industry, government, or private laboratory.

Duration Up to 3 years.

Additional information Fellows work during the summer in a government, industry, or private laboratory. This program is funded by the U.S. National Aeronautics and Space Administration (NASA). The consortium member universities are Bethune-Cookman College, Eckerd College, Embry-Riddle Aeronautical University, Florida A&M University, Florida Atlantic University, Florida Community Colleges, Florida Gulf Coast University, Florida Institute of Technology, Florida International University, Florida Southern College, Florida State University, University of Central Florida, University of Florida, University of Miami, University of North Florida, University of South Florida, and University of West Florida.

Number awarded 3 each year.

Deadline Notices of intent must be submitted by February of each year. Completed proposals are due in March.

[1143]
FORD MOTOR COMPANY FELLOWS PROGRAM

National Association of Latino Elected and Appointed
    Officials
Attn: Internship Coordinator
5800 South Eastern Avenue, Suite 365
Los Angeles, CA 90040-4020
(323) 720-1932, ext. 122   (800) 34-NALEO
Fax: (323) 720-9519   E-mail: ecastillo@naleo.org
Web: www.naleo.org/TTA/Ford/Ford.html

Purpose To provide Latino graduate students and recent graduates from selected states with an opportunity to gain summer work experience on the staff of a member of the U.S. House of Representatives.

Eligibility Applicants must be residents of or attend college in the following states: Arizona, California, Florida, Illinois, Michigan, New Jersey, Texas, and Puerto Rico. They must be a recent graduate of an accredited 4-year institution; graduating college seniors are also eligible and students currently enrolled in graduate and professional school are strongly encouraged to apply. U.S. citizenship or permanent resident status and Latino origin are required. Applicants must be at least 21 years of age, demonstrate leadership potential, and possess a sense of commitment to the Latino community.

Financial data Interns receive transportation, meals, and housing to participate in the annual conference; transportation and housing during their orientation in Washington, D.C.; and a $1,200 stipend for the internship.

Duration 6 weeks during the summer, beginning in June.

Additional information Interns attend the annual conference of the National Association of Latino Elected and Appointed Officials (NALEO) where they meet and network with Latinos who are involved in leadership positions at the municipal, state, federal,

and nonprofit levels; experience a 1-week orientation in Washington D.C. where they meet with Latino elected and appointed officials, White House staff, and congressional staffers; and spend the rest of the time working as a congressional intern with a member of the U.S. House of Representatives. Funding for this program is provided by the Ford Motor Company.

Number awarded 10 each year: 1 from each of the 8 designated states plus 2 selected from a national pool of applicants.

Deadline March of each year.

[1144]
FRANKLIN WILLIAMS INTERNSHIP

Council on Foreign Relations
Attn: Human Resources Office
58 East 68th Street
New York, NY 10021
(212) 434-9489   Fax: (212) 434-9893
E-mail: fellowships@cfr.org
Web: www.cfr.org/public/fp.html

Purpose To provide undergraduate and graduate students with an opportunity to gain work experience in international affairs at the Council on Foreign Relations in New York.

Eligibility Applicants should be currently enrolled in either their senior year of an undergraduate program or in a graduate program in the area of international relations or a related field. They should have a record of high academic achievement, proven leadership ability, and previous related internship or work experience. Minority students are strongly encouraged to apply.

Financial data The stipend is $10 per hour.

Duration 1 academic term (fall, spring, or summer). Fall and spring interns are required to make a commitment of at least 12 hours per week. Summer interns may choose to make a full-time commitment.

Additional information Interns work closely with a program director or fellow in either the studies or meetings program and are involved with program coordination, substantive and business writing, research, and budget management. In addition, they are encouraged to attend the council's extensive meetings programs and participate in informal training designed to enhance management and leadership skills.

Number awarded 3 each year: 1 each academic term.

Deadline Applications may be submitted at any time.

[1145]
FREDRIKSON & BYRON FOUNDATION MINORITY SCHOLARSHIPS

Fredrikson & Byron Foundation
4000 Pillsbury Center
200 South Sixth Street
Minneapolis, MN 55402-1425
(612) 492-7117   Fax: (612) 492-7077
Web: www.fredlaw.com/firm/scholarship.htm

Purpose To provide financial assistance and summer work experience to minority law students who will be practicing in the Twin Cities area of Minnesota.

Eligibility This program is open to African American, Asian American, Pacific Islander, Hispanic, Native American, and Alaska Native students enrolled in their first year of law school. Applicants must be interested in practicing law in the Minneapolis-St. Paul area. Along with their application, they must submit 2 recommendations, a writing sample from their first-year legal writing course, transcripts from undergraduate and law school, and a resume. Financial need is not considered.

Financial data The fellowship stipend is $5,000. The internship portion of the program provides a $1,000 weekly stipend.

Duration 1 year.

Additional information Fellows are also eligible to participate in an internship at the firm's offices in Minneapolis.

Number awarded Up to 2 each year.

Deadline March of each year.

[1146]
G. RICHARD TUCKER FELLOWSHIP

Center for Applied Linguistics
4646 40th Street, N.W.
Washington, DC 20016-1859
(202) 362-0700   E-mail: grace@cal.org
Web: www.cal.org

Purpose To provide an opportunity for graduate students to participate in a research project during the summer at the Center for Applied Linguistics (CAL) in Washington, D.C.

Eligibility This program at CAL is open to candidates for a master's or doctoral degree in any field that is concerned with the study of language. Applicants must be currently enrolled in a degree program in the United States or Canada and must have completed the equivalent of at least 1 year of full-time graduate study. Minorities are especially encouraged to apply. Applicants must be proposing to work with CAL senior staff members on 1 of the center's existing research projects or on a suitable project suggested by themselves; priority is given to proposals that focus on language education, language testing, or language issues related to minorities in the United States or Canada.

Financial data Fellows receive a stipend of $2,400 plus travel expenses up to $1,000.

Duration 4 weeks, during the summer.

Number awarded 1 each year.

Deadline April of each year.

[1147]
GEM M.S. ENGINEERING FELLOWSHIP PROGRAM

National Consortium for Graduate Degrees for Minorities in
   Engineering and Science (GEM)
P.O. Box 537
Notre Dame, IN 46556
(574) 631-7771   Fax: (574) 287-1486
E-mail: gem.1@nd.edu
Web: www.gemfellowship.org

Purpose To provide financial assistance and summer work experience to underrepresented minority graduate students in engineering.

Eligibility This program is open to U.S. citizens who are members of ethnic groups underrepresented in engineering: American Indians, African Americans, Mexican Americans, Puerto Ricans, and other Hispanic Americans. Applicants must be enrolled as at least a junior in an accredited engineering discipline with an academic record that indicates the ability to pursue graduate studies in engineering (including a GPA of 2.8 or higher). Recipients must attend 1 of the 88 GEM member universities that offer a master's degree.

Financial data The fellowship pays tuition, fees, and a stipend of $10,000 over its lifetime. In addition, each participant receives a salary during the summer work assignment as a GEM Summer

Intern, making the value of the total award between $20,000 and $60,000. Employer members reimburse GEM participants for travel expenses to and from the summer work site.

Duration Up to 3 semesters or 4 quarters, plus a summer work internship lasting 10 to 14 weeks for up to 3 summers, depending on whether the student applies as a junior, senior, or college graduate; recipients begin their internship upon acceptance into the program and work each summer until completion of their master's degree.

Additional information During the summer internship, each fellow is assigned an engineering project in a research setting. Each project is based on the fellow's interest and background and is carried out under the supervision of an experienced engineer. At the conclusion of the internship, each fellow writes a project report. Recipients must seek the master's degree in the same engineering discipline as their baccalaureate degree.

Number awarded Varies each year; recently, 327 of these fellowships were awarded.

Deadline November of each year.

[1148]
GEM PH.D. ENGINEERING FELLOWSHIP PROGRAM

National Consortium for Graduate Degrees for Minorities in
   Engineering and Science (GEM)
P.O. Box 537
Notre Dame, IN 46556
(574) 631-7771   Fax: (574) 287-1486
E-mail: gem.1@nd.edu
Web: www.gemfellowship.org

Purpose To provide financial assistance and summer work experience to underrepresented minority students interested in obtaining a Ph.D. degree in engineering.

Eligibility This program is open to U.S. citizens who are members of ethnic groups underrepresented in engineering: American Indians, African Americans, Mexican Americans, Puerto Ricans, and other Hispanic Americans. Applicants must have attained or be in the process of attaining a master's degree in engineering with an academic record that indicates the ability to pursue doctoral studies in engineering (including a GPA of 3.0 or higher).

Financial data The stipend is $14,000 per year, plus tuition and fees; the total value of the award is between $60,000 and $100,000.

Duration 3 to 5 years for the fellowship; 12 weeks during at least 1 summer for the internship.

Additional information This program is valid only at 1 of 88 participating GEM member universities; write to GEM for a list. The fellowship award is designed to support the student in the first year of the doctoral program without working. Subsequent years are subsidized by the respective university and will usually include either a teaching or research assistantship. Recipients must participate in the GEM summer internship; failure to agree to accept the internship cancels the fellowship.

Number awarded Varies each year; recently, 49 of these fellowships were awarded.

Deadline November of each year.

[1149]
GEM PH.D. SCIENCE FELLOWSHIP PROGRAM

National Consortium for Graduate Degrees for Minorities in
    Engineering and Science (GEM)
P.O. Box 537
Notre Dame, IN 46556
(574) 631-7771   Fax: (574) 287-1486
E-mail: gem.1@nd.edu
Web: www.gemfellowship.org

Purpose To provide financial assistance and summer work
experience to underrepresented minority students interested in
obtaining a Ph.D. degree in the natural sciences.

Eligibility This program is open to U.S. citizens who are members of ethnic groups underrepresented in the natural sciences:
American Indians, African Americans, Mexican Americans, Puerto
Ricans, and other Hispanic Americans. Applicants must be
juniors, seniors, or recent baccalaureate graduates in the natural
sciences (biological sciences, chemistry, computer science, earth
sciences, mathematics, and physics) with an academic record
that indicates the ability to pursue doctoral studies in the natural
sciences (including a GPA of 3.0 or higher).

Financial data The stipend is $14,000 per year, plus tuition
and fees. In addition, there is a summer internship program that
provides a salary and reimbursement for travel expenses to and
from the summer work site. The total value of the award is
between $60,000 and $100,000, depending upon academic status at the time of application, summer employer, and graduate
school attended.

Duration 3 to 5 years for the fellowship; 12 weeks during at
least 1 summer for the internship. Fellows selected as juniors or
seniors intern each summer until entrance to graduate school; fellows selected after college graduation intern at least 1 summer.

Additional information This program is valid only at 1 of 88
participating GEM member universities; write to GEM for a list.
The fellowship award is designed to support the student in the
first year of the doctoral program without working. Subsequent
years are subsidized by the respective university and will usually
include either a teaching or research assistantship. Recipients
must participate in the GEM summer internship; failure to agree
to accept the internship cancels the fellowship. Recipients must
enroll in the same scientific discipline as their undergraduate
major.

Number awarded Varies each year; recently, 40 of these fellowships were awarded.

Deadline November of each year.

[1150]
GERALDINE R. DODGE FOUNDATION FELLOWSHIP

College Art Association of America
Attn: Fellowship Program
275 Seventh Avenue
New York, NY 10001-6798
(212) 691-1051, ext. 206   Fax: (212) 627-2381
E-mail: fellowship@collegeart.org
Web: www.collegeart.org/caa/career/fellowship.html

Purpose To provide financial assistance and work experience
to artists or art historians from culturally diverse backgrounds
who are completing graduate degrees and are interested in working in New Jersey.

Eligibility This program is open to artists or art historians who
have been underrepresented in the field because of their race,
religion, gender, age, national origin, sexual orientation, disability,

or history of economic disadvantage. Applicants must be U.S. citizens or permanent residents and able to demonstrate financial
need. They must expect to receive the M.F.A., terminal M.A., or
Ph.D. degree in the year following application and then be interested in working at a cultural institution in New Jersey.

Financial data The stipend is $5,000 per year.

Duration 2 years: the final year of their degree program and the
first year following completion of their degree.

Additional information In addition to receiving a stipend for
the terminal year of their degree program, fellows participate in
an internship in New Jersey during the year following graduation.
The College Art Association helps fellows secure an internship at
a cultural institution, with collections in American art, pre-
Columbian art, Tibetan art, Native American art, textiles, or
numismatics. The Geraldine R. Dodge Foundation subsidizes a
portion of the fellow's salary during their first professional year.
Salaries and terms of employment are determined in consultation
with each fellow and potential host institution.

Number awarded 1 each year.

Deadline January of each year.

[1151]
GOALI GRADUATE STUDENT INDUSTRIAL
FELLOWSHIPS

National Science Foundation
Attn: Directorate for Engineering GOALI Coordinator
4201 Wilson Boulevard
Arlington, VA 22230
(703) 292-8300   TDD: (703) 292-5090
E-mail: lejohnso@nsf.gov
Web: www.eng.nsf.gov

Purpose To provide an opportunity for graduate students to
work in industry as part of the Grant Opportunities for Academic
Liaison with Industry (GOALI) program of the National Science
Foundation (NSF).

Eligibility This program is open to graduate students (preferably Ph.D. students) in science and engineering fields of interest
to NSF. Applicants must be proposing a program of full-time work
in industry in an area related to their research under the guidance
of an academic adviser and an industrial mentor. The program
encourages participation by women, underrepresented minority
students, and those with disabilities.

Financial data Graduate students may receive stipends from
$1,500 to $2,000 per month plus transportation expenses. The
faculty adviser may receive 10% of the total award for research-
related expenses excluding equipment. The sponsoring academic
institution may receive an additional allowance up to 10% of the
total direct cost for administrative expenses in lieu of indirect
costs. The total award may be up to $25,000 for a fellowship for
a single student or up to $75,000 for a graduate student trainee-
ship site (involving several students).

Duration Up to 1 year.

Number awarded Varies each year.

[1152]
HACU NATIONAL INTERNSHIP PROGRAM

Hispanic Association of Colleges and Universities
One Dupont Circle, N.W., Suite 605
Washington, DC 20036
(202) 467-0893   Fax: (202) 496-9177
TTY: (800) 855-2880   E-mail: hnip@hacu.net
Web: www.hnip.net

Purpose To allow Hispanic and other college students to experience the diversity and scope of professional careers available in the federal government and private corporations.

Eligibility This program is open to Hispanic and other college students who are interested in interning at federal agencies in Washington, D.C., at field offices nationwide, or with selected corporate partners. Applicants must be currently-enrolled undergraduate or graduate students who have completed at least the freshman year of college with a GPA of 3.0 or higher. U.S. citizenship or permanent resident status is required. Students who attend colleges that are members of the Hispanic Association of Colleges and Universities (HACU) receive preference. Selection is based on a letter of recommendation from a faculty member or administrator and a 1-page letter by the student explaining why he or she wishes to participate in the internship.

Financial data The salary is $420 per week for sophomores and juniors, $450 per week for seniors, or $520 per week for graduate and law school students. Round-trip travel expenses are included.

Duration 10 weeks during the summer or 15 weeks during the fall or spring semester.

Additional information Assistance in locating housing is available. Internships are available at many agencies of the federal government and with such corporations as the following: Burlington Northern Santa Fe Railroad, Education Testing Service, Goldman Sachs & Company, Marriott International, McDonald's Corporation, PricewaterhouseCoopers, State Fair Foods, and the St. Paul Companies.

Number awarded Varies each year; recently, 611 interns were placed through this program, including 395 in Washington, D.C. and 216 at other locations around the country. Interns included 96 sophomores, 114 juniors, 258 seniors, and 143 graduate students.

Deadline February of each year for summer; June of each year for fall; November of each year for spring.

[1153]
HARVARD SCHOOL OF PUBLIC HEALTH UNDERGRADUATE MINORITY SUMMER INTERNSHIP PROGRAM

Harvard School of Public Health
Division of Biological Sciences
Attn: Administrator
655 Huntington Avenue, Building 1-1204-A
Boston, MA 02115-6021
(617) 432-4470   Fax: (617) 432-0433
E-mail: dbs@hsph.harvard.edu
Web: www.hsph.harvard.edu/sip

Purpose To enable minority college science students to participate in a summer research internship at Harvard School of Public Health.

Eligibility This program is open to members of ethnic groups underrepresented in the sciences (African Americans, Mexican Americans, Chicanos, American Indians, Aleuts, Eskimos, Polynesians, Micronesians, and Puerto Ricans) who are currently college sophomores or juniors majoring in science. Applicants must be interested in participating in a research project related to biological science questions that are important to the prevention of disease (especially such public health questions as cancer, cardiovascular disease, AIDS, malaria, parasites, other infections, lung disease, and nutrition).

Financial data The program provides a stipend of at least $3,100, a travel allowance of up to $475, and free dormitory housing.

Duration 10 weeks, beginning in mid-June.

Additional information Interns conduct research under the mentorship of Harvard faculty members who are specialists in cancer cell biology, immunology and infectious diseases, molecular and cellular toxicology, environmental health sciences, nutrition, and cardiovascular research. Funding for this program is provided by the National Institutes of Health.

Number awarded 16 each year.

Deadline February of each year.

[1154]
HAYWOOD BURNS MEMORIAL FELLOWSHIPS FOR SOCIAL AND ECONOMIC JUSTICE

National Lawyers Guild
143 Madison Avenue, Fourth Floor
New York, NY 10016
(212) 679-5100   Fax: (212) 679-2811
E-mail: nlgno@nlg.org
Web: www.nlg.org

Purpose To provide law students with summer work experience in progressive legal work.

Eligibility This program is open to law students, legal workers, and lawyers interested in working with civil rights and poverty law groups. Applicants must submit essays on their legal, political, educational, and work experience; their reasons for applying; what they expect to gain from the fellowship; the types of legal and political work they hope to do in the future; how this internship will help them in their goals; the kind of work structure with which they are most comfortable; and how they plan to share their summer experience and skills with others. Women and ethnic minorities are particularly encouraged to apply.

Financial data Interns receive a $2,000 stipend. Recipients are encouraged to seek other funding sources, including law school work-study and fellowship programs.

Duration 10 weeks during the summer; renewable the following year.

Additional information Recently, fellowships were available at the following organizations: the Asian Law Caucus (San Francisco, California), Cleveland Works, Inc. (Cleveland, Ohio), Camden Regional Legal Services, Farmworker Division (Bridgeton, New Jersey), Defender Association of Philadelphia (Philadelphia, Pennsylvania), East Bay Community Law Center (Berkeley, California), Florence Immigrant and Refugee Rights Project, Inc. (Florence, Arizona), Georgia Resource Center (Atlanta, Georgia), Harm Reduction Law Project (New York, New York), Lesbian and Gay Community Services Center (New York, New York), Massachusetts Correctional Legal Services (Boston, Massachusetts), Maurice and Jane Sugar Law Center for Economic and Social Justice (Detroit, Michigan), Meiklejohn Civil Liberties Institute (Berkeley, California), National Housing Law Project (Oakland, California), National Whistleblower Center (Washington, D.C.), Northwest Immigrant Rights Project (Seattle, Washington), Protection and

Advocacy, Inc. (Oakland, California), and Southern Arizona People's Law Center (Tucson, Arizona).

Number awarded Approximately 25 each year.

Deadline January of each year.

[1155]
HBA–DC FELLOWSHIPS

Hispanic Bar Association of D.C.
Attn: Foundation
P.O. Box 1011
Washington, DC 20013-1011
(202) 624-2904   E-mail: foundation@hbadc.org
Web: www.hbadc.org/found.htm

Purpose To provide funding to Hispanic law students in Washington, D.C. who wish to gain work experience in public interest law during the summer.

Eligibility This program is open to first- and second-year Hispanic law students at law schools in Washington, D.C. Applicants must be seeking to gain work experience in public law at a nonprofit, non-governmental organization in Washington that provides legal services at little or no cost to clients. They must submit a letter from a sponsoring organization, indicating its willingness to host them as a law student intern.

Financial data The stipend is $3,000.

Duration Summer months.

Number awarded 2 each year.

Deadline March of each year.

[1156]
HEALTH POLICY SUMMER PROGRAM

Harvard Medical School
Office for Faculty Development and Diversity
Attn: Minority Faculty Development Program
164 Longwood Avenue, Second Floor
Boston, MA 02115-5818
(617) 432-4422   Fax: (617) 432-3834
E-mail: jeanette_catherwood@hms.harvard.edu
Web: www.mfdp.med.harvard.edu/cp/hpsp/hpsp.html

Purpose To provide an opportunity for underrepresented minority undergraduate students to engage in research at Harvard Medical School during the summer.

Eligibility This program is open to 1) juniors and seniors at MARC-funded institutions, Hispanic Serving Institutions, Historically Black Colleges and Universities, and Tribal Colleges, and 2) students who have participated in programs sponsored by Harvard Medical School's Minority Faculty Development Program such as Project Success and Biomedical Science Careers Program. Applicants must have completed at least 1 college course in calculus; course work in statistics and/or economics is preferred but not required. Their field of study must relate to health policy or health services research, including biomedical or clinical sciences, public health, epidemiology, statistics, economics, behavioral sciences, and health care administration. Applicants must be interested in working on a research program with senior Harvard faculty.

Financial data Up to $500 is available to provide assistance for transportation costs to and from Boston. A stipend, room, and board are also provided.

Duration 10 to 12 weeks, during the summer.

Number awarded Varies each year.

[1157]
HERBERT SCOVILLE JR. PEACE FELLOWSHIP

Herbert Scoville Jr. Peace Fellowship Program
Attn: Program Director
110 Maryland Avenue, N.E., Suite 409
Washington, DC 20002
(202) 543-4100   Fax: (202) 546-5142
E-mail: scoville@clw.org
Web: www.scoville.org

Purpose To provide an opportunity for college graduates to work with a peace, disarmament, or nuclear arms control organization in Washington, D.C.

Eligibility Applicants must be college graduates who can demonstrate excellent academic accomplishments and a strong interest in issues of peace and security. Prior experience with public-interest activism or advocacy is highly desirable. U.S. citizens receive preference, although foreign nationals residing in the United States are occasionally selected. Complete applications for the fellowship must include 2 letters of reference; a statement describing how the applicant first learned of the program; another essay discussing qualifications, interests, fellowship objectives, and career goals; an essay of up to 1,000 words taking a position on some contemporary, contentious issue; a full curriculum vitae; and transcripts. Preference is given to applicants who have not had substantial prior public interest or government experience in the Washington, D.C. area. Women and people of color are strongly encouraged to apply.

Financial data Fellows receive a stipend of $1,600 per month, health insurance, and travel expenses.

Duration 6 to 9 months, in spring or fall.

Additional information Fellows serve as special project assistants on the staff of 1 of the following 23 participating organizations: Alliance for Nuclear Accountability, Arms Control Association, British American Security Information Council, Center for Defense Information, Center for Nonproliferation Studies, Center for Strategic and Budgetary Assessments, Council for a Livable World Education Fund, Federation of American Scientists, Institute for Energy and Environmental Research, Institute for Science and International Security, Lawyers Alliance for World Security/Committee for National Security, National Security Archive, National Security News Service, Natural Resources Defense Council, Nuclear Control Institute, Peace Action, Physicians for Social Responsibility, Russian American Nuclear Security Advisory Council, Henry L. Stimson Center, 20/20 Vision National Project, Union of Concerned Scientists, Women's Action for New Directions, and World Federalist Association. The program does not provide grant money or scholarships for students.

Number awarded 2 to 4 each semester.

Deadline January of each year for the fall semester; October for the spring semester.

[1158]
HERCULES MINORITY ENGINEERS DEVELOPMENT PROGRAM

Hercules Incorporated
Attn: Human Resources Department
Hercules Plaza
1313 North Market Street
Wilmington, DE 19894-0001
(302) 594-6030   Fax: (302) 594-6483
Web: www.herc.com

Purpose To provide financial assistance and summer work experience to minority undergraduates interested in preparing for a career in engineering.

Eligibility Eligible are minority group members who have completed at least 1 semester of university study before applying, are interested in careers in engineering, have earned at least a 3.0 GPA, and attend 1 of the 5 schools participating in the program (Georgia Institute of Technology, University of Delaware, North Carolina State University, Virginia Polytechnic Institute and State University, and Pennsylvania State University).

Financial data The scholarship stipend is $4,000 per year.

Duration 1 year; renewable for up to 3 additional years.

Additional information Recipients are eligible to work as interns during the summer months throughout their undergraduate years. Information about the scholarship/internship program can be obtained by writing to Hercules Incorporated or contacting the participating university. Candidates must be nominated by their Dean of Engineering.

Deadline Varies from school to school.

[1159]
H.I.S. SCHOLARS PROGRAM

Hispanic College Fund
Attn: National Director
1717 Pennsylvania Avenue, N.W., Suite 460
Washington, D.C. 20006
(800) 644-4223   Fax: (202) 296-3774
E-mail: hispaniccollegefund@earthlink.net
Web: www.hispanicfund.org

Purpose To provide financial assistance and summer work experience to Hispanic American undergraduate students who are interested in preparing for a career in telecommunications.

Eligibility This program is open to U.S. citizens of Hispanic background who are entering their freshman, sophomore, junior, or senior year of college. Applicants must be working on a bachelor's degree in accounting, business administration, computer science, economics, engineering specialties, finance, information systems, management, or other relevant technology or business fields. They must have an interest in telecommunications, have a cumulative GPA of 3.0 or higher, and be available to complete at least 2 consecutive summer internships before graduating from college. Financial need is considered in the selection process.

Financial data Stipends range from $500 to $5,000, depending on need and academic achievement. Funds are paid directly to the recipient's college or university to help cover tuition and fees.

Duration 1 year; recipients may reapply.

Additional information This program is a joint venture of the Hispanic College Fund (which provides scholarships), INROADS (which provides monthly coaching, leadership development, community service, and mentorship), and Sprint (which provides 10- to 12-week paid summer internships).

Number awarded Varies each year.
Deadline April of each year.

[1160]
HISPANIC LINK JOURNALISM FOUNDATION FELLOWSHIPS

Hispanic Link Journalism Foundation
Attn: Executive Director
1420 N Street, N.W.
Washington, DC 20005
(202) 238-0705   Fax: (202) 238-0706
E-mail: Hector@aol.com
Web: www.hispaniclink.org

Purpose To provide work experience in Washington, D.C. to Hispanics who are interested in pursuing a career in journalism.

Eligibility Talented Hispanics interested in pursuing careers in the media are eligible to apply. There are no specific educational, age, or experience requirements. Candidates need not be working as journalists now. Selection is based on writing skills (with emphasis on English language), analytical skills, potential, and commitment to pursue journalism as a career.

Financial data The stipend is $25,000, plus some travel and other benefits.

Duration 12 months.

Additional information The internships include attendance at seminars covering major areas of public policy. Interns work at Hispanic Link News Service in Washington, D.C., covering issues that impact the Hispanic community nationwide.

Number awarded 1 each year.

Deadline June of each year.

[1161]
HP SCHOLAR PROGRAM

Hewlett-Packard Company
Attn: Scholar Program Manager
8000 Foothills Boulevard
MS 5214
Roseville, CA 95747
(916) 785-3809   E-mail: sandy.brooks2@hp.com
Web: www.hp.com/go/hpscholars

Purpose To provide financial assistance and summer work experience to underrepresented minority high school seniors and community college transfer students who are interested in studying computer engineering, electrical engineering, or computer science at designated universities.

Eligibility This program is open to graduating high school seniors and community college students who are members of an underrepresented minority group (African American, Latino, or American Indian). Applicants must be planning to major in electrical engineering, computer engineering, or computer science at the University of California at Los Angeles, San Jose State University, North Carolina A&T University, or Morgan State University. They must be interested in working during the summer at a major Hewlett-Packard (HP) location in California, Colorado, Idaho, Massachusetts, Oregon, or Washington. Selection is based on academic achievement, financial need, family's educational history (priority is given to first-generation students), letters of recommendation, a personal statement (communication skills, personal and professional qualities, community involvement), connections to HP Philanthropy and Education Partnerships, and demonstrated interest in math, science, and engineering.

Financial data The stipend is $3,000 per year. In addition, students receive a salary when they work at HP facilities during the summer. The total value of the award exceeds $40,000 per student.

Duration 4 years of university study plus 3 summers of internships.

Additional information Applications must be submitted to the school the student wishes to attend.

Number awarded Varies each year.

Deadline March of each year.

[1162]
IBM COOPERATIVE FELLOWSHIP PROGRAM

IBM Corporation
Attn: University Relations
P.O. Box 218
Yorktown Heights, NY 10598
E-mail: CFellow@us.ibm.com
Web: www-4.ibm.com

Purpose To provide financial assistance and work experience to students pursuing a Ph.D. in a technical area of broad interest to IBM.

Eligibility Students nominated for this fellowship should be enrolled full time in an accredited U.S. or Canadian college or university and should have completed at least 1 year of graduate study in the following fields: chemistry, computer science, electrical engineering, material sciences, mathematics, mechanical engineering, physics, or related disciplines. They should be planning a career in advanced technology and product development as well as related research areas. Nominations must be made by a faculty member and endorsed by the department head. IBM values diversity and encourages nominations of women, minorities, and others who contribute to that diversity. Selection is based on the nominee's technical excellence and the strong interest of a participating IBM development laboratory in the nominee's desired research areas.

Financial data The fellowship covers tuition and fees as well as providing the recipient a stipend of $15,000. In addition, a small number of Distinguished Fellowships (for recipients who show "exceptional promise") are awarded, with a stipend of $20,000.

Duration 1 year; may be renewed, provided the recipient is renominated and demonstrates continued progress and achievement.

Additional information Recipients are offered an internship at 1 of the IBM's development laboratories as well as the opportunity to interact with IBM technical staff in a variety of settings. As interns, they are given an IBM ThinkPad.

Number awarded 25 each year.

Deadline November of each year.

[1163]
IBM RESEARCH FELLOWSHIP PROGRAM

IBM Corporation
Attn: University Relations
P.O. Box 218
Yorktown Heights, NY 10598
E-mail: RFellow@us.ibm.com
Web: www-4.ibm.com

Purpose To provide financial assistance and work experience to students working on a Ph.D. in a research area of broad interest to IBM.

Eligibility Students nominated for this fellowship should be enrolled full time in an accredited U.S. or Canadian college or university and should have completed at least 1 year of graduate study in the following fields: chemistry, computer science, electrical engineering, material sciences, mathematics, mechanical engineering, physics, or related disciplines. They should be planning a career in research. Nominations must be made by a faculty member and endorsed by the department head. IBM values diversity and encourages nominations of women, minorities, and others who contribute to that diversity. Selection is based on research excellence and the student's overall potential for a research career.

Financial data The fellowship covers tuition and fees as well as providing the recipient a stipend of $15,000. In addition, up to 4 Distinguished Fellowships (for recipients who show "exceptional promise") are awarded, with a stipend of $20,000.

Duration 1 year; may be renewed, provided the recipient is renominated and demonstrates continued progress and achievement.

Additional information Recipients are offered an internship at 1 of the IBM Research Division laboratories and are given an IBM ThinkPad.

Number awarded 25 each year.

Deadline November of each year.

[1164]
ILLINOIS BROADCASTERS ASSOCIATION ENDOWED SCHOLARSHIPS

Illinois Broadcasters Association
2621 Montega, Suite E
Springfield, IL 62704
(217) 793-2636   Fax: (217) 793-5509
E-mail: info@ilba.org
Web: www.ilba.org/minority_intern_program.htm

Purpose To provide funding to minority college students in Illinois who are majoring in broadcasting and interested in interning at a radio or television station in the state.

Eligibility This program is open to currently-enrolled minority students majoring in broadcasting at a college or university in Illinois. Applicants must be interested in a fall, spring, or summer internship at a radio or television station in a small to medium-sized market community in Illinois. Along with their application, they must submit 1) a 250-word essay on how they expect to benefit from a grant through this program, and 2) at least 2 letters of recommendation from a broadcasting faculty member or professional familiar with their career potential and 1 other letter. The president of the sponsoring organization selects those students nominated by their schools who he feels have the best opportunity to make it in the world of broadcasting and matches them with internship opportunities that would otherwise be unpaid.

Financial data This program provides a grant to pay the living expenses for the interns in the Illinois communities where they are assigned. The amount of the grant depends on the length of the internship.

Duration 16 weeks in the fall and spring terms or 12 weeks in the summer.

Number awarded 12 each year: 4 in each of the 3 terms.

[1165]
INDUSTRY-BASED GRADUATE RESEARCH ASSISTANTSHIPS AND COOPERATIVE FELLOWSHIPS IN THE MATHEMATICAL SCIENCES

National Science Foundation
Directorate for Mathematical and Physical Sciences
Attn: Division of Mathematical Sciences
4201 Wilson Boulevard, Room 1025
Arlington, VA 22230
(703) 292-4862   TDD: (703) 292-5090
E-mail: ldouglas@nsf.gov
Web: www.nsf.gov/mps/general.htm

Purpose To provide financial assistance to graduate students in mathematics who want to gain experience in industrial settings.

Eligibility This program is open to graduate students in mathematics who are U.S. citizens, nationals, or permanent residents. Applicants may propose either 1) a research assistantship, in which they conduct research for a master's thesis or doctoral dissertation under the joint supervision of a university faculty member and an industrial scientist, spending part time at the industrial site on a regular basis and the remainder in the classroom or in other campus-based activities; or 2) a cooperative fellowship, in which they work full time as an intern in an industrial setting. Applications are especially encouraged from women, underrepresented minorities, and persons with disabilities.

Financial data The program provides up to 50% (with an upper limit of $20,000) of the total support for each student. The university faculty member involved in the joint supervision of these students may request up to $6,000 as a faculty research allowance.

Duration Up to 1 year.

Number awarded Varies each year.

Deadline November of each year.

[1166]
INROADS NATIONAL COLLEGE INTERNSHIPS

INROADS, Inc.
10 South Broadway, Suite 700
St. Louis, MO 63102
(314) 241-7488   Fax: (314) 241-9325
E-mail: info@inroads.org
Web: www.inroads.org

Purpose To provide an opportunity for young people of color to gain work experience in business or industry.

Eligibility Eligible to apply are African Americans, Hispanics, and Native Americans who reside in the areas served by INROADS and wish to pursue careers in business, computer science, engineering, science, or liberal arts. Applicants should be 1) seniors in high school with a GPA of 3.0 or higher, an ACT composite score of 20 or better, an SAT combined score of 1,000 or better, or a rank in the top 10% of their class; or 2) freshmen or sophomores in 4-year colleges and universities with a GPA of 2.8 or higher.

Financial data Salaries vary, depending upon the specific internship assigned; recently, the range was from $170 to $750 per week.

Duration Up to 4 years.

Additional information INROADS places interns in Fortune 1000 companies, where training focuses on preparing them for corporate and community leadership. The INROADS organization offers internship opportunities through 48 local affiliates in 32 states and the District of Columbia.

Number awarded Approximately 7,000 high school and college students are currently working for more than 900 corporate sponsors nationwide.

[1167]
INSTITUTE FOR INTERNATIONAL PUBLIC POLICY FELLOWSHIPS

United Negro College Fund Special Programs Corporation
2750 Prosperity Avenue, Suite 600
Fairfax, VA 22031
(703) 205-7624   (800) 530-6232
Fax: (703) 205-7645   E-mail: iipp@uncfsp.org
Web: www.uncfsp.org/iipp

Purpose To provide financial assistance and work experience to minority students who are interested in preparing for a career in international affairs.

Eligibility This program is open to full-time sophomores at 4-year institutions who have a GPA of 3.2 or higher and are nominated by the president of their institution. Applicants must be African American, Hispanic/Latino American, Asian American, American Indian, Alaskan Native, Native Hawaiian, or Pacific Islander. They must be interested in participating in policy institutes, study abroad, language training, internships, and graduate education that will prepare them for a career in international service. U.S. citizenship or permanent resident status is required. Preference is given to students interested in pursuing advanced language and area studies in targeted world areas who are supported by Title VI fellowships. Targeted languages include Arabic, Azeri, Armenian, Dari, Hindi, Kazakh, Kyrgyz, Persian, Pashto, Tajik, Turkish, Turkmen, Uzbek, Urdu, and other languages spoken in central and south Asia, the Middle East, and Russia/eastern Europe.

Financial data For the sophomore summer policy institute, fellows receive student housing and meals in a university facility, books and materials, all field trips and excursions, and a $1,050 stipend. For the junior year study abroad component, half the expenses for 1 semester are provided. For the junior summer policy institute, fellows receive student housing and meals in a university facility, books and materials, travel to and from the institute, and a $1,000 stipend. For the summer language institute, fellows receive tuition and fees, books and materials, room and board, travel to and from the institute, and a $1,000 stipend. During the internship, a stipend of up to $3,500 is paid. During the graduate school period, fellowships are funded jointly by this program and the participating graduate school. The program provides $15,000 toward a master's degree in international affairs with the expectation that the graduate school will provide $15,000 in matching funds.

Duration 2 years of undergraduate work and 2 years of graduate work, as well as the intervening summers.

Additional information This program consists of 6 components: 1) a sophomore year summer policy institute based at Clark Atlanta University's Department of International Affairs and Development, comprised of lectures, discussions, and group assignments, complemented by guest speakers and local site visits to international agencies and organizations in Washington, D.C. and New York; the program of study includes international politics, research methods, U.S. foreign policy, international business, economics, and selected area studies; 2) a junior year study abroad program at an accredited overseas institution; 3) a junior year summer institute of intensive academic preparation for graduate school, with course work in economics, mathematics, communication skills, and policy analysis; 4) for students without established foreign language competency, a summer language institute following the senior year; 5) fellows with previously established foreign language competence participate in a post-baccalaureate internship to provide the practical experience needed for successful graduate studies in international affairs; and 6) a master's degree in international affairs (for students who are admitted to such a program). This program is administered by the United Negro College Fund Special Programs Corporation in partnership with the Hispanic Scholarship Fund Institute and the Association of Professional Schools of International Affairs; funding is provided by a grant from the U.S. Department of Education.

Number awarded 20 each year.
Deadline February of each year.

[1168]
INTERNSHIP IN EDUCATIONAL MEDIA

Metropolitan Museum of Art
Attn: Internship Programs
1000 Fifth Avenue
New York, NY 10028-0198
(212) 570-3710　　　　　Fax: (212) 570-3782
Web: www.metmuseum.org/education/er_internship.asp

Purpose To provide work experience at the Metropolitan Museum of Art to graduate students interested in educational media.

Eligibility This internship is available to graduate students in museum studies, design, instructional technology, or related fields. Applicants must be interested in planning, creating, and producing publications for families, teachers, students, and the general museum public. Strong computer skills are required. Applicants of diverse backgrounds (e.g., minorities) are encouraged to apply.

Financial data The honorarium is $20,000.
Duration 12 months, beginning in June.
Additional information The intern will acquire skills in preparing materials for print, electronic, and video production.
Number awarded 1 each year.
Deadline January of each year.

[1169]
INTO THE FIELDS INTERNSHIPS

Student Action with Farmworkers
1317 West Pettigrew Street
Durham, NC 27705
(919) 660-3652　　　　　Fax: (919) 681-7600
Web: www.saf-unite.org

Purpose To provide rural work experience during the summer to students from farmworker families and those attending a college or university in the Carolinas.

Eligibility This program is open to 1) students from farmworker families anywhere in the United States, and 2) students currently attending a college or university in North or South Carolina. Students from outside the Carolinas who are not from farmworker families may apply, but they are not given preference. Spanish skills are required for most placements. Applicants must be interested in working for participating organizations in rural, agricultural areas of North or South Carolina (most placements are in North Carolina).

Financial data Interns receive a stipend of $1,200 to pay for food, gas, electricity, water, telephone and other miscellaneous

expenses, but they are required to raise half of that themselves. The program provides either furnished housing in a family or group setting or (for interns who do not wish to live in such a setting) a partial rent subsidy. It also pays the airfare for students from farmworker families who fly to the Carolinas for the program. Interns who successfully complete the program receive a $1,500 post-service educational award.

Duration Summer months.
Additional information Interns participate in workshops during an orientation session at the beginning of the summer and during a mid-summer and final retreat. Those workshops prepare them for their specific placements and develop their leadership skills. Training sessions familiarize participants with such specific farmworker issues as demographics, legal rights, immigration, education, health, documentary studies, and community and labor organizing. As a final project, interns must either 1) complete a documentary project of the cultural and artistic traditions of farmworkers through direct interviews and photography of farmworkers, or 2) participate in the traveling Levante Theater Group that uses drama to initiate discussion among farmworker students, parents, and educators.

Number awarded Varies each year; recently, 28 of these internships were provided.
Deadline February of each year.

[1170]
INTRODUCTION TO BIOMEDICAL RESEARCH PROGRAM

National Institute of Allergy and Infectious Diseases
Attn: Office of Research on Minority and Women's Health
6003 Executive Boulevard, Room 4B04
Bethesda, MD 20892-7630
(301) 496-8697　　　　　Fax: (301) 496-8729
E-mail: jw25v@nih.gov
Web: www.niaid.nih.gov

Purpose To inform academically talented students from minority groups of career opportunities in the broad field of biomedical research.

Eligibility Deans and faculty from colleges and universities in the United States, Puerto Rico, the Virgin Islands, and Guam may recommend college juniors, seniors, first-year medical students, and first-year graduate students for this program. Nominees must be members of minority groups (American Indians, Alaska Natives, Asians, Pacific Islanders, Blacks, or Hispanics), be U.S. citizens or permanent residents, and have a GPA of 3.0 or better.

Financial data Undergraduates receive per diem expenses and round-trip transportation from the student's academic institution to the National Institutes of Health (NIH) in Bethesda, Maryland. Graduate students also receive a salary.
Duration 5 days, in February.
Additional information The program consists of a series of scientific lectures, interviews, and tours of the NIH facilities. Students have the opportunity to discuss current research initiatives and advances and career concerns with staff scientists as well as summer positions in the NIH Summer Internship Program in Biomedical Research.
Number awarded Approximately 60 each year.
Deadline November of each year.

[1171]
IRTS SUMMER FELLOWSHIP PROGRAM

International Radio and Television Society Foundation
Attn: Director, Special Projects
420 Lexington Avenue, Suite 1601
New York, NY 10170-0101
(212) 867-6650, ext. 306   (888) 627-1266
Fax: (212) 867-6653   E-mail: apply@irts.org
Web: www.irts.org/sfp.htm

Purpose To provide work experience to undergraduate and (upon petition) graduate students interested in working in broadcasting and related fields in the New York City area.

Eligibility Full-time juniors, seniors, and graduate students at 4-year colleges and universities are eligible to apply. They must be either a communications major or have demonstrated a strong interest in the field through extracurricular activities or other practical experience. Minority (Black, Hispanic, Asian/Pacific Islander, American Indian/Alaskan Native) students are especially encouraged to apply.

Financial data Those selected for the program receive air or train fare, housing at a local college dormitory, and a small salary to defray the cost of food, intra-city commuting, and personal expenses.

Duration 9 weeks, during the summer.

Additional information The first week consists of a comprehensive orientation to broadcasting, cable, advertising, and new media. Then, the participants are assigned an 8-week fellowship. This full-time "real world" experience in a New York-based corporation allows them to reinforce or redefine specific career goals before settling into a permanent job. Fellows have worked at all 4 major networks, at local New York City radio and television stations, and at national rep firms, advertising agencies, and cable operations. This program includes the Stephen K. Nenno Inspirational Fellowship, the Barry Sherman Fellowship (established in 2000), and the following, named for broadcast engineers who lost their lives in the World Trade Center on September 11, 2001: the Gerard "Rod" Coppolo Fellowship, the Donald J. DiFranco Fellowship, the Steven Jacobson Fellowship, the Bob Pattison Fellowship, the Isaias Rivera Fellowship, and the William V. Steckman, Sr. Fellowship.

Number awarded Varies; recently, 33 of these fellowships were awarded.

Deadline November of each year.

[1172]
IWPR SUMMER INTERNSHIPS

Institute for Women's Policy Research
1707 L Street, N.W., Suite 750
Washington, DC 20036
(202) 785-5100   Fax: (202) 833-4362
E-mail: iwpr@iwpr.org
Web: www.iwpr.org/employment_intern.html

Purpose To provide work experience opportunities during the summer at the Institute for Women's Policy Research (IWPR) to students interested in women's policy issues.

Eligibility This program at IWPR is open to college students, graduate students, and recent graduates who are interested in economic justice for women. Interns need to have basic research and computer skills and excellent communication skills, both oral and written. An interest in women's issues is also essential; a background in the social sciences and/or statistics is preferred. People of color are encouraged to apply.

Financial data Interns receive a stipend of $100 per week and a local transportation subsidy.

Duration At least 10 weeks; some flexibility can be arranged for starting and ending dates.

Additional information Interns work in Washington D.C. for IWPR, a nonprofit research organization that works primarily on issues related to equal opportunity and economic and social justice for women. They work in 1 of 3 departments: research (reviewing literature, collecting data and resources, gathering information from public officials and organization representatives, and preparing reports and summaries), communications and outreach (handling special requests for public information materials, planning special events, editing and proofreading, and assisting in the maintenance of web activities), and development (grant-writing, nonprofit fund-raising, and direct mail programs). The institute gives special emphasis to issues of race, ethnicity, and class in its projects.

Number awarded Varies each year.

Deadline February of each year.

[1173]
JACKIE JOYNER-KERSEE MINORITY INTERNSHIP

Women's Sports Foundation
Attn: Award and Grant Programs Manager
Eisenhower Park
1899 Hempstead Turnpike, Suite 400
East Meadow, NY 11554-1000
(516) 542-4700   (800) 227-3988
Fax: (516) 542-4716   E-mail: wosport@aol.com
Web: www.womenssportsfoundation.org

Purpose To provide women of color with an opportunity to get a start in a sports-related career.

Eligibility Eligible to apply for these internships at the Women's Sports Foundation are women of color who are undergraduate students, college graduates, graduate students, or women in career change.

Financial data The salary is $1,000 per month.

Duration 4 to 5 months.

Additional information Interns are assigned to the offices of the Women's Sports Foundation on Long Island, New York.

Number awarded 2 or 3 each year.

Deadline Applications may be submitted at any time.

[1174]
JAMES E. WEBB INTERNSHIPS

Smithsonian Institution
Attn: Office of Fellowships
Victor Building, Suite 9300, MRC 902
P.O. Box 37012
Washington, DC 20013-7012
(202) 275-0655   Fax: (202) 275-0489
E-mail: siofg@si.edu
Web: www.si.edu/ofg/intern.htm

Purpose To provide summer internship opportunities throughout the Smithsonian Institution to minority students in business or public administration.

Eligibility This program is open to U.S. minority undergraduate seniors and graduate students majoring in areas of business or public administration (finance, human resource management, accounting, or general business administration). Applicants must have a GPA of 3.0 or higher. They must seek placement in offices, museums, and research institutes throughout the Smithsonian Institution.

Financial data Interns receive a stipend of $400 per week and a travel allowance.

Duration 10 weeks, starting in June.

Number awarded Varies each year.

Deadline January of each year.

[1175]
JAMES H. DUNN, JR. MEMORIAL FELLOWSHIP PROGRAM

Office of the Governor
Attn: Program Director
107 William G. Stratton Building
Springfield, IL 62706
(217) 782-5213   Fax: (217) 524-1677
TDD: (217) 558-2238
E-mail: tammy_payne@gov.state.il.us
Web: www.state.il.us/gov/officeinternship.htm

Purpose To provide recent college graduates with work experience in the Illinois Governor's office.

Eligibility This program is open to recent college graduates. Applicants may have earned a degree in any field and must be interested in working in the Illinois Governor's office or in various agencies under the Governor's jurisdiction. Candidates may be residents of any state and must be able to demonstrate a real commitment to excellence. Selection is based on academic honors, leadership ability, extracurricular activities, and involvement in community or public service areas. Applications are especially solicited from qualified minorities, women, and persons with disabilities.

Financial data The stipend is $2,226 per month.

Duration 1 year, beginning in August.

Additional information Assignments are in Springfield and, to a limited extent, in Chicago.

Number awarded Varies each year.

Deadline January of each year.

[1176]
JEANNE SPURLOCK MINORITY MEDICAL STUDENT CLINICAL FELLOWSHIP IN CHILD AND ADOLESCENT PSYCHIATRY

American Academy of Child and Adolescent Psychiatry
Attn: Department of Research and Training
3615 Wisconsin Avenue, N.W.
Washington, DC 20016-3007
(202) 966-7300, ext. 113   Fax: (202) 966-2891
E-mail: tbrown@aacap.org
Web: www.aacap.org/research/spurlck2.htm

Purpose To provide funding to minority medical students who are interested in working with a child and adolescent psychiatrist during the summer.

Eligibility This program is open to African American, Asian American, Native American, Alaska Native, Mexican American, Hispanic, and Pacific Islander students in accredited U.S. medical schools. Applicants must present a plan for a clinical training experience that involves significant contact between the student and a mentor. The plan should include program planning discussions, instruction in treatment planning and implementation, regular meetings with the mentor and other treatment providers, and assigned readings. Clinical assignments may include responsibil-

ity for part of the observation or evaluation, conducting interviews or tests, using rating scales, and psychological or cognitive testing of patients. The training plan should also include discussion of ethical issues in treatment.

Financial data The stipend is $2,500.

Duration Summer months.

Additional information Upon completion of the training program, the student is required to submit a brief paper summarizing the clinical experience. The fellowship pays expenses for the fellow to attend the academy's annual meeting and present this paper.

Number awarded 5 each year.

Deadline April of each year.

[1177]
JEANNE SPURLOCK RESEARCH FELLOWSHIP IN DRUG ABUSE AND ADDICTION FOR MINORITY MEDICAL STUDENTS

American Academy of Child and Adolescent Psychiatry
Attn: Department of Research and Training
3615 Wisconsin Avenue, N.W.
Washington, DC 20016-3007
(202) 966-7300, ext. 113   Fax: (202) 966-2891
E-mail: tbrown@aacap.org
Web: www.aacap.org/research/spurlck1.htm

Purpose To provide funding to minority medical students who are interested in working with a child and adolescent psychiatrist researcher-mentor during the summer on drug abuse and addiction.

Eligibility This program is open to African American, Asian American, Native American, Alaska Native, Mexican American, Hispanic, and Pacific Islander students in accredited U.S. medical schools. Applicants must present a plan for a program of research training in drug abuse and addiction that involves significant contact with a mentor who is an experienced child and adolescent psychiatrist researcher. The plan should include program planning discussions; instruction in research planning and implementation; regular meetings with the mentor, laboratory director, and the research group; and assigned readings. Research assignments may include responsibility for part of the observation or evaluation, developing specific aspects of the research mechanisms, conducting interviews or tests, using rating scales, and psychological or cognitive testing of subjects. The training plan also should include discussion of ethical issues in research, including protocol development, informed consent, collection and storage of raw data, safeguarding data, bias in analyzing data, plagiarism, protection of patients, ethical treatment of animals. etc.

Financial data The stipend is $2,500.

Duration Summer months.

Additional information Upon completion of the training program, the student is required to submit a brief paper summarizing the research experience. The fellowship pays expenses for the fellow to attend the academy's annual meeting and present this paper. This program is co-sponsored by the National Institute on Drug Abuse.

Number awarded 5 each year.

Deadline April of each year.

[1178]
JEWEL OSCO SCHOLARSHIPS

Chicago Urban League
Attn: Scholarship Coordinator
4510 South Michigan Avenue
Chicago, IL 60653-3898
(773) 451-3567   Fax: (773) 285-7772
E-mail: info@cul-chicago.org
Web: www.cul-chicago.org

Purpose To provide financial assistance for college to Illinois residents of color who are also interested in interning at Jewel Osco.

Eligibility This program is open to Illinois residents of color who are graduating high school seniors with a GPA of 2.5 or higher and planning to enroll as full-time undergraduate students at a 4-year college or university. Applicants must agree to complete a summer internship with Jewel Osco. The selection process includes an interview with a representative of Jewel Osco. Financial need must be demonstrated.

Financial data The stipend is $2,000 per year.

Duration 1 year; nonrenewable.

Additional information This program is offered as part of the Chicago Urban League's Whitney M. Young, Jr. Memorial Scholarship Fund, established in 1970.

Number awarded 2 each year.

Deadline May of each year.

[1179]
JPMORGAN CHASE JUNIOR INTERNSHIPS

JPMorgan Chase
Attn: Recruiting Manager
95 Wall Street, 12th Floor
New York, NY 10005
Web: careers.jpmorganchase.com/ba/jpmc/jpmc_sum.html

Purpose To provide work experience at JPMorgan Chase during the summer to minorities, women, and students with disabilities who are entering their sophomore or junior year in college.

Eligibility This program is open to students at U.S. colleges and universities who are completing their freshman or sophomore year. Applicants must be students of color (Asian American, African American, or Latino), women, or persons with a disability and interested in working at JPMorgan Chase in either internal consulting services or technology application delivery. They must demonstrate analytical, technical, problem-solving, and communication skills; an ability to function well in a fast-paced, team-oriented environment; and (for technology application delivery interns) a working knowledge of C, C++, Visual Basic, and/or Java.

Financial data Competitive stipends are paid.

Duration 10 to 11 weeks, during the summer.

Additional information A goal of the program is to enable the intern to prepare for possible work as a senior intern during the summer following their junior year in college and future employment with the firm.

Number awarded Varies each year.

Deadline JPMorgan Chase representatives interview on many campuses. Students at other colleges and universities may apply online beginning in January. All positions are filled by April.

[1180]
JPMORGAN HONORS PROGRAM

JPMorgan Chase
Campus Recruiting
Attn: Honors Program
277 Park Avenue, Second Floor
New York, NY 10172
Web: careers.jpmorganchase.com/ba/jpm/jpm_sum.html

Purpose To provide work experience at JPMorgan in New York during the summer to minorities, women, and students with disabilities who are entering their sophomore or junior year of college.

Eligibility This program is open to students at U.S. colleges and universities who are completing their freshman or sophomore year. Applicants must be students of color (Asian American, African American, or Latino), women, or persons with a disability and interested in working at JPMorgan in New York in the corporate finance, equity sales and trading, and fixed income sales and trading divisions. Applicants must have strong quantitative, analytical, and technical skills and be able to thrive in a fast-paced, team-oriented environment. Course work in finance or economics is recommended and a GPA of 3.5 or higher is required.

Financial data Competitive stipends are paid.

Duration 10 to 12 weeks, during the summer.

Additional information A goal of the program is to enable the intern to prepare for possible work as a senior intern during the summer following their junior year in college.

Number awarded Varies each year.

Deadline January of each year.

[1181]
JUDITH L. WEIDMAN RACIAL ETHNIC MINORITY FELLOWSHIP

United Methodist Communications
Attn: Communications Resourcing Team
810 12th Avenue South
P.O. Box 320
Nashville, TN 37202-0320
(615) 742-5481   (888) CRT-4UMC
Fax: (615) 742-5485   E-mail: REM@umcom.org
Web: crt.umc.org/rem

Purpose To provide work experience to Methodists who are members of minority groups and interested in a communications career.

Eligibility This program is open to United Methodists of racial ethnic minority heritage who are considering pursuing communications for the United Methodist Church as a career. Applicants must be recent college or seminary graduates who have broad communications training, including work in journalism, mass communications, marketing, public relations, and electronic media. They must be able to understand and speak English proficiently and to relocate for a year. Selection is based on Christian commitment and involvement in the life of the United Methodist Church; achievement as revealed by transcripts, GPA, letters of reference, and work samples; study, experience, and evidence of talent in the field of communications; clarity of purpose and goals for the future; desire to learn how to be a successful United Methodist conference communicator; and potential leadership ability as a professional religion communicators for the United Methodist Church.

Financial data The stipend is $30,000 per year. Benefits and expenses for moving and professional travel are also provided.

Duration 1 year, starting in August.

Additional information Recipients are assigned to 1 of the 65 United Methodist Annual Conferences, the headquarters of local churches within a geographic area. At the Annual Conference, the fellow will be assigned an experienced communicator as a mentor and will work closely with that mentor and with United Methodist Communications in Nashville, Tennessee. Following the successful completion of the fellowship, United Methodist Communications and the participating Annual Conference will assist in a search for permanent employment within the United Methodist Church, but cannot guarantee a position.

Number awarded 1 each year.

Deadline March of each year.

[1182]
KAISER MEDIA INTERNSHIPS IN URBAN HEALTH REPORTING

Henry J. Kaiser Family Foundation
2400 Sand Hill Road
Menlo Park, CA 94025
(650) 854-9400   Fax: (650) 854-4800
E-mail: pduckham@kff.org
Web: www.kff.org/docs/fellowships/internship.html

Purpose To provide summer work experience to minority college or graduate students who want to specialize in urban public health issues and health reporting.

Eligibility Minority college or graduate students studying journalism or a related field may apply for this internship program if their career goal is to be a reporter on urban health matters. Strong writing skills and previous newsroom reporting experience are essential. Reporting experience and/or academic expertise in health, medical, or science-related issues (or urban affairs) is valuable but not required. Applicants must be U.S. citizens or permanent residents.

Financial data This program provides a stipend of at least $500 per week and all travel expenses.

Duration 12 weeks in the summer.

Additional information This program, sponsored by the Henry J. Kaiser Family Foundation, began in 1994. Each participating news organization selects its own intern; recently, those were the *Atlanta Journal-Constitution, Boston Globe, Los Angeles Times, Detroit Free Press, Mercury News* of San Jose, *The Oregonian* of Portland, *Plain Dealer* of Cleveland, *Sun-Sentinel* of Fort Lauderdale, *Milwaukee Journal Sentinel, Orlando Sentinel, Washington Post,* KXAS/5-TV of Dallas-Fort Worth, WAGA/5-TV of Atlanta, and KTVU/2-TV of San Francisco-Oakland. The program begins with a 1-week orientation program in Washington, D.C. at the National Press Foundation in June and concludes with a 1-week wrap-up in Boston at the end of the summer. In between, interns report and write urban health stories at their host papers or television stations.

Number awarded 14 each year: 1 at each participating news organization.

Deadline Applicants to print organizations should submit their applications prior to the end of November; applicants to broadcast organizations should submit their applications in early January.

[1183]
KATU THOMAS R. DARGAN MINORITY SCHOLARSHIP

KATU Channel 2 Portland
Attn: Human Resources
P.O. Box 2
Portland, OR 97207-0002
(503) 231-4222
Web: www.katu.com

Purpose To provide financial assistance and work experience to minority students from Oregon and Washington who are studying broadcasting or communications in college.

Eligibility This program is open to Native Americans, African Americans, Hispanic Americans, or Asian Americans who are U.S. citizens, currently enrolled in the first, second, or third year at a 4-year college or university or an accredited community college in Oregon or Washington, or, if a resident of Oregon or Washington, at a school in any state. Applicants must be majoring in broadcasting or communications and have a GPA of 3.0 or higher. Community college students must be enrolled in a broadcast curriculum that is transferable to a 4-year accredited university. Finalists will be interviewed. Selection is based on financial need, academic achievement, and an essay on personal and professional goals.

Financial data The stipend is $4,000. Funds are sent directly to the recipient's school.

Duration 1 year; recipients may reapply if they have maintained a GPA of 3.0 or higher.

Additional information Winners are also eligible for a paid internship in selected departments at Fisher Broadcasting/KATU in Portland, Oregon.

Number awarded 1 or more each year.

Deadline April of each year.

[1184]
KELL-MUNOZ EDUCATION FELLOWSHIP

Cooper-Hewitt, National Design Museum
Attn: Program Coordinator, Education Department
2 East 91st Street
New York, NY 10128-0669
(212) 849-8380   Fax: (212) 849-8328
E-mail: edu@ch.si.edu
Web: ndm.si.edu/Education/internships.html

Purpose To provide work experience at the Smithsonian Institution's Cooper-Hewitt, National Design Museum in New York City to Latino/Hispanic graduate students and recent graduates interested in a career in the museum profession.

Eligibility Applicants must be of Latino/Hispanic descent and either currently enrolled in a degree-granting graduate program or graduated from a graduate program in the 6 months prior to the start date. They should have a commitment to working in museums. Candidates with experience in arts administration, art history, education, communications, design, or architecture are eligible to apply. Familiarity with office procedures and computer skills are required. Along with their application, they must submit a resume, current transcripts, 2 letters of recommendation, and a 1- to 2-page essay describing their career goals as a museum professional and how the fellowship will help to achieve them.

Financial data The stipend is $10,000.

Duration 10 months, starting in September.

Number awarded 1 each year.

Additional information This program is funded by the Smithsonian Center for Latino Initiatives and Kell-Muñoz Architects.
Deadline July of each year.

[1185]
KNIGHT RIDDER MINORITY SCHOLARS PROGRAM
Knight Ridder, Inc.
Attn: Office of Diversity
50 West San Fernando Street, Suite 1200
San Jose, CA 95113
(408) 938-7734   Fax: (408) 938-7755
Web: www.kri.com/working/interns.html

Purpose To provide financial assistance and work experience to minority high school seniors who are interested in going to college to prepare for a career in journalism.
Eligibility Graduating minority high school seniors are eligible to apply if they are attending a school in an area served by Knight Ridder and are interested in majoring in journalism in college. Candidates first apply to their local Knight Ridder newspaper and compete for local scholarships; selected winners are then nominated for this award.
Financial data The stipend is up to $10,000 per year.
Duration 1 year; may be renewed for up to 3 additional years, if the recipient maintains a GPA of 3.0 or higher.
Additional information Scholarship recipients are offered an internship opportunity at a Knight Ridder newspaper during the summer. At the end of the program, recipients must work at a Knight Ridder newspaper for 1 year.
Number awarded 4 each year.

[1186]
KNIGHT RIDDER MINORITY SPECIALTY DEVELOPMENT PROGRAM
Knight Ridder, Inc.
Attn: Office of Diversity
50 West San Fernando Street, Suite 1200
San Jose, CA 95113
(408) 938-7734   Fax: (408) 938-7755
Web: www.kri.com/working/interns.html

Purpose To offer a training program to young minority journalists who are interested in working on high-profile beats or in specialty departments.
Eligibility Minorities who recently graduated from college with a major in journalism are eligible to apply for internships at selected Knight Ridder newspapers if they are interested in working in an area of the newspaper industry in which minorities are underrepresented, such as high-profile beat assignments, computer-assisted reporting, photojournalism, and graphic arts.
Financial data Salaries are determined by the scale of the participating newspapers.
Duration 1 year.
Additional information Specialty interns are selected by and work at the following Knight Ridder newspapers: the *Detroit Free Press,* the *Miami Herald,* the *Philadelphia Inquirer,* or the *San Jose Mercury News.* Interns are not guaranteed employment following completion of this program.
Number awarded 1 or more each year.
Deadline December of each year.

[1187]
KNIGHT RIDDER ROTATING INTERN PROGRAM
Knight Ridder, Inc.
Attn: Office of Diversity
50 West San Fernando Street, Suite 1200
San Jose, CA 95113
(408) 938-7734   Fax: (408) 938-7755
Web: www.kri.com/working/interns.html

Purpose To offer a training program to young minority journalists who are interested in working at 3 or 4 Knight Ridder newspapers.
Eligibility Minorities who recently graduated from college with a major in journalism are eligible to apply if they are interested in working in a variety of newsrooms, news assignments, and markets.
Financial data Salaries are determined by the scale of the participating newspapers.
Duration 1 year.
Additional information Rotating interns are selected by and work at the following Knight Ridder newspapers: the *News-Democrat* in Belleville, Illinois; the *Contra Costa Times* in Walnut Creek, California; the *Fort Worth Star-Telegram;* the *Kansas City Star;* the *St. Paul Pioneer Press;* or the *Times Leader* in Wilkes-Barre, Pennsylvania. Information is available from each of those newspapers and from Reginald Stuart, Coordinator, Knight Ridder Rotating Internship Program, 13102 Tamarack Road, Silver Spring, MD 20904, (301) 879-0085, E-mail: rstuart5@juno.com. Interns are not guaranteed employment following completion of this program.
Number awarded 1 or more each year.
Deadline December of each year.

[1188]
LANDMARK SCHOLARS PROGRAM
Landmark Publishing Group
Attn: Director of Recruiting
150 West Brambleton Avenue
Norfolk, VA 23510
(757) 446-2456   (800) 446-2004, ext. 2456
Fax: (757) 446-2414   E-mail: csage@lcimedia.com
Web: www.landmarkcom.com

Purpose To provide work experience and financial aid to minority undergraduates who are interested in preparing for a career in journalism.
Eligibility This program is open to minority college sophomores, preferably those with ties to the mid-Atlantic/southern region. Applicants must be interested in pursuing a career in journalism. They must also be interested in internships as reporters, photographers, graphic artists, sports writers, copy editors, or page designers.
Financial data The stipend is $5,000 per year. During the summers between the sophomore and junior years and between the junior and seniors years, recipients are provided with paid internships. Following graduation, they are offered a 1-year internship with full benefits and the possibility of continued employment.
Duration 2 years (the junior and senior years of college).
Additional information The internships are offered at the *News & Record* in Greensboro, North Carolina, the *Virginian-Pilot* in Norfolk, Virginia, or the *Roanoke Times* in Roanoke, Virginia.
Number awarded 1 or more each year.
Deadline November of each year.

[1189]
LASPACE UNDERGRADUATE RESEARCH ASSISTANTSHIPS

Louisiana Space Consortium
c/o Louisiana State University
Physics and Astronomy
371 Nicholson Hall
Baton Rouge, LA 70803-4001
(225) 578-8697   Fax: (225) 578-1222
E-mail: wefel@phunds.phys.lsu.edu
Web: phacts.phys.lsu.edu

Purpose To provide undergraduate science and engineering students in Louisiana with a mentored research experience in the space sciences.

Eligibility This program is open to U.S. citizens who are high school seniors, recent high school graduates, and students currently enrolled at 1 of the Louisiana Space Consortium (LaSPACE) member schools. The consortium is a component of the U.S. National Aeronautics and Space Administration (NASA) Space Grant program, which encourages participation by members of groups underrepresented in mathematics, science, and engineering (women, African Americans, Native Americans, Native Pacific Islanders, Mexican Americans, Puerto Ricans, Alaska Natives, and persons with disabilities). Applicants must be studying or planning to study a space- or aerospace-related field or program at an LaSPACE institution full time. They must coordinate with a faculty member at the institution who will file a joint application with the student and agree to serve as a mentor on a proposed research project. Selection is based on scholastic accomplishments, pertinent science experiences and accomplishments, leadership and recognitions, intellectual abilities, character, and relevance of the proposed research project to a future career in space or aerospace fields.

Financial data Grants are provided in blocks of $5,000. Funding may support 1 or 2 assistants. Funds may be used for wage support for the student(s), travel for a student research presentation, or research supplies.

Duration 12 months.

Additional information The LaSPACE member institutions are Dillard University, Grambling State University, L.S.U. Agricultural Center, Louisiana State University and A&M College, Louisiana Tech University, Loyola University, McNeese State University, Nicholls State University, Northwestern State University of Louisiana, Southeastern Louisiana University, Southern University and A&M College, Southern University at New Orleans, Southern University at Shreveport-Bossier City, Tulane University, University of New Orleans, University of Louisiana at Lafayette, University of Louisiana at Monroe, and Xavier University of Louisiana. This program was established in 2000 as a replacement for the LaSPACE Undergraduate Scholars Program. Funding for this program is provided by NASA.

Number awarded 5 each year.

Deadline May of each year.

[1190]
LAWRENCE WADE JOURNALISM FELLOWSHIP

Heritage Foundation
Attn: Selection Committee
214 Massachusetts Avenue, N.E.
Washington, DC 20002-4999
(202) 546-4400   Fax: (202) 546-8328
E-mail: info@heritage.org
Web: www.heritage.org

Purpose To provide financial assistance and work experience to undergraduate or graduate students who are interested in a career in journalism.

Eligibility This program is open to undergraduate or graduate students who are currently enrolled full time and are interested in a career as a journalist upon graduation. Applicants need not be majoring in journalism, but they must submit writing samples of published news stories, editorial commentaries, or broadcast scripts. Preference is given to candidates who are Asian Americans, African Americans, Hispanic Americans, or Native Americans.

Financial data The winner receives a $1,000 scholarship and participates in a 10-week salaried internship at the Heritage Foundation.

Duration 1 year.

Additional information This program was established in 1991.

Number awarded 1 each year.

Deadline February of each year.

[1191]
LEE ENTERPRISES COLLEGE-TO-WORK SCHOLARSHIP

Wisconsin Foundation for Independent Colleges, Inc.
735 North Water Street, Suite 800
Milwaukee, WI 53202-4100
(414) 273-5980   Fax: (414) 273-5995
E-mail: info@wficweb.org
Web: www.wficweb.org/documents/coll_work.htm

Purpose To provide financial assistance and work experience to minority students majoring in fields related to business or news at private colleges in Wisconsin.

Eligibility This program is open to full-time minority sophomores, juniors, and seniors at the 20 independent colleges and universities in Wisconsin. Applicants may be majoring in any liberal arts field, but they must be preparing for a career in accounting, information technology, computers, graphic design, sales, marketing, news reporting, or communications. They must have a GPA of 3.0 or higher and be interested in an internship at 1 of the 3 Lee newspapers in the state: the *Wisconsin State Journal,* the *La Crosse Tribune,* or the *Racine Journal Times.* Along with their application, they must submit a 1-page autobiography, transcripts, a list of campus involvement and academic honors, a resume including 3 references, and 2 letters of recommendation.

Financial data The stipends are $3,500 for the scholarship and $1,500 for the internship.

Duration 1 year for the scholarship; 10 weeks for the internship.

Additional information The participating schools are Alverno College, Beloit College, Cardinal Stritch University, Carroll College, Carthage College, Concordia University of Wisconsin, Edgewood College, Lakeland College, Lawrence University, Marian College, Marquette University, Milwaukee Institute of Art & Design, Milwaukee School of Engineering, Mount Mary College,

Northland College, Ripon College, St. Norbert College, Silver Lake College, Viterbo University, and Wisconsin Lutheran College. This program is sponsored by Lee Enterprises/Madison Newspapers, Inc. (www.lee.net).

Number awarded 3 each year.

Deadline January of each year.

[1192]
LEIGH COOK FELLOWSHIP

New Jersey Department of Health and Senior Services
Attn: Office of Minority Health
P.O. Box 360
Trenton, NJ 08625-0360
(609) 292-6962
Web: www.state.nj.us/health

Purpose To provide financial support for a summer research assignment to law, public health, and medical students in New Jersey.

Eligibility This program is open to students in the medical sciences, law, or master's of public health programs who are residents of New Jersey attending school in the state or elsewhere. Applicants must be interested in working on a supervised project at the New Jersey Department of Health and Senior Services in Trenton in the areas of minority health, senior services, HIV/AIDS, substance abuse, health insurance, environmental or occupational health, public health, or family health. Minority students are encouraged to apply. Selection is based on commitment to minority and/or public health, as demonstrated by community-based service, volunteer work, personal investment, public health service advocacy, coalition building, and involvement in student organizations that address minority and public health specific issues.

Financial data The stipend is $5,000.

Duration 10 to 12 weeks, during the summer.

Number awarded 1 each year.

Deadline March of each year.

[1193]
LENA CHANG INTERNSHIPS

Nuclear Age Peace Foundation
1187 Coast Village Road, Suite 123
P.M.B. 121
Santa Barbara, CA 93108-2794
(805) 965-3443   Fax: (805) 568-0466
E-mail: wagingpeace@napf.org
Web: www.wagingpeace.org

Purpose To provide work experience at the Nuclear Age Peace Foundation in Santa Barbara, California to ethnic minority undergraduate and graduate students.

Eligibility This program is open to ethnic minority students currently enrolled in undergraduate or graduate course work who can demonstrate financial need and academic excellence. Students from the Santa Barbara (California) area may apply for academic year internships. Summer internships are open to students from anywhere in the United States. Applicants must submit their transcript; 2 letters of recommendation; a letter of intent describing their work experience, educational background, field of study, plans after graduation, and preference for fall, spring, or summer internship; and a copy of their resume or curriculum vitae.

Financial data The stipend is $2,500 for summer; interns are responsible for their own transportation and housing costs. Academic year interns receive $1,250.

Duration The summer internship is 10 weeks of full-time work. Academic year interns are expected to work at least 200 hours.

Number awarded 3 each year: 1 for the summer and 2 for the academic year.

Deadline March of each year for the summer internship; July of each year for fall; December of each year for winter/spring.

[1194]
LIBRARY OF CONGRESS JUNIOR FELLOWS PROGRAM

Library of Congress
Library Services
Attn: Junior Fellows Program Coordinator
101 Independence Avenue, S.E., Room LM-642
Washington, DC 20540-4600
(202) 707-5330   Fax: (202) 707-6269
E-mail: jrfell@loc.gov
Web: lcweb.loc.gov/rr/jrfell

Purpose To provide summer work experience at the Library of Congress (LC) to upper-division and graduate students.

Eligibility This program at the LC is open to applicants with subject expertise in the following areas: American history and literature; cataloging; history of graphic arts, architecture, design, and engineering; history of photography; film, television and radio; sound recordings; music; rare books and book arts; American popular culture; librarianship; and preservation. Applicants must 1) be juniors or seniors at an accredited college or university, 2) be at the graduate school level, or 3) have completed their degree in the past year. Applications from women, minorities, and persons with disabilities are particularly encouraged. Applications must include the following materials: cover letter, Application for Federal Employment (SF 171) or a resume, letter of recommendation, and official transcript. Telephone interviews are conducted with the most promising applicants.

Financial data Fellows are paid a taxable stipend of $300 per week.

Duration 2 to 3 months, beginning in either May or June. Fellows work a 40-hour week.

Additional information Fellows work with primary source materials and assist selected divisions at the Library of Congress in the organization and documentation of archival collections, production of finding aids and bibliographic records, preparation of materials for preservation and service, and completion of bibliographical research.

Number awarded Varies each year.

Deadline March of each year.

[1195]
LIFCHEZ/STRONACH CURATORIAL INTERNSHIPS

Metropolitan Museum of Art
Attn: Internship Programs
1000 Fifth Avenue
New York, NY 10028-0198
(212) 570-3710   Fax: (212) 570-3782
Web: www.metmuseum.org/education/er_internship.asp

Purpose To provide museum work experience at the Metropolitan Museum of Art to disadvantaged graduate students and recent graduates who wish to pursue a career in art history.

Eligibility This program is open to recent college graduates and students enrolled in master's degree programs in art history. Applicants should come from a background of financial need or other disadvantage (e.g., minority status) that will jeopardize their pursuing a career in art history without the support.

Financial data The honorarium is $15,000.

Duration 9 months, beginning in September.

Additional information Interns are assigned to 1 or more of the Metropolitan Museum of Art's departments, where they work on projects that match their academic background, professional skills, and career goals. This program was reestablished in 1998 with funding from Raymond Lifchez and Judith L. Stronach.

Number awarded 3 each year.

Deadline January of each year.

[1196]
LINCOLN LABORATORY SUMMER MINORITY INTERNSHIP PROGRAM

Massachusetts Institute of Technology
Lincoln Laboratory
Attn: Human Resources
244 Wood Street
Lexington, MA 02420-9108
(781) 981-7048   Fax: (781) 981-7086
E-mail: summer@ll.mit.edu
Web: www.ll.mit.edu/careers/summerinternship.html

Purpose To offer undergraduate minority students the opportunity to improve their engineering and scientific skills, supplement their academic course work, and gain unique hands-on work experience at MIT's Lincoln Laboratory during the summer.

Eligibility To be eligible, applicants must have completed their sophomore year in college; be majoring in electrical engineering, computer science, or applied physics; be interested in a research career; be able to demonstrate excellent academic performance; and be U.S. citizens. This program at MIT is specifically for minorities underrepresented in engineering and science careers, i.e., African Americans, American Indians, Mexican Americans, and Puerto Ricans.

Financial data Program participants receive weekly salaries, housing on the MIT campus, round-trip travel to the Boston area, and daily round-trip transportation between the MIT campus and the laboratory.

Duration 10 weeks during the summer, from early June through mid-August. Students who receive successful work and course evaluations, maintain excellent academic averages at their home institutions, and continue to pursue a degree in electrical engineering, computer science, or physics will be reappointed for successive summers.

Additional information The program was established in 1975. Participants have access to the extensive athletic facilities on the MIT campus. Participants who are admitted to MIT after college are eligible to receive substantial support for their graduate education.

Deadline February of each year.

[1197]
LLNL RESEARCH COLLABORATIONS PROGRAM FOR HISTORICALLY BLACK UNIVERSITIES AND COLLEGES AND OTHER MINORITY INSTITUTIONS

Lawrence Livermore National Laboratory
Attn: University Relations Program
P.O. Box 808, L-041
Livermore, CA 94551
(925) 423-1112   E-mail: reed5@llnl.gov
Web: www.llnl.gov/urp/HBCU/homepage.html

Purpose To provide opportunities for research collaborations at Lawrence Livermore National Laboratory (LLNL) to students, postdoctoral researchers, and faculty of Historically Black Colleges and Universities (HBCUs) and other Minority Institutions (MIs).

Eligibility This program is open to undergraduate students, graduate students, postdoctoral researchers, and faculty at HBCUs and other MIs. Applicants must be proposing to conduct research with principal investigators at LLNL in areas of LLNL core competencies, including nonlinear optics, atomic physics, materials science, spectroscopy, plasma diagnostics, and massively parallel computing.

Financial data Students receive stipends based on their discipline, education, and experience; faculty members receive release time from their home institutions.

Duration Most opportunities are in the summer, although some fall and spring assignments may be available.

Additional information Funding for this program is provided from a variety of sources, principally from the Office of Defense Programs of the U.S. Department of Energy.

Number awarded Varies each year.

Deadline Applications may be submitted at any time.

[1198]
LUCENT TECHNOLOGIES BELL LABORATORIES SUMMER RESEARCH PROGRAM FOR MINORITIES AND WOMEN

Lucent Technologies
Attn: Special Programs Manager
283 King George Road, Room B1-D32
Warren, NJ 07059
(732) 559-4267   E-mail: summersearch@lucent.com
Web: www.bell-labs.com/employment/srp

Purpose To provide technical work experience at facilities of Bell Laboratories during the summer to women and underrepresented minority undergraduate students.

Eligibility This program is open to women and members of minority groups (African Americans, Hispanics, and Native American Indians) who are underrepresented in the sciences. Applicants must be interested in pursuing technical employment experience in research and development facilities of Bell Laboratories. The program is primarily directed at undergraduate students who have completed their second or third year of college. Emphasis is placed on the following disciplines: chemistry, communications science, computer science and engineering, data networking, electrical engineering, information science, materials science, mathematics, optics, physics, statistics, and wireless and radio engineering. U.S. citizenship or permanent resident status is required. Selection is based on academic achievement, personal motivation, and compatibility of student interests with current Bell Laboratories activities.

Financial data Salaries are commensurate with those of regular Bell Laboratories employees with comparable education. Interns are reimbursed for travel expenses up to the cost of round-trip economy-class airfare.

Duration 10 weeks, during the summer.

Additional information This program is sponsored by Lucent Technologies and Bell Laboratories.

Number awarded Varies each year.

Deadline November of each year.

[1199]
LUCENT TECHNOLOGIES COOPERATIVE RESEARCH FELLOWSHIP PROGRAM

Lucent Technologies
Attn: Fellowship Programs Manager
283 King George Road, Room B1-D26
Warren, NJ 07059
(732) 559-6971   E-mail: fellowships@lucent.com
Web: www.bell-labs.com/fellowships/CRFP

Purpose To provide financial assistance and summer internships at Bell Laboratories to members of minority groups underrepresented in scientific and technological fields who wish to pursue doctoral studies in designated science and engineering fields.

Eligibility This program is open to U.S. citizens or permanent residents who are members of a minority group currently underrepresented in the sciences (Blacks, Native American Indians, and Hispanics). Applicants must be college seniors who plan to pursue full-time doctoral study in the following fall in chemical engineering, chemistry, communications science, computer science and engineering, electrical engineering, information science, materials science, mathematics, mechanical engineering, operations research, physics, or statistics. U.S. citizenship or permanent resident status is required. Selection is based on scholastic attainment, evidence of ability, and potential as research scientists.

Financial data Fellowships provide full tuition and university fees, a book allowance, an annual stipend of $17,000, and related travel expenses. During their summer internships, fellows receive salaries commensurate with their level of experience and training.

Duration 1 year; may be renewed for up to 3 additional years if the fellow makes satisfactory progress toward the doctoral degree.

Additional information This program is sponsored by Lucent Technologies Foundation and Bell Laboratories. During the summers, fellows conduct research at Bell Laboratories under the mentorship of staff scientists and engineers.

Number awarded 6 each year.

Deadline December of each year.

[1200]
MARIAM K. CHAMBERLAIN FELLOWSHIPS

Institute for Women's Policy Research
1707 L Street, N.W., Suite 750
Washington, DC 20036
(202) 785-5100   Fax: (202) 833-4362
E-mail: iwpr@iwpr.org
Web: www.iwpr.org/employment_fellow.html

Purpose To provide work experience at the Institute for Women's Policy Research (IWPR) to college graduates and graduate students who are interested in economic justice for women.

Eligibility Applicants for this internship at IWPR should have at least a bachelor's degree in social science, statistics, or women's studies. Graduate work is desirable but not required. Applicants should have basic quantitative and library research skills and knowledge of women's issues. Familiarity with spreadsheets and graphics software is a plus. People of color are especially encouraged to apply.

Financial data The stipend is $1,600 per month and includes health insurance and a public transportation stipend.

Duration 9 months, beginning in September.

Additional information The institute is a nonprofit, scientific research organization that works primarily on issues related to equal opportunity and economic and social justice for women. Of the fellows currently being sought, 2 will work as general research assistants on a variety of research projects and reports and 1 will work with the Director of Communications on different aspects of public relations and outreach programs.

Number awarded 2 each year.

Deadline February of each year.

[1201]
MASS MEDIA SCIENCE AND ENGINEERING FELLOWS PROGRAM

American Association for the Advancement of Science
Attn: Directorate for Education and Human Resources
1200 New York Avenue, N.W.
Washington, DC 20005-3920
(202) 326-6760   Fax: (202) 371-9849
E-mail: aking@aaas.org
Web: ehrweb.aaas.org

Purpose To provide internships during the summer to science and engineering students interested in gaining experience in science journalism.

Eligibility The program is open to college juniors, seniors, graduates, and postgraduate students in the natural, physical, health, engineering, and social sciences. Students from underrepresented communities, including Black, Hispanic, Native American, and those with disabilities, are encouraged to apply. Applicants must be interested in working as reporters, researchers, and production assistants at radio and television stations, newspapers, online sites, and magazines. Students majoring in English, journalism, or other nontechnical fields are ineligible.

Financial data Fellows receive a stipend of $450 per week and travel expenses to and from their sites.

Duration 10 weeks in the summer; may be extended, depending upon the interest of the media site.

Additional information Interns work as reporters, researchers, or production assistants in a variety of media. They may be assigned to work for newspapers, magazines, television, or radio. This program began in 1973. It is sponsored by the American Geophysical Union, the American Mathematical Society, the American Physical Society, the American Physiological Society, the American Psychological Association, the American Society for Microbiology, the American Sociological Association, the Burroughs Welcome Fund, the Camille and Henry Dreyfus Foundation, Ford Motor Company, the Foundation for Child Development, the Institute of Food Technologists, and the Institute of Electrical and Electronics Engineers.

Number awarded Varies; generally, 20 to 30 each year.

Deadline January of each year.

[1202]
MASSACHUSETTS SPACE GRANT CONSORTIUM SUMMER JOBS PROGRAM

Massachusetts Space Grant Consortium
c/o Massachusetts Institute of Technology
Building 33, Room 208
77 Massachusetts Avenue
Cambridge, MA 02139
(617) 258-5546   Fax: (617) 253-0823
E-mail: halaris@mit.edu
Web: www.mit.edu

Purpose To provide summer work experience to undergraduate students at space-related firms in Massachusetts.

Eligibility This program is open to undergraduate students at institutions that are members of the Massachusetts Space Grant Consortium (MASGC). Applicants must be interested in employment at participating companies involved in space science and/or space engineering. U.S. citizenship is required. MASGC is a component of the U.S. National Aeronautics and Space Administration (NASA) Space Grant program, which encourages participation by women, underrepresented minorities, and persons with disabilities.

Financial data Stipends are provided.

Duration Summer months.

Additional information Undergraduate member institutions of the MASGC are Boston University, College of the Holy Cross, the Five College Astronomy Department, Harvard University, Massachusetts Institute of Technology, Northeastern University, Tufts University, University of Massachusetts, Williams College, Wellesley College, and Worcester Polytechnic Institute. Recently, the participating companies have included The Aerospace Corporation, Hughes, Lockheed Martin, MIT Lincoln Laboratory, NASA Goddard Space Flight Center, Jet Propulsion Laboratory, Orbital Sciences Corporation, Space Systems Loral, TRW, United Technologies, and Trimble Navigation. This program is sponsored by NASA.

Number awarded Varies each year.

Deadline December of each year.

[1203]
METPRO/EDITING PROGRAM

Newsday
Attn: METPRO/Editing Director
235 Pinelawn Road
Melville, NY 11747-4250
(631) 843-2367   (888) 717-9817, ext. 2367
Fax: (631) 843-4719   E-mail: jobs@newsday.com
Web: www.metpronews.com

Purpose To provide an opportunity for minorities to obtain training for editing positions on daily metropolitan newspapers.

Eligibility Applicants for the Minority Editorial Training Program (METPRO) should be minority (African American, Asian American, Hispanic, American Indian) college graduates with excellent writing skills and an interest in a newspaper career. Selection is based on academic record and potential. Previous professional editing experience is not required.

Financial data Trainees receive a weekly stipend, a monthly housing allowance, and medical benefits for the first year. During the second year, trainees receive compensation and benefits applicable at the newspaper where they are working.

Duration 2 years.

Additional information Participants in this program receive intensive training in editing at *Newsday* during the first year, including a 2-week orientation, 3 weeks or reporting in Queens and on Long Island, 10 weeks of full-time classroom instruction, and 31 weeks of work as editors on *Newsday* copy desks. During the second year, they work for 1 of the 11 Tribune Company newspapers (in Allentown, Pennsylvania; Baltimore, Maryland; Chicago, Illinois; Fort Lauderdale, Florida; Greenwich, Connecticut; Hartford, Connecticut; Los Angeles, California; Melville, New York; Newport News, Virginia; Orlando, Florida; or Stamford, Connecticut).

Number awarded Up to 10 each year.

Deadline January of each year.

[1204]
METPRO/REPORTING PROGRAM

Los Angeles Times
Attn: METPRO/Reporting Director
202 West First Street
Los Angeles, CA 90012
(800) LA-TIMES, ext. 77366
Web: www.metpronews.com

Purpose To provide an opportunity for minorities to obtain training for reporting positions on daily metropolitan newspapers.

Eligibility Applicants for the Minority Editorial Training Program (METPRO) should be college graduates with excellent writing skills and an interest in a newspaper career. Applications by African Americans, Asian Americans, Latinos, and Native Americans are particularly encouraged. Selection is based on essays, a review of written work, college transcripts, recommendations, writing tests, and personal interviews. Previous professional reporting experience is not required.

Financial data Trainees receive a regular stipend for the first year and are furnished housing, utilities, and medical insurance while in the program. During the second year, trainees receive compensation and benefits applicable at the newspaper where they are working.

Duration 2 years.

Additional information This program was established in 1984. Participants spend the first 12 months at the *Los Angeles Times,* beginning with a full-time classroom instruction phase that includes reporting and writing techniques, interviewing, researching, and beat coverage, then several weeks covering a police beat; concluding with work at 1 of the *Times* regional editions. During the second year, they work for 1 of the 11 Tribune Company newspapers (in Allentown, Pennsylvania; Baltimore, Maryland; Chicago, Illinois; Fort Lauderdale, Florida; Greenwich, Connecticut; Hartford, Connecticut; Los Angeles, California; Melville, New York; Newport News, Virginia; Orlando, Florida; or Stamford, Connecticut).

Number awarded Approximately 10 each year.

Deadline January of each year.

[1205]
METROPOLITAN MUSEUM OF ART INTERNSHIPS FOR COLLEGE STUDENTS

Metropolitan Museum of Art
Attn: Internship Programs
1000 Fifth Avenue
New York, NY 10028-0198
(212) 570-3710   Fax: (212) 570-3782
Web: www.metmuseum.org/education/er_internship.asp

Purpose To provide summer work experience at the Metropolitan Museum of Art to college students.

Eligibility These internships are available to college juniors, seniors, and recent graduates who have not yet entered graduate school. Applicants should have a broad background in art history. Freshmen and sophomores are not eligible. Applicants of diverse backgrounds (e.g., minorities) are encouraged to apply.

Financial data The honorarium is $3,000.

Duration 10 weeks, beginning in June.

Additional information Interns are assigned to departmental projects (curatorial, administration, or education) at the Metropolitan Museum of Art; other assignments may include giving gallery talks and working at the Visitor Information Center. The assignment is for 35 hours a week. The internships are funded in part by the Lebensfeld Foundation, the Billy Rose Foundation, the Reed Foundation, and the Ittleson Foundation.

Number awarded 14 each year.

Deadline January of each year.

[1206]
METROPOLITAN MUSEUM OF ART INTERNSHIPS FOR GRADUATE STUDENTS

Metropolitan Museum of Art
Attn: Internship Programs
1000 Fifth Avenue
New York, NY 10028-0198
(212) 570-3710   Fax: (212) 570-3782
Web: www.metmuseum.org/education/er_internship.asp

Purpose To provide summer work experience at the Metropolitan Museum of Art to graduate students.

Eligibility These internships are available to individuals who have completed at least 1 year of graduate work in art history or in an allied field. Applicants of diverse backgrounds (e.g., minorities) are encouraged to apply.

Financial data The honorarium is $3,250.

Duration 10 weeks, beginning in June.

Additional information Interns are assigned to research or writing or to a special exhibition at the Metropolitan Museum of Art, depending upon the needs of the department. The assignment is for 35 hours a week. The internships are funded in part by the Lebensfeld Foundation and the Solow Art and Architecture Foundation.

Number awarded 10 each year.

Deadline January of each year.

[1207]
METROPOLITAN MUSEUM OF ART 6-MONTH INTERNSHIPS

Metropolitan Museum of Art
Attn: Internship Programs
1000 Fifth Avenue
New York, NY 10028-0198
(212) 570-3710   Fax: (212) 570-3782
Web: www.metmuseum.org/education/er_internship.asp

Purpose To provide work experience at the Metropolitan Museum of Art to candidates who can promote diversity in the profession.

Eligibility This program is open to graduating college seniors, recent graduates, and graduate students in art history or related fields. Selection is based on an essay in which applicants indicate how their selection will promote greater diversity in the national pool of future museum professionals and describe their financial need.

Financial data The stipend is $10,000.

Duration 6 months, beginning in June.

Additional information Interns work at the Metropolitan Museum for 35 hours a week.

Number awarded 2 each year.

Deadline January of each year.

[1208]
MIAMI UNIVERSITY MINORITY RESIDENT LIBRARIAN

Miami University
University Libraries
Attn: Dean and University Librarian
King Library, Room 271
Oxford, OH 45056-1878
(513) 529-2800   E-mail: hendribn@lib.muohio.edu
Web: www.lib.muohio.edu

Purpose To provide a residency for minority librarians at Miami University.

Eligibility This program is open to minorities who graduated from library school within the past 2 years and are interested in preparing for a career in academic librarianship. Applicants must have a master's degree from a library school accredited by the American Library Association. They should have a familiarity with and knowledge of advancing technologies, an ability to work collegially in a team environment, possess a knowledge of and interest in academic libraries, and demonstrate the ability to establish and maintain good working relationships with faculty, students, and other library users as well as library staff.

Financial data The stipend is $33,500. Benefits include the standard insurance package.

Duration 1 year; may be renewed for 1 additional year.

Additional information Interns are exposed to all areas of the university library's operations, including public, technical, and administrative services. Actual assignments are based on the interests of the intern and the needs of the library.

Number awarded 1 each year.

Deadline June of each year.

[1209]
MICHAEL CURRY SUMMER INTERNSHIP PROGRAM
Office of the Governor
Attn: Program Director
107 William G. Stratton Building
Springfield, IL 62706
(217) 782-5213   Fax: (217) 524-1677
TDD: (217) 558-2238
E-mail: tammy_payne@gov.state.il.us
Web: www.state.il.us/gov/officeinternship.htm

Purpose To provide undergraduate and graduate students with work experience in the Illinois Governor's office during the summer.

Eligibility This program is open to college juniors, seniors, and graduate students from any academic discipline; law students are also eligible. Applicants must be interested in working in the Illinois Governor's office and in various agencies under the Governor's jurisdiction. They must be residents of Illinois. Applications are especially encouraged from women, minorities, and persons with disabilities.

Financial data The stipend is $1,200 per month.

Duration 2 months, during the summer.

Additional information Assignments are in Springfield and Chicago.

Number awarded Varies each year.

Deadline January of each year.

[1210]
MICKEY LELAND ENERGY FELLOWSHIPS
Associated Western Universities
4190 South Highland Drive, Suite 211
Salt Lake City, UT 84124-2600
(801) 273-8900   Fax: (801) 277-5632
E-mail: info@awu.org
Web: www.awu.org/mlef.htm

Purpose To provide summer work experience at fossil energy sites of the Department of Energy (DOE) to underrepresented minority undergraduate and graduate students.

Eligibility This program is open to full-time African American, Hispanic, and American Indian students who are entering their junior year, senior year, or first year of a master's degree program with a major in mathematics, engineering, or science. Applicants must be U.S. citizens with a GPA of 2.8 or higher. They must be interested in a summer work experience at DOE headquarters, a DOE oil and gas field site, a DOE national laboratory, or industry.

Financial data Weekly stipends are $500 for undergraduates or $650 for graduate students.

Duration 10 weeks, during the summer.

Additional information This program began as 3 separate activities: the Historically Black Colleges and Universities Internship Program established in 1995, the Hispanic Internship Program established in 1998, and the Tribal Colleges and Universities Internship Program, established in 2000. Those 3 programs were merged into the Fossil Energy Minority Education Initiative, renamed the Mickey Leland Energy Fellowship Program in 2000. The oil and gas sites to which interns may be assigned vary each year; recently, they included Department of Energy Headquarters (Washington, D.C.), the Chicago Support Office of the Department of Energy, the Albany Research Center (Albany, Oregon), the National Energy Technology Laboratory (Morgantown, West Virginia and Pittsburgh, Pennsylvania), Lawrence Livermore National Laboratory (Livermore, California), the Naval Petroleum and Oil Shale Reserve (Tulsa, Oklahoma), Strategic Petroleum Reserve sites in Louisiana and Texas, and various opportunities with private industry in the oil, gas, and coal industries in Georgia, Ohio, Texas, and Wyoming. Information is also available from the Department of Energy, Office of Fossil Energy, 1000 Independence Avenue, S.W., Washington, DC 20585. The coordinator for the Historically Black Colleges and Universities program is Dorothy Fowlkes, (202) 586-7421, E-mail: dorothy.fowlkes@hq.doe.gov. The coordinator for the Hispanic and Tribal Colleges and Universities programs is Vanessa Dodson-Cunningham, (202) 586-0445, E-mail: vanessa.dodson@hq.doe.gov.

Number awarded 50 to 60 each year.

Deadline January of each year.

[1211]
MICROSOFT NATIONAL SCHOLARSHIPS
Microsoft Corporation
Attn: National Minority Technical Scholarship
One Microsoft Way
Redmond, WA 98052-8303
(425) 882-8080   TTY: (800) 892-9811
E-mail: scholars@microsoft.com
Web: www.microsoft.com/college/scholarships/general.asp

Purpose To provide financial assistance and summer work experience to undergraduate students, especially underrepresented minorities and women, interested in preparing for a career in computer science or other related technical fields.

Eligibility This program is open to students who are enrolled full time and making satisfactory progress toward an undergraduate degree in computer science, computer engineering, or a related technical discipline (such as math or physics) with a demonstrated interest in computer science. Applicants must be enrolled in their sophomore or junior year and have earned a GPA of 3.0 or higher. Although all students who meet the eligibility criteria may apply, a large majority of scholarships are awarded to female and underrepresented minority (African American, Hispanic, and Native American) students. Along with their application, students must submit an essay that describes the following 4 items: 1) how they demonstrate their passion for technology outside the classroom; 2) the toughest technical problem they have worked on, how they addressed the problem, their role in reaching the outcome if it was team-based, and the final outcome; 3) a situation that demonstrates initiative and their willingness to go above and beyond; and 4) how they are currently funding their college education.

Financial data Scholarships cover 100% of the tuition as posted by the financial aid office of the university or college the recipient designates. Scholarships are made through that school and are not transferable to other academic institutions. Funds may be used for tuition only and may not be used for other costs on the recipient's bursar bill.

Duration 1 year.

Additional information Selected recipients are offered a paid summer internship where they will have a chance to develop Microsoft products.

Number awarded Varies. A total of $540,000 is available for this program each year.

Deadline January of each year.

[1212]
MILDRED COLODNY SCHOLARSHIP FOR STUDY OF HISTORIC PRESERVATION

National Trust for Historic Preservation
Attn: Scholarship Coordinator
1785 Massachusetts Avenue, N.W.
Washington, DC 20036-2117
(202) 588-6124   (800) 944-NTHP, ext. 6124
Fax: (202) 588-6059   E-mail: david_field@nthp.org
Web: www.nthp.org/help/colodny.html

Purpose To provide financial assistance and summer work experience to graduate students interested in working on a degree in a field related to historic preservation.

Eligibility Eligible to apply are students in their final year of undergraduate study intending to enroll in a graduate program in historic preservation and graduate students enrolled in or intending to enroll in historic preservation programs; these programs may be in a department of history, architecture, American studies, urban planning, museum studies, or a related field with a primary emphasis on historic preservation. Applicants must submit an essay in which they discuss their career goals and how their pursuit of a graduate preservation degree relates to those goals, including evidence of their interest in, commitment to, and/or potential for leadership in the field of preservation. Selection is based on the essay, a resume, 2 letters of recommendation, academic transcripts, and financial need. Applications are especially encouraged from people of diverse racial, ethnic, cultural, and economic backgrounds.

Financial data The program provides a stipend of up to $15,000 towards graduate school tuition, a stipend of $5,000 for a summer internship with the sponsor following the student's first year of study, and up to $1,500 towards the student's attendance at a National Preservation Conference.

Duration 1 year.

Additional information Internships may be completed at 1) the sponsor's Washington, D.C. office; 2) a regional office or historic museum site; or 3) the offices of 1 of the sponsor's partner organizations.

Number awarded 1 each year.

Deadline February of each year.

[1213]
MINORITY ACADEMIC INSTITUTIONS UNDERGRADUATE STUDENT FELLOWSHIPS

Environmental Protection Agency
Attn: National Center for Environmental Research
Ariel Rios Building - 8723R
1200 Pennsylvania Avenue, N.W.
Washington, DC 20460
(202) 564-6926   E-mail: boddie.georgette@epa.gov
Web: es.epa.gov/ncer/rfa

Purpose To provide financial assistance and summer internships to undergraduates at minority academic institutions (MAIs) who are interested in majoring in fields related to the environment.

Eligibility Applicants for this program must be U.S. citizens or permanent residents who are enrolled full time with a minimum GPA of 3.0 in an accredited 4-year institution that meets the definition of the Environmental Protection Agency (EPA) as an MAI: Historically Black Colleges and Universities (HBCUs), Hispanic Serving Institutions (HSIs), Tribal Colleges (TCs), Native Hawaiian Serving Institutions (NHSIs), and Alaska Native Serving Institutions (ANSIs). Students must have at least 2 years remaining for completion of a bachelor's degree and must be majoring in environmental science, physical sciences, natural and life sciences, mathematics and computer science, social sciences, economics, or engineering. They must be available to work as interns at an EPA facility during the summer between their junior and senior years.

Financial data The fellowship provides up to $17,000 per year, including up to $10,000 for tuition and academic fees, a stipend of $4,500 ($500 per month for 9 months), and an expense allowance of up to $2,500 for items and activities for the direct benefit of the student's education, such as books, supplies, and travel to professional conferences and workshops. The summer internship grant is $7,500, including a stipend of $6,000, an allowance of $1,000 for travel to and from the site, and an allowance of $500 for travel while at the site.

Duration The final 2 years of baccalaureate study, including 12 weeks during the summer between those years.

Additional information This program began in 1982. It was formerly known as Culturally Diverse Academic Institutions Undergraduate Student Fellowships program.

Number awarded Approximately 25 each year.

Deadline November of each year.

[1214]
MINORITY ADVERTISING TRAINING PROGRAM INTERNSHIPS

Minority Advertising Training Program
6404 Wilshire Boulevard, Suite 1111
Los Angeles, CA 90048-5513
(323) 655-1951   Fax: (323) 655-8627
E-mail: mat@goldenmanagement.com
Web: www.matprogram.org

Purpose To provide internships to minority individuals in southern California interested in a career in advertising.

Eligibility Applicants must be juniors, seniors, master's candidates, or recent graduates of colleges and universities in southern California with a GPA of 2.7 or higher. They must be minority (Alaskan Native, American Indian, Asian, Black, Hispanic, or Pacific Islander) individuals interested in an internship at selected advertising agencies or broadcast outlets in the region.

Financial data The salary is $9 per hour.

Duration Interns work 13 weeks for 20 hours per week.

Additional information The Minority Advertising Training Program (MAT) is a coalition of the Los Angeles Advertising Agencies Association, the Advertising Club of Los Angeles, and TBWA Chiat/Day. This program was established in 1992.

Number awarded Varies each year; since establishment of this program, it has placed more than 400 interns.

Deadline January of each year for spring internships; April of each year for summer internships; August of each year for fall internships.

[1215]
MINORITY FELLOWSHIP IN ENVIRONMENTAL LAW

New York State Bar Association
Attn: Environmental Law Section
One Elk Street
Albany, NY 12207
(518) 463-3200   Fax: (518) 487-5517
E-mail: kplog@nysba.org
Web: www.nysba.org

Purpose To provide an opportunity for minority law students from New York to work during the summer on legal matters for a government environmental agency or public interest environmental organization in the state.

Eligibility This program is open to members of a minority group (African American, Latino, Native American, Alaskan Native, Asian, or Pacific Islander) who are 1) enrolled in a law school in New York or 2) New York residents enrolled in a law school in the United States. Applicants must be interested in summer employment working on legal matters for a government environmental agency or public interest environmental organization in New York. They must submit a resume, transcripts, 2 letters of recommendation, and an essay describing their interest in environmental issues and reasons for wanting to participate in the fellowship.

Financial data The stipend is $6,000.

Duration At least 10 weeks, during the summer.

Number awarded 1 each year.

Deadline December of each year.

[1216]
MINORITY RESEARCH LIBRARY RESIDENCY PROGRAM

University of Iowa
Libraries
Attn: Coordinator for Human Resources and Diversity
    Programs
100 Main Library
Iowa City, IA 52242-1420
(319) 335-5871   Fax: (319) 335-5900
E-mail: susan-marks@uiowa.edu
Web: www.lib.uiowa.edu/hr/mrlrp.html

Purpose To provide professional experience to recently graduated librarians at the University of Iowa in Iowa City.

Eligibility Applicants must hold a recent graduate degree from an accredited program in library and information science; have general knowledge of electronic information sources, the Internet, and the World Wide Web; be able to work in a team environment; have excellent written and oral communication skills; demonstrate an interest in professional development in the libraries and university community; and be interested in an appointment at the University of Iowa's Library. The library is committed to diversity in all aspects of services, including recruitment of racial and ethnic minorities.

Financial data The appointment is at the Librarian I level with an entry-level salary.

Duration 2 years.

Number awarded 1 each year.

Deadline February of each year.

[1217]
MINORITY UNDERGRADUATE RESEARCH FELLOWSHIPS

California Institute of Technology
Attn: Minority Undergraduate Research Fellowship Program
Student-Faculty Programs Office
Mail Code 139-74
Pasadena, CA 91125
(626) 395-2887   Fax: (626) 449-9649
E-mail: murf@its.caltech.edu
Web: www.its.caltech.edu/~murf

Purpose To provide an opportunity for underrepresented minority college juniors to work in a research laboratory at California Institute of Technology (Caltech) or the Jet Propulsion Laboratory (JPL) during the summer under the guidance of scientists and engineers.

Eligibility This program is open to African Americans, Hispanics, Native Americans, Puerto Ricans, and Pacific Islanders who are undergraduate juniors; sophomores may be considered on a case-by-case basis. Applicants must be majoring in astronomy, biology, chemistry and chemical engineering, engineering and applied science, geological and planetary sciences, humanities, mathematics, physics, or social sciences. They must be interested in a program at either Caltech or JPL working on a research project under the supervision of a faculty member and a postdoctoral fellow and/or advanced graduate student. U.S. citizenship or permanent resident status is required.

Financial data Students receive a stipend of $500 per week, round-trip travel expenses, and housing on the Caltech campus at no charge. Meals and other expenses are not covered.

Duration 8 to 10 week, in the summer.

Additional information Support for this program is provided by Northrop Grumman Corporation, General Motors Corporation, Howard Hughes Medical Institute, and the James Irvine Foundation.

Number awarded Up to 15 in biology and chemistry; up to 6 in astronomy, earth and space sciences, engineering, humanities, mathematics, physics, and social sciences.

Deadline December of each year.

[1218]
MISSISSIPPI PSYCHOLOGY APPRENTICESHIP PROGRAM

Mississippi Office of Student Financial Aid
3825 Ridgewood Road
Jackson, MS 39211-6453
(601) 432-6997   (800) 327-2980 (within MS)
Fax: (601) 432-6527   E-mail: sfa@ihl.state.ms.us
Web: www.ihl.state.ms.us/financialaid/map.html

Purpose To provide summer work experience in the field of psychology to students in Mississippi.

Eligibility Current Mississippi residents who are enrolled as full-time undergraduate students majoring in psychology at a Mississippi accredited college or university with a cumulative GPA of 3.0 or higher are eligible to apply for this internship. Special consideration is given to economically disadvantaged, educationally disadvantaged, and/or socially disadvantaged applicants (e.g., minorities).

Financial data Stipends are $500 per month.

Duration 3 months, during the summer.

Additional information Participants engage in research and training in the professional practice of psychology at a Veterans Affairs Medical Center.

Number awarded Varies each year, depending on the availability of funds; awards are granted on a first-come, first-served basis.

Deadline March of each year.

[1219]
MISSOURI SPACE GRANT CONSORTIUM SUMMER HIGH SCHOOL INTERNSHIPS

Missouri Space Grant Consortium
c/o University of Missouri at Rolla
229 Mechanical Engineering Building
1870 Miner Circle
Rolla, MO 65409-0050
(573) 341-4887   Fax: (573) 341-6899
E-mail: kchrist@umr.edu
Web: www.umr.edu/~spaceg

Purpose To provide work experience during the summer to high school students in Missouri interested in a career in an aerospace field.

Eligibility This program is open to Missouri high school students who have just completed their junior or senior year. Applicants must be proposing a specific research or education project in a research laboratory, a computing facility, or the galleries of the St. Louis Science Center. U.S. citizenship is required. The Missouri Space Grant Consortium is a component of the U.S. National Aeronautics and Space Administration (NASA), which encourages participation by women, underrepresented minorities, and persons with disabilities.

Financial data The maximum funding is $2,000.

Duration Summer months.

Additional information This program is funded by NASA.

Number awarded Approximately 10 each year.

[1220]
MODESTO BEE SUMMER INTERN PROGRAM

Modesto Bee
Attn: Executive Editor
1325 H Street
P.O. Box 5256
Modesto, CA 95352
(209) 578-2351   Fax: (209) 578-2207
E-mail: editor@modbee.com
Web: www.modbee.com

Purpose To provide work experience at the *Modesto Bee* (in California) during the summer to students who are interested in a career in journalism.

Eligibility Applicants should have daily journalism experience, either with a university publication or with a daily newspaper. Preference is given to applicants who will be entering their senior year in college, are recent graduates, or are students in master's degree programs. Spanish-speaking applicants are encouraged to apply.

Financial data The stipend is $450 per week.

Duration 10 to 12 weeks, in the summer.

Additional information Assignments at the *Modesto Bee* are available in reporting, editing, photography, and sports reporting.

Deadline November of each year.

[1221]
MONTGOMERY SUMMER RESEARCH FELLOWSHIPS IN LAW AND SOCIAL SCIENCE FOR MINORITY UNDERGRADUATE STUDENTS

American Bar Foundation
Attn: Assistant Director
750 North Lake Shore Drive
Chicago, IL 60611
(312) 988-6580   Fax: (312) 988-6579
E-mail: fellowships@abfn.org
Web: www.abf-sociolegal.org

Purpose To provide on opportunity for underrepresented minority undergraduates to work on a summer research project in the field of law and social science.

Eligibility This program is open to African Americans, Mexicans, Puerto Ricans, and Native Americans who are sophomores or juniors in college, have earned at least a 3.0 GPA, are working on a major in the social sciences or humanities, and are willing to consider a research-oriented career. Applicants must submit a brief essay on the topics to be considered in that year's program, official transcripts, and 1 letter of recommendation from a faculty member familiar with their work.

Financial data Participants receive a stipend of $3,600.

Duration 35 hours per week for 10 weeks during the summer.

Additional information Students are assigned to an American Bar Foundation Research Fellow who involves the student in the design and conduct of the fellow's research project and who acts as mentor during the student's tenure.

Number awarded 4 each year.

Deadline February of each year.

[1222]
MULTICULTURAL ADVERTISING INTERN PROGRAM

American Association of Advertising Agencies
Attn: Manager of Diversity Programs
405 Lexington Avenue, 18th Floor
New York, NY 10174-1801
(212) 850-0734   (800) 676-9333
Fax: (212) 573-8968   E-mail: naip@aaaa.org
Web: www.aaaa.org

Purpose To provide racial minority students with summer work experience in advertising agencies and to present them with an overview of the agency business.

Eligibility This program is open to college juniors, seniors, and graduate students who are Black/African American, Asian/Asian American, Pacific Islander, Hispanic, North American Indian/Native American, or multiracial. Applicants must be majoring in advertising, communications, liberal arts, marketing, or a related area with a GPA of 3.0 or higher. Students with a cumulative GPA of 2.7 to 2.9 are encouraged to apply, but they must complete an additional essay question. Applicants must be U.S. citizens or permanent residents committed to a career in advertising, regardless of their major.

Financial data Interns are paid approximately $350 per week. Interns who do not live in the area of their host agencies stay in housing arranged by the sponsor, but they are responsible for 30% of the cost of housing, travel, and materials.

Duration 10 weeks during the summer.

Additional information Interns may be assigned duties in the following departments: account management, broadcast production, media, creative (art direction or copywriting), interactive technologies, print production, strategic/account planning, or traffic.

Number awarded Varies each year; recently, 69 interns were placed in 37 member advertising agency offices located in Atlanta, Boston, Chicago, Detroit, Irvine (California), Milwaukee, Minneapolis, New York, San Francisco, and Seattle.

Deadline January of each year.

[1223]
MULTICULTURAL UNDERGRADUATE INTERNSHIPS AT THE GETTY CENTER

Getty Grant Program
1200 Getty Center Drive, Suite 800
Los Angeles, CA 90049-1685
(310) 440-6545   Fax: (310) 440-7703
E-mail: summerinterns@getty.edu
Web: www.getty.edu

Purpose To provide summer work experience at facilities of the Getty Center to minority undergraduates from Los Angeles County, California.

Eligibility This program is open to currently-enrolled undergraduates who either reside or attend college in Los Angeles County, California. Applicants must be members of groups currently underrepresented in museum professions and fields related to the visual arts and humanities: individuals of African American, Asian, Latino/Hispanic/Chicano, Native American, and Pacific Islander descent. They may be majoring in any field, including the sciences and technology, and are not required to have demonstrated a previous commitment to the visual arts. Along with their application, they must submit a personal statement of up to 500 words on why they are interested in this internship, including what they hope to gain from the program, their interest or involvement in issues of multiculturalism, aspects of their past experience that they feel are most relevant to the application, and any specific career or educational avenues they are interested in exploring.

Financial data The stipend is $3,500.

Duration 10 weeks during the summer.

Additional information Internships provide training and work experience in such areas as conservation, collections, publications, museum education, curatorship, grants administration, programs, site operations, and information technology.

Number awarded Varies each year.

Deadline February of each year.

[1224]
NACME/NASA UNDERGRADUATE STUDENT AWARDS FOR RESEARCH

National Action Council for Minorities in Engineering
350 Fifth Avenue, Suite 2212
New York, NY 10118-2299
(212) 279-2626   Fax: (212) 629-5178
E-mail: awalter@nacme.org
Web: www.nacme.org/univ/scol/nasa.html

Purpose To provide financial assistance and research internships to undergraduates majoring in science and engineering fields at designated minority institutions.

Eligibility This program is open to students majoring in mathematics, computer science, engineering (aeronautical, astronautical, chemical, civil, electrical, materials, mechanical, metallurgical), environmental sciences (atmospheric sciences, geological sciences), life sciences (agricultural sciences, biological sciences,

environmental biology, medical sciences), and physical sciences (astronomy, chemistry, physics) at 21 designated minority institutions. Applicants must have a GPA of 3.0 or higher, be enrolled full time, have earned no more than 39 credit hours, be able to demonstrate financial need, and be U.S. citizens. They must be nominated by the National Aeronautics and Space Administration (NASA) liaison at their university.

Financial data Awards provide support for tuition during the academic year and for a research internship during the summer.

Duration 1 year; may be renewed up to 3 additional years if the recipient maintains a GPA of 3.0 or higher and satisfactory progress toward a degree in an engineering, mathematics, or science field relevant to the mission of NASA.

Additional information Students submit applications through participating universities; currently, those are California State University at Los Angeles, City College of New York, D-Q University (Davis, California), Gallaudet University (Washington, D.C.), Florida A&M University/Florida State University (Tallahassee, Florida), Fayetteville State University (Fayetteville, North Carolina), LaGuardia Community College (Long Island City, New York), Morgan State University (Baltimore, Maryland), Morehouse College (Atlanta, Georgia), University of New Mexico (Albuquerque, New Mexico), New Mexico Highlands University (Las Vegas, New Mexico), New Mexico State University (Las Cruces, New Mexico), North Carolina A&T University (Greensboro, North Carolina), University of North Carolina at Pembroke, Shaw University (Raleigh, North Carolina), Southern University and A&M College (Baton Rouge, Louisiana), Spelman College (Atlanta, Georgia), Tennessee State University (Nashville, Tennessee), University of Texas–Pan American (Edinburg, Texas), University of Texas at San Antonio, and Winston-Salem State University (Winston-Salem, North Carolina). The National Action Council for Minorities in Engineering (NACME), in consultation with NASA, selects the recipients. NACME has administered this program since 1998, Students are required to participate in a research project at a NASA facility during each summer they receive support from this program.

Number awarded Varies each year.

Deadline Nominations are usually made between the months of March and May.

[1225]
N.A.S.P.A. MINORITY UNDERGRADUATE FELLOWS PROGRAM

National Association of Student Personnel Administrators
1875 Connecticut Avenue, N.W., Suite 418
Washington, DC 20009-5728
(202) 265-7500   Fax: (202) 797-1157
E-mail: office@naspa.org
Web: www.naspa.org

Purpose To provide summer work experience and leadership training to minorities who are completing their second year in college.

Eligibility Eligible to be nominated for this program are ethnic minority students (Native, African, Asian, or Hispanic Americans) who are completing their sophomore year in a 4-year institution or their second year in a 2-year transfer program. Applicants must be able to demonstrate academic promise and be interested in a future in higher education.

Financial data Participants are offered a paid summer internship.

Duration The internship lasts 8 weeks during the summer.

Additional information The program offers 3 main components: 1) participation in a 1- or 2-year internship or field experience under the guidance of a mentor; 2) participation in a summer leadership institute designed to enhance leadership and problem solving skills; and 3) participation in an 8-week paid summer internship designed to encourage the development of future student affairs and higher education administrators.

Deadline Applications for the summer internship must be submitted by March.

[1226]
NATIONAL MUSEUM OF NATURAL HISTORY RESEARCH TRAINING PROGRAM

National Museum of Natural History
Attn: RTP Program Coordinator
NHB, Room W411, MRC 166
P.O. Box 37012
Washington, DC 20013-7012
(202) 357-4548   Fax: (202) 786-2563
E-mail: sangrey.mary@nmnh.si.edu
Web: www.nmnh.si.edu/rtp

Purpose To provide undergraduate students with a summer research training internship at the Smithsonian Institution's National Museum of Natural History in Washington, D.C.

Eligibility This program is open to currently-enrolled undergraduate students interested in pursuing a career in anthropology, botany, entomology, invertebrate zoology, mineral sciences and geology, paleobiology, or vertebrate zoology. Although foreign students may apply, all applicants must be proficient in reading and understanding English. Applications are especially encouraged from women, international and minority students, and persons with disabilities.

Financial data Interns receive a stipend of approximately $3,000, housing, an allowance for transportation to Washington, D.C. (generally $500), and a research allowance (up to $1,000).

Duration 10 weeks, during the summer.

Additional information The heart of the program is a research project, designed by the intern in collaboration with a museum staff advisor. In addition, students participate in a laboratory experience and collection workshop; lectures, discussions, tours, and field trips; and other regular museum activities, such as seminars and special lectures. This program receives support from a number of funds within the Smithsonian and from the National Science Foundation through its Research Experiences for Undergraduates (REU) Program and Louis Stokes Alliances for Minority Participation Program.

Number awarded 20 to 24 each year.

Deadline January of each year.

[1227]
NATIONAL OCEANIC AND ATMOSPHERIC ADMINISTRATION EDUCATIONAL PARTNERSHIP PROGRAM WITH MINORITY SERVING INSTITUTIONS GRADUATE SCIENCES PROGRAM

Oak Ridge Institute for Science and Education
Attn: Education and Training Division
P.O. Box 117
Oak Ridge, TN 37831-0117
(865) 576-9272   Fax: (865) 241-5220
E-mail: babcockc@orau.gov
Web: www.orau.gov/orise.htm

Purpose To provide financial assistance and summer research experience to graduate students at minority serving institutions who are majoring in scientific fields of interest to the National Oceanic and Atmospheric Administration (NOAA).

Eligibility This program is open to graduate students pursuing master's or doctoral degrees at minority serving institutions, including Hispanic Serving Institutions (HSIs), Historically Black Colleges and Universities (HBCUs), and Tribal Colleges and Universities (TCUs). Applicants must be majoring in biology, chemistry, computer science, economics, engineering, geography, geology, mathematics, physical science, physics, social science, or other fields specific to NOAA such as cartography, environmental planning, fishery biology, hydrology, meteorology, or oceanography. They must also be interested in pursuing a training program during the summer at a NOAA research facility.

Financial data During the school year, the program provides payment of tuition and fees, books, housing, meals, and travel expenses. During the summer, students receive a salary and benefits.

Duration 2 years of study plus 16 weeks of research training during the summer.

Additional information This program is funded by NOAA and administered by the Education and Training Division (ETD) of Oak Ridge Institute for Science and Education (ORISE).

Number awarded 5 each year.

Deadline January of each year.

[1228]
NATIONAL OCEANIC AND ATMOSPHERIC ADMINISTRATION EDUCATIONAL PARTNERSHIP PROGRAM WITH MINORITY SERVING INSTITUTIONS UNDERGRADUATE SCHOLARSHIPS

Oak Ridge Institute for Science and Education
Attn: Education and Training Division
P.O. Box 117
Oak Ridge, TN 37831-0117
(865) 576-9272   Fax: (865) 241-5220
E-mail: babcockc@orau.gov
Web: www.orau.gov/orise.htm

Purpose To provide financial assistance and research experience to undergraduate students at minority serving institutions who are majoring in scientific fields of interest to the National Oceanic and Atmospheric Administration (NOAA).

Eligibility This program is open to juniors and seniors at minority serving institutions, including Hispanic Serving Institutions (HSIs), Historically Black Colleges and Universities (HBCUs), and Tribal Colleges and Universities (TCUs). Applicants must be majoring in atmospheric science, biology, cartography, chemistry, computer science, engineering, environmental science, geodesy, geography, marine science, mathematics, meteorology, photogrammetry, physical science, physics, or remote sensing. They must also be interested in pursuing a research internship during the summer at a NOAA site.

Financial data This program provides payment of tuition and fees (to a maximum of $4,000 per year) and a stipend during the internship of $650 per week.

Duration 2 years.

Additional information This program is funded by NOAA through an interagency agreement with the U.S. Department of Energy and administered by the Education and Training Division (ETD) of Oak Ridge Institute for Science and Education (ORISE).

Number awarded 10 each year.

Deadline January of each year.

[1229]
NATIONAL PARK SERVICE SEASONAL REFERRALS

Student Conservation Association, Inc.
Attn: College Diversity Program
1800 North Kent Street, Suite 1260
Arlington, VA 22209
(703) 524-2441   Fax: (703) 524-2451
E-mail: internships@sca-inc.org
Web: www.sca-inc.org/vol/ccdc/ccdcnps.htm

Purpose To provide summer work experience to minority students at facilities of the U.S. National Park Service (NPS).

Eligibility This program is open to minority undergraduate and graduate students who are currently enrolled in college and U.S. citizens. Applicants must be interested in a summer position with the NPS, especially in its Pacific West Region (California, Hawaii, Idaho, Oregon, and Washington) but also at other sites across the country. Applicants who pass an initial screening are referred to park supervisors who make the final selections.

Financial data Seasonal employees are paid at the GS-3 ($7.62 per hour) to GS-7 ($11.85 per hour) level.

Duration Summer months.

Additional information This program began in 1997 when the College Diversity Program of the Student Conservation Association agreed to work with the NPS to increase the diversity of its seasonal applicant pool. Most positions are available as 1) park rangers, who supervise, manage, and perform work in the conservation and use of resources in national parks and other federally-managed areas; 2) visitor use assistants, who collect and account for fees and provide miscellaneous services and information to visitors; and 3) biological technicians, who assist researchers and management staff in collecting and analyzing data on flora and fauna and provide practical technical support in laboratories, field, or other settings. Limited positions are also available in the fields of wildland fire fighting, landscape architecture, law enforcement, trail maintenance, and computer specialist.

Number awarded Varies each year.

Deadline February of each year.

[1230]
NATIONAL PHYSICAL SCIENCE CONSORTIUM GRADUATE FELLOWSHIPS

National Physical Science Consortium
University Village
3375 South Hoover Street, Suite E 200
Los Angeles, CA 90007
(213) 821-2409   (800) 854-NPSC
Fax: (213) 821-2410   E-mail: npschq@npsc.org
Web: www.npsc.org

Purpose To provide financial assistance and summer work experience to underrepresented minorities and women interested in working on a Ph.D. in designated science and engineering fields.

Eligibility This program is open to U.S. citizens who are seniors graduating from college with a GPA of 3.0 or higher, enrolled in the first year of a doctoral program, completing a terminal master's degree, or returning from the work force and holding no more than a master's degree. Applicants must be interested in pursuing a Ph.D. in astronomy, chemistry, computer science, geology, materials science, mathematical sciences, physics, chemical engineering, computer engineering, electrical engineering, environmental engineering, or mechanical engineering. The program welcomes applications from all qualified students and continues to emphasize the recruitment of underrepresented minority (African American, Hispanic, Native American Indian, Eskimo, Aleut, and Pacific Islander) and women physical science and engineering students. Fellowships are provided to students at the 113 universities that are members of the consortium. Selection is based on academic standing (GPA), course work taken in preparation for graduate school, university and/or industry research experience, letters of recommendation, and GRE scores.

Financial data The fellowship pays tuition and fees plus an annual stipend of $16,000. It also provides on-site paid summer employment to enhance technical experience. The exact value of the fellowship depends on academic standing, summer employment, and graduate school attended, but exceeds $200,000.

Duration Up to 6 years.

Additional information Tuition and fees are provided by the participating universities. Stipends and summer internships are provided by 11 private corporations and governmental research facilities.

Number awarded Varies each year.

Deadline November of each year.

[1231]
NATIONAL SECURITY INTERNSHIP PROGRAM

Pacific Northwest National Laboratory
Attn: Science Education Programs
902 Battelle Boulevard
P.O. Box 999, MS K8-15
Richland, WA 99352
(509) 375-2569   (888) 375-PNNL
E-mail: peg.jarretts@pnl.gov
Web: science-ed.pnl.gov/postings/nsip.stm

Purpose To provide undergraduate and graduate students with an opportunity to work on a national security-related science research project at Pacific Northwest National Laboratory (PNNL) during the summer.

Eligibility This program is open to undergraduate and graduate students who have a GPA of 3.0 or higher (preferably 3.4 or higher). Applicants should be majoring in chemistry, computer science, electrical engineering, nuclear science, or physics. They must be interested in working at PNNL on a summer science project related to national security. Women and minorities are encouraged to apply. Selection is based on academic achievement, prior experience, and technical interest.

Financial data Interns receive a stipend (amount not specified).

Duration 8 to 12 weeks, during the summer; may be extended up to 1 year of part-time work during the academic year.

Additional information Tuition reimbursement is available to interns who agree to work as full-time employees at PNNL for a set period of time following graduation. Interns who accept tuition reimbursement and then fail to complete full-time employment for the specified period of time must repay a prorated portion of the educational expenses.

Number awarded 10 each year.

Deadline March of each year.

[1232]
NATIONAL ZOOLOGICAL PARK TRAINEESHIPS

Smithsonian National Zoological Park
Attn: Office of Public Affairs
3001 Connecticut Avenue, N.W.
Washington, DC 20008
(202) 673-0209   E-mail: nationalzoo@nzp.si.edu
Web: www.natzoo.si.edu/Internships/opaintern.htm

Purpose To provide summer work experience in public affairs activities at the Smithsonian National Zoological Park to undergraduate students.

Eligibility This program is open to students majoring in communications, public relations, journalism, biology, life science, or liberal arts. Applicants must be interested in working in the Office of Public Affairs in such activities as maintaining and updating mailing lists, developing new contacts, targeting new audiences, writing and disseminating information materials, and assisting in coordinating special activities and tours. They must submit a resume, a 1- to 2-page statement of their qualifications and interest in the position, a copy of their official college transcript, and 2 letters of recommendation. Minority candidates are especially encouraged to apply.

Financial data The stipend is $3,300.

Duration 12 weeks, during the summer.

Number awarded 1 each year.

Deadline March of each year.

[1233]
NCAA ETHNIC MINORITY AND WOMEN'S INTERNSHIP PROGRAMS

National Collegiate Athletic Association
Attn: Director of Professional Development
700 West Washington Avenue
P.O. Box 6222
Indianapolis, IN 46206-6222
(317) 917-6222   Fax: (317) 917-6888
E-mail: dmoorman@ncaa.org
Web: www.ncaa.org

Purpose To provide work experience at the National Collegiate Athletic Association (NCAA) office to women or minority college graduates.

Eligibility Candidates for this NCAA internship must be women or ethnic minorities who have completed the requirements for an undergraduate degree. They must have demonstrated a commitment to pursuing a career in intercollegiate athletics and the ability to succeed in such a career.

Financial data Interns receive up to $1,600 per month; this includes a $200 monthly housing allowance.

Duration 1 year, beginning in June.

Additional information Interns work at the NCAA national office in Indianapolis.

Number awarded 8 to 10 each year.

Deadline February of each year.

[1234]
NEUROSCIENCE SCHOLARS FELLOWSHIP PROGRAM

Society for Advancement of Chicanos and Native Americans in Science
333 Front Street, Suite 104
P.O. Box 8526
Santa Cruz, CA 95061-8526
(831) 459-0170, ext. 224   Fax: (831) 459-0194
E-mail: neuroscience@sacnas.org
Web: www.sacnas.org

Purpose To provide an opportunity for Native American and Chicano/Latino pre- and postdoctoral students to participate in summer research programs in neuroscience.

Eligibility This program is open to Chicano/Latino and Native American predoctoral students and postdoctoral fellows who are interested in a health and research career in neuroscience.

Financial data As part of the program, fellows participate in summer research at the National Institute of Neurological Disorders and Stroke (NINDS) in Bethesda, Maryland, the Marine Biological Laboratory in Woods Hole, Massachusetts, or other academic research institutions.

Duration Participation extends over 3 years.

Additional information Other benefits of this program include 1) attendance at meetings of the Society for Advancement of Chicanos and Native Americans in Science, the Society for Neuroscience, and other organizations; 2) meetings with prominent neuroscientists to plan a career in basic and clinical research in the neurological sciences; and 3) development of professional networking to augment and strengthen opportunities for productive health and research careers in the field. This program, which began in 1999, is funded by NINDS.

Number awarded 1 or more each year.

Deadline July of each year.

[1235]
NEW JERSEY SPACE GRANT CONSORTIUM UNDERGRADUATE SUMMER FELLOWSHIPS

New Jersey Space Grant Consortium
c/o Stevens Institute of Technology
Edward A. Stevens Hall, Room 130-B
Hoboken, NJ 07030
(201) 216-8964   Fax: (201) 216-8929
E-mail: sthangam@stevens-tech.edu
Web: attila.stevens-tech.edu/njsgc

Purpose To provide financial assistance for summer research experiences in space-related fields to college students in New Jersey.

Eligibility This program is open to undergraduate students who have completed at least 2 years at member institutions of the New Jersey Space Grant Consortium (NJSGC). Applicants must be proposing a program of space-related research in industry or at universities and their affiliated research laboratories. Their field of study may be aerospace engineering, biological science, chemical engineering, computer science and engineering, electrical engineering, material science and engineering, mechanical engineering, natural science, or physical science. U.S. citizenship is required. The New Jersey Space Grant Consortium is a component of the U.S. National Aeronautics and Space Administration (NASA) Space Grant program, which encourages participation by women, underrepresented minorities, and people with disabilities. Selection is based on a biographical sketch, a brief statement of what they hope to accomplish as a space grant fellow, a statement of career goals (including their relationship to aerospace engineering and science), and a description of their plan for the immediate future.

Financial data The stipend is $500 per week, with an additional $500 per student available for laboratory supplies.

Duration 10 weeks, during the summer.

Additional information Members of the NJSGC include New Jersey Institute of Technology, Princeton University, Rutgers University, Stevens Institute of Technology, and the University of Medicine and Dentistry of New Jersey. This program is funded by NASA.

Number awarded Approximately 12 each year.

Deadline March of each year.

[1236]
NEW YORK SPACE GRANT CONSORTIUM UNDERGRADUATE SUMMER INTERNSHIPS

New York Space Grant Consortium
c/o Cornell University
Astronomy Department
517 Space Sciences Building
Ithaca, NY 14853-6801
(607) 255-2710   Fax: (607) 255-1767
E-mail: sfc1@cornell.edu
Web: astro.cornell.edu/SpaceGrant/undergrad.html

Purpose To provide funding for undergraduate students in New York who wish to work as student assistants on space-related research projects during the summer.

Eligibility This program is open to undergraduate students at member institutions of the New York Space Grant Consortium (Cornell University, Barnard College, City College of the City University of New York, Clarkson University, Colgate University, Columbia University, Manhattan College, Polytechnic University, Rensselaer Polytechnic University, SUNY Buffalo, SUNY Geneseo, and Syracuse University). Applicants must be seeking appointments as interns on ongoing research projects sponsored by the U.S. National Aeronautics and Space Administration (NASA). U.S. citizenship is required. The New York Space Grant Consortium is a component of the NASA Space Grant program, which encourages participation by women, underrepresented minorities, and persons with disabilities.

Financial data The stipend is $3,600.

Duration 8 to 10 weeks, during the summer.

Additional information This program is funded by NASA. Most internships are at Cornell, but others are at City College, Clarkson, Columbia, Grumman Aircraft, Ithaco, and the NASA Goddard Space Flight Center.

Number awarded Varies each year; recently, 14 projects offered opportunities for interns.

[1237]
NEWHOUSE SCHOLARSHIP PROGRAM

National Association of Hispanic Journalists
Attn: Scholarship Committee
1000 National Press Building
529 14th Street, N.W.
Washington, DC 20045-2001
(202) 662-7145   (888) 346-NAHJ
Fax: (202) 662-7144   E-mail: nahj@nahj.org
Web: www.nahj.org/scholarship.html

Purpose To provide financial assistance and summer work experience to Hispanic American undergraduate students interested in preparing for careers in the media.

Eligibility College juniors and seniors are eligible to apply if they are of Hispanic descent and are interested in majoring in print journalism. Applicants must submit an official transcript; a 1-page resume with their educational background, work history, awards, internships, other scholarships, language proficiency, and any work done for their school newspaper, radio, and/or television station; samples of their work; 2 reference letters; a 500-word autobiography in third person written as a news story; and documentation of financial need.

Financial data The stipend is $5,000 per year; the program also provides funding to attend the association's convention and an internship during the summer between the junior and senior year.

Duration 2 years.

Additional information This program, which began in 1994, is sponsored by the Newhouse Foundation and administered by the National Association of Hispanic Journalists (NAHJ) as part of its Rubén Salazar Scholarship Fund. The recipient participates in a summer internship at a Newhouse Newspaper.

Number awarded 1 each year.

Deadline January of each year.

[1238]
NONPROFIT SECTOR RESEARCH FUND WILLIAM RANDOLPH HEARST ENDOWED SCHOLARSHIP FOR MINORITY STUDENTS

Aspen Institute
Attn: Director, Nonprofit Sector Research Fund
One Dupont Circle, N.W., Suite 700
Washington, DC 20036
(202) 736-5831   Fax: (202) 467-0790
E-mail: nsrf@aspeninstitute.org
Web: www.aspeninstitute.org

Purpose To provide an opportunity for minority students to learn more about nonprofit activities, including philanthropy and its underlying values, through a summer internship at the Aspen Institute in Washington, D.C.

Eligibility This program at the Aspen Institute is open to minority graduate and undergraduate students. Applicants must be interested in learning about nonprofit organizations by working at the institute, by assisting in preparations for its annual conference, and by engaging in general research and program support for its grantmaking and outreach efforts. Selection is based on research and analytical abilities, background in the social sciences or humanities, writing and communication skills, and demonstrated financial need.

Financial data Stipends range from $2,800 to $4,200, depending on the recipient's educational level, financial need, and time commitment.

Duration 10 to 12 weeks, during the summer.

Additional information This program, established in 1991, is funded by the William Randolph Hearst Foundation.

Number awarded Varies each year.

Deadline March of each year.

[1239]
NOW LEGAL DEFENSE AND EDUCATION FUND GRADUATE INTERN PROGRAM

NOW Legal Defense and Education Fund
Attn: Senior Staff Attorney
395 Hudson Street, Fifth Floor
New York, NY 10014-3684
(212) 925-6635   Fax: (212) 226-1066
Web: www.nowldef.org

Purpose To provide work experience to graduate students interested in working in New York City at the offices of the National Organization for Women (NOW) Legal Defense and Education Fund during the summer.

Eligibility The internship is open to graduate students from a variety of educational backgrounds. Applicants must have a demonstrated interest in women's issues, the law, education, and/or public policy. The sponsor actively recruits people of color, disabled persons, and persons of minority sexual orientation.

Financial data Interns receive a weekly stipend of $420. Applicants are urged to investigate alternative sources of financial support.

Duration Summer months.

Additional information The Legal Defense and Education Fund was founded by members of the National Organization for Women (NOW) but is a separate entity.

Number awarded Varies each year.

[1240]
OFFICE OF BIOLOGICAL AND ENVIRONMENTAL RESEARCH MINORITY INSTITUTIONS STUDENT RESEARCH PARTICIPATION PROGRAM

Oak Ridge Institute for Science and Education
Attn: Education and Training Division
P.O. Box 117
Oak Ridge, TN 37831-0117
(865) 241-3319   Fax: (865) 241-5220
E-mail: kettrell@orau.gov
Web: www.orau.gov/orise.htm

Purpose To provide opportunities for students at minority institutions to participate in health and environmental research at facilities of the U.S. Department of Energy (DOE).

Eligibility This program is open to graduate students at Historically Black Colleges and Universities (HBCUs), Tribal Colleges and Universities (TCUs), and Hispanic Serving Institutions (HSIs) who are interested in conducting research at DOE facilities in the areas of health and the environment. U.S. citizenship or permanent resident status is required. Fields of study include atmospheric sciences, biochemistry, biology, biophysics, bioremediation, biostatistics, chemistry, ecology, genetics, genomics, marine science, molecular and cellular biology, measurement science,

molecular nuclear medicine, nuclear medicine, pathology, physics, physiology, radiation biology, structural biology, terrestrial sciences, toxicology, and other related life, biomedical, and environmental science disciplines.

Financial data The stipend is $650 per week. Participants also receive limited travel reimbursement for round-trip transportation expenses between their home or campus and the research facility.

Duration 10 weeks, during the summer.

Additional information Fellows may conduct research at any of the following participating DOE facilities: Ames Laboratory (Ames, Iowa); Argonne National Laboratory (Argonne, Illinois); Brookhaven National Laboratory (Upton, New York); Ernest Orlando Lawrence Berkeley National Laboratory (Berkeley, California); Lawrence Livermore National Laboratory (Livermore, California); Los Alamos National Laboratory (Los Alamos, New Mexico); Oak Ridge National Laboratory (Oak Ridge, Tennessee); Pacific Northwest National Laboratory (Richland, Washington); Savannah River Site (Aiken, South Carolina); Oak Ridge Institute for Science and Education (Oak Ridge, Tennessee); or Savannah River Ecology Laboratory (Aiken, South Carolina). This program is funded by DOE's Office of Biological and Environmental Research and administered by the Education and Training Division (ETD) of Oak Ridge Institute for Science and Education (ORISE).

Number awarded Varies each year.

Deadline January of each year.

[1241]
OHIO STATE UNIVERSITY LIBRARIES MINORITY INTERNSHIP

Ohio State University Libraries
Attn: Manager, Libraries Administrative Services
110 Main Library
1858 Neil Avenue Mall
Columbus, OH 43210-1286
(614) 292-5863   Fax: (614) 292-7859
E-mail: gonzalez.107@osu.edu
Web: www.osu.edu/Lib_Info/residency.html

Purpose To provide an opportunity for underrepresented minority librarians to gain work experience at Ohio State University.

Eligibility Eligible to apply are recent library school graduates who are interested in working in a university/research library. Members of minority groups underrepresented at Ohio State are the focus of this program (African Americans, Hispanic Americans, and Native Americans).

Financial data The stipend is $32,500 per year, plus benefits.

Duration 2 years.

Additional information The first year of the internship includes introduction/orientation to the various departments and operations within the library; the second year emphasizes 1 or more areas of special interest to the interns.

Number awarded 1 each year.

Deadline December of each year (or until the internship is filled).

[1242]
OREGON STATE BAR CLERKSHIP STIPENDS

Oregon State Bar
Attn: Affirmative Action Program
5200 S.W. Meadows Road
P.O. Box 1689
Lake Oswego, OR 97035-0889
(503) 620-0222, ext. 337   (800) 452-8260 (within OR)
Fax: (503) 684-1366   E-mail: smanabe@osbar.org
Web: www.osbar.org

Purpose To provide job opportunities for minority law students in Oregon and to provide an incentive to prospective employers to hire minority law students in the state.

Eligibility Applicants must be minority law students (African Americans, Asian Americans, Native Americans, or Hispanic Americans) with financial need. They are not required to be enrolled in a law school in Oregon, but they must demonstrate a commitment to practice in the state. Selection is based on economic disadvantage and the potential that the clerkships will help to impact the students' practical experience and networking in Oregon's legal community.

Financial data This program pays a stipend of $5.00 per hour; the employer must then at least match that stipend.

Duration 1 academic year or summer months.

Additional information The selected student is responsible for finding work under this program. The job should be in Oregon, although exceptions will be made if the job offers the student special experience not available within Oregon.

Number awarded 20 each year.

Deadline January of each year.

[1243]
OREGON STATE BAR PUBLIC HONORS PROGRAM

Oregon State Bar
Attn: Affirmative Action Program
5200 S.W. Meadows Road
P.O. Box 1689
Lake Oswego, OR 97035-0889
(503) 620-0222, ext. 337   (800) 452-8260 (within OR)
Fax: (503) 684-1366   E-mail: smanabe@osbar.org
Web: www.osbar.org

Purpose To provide minority law students in Oregon with summer work experience in public interest law.

Eligibility Qualified minority law students are nominated by faculty selection committees at Oregon's 3 law schools (Willamette, University of Oregon, and Lewis and Clark) after the completion of their first year of law school. Nominees must have demonstrated a career goal in public interest or public sector law. Each school may nominate up to 5 students. The sponsoring organization selects the top 2 students from each school on the basis of their economic disadvantage and the potential that the fellowships will help to impact their practical experience and networking in Oregon's legal community. Selected students submit a resume and cover letter to Oregon law firms that offer public interest fellowships. Prospective employers then select students for an interview.

Financial data Fellows receive a stipend of $4,800.

Duration 3 months, during the summer. There is no guarantee that all students selected by the sponsoring organization will receive fellowships at Oregon law firms.

Number awarded 6 each year.

Deadline January of each year.

[1244]
THE OREGONIAN MINORITY INTERNSHIP PROGRAM

The Oregonian
Attn: Director of Recruiting and Training
1320 S.W. Broadway
Portland, OR 97201
(503) 221-8039   Fax: (503) 294-5012
Web: www.oregonian.com/jobs

Purpose To provide work experience at *The Oregonian* in Portland to minority college graduates who are interested in a career in journalism.

Eligibility This program is open to recent college graduates who are African American, Asian American, Hispanic, American Indian, or Pacific Islander. Applicants must be committed to a career in newspapers and be interested in an internship at *The Oregonian* that combines practical experience with professional mentoring in 8 specialized areas: arts reporter/critic; business reporter; copy editor/news editor; graphic artist/page designer; local news reporter; medical/science reporter; sports reporter; or photographer/photo editor.

Financial data A competitive salary is paid.

Duration 2 years.

Additional information Midway through the second year, interns may apply for any position open on the staff of *The Oregonian;* if no opening is available, assistance is provided in finding another job.

Number awarded 3 each year.

Deadline January of each year.

[1245]
PAULINE A. YOUNG RESIDENCY

University of Delaware
Library
Attn: May Morris Director of Libraries
Newark, DE 19717-5267
(302) 831-2231   Fax: (302) 831-1046
E-mail: susanb@udel.edu
Web: www2.lib.udel.edu/personnel/brochure.htm

Purpose To provide full-time professional work experience at the University of Delaware Library to underrepresented minority and other graduates of accredited library schools.

Eligibility This program is open to recent graduates of library schools accredited by the American Library Association Applicants must be able to demonstrate strong written and oral communication skills, an interest in developing a career in academic librarianship, the ability to work independently as well as with colleagues and library users from diverse backgrounds, a willingness to learn, and a desire for professional growth. Members of underrepresented racial and ethnic groups are particularly encouraged to apply.

Financial data Compensation is at the level of assistant librarian; benefits include health coverage, dental insurance, course fee waiver, and relocation assistance.

Duration 2 years; nonrenewable.

Additional information In the first year, residents gain professional experience by rotating through several different areas of the University of Delaware Library. In the second year, they concentrate in 1 area to further specific professional goals. In addition, they are offered opportunities for committee service, specialized training, and professional workshops. Residents are eligible to apply for continuing positions at the library.

Number awarded 1 every other year.
Deadline April of each even-numbered year.

[1246]
PEDRO ZAMORA PUBLIC POLICY FELLOWSHIP
AIDS Action
1906 Sunderland Place, N.W.
Washington, DC 20036
(202) 530-8030 Fax: (202) 530-8031
E-mail: zamora@aidsaction.org
Web: www.aidsaction.org/fellowship.htm

Purpose To provide work experience at AIDS Action to undergraduate and graduate students interested in public policy.

Eligibility This program is open to undergraduate and graduate students who can demonstrate strong research, writing, and organizational skills and experience working in a professional office. Familiarity with HIV-related issues and the legislative process is preferred. Applicants must 1) describe their participation in any school or extracurricular activities related to HIV and AIDS (e.g., peer prevention programs, volunteer activities); 2) describe their participation in any school or extracurricular activities related to advocacy (e.g., lobbying, political campaigns); 3) explain why they wish to receive this fellowship; and 4) explain how they would use the skills they acquire from the fellowship. People of color, women, and HIV-positive individuals are encouraged to apply.

Financial data A stipend is provided (amount not specified).
Duration From 10 to 26 weeks.

Additional information Responsibilities include assisting in researching a variety of public health and civil rights issues related to HIV prevention, treatment, and care; attending Congressional hearings and coalition meetings; monitoring voting records; reviewing the Federal Register and Congressional Record; and preparing correspondence, mailings, and briefing materials. Fellows must commit to a minimum of 40 hours per week at AIDS Action in Washington, D.C.

Number awarded Varies each year.

[1247]
PERFORMING ARTS INITIATIVES INTERNSHIPS
Very Special Arts
Attn: Director of Human Resources
1300 Connecticut Avenue, N.W., Suite 700
Washington, DC 20036
(202) 628-2800, ext. 402 (800) 933-8721
Fax: (202) 737-0725 TTY: (202) 737-0645
E-mail: pauls@vsarts.org
Web: www.vsarts.org/info/interns/performarts.html

Purpose To provide work experience in performing arts at the Very Special Arts program of the John F. Kennedy Center for the Performing Arts.

Eligibility This program is open to students currently enrolled in a college or university who possess a good working knowledge of the performing arts (theater, dance, music). Applicants must have excellent computer and telephone skills and be able to navigate the Internet. Database management skills are also helpful. Candidates must display enthusiasm for working in a fast-paced environment that values personal initiative and teamwork. Minorities and persons with disabilities are encouraged to apply.

Financial data A stipend is paid (amount not specified).
Duration 1 semester or 1 summer.

Additional information Opportunities are available in database management and development, research and writing, program management, and web site development.
Number awarded 1 or more each year.

[1248]
PFIZER/UNCF CORPORATE SCHOLARS PROGRAM
United Negro College Fund
Attn: Corporate Scholars Program
P.O. Box 1435
Alexandria, VA 22313-9998
(866) 671-7237 E-mail: internship@uncf.org
Web: www.uncf.org/Scholarship/CorporateScholars.asp

Purpose To provide financial assistance and work experience to minority undergraduate and graduate students majoring in designated fields and interested in an internship at a Pfizer facility.

Eligibility This program is open to sophomores, juniors, graduate students, and first-year law students who are African American, Hispanic American, Asian/Pacific Islander American, or American Indian/Alaskan Native. Applicants must have a GPA of 3.0 or higher and be enrolled at an institution that is a member of the United Negro College Fund (UNCF) or at another targeted college or university. They must be pursuing 1) a bachelor's degree in animal science, business, chemistry (organic or analytical), human resources, logistics, microbiology, organizational development, operations management, pre-veterinary medicine, or supply chain management; 2) a master's degree in chemistry (organic or analytical), finance, human resources, or organizational development; or 3) a law degree. Eligibility is limited to U.S. citizens, permanent residents, asylees, refugees, and lawful temporary residents. Along with their application, they must submit a 1-page essay about themselves and their career goals, including information about their interest in Pfizer (the program's sponsor), their personal background, and any particular challenges they have faced.

Financial data The program provides an internship stipend of up to $5,000, housing accommodations near Pfizer Corporate facilities, and (based on successful internship performance) a $15,000 scholarship.
Duration 8 to 10 weeks for the internship; 1 year for the scholarship.
Additional information Opportunities for first-year law students include the summer internship only.
Number awarded Varies each year.
Deadline December of each year.

[1249]
PGA TOUR MINORITY INTERNSHIP PROGRAM
PGA Tour, Inc.
Attn: Minority Internship Program
100 PGA Tour Boulevard
Ponte Vedra Beach, FL 32082
(800) 556-5400, ext. 3520 E-mail: MIP@mail.pgatour.com
Web: www.pgatour.com

Purpose To provide summer work experience to minority undergraduate and graduate students interested in learning about the business side of golf.

Eligibility This program is open to full-time undergraduates who have completed their sophomore year and graduate students. All positions are open to men and women of African American, Asian American, Native American, and Hispanic descent.

International students are eligible if they are legally permitted to work in the United States. Although all interns work in the business side of golf, the ability to play golf or knowledge of the game is not required for most positions.

Financial data The salary is $9 per hour for a 40-hour week.

Duration 9 to 13 weeks, during the summer.

Additional information This program was established in 1992. Positions are available in communications, corporate marketing, human resources, information systems, international and domestic television, legal department, retail licensing, tournament operations, and professional services. Most assignments are in Ponte Vedra Beach, Florida.

Number awarded Varies each year; recently, 32 of these internships were provided.

Deadline March of each year.

[1250]
PHILADELPHIA DAILY NEWS INTERNSHIP

Philadelphia Daily News
Attn: New Initiatives Editor
400 North Broad Street
P.O. Box 7788
Philadelphia, PA 19101-7788
(215) 854-2000   Fax: (215) 854-5910
Web: www.phillynews.com/pdn

Purpose To provide summer work experience at the *Philadelphia Daily News* to minority college students interested in journalism as a career.

Eligibility Minority college students are eligible to apply for these internships if they have good academic records and some journalism experience. Internships are available as artists, photographers, copy editors in news or sports, and reporters in news, features, or sports.

Financial data The salary is $656 per week.

Duration Summer months.

Number awarded Varies each year.

Deadline November of each year.

[1251]
PHILADELPHIA INQUIRER MINORITY GRAPHIC ARTS INTERNSHIP

Philadelphia Inquirer
Attn: Oscar Miller, Director of Recruiting
400 North Broad Street
P.O. Box 8263
Philadelphia, PA 19101
(215) 854-5102   Fax: (215) 854-2578
E-mail: inkyjobs@phillynews.com
Web: www.philly.com/mld/philly

Purpose To provide graphic design experience during the summer at the *Philadelphia Inquirer* to minority college students interested in careers in journalism.

Eligibility Minority college students entering their sophomore, junior, or senior year in college are eligible to apply if they are interested in working in the art department at the *Philadelphia Inquirer*. Applicants should submit 5 to 7 samples of their work (published or unpublished), a resume, a cover letter, and references.

Financial data The salary is $573 per week.

Duration 10 weeks beginning in June.

Number awarded 1 each year.

Deadline November of each year.

[1252]
PHILADELPHIA INQUIRER MINORITY PHOTOJOURNALISM INTERNSHIP

Philadelphia Inquirer
Attn: Director of Photography
P.O. Box 8263
Philadelphia, PA 19101-8263
(215) 854-5045   E-mail: cmurray@phillynews.com
Web: www.philly.com/mld/philly

Purpose To provide summer work experience at the *Philadelphia Inquirer* to minority students who are interested in preparing for a career in photojournalism.

Eligibility Minorities who are fully matriculated undergraduate or graduate students with at least 1 prior internship are eligible to apply if they are interested in gaining work experience in photojournalism at the *Philadelphia Inquirer*. Applicants must submit a portfolio with up to 2 pages of slide duplicates showing creativity in news, general features, sports, and environmental portraiture. At least 1 photo essay should be included.

Financial data The salary is $647 per week.

Duration 10 weeks, during the summer.

Additional information A complete set of Nikon equipment is available for use during the internship.

Number awarded 1 each year.

Deadline November of each year.

[1253]
PNNL STUDENT RESEARCH APPRENTICESHIP PROGRAM

Pacific Northwest National Laboratory
Attn: Science Education Programs
902 Battelle Boulevard
P.O. Box 999, MS K9-83
Richland, WA 99352
(509) 375-2569   (888) 375-PNNL
E-mail: kathy.feaster@pnl.gov
Web: science-ed.pnl.gov/precollege/srap.stm

Purpose To provide an opportunity for underrepresented minority students who live within commuting distance of Pacific Northwest National Laboratory (PNNL) to work on a research project at the laboratory during the summer.

Eligibility This program is open to high school students who live within daily commuting distance of the laboratory. Applicants must be at least 16 years of age and of Hispanic, African American, or Native American ethnic origin. They must have an expressed interest in and potential for educational opportunities and careers in science, engineering, mathematics, or computer technology.

Financial data The stipend is $300 per week. Students who commute more than 50 miles each way receive a travel allowance.

Duration 8 weeks, beginning in June. Participants may reapply for a maximum of 3 summer appointments while in high school.

Additional information This program was established in 1979. Students spend 4 days a week assigned to a scientist-mentor in a specific research area. The other day is devoted to educational, career, and leadership development activities involving laboratory demonstrations, field trips, self-esteem, team building, and communications workshops.

Number awarded Varies each year.

Deadline February of each year.

[1254]
POSTBACCALAUREATE INTRAMURAL RESEARCH TRAINING AWARD FELLOWSHIP PROGRAM

National Institutes of Health
Attn: Office of Education
10 Center Drive, Room 1C129
Bethesda, MD 20892-1158
(301) 496-2427   Fax: (301) 402-0483
E-mail: dc26a@nih.gov
Web: www.training.nih.gov

Purpose To provide financial support to recent college graduates for a period of research training in the laboratories of the National Institutes of Health (NIH).

Eligibility This program is open to U.S. citizens and permanent residents who graduated from an accredited U.S. college or university within the last 12 months and plan to apply to graduate or medical school within the next year. Applicants must wish to engage in research studies under the direction of NIH preceptors and use that training to enhance their research skills. The program is particularly intended to provide early training of minorities, women, and persons with disabilities in biomedical research who need additional time to pursue application to either graduate or medical school.

Financial data The annual stipend is $17,600.

Duration 1 year; may be renewed 1 additional year.

Additional information Most NIH laboratories are located in Bethesda, Maryland. All fellows are expected to spend 40 hours per week on their training assignment.

Number awarded Varies each year.

[1255]
PPG SCHOLARSHIPS PLUS PROGRAM

American Chemical Society
Attn: Department of Diversity Programs
1155 16th Street, N.W.
Washington, DC 20036
(202) 872-6250   (800) 227-5558, ext. 6250
Fax: (202) 776-8003   E-mail: scholars@acs.org
Web: www.acs.org/scholars

Purpose To provide financial assistance and summer work experience to underrepresented minority high school seniors from designated communities who wish to pursue a career in a chemically-related science.

Eligibility This program is open to high school seniors in the following communities: Natrium and New Martinsville, West Virginia; Lake Charles, Louisiana; Pittsburgh, Pennsylvania; Shelby and Lexington, North Carolina; Oak Creek, Wisconsin; Cleveland, Ohio; and Houston, Texas. Applicants must be African American, Hispanic/Latino, or American Indian. They must plan to be full-time students pursuing a 4-year degree in either chemistry or chemical engineering. Students planning careers in medicine or pharmacy are not eligible. U.S. citizenship or permanent resident status is required. Selection is based on academic merit (GPA of 3.0 or higher) and financial need.

Financial data The maximum stipend is $2,500 per year.

Duration Up to 4 years.

Additional information In addition to scholarship support, recipients are eligible for summer research assignments at plant sites of PPG Industries (which sponsors this program) near their permanent residences. This program was first offered in 1997.

Number awarded Approximately 10 each year.

Deadline February of each year.

[1256]
PRLDEF LEGAL INTERNSHIPS

Puerto Rican Legal Defense and Education Fund
Attn: Education Division Director
99 Hudson Street, 14th Floor
New York, NY 10013-2815
(212) 219-3360, ext. 223   (800) 328-2322, ext. 223
Fax: (212) 431-4276   E-mail: education@prldef.org
Web: www.prldef.org/education.htm

Purpose To provide work experience to Latino law students interested in a summer internship with the Puerto Rican Legal Defense and Education Fund (PRLDEF).

Eligibility Eligible are law students who have completed their first or second year of study. Applicants must be able to work independently and collaboratively with a legal team and be proficient in computer skills, especially use of Westlaw and Lexis-Nexis. Selection is based on research and writing skills and demonstrated commitment to the Latino community.

Financial data This is a paid internship.

Duration 10 weeks in the summer.

Additional information Interns work closely with PRLDEF's legal staff and do research and writing in support of class action civil rights litigation. Unpaid legal internships are also available during the fall and spring semesters.

Number awarded Varies each year.

Deadline March of each year.

[1257]
PROCTER & GAMBLE RESEARCH AND PRODUCT DEVELOPMENT SUMMER PROGRAM

Procter & Gamble Company
Miami Valley Laboratories
Attn: Doctoral Recruiting Office, Box SI
11810 East Miami River Road
P.O. Box 538707
Cincinnati, OH 45253-8707
(513) 627-1035   Fax: (513) 627-2266
E-mail: doctoral.im@pg.com
Web: www.pg.com/rtci

Purpose To provide summer work experience to doctoral students who are interested in chemical or biological careers.

Eligibility Applicants must be currently enrolled in graduate school or in the senior year of undergraduate study planning to enter graduate school in the fall to work on a Ph.D. in chemical engineering, chemistry, most areas of the life sciences, statistics, toxicology, and regulatory and clinical personnel. U.S. citizenship or permanent resident status is required. Positions are also available to students currently studying or planning to study for a Pharm.D., M.D., D.V.M., or D.D.S. degree. These internships are intended for students who plan to pursue careers as research associates in research and product development. Special consideration is given to applications from underrepresented minority (African American, Hispanic/Latino, Native American) students.

Financial data   Interns receive competitive salaries, depending of their year in school and field of study. Procter & Gamble pays round-trip airfare between school or home and Cincinnati as well as local transportation between university housing and the work site.

Duration   10 to 12 weeks, beginning in June.

Additional information   Interns engage in full-time research at 1 of Procter & Gamble's 4 corporate technical centers in Cincinnati.

Number awarded   15 to 20 each year.

Deadline   February of each year.

[1258]
PROFESSIONAL DEVELOPMENT FELLOWSHIPS FOR ARTISTS AND ART HISTORIANS

College Art Association of America
Attn: Fellowship Program
275 Seventh Avenue
New York, NY 10001-6798
(212) 691-1051, ext. 206   Fax: (212) 627-2381
E-mail: fellowship@collegeart.org
Web: www.collegeart.org/caa/career/fellowship.html

Purpose   To provide financial assistance and work experience to artists or art historians from culturally diverse backgrounds who are completing graduate degrees.

Eligibility   This program is open to artists or art historians who have been underrepresented in the field because of their race, religion, gender, age, national origin, sexual orientation, disability, or history of economic disadvantage. Applicants must be U.S. citizens or permanent residents and able to demonstrate financial need. They must expect to receive the M.F.A., terminal M.A., or Ph.D. degree in the year following application.

Financial data   The stipend is $5,000 per year.

Duration   2 years: the final year of their degree program and the first year following completion of their degree.

Additional information   In addition to receiving a stipend for the terminal year of their degree program, fellows participate in an internship during the year following graduation. The College Art Association helps fellows secure internships at museums, art centers, colleges, or universities and subsidizes part of their salaries. In addition to administrative and/or teaching responsibilities, all fellows' positions must include a curatorial component. Salaries and terms of employment are determined in consultation with each fellow and potential host institution.

Number awarded   Varies each year.

Deadline   January of each year.

[1259]
PUBLIC INTEREST FELLOWSHIP

Alliance for Justice
11 Dupont Circle, N.W., Second Floor
Washington, DC 20036
(202) 822-6070   Fax: (202) 822-6068
E-mail: alliance@afj.org
Web: www.afj.org

Purpose   To provide work experience in public interest law to recent law school graduates.

Eligibility   Candidates must have completed their law degree and possess excellent research, writing, and oral communication skills. They must be interested in working on public interest law at the Alliance for Justice in Washington, D.C. People of color are strongly encouraged to apply. Interested lawyers should send a cover letter, resume, writing sample, transcript, and references.

Financial data   The stipend is $30,000 per year, plus benefits.

Duration   1 year, beginning in September.

Additional information   The Alliance for Justice is a national association of environment, civil rights, women's rights, consumer, and other nonprofit advocacy organizations. Projects for fellows include researching records of judicial nominees, providing technical assistance on laws governing nonprofit advocacy, organizing national conferences to promote interest in public interest law, analyzing legal issues affecting the public interest community, and assisting in lobbying.

Number awarded   2 each year.

Deadline   December of each year

[1260]
PUBLIC INTEREST FELLOWSHIP COMPETITION

San Francisco La Raza Lawyers Association
Attn: Scholarship Committee Chair
P.O. Box 192241
San Francisco, CA 94119-2241
E-mail: Vargumedo@yahoo.com
Web: www.larazalawyers.org

Purpose   To provide summer work experience to law students at nonprofit organizations serving the Latino community in the San Francisco Bay area.

Eligibility   This program is open to law students interested in summer employment with San Francisco Bay area nonprofit organizations serving the Latino community. Applicants must submit 1) the name, address, and telephone number of the community-based legal services provider where they plan to work; 2) a description of legal services to be provided, population to be served, and project objective; 3) a narrative describing their qualifications, statement of need, and anticipated length of the project; and 4) letters in support of their project. Proposals should address at least 1 of the following objectives: projects to develop or expand legal services in the areas of housing, employment, discrimination, immigration, and naturalization; projects to develop materials and training to educate the Latino community about their legal rights and to facilitate their access to the justice system and the courts; and projects providing training, referral, recruitment, and mentoring to law students. Personal interviews are conducted.

Financial data   The stipend is $2,500.

Duration   Summer months.

Number awarded   Varies each year.

Deadline   April of each year.

[1261]
PUERTO RICO LOUIS STOKES ALLIANCE FOR MINORITY PARTICIPATION UNDERGRADUATE RESEARCH STIPENDS

Puerto Rico Louis Stokes Alliance for Minority Participation
c/o University of Puerto Rico at Rio Piedras
Facundo Bueso Building, Office 304
P.O. Box 23334 University Station
San Juan, PR 00931-3334
(787) 764-0000, ext. 5801   Fax: (787) 766-1293
E-mail: a_feliciano@acupr1.upr.clu.edu
Web: www.prlsamp.org

Purpose To provide an opportunity to participate in research projects to students in Puerto Rico studying science, mathematics, engineering, and technology as part of the Puerto Rico Louis Stokes Alliance for Minority Participation (PR-LSAMP).

Eligibility This program is open to undergraduate students at universities in Puerto Rico that participate in the alliance. Applicants must be majoring in such fields as biology, chemistry, physics, engineering, geology, agricultural science, or environmental sciences. They must be interested in participating in a research project at a local or national university or laboratory. Selection is based on financial need and academic performance. Preference is given to students who are both low-income and first-generation college students.

Financial data Stipends range from $500 to $2,000 per year, depending on the need of the recipient.

Duration Recipients participate in research projects during the academic year or summer.

Additional information The PR-LSAMP was established in 1991 with funding from the National Science Foundation.

Number awarded Approximately 300 each year.

[1262]
QEM NETWORK INTERNSHIPS

Quality Education for Minorities (QEM) Network
1818 N Street, N.W., Suite 350
Washington, DC 20036
(202) 659-1818   Fax: (202) 659-5408
E-mail: qemnetwork@qem.org
Web: qemnetwork.qem.org

Purpose To provide underrepresented minority students with an opportunity to work at Quality Education for Minorities (QEM) during the summer to further develop their leadership potential and to enhance their awareness of major issues related to the education of minorities.

Eligibility This program is open to African Americans, Alaska Natives, American Indians, Mexican Americans, and Puerto Ricans who have successfully completed at least the sophomore year in an accredited, degree-granting institution. Applicants must be interested in 1) working on a post-baccalaureate degree; 2) assuming a leadership role at their college/university; and 3) participating in community activities to influence national, state, or local policy as it relates to the education of minorities. They must be interested in working with the staff at the QEM Network, in federal agencies, or on Capitol Hill. Applicants may be studying in any area, but preference is given to majors in computer science, economics, education, engineering, life or physical sciences, mathematics, political science, or public policy.

Financial data The stipend is $3,000 for undergraduates and $4,000 for graduate students. Other benefits include round-trip airfare between home or school and Washington, D.C. and hous-ing for all interns who are not from the Washington, D.C. metropolitan area.

Duration 10 weeks, during the summer.

Additional information Assignments may involve community outreach, parent/youth leadership development, program planning and evaluation, education policy analysis, data collection and analysis, network communications, and the preparation of background papers on major education issues and their implications for the education of minorities. Interns are also expected to become involved in an academic year project at their home institutions. Each intern must identify a faculty advisor and define a specific project that provides quality educational experiences for low-income minority students; interns prepare a written description of the follow-up project, an interim progress report, and a final report on the outcome of the project.

Number awarded Varies each year.

Deadline January of each year.

[1263]
QEM SCIENCE STUDENT INTERNSHIPS

Quality Education for Minorities (QEM) Network
1818 N Street, N.W., Suite 350
Washington, DC 20036
(202) 659-1818   Fax: (202) 659-5408
E-mail: qemnetwork@qem.org
Web: qemnetwork.qem.org

Purpose To provide underrepresented minority students with an opportunity to work during the summer with agencies and organizations involved in making science policy.

Eligibility This program is open to African Americans, Alaska Natives, American Indians, Mexican Americans, and Puerto Ricans who have successfully completed at least the sophomore year in an accredited, degree-granting institution. Applicants must be 1) working on a graduate or undergraduate degree in a mathematics, science (life or physical sciences, political science, or computer science), or engineering field; 2) interested in increasing and affecting the public's understanding of mathematics, science, and engineering issues; and 3) concerned about influencing science-oriented public policy at the national, state, and local levels. U.S. citizenship is required.

Financial data The stipend is $3,000 for undergraduates and $4,000 for graduate students. Other benefits include round-trip airfare between home or school and Washington, D.C. and housing for all interns who are not from the Washington, D.C. metropolitan area.

Duration 10 weeks, during the summer.

Additional information Past assignments have included work in the National Science Foundation, the National Aeronautics and Space Administration, the Smithsonian Institution, the Environmental Protection Agency, and the mathematics, science, and engineering component of the Quality Education for Minorities (QEM) Network. Interns are also expected to become involved in an academic year project at their home institutions. Each intern must identify a faculty advisor and define a specific project that provides quality educational experiences for low-income minority students; interns prepare a written description of the follow-up project, an interim progress report, and a final report on the outcome of the project.

Number awarded Varies each year.

Deadline January of each year.

[1264]
RECORD-JOURNAL MINORITY INTERNSHIP/SCHOLARSHIP

Record-Journal
Attn: Executive Editor
11 Crown Street
Meriden, CT 06450
(203) 317-2370   E-mail: jsmith@record-journal.com
Web: www.record-journal.com

Purpose To provide financial assistance and summer work experience to minority residents of Connecticut interested in a career in journalism.

Eligibility This program is open to minority residents of Connecticut who live within the circulation area of the *Record-Journal.* Applicants must be high school seniors or college students majoring in journalism or a related field and planning to pursue a career in the field. They must submit a completed application, transcripts, an essay, and documentation of financial need.

Financial data The scholarship stipend is $1,500 per year. The program includes an internship at the *Record-Journal,* usually during the summer, that pays up to $3,500.

Duration 1 year; may be renewed up to 3 additional years.

Additional information Recipients are urged to work at the *Record-Journal* after graduation.

Number awarded 1 each year.

Deadline January of each year.

[1265]
RESEARCH AND ENGINEERING APPRENTICESHIP PROGRAM (REAP) FOR HIGH SCHOOL STUDENTS

Academy of Applied Science
1 Maple Street
Concord, NH 03301
(603) 228-0121   Fax: (603) 228-0210
Web: www.aas-world.org/youth_science/reap.html

Purpose To provide an opportunity for disadvantaged high school students to engage in a research apprenticeship in mathematics, science, or technology during the summer.

Eligibility Applicants must be economically and socially disadvantaged high school students who have an interest in mathematics, science, or technology. Recipients are selected on the basis of previously demonstrated abilities and interest in science, mathematics, and technology; potential for a successful career in the field as indicated from overall scholastic achievement, aptitude, and interest areas; recommendations of high school teachers and administrators; and an interview.

Financial data Interns receive a salary in accordance with student minimum wage guidelines.

Duration Summer months.

Additional information The program provides intensive summer training for high school students in the laboratories of scientists. The program, established in 1980, is funded by a grant from the U.S. Army Research Office. Students must live at home while they participate in the program and must live in the area where an approved professor lives. The program does not exist in every state.

Number awarded Varies; recently, approximately 120 students were funded at 52 colleges and universities nationwide.

Deadline February of each year.

[1266]
RESOURCES FOR THE FUTURE SUMMER INTERNSHIPS

Resources for the Future
Attn: Coordinator for Academic Programs
1616 P Street, N.W.
Washington, DC 20036-1400
(202) 328-5060   Fax: (202) 939-3460
E-mail: mankin@rff.org
Web: www.rff.org

Purpose To provide internships to graduate students interested in working on research projects in public policy during the summer.

Eligibility Candidates must be in their first or second year of graduate training, with skills in microeconomics, quantitative methods, or occasionally other social and natural sciences. Outstanding undergraduates may also be eligible. Applicants must be interested in spending an internship in Washington, D.C. in 1 of the divisions of Resources for the Future (RFF): Center for Risk Management, Energy and Natural Resources, or Quality of the Environment. Applicants must be able to work without supervision in a careful and conscientious manner. Women and minority candidates are strongly encouraged to apply. Both U.S. and non-U.S. citizens are eligible, if the latter have proper work and residency documentation.

Financial data The stipend is $375 per week for graduate students or $350 per week for undergraduates.

Duration Summer months; beginning and ending dates can be adjusted to meet particular student needs.

Additional information Interns assist in research projects in complex public policy problems amenable to interdisciplinary analysis, often drawing heavily on economics. Further information on the Center for Risk Management is available from Marilyn Voigt at (202) 328-5077, Fax: (202) 939-3460, E-mail: voigt@rff.org; on Energy and Natural Resources and on Quality of the Environment from John Mankin at (202) 328-5060, Fax: (202) 939-3460, E-mail: mankin@rff.org.

Deadline March of each year.

[1267]
RETAIL MANAGEMENT INSTITUTE INTERNSHIPS

INROADS, Inc.
10 South Broadway, Suite 700
St. Louis, MO 63102
(314) 241-7488   Fax: (314) 241-9325
E-mail: info@inroads.org
Web: www.inroads.org

Purpose To provide an opportunity for young people of color to gain work experience in retailing.

Eligibility Eligible to apply are African Americans, Hispanics, and Native Americans who reside in the areas served by INROADS and wish to prepare for careers in department stores, mass merchant discount stores, specialty stores, consumer electronic stores, supermarkets, or ready-to-wear specialty stores. Applicants must be high school seniors or freshmen or sophomores in accredited 2- or 4-year colleges or universities with a GPA of 2.5 or higher. Students attending a 2-year college must intend to transfer to a 4-year college or university. Some applicants may be asked to take the Retail Readiness Assessment test and achieve a score within the 40 to 60 point range. All applicants must be permanent residents of the United States. Along with their application, they must submit official transcripts, a resume,

SAT or ACT scores (for high school seniors and first-semester college students), and a 250-word essay on why this internship is right for them.

Financial data Salaries vary, depending upon the specific internship assigned.

Duration Up to 4 years.

Additional information INROADS places interns in companies where they receive the necessary pre-professional training and experience to launch a career as a manager of a department, store, district, or chain of stores. The INROADS organization offers internship opportunities through 48 local affiliates in 32 states and the District of Columbia.

Number awarded Varies each year.

[1268]
ROCK HILL HERALD INTERNSHIP PROGRAM

Rock Hill Herald
Attn: Managing Editor
132 West Main Street
P.O. Box 11707
Rock Hill, SC 29731
(803) 329-4060   Fax: (803) 329-4021
E-mail: rrassmann@heraldonline.com

Purpose To provide summer work experience at the *Rock Hill Herald* in South Carolina to minority college students interested in careers in journalism.

Eligibility This program is designed for minority college students, preferably juniors or seniors, but recent graduates may be considered. Applicants must be planning to pursue careers in newspaper reporting, editing, or photography. They must be interested in interning at the *Rock Hill Herald.*

Financial data The salary is at least $250 per week.

Duration 10 weeks, during the summer.

Additional information This program is funded through McClatchy Company and the National Association of Black Journalists.

Number awarded 1 each year.

Deadline January of each year.

[1269]
ROSWELL L. GILPATRIC INTERNSHIP

Metropolitan Museum of Art
Attn: Internship Programs
1000 Fifth Avenue
New York, NY 10028-0198
(212) 570-3710   Fax: (212) 570-3782
Web: www.metmuseum.org/education/er_internship.asp

Purpose To provide work experience at the Metropolitan Museum of Art during the summer to students interested in a museum career.

Eligibility This internship is available to college juniors, seniors, recent graduates, and graduate students who show a special interest in pursuing a museum career. Applicants of diverse backgrounds (e.g., minorities) are especially encouraged to apply.

Financial data The honorarium is $3,000 for undergraduate students and recent graduates or $3,250 for graduate students.

Duration 10 weeks, beginning in June.

Additional information Interns are assigned to departmental projects (curatorial, administration, or education) at the Metropolitan Museum of Art; other assignments may include giving gallery talks and working at the Visitor Information Center. The assign-

ment is for 35 hours a week. The internships are funded in part by the Thorne Foundation.

Number awarded 1 each year.

Deadline January of each year.

[1270]
RUTH CHANCE LAW FELLOWSHIP

Equal Rights Advocates, Inc.
1663 Mission Street, Suite 250
San Francisco, CA 94103
(415) 621-0672   Fax: (415) 621-6744
Web: www.equalrights.org

Purpose To provide work experience at Equal Rights Advocates (ERA) to law school students and recent graduates who are interested in working for the equal rights of women.

Eligibility Applicants for these ERA internships should be third-year law students or recent graduates who are committed to improving the condition of women and women of color. Selection is based on knowledge of and commitment to women's rights and legal issues affecting women, knowledge of and commitment to civil rights and legal issues affecting people of color, ability to work independently, demonstrated commitment and involvement with community concerns, oral and written communication skills, and ability to juggle many and varied tasks. Persons of color and/or bilingual/bicultural individuals are encouraged to apply.

Financial data The annual salary is $32,500; benefits are also provided.

Duration 1 year, beginning in September.

Additional information Equal Rights Advocates is a nonprofit, public interest law firm that is dedicated to combating the disenfranchisement of women, particularly low-income and minority women. The responsibilities of the fellow include overseeing and coordinating an advice and counseling program, assisting staff attorneys with ongoing litigation, and participating in the firm's public policy and education activities.

Number awarded 1 each year.

Deadline January of each year.

[1271]
SACNAS–IBM UNDERGRADUATE RESEARCH SCHOLARSHIP

Society for Advancement of Chicanos and Native Americans
   in Science
333 Front Street, Suite 104
P.O. Box 8526
Santa Cruz, CA 95061-8526
(831) 459-0170   Fax: (831) 459-0194
E-mail: info@sacnas.org
Web: www.sacnas.org

Purpose To provide financial assistance and summer work experience to Native American and Chicano/Latino students majoring in physical science, computer science, or engineering.

Eligibility This program is open to Chicano/Latino and Native American undergraduate students who are currently completing their sophomore or junior years. Applicants must be majoring in chemistry, physics, material science, computer science, or a related engineering field. They must be able to participate in a summer research institute at IBM's Almaden Research Center in San Jose, California.

Financial data The award is $2,500. During the internship period, a stipend is paid.

Duration 1 year, plus a 10-week internship.
Number awarded 1 each year.
Deadline July of each year.

[1272]
SAN ANGELO STANDARD-TIMES INTERNSHIP

San Angelo Standard-Times
Attn: Projects Editor
34 West Harris Avenue
P.O. Box 5111
San Angelo, TX 76902
(915) 653-1221   (800) 588-1884
Fax: (915) 658-6192   E-mail: standard@texaswest.com
Web: www.gosanangelo.com

Purpose To provide summer work experience at the *San Angelo Standard-Times* in Texas during the summer to students who are interested in preparing for a career in journalism.

Eligibility College students who are majoring in journalism are eligible to apply. Preference is given to rising juniors or seniors. Applicants may be from any state. Applications from minority students are encouraged.

Financial data The stipend is at least $250 per week.

Duration 10 weeks, during the summer.

Additional information Interns work in news/editorial.

Number awarded 1 or 2 each year.

Deadline January of each year.

[1273]
SCA DIVERSITY FELLOWSHIP PROGRAM

Student Conservation Association, Inc.
Attn: College Diversity Program
1800 North Kent Street, Suite 102
Arlington, VA 22209
(703) 524-2441   Fax: (703) 524-2451
E-mail: internships@sca-inc.org
Web: www.sca-inc.org/vol/ccdc/ccdcfp.htm

Purpose To provide work experience during the summer to women and students of color at private, nonprofit, state, and federal agencies involved in conservation.

Eligibility This program provides summer internships through cooperating federal, state, private, and nonprofit agencies. It is open to currently-enrolled students who have completed at least the freshman year of college with a GPA of 2.5 or higher. U.S. citizenship or permanent resident status is required. Although all students may apply, the program is designed to allow ethnically diverse and female college students, traditionally underrepresented in the conservation field, to experience the type of careers available to them. Possible placements include interpretation and environmental education; backcountry patrol; recreation management; archival and museum studies; archaeological surveys; cave studies; historical/cultural resource studies; landscape architecture and planning; biological research and monitoring; and wildlife, forestry, and fisheries management.

Financial data The stipend is $100 per week. Participants are also eligible for education awards of $1,500 to $3,000 upon completion of all fellowship requirements. Housing is provided at no cost or through an allotment. Other benefits include a pre-term orientation, transportation to the orientation and the work site, worker's compensation, and accident insurance.

Duration 12 weeks during the summer.

Additional information While participating in the fellowship, students engage in ongoing career counseling, mentoring, personal and career development services, and additional training by the professional staff at each host site. Recently, available positions included Golden Gate National Recreation Area (California), Mammoth Cave National Park (Kentucky), Arlingtonians for a Clean Environment (Virginia), Dinosaur National Monument (Colorado), Lassen National Park (California), and Kenai Fjords National Park (Alaska).

Number awarded Varies each year.

Deadline February of each year.

[1274]
SCIENCE AND ENGINEERING APPRENTICE PROGRAM

George Washington University
Attn: Science and Engineering Apprentice Program
1776 G Street, N.W., Suite 771
Washington, DC 20052
(202) 994-2234   E-mail: seap@gwu.edu
Web: www.gwseap.net

Purpose To provide an opportunity for high school students (especially women, African Americans, and Hispanics) to work during the summer on research projects at selected Department of Defense laboratories.

Eligibility This program is open to high school students interested in careers in science and engineering. A goal of the program is to encourage women, African Americans, and Hispanics to expand their interest in science and engineering careers. Applicants must submit a 1-page statement on their personal goals and why they want to participate in a research project at a Department of Defense laboratory, 1 or 2 letters of recommendation, and a transcript. Most laboratories require U.S. citizenship, although some accept permanent residents. In a few laboratories, security clearance is required. Selection is based on grades, science and mathematics courses taken, scores on national standardized tests, areas of interest, teacher recommendations, and the personal statement.

Financial data The stipend is at least $1,400. Students are responsible for transportation to and from the laboratory site.

Duration 8 weeks, during the summer.

Additional information Funding for this program is provided by the U.S. Department of Defense. Most of the participating laboratories are in the national capital area (including Washington, D.C.; Bethesda, Maryland; Fort Belvoir, Virginia; Alexandria, Virginia; Edgewood, Maryland; Adelphi, Maryland; Aberdeen Proving Ground, Maryland; Quantico, Virginia; Patuxent River, Maryland; Silver Spring, Maryland; Carderock, Maryland; Dahlgren, Virginia; Indian Head, Maryland, and Annapolis, Maryland), Others are in Redstone Arsenal, Alabama; Fort Monmouth, New Jersey; Fort McPherson, Georgia; Natick, Massachusetts; Rock Island, Illinois; Stennis Space Center, Mississippi; Philadelphia, Pennsylvania; and Newport, Rhode Island. In addition, openings are available at defense contractors in Huntsville, Alabama and Arlington, Virginia.

Number awarded Varies each year.

Deadline January of each year.

[1275]

SCMRE GRADUATE ARCHIVAL CONSERVATION INTERNSHIP

Smithsonian Center for Materials Research and Education
Attn: Archives Fellowship and Internship Program
Museum Support Center
4210 Silver Hill Road
Suitland, MD 20746-2863
(301) 238-3700, ext. 147   Fax: (301) 238-3709
E-mail: vanderreyden@scmre.si.edu
Web: www.si.edu/scmre/educationoutreach/internship.htm

Purpose To provide training at the Smithsonian Center for Materials Research and Education (SCMRE) and other Smithsonian facilities to graduate students interested in preservation of archival materials.

Eligibility This program is open to graduate students entering the internship year in a conservation training program or the equivalent with an emphasis on preservation of archival materials. Applicants must be interested in working at SCMRE and with collections in the Smithsonian Institution, undertaking surveys, designing and carrying out rehousing projects, participating in and learning to organize training workshops, initiating training projects for collections managers, and carrying out research. Along with their application, they must submit a statement of expectations for the internship and a curriculum vitae, including references. Minorities are particularly encouraged to apply.

Financial data The stipend is $14,000. An additional $2,000 for travel and research is available. Health insurance can be provided for those without personal coverage.

Duration 1 year.

Number awarded 1 each year.

Deadline February of each year.

[1276]

SCMRE GRADUATE RESEARCH INTERNSHIPS

Smithsonian Center for Materials Research and Education
Attn: Coordinator of Research and Education
Museum Support Center
4210 Silver Hill Road
Suitland, MD 20746-2863
(301) 238-3700, ext. 121   Fax: (301) 238-3709
E-mail: bishopr@scmre.si.edu
Web: www.si.edu/scmre/educationoutreach/internship.htm

Purpose To provide funding to graduate students interested in gaining research experience at the Smithsonian Center for Materials Research and Education (SCMRE).

Eligibility This program is open to graduate students interested in working in an area of SCMRE research programming activity: biogeochemistry; characterizing and preserving natural history collections, photographic materials, and modern materials; preservation science; analysis and characterization of archaeological materials; and conservation treatment and development. Applicants must submit a resume (including transcripts), a statement of experience and intent, and references. Minorities are especially encouraged to apply.

Financial data The stipend is $14,000. Other benefits include a $2,000 travel allowance and health insurance.

Duration 1 year.

Number awarded Varies each year.

Deadline February of each year.

[1277]

SCOTTS COMPANY SCHOLARS PROGRAM

Golf Course Superintendents Association of America
Attn: Scholarship Coordinator
1421 Research Park Drive
Lawrence, KS 66049-3859
(785) 832-3678   (800) 472-7878, ext. 678
E-mail: psmith@gcsaa.org
Web: www.gcsaa.org

Purpose To provide financial assistance and summer work experience to high school seniors and college students, particularly those from diverse backgrounds, who are preparing for a career in golf management.

Eligibility This program is open to high school seniors and college students (freshmen, sophomores, and juniors) who are interested in preparing for a career in golf management (the "green industry"). Women and candidates from diverse ethnic, cultural, and socio-economic backgrounds are particularly considered. Selection is based on cultural diversity, academic achievement, extracurricular activities, leadership, employment potential, essay responses, and letters of recommendation. Financial need is not considered. Finalists are selected for summer internships and then compete for scholarships.

Financial data Each intern receives a $500 award. Scholarship stipends are $2,500.

Duration 1 year.

Additional information The program is funded by a permanent endowment established by Scotts Company. Finalists are responsible for securing their own internships.

Number awarded 5 interns and 2 scholarship winners are selected each year.

Deadline February of each year.

[1278]

SENATOR GREGORY LUNA MEMORIAL LEGISLATIVE SCHOLARS PROGRAM

Senate Hispanic Research Council, Inc.
815-A Brazos
PMB 147
Austin, TX 78701
(512) 499-8606   Fax: (512) 499-8607
E-mail: SHRC@sbcglobal.net
Web: www.tshrc.org/luna.html

Purpose To provide Hispanic undergraduate and graduate students at colleges and universities in Texas with an opportunity to gain work experience at the Texas Senate.

Eligibility This program is open to undergraduate and graduate students who have completed at least 60 semester hours at an accredited 2- or 4-year educational institution in Texas; recent graduates are also eligible. Applicants must demonstrate leadership potential, academic achievement (preference is given to applicants with a GPA of 2.75 or higher), excellent writing and composition skills, and an interest in government, public policy, and Mexican American issues. They should be interested in a career in law, political science, public policy, or communications. Along with their application, they must submit a personal statement on the experiences or activities that led to their interest in government and this internship program, a sample of their best-written work completed for school, and a letter of recommendation.

Financial data Interns receive a stipend sufficient to cover the expense of living and working in Austin.

Duration　Approximately 5 months, during the term of the Texas Senate, beginning in mid-January.

Additional information　This program began in 2002. Interns are assigned to the office of a state senator to perform a variety of legislative tasks, including drafting legislation, floor statements, articles, press releases, legislative research summaries, and hearing agendas. The Senate Hispanic Research Council was established in 1993 to provide educational and leadership opportunities to all segments of the Hispanic community in Texas.

Number awarded　Varies each year; recently, positions were available for 14 interns (11 undergraduates and 3 graduate students).

Deadline　November of each year.

[1279]
SEO CAREER PROGRAM

Sponsors for Educational Opportunity
Attn: Career Program
23 Gramercy Park South
New York, NY 10003
(212) 979-2040　　　E-mail: careerprogram@seo-ny.org
Web: www.seo-ny.org

Purpose　To provide work experience during the summer in selected fields to undergraduate students of color.

Eligibility　This program is open to undergraduate students of color at colleges and universities in the United States. Applicants must be interested in a summer internship in 1 of the following 8 fields: accounting, asset management, corporate law, information technology, investment banking, management consulting, media, or philanthropy. Along with their application, they must submit an essay in which they 1) explain their interest in the field to which they have chosen to apply; 2) comment on their interest in this internship in particular; and 3) elaborate on how relevant work experience, community service, extracurricular activities, and/or course work have influenced their decision to apply.

Financial data　Competitive salaries are offered.

Duration　Summer months.

Additional information　This program was established in 1980.

Number awarded　Varies each year; recently, 275 internships were offered to students at 77 colleges and universities.

Deadline　February of each year.

[1280]
SHELL LEGISLATIVE INTERNSHIP PROGRAM

National Association of Latino Elected and Appointed
　　Officials
Attn: Internship Coordinator
5800 South Eastern Avenue, Suite 365
Los Angeles, CA 90040-4020
(323) 720-1932, ext. 122　　　　　(800) 34-NALEO
Fax: (323) 720-9519　　　E-mail: ecastillo@naleo.org
Web: www.naleo.org/TTA/slip.htm

Purpose　To provide Latino college students from selected states with an opportunity to work with an elected or appointed official from their home state during the summer.

Eligibility　Applicants must be residents of Arizona, California, Colorado, Florida, Illinois, New Mexico, New York, or Texas (but need not attend college in those states), be currently enrolled in an accredited 4-year institution as a junior or senior, be U.S. citizens or legal permanent residents, be of Latino origin, demon-

strate leadership potential, and possess a sense of commitment to the Latino community.

Financial data　Interns receive transportation, meals, and housing to participate in the annual conference; transportation and housing during their week in Washington, D.C.; and a stipend of $1,500 for the internship in their home state.

Duration　4 weeks during the summer, beginning in June.

Additional information　Interns attend the annual conference of the National Association of Latino Elected and Appointed Officials (NALEO), where they meet and network with Latinos who are involved in leadership positions at the municipal, state, federal, and nonprofit levels; experience 1 week in Washington D.C. with federal elected and appointed officials, White House staff, and congressional staffers; and spend the rest of the time working with a Latino elected or appointed official in their home state. Funding for this program is provided by the Shell Oil Company.

Number awarded　14 each year.

Deadline　March of each year.

[1281]
SIGNIFICANT OPPORTUNITIES IN ATMOSPHERIC RESEARCH AND SCIENCE (SOARS) PROGRAM

University Corporation for Atmospheric Research
Attn: SOARS Program Manager
P.O. Box 3000
Boulder, CO 80307-3000
(303) 497-8623　　　　　　　　Fax: (303) 497-8552
E-mail: soars@ucar.edu
Web: www.ucar.edu/soars

Purpose　To provide summer work experience to underrepresented minority undergraduate or graduate students who are interested in preparing for a career in atmospheric or a related science.

Eligibility　Student applicants must 1) be U.S. citizens or permanent residents; 2) be Hispanic/Latino, American Indian/Alaska Native, or African American; 3) have completed their sophomore year of college by the time the internship begins; 4) be majoring in atmospheric science or a related field such as biology, chemistry, computer science, earth science, engineering, environmental science, the geosciences, mathematics, meteorology, oceanography, physics, or social science; 5) have a GPA of 3.0 or higher; and 6) plan to pursue a career in the field of atmospheric or a related science. Along with their application, they must submit an essay on their academic plans, career interests and objectives, community involvement, and significant events or experiences that have influenced their life. The essay is the most important part of the application.

Financial data　Participants receive a competitive stipend and a housing allowance. Round-trip travel between Boulder and any 1 location within the continental United States is also provided. Students who are accepted into a graduate-level program receive full scholarships (with SOARS and the participating universities each sharing the costs).

Duration　10 weeks, during the summer. Students are encouraged to continue for 4 subsequent summers.

Additional information　This program began in 1996. Students are assigned positions with a research project. They are exposed to the research facilities at the National Center for Atmospheric Research (NCAR), including computers, libraries, laboratories, and aircraft. NCAR is operated by the University Corporation for Atmospheric Research (a consortium of 40 universities) and sponsored by the National Science Foundation, the Department of Energy, the National Aeronautics and Space Administration, and the National Oceanic and Atmospheric Administration. Before completing their senior years, students are encouraged to apply to a master's or doctoral degree program at 1 of the participating universities.

Number awarded At least 12 each year.

Deadline February of each year.

[1282]
SMITHSONIAN MINORITY STUDENT INTERNSHIP

Smithsonian Institution
Attn: Office of Fellowships
Victor Building, Suite 9300, MRC 902
P.O. Box 37012
Washington, DC 20013-7012
(202) 275-0655   Fax: (202) 275-0489
E-mail: siofg@si.edu
Web: www.si.edu/ofg/intern.htm

Purpose To provide minority undergraduate or graduate students with the opportunity to work on research or museum procedure projects in specific areas of history, art, or science at the Smithsonian Institution.

Eligibility Internships are offered to minority students who are actively engaged in graduate study at any level or in upper-division undergraduate study. An overall GPA of 3.0 or higher is generally expected. Applicants must be interested in conducting research or working on museum projects in history, art, or science at the institution.

Financial data The program provides a stipend of $350 per week; travel allowances may also be offered.

Duration 10 weeks during the summer or academic year.

Number awarded Varies each year.

Deadline January of each year for summer; June of each year for fall; October of each year for spring.

[1283]
SNPA MINORITY INTERNSHIP PROGRAM

Southern Newspaper Publishers Association
Attn: Foundation
P.O. Box 28875
Atlanta, GA 30358
(404) 256-0444   Fax: (404) 252-9135
E-mail: shannon@snpa.org
Web: www.snpa.org/NF/omf/snpa/interns.html

Purpose To provide an opportunity for minority undergraduates to intern at newspapers that are members of the Southern Newspaper Publishers Association (SNPA) during the summer.

Eligibility This program is open to African American, Hispanic, Native American, and Asian American students who are completing their sophomore year in college or a master's degree. Applicants must be nominated by the SNPA member newspaper where they wish to work. Preference is given to applicants who intend to pursue a career in newspapers, although they do not have to be journalism majors. Along with their application, they must submit a resume that includes part-time and full-time jobs, college transcripts, letter of recommendation from college advisor or major department chair, up to 5 samples of newspaper work, list of college activities and any scholarships or awards received, and a 1-page statement on why they are interested in a newspaper career.

Financial data Newspapers receive $2,500 to be used for the salary of the intern; any expenses in excess of that amount are to be incurred by the newspaper.

Duration 9 weeks, during the summer.

Number awarded 1 each year.

Deadline Nominations must be submitted by March of each year.

[1284]
SPORTS JOURNALISM INSTITUTE

National Association of Black Journalists
Attn: Student Education Enrichment and Development
  Program
8701-A Adelphi Road
Adelphi, MD 20783-1716
(301) 445-7100, ext. 108   Fax: (301) 445-7101
E-mail: warren@nabj.org
Web: www.nabj.org

Purpose To provide student journalists (especially those of color) with an opportunity to learn more about sports journalism during the summer.

Eligibility This program is open to college juniors and sophomores, especially members of ethnic and racial minority groups. Applicants must be interested in participating in a summer program that includes a crash course in sports journalism followed by an internship in the sports department of a daily newspaper. They must submit a current college transcript, 2 letters of recommendation, up to 7 writing samples or clips, and an essay of up to 500 words stating why they should be chosen to participate in the program. Selection is based on academic achievement, demonstrated interest in sports journalism as a career, and the essay. Eligibility is not limited to journalism majors.

Financial data All expenses are paid during the crash course segment. A salary is paid during the internship portion. At the conclusion of the program, participants receive a $500 scholarship for the following year of college.

Duration 10 days for the crash course (at the end of June); 7 weeks for the internship (July through mid-August).

Additional information The crash course takes place during the annual convention of the Associated Press Sports Editors (ASPE), which sponsors this program.

Number awarded 10 each year.

Deadline December of each year.

[1285]
ST. PAUL PIONEER PRESS MINORITY INTERNSHIPS

St. Paul Pioneer Press
Attn: Ruben Rosario
345 Cedar Street
St. Paul, MN 55101-1057
(651) 228-5454   (800) 950-9080, ext. 5454
E-mail: rrosario@pioneerpress.com

Purpose To provide summer work experience at the *St. Paul Pioneer Press* to minority college students interested in journalism as a career.

Eligibility This program at the *Pioneer Press* is open to members of minority groups who are college seniors, journalism school graduates, or postgraduate students. Previous journalism intern experience is preferred, but potential, creativity, and a passion for journalism are essential. Applicants must submit a resume, cover letter, 6 to 8 samples of published work (or published slides for photography candidates), names and contact info for 3 references, and a 2-page essay that provides a general idea of their life pursuits.

Financial data Interns receive a salary of approximately $500 per week and assistance in finding a place to live.

Duration 12 weeks in the summer.

Additional information Interns work in copy editing, reporting, computer-assisted reporting, photography, and graphic design.

Number awarded 4 each year.

Deadline January of each year.

[1286]
SUMMER HIGH SCHOOL APPRENTICESHIP RESEARCH PROGRAM COMMUTER COMPONENT

Modern Technology Systems, Inc.
6801 Kenilworth Avenue, Suite 200
Riverdale, MD 20737-1331
(301) 985-5171   Fax: (301) 985-5176
E-mail: info@nasasharp.com
Web: www.nasasharp.com

Purpose To provide an opportunity for traditionally underrepresented high school students to participate in a research-based mentoring program during the summer at facilities of the U.S. National Aeronautics and Space Administration (NASA) near their home.

Eligibility This program, known as the NASA SHARP Commuter Component, is open to all high school students, but the program's goal is to increase participation by students from groups traditionally underrepresented in science, mathematics, technology, engineering, and geography (SMTEG): women, the disabled, African Americans, Native Alaskans, Native Americans, Hispanics, and Pacific Islanders (natives of the Philippines, Guam, American Samoa, or Micronesia). Applicants must be U.S. citizens; have completed at least 2 college preparatory mathematics courses and 2 college preparatory science courses with an average grade of "B" or better in each discipline and an overall average of "B" or better in all other course work; be at least 16 years of age; demonstrate a strong interest and aptitude for a career in SMTEG fields; and be a permanent resident and attend school within a 50-mile radius of a participating NASA field installation. Selection is based on a 300-word essay on reasons for wanting to participate in SHARP, special talents and hobbies, work experience, honors and awards, community service, extracurricular activities, and SMTEG study and career interests and aspirations; demonstration of excellent oral and written communication skills; 2 recommendations from science and mathematics teachers; and transcripts.

Financial data Students receive a salary.

Duration At least 8 weeks, during the summer. Students may participate only 2 summers.

Additional information The participating NASA field installations are Ames Research Center (Moffett Field, California), Dryden Flight Research Center (Edwards, California), Glenn Research Center (Cleveland, Ohio), Goddard Institute for Space Studies (New York, New York), Goddard Space Flight Center (Greenbelt, Maryland), Independent Verification and Validation Facility (Fairmont, West Virginia), Jet Propulsion Laboratory (Pasadena, California), Johnson Space Center (Houston, Texas), Kennedy Space Center (Kennedy Space Center, Florida), Langley Research Center (Hampton, Virginia), Marshall Space Flight Center (Marshall Space Flight Center, Alabama), Stennis Space Center (Stennis Space Center, Mississippi), and Wallops Flight Facility (Wallops Island, Virginia). Applications must be sent to the NASA field installation where the student wishes to work.

Number awarded Approximately 200 each year.

Deadline February of each year.

[1287]
SUMMER HIGH SCHOOL APPRENTICESHIP RESEARCH PROGRAM RESIDENTIAL COMPONENT

Modern Technology Systems, Inc.
6801 Kenilworth Avenue, Suite 200
Riverdale, MD 20737-1331
(301) 985-5171   Fax: (301) 985-5176
E-mail: info@nasasharp.com
Web: www.nasasharp.com

Purpose To provide an opportunity for traditionally underrepresented high school students to participate in a research-based mentoring program during the summer at designated colleges and universities.

Eligibility This program, known as the NASA SHARP Residential Component, is open to all high school students, but the program's goal is to increase participation by students from groups traditionally underrepresented in science, mathematics, technology, engineering, and geography (SMTEG): women, the disabled, African Americans, Native Alaskans, Native Americans, Hispanics, and Pacific Islanders (natives of the Philippines, Guam, American Samoa, or Micronesia). Applicants must be U.S. citizens; have completed at least 2 college preparatory mathematics courses and 2 college preparatory science courses with an average grade of "B" or better in each discipline and an overall average of "B" or better in all other course work; be at least 16 years of age; demonstrate a strong interest and aptitude for a career in SMTEG fields; and be interested in living on campus at a university to which they are assigned. Selection is based on a 300-word essay on reasons for wanting to participate in SHARP, special talents and hobbies, work experience, honors and awards, community service, extracurricular activities, and SMTEG study and career interests and aspirations; demonstration of excellent oral and written communication skills; 2 recommendations from science and mathematics teachers; and transcripts.

Financial data Students receive a salary.

Duration At least 8 weeks, during the summer. Students may participate only 2 summers.

Additional information The participating universities are California State University at Los Angeles, Georgia Institute of Technology, Hampton University, North Carolina A&T University, Texas A&M University, the University of Michigan, the University of New Mexico, and the University of Wisconsin at Madison. This program is funded by the U.S. National Aeronautics and Space Administration (NASA).

Number awarded Approximately 200 each year.

Deadline February of each year.

[1288]
SUMMER HONORS UNDERGRADUATE RESEARCH PROGRAM

Harvard Medical School
Division of Medical Sciences
Attn: Minority Programs Office
260 Longwood Avenue, Room 432
Boston, MA 02115-5720
(617) 432-1342   (800) 367-9019
Fax: (617) 432-2644   E-mail: SHURP@hms.harvard.edu
Web: www.hms.harvard.edu/dms/diversity/index.html

Purpose To provide an opportunity for underrepresented minority students to engage in research at Harvard Medical School during the summer.

Eligibility This program at Harvard Medical School is open to underrepresented minority college students who have had at least 1 summer (or equivalent) of laboratory research. Applicants should be considering a career in biological or biomedical research.

Financial data The program provides a stipend of approximately $300 per week, dormitory housing, travel costs, a meal card, and health insurance if it is needed.

Duration 10 weeks, during the summer.

Number awarded Varies each year.

Deadline January of each year.

[1289]
SUMMER INTERN PROGRAM IN GEOSCIENCE

Carnegie Institution of Washington
Geophysical Laboratory
Attn: Coordinator, Summer Intern Program
5251 Broad Branch Road, N.W.
Washington, DC 20015-1305
(202) 478-8930   Fax: (202) 478-8901
E-mail: w.minarik@gl.ciw.edu
Web: www.gl.ciw.edu/interns

Purpose To provide an opportunity for undergraduate students to conduct research at the Carnegie Institution of Washington's Geophysical Laboratory or Department of Terrestrial Magnetism during the summer.

Eligibility This summer program at the Carnegie Institution of Washington is open to undergraduate students working on a degree in astronomy, biology, chemistry, geoscience, materials science, physics, or a related field. Applicants must have completed at least 30 semester hours, but graduating seniors are not eligible. U.S. citizenship or permanent resident status is required. Applicants must be interested in conducting research at the laboratory under the supervision of a staff scientist. Women and minorities are particularly encouraged to apply.

Financial data The stipend is $3,000. Also provided are housing and support for travel expenses to Washington, D.C.

Duration 10 weeks, during the summer.

Additional information Funding for this program is provided by a grant from the National Science Foundation's Research Experiences for Undergraduates program.

Number awarded Varies each year; recently, 16 students participated in this program.

Deadline March of each year.

[1290]
SUMMER INTERNSHIP PROGRAM IN BIOMEDICAL RESEARCH

National Institutes of Health
Attn: Office of Education
10 Center Drive, Room 1C129
Bethesda, MD 20892-1158
(301) 496-2427   Fax: (301) 402-0483
E-mail: dc26a@nih.gov
Web: www.training.nih.gov

Purpose To enable students to receive training and participate in ongoing research studies in a variety of laboratory and clinically-related disciplines at the National Institutes of Health (NIH) during the summer.

Eligibility This program is open to graduate, health professions, undergraduate, and high school students who have a strong interest in pursuing studies related to biomedical or behavioral research, including the disciplines of biology, chemistry, physical science, psychology, computer science, biostatistics, mathematics, and biomedical engineering. They must be at least 16 years of age and U.S. citizens or permanent residents. Some internships are available only to underrepresented minority students.

Financial data Salaries depend on the academic level of the recipient, ranging from $990 per month for high school students to $2,200 per month for graduate students with 3 or more years of experience.

Duration At least 8 weeks, in the summer.

Additional information Most components of the National Institutes of Health participate in this program. Some of them reserve positions for interns who are members of minority groups underrepresented in the biomedical and behavioral sciences (African Americans, Hispanics, Native Americans, and Pacific Islanders). Laboratories are located in Bethesda and Rockville, Maryland and in Hamilton, Montana.

Number awarded Varies each year.

Deadline January of each year.

[1291]
SUMMER PROGRAM IN BIOSTATISTICS

Harvard School of Public Health
Department of Biostatistics
Attn: Admissions and Summer Program Coordinator
655 Huntington Avenue, SPH2, Fourth Floor
Boston, MA 02115
(617) 432-3175
E-mail: biostat_diversity@hsph.harvard.edu

Purpose To enable underrepresented minority science undergraduates to participate in a summer research internship at Harvard School of Public Health that focuses on biostatistics.

Eligibility This program is open to members of ethnic groups underrepresented in the sciences (African Americans, Mexican Americans, Chicanos, American Indians, Aleuts, Eskimos, Polynesians, Micronesians, and Puerto Ricans) who are currently college undergraduates interested in biostatistics as a career. Applicants must be interested in participating in a summer program on the use of quantitative methods for biological, environmental, and medical research. They must have some course work in calculus, but prior exposure to statistics is not required. U.S. citizenship or permanent resident status is required.

Financial data Funding covers travel, accommodations, and a modest stipend.

Duration 4 weeks, in June.

Additional information Interns participate in seminars, led by faculty members from various departments at the Harvard School of Public Health and Harvard Medical School, that are designed to broaden a participant's understanding of the relationship of biostatistics to human health.

Number awarded Varies each year.

[1292]
SUMMER RESEARCH INTERNSHIP IN PUBLIC HEALTH

Harvard School of Public Health
Department of Biostatistics
Attn: Admissions and Summer Program Coordinator
655 Huntington Avenue, SPH2, Fourth Floor
Boston, MA 02115
(617) 432-3175
E-mail: biostat_diversity@hsph.harvard.edu

Purpose To enable underrepresented minority science undergraduates to participate in a summer research internship at Harvard School of Public Health that focuses on public health.

Eligibility This program is open to members of ethnic groups underrepresented in the sciences (African Americans, Mexican Americans, Chicanos, American Indians, Aleuts, Eskimos, Polynesians, Micronesians, and Puerto Ricans) who are currently college juniors or seniors interested in pursuing graduate study in public health. Applicants are required to have had some prior exposure to statistics, along with relevant research experience in community-based, sociological, or health research. They must be interested in working on an existing project with a team of researchers, faculty, and graduate students. U.S. citizenship or permanent resident status is required.

Financial data Funding covers travel, accommodations, and a modest stipend.

Duration 10 weeks, beginning in June.

Additional information Interns work independently on various components of the overall project.

Number awarded Varies each year.

[1293]
SUMMER RESEARCH OPPORTUNITIES PROGRAM (SROP)

Committee on Institutional Cooperation
302 East John Street, Suite 1705
Champaign, IL 61820-8146
(217) 265-8005   (800) 457-4420
Fax: (217) 244-7127   E-mail: aeprice@uiuc.edu
Web: www.cic.uiuc.edu/programs/SROP

Purpose To provide an opportunity for minority undergraduates to gain research experience during the summer at academic institutions affiliated with the Committee on Institutional Cooperation (CIC).

Eligibility This program is open to sophomore and junior African Americans, Mexican Americans, Native Americans, Puerto Ricans, and other Latinos. Applicants may be majoring in any field at any university in the United States, but they must be interested in conducting a summer research project under the supervision of a faculty mentor at a CIC member institution.

Financial data Participants are paid a stipend of $2,500, plus up to $1,100 toward room and board and travel to and from the host institution. Faculty mentors receive a $500 research allowance for the cost of materials.

Duration 8 to 10 weeks, during the summer.

Additional information Participants work directly with faculty mentors at the institution of their choice and also engage in other enrichment activities, such as workshops and social gatherings. In July, all participants come together at 1 of the CIC campuses for the annual SROP conference. The CIC member institutions are University of Chicago, University of Illinois at Urbana-Champaign, University of Illinois at Chicago, University of Iowa, University of Michigan, University of Minnesota, University of Wisconsin at Madison, University of Wisconsin at Milwaukee, Indiana University, Michigan State University, Northwestern University, Ohio State University, Indiana University/Purdue University at Indianapolis, Pennsylvania State University, and Purdue University. Students are required to write a paper and an abstract describing their projects and to present the results of their work at a campus symposium.

Deadline January of each year.

Number awarded Varies each year; recently, 529 students participated in this program.

[1294]
SUMMER TRANSPORTATION INTERNSHIP PROGRAM FOR DIVERSE GROUPS

Department of Transportation
Federal Highway Administration
Attn: Office of Human Resources
HAHR-3, Room 4323
400 Seventh Street, S.W.
Washington, DC 20590
(202) 366-1159
Web: www.fhwa.dot.gov/education/stipdg.htm

Purpose To enable students from diverse groups to gain work experience during the summer at facilities of the U.S. Department of Transportation (DOT).

Eligibility This program is open to undergraduate students who are women, persons with disabilities, and members of diverse social and ethnic groups. Applicants must be U.S. citizens currently enrolled in a degree-granting program of study at an accredited institution of higher learning at the undergraduate (community or junior college, university, college, or Tribal College) or graduate level. They must be entering their junior or senior year (students attending a tribal college must have completed their "first year" of school). Students who will graduate during the spring or summer are not eligible unless they have been accepted for enrollment in graduate school. All applicants must be interested in a summer work experience at various DOT facilities. They must have a GPA of 3.0 or higher. Law students must be entering their second or third year and must be in the upper 30% of their class. Selection is based on an expressed interest in pursuing a transportation-related career, GPA or class standing, a reference from a professor or advisor, the endorsement of the department chair, an essay on transportation interests, areas of interest outside of school, and completeness of application package.

Financial data A stipend is paid (amount not specified).

Duration 10 weeks, during the summer.

Additional information Assignments are at the DOT headquarters in Washington, D.C., a selected modal administration, or selected field offices around the country.

Number awarded Varies each year; recently, 17 interns participated in this program.

[1295]
SUN-SENTINEL SUMMER MINORITY PROGRAM

Sun-Sentinel
Attn: Recruitment Editor
200 East Las Olas Boulevard
Fort Lauderdale, FL 33301-2293
(954) 356-4536
Web: www.sun-sentinel.com/opportunities

Purpose To provide summer work experience at the *Sun-Sentinel* in Fort Lauderdale, Florida to minority students who are interested in training to become a journalist.

Eligibility This program is open to high school students (including graduating seniors) who are minorities, residents of Broward, Dade, and Palm Beach counties, and interested in preparing for a career as a journalist at the *Sun-Sentinel.*

Financial data The stipend is $240 per week.

Duration 6 weeks, beginning in June.

Additional information At the mid-point of the program, participants begin writing for the *Sun-Sentinel.* Interns work with experienced reporters, photographers, and artists, producing news stories, photographs, and graphics.

Number awarded 8 each year.

Deadline April of each year.

[1296]
TEACH FOR AMERICA FELLOWSHIPS

Teach for America
315 West 36th Street, Sixth Floor
New York, NY 10018
(212) 279-2080   (800) 832-1230
Fax: (212) 279-2081
E-mail: admissions@teachforamerica.org
Web: www.teachforamerica.org

Purpose To provide an opportunity for recent college graduates to serve as teachers in America's rural and urban public school classrooms.

Eligibility This program recruits students or graduates of colleges for appointments in school districts with severe teacher shortages. A special effort is made to select corps members who are diverse in every respect, particularly with regard to ethnic, racial, and cultural background. All academic majors are eligible, but applicants with a mathematics, science, or engineering major are especially encouraged. No previous education course work is necessary, but a GPA of 2.5 or higher and U.S. citizenship or permanent resident status are required.

Financial data This program covers major expenses for the summer institute, including room and board and academic materials. It also covers room and board during a regional induction. Corps members are responsible for the cost of transportation to the summer institute, and from the summer institute to their placement site. They are also responsible for their own moving expenses, testing fees, and any necessary credits and district fees. During a transitional period before they begin working, they are eligible for grants and no-interest loans ranging from $600 to $4,000, depending on their financial need and cost of living in their assigned region. Teach for America then places recruits in jobs paying $22,000 to $40,000 per year. This program also has a relationship with AmeriCorps that makes participants eligible for forbearance on student loans during their period of service and to receive an AmeriCorps education award of $4,725 for each year of service.

Duration 2 years.

Additional information Once selected for this program, participants attend a 5-week summer institute where they receive additional professional development and support. They then travel to their assigned regions for a 1- to 2-week induction, which helps orient them to the schools, school districts, and communities where they will be teaching. Urban assignments are currently available in Atlanta, Baltimore, Chicago, Detroit, Houston, greater New Orleans, Los Angeles, New Jersey, New York City, Phoenix, the San Francisco Bay Area (especially the east bay), St. Louis, and Washington, D.C.; rural assignments are available in south Louisiana, the Mississippi delta (in Arkansas and Mississippi), an Indian reservation in New Mexico, eastern North Carolina, and the Rio Grande Valley of Texas. There is a $25 application fee.

Number awarded Nearly 2,000 each year.

Deadline February or October of each year.

[1297]
TECHNICIAN TRAINING PROGRAM FOR MINORITIES AND WOMEN AT BROOKHAVEN NATIONAL LABORATORY

Brookhaven National Laboratory
Attn: Diversity Office, Human Resources Division
Building 185A
P.O. Box 5000
Upton, New York 11973-5000
(631) 344-2703   Fax: (631) 344-5305
E-mail: palmore@bnl.gov
Web: www.bnl.gov

Purpose To provide on-the-job training at Brookhaven National Laboratory (BNL) to underrepresented minorities and women who are interested in a career in the field of mechanical technology.

Eligibility This program is open to underrepresented minorities (African American/Black, Hispanic, Native American, or Pacific Islander) and women who are able and willing to participate in an associate (A.A.S.) or baccalaureate (B.S.E.T.) degree program in mechanical technology while working at BNL. Applicants should have previous educational or life experiences, such as trade school or the military.

Financial data Participants receive a competitive salary.

Duration 6 and a half years.

Additional information Trainees at BNL are involved in large and intricate mechanical assembly procedures, the use of machine shop tools, basic electricity, and vacuum procedures. Duties include fabrication of mechanical assemblies, installation of mechanical instruments, and servicing of the instrumentation assemblies.

Number awarded Varies each year.

Deadline Applications may be submitted at any time.

[1298]
TELECOMMUNICATIONS POLICY FELLOWSHIPS

Congressional Hispanic Caucus Institute, Inc.
504 C Street, N.E.
Washington, DC 20002
(202) 543-1771   (800) EXCEL-DC
Fax: (202) 546-2143   E-mail: chci@chci.org
Web: www.chci.org

Purpose To provide Latino graduate students and recent college graduates with the opportunity to apply their academic expertise in the area of public telecommunications policy during a work experience program in Washington, D.C.

Eligibility This program is open to U.S. citizens and permanent residents of Latino background who graduated from a college or university (with a bachelor's or graduate degree) within the past year or are currently-enrolled graduate students. Applicants must be interested in gaining experience in the area of public telecommunications policy. Preference is given to applicants with a GPA of 3.0 or higher. Selection is based on evidence of leadership potential as demonstrated through goal setting, initiative, and responsibility; active interest in community affairs, balanced with academics; and analytical and communication skills (oral and written).

Financial data This program provides transportation to and from Washington, D.C., a monthly stipend of $2,061 (or $2,500 for fellows who already hold a graduate degree), and health insurance.

Duration 9 months, beginning in September.

Additional information Placements are available in congressional offices and federal agencies, advocacy groups, the media, and a broad range of policy-related organizations, but must focus on telecommunications issues.

Number awarded 1 or more each year.

Deadline February of each year.

[1299]
TRAINEESHIPS IN OCEANOGRAPHY FOR MINORITY UNDERGRADUATES

Woods Hole Oceanographic Institution
Attn: Education Office
Clark Laboratory 223, MS #31
360 Woods Hole Road
Woods Hole, MA 02543-1541
(508) 289-2219   Fax: (508) 457-2188
E-mail: education@whoi.edu
Web: www.whoi.edu/education

Purpose To provide work experience to minority undergraduates who are interested in preparing for a career in the marine sciences, oceanographic engineering, or marine policy.

Eligibility This program is open to ethnic minority undergraduates enrolled in U.S. colleges or universities who have completed at least 2 semesters of study and who are interested in the marine sciences, oceanographic engineering, or marine policy. Applicants must be U.S. citizens or permanent residents and African American or Black; Asian American; Chicano, Mexican American, Puerto Rican or other Hispanic; or Native American.

Financial data The stipend is $345 per week; trainees may also receive additional support for travel to Woods Hole.

Duration 10 to 12 weeks during the summer or 1 semester during the academic year; renewable.

Additional information Trainees are assigned advisors who supervise their research programs and supplementary study activities. Some traineeships involve field work or research cruises. This program is sponsored by the Northeast Fisheries Science Center of the National Marine Fisheries Service (U.S. National Oceanic and Atmospheric Administration), the Center for Marine and Coastal Geology (U.S. Geological Survey), and the Office of Naval Research.

Number awarded 4 to 5 each year.

Deadline For a summer appointment, applications must be submitted in February of each year. For the remaining portion of the year, applications may be submitted at any time, but they

must be received at least 2 months before the anticipated starting date.

[1300]
UNCF/HOUSEHOLD CORPORATE SCHOLARS PROGRAM

United Negro College Fund
Attn: Program Services Department
8260 Willow Oaks Corporate Drive
P.O. Box 10444
Fairfax, VA 22031-8044
(703) 205-3490   (866) 671-7237
Fax: (703) 205-3550   E-mail: internship@uncf.org
Web: www.uncf.org/Scholarship/CorporateScholars.asp

Purpose To provide financial assistance and work experience to minority and other students majoring in fields related to business.

Eligibility This program is open to rising juniors majoring in accounting, business, computer science, finance, human resources, or marketing with a GPA of 3.0 or higher. Applicants must be interested in an internship with Household, the program's sponsor, at 1 of the following sites: Bridgewater, New Jersey; Charlotte, North Carolina; Chesapeake, Virginia; Chicago, Illinois; Dallas, Texas; Indianapolis, Indiana; Jacksonville, Florida; Monterey, California; New Castle, Delaware; San Diego, California; and Tampa, Florida. Preference is given to applicants who reside in those areas, but students who live in other areas are also considered. African Americans, Hispanics, Native Americans, and Asian Americans are encouraged to apply. Along with their application, students must submit a 1-page personal statement, a letter of recommendation, and a current undergraduate transcript.

Financial data The students selected for this program receive paid internships and need-based scholarships that range from $5,000 to $10,000 per year.

Duration 8 to 10 weeks for the internships; 1 year for the scholarships, which may be renewed.

Number awarded Varies each year.

Deadline February of each year.

[1301]
UNCF/SPRINT SCHOLARS PROGRAM

United Negro College Fund
Attn: Program Services Department
8260 Willow Oaks Corporate Drive
P.O. Box 10444
Fairfax, VA 22031-8044
(703) 205-3490   (866) 671-7237
Fax: (703) 205-3550   E-mail: internship@uncf.org
Web: www.uncf.org/Scholarship/CorporateScholars.asp

Purpose To provide financial assistance and work experience to minority students who are interested in preparing for a career in telecommunications.

Eligibility This program is open to members of minority groups who are enrolled full time as seniors at a 4-year college or university in the United States. Applicants must have a GPA of 3.0 or higher and be majoring in accounting, communications, computer engineering, computer science, economics, electrical engineering, finance, industrial engineering, information systems, journalism, logistics, marketing, management information systems, public relations, or statistics. They must be interested in a summer internship at Sprint. Along with their application, they must submit a 500-word personal statement describing their career interests and goals. Selection is based on GPA, demonstrated skills and abilities, and interest in pursuing a career in telecommunications. Preference is given to students at the 39 member institutions of the United Negro College Fund (UNCF), other Historically Black Colleges and Universities (HBCUs), and the following schools: Central Missouri State University, DeVry Institutes, Georgia Institute of Technology, Iowa State University, Kansas State University, Northwest Missouri State University, North Carolina State University, Oklahoma State University, Pittsburg State University, Rockhurst University, Southwest Missouri State University, Truman State University, University of Florida, University of Kansas, University of Missouri at Columbia, University of Missouri at Kansas City, University of Missouri at Rolla, University of Nebraska at Lincoln, Virginia Tech, Washburn University, and Wichita State University.

Financial data Each student receives $2,500 as well as additional compensation for the internship, a need-based scholarship up to $7,500, and a travel allowance of $500.

Duration 1 year.

Additional information The corporate sponsor of this program, Sprint, also provides mentorships to the participating students.

Number awarded Varies each year.

Deadline November of each year.

[1302]
UNIVERSITY OF MINNESOTA AFFIRMATIVE ACTION RESIDENCY PROGRAM

University of Minnesota Twin Cities
University Libraries
Attn: Human Resources Director
499 Wilson Library
309 19th Avenue South
Minneapolis, MN 55455
(612) 625-0822   Fax: (612) 626-9353
Web: www.lib.umn.edu

Purpose To provide work experience to minority graduates of accredited library schools.

Eligibility Applicants must be recent graduates from an accredited library school with a master's degree in library or information science, be interested in working in an academic library, have some online experience, and be members of minority groups underrepresented at the University of Minnesota and in academic librarianship (African Americans, American Indians, Asians, and Hispanics). Selection is based on experience and potential.

Financial data Interns receive a salary of at least $35,000 plus benefits and travel support.

Duration 2 years.

Additional information During the first year, the intern receives an introduction and orientation to the various departments and operations; in the second year, the intern focuses on 1 area of personal interest. This program began in 1990.

Number awarded Up to 2 per year.

Deadline The position is available at the beginning of August of each year. Applications are accepted until the position is filled.

[1303]
URBAN FELLOWSHIP PROGRAM

North Central Texas Council of Governments
Attn: Transportation Department
616 Six Flags Drive, Centerpoint Two
P.O. Box 5888
Arlington, TX 76005-5888
(817) 608-2325   Fax: (817) 640-7806
E-mail: lucile@dfwinfo.com
Web: www.dfwinfo.com/trans/fellowship

Purpose To provide financial assistance and work experience to ethnic minorities, women, and economically disadvantaged persons who are interested in obtaining a master's degree in public management and/or planning at a university in Texas.

Eligibility This program is open to ethnic minorities (African Americans, Hispanics, American Indians, Alaskan Natives, Asians, and Pacific Islanders), women, and those who are economically disadvantaged. Only U.S. citizens or permanent residents may apply. Applicants must be interested in obtaining a master's degree at a university in Texas as preparation for a career in public management and/or planning. Full-time enrollment is required. Selection is based on 1) financial need; 2) interest in, and commitment to, a professional career in urban management and/or planning; and 3) the applicant's ability to complete the academic and work placement responsibilities of the program.

Financial data The academic portion of this program pays the cost of tuition and books. The work experience portion of the program pays a salary of $8.50 per hour for 20 hours per week.

Duration 1 year; may be renewed if the recipient maintains a GPA of 3.0 or higher.

Additional information These fellowships are financed by the U.S. Department of Housing and Urban Development in conjunction with local governments in north central Texas (the Dallas/Fort Worth metropolitan area). Fellows are assigned to an internship in a local government in that area. Universities currently participating in the program are the University of North Texas, the University of Texas at Arlington, and the University of Texas at Dallas. Fellows are required to agree to make a good-faith effort to obtain employment in community-building fields for at least 2 consecutive years after graduation.

Deadline July of each year.

[1304]
USDA SUMMER INTERN PROGRAM

Department of Agriculture
Office of Human Resources Management
Attn: Departmental Student Programs Manager
Jamie L. Whitten Federal Building, Room 316-W
1400 Independence Avenue, S.W.
Washington, DC 20250-9600
(202) 720-6104
Web: www.usda.gov

Purpose To provide summer internships at agencies of the United States Department of Agriculture (USDA) to students in college.

Eligibility This internship program at USDA is open to U.S. citizens who are currently enrolled in a college or university and planning to continue enrollment in the following fall. Applicants should be seeking further knowledge about career opportunities and future employment with the department. A special goal of the program is to enhance the diversity of the work force of the department (e.g., by including minorities).

Financial data Students are employed at levels ranging from GS-3 for those who have completed 1 year of college to GS-7 for those who have completed 1 year of graduate work.

Duration 8 weeks, during the summer.

Additional information Interns may select to participate in mentoring programs during their stay in Washington, D.C.; those programs are conducted by the Forum on Blacks in Agriculture and the Hispanic American Cultural Effort. In addition, this program is part of the Work Force Recruitment Program for College Students with Disabilities; interns who are selected as part of that effort are provided with special accommodations, such as sign language interpreting services, microcomputer accessible technologies, telecommunications devices for the deaf, and other special equipment.

Deadline February of each year.

[1305]
VAID FELLOWSHIPS

National Gay and Lesbian Task Force
Attn: Policy Institute
121 West 27th Street, Suite 501
New York, NY 10001
(212) (604) 9830   Fax: (212) 604-9831
Web: www.ngltf.org/about/vaid.htm

Purpose To provide summer work experience related to people of color in the movement for gay, lesbian, bisexual, and transgendered (GLBT) equality.

Eligibility Applicants must be enrolled in a degree program at least half time as a graduate or undergraduate student or have completed a graduate or undergraduate degree within the preceding 12 months. They should have 1) a desire to work in a multicultural environment where commitment to diversity based on race, ethnic origin, gender, age, sexual orientation, and physical ability is an important institutional value; 2) demonstrated leadership in progressive and/or GLBT communities; 3) extensive research, writing, and critical thinking skills; 4) knowledge of, and commitment to, GLBT issues; and 5) computer proficiency in word processing, database work, e-mail, and Internet research. The program supports and recognizes the leadership of people of color and other emerging leaders in public policy, legal, and social science research.

Financial data The stipend is $400 per week. Fellows are responsible for their own housing and living expenses.

Duration 11 weeks, from early June through mid-August.

Additional information The Policy Institute of the National Gay and Lesbian Task Force (NGLTF), founded in 1995, is the largest think tank in the United States engaged in research, policy analysis, and strategic action to advance equality and understanding of GLBT people. Its primary programs are the racial and economic justice initiative, the family policy program, and the aging initiative. In addition to their primary roles of providing research and analysis, all 3 programs work closely with NGLTF colleagues in Washington, D.C. and other allies on advocacy and legislative efforts to actively change laws and policies affecting GLBT people. The main office of the NGLTF may be contacted at 1700 Kalorama Road, N.W., Washington, D.C. 20009-2624, (202) 332-6483, Fax: (202) 332-0207.

Number awarded 1 or more each year.

Deadline February of each year.

[1306]
VILLAGE VOICE MINORITY WRITING FELLOWSHIP

Village Voice
Attn: Editorial Department
36 Cooper Square
New York, NY 10003-7118
(212) 475-3300   E-mail: aforbes@villagevoice.com

Purpose To provide work experience to minority college students interested in interning at the *Village Voice,* a weekly newspaper published in New York City.

Eligibility This program is open to minority college students interested in interning at the *Village Voice.* While journalism experience is not an absolute requirement, candidates should possess research skills, an aptitude for critical thought, and a familiarity with the *Village Voice.* Interested students should submit samples of their written or editorial work, a resume, a letter of recommendation, an application form, and a self-addressed stamped envelope.

Financial data The stipend is $150 per week.

Duration 4 months, usually beginning in January, May/June, or September.

Additional information The *Village Voice* is known for its investigative journalism as well as coverage of cultural events (including reporting on film, art, theater, books, and dance). Interns have the opportunity to work with well-known journalists on the newspaper. College credit may be arranged.

Number awarded Varies each session.

Deadline January for the spring session; March for the summer session; or July for the fall semester.

[1307]
VITO MARZULLO INTERNSHIP PROGRAM

Office of the Governor
Attn: Program Director
107 William G. Stratton Building
Springfield, IL 62706
(217) 782-5213   Fax: (217) 524-1677
TDD: (217) 558-2238
E-mail: tammy_payne@gov.state.il.us
Web: www.state.il.us/gov/officeinternship.htm

Purpose To provide recent college graduates with work experience in the Illinois Governor's office.

Eligibility This program is open to recent college graduates. Applicants may have earned a degree in any field and must be interested in working in the Illinois Governor's office or in various agencies under the Governor's jurisdiction. Candidates must be Illinois residents and able to demonstrate a real commitment to excellence. Selection is based on academic honors, leadership ability, extracurricular activities, and involvement in community or public service areas. Applications are especially solicited from qualified minorities, women, and persons with disabilities.

Financial data The stipend is $2,226 per month.

Duration 1 year, beginning in August.

Additional information Assignments are in Springfield and, to a limited extent, in Chicago.

Number awarded Varies each year.

Deadline January of each year.

[1308]
WCVB-TV SUMMER MINORITY INTERNSHIP PROGRAM

WCVB-TV
Attn: Human Resources Department
5 TV Place
Needham, MA 02494-2303
(781) 433-0461   Fax: (781) 449-6682
E-mail: lwalsh@hearstsc.com
Web: www.wcvb.com

Purpose To provide summer work experience at WCVB-TV in Boston to minorities who are interested in broadcast journalism as a career.

Eligibility Applicants must have completed their freshman year, be majoring in some field of broadcasting, be U.S. citizens, and be minorities or others disadvantaged by economic or social conditions. They must be interested in interning at WCVB-TV in Boston.

Financial data Interns receive the minimum wage for 37.5 hours per week.

Duration 12 weeks during the summer.

Additional information This program at WCVB-TV provides an opportunity for participants to obtain an overview of the television broadcasting field in news, programming, public affairs, or sales. Interns must provide their own transportation.

Number awarded 5 each year.

Deadline April of each year.

[1309]
WILLIAM KELLY SIMPSON INTERNSHIP FOR EGYPTIAN ART

Metropolitan Museum of Art
Attn: Internship Programs
1000 Fifth Avenue
New York, NY 10028-0198
(212) 570-3710   Fax: (212) 570-3782
Web: www.metmuseum.org/education/er_internship.asp

Purpose To provide summer work experience at the Metropolitan Museum of Art to graduate students interested in ancient Egyptian art.

Eligibility This internship is available to graduate students who have completed the course work for a master's degree in Egyptology or in art history with a main emphasis on ancient Egyptian art. Applicants of diverse backgrounds (e.g., minorities) are encouraged to apply.

Financial data The honorarium is $3,250.

Duration 10 weeks, beginning in June.

Additional information The intern works with the curatorial staff at the Metropolitan Museum of Art on projects related to the museum's Egyptian collection or a special exhibition. This internship is funded by the Marilyn M. Simpson Charitable Trust

Number awarded 1 each year.

Deadline January of each year.

[1310]
WISE PROGRAM

Washington Internships for Students of Engineering
Attn: Anne Hickox
400 Commonwealth Drive
Warrendale, PA 15096-0001
(724) 776-4841, ext. 7476   Fax: (724) 776-2103
E-mail: anne@sae.org
Web: www.wise-intern.org

Purpose To provide summer work experience in the Washington D.C. area to engineering students.

Eligibility This program is open to third- and fourth-year undergraduate engineering students and recent graduates beginning study in an engineering policy-related master's program. Interns learn about the operation of government and the interaction between the engineering community and the government in matters of public policy, as well as the way in which engineers can and do contribute to public policy decisions in complex technological matters. Minority students are encouraged to apply. U.S. citizenship is required.

Financial data The stipend is $1,800; lodging and travel expenses are also covered.

Duration 10 weeks, in the summer.

Additional information This internship program is sponsored by a number of engineering and scientific societies, which select and sponsor the student participants. Sponsors include the American Institute of Chemical Engineers (AIChE), the American Nuclear Society (ANS), the American Society of Civil Engineers (ASCE), the American Society of Mechanical Engineers (ASME), the Institute of Electrical and Electronics Engineers (IEEE), the National Science Foundation (NSF), the National Society of Professional Engineers (NSPE), and the Society of Automotive Engineers (SAE). Interns are under the guidance of an engineering professor and receive academic credit. Applicants seeking sponsorship by ANS, ASCE, ASME, or IEEE must be members of those societies.

Number awarded Up to 16 each year.

Deadline December of each year.

[1311]
WOODS HOLE OCEANOGRAPHIC INSTITUTION MINORITY FELLOWSHIPS

Woods Hole Oceanographic Institution
Attn: Education Office
Clark Laboratory 223, MS #31
360 Woods Hole Road
Woods Hole, MA 02543-1541
(508) 289-2219   Fax: (508) 457-2188
E-mail: education@whoi.edu
Web: www.whoi.edu/education

Purpose To provide work experience to minority group members who are interested in preparing for a career in the marine sciences, oceanographic engineering, or marine policy.

Eligibility This program is open to ethnic minority undergraduates enrolled in U.S. colleges or universities who have completed at least 2 semesters of study and who are interested in the marine sciences, oceanographic engineering, or marine policy. Applicants must be U.S. citizens or permanent residents and African American or Black; Asian American; Chicano, Mexican American, Puerto Rican or other Hispanic; or Native American.

Financial data The stipend is $345 per week; trainees may also receive additional support for travel to Woods Hole.

Duration 10 to 12 weeks during the summer or 1 semester during the academic year; renewable.

Additional information Trainees are assigned advisors who supervise their research programs and supplementary study activities. Some traineeships involve field work or research cruises. This program is sponsored by the Northeast Fisheries Science Center of the National Marine Fisheries Service (U.S. National Oceanic and Atmospheric Administration), the Center for Marine and Coastal Geology (U.S. Geological Survey), and the Office of Naval Research.

Number awarded 4 to 5 each year.

Deadline For a summer appointment, applications must be submitted in February of each year. For the remaining portion of the year, applications may be submitted at any time, but they must be received at least 2 months before the anticipated starting date.

[1312]
Y.E.S. TO JOBS PROGRAM

Y.E.S. to Jobs
P.O. Box 3390
Los Angeles, CA 90078-3390
(310) 358-4922   Fax: (310) 358-4330
E-mail: yestojobs@aol.com
Web: www.yestojobs.org

Purpose To provide summer work experience to minority high school students interested in a managerial career in the music industry.

Eligibility This program is open to minority (African American, Asian American, Hispanic American, and Native American) high school students from 16 to 18 years of age in the following cities: Atlanta, Chicago and surrounding suburbs, Dallas, Detroit, Los Angeles, Miami, Nashville, New York, San Francisco, and Washington, D.C. Applicants must have a GPA of 2.5 or higher, a 90% attendance record in school, and an interest in music, media, or business. They must be interested in full-time summer employment in entry level positions at record companies, retail stores, radio and television stations, cable networks, trade publications, film and production companies, public relations and entertainment law firms, or multi-media companies. Selection is based on self-motivation, dependability, and willingness to take initiative and work hard.

Financial data Employers establish the salary they pay interns.

Duration 10 weeks during the summer.

Additional information This program was established by A&M Records in 1987, and became a nonprofit organization in 1994. Y.E.S. stands for Youth Entertainment Summer.

Number awarded Varies each year; recently, more than 250 internships were provided.

Deadline March of each year.

[1313]
ZINA GARRISON MINORITY INTERNSHIP

Women's Sports Foundation
Attn: Award and Grant Programs Manager
Eisenhower Park
1899 Hempstead Turnpike, Suite 400
East Meadow, NY 11554-1000
(516) 542-4700   (800) 227-3988
Fax: (516) 542-4716   E-mail: wosport@aol.com
Web: www.womenssportsfoundation.org

Purpose To give women of color a start in a sports-related career.

Eligibility Eligible to apply for these internships are women of color who are undergraduate students, college graduates, graduate students, or women in career change. The internships take place at the offices of the Women's Sports Foundation on Long Island, New York.

Financial data The salary is $1,000 per month.

Duration 4 to 5 months.

Number awarded 2 or 3 each year.

Deadline Applications may be submitted at any time.

Annotated Bibliography of General Financial Aid Directories

General Financial Aid Directories ●
Subject/Activity Directories ●
Directories for Special Groups ●
Contests and Awards ●
Internships ●
Nothing Over $4.95 ●
Cyberspace Sites ●

General Directories

[1314]

The A's & B's of Academic Scholarships. Annual.

Do you have a "B" average or better? Are your SAT/ACT scores 900/21 or better? If so, you might be able to qualify for a college-based merit scholarship. This paperback lists the major awards offered by 1,200 colleges to students in the top third of their class who have combined SAT scores of 900 or more. Most entries provide information—in tabular form—on number of awards, value range, class standing, study fields, renewability, restrictions, and application date. A short section (generally 4 pages) identifies some noninstitution-based awards. A companion annual paperback issued by Octameron Associates is *Don't Miss Out: The Ambitious Student's Guide to Scholarships and Loans* ($10.00), which outlines strategies for seeking financial aid for college students and provides brief information on a number of funding programs.

Price: $10.00, paper.

Available from: Octameron Associates, P.O. Box 2748, Alexandria, VA 22301. Telephone: (703) 836-5480.

Web site: www.octameron.com/

[1315]

Chronicle Financial Aid Guide. Annual.

When it comes to general financial aid directories, this is one of the better ones. It provides authoritative, clear descriptions of more than 1,800 loans, scholarships, competitions, and internships offered nationally or regionally by 700 private and public organizations to high school and undergraduate students. The financial aid sponsors include private organizations, clubs, foundations, sororities and fraternities, public agencies, and national and international labor unions. The programs are indexed by subject and sponsor.

Price: $24.98, paper.

Available from: Chronicle Guidance Publications, 66 Aurora Street, Moravia, NY 13118-3576. Telephone: (315) 497-0330; toll-free: (800) 900-0454.

Web site: www.chronicleguidance.com/

[1316]

College Student's Guide to Merit and Other No-Need Funding. By Gail A. Schlachter and R. David Weber. Published every even-numbered year.

It's a myth that only the neediest get financial aid. In fact, there are 1,400 college aid programs, open only to college students and students returning to college, that never consider income in the selection process. How do you find out about those programs? Use the *College Student's Guide to Merit and Other No-Need Funding.* This is the only directory to concentrate solely on no-need funding for college students. Here's information on all the financial aid programs that award money—not on the basis of need but on academic record, career plans, creative activities, writing ability, research skills, religious or ethnic background, military or organizational activities, or just pure luck in random drawings. Plus, you can access the listings in the directory by discipline, specific subject, sponsoring organization, program title, where you live, where your school of choice is located, and even deadline date.

Price: $32.00, hardcover.

Available from: Reference Service Press, 5000 Windplay Drive, Suite 4, El Dorado Hills, CA 95762. Telephone: (916) 939-9620.

Web site: www.rspfunding.com/

[1317]

Foundation Grants to Individuals. 12th ed. 2001.

While most foundation grants are for agencies and institutions, some funding opportunities (including a number of scholarships and loans) have been set up specifically for individual applicants. You can find out about these opportunities in the Foundation Center's *Foundation Grants to Individuals.* The current edition (which is also available on CD-ROM and as an online subscription) identifies 2,000 foundations that annually make grants of at least $2,000 to individuals. The work is organized by type of grant awarded (e.g., scholarships, general welfare, medical assistance) and subdivided by eligibility requirements and means of access (including some "Grants to Foreign Individuals" and "Grants to Employees of Specific Companies"). Collectively, these grants total nearly $100 million each year. However, most of these programs are limited geographically and will relate to only small segments of the population.

Price: $65, paper; $75, CD-ROM.

Available from: Foundation Center, 79 Fifth Avenue, New York, NY 10003. Telephone: (212) 620-4230; toll-free: (800) 424-9836.

Web site: www.fdncenter.org/

[1318]

High School Senior's Guide to Merit and Other No-Need Funding. By Gail A. Schlachter and R. David Weber. Published every even-numbered year.

Do you think you or your parents make too much money for you to qualify for financial aid? Not true! This unique guide identifies and describes more than 1,000 merit scholarships and other no-need funding programs set aside just for high school seniors. These programs never consider income level when making awards for college. Here's your chance to get college aid based solely on your academic record, writing or artistic ability, high school club membership, speech-making skills, religious or ethnic background, parents' military or organizational activities, and even pure luck in random drawings. These no-need programs are grouped by discipline (humanities, sciences, social sciences, and any subject area) and indexed by sponsor, program title, geographic restrictions, specific subject coverage, and deadline date.

Price: $29.95, hardcover.

Available from: Reference Service Press, 5000 Windplay Drive, Suite 4, El Dorado Hills, CA 95762. Telephone: (916) 939-9620.

Web site: www.rspfunding.com/

[1319]

Kaplan Scholarships. By Gail A. Schlachter, R. David Weber, and the Staff of Reference Service Press. Annual.

Based on Reference Service Press's award-winning financial aid database and jointly published by Kaplan and Simon & Schuster, this directory identifies more than 3,000 scholarships, grants, and awards that can be used to support study in any discipline in two-year colleges, vocational and technical institutes, four-year colleges, and universities in the United States. A definite plus: no single-school or loan programs are included. All listings offer $1,000 or more per year.

Price: $27.00, paper.

Available from: Simon & Schuster, Attn: Order Department, 100 Front Street, Riverside, NJ 08075. Toll-free: (800) 445-6991.

Web site: www.SimonSays.com/

[1320]

Peterson's Scholarship Almanac. Annual.

Despite the claim of this scaled-down version of *Peterson's Scholarships, Grants & Prizes* ($29.95, annual) that it covers the 500 "largest, most generous student award programs," a number of the listings are under $250 or are available to only 1 or 2 recipients. On the plus side, many of the major programs are described here, the information is quite current, and the price is right. Both private and state-sponsored programs are included. Most entries provide a program summary and specific information on academic/career areas supported, amount awarded, eligibility requirements, application requirements, deadline, number awarded, and contact information. At $12.95, this is a good buy.

Price: $12.95, paper.

Available from: Peterson's Guides, 2000 Lenox Drive, P.O. Box 67005, Lawrenceville, NJ 08648. Telephone: (609) 896-1800; toll-free: (800) 338-3282, ext. 660.

Web site: www.petersons.com/

[1321]

The Scholarship Book. By Dan Cassidy. Annual.

While the program descriptions are rather brief and some of the funding programs listed are quite esoteric, there is still a lot of information here for the money. The directory is compiled by a major figure in the financial aid information field and is taken from his company's scholarship database.

Price: $30.00, paper.

Available from: Prentice Hall, P.O. Box 11075, Des Moines, IA 50336-1075. Toll-free: (800) 947-7700.

Web site: www.phdirect.com/

[1322]

The Scholarship Handbook. Annual.

Described here are more than 3,000 funding opportunities, including private, federal, and state scholarships, fellowships, internships, and loans. This is one of the best financial aid directories, along with *Peterson's Scholarships, Grants & Prizes* and *Kaplan Scholarships* (both described above).

Price: $25.95, paper.

Available from: College Board Publications, Box 886, New York, NY 19191-0886. Telephone: (212) 713-8000; toll-free: (800) 323-7155

Web site: www.collegeboard.org/

[1323]

Scholarships, Fellowships, and Loans. Annual.

Although this directory is too expensive for most students (or their parents) to consider buying, it should not be overlooked; many larger libraries have the title in their reference collection. Described here are 4,000+ scholarships, fellowships, and loans available to undergraduates, graduate students, and postdoctorates in the United States and Canada. Each entry identifies qualifications, funds, purposes, application process, and background. The Vocational Goals Index in the front of the volume summarizes, in chart form, the characteristics of each award (e.g., level

of study, subject of study, geographic restrictions, citizenship requirements).

Price: $199, hardcover.

Available from: Gale Group, 27500 Drake Road, Farmington Hills, MI 48331-3535. Telephone: (248) 699-4253; toll free: (800) 877-4253.

Web site: www.galegroup.com/

Subject/Activity Directories

[1324]

Athletic Scholarships: Thousands of Grants—and over $400 Million—for College-Bound Athletes. 4th ed. 2000.

It's not only the star athletes who receive college scholarships. There are millions of dollars available to college-bound students who have participated in a whole range of sports—ranging from baseball and football to the less common sports of badminton, racquetball, riflery, and skiing. But don't be mislead. This is not a guide to portable athletic scholarships (the kind that student-athletes can use at any school); rather this is a state-by-state listing of 2-year and 4-year colleges which identifies the type of athletic scholarships offered by the schools solely to their own students. Profiles for each school include address, phone number, contact persons, number of grants, amount of aid available at the school, and sports offered for men and women.

Price: $16.95, paper; 38.50, hardcover.

Available from: Facts On File, 132 West 31st Street, 17th Floor, New York, NY 10001. Telephone: (212) 683-2244; toll-free: (800) 322-8755.

Web site: www.factsonfile.com/

[1325]

Directory of Research Grants. Annual.

In the latest edition, more than 4,000 grants, fellowships, and loan programs for research, training, and innovative effort sponsored by 600 organizations are described. The emphasis is on U.S. programs, although some sponsored by other countries are included. Entries are arranged by program title. Annotations include requirements, restrictions, financial data (but not for all entries), contacts, and application procedures. The programs are indexed by subject. The information presented here is also available as an Internet subscription (www.grantselect.com) and in a number of derivative publications, including *Directory of Grants in the Humanities* and *Directory of Biomedical and Health Care Grants*.

Price: $134.95, paper.

Available from: Oryx Press, 88 Post Road West, Westport, CT 06881. Telephone: (203) 226-3571; toll-free: (800) 225-5800.

Web site: www.greenwood.com/

[1326]

Financial Aid for Research and Creative Activities Abroad.

By Gail A. Schlachter and R. David Weber. Published every even-numbered year.

This directory will help Americans tap into the millions of dollars available for research, lectureships, exchange programs, work assignments, conference attendance, professional development, and creative projects abroad. The 1,300 listings cover every major field of interest, are tenable in practically every country in the world, are sponsored by more than 500 different private and public organizations and agencies, and are open to all segments of the population, from high school students to professionals and postdoctorates. A companion volume (described below) identifies funding opportunities for study and training abroad.

Price: $45.00, paper.

Available from: Reference Service Press, 5000 Windplay Drive, Suite 4, El Dorado Hills, CA 95762. Telephone: (916) 939-9620.

Web site: www.rspfunding.com/

[1327]

Financial Aid for Study and Training Abroad. By Gail A. Schlachter and R. David Weber. Published every third year.

If you want to go abroad to study and you need money to do so, this is the directory for you. Described here are more than 1,100 scholarships, fellowships, loans, and grants that Americans can use to support structured or unstructured study abroad, including money for formal academic classes, training courses, degree-granting programs, independent study, seminars, workshops, and student internships. Detailed information is provided for each program: address, telephone number (including fax, toll-free, and e-mail), purpose, eligibility, amount awarded, number awarded, duration, special features, limitations, and deadline date. There's also a currency conversion table and an annotated bibliography of key resources that anyone (interested in study abroad or not) can use to find additional funding opportunities.

Price: $39.50, hardcover.

Available from: Reference Service Press, 5000 Windplay Drive, Suite 4, El Dorado Hills, CA 95762. Telephone: (916) 939-9620.

Web site: www.rspfunding.com/

[1328]

How to Pay for Your Degree in Agriculture & Related Fields. Published every even-numbered year.

How to Pay for Your Degree in Business & Related Fields. Published every even-numbered year.

How to Pay for Your Degree in Education & Related Fields. Published every even-numbered year.

How to Pay for Your Degree in Journalism & Related Fields. Published every even-numbered year.

Majoring in one of these fields? Now you can have information—right at your finger tips—on the billions of dollars available to support students working on one of these undergraduate or graduate degrees. *How to Pay for Your Degree in Agriculture & Related Fields* identifies funding for students majoring in agricultural science, animal science, apiculture, ranching, cooperative extension, dairy science, agricultural economics, crops or soils science, enology/viticulture, horticulture, or other related fields. *How to Pay for Your Degree in Business & Related Fields* describes billions of dollars available to support students working on a degree in such business-related fields as finance, banking, accounting, industrial relations, sales, economics, marketing, and personnel administration. *How to Pay for Your Degree in Education & Related Fields* covers funding for students preparing for a career in preschool education, K-12 education, adult education, special education, guidance, educational administration, and the specialty fields of art education, music education, physical education, etc. *How to Pay for Your Degree in Journalism & Related Fields* covers hundreds of grants, scholarships, fellowships, loans, and awards set aside for students working on a degree in journalism, communications, broadcasting, and similar areas.

Price: $30.00 for each title, comb binding.

Available from: Reference Service Press, 5000 Windplay Drive, Suite 4, El Dorado Hills, CA 95762. Telephone: (916) 939-9620.

Web site: www.rspfunding.com/

[1329]

Money for Graduate Students in the Arts & Humanities. Published every odd-numbered year.

Money for Graduate Students in the Biological & Health Sciences. Published every odd-numbered year.

Money for Graduate Students in the Physical & Earth Sciences. Published every odd-numbered year.

Money for Graduate Students in the Social & Behavioral Sciences. Published every odd-numbered year.

Each of these four titles, which are sold separately, describe funding sources available to support study and research on the graduate school level in a specific discipline. *Money for Graduate Students in the Biological & Health Sciences* covers 1,100 fellowships, grants, and awards for graduate study and research in botany, dentistry, genetics, horticulture, medicine, nursing, nutrition, pharmacology, rehabilitation, veterinary sciences, zoology, etc. *Money for Graduate Students in the Arts & Humanities* describes nearly 1,000 funding opportunities for graduate work in architecture, art, dance, design, filmmaking, history, languages, literature, music, performing arts, philosophy, religion, sculpture, and the rest of the humanities. *Money for Graduate Students in the Physical & Earth Sciences* identifies more than 1,000 graduate funding opportunities in atmospheric sciences, aviation, chemistry, computer sciences, engineering, geology, mathematics, physics, space sciences, technology, and the other related sciences. *Money for Graduate Students in the Social & Behavioral Sciences* covers nearly 1,100 fellowships, loans, grants, and awards for graduate work in accounting, advertising, anthropology and ethnology, business administration, demography and statistics, economics, library and information science, marketing, political science, psychology, sociology, and the other social sciences.

Price: *Money for Graduate Students in the Biological & Health Sciences,* $42.50; *Money for Graduate Students in the Humanities,* $40; *Money for Graduate Students in the Physical & Earth Sciences,* $35; *Money for Graduate Students in the Social & Behavioral Sciences,* $42.50.

Available from: Reference Service Press, 5000 Windplay Drive, Suite 4, El Dorado Hills, CA 95762. Telephone: (916) 939-9620.

Web site: www.rspfunding.com/

[1330]

RSP Funding for Engineering Students. By Gail A. Schlachter and R. David Weber. Published every even-numbered year.

Here, in one place, you can find out about more than 650 funding programs set aside specifically to support study, research, creative activities, past accomplishments, future projects, and travel for both undergraduate and graduate engineering students. All areas of engineering are covered, ranging from general practice to acoustical, agricultural, automotive, chemical, civil, electrical, environmental, industrial, mechanical, nuclear, structural, and dozens of others. Each program description covers: purpose, eligibility, monetary award, duration, special features, limitations, number awarded, and deadline date. Plus, the book is organized so you can search for aid by purpose (study or research), program title, sponsor, residency, tenability, engineering specialty, and even deadline.

Price: $30.00, comb binding.

Available from: Reference Service Press, 5000 Windplay Drive, Suite 4, El Dorado Hills, CA 95762. Telephone: (916) 939-9620.

Web site: www.rspfunding.com/

[1331]

RSP Funding for Nurses and Nursing Students. By Gail A. Schlachter and R. David Weber. Published every even-numbered year.

In all, more than 600 scholarships, fellowships, loans, and grants available to nursing students and nurses to support study, professional activities, and research are described in detail in this biennial directory. Each program description is prepared from current material supplied by the sponsoring organization. Entries are grouped by intended recipient. Using the indexes, you can search for these funding opportunities by title, sponsor, residency, tenability, subject, and deadline date.

Price: $30.00, comb binding.

Available from: Reference Service Press, 5000 Windplay Drive, Suite 4, El Dorado Hills, CA 95762. Telephone: (916) 939-9620.

Web site: www.rspfunding.com/

Directories for Special Groups

[1332]

Financial Aid for African Americans. By Gail A. Schlachter and R. David Weber. Published every odd-numbered year.

If you are a Black or African American looking for financial aid, this is the directory for you. Described here are nearly 1,500 scholarships, fellowships, grants, loans, awards, prizes, and internships—representing billions of dollars—open specifically to Black/African Americans. This money can be used to support a whole range of activities, including study, training, research, creative activities, future projects, professional development, and work experience. The listings cover every major subject area and are sponsored by hundreds of private and public agencies and organizations. This directory is part of Reference Service Press's 4-volume *Minority Funding Set,* which replaced the *Directory of Financial Aids for Minorities* in 1997.

Price: $40.00, hardcover.

Available from: Reference Service Press, 5000 Windplay Drive, Suite 4, El Dorado Hills, CA 95762. Telephone: (916) 939-9620.

Web site: www.rspfunding.com/

[1333]

Financial Aid for Asian Americans. By Gail A. Schlachter and R. David Weber. Published every odd-numbered year.

This directory is aimed at Americans of Chinese, Japanese, Korean, Vietnamese, Filipino, or other Asian ancestry. The book has been designed so that they can quickly identify available funding by specific subject, sponsor, title, residency requirements, where the money can be spent, type of funding, and deadline date. More than 1,000 scholarships, fellowships, loans, grants, awards, and internships set aside for Asian Americans are described here. Full information is provided for each of these programs: purpose, eligibility, financial data, duration, special features, limitations, number awarded, and deadline date. This directory is part of Reference Service Press's 4-volume *Minority Fund-*

ing Set, which replaced the *Directory of Financial Aids for Minorities* in 1997.

Price: $37.50, hardcover.

Available from: Reference Service Press, 5000 Windplay Drive, Suite 4, El Dorado Hills, CA 95762. Telephone: (916) 939-9620.

Web site: www.rspfunding.com/

[1334]

Financial Aid for Hispanic Americans. By Gail A. Schlachter and R. David Weber. Published every odd-numbered year.

One of 4 titles in Reference Service Press's *Minority Funding Set* (which replaced the *Directory of Financial Aids for Minorities* in 1997), this directory identifies more than 1,400 scholarships, fellowships, loans, grants, awards, and internships available to Hispanic Americans, including Mexican Americans, Puerto Ricans, Cuban Americans, and others of Latin American origin. The directory is organized by program type and indexed by sponsoring organization, program title, geographic coverage, subject focus, and deadline date. Detailed program entries provide information on purpose, eligibility, money awarded, duration, special features, number awarded, limitations, and deadline.

Price: $40.00, hardcover.

Available from: Reference Service Press, 5000 Windplay Drive, Suite 4, El Dorado Hills, CA 95762. Telephone: (916) 939-9620.

Web site: www.rspfunding.com/

[1335]

Financial Aid for Native Americans. By Gail A. Schlachter and R. David Weber. Published every odd-numbered year.

Detailed information on 1,500 funding opportunities open to American Indians, Native Alaskans, and Native Pacific Islanders (including Native Hawaiians and Samoans) is presented in this biennial directory. Program entries are arranged by target group and type of funding; additional access is provided by the subject, title, sponsor, residency, tenability, and deadline date indexes. Plus, the directory contains an annotated bibliography of 60 key directories that identify even more financial aid opportunities. This directory is part of Reference Service Press's 4-volume *Minority Funding Set,* which replaced the *Directory of Financial Aids for Minorities* in 1997.

Price: $40.00, hardcover.

Available from: Reference Service Press, 5000 Windplay Drive, Suite 4, El Dorado Hills, CA 95762. Telephone: (916) 939-9620.

Web site: www.rspfunding.com/

[1336]

Directory of Financial Aids for Women. By Gail A. Schlachter and R. David Weber. Published every odd-numbered year.

Are you a woman looking for financial aid? Or, do you know women who need funding for school, research, creative projects, travel, or other activities? If so, take a look at the *Directory of Financial Aids for Women.* Here, in one place, are descriptions of 1,600 funding programs, representing billions of dollars in financial aid set aside just for women. Each of these programs can be accessed by program title, sponsoring organization, geographic coverage, deadline date, and subject. There's also a list of key sources that identify additional financial aid opportunities.

Price: $45.00, hardcover.

Available from: Reference Service Press, 5000 Windplay Drive, Suite 4, El Dorado Hills, CA 95762. Telephone: (916) 939-9620.

Web site: www.rspfunding.com/

[1337]
Financial Aid for the Disabled and Their Families. By Gail A. Schlachter and R. David Weber. Published every even-numbered year.

There are more than 1,000 funding opportunities available to meet the individual needs of America's largest minority: 43 million persons with disabilities and their children or parents. To find out about this funding, use *Financial Aid for the Disabled and Their Families.* All disabilities are covered, including visual impairments, hearing impairments, orthopedic disabilities, learning disabilities, and multiple disabilities. The following information is provided for each entry: program title, sponsoring organization address and telephone numbers, purpose, eligibility, money awarded, duration, special features, limitations, number awarded, and deadline date. To meet the needs of students with visual impairments, information on programs just for them is also available in a large print edition ($30) and on an IBM- or Mac-compatible disk ($50).

Price: $40.00, hardcover.

Available from: Reference Service Press, 5000 Windplay Drive, Suite 4, El Dorado Hills, CA 95762. Telephone: (916) 939-9620.

Web site: www.rspfunding.com/

[1338]
Financial Aid for Veterans, Military Personnel, and Their Dependents. By Gail A. Schlachter and R. David Weber. Published every even-numbered year.

Veterans, military personnel, and their dependents (spouses, children, grandchildren, and dependent parents) make up more than one third of America's population today. Each year, public and private agencies set aside billions of dollars in financial aid for these groups. This directory identifies, in one source, the federal, state, and privately-funded scholarships, fellowships, loans, grants or grants-in-aid, awards, and internships aimed specifically at individuals with ties to the military. More than 1,100 programs are described in the latest edition. These opportunities are open to applicants at all levels (from high school through postdoctoral) for education, research, travel, training, career development, or emergency situations. The detailed entries are indexed by title, sponsoring organization, geographic coverage, subject, and deadline.

Price: $40.00, hardcover.

Available from: Reference Service Press, 5000 Windplay Drive, Suite 4, El Dorado Hills, CA 95762. Telephone: (916) 939-9620.

Web site: www.rspfunding.com/

[1339]
Peterson's Scholarships for Study in the USA & Canada: The Money You Need for the Education You Want. 3d ed. 1999.

The latest edition of this directory identifies scholarships and other funding opportunities for foreign students interested in pursuing an undergraduate or graduate degree in the United States or Canada. While many of the programs described here are open to Americans as well as foreign students, this directory has the distinction of being the only one providing information specifically for foreign students.

Price: $21.95, paper.

Available from: Peterson's Guides, 2000 Lenox Drive, P.O. Box 67005, Lawrenceville, NJ 08648. Telephone: (609) 896-1800; toll-free: (800) 338-3282, ext. 660.

Web site: www.petersons.com/

Contests and Awards

[1340]
Awards, Honors, and Prizes. Annual.

While this massive, 2-volume set is not the kind of publication you're likely to buy for your own financial aid library, you will definitely want to look at it at a library. It contains the most extensive and up-to-date listings of awards, honors, and prizes available anywhere. It covers all subject areas, all areas of the world, and all types of awards, except scholarships, fellowships, prizes received only as a result of entering contests, and local or regional awards.

Price: Volume 1 (United States): $220, hardcover; Volume 2 (Foreign): $245, hardcover.

Available from: Gale Group, P.O. Box 9187, Farmington Hills, MI 48333-9187. Telephone: (248) 699-GALE; toll-free: (800) 877-GALE.

Web site: www.galegroup.com/

Internships

[1341]
The Best 109 Internships. Annual.

Unlike Peterson's *Internships* directory (described below), this listing is selective rather than comprehensive. It describes in detail the "top" 100 or so paid and unpaid internships in America. Information was gathered through questionnaires, interviews with interns, and on-site visits. Each program entry (generally 3 pages) provides information on: application process, selection process, compensation (from nothing to $1,200 or more per week), quality of the work experience, locations, duration, prerequisites, and sources of additional information. The internship profiles are arranged alphabetically by employer. An appendix groups internships by several interesting categories: highest compensation, most selective, etc.

Price: $21.00, paper.

Available from: Random House, 4000 Hahn Road, Westminster, MD 21157. Telephone: (212) 751-2600; toll-free: (800) 733-3000.

Web site: www.randomhouse.com/princetonreview

[1342]
Peterson's Internships. Annual.

Work experience gained through an internship can provide an advantage in a student's job search. Plus, internships can provide cash for college (in stipends, subsequent scholarships, or both). One of the best ways to find out about internship opportunities is with a copy of the latest edition of this directory, which identifies more than 1,300 organizations offering more than 35,000 paid and unpaid on-the-job training opportunities in such fields as architecture, business, communications, and sciences. Program entries describe length and duration of the position, pay, desired qualifications, duties, training involved, availability of college credit, and application contacts, procedures, and deadlines. International internships are also included, as well as information for interns working abroad and non-U.S. citizens applying for U.S. internships.

Price: $26.95, paper.

Available from: Peterson's Guides, 2000 Lenox Drive, P.O. Box 67005, Lawrenceville, NJ 08648. Telephone: (609) 896-1800; toll-free: (800) 338-3282, ext. 660.

Web site: www.petersons.com/

Nothing Over $4.95

[1343]
College Countdown. Annual.

Getting into the right college is one of the most important challenges you'll ever face. Are you doing the right things at the right times? This checklist identifies exactly what high school students need to do to get ready to apply for college and for college aid.

Price: $4.50, paper.

Available from: Reference Service Press, 5000 Windplay Drive, Suite 4, El Dorado Hills, CA 95762. Telephone: (916) 939-9620.

Web site: www.rspfunding.com/

[1344]
College Dollars.

To help students pay for college, State Farm is offering this free scholarship database download to anyone that visits their site (you don't need to be a State Farm customer). The College Dollars database describes nearly 1,800 local and national funding opportunities open to entering or continuing college students. While the directions provided to use the download aren't particularly helpful, and there is no indication of when the information was last updated, this is still a source worth checking. It even comes with application request letters built in.

Price: Free.

Available from: State Farm Insurance, One State Farm Plaza Bloomington, IL 61710-0001. Toll-free: (800) 447-4930

Web site: www.statefarm.com

[1345]
Federal Benefits for Veterans and Dependents. Annual.

This is one of the federal government's all-time best-selling publications. The pamphlet provides a comprehensive summary of federal government benefits (not all of which are monetary) available to veterans and their dependents. It is updated annually and contains information on alcoholism treatment programs, aid for the blind, burial assistance, clothing allowances, compensation for service-connected disabilities, death payments, dental treatment, dependents' education, education and training loans, etc. This publication can also be found online, at the DVA's web site.

Price: $3.50, paper.

Available from: U.S. Government Printing Office, P.O. Box 371954, Pittsburgh, PA 15250-7954. Toll-free: (800) 669-8331.

Web site: www.access.gpo.gov/su-docs/

[1346]
Financial Assistance for Library and Information Studies. Annual.

This tabular summary of fellowships, scholarships, grants-in-aid, loans, and other funding for library education is issued annually (usually in November) by the American Library Association. It lists awards from state library agencies, national and state library associations, local libraries, and academic institutions offering undergraduate and graduate programs in library education in the United States and Canada. For each entry, the following information is given: granting body, level of program, type of assistance, number available, academic or other requirements, application deadline, and contact address. Scholarships of less than $200 are not included.

Price: $4.00, paper.

Available from: American Library Association, 50 East Huron Street, Chicago, IL 60611. Telephone: (312) 280-4277, ext. 4282; toll-free: (800) 545-2433, ext. 4282.

Web site: www.ala.org/

[1347]
Free Application for Federal Student Aid. Annual.

If you are going to be in college next year, you need to fill out the Free Application for Federal Student Aid (FAFSA). By filling out this form, you can start the application process for any of these federal programs: Federal Pell Grants, Federal Supplemental Educational Opportunity Grants, Federal Subsidized and Unsubsidized Stafford Loans, Stafford/Ford Federal Direct Subsidized and Unsubsidized Loans, Federal Perkins Loans, Federal Work-Study, Title VII, and Public Health Act Programs. Fill out this form even if you are not interested in getting (or don't think you can qualify for) federal aid; many privately-sponsored programs require students to have submitted FAFSA before applying for their funding. Help in completing the FAFSA is available online. The address is: www.ed.gov/prog_info/SFA/FAFSA. Students can speed up the FAFSA application process by downloading a free Windows-based program for IBM-compatible computers called FAFSA Express; using it can cut weeks off the application process and eliminate the mistakes and problems that sometimes arise when filling out the paper FAFSA form.

Price: Free, paper or downloadable Windows-based program for IBM-compatible computers.

Available from: To receive a copy, call (800) 4-FED-AID or download FAFSA Express at the following web site:

Web site: www.ed.gov/offices/OPE/express.html/

[1348]
Fulbright and Related Grants for Graduate Study and Research Abroad. Annual.

The Fulbright Student Program is designed to give recent B.S./B.A. graduates, master's degree and doctoral candidates, young professionals, and artists opportunities for personal development and international experience. This annual pamphlet, available without charge from the Institute of International Education, lists Institute-administered Fulbright fellowships and grants available to U.S. graduate students for study and research abroad. The arrangement is by country in which the recipient will study or conduct research. Entries specify recommended fields of study or investigation, language requirements, duration, selection procedures, financial data, application process, special features, and limitations. A similar publication for more advanced applicants is *Fulbright Scholar Program*, also available without charge from IIE.

Price: Free, paper.

Available from: Institute of International Education, 809 United Nations Plaza, New York, NY 10017-3580. Telephone: (212) 883-8200; toll-free: (800) 445-0433.

Web site: www.iie.org/

[1349]

Need a Lift? To Educational Opportunities, Careers, Loans, Scholarships, Employment. Prep. by the American Legion Educational and Scholarship Program. Annual.

What started as just a listing of financial aid offered by American Legion affiliates around the country has grown into a sizeable financial aid publication (each edition is generally 150 pages or more). While American Legion educational assistance on the national and state level is still covered, much more is now presented in each annual issue: information on calculating financial need, a chart describing the major federal programs, some information on funding for veterans and their dependents, and short descriptions of some other types of financial aid. There is even a list of postsecondary schools nationwide, which gives phone numbers, enrollment by gender, SAT scores, tuition costs, costs for room and board, deadlines for admissions and financial aid, and what financial aid forms are required. All this for $3. Quite a bargain.

Price: $3, paper.

Available from: American Legion, Attn: Emblem Sales, P.O. Box 1050, Indianapolis, IN 46206-1050. Telephone: (317) 630-1207; toll-free: (888) 453-4466.

Web site: www.legion.org/

[1350]

Social Science Research Council Fellowships and Grants for Training and Research. Annual.

The Social Science Research Council is an autonomous, nongovernmental, not-for-profit international association devoted to "the advancement of interdisciplinary research in the social sciences." This annual pamphlet, distributed without charge by the Social Science Research Council, provides a listing and short description of grants that the council sponsors either independently or with the American Council of Learned Societies. These programs (dissertation fellowships and advanced research grants) apply to the social sciences and humanities in both the United States and, selectively, abroad. They are open to American and foreign citizens on the advanced graduate or postgraduate levels.

Price: Free, paper.

Available from: Social Science Research Council, 810 Seventh Avenue, New York, NY 10019. Telephone: (212) 377-2700.

Web site: www.ssrc.org/

[1351]

The Student Guide: Financial Aid from the U.S. Department of Education. Annual.

Of the $70 billion in student aid currently available, close to one half of it (approximately $40 billion) will be supplied by the federal government. And, most of the federal funds will be channeled through a handful of programs: Pell Grants, Subsidized and Unsubsidized Stafford Loans, PLUS Loans, Federal Supplemental Educational Opportunity Grants, Federal Work-Study, and Federal Perkins Loans. Get information about these programs straight from the source, in this free booklet issued by the U.S. Department of Education. For each program, official information

is provided on purpose, financial support offered, application procedures, eligibility, recipient responsibilities, and notification process. The *Guide* can also be downloaded from the Department of Education's web site.

Price: Free, paper.

Available from: U.S. Department of Education, c/o Federal Student Information Aid Center, P.O. Box 84, Washington, DC 20044. Toll-free: (800) 4-FED-AID.

Web site: www.ed.gov/prog_info/SFA/StudentGuide/

[1352]

Surfing for Scholarships in Cyberspace. Annual

Use your computer to search for scholarships in cyberspace. This guide will point you in the right direction, by identifying the best internet sites students can use to find money. Best of all, almost all these sites can be searched online without any charge.

Price: $4.50, paper.

Available from: Reference Service Press, 5000 Windplay Drive, Suite 4, El Dorado Hills, CA 95762. Telephone: (916) 939-9620.

Web site: www.rspfunding.com/

Cyberspace Sites

[1353]

CollegeBoard Scholarship Search.

This is a free web version of the College Board's *Scholarship Handbook*. Described here are scholarships, fellowships, loans, internships, and other types of financial aid programs sponsored by 2,000+ federal, state, and private sources. The search interface is relatively easy to use, but the database is limited in scope and only updated annually.

Available on the Internet at: www.collegeboard.org/

[1354]

FASTaid.

Billing itself as the "World's largest and oldest private sector scholarship database," this service is a product of the National Scholarship Research Service, a scholarship search service involved in producing *The Scholarship Book* (described above). Thousands of financial aid programs for undergraduates, graduate students, and beyond are briefly described in the database.

Available on the Internet at: www.fastaid.com/

[1355]

fastWEB: Financial Aid Search Through the Web.

FastWEB advertises itself as "The Internet's largest free scholarship search." It contains concise descriptions of financial aid offered by 3,000+ sponsoring organizations. If you take the time to fill out their multi-page questionnaire online (this can take up to 20 minutes, depending upon connection speed), fastWEB will set up a mailbox for you and deliver a list of scholarships based on the information you supplied.

Available on the Internet at: www.fastWeb.com/

[1356]

FinAid! The SmartStudent Guide to Financial Aid.

Sporting a new look and name, this popular web site (formerly known as the "Financial Aid Information Page") offers a number of short lists of financial aid opportunities available to specific groups, including women, minorities, international students, etc. Much more comprehensive is the bibliography of financial aid resources (print, electronic, and web based), but this area has not been kept up to date.

Available on the Internet at: www.FinAid.org/

[1357]
MACH25.

CollegeNET offers a guide to colleges and universities in the United States (and selected other countries). Its scholarship database, MACH25, contains data from Wintergreen/Orchard House. Information is provided on 8,000 private and school-based financial aid programs offered by 1,500 sponsors. It is updated annually. The database is similar to fastWEB, but not as easy to use. You can view the results of your search in brief or detailed formats, save individual awards in your profile, and generate letters to request additional information. You may get more "hits" with your MACH25 search than with either fastWEB or SRN, but your search results will probably be less precise; so, be prepared to sift through a number of irrelevant "leads" to find ones that exactly match your requirements.

Available on the Internet at:
www.collegenet.com/mach25/

[1358]
Peterson's Scholarship Search

This free Internet search service identifies scholarships, awards, and prizes available to support college study. To conduct a free financial aid search, students must first register and supply a password to enter or reenter the service. After registering, students answer a few questions and then wait for a minute or two for the results. Very brief information for each match is presented on a form, which covers sponsor, type of award, deadline, number awarded, renewability, what's required in the application process, and contact. Some programs also include award descriptions, but many do not.

Available on the Internet at: www.petersons.com/

[1359]
SRN Express.

Sponsored by Scholarship Resource Network (SRN), this web site can be accessed by students directly, without charge. Students have to register (and give out their phone number), but in return they get a chance to search a scholarship database which lists primarily private-sector aid (8,000 programs). Single-school awards are not included. This same database is also available at a web site hosted by SalleiMae: www.wiredscholar.com.

Available on the Internet at: www.srnexpress.com/

Indexes

Program Title Index

If you know the name of a particular funding program and want to find out where it is covered in the directory, use the Program Title Index. Here, program titles are arranged alphabetically, word by word. To assist you in your search, every program is listed by all its known names or abbreviations. In addition, we've used an alphabetical code (within parentheses) to help you determine if the program falls within your scope of interest: S = Scholarships; F = Fellowships; L = Loans; G = Grants; A = Awards; and I = Internships. Here's how the code works: if a program is followed (S) 141, the program is described in entry 141 in the Scholarships section. If the same program title is followed by another entry number—for example, (L) 680—the program is also described in entry 680 in the Loans section. Remember: the numbers cited here refer to program entry numbers, not to page numbers in the book.

S–Scholarships   **F–Fellowships**   **L–Loans**   **G–Grants**   **A–Awards**   **I–Internships**

Barbara Jordan Memorial Scholarship, (S) 33, (F) 406

Barrows Minority Doctoral Student Scholarship. *See* Lionel C. Barrows Minority Doctoral Student Scholarship, entry (F) 505

Barry Sherman Fellowship. *See* IRTS Summer Fellowship Program, entry (I) 1171

Bassett Unified/HSF Scholarship. *See* High School Scholarship Programs of the Hispanic Scholarship Fund, entry (S) 138

Bates Memorial Scholarship. *See* SBC L.C. and Daisy Bates Memorial Scholarship, entry (S) 306

Bates Minority Scholarship Program. *See* Daisy and L.C. Bates Minority Scholarship Program, entry (S) 80

Baum Undergraduate Scholarship. *See* American Meteorological Society Undergraduate Scholarships, entry (S) 16

Bay Area Minority Law Student Scholarships, (F) 407

Bayer Corporation Scholars. *See* Project SEED Scholarships, entry (S) 280

Beaudry Memorial Award. *See* Worldstudio Foundation Scholarships, entries (S) 379, (F) 637

Beaufort Gazette Internship for Minorities, (I) 1097

Beck Fellowship. *See* Stan Beck Fellowship, entries (S) 319, (F) 612

Behavioral Sciences Postdoctoral Fellowships in Epilepsy, (G) 726

Behavioral Sciences Student Fellowships in Epilepsy, (G) 727

Behrend Minority Dissertation Fellowships, (G) 728

Belo Corporation Scholarship. *See* Texas Broadcast Education Foundation Scholarships, entry (S) 336

Belpré Book Award. *See* Pura Belpré Book Award, entry (A) 1063

Bernard Majewski Fellowship, (G) 729

Berrien Fragos Thorn Arts Scholarships for Migrant Farmworkers, (G) 730

Betty A. DeVries Memorial Fund. *See* Associated Colleges of Illinois Scholarship Program, entry (S) 25

Bienstock Fellowship. *See* N.S. Bienstock Fellowship, entry (G) 938

Biloxi Sun Herald Internship for Minorities, (I) 1098

Biomedical Research Training Program for Underrepresented Minorities, (I) 1099

Blaszcak Scholarship. *See* Fleming/Blaszcak Scholarship, entry (S) 114

Blechschmidt Award. *See* Geological Society of America General Research Grants Program, entry (G) 811

Board of Governors Medical Scholarship Program, (F) 408

Bob Pattison Fellowship. *See* IRTS Summer Fellowship Program, entry (I) 1171

Bolin Fellowships for Minority Graduate Students. *See* Gaius Charles Bolin Fellowships for Minority Graduate Students, entry (G) 810

Bolivar Award. *See* Simon Bolivar Lecture Award, entry (A) 1068

Bonner McLane Scholarship. *See* Texas Broadcast Education Foundation Scholarships, entry (S) 336

Booker T. Washington Scholarships, (S) 34

Border Playwright's Project, (A) 1035

Bouchet Award. *See* Edward A. Bouchet Award, entry (A) 1039

Bowen Foundation Internships. *See* Emma L. Bowen Foundation Internships, entry (I) 1133

Bradley Scholarship. *See* Ed Bradley Scholarship, entry (S) 97

Breakthrough to Nursing Scholarships for Ethnic People of Color, (S) 35

"Bright Smiles, Bright Futures" Minority Scholarship. *See* Colgate "Bright Smiles, Bright Futures" Minority Scholarships, entry (S) 59

Bristol–Myers Squibb PRLDEF Corporate Legal Fellowship, (F) 409, (I) 1100

Brock Memorial Scholarship. *See* Cathy L. Brock Memorial Scholarship, entries (S) 48, (F) 415

Brooker Collegiate Scholarship for Minorities. *See* George M. Brooker Collegiate Scholarship for Minorities, entries (S) 130, (F) 462

Brookhaven National Laboratory Minority High School Apprenticeship Program, (I) 1101

Brookhaven National Laboratory Science and Engineering Opportunities Program for Minorities and Women, (I) 1102

Brown COREM Scholarships. *See* Richard and Helen Brown COREM Scholarships, entry (F) 591

Brown Fellowship. *See* Howard Mayer Brown Fellowship, entry (F) 477

Brown Foundation College Scholarships, (S) 36

Brown Memorial Scholarship. *See* Ronald H. Brown Memorial Scholarship, entry (S) 298

Bruce L. "Biff" Reed Award. *See* Geological Society of America General Research Grants Program, entry (G) 811

Buffett Foundation Scholarship Program, (S) 37

Bunche Award. *See* Ralph J. Bunche Award, entry (A) 1064

Bunche Summer Institute. *See* Ralph Bunche Summer Institute, entry (S) 287

Bureau of Land Management Award, (S) 38

Burkhardt Residential Fellowships for Recently Tenured Scholars. *See* Frederick Burkhardt Residential Fellowships for Recently Tenured Scholars, entry (G) 808

Burns Memorial Fellowships for Social and Economic Justice. *See* Haywood Burns Memorial Fellowships for Social and Economic Justice, entry (I) 1154

Burstein Fellows. *See* American Educational Research Association Fellows Program, entry (G) 702

Bushnell Internship Program. *See* Asa S. Bushnell Internship Program, entry (I) 1089

Business Reporting Intern Program for Minority College Sophomores and Juniors, (I) 1103

Byrd Fellowship Program, (G) 731

Byron Hanke Fellowship for Graduate Research on Community Associations, (G) 732

C. Clyde Ferguson Law Scholarship, (F) 410

Cadbury Award. *See* William and Charlotte Cadbury Award, entry (A) 1076

CAHSEE Young Educators Program, (I) 1104

Calder Summer Undergraduate Research Program, (G) 733

California Adolescent Nutrition and Fitness Program Scholarships. *See* CANFit Program Scholarships, entries (S) 43, (F) 413

California Community Service Scholarships, (I) 1105

California Dental Graduate Loan Reduction Program, (G) 734

California Library Association Scholarship for Minority Students in Memory of Edna Yelland. *See* CLA Scholarship for Minority Students in Memory of Edna Yelland, entry (F) 418

California Real Estate Endowment Fund Scholarship Program, (S) 39

Curry Summer Internship Program. *See* Michael Curry Summer Internship Program, entry (I) 1209

Cutler Fellowship in Consumer Studies. *See* Virginia F. Cutler Fellowship in Consumer Studies, entry (F) 629

D. Augustus Straker Scholarship, (F) 427

Daisy and L.C. Bates Minority Scholarship Program, (S) 80

Daisy Bates Memorial Scholarship. *See* SBC L.C. and Daisy Bates Memorial Scholarship, entry (S) 306

Dallas Independent School District/HSF Scholarship. *See* High School Scholarship Programs of the Hispanic Scholarship Fund, entry (S) 138

Dalmas A. Taylor Memorial Summer Minority Policy Fellowship, (I) 1124

Damon P. Moore Scholarship, (S) 81

Daniel Gutierrez Memorial General Scholarship, (S) 82

Dargan Minority Scholarship. *See* KATU Thomas R. Dargan Minority Scholarship, entries (S) 180, (I) 1183

David A. DeBolt Teacher Shortage Scholarship Program, (L) 642

David C. Lizárraga Graduate Fellowships, (F) 428

Davis Legal Memorial Scholarships. *See* Wally Davis Legal Memorial Scholarships, entry (F) 630

Davis Scholarship Fund. *See* Edward Davis Scholarship Fund, entry (S) 101

de La Renta Founders Scholarship. *See* Hispanic Designers Founders Scholarships, entry (S) 143

DeBolt Teacher Shortage Scholarship Program. *See* David A. DeBolt Teacher Shortage Scholarship Program, entry (L) 642

Defense Intelligence Agency Undergraduate Training Assistance Program, (L) 643

Defense Policy Fellowships, (G) 770

Defense University Research Instrumentation Program, (G) 771

Delaware Valley Space Grant College Consortium Graduate Student Fellowships. *See* NASA/DVSGC Graduate Student Fellowships, entry (F) 541

Delaware Valley Space Grant College Consortium Undergraduate Summer Scholarships. *See* NASA/DVSGC Undergraduate Summer Scholarships, entry (G) 911

Delaware Valley Space Grant College Consortium Undergraduate Tuition Scholarships. *See* DVSGC Undergraduate Tuition Scholarships, entry (S) 92

Dell/UNCF Corporate Scholars Program, (S) 83, (F) 429, (I) 1125

Delores A. Auzenne Fellowship for Graduate Study, (F) 430

Denny's Grand Slam Scholars, (S) 84

Dent Student Scholarship. *See* Albert W. Dent Student Scholarship, entry (F) 391

Department of Agriculture Summer Intern Program. *See* USDA Summer Intern Program, entry (I) 1304

Department of Defense Experimental Program to Stimulate Competitive Research, (G) 772

Department of Housing and Urban Development Doctoral Dissertation Research Grant Program. *See* HUD Doctoral Dissertation Research Grant Program, entry (G) 831

Department of State Foreign Affairs Fellowship Program. *See* Thomas R. Pickering Foreign Affairs Fellowships, entry (L) 670

Department of State Student Intern Program, (I) 1126

Department of the Interior Diversity Intern Program. *See* DOI Diversity Intern Program, entry (I) 1128

Developmental Grants for Minority Collaborative Projects, (G) 773

DeVries Memorial Fund. *See* Associated Colleges of Illinois Scholarship Program, entry (S) 25

Dick Hazel Minority Scholarship Award. *See* Pat and Dick Hazel Minority Scholarship Award, entry (L) 664

Dietetic Internship Scholarships, (I) 1127

Dietetic Technician Program Scholarships, (S) 85

DiFranco Fellowship. *See* IRTS Summer Fellowship Program, entry (I) 1171

Dillon Alaska Research Award. *See* Geological Society of America General Research Grants Program, entry (G) 811

Diplomacy Fellowships, (G) 774

Direct Farm Loans for Socially Disadvantaged Persons, (L) 644

Dissertation Fellowship for U.S. Latina/o Scholars. *See* Cesar E. Chavez Dissertation Fellowship for U.S. Latina/o Scholars, entry (G) 746

Dissertation Fellowship Program for Minorities. *See* Ford Foundation Dissertation Fellowship Program for Minorities, entry (G) 805

Dissertation Fellowships for the Study of International Migration to the United States, (G) 775

Dissertation Fellowships in East European Studies, (G) 776

Dissertation Fellowships of the Minority Scholar–in–Residence Program, (G) 777

Dissertation Year Fellowships for Graduate Students of Color in Humanities and Social Sciences, (G) 778

Dissertation Year/Postdoctoral Fellowship for Academic Diversity, (G) 779

District of Columbia Space Grant Consortium Awards, (S) 86, (F) 431

Dixon Woodbury Research Clinical Training Fellowship. *See* Clinical Research Training Fellowships in Epilepsy, entry (G) 757

Doctoral Dissertation Fellowships in Law and Social Science, (G) 780

Doctoral Dissertation Improvement Grants in the Directorate for Biological Sciences, (G) 781

Doctoral Dissertation Research Improvement Grants in the Directorate for Social, Behavioral, and Economic Sciences, (G) 782

DOI Diversity Intern Program, (I) 1128

Don Sahli–Kathy Woodall Minority Student Scholarships, (S) 87

Donald J. DiFranco Fellowship. *See* IRTS Summer Fellowship Program, entry (I) 1171

Donnelley Scholarship. *See* Associated Colleges of Illinois Scholarship Program, entry (S) 25

Douvas Memorial Scholarship, (S) 88

Dr. Juan Andrade, Jr. Scholarship for Young Hispanic Leaders, (S) 89

Dr. Juan D. Villarreal–HDA Foundation Scholarships, (S) 90, (F) 432

Dr. Nancy Foster Scholarship Program, (F) 433

Dr. Pedro Grau Undergraduate Scholarship. *See* American Meteorological Society Undergraduate Scholarships, entry (S) 16

Dr. Scholl Foundation Scholarships, (S) 91

DuBois Fellowship Program. *See* W.E.B. DuBois Fellowship Program, entry (G) 1021

Dunn, Jr. Memorial Fellowship Program. *See* James H. Dunn, Jr. Memorial Fellowship Program, entry (I) 1175

DVSGC Graduate Student Fellowships. *See* NASA/DVSGC Graduate Student Fellowships, entry (F) 541

High School Workshops for Minority Students in Journalism Scholarships, (A) 1046

H.I.S. Scholars Program, (S) 140, (I) 1159

Hispanic Alliance for Career Enhancement National Scholarship Program. See HACE National Scholarship Program, entries (S) 134, (F) 465

Hispanic Alliance for Culture, Education and Recognition/HSF Scholarship. See High School Scholarship Programs of the Hispanic Scholarship Fund, entry (S) 138

Hispanic American Commitment to Educational Resources (HACER) Scholarship Program. See RMHC/HACER Scholarship Program, entry (S) 295

Hispanic Association of Colleges and Universities National Internship Program. See HACU National Internship Program, entry (I) 1152

Hispanic Bar Association of D.C. Fellowships. See HBA–DC Fellowships, entry (I) 1155

Hispanic Business/Professional Association/HSF Scholarship. See High School Scholarship Programs of the Hispanic Scholarship Fund, entry (S) 138

Hispanic Chamber of Commerce Sonoma County/HSF Scholarship. See High School Scholarship Programs of the Hispanic Scholarship Fund, entry (S) 138

Hispanic Church Multiplication Team Scholarships, (S) 141, (F) 470

Hispanic College Fund Scholarships, (S) 142

Hispanic College Fund–INROADS–Sprint Scholars Program. See H.I.S. Scholars Program, entries (S) 140, (I) 1159

Hispanic Designers Founders Scholarships, (S) 143

Hispanic Designers General Scholarships, (S) 144

Hispanic Designers Model Search. See Modelo Mundial–World Model Competition, entry (A) 1055

Hispanic Engineer National Achievement Awards Conference Student Leadership Awards. See HENAAC Student Leadership Awards, entries (S) 135, (F) 468

Hispanic Heritage Youth Awards, (A) 1047

Hispanic Lawyers Scholarship Fund, (F) 471

Hispanic Link Journalism Foundation Fellowships, (I) 1160

Hispanic Outlook Scholarship Fund, (S) 145

Hispanic Outreach In Search of New Scholars. See H.O.R.I.S.O.N.S. Scholarships, entry (S) 148

Hispanic Scholarship Fund/Ford Motor Company Corporate Scholarship Program, (S) 146

Hispanic Scholarship Fund/South Texas Scholarship Program, (S) 147, (F) 472

Hispanic Scholarship Funds. See ABC Hispanic Scholarship Funds, entries (S) 3, (F) 387

Hispanic Theological Initiative Dissertation Year Grants, (G) 828

Hispanic Theological Initiative Doctoral Grants, (F) 473

HIV/AIDS Research Fellowships, (F) 474

Holly A. Cornell Scholarship, (F) 475

Honda Award for Environmental Design. See Worldstudio Foundation Scholarships, entries (S) 379, (F) 637

Hope Scholarship. See American Meteorological Society Undergraduate Scholarships, entry (S) 16

H.O.R.I.S.O.N.S. Scholarships, (S) 148

Horizons/Frameline Film and Video Completion Fund, (G) 829

Horsley Research Clinical Training Fellowship. See Clinical Research Training Fellowships in Epilepsy, entry (G) 757

Household Corporate Scholars Program. See UNCF/Household Corporate Scholars Program, entries (S) 342, (I) 1300

Houston Fellowship for Law Teaching. See Reginald F. Lewis and Charles Hamilton Houston Fellowships for Law Teaching, entry (G) 971

Howard H. Hanks, Jr. Scholarship in Meteorology. See American Meteorological Society Undergraduate Scholarships, entry (S) 16

Howard Hughes Medical Institute Predoctoral Fellowships in Biological Sciences, (F) 476

Howard Hughes Medical Institute Research Training Fellowships for Medical Students, (G) 830

Howard Hughes Medical Institute–National Institutes of Health Research Scholars Program. See HHMI–NIH Research Scholars Program, entry (G) 827

Howard Mayer Brown Fellowship, (F) 477

Howard Research Grants. See Geological Society of America General Research Grants Program, entry (G) 811

Howard T. Orville Scholarship in Meteorology. See American Meteorological Society Undergraduate Scholarships, entry (S) 16

HP Scholar Program, (S) 149, (I) 1161

HUD Doctoral Dissertation Research Grant Program, (G) 831

Hugh J. Andersen Memorial Scholarships, (F) 478

Hughes Medical Institute Predoctoral Fellowships in Biological Sciences. See Howard Hughes Medical Institute Predoctoral Fellowships in Biological Sciences, entry (F) 476

Hughes Medical Institute Research Training Fellowships for Medical Students. See Howard Hughes Medical Institute Research Training Fellowships for Medical Students, entry (G) 830

Hurst Award. See Worldstudio Foundation Scholarships, entries (S) 379, (F) 637

Hyatt Hotel Fund for Minority Lodging Management Students, (S) 150

Ian M. Rolland Scholarship, (S) 151

Ibero American Action League Hispanic Scholarship Endowment, (S) 152

IBM Cooperative Fellowship Program, (F) 479, (I) 1162

IBM Research Fellowship Program, (F) 480, (I) 1163

Idaho Migrant Council Hispanic Scholarship Fund, (S) 153

Idaho Minority and "At Risk" Student Scholarship, (S) 154

Idaho Space Grant Consortium Graduate Fellowships, (G) 832

Idaho Space Grant Consortium Research Initiation Grants, (G) 833

Idaho Space Grant Consortium Scholarship Program, (S) 155

IES Dissertation Grants Program. See AERA/IES Dissertation Grants Program, entry (G) 691

IES Postdoctoral Fellowship Program. See AERA/IES Postdoctoral Fellowship Program, entry (G) 692

IES Research Grants Program. See AERA/IES Research Grants Program, entry (G) 693

Illinois Arts Council Ethnic and Folk Arts Master/Apprentice Program, (G) 834

Illinois Broadcasters Association Endowed Scholarships, (I) 1164

Illinois Consortium for Educational Opportunity Program, (L) 646

Illinois Minority Graduate Incentive Program, (F) 481

Illinois Minority Real Estate Scholarship, (S) 156, (F) 482

IMA Diversity Scholarship Program, (S) 157, (F) 483

Impac Group Award. See Worldstudio Foundation Scholarships, entries (S) 379, (F) 637

John T. Dillon Alaska Research Award. *See* Geological Society of America General Research Grants Program, entry (G) 811

Johnson Award for Unusual Achievement in Mathematics or Science. *See* JoAnne Katherine Johnson Award for Unusual Achievement in Mathematics or Science, entry (A) 1050

Johnson Minority Fellowship in Educational Measurement. *See* Sylvia Taylor Johnson Minority Fellowship in Educational Measurement, entry (G) 1008

Johnson Postdoctoral Fellowship. *See* Lyman T. Johnson Postdoctoral Fellowship, entry (G) 870

Johnson Scholarship. *See* Texas Broadcast Education Foundation Scholarships, entry (S) 336

Jordan Health Policy Scholars Program. *See* Barbara Jordan Health Policy Scholars Program, entry (I) 1096

Jordan Memorial Scholarship. *See* Barbara Jordan Memorial Scholarship, entries (S) 33, (F) 406

José L. Nazar Grants for Latino Projects and/or Latino Filmmakers, (G) 852

José Martí Scholarship Challenge Grant Fund, (S) 173, (F) 493

Joseph E. Murray Award. *See* National Kidney Foundation of Massachusetts, Rhode Island, New Hampshire, and Vermont Research Grants, entry (G) 924

Joseph L. Fisher Doctoral Dissertation Fellowships, (G) 853

Joseph Mattera National Scholarship Fund for Migrant Children. *See* Gloria and Joseph Mattera National Scholarship Fund for Migrant Children, entry (S) 133

Joseph P. Fitzpatrick Scholarships. *See* Father Joseph P. Fitzpatrick Scholarships, entry (F) 442

Joseph Shankman Award. *See* National Kidney Foundation of Massachusetts, Rhode Island, New Hampshire, and Vermont Research Grants, entry (G) 924

Joslyn Medical Fund. *See* Alice Newell Joslyn Medical Fund, entry (S) 8

Joyner–Kersee Minority Internship. *See* Jackie Joyner–Kersee Minority Internship, entry (I) 1173

JPMorgan Chase Junior Internships, (I) 1179

JPMorgan Honors Program, (I) 1180

Juan Andrade, Jr. Scholarship for Young Hispanic Leaders. *See* Dr. Juan Andrade, Jr. Scholarship for Young Hispanic Leaders, entry (S) 89

Juan D. Villarreal–HDA Foundation Scholarships. *See* Dr. Juan D. Villarreal–HDA Foundation Scholarships, entries (S) 90, (F) 432

Juan Eugene Ramos Scholarship, (S) 174

Juanita Robles–Lopez/Pampers Parenting Institute and Procter & Gamble Scholarship, (F) 494

Judge Sidney M. Aronovitz Scholarship, (S) 175

Judith L. Weidman Racial Ethnic Minority Fellowship, (I) 1181

Julia Memorial Scholarship Fund. *See* Puerto Rican Chamber of Commerce Raul Julia Memorial Scholarship Fund, entry (S) 282

Junior Investigator Research Grants in Epilepsy, (G) 854

Junkins Minority Scholarship. *See* Jerry Junkins Minority Scholarship, entry (S) 167

Justicia en Diversidad Scholarship, (S) 176

Kaiser Media Internships in Urban Health Reporting, (I) 1182

Kala Singh Memorial Scholarship, (F) 495

Kansas City Hispanic Scholarship Fund, (S) 177, (F) 496

Kansas Ethnic Minority Scholarship Program, (S) 178

Kansas Space Grant Consortium Program, (S) 179, (F) 497, (G) 855

Kansas Teacher Service Scholarship, (L) 649

Kashiwahara Scholarship. *See* Ken Kashiwahara Scholarship, entry (S) 182

Kathy Woodall Minority Student Scholarships. *See* Don Sahli–Kathy Woodall Minority Student Scholarships, entry (S) 87

KATU Thomas R. Dargan Minority Scholarship, (S) 180, (I) 1183

Kazmierczak Memorial Migrant Scholarship. *See* Frank Kazmierczak Memorial Migrant Scholarship, entry (S) 122

Kell–Muñoz Education Fellowship, (I) 1184

Kellogg Foundation Fellowship Program in Health Research. *See* W.K. Kellogg Foundation Fellowship Program in Health Research, entries (F) 635, (G) 1029

Kemp Memorial Scholarship. *See* Amelia Kemp Memorial Scholarship, entries (S) 10, (F) 392

Ken Inouye Scholarship, (S) 181, (F) 498

Ken Kashiwahara Scholarship, (S) 182

Kennedy Scholarship. *See* Texas Broadcast Education Foundation Scholarships, entry (S) 336

Kenney Scholarship Fund. *See* Monsignor Philip Kenney Scholarship Fund, entry (S) 233

Kentucky Minority Educator Recruitment and Retention Scholarships, (L) 650

Kentucky Space Grant Consortium Graduate Fellowships, (F) 499, (G) 856

Kentucky Space Grant Consortium Research Grants, (G) 857

Kentucky Space Grant Consortium Undergraduate Scholarships, (S) 183, (G) 858

Kern County Hispanic Chamber of Commerce Foundation/HSF Scholarship. *See* High School Scholarship Programs of the Hispanic Scholarship Fund, entry (S) 138

Kilner Leadership Award. *See* C.S. Kilner Leadership Award, entry (A) 1038

King, Chavez, Parks Visiting Professors Program. *See* Martin Luther King, Jr., Cesar Chavez, Rosa Parks Visiting Professors Program, entry (G) 876

King, Jr. Memorial Scholarship Fund. *See* Martin Luther King, Jr. Memorial Scholarship Fund, entries (S) 205, (F) 514

King, Jr. Scholarship. *See* Martin Luther King, Jr. Scholarship, entry (S) 206

Kittrell Fellowship. *See* Flemmie D. Kittrell Fellowship, entry (F) 446

Knight Ridder Minority Scholars Program, (S) 184, (I) 1185

Knight Ridder Minority Specialty Development Program, (I) 1186

Knight Ridder Rotating Intern Program, (I) 1187

Kolovakos Award. *See* Gregory Kolovakos Award, entry (A) 1044

KPMG Minority Accounting Doctoral Scholarships, (F) 500

Lady Bird Johnson Scholarship. *See* Texas Broadcast Education Foundation Scholarships, entry (S) 336

LAGRANT FOUNDATION Scholarships, (S) 185

Landis Scholarships. *See* John and Muriel Landis Scholarships, entries (S) 172, (F) 490

Landmark Scholars Program, (S) 186, (I) 1188

Lang Journalism Minority Scholarship and Internship. *See* C.T. Lang Journalism Minority Scholarship and Internship, entries (S) 77, (I) 1122

Mackin Research Grants. *See* Geological Society of America General Research Grants Program, entry (G) 811

MAES General Scholarships, (S) 203, (F) 511

Maine Space Grant Consortium Graduate Research Fellowships, (G) 871

Maine Space Grant Consortium Undergraduate Research Scholarships, (G) 872

Majewski Fellowship. *See* Bernard Majewski Fellowship, entry (G) 729

MALDEF Law School Scholarship Program, (F) 512

Malice Domestic Grants for Unpublished Writers, (G) 873

Many Voices Multicultural Collaboration Grants, (G) 874

Many Voices Residencies, (G) 875

MARC Faculty Predoctoral Fellowships. *See* Minority Access to Research Careers (MARC) Faculty Predoctoral Fellowships, entry (F) 529

MARC Senior Faculty Fellowships. *See* Minority Access to Research Careers (MARC) Senior Faculty Fellowships, entry (G) 895

Margaret Gonzales Scholarship, (S) 204

Mariam K. Chamberlain Fellowships, (I) 1200

Marie F. Peters Ethnic Minorities Outstanding Achievement Award, (A) 1053

Marriage and Family Therapy Minority Fellowship Program, (F) 513

Marriage and Family Therapy Minority Supervision Stipend Program. *See* MFT Minority Supervision Stipend Program, entry (F) 524

Marshall Minority Scholarships. *See* Jean Marshall Minority Scholarships, entry (S) 166

Martha Atherton Scholarship. *See* Robert and Martha Atherton Scholarship, entry (F) 593

Martí Scholarship Challenge Grant Fund. *See* José Martí Scholarship Challenge Grant Fund, entries (S) 173, (F) 493

Martin Luther King, Jr., Cesar Chavez, Rosa Parks Visiting Professors Program, (G) 876

Martin Luther King, Jr. Memorial Scholarship Fund, (S) 205, (F) 514

Martin Luther King, Jr. Scholarship, (S) 206

Martínez–Márquez Journalism Award. *See* Guillermo Martínez–Márquez Journalism Award, entry (A) 1045

Maryland Space Scholars Program, (S) 207

Marzullo Internship Program. *See* Vito Marzullo Internship Program, entry (I) 1307

Mas Family Scholarship Program, (S) 208, (F) 515

Mass Media Science and Engineering Fellows Program, (I) 1201

Massachusetts Space Grant Consortium Graduate Fellowships, (F) 516

Massachusetts Space Grant Consortium Summer Jobs Program, (I) 1202

Massachusetts Space Grant Consortium Undergraduate Research Opportunity Program, (G) 877

Mathematical Sciences Postdoctoral Research Fellowships, (G) 878

Mathematical Sciences University–Industry Postdoctoral Research Fellowships, (G) 879

Mathematical Sciences University–Industry Senior Research Fellowships, (G) 880

Matos Scholarship. *See* Rene Matos Scholarship, entries (S) 292, (F) 589

Mattera National Scholarship Fund for Migrant Children. *See* Gloria and Joseph Mattera National Scholarship Fund for Migrant Children, entry (S) 133

Maurice Goldhaber Distinguished Fellowships. *See* Gertrude and Maurice Goldhaber Distinguished Fellowships, entry (G) 816

Mayes, Jr. Scholarship. *See* Texas Broadcast Education Foundation Scholarships, entry (S) 336

Mayor Joe Serna, Jr. Scholarship Program, (S) 209

Mayor Joe Serna, Jr./HSF Scholarship. *See* High School Scholarship Programs of the Hispanic Scholarship Fund, entry (S) 138

McCormick Tribune Minority Fellowship in Urban Journalism at the Chicago Reporter. *See* Robert R. McCormick Tribune Minority Fellowship in Urban Journalism at the Chicago Reporter, entry (G) 981

McGraw Foundation Emergency Award. *See* Associated Colleges of Illinois Scholarship Program, entry (S) 25

McGuire Memorial Fund. *See* Associated Colleges of Illinois Scholarship Program, entry (S) 25

McJulien Minority Graduate Scholarship. *See* Wes McJulien Minority Graduate Scholarship, entry (F) 632

McKnight Scholarship. *See* William E. McKnight Scholarship, entry (S) 373

McLane Scholarship. *See* Texas Broadcast Education Foundation Scholarships, entry (S) 336

McLean Award. *See* Franklin C. McLean Award, entry (A) 1042

McLendon Minority Postgraduate Scholarship Program. *See* John McLendon Memorial Minority Postgraduate Scholarship Award, entry (F) 491

McWilliams Award. *See* Carey McWilliams Award, entry (A) 1036

Medical Informatics Research Training Awards, (F) 517, (G) 881

Medical Library Association Scholarship for Minority Students. *See* MLA Scholarship for Minority Students, entry (F) 536

Medlin Scholarships. *See* Geological Society of America General Research Grants Program, entry (G) 811

MEFUSA Scholarships for Latino/as, (S) 210

Mellon Fellowships in Humanistic Studies, (F) 518

Mellon Foundation Early Career Fellowship in Economic Studies. *See* Andrew W. Mellon Foundation Early Career Fellowship in Economic Studies, entry (G) 713

Mellon Postdoctoral Fellowships at Bryn Mawr College. *See* Andrew W. Mellon Postdoctoral Fellowships at Bryn Mawr College, entry (G) 714

Mellon Postdoctoral Research Fellowship at Omohundro Institute. *See* Andrew W. Mellon Postdoctoral Research Fellowship at Omohundro Institute, entry (G) 715

Mendenhall Fellowships for Minority Scholars. *See* Five College Fellowship Program for Minority Scholars, entry (G) 804

Mental Health and Substance Abuse Clinical Fellowship Program, (L) 651

Mental Health and Substance Abuse Services Fellowship, (F) 519

Mental Health Research Fellowship, (F) 520

Mentor Graphics Scholarships, (S) 211

Mentored Clinical Scientist Development Awards, (G) 882

Mentored Clinical Scientist Development Program Awards, (G) 883

Mentored Patient–Oriented Research Career Development Award, (G) 884

Mentored Research Scientist Development Awards, (G) 885

Mentored Scientist Development Award for New Minority Faculty, (G) 886

Mercedes Benz Scholarships, (S) 212

Mercury News Minority Business/Finance Scholarship, (S) 213

Mercury News Minority Journalism Scholarship, (S) 214

Merritt Humanitarian Fund Award. See LeRoy C. Merritt Humanitarian Fund Award, entry (G) 864

Merritt–Putnam Research Clinical Training Fellowship. See Clinical Research Training Fellowships in Epilepsy, entry (G) 757

METPRO/Editing Program, (I) 1203

METPRO/Reporting Program, (I) 1204

Metropolitan Life Foundation Awards Program for Academic Excellence in Medicine, (F) 521

Metropolitan Museum of Art Internships for College Students, (I) 1205

Metropolitan Museum of Art Internships for Graduate Students, (I) 1206

Metropolitan Museum of Art 6–Month Internships, (I) 1207

Mettler–Toledo, Inc. Scholars. See Project SEED Scholarships, entry (S) 280

Mexican American Engineers and Scientists General Scholarships. See MAES General Scholarships, entries (S) 203, (F) 511

Mexican American Engineers and Scientists Presidential Scholarship, (S) 215, (F) 522

Mexican American Grocers Association Scholarship Program, (S) 216

Mexican American Legal Defense and Educational Fund Law School Scholarship Program. See MALDEF Law School Scholarship Program, entry (F) 512

Mexican Fiesta Scholarships, (S) 217, (F) 523

MFT Minority Supervision Stipend Program, (F) 524

Miami University Minority Resident Librarian, (I) 1208

Michael Baker Corporation Scholarship Program for Diversity in Engineering, (S) 218

Michael Curry Summer Internship Program, (I) 1209

Michaels Scholarship Program. See Taylor Michaels Scholarship Program, entry (S) 329

Michele and Peter Willmott Fund for Minority Leadership. See Associated Colleges of Illinois Scholarship Program, entry (S) 25

Michele Clark Fellowship, (G) 887

Michigan Nonprofit Research Program, (G) 888

Michigan Space Grant Consortium Fellowships, (G) 889

Michigan Space Grant Consortium Research Seed Grants, (G) 890

Mickey Leland Energy Fellowships, (I) 1210

Microsoft National Scholarships, (S) 219, (I) 1211

Microsoft Scholarship Program of the Hispanic Scholarship Fund, (S) 220

Mid–career Investigator Award in Patient–Oriented Research, (G) 891

Migrant Farmworker Baccalaureate Scholarship, (S) 221

Mike Carona Foundation Law Enforcement Scholarships, (S) 222

Mildred Colodny Scholarship for Study of Historic Preservation, (F) 525, (I) 1212

Millender Fellowship, (G) 892

Milly Woodward Memorial Scholarship. See Northwest Journalists of Color Scholarship Awards, entry (S) 259

Minnesota Space Grant Consortium Scholarships and Fellowships, (S) 223, (F) 526

Minorities in Government Finance Scholarship, (S) 224, (F) 527

Minorities in Medical Oncology Program Grants, (G) 893

Minority Academic Institutions Fellowships for Graduate Environmental Study, (F) 528, (G) 894

Minority Academic Institutions Undergraduate Student Fellowships, (S) 225, (I) 1213

Minority Access to Research Careers (MARC) Faculty Predoctoral Fellowships, (F) 529

Minority Access to Research Careers (MARC) Senior Faculty Fellowships, (G) 895

Minority Advertising Training Program Internships, (I) 1214

Minority Affairs Committee Award for Outstanding Scholastic Achievement, (A) 1054

Minority Career Advancement Awards. See Career Advancement Awards for Minority Scientists and Engineers, entry (G) 737

Minority Clinical Associate Physician Program. See Clinical Associate Physician Program, entry (G) 755

Minority Community College Transfer Scholarships, (S) 226

Minority Dental Student Scholarship, (F) 530

Minority Dissertation Research Grants in Aging, (G) 896

Minority Dissertation Research Grants in Mental Health, (G) 897

Minority Editing Training Program/Editing. See METPRO/Editing Program, entry (I) 1203

Minority Editorial Training Program/Reporting. See METPRO/Reporting Program, entry (I) 1204

Minority Educational Foundation of the United States of America Scholarships for Latino/as. See MEFUSA Scholarships for Latino/as, entry (S) 210

Minority Engineers Development Program. See Hercules Minority Engineers Development Program, entries (S) 136, (I) 1158

Minority Faculty Fellowship Program, (G) 898

Minority Fellowship in Environmental Law, (I) 1215

Minority Fellowship Program in Mental Health, (F) 531

Minority Geoscience Graduate Scholarships, (F) 532

Minority Geoscience Undergraduate Scholarships, (S) 227

Minority Medical Faculty Development Program, (G) 899

Minority Medical Student Clinical Fellowship in Child and Adolescent Psychiatry. See Jeanne Spurlock Minority Medical Student Clinical Fellowship in Child and Adolescent Psychiatry, entry (I) 1176

Minority Neuroscience Postdoctoral Fellowship Program, (G) 900

Minority Neuroscience Predoctoral Fellowship Program, (F) 533, (G) 901

Minority Nurse Magazine Scholarship Program, (S) 228

Minority Oncology Academic Leadership Award, (G) 902

Minority Opportunities for Research Faculty Development Awards. See MORE Faculty Development Awards, entry (G) 907

Minority Postdoctoral Research Fellowships, (G) 903

Minority Research Library Residency Program, (I) 1216

Minority Research Planning Grants. See Research Planning Grants for Minority Scientists and Engineers, entry (G) 974

Minority Scholarship Award in Physical Therapy, (S) 229

Minority Scholarship Awards for College Students in Chemical Engineering, (S) 230

Minority Scholarship Awards for Incoming College Freshmen in Chemical Engineering, (S) 231

Minority Teachers of Illinois Scholarship Program, (L) 652

Minority Undergraduate Research Fellowships, (I) 1217

Missile Defense Agency Pilot Program for Science and Technology Research at Historically Black Colleges and Universities and Minority Institutions, (G) 904

Mississippi Psychology Apprenticeship Program, (I) 1218

Mississippi Space Grant Consortium Campus Activities, (S) 232, (F) 534

Missouri Minority Teacher Education Scholarship Program, (L) 653

Missouri Society of Certified Public Accountants Minority High School Scholarships. See MSCPA Minority High School Scholarships, entry (S) 236

Missouri Space Grant Consortium Graduate Fellowships, (F) 535

Missouri Space Grant Consortium Summer High School Internships, (I) 1219

Missouri Space Grant Consortium Undergraduate Research Internships, (G) 905

Missouri Vocational Special Need Association Student Scholarship. See MVSNA Student Scholarship, entry (S) 237

MLA Scholarship for Minority Students, (F) 536

Modelo Mundial–World Model Competition, (A) 1055

Modesto Bee Summer Intern Program, (I) 1220

Monsignor Philip Kenney Scholarship Fund, (S) 233

Montagne Fund Award. See Geological Society of America General Research Grants Program, entry (G) 811

Montana Space Grant Consortium Graduate Fellowships, (F) 537

Montana Space Grant Consortium Research Initiation Grants, (G) 906

Montana Space Grant Consortium Undergraduate Scholarships, (S) 234

Montgomery Summer Research Fellowships in Law and Social Science for Minority Undergraduate Students, (I) 1221

Moore Scholarship. See Damon P. Moore Scholarship, entry (S) 81

MORE Faculty Development Awards, (G) 907

Morris Scholarship, (S) 235, (F) 538

Motorola Minority Scholarship. See Associated Colleges of Illinois Scholarship Program, entry (S) 25

Motorola Scholarship. See Associated Colleges of Illinois Scholarship Program, entry (S) 25

Ms. Latina USA, (A) 1056

MSCPA Minority High School Scholarships, (S) 236

Multicultural Advertising Intern Program, (I) 1222

Multicultural Undergraduate Internships at the Getty Center, (I) 1223

Multidisciplinary Research Program of the University Research Initiative, (G) 908

Muriel Landis Scholarships. See John and Muriel Landis Scholarships, entries (S) 172, (F) 490

Murphy Memorial Scholarship. See American Meteorological Society Undergraduate Scholarships, entry (S) 16

Murray Award. See National Kidney Foundation of Massachusetts, Rhode Island, New Hampshire, and Vermont Research Grants, entry (G) 924

MVSNA Student Scholarship, (S) 237

NACME Scholars Program, (S) 238

NACME/NASA Undergraduate Student Awards for Research, (S) 239, (I) 1224

NAEP Visiting Scholar Program. See National Assessment of Educational Progress (NAEP) Visiting Scholar Program, entry (G) 912

NAHJ Photojournalism Competition, (A) 1057

NAHJ Scholarships, (S) 240, (F) 539

NAMEPA Beginning Freshmen Award, (S) 241

NAMEPA Transfer Engineering Student Award. See Transfer Engineering Student Award, entry (S) 340

Nancy Foster Scholarship Program. See Dr. Nancy Foster Scholarship Program, entry (F) 433

NASA Administrator's Fellowship Program, (G) 909

NASA Earth System Science Fellowship Program, (F) 540

NASA Graduate Student Researchers Program, (G) 910

NASA SHARP Commuter Component. See Summer High School Apprenticeship Research Program Commuter Component, entry (I) 1286

NASA SHARP Residential Component. See Summer High School Apprenticeship Research Program Residential Component, entry (I) 1287

NASA Undergraduate Student Awards for Research. See NACME/NASA Undergraduate Student Awards for Research, entries (S) 239, (I) 1224

NASA/DVSGC Graduate Student Fellowships, (F) 541

NASA/DVSGC Undergraduate Summer Scholarships, (G) 911

NASP Minority Scholarship, (F) 542

N.A.S.P.A. Minority Undergraduate Fellows Program, (I) 1225

NATA Undergraduate Scholarships, (S) 242

National Action Council for Minorities in Engineering Scholars Program. See NACME Scholars Program, entry (S) 238

National Action Council for Minorities in Engineering/NASA Undergraduate Student Awards for Research. See NACME/NASA Undergraduate Student Awards for Research, entries (S) 239, (I) 1224

National Aeronautics and Space Administration Administrator's Fellowship Program. See NASA Administrator's Fellowship Program, entry (G) 909

National Aeronautics and Space Administration Graduate Student Fellowships in Earth System Science. See NASA Earth System Science Fellowship Program, entry (F) 540

National Aeronautics and Space Administration Graduate Student Researchers Program. See NASA Graduate Student Researchers Program, entry (G) 910

National Aeronautics and Space Administration Undergraduate Student Awards for Research. See NACME/NASA Undergraduate Student Awards for Research, entries (S) 239, (I) 1224

National Aeronautics and Space Administration/DVSGC Graduate Student Fellowships. See NASA/DVSGC Graduate Student Fellowships, entry (F) 541

National Aeronautics and Space Administration/DVSGC Undergraduate Summer Scholarships. See NASA/DVSGC Undergraduate Summer Scholarships, entry (G) 911

National Assessment of Educational Progress (NAEP) Visiting Scholar Program, (G) 912

National Association of Hispanic Federal Executives Scholarship, (S) 243

National Association of Hispanic Journalists Photojournalism Competition. See NAHJ Photojournalism Competition, entry (A) 1057

National Association of Hispanic Journalists Scholarships. See NAHJ Scholarships, entries (S) 240, (F) 539

National Association of Hispanic Nurses Scholarships, (S) 244, (F) 543

National Association of Minority Engineering Program Administrators Beginning Freshmen Award. See NAMEPA Beginning Freshmen Award, entry (S) 241

S–Scholarships   **F–Fellowships**   **L–Loans**   **G–Grants**   **A–Awards**   **I–Internships**

National Urban League Scholarship for Minority Students. *See* Gillette/National Urban League Scholarship for Minority Students, entry (S) 131

National Urban/Rural Fellows Program, (G) 926

National Zoological Park Traineeships, (I) 1232

NationsBank Minority Student Scholarship. *See* Bank of America Minority Student Scholarship, entry (S) 31

Naval Research Laboratory Broad Agency Announcement, (G) 927

NAVESNP/Piney Mountain Press Student Award, (S) 247

Nazar Grants for Latino Projects and/or Latino Filmmakers. *See* José L. Nazar Grants for Latino Projects and/or Latino Filmmakers, entry (G) 852

NCAA Ethnic Minority and Women's Internship Programs, (I) 1233

NCAA Ethnic Minority Postgraduate Scholarship Program, (F) 551

NEBHE Doctoral Scholars Program in Science, Engineering and Mathematics, (F) 552

Nebraska Space Grant Statewide Scholarship Competition, (S) 248, (F) 553

NEH International and Area Studies Fellowships. *See* ACLS/SSRC/NEH International and Area Studies Fellowships, entry (G) 687

Nenno Inspirational Fellowship. *See* IRTS Summer Fellowship Program, entry (I) 1171

Neuroscience Scholars Fellowship Program, (I) 1234

Nevada Space Grant Consortium Graduate Fellowship Program, (F) 554

Nevada Space Grant Consortium Undergraduate Scholarship Program, (S) 249

New England Board of Higher Education Doctoral Scholars Program in Science, Engineering and Mathematics. *See* NEBHE Doctoral Scholars Program in Science, Engineering and Mathematics, entry (F) 552

New Hampshire Space Grant Consortium Project Support, (G) 928

New Horizons Scholarships, (S) 250

New Jersey Space Grant Consortium Industry/University Cooperative Research Grants, (G) 929

New Jersey Space Grant Consortium Undergraduate Summer Fellowships, (I) 1235

New Jersey Utilities Association Scholarships, (S) 251

New Mexico Alliance for Hispanic Education/HSF Scholarship. *See* High School Scholarship Programs of the Hispanic Scholarship Fund, entry (S) 138

New Mexico Graduate Scholarship Program, (F) 555

New Mexico Minority Doctoral Assistance Loan–for–Service Program, (L) 657

New Mexico Space Grant Consortium Research Opportunities Awards Program. *See* NMSGC Research Opportunities Awards Program, entry (G) 933

New Mexico Space Grant Consortium Training Grants Program. *See* NMSGC Undergraduate Education Enhancement Program, entry (G) 934

New Voices Award. *See* Lee & Low Books New Voices Award, entry (A) 1051

New York Design Center Awards. *See* Worldstudio Foundation Scholarships, entries (S) 379, (F) 637

New York Public Library Fellowships, (G) 930

New York Sea Grant and Hudson River National Estuarine Research Reserve Cooperative Research Fellowship, (G) 931

New York Space Grant Consortium Graduate Fellowships, (F) 556

New York Space Grant Consortium Undergraduate Summer Internships, (I) 1236

New York State Migrant Student Scholarship, (S) 252

New York State Regents Health Care Scholarships, (L) 658

New York State Regents Professional Opportunity Scholarships, (L) 659

Newhouse Scholarship Program, (S) 253, (I) 1237

Newsroom Diversity Scholarship, (S) 254

Next Generation Fellowship Program, (G) 932

Next Generation of Public Servants Scholarship, (S) 255

NHFA Entertainment Industry Scholarships, (F) 557

Nickens, M.D. Minority Faculty Fellowship. *See* Herbert W. Nickens, M.D. Minority Faculty Fellowship, entry (G) 826

Nickens, M.D. Minority Medical Student Scholarships. *See* Herbert W. Nickens, M.D. Minority Medical Student Scholarships, entry (F) 469

NINR National Research Service Award Individual Predoctoral Fellowships, (F) 558

NLN Nurse Educator Scholarship Program, (F) 559

NMF Need–Based Scholarship Program, (F) 560

NMJGSA Scholarships, (S) 256

NMSGC Research Opportunities Awards Program, (G) 933

NMSGC Undergraduate Education Enhancement Program, (G) 934

Noche de Becas Coalition/HSF Scholarship. *See* High School Scholarship Programs of the Hispanic Scholarship Fund, entry (S) 138

Noel Betancourt Award. *See* Association of Cuban Engineers Scholarships, entries (S) 26, (F) 401

Nonprofit Sector Research Fund William Randolph Hearst Endowed Scholarship for Minority Students, (I) 1238

North American Doctoral Fellowships, (F) 561

North Carolina Space Grant Consortium Graduate Fellowships, (G) 935

North Carolina Space Grant Consortium Undergraduate Scholarships, (G) 936

North Carolina Teaching Fellows Scholarship Program, (L) 660

North Carolina Undergraduate Nurse Scholars Program, (L) 661

North Dakota Department of Transportation Educational Grants, (L) 662

North Dakota Space Grant Program Fellowships, (G) 937

North Dakota Space Grant Program Scholarships, (S) 257

Northrop Grumman/HENAAC Scholars Program, (S) 258

Northside Independent School District/HSF Scholarship. *See* High School Scholarship Programs of the Hispanic Scholarship Fund, entry (S) 138

Northwest Journalists of Color Scholarship Awards, (S) 259

Nosotros Scholarship Program, (S) 260

NOW Legal Defense and Education Fund Graduate Intern Program, (I) 1239

N.S. Bienstock Fellowship, (G) 938

NSCA Women and Minority Scholarship, (S) 261

NSF Graduate Research Fellowships, (F) 562

NSF Scholar–in–Residence at NIH Program, (G) 939

NSF Standard and Continuing Grants, (G) 940

Nurse Scholars Program–Undergraduate Program. *See* North Carolina Undergraduate Nurse Scholars Program, entry (L) 661

Nutrition Action Fellowship, (G) 941

S–Scholarships   **F–Fellowships**   **L–Loans**   **G–Grants**   **A–Awards**   **I–Internships**

R. Robert & Sally D. Funderburg Research Scholar Award in Gastric Biology Related to Cancer, (G) 969

Race Relations Multiracial Student Scholarship, (S) 285, (F) 584

Racial Ethnic Educational Scholarships, (S) 286

Racial Ethnic Leadership Supplemental Grants, (F) 585

Rado Watch Scholarship for Design. See Worldstudio Foundation Scholarships, entries (S) 379, (F) 637

Ralph Bunche Summer Institute, (S) 287

Ralph J. Bunche Award, (A) 1064

Ralph W. Ellison Memorial Prize, (A) 1065

Ralph W. Shrader Scholarships, (F) 586

RAND Graduate Student Summer Associate Program, (G) 970

Raul Julia Memorial Scholarship Fund. See Puerto Rican Chamber of Commerce Raul Julia Memorial Scholarship Fund, entry (S) 282

Rawley Prize. See James A. Rawley Prize, entry (A) 1048

Raymond H. Trott Scholarship for Banking, (S) 288

RCA Ethnic Scholarship Fund, (S) 289

RDW Group, Inc. Minority Scholarship for Communications, (S) 290, (F) 587

Recognition Award for Emerging Scholars, (A) 1066

Record–Journal Minority Internship/Scholarship, (S) 291, (I) 1264

Reed Award. See Geological Society of America General Research Grants Program, entry (G) 811

Reeves Jr. Memorial Scholarship. See Garth Reeves Jr. Memorial Scholarship, entry (S) 125

REFORMA Scholarship, (F) 588

Reformed Church in America Ethnic Scholarship Fund. See RCA Ethnic Scholarship Fund, entry (S) 289

Regents Health Care Scholarships. See New York State Regents Health Care Scholarships, entry (L) 658

Regents Professional Opportunity Scholarships. See New York State Regents Professional Opportunity Scholarships, entry (L) 659

Reginald F. Lewis and Charles Hamilton Houston Fellowships for Law Teaching, (G) 971

Reiff Scholarship. See Texas Broadcast Education Foundation Scholarships, entry (S) 336

Reina Feria de las Flores/HSF Scholarship. See High School Scholarship Programs of the Hispanic Scholarship Fund, entry (S) 138

Rene Matos Scholarship, (S) 292, (F) 589

Research and Engineering Apprenticeship Program (REAP) for High School Students, (I) 1265

Research and Training Program on Poverty and Public Policy Postdoctoral Fellowships, (G) 972

Research and Writing Grants Competition in Global Security and Sustainability, (G) 973

Research in Undergraduate Institutions Faculty Research Projects. See RUI Faculty Research Projects, entry (G) 985

Research in Undergraduate Institutions Research Instrumentation Grants. See RUI Research Instrumentation Grants, entry (G) 986

Research Planning Grants for Minority Scientists and Engineers, (G) 974

Research Training Fellowships in Epilepsy, (G) 975

Resources for the Future Summer Internships, (I) 1266

Retail Management Institute Internships, (I) 1267

Revelle Fellowship in Global Stewardship. See Roger Revelle Fellowship in Global Stewardship, entry (G) 984

Rhode Island Space Grant Graduate Fellowship Program, (F) 590, (G) 976

Rhode Island Space Grant Undergraduate Scholarship Program, (S) 293

Rhode Island Space Grant Undergraduate Summer Scholar Program, (G) 977

Richard and Helen Brown COREM Scholarships, (F) 591

Richard and Helen Hagemeyer Scholarship. See American Meteorological Society Undergraduate Scholarships, entry (S) 16

Richard D. Hailey Law Student Scholarships, (F) 592

Richard Gast Fellowship. See EMAF Fellowship Program, entry (F) 439

Richard S. Smith Scholarship, (S) 294

Rio Grande City Consolidated Independent School District/HSF Scholarship. See High School Scholarship Programs of the Hispanic Scholarship Fund, entry (S) 138

Risk Policy Fellowships, (G) 978

Rivera Fellowship. See IRTS Summer Fellowship Program, entry (I) 1171

Rivera Mexican American Children's Book Award. See Tomás Rivera Mexican American Children's Book Award, entry (A) 1074

RMHC/HACER Scholarship Program, (S) 295

Robert and Martha Atherton Scholarship, (F) 593

Robert D. Watkins Minority Graduate Fellowship, (G) 979

Robert J. Hurst Award. See Worldstudio Foundation Scholarships, entries (S) 379, (F) 637

Robert K. Fahnestock Memorial Award. See Geological Society of America General Research Grants Program, entry (G) 811

Robert M. Cover Fellowship in Public Interest Law, (G) 980

Robert R. McCormick Tribune Minority Fellowship in Urban Journalism at the Chicago Reporter, (G) 981

Robert W. Hartley Memorial Fellowship. See Governmental Studies Predoctoral Fellowships, entry (G) 822

Roberts, Sr. Scholarship. See Elliott C. Roberts, Sr. Scholarship, entry (F) 438

Robinson Memorial Prize in Surgery. See James H. Robinson Memorial Prize in Surgery, entry (A) 1049

Robinson Scholarship. See Jackie Robinson Scholarship, entry (S) 162

Robles–Lopez/Pampers Parenting Institute and Procter & Gamble Scholarship. See Juanita Robles–Lopez/Pampers Parenting Institute and Procter & Gamble Scholarship, entry (F) 494

Rock Falls Scholarship. See Associated Colleges of Illinois Scholarship Program, entry (S) 25

Rock Hill Herald Internship Program, (I) 1268

Rockefeller Foundation Humanities Fellowships, (G) 982

Rockwell Corporation Scholarships, (S) 296

Rocky Mountain NASA Space Grant Consortium Graduate Research Fellowships, (F) 594, (G) 983

Rocky Mountain NASA Space Grant Consortium Undergraduate Scholarships, (S) 297

Rod Coppolo Fellowship. See IRTS Summer Fellowship Program, entry (I) 1171

Rodriguez Scholarship. See American Meteorological Society Undergraduate Scholarships, entry (S) 16

Roger Revelle Fellowship in Global Stewardship, (G) 984

Rolland Scholarship. See Ian M. Rolland Scholarship, entry (S) 151

Ronald H. Brown Memorial Scholarship, (S) 298

Ronald McDonald House Charities/HACER Scholarship Program. See RMHC/HACER Scholarship Program, entry (S) 295

Ronald McDonald House Charities/Hispanic American Commitment to Educational Resources Scholarships, (S) 299

Rooks Fellowship for Racial and Ethnic Theological Students. *See* Adrienne M. and Charles Shelby Rooks Fellowship for Racial and Ethnic Theological Students, entry (F) 388

Roosevelt Professional Development Fellowships. *See* Eleanor Roosevelt Professional Development Fellowships, entry (G) 786

Roosevelt Project Implementation Grants. *See* Eleanor Roosevelt Project Implementation Grants, entry (G) 787

Rosa Parks Visiting Professors Program. *See* Martin Luther King, Jr., Cesar Chavez, Rosa Parks Visiting Professors Program, entry (G) 876

Roswell L. Gilpatric Internship, (I) 1269

Roth Manufacturing Engineering Scholarship. *See* Edward S. Roth Manufacturing Engineering Scholarship, entries (S) 102, (F) 436

Roy J. Shlemon Scholarship Awards. *See* Geological Society of America General Research Grants Program, entry (G) 811

Roybal Public Health Fellowship. *See* Edward R. Roybal Public Health Fellowship, entry (I) 1131

RUI Faculty Research Projects, (G) 985

RUI Research Instrumentation Grants, (G) 986

Russell, Jr. Memorial Scholarship. *See* Louis B. Russell, Jr. Memorial Scholarship, entry (S) 198

Ruth Chance Law Fellowship, (I) 1270

Ryskamp Research Fellowships. *See* Charles A. Ryskamp Research Fellowships, entry (G) 748

Sabbaticals for Long–Time Activists of Color, (G) 987

SACNAS Summer Program for Latinos and Native Americans. *See* Summer Research Program for Undergraduates at Cornell University, entry (G) 1006

SACNAS–IBM Undergraduate Research Scholarship, (S) 300, (I) 1271

Sacramento Bee Minority Journalism Scholarships, (S) 301

Sacramento Hispanic Chamber of Commerce Mayor Joe Serna, Jr./HSF Scholarship. *See* High School Scholarship Programs of the Hispanic Scholarship Fund, entry (S) 138

Sahli–Kathy Woodall Minority Student Scholarships. *See* Don Sahli–Kathy Woodall Minority Student Scholarships, entry (S) 87

SALEF Health Scholarship Program, (S) 302, (F) 595

Sally D. Funderburg Research Scholar Award in Gastric Biology Related to Cancer. *See* R. Robert & Sally D. Funderburg Research Scholar Award in Gastric Biology Related to Cancer, entry (G) 969

Saltonstall–Kennedy Grant Program, (G) 988

Salvadoran American Leadership and Educational Fund Health Scholarship Program. *See* SALEF Health Scholarship Program, entries (S) 302, (F) 595

San Angelo Standard–Times Internship, (I) 1272

San Diego County Hispanic Chamber of Commerce Scholarship, (S) 303

San Diego Gas & Electric Scholarship Fund, (S) 304

San Jose GI Forum Scholarships, (S) 305

Sanchez Founders Scholarship. *See* Hispanic Designers Founders Scholarships, entry (S) 143

Santa Clara La Raza Lawyers Scholarship, (F) 596

Sawyer Minority Scholarship. *See* Anna Grace Sawyer Minority Scholarship, entry (S) 19

SBC L.C. and Daisy Bates Memorial Scholarship, (S) 306

SCA Diversity Fellowship Program, (I) 1273

Scholarship for Minority Students in Memory of Edna Yelland. *See* CLA Scholarship for Minority Students in Memory of Edna Yelland, entry (F) 418

Scholarship Research Institute Multicultural Scholarship. *See* SRI Multicultural Scholarship, entry (S) 318

Scholarships for Minority Accounting Students, (S) 307, (F) 597

Science and Engineering Apprentice Program, (I) 1274

Science, Justice, and Public Policy Fellowships, (G) 989

Science Policy and International Security Fellowship Program, (G) 990

Science Teacher Preparation Program, (S) 308, (F) 598

SCMRE Graduate Archival Conservation Internship, (I) 1275

SCMRE Graduate Research Internships, (I) 1276

SCMRE Postgraduate Archival Conservation Fellowship, (G) 991

Scotts Company Scholars Program, (S) 309, (I) 1277

Scoville Jr. Peace Fellowship Program. *See* Herbert Scoville Jr. Peace Fellowship, entry (I) 1157

Scripps Fellowships in Environmental Journalism. *See* Ted Scripps Fellowships in Environmental Journalism, entry (G) 1009

Sean M. Staudt Memorial Scholarship. *See* Associated Colleges of Illinois Scholarship Program, entry (S) 25

Selected Professions Fellowships for Women of Color, (F) 599

Semiconductor Research Corporation Master's Scholarship Program, (F) 600

Senator Gregory Luna Memorial Legislative Scholars Program, (I) 1278

Senior Scientist Awards, (G) 992

SEO Career Program, (I) 1279

Serna, Jr. Scholarship Program. *See* Mayor Joe Serna, Jr. Scholarship Program, entry (S) 209

Serna, Jr./HSF Scholarship. *See* High School Scholarship Programs of the Hispanic Scholarship Fund, entry (S) 138

Sexuality Research Program Dissertation Fellowships, (G) 993

Sexuality Research Program Postdoctoral Fellowships, (G) 994

Shankman Award. *See* National Kidney Foundation of Massachusetts, Rhode Island, New Hampshire, and Vermont Research Grants, entry (G) 924

Sharon D. Banks Memorial Undergraduate Scholarship, (S) 310

Sheldon M. Wolff, M.D. Fellowship in International Health. *See* Diplomacy Fellowships, entry (G) 774

Shell Chemical Company ACS Scholars Program, (S) 311

Shell Legislative Internship Program, (I) 1280

Sherman Fellowship. *See* IRTS Summer Fellowship Program, entry (I) 1171

Sherry R. Arnstein Minority Student Scholarship, (F) 601

Sherry R. Arnstein New Student Minority Student Scholarship, (F) 602

Shlemon Scholarship Awards. *See* Geological Society of America General Research Grants Program, entry (G) 811

Short–Term Training for Minority and Women Dental Students, (G) 995

Shrader Scholarships. *See* Ralph W. Shrader Scholarships, entry (F) 586

Sí TV Playwriting Award, (A) 1067

Sidney B. Williams, Jr. Intellectual Property Law School Scholarships, (F) 603

Steckman, Sr. Fellowship. See IRTS Summer Fellowship Program, entry (I) 1171

Stein Memorial Space Grant Scholarship. See Pennsylvania Space Grant Consortium Scholarships, entry (S) 272

Steinman Clinical Research Award. See National Kidney Foundation of Massachusetts, Rhode Island, New Hampshire, and Vermont Research Grants, entry (G) 924

Stephen H. Coltrin Award for Excellence in Communication Education, (A) 1070

Stephen K. Nenno Inspirational Fellowship. See IRTS Summer Fellowship Program, entry (I) 1171

Sterling/Rock Falls Scholarship. See Associated Colleges of Illinois Scholarship Program, entry (S) 25

Steven Jacobson Fellowship. See IRTS Summer Fellowship Program, entry (I) 1171

Stockton Unified School District/HSF Scholarship. See High School Scholarship Programs of the Hispanic Scholarship Fund, entry (S) 138

Stone, Jr. and Associates Minority Scholarship. See Edward D. Stone, Jr. and Associates Minority Scholarship, entry (S) 100

Strait Minority Stipend. See George A. Strait Minority Stipend, entry (F) 461

Straker Scholarship. See D. Augustus Straker Scholarship, entry (F) 427

Stratton/Tipton Scholarship for Adult Returning Students, (S) 322

Stratton/Tipton Scholarship for High School Seniors, (S) 323

Stronach Curatorial Internships. See Lifchez/Stronach Curatorial Internships, entry (I) 1195

Student CEC Ethnic Diversity Scholarship, (S) 324, (F) 613

Student Conservation Association Diversity Fellowship Program. See SCA Diversity Fellowship Program, entry (I) 1273

Student Opportunity Scholarships for Ethnic Minority Groups, (S) 325

Substance Abuse Training Program for Minority Nurses, (F) 614

Summer High School Apprenticeship Research Program Commuter Component, (I) 1286

Summer High School Apprenticeship Research Program Residential Component, (I) 1287

Summer Honors Undergraduate Research Program, (I) 1288

Summer Institute in Mathematics for Undergraduates, (G) 1005

Summer Intern Program in Geoscience, (I) 1289

Summer Internship Program in Biomedical Research, (I) 1290

Summer Program in Biostatistics, (I) 1291

Summer Research Internship in Public Health, (I) 1292

Summer Research Opportunities Program (SROP), (I) 1293

Summer Research Program for Undergraduates at Cornell University, (G) 1006

Summer Search Foundation/HSF Scholarship. See High School Scholarship Programs of the Hispanic Scholarship Fund, entry (S) 138

Summer Transportation Internship Program for Diverse Groups, (I) 1294

Sun–Sentinel Summer Minority Program, (I) 1295

SUNY Underrepresented Graduate Fellowship Program, (F) 615

Support of Continuous Research Excellence, (G) 1007

SWS Minority Scholar Fund, (F) 616

Sylvia Stein Memorial Space Grant Scholarship. See Pennsylvania Space Grant Consortium Scholarships, entry (S) 272

Sylvia Taylor Johnson Minority Fellowship in Educational Measurement, (G) 1008

Synod of Living Waters Racial Ethnic College Scholarship, (S) 326

Synod of Living Waters Racial Ethnic Seminary Scholarship, (F) 617

Synod of the Covenant Ethnic Full–Time Scholarships, (S) 327

Synod of the Covenant Ethnic Theological Scholarships, (F) 618

TACHE Distinguished Community College Faculty Award, (A) 1071

TACHE Distinguished University Faculty Award, (A) 1072

Tallahassee Democrat/Knight Ridder Minority Scholarships, (S) 328

Taylor Memorial Summer Minority Policy Fellowship. See Dalmas A. Taylor Memorial Summer Minority Policy Fellowship, entry (I) 1124

Taylor Michaels Scholarship Program, (S) 329

Teach for America Fellowships, (I) 1296

Teacher Education Scholarship Program of the Alabama Space Grant Consortium, (S) 330

"Teachers for All" Scholarship. See Utah Jazz "Teachers for All" Scholarship, entry (S) 351

Teachers for Tomorrow Scholarship Program, (S) 331

Tech Force/3M Pre–Engineering Prizes, (S) 332

Technician Training Program for Minorities and Women at Brookhaven National Laboratory, (I) 1297

Ted Scripps Fellowships in Environmental Journalism, (G) 1009

Teen Latina USA, (A) 1073

TELACU Arts Award, (S) 333

TELACU Engineering Award, (S) 334

TELACU Scholarships, (S) 335

Telecommunications Policy Fellowships, (I) 1298

Telemundo Channel 48/HSF Scholarship. See High School Scholarship Programs of the Hispanic Scholarship Fund, entry (S) 138

Telemundo Channel 52/HSF Scholarship. See High School Scholarship Programs of the Hispanic Scholarship Fund, entry (S) 138

Tennessee Minority Teaching Fellows Program, (L) 668

Texas Association of Chicanos in Higher Education Distinguished Community College Faculty Award. See TACHE Distinguished Community College Faculty Award, entry (A) 1071

Texas Association of Chicanos in Higher Education Distinguished University Faculty Award. See TACHE Distinguished University Faculty Award, entry (A) 1072

Texas Association of Chicanos in Higher Education Graduate Fellowship Awards, (F) 619

Texas Broadcast Education Foundation Scholarships, (S) 336

Texas Department of Transportation Conditional Grant Program, (L) 669

Texas Medical Association Minority Scholarship Program, (F) 620

Texas Space Grant Consortium Graduate Fellowships, (F) 621

Texas Space Grant Consortium Undergraduate Scholarships, (S) 337

Texas YES! Scholarships, (S) 338

Theodore I. Steinman Clinical Research Award. See National Kidney Foundation of Massachusetts, Rhode Island, New Hampshire, and Vermont Research Grants, entry (G) 924

Thomas R. Dargan Minority Scholarship. See KATU Thomas R. Dargan Minority Scholarship, entries (S) 180, (I) 1183

Thomas R. Pickering Foreign Affairs Fellowships, (L) 670

Thomas R. Pickering Graduate Foreign Affairs Fellowships, (L) 671

Thorn Arts Scholarships for Migrant Farmworkers. *See* Berrien Fragos Thorn Arts Scholarships for Migrant Farmworkers, entry (G) 730

Tillie Golub–Schwartz Memorial Scholarship for Minorities, (S) 339

TIP Grants. *See* Wisconsin Talent Incentive Program (TIP) Grants, entry (S) 378

Tom Reiff Scholarship. *See* Texas Broadcast Education Foundation Scholarships, entry (S) 336

Tomás Rivera Mexican American Children's Book Award, (A) 1074

Toni S. Smith Scholarship. *See* Associated Colleges of Illinois Scholarship Program, entry (S) 25

Traineeships in AIDS Prevention Studies (TAPS) Program Postdoctoral Fellowships, (G) 1010

Traineeships in Oceanography for Minority Undergraduates, (I) 1299

Transfer Engineering Student Award, (S) 340

Travel Awards for Minority Graduate Students, (G) 1011

Tribune Minority Fellowship in Urban Journalism at the Chicago Reporter. *See* Robert R. McCormick Tribune Minority Fellowship in Urban Journalism at the Chicago Reporter, entry (G) 981

Tucker Fellowship. *See* G. Richard Tucker Fellowship, entry (I) 1146

Tyler Ward Minority Journalism Scholarship, (S) 341

UCSB Library Fellowship Program, (G) 1012

Ullyot Fellows. *See* ASPET Individual Summer Undergraduate Research Fellowships, entry (I) 1090

UNCF/Household Corporate Scholars Program, (S) 342, (I) 1300

UNCF/Pfizer Postdoctoral Fellowships, (G) 1013

UNCF/Sprint Scholars Program, (S) 343, (I) 1301

Undergraduate Scholarship Program for Individuals from Disadvantaged Backgrounds, (L) 672

Undergraduate Scholarship Program of the Alabama Space Grant Consortium, (S) 344

Underrepresented Mental Health Minority Research Fellowship Program, (F) 622

United Church of Christ Fellowship Program in Health and Human Service Management, (F) 623

United Church of Christ Special Higher Education Program, (S) 345

United Methodist Church Crusade Scholarship Program, (F) 624

United Methodist Scholarship Program, (S) 346, (F) 625

United Negro College Fund/Household Corporate Scholars Program. *See* UNCF/Household Corporate Scholars Program, entries (S) 342, (I) 1300

United Negro College Fund/Sprint Scholars Program. *See* UNCF/Sprint Scholars Program, entries (S) 343, (I) 1301

United Parcel Service Scholarship for Minority Students, (S) 347

United States Department of Agriculture Summer Intern Program. *See* USDA Summer Intern Program, entry (I) 1304

United States Department of State Student Intern Program. *See* Department of State Student Intern Program, entry (I) 1126

United States Institute of Peace Senior Fellowships, (G) 1014

Unity Founders Scholarship, (S) 348

University of California at Santa Barbara Library Fellowship Program. *See* UCSB Library Fellowship Program, entry (G) 1012

University of Minnesota Affirmative Action Residency Program, (I) 1302

University of Wisconsin Visiting Minority Scholar Lecture Program, (G) 1015

University Postdoctoral Fellowship Program, (G) 1016

UPS Diversity Scholarships, (S) 349

UPS Scholarship. *See* Associated Colleges of Illinois Scholarship Program, entry (S) 25

Urban Fellowship Program, (F) 626, (I) 1303

U.S. Department of State Foreign Affairs Fellowship Program. *See* Thomas R. Pickering Foreign Affairs Fellowships, entry (L) 670

U.S. Department of State Student Intern Program. *See* Department of State Student Intern Program, entry (I) 1126

USA Funds Access to Education Scholarships, (S) 350, (F) 627

USDA Summer Intern Program, (I) 1304

Utah Jazz "Teachers for All" Scholarship, (S) 351

Vaid Fellowships, (I) 1305

Vann Kennedy Scholarship. *See* Texas Broadcast Education Foundation Scholarships, entry (S) 336

Verizon Scholarship Program, (S) 352

Vermont Space Grant Undergraduate Scholarships, (S) 353

Veterans of Foreign Wars of Mexican Ancestry Scholarship Program, (S) 354

Victor Horsley Research Clinical Training Fellowship. *See* Clinical Research Training Fellowships in Epilepsy, entry (G) 757

Vigil Poster Presentation Awards, (A) 1075

Vikki Carr Scholarship Awards, (S) 355

Village Voice Minority Writing Fellowship, (I) 1306

Villarreal–HDA Foundation Scholarships. *See* Dr. Juan D. Villarreal–HDA Foundation Scholarships, entries (S) 90, (F) 432

Virgil Hawkins Fellowship Program, (F) 628

Virginia F. Cutler Fellowship in Consumer Studies, (F) 629

Virginia Higher Education Teacher Assistance Program, (S) 356

Virginia Medical Scholarship Program, (L) 673

Virginia Nurse Practitioner/Nurse Midwife Scholarship Program, (L) 674

Virginia Society of Certified Public Accountants Minority Undergraduate Scholarship, (S) 357

Virginia Space Grant Aerospace Graduate Research Fellowships, (G) 1017

Virginia Space Grant Aerospace Undergraduate Research Scholarships, (G) 1018

Virginia Space Grant Community College Scholarship Program, (S) 358

Virginia Space Grant Teacher Education Scholarship Program, (S) 359

Virginia Teacher Scholarship Loan Program, (L) 675

Virginia Undergraduate Student Financial Assistance (Last Dollar) Program, (S) 360

Vito Marzullo Internship Program, (I) 1307

Volunteer/Donor Research Award. *See* National Kidney Foundation of Massachusetts, Rhode Island, New Hampshire, and Vermont Research Grants, entry (G) 924

Vouras Dissertation Research Grant. *See* Paul P. Vouras Dissertation Research Grant, entry (G) 951

S–Scholarships F–Fellowships L–Loans G–Grants A–Awards I–Internships

S–Scholarships F–Fellowships L–Loans G–Grants A–Awards I–Internships

Sponsoring Organization Index

The Sponsoring Organization Index makes it easy to identify agencies that offer financial aid primarily or exclusively to minorities. In this index, sponsoring organizations are listed alphabetically, word by word. In addition, we've used an alphabetical code (within parentheses) to help you identify which programs sponsored by these organizations fall within your scope of interest: S = Scholarships; F = Fellowships; L = Loans; G = Grants; A = Awards; and I = Internships. Here's how the code works: if the name of a sponsoring organization is followed by (S) 141, a program sponsored by that organization is described in the Scholarships section in entry 141. If the same sponsoring organization's name is followed by another entry number—for example, (L) 680—the same or a different program sponsored by that organization is described in the Loans chapter in entry 680. Remember: the numbers cited here refer to program entry numbers, not to page numbers in the book.

Michael Baker Corporation, (S) 218
Michigan Space Grant Consortium, (G) 889–890
Microsoft Corporation, (S) 219–220, (A) 1047, (I) 1211
Milken Family Foundation, (G) 791
Minnesota Broadcasters Association, (S) 165
Minnesota Space Grant Consortium, (S) 223, (F) 526
Minority Advertising Training Program, (I) 1214
Minority Corporate Counsel Association, (F) 603
Minority Educational Foundation of the United States of
    America, (S) 210
Minority Nurse, (S) 228
Mississippi Office of Student Financial Aid, (I) 1218
Mississippi Space Grant Consortium, (S) 232, (F) 534
Missouri Department of Elementary and Secondary Education,
    (L) 653
Missouri Department of Health, (L) 666
Missouri Department of Natural Resources, (S) 106, (F) 440
Missouri Society of Certified Public Accountants, (S) 236
Missouri Space Grant Consortium, (F) 535, (G) 905, (I) 1219
Missouri Vocational Special Need Association, (S) 237
Modern Technology Systems, Inc., (I) 1286–1287
Modesto Bee, (I) 1220
Montana Space Grant Consortium, (S) 234, (F) 537, (G) 906
Morris Scholarship Fund, (S) 235, (F) 538
Mudd, (A) 1055
MultiCultural Review, (A) 1036

NACDA Foundation, (F) 491
National Action Council for Minorities in Engineering, (S) 105,
    238–239, 315, 332, (F) 606, (I) 1224
National Association of Black Journalists, (S) 316, (I) 1268, 1284
National Association of Black Journalists. Seattle Chapter, (S)
    259
National Association of Hispanic Federal Executives, (S) 243
National Association of Hispanic Journalists, (S) 76, 240, 253, (F)
    539, (A) 1045, 1057, (I) 1121, 1237
National Association of Hispanic Nurses, (S) 244, (F) 494, 543
National Association of Latino Elected and Appointed Officials,
    (I) 1143, 1280
National Association of Minority Engineering Program
    Administrators, Inc., (S) 241, 340
National Association of School Psychologists, (F) 542
National Association of Schools of Public Affairs and
    Administration, (F) 581
National Association of Social Workers, (F) 425
National Association of Student Personnel Administrators, (I)
    1225
National Association of University Women, (F) 544
National Association of Vocational Education Special Needs
    Personnel, (S) 247
National Athletic Trainers' Association, (S) 242
National Caucus and Center on Black Aged, (G) 918
National Center for Atmospheric Research, (G) 914, (I) 1281
National Center for Education Statistics, (G) 701–702, 704–706
National Collegiate Athletic Association, (F) 551, (I) 1233
National Consortium for Graduate Degrees for Minorities in
    Engineering and Science (GEM), (F) 457–459, (I) 1147–1149
National Consortium on Violence Research, (G) 915–917
National Council of Churches, (F) 561

National Council of Intellectual Property Law Associations, (F)
    603
National Council on Family Relations, (A) 1053
National FFA Organization, (S) 34
National Foundation for Infectious Diseases, (G) 760
National Gay and Lesbian Task Force. Policy Institute, (I) 1305
National Hispanic Coalition of Federal Aviation Employees, (S)
    292, (F) 589
National Hispanic Council on Aging, (G) 918
National Hispanic Foundation for the Arts, (F) 557
National Humanities Center, (G) 808
National Indian Council on Aging, (G) 918
National Kidney Foundation of Massachusetts, Rhode Island,
    New Hampshire, and Vermont, Inc., (G) 924, 953
National Lawyers Guild, (I) 1154
National League for Nursing, (F) 559
National Medical Fellowships, Inc., (F) 478, 521, 560, 635, (G)
    815, 1029, (A) 1042, 1049, 1065, 1076–1077, (I) 1105, 1136
National Minority Junior Golf Scholarship Association, (S) 256
National Opera Association, (A) 1058
National Organization for Women. Legal Defense and Education
    Fund, (I) 1239
National Physical Science Consortium, (F) 548, (I) 1230
National Press Club, (S) 104
National Research Council, (F) 452, 476, (G) 805–806
National Science Foundation, (S) 227, 308, (F) 562, 598, (G) 680,
    688, 701–702, 704–706, 839, 841, 914, 940, 1005–1006, (I)
    1226, 1261, 1281, 1289, 1310
National Science Foundation. Directorate for Biological Sciences,
    (G) 781, 903, 961–962, 1004, 1011
National Science Foundation. Directorate for Education and
    Human Resources, (G) 737, 796, 925, 974, 985–986, (A) 1061
National Science Foundation. Directorate for Engineering, (G)
    820–821, 939, (I) 1151
National Science Foundation. Directorate for Mathematical and
    Physical Sciences, (G) 725, 838, 878–880, 939, (I) 1165
National Science Foundation. Directorate for Social, Behavioral,
    and Economic Sciences, (G) 768–769, 782, 903, 1004, 1011
National Society of Hispanic MBAs, (F) 550
National Society of Professional Engineers, (I) 1310
National Strength and Conditioning Association, (S) 261
National Student Nurses' Association, (S) 35
National Trust for Historic Preservation, (F) 525, (I) 1212
National Urban Fellows, Inc., (G) 926
National Urban League, (S) 131
Native American Journalists Association. Seattle Chapter, (S) 259
NBC Television Stations Division, (A) 1047
Nebraska Space Grant Consortium, (S) 248, (F) 553
Nevada Space Grant Consortium, (S) 249, (F) 554
New England Board of Higher Education, (F) 552
New Hampshire Charitable Foundation, (S) 233
New Hampshire Space Grant Consortium, (G) 928
New Jersey Commission on Higher Education, (F) 410
New Jersey Department of Health and Senior Services, (I) 1192
New Jersey Space Grant Consortium, (G) 929, (I) 1235
New Jersey State Nurses Association, (S) 166
New Jersey Utilities Association, (S) 251
New Mexico Commission on Higher Education, (F) 555, (L) 657,
    667
New Mexico Space Grant Consortium, (G) 933–934
New York Public Library. Center for Scholars and Writers, (G)
    930

U.S. Department of Health and Human Services, (G) 978

U.S. Department of Housing and Urban Development, (F) 626, (G) 831, (I) 1303

U.S. Department of Justice, (G) 989

U.S. Department of Justice. National Institute of Justice, (G) 1021

U.S. Department of State, (L) 670–671, (G) 776, 792–794, 800, (I) 1126

U.S. Department of State. Bureau of Oceans and International Environmental and Scientific Affairs, (G) 774

U.S. Department of the Interior, (I) 1128

U.S. Department of Transportation, (I) 1294

U.S. Department of Transportation. Federal Highway Administration, (S) 103, (G) 785, (I) 1132

U.S. Environmental Protection Agency, (S) 225, (F) 528, (G) 678, 894, (I) 1213

U.S. Food and Drug Administration, (G) 978

U.S. Geological Survey, (I) 1299, 1311

U.S. Health Resources and Services Administration, (G) 797

U.S. Library of Congress, (G) 865, (I) 1084, 1194

U.S. National Aeronautics and Space Administration, (S) 86, 92, 155, 179, 183, 207, 223, 232, 234, 239, 245, 248–249, 257, 263, 266–267, 272, 293, 297, 314–315, 330, 337, 344, 353, 358–359, 365, 369–370, 377, (F) 390, 411, 431, 449, 466, 497, 499, 501, 516, 526, 534–535, 537, 540–541, 553–554, 556, 563–564, 567, 569, 590, 594, 609, 621, (G) 698, 716–717, 735, 763–766, 795, 832–833, 836–837, 855–858, 871–872, 877, 889–890, 905–906, 909–911, 928–929, 933–937, 945, 950, 976–977, 983, 998–999, 1017–1019, 1022–1024, 1026–1028, 1033, (I) 1081, 1085, 1104, 1106, 1115, 1142, 1189, 1202, 1219, 1224, 1235–1236, 1281, 1286–1287

U.S. National Aeronautics and Space Administration. Jet Propulsion Laboratory, (I) 1217

U.S. National Endowment for the Humanities, (G) 686–687, 798, 946

U.S. National Institutes of Health, (F) 572, (L) 655, 672, (G) 679, 756, 799, 827, 868, 884, 891, 922–923, 939, 1001, (I) 1153, 1254, 1290

U.S. National Institutes of Health. Fogarty International Center, (G) 774

U.S. National Institutes of Health. National Cancer Institute, (L) 654, (G) 736, 882, 885, 893, 902, 913

U.S. National Institutes of Health. National Center for Research Resources, (G) 755, 885

U.S. National Institutes of Health. National Eye Institute, (G) 882

U.S. National Institutes of Health. National Heart, Lung, and Blood Institute, (G) 835, 882, 920–921, (I) 1099

U.S. National Institutes of Health. National Human Genome Research Institute, (G) 885

U.S. National Institutes of Health. National Institute of Allergy and Infectious Diseases, (L) 654, (G) 835, 882, (I) 1170

U.S. National Institutes of Health. National Institute of Arthritis and Musculoskeletal and Skin Diseases, (L) 654, (G) 835, 882, 885

U.S. National Institutes of Health. National Institute of Child Health and Human Development, (L) 654, (G) 835, 882

U.S. National Institutes of Health. National Institute of Dental and Craniofacial Research, (L) 654, (G) 835, 882–883, 995

U.S. National Institutes of Health. National Institute of Diabetes and Digestive and Kidney Diseases, (G) 835, 882

U.S. National Institutes of Health. National Institute of Environmental Health Sciences, (G) 835, 882, 885

U.S. National Institutes of Health. National Institute of General Medical Sciences, (F) 529, (G) 712, 895, 907, 1007

U.S. National Institutes of Health. National Institute of Mental Health, (F) 474, 484, 520, 531, 533, 549, 573–574, 580, 622, (G) 835, 882, 885–886, 897, 900–901, 956, 959, 965, 992

U.S. National Institutes of Health. National Institute of Neurological Disorders and Stroke, (F) 533, 573, (G) 761, 882, 885, 900–901, 956, (I) 1234

U.S. National Institutes of Health. National Institute of Nursing Research, (F) 558, (G) 885

U.S. National Institutes of Health. National Institute on Aging, (L) 654, (G) 789, 835, 882–883, 885, 896

U.S. National Institutes of Health. National Institute on Alcohol Abuse and Alcoholism, (F) 484, 549, (L) 654, (G) 773, 835, 882, 885, 992

U.S. National Institutes of Health. National Institute on Deafness and Other Communication Disorders, (L) 654, (G) 835, 882

U.S. National Institutes of Health. National Institute on Drug Abuse, (F) 484, 549, 573, (G) 835, 882, 956, 992, (I) 1177

U.S. National Institutes of Health. National Library of Medicine, (F) 517, 546, (G) 881

U.S. National Park Service, (I) 1123, 1229

U.S. National Security Agency, (L) 656, (G) 1006

U.S. Navy. Naval Research Laboratory, (G) 927

U.S. Navy. Office of Naval Research, (F) 545, (G) 771–772, 908, 942–944, (I) 1299, 1311

U.S. Substance Abuse and Mental Health Services Administration, (F) 519, 614, (L) 651, (G) 968

USA Funds, (S) 350, (F) 627

Utah Education Association, (S) 351

Verizon Foundation, (S) 352

Vermont Space Grant Consortium, (S) 353

Vermont Student Assistance Corporation, (S) 44

Very Special Arts, (I) 1088, 1247

Veterans of Foreign Wars of the United States of Mexican Ancestry, (S) 354

Vikki Carr Scholarship Foundation, (S) 355

Villa I Tatti, (G) 808

Village Voice, (I) 1306

Virginia Department of Education, (L) 675

Virginia Department of Health, (L) 673–674

Virginia Polytechnic Institute and State University. Graduate School, (G) 779

Virginia Society of Certified Public Accountants Education Foundation, (S) 357

Virginia Space Grant Consortium, (S) 358–359, (G) 1017–1018

Virginia. State Council of Higher Education, (S) 356, 360

Wal–Mart, (S) 361

Warner Norcross & Judd LLP, (S) 362–363, (F) 631

Washington Association of School Administrators, (S) 364

Washington Higher Education Coordinating Board, (S) 367–368

Washington Internships for Students of Engineering, (I) 1310

Washington Library Media Association, (F) 492

Washington NASA Space Grant Consortium, (S) 365, (G) 1019

Washington Society of Certified Public Accountants, (S) 366
Washington State University. Graduate School, (G) 1020
Wayne State University, (G) 892
WCVB–TV, (I) 1308
Wells Fargo Bank, (L) 676
West Virginia Space Grant Consortium, (S) 369–370, (G) 1022–1024
William and Flora Hewlett Foundation, (G) 686
William Randolph Hearst Foundation, (F) 561, (G) 888, (I) 1238
William T. Grant Foundation, (F) 581, (G) 1032
William Townsend Porter Foundation, (F) 571
Williams College. Dean of the Faculty, (G) 810
Wisconsin Center for Education Research, (G) 1015
Wisconsin Foundation for Independent Colleges, Inc., (S) 193, (I) 1191
Wisconsin Higher Educational Aids Board, (S) 376, 378, (L) 677
Wisconsin Hispanic Scholarship Foundation, Inc., (S) 217, (F) 523
Wisconsin Institute of Certified Public Accountants, (S) 375
Wisconsin Space Grant Consortium, (S) 377, (G) 1026–1028
W.K. Kellogg Foundation, (S) 380, (F) 635, (G) 888, 1029–1030
Wolverine Bar Association, (F) 636
Women in Film Foundation, (G) 852
Women of the Evangelical Lutheran Church in America, (S) 10, (F) 392
Women's Sports Foundation, (I) 1173, 1313
Women's Studio Workshop, (G) 719–720
Women's Transportation Seminar, (S) 310, (F) 467
Woodrow Wilson National Fellowship Foundation, (F) 518, (L) 670–671
Woods Hole Marine Biological Laboratory, (G) 1025
Woods Hole Oceanographic Institution, (I) 1299, 1311
Worldstudio Foundation, (S) 379–380, (F) 637
Wyeth–Ayerst Laboratories, (G) 694, (A) 1077
Wyoming Department of Education, (S) 88
Wyoming Hispanic Organization, (S) 381
Wyoming Space Grant, (G) 1033

Xerox Corporation, (S) 382, (F) 638

Yale New Haven Hospital, (S) 383
Yale University. International Security Studies, (G) 851
Yale University. Law School. Jerome N. Frank Legal Services Organization, (G) 980
Y.E.S. to Jobs, (I) 1312
YMCA of Greater Seattle, (S) 94
Youth Opportunities Foundation, (S) 384

3M Company, (S) 332

Residency Index

Some programs listed in this book are restricted to residents of a particular city, county, state, or region. Others are open to applicants wherever they may live. The Residency Index will help you pinpoint programs available only to residents in your area as well as programs that have no residency restrictions at all (these are listed under the term "United States"). To use this index, look up the geographic areas that apply to you (always check the listings under "United States"), jot down the entry numbers listed after the program types that interest you (scholarships, fellowships, etc.), and use those numbers to find the program descriptions in the directory. To help you in your search, we've provided some "see also" references in each index entry. Remember: the numbers cited here refer to program entry numbers, not to page numbers in the book.

Aberdeen, Washington: **Scholarships,** 367. *See also* Washington

Adams County, Pennsylvania: **Scholarships,** 9. *See also* Pennsylvania

Addison County, Vermont: **Scholarships,** 339. *See also* Vermont

Alabama: **Scholarships,** 93, 326, 330, 344; **Fellowships,** 390, 617; **Grants,** 698, 772; **Awards,** 1046; **Internships,** 1286. *See also* Southern states; United States; names of specific cities and counties

Alameda County, California: **Scholarships,** 56, 138; **Fellowships,** 417, 521. *See also* California

Alaska: **Grants,** 772; **Internships,** 1081. *See also* United States; names of specific cities

Albany County, New York: **Scholarships,** 339. *See also* New York

Albany, New York: **Fellowships,** 521. *See also* New York

Aransas County, Texas: **Scholarships,** 147; **Fellowships,** 472. *See also* Texas

Arizona: **Scholarships,** 15, 295, 350; **Fellowships,** 627; **Awards,** 1046; **Internships,** 1085, 1143, 1280. *See also* United States; names of specific cities and counties

Arkansas: **Scholarships,** 21, 80, 306; **Loans,** 639–640; **Grants,** 716–717, 772. *See also* Southern states; United States; names of specific cities and counties

Ashtabula County, Ohio: **Scholarships,** 108. *See also* Ohio

Atlanta, Georgia: **Scholarships,** 329; **Fellowships,** 521; **Internships,** 1312. *See also* Georgia

Aurora, Illinois: **Fellowships,** 521. *See also* Illinois

Austin, Texas: **Fellowships,** 521. *See also* Texas

Baltimore, Maryland: **Scholarships,** 170. *See also* Maryland

Bee County, Texas: **Scholarships,** 147; **Fellowships,** 472. *See also* Texas

Bell Gardens, California: **Scholarships,** 50, 333–335; **Fellowships,** 428. *See also* California

Belmont County, Ohio: **Scholarships,** 286. *See also* Ohio

Bennington County, Vermont: **Scholarships,** 339. *See also* Vermont

Berks County, Pennsylvania: **Scholarships,** 9. *See also* Pennsylvania

Berkshire County, Massachusetts: **Scholarships,** 339. *See also* Massachusetts

Boston, Massachusetts: **Scholarships,** 352; **Fellowships,** 521. *See also* Massachusetts

Bridgewater, New Jersey: **Scholarships,** 342; **Internships,** 1300. *See also* New Jersey

Bronx County, New York. *See* New York, New York

Bronx, New York. *See* New York, New York

Brooklyn, New York. *See* New York, New York

Brooks County, Texas: **Scholarships,** 147; **Fellowships,** 472. *See also* Texas

Broome County, New York: **Scholarships,** 339. *See also* New York

Broward County, Florida: **Scholarships,** 138, 282; **Internships,** 1295. *See also* Florida

Caledonia County, Vermont: **Scholarships,** 339. *See also* Vermont

California: **Scholarships,** 1–2, 15, 39–41, 43, 78, 98, 164, 171, 192, 197, 205, 260, 295, 331, 354, 384; **Fellowships,** 413, 418, 489, 503, 514; **Grants,** 734; **Awards,** 1046; **Internships,** 1082, 1143, 1214, 1280, 1286. *See also* United States; names of specific cities and counties

Cameron County, Texas: **Scholarships,** 147; **Fellowships,** 472. *See also* Texas

Canada: **Scholarships,** 17, 109, 224, 285, 324, 347; **Fellowships,** 388, 391, 441, 461, 473, 477, 504, 506, 513, 518, 524, 527, 536, 561, 571, 584, 600, 604, 610, 613; **Grants,** 694–695, 724, 738–739, 757, 759, 788, 803, 808, 811, 828, 845, 969; **Internships,** 1146, 1208. *See also* Foreign countries

Cass County, Missouri: **Scholarships,** 177; **Fellowships,** 496. *See also* Missouri

Tenability Index

Some programs listed in this book can be used only in specific cities, counties, states, or regions. Others may be used anywhere in the United States (or even abroad). The Tenability Index will help you locate funding that is restricted to a specific area as well as funding that has no tenability restrictions (these are listed under the term "United States"). To use this index, look up the geographic areas where you'd like to go (always check the listings under "United States"), jot down the entry numbers listed after the program types (scholarships, fellowships, etc.) that interest you, and use those numbers to find the program descriptions in the directory. To help you in your search, we've provided some "see also" references in each index entry. Remember: the numbers cited here refer to program entry numbers, not to page numbers in the book.

Subject Index

There are hundreds of different subject areas covered in this directory. You can use the Subject Index to identify both the subject focus and the type (scholarships, fellowships, etc.) of available funding programs. To help you pinpoint your search, we've included hundreds of "see" and "see also" references. In addition to looking for terms that represent your specific subject interest, be sure to check the "General programs" entry; hundreds of funding opportunities are listed there that can be used to support study, research, or other activities in *any* subject area (although the programs may be restricted in other ways). Remember: the numbers cited in this index refer to program entry numbers, not to page numbers in the book.

Education, art; General programs; Illustrators and illustrations; names of specific art forms

Art conservation: **Grants,** 991; **Internships,** 1275–1276. *See also* Art; General programs; Preservation

Art education. *See* Education, art

Art history. *See* History, art

Arts and crafts: **Scholarships,** 379; **Fellowships,** 637; **Grants,** 730, 834. *See also* Art; General programs; names of specific crafts

Asian studies: **Grants,** 687, 792–794. *See also* General programs; Humanities

Astronautics: **Fellowships,** 449; **Grants,** 1027; **Internships,** 1142. *See also* General programs; Space sciences

Astronomy: **Scholarships,** 234, 239, 263, 314; **Fellowships,** 449, 466, 537, 548, 556, 563–564; **Grants,** 716–717, 725, 741–742, 905, 910, 928, 945, 999; **Internships,** 1142, 1217, 1224, 1230, 1289. *See also* General programs; Physical sciences

Athletic training: **Scholarships,** 242, 261; **Fellowships,** 393; **Loans,** 659. *See also* Athletics; General programs

Athletics: **Fellowships,** 491, 551; **Internships,** 1089, 1173, 1233, 1313. *See also* Athletic training; Education, physical; General programs; Sports medicine; names of specific sports

Atmospheric sciences: **Scholarships,** 16, 159–160, 239, 246; **Fellowships,** 449, 485, 540; **Grants,** 710, 754, 818–819, 914, 928, 963, 1027; **Internships,** 1142, 1224, 1228, 1240. *See also* General programs; Physical sciences

Attorneys. *See* Legal studies and services

Audiology: **Loans,** 659; **Grants,** 797. *See also* General programs; Health and health care; Medical sciences

Automation. *See* Computer sciences; Information science; Technology

Automobile industry: **Scholarships,** 101, 212. *See also* General programs

Automotive engineering. *See* Engineering, automotive

Automotive technology: **Scholarships,** 212. *See also* General programs; Transportation

Avian science. *See* Ornithology

Aviation: **Scholarships,** 248; **Fellowships,** 553. *See also* General programs; Space sciences; Transportation

Azerbaijani language. *See* Language, Azeri

Azeri language. *See* Language, Azeri

Ballet. *See* Dance

Banking: **Scholarships,** 32, 288; **Internships,** 1095, 1179–1180, 1279. *See also* Finance; General programs

Behavioral sciences: **Scholarships,** 249, 344; **Fellowships,** 390, 452, 484, 531, 545, 549, 554, 572; **Loans,** 654–655; **Grants,** 679, 698, 726–727, 736, 756, 781, 805–806, 810, 868, 895–897, 903, 907, 922–923, 1004, 1011, 1027; **Internships,** 1156, 1290. *See also* General programs; Social sciences; names of special behavioral sciences

Biochemistry: **Scholarships,** 12; **Fellowships,** 476, 606; **Grants,** 716–717, 962; **Internships,** 1240. *See also* Biological sciences; Chemistry; General programs

Biological sciences: **Scholarships,** 53, 106, 225, 234, 239, 246, 249, 251, 255, 263, 273, 344; **Fellowships,** 390, 416, 433, 437, 440, 449, 452, 459, 466, 476, 481, 484, 517, 528, 537, 540, 545, 547, 552, 554, 563–564, 570, 574, 606; **Loans,** 654, 657; **Grants,** 678–681, 684, 697–698, 712, 716–718, 721, 733, 741–742, 762, 770, 774, 781, 805–806, 809, 827, 830, 836–837, 868, 870, 881, 890, 894, 903, 909–910, 914, 928, 939, 945, 954, 959, 961–962, 964, 969, 978–979, 984, 989, 1003–1004, 1006, 1011, 1013; **Awards,** 1075; **Internships,** 1101–1102, 1126, 1128, 1142, 1149, 1153, 1213, 1217, 1224, 1226–1229, 1232, 1235, 1240, 1248, 1257, 1261–1263, 1273, 1281, 1288–1289, 1291–1292. *See also* General programs; Sciences; names of specific biological sciences

Biomedical engineering. *See* Engineering, biomedical

Biomedical sciences: **Fellowships,** 529, 549, 572; **Loans,** 655, 672; **Grants,** 679, 681, 738–739, 756, 759, 799, 845, 884, 895–897, 899, 907, 920–923, 956, 992, 1001, 1003, 1007; **Internships,** 1099, 1136, 1156, 1170, 1240, 1254, 1290. *See also* Biological sciences; General programs; Medical sciences

Blindness. *See* Visual impairments

Botany: **Grants,** 684, 1003; **Internships,** 1226. *See also* Biological sciences; General programs

Brain research. *See* Neuroscience

Broadcast journalism. *See* Journalism, broadcast

Broadcasting: **Scholarships,** 113, 165, 180, 336; **Awards,** 1070; **Internships,** 1133, 1164, 1171, 1183, 1308. *See also* Communications; Radio; Television

Bulgarian language. *See* Language, Bulgarian

Business administration: **Scholarships,** 9, 31–32, 48, 60, 83–84, 94, 103, 107, 112, 117, 127, 131, 140, 142, 146, 151, 208–209, 212–213, 216, 249, 251, 255, 273, 282, 284, 334, 342, 344, 361, 377; **Fellowships,** 390, 415, 424, 429, 438, 515, 550, 554–555, 557, 570, 599; **Loans,** 671; **Grants,** 698, 844, 948, 967, 1020, 1026–1028; **Internships,** 1095, 1110, 1114, 1116, 1120, 1125–1126, 1128, 1159, 1166, 1174, 1248, 1300, 1312. *See also* Entrepreneurship; General programs; Management

Business enterprises. *See* Entrepreneurship

Canadian history. *See* History, Canadian

Cancer: **Scholarships,** 109; **Fellowships,** 441; **Grants,** 736, 893, 902, 913, 947, 969, 1003; **Internships,** 1153. *See also* Disabilities; General programs; Health and health care; Medical sciences

Cardiology: **Grants,** 707–709, 920–921; **Internships,** 1082, 1099, 1153. *See also* General programs; Medical sciences

Caribbean history. *See* History, Caribbean

Cars. *See* Automobile industry; Engineering, automotive

Cartography: **Scholarships,** 246; **Fellowships,** 547; **Internships,** 1110, 1227–1228. *See also* General programs; Geography

Cartoonists and cartoons: **Scholarships,** 380. *See also* Art; General programs; Illustrators and illustrations

Cave studies: **Internships,** 1273. *See also* General programs; Sciences

Chemical engineering. *See* Engineering, chemical

Chemistry: **Scholarships,** 12, 28, 53, 60, 106–107, 132, 207, 225, 234, 239, 246, 251, 263, 273, 277, 280, 300, 311, 334, 356, 382; **Fellowships,** 416, 437, 440, 459, 466, 476, 479–480, 485, 507, 537, 540, 545, 547–548, 552, 563–564, 570, 606, 638; **Loans,** 675; **Grants,** 697, 716–718, 738, 785, 909, 914, 945, 964; **Internships,** 1101, 1114, 1132, 1149, 1162–1163, 1198–1199, 1213, 1217, 1224, 1227–1228, 1230–1231, 1240, 1248, 1255, 1257, 1261, 1271, 1281, 1289–1290. *See also* Engineering, chemical; General programs; Physical sciences

Chicano affairs. *See* Hispanic American affairs

Chicano studies. *See* Hispanic American studies

Early childhood education. *See* Education, preschool

Earth sciences: **Scholarships,** 272, 330, 356, 359, 374; **Fellowships,** 459, 532, 540, 545, 569, 634; **Loans,** 675; **Grants,** 716–717, 818–819, 836–837, 871–872, 910, 928–929, 998, 1019, 1027; **Internships,** 1106, 1149, 1240, 1281. *See also* General programs; Natural sciences; names of specific earth sciences

Eastern European history. *See* History, European

Eastern European studies. *See* European studies

Ecology. *See* Environmental sciences

Economic development: **Scholarships,** 22; **Grants,** 774, 846. *See also* Economics; General programs

Economic planning. *See* Economics

Economics: **Scholarships,** 20, 131, 140, 151, 208, 216, 249, 343–344; **Fellowships,** 390, 424, 443, 515, 547, 554; **Loans,** 671; **Grants,** 686, 698, 704, 713, 726–727, 729, 732, 748, 782, 785, 801–802, 807–808, 822–823, 831, 844, 903, 914, 932, 952, 967, 993–994, 1004, 1011, 1020; **Internships,** 1110, 1120, 1126, 1132, 1156, 1159, 1227, 1262, 1266, 1301. *See also* General programs; Social sciences

Education: **Scholarships,** 21, 33, 36, 70–72, 81, 87, 94, 98, 117, 122, 126, 155, 205, 227, 249, 314, 344, 351, 359, 364; **Fellowships,** 390, 406, 456, 514, 532, 554, 611, 632; **Loans,** 639–640, 650, 653, 660, 664, 667–668, 677; **Grants,** 691–693, 698, 701–706, 763, 784, 786–787, 805–806, 832, 844, 846, 912, 914, 948, 970, 993–994, 999, 1008, 1015, 1020; **Internships,** 1078, 1128, 1130–1131, 1184, 1239, 1262, 1273, 1296. *See also* General programs; specific types and levels of education

Education, administration: **Fellowships,** 619. *See also* Education; Management

Education, art: **Internships,** 1088. *See also* Art; Education; General programs

Education, elementary: **Scholarships,** 163, 308, 330–331, 356; **Fellowships,** 488, 598; **Loans,** 640, 642, 647, 652, 675. *See also* Education; General programs

Education, higher: **Scholarships,** 346; **Fellowships,** 559, 619, 625; **Loans,** 663; **Grants,** 685; **Awards,** 1071–1072; **Internships,** 1119, 1225. *See also* Education; General programs

Education, physical: **Scholarships,** 43, 53, 94, 164, 261; **Fellowships,** 413, 416, 489. *See also* Athletics; Education; General programs

Education, preschool: **Loans,** 642, 652. *See also* Education; General programs

Education, science: **Scholarships,** 308; **Fellowships,** 598. *See also* Education; General programs; Sciences

Education, secondary: **Scholarships,** 163, 308, 330–331, 356; **Fellowships,** 488, 598; **Loans,** 642, 647, 652, 675; **Grants,** 850. *See also* Education; General programs

Education, special: **Scholarships,** 324, 331, 356; **Fellowships,** 613; **Loans,** 648–649, 675. *See also* Education; General programs

Education, vocational: **Loans,** 649. *See also* Education; General programs

Electrical engineering. *See* Engineering, electrical

Electronic engineering. *See* Engineering, electronic

Electronic journalism. *See* Journalism, broadcast

Electronics: **Fellowships,** 600; **Grants,** 697, 718. *See also* Engineering, electronic; General programs; Physics

Elementary education. *See* Education, elementary

Embryology: **Grants,** 741–742. *See also* Biological sciences; General programs; Medical sciences

Emotional disabilities. *See* Mental health

Employment discrimination. *See* Discrimination, employment

Energy: **Grants,** 689, 802, 817, 853; **Internships,** 1210, 1266. *See also* Environmental sciences; General programs; Natural resources

Engineering: **Scholarships,** 9, 11, 26, 49, 53, 60, 84, 112, 121, 126–129, 131, 135–136, 140, 142, 146, 160, 203, 208–209, 215, 218, 225, 232, 238, 241, 245–246, 249, 251, 264, 268, 293, 296–297, 300, 304, 313–315, 334, 338, 340, 365, 369–371, 377; **Fellowships,** 401, 416, 452–453, 456–458, 460, 466, 468, 475, 481, 485, 511, 515, 522, 528, 534, 547, 552, 554–555, 562, 568, 590, 594, 607–608, 611; **Loans,** 657, 659; **Grants,** 679–680, 688, 716–718, 737–738, 762, 770–772, 774, 777, 782, 785, 796, 805–806, 820–821, 839, 867, 869–870, 894, 908, 914, 925, 927, 940, 942–944, 948, 960, 974, 976–978, 983–986, 989, 996, 999, 1020, 1026, 1028; **Internships,** 1102, 1104, 1110, 1114, 1132, 1147–1148, 1151, 1158–1159, 1166, 1196–1197, 1201, 1210, 1213, 1217, 1227–1228, 1253, 1261–1263, 1271, 1274, 1281, 1286–1287, 1310. *See also* General programs; Physical sciences; names of specific types of engineering

Engineering, aeronautical: **Scholarships,** 118, 239, 263; **Fellowships,** 545, 563–564, 606; **Grants,** 945; **Internships,** 1224. *See also* Aeronautics; Engineering; General programs

Engineering, aerospace: **Scholarships,** 86, 92, 105, 155, 179, 183, 207, 223, 232, 234, 257–258, 263, 266–267, 272, 293, 297, 314, 337, 344, 353, 358, 365, 369–370, 377; **Fellowships,** 390, 431, 449, 497, 499, 501, 516, 526, 534–535, 537, 541, 556, 563–564, 567, 569, 590, 594, 609, 621; **Grants,** 698, 763–766, 795, 832–833, 855–858, 871, 877, 889–890, 905–906, 911, 928–929, 933–937, 945, 950, 976–977, 983, 998–999, 1017–1019, 1022–1024, 1026–1028, 1033; **Internships,** 1081, 1085, 1106, 1115, 1142, 1189, 1202, 1219, 1235–1236. *See also* Engineering; General programs; Space sciences

Engineering, agricultural: **Scholarships,** 105–107; **Fellowships,** 440. *See also* Agriculture and agricultural sciences; Engineering; General programs

Engineering, architectural: **Scholarships,** 105. *See also* Architecture; Engineering; General programs

Engineering, automotive: **Scholarships,** 212. *See also* Engineering; General programs

Engineering, biomedical: **Scholarships,** 105, 255; **Fellowships,** 466, 476, 606; **Grants,** 939, 956; **Internships,** 1290. *See also* Biomedical sciences; Engineering; General programs

Engineering, chemical: **Scholarships,** 12, 105–107, 230–231, 234, 239, 255, 258, 263, 277, 280, 332, 382; **Fellowships,** 440, 507, 537, 545, 548, 563–565, 606, 638; **Grants,** 945; **Awards,** 1054; **Internships,** 1199, 1217, 1224, 1230, 1235, 1255, 1257. *See also* Chemistry; Engineering; General programs

Engineering, civil: **Scholarships,** 23, 105–107, 207, 234, 239, 255, 258, 263; **Fellowships,** 440, 537, 563–565, 606; **Loans,** 662, 669; **Grants,** 945; **Internships,** 1123, 1128, 1224. *See also* Engineering; General programs

Engineering, communications: **Fellowships,** 586. *See also* Engineering; General programs

Engineering, computer: **Scholarships,** 83, 96, 105, 149, 207, 211, 219–220, 255, 258, 263, 343, 382; **Fellowships,** 429, 507, 548, 563–564, 606, 638; **Loans,** 656; **Grants,** 945; **Internships,** 1125, 1129, 1161, 1198–1199, 1211, 1230, 1235, 1301. *See also* Computer sciences; Engineering; General programs

Engineering, construction: **Loans,** 662. *See also* Engineering; General programs

Veterinary sciences: **Scholarships,** 273; **Fellowships,** 570; **Loans,** 659; **Grants,** 797, 1020; **Internships,** 1248. *See also* Animal science; General programs; Sciences

Video. *See* Filmmaking; Television

Violence: **Grants,** 823, 915–917. *See also* General programs

Visual arts. *See* Art

Visual impairments: **Loans,** 675. *See also* General programs; Health and health care

Vocational education. *See* Education, vocational

Voice: **Awards,** 1058. *See also* General programs; Music; Performing arts

Water resources: **Fellowships,** 475; **Grants,** 931. *See also* Environmental sciences; General programs; Natural resources

Weather. *See* Climatology

Weaving: **Grants,** 730. *See also* Arts and crafts; General programs

Web design. *See* Internet design and development

Web journalism. *See* Journalism, online

Welfare. *See* Social services

Western European history. *See* History, European

Western European studies. *See* European studies

Wildlife management: **Scholarships,** 106; **Fellowships,** 440; **Internships,** 1128, 1273. *See also* Environmental sciences; General programs

Women's studies and programs: **Grants,** 745, 852, 982, 993–994, 1031; **Awards,** 1077; **Internships,** 1137, 1172, 1200, 1239. *See also* Discrimination, sex; General programs

World literature. *See* Literature

Writers and writing: **Fellowships,** 518, 557; **Grants,** 720, 730, 873–875, 946, 997; **Awards,** 1034–1037, 1040, 1045, 1051, 1059, 1062–1064, 1067, 1074. *See also* General programs; Literature; specific types of writing

Youth. *See* Adolescents; Child development

Yugoslavian language. *See* Language, Macedonian; Language, Serbo–Croatian; Language, Slovene

Zoology: **Internships,** 1128, 1226. *See also* General programs; Sciences; names of specific zoological subfields

Calendar Index

Since most funding programs have specific deadline dates, some may have already closed by the time you begin to look for money. You can use the Calendar Index to identify which programs are still open. To do that, go to the type of program (scholarships, fellowships, etc.) that interests you, think about when you'll be able to complete your application forms, go to the appropriate months, jot down the entry numbers listed there, and use those numbers to find the program descriptions in the directory. Keep in mind that the numbers cited here refer to program entry numbers, not to page numbers in the book. Note: not all sponsoring organizations supplied deadline information to us, so not all programs are listed in this index.